MW01030610

STORIES WITH INTENT

STORIES WITH INTENT

A Comprehensive Guide
to the Parables of Jesus

Klyne Snodgrass

WILLIAM B. EERDMANS PUBLISHING COMPANY
GRAND RAPIDS, MICHIGAN / CAMBRIDGE, U.K.

Published 2008 by

Wm. B. Eerdmans Publishing Co.

2140 Oak Industrial Drive N.E., Grand Rapids, Michigan 49505 /

P.O. Box 163, Cambridge CB3 9PU U.K.

www.eerdmans.com

Printed in the United States of America

17 16 15 14   9 8 7 6 5 4

ISBN 978-0-8028-4241-1

*To my students
at North Park Theological Seminary —
Past, Present, and Future*

and

*To Gabriel and Caeden
who are wonders to behold*

Contents

Contents

Preface

This is unapologetically and quite consciously a selfishly motivated book. This is what I want when preparing to teach or preach on the parables. Hopefully others will find useful what I have collected. This is not a devotional book or a book to be read through at one sitting. It is a resource book for the parables.

Are parables so complex that they require a comprehensive guide? I do believe that Jesus' parables can be understood by average readers and without special helps and instructions. They are not jigsaw puzzles. Some are enigmatic — like the Unjust Steward — but many are clear and compelling or they would not have been loved as much as they are. At the same time, the parables were told in a complex context, one enlightened by numerous parallel texts, and they assume familiarity with an ancient culture. They involve questions dealing with a variety of subjects: ancient agricultural assumptions, wedding customs, relations of slaves and masters, and Judaism and its history, to name only the most obvious. The parables have been placed in a context of scrutiny by scholarship, again involving an array of subjects. Anyone who desires to understand the light offered by the first-century context and to follow the scholarly discussions needs a guidebook like this. Anyone who is going to preach or teach the parables should be fully informed about the world of the parables, the intent of their teller, and the discussions about them in modern literature. I have tried to convey the complexity of discussions by NT scholars because I feel people should be as fully informed as possible and because such discussions become a platform for reflection. I am well aware how easy it is to misrepresent someone, and if I have done so, I apologize in advance.

We live in a day when bibliographies can be electronically produced and updated easily, so I have chosen to list resources in the notes and to include a complete bibliography for the book, rather than a full bibliography for each parable. In the further reading section for each parable, I have not included obvious works on parables or commentaries except where they were especially helpful. I have not chosen contributions that I think are most correct but those that are most helpful in understanding the issues and discussion of each parable.

The gestation period for this book has been quite lengthy, and I have had marvelous support. Thanks is expressed for a grant from the Pew Evangelical Scholars program. I am extremely grateful for unparalleled support from the institution I serve, North Park Theological Seminary. The president, Jay Phelan, and the dean of faculty, Stephen Graham, and my faculty colleagues have backed my work at every point. Their conversations have been helpful and enjoyable. I have had a number of teaching assistants, most for more than one year, who have not only been a great help but who have become good friends: Nathan Pawl, Cindy Reinhart, John Madvig, Sarah Frisk Eix, Rebekah Ecklund, James Amadon, Lars Stromberg, Chris Nelson, and Nathanael Putnam — all salt of the earth people. Chris Nelson has also made the substantial contribution of preparing the indexes. The library staff at North Park University has been very accommodating and helpful. Several good friends have read and commented on one or more chapters: Bruce Chilton, Jan DuRand, John Painter, Roger Aus, Stephen Chester, Glenn Palmberg, and Mike Fitzgerald. I appreciate their contribution, but any shortcomings in the work are, of course, my own.

Sofija Burton, a good friend, assisted significantly with reading German. Bernice Brandel has been a support and friend for many years; her inquisitive mind and her commitment to the life of the church are always encouraging. The people at Eerdmans have been extremely patient and helpful, and special thanks are expressed to Jon Pott, John Simpson, and Reinder Van Til. It has been a pleasure to work with friends in the preparation of this book. Most significant of all has been the support of my wife Phyllis, whose patience, tolerance, and assistance are a gift.

Holy Week, 2007

Abbreviations

AB	Anchor Bible
ABD	D. N. Freedman, ed., *Anchor Bible Dictionary* (6 vols.; New York: Doubleday, 1992)
AFLNW	*Arbeitsgemeinschaft für Forschung des Landes NordRhein-Westfalen*
AGJU	*Arbeiten zur Geschichte des antiken Judentums und des Urchristentums*
AJT	*American Journal of Theology*
AnBib	Analecta biblica
ANET	J. B. Pritchard, ed., *Ancient Near Eastern Texts Relating to the Old Testament* (3d ed.; Princeton: Princeton University Press, 1969)
ANF	*Ante-Nicene Fathers*
ANRW	*Aufstieg und Niedergang der römischen Welt*
Ant.	Josephus, *Jewish Antiquities*
Ant. Rom.	Dionysius of Halicarnassus, *Antiquitates Romanae*
Apoc. Jas.	*Apocryphon of James*
Apoc. Zeph.	*Apocalypse of Zephaniah*
As. Mos.	*Assumption of Moses*
ASCE	*The Annual of the Society of Christian Ethics*
ASTI	*Annual of the Swedish Theological Institute*
AThRSS	*Anglican Theological Review* Supplementary Series
ATR	*Australian Theological Review*
AusBR	*Australian Biblical Review*
AUSS	*Andrews University Seminary Studies*
b.	*Babylonian Talmud*
BAR	*Biblical Archaeology Review*
2-3 Bar.	*2-3 Baruch*
Barn.	*Epistle of Barnabas*
BBB	Bonner biblische Beiträge

BBR	*Bulletin for Biblical Research*
BDAG	W. F. Bauer, F. W. Danker, W. F. Arndt, and F. W. Gingrich, *Greek-English Lexicon of the New Testament and Other Early Christian Literature* (3rd ed.; Chicago: University of Chicago Press, 1999)
BETL	Bibliotheca ephemeridum theologicarum lovaniensium
BEvT	Beiträge zur evangelischen Theologie
BGU	*Aegyptische Urkunden aus den Königlichen Staatlichen Museen zu Berlin. Griechische Urkunden* (Berlin: 1895-1983)
Bib	*Biblica*
BibInt	*Biblical Interpretation*
BibLeb	*Bibel und Leben*
BiblScRel	Biblioteca di scienze religiose
BJRL	*Bulletin of the John Rylands University Library of Manchester*
BL	*Bibel und Liturgie*
BN	*Biblische Notizen*
BNTC	Black's New Testament Commentaries
BO	*Bibliotheca orientalis*
BR	*Biblical Research*
BSac	*Bibliotheca Sacra*
BT	*The Bible Translator*
BTB	*Biblical Theology Bulletin*
BVB	Beiträge zum Verstehen der Bibel
BZ	*Biblische Zeitschrift*
BZNW	Beihefte zur *Zeitschrift für die neutestamentliche Wissenschaft*
CahRB	Cahiers de la *Revue biblique*
CBQ	*Catholic Biblical Quarterly*
CBQMS	*Catholic Biblical Quarterly* Monograph Series
Cher.	Philo, *De Cherubim*
1-2 Clem.	*1 Clement*
ConBNT	Coniectanea neotestamentica/Coniectanea biblica: New Testament Series
Conf.	Philo, *De Confusione Linguarum*
Congr.	Philo, *De Congressu Eruditionis Gratia*
CRINT	Compendia rerum iudaicarum ad Novum Testamentum
CSR	*Christian Scholar's Review*
CTQ	*Concordia Theological Quarterly*
Det.	Philo, *Quod Deterius Potiori Insidiari Soleat*
Diatr.	Epictetus, *Diatribai (Dissertationes)*
DJD	Discoveries in the Judaean Desert
DSD	Dead Sea Discoveries
EgT	*Église et théologie*
EKKNT	Evangelisch-katholischer Kommentar zum Neuen Testament
1-2 En.	*1-2 Enoch*

Enc	*Encounter*
Ench.	Epictetus, *Enchiridion*
ETL	*Ephemerides theologicae lovanienses*
ETR	*Études théologiques et religieuses*
EvQ	*Evangelical Quarterly*
EvT	*Evangelische Theologie*
ExpTim	*Expository Times*
FB	Forschung zur Bibel
FFF	*Foundations and Facets Forum*
FRLANT	Forschungen zur Religion und Literatur des Alten und Neuen Testaments
Fug.	Philo, *De Fuga et Inventione*
Gos. Thom.	*Gospel of Thomas*
Haer.	Irenaeus, *Adversus Haereses*
HBT	*Horizons in Biblical Theology*
HeyJ	*Heythrop Journal*
HibJ	*Hibbert Journal*
HTKNT	Herders theologischer Kommentar zum Neuen Testament
HTR	*Harvard Theological Review*
IBS	*Irish Biblical Studies*
ICC	International Critical Commentary
Inst.	Quintilian, *Institutio Oratoria*
Int	*Interpretation*
ITQ	*Irish Theological Quarterly*
J.W.	Josephus, *Jewish War*
JAAR	*Journal of the American Academy of Religion*
JBL	*Journal of Biblical Literature*
JBLMS	*Journal of Biblical Literature* Monograph Series
JCS	*Journal of Cuneiform Studies*
JES	*Journal of Ecumenical Studies*
JETS	*Journal of the Evangelical Theological Society*
JJS	*Journal of Jewish Studies*
Jos. Asen.	*Joseph and Aseneth*
JPFC	S. Safrai and M. Stern, eds., *The Jewish People in the First Century: Historical Geography, Political History, Social, Cultural and Religious Life and Institutions* (2 vols.; CRINT 1; Philadelphia: Fortress, 1974, 1976)
JQR	*Jewish Quarterly Review*
JSJ	*Journal for the Study of Judaism in the Persian, Hellenistic, and Roman Periods*
JSNT	*Journal for the Study of the New Testament*
JSNTSup	*Journal for the Study of the New Testament* Supplement Series
JSOT	*Journal for the Study of the Old Testament*

JSOTSup	*Journal for the Study of the Old Testament* Supplement Series
JSP	*Journal for the Study of the Pseudepigrapha*
JTS	*Journal of Theological Studies*
JTSA	*Journal of Theology for Southern Africa*
J.W.	Josephus, *Jewish War*
Jub.	*Jubilees*
KEK	Kritisch-exegetischer Kommentar über das Neue Testament
KJV	King James Version
L.A.B.	Pseudo-Philo, *Liber Antiquitatum Biblicarum*
L.A.E.	*Life of Adam and Eve*
LB	*Linguistica Biblica*
LCL	Loeb Classical Library
Leg.	Philo, *Legum Allegoriae*
LSJ	H. G. Liddell, R. Scott, and H. S. Jones, *A Greek-English Lexicon* (9th ed.; Oxford: Oxford University Press, 1996)
LTPM	Louvain Theological and Pastoral Monographs
LUÅ	Lunds universitets årsskrift
m.	*Mishnah*
4 Macc.	*4 Maccabees*
Mand.	Hermas, *Mandates*
Midr.	*Midrash*
Mor.	Plutarch, *Moralia*
MTZ	*Münchener theologische Zeitschrift*
Mut.	Philo, *De Mutatione Nominum*
NAC	New American Commentary
NEB	New English Bible
Neot	*Neotestamentica*
NewDocs	G. H. R. Horsley and S. Llewelyn, eds., *New Documents Illustrating Early Christianity* (Grand Rapids: Eerdmans, 1981-)
NICNT	New International Commentary on the New Testament
NIGTC	New International Greek Testament Commentary
NIV	New International Version
NLT	New Living Translation
NovT	*Novum Testamentum*
NovTSup	*Novum Testamentum* Supplements
NPNF1	*Nicene and Post-Nicene Fathers,* Series 1
NRSV	New Revised Standard Version
NRTh	*La nouvelle revue théologique*
NSBT	New Studies in Biblical Theology
NTAbh	Neutestamentliche Abhandlungen
NTL	New Testament Library
NTOA	Novum Testamentum et Orbis Antiquus
NTS	*New Testament Studies*

Opif.	Philo, *De Opificio Mundi*
OTP	J. H. Charlesworth, ed., *Old Testament Pseudepigrapha* (2 vols.; New York: Doubleday, 1983)
P. Cair. Zenon	Zenon Papyri
P. Flor.	*Papiri Florentini*
P. Mich.	Michigan Papyri
P. Oxy.	Oxyrhynchus Papyri
PL	Patrologia Latina
Plant.	Philo, *De Plantatione*
Praem.	Philo, *De Praemiis et Poenis*
Prov.	Philo, *De Providentia*
PRSt	*Perspectives in Religious Studies*
Pss. Sol.	*Psalms of Solomon*
PW	A. F. Pauly and G. Wissowa, eds., *Paulys Realencyclopädie der classischen Altertumswissenschaft* (new ed.; 49 vols.; Munich, 1980)
Q.E.	Philo, *Quaestiones et Solutiones in Exodum*
QG	Philo, *Quaestiones et Solutiones in Genesin*
Quaest. Ev.	Augustine, *Quaestiones Evangelicarum*
Rab.	*Rabbah*
RB	*Revue biblique*
ResQ	*Restoration Quarterly*
RevExp	*Review and Expositor*
RevQ	*Revue de Qumran*
Rhet.	Aristotle, *Rhetorica*
Rhet. Her.	*Rhetorica ad Herennium*
RHPR	*Revue d'histoire et de philosophie religieuses*
RSR	*Recherches de science religieuse*
RSV	Revised Standard Version
Sacr.	Philo, *De Sacrificiis Abelis et Caini*
SANT	Studien zum Alten und Neuen Testaments
SBET	*Scottish Bulletin of Evangelical Theology*
SBLDS	Society of Biblical Literature Dissertation Series
SBT	Studies in Biblical Theology
ScEccl	*Sciences ecclésiastiques*
SE	*Studia evangelica*
SEÅ	*Svensk exegetisk årsbok*
SecCent	*Second Century*
Sib. Or.	*Sibylline Oracles*
Sim.	Hermas, *Similitudes*
SJT	*Scottish Journal of Theology*
SNTSMS	Society for New Testament Studies Monograph Series
SO	*Symbolae osloenses*
Spec. Leg.	Philo, *De Specialibus Legibus*

ST	*Studia theologica*
Str-B	H. L. Strack and P. Billerbeck, *Kommentar zum Neuen Testament aus Talmud und Midrasch* (6 vols.; Munich, 1922-61)
SUNT	Studien zur Umwelt des Neuen Testaments
SwJT	*Southwestern Journal of Theology*
t.	*Tosefta*
T. Ab.	*Testament of Abraham*
T. Benj.	*Testament of Benjamin*
T. Dan	*Testament of Dan*
T. Gad	*Testament of Gad*
T. Iss.	*Testament of Issachar*
T. Job	*Testament of Job*
T. Jos.	*Testament of Joseph*
T. Levi	*Testament of Levi*
T. Sol.	*Testament of Solomon*
T. Zeb.	*Testament of Zebulon*
TBei	*Theologische Beiträge*
TD	*Theology Digest*
TDNT	G. Kittel and G. Friedrich, *Theological Dictionary of the New Testament* (trans. G. W. Bromiley; 10 vols.; Grand Rapids: Eerdmans, 1964-76)
TGW	*Theologie der Gegenwart*
TJ	*Trinity Journal*
TJT	*Toronto Journal of Theology*
TLG	*Thesaurus Linguae Graecae*
TLZ	*Theologische Literaturzeitung*
TS	*Theological Studies*
TU	Texte und Untersuchungen
TynBul	*Tyndale Bulletin*
TZ	*Theologische Zeitschrift*
USQR	*Union Seminary Quarterly Review*
VC	*Vigiliae christianae*
Vis.	Hermas, *Visions*
WBC	Word Biblical Commentary
WD	*Wort und Dienst*
WTJ	*Westminster Theological Journal*
WUNT	Wissenschaftliche Untersuchungen zum Neuen Testament
y.	*Jerusalem Talmud*
ZDPV	*Zeitschrift des deutschen Palästina-Vereins*
ZNW	*Zeitschrift für die neutestamentliche Wissenschaft und die Kunde der älteren Kirche*
ZTK	*Zeitschrift für Theologie und Kirche*

Introduction to the Parables of Jesus

Jesus' parables are among the best known and most influential stories in the world. Even if people know nothing of Jesus, they either know about his stories or have encountered their impact in expressions like "prodigal" or "good Samaritan." The importance of the parables of Jesus can hardly be overestimated. At no point are the vitality, relevance, and usefulness of the teaching of Jesus so clear as in his parables. Jesus was the master creator of story, and nothing is so attractive or so compelling as a good story. Children (and adults) do not say, "Tell me some facts"; they want a story. Stories are inherently interesting. Discourse we tolerate; to story we attend. Story entertains, informs, involves, motivates, authenticates, and mirrors existence. By creating a narrative world, stories establish an unreal, controlled universe. The author abducts us and — almost god-like — tells us what reality exists in this narrative world, what happens, and why.

Stories are one of the few places that allow us to see reality, at least the reality the author creates. There, to a degree we cannot do in real life, we can discern motives, keep score, know who won, and what success and failure look like. Life on the outside virtually stops; we are taken up in the story. The storyteller is in control so that we are forced to see from new angles and so that the message cannot be easily evaded. Hearers become willing accomplices, even if the message is hostile. From this "other world" we are invited to understand, evaluate, and, hopefully, redirect our lives. Apart from personal experience, stories are the quickest way to learning. We learn most easily in the concrete, but, because we cannot easily remember hundreds of concrete accounts, our brains store most easily in the abstract. In teaching and preaching the shortcut is to repeat the abstract idea we already know, forgetting that others still need to learn

1

in the concrete. We would do better, at least frequently, to clothe the abstract in concrete experience and story, just as Jesus did.

Story pulls us into a narrative world where there are development, plot, *and* resolution. Without resolution — which is often how NT scholarship seeks to view the parables — we feel frustrated and ask, "Why this story?" We expect something interesting and insightful, maybe even unique, but certainly something that merits the time the teller asks of us. The teller has an agenda, an intent, and thinks the story is important, or the story would never be told. The intent may be merely to entertain or much more pointedly to convey truth, convince, and motivate. Stories are not inherently Christian and do not automatically convey truth. They can be used to communicate any religion, ideology, or even any falsehood. Unfortunately, even good stories can be, and are, subverted to promote evil. Understanding the truth in a story depends on the truth inherent in the framework to which it refers and the degree to which the story corresponds to and creatively discloses truth.

However, a parable is not merely a story. "Parable" in its broadest sense refers to an expanded analogy.[1] For example, God forgives and receives sinners as a loving father forgives and receives a wayward son. Such analogies first and foremost are comparisons or contrasts *used to explain or convince.* Parables by their very nature seek to make a rhetorical point.[2] Further, some parables are not stories at all. While the English word "parable" usually refers to a short narrative with two levels of meaning, the Greek and Hebrew words for "parable," as we will see, are much broader and cover a variety of literary forms.

The parables of Jesus presuppose the kingdom they seek to disclose.[3] Imagine having only the stories of Jesus and no sense of their referent. The parable of the Prodigal and his elder brother is moving only because of knowledge that the story mirrors God's reception of sinful people and contrasts God's reception with the frequent disdain some people have for sinners.

Jesus' parables have been described as both works of art and weapons in his conflict with opponents. They are both and more. From the day they were first told right to the present, they have brought delight and instruction to countless people and offence to others. Parables were the means Jesus used most frequently to explain the kingdom of God and to show the character of God and the expectations that God has for humans. That message has often been subverted. Jesus' parables have been abused and forced to serve various purposes — from ancient theological purposes to modern ideological and pastoral ones. Some interpreters treat the parables like modeling clay to be shaped to the interpreter's whim. Others attempt to domesticate the parables so that they always follow prescribed rules and give meanings we can tolerate. Neither approach can succeed. The intent of the teller — Jesus himself — with all the power and creativity of his teaching must be the goal of our interpretive work. These are stories *with intent,* the communicative intent of Jesus.[4] Anything else is a rewriting of Jesus' parables. The ancient church and modern Christians have often rewritten them to create a new intent. I do not seek the intent of the church, a psychologist, a sociologist, a feminist, or any other such rewriting, common as they are. I seek to hear the intent of Jesus to his contemporaries — his disciples and his fellow Jews.

However, these "simple" stories of Jesus, these gems of articulation about life and God, have proven to be anything but simple, and their intent is not narrowly conceived. The work of deciphering Jesus' intent is sometimes difficult. We have the parables of Jesus *only* as they are remembered by the early church and communicated by the Evangelists. On the other hand, the task is not as impossible as some have suggested and sometimes is not difficult at all. The parables do not need to be curtailed, rewritten, domesticated, psychologized, theologized with foreign christological and atonement contributions, decontextualized, or controlled. They need to be allowed to speak, and they need to be heard. Some parables are as clear as bells, and, while we may discuss nuances and backgrounds in lengthy treatises, they do not need explanation so much as implementation. They in effect say to us, "Stop resisting and do it," or "Believe it." We do not need much commentary to know the intent of the parable of the Good Samaritan. Despite the numerous studies of this parable — studies which I will treat — the parable compels us to stop resisting and live its message.

In seeking the communicative intent, i.e., the function of the parable, I am not suggesting that we may psychologize Jesus. In effect, speech act theory is part of the presupposition of my approach. Communication is not about abstract meaning; it acts and seeks to change things. The question for each parable is: How did Jesus seek to change attitudes and behaviors with this parable?[5]

The parables of Jesus deserve a fresh hearing from people who are ready to learn and follow his instruction. Numerous studies of the parables exist, as the bibliography and endnotes here testify, but if any area in NT studies exists where further publication is needed, surprisingly it is the parables of Jesus. Despite the voluminous amount of material written on parables, relatively little exists that offers good and *comprehensive* help for pastors and teachers.[6] Many treat only select parables that match their own concerns. Many of the studies available are so esoteric or skewed by methodological and philosophical assumptions that they are difficult to use for those attempting to make sense of Jesus' teachings. Much helpful information and numerous insights are given, but in the end modern parable interpretation has been tried and found wanting. Over and over we will see this is the case with the analysis of individual parables.

Necessary History

A history of interpretation is virtually a prerequisite for studying Jesus' parables. That history has been told many times and does not need to be repeated here,[7] but two essential pieces of the story must be mentioned, for they determine in one way or another nearly all modern interpretation of the parables. First, the tendency of most interpreters until the end of the nineteenth century was to *allegorize* the parables.[8] Allegorizing (or allegoresis) is the interpretive practice of turning into allegory what was *not* intended to be allegory. That is, people have read *into* the parables elements of the church's theology that had little to do with Jesus' intent. A frequently cited and most revealing example of allegorizing is Augustine's interpretation of the parable of the Good Samaritan (Luke 10:30-37), in which virtually every item is given theological significance: the man is Adam; Jerusalem is the heavenly city; Jericho is the moon, which stands for our mortality; the robbers are the devil and his angels who strip the man of his immortality and beat him by persuading him to sin; the priest and levite are the priesthood and the ministry of the OT; the good Samaritan is Christ; the binding of the wounds is the restraint of sin; the oil and wine are the comfort of hope and the encouragement to work; the donkey is the incarnation; the inn is the church; the next day is after the resurrection of Christ; the innkeeper is the Apostle Paul; and the two denarii are the two commandments of love or the promise of this life and that which is to come.[9] With this we are not very close to Jesus' intent! As another example, in the parable of the Barren Fig Tree (Luke 13:6-9) the three times the owner came looking for fruit was taken to stand for God's coming before the law was given, his coming at the time the law was written, and his coming in grace and mercy in Christ. The vinedresser represents those who rule the church, and the digging and dung refer to the rebuking of unfruitful people and the remembrance of sins.[10]

The practice of allegorizing did not start with the church; it appears in some Qumran writings, such as 1QpHab 12.2-10 (interpreting Hab 2:17), is frequent in the writings of Philo, and was also used by Hellenistic interpreters of Homer and Plato. The later allegorizing of the church was based on the assumption that Scripture could yield a fourfold meaning: the literal meaning, an allegorical-theological meaning, an ethical meaning, and a heavenly meaning that reflected future bliss.[11] Competing allegories of the same text could be accepted. Complaints about allegorizing appeared early in the church's history, even from allegorizers,[12] but as we will see with virtually every parable, allegorizing was the assumed key to parable interpretation.

Allegorizing is more meditation on the text than interpretation of it, and caution should be used in evaluating those who allegorized. People like Augustine were not ignorant, and those who allegorized enjoyed a life relation to the text and were convinced that the text had power to direct their lives. Further, they did *not* base doctrine on allegorical exegesis, and they set up controls to prevent excesses by limiting those who could participate in such interpreting and the boundaries within which they must operate.[13] Still, allegorizing is *not* a legitimate means of interpretation. It obfuscates the message of Jesus and replaces it with the teaching of the church or some ideology. Such an interpretive procedure assumes one knows the truth before reading the text and finds truth paralleled by the text being read, even if the text is about another subject. It does not take a genius to guess that modern scholars would reject allegory with a vengeance, but even with those rejecting the practice, allegory often finds its way back in interpretation.

No one rejected allegory and allegorizing more vehemently than Adolf Jülicher, a German NT scholar, and his influence is the second essential piece to understanding the history of parable interpretation. Jülicher's two-volume work on the parables from the late nineteenth century has dominated parable studies even though it has never been translated.[14] In his war against allegorizing Jülicher completely rejected both allegorizing *and* the genre of allegory. He denied that Jesus used allegory, which he defined as a series of related metaphors, or allegorical traits, where a point in a story "stands for" something else in reality. Although he knew the OT had allegories, he argued that allegory was too complex for Jesus, the simple Galilean preacher. Instead, Jesus' stories were *simple* comparisons which were self-evident and *did not need interpretation.* Therefore, the allegorizing interpretations of the church were totally rejected. Further, where allegory or allegorical traits appear, such as in the parable of the Sower and the parable of the Wicked Tenants, the Evangelists are to blame. Because of the influence of Hellenistic Jewish views of parables, the Evangelists, in Jülicher's opinion, misunderstood Jesus' parables, assumed that parables have a concealing function (e.g., Mark 4:10-12), and turned them into dark and mysterious sayings.[15] Jülicher thought parables are expanded similes, whereas allegories are expanded metaphors. He viewed simile and parable as literal speech which is easily understood, while metaphor and allegory are nonliteral,[16] saying one thing and meaning another. He thought metaphor and allegory are indirect speech, hide, and need to be decoded, and he allowed no mingling of parable and allegory, no "mixed forms." There could be no question of several points of comparison between image *(Bild)* and the object *(Sache)* portrayed, as happens with allegory, since Jesus' parables could have only *one* point of contact (one *tertium comparationis*) between image and object. That one point is usually a general religious maxim. Jesus' purpose was not to obscure, and therefore, his parables cannot be viewed as allegories. On this approach Jesus' teaching was reduced to pious moralisms about God and the world. Further, by arguing that the Evangelists had altered Jesus' parables, Jülicher opened the door for attempts to reconstruct the original versions of the parables.[17]

The attacks on Jülicher's position came quickly and have continued right to the present. Valid arguments against Jülicher were deflected for decades, but that was like bailing out a sinking ship. Today most of Jülicher's argument has been set aside. Hardly anyone today follows Jülicher, even when they affirm or appear to affirm his efforts. Early on Paul Fiebig argued that Jülicher derived his understandings of parables from Greek rhetoric rather than from the Hebrew world, where allegorical parables and "mixed forms" are common.[18] The more attention one pays to Jewish parables, the less impressed one is with Jülicher's explanations. Parables are not necessarily simple, and *no literature is self-interpreting.* A number of scholars recognized that Jülicher had thrown out *allegory,* a literary form, while the problem was *allegorizing,* the interpretive procedure of reading into the parables a theology that Jesus did not intend.[19] Some argue that allegory is not a literary genre at all but a way of thinking that can be present in various genres.[20] Others argue quite openly for allegory, some are guilty of their own allegorizing, and as we will see, even Jülicher could not avoid finding multiple correspondences in some parables.[21] Few today would accept Jülicher's descriptions of metaphor, for most would see a parable as an expansion of metaphor, not simile.[22] And virtually no one accepts Jülicher's argument that the parables give general religious maxims.

Despite the inadequacy of Jülicher's arguments, the clash between the church's allegorizing and Jülicher's rejection of allegorizing *and* allegory set a framework within which parable interpretation still operates — even if one has never heard of Adolf Jülicher. The key question is and always has been how much of a parable is significant for understanding. Do elements within the parable "stand for" something in reality? If some "correspondence" between image and reality exists, should it be assigned to the Evangelists? Fear of allegory frequently has led to rewriting the parables, often resulting in elimination of their introductions and conclusions. Such scholarly reconstructions are common now, even when the people performing them complain about their hypothetical nature.[23]

The analysis of each parable in the chapters that follow will reveal parts of this story of parable interpretation, but regardless of the approach one takes, the parables are among the most abused and mistreated stories ever told. They have been twisted, shortened, subverted, realigned, and psychologized for centuries by pastors and scholars alike. If it is true that Jesus is the receptacle into which every theologian pours his or her ideas, parables are the pitcher they often use to do the pouring. The church has made them mirror theologies Jesus did not intend. Scholars have rewritten them to achieve a supposed original and more compatible form and to understand the Evangelists' communities. Scholars and pastors have shifted them from their purpose in order to promote sociological or homiletical agendas. Parables are, if not fragile, at least vulnerable and have been manipulated for all kinds of theological, political, social, and personal purposes. But the parables of Jesus do not go quietly into the night; they powerfully and stubbornly keep demanding new attention and keep expressing their message. Ultimately they are resistant, saying in effect, "Read me again."

What Is a Parable?

Hardly anything said about parables — whether defining them or explaining their characteristics — is true of all of them. For this reason every parable must be approached in its own right and not assumed to look like or function like other parables. A parable is often defined as an illustration due to the "root fallacy" of deriving the meaning from *paraballō*, which means literally "to throw alongside." From this people have viewed parables as earthly stories with heavenly meanings. Although there is some truth in this saying, this approach to understanding NT parables will *not* do. Parables are much more than illustrations, and although some are concerned with future eschatology, they are not about heaven. They are directed to life on this earth.

In fact, possibly no definition of parables will do, for any definition that is broad enough to cover all the forms is so imprecise that it is almost useless. Some well-known definitions deserve mention. T. W. Manson suggested "A parable is a literary creation in narrative form designed either to portray a type of character for warning or example or to embody a principle of God's governance of the world and men [sic]."[24] Parables do tell about God and humanity, but not all are narratives. C. H. Dodd said parables "are the natural expression of a mind that sees truth in concrete pictures rather than conceives it in abstractions,"[25] and his definition is repeated frequently: "At its simplest the parable is a metaphor or simile drawn from nature or common life, arresting the hearer by its vividness or strangeness, and leaving the mind in sufficient doubt about its precise application to tease it into active thought."[26] Technically speaking, a parable is much more than a metaphor or simile, and although this definition is helpful for many parables, for others it will not work. Some parables are neither vivid nor strange (e.g., Mark 13:28), and some leave no doubt about their application. Paul Ricoeur described parables as "the conjunction of a narrative form and a metaphoric process."[27] Again helpful, but some parables, especially given the way the NT uses the word *parabolē*, are not narratives, and some are not metaphorical, or at least it is debated whether they are. Better is Theon's (first century) definition of fable *(mythos)* — the genre to which parables belong — as "a fictitious saying picturing truth,"[28] or best of all, to adopt the words of a modern poet, parables are imaginary gardens with real toads in them.[29] They create an imaginary world that reflects reality. Of fables it has been said that they are a tactical maneuver to prompt new thinking and that their author engages to manipulate.[30] That is also the case with parables. Quite in line with this is the definition of *mashal* (the Hebrew word corresponding to the Greek *parabolē*) as "an allusive narrative which is told for an ulterior purpose."[31] Parables are a form of indirect communication intended to "deceive the hearer into the truth."[32] Rabbis spoke of parables as handles for understanding Torah; before parables no one understood the Torah, but when Solomon and others created parables, then people understood.[33] Analogously we may say that Jesus' parables are handles for understanding his teaching on the kingdom.

Søren Kierkegaard's treatments of indirect communication deserve careful reflection.[34] He helps us see that direct communication is important for conveying information, but learning is more than information, especially when people think they already understand. People set their defenses against direct communication and learn to conform its message to the channels of their understanding of reality. Indirect communication finds a way in a back window and confronts what one thinks is reality. Parables are indirect communication.

If meaning is the value assigned to a set of relations, parables provide new sets of relations that enable us (or force us) to see in a fresh manner. Parables function as a lens that allows us to see the truth and to correct distorted vision. They allow us to see what we would not otherwise see, and they presume we *should* look at and see a *specific* reality. They are not Rorschach tests; they are stories with an intent, analogies through which one is enabled to see truth. Except for five of Jesus' parables . . . they are stories with two levels of meaning, the story level through which one sees and the truth level, the reality being portrayed.[35]

The immediate aim of a parable is to be compellingly interesting, and in being interesting it diverts attention and disarms. A parable's ultimate aim is to awaken insight, stimulate the conscience, *and* move to action. The primary reason Jesus' parables are stories with intent is, as we will see, that they are prophetic instruments, the tool especially of those who have a message from God. They do not occur in sections of the Bible focused on Torah or history or in the writings of the early church.[36] They are used by those who are trying to get God's people to stop, reconsider their ways, and change their behavior. Biblical parables reveal the kind of God that God is and how God acts, and they show what humanity is and what humanity should and may become.[37] Parables are not merely informative. Like prophets before him, Jesus told parables to prompt thinking *and stimulate response* in relation to God.[38] Parables usually engage listeners, create reflection, and promote action. They are pointed and clinching arguments for a too often slow-minded or recalcitrant audience.[39] They seek to goad people into the action the gospel deserves and the kingdom demands. One of the major problems of Christian churches, of Western Christianity in particular, is our stultefying passivity. The parables compel us — for Christ's sake literally — to do something! Parables do not seek the "mild morality" about which Kierkegaard lamented but radical cross-bearing, God-imitating response worthy of the name "conversion."

In most cases then *a parable is an expanded analogy used to convince and persuade.* As we will see, this is the way ancient Greeks also used the term, and it is sufficiently broad to cover the majority of the ways the Evangelists use the word. The logic of Jesus' parables is proportional analogy.[40] Corresponding to the German terms *Sache* and *Bild,* the English terms *tenor* and *vehicle* are used to explain how analogy functions. *Tenor* refers to the theme being compared, the item for which insight is sought, and *vehicle* refers to the pictorial image, the parable, the instrument by which insight is conveyed. An analogy explicitly or implicitly draws one *or more* points of resemblance. For example, a disciple is to God *(tenor)* as a slave is to a master *(vehicle)* with respect to unsurpassable obligation *(point of resemblance).*[41] According to John Sider every parable labeled as a parable in the Gospels involves more than one point of resemblance — the exact opposite of Jülicher.[42] Analogy by its very nature can easily become "allegorical."

How Should Parables Be Classified?

Not all parables are alike. Classification of parables into different categories is not a pedantic exercise,[43] nor are we necessarily imposing Hellenistic forms onto Jewish parables if we recognize that different kinds of parables exist. Classifications do get us into trouble, for the parables feel no need to conform to our categories; even within a category they are as varied as language itself. On the other hand, classifications provide understanding as we pick up clues from related parables to know how interpretive moves should be made. The classifications are ours, not Jesus' or the Evangelists', but the more clearly we understand how parables are similar or dissimilar, the more we understand how they function and the more we can be alert to their characteristics. No classification scheme is perfect, and other descriptions could be used besides those I have adopted.[44] Unfortunately, even when people use the same words, they do not always mean the same things.

Before describing parable classifications we need to understand that the Greek word *parabolē* has a much broader meaning in the Gospels than the English word "parable." As a result, in biblical studies the word "parable" has at least three different uses. First, *parabolē* can be used of almost any comparative saying intended to stimulate thought. It is used of a proverb such as "Physician, heal yourself" (Luke 4:23),[45] a riddle like "How can Satan cast out Satan? (Mark 3:23), a comparison (Matt 13:33), a contrast (Luke 18:1-8), and both simple stories (Luke 13:6-9) and complex stories (Matt 22:1-14). If "allegory" is a genre, *parabolē* is also used of full allegories (Mark 4:3-9). (See Appendix 1 for a list of the 50 occurrences of *parabolē* in the NT.) This range of meaning derives from the Hebrew noun *mashal*, which is usually translated by *parabolē* in the LXX (28 of 40 occurrences) and is even broader than *parabolē*. In addition *mashal* can be used of a taunt, a prophetic oracle, or a byword. A *mashal* is any dark saying intended to stimulate thought. (See Appendix 2 for occurrences of the noun and verb forms of *mashal* in the OT and Appendix 3 for the occurrences of *parabolē* in the LXX.) In fact, B. Gerhardsson labels virtually all of Jesus' sayings as *meshalim* (the plural of *mashal*) and divides them into aphoristic *meshalim* and narrative *meshalim*,[46] but we need greater precision than this, as Gerhardsson himself grants.

Second, "parable" can also be used in a more restricted sense to refer to any analogy (whether a story with a double meaning or not), a definition that would exclude proverbs, riddles, and nonnarrative forms. Third, an even more restricted meaning of "parable" derives from Adolf Jülicher's work and distinguishes parables (German, *Gleichniserzählungen*) from similitudes *(Gleichnisse)*, example stories *(Beispielerzählungen)*, and allegories *(Allegorien)*, the last of which, of course, Jülicher rejected. Thus while similitude, example story, and allegory are all parables under definition one above, technically and under this more restricted definition there is a difference. These four categories are still used, but there is a fair amount of confusion. There is considerable debate about whether allegory and example story are legitimate categories, about what qualifies as a similitude, and whether similitudes and parables can always be distinguished.

If we set aside for the moment the debated categories of example stories and allegories, we are left with similitudes and narrative parables, and some are content to use just these two categories.[47] There is attraction to this simplicity, but it does not do justice to the variety of forms. Even with the word "similitude" there is confusion. Jülicher used the German word *Gleichnis*, which is usually translated "similitude," to cover parabolic sayings (such as the blind leading the blind in Matt 15:14/Luke 6:39),[48] the proverb "Physician, heal yourself" (Luke 4:23), and the parables of the Tower Builder and Warring King (Luke 14:28-32).[49] Most people today rightly use the term "similitude" in a much more limited sense and refer to parabolic or aphoristic sayings as a separate category.[50] These briefer aphoristic sayings are usually simple comparisons, such as "No one is able to serve two masters" (Matt 6:24/Luke 16:13), and will not be treated in this book.

If, as Kierkegaard argued, parables are a means of indirect communication,[51] most of Jesus' parables are *double indirect communication,* whether similitudes or narrative parables. Direct communication addresses the hearer about the subject at hand. For example, direct communication about the kingdom might say "The kingdom is of supreme value and is worth everything you could give." The parable of the Treasure in the Field is double indirect communication in that it does not speak of the hearer/reader or the subject at hand. It uses another person (the one who finds) and another subject (the treasure) to address the hearer indirectly. The story of the Prodigal and the Elder Brother is double indirect communication. It is about a man and his sons, not the hearers/readers, but it uses these other people and another subject (their relations) to speak of God, relation with God, and relations among humans. We will see this double indirection over and over.

I suggest the following classification is less confusing and more helpful for treating parables:

aphoristic sayings
similitudes (double indirect)
interrogative parables (double indirect)
narrative parables, of which there are three further distinctions
    double indirect narrative parables
    juridical parables, a particular type of double indirect narrative
      parables
    single indirect narrative parables
"How much more" parables

Since aphoristic sayings will not be treated, for practical purposes we end up with six designations for parables: similitudes, interrogative parables, double indirect narrative parables, juridical parables, single indirect parables, and "how much more" parables. All are double indirect forms of communication except those labeled single indirect. These categories are determined both by form and by function. Except for the "how much more" parables and the juridical parables, the categories are mutually exclusive. Juridical parables are a type of double indirect parables, and the "how much more" logic can be used with other categories. These six kinds of parables deserve to be distinguished, and their characteristics must now be made explicit.

Similitudes. If a simile is an explicit comparison using "like" or "as" (such as "They are like sheep without a shepherd"), similitudes are extended similes. Often it is said that they relate a *typical or recurring* event or process in real life and are expressed in the present tense, but neither is true. Tense is *not* a factor in distinguishing forms. Some have two or more tenses, and some use the aorist (e.g., the Leaven in Matt 13:33).[52] Nor is a similitude necessarily a typical or recurring event. Is finding a treasure typical or recurring? The marker of a similitude is that it is an extended analogy which *lacks plot development.* It is more than a simple comparison and may involve several actions and a period of time. For example, the kingdom is like a woman who took leaven and hid it in three measures of dough until the whole was leavened. There is action but no plot, no problem needing resolution or development of the situation so that one has a story.[53] Similitudes, sometimes called parables in a narrow sense, typically are more straightforward, less confrontive, and less representational than other more developed forms. That is, they do not depend on correspondences between individual features and reality to make their point. (E.g., the man in the parable of the Growing Seed, who sleeps and rises and does not understand growth, corresponds neither to God nor to any other specific person.)

Interrogative Parables.[54] Even though these parables are like similitudes in that they do not have plot development and may logically function the same way, their form is different. Questions are one of the major ways that parables create interest and draw us in. Some parables have questions in their introductions such as "To what shall I liken this generation?" (Matt 11:16/Luke 7:31) or "What do you think?" (Matt 21:28). Some have questions within their narrative, and others conclude with questions, especially juridical parables (see below, p. 13). However, the *category* of interrogative parables concerns more than introductory and internal questions; rather it groups those parables that *are presented entirely as questions.* A number of these parables are "Who from you?" *(tis ex hymōn)* parables, and the form is common enough and different enough that it deserves to be recognized. Obvious examples include the parables of the Lost Sheep and the Friend at Midnight. The "Who from you?" questions are often lost in translations. The NIV and NRSV typically render these questions as "Suppose one of you," which is unfortunate (see Luke 11:5). Interrogative parables are not far from juridical parables, for they set up a hypothetical situation, force the hearer/reader to answer a question, and obligate one to transfer that answer to another arena. (Juridical parables carry additionally an accusatory element.) The question "Who from you?" always expects a negative answer: no one would act as the parable describes.[55]

Double Indirect Narrative Parables. Narrative parables, parables in the restricted sense, are metaphors (*contra* Jülicher) extended into narrative analogies *with plots*. If a metaphor is an implied comparison not using "like" or "as" (such as "You are the salt of the earth"), a parable is a fictitious story which narrates a *particular* event, is usually told in the past tense, and is intended to convey a moral or spiritual truth (e.g., the Prodigal Son). Narrative parables of all three types have *plot development*.[56] Something happens in the narrative that creates a problem or possibility, and then other acts happen that bring, or potentially bring, resolution or closure. The parable of the Banquet (Luke 14:15-24) is an obvious example. If there is resolution, dialogue in the parable often signals the place where resolution starts to occur. Some parables are intentionally open-ended, forcing the hearer/reader to ponder what should happen, as, for example, is the case with the parable of the Fig Tree (Luke 13:6-9). Some people think the distinction between similitudes and parables is not clear-cut,[57] but the presence or absence of plot development is a reliable basis for distinction. However, the distance between parable and reality varies drastically from parable to parable.

Juridical Parables. As a subset of double indirect narrative parables[58] these are among the best known and most forceful parables. By hiding their referent, juridical parables elicit a self-condemnation from the hearer(s) through the aid of an image. The hearer is forced to judge the circumstances of the parable, and then the lens drops and one realizes that he or she has judged him or herself.[59] Kierkegaard described indirect communication as "thoughts which wound from behind,"[60] an especially apt description of juridical parables. The best-known juridical parable is Nathan's parable of the Ewe Lamb told to David (2 Sam 12:1-14).[61] I will argue that Jesus' parables of the Two Sons (Matt 21:28-32), the Wicked Tenants (Matt 21:33-45/Mark 12:1-12/Luke 20:9-19), and the Two Debtors (Luke 7:40-47) are juridical parables. Juridical parables nearly always and almost by necessity require concluding explanations, something that points the accusing finger at the hearer and makes explicit how the person has erred. The parable of the Good Samaritan is a single indirect parable, but it comes very close to being a juridical parable. Jesus' concluding question to the scribe requires an answer that is self-condemning.[62]

Single Indirect Parables. Most of these parables have traditionally been called *example stories*. The usual explanation is that the primary purpose of these parables is to present a positive or negative character (or both) who serves as an example to be imitated or whose traits and actions are to be avoided. Either explicitly or implicitly the example story says, "Go and do [or do not do] likewise" (cf. Luke 10:37). Typically only four Gospel parables, all in Luke, are identified as example stories: the Good Samaritan, the Rich Fool, the Rich Man and Lazarus, and the Pharisee and the Toll Collector.[63] A number of scholars reject this category because they are unimpressed with what they see as moralistic teaching in example stories, because other parables also give examples to follow or not follow, and especially because they presuppose that all parables must be metaphorical. In their estimation either these four accounts were originally metaphorical too, or they are not parables, and if they were originally metaphorical stories, they have been changed into moralistic accounts by the Evangelists. D. Via excludes them from the category of parables.[64] J. D. Crossan thinks all four were originally parables of reversal to emphasize that the kingdom brings reversal, but have been turned into moral injunctions by the tradition.[65] For example, in Crossan's opinion the Good Samaritan at the literal level causes the hearers' world to be turned upside down, and the metaphorical point is that the kingdom breaks abruptly into one's consciousness and demands the reversal of values.

I confess that for some time I tried to keep the category example story, but in the end this label is both inadequate and inappropriate. Other parables clearly give examples of behavior to be imitated or avoided. One thinks immediately of such examples as the Unforgiving Servant, the Two Builders, the Faithful and Unfaithful Servant, the Treasure in the Field, the Two Sons, and the Tower Builder and Warring King. No features of their form or content distinguish the so-called example stories from other parables.[66]

Still, the attempt to show that they were originally metaphorical pictures of the reversal of the kingdom cannot suffice. This explanation is noticeably lacking in specificity and unconvincing. Would hearers really see in the Samaritan a reversal of values and draw the *implicit* conclusion that *the kingdom* must have such a reversal, especially when the parable does not mention the kingdom? A reversal of values can be effected by a single indirect story as easily as by a metaphorical/double indirect parable.

These four parables do *function* differently, and I would add a fifth, the parable of the Unjust Steward. These stories have developed plots, but they are not metaphorical in the way that other parables are. Other parables are analogies dealing with two different realms and with two levels of meaning; they are double indirect stories. Through them one sees a subject different from what is in the narrative; i.e., they are not really about seeds, treasure, masters, and servants but about God, the kingdom, and God's people. Interpretation of other parables involves a transfer from the subject in the narrative to some other topic. These five stories do not juxtapose different realms; they are about the subjects they narrate: a Samaritan's aid, the wealth of a rich fool, etc. No transfer is required to another arena, and, therefore, we are justified in speaking of their "relative peculiarity."[67] They address the reader indirectly by telling of another person but directly *by treating the subject at hand.* The parable of the Rich Fool addresses the reader indirectly through the rich man but directly treats the subject of wealth. They are staged portraits of reality.[68] These five parables require a different label, and the best alternative is to call them what they are — single indirect narrative parables.[69] More detailed treatment of the debate over "example stories" appears in connection with the discussion of the parable of the Good Samaritan,[70] but the label "example story" is both inadequate and inappropriate.

"How Much More" Parables.[71] This category is not determined by form but by function, and "How much more" parables — for lack of a better term — will also belong to another classification as well. Some are interrogative parables without plot development, and some are narrative parables with plot development. Most of them explicitly or implicitly contrast human action with God's action. The logic, which is well known in rabbinic writings,[72] is that found in Matt 7:11/Luke 11:13: If a human father knows to give good gifts to his children, how much more will the heavenly Father give good gifts? Contrast between two persons or entities (such as the contrast between the Two Builders) is a feature of many parables,[73] but "How much more" parables function to say that God's action far exceeds or is not at all like the person depicted in the parable.[74] They may not have explicit signals to warn that the parable functions to contrast human behavior with God's, but the context, the conclusion, or the nature of the parable usually leaves little doubt. An obvious example is the parable of the Unjust Judge, who is not like God at all. It is also possible for the contrast to be between human action and the action expected of God's people. (See the discussion of the Unjust Steward, pp. 401-19 below.)

What about Allegory?

I have not included Jülicher's fourth category, *allegory,* as a distinct kind of parable. This is the term that has caused horrendous debate. Typically an allegory is defined as a series of related metaphors,[75] and the parable of the Sower would be an obvious example. But life is never so simple, and in addition Jülicher thought allegories are obscure and need to be decoded. They are supposedly more obfuscating than revealing. Consequently, in biblical studies (but also in eighteenth- and nineteenth-century literary studies) allegory has frequently been viewed with disdain and suspicion. The claim is made that allegory says something other than what it means by placing pictures in front of reality, but *parable does the same thing.* Both are framed on the reality they seek to portray. The claim that other forms enhance understanding while allegory presupposes understanding is absurd. When people speak of allegory, they frequently refer to extreme examples like John Bunyan's *Pilgrim's Progress,* but allegories can be as varied as parables. Few people are even aware that *The Wizard of Oz* is an elaborate political allegory about conditions at the beginning of the twentieth century in the U.S.A., with "Oz" (the abbreviation for "ounce") and the yellow brick road both referring to the gold standard (which was debated at the time), the scarecrow representing the farmers, the tin man the industrial workers, and the cowardly lion reformers, especially William Jennings Bryan. It is a perfectly good story understandable in its own right, but both enjoyable and powerful when the lens of its intent is in place.

Tremendous effort has been expended trying to distinguish parable and allegory, but in the end we must admit that the effort is a *complete* failure, despite the gallons of ink expended. Among the most frequently repeated distinctions are Paul Ricoeur's assertion that allegory is a rhetorical procedure that can be eliminated once it has done its job, while metaphor (and parable) cannot be reduced to abstract language,[76] and Dan Via's assertion that the features in allegories are related directly to the outside and only loosely to each other, whereas features of parables relate first of all to each other internally and are not determined by events or ideas outside.[77] Such statements sound impressive until one reflects on them. Whether parables are incapable of being translated is debatable,[78] but they certainly can be explained, and allegory is no more liable to elimination after doing its job than parable. Nor can one show that allegory relates more externally while parable relates internally or that allegory is necessarily more obscure. A glance at *The Wizard of Oz* or any number of other "allegories" shows how little credence should be given to these assertions. The same holds true for other attempts to distinguish the two forms.[79] Jülicher's approach has been set aside,[80] but his disdain for allegory is still around.[81] Jesus does not need to be saved from allegory. Parables are allegorical, some more so than others. Parables refer outside themselves, or they — except for the single indirect stories — are not parables. If something is thought to stem from the early church, that must be determined on other grounds than that some feature is allegorical.

A number of scholars have no hesitation in describing Jesus' parables as allegories,[82] and keeping allegory as a category of parables is possible, if one so chooses, even if the category is confusing. On the other hand, literary theorists argue that allegory is not a genre at all but rather is a way of thinking.[83] Because no clear distinction can be made between allegory and parable and since all parables except example stories are allegorical to varying degrees,[84] I do not view allegory as a category of parables.

However, the allegorical features of parables *do not give license to allegorize.* The practice of turning parables into allegories that Jesus never intended must be resisted at every point. We seek the illocutionary intent of a parable, the communicative intent and purpose for which it was told. How this can be done is discussed below.

By way of summary, parables should be classified as *similitudes, interrogative parables, double indirect narrative parables, juridical parables (as a specific type of double indirect narrative parable), "How much more" parables, and single indirect parables* (see Appendix 5). All parables except the single indirect ones are metaphorical/allegorical in that they mirror a reality outside themselves. Similitudes and interrogative parables do not have developed plots; double indirect narrative parables, juridical parables, and single indirect parables all have developed plots. "How much more" parables may or may not have developed plots.

Characteristics of Jesus' Parables

1. *Jesus' parables are first of all brief,* even terse. Parables use no more words than necessary. They are as straightforward as they can be. B. Gerhardsson identifies fifty-five narrative *meshālim,* thirty-three of which (60%) have four verses or less and only nine of which (16%) have ten verses or more.[85] They range from one verse to twenty-two in length. Their brevity excludes unnecessary details — *usually.* Unnecessary people and descriptions are omitted, and motives are rarely treated. Questions we deem important are ignored. The descriptions of people are "thin descriptions," to use the language of narratologists. That is, little detail is given of any character, their appearance, history, or psychology so that one can actually picture the person. Except for Lazarus and Abraham in the parable of Lazarus and the Rich Man (Luke 16:19-31), all the *characters are anonymous.* Given this brevity, it is out of bounds to ask where the mother is in the parable of the Prodigal. Brevity also means that actions are omitted or compressed, leaving it to the reader to fill in the obvious. Note how the narrative of the parable of the Feast (Luke 14:16-24) is compressed between vv. 21 and 22; the hearer/reader must assume that the command given in v. 21b to invite the underprivileged is accomplished by the servant, who in v. 22 reports that he is ready for the next step.

2. *Parables are marked by simplicity and symmetry.* Never are more than two persons or groups together in the same scene.[86] We do not see the father relating to the prodigal and the elder brother at the same time but to each separately. The simplicity and symmetry of parables are evident in that they, like

folklore elsewhere, focus on two or three characters (or groups), even if a larger number is mentioned. Note again the parable of the Feast, which tells of a man who invited many people to a banquet, but the narrative mentions only three and treats them as if they were the entire list of guests. The descriptions of the characters and actions in parables often make use of balanced structures, contrasts, repetitions, and parallels so that patterns of symmetry are obvious. Note, for example, the symmetry in the parables of the Unforgiving Servant (Matt 18:23-35) and the Talents (Matt 25:14-30). Attention to symmetry is key in interpreting, but symmetry should not be forced onto parables.

3. *Jesus' parables focus mostly on humans.* Except for the Markan version of the Mustard Seed (4:30-32), even the parables comparing the kingdom to a seed include a human sowing the seed. On the surface Jesus' parables are not accounts describing God or the world of animals and nature. They are "narratives of normalcy"[87] and mirror the commonness of first-century Palestinian human life, the life of farmers, shepherds, servants and masters, women, fathers and sons, and occasionally kings. Their humanness makes them interesting in their own right, but by mirroring they seek to change behavior and create disciples. *Their main purpose is to goad people into response.*

4. *The parables are fictional descriptions taken from everyday life,* but they do *not* necessarily portray everyday events. Quite the contrary. While some are realistic, some are not.[88] A few may draw on historical events, but they do not depict true stories. Because of hyperbole and elements of surprise or improbability, parables often are *pseudo-realistic* and have elements that shock.[89] For example, it is unlikely that anyone in first-century Palestine would owe a 10,000 talent debt (millions of dollars) as in the parable of the Unforgiving Servant (Matt 18:23-35). Further, the events of the parable of the Workers in the Vineyard with its five times the owner goes out to hire are virtually impossible unless the vineyard is next door to the marketplace. However, the shock element of parables has been overemphasized so that all parables are assumed to be counterintuitive and "world shattering."[90] Yes, some shatter worlds, but many do not. Parables must not all be forced to function the same way.

5. *Parables are engaging;* they were told to create interest, and various schemes are used to draw hearers in and compel dealing with the issues at hand. Shock and surprising elements have already been mentioned. Parables also use soliloquy (especially in Luke), dialogue, exaggeration, and concrete details. Parables elicit thought and require decision. Often they require the hearer/reader to pass judgment on the events of the story and then require him or her to make a similar judgment about religious matters. Twenty-two of the parables start with a *question* such as "Who from you . . . ?" "What do you think?" or "How. . . ?"[91] Others have questions at the end of the story. Even

when explicit questions are not present, parables are intended to answer questions. *Finding the implied question a parable addresses is key in interpretation.* Often Jesus' parables come as a response to a statement someone else makes. The intent of parables is to force thought, usually new and unexpected thought, so as to gain insight and bring about response. A number of parables end with the statement "Let the person who has ears to hear hear" or something similar, which is a call to move past superficial thinking, to discern, and to understand the impact of the parable. Implicitly many parables oppose Jesus' opinion to that of his hearers. Not surprisingly, parables frequently spawn questions without giving hints for the answers. What would the good Samaritan do if he had come along while the robbers were still beating their victim? In this way parables — beyond their communicative intent — are tools for reflection and theology, but care should be taken, for this is also where the parables can be distorted.[92]

6. Since they frequently seek to reorient thought and behavior, in keeping with Jesus' teaching elsewhere *parables often contain elements of reversal.*[93] Not all parables implement reversal, but when they do, they are among the most powerful instruments for change that Jesus used. When parables cause reversal, they force unexpected decisions and associations. The tax collector is righteous, not the Pharisee; the Samaritan is neighbor, not the Jewish elite; David is the guilty party, not some terrible person anyone would condemn.

7. With their intent to bring about response and elements like reversal, *the crucial matter of parables is usually at the end,* which functions something like the punch line of a joke. Interpreters legitimately invoke "the rule of end stress" which requires that interpretations focus on the end of the parables. Of course, some parables are so short that this guideline is irrelevant, and the rule does not mean the rest of a parable may be ignored. The rule is marginally relevant — if at all — for parables set up as contrasts (like the Two Builders in Matt 7:24-27/ Luke 6:47-49) and is less pertinent for others (such as the interrogative parables). Each parable must be interpreted in its own right. Still, the rule of end stress is a good guideline.

The focus on the end of the parable raises the question of the legitimacy of the explanations that occur as clinching words at the end of parables, explanations frequently jettisoned by NT scholars. While some parables do not have explanations, many do. Explanations are both natural and frequently necessary because in many cases the analogy is not complete or clear until some indication of the referent is given. This is usually accomplished by statements beginning "Thus also . . ." *All* the story parables in the OT have an explanation either before or after, and such conclusions are regular features in rabbinic parables. Unless one thinks Jesus was a teller of conundra, justice must be done to the explanations as well. Particularly with polemical parables, the story has no barb until the referent is made clear. The only times someone would tell a polemical parable and leave the barb out would be if the teller thought the intent was obvious or the confrontation was too threatening to be explicit.

8. *Parables are told into a context.* Unlike Aesop's fables, Jesus' parables are not general stories with universal truths. At least partly they are framed on the reality they seek to show, or they cannot make their point.[94] They are addressed to quite specific contexts in the ministry of Jesus. This is also true of most rabbinic and Greco-Roman parables. Parables do not serve themselves; a parable is not told for its own purpose, but to serve a specific teaching purpose and to bring about change in people's beliefs and actions.[95] This raises one of the most significant and debated points about parable interpretation. To what degree is the context given by the Evangelists the proper framework for interpreting? Clearly the specific context for many parables has not been preserved, as the thematic arrangements (witness Matthew 13) and redactional work of the Evangelists show. For other parables quite specific contexts seem to have been preserved (witness the parable of the Wicked Tenants). We will discuss this problem later and also in connection with each individual parable, but my primary concern here is to underscore the *general* context of the ministry of Jesus in first-century Palestine. Jesus' parables may not legitimately be torn from that context and placed elsewhere.[96] To do so will not allow interpretation of *Jesus'* parables, nor allow hearing him, but *will make one a creator of a new parable with absconded materials.*

9. *Jesus' parables are theocentric.* I have already indicated that parables seek to change behavior and create disciples, but they do so by telling about God and his kingdom, the new reality God seeks to establish on earth. The attempts to deny that parables reference the kingdom are without basis. How much Jesus' own life and work are reflected in his parables is a matter of debate among exegetes and will be dealt with in connection with individual parables.[97] But while a few parables, such as the parable of the Wicked Tenants, may have christological reference, *most are not directly about Jesus.* They are about God, God's kingdom, and God's expectations for humans. Many parables are "monarchic"; i.e., they are dominated by the figure of a father, master, or king, who is generally an archetype of God. Some deny that these monarchic figures reference God,[98] but these attempts misunderstand how parables function, fail to do justice to the OT and Jewish context in which the parables were told, and render Jesus' parables lame and ineffective. The monarchic figures can easily be distorted, if one forgets that they appear in *parables,* but that does not change the fact of their pointing to God.

10. *Parables frequently allude to OT texts.* While Jesus' parables are not

exegetical in the way rabbinic parables are, some of them adapt OT themes, and, more than is recognized, a number of them address specific OT texts and ideas.[99]

11. *Most parables appear in larger collections of parables.* In addition, they are sometimes arranged as doublets (e.g., the Mustard Seed and the Leaven) or triplets (the parables of lostness in Luke 15 or the parables about Israel in Matt 21:28–22:14). Doublets and longer combinations strengthen and explore a theme by using two or more images to make the same or related points. For example, salt and light are both used to explain the character of discipleship (Matt 5:13-16). Such collections are paralleled frequently in rabbinic writings. The arrangements often appear to be the redactional work of the Evangelists, but some pairings likely stem from Jesus. In Luke a number of parables are set in a chiastic parallel by the way the "travel narrative" is arranged (e.g., the Friend at Midnight in 11:5-8 and the Unjust Judge in 18:1-8).

Besides this list of general characteristics, we must also recognize that there are characteristics specific to each of the Evangelists. The redactional tendencies of each Evangelist extend, of course, to their parables, so the themes of interest to each (such as Luke's concern for money) appear in his parables. The characteristics of Mark's parables are harder to identify since he has so few. The characteristics of parables in Luke are the easiest to identify. Luke shows a preference for soliloquy, for parables that begin with *anthrōpos tis* ("a certain man"), and for *tis ex hymōn* ("Who from you") parables. Goulder argues that Luke's parables are primarily imperative while Matthew's tend to be indicative, a distinction which is overdrawn, for several of Matthew's parables carry an imperatival emphasis.[100] Matthew's parables are judged by Goulder and others to be more allegorical, but much of this results from imposing allegory on Matthew that he probably never intended.[101] Matthew does tend to operate on a grander scale with regard to numbers and the social status of his characters, but gives less specific description of them than Luke does for his. Specific reference to the kingdom is less frequent with Luke's parables than with Mark and especially with Matthew.[102]

A good parable creates distance, provokes, and appeals.[103] By creating distance it gives the hearer/reader space to reconsider; one has no sense of needing to defend one's turf. By provoking the parable requires new channels of thought, and by appealing the parable seeks decisions that bring behavior into line with the teller's intent.

With this said, however, not all parables operate the same way. Parables have varying levels of opacity; i.e., the ease with which one sees their lens-like character varies from parable to parable. Some are diaphanous and the hearer/reader knows easily a given story is a lens, and the reality it shows is obvious from the first. This is most often the case when the teller and the hearers share considerable agreement or when the parable is a prophetic accusation.[104] The more one is trying to make a strong point, the more likely the reality is to show through. Ezekiel condemns the harlotry of the two sisters Oholah and Oholibah for 49 verses (ch. 23), but already in v. 4 they are explicitly identified as Israel and Judah. In Hosea 2 the prophet's wife Gomer is a thin veil for Baal-serving Israel.[105] Obviously such examples render absurd any desire to delete anything in a parable with external reference. The more a parable is a *prophetic* instrument the more we should expect the reality to show through. Matthew's parable of the Wedding Feast (22:1-14) is an example of a diaphanous parable. One knows quickly that this cannot be a story of an actual wedding; rather it depicts the failure of Israel. To treat it as if it were a realistic picture is a huge distortion. Other parables are surreptitious; they do not reveal their target until self-incriminating judgments have been made. Then, a *nimshal* is added, an explanation that hammers home the intent. Nathan's parable to David (2 Sam 12:1-12) and the parable of the Wicked Tenants (Matt 21:33-46 and parallels) are classic examples. Still other parables are neither diaphanous nor surreptitious; they merely hold forth an analogy that may or may not be clear until the account is completed. Some in their present forms are no longer clear and are heavily debated. The Laborers in the Vineyard (Matt 20:1-16), for example, does not yield itself to easy explanation. Clearly each parable must be analyzed in its own right to determine how it functions.

Distribution of the Parables

The parables make up about thirty-five percent of Jesus' teaching in the Synoptics. If one accepts the four-source theory of Synoptic origins, parables make up about sixteen percent of Mark, twenty-nine percent of Q, forty-three percent of M, and fifty-two percent of L. There is little agreement about the number of parables, with estimates ranging from thirty-seven to sixty-five. Determination depends on how one defines "parable," on judgments about specific forms, and on whether similar parables such as those of the Talents and of the Pounds are one parable or two.[106] I treat thirty-three parables (counting the parables of the Talents and of the Pounds separately and the Feast and the Wedding Banquet separately). Obviously there are other parabolic sayings and a few short parables that I have chosen not to treat,[107] partly because they seem obvious enough and partly because of space.

In the technical sense there are no parables in John. There are *meshalim* such as the Door to the Sheepfold or the Good Shepherd, but nothing like the

Synoptic similitudes, double or single indirect narratives, juridical parables, or interrogative parables. John does not use the word *parabolē*, but he does use *paroimia*, often translated as "proverb" or "dark saying," in 10:6 and 16:25 (twice) and 29. In fact, the word *parabolē* does not occur in the NT outside the Synoptic Gospels except in Heb 9:9 and 11:19, where it has the meanings "illustration" and "figure" respectively.

There are relatively few parables in Mark. He records only four narrative parables, the first three of which are in a collection of parables in ch. 4: the Sower, the Seed Growing Secretly (unique to Mark), and the Mustard Seed. Then in ch. 12 he has the parable of the Wicked Tenants. Some also count the Doorkeeper in 13:34-37 and the Fig Tree in 13:28-29.

Of Mark's parables Matthew and Luke have the Sower, the Mustard Seed, the Wicked Tenants, and the Fig Tree. Matthew and Luke also have a few parables in common that are not in Mark. Both have the Leaven, the Lost Sheep, the Two Builders, the Faithful and Unfaithful Servants, the Thief, and the Children in the Market. Both also have parables of refused invitations to a banquet and of servants entrusted with money, but whether these accounts are parallels or merely similar stories is debated.

For the rest of the parables, ten are unique to Matthew and eighteen are unique to Luke. About two-thirds of the parables are in Luke. Matthew's parables mostly appear in chs. 13, 18, 20–22, and 24–25 and are thematically arranged. Most of Luke's parables appear in chs. 10–20 and are thematically arranged within the travel narrative. A good case can be made for a chiastic arrangement of Luke's travel narrative, and many accept that Luke had a parable source from which he adapted his material.[108]

The *Gospel of Thomas* has parallels to eleven of the Synoptic parables, nine of which are not debated: the Sower (logion 9), the Mustard Seed (logion 20), the Weeds (logion 57), the Rich Man (logion 63), the Banquet (logion 64), the Wicked Tenants (logion 65), the Pearl (logion 76), the Leaven (logion 96), and the Lost Sheep (logion 107). The Wise Fisherman (logion 8) and the Hidden Treasure (logion 109) are probably parallels to the Synoptic counterparts, but they diverge enough that some see them as independent and previously unknown parables. *Gos. Thom.* version of these eleven is given in the discussion of individual parables, and each will be assessed in the appropriate context. In addition, *Gos. Thom.* has three previously unknown parables: the Little Children in a Field (logion 21a), A Woman Carrying a Jar of Meal (logion 97), and A Killer's Test (logion 98).[109] Note that both *Gos. Thom.* 1–2 and *Apocryphon of James* 1:9–2:39 stress the secret and esoteric nature of the contents of their work. *Apoc. Jas.* also reports sayings supposedly from the risen Christ, mentions seven (or possibly six) parables by name, presumably all known from the Synoptics,[110] and records three previously unknown parables: the Date Palm (7:24-35), the Grain of Wheat (8:16-28), and the Ear of Grain (12:22-30).[111]

For all intents and purposes, the early church did not tell parables, not in the canonical material and not in the early or later writings after the apostolic period. The closest accounts similar to parables are the long allegorical treatments in the *Shepherd* of Hermas, but they are not close to Jesus' parables, even though they use the word *parabolē* and have occasional similarities. (See pp. 51-53 below.) After the resurrection of Jesus the parabolic mode, which is a prophetic mode, appears to have been dropped in favor of more direct avenues of gospel proclamation.

How Should Parables Be Interpreted?

There have been those who said parables do not need to be or cannot be interpreted.[112] Of course, these same people write books explaining the parables. Jülicher argued that parables do not need to be interpreted because they are literal[113] language and say what they mean. But no communication is self-interpreting, and Jülicher's comments are at best an exaggeration. Those who argue that parables cannot be interpreted sometimes see parables as "language events"[114] or have been impacted by modern reader-oriented approaches. There is validity in the focus on parables as language events that create new situations, and there is truth in saying that parables are not reducible to meaning and must be experienced. They cannot be abstracted and then, with meaning in hand, left behind. But no one explaining the parables wants to leave them behind. Instead, we seek to make them fully present. R. Stein points out that all language has both referential and commissive/affective dimensions.[115] All language, parables included, *must* be interpreted, and especially the referential aspects of parables can be explained in other ways, but the affective aspects, while they can be described, need to be felt.[116]

The primary stance in interpreting is the *willingness to hear and respond appropriately,* a point made specifically by the parable of the Sower, but even the willingness to hear does not guarantee objectivity and right hearing. I will be the first to grant that objectivity when interpreting parables is difficult. Parables are not lists of information; they are stories, but they may not be the stories we think they are. Each must be approached and dealt with on its own grounds, not with some predetermined view as to what parables must look like and do. Stories create worlds. By reading a story we, at least temporarily, inhabit that world. If we bring too much of ourselves into that world, we reshape it and rearrange its landscape. But if we do that, we have created a world other than what the story portrays. Further, parables mirror pieces of reality and sometimes mirror the lives and histories of their readers. They may contain a plot we have already lived. They reveal us and at the same time call us to embrace a plot in order to be taken up in the plot (or, if negative, to choose another plot). We are asked not to be objective and distant but to embody the parable's intent.

After this emphasis on the role of hearing, we should state the obvious fact that all the regular practices for good interpretation of texts are in force when interpreting parables:

1. *Analyze each parable thoroughly.* To state the obvious, if it appears in more than one Gospel, do a comparative analysis of the various accounts. Pay particular attention to the structure of the parable and the development of its thought. Pay close attention to symmetry or parallelism between various components.

2. *Listen to the parable without presupposition as to its form or meaning.* No attempt should be made to force symmetry on the parables or to assume that a parable must conform to some theory of parables or must teach a particular theology.

3. *Remember that Jesus' parables were oral instruments in a largely oral culture.* Most of them would have been told numerous times, in various contexts, and with small and sometimes not so small variations. Everyone admits this, but few do it justice. Parables would have been constructed with similar features, themes, and formats. They would also often have been repeated orally among Christians, again with variations. Therefore, any attempt to reconstruct the original version of a parable is misguided. Any thought of slavish literary dependence as the only way to account for Synoptic relations is ill-informed.[117] E.g., it is difficult to believe that the first time Matthew encountered the parable of the Sower was when he read it in Mark — if indeed he used Mark.

4. *If we are after the intent of Jesus, we must seek to hear a parable as Jesus' Palestinian hearers would have heard it.*[118] Any interpretation that does not breathe the air of the first century cannot be correct. That requires listening in a context not our own and presumes some familiarity with that context. We cannot archaize ourselves, but we can be sensitive enough to the biblical culture to understand what we read. For this reason analysis of each parable in this book will include treatment of cultural factors pertinent for understanding. Especially important will be ideas and metaphors from the OT and Jewish religious life. Jesus was not the first Jew to tell parables. He may have drawn on a common fund of parables in use among Jewish teachers. Although there are significant problems in using the rabbinic materials, rabbinic parables can provide both cultural insight and understanding of how parables function. (See the next chapter.)

25

5. Note how each parable and its redactional shaping fit with the purpose and plan of each Evangelist. This will include looking for help in the context in which a parable appears, but with the recognition that the specific context of many of the parables has not been preserved. The parables are stories used twice — once by Jesus and then again by the Evangelists. They are stories within larger stories, parables woven into the Gospel narratives. The narratives provide an interpretive field within which both the parables and the larger narrative shed light on each other.[119] The parables were remembered because of their relevance in understanding the larger story. We must read stereoscopically for both the intent of Jesus and the intent of the Evangelists. Those intents are not identical, but if they are not coordinate or at least reconcilable, we have no hope of understanding Jesus.

Such practices are givens and apply to any text in the Gospels, but guidelines specific to parables are both more instructive and more critical:

6. Determine specifically the function of the story in the teaching of Jesus. This is the crux of the matter, and several issues need to be addressed. I start with closer attention to the phrase "in the teaching of Jesus" — the context of the parables. If we cut the parables out of the context of Jesus' teaching, we can make them mean anything, which is precisely what has happened with a number of studies.[120] While the specific context of many parables has not been preserved, the general context in the teaching of Jesus has. I think we must insist upon the *general* context of Jesus, not existential thought, not the plight of the poor — as pained as I am with this tragedy, not Freudian psychology, or any of the number of other contexts into which Jesus' parables have been placed. Context is a determiner of meaning — in the end the only determiner of meaning, for words themselves have only possible meanings apart from context. If the goal is to hear the voice of Jesus, some other context cannot work. If we place parables in contexts of our choosing, we change them into something other than Jesus' communicative intent. If the general context in which parables have been placed is not to be trusted, then we should give up ever hoping to understand them.

We must interpret each parable as a whole to determine *how the analogy works.* If meaning is the determination of, and value placed on, a set of relations,[121] parables provide a picture that enables — sometimes forces — an understanding of the relations in question, the relations of Jesus' and his contemporaries to God and God's purposes. Through those relations we understand the realities pertaining to our own relations with God and God's purposes. The crucial issue is how much of the parable is pertinent. There may be more than one climax and more than one point of comparison. Jülicher's limits do not work.[122] But recognizing multiple relevant features is *no* license to allegorize. Give up the need to find allegorical correspondences. The concern in parable interpretation is not "What does this element stand for?" or "How many correspondences are there?" even though correspondences may exist and may be identified. With some parables (e.g., the Unjust Steward in Luke 16:1-9) attempts to find correspondences for the features lead to ruin.[123] The only reason to identify correspondences is to know to what the analogy refers. Parables, however, are *not* one-for-one analogies. They picture actual realities *partly,* but are intended to make people think and question and often do so through hyperbole, surprise, and *inexactness.*[124] A point in a parable may be intended, *not* to mirror theological realities, but to force reflection and analysis. For example, God does not have torturers (Matt 18:34), nor should we conclude that God is harsh and reaps where he did not sow (Matt 25:24/Luke 19:21). Both statements serve as hyperbolic warnings. Sometimes there is unevenness between parable and reality, both with Jesus' parables and those of rabbis. Sometimes the reality is hidden behind the parable, and sometimes the reality seems almost in front of the parable. Such differences are to be expected. Correspondences may line up exactly, or they may be part of the parable's veiling to deceive us into the truth. In Nathan's parable to David, the rich and poor men and the sheep correspond to David, Uriah, and Bathsheba, but it is Uriah who dies, not Bathsheba.[125]

Analogies have correspondences by necessity, but understanding parables results usually from obvious givens in the analogy or from a flash of insight given in a revealing statement (such as Nathan's "You are the man"), not from deducing correspondences. The more you spend time trying to deduce correspondences the more likely you will miss the force of the parable. The power of a parable is in the moment when the obvious givens of the analogy or insight about the analogy effects transference. At such moments correspondences are obvious. David did not deduce the correspondences of Nathan's parable until Nathan forced the insight. The same is the case even with parables that are not juridical or parables that do not have explicit explanations.

Parables have correspondences, but they have much more besides. They also have features that convey significance even though they do not "stand for something." The swine in the parable of the Prodigal Son do not stand for some "fact" in life but are mentioned to express the depths to which the boy had sunk. Some features of a parable, because of common metaphorical associations, set off resonances that may be clarifying *or* veiling, depending on the purpose of the story. Parables about vineyards raise the expectation that the subject is God and God's people, but the outcome is often different from what was expected.

John Sider rightly says that the ability to determine symbolic significance in parables is a grace that lies beyond rules, but he also offers criteria for making decisions about the significance of features in parables. A discussion of such criteria, however, applies in most cases only to double indirect narrative parables, not to similitudes, interrogative parables, and single indirect parables. Sider's criteria are:[126]

> the criterion of proportion: In general, the more central a feature is, the more likely it is to be symbolic; the more marginal, the less likely.
> the criterion of similarity: If the criterion of dissimilarity seeks to find what is unique to Jesus, a criterion of similarity focuses on symbolic possibilities that cannot be easily denied to Jesus because they are so characteristic of his message.
> the criterion of indispensability: Is the element required to make the story work or merely "part of the machinery" of the story? Is the element so central or unusual that it must have symbolic significance?
> the criterion of analogy: Knowledge of part of the analogy sheds light on other elements of the analogy. If the Great Supper is eschatological, the coherence of the picture sheds light on the identity of the characters in the story.

I would only caution that these criteria are easily open to abuse. Determining how an analogy functions does not follow some formula or list of rules. It requires the understanding and intuition to discern how language functions in a given context, i.e., how words convey the significance of the sets of relations being depicted. I do not think we can say a parable has one point per main character as C. Blomberg does;[127] rather, each parable must be allowed to function as it will and to make as many points as it wishes in its own context.

We will continually encounter the question of how much of a given parable has metaphorical significance. *The key is knowing when to stop interpreting.* As with metaphor, *parable interpretation is about understanding the limits — and the significance — of the analogy.* Wendell Berry comments with regard to metaphor, "But the legitimacy of a metaphor depends upon our understanding of its limits. . . . When a metaphor is construed as an equation, it is out of control; when it is construed as an identity, it is preposterous."[128] This is precisely the case with parables, but interpreters want them to be theological identities — complete pictures of theology. Over and over parables have been forced to address ideas not their concern or critiqued because they do not. No single parable does everything, not even everything about a given topic. This insensitivity to the limits of analogy invariably leads to ruin in understanding. Parables do not have equal signs making them identical to the reality they portray. Parables only partially overlap the realities they seek to reveal.

We must do justice to both the strength and limitations of metaphors and parables.[129] Metaphors convey pictures that abstract language cannot rival. Because of their strength they are often used for hyperbole. They are not invitations for us to think of all the possible meanings that could apply (as has often happened with the statement "You are the salt of the earth"). They are invitations to understand them within their set of relations. Some metaphorical ideas are at the heart of the parables in which they occur — such as the relation of master and slave; some are peripheral and used for effect rather than to convey precise theological information. For example, we surely should not think that in the kingdom Christians will literally be placed over cities (in Luke 19:17 and 19) or that God dichotomizes people (Matt 24:51/Luke 12:46).

Determining the function of a parable also entails the realization that introductions such as "The kingdom is like a man" (or a woman or seed, etc.) do not compare the kingdom to the characters or objects but *to the whole process of the narration.* E.g., the kingdom is not compared to a mustard seed but to what happens in the whole process of this "smallest seed" being planted and growing quite large. We will see over and over that the whole narrated process is in view, not just the first item mentioned.[130]

In short, some parables make one point, and some make several points. A formulaic approach to parable interpretation, as for all biblical studies, just does not work. One must discern from context the intent of the analogy.

7. *Interpret what is given, not what is omitted. Any attempt to interpret a parable based on what is not there is almost certainly wrong.* All parables — as all other written material — have gaps, jumps that the author feels are safe to make without loss of understanding. The more attention one gives to what is not there without evidence that the author intended some conclusion to be drawn the more one is almost certainly wrong. Note the gap between Luke 15:21 and 22. The father ran out to meet the son and, after the son's statement, gave a command to the servants. Did servants run out with him, or before the request have the father and son returned to the house? From the teller's perspective it does not matter, and to give attention to such a detail would be pedantic and diminish the drama. What matters is the meeting and the command to start the celebration.

8. *Do not impose real time on parable time.* The narrative time of parables is not real time chronology, and the effort to make it so almost certainly distorts. Note the parable of the Wedding Feast in Matt 22:1-14 or the Banquet in Luke 14:15-24. The former has an extended chronology that allows a war in the middle of a feast, apparently without the food getting cold, and the latter has a truncated chronology that assumes that the servant has gone out, done as instructed, and returned. The attempt to lay the real chronology of Jesus or the church's mission on either of these parables creates enormous problems, as in the suggestion that the invitation to the poor only occurs after the wealthy have

declined.[131] Also, there is no "logical time" that extends beyond the narrative time of the parable. When the parable is over, the narrative time is over. Thus to ask about events outside the story time — such as asking what the pearl merchant did after he sold all he owned and bought the one pearl[132] — destroys the parable and demonstrates misunderstanding about how analogies and parables work.

9. *Pay particular attention to the rule of end stress.* Some parables have crucial material spread over the parable, such as the parables of the Sower and of the Wicked Tenants. Even with those, however, the most important material is at the end. Some parables are so short that it is meaningless to speak of the rule of end stress, but this guideline is still worth heeding. For most parables what comes at the end is the clinching indicator of intent. How this relates to critical concerns about the authenticity of conclusions to the parables is treated below (see pp. 33-35).

10. *Note where the teaching of the parables intersects with the teaching of Jesus elsewhere.* This extremely important guideline is merely a variation of the *criteria of multiple attestation and coherence,* but it will help prevent errors in interpretation. If you cannot validate the teaching you think is in the parable from nonparabolic material elsewhere in the Gospels, you are almost certainly wrong.[133] Some aspects of Jesus' teaching do not appear in the parables. The parables do not address sabbath-keeping, food laws, miracles, exorcisms, the suffering disciples can expect,[134] the cross (though it is mirrored in the Wicked Tenants), or the resurrection. They do not show Jesus' teaching on nonretaliation, divorce, oaths, or faith (at least directly), but it seems that all the subjects addressed in the parables are in some measure addressed in nonparabolic material.

11. *Determine the theological intent and significance of the parable.* This does *not* assume that parables or metaphors may be reduced to literal speech without loss of cognitive content or affective force. It does assume that the same teaching can be presented in different formats and especially that parables are not the focus of their own telling. They are told to teach and convince about another and more important reality. They are referential, and they are useless if we do not determine what they refer to, what they teach, and what we should do with such knowledge. While some have tried to deny that they are referential, others have tried to limit their theological significance, saying sometimes explicitly that we cannot do theology from parables,[135] which if taken absolutely would be an intolerable conclusion. The parables are a different kind of theological argument from what one finds in Romans, but they are *just as theologically relevant.* Without them we would be theologically impoverished. I have argued against seeing parables as straight-line pictures of theological reality. They are mirrors of reality — angled at different degrees — designed often

to shock and arrest and move people to response. For example, the harshness of some parables of judgment (e.g., Matt 18:34 or 24:51) is offensive and troublesome to some, but these parables are not realistic descriptions of judgment. Rather, they warn about the reality and seriousness of judgment. The parables of Jesus do not reveal the whole of Christian theology by any means. Without the cross and resurrection Christian theology would not exist. However, the parables provide material for a compelling and convincing picture of Jesus' teaching on the kingdom, his understanding of God, and the kind of life expected of his disciples, whether they live in the first or the twenty-first century. The theology of these stories merits our investment in them. It is one thing to ask what some feature in a parable stands for, as if it were to be allegorized, but it is quite another to ask what the elements of the parable signify for the teller. For example, the far country or other features in the parable of the Prodigal do not stand for some theological reality, but they are significant in describing the *theological* issues the parable addresses. No formula exists for determining whether an element is theologically significant. That will have to be determined from the whole of the parable and the whole of Jesus' teaching.

NT Criticism — Assumptions and Hesitations, Method and Procedure

I am not proposing a new theory of parable interpretation, but my approach is different from that taken in a number of recent studies of parables. Several comments regarding issues pertaining to technical NT studies may assist in understanding the analysis of individual parables that follows.

With regard to the authenticity of the parables, virtually everyone grants that they are the surest bedrock we have of Jesus' teaching.[136] Still, authenticity will be an issue for a number of parables because of assumptions some make about the nature of the Gospel material, about the form of parables, or their personal dislike for the theology of certain parables. Where authenticity is an issue for a specific parable, it will be discussed. I am convinced, however, that the parables are indeed the surest place where we have access to Jesus' teaching. As indicated earlier, as far as we can tell, the early church hardly ever told parables.[137] Parables fit Jesus' prophetic stance, and the teaching in the parables can be corroborated in nonparabolic material.

More problematic is the attempt of some scholars to reconstruct earlier, simpler versions of the parables than those preserved by the Evangelists. Without question the Evangelists have shaped their material, as can be seen easily in comparisons of parallel accounts. They have placed the parables in their narratives for theological and rhetorical effect. They have nuanced the wording to assist the reader in understanding the intent of Jesus or to emphasize the significance of his teaching. The original contexts have sometimes not been preserved. Unfortunately, however, the reconstructions of parables offered to us by NT scholars *never* have sufficient basis to inspire confidence. They convince only a few at best and never have sufficient breadth to become the basis of ethical thinking or the authority to instruct the church or those seeking to understand Jesus. These reconstructions are not so much interpretations of the parables as they are rewritings of the parables as someone thinks they should have been, and in this they tend to reveal more about their proposers than about the parables of Jesus. Reconstructions pretty well permit any conclusion desired. As U. Luz comments, "It is amazing what can be surmised with a hypothetically reconstructed Jesus text!"[138] Several scholars with quite different views have bypassed attempts at reconstruction and seek to understand the broader picture painted by the Gospels.[139]

Several very questionable assumptions stand behind reconstruction attempts:

that there was "an original" form,
that items with allegorical significance were probably added,
that the handing on of traditional material follows certain "laws" so that the shorter is earlier, the more detailed is later, etc.,
that stylistic traits of the Evangelists demonstrate the origin of the material,[140]
that the parables can be read as mirror images of what was happening in the Evangelists' communities, i.e., indirect communication mirroring the church rather than direct communication from Jesus, and
that the Evangelists' contexts, the introductions and conclusions of parables, and interpretations of the parables may be dismissed.

These assumptions require some comment, but none of them is a valid basis for reconstructing parables. There are a few parables so contextually fixed (such as the Wicked Tenants and the Two Debtors) that they *may* have been told only once, but most parables would have been told numerous times with slight variations. The idea of reconstructing an original is not even a legitimate goal, and the more one takes seriously the nature of oral tradition, the less one can think of reconstructing an original. It will not do either to think of reconstructing only the originating structure,[141] for the same illegitimate assumptions are at play, and the versions offered are subjective, truncated, and colorless, quite unlike anything Jesus likely told — at least as far as the evidence indicates.

I have said enough about parables having correspondences and allegorical features that it is clear no one should reject a feature of Jesus' parables because it has allegorical significance. If Jesus' figures did not bear some relation to reality, he would have no reason to use them. Parables do function as lenses onto another reality, and without question more than one point of comparison may exist between story and reality. Many of Jesus' images were stock metaphors from the OT and Judaism (e.g., a vineyard, servants, masters, etc.). No cause for concern with allegorical features should exist unless the feature in question could not have been used by Jesus. Further, those most eager to reject allegorical features quite regularly reinsert them in interpretation.[142]

E. P. Sanders long ago dispelled the notion that there were fixed laws of tradition so that earlier forms could be discovered.[143] With regard to parables, Jeremias's "ten principles of transformation" are highly debatable.[144] Only the translation of parables from Aramaic into Greek, the adaptation at times to Hellenistic culture, and to some degree the collecting of parables thematically are obvious and substantive, but these are issues required for communication. Even with these, however, there is debate about specifics.

Evidence of an Evangelist's style is *not* a determiner of origin or validity, and in fact we would be shocked if an Evangelist's style did not show through. Some parables may reveal an Evangelist's hand more than others, but that does not tell us whether or not he has faithfully rendered the content and intent of Jesus' telling. If, as virtually anyone studying the Gospels grants, we do not have the *ipsissima verba*, the very words of Jesus, why should we be surprised at evidence of the shaping of the material? Shaping of the material does not necessarily mean distortion of it.

That the parables mirror the situation of the Evangelists' communities is a gratuitous assumption. I find it unlikely that any of the Gospels was written for a specific local community or serves *primarily* to address the problems of such a community. The Gospels are not veiled histories of Christian churches or indirect communication addressing the problems of a local community. They are direct communication written for a broad audience[145] to convey material about the teaching and life of Jesus in order to create followers of Jesus. Again to focus on oral tradition, the more we do justice to oral tradition, the less we focus on the Gospels as windows on Christian communities. The theological and parenetic concerns of the Evangelists are real, of course, but no evidence shows that those concerns were dictated by the conditions of local or even regional churches.

Most important of all is the question concerning the introductions, conclusions, and interpretations of the parables. The tendency of some scholars to lop off introductions, conclusions, and explanations as standard operating procedure is unacceptable. Repeatedly scholars have reduced the artful stories in the Gospels to colorless plot structures with meanings so banal that one wonders why they would have ever been told.[146] The parables of Jesus are not like Aesop's fables, which were collected by themselves virtually without order and were told for entertainment and general instruction in wisdom. Jesus' parables serve a larger and prophetic purpose within a comprehensive narrative scheme to engage people with God's kingdom. Since Jesus' parables were told into a context, the Evangelists' situating them within that general context and showing how they relate to it are both natural and necessary. The introductions, whether based on a comment from Jesus or part of the narrative, provide a framework for understanding. Many of the introductions are stereotypical and have exact parallels in rabbinic material. Each parable will have to be analyzed individually to determine whether the introduction and also any conclusion and interpretation express Jesus' intent or reveal a misapplication of the parable by the Evangelists. Since the Evangelists have arranged their material thematically, a change in emphasis or audience is possible and has been argued for parables such as the Workers in the Vineyard (Matt 20:1-16) and the Unjust Judge (Luke 18:1-8). Both are difficult parables. At least for most of the parables though, the context provided by the Evangelists is not a distortion but the necessary help needed to understand them. My concern is *not* for a *specific* historical context but the proper frame of reference within Jesus' ministry for understanding the specific parable.

Only three parables are provided a detailed explanation in which the features of the account are assigned allegorical significance: the Sower, the Wheat and the Weeds, and the Net. Some parables are left without an explanatory conclusion, a *nimshal* making explicit the nature of the analogy. They are either clear enough without a *nimshal* or are intended to illicit thought so that in effect the reader supplies the *nimshal* (e.g., the Prodigal Son, Luke 15:32). Other parables — following OT, apocalyptic, and rabbinic forms — include a *nimshal*, usually introduced with "thus" (*houtōs*, e.g., Matt 18:35) or "I say to you" (e.g., the Lost Sheep, Luke 15:7). Juridical parables by their very nature virtually require a *nimshal*. It may well be that parables that did not need a *nimshal* when originally told by Jesus required one when placed by the Evangelists in a narrative (or vice versa). If a *nimshal* has been provided, it may have been to emphasize Jesus' intent, but the only serious question regarding any *nimshal* is whether it fits the purpose of the parable. The important fact is that many parables *need* conclusions and explanations to make their point.[147] All the OT parables either have a concluding explanation or an introduction that explains the analogy at the beginning. Apocalyptic parables are often framed to be mysteries until an explanation is given.[148] Greco-Roman parables have explanations, and rabbinic parables often have lengthy explanations detailing the intent of the analogy, as even a casual glance shows. To argue that Jesus' parables do not need interpretation or that the interpretations are later additions shows a bias against reality and argues against everything discerned about parables elsewhere.[149]

We do not have the *ipsissima verba* of Jesus, nor should we expect them, and attempted reconstructions are not going to supply them. James Dunn is right; the only Jesus accessible to us is the remembered Jesus, Jesus as he impacted his disciples.[150] Dunn's position is reminiscent of Martin Kähler's: the only Jesus that exists is the historic, biblical Christ.[151] Anything else is a figment of the imagination. This is not to side with those who would deemphasize the historical analysis of Jesus, but it is a recognition of the nature of our documents.

None of these comments is intended to cut short the investigation. Each parable has to be analyzed in its own right with regard to form and content, redactional shaping, fit with its context, or any other critical question that emerges in the course of investigation, and the following pages seek to give that kind of attention to each parable treated. Theories about which account of a parable is the earliest must be determined from an analysis of the accounts, not from any theory of Synoptic relations and certainly not from a theory of an early date for *Gos. Thom.* The "two-document" hypothesis may be correct, but I am not convinced, and I do not want a theory about the text to determine analysis of the text. The places where people argue Matthew and Luke used different versions of Mark and Q or a version of Mark that we do not have[152] do not instill confidence. The picture may be — and I think is — much more complicated than introductions to NT study imply. I am convinced that *Gos. Thom.* originated in the second century as a product of secondary orality. It is not directly dependent on any of the canonical Gospels, but it is dependent on the canonical Gospels tradition, which in large part would have circulated orally.[153] But a theory of origins does not resolve the issue. Any Gospel, no matter how late, conceivably could preserve the earliest account of a parable, and the only solution is analysis of each parable and its issues. That analysis will follow after an investigation of parables in the ancient world.

Parables in the Ancient World

Jesus was not the first person to tell parables, and despite his originality and creativity, the forms he used were not new.[1] Parables of various types are known in virtually all cultures and appear in various kinds of literature. The oldest parable-like or parabolic material of which I am aware is from about the twenty-fourth century B.C.,[2] but older examples may exist. To some degree Christian and Jewish scholars have been guilty of provincialism and cultural imperialism in studying the parables, for often they have ignored or downplayed parables from other contexts. As important as rabbinic parables are, we need a much broader field of vision in analyzing parables similar to those of Jesus. Parabolic speech is a common human way of thinking, known in all cultures. Buddhist and Chinese parables especially had a wide influence. The Aesopic fables of the Greek world are clearly similar, even if told for different purposes and even if *usually* about plants and animals. In fact, A. Jülicher categorized Jesus' narrative parables as fables.[3] The differences are obvious, but one is dealing with the same process of thought. These stories did not suddenly grow on Greek soil either, as the collectors of Aesop's fables were aware, for they themselves point to a "Syrian" origin.[4] Some scholars suggest influence from Buddhist stories on Aesop's fables and rabbinic parables.[5]

But, if parabolic thinking is pervasive in all cultures, as far as we know no one prior to Jesus used parables as consistently, creatively, and effectively as he did. Nor has anyone since, but that is not to ignore or detract from the value of others who used the parabolic method, whether Ahiqar, Jewish rabbis, Epictetus, Blaise Pascal, Søren Kierkegaard, or a host of others in various cultures and times. We cannot deal with parables in general, but we do need to survey the religious and cultural contexts pertinent to studying Jesus' parables, and that includes the OT, early Jewish writings, the Greco-Roman context, the early church, and later Jewish writings.

The Old Testament

The primary influence on Jesus' use of parables is the OT. The form of Jesus' parables, the parabolic way of thinking, the images used, and the use of parables in wisdom literature and especially as prophetic instruments all point in that direction.[6] This obvious source for Jesus has often been undervalued,[7] but we have no evidence of other sources influencing him or of other parables prior to Jesus demonstrating anything close to his use. We will see that there are related forms, but outside the OT not much is really close to the form of Jesus' parables. Narrative parables do not occur in the Dead Sea Scrolls, nor do they appear in the Apocrypha and Pseudepigrapha that predate the ministry of Jesus. If we follow Jacob Neusner in saying "what we cannot show, we do not know," we must be much more cautious about merely latching onto rabbinic parables as the key to understanding Jesus,[8] as important as the rabbinic parables may be. Further, to focus merely on the rabbinic writings ignores the larger question of the relation of the parables of Jesus and the rabbis to similar types of discourse in virtually every culture. From where did the rabbis develop the procedure? For them, too, whatever else is involved, the OT was a primary source.

Without neglecting later Jewish writings and the culture of the first century and without diminishing the creativity and uniqueness with which Jesus taught, the one sure direct influence on him was the OT. If much of his thought and the evidence substantiating his preaching came from the OT, it should occasion no surprise that his method and way of thinking are influenced by it as well. Closer analysis of *mashal* and of OT parabolic forms offers crucial insight for understanding Jesus' parables.

We have already noted the breadth of the Hebrew word *mashal*.[9] The older Brown, Driver, and Briggs lexicon actually lists three different verbs spelled *mashal*: "to be like," "to use a proverb or parable," and "to rule."[10] Some trace all three ideas back to one common word, but most see two distinct and unrelated verbs, coincidentally spelled the same way, one meaning "to be like," which was adapted to refer to proverbial speech, and the second meaning "to rule."[11]

Even if we exclude "to rule" as from an unrelated word, *mashal* still covers a wide semantic range. (See Appendix 2, p. 570, below for a list of occurrences.) The seventeen occurrences of the verb form all fall easily into two categories:

seven (all in Psalms, Job, and Isaiah) that involve a comparison, such as Ps 28:1 ("I will be like those who go down to the pit"), and ten (Num 21:27; Job 17:6;[12] and eight in Ezekiel) that refer to speaking parables or proverbs, such as Ezek 16:44 ("Everyone will quote this proverb"). The noun form occurs forty-one times, and here the meanings proliferate. The most frequent reference is to a proverb, such as "Is Saul also among the prophets" (1 Sam 10:12) or "Out of the wicked comes forth wickedness" (1 Sam 24:13[14]). The title of the book of Proverbs *(mishle Shelomoh)* uses the plural construct form of *mashal.* In Prov 1:6 the wise man is said to be able to understand a proverb *(mashal),* a figure, sayings of the wise, and their riddles.[13]

Mashal can also refer to a "taunt" or "byword," such as the taunt against the king of Babylon "How the oppressor has ceased!" (Isa 14:4) or the accusing taunt "Woe to him who increases that which is not his" (Hab 2:6).[14] Related are references to a "lament," such as "We are utterly ruined" (Mic 2:4). In Ezek 14:8 God's punishment of idolators makes such people a *mashal* and "sign," symbols of the error of their ways. Unexpectedly, *mashal* can refer to Balaam's oracles (Num 23:7)[15] or to the extended discourses of Job (27:1 and 29:1). In Pss 49:4[5]; 78:2; and Ezek 17:2 *mashal* appears in parallelism opposite "riddle" *(ḥidah).* However, *mashal* is *not* used of the stories that are most similar to Jesus' parables, such as Nathan's parable to David (2 Sam 12:1-7). On the other hand, Ezekiel does use it of longer forms such as an elaborate allegory (17:2-10, the Eagle and the Vine), a prophecy (20:44-49 [21:1-5], the Devouring Fire), and of an extended comparison (24:3-5, the Cauldron).

Why such a broad array of meanings can be indicated by one word is not obvious. The idea of comparison apparently is the dominant idea, but in the end we have to conclude that a *mashal* is any saying meant to stimulate thought and provide insight.

In the Septuagint *parabolē* is used most of the time to translate all these different nuances,[16] and it is not used to translate any other Hebrew word. In fact, in some ways it is surprising that *parabolē* was chosen to cover this range of meaning, for its primary meaning in Greek usage was "comparison," and it was not a particularly common word prior to the end of the first century A.D. Josephus uses *parabolē* only twice and Philo only three times. Plato has it only twice, and Aristotle fourteen times. Other words such as *ainos* ("tale" or "story," but also "riddle" and "proverb") could have been used to cover the broad range of *mashal.* By choosing *parabolē* the translators of the Septuagint brought into prominence a word the Evangelists would catapult to notoriety. It is worth repeating that the broad range of *mashal* in the OT is mirrored by *parabolē* in the NT.

Not many OT precursors to the longer narrative parables of Jesus exist, and scholars disagree as to which accounts should be included. Birger Gerhardsson identifies only five parables from the Hebrew Scriptures, but also lists ten additional borderline cases.[17] T. W. Manson lists nine parables and two fables,[18] some of which are not in Gerhardsson's two categories. By contrast, Claus Westermann surveys, not just parables, but comparisons, which may be a single word, a sentence, or an extended narrative, only the last of which would be labeled as parables.[19] Westermann emphasizes that parabolic language appears rarely in legal texts and historical narrative but abounds in the prophetic literature, psalms, and proverbs. The majority of comparisons and parables occur in contexts of judgment and indictment.[20] The sayings identified as parables in the various lists appear primarily in the mouth and writings of prophets.

Several OT passages are obvious counterparts to the parables of Jesus. Two are juridical parables (see above, p. 13) that force hearers to make judgments in the world of the parable that end up being self-condemnations: *the parable of the Ewe Lamb,* which Nathan tells David (2 Sam 12:1-14), and *the parable of the Vineyard* (Isa 5:1-7), which expresses judgment on the house of Israel and the people of Judah for being so unproductive.[21] Two more passages are juridical parabolic dramas: *the parable of the Widow and the Avengers,* which Joab arranges for a wise woman from Tekoa to tell David (2 Sam 14:1-20),[22] and *the parable of the Fake Injury,* by which an unnamed prophet confronts Ahab (1 Kgs 20:35-42).

The OT has two political fables about trees and plants, Judg 9:7-15 and 2 Kgs 14:9-10, but the NT has no parallel to such accounts. The focus in the NT is on humans and their relation to God and his kingdom.

All the other story type parables appear in Ezekiel, which has more use of parabolic forms than any other OT book. At least six passages in Ezekiel are narrations — some would call them allegories[23] — presenting Israel's history in figurative form: 16:1-54, *Jerusalem the Prostitute;* 17:2-24, *the Eagle and the Vine* and its explanation;[24] 19:2-9, *the Lioness and her Cubs;* 19:10-14, *the Transplanted Vine;* 23:1-49, *the Two Sisters* and its explanation; and 24:3-14, *the Cauldron* and its explanation. New Testament scholarship — probably rightly — draws no connection between Ezekiel's being addressed as Son of Man and Jesus' use of Son of Man (which is derived from Dan 7:13), but one has to wonder about Ezek 20:49 [21:5]: "They say of me, 'Is he not a speaker of parables?'"

All twelve of these OT parables have explicit interpretations,[25] most following the parable but some preceding it. The accounts are not general stories, but context-specific. They were told to mirror specific realities. They are stories with intent, just as is the case with Jesus' parables.

Other passages must also be considered parabolic, even if they are different from what we find with Jesus. Both Ezekiel 34 (an extended narration about the failed shepherds of Israel and a promise that God will be Israel's shepherd) and Ezekiel 37 (the valley of dry bones) are parabolic. Jer 23:1-4 uses imagery of shepherds who scatter the sheep and of God who will bring his flock back to their folds and protect them.[26] Isa 28:23-29 has an interrogative parable about plowing and sowing to teach about the coming judgment of God. Isa 59:16-17 presents God as a warrior putting on his armor to bring salvation. Jer 13:12-14, through a similitude about a wine bottle, depicts the drunkenness and destruction of all the people. This example is virtually a juridical parable. Jer 18:2-13 uses the image of a potter to depict the sovereignty of God. The book of Hosea is largely a parable about God's relation to Israel depicted in the guise of Hosea's relation to his wife. Ps 80:8-17 describes Israel's history as the story of a vine that was brought out of Egypt, was planted, then ravaged and burned. Hab 1:13-17 describes the Babylonians' capture of people with a similitude of a fisherman who catches fish and then sacrifices to his net. Eccl 9:14-18 laments the failure of people to heed wisdom by giving a short single indirect narrative about a poor wise man who delivers a small city besieged by a powerful king, but the wise man is forgotten.

Other analogies might be listed,[27] among which would be acted parables or symbolic acts. What could have been stated as a parable on a figurative level is acted out and then explained in terms of its significance for the life of the people. Jeremiah is probably best known for giving acted parables such as the spoiled loincloth (13:1-11),[28] but Isaiah, Ezekiel, and Nehemiah all have examples.[29]

Also relevant are OT symbolic visions and dreams. With visions and dreams images are shown to a prophet (or someone who needs the prophet's help in interpreting) to depict the reality of the nation's relation to God or an overview of coming events.[30]

Nearly all the passages just mentioned occur in prophetic books or in the mouths of prophets. Parabolic language is a tool of prophets in the conflict they have with Israel and her leaders.[31] They are mirrors of the nation, its king, and the fate that awaits it. Prophets used parables to confront the nation, warn of judgment, and bring about change. These OT examples are important in their own right, but they are also important because they provide Jesus and other tellers of parables the genre, the images, and the forms for constructing parables. Every indication is that Jesus learned the parabolic method from the Hebrew Scriptures, especially the prophets. Sometimes he used parables as the prophets did, to confront the nation, but unlike the prophets Jesus also used parables to portray the kingdom, to confront individuals, and to teach about behavior, compassion, the use of money, and issues of discipleship.

Matthew, at least, was aware of the connection of Jesus' use of parables and his prophetic stance, for he sees Jesus' speaking in parables as fulfillment of what was spoken through "the prophet" in Ps 78:2: "*I* will open my mouth in parables; I will dig out things hidden from the foundation [of the world]" (Matt 13:35). The parabolic themes of hardness of heart and judgment in Jesus' teaching are much more understandable when we do justice to parables as a preferred prophetic discourse. This is the context in which Jesus must be understood.

Early Jewish Writings

I purposely separate early Jewish parabolic material from later rabbinic parables to force awareness of the problem of dating for use of the rabbinic material. We cannot merely lump all Jewish parables together with those from Jesus and ignore the *centuries* that may separate their origins.

Jesus did not create the parabolic method; he honed and mastered it. Others clearly were using parables in first-century Palestine, as even the sayings from John the Baptist attest (e.g., Matt 3:10). One would be surprised if this were not the case, given the popularity of similar forms in the Greco-Roman world. Still, the evidence of parables in early Judaism is sketchy at best, partly due to the character of the documents we have. If we include only what we *know* is prior to or contemporaneous with Jesus,[32] there is important parabolic material, but little that has the character, form, or incisiveness of Jesus' narrative parables. To our knowledge *no one* else used parables as frequently or as forcefully as Jesus does in the Synoptic Gospels. When parabolic material does appear, it often mirrors the prophetic and confrontational stance of the OT parables.

In assessing prior parabolic material the *Story of Ahiqar* deserves first mention. It exists in various versions, was popular among Jews, and influenced Aesop's fables. The later versions have some narrative parabolic material, but the earliest account (that found at Elephantine) is fragmentary and has only a few sayings that qualify for consideration.[33] The later versions are difficult to date and should be used with caution. Whether the sayings in later versions that are closest to Jesus' parables were included in the Elephantine account cannot be known. Still, the influence of the *Ahiqar* traditions on parable production[34] and possibly on Jesus should not be ignored and will be considered where influence on Jesus is possible.[35] The *Story of Ahiqar* is wisdom material used in a confrontational setting.

Very little exists in the Qumran material that contributes to our analysis. There are no accounts similar to Jesus' parables. The evidence does show that the broad range of meanings for *mashal* still existed.[36] At least four parabolic accounts should be considered. First, *Genesis Apocryphon* 19.14-21 (50 B.C. to

A.D. 50) relates Abraham's dream of a cedar tree and a palm tree, in which some men were going to cut and uproot the cedar, but the palm objected that both were from the same root and thus saved the cedar. The interpretation explains that the trees refer to Abraham and Sarai. Second, the text of 4Q302 is fragmentary, but it is labeled an admonitory parable. Fragment 2, col. 2 of this document tells of a good tree that is well cared for, but the next column indicates that wild boars will gnaw it and it will be cut down. This is a probably a parable of judgment on God's people similar to Isa 5:1-7 and Ps 80:8-19. Third, fragment 3, lines 4-5 of 4Q424 has a comparative *mashal:* "Like him who winnows in the wind [grain] which does not separate out, so is he who speaks to an ear which does not listen or he who recounts to someone asleep. . . ." Fourth, 4QFour Kingdoms[a,b] (4Q552 and 553) is fragmentary in both manuscripts, but it is clear that four trees are interpreted as four kingdoms. Elsewhere analogies, even extended ones, are used in the Qumran documents,[37] but there is little that is close to the forms Jesus used.

The issue of dating is problematic for several documents in the Apocrypha and Pseudepigrapha,[38] especially the *Similitudes* of Enoch (*1 En.* 37–71), and it may be better to list some items with Later Jewish Writings instead of here under Early Jewish Writings. If the first part of the second century can be used as a boundary for the early writings, then the following documents deserve attention in attempting to understand parabolic thinking before or just after Jesus' teaching.

Jub. 37:20-23 uses several analogies to show that Esau does not intend to forgive Jacob (e.g., "And if the lion becomes a friend of the ox, . . . then I will make peace with you"). Such analogies appear in various documents but do not contribute much to studying parables.

1 En. 1:2-3 identifies the whole document as a parable (Aramaic *mĕtal,* Greek *parabolē;* cf. 93:1 and 3). This is not the way we use the word "parable," but it is in keeping with the breadth of the Hebrew word *mashal,* which is used of Balaam's oracles and Job's discourses. The *Similitudes* are from a later date, the first or possibly even the third century A.D. This section has a series of visions which are referred to as "parables" (37:5; 38:1; 43:4; 45:1; 57:3; 58:1; 60:1; 68:1; 69:29).[39] In the final sections of *1 Enoch,* which are pre-Christian, chs. 85–90 present an apocalypse of the animals, which, while not called a parable, is an extended allegory of the history of the world in the guise of animals, a "zoomorphic" history in J. T. Milik's words.[40] The history of Israel is presented as a history of sheep in ch. 89. In *1 En.* 101:4-9 there is an extended analogy of sailors who rightly fear the sea, a sea which is controlled by God, but, we are told, even though sailors fear the sea, sinners do not fear God.

4 Macc 1:28-30 is closer to being a similitude, for it views pleasure and pain as two plants growing from the body and soul, with reason as the master cultivator who weeds, prunes, etc., to tame the jungle of habits and emotions.

In *Joseph and Aseneth* 12:8 one finds an analogy similar to some from Jesus:

> For (just) as a little child who is afraid flees to his father, and the father, stretching out his hands, snatches him off the ground, and puts his arms around him by his breast, and the child clasps his hands around his father's neck, and regains his breath after his fear, and rests at his father's breast, the father, however, smiles at the confusion of his childish mind, likewise you too, Lord, stretch out your hands upon me as a child-loving father, and snatch me off the earth.

In 15:7-8 and 19:5-6 Aseneth is renamed "City of Refuge" and interpreted allegorically as sheltering behind her walls many people who attach themselves to the Most High God.[41]

Testament of Naphtali 2:2-4 has an extended analogy: just as a potter knows the pot, how much it holds, etc., so the Lord forms the body in correspondence to the spirit, etc., and just as the potter knows the use of each vessel, so the Lord knows the body and whether it will persist in goodness or be dominated by evil.[42]

Testament of Job 18:6-8 comes closer to what we find in the Gospels. The author, like one on a ship willing to sacrifice everything in order to enter a city, considers his goods as nothing compared to the city about which an angel has informed him.[43] (See p. 237 below for the full text.)

4 Ezra, which is probably from the end of the first century,[44] has several passages that are close to the Gospel parables:

4:13-21 is a juridical parable of a conflict between the forest and the sea.
4:28-32 is a parable about evil being sown and harvested.
4:38-43 is a parable comparing the fact that a pregnant woman at the end of nine months cannot delay birth with the reality that the end of the age cannot be delayed.
7:49-61 is a parable of judgment comparing the greater value of rarer metals to the greater value of the few who are saved.
8:1-3 retells in shorter form the parable of the metals.
8:41-45 is a parable about a farmer sowing seeds, not all of which come up, to demonstrate that not all sowed into the earth will be saved.
9:30-37 is a parable of contrast to show that those who do not keep the law perish, unlike the earth (or other items) that remains even when what was sowed or placed in it is destroyed.[45]

The similarity of some of these to Jesus' parable of the Sower is obvious. In this document parables are always used by the divine speaker, not Ezra. The parables express divine secrets, but they are not revelatory by themselves. *They require interpretation for the meaning to be known.*[46] This is often the case with other parables in other sources.

Pseudo-Philo, *Biblical Antiquities* 37.1-5 recounts the fable of the trees and bramble bush from Judg 9:1-21. More significantly, 47:1-10 tells a fable of animals not provoked by the failures of a lion until many animals are destroyed. This fable mirrors the failure of people to be provoked by Micah until many of them were destroyed (describing Judg 20:1-48).

2 Baruch 22–23 reminds one of interrogative parables, for in them Baruch is asked a series of questions (e.g., "Who starts a journey and does not complete it?"), which are answered negatively, and then he is asked why he is disturbed about what he cannot know. Chs. 36–40 have a detailed allegorical depiction of the forest, the vine, the fountain (the Messiah), and the cedar and an equally detailed interpretation. Chs. 53–74 are an apocalypse of waters accompanied by a detailed historical-eschatological explanation. These are closer to apocalyptic revelations than parables, somewhat like the visions in the *Shepherd* of Hermas, but their allegorical character cannot be ignored.

4 Baruch 7:26-27 is a similitude which Jeremiah offers to Baruch: "For (it is) just as (when) a father has an only son and he is handed over for punishment; those who . . . (are) consoling him cover his face so he will not see how his son is being punished. . . . For God similarly had mercy on you and did not allow you to come into Babylon so that you would not see the oppression of the people."

Possibly some rabbinic parables stem from as early as the first century, but this is difficult to demonstrate with specific cases. David Instone-Brewer suggests *t. Pe'ah* 3:8 is a parable from a time when the temple was still in existence, for in it a man asks his son to make two animal sacrifices on his behalf.[47] This is not a parable, but, as it is labeled, a *ma'aseh*, a case or precedent. There is some similarity to a Greek *paradeigma*, an example, but precedents and examples are not the same genre. This is merely a story about a pious man who was extremely scrupulous about keeping the law. It is presented as a historical precedent, which is not like any of the stories of Jesus, none of which purport to be historical. D. Flusser has said that *m. 'Abot* 1:3, a parable about work attributed to Antigonus of Socho (about 180 B.C.), is the oldest evidence of Jewish parables.[48] He, of course, uncritically accepts the attribution of the saying to this rabbi. Parables are attributed to other early rabbis such as Hillel the Elder (ca. 30 B.C.; *Lev. Rab.* 34:3),[49] Johanan ben Zakkai (ca. A.D. 80; see, e.g., *b. Šabbat* 153a below, pp. 303-4), or Gamaliel the Elder (ca. A.D. 40; e.g., *'Abot de Rabbi Nathan*

40:10) and could stem from the first century, but again the uncertainty of the attributions vitiates any sure knowledge about date.[50]

What is striking in this early Jewish material is that, while there are forms clearly using parabolic modes of thinking, there is relatively little that is close to Jesus' narrative parables.

Greco-Roman Writings

A significant number of books have been written on Jewish and rabbinic parables, but relatively little has been written on Greco-Roman parables. This is unfortunate, for Greeks and Romans used analogies, parables, and parable-like sayings as much as anyone else. Several rhetoricians discuss the form and use of parables and related genres. Further, the intermingling of Jewish and Gentile cultures in the first century is a given. While Greco-Roman parabolic material has significant differences from the parables of Jesus, some of it clearly is of the same pattern. Those claiming that Jesus' parables are something new could learn from a closer look at Greco-Roman materials. Those items closest to Jesus' parables are from philosophers or others confronting people for their failures, an obvious kinship with the prophetic use of parables in the OT and by Jesus.

The semantic field of the word *parabolē* in this context is not nearly as broad as that of the Hebrew word *mashal* or of *parabolē* in the NT. Most often it refers to a simple comparison, occasionally a more developed form, or it may have a meaning bearing no relation to our concerns.[51] *Parabolē* does not occur frequently, and other words also are used for comparisons and for parabolic forms: *eikōn, ainos, mythos, logos,* and *paradeigma.* One of the large questions is why the translators of the LXX chose *parabolē,* which mostly meant a simple comparison, to render *mashal* when it referred to longer forms, and even more why the Gospel tradition uses *parabolē* of longer narrative forms, for which there was little precedent.

Justice cannot be done here to Greco-Roman parables,[52] but the frequency of such forms must be recognized. Sometimes people speak of parables in Homer, but the examples referred to are not like Jesus' parables. They are instead symbolic or allegorical narratives such as the accounts of Polyphem the cyclops (*Odyssey* 9.166-566) or of the oarsmen and the sirens (12.37-200) or the description of prayers as the daughters of Zeus (*Iliad* 9.502-514).[53] Extended similes occur frequently in Homeric writings,[54] but they are more poetic descriptions than anything like the similitudes of Jesus. As more pertinent examples of parables I list the following accounts gleaned from a variety of sources.

Often given as first witness in rhetorical manuals is a parable Herodotus (*Histories* 1.141, 5th century B.C.) tells of King Cyrus's failed attempt to get the Ionian and Aeolian cities to join in a revolt against Croesus. After the defeat of Croesus these cities sent messengers offering to be Cyrus's subjects on the same terms under which they had served Croesus, an offer Cyrus rejected with this story:[55]

> Once, he said, there was a flute-player who saw fishes in the sea and played upon his flute, thinking that so they would come out on to the land. Being disappointed of his hope, he took a net and gathered in and drew out a great multitude of the fishes; and seeing them leaping, "You had best," said he, "cease from your dancing now; you would not come out and dance then, when I played to you."

The parable was an expression of anger that did not need explanation. On receiving his message the cities fortified themselves for war. The correspondences in the analogy are obvious: Cyrus corresponds to the flute player, the cities to the fish, their refusal to dance to the refusal to revolt with Cyrus, and their leaping into the nets to their present attempt to please Cyrus, but no one needed to deduce or spell out the correspondences. They were obvious because, like Jesus' parables, this story was told into a context. Later this parable was taken over by Aesop (*Babrius* 9), but without its context and original intent, and given an insipid, generic application.[56] It has minimal value without its historical context. Its true force depends on that context.

Livy (59 B.C.–A.D. 17) tells of Agrippa Menenius, an eloquent man, being sent to quell a rebellion in 494 B.C. (*Ab Urbe Condita* 2.32):

> On being admitted to the camp he is said merely to have related the following apologue, in the quaint and uncouth style of that age: In the days when man's members did not all agree amongst themselves, as is now the case, but had each its own ideas and a voice of its own, the other parts thought it unfair that they should have the worry and the trouble and the labour of providing everything for the belly, while the belly remained quietly in their midst with nothing to do but to enjoy the good things which they bestowed upon it; they therefore conspired together that the hands should carry no food to the mouth, nor the mouth accept anything that was given it, nor the teeth grind up what they received. While they sought in this angry spirit to starve the belly into submission, the members themselves and the whole body were reduced to the utmost weakness. Hence it had become clear that even the belly had no idle task to perform, and was no more nourished than

it nourished the rest, by giving out to all parts of the body that by which we live and thrive, when it has been divided equally amongst the veins and is enriched with digested food — that is, the blood. Drawing a parallel from this to show how like was the internal dissension of the bodily members to the anger of the plebs against the Fathers, he prevailed upon the minds of his hearers.

Among many examples from Seneca (4 B.C.–A.D. 65) is an interrogative parable with an explanation:

> And so there is no reason for you to think that any man has lived long because he has grey hairs or wrinkles; he has not lived long — he has existed long. For what if you should think that that man had had a long voyage who had been caught by a fierce storm as soon as he left harbour, and, swept hither and thither by a succession of winds that raged from different quarters, had been driven in a circle around the same course? Not much voyaging did he have, but much tossing about. (*De Brevitate Vitae* 7.10).

Seneca also asks, "Would anyone want to stab an enemy with such force as to leave his own hand in the wound and be unable to recover himself from the blow? But such a weapon is anger; it is hard to draw back" (*De Ira* 2.35.1). Similar to Jesus' saying about finding a log in a brother's eye, Seneca writes, "You look at the pimples of others when you yourselves are covered with a mass of sores" (*De Vita Beata* 27.4).[57]

Plutarch (A.D. 46 to just after 120) frequently uses comparisons and parabolic forms. He tells the story of the sun defeating the north wind in getting a man to remove his cloak. The harshness of the wind made the man hold his garment more tightly, but the warmth of the sun caused him to strip it off. The story is applied to women whose husbands try to remove their extravagance. If husbands use force, the wives fight continually, but if they use reason, the wives practice moderation (*Mor.* 139D-E, "Advice to Bride and Groom"). The same document tells of a runaway slave caught hiding in a mill where slaves work and whose master says, "Where else could I have wished to find you rather than here?" The application is a warning to a woman who on account of jealousy files for divorce, since her rival would want nothing more (144A). Plutarch also refers to Aesop's hen in a situation of enemies inquiring about a man's conflict with his brother. The hen replies to the cat who inquires about the sick bird's welfare, "Very well, if you keep away." Plutarch adds — very much like the *nimshal* in a NT or Jewish parable — "so *(houtōs)* one would say to the sort of person who brings up the subject of the quarrel and makes inquiries and tries to dig up some secrets" (*Mor.* 490C, "On Brotherly Love").[58]

Epictetus's *Discourses* and *Enchiridion* (A.D. 55-135) are full of comparisons and parable-like sayings. Like several other writers, Epictetus has interrogative parables close to the form of Jesus' interrogative parables (e.g. *Diatr.* 1.27.19: "Who among you when he wishes to go to a bath goes to the mill instead?").[59] He compares people failing to reach excellence because they were satisfied with achievement to someone going on a trip but staying at a nice inn and never reaching his goal (2.23.36-41). In a parable reminiscent of Jesus' parable of the Strong Man, Epictetus compares one investigating Cynicism with an intruder claiming to be the master of the house and offers an explanation of the analogy introduced by "thus" *(houtōs)* (3.22.1-5). The duties of life are compared to tasks on a boat or those of a soldier (3.24.32-37). The body is compared to a poor loaded-down donkey, and numerous correspondences are detailed about the donkey and its little bridles, little pack-saddles, etc. (4.1.78-80). People are urged to keep their philosophy to themselves for a while, which is how fruit is produced in plants, with the seed buried and hidden and allowed to grow slowly. The image is extended at length describing premature blossoming and hazards of the weather, and the correspondences serve as a warning of what can happen to people (4.8.36-40). Life is compared to a voyage on a ship when one is allowed to go on shore for a while. Several correspondences exist between what one may find on the shore and what one has in life (*Ench. 7*).[60]

Aesop's fables bear an obvious if distant relation to biblical parables, but numerous others told fables as well.[61] In fact, "Aesop" is as much a generic label as a reference to a person. We usually think fables are moralistic tales about animals and plants speaking and acting as humans. They are moralistic, but not all are about plants and animals. Many deal with the actions of humans, and some are about gods.[62] Although formally related in terms of structure, Aesop's fables are in many ways *unlike* the parables of Jesus. The primary difference is in terms of content and context. The fables were written and collected first to provide entertainment and second to teach wise counsel, often in a witty, satirical way. They were told for their own interest and did not serve a larger narrative or a specific context.[63] This is very unlike Jesus' parables, which were told into the context of his own ministry and served to explain his message. Jesus' parables may have been humorous at times, but they were intended more to provoke than to entertain.

The prologues of the various books of *Phaedrus* and *Babrius,* the two collections in which Aesop's fables are preserved, are especially instructive, but one must remember that the collections are *hundreds* of years later than Aesop himself. *Phaedrus* and *Babrius* are from the early and late first century respectively, but Aesop is believed to have lived in the early sixth century B.C. Both collectors indicate that they are using Aesop's form for their own contributions, and "Phaedrus" assures his readers that he tries to preserve the spirit of the "famous old man," even if he inserts something of his own. Later he claims with his own contributions to have built a highway where Aesop made a footpath.[64] Promythia, identifications of the subject, were added at the beginnings of fables, apparently for indexing purposes, and epimythia, morals and applications, follow the fable to show its intent. Some of the epimythia do not fit very well, and most are assumed to be secondary additions. This should not be presumed, for some claim to be from the author himself (*Phaedrus* 4:11; 5:10), and such explanations were at times necessary (e.g., *Babrius* 74).[65]

More important than Aesop's fables is Theon's *Progymnasmata* because of what these exercises reveal about attention to the genre of fables/parables. Theon is probably from the first century A.D., and progymnasmata were textbooks providing preliminary exercises for instruction in rhetoric. Discussions of fables, chreia, and other forms were designed to help students understand the genre of each and its use in argumentation and become adept in composition. In addition to reciting the fable, combining it with a narrative, expanding it and condensing it, students inflected the parable. That is, they were required to tell the parable using various cases and numbers of the Greek language.[66]

Attention should be given as well to chreiai and their elaborations. A chreia (the Greek word for "need" or "what should be supplied") is a pithy saying introduced by a crisp description of the situation in which it was purportedly spoken by some well-known historical figure. For example, Isocrates said, "The root of education is bitter, but its fruits are sweet." Collections of such "useful sayings" appear as early as the fourth century B.C. Education regularly included exercises *(progymnasmata)* for elaborating and defending chreiai, and while various schemes existed for such elaborations, at least from the second century A.D. analogy *(ek tou parabolēs* [sic]) is a regular part of the elaboration, usually the fifth stage, followed by a specific historical example *(paradeigma)*.[67] This form of argumentation is much older than the second century[68] and only underscores how important parables and fables were in the ancient Greco-Roman world.

Earlier descriptions of parables and their rhetorical function are also important for understanding their role in the ancient world. Works on rhetoric are manuals for argumentation and persuasion, and they detail the components of persuasion. Examples and parables are regularly viewed as forms of argumentation. In his *The "Art" of Rhetoric* Aristotle distinguished two kinds of examples *(paradeigmata)*, historical and invented,[69] with the latter subdivided into comparisons *(parabolē)* and fables *(logoi)*. His example of a *parabolē* is Socrates' argument that magistrates should not be chosen by lot any more than athletes or the helmsman of a ship should be chosen by lot.[70] He adds that it is easier to invent examples than find historical examples, but the latter are more useful.[71]

Not everyone followed Aristotle's explanation by any means. More detailed and instructive descriptions of comparison (with examples) appear in *Rhetorica ad Herennium* and in Quintilian's *Institutio Oratoria*. The former lists four aims of comparison and four corresponding forms of presentation.[72] The author recognizes both multiple points of comparison and that the resemblance need not apply throughout the comparison.[73] Quintilian offers a long discussion of proof by comparison in *Inst.* 5.11.1-44. Although Roman writers preferred the Latin word *similitudo* ("comparison") to translate Greek *parabolē* and *exemplum* ("example") to translate Greek *paradeigma*, Quintilian preferred, like many Greeks, to apply *paradeigma* ("example")[74] to all comparisons. He viewed examples — whether real or assumed — as the most important proofs by comparison. He knew parallels may be partial or complete and that parables compare things whose resemblance is not obvious.[75] He had less appreciation for fables because they are especially attractive to rude and uneducated minds (5.11.19).[76] He discussed metaphor, the supreme ornament of oratory, at length (8.2.6 and 8.6.4-18), and while modern theorists reject his substitution theory of metaphor, his treatment is still valuable. Unlike modern scholars, he viewed allegory as a legitimate form of argument that is frequently used in oratory and is quite natural even with those of little ability. His examples are not narratives as lengthy as the allegorical parables in the Gospels, but his examples show that he would not have raised an eyebrow about the form of Jesus' parables. Other parts of the modern debate about NT parables are anticipated by Quintilian. He distinguished between pure allegories and mixed forms (partly metaphorical and partly literal), warned against obscurity in parables, and reported debates whether his examples are allegory or whether allegory by necessity involves obscurity. He also argued that allegory can be a way to disguise bitter taunts in gentle words by way of wit.

The importance of the material from the rhetoricians is only partly in their attempts to categorize and instruct about the function of different forms. This material also shows the popularity of parables and parabolic sayings in the Greco-Roman world and the fact that people seriously investigated their effectiveness. Jesus' parables would not have seemed strange to Gentiles.[77]

The Early Church

Relatively little needs to be said about parables in the early church, for parables hardly occur. Within the NT letters analogies occur (e.g., 1 Cor 9:26-27), and

Paul gives an allegorical reading of the story of Sarah and Hagar (Gal 4:21-31), but nothing exists that is close to the Synoptic parables. The word *parabolē* occurs in Heb 9:9: the Day of Atonement was a *symbol* or *illustration* of the ineffectiveness of the old order, and in 11:19: *figuratively* Abraham received Isaac back from the dead.

1 Clem. 23:4-5 and *2 Clem.* 11:2-3 use the analogy of the growth stages of a vine as an argument against those who say all things continue as before. *1 Clem.* 24:1-5 alludes to Jesus' parable of the Sower but uses the sowing of seeds, their decay, and their being raised as an argument for the resurrection.

The word *parabolē* occurs thirty-four times in the Apostolic Fathers, all but two in the *Shepherd* of Hermas (see Appendix 5, p. 575). *Barnabas* 6:10-17 says regarding the expression "a land flowing with milk and honey"(Exod 33:3) that "the prophet speaks a parable of the Lord [*parabolēn kyriou*]." Several OT texts are then understood allegorically of the new creation in Christ, with Christians being those who enter the good land and "milk and honey" understood as the nourishment of faith in the promise and by the word. *Barnabas* 17:2 uses the plural *parabolai* to indicate that if he writes concerning things present or future, the reader will not understand, for they are hid in parables.

Many of the occurrences of *parabolē* in the *Shepherd* of Hermas refer to elaborate allegorical descriptions. *Vis.* 3.2.4–3.8.11 has a long description of a tower of stones built on the water, which is specifically labeled "the parables of the tower" [*tas parabolas tou purgou*] (3.3.2). The tower is interpreted as the church — built on water because Hermas is saved through water. Six young men building and other people bringing stones are interpreted as angels, and the various stones are interpreted in detail of people in various relations to the church, whether apostles, church leaders, the upright, sinners for whom repentance is still an option, the wicked, etc. Seven women around the tower represent faith, continence, and other virtues. *Parabolē* is also used of briefer forms. *Vis.* 3.12.1-3 relates a parable of one in old age being rejuvenated by an inheritance, which is interpreted of Hermas's renewal on hearing revelation.[78] *Mand.* 11:18-20 uses *parabolē* with reference to the impossibility of throwing something into heaven (virtually a riddle) to make the point that things on earth have little power, whereas the smallest things from above (such as hail or water) have great power, just as does the Spirit.

The third major section of the *Shepherd* of Hermas is, of course, usually labeled *Similitudes,* and the word *parabolē* occurs as the title of subsections within this part of the book.[79] Ten parables are designated, but they are more like images or visions than anything we would call a parable, and they receive explanations similar to explanations of apocalyptic visions, explanations that are far longer than those attached to parables in the Gospels or the rabbinic material. Two parables are especially noteworthy: the parable of the elm and the vine (*Sim.* 2.1-10) and the parable of the field and the servant (*Sim.* 5.2.1–5.7.3). The dependence of the vine on the elm to produce good fruit is understood as reflecting the dependence of the rich on the poor to be truly productive. The parable of the field and the servant, which is influenced by Jesus' parable of the Wicked Tenants (Matt 21:33-45/Mark 12:1-12/Luke 20:9-19), tells of a servant who goes well beyond his master's command to care for a vineyard. In the detailed, lengthy explanation the servant is the Son of God, the vines are God's people, fences are angels, weeds are iniquities, and several other items are given theological significance. Parable 9 is a picture of twelve mountains, and the explanation returns to the images of the tower and the stones of *Vis.* 3.2.4–3.8.11 to give an even more detailed allegorical description of the church and of God's assessing the validity of its components. Several texts make the point that parables must be interpreted.[80]

For the sake of completeness we should add *Acts of Philip* 135, which has a collection of nine parable-like questions,[81] and *Acts of John* 67, which offers four analogies to show that the validity of faith is seen only at the end of life.

Before leaving this material some evaluation is in order. None of the items encountered is close to the Synoptic parables. The writers expect that parables need explanation, and detailed correspondences between image and reality are presumed. But, as far as the evidence exists, no Christian imitates Jesus in telling parables like his.

Later Jewish Writings

With later Jewish writings we are dealing with material ranging from the second to the seventh centuries A.D. or even later. Possibly some of the material in the section above on early Jewish writings belongs here, but the real focus at this point is on the rabbinic writings.

With the rabbinic parables suddenly the discussion is different. Here there is an abundance of material,[82] and some of it is identical or very close to the parables of Jesus in structure, introductory formulas,[83] images used (masters, servants, etc.), plots, interpretations, and formulas used to transition to the interpretations.[84] The similarities are so strong that scholars often assume that Jesus drew from a stock of rabbinic parables. That is possible, even likely, but it cannot be demonstrated, for none of these later rabbinic parables with certainty can be shown to have existed prior to Jesus' ministry. Further, the Mishnah, the earliest document among the rabbinic materials, does not have *any* narrative parables. Caution must be exercised, for even where there is similarity, there are also significant differences between Jesus' parables and those of rabbis, primarily with regard to motives and theology. Rabbinic parables usually are intended to explain Scripture passages or halakhic rulings for everyday life, whereas Jesus' parables explain and proclaim the kingdom.[85] R. M. Johnston suggested that many of Jesus' parables seem intended to reverse conventional values, while the rabbinic parables are intended to reinforce them, which merits reflection but is only partly true, as Johnston acknowledges.[86] Rabbinic parables often do not have the prophetic character of the parables of the OT and of Jesus and are less confrontational. Regardless of the differences, the similarity of the rabbinic parables to sayings of Jesus precludes any idea of ignoring this material.

A preliminary question must be treated — the question of the original language of rabbinic parables. David Flusser points out that rabbinic parables generally stem from Palestinian Judaism, not from the Babylonian diaspora, from which we have the Babylonian Talmud, and asserts that there are only Hebrew parables, not Aramaic parables.[87] Even if a rabbi spoke Aramaic, in telling parables he switched to Hebrew. Flusser knew that Aramaic expressions and dialogue do occasionally occur, but he thought the frames of the parables were always in Hebrew. He implies from this that Jesus also taught his parables in Hebrew.[88] C. Thoma and S. Lauer give a slightly different perspective. They indicate that of 133 parables in *Pesiqta de Rab Kahana* thirty-six contain Aramaic sentences or expressions, primarily in direct speech, and that two parables are almost entirely in Aramaic and another in a parable series is in Aramaic.[89] They suggest that Aramaic occurs in direct speech to fashion the parable (or at times the *nimshal*, the explanation) in popular language, but they do not trace all the Aramaic to popular speech. They suggest there was a Hebraic renaissance about A.D. 500, at which time Aramaic parables were re-Hebraized.[90] Debate about the reason parables appear almost always in Hebrew will continue,[91] but I do not think the language of the rabbinic parables gives us any information about the language in which Jesus taught his parables. First-century Palestine was for all intents and purposes trilingual,[92] and Jesus could have taught some in Hebrew. Even so, I would expect that Aramaic was the language in which he did most of his teaching, and his parables were assumedly given in Aramaic as well.

The following chapters gives primary source material from various quarters that is parallel to and sheds light on Jesus' parables. Rabbinic parables frequently provide such parallels. Sometimes a Jewish parable is so similar to a parable of Jesus that dependence of one on the other is suggested. I do not, however, present primary source material because I think there is dependence in either direction or any kind of genetic relation.[93] Except for the Hebrew Scriptures and a few other places where a parable of Jesus may allude to a Jewish writing, my concern is to show a way of thinking and how parables function, not some theory of dependence. Further, the lateness of some material urges us to use it with extreme caution. No straight line can be drawn from a specific rabbinic parable or from rabbinic parables generally to the parables of Jesus. Still, a great deal can be learned from rabbinic parables about parabolic form and function, about the process of analogical thinking, and about Jewish culture. More attention to these parables could have prevented the exaggerations Jülicher and others made popular. A huge amount of material could be considered at this point, but I will mention only the most important and representative material, and other relevant material will be given in the discussions of individual parables.

Reminiscent of Aristotle's distinguishing two kinds of examples (the historical and invented, see p. 50 above), rabbinic materials make use of two kinds of proof: the *ma'aseh* (precedent) and the *mashal* (analogy/parable). A world of difference exists, however, between Aristotle's argumentation and that of the rabbis because of the worldview and concerns of each. One may be tempted to see so-called "example story" and similitude/parable behind *ma'aseh* and *mashal* respectively, but that would be a mistake. Similarities exist, but with the so-called "example stories" — better called single indirect narratives (see pp. 13 and 15) — Jesus was not providing precedents the way rabbis gave precedents for halakhic rulings, and he was not giving purportedly historical incidents. One has only to check the places where *ma'aseh* is used to see how different Jesus' stories are.[94] Jesus' indirect speech about a topic of concern is not the equivalent of providing a precedent for a rabbinic decision.

Also, and of primary importance, is the recognition that *ma'aseh* and *mashal* take on different meanings in the various rabbinic documents. In a detailed analysis of rabbinic parables and precedents Jacob Neusner has documented the development both words went through and has shown that we may not speak generically of rabbinic parables.[95] The meaning of *mashal* ranges from a simple simile to an extended simile to a narrative with a developed plot. As with the parables of Jesus, a *mashal* in rabbinic writings does not name specific people or specific contexts or appeal to authoritative texts, unlike the *ma'aseh* in early documents, which does all three.[96] *Ma'aseh* is used in halakhic contexts, and *mashal* is used in haggadic contexts. In later documents *ma'aseh* loses its distinctiveness and is close to *mashal* in function.[97]

Neusner makes several other very important points. He finds little support for the idea that a corpus of autonomous parables circulated and were appropriated to situations. They are not "off the rack" parables; rather, most parables were generated by the text they serve. They are context-specific and built in relation to their *nimshalim*, the interpretive explanations that follow most rabbinic parables. Some few show unevenness between *mashal* and *nimshal,* but most show direct, even allegorical, correlation.[98] If one argues that Jesus' parables are open-ended, do not have interpretations, and are not context-specific, i.e., not created for the contexts in which they appear, then it is at least incumbent to give evidence validating such an approach and also to explain why Jesus' parables are so different from OT and rabbinic counterparts.

If we start with the earliest rabbinic document, the Mishnah (second century A.D.), except for *m. 'Abot* ("Sayings of the Fathers"), little that is parabolic appears. Only three passages merit attention: *m. Sukkah* 2.9;[99] *m. Niddah* 2.5;[100] and 5.7.[101] All are rather rudimentary and more akin to similitudes. Narrative parables with developed plots do not appear. *M. Soṭah* 9.15 adds as an honorific exaggeration that when Rabbi Meir died there were no more makers of parables, but the intent with "parables" *(meshalim)* is not clear.[102] Given the halakhic nature of the Mishnah, the paucity of parables is not surprising, for they occur primarily in haggadah.

If we include *'Abot,* several other passages are instructive, even though *'Abot* does not use the marker *mashal* and does not have narrative parables with developed plots.[103] The parable attributed to Antigonus of Socho (1.3) was mentioned above (p. 45). Six additional texts are similar to the similitudes of Jesus. *'Abot* 2.15 has an eschatological slant: "The day is short and the task is great and the labourers are idle and the wage is abundant and the master of the house is urgent." The similarity to Jesus' parable of the Workers in the Vineyard is obvious. An eschatological slant is present also at 3.17 with an analogy of a shopkeeper giving credit and collectors exacting payment with all being made ready for the banquet (see p. 484 below). Similar to Jesus' parable of the Two Builders, two analogies in *'Abot* 3.18 refer to the relation of wisdom and works: a tree whose branches are abundant and roots are few and that the wind destroys and a tree whose branches are few and whose roots are many that the wind does not move (see pp. 327-38 below). Another eschatologically oriented parable appears in 4.16: "This world is like a vestibule before the world to come: prepare thyself in the vestibule that thou mayest enter into the banqueting hall." At 4.20, using the question "To what is he like?" learning as a child or an old man is likened respectively to ink written on new paper and ink written on paper that has been blotted out, and those who learn from the young or from the old are likened respectively to one who eats unripe grapes and drinks from his winepress and to one who eats ripe grapes and drinks old wine, to which another rabbi cautions that one should look not on the jar but on what is in it. At 5.15 a fourfold analogy appears to describe four types of people who sit before the sages: the sponge, the funnel, the strainer, and the sifter (see p. 149 below). The similarity to the four soils in the parable of the Sower is obvious.

After the Mishnah parables proliferate. The first *narrative* parables that we encounter in the rabbinic materials are in the Tosefta (about A.D. 300), but then subsequently they appear in virtually all the materials: both Talmuds, the various midrashic writings, and the collections of sayings. The same parable may appear in various documents with variations. Six different parables are given to demonstrate that parables are handles for understanding Torah in *Song Rab.* 1.8. Before Solomon gave parables, people did not understand the Torah, but by creating *meshalim* he made understanding accessible.

With rabbinic parables usually a fairly stereotyped structure is followed: (1) the point to be illustrated, (2) an introductory formula, (3) the parable, (4) the application, usually introduced by "thus" or "so," and (5) a scriptural quotation, often introduced by "as it is written."[104] Sometimes one or more of these items are missing.

No justice can be done to the voluminous number of parables in the various rabbinic documents. At this point a few examples will suffice to give a flavor of what we will see with the analysis of individual parables that follows.

t. Berakot 1.11:

Remember not the former things, nor consider the things of old (Isa 43:18). . . . They drew a parable, to what may the matter be compared? To one who was walking in the way and a wolf attacked him, but he was saved from it. He would continually relate the incident of the wolf. Later a lion attacked him, but he was saved from it. He forgot the incident of the wolf and would relate the incident of the lion. Later still a serpent attacked him, but he was saved from it. He forgot the other two incidents and would continually relate the incident of the serpent. So, too, are Israel: the recent travails make them forget about the earlier ones.

y. Berakot 2.7:

When R. Bun bar Hiyya died [at a young age], R. Zeira came up and eulogized him [by expounding Eccl 5:12]. . . . To what [story] may [the life of] R. Bun bar R. Hiyya be compared? [To this story.] A king hired many workers. One worker excelled in his work. What did the king do? He took him and walked with him back and forth [through the rows of crops and did not let him finish his day's work.] Toward evening, when all the workers came to be paid, he gave him a full day's wages along with [the rest of] them. The workers complained and said, "We toiled all day, and this one toiled only two hours, and he gave him a full day's wages!" The king said to them, "This one worked [and accomplished] more in two hours than you did in a whole day."

So R. Bun toiled in the study of Torah for twenty-eight years, [and he learned] more than an aged student could learn in a hundred years.

b. Roš Haššanah 17b (concerning a question a woman put to Rabban Gamaliel about the seeming contradiction of Deut 10:17 and Num 6:26):

R. Jose the priest joined the conversation and said to her: I will give you a parable which will illustrate the matter. A man lent his neighbour a *maneh* and fixed a time for payment in the presence of the king, while the other swore to pay him by the life of the king. When the time arrived he did not pay him, and he went to excuse himself to the king. The king, however, said to him: The wrong done to me I excuse you, but go and obtain forgiveness from your neighbour. So here: one text speaks of offences committed by a man against God, the other of offences committed by a man against his fellow man.

Mekilta Beshallaḥ §4 (on Exod 14:15):

R. Absalom, the elder, giving a parable, says: To what is this like? To a man who got angry with his son and drove him out of his house. His friend came to him, requesting that he allow the son to come back to the house. He said to his friend: You are only asking me on behalf of my own son. I am already reconciled to my son. So also did the Holy One say to Moses: Wherefore criest thou? Is it not on behalf of My own sons? I am already reconciled to My sons.

Sifra Behuqotai 262.9 (on Lev 26:9):

There is a parable: to what is the matter comparable? It is to be compared to the case of a king who hired a large work force, and there was there a certain worker, who did work for him over a long period of time. The workers came to collect their wages, and that worker came with them. The king said to him, "My son, I shall turn to you [and pay you special attention]. These young workers who have worked for me have done a fair amount of work, so I shall give them a modest wage, but to you I am going to make a substantial settlement." So the Israelites are in this world: They seek their reward before the Omnipresent, and the nations of the world seek their reward before the Omnipresent. The Omnipresent says to the Israelites, "My children, I shall pay attention to you. The nations of the world who have worked for me have done a fair amount of work, so I shall give them a modest wage, but to you I am going to make a substantial settlement."

*   *   *

Several points should be clear from our overview of parables in the ancient world. Jesus was not the first or the only person using parables; parables are and virtually always have been a human means of persuading and enlightening. At the same time, except for the OT forms and a limited group of examples from elsewhere, not many precursors of Jesus' narrative parables are evident. Some rabbinic examples may reach back into the first century, but that is uncertain. Jesus' parabolic teaching is not unique, but we do not have evidence that anyone prior to him used parables so frequently or forcefully as he did.

Other insights may be drawn without overstepping the evidence. Except for collections of fables such as Aesop's, parables are context-specific and are effective *because of their contexts. Parables regularly have interpretations.* Sometimes the context in which they are placed makes the communicative intent obvious without an interpretation, but by far the majority of parables have interpretations. Also, parables regularly have multiple points of contact, sometimes detailed ones, with the reality they portray. Sometimes correspondences fit exactly and sometimes they do not. But again, even though rabbinic interpretations regularly detail correspondences, parable interpretation is not so much about assigning correspondences as it is about understanding how the analogies work.

Grace and Responsibility

The two parables in this chapter, especially the parable of the Unforgiving Servant, are the most revealing and compelling of all Jesus' parables. They reveal both the nature of parables and the essence of Jesus' kingdom message. They focus primarily on grace and responsibility but could be grouped with parables of the present kingdom or parables of discipleship.

THE UNFORGIVING SERVANT
(Matt 18:23-35)

Adolf Jülicher thought this was one of the simplest and clearest parables we have from the mouth of Jesus.[1] Others devalue this parable because of the contradictory and unflattering picture of God it offers, with the result that what Jülicher thought was simple has unnecessarily become a theological briar-patch.[2] The focus on judgment in this parable should be compared to other parables of judgment, especially the parables of the Wheat and the Weeds and of the Rich Man and Lazarus and the parables of future eschatology.

Parable Type

This parable, which appears only in Matthew, is a two-stage double indirect narrative[3] parable with a plot development of four components. It has a balanced three-part structure presenting the three scenes of the narrative followed by a *nimshal* (an explanation): vv. 23-27: the merciful decision of the king; vv.

28-30: the unmerciful decision of the first servant: vv. 31-34: the king's response; and v. 35: the explanatory *nimshal.* Vv. 23-27 could function as a parable by themselves. Note the way the three scenes develop:

	Scene 1	Scene 2	Scene 3
Introduction	vv. 23-25	v. 28	v. 31
Words	v. 26	v. 29	vv. 32-33
Action	v. 27	v. 30	v. 34
Explanation	v. 35[4]		

Issues Requiring Attention[5]

1. The relation of the parable to its context, especially vv. 15-20 and 21-22.
2. How much is intended with "10,000 talents"? Is this amount Matthean hyperbole?
3. Are the characters depicted as Gentiles, and if so, what is the relevance of that? Has Matthew elevated the master by giving him the title "king"?
4. Does the parable end with v. 33, or are vv. 34-35 an integral part of the original account?
5. What does the parable teach? Is God like or not like the king in the parable?
6. Does this parable teach a form of "works righteousness" which argues that one's forgiveness of others is a precondition for experiencing divine forgiveness?
7. To what degree is the parable christological?
8. Is God bound by the unlimited forgiveness of vv. 21-22?

Helpful Primary Source Material

See also relevant primary source material under the parable of the Two Debtors (pp. 78-79).

Canonical Material

- OT: Gen 4:24; 2 Kgs 4:1; Neh 5:5; Ps 103:8-13
- NT: Matt 5:7, 25-26/Luke 12:57-59; Matt 6:12/Luke 11:4; Matt 6:14-15; 7:1-2; 10:8; Mark 11:25; Luke 7:36-50; 17:3-4; Eph 4:32

Early Jewish Writings

- Sir 28:2-4: "Forgive your neighbor the wrong he has done, and then your sins will be pardoned when you pray. Does anyone harbor anger against another, and expect healing from the Lord? If one has no mercy toward another like himself, can he then seek pardon for his own sins?"
- Sir 33:26: ". . . for a wicked slave there are racks and tortures."
- Wis 2:19 speaks of the ungodly testing the righteous with insult and torture.
- Wis 11:9 reports that the Israelites learned "how the ungodly were tormented *(ebasanizonto)* when judged in wrath."
- Wis 12:23 says that God tormented *(ebasanisas)* the unrighteous through their own abominations.
- 2 Macc 7.17: A foreign king is warned that God's mighty power will torture *(basaniei)* him and his descendants.
- *T. Zeb.* 5.1-3: The *Testament of Zebulon* is about compassion and mercy, both of which are encouraged in this passage, for "whatever anyone does to his neighbor, the Lord will do to him."
- *T. Gad* 6.3 encourages love from the heart and forgiveness.
- Josephus, *Ant.* 12.155-85 recounts how wealthy people purchased the right to farm taxes and how Joseph the son of Tobias rescued the people from difficulty by promising to pay double the 8,000 talents bid for the right to collect taxes in Coele-Syria, Phoenicia, Judea, and Samaria.
- *T. Ab.* 12.18 describes a judgment scene in which one person is neither turned over to the torturers nor placed among those being saved.

Greco-Roman Material

- Diogenes Laertius, *Bion* 4.46 narrates Bion's account that his father had cheated on taxes with the result that he and all his family were sold into slavery.
- Quintilian, *Inst.* 6.3.93: "Again when his [Afer's] steward, being unable to account for certain sums of money, kept saying, 'I have not eaten it: I live on bread and water,' he replied, 'Master sparrow, pay what you owe.'"
- Juvenal, *Satirae* 14.274 offers a complaint about a merchant who runs risk for the sake of a thousand talents or a hundred mansions.

Later Jewish Writings

- *m. Soṭa* 3.8: ". . . a man may be sold [to make restitution] for what he has stolen, but a woman cannot be sold [to make restitution] for what she has stolen."

- *m. Giṭṭin* 4.9: "If a man sold himself and his children to a Gentile, they may not redeem him. . . ."
- *m. Baba Batra* 10.8: "If a man seized a debtor by the throat in the street. . . ."
- *t. Yoma* 4.13: "[If] a man sins two or three times, they forgive him. [But on the] fourth, they do not forgive him." On the basis of Amos 2:6 and Job 33:28-29 this is assumed to be God's procedure as well. (Cf. *'Abot de Rabbi Nathan* 40: "But if one says, 'I shall sin and then repent,' he is forgiven up to three times but no more"; *b. Yoma* 86b: "If a man commits a transgression, the first, second, and third time he is forgiven, the fourth time he is not forgiven." The subject is forgiveness by God.)
- *t. Soṭah* 2.9: "A man is sold as a Hebrew slave, but a woman is not sold as a Hebrew slave."
- *Sifre Deut.* 26: "A parable: A man borrowed from the king a thousand *kor* of wheat per year. Everyone said, 'Can it be possible for this man to manage a loan of one thousand *kor* of wheat in one year? It must be that the king has made him a gift of it and has written him a receipt!' One time the man had nothing left over and could not repay anything to the king, so the king entered the man's house, seized his sons and daughters, and placed them on the auction block, whereupon everyone knew that the man had received no pardon from the king. So also all the punishments which came upon David were made multiple. . . ."
- *b. Roš Haššanah* 17b describes an oath on the life of the king to pay a debt to a neighbor, and when the debt cannot be paid, the king forgives the infraction but directs the man to get forgiveness from his neighbor (see above, p. 58).
- *b. Ketubbot* 102a: "'Behold,' he replied, 'this is just as if [a creditor] were [in the act of] throttling a debtor in the street . . .'" (also in *b. Baba Batra* 175b-176a).
- *Midr. Tanḥumah Mishpatim* 6.7 indicates that God is not like a human who demands what he is owed.
- *Midr. Tanḥumah Emor* 8.30 (on Lev 23:39-40) has a long parable about a province which owed taxes to a king. The people did not pay when the king sent repeated emissaries. The king and his courtiers went themselves. As he approached, three successive delegations met him asking that the amount be forgiven. He forgave half, half more, and then the entire debt. The explanation is that the king is the Holy One and the people of the province are Israel, whose sins are forgiven at the festivals throughout the year. The multiple correspondences between parable and explanation are obvious.

- *Exod. Rab.* 31.1: "There is no creature that is not indebted to God, but being gracious and merciful, He forgives all former misdeeds, as it says, *Remember not against us the iniquities of our forefathers* (Ps 79:8). It can be compared to one who had borrowed from a money-lender and forgot about it. After a time, he appeared before his creditor and said: 'I know that I am your debtor.' The other replied: 'Why do you remind me of the first debt; I have long since completely dismissed it from my mind.' So is the Sovereign of the Universe. Men sin before Him; and He, seeing that they do not repent, forgives them sin after sin, and when they come and remind Him of the debt they contracted previously, He says to them: 'Do not remind yourselves of the former sins.'" For God viewed as a creditor and sins as debts, see also *m. 'Abot* 3.16; *Gen. Rab.* 85.2; 92.9.
- *Midr. Pss.* 79.5, however, contrasts a human owed money who cannot collect from a friend who has no money with God who makes the soul pay.

Textual Features Worthy of Attention

Matthean stylistic features are abundant, such as beginning a sentence with a participle and use of "then" *(tote)*, "be like" *(homoioō)*, "worship"/"do obeisance to" *(proskyneō)*, and "exceedingly" *(sphodra)*. Matthew has a redactional focus on "mercy" (*eleos* and related words): *eleos* in 9:13; 12:7 (quotations of Hos 6:6); 23:23; *eleeō* in 5:7; 9:27; 15:22; 17:15; 18:33 (two); 20:30, 31; *eleēmosynē* in 6:2-4; and *eleēmōn* in 5:7. He also stresses the importance of the heart (*kardia* occurs 16 times — e.g., 5:8, 28; 13:15, 22:37) and forgiveness (the verb *aphiēmi* occurs 15 times with the meaning "forgive," but the noun *aphesis* only at 26:28).[6] Some suggest that Matthew was the first to put this parable in written form.[7]

Matt 5:7; 6:12, 14-15 are directly relevant to this parable. 5:7 emphasizes mercy, and 6:12, 14-15 stress the direct link between forgiveness and being forgiven. Cf. also 5:23-26/Luke 12:57-59; Matt 5:48; and 7:1-2.

Ch. 18, Matthew's "ecclesiastical discourse," is carefully arranged. Vv. 1-5 emphasize the question "Who is [will be] great in the kingdom?" (i.e., in what does greatness consist?), with the resulting focus on humility; vv. 6-9 focus on temptations to sin; vv. 10-14 give the parable of the Lost Sheep; vv. 15-20 give instructions for dealing with sin in the community; vv. 21-22 deal with the question about the limits of forgiveness; and vv. 23-35 are the parable of the Unforgiving Servant. Vv. 15-20 are the central theme, and the rest of the discourse is provided as commentary and for balance in dealing with the subject.

The requests of the two servants for patience (vv. 26 and 29) are almost identical.

Compassion (*splanchnistheis* in v. 27) has an important role in Jesus' ministry.[8] In my estimation it is one of the four main features of Jesus' message.[9] It is also mentioned explicitly in the parables of the Good Samaritan and the Prodigal (Luke 10:33 and 15:20).

All five of Matthew's "discourses" end with a focus on judgment, most in the form of a parable.

Cultural Information

Most of Jesus' sayings about slaves envision slaves performing managerial tasks, not menial tasks.[10]

We are told that, at least theoretically, in the Jewish context a wife could not be sold, that no institution of slavery for debt existed, and that torture was not permitted.[11] However, although often repeated, the evidence is not so clear. *M. Soṭah* 3.8 concerns selling a woman for restitution for *theft. T. Soṭah* 2.9 is more explicit but brief (see above, p. 64). Further, the OT is well aware of people being sold for debt (2 Kgs 4:1; Neh 5:5; Isa 50:1; Amos 2:6), a practice that was common throughout the Mediterranean world. Laws, of course, are written down because there are violations. Herod the Great was known to have torturers.[12] Certainly the first-century Palestinian world was well aware of families being sold or imprisoned for their debts and of torture at the hands of various oppressors.

A "talent" is a measurement of weight of gold, silver, or copper. It varied but was between approximately 60 and 90 pounds. Ten thousand talents would be about 204 metric tons.[13] Depending on which metal was used, a talent was the equivalent of about 6000 denarii, which would make the first servant's debt 60,000,000 denarii, and at one denarius a day (as in Matt 20:2) would require a day laborer over 164,000 years to repay![14] The annual salary of Herod the Great was reportedly 900 talents: 200 talents being the tax revenue for Galilee and Perea, 100 talents the tax revenue from the regions assigned to his son Philip, and 600 talents the tax revenue for the areas controlled by Archelaus (see Josephus, *Ant.* 17:318-20).

The price of a slave usually ranged from about 500 to 2000 denarii.[15]

Explanation of the Parable

Options for Interpretation

The parable depicts the forgiveness of God, the necessity of humans forgiving because God forgives, and the warning of judgment for those who fail to forgive.

The church allegorized this parable less than others, but some struggled with its difficulties. Augustine understood the debts as sins against the Law with the debtor's wife and children being cupidity (excessive desire) and works respectively. Some viewed the greater and lesser debtors as Jews and Gentiles respectively.[16]

B. Scott suggests the parable is intended to reject Jewish notions of superiority and also points to the realization that entanglement with evil is part of the kingdom and leads to repentance.[17]

Because of the unflattering picture of God the parable suggests, a number of people attempt to read it as a confrontation with the oppression and violence of this world. For example, W. Herzog reads this parable as showing the inadequacy of messianic hope and of kingship. People must look elsewhere to reshape their world.[18]

Decisions on the Issues

1. The relation of the parable to its context, especially vv. 15-20 and 21-22. The importance of this parable should not be underestimated, for its climactic position at the end of the ecclesiastical discourse marks it as the hermeneutical key to the whole chapter.[19] Jesus addresses his followers who have experienced the kingdom, not Jews in general,[20] and Matthew has framed this section to emphasize what it means to follow Jesus as it relates to sin and forgiveness.

Several interpreters complain that the parable, which is about the necessity of forgiveness, is not a suitable example of vv. 21-22, which rejects limits for forgiveness.[21] Often vv. 21-22 are deleted from consideration of the parable, and understandably so, for the parable is *not* an illustration of limitless forgiveness. Surely Davies and Allison are right, though, in saying that Matthew joined the parable to vv. 21-22 not because both units teach the same thing, but because both treat the topic of forgiveness, even though with two different emphases.[22] As they point out, the structure of the ecclesiological discourse reveals Matthew's intent in vv. 21-35. He sought to provide a hedge against rigidity and absolutism and to balance the hard teaching of the previous paragraph on church discipline. Further, he sought to avoid statistical accounting and to engender proper attitudes in correcting others (cf. 7:1-5).[23] The parable is *not, and was not intended to be,* an illustration of 18:21-22. In keeping with Matthew's use, *dia touto* ("because of this") in v. 23 indicates a connection rather than an example or proof. This is the case in seven of the ten times he uses the phrase.[24] It picks up only part of the subject of forgiveness, the necessity to forgive.

2. How much is intended with "10,000 talents"? Is this amount Matthean hyperbole? The amount of money owed by the first servant (see above, p. 66) is so large that some have argued that it must be Matthean hyperbole.[25] Certainly the debt is enormous and strains credulity, but parables often contain hyperbole and tend to be *pseudo-realistic.* The numbers are not, however, unthinkable. Esth 3:9 recounts Haman's promise to pay 10,000 talents into the treasury to bring about the destruction of the Jews, and other texts report such high numbers as well, not least of which is Josephus's report that Pompey exacted more than 10,000 talents from the Jews after his conquest.[26] The hyperbole as likely stems from Jesus as from Matthew. The main point is that the debt is so high that no possibility exists of the servant ever paying it.

The parable does not specify the circumstances, but the most probable scenario is that the servant is a "tax farmer." That is, he has contracted to collect taxes for a specific region.[27] Is the servant a slave or an "official," a tax minister? The word in question is *doulos,* regularly used of slaves, but it is also used of tax ministers or other officials.[28] Slaves with ability were often given responsibility for financial oversight, and this could be the situation here.[29] On the other hand, the man and his family are to be sold *into slavery* (v. 25). Is it punishment to sell a slave into slavery? In the end, conclusions about the parable do not depend on whether he is literally a slave, but more likely he is a contracted agent.

The word "loan" *(daneion)* seems odd to some, but it does not require that the king converted the debt to a loan and later forgave it.[30] Even if the word *daneion* is unexpected, it *was* used for debts. Of most significance is its use by Josephus (*Ant.* 3.282) of *debts forgiven at the time of the Jubilee* and in 4 *Maccabees* 2:8 of forgiving debts at the end of seven years. The parable's intent with the description of the first debt is to achieve maximum effect in underscoring the enormity of the king's act of forgiveness.[31] Matt 6:12 uses "debts" *(opheilēmata)* and "debtors" *(opheilētēs)* in reference to sin and sinners, which is in accord with Jewish sources as well.[32] No one should be surprised that an intended reference to God and the forgiveness of sins shows through. Parables are constructed on the reality they seek to portray (e.g., Nathan's parable to David). This does not mean that every feature has to fit, but the analogy does have to correspond well enough to work.

3. Are the characters depicted as Gentiles, and if so, what is the relevance? Has Matthew elevated the master by giving him the title "king"? Several interpreters think the description of the king indicates he was a Gentile king.[33] This assumption leads B. Scott to think the parable is told in the context of attitudes of Jewish superiority and entraps the reader in a chaotic situation in which forgiveness can be taken back and in which the fellow servants behave the same way the first servant did by failing to forgive him. For Scott the parable leads to a parabolic experience of evil and teaches that the ability to acknowledge one's entanglement in evil is part of the experience of the kingdom. It is an imitation of the petition in the Lord's Prayer, "let us not succumb to the test," and requires the Jewish reader to surrender Jewish superiority.[34]

A bridge between the parable and Scott's view does not exist. Such a reading is a distortion of the parable, expects far too much of readers, and certainly is not a convincing reading, even if one assumes that the king is a Gentile, which is by no means clear.[35] That *proskynei* (often translated as "worship") is used is no indication of a Gentile context, as a cursory glance at Septuagint uses of the word shows.[36] The word is often used of obeisance by an inferior to a superior. A family being sold into slavery and the mention of torturers do not necessarily indicate a Gentile context either. *Sifre Deut* 26, quoted above, is similar to our parable, with children being sold for debt, but it does not assume a Gentile king, or at least does not care. Such brutality was all too well known in ancient Palestine and the surrounding area.[37] To think that ancient Jews were above torture is a romanticist's view which forgets that many Jews were viewed as "ungodly," and zeal for the Torah led to forced circumcision and destruction of the ungodly.[38]

Some suggest that Matthew enhanced the parable by changing an original focus on a master to a focus on a king, but if this was originally a kingdom parable, the use of the king metaphor is natural, even if infrequent.[39] The understanding of God as king is a common OT and Jewish theme.[40] Further, the size of the debt is more appropriate for a king and his ministers and almost invites one to move beyond a surface reading. The shift from "king" to "master" *(kyrios)* in vv. 25-34 is natural in that "master" corresponds to the mention of servants. Rabbinic parables often compare God to a king,[41] even though any king in recent memory would have been a Gentile, but that does not hamper the analogies. I doubt that a Gentile king is implied, but if that is the case, it makes no difference for the parable. We should remember, however, that the kingdom of heaven is not merely like a king, but like the whole sequence of actions in vv. 23-34.

4. Does the parable end with v. 33, or are vv. 34-35 an integral part of the original account? The suggestion that the parable should stop with v. 33 or even earlier[42] has little in its favor. If it did end with v. 33, the reader rather than the storyteller would have to make the judgment, which would make this a juridical parable, but not all parables leave decision making to the hearer. The parallel structure of the three acts in the story demonstrates that v. 34 belongs,[43] and "thus" *(houtōs)* in v. 35 follows typical Jewish practice in the application of the parable. At the narrative level the master's rhetorical question (v. 33) requires an answer, and every reader wants to know what will happen to the servant.[44] The *nimshal* in v. 35 only does the necessary job of explaining the referent of the parable. The language may underscore Matthean concerns such as the themes of judgment and integrity of action done from the heart, but the parable, however shaped by Matthew, is incomplete without its concluding section. The attempts to reconstruct the parable without the closing verses seem to be clear attempts to distance Jesus from the idea of judgment.[45]

5. *What does the parable teach? Is God like or not like the king in the parable?* The problem with this parable is that the king is both very attractive as a magnanimous figure and problematic in that he can renege on his forgiveness and send his servant to the torturers. The discomfort at the actions of the king in the parable arise not merely from modern concerns for political correctness. At least since the Middle Ages people have wrestled with the parable's question whether the God who forgives might still be encountered as the God who judges, whether judgment can negate grace.[46] This question is paramount with this parable, but it is present throughout the NT, not least in the focus on judgment according to works even though salvation is by grace (e.g., Rom 2:6; 14:10-12).

The difficulty of this question and discomfort with any idea of a judging God have caused a number of interpreters to argue that the king in the parable is intended to portray what God is *not* like. Luise Schottroff argues that the hearers would know that God is not to be equated with a human oppressive king and that to identify God with the king in the parable would be blasphemy. To avoid any direct analogy with God she translates *houtōs* ("thus") in v. 35 as "How is this, then, to be compared to the kingdom of God?" Like Jülicher, she limits the parable to one point, the imperative of forgiveness among humans, and argues that nothing is said explicitly about God. She concludes that God will call people to account at judgment if they do not forgive each other.[47] The problems are self-evident. The meaning Schottroff assigns to *houtōs* is not valid, and in the end she still concludes that *God* will hold people accountable. She tries to make her case from a rabbinic parable about a city that could not pay taxes to a king,[48] which is understood of God forgiving Israel, but even though she grants that the parable identifies the king as the King of kings, she denies that the king is an image of God.[49]

W. Herzog's approach fails equally. He paints the king as a ruthless figure, but if the king is ruthless, why should he care if the second servant is mistreated? He describes the king's first act as a "messianic act of forgiveness of debt . . . meant to initiate further acts of forgiveness of debt."[50] But if the king is a ruthless oppressor not representing God, from where does any expectation of messianic forgiveness come, and what would motivate such a costly act? Most tragic of all for such approaches, the wonderful picture of the magnanimous grace of God is lost.

On the other hand, if the king does represent God, do we not have just as many problems? Besides selling a family into slavery and sending the servant to the torturers, does God not know beforehand that the first servant will not show mercy? Does God need someone to tell him what happened, as v. 31 might suggest, or do we conclude that sins against brothers and sisters are exceedingly worse than sins against God, as if they could be separated? Should we conclude from this parable that an atonement theology is unneeded because forgiveness is granted outright? All such questions are out of bounds and violate the character of parables.

Part of the value in this parable is in what it demonstrates about interpreting parables.

The problem is with reading parables as if they were equations,[51] as if every part of the parable was to be a mirror of reality. Parables are not equations, and that is why parable interpretation is not about listing correspondences or about tracing the reflection of a theology. "There is always an 'is' and an 'is not' to metaphors."[52] Parables must be interpreted as analogies, analogies that show *pieces* of reality but may contain other elements for a variety of purposes. Interpreters want parables to serve up whole theological structures on a platter, but parables are not theologies. They *are* theological, and we are greatly impoverished if their theology is neglected, but they must be allowed to do what they intend and not be pushed beyond their purposes. We ruin a parable if we forget the "is not" character of metaphor.[53] There would be safety in saying this parable makes only one point, but there would be great loss. What does this parable seek to do, and how does it accomplish its purpose?

The debt picture, even if hyperbole, depicts a well-known reality. There is no suggestion — despite claims — that the king or either of the servants is part of an oppressive system,[54] as much as all of us should stand against every oppression. In Jewish parables the image of a king is regularly identified with God. Jesus used the image much less, but hearers early on would probably assume that the parable provided *an analogy for God, not a picture of God*, especially since "debts" was regular language to refer to sins.[55] Hearers naturally would identify with the plight of the first servant and be relieved on hearing that his predicament was solved. The parable's picture of astonishing forgiveness reflects expectations associated with the end-time Jubilee, and like Luke 4:18-21, implies that Jesus was in effect announcing the Jubilee.[56] So the first part of the parable points to the enormous, unpayable debt of sin and God's stunningly gracious forgiveness.

Matthew's use of *homoiōthē* ("has become like") in v. 23 probably is a marker for the presence of the kingdom.[57] The forgiveness is already being dispensed in Jesus' ministry because the kingdom is present. While this parable is not grouped with parables of present eschatology, it could have been, and it also obviously fits with parables of future eschatology. Our categories for studying parables rarely do justice to the parables themselves.

Hearers would also have identified with the first servant if the story had started with his demand that his colleague pay what he owed, for he was fully within his rights to demand to be paid. What makes his action reprehensible and shifts the allegiance of hearers is the contrast between the treatment he received and the treatment he gave.[58] The contrast is heightened by the similarity of wording in the two requests for mercy (vv. 26 and 29). The intent of the parable is that God's prior action of mercy and forgiveness is to be extended to other people (cf. Matt 10:8). The complaint that such imitation of God encourages legalism and guilt is unjustified.[59] If Judaism and Christianity are not about the imitation of God, what is the relevance of such language as "image of God" and "covenant"? The expectation that humans conform their lives to the character of God is present throughout Scripture.[60] The instruction of this kingdom parable — as elsewhere in Scripture — is "Do unto others as God has done to you." The ethic is responsive and reflective — responding to God's prior action and reflecting God's character. As everywhere with NT ethics, the indicative precedes the imperative. *The kingdom comes with limitless grace in the midst of an evil world, but with it comes limitless demand.* Nowhere is that more obvious than in this parable. God acts, and his people are expected to act in accordance with his actions and character.

The third scene in the parable (vv. 31-34) makes explicit what is already implied, but it also brings two additional features dear to Matthew, mercy and judgment. We have already seen that Matthew ends each of his major discourses with a focus on judgment, which is the case here in ch. 18. The failure of the first servant to show mercy is met with rebuke, and then in v. 33 comes the primary instruction of the parable. English translations often lose the force of v. 33, for the text has: "Is it not *necessary* for you also to show mercy to your fellow servant as I have shown mercy to you?" Mercy is a requirement for disciples of the kingdom. Marcus Borg's statement that Jesus substituted the mercy code for the holiness code[61] may be an exaggeration, but not much. Mercy marks the ministry of Jesus, and it must mark the lives of his followers. If Jubilee is in effect and you are or should be celebrating release, how could you possibly be hardhearted and uncaring about someone minimally indebted to you? This is a new emphasis derived from the focus on the present kingdom, for forgiving others is not emphasized in the OT or first-century Judaism.[62]

Along with the focus on mercy in both Matthew and Jesus is a focus on judgment. Should the master have done nothing when he heard what happened? As much as people recoil from the theme of judgment, it is an integral part of Jesus' kingdom message. The kingdom cannot be present if evil is not being named and defeated. If there is no judgment, salvation is not needed. The judgment language is hyperbole (e.g., Matt 5:29-30 par.), not a description of actuality, but it assures people that there will be a reckoning and that God will vindicate the oppressed.[63]

That the man is given over to the torturers until all is paid is strong language within the story world to emphasize the seriousness of the failure to show mercy and the reality of judgment. God does not have torturers,[64] and the story cannot be pushed to yield information about the nature of judgment. Here the principle that the teaching of the parables must be verified from nonparabolic material is of obvious relevance.[65] Sometimes the elements of a parable are there not just to deceive the hearer into truth but, rather, to *shock* the hearer into the truth, and that is the case here. As the *nimshal* in 18:35 shows, the concern of the story is twofold: the necessity of mercy and forgiveness and the seriousness of any failure to show mercy and forgiveness. This parable warns of judgment for the failure to show mercy. Similar emphases appear in the Beatitude on mercy (5:7) and in the Lord's Prayer (6:12), with the petition for forgiveness being the only one that receives commentary (6:14-15). The similarity of the parable to 5:25-26 (handed over to the judge, to the jailer, and thrown into prison until the last penny is paid) is striking.

The king's compassion is an expression of amazing grace, but such language is unusual in the Gospels. "Grace" *(charis)* is not explicit in the parable, and except in John 1:16 *charis* with the meaning "grace" does not occur in the Gospels. Further, while we might summarize much that Jesus does by speaking of grace, relatively few of his parables focus predominately on a theology of grace: only this parable, the Two Debtors (Luke 7:41-42), and the three parables of Lostness in Luke 15. Most instead focus on the character of the kingdom or the response required.[66]

This parable is also instructive for thinking about Jülicher and how parables function. If one tried to follow Jülicher and limit this parable to one point, a great deal would be lost. The analogy necessarily has several correspondences between the story and reality, and it teaches several points: the enormous debt of human sin, the compassion and forgiveness of God made available in the kingdom ministry of Jesus, the release expressed in terms of Jubilee, the necessity of mirroring God's mercy, and the warning of judgment for those who do not. It is not allegorizing to see these "multiple points," for they arise from the parable and express its intent.[67] The issue is always how the analogy works, not deciphering correspondences or expecting every feature to stretch on a theological or chronological grid. Attempts to find significance in details such as the report of the fellow servants or the torturers is misguided, for they violate the character of parables or do not fit Jesus' nonparabolic teaching. The second servant is forgotten in prison, for his fate is not the concern of the parable. The servants who report to their master have no relevance in interpretation either. God does not have torturers and does not need anyone to report on the failure of his people. Parables are analogies, not pictures of reality.

This text is a clear example of the tension between two or more truths that are always present in Christian theology. The community cannot tolerate sin without confrontation and reproof, but must always love and forgive without limits. Deciding what should be done is always a matter of wisdom. Sin has disastrous and eternal consequences, confrontation and discipline are necessary, and excommunication from the community is a real possibility. At the same time, God searches out those who stray and wills that none be lost, and the community can lay no bounds to its forgiveness or forget that its forgiveness is modeled on God's forgiveness of its members' own much larger debt. The biblical and Jewish traditions do not feel the tension we feel between reproof and love. Rebuke of the neighbor and love of the neighbor stand together in Lev 19:17 and *T. Gad* 6.3-4. By framing Jesus' teaching as he has, Matthew has insisted that the community address seriously issues of obedience and sin, if possible in discrete ways, even if that leads to starting all over with those it rebukes, treating them as outsiders. At the same time Matthew has insisted that humility and forgiveness dominate the efforts.

The parable prevents any presuming on grace. The church has often presented a grace that did not have to be taken seriously, but biblical grace is transforming grace. When you get the gift, you get the Giver,[68] who will not let you go your way.

6. Does this parable teach a form of "works righteousness" which argues that one's forgiveness of others is the precondition for experiencing divine forgiveness? To ask whether the parable teaches "works righteousness" is to force a Pauline agenda on a Matthean text. Neither Matthew nor Jesus is legalistic, neither promotes salvation by works, neither faces Paul's problem, but both insist that discipleship includes obedience. All the focus on obedience, however, is based in God's prior action. The indicative of God's forgiveness precedes the imperative of our response. In Matthew, as elsewhere in both Testaments, the ethic is a responsive ethic, a response to God's grace and calling. That is obvious with this parable's first scene, the depiction of the master's mercy, but it is also true even in texts that seem to say that human obedience causes God's response (e.g., 6:14-15). In such texts God's presence is presumed precisely because the kingdom is present in the ministry of Jesus.

The fear of works righteousness is far too exaggerated. Would that there were an equal fear of being found inactive. Works righteousness is not the problem of most modern Christians. We would do better to realize that if we do not work, we are not righteous.

7. To what degree is the parable christological? Is the king in the parable a "God figure" or a "Christ figure"? If one does not discount the *nimshal* in v. 35, it indicates that the parable refers to the Father's mercy and judgment, rather than to the mercy of Jesus. Even without v. 35 the reference is to God. However, no gulf should be forced between what God does and what Jesus as God's agent does. As the Davidic king rules in the kingdom of God in the OT, so the Messiah functions as king in God's kingdom. If so, the parable has christological implications.[69] It focuses on the forgiveness available in the kingdom, a forgiveness often extended by Jesus himself. Further, of the five times the verb "have compassion" *(splanchnizomai)* appears in Matthew, the other four have Jesus as the subject.[70] At best, though, the christological thinking is implicit and is not the focus of the parable.

8. Is God bound by the unlimited forgiveness of vv. 21-22? Some are offended that God does not seem bound by the demand for limitless mercy in vv. 21-22, but this is a distortion caused by the failure to stay within the narrative world. Asking about the limits of God's mercy is certainly legitimate, but it is not the concern of this parable. In the end we should recognize that God is the only one who ultimately can hold humanity accountable. The concern of the parable is God's forgiveness and the seriousness of failing to mirror God's mercy, not an atonement theology or a general discussion of judgment. At least within Scripture a focus on the boundless mercy of God does not preclude judgment, even if mercy is given more emphasis (cf. Jas 2:13). The comment of E. Fuchs is appropriate: "God does not insist upon his pound. . . . But God insists upon the dignity of his mercy."[71] God's mercy must not be treated cavalierly. Mercy is not effectively received unless it is shown, for God's mercy transforms. If God's mercy does not take root in the heart, it is not experienced. Forgiveness not shown is forgiveness not known. As Jeremias and others correctly indicate, the parable teaches "Woe to you if you stand on your rights, for God will then stand on his and see that judgment is executed"[72] (cf. Matt 7:1-5; 10:8).

This parable then pictures the magnanimous and limitless grace of God in forgiving the incalculable debt of sin. This Jubilee forgiveness is made available in Jesus' present kingdom, but grace always brings with it responsibility. The forgiveness of God must be replicated in the lives of the forgiven, and the warning is clear. Where forgiveness is not extended, people will be held accountable.

Adapting the Parable

Discussion of the procedure for church discipline in 18:15-20 rarely does justice to the framing of Matthew. All too often these verses are lifted from their context and used in legalistic and insensitive ways, which could not be further from Matthew's intent. What if church leaders merely followed the order of the chapter and looked in humility to themselves first, looked at the causes of sin in the world, took seriously God's care and seeking for those who stray (knowing that it is not God's will that one of these least ones is destroyed), spoke truth taking care to guard the privacy of the offender as much as possible without ignoring the sin, set no limits for forgiveness, and emphasized the necessity of a forgiveness modeled on God's own forgiveness, knowing that judgment is severe for those who do not forgive?

The message of this parable is badly needed by churches and individuals who live in a society where people insist on standing on their rights and division marks our churches, families, and societies. The teaching of the parable is counterintuitive, but it is possibly the most forceful expression of how Christians should live. Christian living — rather than insisting on rights — should be a continual dispensing of mercy and forgiveness, mirroring God's own character and treatment of his people. The NT ethic is a responsive, reflective ethic, one that responds to God's prior acts of mercy and reflects his actions in human lives. Unfortunately forgiveness and mercy are often least at home in our churches, and our society views forgiveness as weakness. But, as Mahatma Gandhi reportedly said, only the strong can forgive. Society also cheapens forgiveness so that sin is treated lightly, but the focus on judgment in Jesus' parables warns that forgiveness brings with it a call for reform. If forgiveness does not effect change, it is not experienced.

Further, it would be wrong to keep this parable on the "spiritual" level and ignore its implications on the economic level. Surely mercy extends beyond forgiveness for wrongs done to compassion for people in desperate economic situations. There are right ways and wrong ways to theologize about parables, and it is wrong to read this parable as an allegory of modern economic circumstances.[73] On the other hand, the theology of the parable, which is rooted in a *required* compassion and mercy, must be applied in all circumstances. What better witness to the kingdom than release from enslaving debt by those who can provide such release? The mercy of the kingdom is evident when people are assisted out of desperate situations, whether economic or otherwise.

For Further Reading

W. D. Davies and Dale C. Allison, *A Critical and Exegetical Commentary on the Gospel According to Saint Matthew* (3 vols.; ICC; Edinburgh: T. & T. Clark, 1988-97), 2:791-807.

Thomas Deidun, "The Parable of the Unmerciful Servant (Mt 18:23-35)," *BTB* 6 (1976): 203-24.

Joachim Jeremias, *The Parables of Jesus* (2d ed., trans. S. H. Hooke; New York: Charles Scribner's Sons, 1963), pp. 210-14.

Peter Rhea Jones, *Studying the Parables of Jesus* (Macon, Ga.: Smyth & Helwys, 1999), pp. 263-93.

William G. Thompson, *Matthew's Advice to a Divided Community: Mt. 17,22–18,35* (AnBib 44; Rome: Biblical Institute Press, 1970), pp. 203-37.

THE TWO DEBTORS
(Luke 7:41-43)

Claude Montefiore, a Jewish NT scholar, described "this exquisite story [as] . . . one of the treasured religious possessions of the Western world."[74] Although neglected,[75] it deserves to be ranked with the most revealing stories of the Christian faith. While it is not as explicit as the parable of the Unforgiving Servant, the same themes of grace and responsibility show through clearly.

Parable Type

This small parable is a juridical parable, the type of double indirect narrative parable that elicits a self-judgment. It is a typical three-pronged, brief analogy enclosed within a narrative. The analogy sets forth a reality and concludes with a question requiring a decision, which is provided by the Pharisee. As with many parables, the answer to the question must be transferred to the circumstances being discussed, and in this regard vv. 44-46 function as an extended *nimshal.*

Issues Requiring Attention

1. What is the relation of this account to the anointing stories in the other Gospels?

2. Was this parable originally told in the context of a meal with a Pharisee, or were the parable and the meal narrative independent units that have been joined later?
3. What elements originally made up the meal narrative?
4. What is the meaning of the parable? Specifically what should we understand takes place in the narrative and in the parable?
5. What is the relation of the woman's acts and her forgiveness? Did she act because she was forgiven, or was she forgiven because of her acts?
6. What is the relation of love and faith?

Helpful Primary Source Material

See the sources listed under the parable of the Unforgiving Servant (pp. 62-65).

Canonical Material

- OT: Lev 25:8-55; Deut 15:2; Neh 10:31
- NT: Matt 6:12/Luke 11:4 (sin as debts, *opheilēmata;* sinners as debtors, *opheiletais*); Matt 18:21-35; 23:16, 18 (for the idea of being indebted, *opheilei*); Luke 13:4 (which asks if the eighteen on whom the tower fell were greater debtors, *opheiletai*, than others; cf. 13:2, which uses "sinners" as a parallel to "debtors"); 16:5

Early Jewish Writings

- 1 Macc 10:43 and 15:8 report rulers canceling debts in an attempt to gain favor with their subjects, but the message is not taken seriously.
- *4 Maccabees* 2:8 points to the canceling of debts in the seventh year.
- Josephus, *Ant.* 19.358 tells of celebrations at the death of Agrippa which included public feasts with people reclining, wearing garlands, and using scented ointments.
- *Joseph and Aseneth* 7.1 and 20.2-5: Joseph's feet are washed in preparation for a meal.

Greco-Roman Writings

The following items may have no direct relevance for understanding Luke 7:36-50 because they describe much more elaborate affairs than a dinner with a Pharisee.

- Petronius, *Satyricon* 31-78 offers a long description of an extravagant banquet at which slaves serve and care for guests, even washing their hands and paring hangnails. He then reports [70], "I am ashamed to tell you what followed: in defiance of all convention, some long-haired boys brought ointment in a silver basin, and anointed our feet as we lay, after winding little garlands round our feet and ankles."

- Plutarch, *Mor.* 712A (*Quaestiones conviviales* 7.8) says that at banquets of the great a special waiter stands by each guest. Seneca, *De Beneficiis* 3.27.1 is further evidence. But, of course, the dinner of a Pharisee hardly qualifies as a "banquet of the great."

- Plutarch, *Mor.* 148C, *Septem Sapientium Convivium* ("Dinner of the Seven Wise Men") indicates that guests on arriving at luxurious dinners enjoyed a rubdown or bath. See also Xenophon, *Symposium* 1.7-8. Further evidence of slaves washing and attending to the needs of guests is provided by Plato, *Symposium* 175A, 213B.

Later Jewish Writings

- *b. 'Abodah Zarah* 4a: "'I will explain it by a parable,' he replied, 'To what may it be compared? To a man who is the creditor of two persons, one of them a friend, the other an enemy; of his friend he will accept payment little by little, whereas of his enemy he will exact payment in one sum!'" In the interpretation God is the creditor, and Israel is the friend. The enemy has no correspondent in reality.[76]

Comparison of the Accounts

There is no parallel to the parable in Luke 7:41-42, but the similarity of the banquet anointing scene in 7:36-50 to that in Matt 26:6-13/Mark 14:3-9/John 12:1-8 creates a vexing problem. The context of the parallels is "passion week" just prior to the final events which led to Jesus' arrest. Luke does not have an anointing during "passion week." The other Evangelists view the anointing as a preparation for Jesus' burial, concerning which nothing is said in Luke. In Matthew and Mark a woman anoints Jesus' head, but in Luke and John she anoints his feet (Luke and John often converge in the passion narrative). In Matthew and Mark the incident occurs in Bethany in the house of Simon the leper, and the woman is unnamed. In Luke it occurs in an unspecified city *in Galilee* in the house of Simon *the Pharisee,* and the woman is described as a known sinner of the city. In John the anointing occurs in Bethany in an unspecified house, but

Lazarus is there, Martha is serving, and Mary is the woman who anoints Jesus. The designation of Lazarus as "one of those at table" suggests that this is not the house of Lazarus and his sisters, but it could be.[77] Unlike Luke, the other three Evangelists agree in recording both the complaint that this costly perfume should have been sold, with the proceeds given to the poor, and Jesus' defense of the woman.

Obviously the other three Evangelists record the same event, but whether Luke records a different but similar anointing is debated. Simon was a common name and does not necessarily show that Luke records the same event as Matthew and Mark, but it is pushing things to suggest that Simon the leper was a Pharisee. Luke surely would not have described Mary as a known sinner of the city. On the other hand, some agreements suggest that all four accounts point to the same event, especially the description of the perfume as an "alabaster [vase] of perfume" in all three Synoptics and the woman drying Jesus' feet with her hair in Luke and John. From a mechanical standpoint not a lot of agreement exists. The only words Luke has in common with Matthew and Mark are "the house of," "woman," "alabaster [vase] of perfume," and "recline." Luke's only words in common with John are "the feet," "dried with hair," "his feet," and "perfume."

Four explanations are possible: Luke records the same event as the others but alters the location and makes it polemical;[78] Luke records the same event, but the others have shaped the event toward the passion;[79] Luke records a similar but different event;[80] or Luke records a different event but the traditions have influenced each other.[81] While NT scholars have various theories, there is much we do not know and cannot prove. In fact, T. Brodie thinks we have a stalemate on the question of the relation of these accounts.[82] Still, some comments seem valid. Even if Luke were referring to the same event as the others, it is clear that his account is *not directly dependent* on any of them. Also, it is more likely that the anointing of Jesus' feet was changed to the anointing of his head than the reverse. The anointing of the head would more easily convey messianic ideas.[83] Each of the Evangelists should be allowed to tell his own story, but forced to make a choice, I would say that we have two separate events and that the traditions of these events have influenced each other in the course of transmission.[84]

Textual Features Worth Noting

Like Matt 18:23-35 this parable assumes that forgiveness is a gracious release from indebtedness to God. In both these parables and the parable of the Unjust Steward in Luke 16:1-8, money seems of little importance to the person owed.

Luke 7:36-50 is clearly an example of Jesus' (and John's) association with and reception by sinners as discussed in 7:29-30 and 34, but it also illustrates the division between the religious authorities and the sinful people attracted to Jesus.[85] Luke has a special concern for sinners: in addition to this text, note 5:8, 30, 32; 6:32-34; 7:34; 13:2; 15:1, 2, 7, 10; 18:13; 19:7; 24:7.[86]

This is one of three Lukan parables outside the travel narrative of chs. 9–19 (the other two being the Two Builders and the Sower), and the only one unique to Luke that is not in the travel narrative.

The forgiveness/release theme (*aphiēmi* and *aphesis* cover both ideas) is important in Luke. Note 1:77; 3:3; 4:18 (twice); 5:20, 21, 23, 24; 7:47-49; 11:4; 12:10; 17:3-4; 23:34; 24:47. See also the use of *apolyō* in 6:37; 13:12; and *apolytrōsis* ("redemption") in 21:28.[87]

Luke 5, especially vv. 17-26, has a number of parallels with 7:36-50. In 5:8 Peter confesses that he is a sinner *(hamartōlos)*, and in 7:39 the woman who anoints Jesus is described with the same word. In 5:20-24 and 7:48-50 Jesus forgives sins, forgiveness is connected to faith, and people ask who this is who thinks he forgives sins. In 5:22 and 7:40 (by implication) Jesus knows what is in people's hearts. In both texts a Pharisee or Pharisees question Jesus' actions, and in both there is astonishment from onlookers. In 5:29-30 Jesus reclines at a banquet with tax collectors and sinners, which results in grumbling from Pharisees and scribes. In 7:38-39 Jesus reclines at a Pharisee's banquet, and contact with a sinful woman results in unexpressed questioning.

Jesus is also invited to meals with Pharisees in 11:37-54 and 14:1-24, and conflict results.[88] Other passages also have parables used in the context of conflict (10:25-37; 12:13-21, although here the conflict is between brothers, not with Jesus; 15:1-32; 20:1-19).

Some similarity of form exists between this parable and the Good Samaritan. In 7:42 and 10:36 Jesus asks his hearer a "Which of these" question, and in 7:43 and 10:37 the hearer responds with the obvious answer, and Jesus draws a conclusion from the answer.

The parable of the Pharisee and the Toll Collector in 18:9-14 parallels 7:36-50 in that a Pharisee and a sinner are contrasted, and in both cases the Pharisee comes out inferior.

Jesus is presented as a prophet in Luke as strongly as anywhere.[89] Codices Vaticanus and Zacynthius have *ho prophētēs* ("the prophet") in v. 39 instead of merely *prophētēs*. The reading with the article would point to *the* eschatological prophet, an end-time deliverer, but the reading without the article is much more strongly attested and surely correct.[90]

Cultural Information

The Pharisee was not obligated to wash Jesus' feet, anoint him with oil, and greet him with a kiss, but he should have provided water so that Jesus could wash his own feet. A kiss would have been an appropriate greeting and a way to honor a guest.[91]

Kissing someone's feet was the ultimate way to express honor, gratitude, and submission,[92] but it was also an act of deep humility.[93]

Anointing with oil was a common procedure (cf. Deut. 28:40; Ruth 3:3; Ps. 23:5), but anointing with costly perfume (*myron*, the word in Luke 7:37) was unusual.[94] The LXX at Exod 30:25-28 uses *hagion myron* to describe the perfumed ointment for anointing the tabernacle furniture, Ps 133:2 speaks of anointing the head with precious oil (LXX *myron*), and Song 1:3 speaks of fragrant anointing oils of the male lover. Josephus, *Ant.* 19.239 reports that Claudius Agrippa, when summoned to the Roman senate, anointed his head with perfumes *(myrois)* as if he had arrived from a banquet, which suggests that such anointings may have been customary at luxurious banquets in Rome,[95] but it would be hazardous to transfer such a custom to first-century Palestine.[96]

Anointing the feet would have been highly unusual,[97] and anointing them with perfume would have also been an extravagant and almost certainly offensive act, especially from a sinful woman. *If* the woman was a prostitute, which is probable but not the only possiblity,[98] the perfumed ointment would have been used in her profession.[99] Jesus' attitude toward prostitutes is in marked contrast to Sir 26:22: "A prostitute is regarded as spittle. . . ."

For a woman to let her hair down in public was usually considered a shameful and seductive act, something no respectable woman would do.[100] To anoint Jesus' feet, kiss them repeatedly,[101] and dry them with her hair would all have been viewed as erotic and shameful acts, *if* it were not for her tears, and clearly the woman did not intend the acts to be erotic.[102] Women sometimes let their hair down for other reasons, especially to show religious devotion/gratitude or grief, either of which could be operative here.[103]

Meals have always been important times for conversation. In the Greco-Roman world a long-standing tradition of symposia as a place of philosophical exchange (and less exalted exchanges) is evidenced in various writings.[104] Scholars often suggest that Luke mirrors Greco-Roman symposia with his meal settings,[105] but the more one reads about symposia the less likely this appears true.[106] Accounts of symposia are usually long narratives with all those in attendance expected to offer a discourse on the topic at hand, and symposia are often depicted as bawdy drinking parties.[107] None of this fits the meals Jesus attended. Not every meal was a symposium, and the verbs used for reclining (*anaklinō, kataklinō, katakeimai*) do not by themselves refer to a symposium meal. These verbs, not verbs for sitting, are used for meals in general, including the feeding of the five thousand (Matt 14:19/Mark 6:39/Luke 9:14). Furthermore, the only two occurrences of *symposion* in the NT are in Mark 6:39, where it cannot possibly have any relation to a Hellenistic symposium. Luke 5:29-32, a parallel account of Jesus eating with sinners, surely is not to be viewed as mirroring a symposium.

Particularly within a Jewish context, if not a meritorious act, it was at least an honor to have a respected teacher as a guest for a meal. In calling Jesus a teacher the Pharisee gave him a title of respect and honor, as is clear from Matt 23:8-10 and other texts. Pharisees viewed meals as an opportunity for study with *ḥaberim* (partners in purity), if "Pharisee" and "*ḥaber*" are synonymous. They were extremely concerned with ritual purity at meals.[108] This only heightens for Jesus' Pharisaic host the offensive character of the woman's actions. Defilement was a much more serious matter among ancient Jews than we can imagine. *T. Yoma* 1.12 argues that uncleanness is worse than bloodshed. (Note that 2 Sam 11:4 already has a concern for purity in the midst of David's committing adultery.)

That the people reclined at the meal indicates that it was a relatively formal occasion. Women did not usually eat with men at banquets, but the woman's presence is not completely out of the ordinary, especially in narratives about Jesus.[109] In the Middle East banquets tended to be less private than we might expect. Houses were more open, and uninvited people could come in and observe from the sidelines and among the servants.[110] The guests would have reclined at table angling away from the food so that their feet would have been on the perimeter of the meal configuration. Women and slaves or uninvited watchers would have stood outside the circle and near the feet of the guests.

A denarius is one day's wage for a common laborer. Therefore, the first debtor in the parable owes a little more than a year and a half's wages, and the second owes about two months' wages. Indebtedness was a terrible social problem in the ancient world. When the temple was taken over in the revolt against Rome, the first act was to destroy the records of debt.[111]

Explanation of the Parable[112]

We do not need to list the options for interpretation for this parable, for, although differences in interpretation exist, the parable is clear and rather straightforward. Questions exist about theories of redaction and about nuances, but the parable's message of grace and forgiveness is compelling and obvious.

Decisions on the Issues

1. *The relation of this account to the anointing stories in the other Gospels* has already been treated in the section on the comparison of accounts (see above, pp. 79-80).

2. *Was this parable originally told in the context of a meal with a Pharisee, or were the parable and narrative independent units that have been joined later?* Supposed areas of unevenness between the parable and the meal narrative suggest to some that the parable was originally independent of the narrative. Evidence offered for this view includes: the meal story tells about forgiveness of sins, the parable about remission of debts; the story contrasts everything and nothing, but the parable contrasts much and little; and in the meal story love has to do with forgiveness, but in the parable love is the point of comparison.[113] These contrasts are overdrawn. The parable does not contrast much and little; it asks a question about two debtors. Further, the supposed contrasts ignore the metaphor of debts for sins and presume that parables must look exactly like the reality they mirror. They do not. There is no basis for arguing the parable had an independent life separate from this narrative. The parable and narrative not only belong together, but the parable has its origin in and derives its meaning from the specific occasion. If vv. 41-43 are removed, the reply to the Pharisee's thoughts and the transition to the idea of forgiveness make little sense.[114]

3. *What elements originally made up the meal story?* Several theories have been offered about the tradition history of this pericope, none of them compelling.[115] Often v. 47 and especially vv. 48-50 or portions of them are seen as later additions to the original story. Part of the concern leading to the rejection of v. 47 is theologically motivated to avoid the suggestion that the woman earned forgiveness by her actions rather than acted because she was forgiven. Part of the concern derives from the awareness of parallels to the question "Who is this who forgives sin?" (v. 49; see 5:21 but also Mark 2:7; 4:41) and to the statement "Your faith has saved you; go in peace," which introduces faith, a subject not in the earlier part of the pericope but paralleled exactly in the miracle story of the woman with the issue of blood.[116] The tensions in the text are real, at least from our standpoint, but in the end none of the tradition histories is convincing, and v. 46 is not an appropriate stopping place. Some conclusion such as v. 47 and some response to the woman from Simon or the onlookers such as is found in vv. 48-49 are necessary. The story is surely incomplete without such responses. Still, this section bears a strong Lukan stamp.

The only verse not fitting easily in the context is v. 50. Whether it is what Jesus said about the woman's faith or a saying shaped by Luke to draw an analogy with the miracle stories cannot be easily determined. John Kilgallen argues against seeing v. 50 as an addendum,[117] but the language is Lukan. In any case, v. 50 is an appropriate narrative ending, and "Your faith has saved you; go in peace" fits as well for metaphorical healing as for literal healing.

Awareness of how infrequently "faith" *(pistis)* is treated in the Gospels is enlightening. John, of course, never uses the word. In the Synoptics it is most often used in connection with miracle stories, especially healings, and in rebukes of the disciples for being people of little faith. Outside these contexts *pistis* is used sparingly: in discussions about the efficacy of even a little faith (Matt 17:20/Luke 17:5-6; Matt 21:21-22/Mark 11:22-24); faith/faithfulness as one of the weightier matters of the Law (Matt 23:23), in the question whether the Son of Man will find faith when he returns (Luke 18:8), and in Jesus' prayer for Simon Peter's faith (Luke 22:32). Regardless of a decision about the origin of 7:50, its connection of faith, forgiveness, and salvation is unparalleled in the Gospels.[118]

4. What is the meaning of the parable? Specifically what should we understand takes place in the meal narrative and in the parable? The meal story partly illustrates the contrast in 7:29-34 between Jesus' (and John the Baptist's) reception by and association with sinners and the rejection of both John and Jesus by "the children of this generation" (especially Pharisees), but the story goes well beyond this contrast.[119]

The suggested structure of three cases of report and evaluation (vv. 36-38, 39; 40-42, 43; and 44-46, 47) followed by vv. 48-50 as an epilogue is the most helpful.[120]

Nothing sinister should be attached to the fact that a Pharisee invited Jesus for a meal.[121] Pharisees invite Jesus to meals elsewhere in Luke (11:37; 14:1) and also warn Jesus that Herod wants to kill him (13:31).[122] Further, explanations that see the Pharisee as deliberately insulting Jesus by not providing the hospitable acts described in vv. 44-46 go too far.[123] The Pharisee may have been insensitive or less than gracious, but his failures do not constitute antagonism prior to the woman's actions.

Since the woman brought the ointment with her, she almost certainly came with the intent to anoint Jesus' feet. Occasionally she is identified with Mary Magdalene, but no justification exists for this. Her identity is not known, other than the fact that the townspeople knew that she was a sinner, presumably a prostitute but that is not certain. An Aramaic wordplay lies behind the text. The words for sinner *(ḥayyabta)*, lender *(mar ḥoba)*, debtor *(bar ḥoba or ḥayyab)*, sin *(ḥoba)*, and love *(ḥabeb or 'aḥeb)* are all obviously similar.[124] The woman's tears fell on Jesus' feet sufficiently that she felt that they should be wiped off. The motive for her tears cannot be determined,[125] but as likely as any explanation is that they are tears of joy. Almost certainly the woman had either heard Jesus or had heard a great deal about him. This meal cannot have been her first awareness of who he was. Jeremias justly assumes we may infer that Jesus' preaching had been heard by the host, the guests, and the woman.[126] By letting her hair down, touching Jesus' feet even with her hair, and anointing his feet with perfume she contravened every social convention of the day. Were it not for her tears, the acts would border on the obscene. Letting her hair down could be interpreted as a sign of grief or religious devotion.[127] No doubt the act was spontaneous rather than thought out, and while devotion is surely present, a variety of motives may be involved.

Pharisees had a concern for purity at meals that we can hardly appreciate. With such purity concerns Simon, the host, was convinced that Jesus' tolerance of contact with this known sinner proved that he could be neither righteous nor a prophet. Two passages from Sirach help to understand the Pharisee's conclusion: 12:14, "So no one pities a person who associates with a sinner and becomes involved in the other's sins"; and 13:17, "What does a wolf have in common with a lamb? No more has a sinner with the devout." One of the most certain facts about Jesus is that he associated with the wrong people, people others thought caused defilement, but Jesus did not fear becoming unclean by contact with the unholy. He thought holiness was stronger and more contagious than defilement,[128] and he accepted the woman's actions as righteous and loving.

Underneath this narrative are questions of identity. Most obvious is the identity of Jesus. To the Pharisee, Jesus could not be a prophet since he did not understand what kind of woman touched him, but, with some irony in the narrative, Jesus shows that he is a prophet because he knows what is in the Pharisee's heart, and more than a prophet because he announces forgiveness of sins. The identity of the woman is at issue. The Pharisee is sure she is a sinner; Jesus is sure she is a forgiven sinner. The Pharisee's identity is also in question. Is he as pure and right before God as he thinks? Directly related to issues of identity are issues of value and honor. Jesus' understanding of the value and honor of people is at direct odds with that of Simon.[129] The sinner woman is better than the Pharisee.

In response to the Pharisee's doubts about Jesus and his certainties about the woman, Jesus tells the cryptic, bare, little parable in vv. 41-42. Such simple, straightforward parables can teach us a lot about how parables function. This is not explicitly a kingdom parable, but surely this parable as much as any demonstrates what the kingdom preaching of Jesus was about.[130] The parable makes two main points by a three-part analogy. The two main points are: God forgives sin freely, and one forgiven more will love more.[131] At least one forgiven more *should* love more, but gratitude is not automatic, as the parable of the Unforgiving Servant attests. The idea that sins are debts to God is well known in Judaism and appears elsewhere in the teaching of Jesus.[132] Canceling of debts may have been subversive to some since it went against the inequality and hierarchy of the client-patron relationship,[133] but it would *not* have been subversive to Jews familiar with Deut 15:1-3 and the year of Jubilee (Lev 25:10-55), both of which call for the canceling of debts. Jesus' adaptation of Isaiah 61 recorded in Luke 4:16-21 is almost certainly to be understood as an announcement of the eschatological Jubilee,[134] and this parable, like the parable of the Unforgiving Servant, assumes that the Jubilee *has begun* and that God is in the process of canceling debts, i.e. forgiving sins.[135] This parable expresses the grace and goodness of God. When it comes to forgiveness, God is like a moneylender who does not care about money.

The word used for the cancellation of debts — *charizomai* — is rarely used of canceling of debts, although parallels do exist.[136] It is formed from the word *charis* ("grace"), often means "give graciously," and is used in the Pauline letters for forgiveness of sins. Luke's only other use of it is in 7:21 in connection with Jesus *granting* sight to many blind people, which provides another connection between this account and miracle stories in Luke.

Clearly this parable has correspondences between image and reality: the creditor corresponds to God (or Jesus), debts correspond to sins, canceling of debts to forgiveness of sins, the woman to the debtor who owed more, and Simon to the debtor who owed less.[137] Again, parable interpretation is not about finding correspondences, even when they exist; the issue is how the analogy works. Still, analogies cannot work without correspondences, and it is not allegorizing to recognize correspondences where they exist. The numbers five hundred and fifty do not have a specific function other than to mark one debt as greater than another. To even ask to what such details refer is to derail the intent of the parable. Not to notice the obvious correspondences is to blindfold oneself to how the analogy functions.

Like many parables, this one ends with a question requiring that the hearer pass judgment. The answer to the question is so obvious that it is almost pedantic, but when Simon gives the answer he sets himself up to be "wounded from behind." Once the answer is granted, the relevance of the conclusion cannot be evaded. Obviously the person forgiven the greater debt (or at least aware of the greater size of the debt forgiven) *should* love more — or possibly be more grateful — in return. J. Jeremias argued that no word for "thank" or "thankfulness" existed in Aramaic, and therefore the Greek word for love *(agapan)* was used in the sense of "gratitude" or "grateful love."[138] However, Hebrew *yadah* and related words were used to express thanksgiving, and there is an advantage in retaining the focus on love.[139] Furthermore, does not love, at least human love, contain gratitude, even if often proleptic?

After Simon answers correctly, Jesus asks if he sees "this woman." Clearly Simon sees her reputation, not her, and is this not frequently still the problem, that we see systems and concerns but not people? This is not to say that concerns about sin or other issues are unimportant, but if Jesus did anything, he actually saw people.

Jesus' contrast of the actions of the woman and of Simon marks out that Simon has done nothing to express any care at all, whereas the woman was extravagant in her love. This extravagance Jesus took as either evidence of, or grounds for, forgiveness. The contrast places the woman in a much more honorable position than Simon and marks him as one who loves little. How is the proverb in v. 47c (note the present tenses) to be understood? "The one forgiven little loves little." Should we understand that Simon was forgiven little because he actually needed but little forgiveness? Certainly he corresponds to the debtor owing the smaller amount in relation to the woman, but the parable is an analogy, not a picture of reality. Once again problems are caused by those who want parables to be perfect reflections of theology. Simon has shown no evidence of love. Has he been forgiven at all? Or to stay with the thought of the proverb, is the one who loves not at all forgiven not at all? The narrative is left open, and surely Jesus' words were intended as a challenge to Simon to reconsider both his own stance — maybe he is not so small a debtor — and his attitudes toward both the woman and Jesus. He cannot be righteous if he does not show the compassion of God.

5. *What is the relation of the woman's acts and her forgiveness? Did she act because she was forgiven, or was she forgiven because of her act?* Are her acts evidence of remorse and repentance? Enormous attention has been given to vv. 47-48 and their implications and especially to *hoti* ("because" in some sense) in v. 47. Vv. 47a and 48 could be taken to mean that she is forgiven because of her acts of love. V. 47b ("The one forgiven little loves little"), however, implies that the woman's love is a consequence of her forgiveness. Often this is pitched as a disagreement between Catholics and Protestants, with the former seeing the woman's love as the basis of her forgiveness (taking *hoti* as "because") and the latter arguing that the woman's love stems from her previous forgiveness (taking *hoti* as "in recognition of the fact that").[140]

The attempt to guard against salvation by works motivates much of the discussion, and we can agree with Jülicher that the discussion is loaded with prejudice.[141] Before deciding on this issue, we should recognize that, as far as we can tell, neither Jesus nor the Evangelists were as anxious as we are about avoiding any thought of salvation by works. Other texts display a similar "strangeness" of order or lack of concern about the order of salvation. The merciful receive mercy (Matt 5:7), those who forgive are forgiven (Matt 6:12/Luke 11:4), and people are told to obey in order to have eternal life (Luke 10:25-28; 18:18-23). In Luke 17:19 the cleansed leper who returns is told that his faith has saved him, language that elsewhere is used of healings, but the other nine lepers were healed too. In any case, the statement is a consequence of the leper's action. None of these texts is urging salvation by works. F. Bovon is correct to say that in 7:36-50 Luke is not posing the theological question of the relation of God's initiative and human response and that for Luke both are active in reconciliation. For Bovon the woman's actions are simultaneously indications of and reasons for her forgiveness.[142] Although we are unduly exercised over this issue, several points can be mentioned that strengthen the case that forgiveness precedes the woman's love:

> The logic *of the parable* assumes that forgiveness comes first and without any reason in the debtor and that love flows from forgiveness.
> Something prior caused the woman's actions. From the standpoint of the narrative the woman's actions are a response to Jesus being a friend of sinners (7:34).[143]
> The statements about forgiveness in vv. 47a, 48 use the perfect tense ("have been forgiven"), indicating that forgiveness preceded the acts of love.
> *Hoti* can mean "in recognition that."

That said, however, the parable emphasizes the interrelation of love and forgiveness. Luke is not concerned to answer our questions about the woman's remorse or repentance. He assumes that if the reader understands forgiveness granted and love expressed, remorse and repentance will take care of themselves.[144] Repentance in this text is assumed, certainly for Luke, or talk about "her many sins" and forgiveness makes no sense. The context of faith and peace does not leave her in her sin. Neither the parable nor the narrative does everything, and neither should be expected to. What Luke emphasizes for his reader is that with Jesus forgiveness — the Jubilee release — is being dispensed, and people like this sinful woman took full advantage of it and found peace and salvation, even while people like the Pharisee could not understand or accept what was happening. In that regard, it may be that the woman's actions were part of the celebration inherent in Jesus' message.

Obviously this narrative and parable have christological implications.

The implication is that Jesus is the one who forgave since he is the one who receives the love. At the very least, he validates his prophetic stature and that he is the agent announcing God's forgiveness, but much more seems intended than that. Further, that Jesus is viewed as forgiving sins carries with it suggestions that he is replacing the temple functions or at least that his actions are on a par with the temple (cf. Matt 12:6).

With regard to Simon the narrative is left open. The parable functions as a warning and a challenge to Simon, but we do not know how he responded.

6. *What is the relation of love and faith?* This pericope forces us to bring faith and love closer in relation than we usually do. For us faith is a head matter, whereas love is a heart matter, but Scripture does not know this bifurcation. In this passage love is understood as the expression of faith (cf. Gal 5:6), and properly understood it is difficult to imagine faith that does not involve love. To love God with the whole heart, mind, and strength is not something less than faith, and faith cannot accomplish more. Faith will love, or it is not faith (cf. the discussion of Luke 10:25-37; pp. 338-62 below).

Cancellation of debts is pure grace, but it is grace that transforms, creates love and relationship, and requires — even demands — a response. Jesus' parable and the dialogue accompanying it demonstrate the presence of the kingdom, the forgiveness made available to sinners, and the responsibility that comes with grace.

Adapting the Parable

For both this parable and that of the Unforgiving Servant one central focus is response. The kingdom comes with limitless grace in the midst of an evil world, but grace that does not bring forth a response is grace unknown. Christians today too frequently think grace can be received without effect and without response. That is impossible. Is the tepidness of our commitment to God because we have a very small sense of a huge debt forgiven? If we care about what God has done for us, gratitude that responds and acts will be present.

Part of that response will be to develop the ability actually to see people. If anything was true of Jesus, he could see people — not just look at them. We need to be able to see beyond the obvious and the form of people to see who they actually are, what their needs are, and what their potential is. Only then can the love of God find an avenue through us. The ability to see also involves the ability actually to see and evaluate our culture.

Particularly in white North American culture, people are taught to guard against emotion in their responses, but nothing great happens without emotion.[145] The woman in this parable teaches us the importance of emotion, of not taking forgiveness for granted but having some sense of its value. This is what gave her a deep love and commitment to Jesus. We should not downplay the importance of this woman's response. The similarity of her act of anointing Jesus' feet and drying them with her hair to his act of washing the feet of the disciples and drying them with a towel is obvious, especially as love is marked as the motivation for both (Luke 7:47 and John 13:1). Jesus was the recipient of such an act of love and humility prior to extending it to his disciples. The woman modeled the humility Jesus expressed.

Questions of identity obviously must be faced. Christological implications must be drawn, but especially questions about our own identity in relation to God and to other people must be faced. We are debtors, and potentially, if we are willing to respond, forgiven debtors, and we are all in that category. None of us actually fits in a "lesser debtor" category. This means that disdain for others and attitudes of superiority have no place with Christians. The parable does not portray the whole chain of events, but a glance at human society shows that arrogance leads to disdain, which leads to strife, which often leads to violence.[146]

The implications of this parable for issues of separation from sin and "the world" are large. Clearly separation cannot entail separation from people. Christians do not have the right to reject "outcasts." Even when rejecting specific actions, Christians must be willing to embrace sinners without affirming actions or events that are clearly wrong. Holiness, at least true holiness, is stronger and more contagious than sin.[147] Sin is to be avoided, not feared. A wideness of soul *(makrothymia)* is extended to people to help them move toward faith and obedience.

Grace and responsibility are not about cheap grace, nor is grace ever without responsibility. People and churches want grace without responsibility. Forgiveness is without limits but not without responsibility, confession, truth, and even restitution. These two parables are only two pictures of the many-sided subject of forgiveness.

For Further Reading

Kenneth E. Bailey, *Through Peasant Eyes: More Lucan Parables, Their Culture and Style* (Grand Rapids: Eerdmans, 1980), pp. 1-21.

François Bovon, *Luke 1: A Commentary on the Gospel of Luke 1:1–9:50* (trans. Christine M. Thomas; Minneapolis: Fortress, 2002), pp. 289-98.

Hans Drexler, "Die große Sünderin Lucas 7:36-50," *ZNW* 59 (1968): 159-73.

Joseph A. Fitzmyer, *The Gospel According to Luke (I–IX): Introduction, Translation, and Notes* (AB; Garden City, N.Y.: Doubleday, 1979), pp. 683-94.

John Nolland, *Luke 1–9:20* (WBC; Dallas: Word, 1989), pp. 349-62.

James A. Sanders, "Sins, Debts, and Jubilee Release," in *Luke and Scripture: The Function of Sacred Tradition in Luke-Acts* (ed. Craig A. Evans and James A. Sanders; Minneapolis: Fortress, 1993), pp. 84-92.

Reinhard von Bendemann, "Liebe und Sündenvergebung. Eine narrativ-traditionsgeschichtliche Analyse von Lk 7,36-50," *BZ* 44 (2000): 161-82.

Parables of Lostness

The closely related parables of the Lost Sheep, the Lost Coin, and the Two Lost Sons in Luke 15 deal with loss and recovery. They reflect Jesus' use of a specific theme to speak about the presence of the kingdom and the compassion of God. They should be seen first in relation to the parables of grace and responsibility because of what they reveal about God. They should also be set in relation to the parables of the present kingdom.

The Arrangement of Luke 15

Luke has clearly arranged ch. 15 for rhetorical effect, and an understanding of how this section functions assists in interpreting the individual parables. The flow of the chapter is easily discernible:

> vv. 1-3 — an editorial description of the reason for these parables in the grumbling of the Pharisees and scribes at Jesus' reception of and eating with sinners (though in v. 3 the word "parable" is singular)[1]
> vv. 4-7 — the parable of the Lost Sheep
> vv. 8-10 — the parable of the Lost Coin
> vv. 11-32 — the parable of the Two Lost Sons

Matthew places the parable of the Lost Sheep in a completely different context, and *Gos. Thom.* also has this parable, but the other two parables have no parallel.

Virtually every possible explanation of the origin of this collection has representatives. Some argue that Luke's tradition had already joined these three parables, some that he is responsible for bringing them together. Some argue that the Lost Sheep and Lost Coin were told at the same time or were brought together before Luke, others that they were not. Some argue that both parables were in Q and that Matthew omitted the Lost Coin, and others that the Matthean and Lukan versions are from M and L respectively. None of the theories are demonstrable or contribute much to understanding.[2]

What is demonstrable is how this section of Luke achieves its rhetorical effect. At least ch. 15, if not the whole of 14:1–17:10, is focused on the gospel for the outcasts.[3] This chapter is the heart of Luke's travel narrative, in which he presents the bulk of Jesus' teaching and, for that matter, the heart of his whole Gospel. Grouping three or even more parables together for an effective argument has parallels in rabbinic literature and in Greek chreiai.[4] Without diminishing the importance of the Lost Sheep and the Lost Coin, these two interrogative parables function almost as a prelude to the longer and more complex parable of the Two Lost Sons.[5] The movement from one hundred sheep to ten coins to two sons supports the climactic nature of the structure. Ch. 15 has connections with ch. 14 in the Pharisaic attitude toward Jesus' actions (14:1-6 and 15:1-2), in Jesus' concern for the outcasts (14:13, 23 and 15:1-2), and in the repetition of the word "hear" (14:35 and 15:1), which is especially important. The three parables in ch. 15 challenge those with ears to hear to join in the rejoicing. There are connections with ch. 16 in the identical beginnings of the parables in 15:11 and 16:1 ("A certain man had," *anthrōpos tis eichen*), use of the word "squander" (*diaskorpizein*, 15:13 and 16:1), and in parables about a person dealing with a crisis of no resources (the prodigal in 15:14-16, the unjust steward in 16:3, Lazarus in 16:20-21, with "desiring to be filled" *(epithymein chortasthēnai)* used of both the prodigal and Lazarus). Such connections are not keys to interpretation, and some may result merely from standard expressions. They would, however, have assisted hearers processing oral material.

More important are the subject matter addressed and the internal relations within ch. 15. Jesus' association with toll collectors and sinners is one of the surest — and to the religious authorities most unacceptable — features of his ministry.[6] Jesus considered that his mission was to seek and to save the lost (Luke 5:32; 19:10; see also Matt 10:6; 15:24; Luke 15:1-10). Parallel to the grumbling of the Pharisees and scribes in 15:2 and the grumbling and jealousy of the elder brother is the grumbling of the workers in the parable of the Vineyard Workers (Matt 20:11-12),[7] the attitude of Simon toward the sinful woman who anointed Jesus (Luke 7:36-50), the disdain of the Pharisee in the parable of the Pharisee and the Toll Collector (Luke 18:11), the grumbling that occurs when Jesus eats with Zacchaeus (Luke 19:7), and most importantly, the grumbling of the Pharisees and their scribes at Jesus' eating and drinking with toll collectors and sinners at the banquet put on by Levi (5:27-32). The similarity of 5:29-32 to 15:1-2, 7 marks the importance of this theme for Luke.

Regarding connections within ch. 15, an inclusio exists between the grumbling of the Pharisees in vv. 1-2 and the grumbling of the elder brother in vv. 29-30. The claim of the elder son to have never transgressed a command (v. 29) parallels the righteous who do not need to repent (v. 7). The joy and celebration in vv. 5-7 and 9-10 parallels the rejoicing and celebration at the return of the prodigal (vv. 22-27 and 32). In fact, celebration and joy are the dominant motifs in the chapter. The first two parables focus on what was lost and then found, which is picked up in the refrain "was lost and has been found" regarding the prodigal (vv. 24, 32). There can be little doubt that the three parables carry the same essential message, but there are differences. No fault is assigned to the sheep or coin, even though the applications of both parables focus on repentance, but the prodigal twice says "I sinned" (vv. 18, 21). The shepherd and the woman both search for what is lost, but the father does not. From this some conclude that the first two parables emphasize divine initiative while the third emphasizes human response,[8] but this distinction will not suffice. While the father does not search for the prodigal, he does go out to both sons. There are virtually identical phrases in the parables of the Lost Sheep and Lost Coin,[9] but there are also differences. The shepherd's leaving the ninety-nine has no parallel in the Lost Coin. The latter has much more description of the effort in searching than does the parable of the Lost Sheep, the two descriptions of joy differ, and the parable of the Lost Coin has no parallel to the idea of some not needing repentance.

I have argued elsewhere that the four dominant components of Jesus' gospel are celebration, compassion, the restoration of Israel, and the present and future kingdom of God.[10] The parables in ch. 15 are primary evidence of Jesus' gospel of celebration and compassion. The other two themes are only implicit, but they are there. As a result, this chapter is the most forceful description that exists of God seeking sinners and reveling in their return.

THE LOST SHEEP
(Matt 18:12-14/Luke 15:4-7)

Parable Type

In both Matthew and Luke this is an interrogative parable. In Matthew an introductory question ("What do you think?") is followed by hypothetical circumstances, which are followed by a parable question ("Will he not leave?").

The *condition* of finding (v. 13: "and if he finds it") is followed by a statement of consequences and an explanatory *nimshal*. In Luke this is a "Who from you?" parable (literally "What man from you?") followed by statements of consequence and a *nimshal*. Some label this account a similitude, and some argue that it was originally a parable referring to a specific event.[11] There is no developed plot, so this is not a parable in the technical sense. At most it is an implied similitude, as if to say, "My association with sinners is like the circumstance of a shepherd recovering a lost sheep and happily rejoicing with friends over the recovery." However, in the interests of clarity it is best to label it according to its form as an *interrogative parable*. Interrogative parables are not far from juridical parables, for they set up a hypothetical situation, force the hearer/reader to answer a question, and obligate one to transfer that answer to another arena. (Juridical parables carry additionally an accusatory element.)

Issues Requiring Attention

1. What are the original form and context of the parable? Is Matthew or Luke closer to the words of Jesus and the original *Sitz im Leben?* What significance does the relation of the two have for understanding?
2. Would a shepherd abandon the ninety-nine other sheep? What relevance does this decision have for understanding the parable?
3. Has the parable been framed on one or more OT texts? Specifically, is Bailey correct to see Luke 15 as an expansion of Psalm 23?
4. Do the features represent theological realities? Should the shepherd be identified with God, Jesus, the disciples, or someone seeking the kingdom? Does the parable have christological implications?
5. What is to be learned here about repentance? Do some not need repentance?
6. What does the parable teach?

Helpful Primary Source Material

Canonical Material

- OT: Gen 48:15; 49:24; Pss 23; 119:176; Isa 40:10-11; 53:6; 60:4; Jer 23:1-4; 50:6; Ezek 34
- NT: Matt 10:5-6; 12:11-12; John 10:1-18; Acts 20:28-30; Heb 13:20; 1 Pet 2:25; 5:4; Rev 7:17

Early Jewish Writings

- From Qumran, CDA 13.7-10: "And this is the rule of the inspector of the camp. . . . He shall have pity on them like a father on his sons, and will heal all the <afflicted among them> like a shepherd his flock. He will undo all the chains which bind them, so that there will be neither harassed nor oppressed in his congregation" (also 4Q269 frag. 11.4-8).
- CDB 19.5-11: "But (over) all those who despise the precepts and the ordinances, may be emptied over them the punishment of the wicked, when God visits the earth, when there comes the word which is written by the hand of the prophet Zechariah [Zech 13:7] 'Wake up, sword, against my shepherd, and against the male who is my companion — oracle of God — strike the shepherd, and the flock may scatter, and I shall turn my hand against the little ones.' Those who revere him are [Zech 11:11] 'the poor ones of the flock.' These shall escape in the age of the visitation; but those that remain shall be delivered up to the sword when there comes the Messiah of Aaron and Israel."
- 4Q171 3.5-6: "'Whoever loves YHWH will be like precious lambs' (Ps 37:20). [Its] interpretation [concerns . . .] who will be chiefs and princes over [the whole congregation, like shepherds] of ewes in among their flocks."

Early Christian Writings

- *Gos. Thom.* 107: "Jesus said: The kingdom is like a shepherd who had a hundred sheep. One of them went astray; it was the largest. He left the ninety-nine (and) sought for the one until he found it. After he had exerted himself, he said to the sheep, I love you more than the ninety-nine."
- *Gospel of Truth* 31-32: "He is the shepherd who left behind the ninety-nine sheep which were not lost. He went searching for the one which was lost. He rejoiced when he found it, for ninety-nine is a number that is in the left hand which holds it. But when the one is found, the entire number passes to the right (hand). Thus (it is with) him who lacks the one; that is, the entire right which draws what was deficient and takes it from the left-hand side and brings (it) to the right, and thus the number becomes one hundred. . . . Even on the Sabbath, he labored for the sheep, which he found fallen into the pit. He gave life to the sheep, having brought it up from the pit in order that you might know interiorly . . . what is the Sabbath. . . ."

Later Jewish Writings

- *Test. Sol.* D and E have the contrast between ninety-nine and one sheep in connection with the parable spoken by Nathan to David.[12]
- *m. Baba Meṣiʿa* 7.8-9 has a number of regulations for dealing with loss of an animal, depending on the circumstances.
- *m. Baba Qamma* 6.2 has regulations concerning a shepherd leaving a flock or handing it over to someone else. "If he left the flock in the sun, or if he delivered it to the care of a deaf-mute, an imbecile, or a minor, and it came out and caused damage, he is culpable. If he delivered it to the care of a herdsman, the herdsman stands in the place of the owner." *b. Baba Qamma* 55b, 56b explain: ". . . that 'he handed it over to a shepherd' means [the shepherd handed it over] to his apprentice, as it is indeed the custom of the shepherd to hand over his sheep to [the care of] his apprentice." See also *t. Baba Qamma* 6.20.
- *Exod. Rab.* 2.2: "Also Moses was tested by God through sheep. Our Rabbis said that when Moses our teacher, peace be upon him, was tending the flock of Jethro in the wilderness, a little kid escaped from him. He ran after it until it reached a shady place. When it reached the shady place, there appeared to view a pool of water and the kid stopped to drink. When Moses approached it, he said: 'I did not know that you ran away because of thirst; you must be weary.' So he placed the kid on his shoulder and walked away. Thereupon God said: 'Because thou hast mercy in leading the flock of a mortal, thou wilt assuredly tend my flock Israel.'"[13]
- *Midr. Ps.* 119.3 understands "I have gone astray like a sheep" (Ps 119:176) to point to David's innocence since strayed sheep are innocent. David is then understood as asking God to seek him as a shepherd seeks lost sheep.

Comparison of the Accounts

Matthew and Luke have relatively little in common in this parable, and their accounts display a surprising phenomenon in Synoptic relations. As we might expect, triple tradition material is usually closely related, but double tradition material is either extremely close (e.g., the parables of the Two Builders in Matt 7:24-27/Luke 6:47-49, the Leaven in Matt 13:33/Luke 13:20-21, and the Faithful and Unfaithful Servant in Matt 24:45-51/Luke 12:41-48) or so unalike as to raise questions whether the accounts are related at all (e.g., the Banquet/Feast parables of Matt 22:1-14 and Luke 14:15-24 and the parables of the Talents/Pounds in Matt 25:14-30 and Luke 19:11-27). The two accounts of the Lost Sheep fit in the latter category. Of the sixty-five words in Matt 18:12-14 and eighty-nine in Luke 15:4-7 only fourteen are identical in both accounts, with four more words shared but with different grammatical forms. The words in common are basic components such as "one hundred sheep," "one from them," and "the ninety-nine," but for nearly everything else each Evangelist has his own wording. Among the most significant differences are:

In Matthew	In Luke
the parable is told to disciples (18:1), is part of Matthew's ecclesiastical discourse, and concerns erring disciples	the parable is told as Jesus' response to the grumbling of Pharisees and scribes at his reception of and eating with sinners (15:1-2)
the sheep strays *(planēthē)*	the sheep is lost *(apolesas)*
the word for "leave" is *aphēsei*	the word for "leave" is *kataleipei*
the ninety-nine are left on the mountains *(ta orē)*	the ninety-nine are left in the "wilderness" *(en tē erēmǭ)*
"*if* he should find"	the man searches until he finds
the parable is briefer	the parable is more expansive. The man puts the sheep on his shoulders and rejoices. When he arrives at home he calls his friends to rejoice with him.
the conclusion stays within the parable plane and says that the man rejoices more over the recovered sheep than over the ninety-nine	the conclusion moves to the theological plane and explains that there will be more joy in heaven over one repentant sinner than over ninety-nine righteous who do not need it
the text then moves to the theological plane and concludes that it is contrary to God's will that one of these little ones should be lost *(apolētai)*	Luke has no parallel

On the significance of these differences see below, pp. 103-4.

Hardly anyone argues that *Gos. Thom.* 107 is earlier than the Synoptic versions or has a preferable account of this parable,[14] even if it is not dependent on the canonical accounts.[15] In *Gos. Thom.* the parable is explicitly a kingdom parable. The shepherd leaves the ninety-nine because the one lost sheep is the largest and the shepherd loves it more than the ninety-nine, which is usually taken as a reference to the superior status of the Gnostic. Similarly, in *Gos. Thom.* 8 a fisherman keeps the one large fish and lets all the little ones go. *Gos. Thom.* 109 and 110 are closely related parables and deal with the theme of finding something of immense value that bestows superior status. Once again *Gos. Thom.* is clearly secondary and, in my opinion, if not Gnostic, at least proto-Gnostic.[16]

Textual Features Worth Noting

Matt 18:11 is with good reason omitted from most modern editions of the NT on both external and internal grounds. The variant has two forms: "the Son of Man came to save the lost" and "the Son of Man came to seek and to save the lost," with the former more widely attested. The verse is omitted by several manuscripts, most notably Sinaiticus and Vaticanus (fourth-century uncials), 33 (the "queen of the minuscules"), and several early versions and church fathers. It appears to have been copied from Luke 19:10. It is difficult to imagine a scribe omitting this verse had it been original.

Matt 18:10-14 has a possible chiasmus:

10a	one of these little ones
10b	my Father who is in heaven
12b	has gone astray
12c	the ninety-nine
12c	the one that went astray
13b	the ninety-nine
13b	went astray
14	your (or my) Father who is in heaven
14	one of these little ones[17]

Laying out the text in this fashion is instructive but it leaves out of consideration a good deal of the text. If this is a chiasmus, it is certainly unbalanced. But there is at least an inclusio between vv. 10 and 14 which marks this section off as a unit. A similar chiastic arrangement is suggested for Luke 15:4-7, but that appears to be forced.[18]

The references to angels in Matt 18:10 (the Lost Sheep) and Luke 15:10 (the Lost Coin) are similar.

Among several key words connecting the sections of Matthew 18 is "little ones" *(mikroi)* in vv. 6, 10, 14.

Matt 12:11-12 has a quite similar interrogative parable about a sheep and whether one would not draw it out from a pit on the Sabbath. It expects an affirmative reply and draws a theological conclusion.

The introductory question "What do you think?" *(ti hymin dokei)* in Matt 18:12 is paralleled in Matt 21:28; 22:42; 26:66 and in 17:25; 22:17 with the singular pronoun *(ti soi dokei)*. Outside Matthew this form appears in the NT only in John 11:56, but whether such a general phrase should be labeled a Mattheanism or attributed to Matthew is debatable, especially since a very similar construction occurs in Luke 10:36 *(tis . . . dokei soi)*[19] and has Semitic parallels.[20] Questions were a regular feature of Jesus' teaching. Dio Chrysostom, *Oratio* 70.5 displays a similar use of questions that require a choice ("Which of the two will you say . . . ?) and draw a conclusion from the answer.

The interrogative form of the parable in Luke "What man from you?" *(tis anthrōpos ex hymōn)* is paralleled (with slight variation) in Matt 7:9 and 12:11. The shortened form "Who from you?" *(tis ex hymōn)* is paralleled in Matt 6:27; Luke 11:5 (the parable of the Friend at Midnight), 11; 12:25; 14:28 (the parable of the Tower Builder); 15:8 (the parable of the Lost Coin); and 17:7 (the parable of the Slave at Work); cf. also the shortened form at Luke 14:5.[21] An examination of the contexts shows that the expected answer in all these cases is "No one," which, since the question in 15:4 is asked as a negative ("will he not leave?"), means that *any* shepherd would leave the ninety-nine and go find the lost sheep. The logic of these parables is from the lesser to the greater, either of humans (e.g., if a human will save an animal on the Sabbath, how much more appropriate is it to heal a human!) or of God (e.g., if humans behave in such a reasonable way as giving good things to their children, how much more will God act similarly!).[22] It is possible that the question in Luke 15 extends all the way to the end of v. 6, or, as the punctuation of most editions indicates, only through the end of v. 4.

Luke 15:6 and 9 are close in wording.

Cultural Information

Besides the evidence of the NT,[23] the Pharisaic refusal to associate with sinners is reflected in various sayings. E.g., *Mekilta Amalek* 3.55-57 (on Exod 18:1) says, "In this connection the sages said: Let a man never associate with a wicked person, not even for the purpose of bringing him near to the Torah." The feelings were at times intense.[24] The importance of meals for marking identity boundaries was especially important in ancient Palestine[25] and is evident in NT texts, especially in Luke (e.g., 14:7-14).[26]

Shepherding was a despised trade. E.g., *Midr. Ps.* 23.2: "R. Jose bar Ḥanina taught: In the whole world you find no occupation more despised than that of the shepherd, who all his days walks about with his staff and his pouch. Yet David presumed to call the Holy One, blessed be He, a shepherd!" (which is explained from Gen 48:15). *M. Qiddušin* 4.14 assumes that shepherds are robbers because they lead sheep onto other people's lands, *b. Sanhedrin* 25b lists herdsmen among those ineligible to be witnesses and associates them with tax collectors, and *b. Baba Qamma* 94b says that it is difficult for shepherds to repent and make resitution.[27] Jesus' question, "What man of you having one hundred sheep?" would have caused the Pharisees and scribes, people immensely concerned about cleanness, to imagine themselves involved in a trade they considered unclean. The anomaly would not go unnoticed and was probably an intended rhetorical strategy.[28] Yet the shepherd image is used of God's tender care of his people[29] and for leaders of the people in the OT and Judaism, including the eschatological deliverer.[30] Leaderless or poorly led people are described as sheep without a shepherd.[31]

The shepherd in the parable appears to be the owner of the flock, and the size of the flock would indicate someone who was reasonably well off. He was not rich, but one hundred sheep was a flock of considerable size. *T. Baba Qamma* 6.20, in discussing the culpability of a shepherd handing over his flock to someone else, says that he is exempt from blame in handing them over even if he has responsibility for three hundred sheep, in this context an exaggerated number. By comparison, Job had seven thousand sheep at first and later was blessed with fourteen thousand (Job 1:3; 42:12), and Jacob gave Esau, among other things, two hundred twenty sheep as a gift (Gen 32:14).

A lost sheep, we are told, usually lies down and gives up and will not find its way back.[32] Possibly this is why the shepherd carries the sheep on his shoulders, but more likely it is intended to convey the care of a good shepherd. Images of shepherds carrying sheep are known from the various cultures long before Jesus.[33]

Repentance is a central pillar of Jewish thinking.[34]

The parable is realistic except for the calling of friends and neighbors, which seems to be an exaggeration. This is especially true for the parable of the Lost Coin. Presumably calling the neighbors in to celebrate required some expenditure for food, which would add some financial cost to the recovery. This exaggeration draws the parable closer to the reality of Jesus eating with sinners and emphasizes the theme of rejoicing.[35]

Explanation of the Parable

Options for Interpretation

The early church most often understood the shepherd's going to find the sheep as a reference to the incarnation to recover lost humanity, with the ninety-nine understood as the angels.[36] Most modern interpretations focus on some sense of God's or Christ's seeking to restore the lost. Usually both the searching and the celebration at finding are emphasized. Within this framework a variety of nuances are suggested. A few argue instead that the parable was originally more like the parable of the Hidden Treasure and referred to people seeking the kingdom.[37]

Decisions on the Issues

1. *What are the original form and context of the parable?* Is Matthew or Luke closer to the words of Jesus and the original *Sitz im Leben?* What significance does the relation of the two have for understanding? The authenticity of this parable is rarely questioned, but parts of it are typically ascribed to the editorial work of Matthew and Luke.[38] Luke's editorial arrangement of the chapter and his framing of the introduction in 15:1-3 to mirror 5:29-32 are readily acknowledged. Matthew's version of the parable is thought to be more original because it is briefer and less refined and because the finding of the sheep is uncertain, which is not likely to have been introduced later.[39] The explanations of the parable in both Matt 18:14 and Luke 15:7 are considered secondary and as going beyond what it teaches. Matthew is believed to have applied a parable originally about God's acceptance of sinners to a church context to instruct church leaders about God's care for insignificant or weak believers, a care leaders should mirror in their own conduct. Luke shifts from divine initiative in the parable to joy over the human response of one person repenting, but repentance is not in the parable.[40]

From these conclusions some attempt to reconstruct a shorter version of the parable, which is a perilous task.[41] At any rate, such an explanation of the relationship of the accounts is not certain, and scholars have tended to assert more than the facts demonstrate. Now that people are starting to consider more the oral character of the tradition, yesterday's certainties are not so clear. We cannot show which account is "more original." Some discomfort should be felt that interpreters tend to prefer Matthew's wording in 18:12-13 but Luke's context. That there is so little verbal agreement between the two accounts suggests that we are dealing with two independent and equally valid traditions, and it is reasonable to think that Jesus told this parable several times and quite possibly for different purposes.[42] Why would it be surprising if he told his disciples a parable addressing their relationships that he also told Jews, addressing theirs? Both accounts agree on the essential points of God's effort and attitude toward recovering the lost.

As J. Dupont notes, Matthew's conclusion relates to the first part of the parable (the seeking) and Luke's to the second part, the joy.[43] Matthew's is straightforward and stays in line with the parable:[44] if a shepherd is not willing to lose a sheep but searches for it and rejoices when he finds it, by analogy the same is true of God, who like the shepherd is not willing that any be lost. Matthew may well have added this application, but it is perfectly legitimate, and the parable is still addressed to the whole community, not just to leaders.[45]

If Luke is responsible for 15:7, he has merely drawn a conclusion inherent in the parable. He gives it a communal focus with the rejoicing functioning almost as an invitation for the hearer/reader to join in. He emphasizes that the joy is God's and that it responds specifically to *repentance* of one sinner. He could have merely said "Likewise, there will be joy in heaven over the recovery of one sinner." Instead, he has highlighted the way recovery takes place. This application is not merely an explanation but a deduction, which makes an additional point on the basis of the parable.[46] It is actually closer to Matt 18:13 than many have noticed and, like Matt 18:10, emphasizes the value of the lost/little ones before God.

Nimshalim (explanations) most often stay in line with their parables, but not always.[47] The introductions and the conclusions may not be jettisoned; at least one — either an introduction or a conclusion — is necessary to indicate the referent of the parable, or interpretation would be almost impossible.

In short, any quest for an original form should be abandoned. We have two forms of the parable, probably two independent oral traditions. Luke's context is the most likely,[48] but both contexts may reflect situations in the life of Jesus. Both forms of the parable make essentially the same point, but the enhancement brought by the differences should be recognized. In addition to the differences mentioned, the words "strayed" and "lost" convey the same thing about a sheep but have different nuances when referring to humans. Matthew, with "strayed" *(planēthē)*, uses a word that is most appropriate for someone in the community and that places responsibility on the person.[49] No significance attaches to the fact that Matthew says that the ninety-nine are left on the mountains/hills, while Luke says that they are left in the wilderness. Both terms could be used of the same area.

2. *Would a shepherd abandon the ninety-nine other sheep? What relevance does a decision here have for understanding?* A number of commentators are sure the shepherd abandoned the ninety-nine sheep and interpret the parable accordingly as absurd,[50] as showing that God's mercy is a mystery[51] or that the

shepherd is irresponsible,[52] or as making the shepherd a symbol of risk-taking.[53] This approach violates both cultural and literary sensitivities. Care for one sheep does not preclude care for all the sheep, and certainly some provision would be made for the ninety-nine, to leave them either in some enclosure or more likely with another shepherd.[54] A flock this size may have had more than one shepherd anyway. If one assumes the ninety-nine are abandoned in the wilderness, then Luke's account is even more problematic. Did the shepherd carry the lost sheep home and leave the ninety-nine in the wilderness? Should we think he took the lost sheep back to the ninety-nine? What did he do with the sheep when he celebrated with his neighbors?[55] Parables are marked by focus and brevity and do not care about unnecessary issues. Like all literature they often have gaps. This parable does not care about any of these questions, for it is focused on the certainty of searching and the celebration at finding. Nothing else counts, and to make such issues matters of interpretation is catastrophic. Interpretation based on elements not there is almost certainly wrong. Two other facts show that any focus on the ninety-nine is misplaced. First, in both accounts the hearer/reader is expected to agree that the shepherd should indeed leave the ninety-nine and search for the lost.[56] Second, no parallel to the idea of abandonment appears in the parables of the Lost Coin or the Two Lost Sons.[57] Valid interpretation should not focus on the ninety-nine at all.

3. *Has the parable been framed on one or more OT texts? Specifically, is Bailey correct to see Luke 15 as an expansion of Psalm 23?* As indicated above (see p. 102), OT shepherd imagery frequently refers to God or to leaders of God's people. Ezekiel 34 is particularly striking because of the similarity of some phrases to the wording of the parable. Whereas Matthew and Luke differ in describing the one sheep as having strayed or become lost, Ezek 34:4, 16 uses both words *(planaō* and *apollymi)* in parallelism to describe lost sheep. Ezekiel 34 mentions sheep wandering on the mountains and hills (v. 6) and says that God himself will search for his sheep (v. 11), care for them (v. 16), judge their oppressors (vv. 17, 20, and 22), and set a Davidic shepherd over them to care for them (vv. 23-24). In addition, God will judge the shepherds who have failed to care for the sheep. Other texts have the same thoughts and hopes that God will shepherd his people and/or appoint a Davidic deliverer to shepherd them. Ezekiel 34 is only one of several texts carrying this shepherd theology.[58] Whether the connection is to Ezekiel 34 or to the larger shepherd tradition cannot be determined with certainty, but at the very least the parable has been framed on the OT shepherd tradition which Ezekiel 34 expresses so forcefully.[59] This underscores the importance of the OT in the formation of the parables, but two other important results emerge. First, this parable is an implicit complaint against the religious authorities for failing in their role as shepherds of Israel who should seek for the lost. Second, at some

level Jesus saw himself as taking up the task described in Ezekiel 34 and other texts which focus on a deliverer from God who will shepherd the people as God intends (on which see below, p. 107).

If dependence on these (mostly prophetic) texts is clear, the case with Psalm 23 is different. K. Bailey argued that Luke 15 has numerous parallels with Psalm 23 and that the three parables in this chapter are Jesus' detailed expansion of the psalm.[60] Bailey's approach is rather complex. In addition to Psalm 23 he finds numerous parallels with Jer 23:1-8 and Ezekiel 34. With the parable of the Lost Sheep he thinks the shepherd is first a bad shepherd, and with this image Jesus accuses the Jewish leaders. Then the shepherd becomes a good shepherd and reflects Jesus' own ministry. Bailey understands Ps 23:3, usually translated as "He restores my soul," as "He brings me back" and as at least implying "He causes me to repent." Repentance is then understood as "the acceptance of being found." Further, Bailey finds allusions to the incarnation in these texts and understands the shepherd's carrying the sheep as a reference to Jesus' own suffering and as implying a significant understanding of the atonement.[61] In later works Bailey adds numerous parallels between Luke 15 and the Jacob story.[62]

I find this highly imaginative and none too convincing. The supposed parallels with Psalm 23, apart from the most general terms, just are not there. The parable does not present a bad shepherd first, for the shepherd could be viewed negatively only if he did not go and search for the lost sheep. Psalm 23 does not speak of a lost sheep; rather the whole point is that God is like a shepherd who gives careful attention to the sheep *to keep it from getting lost* or into trouble. Bailey's argument that repentance is referred to in Ps 23:3 has no basis, for the words in question, *napshî yěshôbēb* do not mean merely "He brings me back." These two words (*nepesh*, "life" or "soul," and *shûb*, "return" or "restore") are used together several other times with the sense of reviving life, both literally and metaphorically.[63] The traditional understanding of Ps 23:3 ("He restores my soul," in the sense of either "refresh me" or "rescue me") is correct. If the shepherd imagery is traditional language about God and leaders, any use of the imagery is bound to have language in common with other texts, but there is virtually nothing here to build the kind of case Bailey does. To say this does not diminish the importance of the OT texts about shepherds. They provide the wording and the context for Jesus to paint a forceful picture, one that implicitly accuses leaders of failing and points to the character of God and the nature of his own ministry.

4. Do the features represent theological realities? Should the shepherd be identified with God, Jesus, the disciples, or someone seeking the kingdom? And especially, does the parable have christological implications? We have seen that K. Bailey and the early church saw the incarnation depicted in the parable and that Bailey found the atonement reflected in the shepherd's effort. J. Bengel even found the shepherd's returning home to refer to Jesus' ascension.[64] Such theological allegorizing is out of bounds, but parables generally, and this one specifically, *do* teach theology. Otherwise they would be useless. Once again we face the primary question with parables. How much of the parable is theologically significant? The key, as always, is determining how the analogy works. Care in the use of language is important. This parable is not saying that God is a shepherd, nor do the following parables make God a woman or a father.[65] These parables are implied *analogies.* The actions and attitudes portrayed — not the people themselves — mirror the actions and attitude of God. The parable of the Lost Sheep is an analogical "how much more argument." The shepherd is not God, Jesus, or anyone else, and the sheep is not a person or group. These figures reside in and stay in the story. Certainly the mountains/wilderness and the friends do not "stand for something." At the same time, images selected for stories are not chosen at random; they are specifically chosen to set off resonances, and reference to a shepherd and sheep would bring to mind the OT use of these images for God, leaders, and hope for God's people. Nothing supports the suggestion that reference is to someone seeking the kingdom.[66] The logic of the parable is this: If, as surely you would agree, a shepherd will go after a lost sheep and rejoice when he finds it, how much more will God search for a lost/strayed person and rejoice when he recovers that person? Both Evangelists point to God as the analogue of the shepherd in the way they frame the parable,[67] which fits with the OT imagery.

Still, the parable is significant christologically. The OT associations include the tantalizing hope that God will set a Davidic shepherd over his people.[68] If Jesus defends his eating with sinners by pointing to God's character and saying that God is like a shepherd searching for the lost, then he implicitly claims that he is doing God's work.[69] At least with respect to Luke, the analogy of the shepherd refers to both the character of God and the activity of Jesus. The parable by itself is not specific enough to make it certain that Jesus claimed the role of the Davidic shepherd, but within the larger context of Jesus' teaching this seems clear.[70] As Jan Lambrecht comments, without this eschatological and christological dimension every explanation of the parable is superficial.[71]

5. *What is to be learned about repentance? Do some not need repentance?* I indicated above that no basis exists for K. Bailey's argument that Ps 23:3 is mirrored by the parable and means "He causes me to repent." Bailey's further argument, based especially on the story of the Prodigal but also on the Lost Sheep, that repentance in Luke 15 means the acceptance of being found is also baseless.[72] This theory emerges partly from needless anxiety about repentance being viewed as a human work. *Humans act or nothing happens pertaining to life with God,* however much we emphasize rightly that salvation is entirely the act of God. But repentance is not part of the parable. This parable neither defines

repentance nor blames the sheep. It portrays an analogy to the attitude and actions of God. Repentance appears only in Luke — it is not in Matthew — when the point of the analogy, God's joy at restored people, is described *and extended.* Especially for Luke,[73] restoration of sinners involves repentance, and the concern of the passage *is* the restoration of sinners. Further, repentance is a major feature of Jesus' message[74] and should not be slighted.

The more troublesome part of the discussion of repentance is the reference in Luke 15:7 to the ninety-nine righteous who do not need repentance. Since theologically it is assumed that no such people exist and since the Gospels imply that Pharisees do need to repent, this statement is often taken as irony, exaggeration, or sarcasm.[75] I do not think that this is the solution to the text. Judaism did ascribe sinlessness to a very few people,[76] but "righteous" does not mean "sinless." It merely refers to those in good standing before God. Repentance is so central to Jewish thinking that it is hard to imagine Jews thinking of themselves, of the majority of the people, or even of ninety-nine specific people as not needing repentance. Ideas parallel to not needing repentance appear in Luke 5:31-32 (the sick, not the well, need a doctor; Jesus did not come to call the righteous but sinners to repentance) and in 15:29 (the elder son's claim not to have broken a command is left unchallenged). Yet, Luke 13:3 warns that all must repent or perish. Church fathers got around the difficulty by saying that the ninety-nine referred to angels. Several scholars legitimately question whether Pharisees are in view with the ninety-nine.[77] Some suggest that *mallon* ("more") is to be supplied so that the meaning is "more than" instead of "rather than" — i.e., joy will be in heaven over one sinner repenting more than over ninety-nine righteous, since God is pleased with the righteous too (e.g., 1:6).[78] If we focus on the function of these words, they are a forceful expression of God's valuing the lost and despised and, therefore, a defense of Jesus' actions, *not* an assessment of the state of the ninety-nine.[79] The importance of this statement is escalated by the introductory "I say to you," which Jesus used to underscore the truth of a saying.[80] A paraphrase might be "One repentant sinner brings pleasure to God more than ninety-nine people in good standing with God" — or should it be "than ninety-nine sinners in good standing with God"? That the point is the value of the lost is confirmed by Matthew's reference to the angels of the "little ones" continually seeing God's face (18:10), a metaphorical way to stress how important the little ones are.[81]

In other words, the parable teaches virtually nothing about the nature of repentance, but does emphasize how much God values repentance.

6. *What does the parable teach?* The primary function of this parable for Jesus was a defense of his deliberate association with and eating with people known to be sinners.[82] By his reception and eating with such people he demon-

strated the presence of the kingdom and the forgiveness available to all. Indirectly this is a kingdom parable,[83] for with this parable Jesus asserts that the promised activity of God to shepherd his own people was taking place. Further, with the parable he showed those complaining about his actions that their attitude did not match the character and desires of God, and in effect, invites them to join in the kingdom celebration of the forgiveness being dispensed. Luke wants his readers to understand Jesus' gospel and to adopt the same attitude. Implicitly there may also be the charge that the religious leaders were not doing their job in seeking the lost. Matthew — regardless of whether Jesus or Matthew applied the parable to disciples — wants his readers to apply the character and desires of God to their relations in the community, especially to those who appear to be marginal. If the *nimshalim* are redactional, still they have it correct, merely making explicit that the controlling factor is the character of God. However, this is not an abstract theological discussion; the parable portrays the character of God *as it is specifically revealed in the ministry of Jesus.*

What is revealed about the character of God is the value he places on even the least deserving and the care he extends to such people. God is not passive, waiting for people to approach him after they get their lives in order. He is the seeking God who takes the initiative to bring people back, regardless of how "lost" they are. C. G. Montefiore, a Jewish NT scholar, said that this focus on God's direct seeking of sinners was a new element with Jesus, something not in the OT or rabbinic teaching.[84] This is at least an exaggeration, for certainly the OT knows that the initiative for forgiveness always lies with God. Whether new or not, the God revealed by Jesus is a caring God who values even those without value and seeks them.[85] If the kingdom comes with limitless grace and limitless demand, this parable emphasizes the limitless grace. Unquestionably, God will seek the lost and restore them. Seeking and joy are the twin pillars of the parable, and God's seeking does not come with conditions attached.[86] The joy reflects both the attitude of God at recovering the lost and the celebration of the kingdom with its good news that God's promised redemption has begun. The joy is communal, and Jesus' hearers should join the celebration.[87]

Adapting the Parable

This parable is both theological and christological, and the most important thing in adapting the parable is understanding what God is like and what the nature of Jesus' ministry was. Few things are more important than our perception of God, for from that understanding we perceive our own identity, how we should think and act, and how the world ought to be. If God is a seeking, caring

God, then his grace should characterize our self-perception and our treatment of other people. The awareness that God seeks us brings freedom and confidence to life. That his grace is to determine how we treat others should cause us to be caring and sensitive. We tend to know these truths abstractly, but they are not translated into practice either in how we view ourselves, in how we treat others, or in how we arrange church life. We are more likely to assume that God must be much more harsh, and we are more likely to look for the ninety-nine than the lost one. Do lost, disobedient to God, and "insignificant" people have any sense from us that God really cares about and seeks them? Or that we do? The Matthean text reminds us that God cares not only for "sinners" outside the community but also for the marginal and questionable in the community. We are more likely to show grace to those we seek to bring in than to those with whom we must work in the church. God's grace, his seeking and care, applies to all, and our mirroring God's care must be extended within the community as well.

The Lukan text stresses the value of repentance, and repentance is a necessary and ongoing task for all of us. We do not need to fear that repentance exposes us to an attempt at salvation by human effort. The whole of Scripture underscores that God is the one who takes the initiative. Any action of humans is a response to the grace of God. Yet, the whole of Scripture also insists that humans do indeed act. Salvation is entirely the work of God, in which we are entirely involved. There is a huge difference between responding to the grace of God and trying to make oneself look right.

Another level at which this parable deserves attention is its focus on joy. Christian worship often lacks any sense of joy. It may have form, tradition, energy, or novelty, but joy is in short supply. Joy deserves focus as the true mark of Christianity,[88] for it is directly connected with the theological awareness of the character and attitude of God as one who seeks and celebrates recovery. At some level Christian worship entails entering into God's own attitude at finding and establishing a people for himself. Join the celebration!

For Further Reading

Kenneth Bailey, *Finding the Lost: Cultural Keys to Luke 15* (St. Louis: Concordia, 1992), pp. 54-92.

————, *Jacob and the Prodigal: A Study of the Parable of the Prodigal Son in the Light of the Saga of Jacob* (Downers Grove, Ill.: InterVarsity, 2003), pp. 65-85.

W. D. Davies and D. C. Allison, Jr., *A Critical and Exegetical Commentary on the Gospel According to Saint Matthew* (ICC; Edinburgh: T. & T. Clark, 1988-97), 2:768-80.

J. Dupont, "Les implications christologiques de la parabole de la brebis perdue," in *Jesus aux Origines de la Christologie* (BETL 40; Leuven: Leuven University Press, 1975), pp. 331-50.

Greg W. Forbes, *The God of Old: The Role of the Lukan Parables in the Purpose of Luke's Gospel* (JSNTSup 198; Sheffield: Sheffield Academic Press, 2000), pp. 109-24.

Arland Hultgren, *The Parables of Jesus* (Grand Rapids: Eerdmans, 2000), pp. 63-70.

Peter Rhea Jones, *Studying the Parables of Jesus* (Macon, Ga.: Smyth & Helwys, 1999), pp. 196-214.

Adolf Jülicher, *Die Gleichnisreden Jesu* (2 vols.; Freiburg i. B.: Akademische Verlagsbuchhandlung von J. C. B. Mohr, 1888-89), 2:315-33.

THE LOST COIN
(Luke 15:8-10)

This brief parable is often neglected because of its similarity to the longer and more favored parable of the Lost Sheep. This is understandable, and much that is common to the two parables does not need to be repeated here. On the other hand, while the parables are twins, they are not identical, and this one has its own message. At first glance it seems rather common, common enough to be labeled one of the homeliest and quaintest of Jesus' parables,[89] but it also carries vital revelation about the character of God. For each section below see the corresponding treatment for the parable of the Lost Sheep.

Parable Type

Like the parable of the Lost Sheep, this is an interrogative parable which functions as an implied simile. Its question is followed by a statement of consequences and an explanatory *nimshal*.[90] There are no parallels.

Issues Requiring Attention

1. What is the significance of the fact that the parable is about a woman? Is the woman an image for God? What does the parable imply about the role of women today?

2. What does the parable teach? In particular, how much theology is mirrored by the parable?

Helpful Primary Source Material

Greco-Roman Writings

- Dio Chrysostom, *Oratio* 20:5 complains about people who pay no attention to how they spend their money and time yet become distressed if they lose one drachma.

Later Jewish Writings

- *Song Rab.* 1.1.8: "Our Rabbis say: Let not the parable be lightly esteemed in your eyes, since by means of the parable a man can master the words of the Torah. If a king loses gold from his house or a precious pearl, does he not find it by means of a wick worth a farthing? So the parable should not be lightly esteemed in your eyes, since by means of the parable a man arrives at the true meaning of the words of the Torah." Note that this parable's introduction and conclusion frame it with explanations of its meaning.
- *Song Rab.* 1.1.9: "If a man loses a selaʿ or an obol[91] in his house, he lights lamp after lamp, wick after wick, till he finds it. Now does it not stand to reason: if for these things which are only ephemeral and of this world a man will light so many lamps and lights till he finds where they are hidden, for the words of the Torah which are the life both of this world and of the next world, ought you not to search as for hidden treasures?"

Textual Features Worth Noting

See pp. 93-95 above on the arrangement of Luke 15.

Luke frequently pairs accounts dealing with both men and women.[92] While some downplay the significance of this, it is part of a Lukan strategy to underscore the role of women and Jesus' relation to them.

The form of the questions "Who from you having 100 sheep . . . ?" and "What woman having ten drachmas . . . ?" does not suggest that the implied reader is male.[93] The questions take their form because in the narrative they are addressed to the Pharisees and scribes, all of whom would have been male.

However, women were clearly included among the sinners with whom Jesus associated.

The question in v. 8 assumes an affirmative answer. Any woman would search for a lost coin, especially if she had only ten coins in her possession. The logic is from the lesser to the greater, a "How much more!" logic. If a woman will search diligently for a lost coin and rejoice at finding it, how much more will God search for a lost person and rejoice at recovering that person!

Vv. 8-9 could constitute one continuous question,[94] but this is not likely. If v. 9 were also part of the question, the negative *ou* would have been repeated before "calls" (*synkalei*).

The gender of "friends" (*tas philas*) is feminine,[95] and we should think of celebration among women. Correspondingly we should think of the shepherd's celebration as celebration among men.[96]

While this parable is closely related to that of the Lost Sheep and the two make similar points, they are not synonymous. The introductory *ē* ("or") does not mean the two are identical. Cf. 13:4 and 14:31.

The authenticity of this parable is rarely questioned,[97] although v. 10 is often viewed as a Lukan addition. While the verse is certainly shaped by Luke, some such ending is required. Otherwise, the direction of the parable would be unknown.[98]

The main differences between this parable and that of the Lost Sheep are the emphasis on the woman's diligent search (lighting a lamp, sweeping, seeking), the lack of any parallels to leaving the ninety-nine sheep, carrying the lost sheep, and the joy over one sheep being greater than the joy over the ninety-nine. These differences are not just to avoid monotony[99] but result partly from what is appropriate to the image and partly from a stronger emphasis on the diligence of the search.

Cultural Information

The word "drachma" occurs in the NT only here in vv. 8 and 9 and only seven times in the LXX.[100] In the first century a drachma was about the equivalent of a denarius, usually one day's pay for a day worker (see Tob 5:14).[101] Some suggest that a woman would have received only half a drachma for a day's wage.[102] The woman is usually viewed as fairly poor, which may be overstated; a day's wage is not a small amount. She is probably just a typical woman one would find in any Galilean village.[103]

Houses typically were small and, if they had windows, the windows would be small, so light would be limited. The floors were either beaten earth or stone. Near Capernaum where basalt stone is plentiful, such stones were used for some floors. In fact, coins were found by archaeologists in the cracks of the floor in "Peter's house" in Capernaum.[104]

The suggestion that the coin is from a headdress or necklace is ill-founded.[105] The only evidence early enough to support this is *m. Kelim* 12.7,[106] but this passage assumes that the coin had already become defective and had lost its value as a coin. Defacing a coin to use it as jewelry would have reduced its value or rendered it useless.[107]

Explanation of the Parable

Options for Interpretation

Augustine set the tone for many when he allegorized the coin as humans made in God's image and the woman as Christ, the Wisdom of God. The friends and neighbors and even the nine coins were sometimes understood to refer to angels.[108] The identification of the woman as Christ, the Wisdom of God, is also found among modern feminist interpreters.[109] A very few interpret this parable in relation to the parable of the Hidden Treasure as pointing to the crisis of and joyful response to the proclamation of the kingdom.[110] The primary option for interpretation is to understand the parable as an analogy of God's actions and attitude toward the lost similar to the parable of the Lost Sheep.

Decisions on the Issues

1. *What is the significance of the fact that the parable is about a woman? Is the woman an image for God? What does the parable imply about the role of women today?* A great deal is made of the fact that a woman is the central character in the parable, sometimes without much care about language. Luke's use of male-female pairs was mentioned above. It is less than accurate to say that the woman is a *symbol* for Jesus,[111] and there is no basis for identifying her with divine Wisdom. The parable is a "How much more?" *analogy.* If a woman will search diligently for a lost coin, how much more will God diligently search for his lost people? The woman corresponds to God in the analogy, just as other female actions or attitudes are compared to God's in the OT (such as the comfort a mother gives her children, Isa 66:13). A comparison is not the same as a symbol. The use of the woman *is* significant but should not be exaggerated. She is evidence of attention to and value of women in a strongly patriarchal society. Jesus' sensitivity toward women and the presence of women among his disci-

ples are something new, even surprising,[112] and of major significance for the life of the church both in the first century and now.

For some people, however, the woman in this parable is of negligible significance. Some are sure that Matthew omitted this parable because the woman was not a fitting symbol for church leadership,[113] but this is a gratuitous assumption. Did Matthew even know the story? This and similar stories are viewed by some as too patriarchal and, it is said, should not be read at all or should be rewritten with a feminist agenda.[114] That is precisely the problem. People bring their agendas to the text and expect the text to conform to us, rather than listening to the text, even in its foreignness, and appropriating its message. The text is not to us, even though it is for us. *The first step in interpreting the text is allowing it to be what it is — an ancient text.* Only when the text is allowed to be what it is can it confront us in legitimate ways and have a chance of transforming us. Ancient texts should not be asked to deal with all our issues. Problems such as the abuse of women are horrendous, and churches must address them, but the biblical text must be allowed to do its task, not forced to do ours or to treat every subject we know.[115] It is not easy to be biblical, particularly with issues such as the role of women, but the biblical message properly understood provides a platform for the equal status and unrestricted function of women in the Christian community.

2. What does the parable teach? How much theology is mirrored by the parable? With all the parables it is easy to lay our own theology on the text and then triumphantly find it there. This parable does not liken human sin to a lifeless coin, nor does it carry an atonement theology,[116] and the candle is not the divine light.[117] Nor is the parable a burlesque with the kingdom scandalously presented as an unclean woman searching for something of little intrinsic value.[118] The woman is not implicitly blamed that the coin is lost, and certainly the coin is not.

The woman's searching is an analogy of God's initiative and diligence in seeking to recover his people. The verbs of action, that she seeks carefully,[119] and her persistence until she finds underscore the effort to which she goes. This diligence is the new factor only hinted at in the other two parables of Luke 15. If a woman will expend herself until she finds something lost and rejoice when she finds it, will not God much more expend himself and rejoice at finding his lost people?[120] Both the searching and the joy are essential features; parables cannot be limited to one point. Like the celebration of the shepherd, the celebration of the woman with her friends is exaggerated to bring the picture more closely in relation to the reality of the celebration of Jesus eating with sinners.[121]

Implicitly, as with the parable of the Lost Sheep, this is a kingdom parable.[122] Both parables function the same way. Both assume the presence of the kingdom and that in Jesus' ministry God is at work to redeem his people and to fulfill his promises to restore Israel. Both present a defense of Jesus' association with tax collectors and sinners and show that those complaining about his actions reveal their lack of understanding of God's attitude and actions. God is the diligent searcher, the one who takes the initiative to recover what is his. He gives no grudging or hesitant acceptance of sinners but eagerly seeks them and finds cause to celebrate at their recovery. The kingdom comes with limitless grace, even for those that others denigrate.

The explanation in 15:10 makes the same two shifts as the explanation of the parable of the Lost Sheep (15:7): it is *God's* joy, and the cause of the joy is repentance, the way the recovery takes place. Jesus does not merely say "I am celebrating like a woman who found a lost coin." He implicates God in the celebration — "Joy will be in the presence of the angels of God for one sinner repenting."[123] God rejoices over what is happening in Jesus' reception of sinners. With the theme of repentance the explanation moves beyond the parable to make an additional point, but it is a necessary and legitimate point. The suggestion that repentance means "allowing oneself to be found" has even less viability with the coin.[124]

Adapting the Parable

This parable is less significant christologically than that of the Lost Sheep because it does not have resonances with OT promises the way the shepherd image does, but its picture of God diligently searching is poignant. If that is the character of our God, it should be our own character as well. These parables do not tell us how to search for the lost, but they do imply that we should. Unfortunately we have strange ideas of what it means to search for the lost. We more likely have images of accosting people than images of the limitless grace in Jesus' reception of sinners. Christians worry that sinners do not change fast enough or, even worse, that association with sinners will give Christians a bad reputation or be a bad influence on them. The necessity of separating from sin is a reality, but so is the necessity of being involved in seeking the lost. What wisdom will suffice to guide both necessities? Jesus neither condoned sin, left people in their sin, nor communicated any disdain for sinners. He mirrored the image of his Father and invited them to receive God's forgiveness and participate in God's kingdom. Whatever else we say, the initiating grace and acceptance of God displayed by Jesus must be evident in all we do.

The image of the woman is not the heart of the parable's message. She is a building block in the analogy, but her appearance reminds us of Jesus' valuing of women. Even when Christians disagree about the roles of women, they still must show the same sensitivity Jesus had toward women, their equality, and their ability to function on the same level as men. We live in a world where women are demeaned, denigrated, and abused. Christians should weep for the abuse of women in both the ancient and the modern worlds, but we must move past weeping. The way women are treated in our homes, churches, and society and the way we seek justice for women should be expressions of the limitless grace of God's kingdom, a grace that refuses to accept sinful treatment of others, whether it be Pharisaic disdain or physical abuse. Grace creates room, whether it is God's creating room for us or our creating room for people who think that they do not belong. The kingdom comes with limitless grace — God diligently searching for his people — and with limitless demand — the expectation that God's grace will be replicated in the lives of his people.

Once again, the note of joy, an essential feature of the kingdom, cannot be neglected. Where joy is absent, the kingdom is absent.

For Further Reading

Kenneth Bailey, *Finding the Lost: Cultural Keys to Luke 15* (St. Louis: Concordia, 1992), pp. 93-108.

————, *Jacob and the Prodigal: A Study of the Parable of the Prodigal Son in the Light of the Saga of Jacob* (Downers Grove, Ill.: InterVarsity, 2003), pp. 86-94.

Arland Hultgren, *The Parables of Jesus* (Grand Rapids: Eerdmans, 2000), pp. 63-70.

Carol Schersten LaHurd, "Rediscovering the Lost Women in Luke 15," *BTB* 24 (1994): 66-76.

Susan Marie Praeder, *The Word in Women's Worlds: Four Parables* (Wilmington: Michael Glazier, 1988), pp. 36-50.

THE COMPASSIONATE FATHER AND HIS TWO LOST SONS
(Luke 15:11-32)

This parable and that of the Good Samaritan are the most influential and best loved of all the parables. For some it is the gospel within the gospel, or even the most beautiful short story ever told. This parable has been painted by a host of artists, most notably Rembrandt, made the subject of plays — or has provided the themes for plays, most notably those of Shakespeare — been set to music, and made the subject of movies.[125] On the other hand, Marcion excised this parable from his truncated version of Luke.[126]

Most grant that the traditional title "the parable of the Prodigal Son" is not adequate since this ignores the parable's second half. Some suggest focusing on the father with titles like "the parable of the Waiting Father" or "the parable of the Father's Love,"[127] either of which is an improvement but still excludes the elder son. At least as Luke presents the parable, it is best labeled "the parable of the Compassionate Father and His Two Lost Sons,"[128] even though for reasons of brevity it no doubt will still be called the parable of the Prodigal or of the Two Lost Sons.

Parable Type

This is a two-stage, double indirect narrative parable. In its two stages are two "discourses." It is the longest of Jesus' parables and has more discourse than any other parable. There is no *nimshal*.[129] Like all the parables except the single indirect stories, it is a double indirect parable. The subject matter and the people in question are both changed to enable sight from a new perspective.

Issues Requiring Attention

The authenticity of this parable is rarely questioned,[130] especially because of its artistry and power, the parallels between the grumbling of the elder brother and the parable of the Vineyard Workers (Matt 20:1-16), and the fact that no early Christian would describe the Pharisees with the positive comments made about the elder brother.[131] His claim not to have violated a command and the father's "you are always with me and all my things are yours" hardly express early church attitudes toward the Pharisees. Some argue, in fact, that the parable has been only lightly edited.[132] The parable itself is relatively straightforward. What scholars often do to the parable is not. Issues include:

1. Was this parable originally shorter?
2. Does it have any relation to Matthew's parable of the Two Sons?
3. Against what background should one read? Suggestions include several different OT texts, various Greco-Roman influences, and rabbinic discussions.
4. How should cultural factors inform the reading of the parable? In particular, how do cultural and legal factors pertaining to the younger son's re-

quest and the father's division of his property influence understanding? What is the younger son's sin?

5. Does the parable depict the human condition generally, the exile and restoration of Israel, or specific groups listening to Jesus? To what is analogy being made? Is Luke's context for the parable correct?

6. What does the parable teach about the Pharisees? If the elder son represents the Pharisees and scribes, why are the father's comments to the elder son so positive? What does the parable imply about the relation of the Pharisees to God and their inclusion in the kingdom since the father says the elder son is always with him and owns all things with him?

7. What is the theological significance of the parable? Does it have "allegorical" correspondences? What conclusions should be drawn about repentance, christology, or the atonement?

8. What is the purpose of the parable?

Helpful Primary Source Material

Additional material relative to specific cultural issues is listed under the section on cultural background. Other OT texts are discussed in the section dealing with the appropriate background against which to read the parable. The primary sources listed here, many of which are later than the NT, *do not bear any direct relation* with Jesus' parable. They show instead the thought world, themes, attitudes, and concerns that were prevalent throughout the ancient Mediterranean world.

Canonical Material

- OT: Genesis 33; Deut 21:17-21; Psalms 103 and 133; Prov 24:30-34; 27:10; 28:7, 19; Jer 31:18-20; Mal 3:7
- NT: Luke 5:29-32; 7:39; 19:7, 10

Early Jewish Writings

Concerning Division of Property during One's Life
- Tob 8:21: "Take at once half of what I own and return in safety to your father; the other half will be yours when my wife and I die."
- Sir 33:20-24: "To son or wife, to brother or friend, do not give power over yourself, as long as you live; and do not give your property to another, in case you change your mind and must ask for it. While you are still alive

and have breath in you, do not let anyone take your place. For it is better that your children should ask from you than that you should look to the hand of your children. . . . At the time when you end the days of your life, in the hour of your death, distribute your inheritance."

Concerning Attitudes toward Prodigals, Parents, and God's Forgiveness

- Sir 2:11: "For the Lord is compassionate and merciful; he forgives sins and saves in time of distress."
- 11QTemple 64.2-6 treats the rebellious son of Deuteronomy 21. Stoning him will eradicate evil and all Israel will hear and fear.[133]
- *T. Iss.* 3.1-8 relates Issachar's boasting of his integrity working as a farmer for the benefit of his father and brothers.
- *T. Iss.* 6.1-4: "Understand, my children, that in the last times your sons will abandon sincerity and align themselves with insatiable desire. Forsaking guilelessness, they will ally themselves with villainy. Abandoning the commands of the Lord, they ally themselves with Beliar. Giving up agriculture, they pursue their own evil schemes; they will be scattered among the nations and enslaved by their enemies. Tell these things to your children, therefore, so that even though they might sin, they may speedily return to the Lord, because he is merciful: He will set them free and take them back to their land."
- *Jos. Asen.* 12.8: "For (just) as a little child who is afraid flees to his father, and the father, stretching out his hands, snatches him off the ground, and puts his arms around him by his breast, and the child clasps his hands around his father's neck, and regains his breath after his fear, and rests at his father's breast, the father, however, smiles at the confusion of his childish mind, likewise you too, Lord, stretch out your hands upon me as a child-loving father, and snatch me off the earth."
- Philo, *Prov.* 2.2-6 compares God as king to a father in his relation to his human children. Parents do not lose thought for their wastrel children, but show them pity and care. Parents often lavish kindness on wastrels more than on the well-behaved, knowing the latter will make it on their own.[134]
- Philo, *QG* 4.198 (on Gen 27:3-4) says of Esau and Jacob that Isaac blesses the son worthy of blame, not because he honors him more than the virtuous, but because he knows that the latter can make it on his own.

Greco-Roman Writings

- Seneca the elder, *Controversiae* 3.3 presents a case for debate about a man who adopted his disinherited brother and was himself to be disinherited.

"When a man reaches the age of thirty, his father must divide his property with him.¹³⁵ A father had two sons, a good one and a debauched one." The father disinherits the latter but the other is captured by pirates but then redeemed by the debauched son. The good son returns and adopts the disinherited and is being disinherited himself. Arguments are presented for the sons and for the father, who claims to have shared his estate with one son and had it squandered by another.

- Quintilian, *Declamatio* 5 is a variation on the same theme: "Children are obligated to support their impoverished parents, or they deserve to be imprisoned. There once was a man who had two sons. The one was a good manager, the other a spendthrift. Both traveled into a far country and were captured by pirates." According to the rest of the story, the spendthrift became sick, and both sons wrote their father asking to be ransomed. The father converted all his assets into cash to redeem them. The pirates said his funds were sufficient to ransom only one son and he had to choose which. He chose the sick son, who then died. The other son escaped, and the impoverished father asked his son for support. The son refused. As part of his plea the father claims not to have loved the sick son more.

- Quintilian, *Inst.* 5.10.48: "He was a prodigal, for he squandered his patrimony."

- Quintilian, *Inst.* 5.10.97: "There is a law to the effect that 'the man who refuses to support his parents is liable to imprisonment.'"¹³⁶

- Plutarch, *Mor.* 479F-480A *(On Brotherly Love)*: "Nor is there, again, a greater exhibition of an impious nature than neglect of parents or offences against them. . . . if we do not always afford, both in deed and in word, matter for their pleasure, even if offense be not present, men consider it unholy and unlawful."

- *Mor.* 482E-483A says that a son who sees his father angry with his brother should take his share of the anger and act as a mediator to restore the brother.

- Aeschines, *In Timarchum* 30-47 states that among those not permitted to speak before the people is the man who has squandered his patrimony or other inheritance. Timarchus is accused of disgracefully squandering his patrimony and is described as one not ashamed to abandon his father's house.¹³⁷

- *Select Papyri* (LCL) 1:316-19 (a second-century papyrus from Fayûm): "Antonis Longus to Nilous his mother, very many greetings. I pray always for your health; every day I make supplication for you before the lord Serapis. I would have you know that I did not expect that you were going up to the metropolis; for that reason I did not come to the city myself. I was ashamed to come to Karanis, because I go about in filth. I wrote to you that I am naked. I beg you, mother, be reconciled to me. Well, I know what I have brought upon myself. I have received a fitting lesson. I know that I have sinned. . . ."[138]

- *P. Flor.* 99.6-7 (a first- or second-century public notice of parents against a prodigal): "Since our son Castor along with others by riotous living has squandered all his own property, and now has laid hands on ours and desires to scatter it, on that account we are taking precautions lest he should deal despitefully with us, or do anything else amiss — we beg, therefore, that a proclamation be set up (that no one any longer should lend him money). . . ."[139]

Later Jewish Writings

Concerning Division of Property during One's Life

- *m. Baba Batra* 8.7: "If a man assigned his goods to his sons he must write, 'From today and after my death.' . . . R. Jose says: He need not do so. If a man assigned his goods to his son to be his after his death, the father cannot sell them since they are assigned to his son, and the son cannot sell them since they are in the father's possession. If his father sold them, they are sold [only] until he dies; if the son sold them, the buyer has no claim on them until the father dies. The father may pluck up [the crop of a field which he has so assigned] and give to eat to whom he will, and if he left anything already plucked up, it belongs to [all] his heirs."

- *b. Baba Meṣiʿa* 75b: "Our Rabbis taught: Three cry out and are not answered. Viz., he who has money and lends it without witnesses; he who acquires a master for himself; and a henpecked husband. 'He who acquires a master for himself'; what does this mean? — Some say: He who attributes his wealth to a Gentile; others: He who transfers his property to his children in his lifetime. . . ."

- *b. Ketubbot* 49b-50a: "Come and hear: R. Ḥanina and R. Jonathan were once standing together when a man approached them and bending down kissed R. Jonathan upon his foot. 'What [is the meaning of] this?' said R. Ḥanina to him. 'This man,' the other replied, 'assigned his estate to his sons in writing and I compelled them to maintain him.'"

Concerning Attitudes toward Prodigals, Parents, and God's Forgiveness

- *Mekilta Beshallaḥ* 4.35-41: "R. Absalom, the elder, giving a parable, says: To what is it like? To a man who got angry with his son and drove him out of his house. His friend then came to him, requesting that he allow the son to come back to the house. He said to his friend: You are only asking me on behalf of my own son. I am already reconciled to my son. So also did the Holy One say to Moses: Wherefore criest thou? Is it not on behalf of My own sons? I am already reconciled to My sons."

- *Lam. Rab.* 1.34 (on 1:7): ". . . the Palestinian Rabbis say: When the son goes barefoot he recalls the comfort of his father's house."
- *Lev. Rab.* 35.6: "Israel needs carobs [poverty] to lead them to repentance."
- *Deut. Rab.* 2.24 (on Deut 4:30): "This can be compared to the son of a king who took to evil ways. The king sent a tutor to him who appealed to him, saying, 'Repent, my son.' The son, however, sent him back to his father [with the message], 'How can I have the effrontery to return? I am ashamed to come before you.' Thereupon his father sent back word, 'My son, is a son ever ashamed to return to his father? And is it not to your father that you will be returning?' Similarly, the Holy One, blessed be He, sent Jeremiah to Israel when they sinned, and said to him: 'Go, say to My children, "Return."'"[140]
- *Pesiqta Rabbati* 44.9: "Consider the parable of a prince who was far away from his father — a hundred days' journey away. His friends said to him: 'Return to your father.' He replied: 'I cannot: I have not the strength.' Thereupon his father sent word, saying to him: 'Come back as far as you can according to your strength, and I will go the rest of the way to meet you.' So the Holy One, blessed be He, says to Israel: *Return unto Me, and I will return unto you* (Mal 3:7)."
- *Apocalypse of Sedrach* 6.1-8 is on the sinfulness of man who took God's gifts and became an alien, an adulterer, and a sinner. 6.4 asks what sort of father would give an inheritance to his son, who would leave his father and become an alien and serve aliens. In this case the father retrieves his wealth and banishes his son. There is no return and loving acceptance. Ch. 8 does focus on the love of God.

Textual Features Worth Noting[141]

See pp. 94-95 above on the arrangement of Luke 15.

The ending of this parable is similar to the ending of the parable of the Unforgiving Servant:

Luke 15:32: "It was necessary *(edei)* to celebrate and rejoice. . . ."
Matt 18:33: "Was it not necessary *(edei)* also for you to show mercy. . . ."

Cf. also Matt 25:27 and Luke 13:16.

This is the longest parable, has the most discourse, and is the one that is most obviously a two-stage parable. Other two-stage parables — at least in their present form — include the Unmerciful Servant (Matt 18:23-35), Matthew's version of the Banquet (22:1-14), Lazarus and the Rich Man (Luke 16:19-31), and Luke's parable of the Pounds (19:11-27).

Other parables contrast the actions of two persons or groups: the Two Builders, the Two Debtors, the Wheat and Tares, the Dragnet, the Two Sons, the Pharisee and the Toll Collector, the Unmerciful Servant, the Faithful and Unfaithful Servants, the Wise and Foolish Virgins, the Sheep and the Goats, and the Sower. The Unforgiving Servant, the Two Debtors, and the Pharisee and the Toll Collector are especially close. Contrasting positive and negative characters is a universal teaching method. This parable is one of several "triangle" parables, what the Germans call a *dramatisches Dreieck*,[142] in which an authority figure relates to two subordinate and contrasted persons or groups.

Possessions in 12:16-21 and 14:33 and celebration in 12:19 and 16:19 (using *euphrainein* for celebrating) are viewed negatively, but the father's possessions and his celebration in this parable (again using *euphrainein*, vv. 23, 24, 29, 32) are viewed positively.

Note the connections to the material in ch. 14 and ch. 16. "Hear" *(akouein)* in 15:1 connects to the same verb in 14:35. The toll collectors and sinners willingly hear, whereas others do not. The banquet theme is common to all three chapters. Both the prodigal and the unjust steward squandered *(diaskorpizein*, 15:13; 16:1), and both the prodigal and Lazarus desire to be filled *(epithymein chortasthēnai*, 15:16; 16:21).[143]

The structure of the two halves of the parable seems intentionally to draw parallels between the two sons.[144] Both are in the field (vv. 15, 25) and both lack. Neither is given anything (vv. 16 and 29). Both assess their own state: one sinned and the other claims not to have transgressed one command (vv. 18, 29). One wants to be a hired hand; the other claims to have served (vv. 19, 29). One goes and one refuses to go (vv. 20, 28). The father goes out to both (vv. 20, 28). Both choose to celebrate without the father (vv. 13, 29).

The closing element of the second half is omitted, which forces the reader to reflect on whether the elder son went in to the banquet.

Most often scholars suggest a three-part sequence but disagree over whether the first section should include vv. 11-16, 11-19, or 11-20a.[145] More helpful is a four-part arrangement: vv. 11-12 (introduction), vv. 13-20a (the younger son), vv. 20b-24 (the father's reception), vv. 25-32 (the elder son and the father).[146]

Some Lukan stylistic traits are evident: "And he said" (*eipen de*, v. 11), "he said to" (*eipen pros*, v. 22), the litotes "not long afterward" in v. 13 (litotes is used by Luke at least seventeen times), "having risen" (*anastas*, vv. 18, 20), "he was lost" (*apolōlōs*, vv. 24 and 32), "he inquired" (*pynthanesthai*, v. 26), and the optative mood in v. 26 ("what these sounds are about").[147]

Much of the story is told with coordinate sentences; the action is typically expressed in paired ideas (e.g., "the younger son departed . . . and squandered . . . ," v. 13).

As with all written material, parables have gaps, jumps that the author feels are safe to make without loss of understanding. Note the gap between vv. 21 and 22. The father ran out to meet the son, and after the son's statement, gave a command to the servants. Did servants run out with him, or before the request have the father and son returned to the house? From the teller's perspective it does not matter and to give attention to such a detail would be pedantic and diminish the drama.[148] What matters is the meeting and the command to start the celebration. Similarly, how did the elder brother know that his brother was in economic distress and had wasted his inheritance on harlots? Had reports been brought back by travelers? Did the father not know these things? To ask such questions is misguided. The *hearer/reader* knows the prodigal is penniless, and that is all that is necessary for the story to function. The charge of using prostitutes is assumed as something true of those who live "riotously" (*asōtōs*).[149]

None of the parables appearing only in Luke is explicitly a kingdom parable, yet God is reflected in all of them directly or indirectly. G. Forbes argues that each of the Lukan parables confronts a view of God that has either distorted or departed from the OT portrait of God.[150]

If one accepts C. F. Evans's view that Luke's travel narrative parallels Deuteronomy,[151] then Luke 15:1-32 corresponds to Deut 21:15–22:4, which includes regulations for dealing with rebellious sons.

Cultural Information

Some cultural factors will be treated in the explanation section below.

Agricultural work was highly valued, and at least in the minds of some, abandoning agricultural work brought loss of respect.

As the primary sources above show, in the ancient world disrespect toward parents (especially fathers) or failure to care for parents was condemned, even to the point of saying that neglect of parents was an imprisonable offense. Even if such imprisonment was not true specifically in Palestine, it shows how deeply respect of parents was associated with respectability, honor, and, conversely, shame. According to Deut 21:18-21 rebellious sons were to be stoned.[152]

Inheritance problems were common, as indicated in Luke 12:13 and in numerous accounts in both the Jewish and Greco-Roman worlds.[153]

Particular responsibility fell to the eldest son in a family, but he also got a double portion of the inheritance since the primary care of the parents would fall to him. Other children still had responsibility for their parents. The eldest son was also expected to take a leadership role in other family matters.[154]

Attitudes toward prodigals were strongly negative, as demonstrated in the texts above. According to Lucian prodigality was a crime that entitled a father to disown his son and, along with neglect of the father, a basis for censure by society.[155] Although later and removed from first-century Palestine, his words express the sentiments of most of the ancient Mediterranean world.

Famines were frequent and often severe in the ancient world.[156]

Taking care of swine was viewed with disdain even in the Greco-Roman world, but Jews were prohibited from raising swine at all since the OT labels them as unclean, to be neither eaten nor touched.[157] The Mishnah states explicitly "None may rear swine anywhere" (*m. Baba Qamma* 7.7), to which the Talmud adds "Cursed be the man who would breed swine and cursed be the man who would teach his son Grecian Wisdom" (*b. Baba Qamma* 82b). The analogy between the prodigal who joined himself to a Gentile to feed pigs and tax collectors who joined themselves to the Romans is obvious.[158]

Carob pods were known throughout the Mediterranean region as fodder for animals and the food of desperation for humans. Usually the reference is understood to be pods from an evergreen tree *(ceratonia siliqua)* which, when ripe, contained sweet seeds.[159]

Respected older men avoided running because it was viewed as shameful to show one's legs and to appear so undignified.[160]

Being without shoes was a mark of degradation (or mourning).[161] Putting shoes on someone else is the work of a slave and acknowledges the other person as one's master.[162]

Meat was usually eaten only on festive occasions, and the banquet underscores the elation of the father at his son's return.[163] Hultgren estimates that the price of a goat was one-tenth that of a cow.[164]

Explanation of the Parable

Options for Interpretation

This parable has at times been treated in strange ways, even more in the modern period than in earlier times. The patristic allegorical interpretations of this parable were determined primarily by Jerome, Ambrose, and Augustine. Two main approaches were taken, both seen as valid. The elder and younger sons were understood to represent either Jews and Gentiles or the ostensibly just person and the penitent sinner. Augustine discusses only the Jews and Gentiles option, whereas Jerome and Ambrose mention both. Jerome concentrated on the former and Ambrose the latter, particularly as it related to Christians who depart from the church and arrogant Christians who demean the penance and reconciliation of sinners. Other parts of the parable were assigned significance. The father is always understood as God, and the feast is understood as referring to the Eucharist. The Holy Spirit was seen in either the ring or the robe. Some identified the fatted calf with Christ (e.g., Jerome), and the father's going out to the prodigal was identified with Christ's incarnation (e.g., Jerome and Augustine). These early interpreters were aware of the difficulty caused by the positive comments about the elder son. They solved the problem by saying that the elder's claim not to have transgressed a command simply was not true or referred only to those Jews not guilty of idolatry. The statement that all things were his would be true only *if* he entered the house.[165]

A psychological approach is offered by several scholars and therapists. With such approaches the parable is seen as mirroring human relations generally or some aspect of psychoanalytic theory. G. V. Jones thinks the parable is about the human predicament and such human dynamics as estrangement, longing, and reconciliation.[166] J. Breech thinks the story explores the basic problem of triangular human relationships and presents an absurdist drama in which people talk but do not communicate. He views the father as a negative figure and the return of the younger son as a most tragic story.[167] M. Tolbert offers two conflicting Freudian interpretations (both valid in her estimation). One sees in the three figures Freud's id, superego, and ego (the father). According to the other, the parable expresses emotional ambivalence toward those one is closely related to (with the father's excessive actions toward the prodigal evidencing his hostility and ambivalence).[168]

A sociological approach is offered by R. Rohrbaugh, who argues that the parable is about propriety and shame in a dysfunctional family and that the father must not only reconcile his sons but the whole village. The banquet is held to reconcile the village, not celebrate the return of the prodigal, and the contrast is between the villagers and the elder brother, not between the two sons. On Rohrbaugh's approach Jesus told the story to promote reconciliation among quarrelsome disciples and to point to a kingdom in which prudence is not the highest value.[169]

A metaphorical clash of worlds is offered by a few as the intent of the parable. The father's behavior is so exaggerated and unexpected that the hearer/

reader with any conventional sensitivities must protest. This protest is expressed by the elder son and sets up a clash of worlds. Through this clash of worlds the hearer is enabled to contemplate the character of the kingdom.[170]

According to N. T. Wright the parable portrays the exile and restoration of Israel; it is Israel's story in miniature. The background of the parable is Jer 31:18-20, a text about exile and repentance that refers to Israel as God's dear son. The references to resurrection in 15:24 and 32 are metaphors for return from exile, and the elder brother represents the mixed multitude (especially the Samaritans) who resisted Israel's return. Those who grumble at what is happening in Jesus' ministry position themselves virtually as Samaritans. The parable acts to create a new world, and with it Jesus announces that God is restoring his people after the long exile.[171]

The parable depicts God's reception of the repentant and challenges those who object. A number of variations and implications exist with this approach, but usually the parable is seen as a defense of Jesus' eating with sinners.[172] In the modern period this is the most common interpretation.

Decisions on the Issues

1. Was this parable originally shorter? Occasionally interpreters have argued that vv. 25-32 (the section about the elder brother) were not originally part of the parable. Obviously vv. 11-24 function well enough as a parable, and the second section has often been ignored. Vv. 25-32 also supposedly have more Lukan traits. Further, the tension between the division of goods to both sons in v. 12 and the father's continued authority over the goods coupled with the elder son's complaint that not even a kid was provided for him (vv. 29-31) is offered as evidence that Luke added the second part.[173]

This tension is present for any approach and will be dealt with below, but the theory that Luke added the second part does not explain the tension. That the second part has more Lukan traits has been discredited.[174] More important are factors showing the second part was always an integral part of the parable. Clearly vv. 11-12 indicate that the story is about *two* sons and that the father divided his possessions to them both. The hearer/reader expects to hear the actions of the two sons contrasted. Further, the parallels between the two sons listed above (see p. 124) almost assures that this was always a two-part parable, as most scholars acknowledge.[175]

2. Does this parable have any relation to Matthew's parable of the Two Sons? This question can be dealt with quickly. A few suggest that Luke created his parable of the two sons from his knowledge of Matthew's parable.[176] Evidence for the suggestion does not exist. Hardly anything corresponds between the two parables. Even the words for "sons" are different.[177] That both Gospels have a parable about two sons is not in the least surprising. Stories contrasting two sons were a common means of instruction and frequent in the OT, Jewish parables, and Greco-Roman stories and declamations.[178] Further, as Hultgren points out, the insolence of the first son in Matthew has no place in Luke's description of the elder brother.[179]

3. Against what background should one read? The debate here is more complex, for a case can be made for finding the background in one of several different OT texts, in various Greco-Roman influences, or in rabbinic discussions. Suggestions for an OT background include: Jacob's reception by Esau (Genesis 33),[180] Joseph's elevation with Pharaoh's ring and fine clothes and his reception of his brothers (Genesis 41 and 45),[181] commands concerning rebellious sons (Deut 21:18-21),[182] Psalm 23,[183] Psalm 103,[184] Jer 31:10-20,[185] or an amalgam of several texts.[186] Each of these options shares features with the parable, and, if read in isolation and without drawing tenuous connections, is plausible. All these texts provide insight concerning general cultural or theological features, but none of them (or combination of them) shows enough similarity to justify seeing it as the source of Jesus' parable and its wording. That so many lines can be drawn between the parable and other texts should engender caution.

K. Bailey marks out thirteen parallels between the three parables in Luke 15 and Psalm 23 and argues that Jesus' three parables can be seen as an expansion of the psalm.[187] Later, with little reference to Psalm 23, Bailey marked out fifteen similarities (and sixteen dissimilarities) with the Jacob story and argued that Jesus took the story of Jacob and retold it.[188] In still another work Bailey found fifty-one parallels between the parable and the Jacob story.[189] Many of Bailey's parallels to both Psalm 23 and the Jacob story are superficial or exaggerated.

With regard to suggestions of rabbinic influence, R. Aus lists fourteen motifs of this parable paralleled in Jewish traditions about Joseph. He concludes that Jesus drew from these traditions in composing his parable.[190] K. Rengstorf argues that the parable presupposes that the younger son was subjected to the legal act of separation or disowning *(qetsatsah),* which is why he is described as dead. The father's extreme actions provide a legal reinvestiture so that the son is restored with his former clothes and marks of authority.[191] Rengstorf's view presupposes too much not specified in the parable and has not found much acceptance.

D. Holgate and W. Pöhlmann point instead to parallels in various Greco-Roman narratives about prodigal sons (see above, pp. 120-22). Holgate argues that Luke's version of Jesus' parable has similarities with the Greco-Roman topos "On Covetousness" and is designed to provide moral instruction on covetousness, liberality, and stinginess.[192] Pöhlmann thinks the parable pictures the "wisdom ethos of the household" — domestic attitudes about morality, which with the elder's protest from such a perspective enables the hearer to perceive the kingdom.[193] Neither approach is satisfactory, for both neglect the Palestinian context of Jesus' ministry (to say nothing of Luke's context). We may agree with Holgate (and others) that the right use of possessions is a subsidiary theme in the parable,[194] but the parable is about much more than covetousness, liberality, and meanness. With regard to Pöhlmann, the elder's protest is based on conventional morality, but Pöhlmann is none too clear on how the kingdom is perceived from this vantage. Surely the parable is more than a picture of conventional "household" morality against which one may perceive the kingdom. What is important about these two studies is their collection of Greco-Roman stories on fathers with two sons, prodigals, and inheritance issues.

The fact is that one can point to parallels with a host of traditions from various times and cultures, but none of them can make a claim to be the starting point of the parable or the lens through which it should be read. Such stories were far too common for these arguments to be convincing without much more specific evidence. That a text has a focus on God as Father or Israel as a wayward son or on acts such as the reconciliation of Jacob and Esau or Pharaoh's honoring of Joseph is interesting, even generally informative, but does not demonstrate the origin of the parable or provide the hermeneutical key for interpretation. None of these suggestions is more than background music for interpreting the parable. No specific text or group of texts provides *the* background. At the same time, understanding this parable is enhanced by knowledge of conventional stories of a father and two sons, one good and one prodigal, of attitudes toward rebellious sons, of OT themes of mercy and reconciliation, and of the cultural significance of the details of the parable.

More important than any of the suggestions offered is a specific aspect of Jesus' ministry and message. J. Fitzmyer rightly points to the Jubilee as a backdrop for reading the parables in this chapter,[195] just as we saw with the parables of grace and responsibility. In first-century Judaism Jubilee themes were associated with eschatological deliverance and the coming of the Messiah.[196] With the forgiveness and restoration of the prodigal and the insistence on joy and celebration the parable exemplifies the proclamation of the year of the Lord's favor (cf. 4:18-22). Grumbling in the face of such restoration only attests that one does not understand what is happening.

4. How should cultural factors inform the reading of the parable? The cultural and legal factors pertaining to the younger son's request and the father's division of his property lead one into a morass of detail, and regardless of what else is said, we must remember that this is a *story*, not a legal code, and that the story works quite well. Still, this parable more than any other assumes familiarity with the cultural significance of its components. The nuance of many of the cultural factors can be demonstrated from early sources, but for others there is less clarity. Is this a story of everyday events or of something unusual? Do the events portrayed conform to legal practice, or are they artificially contrived for theological purposes? If the father divides his goods to both sons, why is he still in control of those goods at the return of the prodigal?

Most scholars assume that the younger son's request was unusual, with some going so far as to say that he should have been beaten for the request or that he in effect wishes his father were dead. Others think the request was common enough, possibly motivated by the fact that small family farms were not sufficient to maintain younger sons, who consequently had to strike out on their own.[197] The parable gives no basis for thinking any necessity led to the younger son's request, but there is some evidence of people getting their share of an inheritance while the relative is still alive, most notably *m. Baba Batra* 8.7.[198] The request is imaginable, but at the very least we must recognize that the boy's request and especially his departure would have been viewed negatively by all Mediterranean societies.[199] It is no accident that v. 12 reads literally "He divided to them *the life (ton bion)*" (cf. "your life" in v. 30), for these resources were the father's means of maintaining his life, especially in old age. The boy may not have literally wished his father dead, but his actions show that he did not really care for his father or desire a relationship with him. He wanted the father's money, not the father. Even with the division of goods, the younger son would still have had responsibility to help care for his father,[200] a responsibility he ignores by leaving.

This raises a question: What was the prodigal's sin against heaven and his father? Several answers have been given: the request for his share of the possessions,[201] his covetousness,[202] his leaving,[203] his squandering,[204] his lifestyle,[205] or his neglect of his father.[206] From an OT perspective the prodigal would have been guilty of violating the command to honor one's parents (Exod 20:12), but I do not think a choice has to be made on this issue. The request itself may not have been a sin, and I doubt that covetousness is in view, but first-century Jews and Greeks alike would have considered all the other factors as reprehensible and unethical.

On the basis of Deut 21:15-17 the elder brother would be given two-thirds of the property,[207] and the primary responsibility for the care of the parents would fall to him. We cannot assume that the younger son would receive one-third of the family *land*. The language allows for reference to the land, but that the boy would be given the right to dispose of the land is unlikely.[208] The best estimate is that he received possessions equivalent to two-ninths of the estate,[209] but even that may be too high.

Whether the elder son's portion was given to him when the younger son received his part or was only designated for him to receive later is not clear, despite Luke's "he divided *to them* the life" (15:12). D. Daube argues that the elder son did not receive his portion, while D. Derrett argues that he did.[210] If the division was actually made to both sons, the complaint of the elder hardly makes sense. The evidence suggests that the younger son obtained his property in advance and would have no further claim at his father's death. The elder's portion would have been designated (in this case almost by default since there were only two sons), but the father would have retained oversight and control. According to *m. Baba Batra* 8.7 (see above, p. 122), if property was assigned before death, neither the father nor the elder son could sell it since it was assigned to the son but possessed by the father. Actual transfer of the property to the elder son would not occur until the death of the father,[211] which is why the father could still reinstate the younger son and give commands concerning the banquet. The "poverty" of the elder son is enlightened by a talmudic comment: "as the first-born has nothing while his father is alive, so has this one also nothing while his father is alive."[212] The father's assuring him that "all my things are yours" is verification that his portion of the inheritance will not be decreased by his brother's return, but the father also seeks recognition of the younger brother as a brother, which, if taken seriously, would have consequences for assisting the younger brother.[213]

The elder brother had family responsibilities beyond caring for aged parents. He should have taken a leadership role at important occasions or difficult times and should have mediated relational conflicts.[214] This expectation intensifies how embarrassing the elder's refusal to enter the banquet would be.

Awareness of such cultural expectations is illuminating, but fascination with the culture can cause one to read into the parable aspects that are not there. K. Bailey's contribution from his experience as a missionary to Middle Eastern peasants is often insightful, but he uncritically assumes a continuity between first-century Jewish Palestine and modern Middle Eastern peasants impacted by centuries of Islamic rule. Attitudes may have remained the same, but that cannot be presupposed. Further, Bailey and others who focus on sociological approaches become more intrigued with the culture than with the parable, more with what is not there than with what is. Once again the principle is demonstrated: the more an interpretation focuses on what is not explicit in the parable the more likely it is to be wrong.

Bailey's cultural psychologizing of the parable is evident in his thinking that the son has been disowned, that he has either endured the cutting off ceremony of *qetsatsah* or that he will be liable to this ceremony as soon as the villagers see him.[215] Bailey interprets the father's actions of running to the boy and hugging and kissing him as an effort to protect him from the villagers and signal his reinstatement. Bailey's reconstruction presents a poignant picture, but one that does not find much basis in the parable itself. He must presuppose that the farm was next to a village eager to punish offenders, but the parable has no mention of any of this, and no evidence exists that the *qetsatsah* is even remotely in the background of the parable.[216]

R. Rohrbaugh is equally guilty of misapplying cultural information when he argues that the parable is about propriety and shame in a dysfunctional family with the father and both sons acting shamefully and the father then seeking to reconcile his sons and the family with the village.[217] Nothing in the parable suggests that the father acted shamefully or that the village needs to be reconciled. The village plays at best a minor role in the parable, if any, and it is difficult to discern any reason to think the contrast is between the villagers and the elder son instead of the father and the elder son.

One further point needs to be made. The father's actions are not so exaggerated and unexpected that they fall outside the range of human behavior. While some fathers may reject prodigals or require conditions for acceptance, others express tenderness and love, as some of the primary sources above demonstrate.[218]

5. Does the parable depict the human condition generally, the exile and restoration of Israel, or specific groups listening to Jesus? To what is analogy being made? Is Luke's context for the parable correct? Determining the point of the analogy depends to some degree on whether one thinks Luke's context for the parable is correct. Jesus does at times teach generally about the human condition (e.g., Matt 6:24/Luke 16:13; Matt 15:10-20/Mark 7:14-23), and this parable mirrors human need and forgiveness poignantly. We can understand why people have reflected on the parable's anthropological and psychological insight, but there is a big difference between reflecting on the broader applicability of the parable and discerning the communicative intent of Jesus' analogy. I find it hard to believe that with this parable Jesus was concerned first with the general human condition rather than the context of his own mission. Virtually all the parables are pointed pictures of circumstances and realities in his ministry. The parable of the Pharisee and the Toll Collector possibly comes closest to providing an analogy of humans generally, but it, too, springs from specific tensions created by Jesus' ministry. The proximity of that parable to the Prodigal bears reflection. Both are directed at those who assume their own good standing and reject other people as inadequate. In neither parable is the analogy merely about the human condition; it is about the impact of Jesus' ministry of the kingdom and the attitudes expected of his followers. The attempts to read the parable as reflecting general or dysfunctional human relations are abortive.

N. T. Wright argues that this parable — as he does for most of Jesus' parables — is Israel's story in miniature.[219] Other parables do indeed present Israel's story in miniature; the Fig Tree and the Wicked Tenants are among the most obvious examples. Also, one may take the theology of repentance in this parable — a theology shared with much of the OT — and apply it to Israel, which is what Wright has done. The same procedure Wright uses to apply the story to Israel he also uses to apply it to modern NT scholarship.[220] Wright can make the first half of the parable fit the story of Israel easily because the cycle of forgetting God and repenting is Israel's story, but his attempt to say the elder brother represents the Samaritans who do not want Israel to return from exile is not the least convincing and shows that his explanation of the parable cannot be followed.

Almost by necessity we are forced to see that the parable reflects the realities of those listening to Jesus.[221] The arrangement of the chapter is probably Lukan,[222] but the frequent objections to Jesus' associates and meal partners is not merely a Lukan idea.[223] Those who reject Luke's context do not offer any convincing alternative, or they still find the parable applied to the Pharisees.[224] The original audience probably included both the sinners and those objecting to them, but the primary target appears to be the latter. The first two parables in this chapter focus on the searching and the joy and celebration at finding. Both also compare the joy of finding with the joy accompanying repentance. The third parable develops the theme of joy and celebration even more but contrasts the attitude of the father and that of the elder son. This contrast mirrors the attitude of God toward repentant sinners and the attitudes of those who refuse to rejoice and instead disparage repentant sinners.

Any claim from Jesus that the kingdom of God was present or even that God was at work would be viewed with suspicion as long as those around him were obvious sinners like toll collectors, the ceremonially unclean, and the disreputable. The attitude of Simon the Pharisee toward Jesus and the woman who washed his feet (7:36-39) is one more example of the response of the righteous to Jesus' associates. Such passages and the parables in ch. 15 point to a conflict between Jesus' claims and the expectations of the Pharisees and others of what should happen if those claims were true. The parable contrasts the acceptance of sinners by God and the suspicion of groups like the Pharisees.

6. *What does the parable teach about the Pharisees? If the elder son represents the Pharisees and scribes, why are the father's comments to the elder son so positive? What does the parable imply about the relation of the Pharisees to God and their inclusion in the kingdom since the father says the elder son is always with him and owns all things with him?* The parable's teaching on the Pharisees is at first glance surprising. If the elder son represents the Pharisees and scribes, we would have expected the elder's claim never to have violated a command to be

challenged,[225] and we would not expect the father to say that the elder is always with him and owns all things with him. While patristic interpreters decided the claim was not true and that the father's comments were conditioned on the right response, B. Scott argues the parable does not fit well with Luke's understanding of salvation and that identification of the elder son with the Pharisees has miscued interpretation. Why should the Pharisees respond to Jesus' gospel if indeed they have everything already? Scott argues that the parable subverts the use of the mytheme of two sons to explain who is chosen and who is rejected (e.g., Mal 1:2-3 and Gal 4:21-31). In this parable no one is rejected; both are chosen. On Scott's view the kingdom (the metaphor for which is the father's going out) does not divide but unifies, and Jesus rejects any apocalyptic notion of some group's rejection. The kingdom is universal, not particularist.[226]

Certainly the parable is not an attack on the Pharisees, and the missing conclusion to the story functions as an invitation for them to change their attitude. But Scott's view makes the parable carry a heavy burden, one that flies in the face of many of Jesus' other sayings and parables in which the kingdom is indeed about judgment and separation.[227] If the meaning suggested for a parable cannot be verified in non-parabolic material, it has little reason to be accepted.

No doubt, the claim that the elder son has never violated a commandment (v. 29) borders on breaking the boundaries of the story. These words function to solidify the connection between him and the Pharisees or others who considered themselves righteous keepers of the Law. Hearers may have gone along with the elder's claim, or they may well have viewed it as invalid because of the elder son's attitude toward his father. By not going in to the banquet he has shamed his father and violated the commandment to honor his father.[228]

In reality, however, the question why such positive things can be said of the elder son, if he represents the Pharisees, is misguided. It assumes that the parable is a complete picture of the reality it portrays, says everything that should be said about the Pharisees, and has the kind of detailed correspondences that most say they find questionable. This parable has no intention of describing the Pharisees' relation to God or their status with regard to the kingdom. It contrasts the *attitude* of the father (God) and the *attitude* of the elder son (the Pharisees) *toward the repentant*.[229] The contrast is between celebration and disdain. Parables are not photographs of reality, even though interpreters often try to make them so. The question is always how much of a parable intends to portray the reality, and the answer must be decided on a case-by-case basis. No formula exists for answering the question; an interpreter can only rely on some intuitive sense of how the story functions in its context and what the boundaries of its purposes are. If this parable had mirrored Jesus' relation to the Pharisees or depicted the rejection of the Pharisees by the punishment or banishing of the elder son, the story would have been artificial and could hardly have functioned as a story. A story of a father throwing out the elder son would not be unheard of, but it would hardly fit with the attitudes portrayed in this parable or the call to celebrate the return of the repentant. While other parables focus on judgment, this one serves to contrast celebration and disdain for the repentant. Jesus could have argued abstractly from Jewish ideas of repentance that the attitude of the Pharisees was wrong; he did not. He confronted them with a compelling picture of the narrowness of their thinking and with the open question about whether the elder son will enter the house and join the celebration. In effect, Jesus invites the Pharisees to adopt God's attitude, forgive those they disdain as sinners, and join the celebration accompanying his proclamation of the kingdom.

7. *What is the theological significance of the parable? Are there "allegorical" correspondences and teachings about repentance, christology, or the atonement?* How far theological significance should be drawn from the details of the parable is determined by some sense of the purpose and boundaries of the story. We cannot deny that there are correspondences between image and reality.[230] Even those who reject any thought of allegory still see correspondences between image and reality. Jülicher, for example, admits that the parable has an intended double meaning (which is, of course, what makes it a parable), but still says it is not an allegory. He understands the parable to say that God does not allow the righteous to complain when he accepts the sinners,[231] which assumes that the father, the elder son, and the prodigal represent God, the righteous, and sinners respectively. Schottroff refuses to see God represented by the father, but she still sees the parable as teaching about God's forgiveness of sins.[232] People may say they reject allegory, but they cannot make sense of parables without determining how they mirror the reality they seek to convey. Again, I see little value in thinking allegory is a literary genre, but parables (excluding the single indirect stories) to one degree or another are allegorical; that is, they mirror, however imperfectly, a reality on a different plane.

Nearly all admit or assume the straightforward associations of the parable with God, sinners, and the "righteous."[233] It is hard to avoid such connections. It is also fair to assume that the details of the parable *do* have purpose — they are not mere window dressing; but they are *not* allegorical representations. The specifics of the prodigal's plight do not stand for theological realities; they paint a picture of degradation and need, especially for Jewish hearers. The father's extravagant action in receiving the prodigal paints a picture of eager reception, but the individual actions do not stand for theological ideas. Similarly, the description of the restoration of the prodigal with robe, ring, shoes, and fatted calf for celebration paints a picture of joy and full acceptance, but these items do not have individual referents.[234] The hearer/reader does not even have time for such associations, for the story proceeds at a lively pace. People may justly debate whether the celebration hints at the messianic banquet, given the importance of that theme, but the parable does not give much basis for thinking future eschatology is in mind. The focus is on the present celebration that should be taking place. If anything, realized eschatology is at work here.

Problems arise when people attempt to extract more theology from the parable than is justified. For K. Bailey and H. Weder it is not enough to say that the father mirrors God's eager acceptance of returning sinners. For them the father mirrors *both* God and Jesus.[235] Like patristic interpreters, they view the father's going out to the prodigal as a picture of the incarnation. Luke 15, like much of Scripture, presents God as a seeking and gracious God, which is certainly in line with the theology of the incarnation, but to think that the parable intentionally conveys this overburdens the parable. Any double referent would require too much from hearers and readers. Some even find Jesus as the prodigal who goes out and returns to the father,[236] but surely that is a forced reading, something founded in the interpreter's desire rather than in the story itself.

Equally misguided are those who take offense because there is no mother in the parable[237] and those who find a feminine emphasis in the actions of the father or some other aspect of the story.[238] To complain that there is no mother in the story is to foist one's own agenda on the parable and ignore the fact that parables virtually always leave out characters unnecessary to the plot.[239] What narcissism drives the feeling that we or our kind have to be found in every text? To find the feminine implied in the famine,[240] in the parable's focus on nourishment (vv. 16 and 23), or in the father's kiss[241] cannot be defended from the culture or on any other basis. Other texts speak of God in feminine terms, but this parable has no relevance for feminist concerns.

Similarly, interpreters have discussed whether the atonement is alluded to in the story. K. Bailey and others find the atonement in the costly actions of the father or in the calf.[242] It is one thing to see God's saving activity as costly or requiring effort on his part and quite another to think that this parable attempts to mirror atonement thinking. I see no justification for pushing the parable that far. On the other hand, Jülicher finds it significant that this parable has no room for a dying mediator and sees salvation as dependent only on the character of God,[243] a conclusion beyond the parable's purpose. We do not ask about an atonement and a mediator with most parables; why should we here? Is it not because of the tradition that this parable is the gospel within the gospel?[244] This parable is obviously a powerful presentation of the saving grace of God, but to make it carry the weight of picturing the whole gospel is absurd. Neither this nor any other parable is a full compendium of theology, even though we often try to make them that.

Is the parable christological? I do not think christology is internal to the parable, but there are christological implications. If Jesus used the parable to defend his association with sinners and his proclamation of forgiveness to them, then indirectly the parable is a claim that he is God's agent announcing forgiveness. If the parable mirrors the Jubilee themes of restoration and forgiveness, then it assumes that Jesus is the one announcing the Jubilee. Jesus is not in the parable, but the context of the parable carries with it christological implications.[245]

Another arena where theological questions arise is the parable's teaching on repentance. Here as elsewhere, biases about the order of repentance and forgiveness often unfairly dictate the contours of the discussion. The first question is whether the prodigal's confession and return were sincere acts of repentance or, as J. Breech and a significant number of others argue, merely a self-centered attempt to get food, a "soup kitchen conversion."[246] The similarity of the prodigal's confession in v. 18 to Pharaoh's confession in Exod 10:16 is proof enough for Bailey that the repentance is a charade and that the boy has no remorse.[247] But could hearers have been expected to make that connection, particularly when "I have sinned" is the way sincere confession is expressed in many OT passages?[248] Bailey and others seem to have been motivated by the desire to emphasize God's initiative in saving and to deemphasize human responsibility, for by a specious connection to Ps 23:3 he seeks to define repentance in Luke 15 as something done for the believer. "Repentance is the acceptance of being found."[249] This desire to avoid human effort reads soteriological anxieties into Jesus' parable that are not there and that Jesus did not have.

Although some, on the basis of Semitic evidence, think "when he came to himself" *(eis heauton de elthōn)* means repentance,[250] all it really means is "he came to his senses."[251] The repentance itself is expressed in the confession in vv. 17b-19 and 21. On the other hand, "came to his senses" must be taken seriously, for it is the prerequisite to or first step of repentance.[252] The parable does not mention repentance; it speaks only of the prodigal's coming to his senses, his confession, and his return. No doubt for any Jew those were valid aspects of repentance, even if they do not cover everything involved. The prodigal's confession and change must be seen as sincere.[253] Certainly Luke takes the repentance as sincere, or he would not have structured the chapter as he has. The celebration of the recovery of the lost son in this parable parallels the celebration of the recovery of the lost sheep and the lost coin, both of which are explicitly connected to repentance.

This parable is different from the other two. In the others the sheep and the coin do not do anything, yet the celebration at their being found mirrors heaven's joy over the repentant. In this parable the prodigal acts first. It is true that the father's actions occur before the son has time to confess and that the father's actions are determined by his character rather than that of his sons.[254] Once again we have a parable that mirrors the limitless grace of God, but it is also true that in this parable the father does *not* go seeking for the lost son. The son's return prompts the father's going out.

What should we conclude about repentance from these parables? Should we conclude that repentance is only the acceptance of being found, as Bailey? Should we think that the first two parables of this chapter reflect divine sovereignty and the last reflects human responsibility?[255] Should we be concerned about the parable's *ordo salutis,* its order of salvation, and whether God's action is dependent on human response first?[256] To me such questions push beyond the concerns of the parable and forget story to theologize. The first two parables do not portray repentance but joy over the *recovery* of the repentant. Nor does the prodigal portray a *full* theology of repentance. Certain aspects of repentance are present, but we may no more draw an accurate picture of repentance from it than draw guidelines on inheritance questions from it. The issue once again is how the analogy functions, and the purpose of the analogy is to contrast the father's attitude of celebration with the elder son's disdain. We may focus on the theological significance of the three acts of coming to oneself, confession, and return, items that are explicit, but the parable is not intended to work out a theology of repentance or establish a picture of an *ordo salutis.*

Still others, like patristic interpreters before them, seek theological referents behind the two sons, the elder standing for the Jews or Jewish Christians and the younger for Gentiles or Gentile Christians.[257] Certainly none of this works for Jesus' telling of the parable,[258] and it is just as unlikely for Luke. As several point out, the prodigal does not reflect the situation of the Gentiles, for he *starts out* in the father's house.[259] There is no basis for seeing any more in the *analogical* referent of the two sons than the sinners who gathered around Jesus and those who disparaged such people.

Similarly, some see Luke's *community* portrayed by the parable so that the story describes the conflict between the Lukan community and the synagogue or between rigorists in Luke's community who questioned acceptance of the Gentiles and those ready to accept Gentiles.[260] Certainly Luke wanted to teach his readers about self-righteous attitudes, but nothing in this chapter provides *any* evidence for describing the situation of Luke's community. Such conclusions are gratuitous assumptions.

8. What is the purpose of the parable? From the discussion so far it should be evident that we must speak not merely of the purpose of this parable but of its *purposes.* Which of the three characters is the central figure is an unnecessary question, for the parable needs all three to accomplish its goals.[261] While conventional stories of two sons would lead us to focus on a contrast between them, the real contrast here is between the father and the elder son. *The first purpose* of the parable is to emphasize the compassion[262] — one of the four major features of Jesus' message and work — and the unquestioning love of the father, who mirrors analogically the attitude of God. V. 20 underscores that the prodigal did not merely return home: he returned to his father. The eagerness of the father to recover and restore the erring son is poignantly and tenderly described. The parable is a narrative demonstration of the grace with which God reaches out to embrace sinful people.[263] Jesus did not need to introduce the idea that God accepts sinners, but his message of the kingdom emphasized that *he* was restoring Israel, that end-time forgiveness was being offered now, and that this was the critical time for repentance. The God that Jesus represents and proclaims is precisely the forgiving and merciful God reflected in the parable. Our familiarity with the message should not keep us from appreciating it.

Less emotionally laden language is used of the father's entreating the elder son (no doubt, because no sense of loss was present), but the father did go out to both sons and addressed the elder affectionately as "son" (or "child," *teknon*) and reassured him of his place.[264] Because of the several parallels between the two sons, the parable is about two lost sons, one who wanted to be a servant and the other who felt like one,[265] but the father insisted that both are sons *and brothers* to each other. The inability of the elder son to perceive reality is marked by the opposition of his "never" and the Father's "always."[266] The equally dramatic contrast of language used by the elder son ("this son of yours," v. 30) and that of the father ("this brother of yours," v. 32) calls for recognition of the familial relation and of the need to celebrate. If the elder son accepts the father's invitation, his return will have sociological consequences: he will gain a brother.

A second purpose of the parable is the invitation to celebrate and rejoice, which is explicit in vv. 23-24 and 32.[267] Some would even say that joy is the primary concern of the parable.[268] If God rejoices at the return of sinners, can God's people do less? As E. Linnemann pointed out, in response to the Pharisees' question how Jesus could celebrate with such sinful people, Jesus answered, "The lost is found. This must be celebrated. I am joining in celebrating God's feast. And what are you doing?"[269] Like the parable of the Banquet in 14:16-24 this parable in effect says "God is giving a party, are you going to come?" The forgiveness enacted with Jesus' proclamation of the Jubilee must be celebrated.

The parable functions *with a third purpose* then as a defense of Jesus' association with sinners.[270] If God accepts such people — not just generally, but specifically because of the presence of the kingdom, and if Jesus' eating with these sinners enacts God's forgiveness and mercy, then complaints about his actions are clearly misguided and out of touch with what God is doing. But more is involved than defense. The parable, especially with its incomplete ending, functions as an invitation for the hearers to take the same attitude toward sinners as the father toward the prodigal.[271] That change of attitude carries with it a missional force so that one is motivated not only to accept sinners but also to find them.[272]

Adapting the Parable

No parable provides as much material for theological reflection as this one. Its use of metaphors and ideas for distance is instructive. The prodigal does not belong in the far country and in the alliance he has made. He is distant from himself, but both he and his brother are distant from their father in different ways. Most of us also live fractured lives, knowing neither unity within ourselves nor the familial relationship with God that has been offered to us. The specter of death haunts the parable as well. The parable's message is that both sinners and seemingly righteous people — both the irreligious and the religious — have a home with God. They belong at home in God's family. The parable is more than theological ideas about God's character; it is an invitation to recognize our estrangement and bankruptcy. For good reason Rembrandt's painting of the prodigal in Dresden's Zwinger Gemäldegalerie is a self-portrait of Rembrandt with his girlfriend Saskia. The prodigals are not the other people. At the same time, the parable is an invitation to return to our true selves — to come to ourselves (v. 17), return to God, and be willing to be embraced by God. With such ideas the parable is fertile ground for reflection on conversion and reconciliation. Conversion often occurs in a context of crisis, but must "famine" be present before conversion occurs? Is it possible to return to our senses before we hit bottom?[273] The first step to conversion and reconversion (for conversion is a process) is coming to ourselves. God's grace allows us to come to ourselves; only there do we know who we are and are able to speak the truth, truth without which we cannot live.

If Scripture seeks to give us an identity, which it does, this parable is a prime identity-shaping text. It says, in effect, that humans are not legitimately inhabitants of the far country, that they are not prodigals or slaves. Rather, they are children of their father and belong with their father. The prodigal declares that he is not worthy of his own identity and wants something less, but he is no hired hand. Grace lets you be who you are supposed to be even though you do not deserve to or may not want to. The elder son is suspicious of joy and sees himself as equivalent to a servant, but the father insists that he is a son as well.

Boundaries or the rejection of them dominates the passage. The younger son feels that his home is a boundary prohibiting him. The elder son creates a boundary by refusing to enter, but the father seeks to nullify the boundary. The elder son has excluded his brother, but their father reintroduced the younger son. The elder son was jealous and judgmental and felt deprived, but the father says that he is privileged, that he belongs to the inner circle, and that all things are his.

The parable sounds a note of joy that should mark disciples of the kingdom. If the kingdom is present and forgiveness is being dispensed, even if evil is still in the world, joy should characterize those who recognize what is happening. Christians sometimes are not a joyful lot. They either take faith for granted or forget what they have, or worse, like the elder son who hears music and does not want to get too close, they are suspicious of joy. H. Thielicke reminds us how wretched it is to call oneself a Christian and yet be a stranger and grumbling servant in God's house.[274] Joy is not an optional feature of the faith, nor can it be attained by smiling more and singing louder. It must emerge from an awareness of the mercy and forgiveness of God enacted in the kingdom.

One of the more striking theological adaptations of this parable is M. Volf's *Exclusion and Embrace*.[275] Volf writes from his experience as a Croatian struggling with the results of war with Serbians and with injustice and oppression more generally. He uses the story of the prodigal and of the father's reception of the prodigal to address the themes of distance, otherness, exclusion, belonging, and embrace of one's enemies. He rightly sees that this parable is not merely about relations with God but that it sets the pattern for dealing with human relations and estrangement as well. We cannot claim to be returning to the Father without displaying the same kind of forgiveness and willingness to embrace which the Father displays. Tertullian, because of the problem of dealing with Christians who denied the faith under persecution, argued that this parable should never be applied to Christians.[276] This sounds like the complaint of the elder son. If conversion is a process, which it certainly is, then God is always welcoming back his erring children at the same time that he holds them accountable. Grace cannot be confined within boundaries.

As noted above, the parable has missional overtones. If God is receiving sinners so eagerly, then that message needs to be shared, and people need to be invited home.

For Further Reading

Kenneth Bailey, *Finding the Lost: Cultural Keys to Luke 15* (St. Louis: Concordia, 1992).

————, *Jacob and the Prodigal: A Study of the Parable of the Prodigal Son in the Light of the Saga of Jacob* (Downers Grove, Ill.: InterVarsity), 2003.

————, "The Parable of the Prodigal," *Christianity Today* (Oct. 26, 1998): 32-69 (special section on this parable with contributions by Kenneth E. Bailey, Miroslav Volf, Barbara Brown Taylor, and Christopher A. Hall).

————, *Poet and Peasant: A Literary Cultural Approach to the Parables in Luke* (Grand Rapids: Eerdmans, 1976), pp. 158-206.

Greg W. Forbes, *The God of Old: The Role of the Lukan Parables in the Purpose of Luke's Gospel* (JSNTSup 198; Sheffield: Sheffield Academic Press, 2000), pp. 109-51.

David A. Holgate, *Prodigality, Liberality and Meanness in the Parable of the Prodigal Son: A Greco-Roman Perspective on Luke 15:11-32* (JSNTSup 187; Sheffield: Sheffield Academic Press, 1999).

Arland Hultgren, *The Parables of Jesus* (Grand Rapids: Eerdmans, 2000), pp. 70-91.

Joachim Jeremias, *The Parables of Jesus* (New York: Charles Scribner's Sons, 1963), pp. 128-32.

John Nolland, *Luke 9:21–18:34* (Word Biblical Commentary 35b; Dallas: Word, 1993), pp. 777-91.

Wolfgang Pöhlmann, *Der verlorene Sohn und das Haus. Studien zu Lukas 15, 11-32 im Horizont der antiken Lehre von Haus, Erziehung und Ackerbau* (Tübingen: Mohr-Siebeck, 1993).

Eckhard Rau, *Reden in Vollmacht. Hintergrund, Form, und Anliegen der Gleichnisse Jesu* (FRLANT 149; Göttingen: Vandenhoeck & Ruprecht, 1990).

Miroslav Volf, *Exclusion and Embrace: A Theological Exploration of Identity, Otherness, and Reconciliation* (Nashville: Abingdon Press, 1996), pp. 156-65.

N. T. Wright, *Jesus and the Victory of God* (Minneapolis: Fortress, 1996), pp. 125-31.

The Parable of the Sower
and the Purpose of Parables
(Matt 13:3-23; Mark 4:3-20; Luke 8:5-15)

This parable is among the best known but is not nearly as easy as some have thought. The parable of the Sower and its surrounding context have a foundational role in all three Synoptic Gospels. It is the first substantive parable in all three and, other than Matthew's parables of the Wheat and the Weeds and of the Net, is the only parable given a detailed interpretation.[1] It and the Wheat and the Weeds are the only two parables given a title (Matt 13:18 and 36). The Sower is unique in that it is given pride of place in each Gospel at the beginning of crucial instruction on parables and the kingdom (Matt 13:1-52/Mark 4:1-34/ Luke 8:1-18). It is *the* parable about parables.

All three Synoptic Evangelists place an explanation of the purpose of Jesus' parabolic teaching between the parable and its interpretation. In all three at least a portion of Isa 6:9-10 is quoted. Particularly for Matthew and Mark, the arrangement of their parable collections is carefully structured. After the Sower and its interpretation Matthew presents a collection of seven parables on the kingdom (eight if one counts 13:52 as a parable) and further discussion of the purpose of parables (13:34-35).[2] Mark joins to the Sower and its interpretation several sayings related to parables in 4:21-25, gives two more parables (the Growing Seed and the Mustard Seed) and concludes his parables discourse with a summary statement on Jesus' teaching in parables. Luke does not have a discourse on kingdom parables since in this context he offers only the Sower and its interpretation. He does follow the same basic story line and does parallel Mark 4:21-25 in including the sayings related to parables (Luke 8:16-18), but he places the parables of the Mustard Seed and the Leaven at 13:18-21 with no connection to any discussion of parables. Several of the parables in these collections are sometimes labeled parables of growth.

Questions about the authenticity of the Sower are rarely raised.[3] Since the interpretation looks like an allegorical reading of the parable, those taking their cue from Adolf Jülicher have rejected unreservedly any possibility that the interpretation is from Jesus, and until recently the majority of NT scholars just followed in lockstep agreement. With some, however, the interpretation is surreptitiously reintroduced when scholars give their own explanations of the parable.[4] If the interpretation is truly left out of consideration, little direction remains for determining the meaning, so much so that Bultmann and a few others despaired of finding the original intent.[5] The ambiguity has led to controversy, to a voluminous bibliography of contributions on this parable, and to a variety of understandings.

Scholars did not cause the problems though in understanding this passage, for real difficulties and anomalies exist in the Synoptic accounts. Despite its crucial role in all three Synoptics, this is a difficult parable, especially in Mark.

Parable Type

This parable is not like most others in that it is neither brief and simple nor does it have a developed plot. It presents three incidents of unsuccessful sowing and one successful, followed by an appeal for hearing. People disagree over how to categorize this parable. If the sowing and plowing are viewed as everyday occurrences, then the story is viewed as a similitude.[6] If the sowing and plowing are viewed as a specific and unusual instance, the story is viewed as a parable.[7] For some it is clearly an allegory or an allegorical parable.[8] The best approach is to view the parable as a composite of four images, *a fourfold similitude.*[9] Parallels with such composite features are common.[10]

Issues Requiring Attention

1. What is the significance of the structure of Mark 4, Matthew 13, and Luke 8? A variety of related questions demand attention. Most importantly, why does Mark 4 seem so disorganized with Jesus in the boat at 4:1 and at 4:36 back in the boat at the end of the day ready to disperse the crowd, but in 4:10 alone with his disciples? And especially, what is the relevance of the seemingly unrelated sayings in Mark 4:21-25/Luke 8:16-18, which in Matthew, except for the saying in 13:12, are placed in other contexts?
2. How are the difficult words of 4:10-12 to be understood? A host of questions cry out for treatment: Why would Mark or Jesus suggest that para-

146

bles were told to prevent understanding? Does Mark have a theory of parables that sees them as obscurities that derives partly from his view of the messianic secret? Is this text about "double predestination"? Who are those on the "outside" in Mark and how does one get inside? What is the significance of the use of Isa 6:9-10? What is the meaning of *hina* (usually "in order that") and *mēpote* (either "lest," "whether," or "perhaps") in Mark 4:12? What is the intent with such words as "parables" in the *plural* (Mark 4:10), *mystērion* ("mystery," v. 11), and *ta panta* ("all things," v. 11)? The statement "To those outside all things come in parables" is especially unsettling because in all three Synoptics Jesus has been teaching the crowds without parables and has been understood as one teaching with authority, most obviously in Matthew and Luke with their Sermons on the Mount/Plain, but also in Mark 1:15, 21-22, 38-39.

3. Does the interpretation belong originally with the parable or is it a result of early church allegorizing? Do correspondences always point to the work of the early church? Is the interpretation from Jesus, or is Jeremias correct in pointing to numerous features in the interpretation that show that it derives from the early church?[11] How can both the word and people be sown (Mark 4:14, 15-20)?

4. Would anyone sow seed this way? Should we assume that the sower is careless and sows with abandon or that this is just what happens with sowing in the ancient world?

5. Is the analogy about God sowing people in Israel or God sowing his word?

6. What is the meaning and significance of this parable and its context? Is the focus on the sower, the seed, the soil, or the harvest? Specifically, what does it tell us about the kingdom?

7. How has the redactional shaping of each Evangelist impacted the nuance of the parable?

Helpful Primary Source Material

Only obvious parallels are listed here. Other primary sources are included in the discussion that follows.

Canonical Material

- OT: Isa 6:1-13; 30:8-26; 55:10-11; Jer 4:3-4; 5:21; 23:8; 31:27-28; Ezek 12:2; 36:9; Hos 2:22-23

- NT: Matt 7:24-27/Luke 6:47-49; Matt 9:35-38; 11:25-26/Luke 10:21-24; Mark 7:14; 8:17-18; John 8:43; 9:39; 12:39-40; Acts 28:26-28

Early Jewish Writings

- *4 Ezra* 4:28-32: "For the evil about which you ask me has been sown, but the harvest of it has not yet come. If therefore that which has been sown is not reaped, and if the place where the evil has been sown does not pass away, the field where the good has been sown will not come. For a grain of evil seed was sown in Adam's heart from the beginning, and how much ungodliness it has produced until now — and will produce until the time of threshing comes! Consider now for yourself how much fruit of ungodliness a grain of evil seed has produced. When heads of grain without number are sown, how great a threshing floor they will fill!"
- *4 Ezra* 8:41-44: "For just as the farmer sows many seeds in the ground and plants a multitude of seedlings, and yet not all that have been sown will come up in due season, and not all that were planted will take root; so also those who have been sown in the world will not all be saved. I answered. . . . If the farmer's seed does not come up, because it has not received your rain in due season, or if it has been ruined by too much rain, it perishes. But people, who have been formed by your hands and are called your own image because they are made like you, and for whose sake you have formed all things — have you also made them like the farmer's seed?"
- *4 Ezra* 9:30-35: "Hear me, O Israel. . . . For I sow my law in you, and it shall bring forth fruit in you, and you shall be glorified through it forever. But though our ancestors received the law, they did not keep it and did not observe the statutes; yet the fruit of the law did not perish — for it could not, because it was yours. Yet those who received it perished, because they did not keep what had been sown in them. Now this is the general rule that, when the ground has received seed, or the sea a ship, or any dish food or drink, and when it comes about that what was sown or what was launched or what was put in is destroyed, they are destroyed, but the things that held them remain; yet with us it has not been so."

Greco-Roman Writings

- Seneca, *Epistlae Morales*, 38 ("On Quiet Conversation").2: "Words should be scattered like seed; no matter how small the seed may be, if it has once found favorable ground, it unfolds its strength and from an insignificant thing spreads to its greatest growth. . . . precepts and seeds have the same quality; they produce much, and yet they are slight things."

Early Christian Writings

- *Gos. Thom.* 9: Jesus said: "Behold, the sower went out, he filled his hand, he sowed (the seed). Some (seeds) fell on the road. The birds came (and) gathered them up. Others fell on the rock and did not send a root down into the earth, and did not send an ear up to heaven. And others fell among thorns. They choked the seed, and the worm ate it (literally "them"). And others fell upon the good earth; and it brought forth good fruit up to heaven. It bore sixty-fold and one-hundred-and-twenty-fold."
- *1 Clem* 24:5 (as an example of the resurrection): "Let us take the crops: how and in what way does the sowing take place? 'The sower went forth' and cast each of the seeds into the ground, and they fall on the ground, parched and bare, and suffer decay; then from their decay the greatness of the providence of the Master raises them up, and from one grain more grow and bring forth fruit."[12]
- Justin, *Dialogue* 125:1-2 (on the meaning of the name Israel in a context of suspicion that Jews will not admit what they know): ". . . but I speak all things simply and candidly, as my Lord said, 'A sower went forth to sow . . .' [summarizes where seed fell]. I must speak, then, in the hope of finding good ground somewhere. . . ."

Later Jewish Writings

- *m. 'Abot* 3.18: "He whose wisdom is more abundant than his works, to what is he like? To a tree whose branches are abundant but whose roots are few; and the wind . . . uproots it. . . . But he whose works are more abundant than his wisdom, to what is he like? To a tree whose branches are few but whose roots are many; so that . . . it cannot be stirred from its place. . . ."
- *m. 'Abot* 5.15: "There are four types among them that sit in the presence of the Sages: the sponge, the funnel, the strainer, and the sifter. 'The sponge' — which soaks up everything; 'the funnel' — which takes in at this end and lets out at the other; 'the strainer' — which lets out the wine and collects the lees; 'the sifter' — which extracts the coarsely-ground flour and collects the fine flour." Cf. *t. Soṭah* 5.9, which has four analogies of men who have a fly around or in their cup, each symbolizing a different attitude of a man to a particular kind of wife. *b. Giṭṭin* 90a-b repeats three of the analogies.

Comparison of the Accounts

Since the structure of each Evangelist's parable collection is determinative for understanding the parable, especially in Mark, the structure will be treated under the explanation of the parable. See below, pp. 156-57, 173-74, and 175. If we compare the wording of the different accounts (without listing every detail) we find the following.

Matthew and Mark have Jesus speaking many parables from a boat, whereas Luke refers to *a* parable (he does not present other parables here) and has Jesus teaching from a boat at Luke 5:1-3. Matthew says Jesus spoke while Mark and Luke say he taught (some see this as significant; see below, p. 172).

Mark begins the parable with an appeal to hear and see (*akouete, idou* 4:3; NRSV translates the first word as "Listen!" and omits the second); Matthew has only the appeal to see (*idou* 13:3b, which the NRSV also translates as "Listen!"). Luke omits both words.

Neither Matthew nor Mark uses the word "seed," and Luke has it only twice (8:5, 11). Matthew refers to the seeds with plural pronouns in the parable and singular pronouns in the interpretation. Mark uses singular pronouns for the first three seeds in the parable and then switches to plurals for the fourth seed and for all references in the interpretation. Luke uses singulars in the parable and plurals in the interpretation, but in vv. 14 and 15 uses both singular and plural pronouns (*to de . . . peson . . . houtoi;* "that which fell . . . , these are . . ."). Are singular pronouns used because *sporos* ("seed") is a collective noun?

Matthew and Luke agree against Mark in

the wording of the sowing of that which fell by the road (Matt 13:4/Luke 8:5),

the expression "know the mysteries" (Matt 13:11/Luke 8:10; Mark 4:11 does not use "know" and has singular "mystery"),

using the "measure" saying in relation to judging others (Matt 7:2/Luke 6:38), while Mark 4:24b understands it of receiving parables,

using *blepein* instead of *idein* to express "not seeing" (Matt 13:13b/Luke 8:10b),

omitting "lest they turn and it be forgiven them" (Mark 4:12), although Matthew does include a non-Markan version of this clause when he repeats and extends the quotation (Matt 13:15), and

the focus on the heart (Matt 13:19/Luke 8:12).

Matthew and Mark agree against Luke in

the description of the shallow soil among the rocks and the rising and the
   heat of the sun (Matt 13:5-6/Mark 4:5-6), which Luke omits, and the
   corresponding interpretation referring to tribulation and persecution
   (Matt 13:21/Mark 4:17), which Luke reduces to temptation, and
the description of the seed sown among the thorns (Matt 13:7/Mark 4:7).

Mark and Luke agree against Matthew in

using *hina* ("in order that," 4:12/8:10b), whereas Matt 13:13 uses *hoti* ("because" or "that"), and
including three sayings after the parable's interpretation (Mark 4:21-25/
   Luke 8:16-18). Mark's fourth saying (4:24b) is in the Sermon on the
   Mount/Plain (Matt 7:2/Luke 6:38). Matthew places the saying about
   "the one who has" at 13:12 prior to the interpretation of the parable
   and at 25:29. He uses the other sayings in other contexts and interprets
   them differently (Matt 5:15; 7:2; and 10:26). Luke reuses some of these
   sayings in other contexts as well; see 11:33; 12:2; and 19:26.

After initially quoting part of Isa 6:9 in 13:13, in vv. 14-15 Matthew quotes
all of Isa 6:9b-10. Only Matthew specifies that this is the parable of the Sower
(13:18) and that "the word" is the word of the kingdom (13:19).

Matthew lists the increase in descending order (100, 60, 30), Mark has an
ascending order (30, 60, 100), and Luke lists only 100-fold.

All these differences are relatively minor but still of interest. The relationships are unusual enough, especially the agreements of Matthew and Luke
against Mark, that U. Luz argues for a deutero-Markan reworking of Mark's
text.[13] In other words, for Luz the text of Mark used by Matthew and Luke is
not the Mark we have. Similarly, Nolland argues that Luke had a second source
besides Mark for the parable (but not for the interpretation).[14] Such theories
ought to make us much more cautious about explaining Synoptic tradition and
redaction from simple assumptions of Markan priority.

Gos. Thom. 9 lacks descriptive detail and is much more cryptic than the
Synoptic accounts. For the seed on the rock, rather than being told it sprang up
because there was no depth of soil, we are told that it did not send a root down
to the earth and did not send an ear up to heaven, something not attested in the
Synoptics. *Gos. Thom.* also adds that a worm ate the seed among the thorns and
that the seed on good soil bore good fruit up to heaven. Two rates of increase
are offered, 60 and 120.

Textual Features Worth Noting

Mark 4 is framed redactionally in a surprising way. Jesus is in a boat addressing the crowd (4:1-2; cf. 3:9), then alone with his disciples (4:10), and then with his disciples back in the boat and only at this point are they leaving the crowd (vv. 35-36). Clearly 4:35-36 connects chronologically with 4:9, and 4:10-34 has been inserted redactionally into the narrative. Matthew 13 is just as obviously a redactional arrangement.

The redactional emphases of each author are striking, even if one accepts (as many do) that the material in Mark is from a pre-Markan tradition. *In all three the dominant idea is hearing.* In Mark's account the verb *akouein* ("hear") appears thirteen times (4:3, 9 [twice], 12 [twice], 15, 16, 18, 20, 23 [twice], 24, 33). In Mark the parable begins and ends with a focus on hearing, thus forming an inclusio. *The parable of the Sower is a parable about hearing the message of the kingdom.* Matthew has *akouein* fifteen times but also uses the verb *sunienai* ("understand") in 13:13, 14, 15, 19, 23, 51. The reason Matthew somewhat redundantly quotes Isa 6:9b-10 in vv. 14b-15 is surely to include the phrase "understand with the heart." Whereas Mark asks "Do you really hear Jesus' message?" Matthew asks "Do you really understand with your heart?" Luke has streamlined the whole section, as is his custom, but still has *akouein* nine times. He emphasizes that "the word" is the word of God (8:11).

This is the only parable to which all three Synoptists attach the saying "Let the one who has ears to hear hear." The expression also appears in Matt 11:15; 13:43; Mark 4:23; 7:16 (as a variant); Luke 14:35; Rev 2:7, 11, 17, 29; 3:6, 13, 22; 13:9. The origin appears to be Ezek 3:27.

Three OT parables begin like Mark with the injunction to hear (Jdg 9:7; Isa 28:23; Ezek 20:47 [21:3]; cf. *1 En.* 37:2). Elsewhere the imperative "Hear" is used to introduce material at Matt 15:10; 21:33; Mark 7:14; 12:29 (in quoting the Shema); Luke 18:6; Acts 2:22; 7:2; 13:16; 15:13; 22:1; Jas 2:5.

In all three Synoptic accounts the aorist tense is used of what happened with the seed that failed, which Luke also uses for the productive seed. Matthew and Mark, however, switch to the imperfect tense for the productive seed. For all three the present tense is used throughout the interpretation.

Some sayings connected to parables by one Evangelist have a different focus with another Evangelist. The saying about light in Mark 4:21/Luke 8:16 is similar to Matt 5:15, but in Matthew the light that cannot be hidden concerns discipleship and the evidence of good works, whereas in Mark and Luke the parables are the light that brings revelation. Luke repeats a form of this saying in 11:33 in connection with a warning against hypocrisy. The saying about measuring in Mark 4:24 is parallel to Matt 7:2/Luke 6:38, but in Matthew and Luke it has to do with judging others, whereas in Mark it has to do with how one judges and thus receives the message of the kingdom. Mark's statement in 4:25 ("the one who has receives more and the one who does not have will have taken from him even what he has") appears in Matt 13:12 (before rather than after the interpretation of the parable of the Sower) but also in Matt 25:29 at the conclusion of the parable of the Talents.

All three Synoptists indicate that Jesus taught the crowds and then gave further instruction in private to his disciples, often in response to their questions (Mark 7:17-23; 9:28; 10:10; 13:3-36; Matt 13:36; 15:12; 17:10; 17:19; 19:23; Luke 10:23; 11:1; 17:22). In Mark this private teaching usually takes place in a house. General teaching to the crowds and additional private teaching to those who respond were, no doubt, a pattern in Jesus' ministry.

Isa 6:9b-10 is not quoted but summarized and is changed in the process. The Hebrew has second person imperatives "hear" and "see" and second person *qal* imperfects for "comprehend" and "understand" in v. 9. The LXX changed "hear" and "see" to second person future indicatives and used the subjunctive with an emphatic double negative for "comprehend" and "understand." In doing so it softened the hardening focus and shifted the responsibility from God to Israel. All three Evangelists summarize Isaiah's words in a non-LXX form. They reverse the order so that "seeing" comes first, use participles for "hear" and "see," and use a single negative. Matthew introduces the saying with *hoti*, uses third person plural indicatives (*hoti blepontes ou blepousin . . .* "because seeing they will not see . . ."), a fulfillment formula, and then gives the full LXX text of Isa 6:9b-10.[15] Mark introduces the saying with *hina*, has additional verbs from Isaiah, uses third person plural subjunctives (*hina blepontes blepōsin kai mē idōsin . . .* "in order that seeing they may see and not see . . ."), and includes from Isa 6:10 *mēpote epistrepsōsin kai aphethē autois* ("lest they turn and it be forgiven them"). The use of "forgive" rather than "heal" parallels the wording of the Targum on Isaiah (as does the use of the second person plurals). Luke, like Mark, has *hina* and third person plural subjunctives, but like Matthew omits the additional verbs and Isa 6:10b. Matthew and Luke may be seen as less harsh than Mark's hardening motif, but not by much.

Mark, unlike Matthew and Luke, preserves at the beginning of the parable (4:3) both the words "hear" and "see" (*akouete* and *idou*), which appear in the quotation of Isa 6:9-10 in 4:12.

Jer 5:21 and Ezek 12:2 adopted the words of Isa 6:9-10 to express hardness of heart and judgment, and Isaiah's words play an important role elsewhere in the NT. Isa 6:10 is alluded to in John 9:39 and quoted at John 12:40 to describe Jesus' ministry and the hardness of heart of those who do not respond to his preaching. Isa 6:9-10 is also quoted at Acts 28:26-27 to describe the hardness of heart of those who rejected Paul's message.

Mark has the hardening of heart theme in 3:5; 6:52; and 8:17-21. Mark 8:18 uses language of having eyes and not seeing and ears and not hearing similar to Isa 6:9, but actually the wording derives from either Jer 5:21 or Ezek 12:2, both of whom borrowed the language from Isaiah. This time, however, the hardness of heart language is used not of "outsiders" but of Jesus' disciples.

Matthew also has several passages demonstrating resistance to the message of Jesus: 11:16-19 (uncooperative children in the marketplace); 11:20-23 (woes on unrepentant cities); 12:1-8 (picking grain on the Sabbath: "If you knew . . . you would not have condemned the innocent"); 12:9-14 (the desire to accuse and then destroy Jesus over healing on the Sabbath); 12:22-32 (the Beelzebul controversy); 12:38-42 (the only sign granted is the sign of Jonah, and the Ninevites who repented at preaching will judge this generation). Matthew, unlike Mark and Luke, brackets his parables discourse with scenes concerning Jesus' family: 12:46-50 indicates that his true family are those who do the will of the Father, and 13:53-58 shows that Jesus — like all prophets — is rejected by his own.

The importance of the parable of the Sower is especially evident in Mark. Mark has only two parable sections, the three parables in ch. 4 and the parable of the Wicked Tenants in ch. 12. The centrality of the Sower is obvious from 4:13. M. Tolbert argues the parables in ch. 4 open the first main division of the Gospel and that the parable of the Tenants opens the second main division. For her these two parables summarize the Gospel's view of Jesus as the sower of the word and the heir of the vineyard. The two parables thus make up this Gospel's basic narrative christology and summarize Mark's primary message.[16]

The themes of the parable are mirrored in the Gospel narratives.[17] Those scandalized by the word during persecution (Matt 13:21/Mark 4:17/Luke 8:13) are reflected in Matt 11:6/Luke 7:23; Mark 6:3; Matt 15:12; 24:10; and Matt 26:31/Mark 14:27. Those deceived by the cares of the age, wealth, and other desires (Matt 13:22/Mark 4:18-19/Luke 8:14) are reflected in Matt 6:19-34/Luke 12:22-34; the accounts of the rich young ruler (Matt 19:16-22/Mark 10:17-22/Luke 18:18-23); and the parable of the Banquet (Luke 14:15-24).

Matt 7:24-27/Luke 6:46-49 (the parable of the Two Builders) has the same focus on the importance of hearing that is not mere hearing but hearing that leads to action. Cf. the parable of the Two Sons (Matt 21:28-32).

Cultural Information

Images of seeds, sowing, failure of crops, and fruitful harvest are among the most common metaphors to describe life with its hardship and its prosperity, instruction, and the judgment and blessing of God. This has probably always been the case, but it is certainly true for the OT, the NT, and the Greco-Roman world.[18]

Whether the parable implies that sowing preceded or followed plowing is discussed below, pp. 166-67.

The size of the yield has caused debate. Is one hundredfold an exaggerated harvest signifying an eschatological harvest or merely a good harvest?[19] The evidence is somewhat confusing, especially because some think reference is to the yield of individual seeds[20] while others assume reference is to the yield of the whole field.[21] Estimates of normal yields in the ancient world range from 3.75-fold to 7.5-fold, if referring to the yield of fields,[22] and from 7.5 to 33-fold, if referring to individual seeds, with yields as high as 150-fold being reported.[23] While some uncertainty exists, two factors indicate that a bountiful harvest, not an eschatological one, is in mind. First, in Gen 26:12 we are told that Isaac's field yielded 100-fold, a bountiful harvest showing God's blessing. A miraculous yield is not intended. Second, in other texts where reference is to harvests in the eschaton the numbers are clearly phenomenal — 1000-fold, or even 1,500,000-fold.[24] It seems best to conclude that we are dealing with the bountiful yield of individual seeds, a prosperous harvest, not an exaggerated one.

Even in Galilee Palestine is blessed with an abundance of rocks. In places the soil may look fine but merely provides a shallow covering for rock underneath. The temperature of the soil is warm, which leads to seeds sprouting quickly but dying because of inadequate roots.

Explanation of the Parable

Options for Interpretation[25]

To some degree interpretation of the parable is determined by whether one focuses on the sower, the soil, the seed, or the harvest. So many nuances have been suggested that sorting them out is akin to sorting hay in a haystack. The most significant options are:[26]

1. The parable points to the miracle that, despite hopelessness and failure, God's eschatological overflowing of divine fullness brings the triumphant end he has promised.[27] Focus with this view is on the contrast between

failure and success and on grace and overcoming hopelessness. This eschatological approach assumes the yield of the seed is unrealistic and usually involves the rejection of the canonical interpretation and of any relevance of the Isaiah quotation. Other options often reject the interpretation and the relevance of the Isaiah quotation as well.

2. The parable gives the disciples encouragement despite failures.[28]
3. The parable explains why Israel has rejected the Messiah.[29]
4. The parable reflects the experience of Jesus in his own proclamation.[30]
5. The parable emphasizes the effectiveness of the proclaimed word and the certainty of a good result, despite the lack of success with some.[31]
6. The seed is understood as representing the remnant of Israel. The exile is over since God is sowing the true Israel in her own land. Implicit is a focus on Jesus' role in proclaiming the good news of the kingdom.[32]
7. The parable and the interpretation are a midrash on Isa 6:9-10. On this approach the parable was framed with Isaiah 6 in mind, and the parable, the interpretation, and the quotation are unified.[33]
8. The parable focuses on the responsibility of hearing, understanding, and responding to Jesus' message.[34]

These options are not mutually exclusive, but the first three, and especially the first, have little in their favor as expressing the purpose of the parable. Clearly the story gives prominence to the failures by the amount of space but by the end gives stress to the successful sowing. Any explanation of this passage must do justice to both failure and success and the way these relate to Jesus' ministry, but the keys to right understanding are in options six, seven, and eight. This parable, as we will see, is about God sowing his people in the land in fulfillment of his promises, which is directly tied to Isaiah 6 and its message about how people hear and respond to God's message.

Decisions on the Issues

Since this parable and its context in each Gospel are so involved and since Mark's account is the most difficult and the most revealing, it will be easier to deal with Mark's Gospel first and then treat Matthew and Luke separately.

1. What is the significance of the structure of Mark 4, of Matt 13, and of Luke 8? The structure of Mark 4 is absolutely crucial to understanding the parable and its intent. The structures in Matthew and Luke are similar to Mark's at points but are not as precise. Their structures will be dealt with in the section on redactional shaping. While several interpreters have suggested a five-part chiasmus for Mark 4:1-34,[35] a seven-part chiasmus is more accurate:[36]

The Parable of the Sower and the Purpose of Parables

A   4:1-2 Narrative Introduction
B   4:3-9 A Seed Parable (the Sower)
C   4:10-12 General Statement on the Purpose of Parables
D   4:13-20 Interpretation of the Sower
C′   4:21-25 General Statements Applied to Parables
B′   4:26-32 Two Seed Parables
A′   4:33-34 Narrative Conclusion on the Use of Parables

Clearly this chapter is artfully arranged and has not been put together in a disorganized fashion. Mark abandons his narrative sequence at 4:9 (where Jesus was teaching in a boat, vv. 1-2)[37] and does not begin it again until 4:35 (where Jesus is back in the boat and leaving the crowd). In between Mark inserts redactionally a discussion of parables (4:10-34) while Jesus is alone with his disciples, at least for 4:13-25.[38] The interpretation of the Sower is the center of the chiasmus and the primary focus. The parallel elements of the chiasmus are not identical but do shed light on each other. Clearly 4:21-25 is not — as it appears at first sight — a collection of unrelated sayings but is central to understanding Mark's thought. These verses are parallel to and provide commentary on 4:10-12 and underscore the themes of the Sower. Nothing is hidden except that it should be made clear; that is, nothing is placed in parables except in order to reveal. *The parables hide in order to reveal.* Vv. 23-24 challenge people to hear and warn them to be careful how they hear, just as the parable does. Vv. 24-25 provide insight regarding 4:12, as we will see.

Further, Mark uses the technique of *intercalation;* that is, he *brackets* a section before and after with material that provides help in understanding.[39] Three brackets are evident in this passage: 3:31-35 (the pericope about Jesus' true family) and 4:10-12 bracket the parable with their focus on those *outside;* 4:1-9 and 13-20 bracket 4:10-12 with emphasis on hearing; and 4:10-12 and 21-25 bracket the interpretation to underscore hearing and response. Both 3:31-35 and 4:10-12 are concerned with those who are outside, and those outside are clearly *not* the crowds who have responded and gathered around Jesus ready to do God's will (3:34-35). Those around Jesus ready to do the Father's will mirror the good soil in the parable of the Sower. Those outside are Jesus' mother and brothers in 3:31-35, who are symbolic for those who should have responded and did not (cf. 6:1-6). Surely a broader "outside" group is in view in 4:11, but, whoever else is included, they are those who should have responded and did not.

2. How are the difficult words of 4:10-12 to be understood? The material in 4:10-12 with its adaptation of Isa 6:9-10 has created enormous debate but is the key to understanding this parable. It would be easier to ignore these verses. The language is difficult and harsh and appears to say that Jesus tells parables to

157

keep people from understanding so that they will not repent and be forgiven — the exact opposite of everything we think we know both about Jesus and parables. Not surprisingly, these verses are omitted in the standard lectionary for preaching, and among scholars their authenticity as sayings of Jesus is frequently denied. The verses are assigned to Mark or his tradition and viewed as an attempt to explain why the Jews did not believe. The Evangelists are blamed for any idea that the parables conceal since it is presumed that Jesus' purpose with parables was only to be clear and convincing.[40] Dan Via goes so far as to conclude that Mark thinks parables are useless,[41] which is hard to imagine.

Various explanations seek to soften the language or present it in a more palatable way. Jeremias and others argue that vv. 11-12 were spoken by Jesus, but not in this context nor specifically about parables. Instead, these verses deal with Jesus' preaching generally and teach that the presence of the kingdom has been revealed to the disciples, but to outsiders remains obscure[42] because they do not recognize his mission and repent. *Hina* in v. 12 is understood, not as "in order that," but as if it were *hina plērōthē*, "in order that [the Scripture] might be fulfilled." The difficulty of *mēpote* ("lest"; NRSV: "so that . . . not . . ."; NIV: "otherwise") is removed by noting the similarity of Mark 4:12 to the Targum rendering of Isa 6:10,[43] which has Aramaic *dilma'* ("unless"), and arguing that Mark meant "unless" as well, so that the passage is really a promise of forgiveness.[44] This solution is almost ingenious, but we are left with the impression that we have "fixed" the text. Further, if Jesus could have held such ideas about revelation to his disciples while others were left in the dark for his *teaching* on the kingdom, why could he not have also had such ideas about his teaching in parables?

T. W. Manson thought that Mark 4:12 is simply absurd and argued that Mark misunderstood an ambiguous Aramaic *de* as *hina* when it should have been understood as *hoi,* the relative pronoun "who." The passage only describes the hardness people already have, not the purpose of Jesus in telling parables.[45] Others point to Matthew's use of *hoti* ("because"), not *hina,* in 13:13 and to the fact that *hina* can mean "because" (e.g., Rev 14:13; 22:14).[46] Still others argue for the meaning "so that" which is also a legitimate meaning of *hina* (e.g., John 9:2; Gal 5:17).[47] T. Weeden even concluded that these verses (along with most of ch. 4) belonged to Mark's opponents,[48] a position that is difficult to fathom.

This is a formidable, even harsh, text, but does it seem absurd only because we read it in a crassly literal way[49] and pay insufficient attention to its background? Jesus did *not* tell parables to prevent understanding, although parables are not pious little stories and some are enigmatic. Nor does Mark have a theory that parables are not understandable and obfuscate. Mark has relatively little extended teaching from Jesus, but one of his two major blocks of teaching is the *parables* in ch. four. Further, Mark has only four narrative parables — not much on which to base a theory, and one of them is understood quite well by Jesus' opponents (12:1-12). Besides, as has been pointed out since Chrysostom at least,[50] if Jesus wanted to prevent understanding, it would have been easier just to remain silent. The same is true for Mark.

Jesus did not haphazardly choose parables as the medium of communication. *Parables are prophetic instruments,* the language of the OT prophets, which occur especially in contexts of judgment and indictment.[51] Later they become apocalyptic instruments and still later with the rabbis exegetical tools, but with Jesus they are primarily a prophetic mode of communication. Parables enlighten and instruct, but often with a message that people do not want to hear. Jesus consciously presented himself as a prophet, a point N. T. Wright has correctly emphasized,[52] and Jesus' use of parables is a fitting and effective means of presenting his prophetic message. Matt 13:34-35 points precisely to this idea by quoting Ps 78:2 to show that Jesus' teaching in parables fulfills the word of the *prophet:* "I will open my mouth in parables; I will proclaim things hidden from the beginning."[53] Certainly Jesus saw himself as more than a prophet,[54] but the initial model for understanding him is that of a prophet. Like the OT prophets he announced both the judgment and deliverance of God. He presented himself through the language of the prophets (e.g., Luke 4:18-19; Mark 11:17) and in explicit comparison to them (e.g., Luke 4:25-27), and he performed symbolic acts like them (both miracles and actions like the triumphal entry). Unlike the prophets his message was that the long awaited kingdom was already at work, and with his proclamation of the kingdom he called for repentance and the reconstitution of the nation under his own leadership. Understanding of Mark 4:10-12 starts with a recognition of Jesus' role as a prophet.

Nor was Isa 6:9-10 chosen haphazardly. If we think Mark 4:10-12 is difficult, the problem in Isa 6:9-13 is even worse. If Mark wanted to emphasize that Jesus taught to prevent understanding, he could have used the even harsher words from Isaiah 6 that he omitted: "Make the mind of this people dull, and stop their ears, and shut their eyes, so that they may not look . . . and listen . . . and comprehend . . . and turn and be healed." These words do not merely reflect the results of Isaiah's preaching viewed from the end of his life.[55] They are at least, as C. F. D. Moule argued, a vigorous way of stating the inevitable — that Israel will not listen and repent — and a hyperbolic description of the conditions of the ministry of Isaiah.[56] But even more, they express a common theme of the prophets: Israel is too far gone and judgment is already decreed. The nation has refused the appeals of Yahweh, and Isaiah's call presupposes that the hardening has already occurred and judgment is coming — points made repeatedly in Isaiah 1–5.[57] Such harsh words about the rebelliousness of Israel and the certainty of judgment are regular features of prophetic material.[58] The intent is not that Isaiah actually should do what these verses say, and he does not. The lack of hearing and seeing has already been accomplished. Still, even though the nation is too far gone, Isaiah urges people to stop being rebellious and to return to God.[59]

Whether we call Isa 6:9-10 irony,[60] an attempt to shock into repentance, or reverse psychology,[61] these words are not literalistic. Their illocutionary effect is *to urge hearing in a context where judgment is assured* and where there are promises that a remnant will return and blessing will come from Yahweh.[62] The ideal reader wants to be part of that remnant. Further, reversing the images of Isa 6:9, the promise for the future is that the deaf will hear and the blind will see (Isa 29:18; 35:5). The use of the words of Isa 6:9-10 by later writers shows that this passage became *the* classic depiction of the refusal to hear.[63]

Despite the message of judgment and the expectation that the people will not respond, still the word of God is to be proclaimed. Even the harsh message of Isaiah seeks hearers and gains disciples (8:16-18). The function of this language is both a warning of what is happening — that judgment is inevitable, that the people have not responded and will not — and also a challenge and an invitation for people not to remain in such insensitivity but to hear the word and repent.[64]

Four things are obvious: (1) the harsh language of Isa 6:9-10 is a prophetic instrument for warning and challenge; (2) it expresses the certainty of God's coming judgment for a people who are past hearing; (3) the words of Isa 6:9 became the classic expression to speak of the people's hardness of heart; and (4) the proclamation still expects and seeks some to hear and follow.

Since Jesus identified himself as a prophet and since Isa 6:9-10 is a classic expression of what happens with prophets, the quotation becomes understandable. Drawing a parallel between himself and Isaiah, Jesus took these words about hardness of heart to describe his own ministry, just as Jeremiah and Ezekiel had done. Jesus drew an intended parallel between his ministry and the book of Isaiah[65] so that there is a correspondence in history between the prophet Isaiah and the prophet Jesus.[66]

Still more, Isa 6:9-10 has greater significance for this whole context than is often realized. The parallel of Mark 4:10-12 with both 3:31-35 and 4:21-25 signaled by bracketing and the strategic location of these verses between the parable of the Sower and its interpretation shows that the quotation of Isa 6:9-10 has been the *starting point and reference point* for the organization of this section of Mark.[67] Mark ties the parable to the quotation of Isa 6:9-10 more strongly than the other Evangelists, even though his connection is lost in translations. Mark starts the parable with "hear, see" *(akouete, idou),* both of which occur in v. 12 in the quotation of Isaiah. Even so, the quotation from Isa 6:9-10 is not merely a Markan instrument, a disruption between parable and interpretation, possibly referring to Jesus' teaching in general. Every indication is that *the parable of the Sower is based on the ideas in Isa 6:9-13*. It is odd that so many ignore the fact that Isaiah 6 deals with hearing and explicitly refers to the remnant with the image of the "holy seed" (Isa 6:13c),[68] a reference the Targum interprets as the return of the exiles.[69] This set of relations is hardly a coincidence.

John Bowker argued that the parable of the Sower and its interpretation should be understood as an exposition of Isa 6.[70] Similarly, N. T. Wright argued that the parable of the Sower depicts Yahweh again sowing true Israel, the remnant, in her own land, and in the process the parable *acts* by creating the situation where having ears to hear is one of the marks of the true remnant. For Wright the parable is a story of the return from exile taking place in Jesus' own work.[71] While Wright at times reads too much into the parables,[72] his instincts on the Sower are correct. By adapting Isaiah 6 the parable points to the fact that God's seed is being sown in the proclamation of the kingdom. Involvement in the kingdom depends on the reception the proclaimed seed receives in human ears and hearts. Some people close off hearing just as in Isaiah's day and place themselves outside what God is doing. Such an approach does not presuppose that Mark 4:3-20 was originally a unit;[73] it presupposes only that Isaiah 6 is the origin of the thinking that led to the creation of the parable.

One further point is crucial: as E. Lemcio and others have noticed, the sequence of parable (or revelation), statement of difficulty in understanding or request for explanation, then interpretation follows an apocalyptic/revelation pattern.[74] Although many parables do not fit this apocalyptic/revelational scheme, this is precisely the pattern in Mark 4:3-20. This pattern also includes the idea that the truth in the parable will remain unseen for some, with 2 *Bar.* 51:1-6 even contrasting the righteous who have *planted* the root of wisdom in their hearts with the guilty who despised the Law and *stopped their ears* lest they hear wisdom and receive intelligence.[75] This last text offers a parallel for understanding *mēpote* ("lest") in Mark 4:12/Matt 13:15. It is not God who seeks to thwart turning and forgiveness but the people.[76]

The words of Isa 6:9-10 are to be understood not literally but forcefully. They express by hyperbole what has already happened due to hardness of heart and unwillingness to hear. They function as irony, as provocation *to bring about hearing and obedience*.[77] Jesus' use of the quotation and his parable formed on it both have the same function.

With this framework several of the questions from Mark 4:10-12 may be reconsidered. The attempt to lessen the impact of *hina* is unnecessary. It may be an abbreviation for *hina plērōthē* ("in order that it might be fulfilled"), but if so, the intent is to say that what happened with Isaiah is happening again with Jesus. To say that *hina* indicates cause or result is not so much wrong as inappropriate because the shock of the wording is lost. Jesus draws a parallel here with the recalcitrance of Israel in Isaiah's time to warn and to stimulate hearing in a context of judgment. His message of the kingdom *is* partly a message of judgment. Mark's redaction shows that he also seeks to stimulate hearing. Nor is there any necessity to interpret *mēpote* as if it meant "perhaps" and held out hope. There is hope, but only if the shock of the Isaiah quotation has its illocutionary effect to cause hearing.

A number of questions still remain. Who are those outside? Only Mark uses this description at this point. Most interpreters jump to the conclusion that "those outside" are the crowds while the disciples are the ones inside. This seems to fit 4:34 at first glance, but it does not fit well with Mark's Gospel overall. The crowds around Jesus hear him gladly; the opposition to Jesus comes from the religious leadership and his own family (note esp. 3:21-32 and 7:6-7).[78] That the distinction is not between the disciples narrowly conceived and the crowds is evident in Mark's expression "those around him with the twelve" (4:10).[79] A larger group of followers is in view. "Those around him" is precisely the expression used in 3:34 of the obedient. This rules out an anti-Semitic interpretation that would see Jews as outsiders and Christians as insiders.[80] The expression "those outside" does not refer to the crowds in general — some predetermined group — but to people like Jesus' family and the religious leaders who are not ready to hear and do the will of the Father.[81] It is the stance of willingness to hear and obey that determines whether one is outside or inside.[82]

Does Mark see parables as obscurities that keep some people outside? This is the way "parables" in 4:11 is usually understood, but this is odd and goes against all we know about the function of parables to demonstrate and enlighten. It also creates difficulty with 4:33 where clearly parables are meant to enable hearing ("even as they were able to hear"). At 3:23 Jesus *with parables* "summons," "invites" *(proskalesamenos)* his opponents to change their thinking. J. Bowker suggests taking *en parabolais* ("in parables") in 4:11 "*not* in the sense 'enigmatically,' but 'in clearest possible illustration,'" in order to leave "no possible illusion about those who have failed to receive or come inside the kingdom of God." They make clear the nature and character of those who hear.[83] Parables do that; they confront, engage, force thought, and promote action, but it is too narrow to understand *en parabolais*[84] as "in clearest possible illustration." Parables by their very metaphoricity have a veiling quality, some more than others, and especially in a context of opposition they say indirectly what cannot be said openly. They can be mysterious, but if so, it is to stimulate thought.[85] They both hide and reveal, and to say "to those outside all things happen in parables" is to say what 4:33 and 3:23 imply: Jesus taught in parables, like any good prophet, to appeal and to enable hearing. Where parables find a willing response, further explanation is given. Where there is no response the message is lost.

Mark is not the only one who says Jesus' message is hidden from some and revealed to others or that some people refuse to hear or hear with difficulty. Revelation from God is not merely thrown out and grasped on the run. In Matt 11:25-26/Luke 10:21-22 Jesus thanks the Father for hiding "these things from the wise and understanding and revealing them to infants" (cf. 1 Cor 2:6-16). In Luke 19:41-42 Jesus weeps over Jerusalem because the things of peace have been hid from her eyes. In John 6:60 in response to difficult teaching from Jesus some of his disciples ask, "Who is able to hear him?" In John 8:43 Jesus asks why the people do not understand what he says and answers, "because you are not able to hear my word," which in the context clearly means that they are not willing to hear. In John 12:39-40 at the close of Jesus' public ministry Isa 53:1 and 6:10 are quoted to explain the unbelief of the Jews, and just prior to the quotation of Isa 6:10 the Evangelist notes: "Because of this, they were not able to believe." The language of being able to hear or believe is reminiscent of Mark 4:33: "With many such parables he was speaking the word to them even as they were able to hear." Finally, Luke quotes Isa 6:9-10 at the end of Acts to explain the failure of the Jews in Rome to believe Paul's preaching.

Neither these passages nor Mark is about "divine hardening" and certainly not about ideas of predestination. The focus is on *human responsibility* and willingness to hear and on not repeating the pattern of Israel's refusal to hear the messengers of God (cf. 12:1-12).[86] People place themselves inside or outside by the way they respond to the message, and their position is *not* then permanently determined. The same language of hardness of heart and of having eyes and not seeing and having ears and not hearing is used of *the Twelve* in 8:17-18 (cf. 6:52 and also 3:5). The issue is whether people — disciples or otherwise — respond to the message or are guilty of a hardness of heart that prevents understanding. In fact, given the rest of Mark's Gospel, the interpretation of the parable of the Sower seems to be *a warning to the disciples as much as it is a description of Jesus' ministry generally.*

Parables are not always obvious and self-explanatory, but even when enigmatic, their purpose is to enlighten. The very uncertainty of their reference is part of their appeal and often the means of their effectiveness, but they are not meant to obfuscate. That is not what Mark means with *mystērion* (NRSV: "secret") in 4:11. "Mystery" in the Semitic world does not refer to what is mysterious and unknown, but to revelation, to what would be unknown if God had not revealed it.[87] To say "the mystery of the kingdom of God has been given to you" is to say that *revelation* from God about the kingdom has been given to you.[88] (Cf. Matt 13:16-17/Luke 10:23-24.[89]) The concept of God's mystery inherently has to do with people's reception of the message. M. Boucher comments, "The mystery has to do entirely with one's willingness to receive the eschatological and ethical teaching of Jesus."[90] Jesus' parables reveal the kingdom of God and give handles for grasping it. The content of the revelation focuses on the present working of the kingdom in the ministry of Jesus,[91] but it also includes — as other parables and texts attest — the hidden character of the kingdom and that one finds life by losing it.

More remains to be said about the meaning of the parable and this whole section, but it should be clear that the quotation of Isa 6:9-10 is the key to understanding and is indeed the origin of the parable.

3. Does the interpretation belong originally with the parable or is it a result of early church allegorizing? Since Jülicher's work a good deal of NT scholarship has rejected the interpretation as early church allegorizing. Several assumptions led to this conclusion: the disdain for allegory, an assumption that parables do not need explanations, the fact that *Gos. Thom.* does not have the interpretation, the inconsistency of the seed being both the word and people (Mark 4:14 and 15-20), a lack of Semitisms in the interpretation, and a conviction that the vocabulary of the interpretation was the vocabulary of the early church. Many have just assumed that Jeremias demonstrated beyond question that the language in the interpretation — unlike the wording of the parable — is that of the early church. Today, however, a significant change has clearly taken place. Many now argue that the canonical interpretation is authentic or at least possibly authentic. Included in this number are the four most significant recent commentaries on Matthew and several on other Gospels.[92] U. Luz's comments are striking: "Along with others I assume that the fourfold parable of the seed was meant exactly as it was interpreted in Mark 4:13-20. From the beginning it was a 'parable about parables,' or *a meditation about the various hearers of Jesus' proclamation.* The interpretation fits the original character of the fourfold parable exactly."[93]

This change results from several developments. Although it has taken time and effort, Jülicher's theories about parable and allegory have been discredited.[94] Parables — whether OT, Jewish, or Greek — quite regularly have explanations. Parable forms are quite varied, and not all parables have detailed interpretations, but many do. Allegory is not seen as a separate genre by some, but in any case, is no longer rejected as a valid form.[95] *Gos. Thom.* is increasingly seen as coming from the second century and dependent in some way on the canonical Gospels and has little claim to possess an earlier version of this parable.[96] The tension of the seed being both word and people is viewed as natural,[97] and Jeremias's seemingly impressive list of linguistic proofs is shown on closer examination to be a house of cards. Also contributing to this change is the recognition of the role of Isaiah 6 and the apocalyptic/revelation pattern mentioned above, which show how Mark 4:3-20 functions as a unit.

Some exaggerate the eschatological harvest in the parable and contrast it with the parenetic concerns of the interpretation,[98] but whatever else is said, the interpretation fits the parable. To what degree the parable is eschatological is debated, but any interpretation that focuses only on the successful seed neglects the bulk of the narrative. Even Jülicher granted that the parable is structured for the interpretation, going so far as to allow that both might go back to Jesus but finally concluding the parable was augmented when the interpretation was added.[99] Several grant that the parable is not understandable without the interpretation, even when they reject the latter,[100] and others concede that the interpretation is close to the parable's intent.[101]

While some parables are left unexplained, we have seen that in the OT, Judaism, and the Greco-Roman world explanations or interpretations are usually explicit, even if only providing a short statement, a *nimshal,* to make the point of the parable clear.[102] Anyone who doubts this just has not read the material or is guilty of a blind refusal to admit what is obvious: correspondences are at the very heart of analogical argument.[103] Identifications of the referents of a parable are sometimes implicit because the analogy is obvious. Extended allegorical identifications as with the Sower are less frequent, especially in the NT, but are still very much at home in ancient parables, as a glance at the primary source sections of this book show.[104] Sometimes identifications specifically use expressions such as "this is" or "these are." If dreams and visions in the OT have point-for-point correspondences, if *1 En.* 89.10–90.39 can have an elaborate "zoomorphic" history of the world, if 1QpHab 12.2-10 can interpret Hab 2:17 allegorically,[105] if early and late Jewish sayings and parables and early Christian "allegories" can have point-for-point explanations,[106] on what grounds do we say that Jesus' parables did not do the same? In fact, what we have with this parable is not one parable but four similitudes, and if any one of the seed-soil pictures was presented and explained by itself, no one would have raised an eyebrow. We have four parabolic pictures spliced together in order to contrast two kinds of hearing, unsuccessful and successful.[107] The Sower, like many parables, needed an explanation, and the interpretation provided is not suspicious merely for being an interpretation or for having "allegorical" features. At the same time we should note that two of the features most relevant to the life of the church are not explained in the interpretation: the identity of the sower and the meaning of the fruit.[108] This hardly fits an origin in the church. Nor does Matthew or Luke give any explanation of the variations in yield.[109]

The other basis most used to reject the interpretation has been Jeremias's linguistic argument that the interpretation is the language of the early church, but this is another case where a litany of detail is an illusion, which some adopt without analysis. Jeremias took particular offense at the absolute *ho logos* ("the word") used as a technical expression for the gospel, which Jeremias claims occurs in Jesus' sayings only in the interpretation of this parable, but it is Jeremias — not Mark — who interprets *ho logos* this way. In fact, the Evangelists do not think *ho logos* is a technical term at all.[110] Further, is it fair to make so much of the absolute *ho logos?* Is it so different from expressions such as "my words," "these words," or "the word of God"?[111] *Logos* and *ho logos* (or the Hebrew and Aramaic *dabar*) are typical ways to refer to a message, speech, or teaching, especially a prophetic message.[112] What other word should Mark have used to refer to Jesus' teaching? Redactional shaping has obviously occurred, but *ho logos* does not demonstrate that the interpretation is an early church formulation.

Many of the words that Jeremias lists occur rarely in the NT, as his own footnotes attest, and can hardly be called *common* early church language.[113] For example, he points to parallels with "received the word with joy," but this expression occurs only in 1 Thess 1:6, which for "receive" uses *dechesthai* (as in Luke), not *lambanein,* as in Matthew and Mark.[114] *Speirein* ("sow") with the meaning "preach" occurs only at 1 Cor 9:11. Jeremias finds parallels to *riza* ("root") as a metaphor for inward stability only at Eph 3:17 and Col 2:7, even though both epistle texts have a participle. But this metaphor is common in the OT and elsewhere, and its origin cannot be assigned to the early church.[115] *Proskairos* ("temporary") occurs elsewhere in the NT only at 2 Cor 4:18 and Heb 11:25, neither in connection with reception of the word. Other examples could be given, but this should suffice to show that Jeremias's list proves nothing. His complaint that the eschatology of the parable has been changed to exhortation by the church overlooks the fact that this metaphorical field was used for parenetic purposes for centuries. The language of the interpretation fits the subject matter and the context of Jesus' ministry as easily as it fits the context of the early church's preaching.[116]

The sayings of Jesus were shaped both in the oral tradition and by the Evangelists, but the interpretation fits the parable and has every claim to be in some form the explanation Jesus gave his disciples.

4. Would anyone sow seed this way? Does the sower sow carelessly and with abandon, possibly mirroring an indiscriminate proclamation of the message, or is his sowing realistic practice in the ancient world? More ink has been spilled on this question than it deserves, but some attention must be given here because the sower's actions seem odd, at least from modern farming practices. J. Jeremias argued that the parable tells of a normal sowing procedure which presumes that sowing precedes plowing[117] and that no seed is wasted or thrown carelessly. K. D. White offered evidence that plowing preceded sowing.[118] Jeremias responded with a more nuanced discussion saying that sowing is most often done prior to plowing, except for the late sowing, in which case occasionally plowing is done both before and after the sowing. Jeremias stuck with his assertion that in any case after sowing the seed is plowed into the ground.[119]

The evidence shows that plowing occurred both before and immediately after sowing.[120] Plowing before sowing was recommended but not always done. Regardless of what preparations were made before sowing, plowing would have followed sowing immediately in order to bury the seed.[121] We do not know whether plowing preceded in this case or not, and the parable does not care. Parables do not give unnecessary details. Nor is the point that the sower sows haphazardly or with abandon, even on the road where seed will not grow,[122] and no theological conclusions should be drawn along these lines. The point is that the sower sowed and his seed had various results. The farmer does not intentionally sow seed on the road; rather some seed falls *alongside* the road.[123] That some seed is sown among the thorns could mean the seed is sown among dried thorns from the preceding year that will be plowed under, or it could be merely a brief way to express that seed is sown in a plowed field where thorns will later grow.[124] No attempt is made to explain why birds ate only the seed by the road and not that sown in the field, but if, as the evidence indicates, the person plowing follows right behind the sower, the seed in the field would have been covered before the birds could get to it.[125] In the end, however, these questions are not important for understanding the parable.[126]

Nor should we conclude, as some commentators do, that three-fourths of the seed was lost. There is a balance between three circumstances of loss and three levels of success, and considerable emphasis is placed on the danger of loss, but the amount of seed in each case is not specified. Mark uses the singular *ho* and *auto* (the neuter relative pronoun and neuter personal pronoun respectively) to specify the unproductive seed (4:4-6) but uses the plural in 4:8 for the productive seed. Apparently the change to the plural indicates for Mark the larger amount of productive seeds.[127] However, Mark uses the plural throughout the interpretation, Matthew uses the plural in the parable and the singular in the interpretation, and Luke has the singular throughout the parable (including 8:8) and the plural in the interpretation. In none of the accounts, though, is there any indication of a farmer disappointed with his losses.[128] The picture is a realistic portrayal of ancient farming practice where incidental losses occurred, particularly in Palestine with its shallow earth and plentiful thorns, but also where a bountiful harvest resulted.

5. Is the analogy about God sowing people in Israel or about God sowing his word? The real issue here is to what degree the OT background — and which OT background — determines the meaning of the parable. Some suggest that the seed is a fixed metaphor for God's word and that people would not have needed an explanation,[129] but this is not the case. Others argue that the audience would not know the intent of the seed metaphor until it was explained.[130] How much the audience would have been in the dark is unclear, but there certainly was no fixed use of the metaphor. As noted above, sowing seeds was used metaphorically for instruction in both the Greco-Roman and the Jewish worlds.[131] The occurrence of the expression *logos spermatikos* ("generative word/principle") underscores just how common the metaphor was for some. Sowing could be used metaphorically of scattering or distributing (e.g., Zech 10:9) but is used more frequently of depositing for future increase, "investing," whether with regard to children or positive or negative entities. It was used of sowing God's word (or Law), God's secrets, human teaching, goodness, peace, righteousness, and charity,[132] but also of sowing trouble, evil, and deceit.[133] Obviously in some NT parables the seed is a metaphor for the kingdom.

The metaphor of God sowing (or planting) people[134] is used in the OT often to refer to God causing his people to prosper and especially of God restoring Israel after the exile.[135] G. Lohfink emphasizes this background of God sowing people to bring about the restoration of the exiles to argue against a focus in the parable on God sowing his word. Jesus in telling the parable would, then, be picturing the sowing of the end-time community.[136] It must be granted that it is much easier in the OT to demonstrate *God's* sowing is a metaphor for restoration of the exiles than for proclamation of the word. Perhaps the strongest text is Hos 2:21-23 (23-25): ". . . they will respond to Jezreel [Jezreel means 'God sows']. I will plant her for myself . . . ,"[137] but other texts express the same idea. Note the following:

> 2 Kgs 19:30; Isa 37:31: The remnant of Judah will take root downward and bear fruit upward.
> Isa 27:6: Jacob will take root and fill the earth with fruit.
> Isa 43:5: "I will bring your seed from the east."
> Isa 60:21: "Your people will all be righteous; they will possess the land forever. They are the shoot that I planted. . . ."
> Jer 24:5-7: ". . . so I will regard as good the exiles from Judah. . . . I will plant them. . . . I will give them a heart to know that I am the LORD."
> Jer 31:27-28: "The days are coming, says the Lord, when I will sow the house of Israel and the house of Judah with the seed of humans. . . ."
> Cf. Ezek 36:9; Hos 14:5; *1 En.* 62:8; *4 Ezra* 8:41-44; *2 Bar.* 70:2

J. Liebenburg, however, argues that Lohfink does not do justice to the three failures in the parable and insists that the metaphor is "sowing is preaching." Liebenburg grants that little evidence exists in the OT for the image of *God sowing his word*. Most mention only Isa 55:10-11, but this text speaks of God's word being like the rain that gives seed to the sower, not of God sowing his word. The only other relevant text is Isa 5:24 (". . . so their root will become rotten, and their blossom go up like dust; for they have rejected the instruction of the LORD of hosts, and have despised the word of the Holy One of Israel").[138] What clinches for Liebenburg the conclusion that the parable is about the preaching of Jesus are the parable's structure, its conventional metaphors, and the context (especially Mark 4:3 and 9), which emphasizes hearing. Certainly for the Evangelists the image is of Jesus as God's agent sowing God's word.

However, pitting God's eschatological sowing of people and God's sowing his word against each other creates a false antithesis. An eschatological sowing of people presupposes people who listen and respond obediently to God's word or are enabled by God to respond, as is explicit in Jer 24:5-7 and 31:31-34. Isaiah 6 is the *one* text that brings together the concern for hearing the word of God and the idea of the remnant as a holy seed. If we are correct that Isaiah 6 is the frame on which the parable was formed, then there is no need to drive a wedge between God sowing his people and God sowing his word. It is by sowing the word that the end-time people is planted.[139]

6. What is the meaning and significance of this parable and its context? Is the focus on the sower, the seed, the soil, or the harvest? Specifically, what does it tell us about the kingdom? By this point the meaning and significance of this parable should be clear. Despite the title given the parable by Matthew, the focus is not on the sower, who is not identified in any of the interpretations.[140] The seed and the harvest are both important, but are not the focus. Other hazards to growth (such as drought and disease) are not mentioned and the cause of failure is not with the seed. The only variable determining failure or success is the soil on which the seed falls.[141] Further, any valid interpretation must do justice — not merely to the harvest — but to the emphasis given the threefold failure, failure that occurs at increasingly later stages in the growth process. Despite the popularity of an interpretation focused on an eschatological harvest, such an explanation is too narrow and misguided.[142] The emphasis has to be on the receptivity and conditions of the soil. To determine what Jesus' original hearers would have understood is impossible because we do not know what other comments were made or information was given in connection with the parable. If attention was directed to the proclamation of the kingdom,[143] people may have understood the parable as referring to response to the message. Some, because of their familiarity with the image of teaching as seeds being sown, probably picked up on this idea. The challenge for the one with ears to hear would have given a further clue that the focus was the reception of the word, but without reflection many, including the disciples, may not have grasped the intent. Even if people knew the parable was about hearing God's word, they would not have seen how significant the parable was until the connection with Isaiah 6 was made explicit.

The parable is a description of various responses to hearing God's word and surely depicts the responses Jesus encountered in his own ministry.[144] To ask whether it depicts God sowing or Jesus sowing is to make a false distinction. Whether we think of Jesus' words or of the Evangelists' redactions, the assumption is that Jesus is the agent communicating the words of God. The parable warns against superficial hearing, but it also anticipates real and productive hearing. Real hearing is hearing that leads to obedience, and we should not forget that the Hebrew verb for hearing *(šāma')* is often translated in English as "obey."[145]

In response to further inquiry about the parable by those ready to obey, Jesus pointed to the hardness of heart motif and the parallels between his ministry and that of Isaiah. No other interpretation is even attractive. As U. Luz notes, the modern interpretation of this parable as a parable of contrast corresponding with the Reformation's theology of grace and helping people escape hopelessness does not correspond to the parable.[146] The complaint that soil is passive and that only a foolish farmer would exhort his soil[147] is off track and assumes identity between the parable and reality rather than that parables argue by analogy. Not every part of the metaphor is mapped onto the reality.

The Evangelists — especially Mark — have underscored the idea of hearing, receptivity of the message, as the main concern. The parable and its context sound the resonances of traditional language about hardness of heart to serve as a challenge and a warning about how people respond to the message of Jesus by which God is doing his sowing work of restoration.[148] What Mark really intends, which is quite in keeping with Jesus' intent, is clear when one sees how the whole passage works. V. 3, with its call to hear, summons attention. The parable's ending — "Let the one who has ears to hear hear" — urges the hearer to depth listening, to moving beyond the surface of the words to understand what is really being talked about. Vv. 10-12 describe what typically happened — note the imperfects (*ērōtōn,* "they were asking"; *elegen,* "he was saying").[149] When people responded to the message of the parables by joining themselves to Jesus and seeking further understanding, further revelation and explanation about the kingdom were given; to those whose hearing remained at a superficial level no further revelation was given. They were left with parables which did not achieve their goal of enlightening. The lack of receptivity prevented further progress.

The stress on reception of the message is verified by 4:21-25 and Mark's summary statement in 4:33-34. Vv. 21-25 show that God's message is "hidden" in parables in order that it should be made clear.[150] Parables hide in order to reveal[151] — or as Kierkegaard observed, they deceive a person into the truth.[152] It is fair to say that v. 22 expresses the intention of the whole section on parables: nothing is hidden in parables except that it should be brought into the open.

In v. 23 people are urged to move beyond the surface of the words to really hear, and vv. 24-25 warn that people must be careful how they hear, for their hearing will determine their fate. With the measure they measure it will be added to them, and the person who has will be given more, while the person who does not have loses even what he or she has. This on the surface unfair treatment describes exactly what vv. 10-12 describe, the process of hearing. How people respond to the parables determines whether additional revelation is given. Those who respond with real hearing receive added revelation. For those who respond with superficial hearing, even what they have heard is of no effect.[153] The parables were intended to meet people at their level and draw them to a deeper message. Some parables appeal, some enlighten, some challenge, and some are pointed and clinching arguments for a too often slow-minded, inattentive, or recalcitrant audience to move them to action. But they all seek a response and all are revelatory to some degree.

The summary statement in Mark 4:33-34 indicates that Jesus was telling parables *even as people were able to hear*. It is clear from these two verses that *Mark thought parables were meant to enable hearing*, not prevent it, but also that hearing the parables was only stage one on the road to understanding.[154]

For all three Evangelists this is *the* parable for understanding the kingdom,[155] and it makes three significant points. First, the kingdom is a kingdom of the word;[156] it involves a proclamation about God and God's purposes and actions. Language creates a world, and the proclamation of the kingdom makes a new reality available. This is precisely what was happening with Jesus' preaching. The kingdom was being made a reality. Second, the kingdom presents a challenge for perception and reorientation of life. People must hear and respond with a lifestyle that "bears fruit," that is, a lifestyle marked by obedience to God as revealed in the message of Jesus. Third, the kingdom is presently at work and is established *partly* as people respond with believing obedience and inhabit the world created by the proclamation. *By "sowing" such people God is fulfilling the promise to restore Israel.* The real focus is on bearing fruit. The only valid hearing is hearing that produces. Anything else falls under the indictment of Isa 6:9-10.

Parables address both individuals and the nation, and nowhere is this more true than with the parable of the Sower and the other parables in Mark 4. Obviously the Sower addresses the responsibility of the individual to hear. But at least implicitly it warns the nation not to repeat the failure of Israel in Isaiah's time, and it also proclaims that God is at work in the ministry of Jesus to restore Israel. The Sower is a foundational parable which assumes that the kingdom is present and at work, a parable that virtually pleads for responsible and productive hearing.

7. *How has the redactional shaping of each Evangelist impacted the nuance of the parable?* Mark's redactional shaping has already been discussed. The parable functions similarly in Matthew and Luke to emphasize hearing, but less pointedly than in Mark. Matthew's redactional shaping (regardless of the question of originality) is just as strongly pronounced as Mark's, while Luke's redaction accomplishes less. The differences of the three accounts in the wording of the parable, its interpretation, and the intervening material about the purpose of parables are rather insignificant. Luke, as is his custom, has streamlined this material, but the meaning and function remain essentially the same in all three accounts. Matthew and Mark underscore persecution because of the word, likely reflecting early church experience, but the efforts to see specific aspects of the church's life and theology reflected in the differences of wording are guesswork at best.[157]

The accounts in Matthew and Luke are less harsh than Mark 4:10-12. This is evident in Matthew's using *hoti* instead of *hina* and in his omission of Mark 4:12c ("lest they turn and it be forgiven them") in 13:13, although he does include a different form of these words in his quotation of Isa 6:9-10 in 13:15. Luke uses *hina* but does not include Mark 4:12c at all. One could think that the repetition of the divine passive *dedotai* ("given") in Matt 13:11 sharpens the predestination teaching (Mark and Luke have it only once).[158] But this presupposes that the passage says something about predestination, even though it does not ask *why* knowlege of the mysteries of the kingdom has been given to some and not to others. The focus in all three accounts is not predestination[159] but revelation and whether one responds to revelation. This is to take nothing away from the sovereignty of God or God's involvement in enabling people to hear, but *this* whole context and especially the allusion to Isaiah 6 put the focus on human responsibility.[160]

Regarding *Matthew's redaction,* it is not true that Matthew views parables as a means of punishment rather than a means of teaching, a conclusion some draw partly because Matthew does not use *didaskein* ("teach"), which Mark has twice in 4:1-2.[161] For Matthew Israel's rejection of Jesus is an established fact, not something caused by the parables.[162] Nor are the parables merely a condemnation of hardness of heart; they seek to move people to hearing. The force of the negative statements in 13:10-15 is somewhat surprising, a result no doubt of Matthew's thematic arrangement, but it is not true that in the narrative to this point the multitudes are only viewed positively. Several passages indicate some people lived in illusion or that "this generation" was unwilling to receive Jesus' message (8:12, 21-22; 10:34-39; 11:16-24; 12:38-42). The parable chapter reflects this unwillingness to hear but also seeks to persuade people to hear by both positive statements about the value of the kingdom and negative statements about judgment.

Matthew's arrangement of this material emphasizes not merely hearing but understanding. Five times he uses the verb *syniēnai* ("understand") in connection with the parable (13:13, 14, 15, 19, 23), and then at the end of the parables discourse Jesus asks his disciples if they understand these things (13:51). Real hearing for Matthew means understanding in a way that transforms one's identity and is evident in obedience.

Where Matthew's theological influence is most at work is in the structure of his parables discourse (13:1-52). The contents of the discourse include much more than Mark and Luke and unfold as follows:

13:1-3a	setting
13:3b-9	parable of the Sower
13:10-17	the purpose of the parables, which in Matthew is longer and focuses on present fulfillment in vv. 16-17
13:18-23	interpretation of the Sower
13:24-30	parable of the Wheat and the Weeds
13:31-33	parables of the Mustard Seed and the Leaven
13:34-35	the use of parables
13:36-43	interpretation of the Wheat and the Weeds
13:44-46	parables of the Treasure and the Pearl
13:47-50	parable of the Dragnet
13:51-52	treasures new and old

Of these Mark has only the Sower and the Mustard Seed, and he alone has the Growing Seed. Luke has only the Sower, the Mustard Seed, and the Leaven but has placed the Mustard Seed and the Leaven in a different context after the healing of the woman bound by Satan (13:18-21). Note that Matthew has three parable "twins" in ch. 13: the Wheat and the Weeds and the Dragnet, the Mustard Seed and the Leaven, and the Treasure in the Field and the Pearl of Great Price.

Some divide Matthew's parables discourse into two similar sections (vv. 1-35 and 36-52). Each section has four parables (if 13:52 is a parable), a description of the setting (vv. 1-3a and 36a), an excursus containing a detailed interpretation (vv. 10-23 and 36b-43), and an appropriate conclusion (vv. 34-35 and 51-52).[163] The main drawback to this approach is that the parable of the Wheat and the Weeds and its interpretation are placed in two different sections. More convincing is a threefold division: vv. 1-23, 24-43, and 44-52. Each section has at least one parable (vv. 1-9, 24-33, and 44-48), a statement about parables (vv. 10-17, 34-35, and 51-52), and an interpretation of a parable (vv. 18-23, 36-43, and 49-50).[164]

By placing these eight parables together Matthew depicts several features of the kingdom, a summary of which must await analysis of the remaining parables. At this point though it seems obvious that Matthew would say that the kingdom involves a proclamation that must be received and lived out. The proclamation is an assertion about reality that is to be believed and allowed to have defining force. Matthew would also say that the kingdom's coming does not now obliterate evil but one day will involve separation of the just and the unjust, that the kingdom appears as discouragingly small and unseen but will have overwhelming impact, and that the kingdom is valuable beyond all else and incorporates both the new and what is good from the old.

Matthew not only describes the character of the kingdom; he also focuses on Israel's rejection of Jesus' message. Whereas Mark places the pericope contrasting Jesus' family outside the circle with his true family prior to his parables discourse and Luke has this pericope after the parallel material, Matthew alone frames his parables discourse *before* with a pericope about Jesus' family being outside (12:46-50) *and after* with a pericope about Jesus' family and hometown being offended at him (13:53-58). In Matthew this second pericope records the last time Jesus taught in "their synagogue" (13:54). This discourse does *not* mark Israel's rejection of the message and Jesus' turn from Israel to the disciples.[165] The rejection theme is already at work from the beginning of ch. 11, especially from v. 16 on. The framing pericopes about response to Jesus' message help the parables fulfill their functions. Matthew intends the parables to warn readers not to repeat Israel's failure to respond to the kingdom message and also to help people understand why Israel rejected Jesus' message: hardness of heart, the efforts of the evil one, the world's cares and money, and the seeming insignificance of the kingdom.[166] Matthew also places here an emphasis on the privilege of the disciples who see and hear what others have longed to see and hear (13:16-17/Luke 10:23-24).[167] The purpose is not to exalt the disciples but to mark the eschatological significance of Jesus' preaching.

Luke's redaction does more than streamline, and like Matthew his arrangement of his material is the method used to nuance the discussion. He does not have Jesus teaching from a boat, apparently to avoid the redundancy with 5:3.[168] Like Matthew and Mark, Luke separates the parable and its interpretation with the discussion of the purpose of the parables and the use of Isa 6:9. His treatment unfolds as follows:

8:4	setting (different from the other accounts)
8:5-8	parable of the Sower
8:9-10	the purpose of the parables
8:11-15	interpretation of the Sower
8:16-18	related sayings about light and hearing
8:19-21	Jesus' family is those who hear and do God's word
	(*precedes* the parable of the Sower in Matthew and Mark)

Luke does not emphasize that Jesus discussed the purpose of parables and the interpretation of the Sower *in private*. In addition to the focus on the kingdom in the statement on the purpose of the parables (8:10), he places the parable in a context of Jesus' preaching about the kingdom (8:1). He states explicitly that the seed is the word of God and emphasizes the challenge to hear by saying Jesus "cried out" when he said "Let the one who has ears to hear hear." He also adds the need for holding fast to the word with endurance (8:15), a theme that reappears later.[169]

Adapting the Parable

This parable and its interpretation are important because they give the most extended treatment of the reception of the word of God. The kingdom is a kingdom of the word, and the parable is a parable about receiving that word. To be a disciple of the kingdom means hearing and remaining focused on the message of the kingdom in such a way that one is defined by it.[170] The key to spiritual formation is the willingness to listen, the practice of the discipline of listening, and responding appropriately to the received word.

The content of the message is not treated in the parable, but it is presupposed that the kingdom is present and brings newness and potential as surely as a farmer injects something new and with potential in planting seeds. This new thing can be lost, undervalued, or received, but if received it has its effect. Some will receive it and implement it to great success. The message functions as a *promise* about who God is and what God is doing and will do in Jesus' actions. The sowing of seed in Jesus' proclamation is restoring Israel and establishing God's kingdom, but the parable is also a warning for hearers not to fail as Israel failed with Isaiah. One greater than Isaiah is here. This message cannot be satisfied with casual or temporary attention; rather, it is all-encompassing and will not share the stage with wealth and mundane cares about life. The failures must be given attention, but the parable is not about failure and does not presume that failure is more frequent than success. It is a warning against failure to hear and produce.

The word we proclaim is not the same word Jesus proclaimed, and our time is not his time. He proclaimed the present and future kingdom with a warning and promise to Israel. Those features are still present for us but are altered in light of the death and resurrection of Jesus. The word still focuses on the revelation of God made known in Jesus, and the dynamics of hearing, reception, hardness of heart, and productivity are still the same.

The parable emphasizes both receptivity and bearing fruit. Two of the three sowings that fail describe people who respond *positively* to the message. They even hear the message with joy, but their hearing is still superficial. Receiving the kingdom with joy is not enough — a message the modern church desperately needs to hear. Faith that is temporary and unproductive is not true faith. Most pastors would be quite happy if people received the word with joy or made claims about faith, but this parable asserts that people can receive the word with joy and still be guilty of hardness of heart. Any hearing that does not result in productive living in relation to the Father is not valid hearing. As C. Keener observes, "the only conversions that count in the kingdom are those confirmed by a life of discipleship."[171] Fear that a concern for productive living leads to legalism only shows how much people have misunderstood Jesus' message.[172] Does initially receptive hearing that eventually fails raise the question of eternal security? People are overly vexed with the question of eternal security because of inadequate understandings of faith. This parable does not address the question of eternal security; it raises the question of inadequate and unproductive hearing. Churches should not be complicit in allowing people to think an initial response unaccompanied by productive living is saving faith.

The parable of the Sower is eschatological because it embodies the activity of God sowing his restored people through the preaching of Jesus. To suggest that the parable teaches how to manage despair or shows that in failure and everydayness lies the miracle of God's activity[173] is to domesticate the parable, remove it from the context of Jesus' life and ministry, and ignore the emphasis on hearing. The parable is about hearing that leads to productive living, and adapting the parable will mean enabling people to move past merely hearing words — even with joy — to hearing that captures the whole person. People think they can look like giant oaks without putting down deep roots. When they realize how much effort it takes to put down deep roots, they too often settle for being bramble bushes.

For Further Reading

Madeleine Boucher, *The Mysterious Parable: A Literary Study* (CBQMS 6; Washington, D.C.: Catholic Biblical Association of America, 1977), pp. 42-85.

John W. Bowker, "Mystery and Parable: Mark iv.1-20," *JTS* 25 (1974): 300-317.

W. D. Davies and Dale C. Allison, Jr., *A Critical and Exegetical Commentary on the Gospel According to Saint Matthew* (3 vols.; Edinburgh: T. & T. Clark, 1988-97), 2:373-406.

Craig A. Evans, *To See and Not Perceive: Isaiah 6.9-10 in Early Jewish and Christian Interpretation* (JSOTSup 64; Sheffield: Sheffield Academic Press, 1989).

Greg Fay, "Introduction to Incomprehension: The Literary Structure of Mark 4:1-34," *CBQ* 51 (1989): 65-81.

R. T. France, *The Gospel of Mark* (NIGTC; Grand Rapids: Eerdmans, 2002), pp. 181-207.

Joachim Jeremias, *The Parables of Jesus* (2d ed.; trans. S. H. Hooke; New York: Charles Scribner's Sons, 1963), pp. 77-79, 149-51.

Jacobus Liebenberg, *The Language of the Kingdom and Jesus: Parable, Aphorism, and Metaphor in the Sayings Material Common to the Synoptic Tradition and the Gospel of Thomas* (Berlin: Walter de Gruyter, 2001), pp. 350-414.

Ulrich Luz, *Matthew 8–20: A Commentary* (trans. James E. Crouch; Minneapolis: Fortress, 2001), pp. 228-51.

C. F. D. Moule, "Mark 4:1-20 Yet Once More," in *Neotestamentica et Semitica: Studies in Honor of Matthew Black* (ed. E. E. Ellis and Max Wilcox; Edinburgh: T. & T. Clark, 1969), pp. 95-113.

Klyne Snodgrass, "A Hermeneutics of Hearing Informed by the Parables with Special Reference to Mark 4," *BBR* 14 (2004): 59-79.

N. T. Wright, *Jesus and the Victory of God*, vol. 2 of *Christian Origins and the Question of God* (Minneapolis: Fortress, 1996), pp. 230-39.

Parables of the Present Kingdom
in Matthew 13, Mark 4, and Luke 13

Any number of parables could be labeled parables of the present kingdom, and to some degree all the parables presuppose that the kingdom of God is present in the activity of Jesus, even where the kingdom is not explicitly in view. Obviously parables like the Sower or the parables of Israel are parables of the present kingdom and must be included for any wholistic view of Jesus' teaching on the kingdom. The parables treated in this chapter are those that Matthew and Mark have placed after the Sower to emphasize the present kingdom. Luke places his two parables from this collection in a different place,[1] but in doing so he emphasizes in his own way the presence of the kingdom. The phrase "present kingdom" does not mean that the end of the world was present; it means that the promises of the OT Scriptures, especially the prophets, had begun with Jesus' actions and words.

THE GROWING SEED
(Mark 4:26-29)

This parable occurs only in Mark and is one of only thirteen Markan texts B. H. Streeter lists as neither in Matthew nor Luke.[2] It is the only Markan parable not recorded in Matthew, Luke, or Thomas (although *Gos. Thom.* 21 looks like a shortened adaptation).[3] Interpreters have suggested that Matthew and Luke omitted this parable because it was enigmatic and not particularly helpful and because it went against Luke's emphasis on doing and productivity. Some suggest that Matthew did not omit it but has expanded it into his parable of the Wheat and the Weeds, a suggestion with little support.[4] Why this parable is omitted cannot be demonstrated.[5]

Parable Type

This is a good example of a similitude. It is an extended simile which depicts a recurring event, mostly in the present tense,[6] for the sake of an analogy. There is no developed plot.

Issues Requiring Attention

1. What is the relation of this parable to the parables of the Sower and of the Mustard Seed?
2. Is the depiction of the man determinative? Should he be described as inactive between the sowing and the harvest? What is the significance of his not knowing?
3. What is the significance of the word *automatē* ("of itself")?
4. Is there an allusion to the harvest imagery of Joel 3:13 (Hebrew 4:13) and, if so, with what intent? Does the harvest refer to final judgment or, as some suggest, the time of Jesus' own ministry or that of his disciples?[7]
5. Is the focus of the parable on the man, the seed, or the harvest? Are the features in this account to be identified so that the man refers to God, Jesus, or Jesus' disciples, the stages of growth refer to specific time periods, sleeping and rising refer to death and resurrection, and the harvest refers to judgment?
6. What wrong idea does the parable seek to correct and what understanding does the parable seek to promote?

Helpful Primary Source Material

Canonical Material

- OT: Joel 3(Hebrew 4):13
- NT: cf. 1 Cor 3:6-7; Jas 5:7-8; Rev 14:14-19

Greco-Roman Writings

- Epictetus, *Diatr.* 4.8.38-40, 43 uses plant imagery of the development of humans and complains about some who have bloomed too quickly. "Allow us . . . to ripen as nature wishes. . . . Let the root grow, next let it acquire the first joint, and then the second, and then the third; and so finally the fruit will forcibly put forth its true nature, even against my will."

Early Christian Writings

- *1 Clem.* 23:4-5: "Oh, foolish men, compare yourself to a tree: take a vine, first it sheds its leaves, then there comes a bud, then a leaf, then a flower, and after this the unripe grape, then the full bunch. See how in a little time the fruit of the tree comes to ripeness. Truly his will shall be quickly and suddenly accomplished. . . ." Almost the same wording appears at *2 Clem.* 11:3.
- *Gos. Thom.* 21: "May there be a man of understanding among you! After the fruit ripened, he came quickly with his sickle in his hand [and] reaped it."

Later Jewish Writings

- *b. Megillah* 14b: "Also, O Judah, there is a harvest appointed for thee, when I would turn the captivity of my people." Similarly *b. ʿArakin* 33a.
- *Midr. Ps.* 8.1 uses the judgment language of Joel 3(4):12-13 with its mention of a winepress to explain the words "treading the winepress" *(gittith)* from Ps 8:1. The harvest is understood of the fall of Babylon, but shortly after that is the comment: "In Scripture, you find redemption described by four metaphors: as a grape-gathering, as a harvest [again with reference to Joel 4:13], as a pregnant woman, and as spices." *Midr. Ps.* 8.8 interprets Joel 3(4):13 of God's judgment on the nations. *Song Rab.* 8.19 is similar.

Textual Features Worth Noting

The narrative connection "And he was saying" *(kai elegen)* is a Markan stylistic device (which some would attribute to his source). It occurs seven times in his parables discourse (4:1-34) and ten additional times in his Gospel. Mark has used it in the parables discourse as a way to link sayings.

The introduction "Thus the kingdom of God is as . . ." *(houtōs estin hē basileia tou theou hōs)* occurs nowhere else, and no other parable begins with *houtōs . . . hōs.*[8] *Houtōs* ("thus, so") more frequently occurs at the ends of parables in the explanation (the *nimshal*),[9] but can be and is used elsewhere, not in reference to what precedes, but with reference to what follows. Possibly the nuance is "It's like when. . . ."[10] A decision about whether "thus" ties the parable in any determinative way to the preceding sayings, especially the parable of the Sower, is crucial. I do not think it does, particularly because "thus" is preceded by "and he was saying" *(kai elegen),* which seems to distance what follows from any logical connection to what precedes. The connection of the parables here is no more than that all three use the growth of seeds as pictures of the kingdom.

Mark explicitly connects the kingdom only to this parable and that of the Mustard Seed. (Mark 4:11 does connect the parable of the Sower to the kingdom by implication.)[11]

Little evidence points to Markan redaction with the possible exception of "immediately" *(euthys).*[12]

V. 26 introduces the man, the seed, and the earth, and the rest of the parable develops these three features. The parable focuses on:

the actions of the man in vv. 26b and 27a (fourteen words),
the process of growth in vv. 27b-29a (twenty-nine words, of which ten describe the activity of the seed and the man's not understanding, v. 27b, and nineteen describe the earth and its effect, vv. 28-29a), and
the actions of the man occasioned by the readiness of the harvest in vv. 29b-c (eight words).[13]

The parable views the process of growth twice, once of the seed's activity (sprouting and growing) and once of the earth's (bearing fruit detailed as the blade, the ear, the grain in the ear, then the ripe fruit and harvest).

If this is a parable of contrast, the contrast is between the activity of the man in sowing and harvesting and the activity of the seed during the growing process. Some suggest that the contrast is between either the seed's activity and the man's inactivity during growth[14] or between the two attitudes of the man in working and not working.[15] However, the parable does not emphasize the man's inactivity. Does the mention of his sleeping and rising indicate that he did nothing else, or does it convey the passing of time? I would suggest the latter.

Note the parallel between sleeping and rising in vv. 27 and 38.

Cultural Information

Little treatment is required here other than to mention that in Judaism the day begins at sundown, which explains the order "night and day" in v. 27. Cf. Esth 4:16; Isa 34:10.

Explanation of the Parable

This has to be ranked as one of the more enigmatic parables, even though its overall intent is clear enough. Virtually all agree the parable's focus is on the present kingdom, but how it works creates consternation among commentators. On the other hand, this parable has much to teach about parable interpretation and, if heeded, may require changes in how parables are treated.

As is evident elsewhere, the title given a parable prejudices the way it is read.[16] The traditional title, the Seed Growing Secretly, has the advantage that it emphasizes the seed and its growth, but the idea of secrecy is not in the text. Other suggested titles are no more compelling and are often conditioned by questionable readings of the parable. Suggestions include the parable of the Patient Husbandman,[17] of the Earth Producing of Itself,[18] of the Carefree Sower,[19] or of the Unbelieving Farmer.[20] The emphasis is caught if we call it merely the parable of the Growing Seed.

The authenticity of this parable is rarely questioned.[21] Some suggest that it was in a collection of seed parables prior to its adaptation by Mark,[22] but, although plausible, this cannot be demonstrated. A few have attempted to delete the introduction in v. 26,[23] and a few others have argued against the authenticity of the reference to the harvest in v. 29.[24] Such suggestions are based more on how these elements fit with prior assumptions about the kingdom than on any basis in fact. The harvest is virtually required by the sequence of growth to maturity. Most accept the unity of the parable as Mark presents it and find little evidence of Markan redaction.[25]

Mark presents the parable without indication of its audience, and no marker of the audience has appeared in his account since reference to the disciples in 4:10. Vv. 33-34 indicate, however, that the parables in vv. 26-32 were told to the crowds, and, although a bit unexpected, that is what we should assume.

Major Options for Interpretation[26]

Medieval allegorizing took this parable to refer to Christ implanting the divine seed in human hearts with the growth representing the development of Christian work and the harvest pointing to judgment.[27]

The older liberal interpretation thought the parable described the gradual evolution of the kingdom of God in human society.[28]

Some focus on the harvest as the apocalyptic end time. The focus would then be on an imminent end or on dealing with a delay.[29]

The parable is also understood of Jesus' immediate situation as one who is standing in a field ready to harvest. The sowing and growth show God's prior activity throughout history.[30]

Some think the parable was told to dampen the impatience of disciples or zealots who thought more should be happening than they saw with Jesus' ministry.[31]

The parable is frequently understood as showing that the kingdom of God is a miraculous event and does not result from human activity.[32]

A few have thought the parable stressed that time has been given to us.[33]

Some view the seed as the word with the result being that the proclaimer is free from worry since the power is inherent in the word and will accomplish its goal.[34]

Most of these options are not mutually exclusive. Interpretations diverge because of differences over which is the main feature. If one thinks the seed is the focus, one will think the parable is either about confidence in proclaiming the word or assurance about the harvest. If one focuses on the sower, the meaning will be sought in the man's inactivity or in his activity at harvest time. Obviously determinative here will be any decision about who is represented by the man. If one focuses on the earth, meaning will be found in the fact that the man does not produce the growth. If the growth itself is emphasized, then development of the kingdom comes to the fore. However, isolating one feature leads to distortion, and all the elements must be taken into account. As we have seen with other parables, an introduction such as "the kingdom is like a man" must be understood to mean the kingdom is like the *whole process* narrated by the parable.[35]

Decisions on the Issues

1. What is the relation of this parable to the Sower and the Mustard Seed? Several scholars think this parable forms a pair with that of the Mustard Seed and makes the same point or at least a similar point. Some see the similarity as the contrast between the small beginning and the large harvest.[36] G. Caird thinks the Mustard Seed provides the clue for a realized eschatological interpretation which sees the climax of the parable, not as an apocalyptic event at the end of history, but as the success of a world mission.[37] Some point instead to the connection with the Sower and see this parable as repeating its themes so that the focus then is on the power of the word and the discipleship that results.[38] Clearly a close connection exists for the three parables in Mark 4 with all of them having seeds, sowing, and the earth *(gē)*, but that does not mean that they all have the same message or function in the same way. Obviously, too, Matthew and Luke both paired the Mustard Seed with the Leaven, not with the Growing

Seed. Rather than force this parable to conform to one of the others, each must be understood in its own right. I would suggest though that all three deal with the same problem, the problem of why things appear as they do if the kingdom is indeed present. Other than that there is no direct relation to the other parables, and they do not provide the key to interpretation of this one.

2. Is the depiction of the man determinative? Should he be described as inactive between the sowing and the harvest? What is the significance of his not knowing? This similitude, like all parables, presents its case in streamlined form. The man sows, sleeps and rises, and sends the sickle. Interpreters regularly conclude from this that the focus is on the man's inactivity. Farmers do more than sow seed. Tilling the soil, weeding, irrigating, and protecting are all necessary if there is to be a harvest. From the omission of such labors people have drawn all kinds of conclusions: that the parable is unrealistic, that the farmer is incompetent or lazy, and that his inactivity is the focus. From such assumptions the parable has been thought to teach passivity, an ostentatious indifference so that overactivists learn to wait on God, wait with a carefree attitude, or take time to sleep and relax, or even that those who hear the word need no further nurture and care from Jesus.[39] Surely such conclusions are out of bounds and cannot meet the test of being verifiable from the nonparabolic teaching of Jesus. We cannot assume that the farmer was inactive, for the comment about sleeping and rising night and day is better understood as marking the passage of time.[40] The man's inability to contribute to the growth is the presupposition of the narrative but not its point. To focus on the man's inactivity — which is not mentioned — is erroneously to determine the parable's meaning from something that is not there.[41] The implications of the lack of focus on the man's activity must be assessed below.

That the man does not know how growth happens does underscore that the process of growth is not dependent on him and is beyond his understanding, and while this may have implications, it is not the focus of the parable. Attempts to connect the man's not knowing to Jesus' not knowing the time of the parousia (Mark 13:32) or to the disciples' blindness in Mark are unjustified.[42] The depiction of the man is not the determinative feature.

3. What is the significance of automatē *("of itself")? Automatē* is used of that which happens spontaneously, such as growth during a sabbatical year (Lev 25:5, 11) or a gate opening spontaneously (Acts 12:10).[43] Here it clearly does not refer to sabbatical growth, for the man sows the seed.[44] It refers to that which grows or happens without human intervention. It does not necessarily mean "effected by God" or designate something as a "miracle,"[45] nor is the word necessarily eschatological. Still, *automatē* is a key word — maybe *the* key word — for understanding the parable. The "automatic" earth produces the growth. While the passivity of the man is not emphasized, this word under-scores that growth happens without human intervention.

The parable is not teaching how humans should act; it is showing what the kingdom is like. Just as sowing begins a seemingly spontaneous process, so the kingdom is like a process of growth that will move automatically to harvest. It is fair to conclude that the kingdom does not depend on human effort, but that is not a point many in the first century would have contested.[46]

4. Is there an allusion to the harvest imagery of Joel 3:13 (Hebrew 4:13), and if so, with what intent? Does the harvest refer to end judgment or to the time of Jesus' own ministry? Some seek to avoid an allusion to Joel or see it as present only in a secondary expansion because the reference there is to harvest as a judgment on the nations, whereas here the harvest is viewed positively.[47] Several argue legiti-mately that the allusion to Joel may be only an evocative use of harvest lan-guage without any intent to make the same point.[48] As indicated earlier, the harvest image is virtually required by the detailed stages of growth. It would be strange to list the stages and stop short of the harvest. There is no objective rea-son to delete the language of "sending the sickle," which *is* an allusion to Joel. Sickle and harvest language describes final judgment in Rev 14:14-20, and the allusion to Joel 3:13 is certain there because Joel's language of treading out the vintage in the winepress is also present. I do not think an allusion to Joel 3(4):13 in Mark 4:29 can be avoided, as a comparison of the passages shows:

Joel 4:13	*šilḥû magāl ki bāšal qāṣîr*
	"send a sickle because the harvest is ripe"
LXX Joel 4:13	*exaposteilate drepana hoti parestēken trygētos*
	"send forth sickles because the vintage is here"
Mark 4:29b	*euthys apostellei to drepanon hoti parestēken ho therismos*
	"immediately he will send the sickle because the harvest is here"

Whether Mark has been influenced by the LXX or alludes to the Hebrew text is debated,[49] but the allusion is clear. Other references using images of harvest and a sickle also point to judgment.[50]

Jesus used the harvest image of his own ministry (Matt 9:37-38/Luke 10:2; John 4:35) and of future judgment (Matt 13:30, 39). Some, most notably C. H. Dodd, think he refers here to the harvest happening in his own ministry.[51] This seems unlikely because the Joel citation more naturally points to final judg-ment, because *hotan* ("when") seems to point to the future,[52] and because the parable's purpose is to explain why the appearance of the kingdom is not more obvious, which does not fit if the intent is to point to a successful harvest in the present. This is especially the case if the parable has any nuance encouraging patience.[53] The purpose of the allusion then is to point to final judgment.

5. Is the focus of the parable on the man, the seed, or the harvest? Are the features in this account to be identified so that the man refers to God, Jesus, or Jesus' disciples, the stages of growth refer to specific time periods, sleeping and rising refer to death and resurrection, and the harvest refers to judgment? Despite Jülicher and claims of rejecting allegory, scholars still allegorize. This parable has been allegorized in multiple directions, even to the point of absurdity. For C. H. Dodd God is the one who sows in his prevenient grace, the stages of growth refer to the OT era, and the harvest points to the crisis of Jesus' ministry.[54] With some the seed is identified with the word and its sowing with the ministry of John the Baptist, of Jesus, and of the disciples.[55] Some understand the sower as Jesus and the sleeping and rising as a reference to Jesus' death and resurrection, and even take the sowing of the seed in the ground as referring to the sacrifice of the Son of Man.[56] Some take the sower as God or the disciples or both.[57] The man's not knowing has been understood both of Jesus' not knowing the time of the parousia (13:32) or the disciples' blindness.[58] The stages of growth have been taken to refer to the growth of the crowds around Jesus or to the time of Jesus' ministry, the time of the church's ministry, and the parousia.[59]

Such identifications lead swiftly to difficulty. The man's not knowing hardly fits what Mark would say of either God or Jesus, and the parable is not about the need for disciples to proclaim the kingdom and wait on God. Conclusions drawn from such identifications simply do not work. Is either God or Jesus uninvolved or uninterested in the growth of the kingdom?[60] Because of the difficulty of the identifications, R. Guelich argued that the sower of vv. 26-27 and the divine reaper of v. 29 were not the same person, a change posited long ago by medieval allegorists.[61]

These approaches are a mixture of allegorizing and theologizing. With analogies we look for correspondences, and if the brain cannot see them easily, it will create them. Also, people seek to make each parable a complete theological picture, one that fits their own assumptions. Parables do not give complete pictures, and certainly not complete pictures of theology. We should know by now that parables do not all work the same way and that each parable must be dealt with individually. Some have multiple correspondences, and some do not. Some use stock metaphors, but metaphors are always capable of being used in novel ways. Determining where an image has a direct correlation (such as the storms to God's judgment in the parable of the Two Builders or the vineyard to the relation of God and God's people) and where images do not (such as the man here) is key to correct interpretation. While no formulaic approach will resolve the issues, it seems clear that similitudes, single indirect narratives, and "who from you" parables do not rely on identification of outside referents, whereas the longer narrative parables usually depend on recognition of such referents. All these parabolic forms are analogies, but similitudes are more streamlined in accomplishing their task. The man in this parable stands for no one,[62] and understanding the analogy requires identification of the man no more than interpretation of the parable of the Leaven requires identifying the woman in Matt 13:33/Luke 13:21 (or other characters in similitudes). The analogy is not with one feature (such as the man) but with the entire process. The images may set off resonances, as the harvest does with final judgment, but the individual features do not "stand for something." We cannot legitimately argue that the salient point is the seed or the harvest, for the entire process is required to make the point. The kingdom is like a farmer who sows, goes about his life, and the "automatic" earth produces a plant and its fruit, and then comes the harvest.

6. *What wrong ideas does the parable seek to correct and what understanding does it seek to promote?* There is general agreement that "parables of growth" (the Sower, the Growing Seed, the Mustard Seed, the Leaven, the Wheat and Weeds) answer questions and challenges to Jesus' proclamation of the kingdom.[63] To Jesus' announcement of salvation and the presence of the kingdom (e.g., Matt 12:28; Mark 1:15; 4:11) the obvious response was Where? Could Jesus be the coming one if expectations about the kingdom and the redemption of Israel were not taking place? How could this itinerant and his small group of disciples be the kingdom? Some think Jesus is addressing the kingdom ideas and activist desires of zealots and Pharisees,[64] but while this parable could be applied to such misunderstandings, that does not seem to have been its origin. If people expected deliverance from Rome's subjugation, the removal of evil, the establishment of righteousness, and material blessing (as e.g., *Pss. Sol.* 17–18), it was not happening on any acceptable scale, but one point of the parable is that the kingdom's coming is more complex than that. From the parable people would have to expand their understanding of the kingdom to allow for its not being so obvious and for some passing of time before it was fully in effect.

Often overlooked is the importance of this parable for understanding Jesus' eschatological teaching. In the chapter on parables of future eschatology the overview of Jesus' eschatological teaching will point to Jesus' expectation of an interval between the events of his life and the events of the end time (see pp. 477-564 below). Obviously this parable, whose authenticity hardly anyone doubts, assumes such a view in that it anticipates some length of time between Jesus' present and the end-time appearing of the kingdom. The kingdom involves the passing of time.[65] No hint is given as to how long that time might be, but this parable should at least slow down any overemphasis on a soon appearing kingdom. This and other parables assume at least two stages of the kingdom, a time of sowing and growth and the time of harvest.[66]

The understanding which the parable promotes includes at least three items: the presence of the kingdom, a point more assumed than taught, which is itself a significant fact; some length of time for growth; and the certainty of the harvest. The sowing took place in the ministry of Jesus, a point expressed by the use of the aorist. The growth and the harvest are both emphasized by the use of the present tense, the amount of space given to them, and, for the harvest, the use of the word "immediately." *Jesus' ministry has inaugurated a sequence of action leading to the fullness of God's kingdom just as surely as sowing sets in play a spontaneous process leading to harvest.* Even if hidden (cf. 4:22) and unrecognized, the kingdom is present and will be fully revealed in God's time.[67] The point is not merely that the kingdom is coming, for most Jews would assume that. The parable asserts that the kingdom process is already under way with Jesus' teaching and activity and that the glorious revelation of the kingdom has its beginning in, and is directly tied to, what he is doing.[68]

Interpreters often recoil at the idea of the growth of the kingdom because of the older evolutionary understandings of humanity's progress toward the final kingdom and because Judaism and Jesus elsewhere do not teach anything of a developing kingdom.[69] But, even if we rightly reject any ideas of a straight-line, evolutionary development, this parable, the Mustard Seed, and the Leaven *do* focus on growth. The kingdom Jesus proclaimed necessarily involves growth, even if his teaching does not detail how that growth happens. In effect the parable says, "What you see is not all that will happen before the certain coming of the kingdom."[70]

The parable does not address what humans can or should do. The "automatic earth" produces the growth. The kingdom is God's kingdom and humans do not understand or cause its process,[71] but that process is as inevitable as seed growing and producing fruit for harvest. The parable then is optimistic; in spite of appearances people may be confident that what has begun with Jesus will lead to the full realization of the kingdom. Although they are not mentioned in the text, patience and encouragement are results flowing from this parable.[72]

Adapting the Parable

Not every parable is a compelling practical lesson, and interpreters should be content to let this parable do its job without being forced. It does not instruct people about what they should or should not do and should not, therefore, be seen as addressing works righteousness, psychologized to address the problem of workaholism,[73] or viewed as an encouragement to passivity. It is not to be spiritualized into some developmental hypothesis of the spiritual life, and it is not about the power of preaching.[74] People need to remember that this is a kingdom parable. Claims about the presence of the kingdom are no more compelling now than earlier, probably less so. People may still know that despite appearances the kingdom process has already been set in motion and will reach its goal. While people go about their daily routines, the kingdom is present and at work, and God's harvest with his judgment will certainly follow. Humans do not bring in the kingdom; they are servants of the kingdom, not its cause. The parable illustrates the proper attitudes toward the kingdom and its eschatological harvest: patience — it will come when God's time is ripe, confidence despite appearances because God is the one at work, and comfort knowing that all is in God's hands. These attitudes are not explicit in the parable but logical deductions from what the parable teaches.

For Further Reading

Aloysius M. Ambrozic, *The Hidden Kingdom: A Redaction-Critical Study of the References to the Kingdom of God in Mark's Gospel* (Washington, D.C.: The Catholic Biblical Association of America, 1972), pp. 106-22.

Nils Dahl, "Parables of Growth," in *Jesus in the Memory of the Early Church* (Minneapolis: Augsburg, 1976), pp. 141-66.

C. H. Dodd, *The Parables of the Kingdom* (London: Nisbet, 1936), pp. 176-80.

Jacques Dupont, "Encore la parabole de la Semence qui pousse toute seule (Mc 4,26-29)," in *Jesus und Paulus. Festschrift für Werner Georg Kümmel zum 70. Geburtstag* (ed. E. Earle Ellis and Erich Gräßer; Göttingen: Vandenhoeck & Ruprecht, 1975), pp. 96-108.

Robert H. Gundry, *Mark: A Commentary on His Apology for the Cross* (Grand Rapids: Eerdmans, 1993), pp. 219-26.

Peter Rhea Jones, *Studying the Parables of Jesus* (Macon, Ga.: Smyth & Helwys, 1999), pp. 100-122.

Eckhard Rau, *Reden in Vollmacht. Hintergrund, Form, und Anliegen der Gleichnisse Jesu* (Göttingen: Vandenhoeck & Ruprecht, 1990), pp. 119-71.

THE WHEAT AND THE WEEDS
(Matt 13:24-30, 36-43)

This parable, which is often called the parable of the Wheat and Tares, is one of only three given a detailed interpretation, and other than the Sower is the only one to be given a title. The detailed allegorical interpretation in vv. 36-43 is given in response to the disciples' request for an explanation. The interpretation ends, as a few parables and other sayings do,[75] with a call for hearing, which underscores the importance of the parable for Matthew and serves as a warning to take its message seriously. The parable is separated from its interpretation by the parables of the Mustard Seed and the Leaven and a short statement on the purpose of parables. The differences between the parable and its interpretation in Matthew make this one of the more difficult parables.

Parable Type

This is a double indirect narrative parable. It has a developed plot and is introduced by an explicit statement that the kingdom is like the process narrated in the parable.

Issues Requiring Attention

1. Was this parable derived either from an earlier, shorter parable similar to the parable of the Dragnet or from the parable of the Growing Seed?
2. What is the relation of *Gos. Thom.* 57 to the parable in Matthew?
3. Is this a realistic story of agricultural life, or are several features artificially constructed allegory?
4. Is this a parable about the mixed character of the church, as is often assumed? Is it about the mixed nature of the individual, which inherently includes both good and evil?
5. Does this parable reflect a conflict between Matthew's church and the synagogue?
6. Does this parable have anything to do with Jesus' stance of non-retaliation or with his association with toll collectors and sinners? Who or what is indicated by the seed sown by the enemy?
7. To what question does the parable provide an answer?
8. Does "Sir" (v. 27), *kyrie*, which can also be translated as "Lord" or "master," have christological significance?

9. Do the parable and its interpretation stem originally from Jesus, or is one or both of them a creation of Matthew or his tradition?

10. What is the relation of the kingdom of heaven (v. 24), the world (v. 38), the kingdom of the Son of Man (v. 41), and the kingdom of the Father (v. 43)? Is "the kingdom of the Son of Man" a reference to the church? Does this parable tell us of the relation of the kingdom, the church, and the world?

11. What does this parable teach?

Helpful Primary Source Material

Canonical Material

- OT: Dan 3:6; 12:3; Zeph 1:3; Mal 4:1-2 (Hebrew 3:19-20)
- NT: Matt 15:12-13; 24:30-31; 25:31-33; 1 Cor 4:5

Early Jewish Writings

- Wis 4:3: The children of the ungodly are described as illegitimate seedlings.
- 1QS 3.19-23 describes the spirits of truth and deceit that dwell in humanity. "From the spring of light stem the generations of truth, and from the source of darkness the generations of deceit. And in the hand of the Prince of Lights is dominion [*mmšlt*] over all the sons of justice; they walk on paths of light. And in the hand of the Angel of Darkness is total dominion over the sons of deceit; they walk on paths of darkness. From the Angel of Darkness stems the corruption of all the sons of justice . . . and their offensive deeds are under his dominion in compliance with the mysteries of God, until his moment [or "end," *qšo*]. . . ."
- 1QS 4.15-26 describes the two divisions of humans (the children of truth/light and the children of deceit/darkness) God has set until the last time (*qṣ*), the time of visitation when he will obliterate injustice.
- 1QM 1.8-9: "And [the sons of jus]tice shall shine to all the edges of the earth, they shall go on shining, up to the end of all the periods of darkness; and in the time of God, his exalted greatness will shine for all the et[ernal] times, for peace and blessing, glory and joy, and length of days for all the sons of light."
- Philo, *Prov.* 2.35-36 discusses the delay in divine punishment.
- Philo, *Leg.* 3.106 says that God does not punish sinners immediately but allows time for repentance.

- *Pss. Sol.* 17:21-32: The Messiah is expected ". . . to purge Jerusalem from gentiles . . . to drive out the sinners from the inheritance; to smash the arrogance of sinners . . . ; to destroy the unlawful nations . . . ; at his warning the nations will flee from his presence; and he will condemn sinners by the thoughts of their hearts. He will gather a holy people whom he will lead in righteousness. . . . He will not tolerate unrighteousness (even) to pause among them. . . . the alien and the foreigner will no longer live near them. . . . There will be no unrighteousness among them in his days, for all shall be holy, and their king shall be the Lord Messiah."

- *4 Ezra* 4:28-32: "For the evil about which you ask me has been sown, but the harvest of it has not yet come." The text goes on to say that reaping must occur and the place where evil has been sown must pass away before the field where good has been sown will come. A grain of evil seed was sown in Adam's heart and it has produced and will produce much ungodliness until the time of threshing comes.

- *2 Bar.* 70.2: "Behold, the days are coming and it will happen when the time of the world has ripened and the harvest of the seed of the evil ones and the good ones has come. . . ."

- *T. Ab.* A 10-14: This passage describes the archangel Michael taking Abraham in a chariot above the whole earth so that he can see all that happens. When he saw sinners he called down destruction on them until a voice from heaven stopped him for his lack of mercy. God does not want to destroy but delays death so that people may repent. Abraham is allowed to witness the judging process in which angels conduct souls to judgment and carry out the decisions. Abraham prays for the souls he destroyed previously, and they are restored.

Early Christian Writings

- Hermas, *Sim.* 5.2.1-10 records a parable of a man who had a vineyard in a field and a servant who had the responsibility of fencing the vineyard. When the servant completed the fence, he pulled out all the weeds. The master was so pleased that he made the servant joint heir with his son and had a great feast. After lengthy discussion of the difficulty of interpreting this parable and requests for explanation (5.3-4), not unlike the separation of parable and interpretation in Matthew, 5.5.1-5 gives a detailed interpretation of each of the elements in the story. The field is the world, the Lord of the field is the Creator, the servant is the Son of God, the vines are the people he planted, the fences are the angels who support the people, the weeds are the iniquities of the servants of God, and the food from the feast is the commandments. This parable may have been influenced by Matthew's parable of the Wheat and the Weeds.

- *Gos. Thom.* 57: "Jesus said: The kingdom of the Father is like a man who had [good] seed. His enemy came by night (and) sowed a weed among the good seed. The man did not allow them to pull up the weed. He said to them, lest you go to pull up [literally "that we may pull up"] the weed, and you pull up the wheat along with it. For on the day of the harvest the weeds will appear; they will be pulled up and burned."

Later Jewish Writings

- *m. Kil'ayim* 1.1: "Wheat and tares are not accounted Diverse Kinds." Cf. the laws against sowing fields with two kinds of seeds in Lev 19:19 and Deut 22:9.
- *m. Terumot* 2.6: A heave offering is valid even if given from the worse of two kinds of produce that are not diverse kinds, "save only when tares are given instead of wheat, since they are not food."
- *b. Baba Meṣi'a* 83b: R. Eleazar arrested some Jewish thieves for the Romans. "Thereupon R. Joshua, son of Ḳarḥah, sent word to him, 'Vinegar, son of wine! How long will you deliver up the people of our God for slaughter!' Back came the reply: 'I weed out thorns from the vineyard.' Whereupon R. Joshua retorted: 'Let the owner of the vineyard himself [God] come and weed out the thorns.'"
- *Gen. Rab.* 28.8: "*For all flesh had corrupted their way,* etc. (Gen 6:12). R. Julian [Lulianus] b. Tiberius said in R. Isaac's name: Even the earth acted lewdly; wheat was sown and it produced pseudo-wheat, for the pseudo-wheat we now find came from the age of the deluge." A wordplay exists between "act lewdly" *(zānāh)* and "pseudo-wheat" *(zônīn)*, the *zizania* of the parable. The wordplay appears also in *y. Kil'ayim* 1.3.
- *Num. Rab.* 1.4: "Israel has been compared to a heap of wheat. As the measures of wheat are counted when carried into the barn . . . shall Israel be numbered on all occasions. . . . The straw and the stubble, however, are neither numbered nor measured. So are the heathens likened unto straw and stubble, as it is said, *Make them . . . as stubble before the wind* (Ps 83:14). . . . *All the nations are as nothing before Him* (Isa 40:17)." This is paralleled in *Pesiqta Rabbati* 10.3-4.
- *Num. Rab.* 4.1: "The Holy One, blessed be He, said: 'Thou art precious in My sight, since I gave no numbering to any of the nations of the world, but to thee I gave a numbering.' This may be illustrated by a parable. A king had numerous granaries all of which contained much refuse and

were full of rye-grass. He was consequently not particular about the quantity of the contents. He had, however, one particular granary which he perceived to be a fine one. Said he to a member of his house: 'Those granaries consist of refuse and are full of rye-grass. Be not, therefore, particular about the quantity of the contents. As regards this one, however, ascertain how many *kors,* how many sacks, how many *modii* it contains.' Thus, 'the king' is the supreme King of kings, the Holy One, blessed be He; 'the granary' is Israel — *O thou my threshing, and the winnowing of my floor* (Isa 21:10). . . . The Holy One, blessed be He, said to Moses: 'The idol worshippers are worthless grain' . . . (Isa 33:12). Be not, therefore, particular about their numbers. Israel, however, are righteous; they are all wheat fit for storage. . . ."

- *Song Rab.* 7.3.3: A parable demonstrates that Israel is as wheat which God planted (Jer 32:41) and the nations as nothing: "The straw, the chaff, and the stubble were arguing with one another, each claiming that for its sake the ground had been sown. Said the wheat to them: 'Wait till the threshing time comes, and we shall see for whose sake the field has been sown.' When the time came and they were all brought into the threshing-floor, the farmer went out to winnow it. The chaff was scattered to the winds; the straw he took and threw on the ground; the stubble he cast into the fire; the wheat he took and piled in a heap, and all the passers-by when they saw it kissed it, as it says, *Kiss ye the corn* (Ps 2:12). So of the nations some say, 'We are Israel, and for our sake the world was created,' and others say, 'We are Israel, and for our sake the world was created.' Says Israel to them: 'Wait till the day of the Holy One, blessed be He, comes, and we shall see for whose sake the world was created'; and so it is written, *For, behold, the day cometh, it burneth as a furnace,* etc. (Mal 3:19)." This is paralleled in *Gen. Rab.* 83.5 and *Pesiqta Rabbati* 10.4.[76]

Comparison of the Accounts

The *Gos. Thom.* account is obviously abbreviated, regardless of its origin. The sowing of good seed in the field is merely assumed. Matthew's "while people slept" is "by night" in *Gos. Thom.,* and the enemy's leaving is assumed. Several items in Matthew are omitted in *Gos. Thom.:* the growth sequence of the seed, the servants' questions, the first response of the owner explaining the origin of the weeds, the command to let both grow together, the directions to the reapers, and the gathering of the wheat into the barn. But the servants' question whether they should pull out the weeds is assumed. No interpretation is provided in *Gos. Thom.* For further discussion of *Gos. Thom.*, see below, p. 200.

Textual Features Worth Noting

The section of Matthew in which this parable appears (9:35–16:20) tells largely about Jesus' mission to Israel and his frequent rejection. See particularly 12:33-37, but the harvest image in 9:37-38 is used of Jesus' ministry, not the consummation of the age.

This parable follows that of the Sower and its interpretation and precedes the parables of the Mustard Seed and the Leaven. Together these parables present a view of the kingdom as present, but unexpectedly evil is still present too, and the kingdom is not visibly overwhelming.

Two other parables begin the same way as this one ("the kingdom of heaven has become like . . . ," aorist passive of *homoioun* and the dative): Matt 18:23 and 22:2. The aorist passive is probably a marker for the presence of the kingdom.[77] The future passive of *homoioun* and the dative introduce parables in Matt 7:24, 26; 25:1. The active of *homoioun* and the dative introduce parables in Matt 11:16; Mark 4:30; Luke 7:31; 13:18, 20. Note also "is like" (*homoia estin* or *homoios estin*) in Matt 11:16; 13:31/Luke 13:19; 13:33/Luke 13:21; 13:44, 45, 47, 52; 20:1; Luke 6:47, 48, 49; 7:31, 32; 13:18, 19, 21. Such language is similar to introductions to rabbinic parables.

After the introduction in v. 24a the parable has five movements: good sowing (v. 24b), hostile sowing (v. 25), growth (v. 26), first question and answer (vv. 27-28a), second question and answer, the latter consisting of directions for the present and an explanation of future action (vv. 28b-30). The interpretation consists of three parts: a narrative introduction (v. 36), a list identifying seven items from the parable (vv. 37-39), and an apocalyptic explanation (vv. 40-43). Several items from the parable are not mentioned in the interpretation: sleeping, the departure of the enemy, fruit, the servants and their questions, and, surprisingly, the answer of the owner to let both wheat and weeds grow together, which appears to be the primary concern of the parable. The list of seven items primarily just sets the stage for the real focus of the interpretation, the harvest metaphor, which is given much more attention than it had in the parable. *On any estimation the interpretation goes beyond the parable and shifts the focus* by emphasizing the "consummation *(synteleia)* of the age" (cf. 13:39, 40),[78] a closer description of the angels gathering all offenses and doers of lawlessness and throwing them into a furnace of fire, and a description of the righteous shining like the sun (which has no parallel in the parable).

Prominence is given to "gather" *(syllegō)*, which appears in vv. 28, 29, 30, 40, and 41.

Several themes in this parable appear elsewhere in Matthew, especially the focus on "good" and "bad" together[79] and on the "weeping and gnashing of teeth" at judgment.[80]

The saying of John the Baptist at Matt 3:12/Luke 3:17 is similar: the "coming one" will gather his wheat into his barn and will burn the chaff with unquenchable fire.

Themes and ideas in this parable are paralleled in other parables of Jesus. These parables show that agricultural themes were reworked in several directions to demonstrate aspects of his teaching on the kingdom. Elements in common with the parable of the Sower and its interpretation include kingdom, someone sowing, good, production of fruit, the evil one/devil, and an appeal to hear. With the Growing Seed (Mark 4:26-29) this parable shares kingdom, a man, sowing seed (Matthew: *speiranti kalon sperma;* Mark: *balē ton sporon*), sleep, sprout, fruit (Matthew: *karpon epoiēsen;* Mark: *karpophorei*), blade, wheat (or grain: *sitos*), and harvest. Like Luke's parable of the Fig Tree (13:6-9) this parable mentions fruit and has a dialogue between a servant and an owner. Both parables say that no immediate action should be taken, that the crop should be left *(aphiēmi)* until harvest or the tree left *(aphiēmi)* until sufficient time for fruit. Both also have the theme of judgment. Matthew's parable of the Net (13:47-50) is so similar to the interpretation of the Wheat and the Weeds that it is often viewed as a twin parable, which unjustly ignores the differences, but note the following common elements: kingdom of heaven, gather, good, "thus will be the consummation of the age," angels assisting at judgment, evil, righteous, and "they will cast them into the furnace of fire; there will be weeping and gnashing of teeth." The interpretation of the Wheat and the Weeds and the parable of the Net bracket the twin parables of the Treasure and the Pearl with the theme of eschatological judgment.

This parable and the parables of the Sower and the Net are the only parables given a detailed, itemized explanation.[81] With the rest of the parables Matthew is content to give a short explanation ("Thus it is . . .") or to leave the parable without comment. With the Sower the explanation of each soil is independent of the others, whereas with the other two parables the features function together to form one explanation. The interpretations are given only to Jesus' disciples. The framing and attention given to the parables of the Sower and of the Wheat and the Weeds suggest that in Matthew's mind these two are the most revealing about the nature of the kingdom.

Cultural Information

Most of the information on the cultural background will be treated below in the discussion of whether the parable is realistic or not (pp. 200-202).

Nearly all commentators think *zizania* ("tares" or "darnel") should be identified as *lolium temulentum,* an annoying weed that looks very much like wheat, especially before maturity, and can carry a poisonous fungus. If it is harvested and ground together with wheat, the resulting flour is spoiled.[82]

G. Dalman observed that in Palestine a week before the ears the leaves of the tares are two to three millimeters wide while the wheat is four to five millimeters wide. Fully developed the blades are three millimeters wide and the wheat six to twelve. At the time of the ears the roots of both are fully developed and entangled. Dalman also reported observing a variety of methods among Palestinian farmers for dealing with the weeds.[83]

Explanation of the Parable

This is a difficult parable made more difficult by fundamental disagreement among scholars on core issues such as hermeneutics, critical method, and ecclesial practice. Many of the problems here as elsewhere are caused by the attempt to wring more theology and direction for church practice from the parable than is warranted.

Options for Interpretation

Historically this parable has had an important role in discussions of a Christian response to evil, especially evil in the church.[84] Hippolytus relates that Callistus justified lax attitudes toward those indulging in sin by saying "Let the tares grow along with the wheat" (Matt 13:30).[85] Augustine used this parable to argue against the Donatists (who insisted on a pure church uncontaminated by those who had recanted during persecution), but the Donatists insisted that the parable was irrelevant to the debate since the field in which tares were sown was the world, not the church (v. 38).[86] Later, regrettably, this discussion centered around whether the parable allowed or prohibited killing of heretics.[87]

This parable is so difficult that some despair of recovering Jesus' intent.[88] Despite the difficulty, the options for interpretation are rather limited.[89]

One may view this parable as addressing the church as a *corpus permixtum* consisting of good and evil. The parable has often been in-

terpreted as giving the church direction for dealing with heretics
within its own body.

Surprisingly similar is the modern critical approach that views the parable as Matthew's dealing with the problem of his mixed community,
either to warn his Christian readers against separation from Judaism
or to warn them against trying to purify the church of wrongdoers.
Both the traditional and modern critical approaches see the parable as
a call to patience or as a warning about judgment for the church. Neither approach pays attention to the context of the historical Jesus, the
first because its concern is primarily ecclesiological, the second because of assumptions about Matthew and his procedure.

A less frequent approach says the parable addresses the conflict of good
and evil within the individual.

Some view the parable (with or without its interpretation) as Jesus' explanation of why the kingdom he proclaims does not fit Jewish expectations of immediate glory.

Decisions on the Issues

1. *Was this parable derived either from an earlier, shorter parable similar to the
parable of the Dragnet or from the parable of the Growing Seed?* Hans Weder is
typical of a few who argue for an original, shorter version. In his estimation the
parable is from Jesus but included only vv. 24b (without *kalon*, "good"), 26, and
30b. This leaves an account parallel to the parable of the Dragnet (13:47-48).[90]
The assumption is not only that the Wheat and Weeds and the Dragnet are
"twins" but that they must be identical twins. Even parables usually considered
twins, such as the Treasure and the Pearl, do not conform in every respect. If the
reconstructed form omits v. 30a (the command to let both grow together), this
shortened form is merely a judgment parable. While such a parable fits easily in
Jesus' teaching, the reconstruction does not inspire confidence.[91] Further, the
command to let wheat and weeds grow together, which many would view as the
key element, fits with Jesus' teaching elsewhere on judgment being temporarily
delayed, as in the parable of the Fig Tree (Luke 13:6-9).

A more common suggestion is that this parable is a restructuring of the
parable of the Growing Seed (Mark 4:26-29).[92] *If* one accepts that Matthew
used Mark, then Matthew has included most of Mark's account, usually in the
same order. But Matthew deviates from Mark 4:21-29, the material between the
interpretation of the parable of the Sower and the parable of the Mustard Seed.
Matthew uses Mark 4:21-25 at other places in his Gospel, but he and Luke both
omit the parable of the Growing Seed. Was it missing in their manuscripts of

Mark?[93] Did they think the passage was too passive and bypassed human responsibility?[94] This oddity and the common words between Mark's parable and Matthew's parable of the Wheat and Weeds (see above, p. 197) have led to the suggestion that Matthew has rewritten Mark's parable for his own purposes. The parallels between the two parables are, however, not that close. Different Greek words are used for the sowing process and for bearing fruit. Other than the stages of growth and the appearance of the word "sleep," there is little to commend this view. That Jesus told several parables around common themes is obvious, themes such as settling accounts, finding something valuable, and various agricultural practices. That being the case, little need exists to try to explain one agricultural parable as originating in another.[95]

2. *What is the relation of Gos. Thom. 57 to the parable in Matthew?* While a few would advocate the independence of *Gos. Thom.* here,[96] this is one of the easiest passages to argue for its dependence on the Synoptic tradition. Even those usually prone to see *Gos. Thom.* as independent elsewhere admit that it is later in this case.[97] The abbreviated story in *Gos. Thom.* presupposes the servants and their question whether the weeds should be gathered and omits the command to let wheat and weeds grow together. This does not prove direct dependence of *Gos. Thom.* on Matthew, but it does demonstrate dependence on a longer form of the parable like that in Matthew.[98] Certainly no justification exists for thinking Matthew's account derived from that of Thomas.

3. *Is this a realistic story of agricultural life, or are several features artificially constructed allegory?* From Jülicher on, those who object to the authenticity of the parable usually argue that several aspects of the parable are not realistic but have been shaped by the allegorical reality. The following features are viewed as unrealistic and allegorical:

> The man would not sow the field himself, but the narrative represents Jesus' sowing the gospel.
>
> The text implies that others slept, but the owner did not, which points to the continual care of the risen Lord.
>
> The action of the enemy is unlikely, but the owner without evidence knows an enemy is to blame. This points to the influence of evil in the church.
>
> The servants would not be surprised at weeds in a field; rather, they would be surprised if there were no weeds. This feature appears only so that the parable can work.
>
> The weeds would be distinguishable earlier, and normal practice was to take weeds out early in the growing process, but the inability to distin-

guish and the presence of both wheat and weeds points to the mixed character of the church.

The man's servants would have done the harvest, not a second group of reapers, but the second group is required to focus on the angels at judgment.

The weeds would not have been bundled but left in the field to be burned.[99]

Parables do sometimes have unrealistic features, and a charge of lack of realism should not necessarily be a threat to authenticity. Parables are pseudo-realistic. Also, parables quite regularly are constructed on the reality they depict. Yet, if there is unrealism in this parable, it is so small it would hardly be noticed. Most of the seven items listed above are a smokescreen and result from overreading. Parables are brief, even cryptic, and often leave out details. They usually give only what is necessary to make the story work. Note that Luke 14:22 just assumes that the servant carried out his master's orders. That Matthew's parable says "A man sowed good seed in his field" does not necessarily mean that the man did the work himself any more than "A man made a great banquet for his son" (Matt 22:2) means the man himself did all the preparations for the banquet. Further, while Matthew sees Jesus as the sower, in 10:5 the disciples are sent out with the same mission, so it is difficult to lodge a charge of unrealism over the statement "A man sowed."

Nor does the text say everyone slept but the man. Surely 13:25 merely means "while people slept," that is, at nighttime, and is not making a point about the Lord never sleeping. This seems to be a case of scholars allegorizing something not intended allegorically.

The action of the enemy is not an everyday occurrence, but people did sabotage the fields of their enemies. *Sib. Or.* 1.396 describes the punishment and exile of the Hebrews, who are slaughtered and who have much darnel mixed in their wheat. The Romans passed laws prohibiting such acts, which only proves that it was a problem.[100] Juvenal complains of those who sabotage fields by sending cattle to eat the crops and says that the number of those bewailing such wrongs and the number of forced selling of fields can scarce be told.[101]

The surprise of the servants and the conclusion drawn by the master both presume something not explicit in the parable, that the number of weeds was far beyond normal. This presumption is again typical of the brevity of parables. The number of weeds resulting from sabotage would far exceed those occurring normally, and if the issue were merely naturally occurring weeds, neither the servants' question nor the master's conclusion would have arisen.

The last two items in the list above are not troubling either. That day laborers would be hired to do the harvest is what one would expect, as in the parable of the Vineyard Workers (Matt 20:1-16; cf. 9:38; Jas 5:4). That the tares are bundled for burning is not strange, although Dalman reported a variety of practices in modern Palestine for dealing with the weeds.[102] The parable assumes that they are tied in bundles to be used as fuel, as were other scraps of agricultural waste in ancient Palestine.[103]

Somewhat more difficult — unless one is a Palestinian wheat farmer — is the decision whether the tares could be distinguished easily and could be removed early in the growing process. Most grant that tares and wheat are almost indistinguishable at the early stage,[104] which is understandable if only a millimeter or two difference in the size of the blades of the leaves exists (see above, p. 198). As far as can be determined, normal practice would be to weed early as much as possible, and this is implied in the servants' question. The decision not to weed can only be based on the large number of tares and the fact that at this stage of growth the roots of the two would have become entangled. Even at an early stage, tares sufficient in number to be recognized as the work of an enemy would not be easily removed without damage to the wheat.

The charge then that the parable is an unrealistic cover for the allegory portrayed cannot be sustained. The circumstances of the parable are not commonplace, but they fit the first-century context.[105]

4. *Is this a parable about the mixed character of the church, as is often assumed?*[106] Is it about the mixed nature of the individual, which inherently includes both good and evil? Decision here is crucial, a parting of the ways concerning whether one is hearing Jesus' preaching to Israel or Matthew's reformulation/creation to address his own community. One must decide whether this parable is a reasonable report of part of Jesus' preaching to Israel, his *prophecy* of a future situation in the church (the implicit assumption of the church fathers), or Matthew's coded message reflecting the situation of his community, if indeed he was writing for *a* community. Great care is needed to read stereoscopically. The Evangelists seek to tell us about Jesus, but they certainly also seek to influence the church.

Of the many who affirm that the parable is about the mixed character of the church, J. Roloff is typical in arguing that virtually everything in Matthew tells about his community. The disciples are transparent for Matthew's community, and the parables are the most immediate manifestation of Matthew's churchly self-understanding. In the parables Matthew makes his community clear, what it is, from where it comes, and what God expects of it.[107] This approach is implicit in numerous studies, but implicit as well is either that Jesus was prophesying about the church or that the parable has been reformulated or created by Matthew. That the parable is a prophecy about the church's future is not impossible, but it is not likely. Nothing in the text suggests Jesus was prophesying or had the church in mind, and consequently most who think the parable is about the church derive this from Matthew.

Those who view the parable as describing the church as a mixed community of good and evil usually argue that it discourages a judgmental attitude and any attempt to root out evil in the church and urges patience until God judges at the end. With this approach Matthew is understood as rejecting any attempt to attain a pure church. D. Patte goes so far as to say a person cannot be a disciple so long as one's vocation is seen as the negative vocation of fighting evil.[108] Some think the message is directed to leaders in the Matthean community to warn against their taking matters in their own hands to deal with dissident members.[109] The parable then would advocate patience and tolerance of evil in the community.

Support for this approach — in addition to the fact that the church has always been a mixture of good and evil — is evidenced in passages that reject judging (5:21-22; 7:1-5), other texts assuming the presence of good and evil together (13:47-48; 22:10), and the fact that in the parable the weeds are sown in an already existing field of good seed (evil is sown in the community, not the community into an evil world).

While initially attractive and accepted by many, problems with this view arise rather quickly. The fact that bad seed was sowed after the good seed raises questions about parable chronology (see below, pp. 213-14) but points at most to negative responses to Jesus' message, not necessarily to the church. The idea of passivity with regard to evil does not sit well either logically or in the context of Matthew. U. Luz and H. Hendrickx both are constrained to argue against the passivity they see in Matthew's parable, Hendrickx even arguing that we must "attack the tares."[110] While Matthew's Gospel prohibits judging, it also creates tension because other texts insist that the differences between good and evil plants/people *can* be recognized and that false prophets — deceptive as they may be — can be recognized (7:15-20; 12:33-37; 15:13-14; cf. 3:7-12). That Matthew would suggest passivity toward evil is difficult to conceive. Twice he reports Jesus' radical teaching that the part of the body causing sin should be cut off (5:29-30; 18:8-9). Also, Matthew records directions for dealing with sin in the community which include both confrontation and excommunication (18:15-17). If one notices as well Matthew's warnings of judgment for all (including Christians), he is anything but passive in confronting evil.[111] The other obvious fact is that the interpretation of the parable says explicitly "the field is the world" (13:38), not the church, a fact ignored by those who think Matthew was referring to his mixed community.[112] Despite the popularity of the mixed church view, it is better to conclude as Davies and Allison that the parable and its interpretation do not address a situation in Matthew's community — neither opposition to its gospel nor the character of its members. Neither idea is expounded in the interpretation, surely the place Matthew would make his point. They rightly advise that "instead of conjuring up some hypothetical Matthean *Sitz im Leben* the text itself and its literary context should be the key to interpretation."[113] The parable is not about the mixed character of the church but about the fact that the righteous and sinners coexist in the world — even when the kingdom is present.[114] The church is indeed of mixed character, tragically so, but that is not what Matthew's parable is about.

The suggestion that the parable or its interpretation is about the mixture of good and evil in the individual has nothing in its favor.[115] That humans have both good and evil impulses is beyond doubt, but neither Jesus nor Matthew is dealing with that subject here. That one should not root out evil in one's own being makes no sense at all.

5. *Does this parable reflect a conflict between Matthew's church and the synagogue?* Jack Kingsbury views the servants' question about rooting out the tares (v. 28) as implying that Matthew's church is seriously occupied with the matter of forcing a formal and irrevocable separation between itself and the rest of Judaism. The parable then cautions against such a separation so as not to harm the Christian mission.[116] To make this work Kingsbury understands the field as Israel and the interpretation as a separate, independent narrative which is not really an explanation of the parable.

Decision on the relation of Matthew's community and the synagogue is notoriously difficult, and whether hints of that conflict are evident in this parable is difficult to determine. Two items speak in favor of such a conclusion. The primary source material above shows that at least from the time of Wis 4:3 (150 B.C.) the ungodly were viewed as illegitimate seedlings and that later rabbinic materials contrast Israel as wheat with other nations as weeds.[117] One can easily imagine debates between Jews and Christians over who constituted the real wheat. More substantive is the parallel with Matt 15:12-14, which implies that the Pharisees may be illegitimate plants that the Father will uproot *(ekrizoun),* the same word as in 13:29, in both places a metaphor for God's judgment.[118]

The problem is that the parable and 15:12-14 do not make the same point. The parable commands the servants to let *(aphienai)* both wheat and tares grow together until harvest, and then the tares are gathered, not uprooted. In 15:12-14 the disciples are told to leave *(aphienai)* the Pharisees since they are blind guides. If the parable hints at the conflict between the church and Judaism, it suggests that the church not separate itself from the synagogue, whereas 15:12-14 would say the opposite.[119] I cannot exclude the possibility that the church's conflict with Judaism is addressed, but I find little to commend it.

6. *Does this parable have anything to do with Jesus' stance of non-retaliation or with his association with toll collectors and sinners? Who or what is indicated by the seed sown by the enemy?* Pheme Perkins suggests the parable promotes non-retaliation,[120] but little in the parable suggests that this is the intent, and she must presume that the owner knows the identity of his enemy. More frequent is the view that this parable is Jesus' apologetic for gathering a mixed community of the righteous and those deemed not righteous.[121] Objections could have come from Jewish expectations (Pharisaic or Essene) that the Messiah would gather a pure community, from circles influenced by John the Baptist, or from among Jesus' own disciples. This approach emphasizes Jesus' open and conditionless invitation, his "more tolerant, humane view of the kingdom,"[122] and his rejection of separatism. Jesus' ministry is the time for sowing, for proclamation, with no attempt to remove the unholy, according to this argument.

Certainly Jesus' association with tax collectors and sinners brought criticism, and clearly both good and bad existed among Jesus' disciples. Judas and disciples who were temporary followers come to mind quickly. The disciples' eagerness to condemn is obvious as well.[123] But while such criticism may be related to the parable (see the next section), the parable is not intended to defend Jesus' gathering toll collectors and sinners. Jesus would not refer to those he viewed as legitimate followers as seed sown by the enemy. To call them "weeds" is the attitude of the Pharisees or other religious purists. Nor does the parable suggest that only at judgment will it be revealed who actually is among the weeds. The weeds are obvious as weeds; only their removal is suspended till judgment day.

A further difficulty with this approach is that it one-sidedly views Jesus as inviting people into his circle but making no demands on them. Jesus' invitation was open, but far from conditionless. The demands on the rich young ruler (Matt 19:16-22/Mark 10:17-22/Luke 18:18-23), the classic statements on discipleship (Matt 16:24-26/Mark 8:34-37/Luke 9:23-25), and the Sermon on the Mount quickly refute any such idea.

7. *To what question does the parable provide an answer?* Every explanation of a parable assumes that there is an implied question to which the parable is a response. If the implied question to which Jesus was responding can be determined, then the path to interpretation is much easier. Determination of the implied question is an issue of fit between the facts of the parable and what can be demonstrated about the context of Jesus within Judaism. I have rejected above the possibility that the implied question behind this parable is either:

What should the church do about evil people in its own body?
Should the church separate from the synagogue?

or

Why does Jesus have impure people in his community?

Like the parables of the Mustard Seed and the Leaven, this parable deals with the mystery of the kingdom, the fact that the kingdom is present, but in an unexpected way. The implicit question behind all three parables is "Can the work of Jesus and his small group really be the kingdom when so much else is still wrong?"[124] More precisely, in this parable the question is "How can this be the kingdom if evil is still present?" Contained in this question are several others: Why have many in Israel rejected Jesus' message (which the Sower also addressed)? Why are the Romans still here? Why is separation of the righteous from the unrighteous not happening? Why is judgment not occurring?

The expectation that the Messiah would separate the wheat from the chaff to establish a pure community is beyond question. People expected that when the Messiah comes the Romans — and all other enemies — will go.[125] John the Baptist expected the Messiah to bring judgment, and when that did not happen he sent messengers to ask Jesus if he were indeed "the coming one" (Matt 3:10-12; 11:3). Possibly most instructive is *Pss. Sol.* 17:21-32 (see above, p. 193), which expects the Messiah to purge Jerusalem of Gentiles, to drive out sinners, to gather a holy people, and to be intolerant of the unrighteous. Zealots, Pharisees, and the Qumran community would all have nodded in agreement. None of these messianic acts was happening in Jesus' ministry, yet he was proclaiming the presence of the kingdom. The parable fits well as a response to questions about how the kingdom could be present if none of the expectations were happening. The parable is, then, directed at doubt arising from Jesus' failure to purge Israel and create a pure community.[126]

8. *Does "Sir" (v. 27), kyrie, which can also be translated as "Lord" or "master," have christological significance?* Parables always present the problem of determining the significance, if any, of the details, and particularly this is true of this parable. Why are some items assigned theological significance and not others? Why does no one make anything of the fact that the enemy is "a man" or that he goes away (vv. 25 and 28)? If christological significance is assigned to *kyrie,* is that merely an attempt to milk as much theology from the story as possible? The important point in interpretation is not the details, but how the analogy works.

Several people argue that *kyrie* (v. 27) would have been read as a christological title, especially because *kyrios* and *oikodespotēs* (which is used of the master in 13:27) are used of Jesus in 10:24-25.[127] J. Kingsbury goes so far as to say that vv. 27-28a "permit Jesus the exalted Kyrios who lives in the circle of his followers . . . to enter into conversation with them."[128] That Matthew knew and valued *kyrios* as a christological title may be assumed, but on the other hand, an explicit christological use of the title is not frequent in Matthew (only 7:21-22; 12:8; 21:3; 24:42; 25:37, 44).[129] When Christian scholars see *kyrie*, they think "Lord" and ignore the obvious fact that this was also the polite form of address for any man. Its use as the correct address to Pilate (27:63) would not cause anyone to think christologically. Similarly, it is the appropriate address of slaves to their masters and almost the only suitable expression that could be used in the parable.[130] Since Matthew makes nothing of either *kyrios* or the servants in the interpretation, neither should we.[131] One wonders if assigning christological significance to *kyrie* in passages like this is not something similar to an illegitimate totality transfer.[132]

9. *Do the parable and its interpretation stem originally from Jesus, or is one or both of them a creation of Matthew or his tradition?* This is in some ways the most important and most difficult question. Underlying this question are the debates on the relation of parable and allegory and methodological assumptions about Gospel studies. It is obvious that some NT scholars do not like this parable. A sizable group rejects both parable and interpretation.[133] A larger group argues that the parable is from Jesus but the interpretation is Matthean.[134] Relatively few academics argue the interpretation is from Jesus. Those who reject the parable do so because they think it is Matthean in character, addresses the problem of a mixed community, is unrealistic and allegorical, and does not fit well with the ministry of Jesus.[135] We have already addressed most of these issues and see no reason to think that the parable does not derive from Jesus. On the contrary, it fits easily in the context of his ministry and conveys important teaching about the kingdom.

The reasons the interpretation is rejected include:

Disdain for allegory is often associated with the assumption that Jesus did not explain his parables or that parables by nature do not need explanation.[136]

The interpretation is believed to contain expressions Jesus could not have used: *kosmos* with the meaning "world," "the evil one" as a designation for the devil, "kingdom" without qualification, "sons of the kingdom" to designate true citizens of the kingdom (in 8:12 it is used of Jews excluded from the kingdom), and "the kingdom of the Son of Man." Further Jeremias listed thirty-seven Matthean linguistic characteristics in the interpretation. Jeremias's work has been so influential that many have just adapted his work without analysis.[137]

Some scholars downplay or reject the judgment motif.[138]

The interpretation views the field as the world, evidencing a universal perspective similar to the church, whereas Jesus confined his attention to Israel (10:5-6).[139]

The interpretation shifts the focus by omitting what most feel is the climax of the parable, the command to let both wheat and weeds grow together (v. 30), and by focusing on judgment, a favorite Matthean theme.

Especially the last item, the interpretation's shift in focus, makes the case against the interpretation both reasonable and attractive. While the rejection of the authenticity of the interpretation is a given for some, the issues deserve a fresh hearing. The case is not as impressive as usually assumed. Is it possible that the interpretation also gives us the voice of Jesus?

Hopefully we have begun to move beyond Jülicher's influence and disdain for allegory. We have seen and will continue to see that multiple correspondences between image and reality are a feature of parables generally. In order to work, analogies require correspondence between image and reality, but the correspondences are not the focus and may not be exact. Furthermore, Jülicher was wrong. Parables usually do require explanation, unless they are riddles, which is certainly not the case with most of Jesus' parables. OT and rabbinic parables nearly always have explanations or detailed interpretations (see pp. 38-59 above). There is no self-interpreting literature. Detailed allegorical interpretations are evident in apocalyptic literature, in rabbinic material, and in the *Shepherd* of Hermas.[140]

With regard to expressions Jesus could not have used, we should remind ourselves that we do not have methods that allow us to recover the *ipsissima verba* of Jesus. The complaints concerning expressions Jesus could not have used imply that it is the *ipsissima verba* that we seek and hear in most sayings. Rather, *all of Jesus' sayings have been translated and shaped by the tradition and the Evangelists*. The issue is not "Would Jesus have used such an expression?" but "Do these Greek words convey the message, the communicative intent, of Jesus?" Those concerned over *kosmos* with the meaning "world" have been influenced by G. Dalman, who doubted that the Aramaic word 'ālam (or 'ôlām) was used for "world" in pre-Christian times or by Jesus (except in Matt 16:26/Mark 8:36/Luke 9:25).[141] But how does Dalman or anyone else know what Aramaic word lies behind *kosmos* in the Gospel sayings? Jesus could have just as easily used 'ar'ā' (the Aramaic equivalent of Hebrew 'ereṣ, the word for "earth" or "land").[142]

The recoil against the expressions involving the kingdom is pedantic, especially the anxiety about the use of "kingdom" without qualification. Such an abbreviation would be quite natural for Jesus or Matthew, but, if by Matthew, such a shortening would neither distort the meaning nor demonstrate the origin of the interpretation.[143] The same is true with regard to use of "the evil one" for the devil. Such a use cannot be excluded for Jesus and, if it is Matthean, could as easily be a legitimate paraphrase of a statement of Jesus as something originating with Matthew.

More influential has been Jeremias's list of thirty-seven Matthean linguistic characteristics.[144] But, characteristics of style do *not* necessarily indicate origin. They can and do show the Evangelist's hand in shaping and emphasizing certain features. *If* Jeremias's list were valid, it would mean at least that Matthew had thoroughly rewritten the interpretation, which would be no surprise. As we have already seen with Jeremias's lists, however, the facts are sometimes not as he presents them. M. de Goedt critiques the list and reduces the number of Matthean characteristics from thirty-seven to seven.[145] I. Jones, in a bit of overkill, reduces the number to only two.[146] Obviously what counts as a Matthean characteristic requires careful analysis, and in the end Jeremias's list is not that impressive. For example, he describes *hoi ochloi* ("the crowds") as a Matthean characteristic,[147] but while thirty of Matthew's forty-eight occurrences of *ochlos* are plural and only one of Mark's thirty-six, of Luke's forty-one occurrences sixteen are also plural. Why is Matthew's use of this word seen as a determining characteristic? Why is *apheis* ("having left," v. 36) listed as a Matthean characteristic when the other Evangelists use the term almost as much (47 occurrences in Matthew, 37 in Mark, 32 in Luke)?[148] If an expression occurs only two or three times, all in Matthew, does that make it a Matthean characteristic, as Jeremias claims?[149] Most of Jeremias's items occur in the narrative introduction (vv. 36-37), where one would expect Mattheanisms, and in vv. 40-43, where several words are drawn from the OT and apocalyptic traditions on judgment. Without question, the interpretation — like the rest of Matthew — evidences Matthean stylistic traits and themes, but that is to be expected and does not show anything about the origin of the material. Matthew has Mattheanisms.

Discussions of stylistic and thematic features rarely ask about their origin. From where did Matthew develop the tendencies he had? How much did Jesus' teaching and traditions about Jesus' teaching influence Matthew's preferences? Matthew has an obvious focus on judgment and uses expressions occurring rarely outside his Gospel such as "consummation of the age" (elsewhere only at Heb 9:26) and "weeping and gnashing of teeth" (elsewhere only at Luke 13:28). But judgment is certainly a key factor in Jesus' preaching, and such expressions (or very similar ones) are found also in apocalyptic and other Jewish writings.[150] In fact, several features of the parable are easily paralleled: the enemy as the evil one,[151] judgment as a harvest or threshing,[152] judgment as fire or a furnace,[153] angels as the agents of judgment,[154] and light as the reward of the righteous.[155] The more the interpretation conforms to apocalyptic expectations of judgment and reward the more difficult it is merely to assign this material to Matthew. Like John the Baptist, Jesus used apocalyptic ideas to express his gospel of the kingdom (although his message differed from John's).[156] Certainly the interpretation is shaped by Matthew, but the content of the interpretation is no ground for denying the interpretation to Jesus.

Nor may we legitimately object to the judgment motif in the parable's interpretation. Our society may wish to ignore judgment, but it is a central feature of Jesus' teaching in all strata of the tradition.[157] Similar descriptions of judgment appear in the OT and in other Jewish writings. How judgment should be understood in actual terms needs careful discussion, for the intent of the metaphorical and apocalyptic language of Scripture is quite different from the assumptions of popular Christianity. Still judgment is an essential aspect of Jesus' agenda for the restoration of Israel and in his understanding of human responsibility. Without judgment there is no need for salvation.

The interpretation's focus on the field as the world at first glance seems contrary to Jesus' limitation of his ministry to Israel. Jesus did not sow the gospel in the world, but only in Palestine.[158] It is quite possible that Jesus' parable used the ambiguous Aramaic word 'ar'ā' (which could mean either "earth" or "land")[159] and that Matthew or the tradition has broadened the focus with the translation "world" *(kosmos)*. On the other hand, apocalyptic views of judgment are not limited to Israel but take in all humanity.[160] Further, Jesus' model prayer is concerned that the will of the Father is done on earth, not just in Palestine (Matt 6:10), the temptation of Jesus concerns all the kingdoms of the world (Matt 4:8/Luke 4:5), the Beatitude speaks of inheriting the earth (Matt 5:5), and the disciples are the light of the world (gē, Matt 5:14). The use of "world" is less important than other issues and is no trump card excluding the interpretation.

Much more significant is the fact that the interpretation omits the climax of the parable (the command to let both weeds and wheat grow together) and focuses on final judgment brought by the Son of Man. This shift parallels the shift in audience from the parable addressed to the crowds to the interpretation being a response to the disciples' request. While this shift could result entirely from Matthew, several facts should be considered.

First, the separation of the interpretation from the parable follows an apocalyptic pattern in which a dream, vision, or parable is followed by a request for explanation or other instruction and then by the interpretation.[161] The separation of the interpretation from the parable of the Weeds may be modeled on and parallel to the parable of the Sower and its interpretation, but this pattern is typical with interpretations.[162] Here the intervening material consists of a statement about the parables being a form of hidden revelation, which is validated by the quotation of Ps 78:2 (Matt 13:34-35)[163] and by the disciples' request for explanation (v. 36). More difficult to answer is why of all the parables in the Synoptic tradition only this parable, the parable of the Sower, and the Net receive detailed interpretations. If the interpretation of these three is not related to the reasons why Jesus spoke in parables, I do not have an answer.

Second, the interpretation, while shifting the focus, offers precisely the information required. Virtually every explanation equates Jesus (or God) with the sower and the enemy with the evil one and assumes that this is a parable dealing with the judgment of the righteous and the evil. As Jülicher pointed out, even without the interpretation the parable would be interpreted this way.[164] Jeremias, though he thinks the interpretation is secondary, even says that it coheres with Jesus' intent.[165]

Both these first two points show that the attempt to treat the interpretation in isolation from the parable is misguided.[166] The interpretation is closely tied to the parable, but it is more than a mere explanation. The interpretation *goes significantly beyond* the parable and places much heavier focus on judgment.[167]

Third, vv. 37-39 specify only the features needed to describe the judgment scene, the primary concern in vv. 40-43. This description of judgment with the Son of Man sending his angels to separate the righteous from the evil is essentially the same picture given in Matt 24:30-31 *and Mark 13:26-27*. It is not merely a Matthean construct. Also, if the interpretation were from the church, one might expect that the servants, sleep, and the defeat of the enemy would receive attention.[168]

As Jülicher and Fiebig both argued long ago, the difference between the parable and the interpretation is not that great.[169] The parable prohibits division before the end (vv. 29-30) while the interpretation describes the division at the end *and* the fate of each group, how bad it is for the evil and how good for the righteous.[170] That Jesus might emphasize one aspect with the crowds and another with his disciples is plausible.[171] The way the material is framed by Matthew allows the two points to be communicated effectively. The implicit commentary provided by the surrounding parables makes the significance of the prohibition of division clear, whereas the parables following the interpretation underline the judgment motif and preparation for it.

Therefore, granted the shaping by Matthew, I think we hear the voice of Jesus in both the parable and its interpretation. The parable fits with his proclamation of the mystery of the kingdom, and the interpretation focuses more intently on the judgment motif and conforms generally with Jewish apocalyptic expectations.

10. What is the relation of the kingdom of heaven (v. 24), the world (v. 38), the kingdom of the Son of Man (v. 41), and the kingdom of the Father (v. 43)? Is "the kingdom of the Son of Man" a reference to the church? Does this parable tell us of the relation of the kingdom, the church, and the world? For some, this parable distinguishes the kingdom of the Son of Man from the kingdom of the Father, the former referring to the church or the world, the earthly kingdom of the Son of Man, and the latter to the end-time reign of God.[172] The distinction of the kingdom of the Son of Man and the kingdom of the Father would fit with Paul's idea of Christ reigning until the last enemy is nullified and then all (including Christ) being subjected to the Father (1 Cor 15:25, 28). "The kingdom of the Son of Man" is not, however, a reference to the church. This has no basis unless one can demonstrate that the parable is directed against the mixed nature of the church, which I have argued against.[173] The church is not the subject. Nor is the kingdom of the Son of Man the world. The world was there before the kingdom and is the arena into which the kingdom comes, but it is not the kingdom. Still, the parable makes an implicit claim for the authority of the Son of Man over the world.

The kingdom of heaven in 13:24 is apparently identical to the kingdom of the Son of Man in 13:41,[174] but the relation of the kingdom of the Son of Man and the kingdom of the Father is not obvious. For some, no distinction is intended.[175] Surely no hard lines should be drawn, for the Son of Man is the Father's agent and the kingdom of the Son of Man will become the kingdom of the Father. Still, *this* passage seems to make a distinction between the two. If the parable is about the presence of the kingdom in the midst of an evil world, the kingdom of the Son of Man is the kingdom that the Son of Man has brought as an incomplete kingdom, a proleptic kingdom which does not yet obliterate evil. This kingdom remains incomplete until the consummation when evil will be removed.[176] Note that both "all offenses" (neuter) and "all those doing lawlessness" (masculine/generic) are removed. The completed kingdom devoid of evil is the kingdom of the Father. This understanding of the kingdom of the Father as the consummation of all things is paralleled in Matt 26:29 ("I will not drink . . . until . . . when I drink it with you new in the kingdom of my Father") and Matt 6:10/Luke 11:2 ("Let your kingdom come"; cf. 1 Cor 15:28).[177]

11. What does the parable teach? While the parable may have implications for patience or serve as a warning, its primary teaching is that the kingdom is present despite the presence of evil *and* that evil will be dealt with at the judgment.[178] The focus is the nature of the kingdom, and implications for human conduct are secondary. The use of the aorist passive "The kingdom *has become* like . . ." is no accident. The kingdom has arrived and is like a field with both wheat and weeds which will one day be separated. It is not merely like a man sowing good seed, but like the whole process described in the parable from sowing to separation. The parable is not a complete picture of the kingdom; no parable is. But it does emphasize the presence of the kingdom and the future judgment.

The sowing and seed metaphors are not always used the same way. The parable of the Sower interprets the seed as the word and the people who hear the word. In the parable of the Growing Seed the seed seems to be the kingdom itself. In the parable of the Wheat and the Weeds both good and bad seeds refer to people. With all three parables, however, sowing is a metaphor for God's sowing Israel at the end time. It is a metaphor for God fulfilling his promises to have a kingdom and a righteous people.[179] All three parables are vignettes of God's sowing that is taking place in the ministry of Jesus.

This parable and that of the Net describe the kingdom as a sifting process,[180] but both describe this sifting as occurring at the consummation of the age, not at the present. The Wheat and the Weeds and its interpretation focus equally on the present and the end-time sifting. The implications of the parable are significant. Jesus presented a crisis to Israel with his warning of judgment, but it is a *delayed* judgment. Unlike the message of John the Baptist, Jesus' message holds judgment back, even while assuring that it is certain. This is verified by the parable of the Fig Tree (Luke 13:6-9).[181] The judgment theme cannot be minimized in Jesus' teaching. Even in the parable — to say nothing of the interpretation — the rule of end stress would require that emphasis is given to the theme of judgment.[182] Accordingly, this is a two-pronged parable, part depicting the kingdom as present in the midst of an evil world and part emphasizing the separation of evil from the righteous at judgment.[183] Legitimate subsidiary points of the parable's teaching may be lifted out with care. The concern — even in this parable where many points are identified — is how the analogy works. The identifications in vv. 37-39 give one the equipment to understand the analogy, but details which the parable does not emphasize should not be pushed. The servants do not "stand for" the church or church leaders,[184] and sleep is not a negative metaphor.[185] We can no more draw such conclusions than decide that God needs to be told about human sin because in the parable of the Unforgiving Servant (Matt 18:31) the fellow-servants tell the master of their colleague's lack of forgiveness.

More difficult is the task of determining how much the chronology of the parable fits the chronology of reality. Does the analogy focus on evil in the world generally (cf. 5:45) or specifically on something new, the emergence of evil people after the sowing of the sons of the kingdom? Parables do not necessarily conform to the chronology of the reality they depict. For example, God does not turn to the poor only after the wealthy have refused his offer, as a strict chronology of Luke's parable of the Banquet would suggest.[186] That bad seed is sown after the good in the parable could point to the rejection of Jesus' message, but this does not fit easily with the idea of sowing.[187] In my estimation the parable does not care about chronology. Rather, it makes the point that evil is still present and active even though the kingdom has arrived. Alongside the power of the kingdom another power, an illegitimate power, is at work. The action of "the enemy" is a prominent feature of Jesus' ministry,[188] particularly in this parable and that of the Sower, but no specific activity of the enemy is referred to with his sowing. Both parables emphasize the victory of God's kingdom, but also unbelief, failure, and opposition. The parable of the Sower focuses primarily on human responsibility for failure, whereas this parable blames the enemy, the devil.[189] Other parts of the parable are irrelevant for interpretation. Nothing should be made of the fact that the enemy is called a man (a favorite Matthean word) nor that the enemy goes away. The parable does not seek to defeat the enemy. These features have no function in the analogy.

The parable does not teach passivity toward evil or non-retaliation.[190] It answers the question "How can this be the kingdom if evil is present?" not "What shall we do about evil?" By excluding any idea that evil will be removed before judgment it does exclude any hint of zealot activity for Jesus or his disciples. It also provides a worldview that accounts for and is not surprised at the presence of evil. With the focus on judgment separating out offenses and those doing lawlessness from the righteous the parable also serves as a warning for all its readers. The parable conveys that judgment belongs to God and his agents, not to humans.[191]

Adapting the Parable

This parable has perhaps been misused more than any other because of the belief that it dealt with the mixture of good and evil in the church, but this is not a parable about church discipline. The parable has been distorted so that a passivity with regard to right living resulted. In light of the teaching of Jesus any thought of passivity toward evil or assertion that the church does not need to be a pure community is bizarre. Granted the difficulty of rooting out evil without becoming evil or making huge mistakes, such ideas are heresy. One cannot imagine legitimately being Christian and taking a passive approach to racism, adultery, and other such evils, whether in the church or in society.

The present church needs to make the same two points the parable teaches. First, the kingdom is present, even though judgment is not taking place, because of the ministry of Jesus and the work of the Spirit. The presence of evil is no evidence that the kingdom is not at work. Second, while this is not the time for judgment, judgment will certainly come. The kingdom will cause a sifting, a separation of good and evil. Obviously the statements on judgment are neither merely descriptive nor vindictive; rather, they provide a warning and seek to change behavior. The judgment saying in 13:43 is also an encouragement, a promise of future blessing.

The parable contributes to discussions of theodicy and helps address our consternation that evil still is at work, that life is not fair, even though Christ and his kingdom have come. God is not the only one at work, and *not all actions in this world can be attributed to God.* God often gets blamed for every event that occurs, but he is not the cause of every event. Evil happens that can only be identified as the work of an enemy. Accordingly, this parable should slow down an overemphasis on the sovereignty of God or a naïveté that attributes every event to God's manipulation.

The parable is also a reminder that Christians should be neither surprised at nor unaware of the fact that evil is active at the same time that God's reign is. *The kingdom comes with limitless grace in the midst of an evil world.* The new age has dawned in the midst of the old, but the old is not removed. The issue is at bottom one of identity. From which reality will we take our identity, the evil of the old age or the righteousness of God's new age? If we take our identity from the kingdom of limitless grace, how will that identity be lived out? God is still sowing a people, and we are called to respond. The challenge "Let the one who has ears hear" in v. 43 is a call for discernment, decision, and right living.

Questions about how we should respond to evil are spawned by the parable, but not addressed. Other texts must be brought in for that discussion, but clearly any idea of doing God's work of judging or any thought that we will obliterate evil are set aside by the parable. The biblical message always leaves us dealing with tension. We cannot be tolerant of evil, but the destruction of all evil is not our task. We must stop being evil, and we must stop evil from destroying, but how can we stop evil without becoming evil in the process? That may well be *the* human question.

For Further Reading

George Beasley-Murray, *Jesus and the Kingdom of God* (Grand Rapids: Eerdmans, 1986), pp. 132-35.

W. D. Davies and Dale C. Allison, *A Critical and Exegetical Commentary on the*

Gospel According to Saint Matthew (ICC; Edinburgh: T. & T. Clark, 1991), 2:406-15, 426-33.

Joachim Jeremias, *The Parables of Jesus* (2d ed.; trans. S. H. Hooke; London: SCM, 1972), pp. 81-85, 224-27.

Ulrich Luz, *Matthew 8–20* (trans. James E. Crouch; Minneapolis: Fortress, 2001), 2:252-56, 267-74.

Ulrich Luz, "Vom Taumellolch im Weizenfeld," in *Vom Urchristentum zu Jesus* (ed. Hubert Frankemölle and Karl Kertelge; Freiburg im Breisgau: Herder, 1989), pp. 154-71.

Robert K. McIver, "The Parable of the Weeds among the Wheat (Matt 13:24-30, 36-43) and the Relationship between the Kingdom and the Church Portrayed in the Gospel of Matthew," *JBL* 114 (1995): 643-59.

THE MUSTARD SEED
(Matt 13:31-32; Mark 4:30-32; Luke 13:18-19)

Parable Type

Because of the use of the present tenses the Markan version of the Mustard Seed is usually labeled a similitude (referring to a recurring event, but Mark also uses the aorist subjunctive twice to refer to the seed's being sown). Luke's use of the aorist tense and Matthew's use of both present and aorist led some to designate their versions as a parable (a specific instance of a seed being sown).[192] *Tense is no ultimate guide* to the distinction between similitudes and parables, as a glance at the different tenses in the parables of the Treasure in the Field and of the Pearl shows. All three forms of the Mustard Seed are *similitudes*. None of the forms has a developed plot; instead each presents an analogy between the mustard seed and plant and the present and future kingdom.

Issues Requiring Attention[193]

1. What is the significance, if any, of the variations in wording in the four accounts?
2. Is there allegorical significance to any of the features?
3. Is there an allusion to one or more OT texts with the reference to birds dwelling in the mustard plant, and if so, what is the significance of the allusion?
4. What question is being addressed and what is the significance of the answer?

5. To what degree is focus placed on some length of time and growth or development and what is the relevance of the parable for thinking about eschatology?
6. Does this text teach universalism?

Helpful Primary Source Material

Canonical Material

- OT: Ps 104:12, 16-17; Ezek 17:22-23; 31:6; Dan. 4:10-12, 20-21
- NT: Matt 17:20/Luke 17:6

Early Jewish Writings

- 1QH 14.14-16: "[Their root] will sprout like a flo[wer of the field f]or ever, to make a shoot grow in branches of the everlasting plantation so that it covers all the wo[rld] with its shade, [and] its [crown] (reaches) up to the skie[s, and] its roots down to the abyss."
- 1QH 16.4-9: "I give [you] thanks, [Lord,] because you have set me . . . a plantation of cypresses and elms, together with cedars, for your glory. Trees of life in the secret source, hidden among all the trees at the water, which shall make a shoot grow in the everlasting plantation, to take root before they grow. . . . On the shoots of its leaves all [the anima]ls of the wood will feed, its trunk will be pasture for all who cross the path, and its leaves for all winged birds."

Greco-Roman Writings

- Seneca, *Epistlae Morales* 38 ("On Quiet Conversation") 2: See above, pp. 148-49.

Early Christian Writings

- *Gos. Thom.* 20: "The disciples said to Jesus: Tell us what the kingdom of heaven is like. He said to them: It is like a grain of mustard seed, smaller than all seeds. But when it falls on the earth which has been cultivated, it puts forth a great branch (and) becomes a shelter for (the) birds of heaven."

See also below under Cultural Information.

Comparison of the Accounts

The four accounts of this parable provide good illustrations of the Synoptic problem and the relation of *Gos. Thom.* to the Synoptics. The "status quo" explanation on this parable is that Mark and Q (represented by Luke) preserve two different traditions of the parable, that Matthew used both, and that *Gos. Thom.* 20 is probably secondary. It is,[194] but other explanations of the Synoptic relations are just as conceivable. Redactional tendencies of each Evangelist are evident. The major aspects of the relations include:

Placement: Matthew and Mark both place this parable in their collection of parables on the kingdom. Luke places it instead after the healing of the woman bound by Satan for eighteen years. Matthew and Luke both present this parable in tandem with the parable of the Leaven. Mark does not have the parable of the Leaven, and *Gos. Thom.* has the two parables, but not together (sayings 20 and 96) and has placed the Mustard Seed in a series of sayings explaining the kingdom and discipleship.

The introduction: Matthew stands alone with his "He placed another parable before them," the same introduction he used in 13:24 (cf. "another parable" at 13:33 and 21:33). Mark starts with "And he said," which he also used at 4:2, 11, 21, 24, 26 (cf. 4:13), and has a double question "How shall we liken the kingdom of God and with what shall we place it in a parable?" Luke, like Mark, has "he said" and the double question, but with slightly different words. In *Gos. Thom.* the disciples ask for a description of the kingdom, which is followed by "he said to them."

The sowing of the seed: Matt 13:31b and Luke 13:19 are identical except that Matthew has "kingdom of heaven" (Luke used "kingdom of God" in v. 18) and "sowed *(speirein)* in his field" (cf. 13:24, 27, 36, 38, 44), whereas Luke has "cast *(ballein)* into his garden." Outside Luke 13:19 "garden" *(kēpos)* occurs elsewhere in the NT only in John 18:1, 26; and 19:41 (twice). Unlike Mark, both Matthew and Luke mention a man doing the sowing. Mark has merely "as" instead of "is like" and "whenever it is sown upon the earth." Mark has emphasized the earth *(gē)* throughout his parables chapter (4:1, 5, 8, 20, 26, 28). The sowing is delayed in *Gos. Thom.*

Description of the seed: Matthew, Thomas, and Mark describe the mustard seed as "the smallest of all the seeds," to which Mark adds "upon the earth." Luke omits the description entirely.

The growth: Matthew has "when it has grown *(auxēthē)*, it becomes greater than all the vegetables and becomes a tree." Mark repeats "when it is sown," uses a different verb for growth *(anabainei)*, agrees with Matthew that it becomes greater than all vegetables, but instead of saying that it becomes a tree says that it makes large branches. Luke is simpler but is close to Matthew in saying "it grew and became a tree." In line with Mark, *Gos. Thom.* describes the sowing at this point ("when it falls on the earth which has been cultivated") and has "it puts forth a great branch."

The conclusion: Matthew and Luke are virtually identical in the final part of the parable. The differences are that only Matthew has "so that," "come," and "and." Mark uses "so that" like Matthew but says the birds are able to dwell under the shadow of the plant, whereas Matthew and Luke have the birds dwelling in its branches. *Gos. Thom.* says merely that the plant becomes a shelter for (the) birds of heaven.

Textual Features Worth Noting[195]

The double question introducing the parable in Mark and Luke is thoroughly Semitic. It appears already in Isa 40:18 (cf. 40:25; 46:5; Lam 2:13) and is used by Jesus in Luke 7:31. Introductory questions appear regularly with rabbinic parables,[196] but, as far as I can determine, the double introductory question is unusual, which suggests that Isa 40:18 is more important than interpreters have realized.[197]

Obviously this parable is a twin with the Leaven. Parable "twins" and triplets are a pedagogical device of Jesus and also appear in rabbinic literature.[198] Such groupings of parables occur already in Ezek 17:2-24 and 19:2-14. One should not assume that parable twins are necessarily identical. They may well be "fraternal" twins and make similar but not identical points.

Various "hooks" exist in Matthew's and Mark's sections on parables of the kingdom that would assist in both hearing and remembering. In Matthew note the repetition of "another parable" (vv. 24, 31, 33), "sow" (some form of *speirein*, vv. 3-4, 18-23, 24-26, 31, 37, 39), "field" (vv. 24, 27, 31, 36, 38, 44), "all" or "every" (some form of *pas*, vv. 19, 32, 34, 41, 44, 46, 47, 51, 52), "seed" (vv. 24, 27, 32, 37, 38). In Mark note the repetition of "and he said" (vv. 2, 21, 24, 26, 30; cf. vv. 13, 35), "earth" or "upon the earth" (vv. 1, 5, 8, 20, 26, 28, 31).

The ideas of hiddenness and revelation in Mark 4:21-22 prepare for and parallel the mustard seed and its growth.

Luke's arrangement is a surprise. His placement of these two parables after the healing of the woman bound by Satan (13:10-17) has no obvious explanation other than to provide an interpretation to emphasize that the kingdom is present and that the woman's healing and the implied defeat of Satan are evidence of this fact.

J. Liebenberg suggests that Luke's travel narrative has three discourse sections (9:51–13:21; 13:22–17:10; and 17:11–19:28), each with a healing narrative closely linked with subsequent discourse on the kingdom.[199]

Cultural Information

In both the Jewish and Greco-Roman world mustard seeds were proverbially known for their small size,[200] even though other seeds, such as the orchid or cypress, were known to be smaller. Those who measure such things report that the mustard seed is one millimeter in diameter and is so tiny it requires from 725 to 760 seeds to equal one gram (one twenty-eighth of an ounce).[201] Since we are dealing with a proverbial use, anxiety about issues of accuracy are out of bounds.[202] The words translated "smallest" *(mikroteron)* and "largest" *(meizon)* in Matthew and Mark actually are both comparative forms, but the comparative is often used for the superlative in NT Greek. Since the comparison is with "all the seeds," a superlative meaning seems required.[203]

Most identify the seed in question as black mustard *(Brassica nigra)*, although other varieties like white mustard are possible. This seed germinates within five days and grows quickly to a height of about ten feet and has large leaves, especially at its base.[204] Mark is more precise in referring to the plant as a vegetable *(lachanon);* it does not really become a tree.[205] Whether Matthew and Luke use language loosely,[206] use hyperbole intentionally, or use "tree" to allude to an OT text will have to be determined in analyzing the possibility of an OT allusion. Pliny viewed mustard as extremely beneficial to health, able to cure a long list of ailments.[207] Such facts are interesting, but for the meaning of the parable all characteristics of the mustard seed are irrelevant except that it grows so high from such a small seed.[208] Birds would have been attracted to the mustard plant because of both its shade and its seeds.

Repeatedly one reads that according to Jewish regulations mustard must be planted in fields and not in a garden so as not to violate the regulation against sowing a field with diverse kinds of seed (based on Lev 19:19). Evidence for this is erroneously drawn from *m. Kil'ayim* 3.1-2, which, however, gives regulations for a small garden bed only two feet square and that presumably would not apply to a larger garden.[209] From this erroneous assumption people have drawn dubious conclusions such as Luke having changed Mark's use of "earth" to "garden" to fit Hellenistic practices[210] or the farmer having violated laws against sowing diverse seeds in the same field, which serves as a symbol of Jesus associating with uncleanness.[211] Halakhic regulations have no relevance for this parable.[212]

It is doubtful, as some assume, that the analogy thinks of a single mustard seed being sown. Those who think that the form in Matthew and Luke is a parable about a specific instance (because of the aorist tenses) are inclined in this direction. However, this is a similitude and the concern is not for the number of seeds sown but for the difference between the small seed and the large plant.[213]

Explanation of the Parable

Options for Interpretation

Historically the church understood this parable most often as referring to the growth and development of the church or of the individual or to the progression of Jesus' life from birth to his burial and resurrection, which take place in a garden. The three approaches could be combined and the details allegorized. Jesus is either the seed or the sower who sows the gospel. If the church is in mind, the parable points to the triumph of Christianity over other religions. If the individual is in mind, it points to maturity of faith. In modern times both the Mustard Seed and the Leaven have been interpreted of the effect of Christianity on the broader society.[214]

From more recent studies other possibilities emerge.[215]

As expected, for C. H. Dodd the parable is a parable of growth so that the kingdom is compared to a harvest. Consequently, the kingdom is present and the birds are flocking to find shelter in response to Jesus.[216]

R. Funk reads the parable against the OT symbolism of the mighty cedar and argues that Jesus created a lighthearted burlesque and satire of all pride, especially Israel's. The kingdom then erupts from weakness and refuses to perpetuate itself by power.[217]

More frequently this parable is understood as a contrast of the apparent insignificance of Jesus' ministry to the resulting great kingdom it will bring[218] or as focusing on some combination of contrast, growth, and continuity between Jesus' ministry and the later glorious kingdom.[219] The certainty of the kingdom's coming is usually emphasized in either case.

Despite disagreement over details and over whether the focus is contrast or growth,[220] there is surprising agreement about the intent of the parable. Here, virtually unquestioned, we hear the voice of Jesus asserting a vital and central element of his eschatology, his understanding of what God was doing to set things right. Whatever else is debated, this parable pictures the presence of the kingdom in Jesus' own ministry, even if others do not recognize it, and Jesus' expectation of the certain full revelation of the kingdom to come. In Matthew and Mark the persons addressed by this parable are the crowds (13:34/4:33). Presumably the same is the case in Luke, but no specific indication is given. The point of the parable would have been effective both for adherents and opponents.

Decisions on the Issues

1. What is the significance, if any, of the variations in wording in the four accounts? Enormous energy has been expended on the relationship of the accounts but with little agreement on conclusions. Some think Mark's account is the earliest and best preserved,[221] others that Q is (usually as preserved by Luke with Matthew combining Mark and Q).[222] Some attempt to rewrite the original version of the parable based on Mark or the original version of Q, often with explanations of why each of the Evangelists edited as he did.[223] Little is gained from these discussions. I am not convinced of the existence of Q, but even if it did exist in some form, the procedure used in reconstructing or determining original forms is not trustworthy. Hypotheses on these matters cannot be demonstrated and often show more about the scholars' assumptions than anything about the tradition history. With some sayings of Jesus the facts seem clear enough to show that one account is earlier, but often the argument can go either way, as the disagreements on this parable show.[224] Especially if we take seriously the oral tradition, as we must,[225] such efforts are misguided. Surely, if any of Jesus' parables were told more than once — and not all were — the parables of the kingdom were. If there were multiple tellings of a parable, the attempt to find an original form is beside the point.

The differences among the accounts are interesting, but they — apart from the possible significance of the "tree" — do not constitute a difference in meaning. The smallness of the seed is mentioned in Mark and Matthew and assumed in Luke, and whether it is sown in a field, the earth, or a garden changes nothing in terms of the parable's intent. In the end there is not much significance to the variations in wording.

Commentators disagree as well on whether the parable of the Leaven was originally connected to the Mustard Seed.[226] Mark does not have the Leaven, and the two are separate in *Gos. Thom.*[227] Mark may have received this parable in a collection of seed parables, which could be a reason the Leaven is omitted. The two could have been joined at some stage of the tradition, or they could have been joined originally. Parabolic twins appear to have been used by Jesus, but that does not prove that these two were joined originally.

2. Is there allegorical significance to any of the features? A surprising amount of allegorical significance is assigned by scholars to the details of this parable. Three sources contribute to allegorical interpretation: the supposed connection to other parables with allegorical correspondences such as the Sower or the Wheat and the Weeds, the assumed allusion to OT imagery of birds in trees, and redaction-critical readings of the parable — that is, readings that assume that the situation of the Evangelist's community is mirrored in the wording. As a result, significance is assigned to details that rival any reading of the medieval church. The sowing of the seed in the "land" in Mark and Matthew is understood of Jesus' sowing the word in the people,[228] the birds in the tree are understood as Gentiles in the kingdom,[229] the large size of the tree is understood of the magnitude of the kingdom in Jesus' ministry or later at the parousia,[230] and the smallness/hiddenness theme in this parable and in the Leaven is understood as symbolic of the Q community's strategy of secrecy in missionizing (i.e., while traveling they had to remain hidden to avoid "wolves" — robbers or perhaps Roman soldiers).[231] None of this has much basis, apart from the possible OT allusions to birds and trees, which will be considered next.

At issue here is again how parables and similitudes function. This similitude does point to Jesus' ministry, but it does not depict specifically his preaching or any other aspect of his work. The concern of the similitude is to provide an analogy to the kingdom. That Matthew interpreted the sower in the Wheat and the Weeds as the Son of Man and the field as the world does not show that the man and the field here have the same meanings. While this seems attractive at first glance, such connections are not explicit, and I think they are unlikely. By extension this approach would mean that the woman in the parable of the Leaven was a symbol for Christ as well. Some draw this conclusion, but that does not seem to be Jesus' intent or the Evangelists'. The point is not that Jesus is like a man who sowed mustard seed or a woman who hid leaven but that the kingdom is like the *process* described. Jesus was not setting up allegories here. The Mustard Seed similitude gives an *analogy,* and it needs to be left as an analogy. The point of the analogy is this: unexpectedly as far as Jews were concerned, like a mustard seed God's kingdom starts as something insignificant but becomes something quite large. Yes, the mustard seed is analogous to Jesus' proclamation of the kingdom and the insignificant beginnings of his ministry, but it is allegorizing to label the details of the similitude.

3. Is there an allusion to one or more OT texts with the reference to birds nesting, and if so, what is the significance of the allusion? This is the most difficult question for this parable. Mention of birds dwelling in the mustard plant or especially the "tree" of Matthew and Luke, may allude to one of several OT texts: Ezek 17:23; 31:6; Dan 4:9, 18 (12, 21 in Theodotion and LXX); or Ps 104:12. A tree in whose shade animals or birds find shelter and sustenance is an OT image of a powerful kingdom sheltering nations.[232] Because of this, many conclude that the birds dwelling in the plant/tree point to the kingdom and the inclusion of the Gentiles.[233] Jeremias even argues that "dwell" *(kataskēnoun)* is an eschatological term,[234] but there is little evidence for this. The verb *kataskēnoun* is often translated "nest" but merely means "dwell."

Some deny that there is an OT allusion at all,[235] for the wording is not close enough to identify one text to which allusion is made. Ps 104:12 may be excluded, for although it has the words "the birds of heaven will dwell" *(ta peteina tou ouranou kataskēnōsei)*, it has no reference to a kingdom. It merely describes the provision available in water God supplies. Ezek 17:23 has specifically a cedar *(kedron)*, not a tree *(dendron)*, and the only words in common with the NT are "bird" (singular, unlike the Gospels) and "under its shadow" (which appears only in Mark 4:32). Ezek 31:6 has only "the birds of heaven" and "its branches" (which appears in Matt 13:32/Luke 13:19). Dan 4:9 and 18 have only "in" (as in Matthew and Luke) and "the birds of heaven." This is not much to base an allusion on, and it may be that J. Liebenberg is correct in arguing that the expression "birds of heaven" is just a way to refer to non-domesticated birds and that the intent is merely to show the large size of the plant.[236] If there is an allusion, it is not to a particular text but to the general idea of a sheltering tree symbolizing a kingdom.[237] That is probably the case, which is significant, but how much this imagery would have been recognized by Jesus' hearers or the Evangelists' readers is unclear. The Evangelists have certainly not made the connection clear. If there is an allusion to the kingdom with empire language, the political implications in relation to Rome and Jewish messianic expectation should not be ignored.[238] One can see how people jump to the conclusion that the birds represent the Gentiles, but that is going too far.[239]

If there is an allusion to this OT imagery, why not make the point with a parable about the cedars of Lebanon? R. Funk answered that question with his theory that Jesus' mustard plant is a caricature of the cedar image and was directed against human notions of pride and power.[240] While Jesus certainly rejected human ideas of pride and power, that is not his point with this parable, and any toying with the cedar imagery does not fit with the accounts of either Mark in particular with its reference to vegetables or the other Evangelists.[241] The mustard seed is not chosen to create a parody, but because of its small size.

At least part of the concern of the parable is the contrast between the small beginning and the large result.

In the end whether this parable alludes to the OT tree symbolism or not does not affect the meaning. Any idea of empire and provision for the nations is already inherent in the mention of the kingdom of God. The beginning of the parable is more important in this respect than the end, and if there is an allusion to the OT, it only strengthens what is already assumed.

4. What question is being addressed and what is the significance of the answer? Parables address questions, whether the questions are explicit or implicit. Nearly all agree that this similitude addresses the implicit question about the unimpressive and unexpected nature of the kingdom Jesus claimed was already present. Could what was happening with Jesus and his disciples really be the establishment of God's kingdom?[242] Was not the kingdom supposed to be a mighty display of God's defeat of evil and the removal of nations afflicting Israel?[243] Jesus' miracles are nice, but where is the rest of the story? Such questions would have gone through the mind of many of Jesus' hearers, whether friend or foe. The Mustard Seed similitude urges, possibly warns, that no one should be put off by what appears unimpressive. Like the tiny mustard seed which grows to a large plant, so the kingdom is present, even if hidden, unnoticed, or ignored, and its full revelation with its benefits will come.

Interpreters have often focused only on the contrast between the small seed and the large plant and have argued against other nuances.[244] They have done this to avoid any idea of the development of the kingdom, which is treated next, but more is involved with this similitude than merely contrast. Contrast is assumed, but it is not the point and is present only because of the nature of things at the beginning of Jesus' ministry. No one thought what was happening in Jesus' ministry was the totality of the kingdom. The question was whether his ministry had *anything* to do with the appearing of God's kingdom. Recent interpreters have opted for a both-and approach, arguing that this similitude is about both contrast and growth[245] or contrast and continuity[246] or the organic unity of the beginning and the end.[247] Growth is assumed and is not a bad thing,[248] but it is not the point either. The point is that what one sees with Jesus will lead to what one hopes for in the kingdom.[249] The focus is on the *organic unity* between Jesus' present ministry in Israel and the coming kingdom of God. The end, the end that everyone knows and longs for, is already in the beginning, the beginning inaugurated by Jesus and now at work.[250] What is at stake with this similitude is a restructuring of Jewish expectation. The kingdom, which has already begun with Jesus, does not come with a glorious bang and the defeat of Rome; rather, it comes unexpectedly, almost unnoticed. But all that is necessary is already there, and the end is present in the beginning. The focus on the birds dwelling in the branches or shade of the tree should not be lost, regardless of the origin of the idea. In the end the greatness and benefit of the kingdom will be a pleasant and wonderful reality.

The message is not merely about the certainty of the coming of the final kingdom, as important as that is.[251] Jews, disciples of Jesus or otherwise, did not need to be told the kingdom was coming. What they needed to know was that the future kingdom was already present in Jesus' teaching and work. God's longed-for kingdom has begun; it has started and will come to fulfillment. With that conviction come hope, confidence, and encouragement, but with it as well is implied a challenge to make sure that one is identified with this kingdom rather than seen as in opposition to it.

5. *To what degree is focus placed on some length of time and growth or development, and what is the relevance of the parable for thinking about eschatology?* The similitudes of the Mustard Seed and the Leaven imply an interval for the transition from the small beginning to the large result. This is often denied, but what else would words like "until" *(heōs hou)* in the parable of the Leaven mean (Matt 13:33/Luke 13:21)? Both parables presume an interval. Of what significance is this interval for theology? The point is frequently made that the kingdom does not grow,[252] and in one sense this claim is justified. If the kingdom is defined as God coming to be king in fulfillment of the OT promises, growth is obviously not pertinent. The kingdom — God's coming — needs no growth. Resistance to the idea of growth is understandable in light of the evolutionary ideas of the past, especially when the growth of the kingdom was associated with the growth of the church.[253]

On the other hand, the protests against growth and time do not derive from the text but are driven by the history of interpretation and theological concerns. These parables do stress growth and a power at work effecting God's purposes over a period of time, but they do not imply anything about the length of time. No implications should be sought in the fact that mustard is a fast-growing plant or that leavening takes place overnight. Description of the time is not the issue; rather, the parable points to the transformation of the plant and the flour from a stage of smallness or imperceptibility to a large result. The parables do not tell us whether the full growth and leavening are viewed as happening in Jesus' lifetime or over a much longer period.

Since an interval is assumed, some have thought that these parables deal with the delay of the parousia.[254] I see no basis for such a conclusion. The only delay the parables deal with is the unanticipated delay between the kingdom's inauguration and its full revelation. Parables should not be forced to answer questions they do not address. We may want to discuss those issues in light of the parables, but the parables do not supply the answers. What is clear concerning time, especially with the aorists in Matthew and Luke but for Mark as well, is that kingdom time has begun, even if it does not look like it, and will come to complete fulfillment.

6. Does this text teach universalism? This may seem an odd question, and it would not be raised apart from the fact that a few have argued that the similitudes of the Mustard Seed and the Leaven teach universal salvation.[255] This question is more pertinent for the Leaven, but both are lumped together in these discussions as teaching the same thing, so they will be treated together here. The suggestion of universalism is based on one word, the word "whole" in the description of the effect of the leaven. If the kingdom is like a woman hiding leaven in dough until the whole is leavened, what is the whole? Those arguing for universalism think "of the world" or "of humanity" should be supplied.[256] The similitude obviously is not explicit as to the referent with "whole," and people can only conclude that the passage teaches universalism by assuming their conclusion.[257] Nothing supports this view, and it is at odds with the rest of Jesus' teaching. "The whole" could refer to the totality of God's purpose for Israel[258] or for the people of God, or most likely merely to the full manifestation of the kingdom with no other entity in view. If so, the analogy says that the leaven is to the beginning of the kingdom as the completely fermented dough is to the full reality. That is all. Jesus was not comparing the kingdom to the world, and any thought of universalism is a gratuitous leap.

Adapting the Parable

This parable is less direct in its application than some because it is so focused on addressing the doubts of Jesus' contemporaries about the nature of his ministry. Its most important point is that the kingdom is indeed present in his ministry, and, if that is so, the obvious import and next question are about one's stance toward the kingdom. If the Mustard Seed similitude is an apologetic that the kingdom has come, it is also comfort and exhortation with regard to one's identity.[259] It is wrong to think this parable is about the spiritual growth of the individual; it is not wrong to understand the dynamic of God's working and apply it to the individual or to other circumstances. It is not only with Jesus' ministry that things may look small and insignificant and yet yield huge results. We see it later with the crucifixion, and this dynamic seems to be a regular practice of God (cf. 1 Cor 1:26-31). Like the cross, the Mustard Seed parable is a challenge to human perception and judgment about smallness and significance. We see through a glass darkly and too often fail to recognize a seed planted by God. We should expect and implement "mustard seed" thinking, neither disparaging insignificance nor doubting what God can do and does do with small beginnings. The christological implications of the parable should not be ignored. It is in Jesus' word and work that the kingdom has made its entrance.

For Further Reading

Nils Dahl, "The Parables of Growth" in *Jesus in the Memory of the Church* (Minneapolis: Augsburg, 1976), pp. 141-66.

Arland J. Hultgren, *The Parables of Jesus: A Commentary* (Grand Rapids: Eerdmans, 2000), pp. 392-403.

Adolf Jülicher, *Die Gleichnisreden Jesu* (2 vols.; Freiburg i. B.: Akademische Verlagsbuchhandlung von J. C. B. Mohr, 1888-89), 2:569-81.

Jack Dean Kingsbury, *The Parables of Jesus in Matthew 13: A Study in Redaction-Criticism* (Richmond: John Knox, 1969), pp. 84-88.

Jacobus Liebenberg, *The Language of the Kingdom and Jesus: Parable, Aphorism, and Metaphor in the Sayings Material Common to the Synoptic Tradition and the Gospel of Thomas* (BZNW 102; Berlin: Walter de Gruyter, 2001), pp. 276-349.

THE LEAVEN
(Matt 13:33; Luke 13:20-21)

Parable Type

This is a similitude despite the use of the aorist tense to describe the woman's actions. A developed plot, not tense, is the factor that distinguishes parables from similitudes. There is no developed plot here; rather we have an analogy based on a typical everyday occurrence. The aorist is used to point to the fact that the action inaugurating the kingdom has already occurred.

Issues Requiring Attention

1. What is the relation of this parable to that of the Mustard Seed and what relevance does this relation have for interpretation?
2. Is leaven always a negative symbol?
3. Is there allegorical significance to any of the features?
4. Is there an allusion to Gen 18:6, and if so, what is its significance?

5. What question is being addressed and what is the significance of the answer?
6. To what degree is focus placed on some length of time and growth or development, and what is the relevance of the parable for thinking about eschatology?
7. Does this text teach universalism?

Helpful Primary Source Material

Canonical Material

- OT: Gen 18:6; Exod 12:15-20; 13:3-7; 23:15, 18; 34:25; Lev 2:11; 6:17 (Hebrew 6:10); 7:13-14; Num 28:16-25; Deut 16:2-8; Amos 4:5
- NT: Matt 16:6, 11-12/Mark 8:15/Luke 12:1; 1 Cor 5:6-8; Gal 5:9

Early Jewish Writings

- Philo, *QE* 1.15 (on Exod 12:8): "But as for the deeper meaning, this is worth noting, (namely) that that which is leavened and fermented rises, while that which is unleavened is low. Each of these is a symbol of types of soul, one being haughty and swollen with arrogance, the other being unchangeable and prudent. . . ."
- Philo, *QE* 2.14 (on Exod 23:18): "He indicates through two necessary symbols that one should despise sensual pleasures, for leaven is a sweetener of food but not food (itself). And the other thing (indicated) is that one should not be uplifted in conceit by common belief. For both are impure and hateful, (namely) sensual pleasure and arrogance (or) foolish belief, (both being) the offspring of one mother, illusion." See also *Congr.* 161-62.
- Philo, *Spec. Leg.* 2.184-85: "But leaven is also a symbol for two other things: in one way it stands for food in its most complete and perfect form, such that in our daily usage none is found to be superior or more nourishing. . . . The other point is more symbolical. Everything that is leavened rises, and joy is the rational elevation or rising of the soul."

Greco-Roman Writings

- Plutarch, *Quaestiones Romanae* 109 (289F): "Why was it not permitted for the priest of Jupiter, whom they call the *Flamen Dialis*, to touch either flour or yeast? . . . Yeast is itself also the product of corruption, and produces corruption in the dough with which it is mixed; for the dough becomes flabby and inert, and altogether the process of leavening seems to be one of putrefaction; at any rate if it goes too far, it completely sours and spoils the flour."

Early Christian Writings

- *Gos. Thom.* 96: Jesus [said]: The kingdom of the Father is like [a] woman; she took a little leaven, [hid] it in dough, (and) made it into large loaves. He who has ears, let him hear.

Later Jewish Writings

- *m. Menaḥot* 5.1: "All Meal-offerings were offered unleavened, excepting the leavened [cakes prescribed] for the Thank-offering and the Two Loaves [at Pentecost], which were offered leavened."
- *b. Ketubbot* 10b: "As the leaven is wholesome for the dough, so is blood wholesome for a woman. And one has [also] taught in the name of R. Meir: Every woman who has abundant blood has many children." The same tradition is at *b. Niddah* 64b.

Comparison of the Accounts

Passages like these are the reason some people believe in Q, the sayings source supposedly used by Matthew and Luke. Apart from the introductory material, the wording of the two accounts is virtually identical. Matthew uses "He spoke another parable to them" in conformity with the way he has introduced other parables (cf. 13:3, 24, 31), whereas Luke has merely "And again he said." Matthew has "The kingdom of heaven is like leaven," whereas Luke has "To what shall I liken the kingdom of God? It is like leaven." From that point on the wording is identical.[260] Some assume that Luke has the more primitive form because he does not frequently use the word "again" (*palin*, v. 20),[261] which is slim evidence for any conclusion.

Gos. Thom. 96 has changed the parable so that the point of comparison is not the leaven but the woman. What was intended by the change is not obvious, especially given the negative view of women in *Gos. Thom.* 114, but this parable is placed as the first of three parables of the kingdom, two of which are about women. These parables are followed by the disciples telling Jesus that his family is standing outside and his reply that those who do the will of his Father are his brothers and mother and will enter the kingdom (saying 99). Luke placed this pericope about Jesus' family *after* parables of the kingdom (8:19-21), whereas Matthew and Mark have it preceding their parables discourse. Most do not view Thomas as the best preserved account.[262]

Textual Features Worth Noting

See also pp. 219-20 on the Mustard Seed.

"Hidden" is unexpected language and is intentionally used to draw attention to the hiddenness of the kingdom. The word "hidden" reappears in Matt 13:35 and 44.[263] Cf. also Matt 11:25/Luke 10:21; 18:34; 19:42. The kingdom Jesus proclaimed is a hidden kingdom.[264]

Unlike the parable of the Mustard Seed, neither of the versions of this parable explicitly mentions contrast.[265]

Cultural Information

Leaven was, of course, viewed negatively because of Passover and the necessity of eating unleavened bread for seven days. In preparation for Passover, "on the night of the 14th [of Nisan] the *ḥameṣ* must be searched for by the light of a lamp" (*m. Pesaḥim* 1.1), and anything containing or made from a fermentation process must be removed. Numerous regulations about removing leaven appear in various texts, most notably *b. Pesaḥim* 2a-116a. Whether leaven is negative in this parable is discussed below.

Leaven is not the same as yeast, the small substance we use to cause leavening. In the ancient world leaven was merely fermenting dough.[266] Some fermented dough is kept back from baking and used to ferment the next batch.

Since most houses were small (approximately fifteen feet square), baking was often done in courtyards and may have been performed as a communal act. Possibly the large quantity envisioned by this parable results from the assumption the woman was kneading dough for her group. Professional bread bakers did exist, but this task was work expected of women, one of seven responsibilities the Mishnah (*m. Ketubot* 5.5) requires wives to do for husbands. In Jer 7:18 baking bread is viewed as a family task.[267]

The similitude mentions three measures *(sata)* of flour, and a *saton* is understood as equivalent to the Hebrew *sĕʾāh*. However, *saton* ("measure") is *not* used in the LXX to translate *sĕʾāh*. Precision is not available for ancient measurements, but from the evidence available a *saton* is usually understood to be equivalent to about three gallons or thirteen liters dry measure. Three *sata* would be almost a bushel of flour and would be about all one woman could knead. It would obviously make a lot of bread, enough to feed from 100 to 150 people, *if the measurements have been understood appropriately.* The amount of leaven required to ferment that amount of flour is estimated at three or four pounds.[268]

Explanation of the Parable

Options for Interpretation

As expected, the church allegorized virtually every feature of this parable in a variety of ways. The woman was understood to be Mary, the church, or negatively the synagogue, which killed Christ the leaven. The leaven was also understood to be the twelve apostles, Christian doctrine, and knowledge of Scripture. Stephen Wailes reports that the three measures were given seventeen different identifications ranging from the trinity to specific moral virtues to Asia, Africa, and Europe.[269] This tells us more about the church than it does about the parable.

Recent scholarship has its own array of options for dealing with this one-verse similitude.[270] The following should be mentioned:

C. H. Dodd — no surprise — views the dough as completely leavened with Jesus' ministry, or if this parable was not originally with the Mustard Seed, it is about the "power of God's kingdom . . . mightily permeating the dead lump of religious Judaism in [Jesus'] time."[271]

The association with the Mustard Seed leads some to the assumption that the parable is about contrast.[272]

Some view the leaven as negative and focus on the kingdom as a subversive force and on the inclusion of outcasts in Jesus' ministry.[273]

Frequently people focus on the kingdom as a hidden but pervasive and irresistible power.[274] Sometimes this is associated with Gen 18:6, the context of which concerns divine visitors to Abraham, and ideas of revelation and epiphany.[275]

A few argue that the parable is about God's providential care.[276]

A few think the parable points to the involvement of women in leadership of the church.[277]

Decisions on the Issues

1. What is the relation of this parable to that of the Mustard Seed and what relevance does this relation have for interpretation? These two similitudes are twins, but not identical twins. While they should be read together, each must be understood in its own right. The idea of contrast is not explicit with the Leaven and should not be made the focus, certainly not if I am correct that contrast is not the central point of the Mustard Seed either. It has often been said that the Mustard Seed depicts extensive growth and the Leaven intensive transformation,[278] but both similitudes have both elements, so this distinction does not work.[279] Both parables emphasize an intentional process with an explicit goal,[280] and both portray the surprising large effect of something small or unobservable. In that sense they provide two different pictures of the same reality and make the point more strongly than either could alone. Both are addressed to the same doubt about the kingdom's presence.

2. Is leaven always a negative symbol? As the primary sources above show, leaven is commonly viewed negatively, but other texts show positive uses, especially in peace offerings, offerings of firstfruits to God, and thank offerings (Lev 7:13-14; 23:17; *m. Menaḥot* 5.1). Leaven is not to be used with burnt offerings, but neither is honey. No one concludes that honey is negative. When leaven is used negatively, the context makes that clear, whether in Scripture or elsewhere. Nothing in the context here suggests anything but a positive use. Any attempt to see the kingdom as an "epiphany of corruption" and the parable as an attempt to subvert hearers' ready dependence on the rules of the sacred has nothing in its favor.[281] If leaven is not viewed negatively here, then also excluded are interpretations that emphasize subversive aspects of the kingdom and the inclusion of outcasts. Those themes are present elsewhere, but not here.

3. Is there allegorical significance to any of the features? The allegorical identifications of the medieval church seem odd today, but some still want to find identifications for the features of the parables. If there were not correspondences between the image and the reality, an analogy would not work, but correspondences are not the same as allegorical identifications. The analogy is this: leaven which ferments a large amount of dough corresponds to (or shows analogously) the relation of Jesus' ministry and the full manifestation of the kingdom. The woman is not a symbol for Jesus; the concern is not the woman but the process of leaven fermenting a huge amount of dough. Since Jesus compares himself to a mother hen (Matt 23:37), presumably he would not hesitate to compare himself to a woman, but such comparisons do not accomplish much regarding the value of women or chickens. Our society needs a much better valuation of women and their leadership than it has, but this parable is not the basis for that discussion.

4. Is there an allusion to Gen 18:6 and if so what is its significance? As with the Mustard Seed, there is the possibility of an allusion to an OT text that could have major implications for the purpose of the parable. In Gen 18:6 Abraham tells Sarah to take three measures of flour and quickly make cakes for the visitors. Other than the three measures of flour, not much suggests an allusion in Jesus' parable. The Genesis text does not mention leaven, and if an allusion is made, there is no influence from the LXX text. Even the words for "measures" are not the same.[282] Some point to the word *enkryphias* ("cakes") in LXX Genesis because it sounds like *kryptō* ("hide") in the Gospel parable, which is then believed to be a play on words.[283] This is not very impressive and looks more like coincidence than wordplay. Because of the need for haste, it may well be that the cakes Sarah prepared were *unleavened* (cf. 1 Sam 28:24), particularly since in Judg 6:19, another divine visitation text, Gideon prepares unleavened cakes from an ephah of flour (the same quantity as three measures; see also 1 Sam 1:24).

Those who see an allusion to Gen 18:6 in the parable think the three measures of flour would be recognized as an offering for an epiphany and would understand the parable then to be pointing to revelation, the sacramental power of the kingdom, and to the inversion of the sacred and profane, implicitly a negation of the temple.[284] That is a lot to conclude from "three measures," and in the end I think the likelihood of an allusion to Gen 18:6 is minimal at best. The three measures still could be taken as symbolic of the kingdom, possibly pointing to the eschatological banquet,[285] if estimates are correct that this amount of flour was enough to feed 100 people or more. As some warn, however, three measures may be merely a conventional amount. At least we should be cautious about conclusions drawn about the symbolic value of the amount of flour.[286]

5. What question is being addressed and what is the significance of the answer? (See also the similar discussion of the Mustard Seed.) As indicated above, this similitude is directed at doubts concerning Jesus' proclamation of the presence of the kingdom. What people thought should be happening was not happening, even though parts of Jesus' ministry did fulfill expectations. A parallel context is evident in the question of John the Baptist whether Jesus was "the one" and Jesus' answer pointing to works fulfilling OT expectations (Matt 11:2-6/Luke 7:18-23).[287] Luke's tying the parable to the healing of the crippled woman strengthens the association. The point again is that what you see with Jesus is the beginning of what you hope for in the kingdom and will surely lead to it. The focus is not the contrast of small and large but the hidden beginning which will result in the completion of God's work in the kingdom, the leavening of the whole. Something has happened (note the aorists) and will have its full effect. A hidden power, hardly discernible to some, is already and irresistibly working. The kingdom in Jesus' ministry has its beginning and is at work, even if in a hidden or unanticipated way.[288] Acceptance of the parable's point instills confidence and hope.

For questions six and seven *(To what degree is focus placed on some length of time and growth or development, and what is the relevance of the parable for thinking about eschatology? and Does this text teach universalism?)* see the treatments under the parable of the Mustard Seed (pp. 226-27).

Adapting the Parable

See also pp. 227-28 above on the Mustard Seed.

The presence of the kingdom is possibly the most important aspect of Jesus' message. History is changed by his word and work. That claim must be treated more broadly at the end of this chapter, but clearly the whole point of this parable is that the kingdom is already underway and will not be stopped. The christological assumptions are obvious. The challenge to human perception and judgment about smallness and significance is present here too. Many people know insignificant beginnings in their lives that God has brought to completion. That dynamic is part of life and should be savored and protected both for ourselves and others. Confidence and hope are the result of the parable. If people are given over to God's purposes, small beginnings still come to fruition. God seems to be about the business of leavening — magnifying — what seems insignificant.

For Further Reading

Robert W. Funk, "Beyond Criticism in Quest of Literacy: The Parable of the Leaven," *Int* 25 (1971): 149-70.

Jacobus Liebenberg, *The Language of the Kingdom and Jesus: Parable, Aphorism, and Metaphor in the Sayings Material Common to the Synoptic Tradition and the Gospel of Thomas* (Berlin: Walter de Gruyter, 2001), pp. 276-349.

Susan Marie Praeder, *The Word in Women's Worlds: Four Parables* (Wilmington, Del.: Michael Glazier, 1988), pp. 11-35.

Elizabeth Waller, "The Parable of the Leaven: A Sectarian Teaching and the Inclusion of Women" *USQR* 35 (1979-80): 99-109.

THE TREASURE
(Matt 13:44)

Parable Type

We have seen with the Mustard Seed and the Leaven that tense alone is not the factor that distinguishes between similitudes and parables. Comparison of the Treasure (which uses the aorist for "hid," *ekrypsen,* and then uses the present tense) with the Pearl (which uses the perfect tense for "sold," *pepraken,*[289] the imperfect for "had," *eichen,* and the aorist for "bought," *ēgorasen*) verifies that tense is no basis for distinction. Clearly the Treasure and the Pearl are the same type. Both are similitudes similar in form to the Leaven. Although there is movement, there is not a developed plot.

Issues Requiring Attention[290]

1. What is the relation of the parables of the Treasure and of the Pearl and the significance of that relation? Is there any difference in nuance because of the differences in tense?
2. Was the finder's action unethical, and if so, is this relevant for interpretation?
3. Do the features have allegorical significance?
4. What does the similitude teach, the value of the kingdom or the cost of discipleship? Does this parable have anything to do with salvation by grace?

Helpful Primary Source Material[291]

Canonical Material

- OT: Deut 33:19
- NT: Matt 6:33; Matt 16:24-26/Mark 8:34-37/Luke 9:23-25; Matt 19:21, 27/ Mark 10:21, 28/Luke 18:22, 28; Luke 14:26-33

Early Jewish Writings

- Sir 40:18: "Wealth and wages make life sweet, but better than either is finding a treasure."

- Philo, *De Deo* 91: "On the other hand, it is a common experience that things befall us of which we have not even dreamt, like the story of the husbandman who, digging his orchard to plant some fruit-trees, lighted on a treasure, and thus met with prosperity beyond his hopes." Philo has in mind the treasure one finds in God's wisdom.

- *T. Job* 18.6-8: "And I became as one wishing to enter a certain city to discover its wealth and gain a portion of its splendor, and as one embarked with cargo in a seagoing ship. Seeing at mid-ocean the third wave and the opposition of the wind, he threw the cargo into the sea, saying, 'I am willing to lose everything in order to enter this city so that I might gain both the ship and things better than the payload.' Thus, I also considered my goods as nothing compared to the city about which the angel spoke to me."[292]

Greco-Roman Writings

- Horace, *Satires* 2.6.10: "O that some lucky strike would disclose to me a pot of money, like the man who, having found a treasure-trove, bought and ploughed the self-same ground he used to work on hire, enriched by favor of Hercules!" Hercules was known as the god of the treasure trove.

- *Aesop's Fables* 42, "The Farmer's Treasure and His Sons": "A farmer who was about to die wanted his sons to be knowledgeable about the farm, so he summoned them and said, 'My children, there is a treasure buried in one of my vineyards.' After he died, his sons took plows and mattocks and dug up the entire farm. They did not find any treasure, but the vineyard paid them back with a greatly increased harvest. Thus they learned that man's greatest treasure consists in work."[293]

- Philostratus, *Apollonius* 6.39: A man sacrifices to Mother Earth in hope of finding a treasure. He prays to Apollonius, and after discussion about his wealth, lack of work, and need for dowries for four daughters, Apollonius has compassion and says he and Mother Earth will provide. He shows the man an estate. The man buys it and then finds a jar containing 3000 darics, and has a good crop too. He praises the sage, and his house is crowded with suitors for his daughters.

Early Christian Writings

- *Gos. Thom.* 109: "Jesus said: The kingdom is like a man who had a treasure [hidden] in his field, without knowing it. And [after] he died, he left it to his [son. The] son knew nothing (about it). He accepted that field (and) sold [it]. And he who bought it came, (and) while he was plough-ing [he found] the treasure. He began to lend money at interest to [whomever] he wished."

Later Jewish Sources

- *m. Baba Batra* 4.8-9: "If a man sold a field he has sold also the stones that are necessary to it, and the canes in a vineyard that are necessary to it, and its unreaped crop. . . . But he has not sold the stones that are not necessary to it or the canes in a vineyard that are not necessary to it or the produce that is already gathered." Various regulations follow, most presuming if something was sold, everything part of it was sold too.
- *T. Sol.* 12.4: A demon under Solomon's control tells him that much gold is buried at the temple building site and that Solomon is to dig it up and take it.
- *Mekilta Beshallaḥ* 2.149-55 (on Exod 14:5): "Another interpretation: R. Si-mon the son of Yoḥai, giving a parable, says: To what can this be com-pared? To a man to whom there had fallen as an inheritance a residence in a far-off country which he sold for a trifle. The buyer, however, went and discovered in it hidden treasures and stores of silver and of gold, of pre-cious stones and pearls. The seller, seeing this, began to choke with grief. So also did the Egyptians, who let go without realizing what they let go. For it is written: 'And they said: What is this we have done that we have let Israel go.'" *Pesiqta de Rab Kahana* 11.7 also has a three-fold analogy on this theme; cf. *Song Rab.* 4.12.1; *Exod. Rab.* 20:2.
- *y. Baba Meṣiʿa* 2.5, 8: "Simeon b. Shetah was employed in flax [to support himself]. His disciples said to him, 'Rabbi, remove [this work] from your-self, and we shall buy for you an ass, and you will not have to work so much.' They went and bought him an ass from a Saracen. Hanging on it was a pearl. They came to him and told him, 'From now on you do not have to work any more.' He said to them, 'Why?' They told him, 'We bought you an ass from a Saracen, and hanging on it was a pearl.' He said to them, 'Did its master know about it?' They said to him, 'No.' He said to them, 'Go, and return it.'" Several other incidents are reported of Jews re-turning lost merchandise to Gentiles so they will bless the God of the Jews. "Said R. Huna, 'All concur that if [one found] a pouch of money, he should not touch it.'" Tarfon and Aqiba agree that in this case the finder leaves the money alone and does not make use of it.
- *y. Horayot* 3.4: A man supporting rabbis lost money and was encouraged by his wife to sell one half of their only remaining field and give the pro-

ceeds to them. "He went and did just that. He came to our rabbis, and he gave them the proceeds. Our rabbis prayed in his behalf. They said to him, 'Abba Judah, may the Holy One, blessed be He, make up all the things you lack.' When they went their way, he went down to plough the half field that remained in his possession. Now while he was plowing . . . his cow fell and broke a leg. He went down to bring her up, and the Holy One, blessed be He, opened his eyes, and he found a jewel. He said, 'It was for my own good that my cow broke its leg.'" This story is repeated with variations in *Lev. Rab.* 5.4 and *Deut. Rab.* 4.8.

■ *Lev. Rab.* 27.1: "He [Alexander] marched away to another province named Africa. They came out to meet him with golden apples, golden pomegranates, and golden bread. 'What is the meaning of this?' he cried, 'do they eat gold in your country?' They answered him: 'Is it not so in your country?' He said to them: 'It is not your possessions I have come to see but your laws.' As they were sitting, two men came before the king for judgment. One said: 'Your majesty! I bought a carob-tree from this man, and in scooping it out I found a treasure therein, so I said to him: "Take your treasure, for I bought the carob-tree but not the treasure."' The other argued: 'Just as you are afraid of risking punishment for robbery so am I. When I effected the sale I sold you the carob-tree and all that is therein.' The king called one of them and said to him: 'Have you a son?' 'Yes,' he replied. He called the other and asked him: 'Have you a daughter?' 'Yes,' he replied. 'Go,' said the king to them, 'and let them get married to one another and let them both enjoy the treasure.' Alexander of Macedon began to show surprise. 'Why,' the king asked him, 'are you surprised? Have I not judged well?' 'Yes,' he assured him. 'If this case had arisen in your country,' he asked him, 'what would you have done?' He replied: 'We should have removed this man's head and that one's, and the treasure would have gone to the king.'" Alexander's logic is refuted from Ps 37:7. The same account with variations is at *Pesiqta de Rab Kahana* 9.1; *Gen. Rab.* 33.1; *y. Baba Meṣiʿa* 2.5; and *Midr. Tanḥuma Emor* 9.

■ *b. Baba Meṣiʿa.* 10a: "If a man lifts up a found object for his neighbor, the neighbor does not acquire it. . . . A laborer's find belongs to himself. This decision only applies to a case where the employer said to the laborer: 'Weed for me to-day,' [or] 'Hoe for me to-day.' But if he said to him: 'Do work for me to-day,' the laborer's find belongs to the employer! He [R. Nahman] answered him: 'A laborer is different, as his hand is like the hand of his employer!'" Similar instruction is at 12b and 118a.

■ *b. Baba Meṣiʿa* 25a: Money found in front of a purse belongs to the finder. Stacked coins must be proclaimed; scattered coins belong to the finder.

- *b. Baba Meṣiʿa* 25b: "If a man finds a vessel in a dungheap: if covered up, he must not touch it; if uncovered, he must take and proclaim it." [Debates regarding this ruling follow.] ". . . A Tanna taught: Because he [the finder] can say to him, 'They belonged to Amorites.' Do then only Amorites hide objects, and not Israelites?"

Comparison of the Accounts

Neither Mark nor Luke has this parable, *Gos. Thom.* 109 does, although the Thomas account is closer to *Mekilta Beshallaḥ* 2.149-55 and its parallels (see above) than to Matthew. Some, like Jeremias and Crossan,[294] think with good reason that the Jewish parable has influenced *Gos. Thom.* Matthew compares the kingdom to the treasure found and purchased; *Gos. Thom.* compares the kingdom to a man and his heir, neither of whom knows about the treasure, and focuses on the heir's loss. Matthew has the finding before the purchase, whereas *Gos. Thom.* has it after. Matthew mentions the finder's hiding the treasure, his joy, his selling all he has, and his purchasing the field, none of which are in *Gos. Thom.* Unlike Matthew, the Thomas account reports that the finder began to lend money at interest to whomever he wished, which does not fit with the disdain of businessmen and creditors elsewhere in *Gos. Thom.*[295] The account in *Gos. Thom.* is almost certainly secondary, a point recognized by nearly all,[296] and possibly dependent at least partly on Matthew.[297]

Textual Features Worth Noting

J. C. Fenton suggests a six-part chiasmus in Matt 13:34-52: A^1 speaking in parables as fulfillment of prophecy, B^1 explanation of the weeds, C^1 Treasure, C^2 Pearl, B^2 the Net and its explanation, A^2 the saying about old and new.[298]

Matt 13:45 and 47 begin identically with "Again the kingdom of heaven is like . . . ," and v. 44 begins the same way except that it lacks "again."[299] This introduction ("*x* is like") is a standard Jewish parable introduction.

Forms of the word "hide" *(kryptein)* appear in vv. 33 and 35 and twice in v. 44. From v. 35 (the quotation of Ps 78:2) it is clear that parables are the means to disclose what is hidden, and in this chapter the kingdom is the hidden entity. The parables disclose the hidden kingdom of heaven. The idea that the kingdom could be hidden is itself a revelation.

The word "treasure" *(thēsauros)* appears again in v. 52, but while the repetition may assist the oral conveyance of the material, the two treasures do not seem to be related. In v. 44 the kingdom is like hidden treasure found and from joy acquired, despite the cost. In v. 52 the scribe discipled for (or by) the kingdom is like a householder who brings both new and old things from his storeroom (treasure), benefiting, apparently, from both the kingdom and God's prior revelation in Israel.

I do not think there is any substantive connection to the word "field" *(agros)* in the parables of the Wheat and Weeds and of the Mustard Seed (vv. 24, 27, 31, 36, 38). Obviously the repetition of the word would have assisted in conveying the material orally.

The positive and celebrative message of the parables of the Treasure and the Pearl is bracketed by the judgment message of the Wheat and the Weeds and of the Net. The good news of the kingdom, especially in Matthew, is ignored at one's peril.

Other than the expression "the kingdom of heaven is like" (13:31, 33, 44, 45, 47; 20:1), the suggested Mattheanisms (such as "treasure," "joy," "hide,")[300] are not very impressive.

Other parables focus on finding and joy such as those of the Lost Sheep, the Lost Coin, and the Two Lost Sons in Luke 15, as do sayings such as Matt 10:39; 16:25.

Cultural Information

In all cultures, including modern ones, people have hidden money and other valuables in the ground, especially during uncertain times such as war. Josephus tells of wealth hidden by Jews and the efforts of Romans to find it.[301] The servant who hid his talent in the ground (Matt 25:18, 25) shows the same practice at less troublesome times. The most striking evidence is the Copper Scroll at Qumran (3Q15). This scroll is literally copper leaf, and engraved on it is a list of various treasures, mostly gold and silver, and their respective hiding places in cisterns, under stones, in fields, and in burial mounds. Also, not long ago a jar with almost twenty pounds of silver was found; it had been buried since about the eleventh century B.C.[302] Finding such a treasure in the ancient world was the equivalent of winning the lottery.[303]

On the question of the morality of the man's hiding the treasure and buying the field, see below, pp. 243-44.

Explanation of the Parable

Options for Interpretation

The early church quickly identified the treasure in the field as Christ either in the world, in the Scriptures, or in the flesh.[304] However, the treasure was also deemed plurisignificant and later was identified as the Bible, virginity, heaven, or various virtues, especially wisdom. The idea of selling all was sometimes associated with almsgiving but more frequently with personal perfection and the rejection of worldly values.[305]

In the modern period much of the debate is whether this similitude is about the value of the kingdom or the cost of discipleship. Is its purpose indicative or imperative?[306] For a few, notably Jeremias, the focus is the joy in finding.[307] All three of these options include recognition of the presence of the kingdom. A few, fearing some focus on salvation by works, see this similitude as a parable on Christ's atoning work.[308] Conclusions that the finder's actions were immoral have led to some other strange twists (concerning which see below, pp. 243-44.)

Decisions on the Issues

As with other parables starting with "The kingdom is like . . . ," the analogy is not merely between the kingdom and the treasure. The analogy is with the whole process described in the similitude: The kingdom of heaven is like the case of a man who finds a treasure, covers it, and because of joy goes, sells all, and purchases the field. The kingdom encompasses all these aspects.

1. *What is the relation of the parables of the Treasure and the Pearl and the significance of that relation?* These two parables begin and end almost identically except that the first uses the present tense and the second uses the imperfect and aorist. The middle sections of the two parables are considerably different:

> In the first the treasure (the thing found) is the entry point of the analogy, but in the second it is the merchant (the finder).
> Joy is emphasized in the first but omitted in the second.
> The man in the first parable was not looking for treasure, but the merchant in the second was seeking good pearls.
> The first parable twice mentions that the treasure was hidden, but this theme plays no part in the second.

Obviously these are twin similitudes, but not identical twins. Matthew connects them with "again," but this is *not* an indicator that they mean the same thing, for the next parable, the Net (v. 47), is quite different but begins the same way. The Treasure and the Pearl may point to the same reality but they do so with different nuances.

The change of tense and the fact that *Gos. Thom.* has these two parables in different locations suggest to some that they were not told at the same time. What Thomas does is insignificant, of course, if as I think likely, that Gospel is dependent on the canonical Gospels, at least indirectly. Whether the parables were told together originally cannot be demonstrated either way, and the decision makes little difference. Without question Matthew has arranged his material thematically, and these two parables are so central to Jesus' teaching on the kingdom that they were surely told more than once. They may have been told together on one occasion and separately on another.

The parables are enough alike that, even if not told together originally, they quickly were joined and together emphasize more strongly than either could alone that the kingdom is a fortuitous find deserving total investment. Their common message does not mean that the differences are irrelevant. With their different nuances they strengthen the teaching about the kingdom. The absence of joy from the second parable is noteworthy, but especially given Matthew's arrangement and the story itself, it would be foolish to argue that joy is not present in that parable as well. No one goes and sells all for something that does not cause the adrenaline to flow. The absence of hiddenness in the second parable likewise is not a major factor and at least finds a coordinate idea with the mention of seeking, which is absent in the first parable. We cannot say that this seeking is unimportant. If the first parable provokes the desire to be so fortunate in finding, it answers that the kingdom is the means to that end, but the second implies "You should be seeking the kingdom." The remaining difference, the change of tense, appears to have minor significance. It would be hard to argue for some temporal difference between the two with respect to the kingdom, and the action is viewed as past in both parables. If there is any significance, it appears to be that the historical presents in the parable of the Treasure are used for vividness and to highlight the appropriate response to the kingdom.[309]

2. Was the finder's action unethical, and if so, is this relevant for interpretation? As Crossan points out, the sequence in Jesus' parable of finding, acting, and buying differs from the sequence in some other Jewish treasure stories where the sequence is buying, acting, and finding.[310] The sequence in Jesus' story raises ethical questions for modern readers. Was it moral to purchase the field knowing what the owner did not, that a treasure was in it? For some, especially Crossan and Scott, the finder's actions are immoral, and this leads to unexpected meaning. Crossan thinks this parable shows that the kingdom demands the abandonment of our goods, our morals, and even of this parable with the intended result that the parable shows that the kingdom cannot be explained.[311] Scott thinks the parable ends with lawless narcissism and the man impoverished because he has sold everything yet cannot dig up the treasure without facing the question of its origin. For him the parable points to the corrupting nature of the kingdom.[312] It is very difficult to think either of these options represents the intent of Jesus or something hearers could discern, to say nothing of Scott's violation of the parable's narrative time by saying the hearer must project beyond the story to ask what the man will do with the treasure.[313] This violation of parable time ignores that this is a similitude, a form with an undeveloped plot, not an instance in a man's life.

J. Derrett argues that the man's actions are moral and legal because of rabbinic regulations about finding and "lifting."[314] The owner of the land had not lifted the treasure, that is, taken possession of it, and therefore did not own it. Rabbis and other ancient sources do discuss ownership of found items, particularly whether they belong to a workman or the person who has hired him and what must be proclaimed if found and what need not be.[315] Apparently Roman law was undecided about the ownership of found treasure. Derrett is helpful in pointing to the rabbinic discussions, but unfortunately they are not specific enough to answer the questions about Jesus' parable.

If the man's actions are immoral, this is irrelevant to the point of the parable.[316] If illegality had anything to do with the point of the parable, it would have received some attention. Once again the principle can be invoked: any attempt to interpret a parable by what is not there is almost certainly wrong. The absence of any thought of illegality in the parallel parable of the Pearl strengthens the case that it is not a concern here either.[317] More than likely though, the actions would have been considered legitimate and would not have caused difficulty for the hearers. The treasure obviously had no relation to the owner and may have been in the ground for centuries (as with the silver horde from the eleventh century B.C. and *b. Baba Meṣi'a* 25b's claim that valuables were hidden by the Amorites, pp. 241 and 240 above). If the finder had just taken the treasure, a claim could be lodged against him. By buying the field he established a legitimate claim to own the treasure (cf. *m. Baba Batra* 4.8-9 above).

3. Do the features have allegorical significance? As seen above, the church assigned allegorical significance to the details of this similitude, but with good reason most scholars do not. Some assume that Matthew read the field as the world because of this identification in 13:38,[318] but this will not work. It would mean that the finder sold all he had to buy the world, surely not anyone's intent. The significance of a metaphor in one parable does not determine its meaning in another, and the field in this parable has no specific reference. When allegorical significance has been sought, it is usually because an interpreter sees this similitude as a description of Jesus' own sacrifice. Jesus is the one who sells all to acquire the treasure, his disciples, and the finding refers to God's activity in Jesus to retrieve the lost.[319] It is hard to believe this was Jesus' aim or Matthew's, and such an approach is unnecessarily motivated by the desire to avoid any thought of salvation by works. Neither the man, the finding, nor the field requires or should receive specific identification. If we remember that the intent of the introduction is "The kingdom is like the situation [of such a finding]" and that this is an analogy, then identification of details is uncalled for. Similitudes do not focus on correspondences. The analogy is not about Jesus; it is about the value and joy of finding the kingdom.

4. *What does the similitude teach, the value of the kingdom or the cost of discipleship? Does this parable have anything to do with salvation by grace?* If Matthew has this parable addressed to the disciples, which is not as clear as is often assumed, it would suggest that the focus is the cost of discipleship, but a prior question must be asked. Was this parable originally addressed only to disciples or only to the Jewish crowds, or, as is likely, told on more than one occasion and to various audiences? There is no specific indication of the audience of this parable, just as there is not for all the other parables in the chapter except for the Sower (13:1-2). The only way we know that the Wheat and the Weeds, the Mustard Seed, and the Leaven were addressed to the crowds is that Matthew mentions this *after the fact* (13:24). He does not do this for the Treasure and the Pearl.[320] Nothing about this parable or the Pearl makes it suitable only for disciples or indicates that Matthew limited it to them. Both parables are at least partly about discipleship, but their addressees cannot be limited to "believers."[321] These parables are as much as anything a *call* to discipleship, and the message of both similitudes is at least as pertinent for hearers in general as it is for disciples.

A choice between the value of the kingdom and the cost of discipleship is not necessary. Both themes and the theme of joy deserve emphasis and, in fact, are interrelated. No one pays the cost of discipleship without some sense of the value to be gained and without joy accompanying such an awareness. It is not true as some suggest that no one needed to be told of the value of the kingdom. If the previous parables have convinced that the kingdom is hidden, this parable underscores the value of this hidden kingdom, a value many do not recognize. Value is inherent in the very word "treasure" and in the man's actions (and is explicit in the parable of the Pearl), but Jesus did not merely say "The kingdom is like a treasure." The point of the similitude is in the *behavior* of the finder; he found something hidden worth all he had, and he took all necessary measures to acquire it. The hidden kingdom is like that, beyond compare and worth whatever is required to participate in it.[322] E. Linnemann legitimately points out that the parable is not about sacrifice, for the finder receives something of much greater value.[323] Some suggest that Jesus' words "sold all he had" are to be understood literally of selling all one's possessions and giving the proceeds to the poor,[324] but that is pushing this parable beyond its intent. While the words resonate with the call in other texts to sell all literally (e.g., 19:21; Luke 12:33),[325] here they only express "ultimate value." The similitude is even more reminiscent of passages describing the disciples as those who have found the treasure of the kingdom and abandoned all to follow Jesus (Matt 4:20-22; 19:27; see also Matt 10:37-39/Luke 14:25-27; Matt 16:24-26/Mark 8:34-37/Luke 9:23-25 and contrast Matt 8:19-22/Luke 9:57-62).

This parable has nothing to do with salvation by grace. The kingdom is not expressed here as sheer gift[326] since the man sells all he has. That the man was not seeking treasure while the pearl merchant in the next parable is seeking pearls indicates that neither parable explains how one finds the kingdom.[327] At least neither seeking nor not seeking is central. Nor does one need to worry that this parable requires "works" since the man did something. The kingdom or any action of God for us always requires response, but it is a distortion of the parable to force the grace vs. works discussion onto it.

The parable presupposes that the kingdom is hidden and available to be found. Put another way, the kingdom is present and awaiting recognition of its value and the radical action it deserves. It is not about reward in heaven or the age to come.[328] Jesus told this story to announce the presence of the kingdom and to elicit the joy of discovery and the radical action of following him.

In my estimation the gospel of Jesus includes four primary items: joy, compassion, fulfillment of the promises to Israel, and the presence of God's kingdom.[329] This parable involves two of these themes explicitly and offers quick insight into Jesus' ministry and message. The parable urges a recognition of what time it is. With Jesus' ministry the kingdom is present, and it is time to celebrate and participate in that kingdom at any cost.

Adapting the Parable

According to the TV news a man named Roy Whetstine had a "treasure in the field, exceedingly valuable pearl" experience. Roy was a rock collector whose two sons each had given him five dollars to buy a rock for them at a rock show. He found a potato-sized rock in a tupperware container with a lot of agates around it. The sign said "Any stone $15." He picked up the potato-sized rock and said, "You want fifteen dollars for this?" The man said, "I'll give it to you for ten, since it is not as pretty as the agates." Roy bought it and got a receipt and could hardly contain himself until he got outside. He had just purchased the largest known star sapphire — 1509 ct. — valued at 2.5 million dollars uncut and about 10 million cut. The analogy is obvious. A lot of us spend our time looking for pretty agates and miss the sapphires of life in God's kingdom.

All of life is a seeking after value. Sometimes we find value fortuitously and sometimes with great effort, but often our sense of value is skewed. We need to aim higher. Our relation with God is the most important part of life. All our other pursuits are trivial by comparison. More specifically, understanding what God has done in Christ and following Christ are more valuable than all else we possess or seek. It is clear too that we cannot be focused on "our things" and do justice to God's kingdom. God's call trumps all else in life — and it is worth it.

We also need to realize what time it is. If the kingdom is present, radical response is needed *now*. If the kingdom is worth all we have, then joy and celebration should accompany our finding and involvement with the kingdom. The problem with most of us is that we would like a little of the kingdom as an add-on to the rest of our lives. We want to hedge our bets. You cannot hedge your bets with the kingdom. This parable urges us to abandon what we thought was the focus of life and focus entirely on what God is doing with the kingdom.

We must face the reality though that to many people any talk about Christianity partaking of a treasure borders on the ludicrous. Christians have so frequently failed to live their own gospel and have identified with certain cultural and political ideas that Jesus' message has been lost. The gospel we proclaim must deserve and explain the label "treasure," and our lives must express the ultimate value found in Christ.

For Further Reading

John Dominic Crossan, *Finding Is the First Act: Trove Folktales and Jesus' Treasure Parable* (Philadelphia: Fortress, 1979).

W. D. Davies and D. C. Allison, Jr., *A Critical and Exegetical Commentary on the Gospel According to Saint Matthew* (ICC; Edinburgh: T. & T. Clark, 1991), 2:434-37.

Arland J. Hultgren, *The Parables of Jesus: A Commentary* (Grand Rapids: Eerdmans, 2000), pp. 409-16.

Jack Dean Kingsbury, *The Parables of Jesus in Matthew 13: A Study in Redaction-Criticism* (Richmond: John Knox, 1969), pp. 110-17.

John W. Sider, "Interpreting the Hid Treasure." *CSR* 13 (1984): 360-72.

THE PEARL
(Matt 13:45-46)

Although this parable deserves to be treated in its own right and not merely subsumed under the Treasure in the Field, obviously the discussion of the two overlaps considerably.

Parable Type

This is a similitude. See the corresponding section for the Treasure (p. 236).

Issues Requiring Attention[330]

1. What is the relation of the parables of the Treasure and the Pearl and the significance of that relation? Is there any difference in nuance because of the difference in tense?
2. Do the features have allegorical significance?
3. What does the similitude teach?

Helpful Primary Source Material

Canonical Material

- NT: Matt 6:33; 7:7-8/Luke 11:9; Rev 17:4; 18:12, 16; 21:21

Greco-Roman Writings

- Pliny, *Natural History* 9.106 describes pearls as having the "topmost rank among all things of price." In 9.119 he tells of two pearls owned by Cleopatra that were the largest in history and worth ten million sesterces.
- Suetonius, *Caesar* 50: Caesar gave the mother of Brutus a pearl worth 6 million sesterces.

Early Christian Writings

- *Gos. Thom.* 76: "Jesus said: The kingdom of the Father is like a merchant who had merchandise (and) who found a pearl. This merchant was prudent. He got rid of (*i.e.* sold) the merchandise and bought the one pearl for himself. You also must seek for the treasure which does not perish, which abides where no moth comes near to eat and (where) no worm destroys."

- *Acts of Thomas* 108-13 tells of a journey to obtain the one pearl which is in the midst of the sea in the abode of a loud-breathing serpent. After some trials Thomas snatches the pearl and takes it to the king of kings.

Later Jewish Writings

- *'Abot de Rabbi Nathan* 18: "... *Assemble the people, the men and the women and the children* (Deut 31:12). 'And how did he interpret it?' he asked them. They said to him, 'This is how he interpreted it: As to *the men*, they come to study; as to *the women*, they come to listen. Why do *the little ones* come? So that a goodly reward might be given to those who bring them.' Said Rabbi Joshua to them: 'A precious pearl was in your hands, and you were about to deprive me of it! Had you gone to hear no more than that, it would have been enough.'" A pearl is used to describe a valuable teaching; this tradition appears also at *Num. Rab.* 14.4. *Midr. Ps.* 28.6 has a parable in which the Torah is compared to a pearl.
- *Song Rab.* 1.1.8, on the value of parables: "If a king loses gold from his house or a precious pearl, does he not find it by means of a wick worth a farthing? So the parable should not be lightly esteemed in your eyes, since by means of the parable a man arrives at the true meaning of the words of the Torah."
- *Ruth Rab.* 3.4 tells a story of a poor rabbi who does not have provisions for a festival but prays and a hand extends to him a priceless pearl. He makes preparations for the feast, but his wife makes him take the provisions back and return the pearl so that he will not have one pearl less in his canopy in the world to come.
- *Pesiqta Rabbati* 23.6 tells a story of a pious tailor who outbids the governor's servant for the only fish in the market and pays a denar per pound. The Governor thinks the man must be rich and calls him in to take his money. The Jew explains the value of the Sabbath and that he honored that day with his purchase. God caused the tailor to find in the fish a gem of purest ray, a pearl, and on the money he got for it he sustained himself all the rest of his days. Similar stories appear at *b. Šabbat* 119a and *b. Baba Batra* 133b.[331]

Comparison of the Accounts

Neither Mark nor Luke has this parable, but *Gos. Thom.* 76 does. This parable, the Treasure, the Net, and the Wheat and the Weeds appear only in Matthew and *Gos. Thom.* The differences in the accounts of the Pearl are:

> The merchant in Matthew seeks good pearls; in *Gos. Thom.* he neither seeks nor was specifically looking for pearls, but is described as prudent.
>
> Matthew has the merchant find *one extremely valuable* pearl;[332] *Gos. Thom.* has no description of the pearl.
>
> Matthew has the merchant depart to sell all his possessions; *Gos. Thom.* omits the departing and has the merchant sell his merchandise (omitting "all").
>
> *Gos. Thom.* attaches a variation of Matt 6:19-20/Luke 12:33, almost certainly because of the catchword "treasure," even though the treasure parable is placed at saying 109.

Because of the connection to the treasure saying and the apparent Gnostic interpretation of the pearl as the inner self, most view *Gos. Thom.* 76 as secondary, if not directly dependent on Matthew.[333]

Textual Features Worth Noting

The merchant is seeking good pearls. For other significant occurrences of "seek" (*zētein*) in Matthew see 6:33; 7:7-8; 18:12. See further under this heading for the Treasure (pp. 240-41).

Cultural Information

Neither the OT nor the LXX explicitly mentions pearls. Where translations use the word "pearl," the Hebrew word actually refers to jewels in general or to coral. See Job 28:18; Prov 3:15; 8:11; 20:15; 31:10; Lam 4:7.

Pearls were regarded as the most valuable objects in existence, so they became a figure of speech for something of supreme worth,[334] which is the basis of this similitude.

The risks and rewards of being a merchant were both great.[335] Some in the ancient world had little respect for merchants, as Sir 26:29 attests: "A merchant can hardly keep from wrongdoing, nor is a tradesman innocent of sin."

Most accept that the parable is about a wholesale dealer.

Explanation of the Parable

Options for Interpretation

The church often focused on Christ as the extremely valuable pearl with the good pearls the merchant sought understood as good humans or human knowledge prior to the incarnation.[336] Jerome interpreted the pearl as Christianity and the good pearls as people who did business with the Law and prophets.[337] The pearl was also identified as moral precepts, love, and the word of God. A few took the merchant as Christ and the pearl as the church, which Christ purchased with his blood. The idea of selling all was understood as abandoning old practices or relinquishing the earthly for the sake of the heavenly, and so, like the Treasure, the parable was understood as describing the pursuit of Christian perfection.[338] It is easy to see why interpreters made such moves, but identifications like this do not show what Jesus was trying to communicate about the kingdom.

Decisions on the Issues

1. What is the relation of the parables of the Treasure and the Pearl and the significance of that relation? Is there any difference in nuance because of the difference in tense? See the treatment of this question in the explanation of the Treasure in the Field (pp. 242-43).

2. Do the features have allegorical significance? Partly because of the past tense of verbs in this parable, O. Glombitza argued that the merchant stood for God who seeks people and has given all for them in his one-time act of redemption.[339] Nothing justifies such a conclusion, and as with the Treasure, there is no basis for assigning allegorical identification to any of the parable's features.

3. What does the similitude teach? The explanation of the teaching of the Treasure in the Field is relevant here and most aspects will not be repeated. Worthy of repetition is that those who ignore the boundaries of parable time and think the purchase of the pearl leaves the merchant impoverished violate how analogies and metaphorical language work.[340] As with the Treasure the similitude suits a general audience as easily as the disciples, and nothing inherent in the parable suggests that it was told only to disciples. It functions to strengthen the message of the Treasure in urging recognition of the significance of the presence of the kingdom and the radical obedience required to participate in that kingdom. Nothing is more significant or valuable for Jesus' Jewish audience than what he offers with the kingdom.

The fact that the merchant was seeking ought not be either overemphasized or underappreciated. Neither parable is a plan on how to find the kingdom, but surely that the merchant was seeking pearls implies for hearers that they too should be seeking what is truly worthwhile.

That the merchant sold all may be hyperbole, a standard feature of parables, but if so, the hyperbole underscores that the kingdom cannot be fitted into some previously existing system. All other systems have to be given up in order to experience the kingdom.

Adapting the Parable

See the corresponding section for the Treasure (pp. 246-47). I do not think this parable describes a different group of people (such as those terribly earnest about finding ultimate meaning) or that it teaches that joy is not enough.[341]

For Further Reading

W. D. Davies and D. C. Allison, Jr., *A Critical and Exegetical Commentary on the Gospel According to Saint Matthew* (ICC; Edinburgh: T. & T. Clark, 1991), 2:437-40.

Arland J. Hultgren, *The Parables of Jesus: A Commentary* (Grand Rapids: Eerdmans, 2000), pp. 416-23.

R. Schippers, "The Mashal-Character of the Parable of the Pearl," *SE* 2 (= *TU* 87) (1964): 236-41.

*　　　*　　　*

Other parables contrast the old to the new reality that has come with Jesus and emphasize the celebration that should be occurring: the analogies of the Old Garment and the New Patch and of the Old Wineskins and the New Wine and the parables of the Banquet and of the Two Lost Sons. If we know anything of Jesus' message, surely it is that he preached the present and coming kingdom and the newness that was already making its way. While kingdom and power language can be abused, such language is not oppressive if we refer to God's kingdom. The kingdom of the God of grace is not oppressive, even if we must also speak of judgment with kingdom language. The authority of the kingdom is inherent in the very being of God.[342]

We cannot avoid a focus on time and its change with the historical Jesus. But, was the kingdom really present? Did history really change? Christians have no doubt about answering both questions affirmatively. Is the kingdom *still* present, and, if history changed, how did it change? What was and is really new? Two items must be mentioned: the Holy Spirit and the resurrection. Neither is directly pertinent for discussing parables, but both are of supreme significance for discussing Jesus and newness. If the kingdom was present with Jesus, it was only because the Holy Spirit endowed his ministry from the first. If any claim can be made that the kingdom still is present, it is because the Spirit was poured out by the resurrected Christ.

The problem with any claim for newness, the presence of the kingdom, and real change in history, however, is the continued presence of evil and the failure of the Christian church. We have seen that some parables address the presence of evil and the hiddenness (if not invisibility) of the kingdom during Jesus' lifetime (the Wheat and the Weeds, the Growing Seed, the Mustard Seed, and the Leaven), and the point of those parables is still as relevant as ever. Yet, if the church has any viable message and is not to be laughed out of existence, it has a responsibility to demonstrate the presence of God's kingdom. The church does not bring in the kingdom. It witnesses to, is a servant of, and demonstrates the presence of the kingdom. Christians have the task of showing the reality of the new age right in the midst of the old. That same Holy Spirit active with Jesus must be evident showing the compassion, the acceptance, the forgiveness, the justice, and the joy that marked Jesus' own ministry. Without that, we have no right to speak of the presence of the kingdom.

Parables Specifically about Israel

The categories into which the parables are placed never totally suffice. One can easily argue that other parables should be included in a particular category, or sometimes parables may overlap two categories. With regard to the parables mirroring Israel, part of the Lukan version of the parable of the Pounds, with its allusions to Archelaus, is surely about Israel, even though for other reasons it is treated in this volume with parables on future eschatology. N. T. Wright, of course, would see almost all of Jesus' parables as parables of Israel, but in my opinion he has forced a number of parables into this category.[1]

THE BARREN FIG TREE
(Luke 13:6-9)

Parable Type

This is a double indirect narrative parable. It has a developed plot, but is left without a resolution or a *nimshal*. It is one of nine parables that end without an explicit explanation. The need for a *nimshal* is lessened by the preceding material, which functions implicitly to indicate the intent.

Issues Requiring Attention[2]

1. What is the relation between this parable and the incident of the cursing of the fig tree (Matt 21:18-22/Mark 11:12-14, 20-25) and the parable of the fig tree in Matt 24:32-33/Mark 13:28-29/Luke 21:29-31?

2. To whom was the parable originally addressed?
3. Is the connection between the parable and its context original?
4. What metaphorical associations — if any — are intended with the three years, the fig tree, the owner, and the vinedresser?
5. Is the focus on mercy and delay or on the present crisis, and how do these factors relate to the ministry of Jesus?
6. Does the impending judgment point to the destruction of Jerusalem or to final judgment?

Helpful Primary Source Material

Canonical Material

- OT: Isa 5:1-7; 10:34; Jer 8:10-13; Hos 9:10, 16; Mic 7:1-7; Hab 3:16-17
- NT: Matt 3:10/Luke 3:9; Matt 21:18-22/Mark 11:12-14 and 20-25; Matt 24:32-35/Mark 13:28-31/Luke 21:29-33

Early Jewish Writings

- *L.A.B.* 12.8-9: Moses, after the golden calf incident, describes God as wanting to uproot a vine he has planted because it has lost its fruit. Moses pleads for mercy and for the restraint of God's anger from destroying the vine. This account seems to be adapted by the parable in *Exod. Rab.* 43.9 printed below.
- *L.A.B.* 37.3 recounts the Jotham fable of Judges 9: ". . . and the fig tree signifies the people, and the vine signifies those who were before us."

Greco-Roman Writings

- Appendix 299 (Perry, *LCL*) of Aesop's Fables tells of a tree that yielded no fruit. The farmer wanted to cut it down in spite of the protests of the birds and cicadas who lived there, but when he struck the tree three times with his axe, he found a beehive and honey, which resulted in his sparing the tree and tending it carefully.

Early Christian Writings

- *Apocalypse of Peter* 2: "'And ye, *receive ye the parable of the fig-tree* thereon: as soon as *its shoots* have gone forth and *its boughs* have *sprouted*, the end of the world will come.' And I, Peter, answered and said unto him, 'Explain to me concerning the fig-tree, [and] how we shall perceive it, for throughout all its days does the fig-tree sprout and every year it brings forth its fruit [and] for its master. What (then) meaneth the parable of the fig-tree? We know it not.' — And the Master answered and said unto me, 'Dost thou not understand that the fig-tree is the house of Israel? Even as a man *hath planted a fig-tree in his garden* and it brought forth no fruit, and he *sought its fruit for* many years. When he *found it not, he said to the keeper of his garden,* "*Uproot the fig-tree* that *our land may* not be unfruitful for us." And the gardener *said to God,* "*We thy servants (?) wish to clear it (of weeds) and to dig the ground around it and to water it. If it does not then bear fruit,* we will immediately *remove* its roots from the garden and plant another one in its place." Hast thou not grasped that the fig-tree is the house of Israel?'"[3]

- *Pistis Sophia* 3.122: "Mary answered [concerning a woman whom Jesus had baptized three times and who still had not acted worthy of the baptisms] and said: 'My Lord, I have understood the mysteries of the things which have fallen to this woman's lot. Concerning the things then which have fallen to her lot, thou hast spoken unto us aforetime in similitude, saying: "A man owned a fig-tree in his vineyard; and he came to look for its fruit, and he found not a single one on it. He said to the vine-dresser: Lo, three years do I come to look for fruit on this fig-tree, and I have not any produce at all from it. Cut it down then; why doth it make the ground also good for nothing? But he answered and said unto him: My lord, have patience with it still this year, until I dig round it and give it dung; and if it beareth in another year, thou hast let it, but if thou dost not find any [fruit] at all, then hast thou [to] cut it down." Lo, my Lord, this is the solution of the word.'"[4]

Later Jewish Writings

Numerous rabbinic stories about vineyards and gardens exist; see the examples given with the parables of the Workers in the Vineyard, the Two Sons, and the Wicked Tenants.

- The Arabic version of *Ahiqar* 8.30 compares Ahiqar's nephew to a fruitless tree by the water (the most fertile location), which on the threat of being cut down asks to be moved to another place and given a last chance, a request that is rejected. While this story is old, the Arabic version in which this account appears is of a questionable and probably quite late date. J. Jeremias has influenced a number of commentators to assume that Jesus knew and adapted the parable from *Ahiqar,* but the evidence is too late to be credible.[5]

- *Exod. Rab.* 43.9: "It can be compared to a king who had an uncultivated field and who said to a tenant-labourer: 'Go improve it and convert it into a vineyard.' The labourer departed and tended the field and planted it as a vineyard. The vines grew and produced wine, which, however, became sour. When the king saw that the wine had become sour, he said to the labourer: 'Go and cut it all down; what is the use to me of a vineyard which produces vinegar?' But the labourer pleaded: 'O my lord and king, consider what sums thou didst lay out before the vineyard was planted, and now thou seekest to cut it all down.'" The laborer explains that the sourness is due to the newness of the vineyard and that new vineyards cannot produce good wine. The parable is interpreted of Moses interceding for Israel after the incident of the Golden Calf.[6]
- *b. 'Erubin* 21a-b describes the righteous as good figs and the wicked as bad figs, but holds out hope that the bad figs will yet be profitable. This is drawn from Jer 24:1-10.

Textual Features Worthy of Attention

Luke 12 emphasizes the themes of real vs. false security, focusing on the kingdom rather than possessions, readiness for the return of the Master, and judgment. *Discerning the time* is the focus in vv. 35-56, and in vv. 57-59 the focus is on the need to settle with one's accuser rather than face judgment. The parable and its context emphasize both discerning the time and avoiding judgment. Note the focus on time *(kairos)* in 12:56 and 13:1.

The sequence of problem, answer, parable in 13:1-9 mirrors the same sequence in 12:13-21, and the wording of 13:2-5 *(dokeite . . . ouchi, legō hymin all')* mirrors that of 12:51.

The preceding narrative about Pilate's slaughter of worshipers and about those who died when a tower fell provides a warning and call for repentance. This preceding context functions as an introductory explanation of the parable, much like the Lukan introductions at 18:1, 9; 19:11.

Resonances from the parable also reverberate in the following account about the healing of the crippled woman (13:10-17). She has been in a weakened condition for a long time (eighteen years). Jesus' ministry of restoration is effective for her, but others resist. She is healed; will Israel be restored? The number eighteen from v. 4 reappears in v. 11 and functions like a magnet to keep the texts closely connected and easily transmitted in an oral context.

The gardener tells the owner that he will dig around the tree and put manure on it to see if it produces fruit in the future; if it does not, "*you* will cut it down."[7] The owner, not the gardener, will do the cutting or at least give the order to do so.

The story is left without resolution.[8] Other parables sometimes end at the conclusion of a dialogue.[9] The parable does not state explicitly that the owner accepted the vinedresser's advice, but this is assumed. At the narrative level the question remains open whether Israel will respond, even though at the time of writing Luke knew the outcome, at least for most of Israel. Contrast the openness of the parable with Luke's two laments over Jerusalem (13:34-35 and 19:41-44).

The parable of the Wheat and the Weeds is similar to this parable in several respects: both report a problem with plants, someone suggests immediate action, someone else urges delay, and both have reference to judgment for sin.[10] A parallel also exists with the parable of the Unforgiving Servant in that a harsh decision is altered after a request for leniency (Matt 18:25-27).[11]

To some degree this parable mirrors 13:32-35, Jesus' assertion that he is completing his work today, tomorrow, and the third day and his lament over Jerusalem.

The double tradition material has a focus on "fruit." See especially Matt 3:8-10/Luke 3:8-9; Matt 7:16-20/Luke 6:43-44.

Cultural Information

The fig tree is not as clear a symbol for Israel as a vine or a vineyard, but a fig tree and figs are used several times in connection with Israel (Jer 24:1-10; Hos 9:10; Mic 7:1; *L.A.B.* 37.3; *Exod. Rab.* 36.1). Fig trees and vines were associated with peace and prosperity, and their absence was seen as a curse and punishment (Deut 8:8; 2 Kgs 18:31; and Num 20:5 respectively). The idea of sitting under one's own vine and fig tree became virtually a symbol for the messianic age. The eschatological associations of the fig tree are important (for the origin of such thinking see 1 Kgs 4:25; Isa 34:4; Mic. 4:4; Zech 3:10; cf. Rev 22:2).[12] Conversely, unproductive plants are frequent images of the unfaithful nation or individuals (Isa 5:1-7; Jer 8:13; Mic 7:1-2; Hos 9:16; Wis 4:5; 10:7; Matt 7:16-20/Luke 6:43-45; Jude 12), and the destruction of vines and fig trees is a metaphor for judgment (Ps 105:33; Jer 29:17; Ezek 17:9; 19-12-14; Hos 2:12[14]; Joel 1:7, 12; Amos 4:9). Putting manure on trees is not mentioned in the OT.

Fig trees bear the early figs in May and June and the late or summer figs from August to October. Josephus exaggerates in saying that fig trees in Galilee bore fruit ten months of the year (*J.W.* 3.519).

That a fig tree is planted in a vineyard is not unusual.[13] Fig trees and vine-yards are associated in several OT texts (e.g., Ps 105:33; Song 2:13; Jer 8:13; Joel 1:7, 12; Mic. 4:4). In fact, vines are allowed to grow on fig trees for support of the vine (Pliny the Elder, *Naturalis Historia* 17.35.199-200). Athenaeus, quoting Hipponax, even says that the black fig tree is sister of the vine (*Deipnosophistae* 3.78b).[14]

Atrocities committed by Pontius Pilate are well-attested, but efforts to identify the event recounted in Luke 13:1 with a specific report from Josephus or others are unsuccessful.[15]

Explanation of the Parable

Options for Interpretation

This parable has been an easy target for the church's allegorizing, which devel-oped primarily along three lines, seeing the parable as a description of the Jews, of human morality, or, less frequently, of the church. Ambrose viewed the vine-yard as the Jewish people, the fig tree as the synagogue with the Lord coming three times seeking fruit (with Abraham, with Moses and the Law, and with the incarnation), and the vinedresser as Peter. Augustine understood the vineyard as the world, the fig tree as the human race, the three times coming as God's re-lation with humanity before the Law, under the Law, and under grace, the gar-dener as saints in the church, and the cultivation and fertilization as teaching on humility/penitence and sorrow for sin. Later the vineyard was understood of the church, the fig tree either of a person or a monastery, and the three visits of the stages of human life: the times before the Law, under the Law, and under grace; or the three years of Jesus' ministry.[16] The three-year time frame for Je-sus' ministry is, of course, from John, not Luke, and the request for additional time would include a fourth year, which precludes any reference to Jesus' three-year ministry.

The parable is now most often seen as a warning and a call to repentance, either to Israel or, from Luke's standpoint, to both Israel and early Christians. This approach does not depend on whether one finds allegorical representation or not, and various nuances are possible. Other options have been offered but have little in their favor.[17]

Decisions on the Issues

1. What is the relation between this parable and the acted parable of the cursing of the fig tree (Matt 21:18-22/Mark 11:12-14, 20-25) and the parable of the fig tree in

Matt 24:32-33/Mark 13:28-29/Luke 21:29-31? The *Apocalypse of Peter* already joined our parable to Matt 24:32-33/Mark 13:28-29/Luke 21:29-31 (see above, pp. 256-57), but there is little connection between the two accounts other than the mention of a fig tree. More pertinent is the question of the relation of the parable to the cursing of the fig tree. Since Luke does not have the cursing incident, people have sometimes suggested that this parable has been made into the cursing event by Matthew and Mark or that the cursing has been turned into a parable by Luke.[18] Both accounts deal with the lack of fruit, but the accounts go in quite different directions. Nothing in the accounts of the cursing parallels the request for leniency and additional time. Further, little verbal similarity exists other than the words in Luke 13:6 "fig tree," "came," "on it," and "did not find." The leaves are not mentioned in the parable, but they are a crucial point in Matthew and Mark.[19] There is little reason to see any direct connection between the accounts, and few recent scholars argue for a direct connection. From a redactional standpoint, having used the parable, Luke would not have had much impetus to include the cursing incident.[20]

2. To whom was the parable originally addressed? Two questions are involved here. First, is the parable addressed to the crowd generally or to the leaders? Second, is it addressed to the nation or to the individual? The first question would not have arisen apart from K. Bailey's assuming Isa 5:1-7 as the background of this parable. Since the Isaiah text is used in the parable of the Wicked Tenants to address Israel's leaders, Bailey concludes that this parable is also addressed to the leaders.[21] However, any connection of this parable to Isaiah 5 is remote at best. From Luke 11:29 on the concern is the failure of "this generation," even when the Pharisees are being denounced (11:49-51). In ch. 12 Jesus addresses his disciples in the presence of the crowds. There is no change of time or place after 12:1 until 13:10. Between 12:1 and 13:10 Jesus addresses the disciples (vv. 1-12), someone in the crowd (vv. 13-14), "them" (vv. 15-21, presumably the crowd), the disciples (vv. 22-53, but Peter in v. 41 asks if the parable is for them or for all), the crowds (vv. 54-59), and the ones who bring the question about Pilate (13:1). Nothing suggests that the leadership is in view with the parable; rather it is addressed to a general audience. That is Luke's intent, and nothing in the parable suggests otherwise for Jesus. Jesus' message of repentance, like that of John the Baptist, was directed to the nation and not just to its leaders.

Some would limit the address of the parable, at least for Luke, to the individual, not the nation.[22] In some ways this is a false dichotomy, for if the concern is for the nation, it is individuals within the nation who must effect change. Luke, no doubt, wants his Christian readers to know that "fruit" is expected from them, even though the context is entirely about Israel, but we may safely conclude that Jesus' concern is with the nation.

3. Is the connection between the parable and its context original? Several parables in Luke are introduced by comments from individuals or by a dialogue between an individual and Jesus.[23] The report of Pilate killing Galileans while they were sacrificing was intended to elicit a response from Jesus which would reveal his stance either toward the Roman occupation and Zealot tendencies or toward the relation of catastrophe and sin. Whatever the motivation of the announcement, Jesus declined the invitation and added another example, that of eighteen killed when a tower fell in Jerusalem (v. 4). The two examples are presented almost as synonymous parallelism. Many in the ancient world (as also the modern world) presumed that catastrophe was an indication of the sinfulness of the victim,[24] a connection that Jesus did not accept as necessary. He rejected the notion of direct retributive justice and that the calamities mentioned proved the greater sinfulness of the victims. Instead he warned that destruction faced all who do not repent (13:3, 5). As elsewhere when people asked Jesus about someone else, his response was "Look to yourself first."[25]

There is no inherent necessity that the parable was initially told immediately after the warning in 13:1-5. Within Luke's narrative the warning functions as an introduction to the parable, which renders an explanation of the parable unnecessary. Without this introduction, the intent might still have been clear, if people discerned easily that the fig tree was a metaphor for Israel. The parable would still be an analogy of impending but delayed judgment. Whether the parable was told originally in its present context is impossible to determine. Luke may be responsible for bringing the two accounts together, as would be supported by the parallels with other dialogues introducing parables. On the other hand, that the two were connected in the tradition before Luke or by Jesus cannot be excluded.[26] Commentators often note that the parable fits its context well and seems to require, if not this context, at least some similar occasion.[27] What is clear is that Luke wants the two passages read together.[28] Both show that something is terribly wrong and provide a warning of judgment and call for repentance, but the parable is not merely a repetition of the warning in vv. 1-5. The preceding verses express only crisis, but the parable tells of coming to the brink of crisis and the crisis being pushed back. The crisis is delayed, and hope is aroused that destruction will not be necessary.

4. What metaphorical associations if any are intended with the three years, the fig tree, the owner, and the vinedresser? The church's allegorizing took the parable out of its context in Jesus' ministry and may be set aside, but what did Jesus and Luke intend with these images? Decisions are not easy, but a great deal can be learned from this parable about method. Once again, parable interpretation is not about finding correspondences but about determining how an analogy works, yet analogies do have correspondences. We cannot begin to interpret this parable without finding metaphorical significance, but how far should we push the images? A. Jülicher, as expected, denied any representational significance, including interpreting the fig tree as Israel. He thought the parable reinforced the warning in vv. 1-5 but, although he denied that the tree stands for Israel, he had to grant that Jesus spoke the parable in view of Israel. The tree is not Israel but is applied to Israel so that Israel finds itself already in the position of the fig tree.[29] This looks like double-talk, but on the other hand, surely Jülicher is correct to argue the parable does not reflect a dialogue between the Father and the Son so that God's wrath is softened by the request. Similarly B. Heininger thinks Jesus brings to expression in a parabolic way his sending to Israel and that his appearance and preaching mean a last time of grace for Israel. The tree is interpreted as Israel, but Heininger denies that the owner refers to God, the gardener to Jesus, and the three years to the time since the ministry of John the Baptist, even if the logic of the fertilization may contain an allusion to the ministry of Jesus.[30] This too sounds like double-talk and shows how difficult it is to maintain a denial of metaphorical significance to parables.

Again, the important point is knowing when to stop interpreting. Not all aspects of the source domain are mapped onto the target domain. As J. Liebenburg points out, two assumed metaphors are operative in this parable: people are plants and fruits are actions. For him the similarities between vv. 1-5 and vv. 6-9 governs how the mapping takes place, with the result that the people are mapped by the plant, the lack of deeds is mapped by the lack of fruit, God is mapped by the man, and Jesus is mapped by the caretaker.[31] At least the first three must be granted. From OT and Jewish texts on fig trees,[32] the symbolism of the fig tree for Israel is obvious, and if that is the case, the parable unavoidably depicts the failure of the nation in its relation to God. The intervention of the gardener is more difficult to assess. It may be that Jesus intends a self-reference,[33] or the gardener may only dramatize the brevity of time available for change. Not much is gained by a self-reference since in any case Jesus is the one announcing the delay and the present crisis. His ministry is a call for the nation to return. The difference of opinion between the owner and the gardener and the acts of digging and fertilizing do not map onto reality and cannot be paralleled from Jesus' non-parabolic teaching.

The three years have no specific referent. Because of Lev 19:23-24, which indicates that the fruit of a tree's first three years is forbidden and the fruit of the fourth year is holy to the Lord, interpreters have debated the age of this tree, with six, seven, and nine years being suggested.[34] The age of the tree is not stated and is irrelevant. The three years only indicate the complete failure and seeming hopelessness of the tree.

5. Is the focus on mercy and delay or on the present crisis, and how do these factors relate to the ministry of Jesus? The parable up through v. 7 is very close to the statement of John the Baptist that the axe already lies at the root of the tree (Matt 3:10/Luke 3:9), which has the only occurrence of *ekkoptō* ("cut out") in Luke-Acts outside 13:6-9. But vv. 8-9 of the parable mark out a major distinction between the messages of John and Jesus. The crisis announced by John is not lessened, but it is temporarily suspended to see if productivity can be established. If John said "Judgment is here," Jesus says, "There is still time, but not much."

Like Abraham interceding for Sodom, the gardener intercedes for the fig tree.[35] Fig trees normally do not require much attention, but the gardener proposes unusual care and effort. The parable points to the situation of Jesus' ministry, both the crisis of judgment announced on the nation and the granting of God's mercy. Jesus' ministry takes place on the edge between mercy and judgment; it is a display of mercy in view of the coming crisis. With this parable though, "mercy" may be inaccurate, and it would be wrong to overplay the focus on compassion,[36] even though compassion is a major component of Jesus' gospel. Judgment is not canceled in the parable; it is merely postponed, and the delay is a call for repentance. As Jülicher pointed out, the thought of the parable is close to that of Rom 2:4: the kindness of God is meant to lead to repentance.[37]

The message of the first part of this parable does parallel the theology of the song of the vineyard in Isaiah 5 (cf. Hos 9:16). *If the privilege of being God's people does not lead to productivity, it leads to judgment.*[38] Especially for Luke, conversion involves both a break from sin and production of fruit,[39] that is, life lived in obedience to the will of God. With this parable Israel is depicted as in a perilously similar position to the fruitless vineyard. Israel should have been like a fruitful fig tree, the very symbol of divine prosperity; instead she was fruitless and faced judgment. Rather than immediate destruction, which would be justified, a delay is in effect to provide a last chance to produce. There is still time, but not much.[40] The difference between the tone of this parable and the laments over Jerusalem (13:34-35; 19:41-44) suggests that this parable belongs to the beginning or middle of Jesus' ministry.[41]

6. Does the impending judgment point to the destruction of Jerusalem or to final judgment? What Jesus or Luke intended with this judgment is not specified. In view of 13:34-35 we probably should think of the destruction of Jerusalem, but as is evident elsewhere, the two options are not always kept separate. The concern is for the reality of judgment, not the description of it. One might hope that it is unnecessary, but we should add that this parable is not anti-Semitic. It is not a rejection of Israel but a warning of judgment because of the lack of productivity.[42]

Adapting the Parable

The parable asserts that the lack of productivity is a cause of judgment. Jesus pointed to his own ministry as a time of delay, of warning, before judgment comes. In our day we have little awareness of judgment and certainly no sense of the time of judgment or any sense of crisis. We are insulated from such ideas. Even so, life is lived in the tension of the offer of mercy and the reality of judgment, even if the parable is more about delay than mercy. We do not know when we will be called to account for our lives. We need to recover some sense that our actions really are significant and remember that the gospel includes judgment, mercy, and a call for repentance and productive living. Lack of productivity still stands under indictment before God. If the privilege of being God's people does not lead to productivity, it still leads to judgment. The Christian church stands under the indictment of this parable as much as Israel ever did. Further, as F. W. Young points out, whatever else is involved in repentance, a radical new understanding of time is required, a discerning of time and an understanding of how time impacts one's own life.[43]

For Further Reading

Kenneth Ewing Bailey, *Through Peasant Eyes: More Lucan Parables, Their Culture and Style* (Grand Rapids: Eerdmans, 1980), pp. 74-87.

Josef Blinzler, "Die letzte Gnadenfrist. Lk 13,6-9," *BL* 37 (1963-64): 155-69.

Greg W. Forbes, *The God of Old: The Role of the Lukan Parables in the Purpose of Luke's Gospel* (JSNTSup 198; Sheffield: Sheffield Academic, 2000), pp. 88-93.

H.-Konrad Harmansa, *Die Zeit der Entscheidung. Lk 13,1-9 als Beispiel für das lukanische Verständnis der Gerichtspredigt Jesu an Israel* (Erfurter Theologische Studien 69; Leipzig: Benno, 1995).

Charles W. Hedrick, "Prolegomena to Reading Parables: Luke 13:6-9 as a Test Case," *RevExp* 94 (1997): 179-97 (surveys a number of approaches and isolates methodological questions).

Peter Rhea Jones, *Studying the Parables of Jesus* (Macon, Ga.: Smyth & Helwys, 1999), pp. 123-41.

William R. Telford, *The Barren Temple and the Withered Tree* (JSNTSup 1; Sheffield: JSOT Press, 1980), 224-39.

THE TWO SONS
(Matt 21:28-32)[44]

This seemingly simple parable has caused considerable disagreement. Even so, scholars express themselves confidently on key issues as if there were no debate. One has the impression at times that arguments are created to verify conclusions already reached.

Parable Type

This is a *juridical parable,* a particular kind of double indirect narrative parable. It is similar to Isaiah 5 and other OT texts in which a prophet announces judgment by eliciting a self-condemnation from the hearer(s) through the aid of some image. The parable of Nathan to David in 2 Sam 12:1-10 is the classic example of this genre.[45] Matt 21:31b reveals that the hearers have condemned themselves, and v. 32 explains why this judgment is valid.

Issues Requiring Attention

1. Since there is a divided textual tradition on the wording of this parable, what is the original sequencing of the parable in vv. 29-31?
2. What is the original form of the parable, and is it from Jesus or Matthew? Were v. 31b (the statement about toll collectors and prostitutes) and v. 32 part of the original version of the parable or later additions? Or to ask the question another way, did the parable originally refer to John the Baptist? Is Luke 7:29 a parallel to v. 32?
3. Does the parable belong originally in its present context?
4. How should v. 31 and especially *proagousin* ("are going . . . ahead [of you]") be understood? Does *proagousin* mean the high priests and elders are excluded from the kingdom, or is the kingdom still open for them too? Further, were the toll collectors and prostitutes entering the kingdom during Jesus' ministry, or is *proagousin* a futuristic present indicating that the toll collectors and prostitutes will precede the hearers into the end-time kingdom? That is, is this a parable about present or future eschatology?
5. Is this parable christological?
6. Is this parable anti-Semitic?
7. What is the meaning of the parable?

Helpful Primary Source Material

Canonical Material

- OT: Isa 29:13; Ezek 33:31
- NT: Matt 7:21-27/Luke 6:46-49; Matt 8:11-12/Luke 13:28-30; Matt 11:16-19/ Luke 7:31-35; Mark 7:6/Matt 15:8; 23:3; Luke 7:29-30

Early Jewish Writings

- Philo, *Praem.* 79-84 emphasizes doing the commands as opposed to merely hearing them or treating them lightly. See the text on pp. 328-29 below.

Greco-Roman Writings

- Dio Chrysostom, *Oratio* 70.5 contrasts two persons, one who says that he intends to sail and gain from trading but makes no provision to do so and the other who plans and prepares the ship. He then asks: "Which of the two will you say is seriously interested in trading?" When the answer is given, "I should say the latter," the conclusion is drawn, "In every matter, then, will you consider that the word alone, unaccompanied by any act, is invalid and untrustworthy, but that the act alone is both trustworthy and true, even if no word precedes it?" The answer is given, "Just so."

Early Christian Writings

- Justin, *1 Apologia* 16.10 also underscores the necessity of doing as opposed to merely professing Christ. See the text on p. 329 below.

Later Jewish Writings

Numerous rabbinic stories about vineyards and gardens exist, several of which are printed below with the parable of the Wicked Tenants (pp. 278-80). Also numerous stories exist about two sons whose behavior is contrasted. See above, pp. 120-21; 128-29 especially n. 178; and 129-30.

- *b. Baba Meṣiʿa* 87a: "This teaches that righteous men promise little and perform much; whereas the wicked promise much and do not perform even little."
- *Exod. Rab.* 27.9: "When God was about to give the Torah, no other nation

but Israel would accept it. It can be compared to a man who had a field which he wished to entrust to métayers. Calling the first of these, he inquired: 'Will you take over this field?' He replied: 'I have no strength; the work is too hard for me.' In the same way the second, third, and fourth declined to undertake the work. He called the fifth and asked him: 'Will you take over this field?' He replied 'Yes.' 'On the condition that you will till it?' The reply again was 'Yes.' But as soon as he took possession of it, he let it lie fallow. With whom is the king angry? With those who declared: 'We cannot undertake it,' or with him who did undertake it, but no sooner undertook it than he left it lying fallow? Surely, with him who undertook it. Similarly, when God revealed Himself on Sinai, there was not a nation at whose doors He did not knock, but they would not undertake to keep it; as soon as he came to Israel, they exclaimed: *All that the Lord hath spoken will we do, and obey* (Exod 24:7)."

- *Deut. Rab.* 7.4: "R. Simeon b. Ḥalafta said: If one learns the words of the Torah and does not fulfil them, his punishment is more severe than that of him who has not learnt at all. It is like the case of a king who had a garden which he let out to two tenants, one of whom planted trees and cut them down, while the other neither planted any [trees] nor cut any down. With whom is the king angry? Surely with him who planted [trees] and cut them down. Likewise, whosoever learns the words of the Torah and does not fulfil them, his punishment is more severe than that of him who has never learnt at all."

Textual Features Worthy of Attention

Like at least twenty-two of Jesus' parables, this one begins with a question. With the exception of John 11:56, the question in this exact form occurs only in Matthew, but there are close parallels. A second question in v. 31 entices the hearers to a self-condemning decision.

The words "finally repented" in v. 29 *(hysteron de metamelētheis)* are repeated in v. 32 *(metemelēthēte hysteron)*, forming an *inclusio*.

Obvious similarites exist between this parable and the parable of the Prodigal Son, but there are also differences.

The parable is connected with the preceding questioning of Jesus' authority by the focus in both on believing John the Baptist (vv. 25 and 32).

Matthew has placed three parables together here to mark the obstinacy of the Jewish leadership: the Two Sons, the Wicked Tenants (paralleled in Mark and Luke at the same place), and the Wedding Feast (Luke has a similar parable in a different context, 14:15-24). The three parables form a progression of increasingly strong denunciation. The wording of the three parables has been shaped in Matthew so that the wording of each has been influenced by the others. The parable of the Two Sons is tied to the parable of the Wicked Tenants by the use of "man" *(anthrōpos)*, "vineyard" *(ampelōn* in vv. 28, 33, 39, 40), "finally" *(hysteron* in vv. 29, 32, 37), "likewise" *(hōsautōs,* NRSV "the same," in vv. 30, 36), "sir/lord" *(kyrios* in vv. 30, 40), "Jesus said to them" (vv. 31, 42), the replacement motif (vv. 31, 41, 43), "kingdom of God" (vv. 31, 43, two of Matthew's four uses of this phrase[46]) instead of Matthew's more typical "kingdom of heaven," and "seeing" *(idontes* in vv. 32, 38). The parable of the Two Sons and that of the Wedding Feast are connected minimally by *apokritheis eipen* ("Answering he said") and *apēlthen/apēlthon* ("went"). For the connections between the other two parables see below, p. 283. A significant difference is that the Two Sons uses *tekna* and *teknon* ("children" and "child") whereas the other two parables have *huios* ("son").

In v. 30 the second son even says "Sir" *(kyrie),* showing significant deference.[47]

The verb in v. 31 "going before [you]" *(proagousin)* is present tense.

The parable of the Two Builders and its preceding context (7:15-27) and the parable of the Sower provide close parallels to the parable here.

"Toll collectors and prostitutes" *(hoi telōnai kai hai pornai)* appears only here. Whereas the word translated "toll collector" *(telōnēs)* occurs twenty times in the Synoptics, the only other occurrence of "prostitute" *(pornē)* in the Gospels is in the charge of the elder brother against the prodigal (Luke 15:30).

Several Mattheanisms appear in these verses:[48] *proserchesthai* ("come to"), *amēn legō hymin* (more than twice as often in Matthew as in Mark, and Luke has it even less), *hysteron* ("finally," but five of the seven occurrences are in parables), *dikaiosynē* ("righteousness," seven times in Matthew, none in Mark, and one in Luke), and possibly "What do you think?" *(ti hymin dokei),* although there are only six occurrences (two with the singular pronoun), and Jewish parallels exist.[49] On the other hand, some supposed Mattheanisms at least need to be discussed. Is it fair to say that *apokritheis eipen* ("answering he said") is Matthean (forty-one occurrences) when Luke has it twenty-five times? Is *hōsautōs* Matthean when it only occurs four times, while Mark has it twice and Luke three times? Is *metamelesthai* ("change the mind, repent") Matthean when outside this parable it occurs only once (27:3)?

Cultural Information

Little needs to be said here other than the reminder of the almost absolute authority that fathers possessed in the ancient world and of the stereotypically debased position of toll collectors and prostitutes.[50] The religious leaders with whom Jesus conversed would have had extreme disdain for both.

Explanation of the Parable

Options for Interpretation

From the time of Jerome the church allegorized the two sons as Gentiles who rejected the natural law but later obeyed Christ and Jews who vowed obedience but did not obey.[51] Jerome also accepted a straightforward reading so that the reference is to sinners who accepted John's message and pharisaic persons who rejected it.[52]

A. Jülicher thought this parable was one of the clearest and simplest and that it emphasized the discrepancy between saying and doing and the necessity of obedience.[53]

J. Lambrecht thinks the "yes-sayers" refer to people initially sympathetic to Jesus who later were unfaithful. He finds in the parable a hidden christological dimension since it deals with the new order God presents in Christ. It is an "eminently christological parable."[54]

B. Scott argues that both sons shamed and honored their father, the one by refusing and then going, the other by appearing to be a good son but doing nothing. He interprets the parable as a parable of the kingdom, which is like a family, an imperfect family.[55]

Others say that the parable describes two groups of Israelites: outcasts who have responded positively to the message of John the Baptist and the religious leaders who did not. By implication both groups respond to Jesus the same way they responded to John.[56]

Decisions on the Issues

1. *Since there is a divided textual tradition on the wording of this parable, what is the original sequence of the parable in vv. 29-31?* The textual problem in this passage is fairly complex in that the manuscript evidence supports three forms of the story.

(1) The first son refused to go to the vineyard, but changed his mind and went. The second son agreed to go but did not. The first is the one who did the father's will. This reading is supported by ℵ*, C*, L, W, X, Z, Δ, f¹, and the majority of the minuscules.

(2) The first son refused to go to the vineyard, but changed his mind and went. The second son agreed to go but did not. The second is the one who did the father's will. This reading is attested only by Codex Bezae, several Old Latin versions, and the Sinaitic and Curetonian Syriac.

(3) The first son agreed to go and did not. The second son refused to go, but changed his mind and went. The second is the one who did the father's will. With some variations this reading is supported by B, Θ, f¹³, 700, and a few other texts.

Somewhat surprisingly, all three of these readings have their defenders. Even though the second is the most difficult, relatively few argue it is the right reading since it makes no sense. Jerome knew of this reading and suggested that the Jews perversely and intentionally gave the wrong answer. But if it were the correct reading, one would expect a refutation of the answer in the text. This reading can be set aside.[57] Either of the other readings works, and they could be the result of different oral performances of the parable. Most investigating this question rightly accept the first reading as the original: the first son refuses to go, changes his mind, and then goes. The reverse order in the third reading emerged apparently to bring the two sons in line with the actual course of events: the Jews agreed to obey God but then did not, but the Gentiles, who at first refused, later accepted the gospel.[58]

2. What is the original form of the parable, and is it from Jesus or Matthew? Were v. 31b (the statement about toll collectors and prostitutes) and v. 32 part of the original version of the parable or are they later additions? Or to ask the question another way, did the parable originally refer to John the Baptist and is Luke 7:29 a parallel to v. 32? There are four main positions held on the origin and authenticity of vv. 28-32:

(1) The entire section is a Matthean creation. This is argued by relatively few.[59]

(2) Except for the initial question, vv. 28 through 31b (the answer) are from Jesus, and vv. 31c-32 are from Matthew or his tradition.[60]

(3) All of vv. 28-31 are from Jesus, and v. 32 is from Jesus but originally belonged in another context.[61]

(4) Vv. 28-32 form a coherent whole and belong together as a parable from Jesus.[62]

Positions two and three usually assume that the original parable ended with something like Matt 7:21 with its focus on doing the will of the Father.

No one doubts that Matthew has shaped the material, but indications of an Evangelist's style do not necessarily indicate origin. The words attributed to Jesus in vv. 31 and 32 are questioned for these reasons:[63]

(1) The parable's contrast between hearing and doing is not present in v. 31.
(2) V. 32 appears to be a reshaping of an independent logion found in Luke 7:29-30.
(3) The parable depicts a change of mind in the obedient son, whereas nothing is known of a change of mind for either the Jewish leaders or the sinners in relation to John the Baptist.
(4) The present arrangement assumes that John the Baptist is compared to the father in the parable, but a father with two sons and a vineyard is not a fitting image for the ascetic prophet.

The complaint that the contrast between hearing and doing is not present has force only if one has already rejected v. 32. With v. 32 in place the contrast between some who appear righteous but do not demonstrate it and others who appear unrighteous but repent and show themselves righteous is very much present. Matt 21:32 has little in common with Luke 7:29-30 and is not a reshaping of it, which is acknowledged even by some who disconnect v. 32 from the parable.[64] The only words in both Matt 21:32 and Luke 7:29-30 are "John," "toll collectors," and "him."[65] Both the third and fourth reasons assume that the parable must be a thin allegorical representation of reality rather than an analogy. The charge that no change of mind takes place toward John by either group misses the point, for the change in mind is not in relation to John but in relation to *God*. John is not mirrored by the image of the father; he is merely the occasion to which obedience and refusal are responses. The issue is that people who initially seemed disobedient repented and believed, while those who claimed obedience really did not obey. The assumption, of course, is that John was a messenger from God who should be heeded. Matthew has not previously made the point that outcasts followed John — only that the people he baptized were confessing their sins, but he has mentioned the conflict between John and the Pharisees and Sadducees in 3:7-12.[66]

The primary disjunction between v. 32 and the parable is that the parable focuses on obedience to the will of the father whereas v. 32 focuses on belief. This could be part of Matthew's shaping of the parable to the context, but it is an appropriate summary unless one has driven a wedge between belief and practice. In fact, the parable, with or without v. 32, fits well with the Matthean emphasis on actual obedience to the will of God as opposed to merely claiming to serve God (e.g., 7:15-27, especially 21-23; and 19:16-22).

There are also positive reasons to see vv. 31-32 as originally joined to the parable. First, as J. Lambrecht admits, without the explanation in vv. 31c-32 the parable is puzzling;[67] the story is left incomplete, without direction and force. No one would have gotten its message. Second, "kingdom of God" in v. 31 is not Matthew's typical language and cannot be written off to redaction as easily as some attempt.[68] Third, and most significantly, I find it very unlikely that Matthew or any other early Christian would have changed the parable so that it focused on believing John the Baptist to enter the kingdom.[69] What would be gained by shifting the focus from Jesus and the will of the Father to John? Fourth, the *inclusio* established between vv. 29 and 32 favors the view that v. 32 belonged with the parable from the first. V. 32 serves well as an explanation for the reversal found in v. 31, and in my opinion is a necessary part of the parable.

3. Does the parable belong originally in its present context? Whether the parable was originally spoken in this context or has been placed here by Matthew depends largely on one's understanding of v. 32. If v. 32 belonged with the parable originally, the parable would necessarily have emerged in some such discussion about John the Baptist and fits well in its present context.[70] The narrative in Matthew works well, and the parable is not a disruption between the question of authority and the parable of the Wicked Tenants.[71] If v. 32 is a later attachment, the parable in vv. 28-31 would fit in any discussion between Jesus and his Jewish opponents.

In this context the parable is an indictment of the Temple authorities for their failure to participate in the repentance movement started by the Baptist. This assumes that what John the Baptist began Jesus is continuing and that to reject one is to reject the other.

4. How should v. 31 and especially proagousin *("are going . . . ahead [of you]") be understood? Does* proagousin *mean that the high priests and elders are excluded from the kingdom, or is the kingdom still open for them too? Further, were the toll collectors and prostitutes entering the kingdom during Jesus' ministry, or is* proagousin *a futuristic present indicating that the toll collectors and prostitutes will precede the hearers into the end-time kingdom? Is this a parable about present or future eschatology?* With equal confidence scholars affirm both that *proagousin* means that the religious authorities are excluded from the kingdom and that the way is still open for them.[72] I do not think the mere use of this word allows us to say, and in fact, framing the question this way seeks more from the word than is justified. The next parable may indicate that Matthew thinks of exclusion, but that cannot be determined from the present parable. The intent is merely to indicate how far off base the religious authorities are in their attitudes toward Jesus and John. Even the people they would despise most are more in line with God's purposes than they are.

With regard to whether the present tense *proagousin* points to the present or the future, I am inclined to see a reference to the presence of the kingdom. That would make sense in terms of the emphasis on the presence of the kingdom elsewhere and also because of the response of the outcasts to Jesus, but in reality the tense of this verb does not permit a firm conclusion. The reference could be to the future kingdom just as easily.[73]

5. *Is this parable christological?* This question probably would not be asked were it not for the attempts of J. Lambrecht and H. Weder to interpret the parable christologically. Having set aside v. 31 (in part), v. 32, and the Matthean context, they reconstruct a supposed original and find in it a christological claim.[74] Nothing in the parable suggests a christological reference. The word "son" *(huios)* is not used,[75] and no reference is made to Jesus in any way. At most one might find an implicit christological claim in that Jesus decides who takes precedence in entering the kingdom, but that does not prove messianic identity.

6. *Is this parable anti-Semitic?* The parable is not anti-Semitic and does not have the Jews as an ethnic group in mind. The parable is directed against the high priests and the elders, not the whole nation. The toll collectors and prostitutes are not a metaphor for Gentile Christians. The sinners who were entering the kingdom were also Jews who had responded to John's message.

7. *What is the meaning of the parable?* The vineyard is *not* Israel, which would make no sense; rather it stands for God's purposes generally. To work in God's vineyard is the equivalent of being engaged with God's purposes. The parable breaks the stalemate over the question of authority (vv. 23-27) by enticing the Jewish leaders to judge themselves. By analogy they are accused of not having been engaged with the work God was doing with John the Baptist. Quite clearly what counts is obedience, actual performance of God's desires, not mere profession. The expression "way of righteousness" in v. 32 has caused considerable debate, but whether the focus is merely on proper conduct or points more comprehensively to the purpose and plan of God for salvation,[76] the assumption is that John came in the way marked out by God, and the leaders did not join him in that way. Twice in v. 32 it is said that the leaders did not believe John: they did not believe at first and even when they saw sinners believing they still did not change their minds and believe him. In what way they failed to obey God is not specified by the parable, but one would presume that Jesus' complaints about emphasizing ritual purity and the traditions of the elders rather than mercy and love lie behind the charge of disobedience.[77]

The parable then is an accusation that the leaders of Israel claim to serve God but do not (cf. 23:3, where the Pharisees are accused of saying and not doing). It is also an assertion that the repentance movement begun by John the Baptist and continuing with Jesus is the work of God that leads to the kingdom. Implicitly it is also a defense of Jesus' identification with sinners.

Adapting the Parable

The primary feature of this text is clear. God requires productive and obedient living from his people. Claims and concerns for appearance are not enough. Churches often push for membership and professions of faith but allow (or even foster) a separation between believing and doing. How did people ever get the idea that obedience to the will of God is optional? Many parables, and especially this one, push for an integrity of life before God. Talk and external appearance are cheap; what counts is actually doing the will of the Father from the heart (cf. Matt 7:15-27). Any separation of believing and doing is a distortion of the gospel message and is directly confronted by this parable. A person cannot believe apart from obedience.

This parable should caution us against assuming that involvement in religious life and claiming religious authority are guarantees of legitimacy or theological accuracy. Those of us engaged in religious life should be the least presumptuous both about ourselves and about those we think are "outside." The parable also encourages us to remember that initial responses are not ultimate responses. An initial refusal does not have to stay a refusal,[78] and an initial agreement is not enough. It must be lived.

For Further Reading

Arland J. Hultgren, *The Parables of Jesus: A Commentary* (Grand Rapids: Eerdmans, 2000), pp. 218-25.

Ulrich Luz, *Matthew 21–28* (trans. James E. Crouch; Minneapolis: Fortress, 2005), pp. 25-33.

Wesley G. Olmstead, *Matthew's Trilogy of Parables: The Nation, the Nations, and the Reader in Matthew 21:28–22:14* (SNTSMS 127; Cambridge: Cambridge University Press, 2003), pp. 99-108 and 167-76.

THE WICKED TENANTS
(Matt 21:33-46; Mark 12:1-12; Luke 20:9-19; *Gos. Thom.* 65–66)

This is one of the most significant, most discussed, and most complicated of all the parables, and not surprisingly, one about which there is enormous debate. For some the parable says too much for them to be comfortable that it represents the view of Jesus, but the attempts to make it say less render it banal. If it is taken out of the sphere of Jesus' confrontation with Israel's leaders, the interpretations seem odd, especially for first-century Palestine, and are unconvincing. The stakes are high, for, unlike most parables, this one is of direct and major christological significance.

Parable Type

This is a double indirect narrative parable with several correspondences between image and reality. The form varies in the different accounts, but in Matthew, like the parable of the Two Sons, this is a *juridical parable* similar to Isaiah 5 and other OT texts in which a prophet elicits a self-condemnation from the hearers through the aid of an image.[79] In Mark and Luke the juridical character of the parable is implicit. In all the Synoptic accounts the quotation of Ps 118:22 serves as a *nimshal* explaining the intent of the parable. The quotation is also in *Gos. Thom.* 66, immediately after the parable.

Issues Requiring Attention

1. Does Matt 21:44 belong in the text?
2. Does the parable belong in its present context?
3. What was the original form of the story? A number of questions are involved. Does the allusion to Isaiah 5 in Matthew and Mark belong to the parable? How many servants were sent before the son, and how were they treated? Where does the parable end? Is the judgment statement included? Did the quotation of Ps 118:22-23 (only 118:22 in Luke) belong to the parable originally, or does it stem from the early church? Does Matt 21:43 with its statement that the kingdom is taken away and given to others stem from Jesus? Does the second stone quotation in Luke 20:18 and most manuscripts of Matt 21:44 belong to the parable? Can the parable's transmission history be traced?
4. Is this story realistic, and how realistic must it be? What landowner would

act as this one does, particularly in Mark's Gospel, in sending servants repeatedly to be abused and then in sending his own son into such a situation? Do relevant cultural factors exist to make this story understandable?

5. Is this parable an allegory and, if so, do *all* the features in the story have some parallel in reality? What is the resultant meaning of the parable?
6. Does the parable stem from Jesus or from the early church? If from Jesus, what is its significance for his own sense of his mission and identity?
7. Does this parable, particularly in its Matthean form, teach that God has rejected Israel by giving the kingdom to Gentiles?

Helpful Primary Source Material[80]

Canonical Material

- OT: Isa 5:1-7; Ps 118:22-23; and Dan 2:44-45 are alluded to or quoted in the parable. See also 1 Kgs 21:1-29; 2 Chron 24:17-21; 26:10; Ps 1:3; Isa 3:14-15; Jer 12:7-17; Song 8:11-12. Is Gen 37:20 relevant?
- NT: Matt 23:37-39/Luke 13:34-35

Early Jewish Writings

- Wis 2:10-20 gives the words of the evil against the righteous person. In v. 13 the righteous man is said to call himself a child of the Lord *(paida kyriou)*. Then the evil say (vv. 16-20), "We are considered by him as something base, and he avoids our ways as unclean; he calls the last end of the righteous happy, and boasts that God is his father. Let us see if his words are true, and let us test what will happen at the end of his life; for if the righteous man is God's child *(huios theou)*, he will help him, and will deliver him from the hand of his adversaries. Let us test him with insult and torture, so that we may find out how gentle he is and make trial of his forbearance. Let us condemn him to a shameful death, for, according to what he says, he will be protected."
- Josephus, *J.W.* 5.272 describes the Romans' using war machines to lob large stones into Jerusalem during the siege of the city: "Watchmen were accordingly posted by them on the towers, who gave warning whenever the engine was fired and the stone in transit, by shouting in their native tongue, 'The son is coming' *(ho huios erchetai)*;[81] whereupon those in the line of fire promptly made way and lay down, owing to which precautions the stone passed harmlessly through and fell behind them."

- Josephus, *Ant.* 9.264-67 recounts how Israelites mocked and finally killed ambassadors from Hezekiah who invited them to come to Jerusalem to observe the feast of Unleavened Bread.

Greco-Roman Writings

- Plutarch, *Mor.* 236A *(Sayings of the Spartans):* The Spartans killed heralds sent from King Xerxes of Persia. To atone for this treachery, at the direction of an oracle two Spartan soldiers volunteered to go to Xerxes to be killed in any way he desired. He let them go free because of their bravery.

Early Christian Writings

- *4 Ezra* 1:32-35: "I sent you my servants the prophets, but you have taken and killed them and torn their bodies in pieces; I will require their blood of you, says the Lord. 'Thus says the Lord Almighty: Your house is desolate; I will drive you out as the wind drives straw; and your sons will have no children, because with you they have neglected my commandment and have done what is evil in my sight. I will give your houses to a people that will come, who without having heard me will believe. Those to whom I have shown no signs will do what I have commanded.'" This is part of the Christian addition to *4 Ezra* and is apparently shaped by Jesus' parable.
- *Gos. Thom.* 65–66: "He said: A good [*chrēstos*, or "rich," *chrēstēs*][82] man had a vineyard. He gave it to tenants that they might cultivate it and he might receive its fruit from them. He sent his servant so that the tenants might give him the fruit of the vineyard. They seized his servant (and) beat him; a little more and they would have killed him. The servant came (and) told it to his master. His master said, Perhaps he did not know them. He sent another servant; the tenants beat him as well. Then the owner sent his son. He said, Perhaps they will respect my son. Since those tenants knew that he was the heir of the vineyard, they seized him (and) killed him. He who has ears, let him hear. Jesus said: Show me the stone which the builders rejected. It is the cornerstone."[83]
- Hermas, *Sim.* 5.2.1–5.7.3 has a long allegorical parable constructed from this parable. See above, p. 53.

Later Jewish Writings.

Numerous rabbinic stories about vineyards and gardens exist, of which only the most obvious are mentioned here.[84]

- *Sifre Deut.* §312 (on 32:9): "A parable: A king had a field which he leased to tenants. When the tenants began to steal from it, he took it away from them and leased it to their children. When the children began to act worse than their fathers, he took it away from them and gave it to (the original tenants') grandchildren. When these too became worse than their predecessors, a son was born to him. He then said to the grandchildren, 'Leave my property. You may not remain therein. Give me back my portion, so that I may repossess it.'" In the accompanying explanation of the parable God is the king, Abraham is represented by the first tenants and Isaac by the second. These two were rejected because something objectionable was found in them, their sons Ishmael and Esau. The third group of tenants is not explained. The son in the parable represents Jacob, none of whose descendants were objectionable.
- *Midr. Tanḥuma Beshallah* 4.7 (on Exod 13:17): "To what is the matter comparable? To a king who had a small son. He also had an *ousia* [i.e., an orchard]. Now he wanted to go away overseas, <so> he told a certain tenant to take care of it and eat of its fruit until his son became mature. When the king's son grew up, he sought the *ousia*. The tenant immediately began to cry: Alas. Similarly, while Israel was in Egypt, the Canaanites dwelt in and took care of the land of Israel. They also ate of its fruits. As soon as they heard that Israel had left Egypt, they began yelling: Alas."
- *Midr. Tanḥuma Emor* 8.30 (on Lev 23:39-44) has a long parable about a province which owed taxes to a king. They did not pay when the king sent repeated emissaries. The king and his courtiers went themselves. As he approached, three successive delegations met him asking that the amount be forgiven. He forgave half, half more, and then the entire debt. The explanation is that the king is the Holy One and the people of the province are Israel, whose sins are forgiven at the festivals throughout the year. The multiple correspondences between parable and explanation are obvious.
- *Exod. Rab.* 30.17: "Because Egypt enslaved Israel, she was punished and justice was exacted both in Egypt and at the sea. They were like robbers who had broken into the king's vineyard and destroyed the vines. When the king discovered that his vineyard had been destroyed, he was filled with wrath, and descending upon the robbers, without help from anything or anyone, he cut them down and uprooted them as they had done to his vineyard."[85]
- *Lev. Rab.* 11.7: "This may be compared to the case of a province which owed tax arrears to the king, who sent a collector of the [king's] treasury to collect [the debt]. What did the people of the province do? — They rose and mulcted him and hanged him. People said: 'Woe to us, should

the king become aware of these things. That which the king's emissary sought to do to us, we did to him.'" This is also found in *Gen. Rab.* 42.3.

Comparison of the Accounts

This parable is a good example both of the essential fidelity of the Gospel writers to the tradition they received *and* the freedom with which they adapted it. Clearly the early church was not interested in verbatim reporting, and the Evangelists felt free to shape the material to their own purposes. The story is essentially the same in all accounts, but there are significant differences. Despite numerous attempts by NT scholars, one cannot with any confidence reconstruct a primitive version of the story, but one can trace movement within the tradition.

Gos. Thom. 65–66

The *Gos. Thom.* account is less obviously theological and is much shorter and simpler than the Synoptic accounts, and for this reason a number of scholars argue that it is earlier than the Synoptic accounts or is the original version. Despite the popularity of this view among some, almost certainly the *Gospel of Thomas* is dependent on the canonical Gospels, both generally and for this parable.[86] I would not argue that the author copied directly from the canonical Gospels; the compiler of these sayings did not rely on written copies. Rather, *Gos. Thom.* is evidence of a "secondary orality," a later tradition drawn from the canonical Gospels and influenced by oral transmission of the gospel stories until written down in the middle to late second century.

In this parable *Gos. Thom.* shows the influence of Luke in the words "they will give to him" (Luke 20:10) and "perhaps" (*isōs*, Luke 20:13).[87] The latter occurs nowhere else in the NT, and its appearance in Thomas must arouse suspicion. Further, the old Syriac translations of the Gospels have a twofold sending of individual servants like *Gos. Thom.*, but this twofold sending derives from attempts to harmonize the Synoptic accounts (Matthew has a twofold sending of several servants). *Gos. Thom.* has a Syrian provenance and seems dependent on such harmonizing traditions.[88] As in the Synoptics, the stone saying from Ps 118:22 follows the parable in *Gos. Thom.* as the next saying, but neither its OT source nor its connection to the parable is recognized. That the connection (explained below) is not understood argues that *Gos. Thom.* is dependent on the canonical tradition.

J.-M. Sevrin argues further for the secondary nature of the *Gos. Thom.* account because of its treatment of the theme of riches. The parable of the Wicked Tenants is preceded by the parables of the Rich Fool and the Great Banquet, which *Gos. Thom.* directs against buyers and merchants (logia 63-64). All three parables begin the same way and are grouped together to show the futility of attempting to amass wealth since riches are an impediment to salvation. Sevrin argues that the parable is altered to emphasize the servant's lack of knowledge ("Perhaps *he* did not know *them*") and the tenants' possession of knowledge. With this emphasis the author has made the tenants positive characters and the servants negative characters. Sevrin also argues that the first line of the parable should not be restored to read a "good" *(chrēstos)* man (only the first three letters and the last letter remain in the text). Rather, the text should read "lender" (or "usurer": *chrēstēs*). On this reading the proprietor represents not God but a man of wealth whose riches lead to destruction,[89] which is then the theme of all three parables in this grouping.

The parallels between the parable of the Rich Man in logion 63 and that of the Wicked Tenants in logion 65 deserve attention. Both focus on a man of wealth and on fruits, end abruptly with death, and have the appended saying "He who has ears, let him hear." Further *Gos. Thom.* expands and changes the parable of the Feast[90] so that it is no longer about Israel but is directed against buyers and merchants and similarly changes the parable of the Wicked Tenants. That *Gos. Thom.* reinterprets the Synoptic parable is difficult to resist, given Sevrin's explanation of the intent of this grouping. If the reading "lender" is correct, this conclusion is overwhelming, even though J. Kloppenborg still argues for the originality of *Gos. Thom.*[91]

Differences among the Synoptic Accounts

The context and setting of the parable are the same in all three Synoptic accounts: after the question of authority from the chief priests and elders and before the question about paying taxes to Caesar. Matthew has added a parable on each side of this one to form a trilogy of parables mirroring Israel. Neither Mark nor Luke has the parable of the Two Sons (Matt 21:28-32). Luke's parable of the Great Banquet (14:15-24), which is similar to Matthew's parable of the Wedding Feast (22:1-14), is in a different context. Matthew and Mark allude to Isa 5:2 in detailing the construction of the vineyard. Luke has only "A man planted a vineyard." *Gos. Thom.* does not have the allusion to Isaiah 5.

The owner's sending of servants and the son to the tenants is quite different in each of the four accounts. Matthew has an intensification in both the importance of the envoys and their mistreatment. Mark has an intensification of the mistreatment, but it is of little consequence since many are killed. Emphasis

Matthew	Mark	Luke	Gos. Thom.
his servants, one beaten, one killed, one stoned	a servant, beaten and sent away	a servant, beaten and sent away empty	his servant, beaten
a larger group of servants, the same treatment	a servant, beaten on the head and dishonored	a servant, beaten, dishonored, and sent away empty	a servant, beaten
	a servant, killed	a servant, wounded and cast out	
	many others, some beaten and some killed		
"Finally *(hysteron)* he sent his son, cast out of the vineyard and killed"	"an only [or 'beloved'] son *(huion agapēton)* sent last *(eschaton),* killed and cast out of the vineyard."	"my only [or 'beloved'] son *(ton huion mou ton agapēton),* cast out of the vineyard and killed."	his son, seized and killed

is placed on the son in Mark by the description. Luke has a climactic three plus one formula and also emphasizes the son by the description. Luke has similarities to both Mark (especially in the use of "only" [or "beloved"] to describe the son) and Matthew (especially in the agreement that the son was cast out and then killed and in the second stone saying, if Matt 21:44 belongs in the text).

In Mark and Luke Jesus answers his own question as to what the owner will do. In Matthew the religious authorities answer. Ps 118:22-23 is provided for interpretation in Matthew and Mark, whereas Luke includes only 118:22. Matthew has a further explanation (21:43) and second stone saying (21:44), which is omitted in a few manuscripts; Luke has the second stone saying, but not the explanation.

Although differences in wording exist, all three Synoptic accounts agree in substance in the conclusion of the narrative. The religious authorities, the priestly establishment in particular,[92] know that Jesus has spoken the parable against them. They seek to seize him, but fear the crowd.

Interpreters make of these differences what they will. Some assume the priority of Mark,[93] but even so view Mark 12:5b (the mistreatment of numerous servants) and the christological language of 12:6 as later embellishments. Luke's account is championed by some because it reserves killing for the son, does not so clearly identify the servants as the prophets, and appears not to allude to Isa 5:2. Some think Luke is not dependent on Mark and has access to other traditions, of which at least one goes back to a Hebrew narrative.[94] That is not impossible, but it has not been proven. Luke's version shows his own redactional shaping.[95] The agreements between Luke and Matthew may point to a double tradition account independent of Mark, unless Luke used Matthew.[96] Matthew is often accused of having the most allegorical version of the parable, but this reflects assumptions about Matthew more than anything that comes from the text.[97]

Matthew's account, taken for itself, is the least allegorical,[98] makes the most sense as a story, and could be the earliest account, granted of course that Matthew has his own redactional shaping.[99] Matthew has two groups of servants and the son sent to the vineyard — which is realistic. He does not refer to the son as "beloved," although the title is christologically significant for him elsewhere (3:17; 12:18; 17:5). *This fact must be given sufficient weight.* I have yet to see a convincing explanation why Matthew has omitted Mark's christological underlining, if indeed he followed Mark. Matthew's account preserves explicitly the form of a prophetic-juridical parable that leads the hearers to judge themselves (very much like the parable of Nathan to David in 2 Sam 12:1-7).

Textual Features Worthy of Attention

The lament over Jerusalem (Matt 23:37-39/Luke 13:34-35) reflects the thought of the parable, and it is striking that both the lament and the parable quote Psalm 118.

The passion predictions in Mark 8:31; Luke 9:22; 17:25 appear to be constructed from Ps 118:22, especially in the use of "rejected" *(apodokimazein).*

Several connections exist among the three parables in Matt 21:28–22:14. For the connections with the parable of the Two Sons see above, p. 269. The parable of the Wicked Tenants is connected to that of the Wedding Feast by the words "man," "parables," "kingdom," "son," "those," and "seized," identical language for the twofold sending of servants, and quite similar language for the fact that some of them were beaten and killed *(edeiran . . . apekteinan* and *hybrisan kai apekteinan).* One very important difference is that in the parable of the Wedding Feast the son is merely mentioned; he does nothing and is *not* killed.

Luke's parable is addressed to the people, in keeping with his tendencies, whereas Matthew and Mark both have the parable addressed to the religious leaders. Yet at the conclusion Luke also says that the religious leaders knew the parable was directed against them.

Cultural Information

Examples of land cared for by tenants and of leases between tenants and owners are well known.[100] Tensions and conflicts between the two parties are also well attested, right down to arguing over who got the twigs left over after pruning.[101] M. Hengel pointed to the importance of the Zenon papyri (about 260 B.C.) for understanding this parable. Distant owners, lease arrangements, elaborate care for vineyards and wine production, tensions with groups of tenants, and repeated requests for justice are all chronicled.[102] That the owner departs does *not* necessarily indicate that he was a foreigner.[103]

The judicial system of the ancient world often led to repeated requests for justice, as Luke 18:1-9 illustrates. If the owner had used force, he would only have created more trouble and would have had to find other tenants to care for the vineyard. As both M. Hengel and Craig Evans demonstrate, in such conflicts pleading, repeated requests, and violence are all attested.[104] This is less a factor for Matthew's account, which has only two sendings of servants.

Regulations prohibited tenants from the usual right of owning land after three years of undisputed possession.[105] It is doubtful that the tenants were concerned with legal ownership; they were interested in possession and use. The Greek word *klēronomia* often means "possession" rather than "inheritance." The LXX account of Ahab taking possession of Naboth's vineyard uses just this language: Ahab "inherits" *(klēronomei)* Naboth's vineyard (3 Kgdms 20[21]:15-16). Josephus likewise uses inheritance language *(klēronomein)* to describe the same event.[106]

For further information on cultural matters see below, pp. 291-92.

Explanation of the Parable

Options for Interpretation[107]

This parable was easily and consistently viewed as an allegory of salvation history depicting the patience of God, his sending of the prophets and finally of his son (who was cast out of Jerusalem and then killed), the rejection of the Jews, and the calling of the Gentiles. At times smaller details of the parable were allegorized as well. For example, the hedge around the vineyard was understood as the help of the angels, the tower as the Temple, and the owner's leaving as human free will. Later the parable was interpreted of the individual (each person receives a vine at baptism to tend and the sendings are the Law, the Psalms, and the Prophets) and spiritual development.[108]

Some argue that the parable is an allegory from the early church. A. Jülicher thought the story to be a completely unrealistic account and clearly an allegory of God's sending of his son to the leaders of Israel. He viewed everything after Mark 12:9 as a later addition: the stone quotation, the explanation in Matt 21:43, and the second stone quotation in Matt 21:44/Luke 20:18. Matthew and Luke were seen as adaptations of Mark. Jülicher accepted that there could be a parable from Jesus behind Mark 12:1 and 9 but thought it could not be recovered. In his estimation the parable as we have it is from the first Christian generation.[109] W. G. Kümmel argued that the son would not have had messianic significance in pre-Christian Judaism, a further indication of the origin of the parable in the church.[110]

Some ascribe the parable in a shorter and simpler form to Jesus. On this approach, if one removes the allusions to Isaiah 5, Mark 12:5b (the mistreatment of many servants), the judgment saying in v. 9, and the quotation of Ps 118:22-23, a realistic story remains, with the coming of the son required logically rather than theologically. The early and strongest advocates for this kind of approach were C. H. Dodd and Joachim Jeremias,[111] but it has become fairly standard.[112] In fact, by de-allegorizing the story the way Dodd and Jeremias suggested, one is left with a version very much like that of *Gos. Thom.*, which had not been discovered when they first made their suggestions.[113] A major problem is that both Dodd and Jeremias still attached allegorical significance to the story and particularly to the son,[114] but then any attempt to stay with the story finds it difficult to avoid allegorical significance.

In recent years dissatisfaction with the three options above has led to an array of suggestions, but none of these more recent attempts to find an alternative inspires any confidence. Because the previous parable focused on John the Baptist and to avoid any thought that Jesus referred to himself with the son in this parable, a few have suggested that the son is a reference to John.[115] J. D. Crossan argued first that the parable is an example of the prudent grasping of one's immoral chance as in the parable of the Unjust Steward[116] and later that the parable depicts a terribly foolish action by the owner, as in the parable of the Rich Fool.[117] Pheme Perkins, having set aside the conclusion of the parable, suggested that Jesus was showing what is involved in his teaching of nonviolence and love for one's enemy.[118] Somewhat related, others have taken a sociological approach and argued that the parable is about the revolt of peasants against a rich creditor, a despot who has wrongly taken their land, and shows the futility of violence under these circumstances.[119] B. B. Scott argued that the parable views the kingdom as an object of tragedy with both the inheritance and the owner's fate being in doubt.[120] J. Kloppenborg argues that the Synoptic tradition, by adding the allusion to Isa 5:1-7, turned the parable into a theological allegory of the relation of God and his people. He objects to the lack of realism in the Synoptic versions, especially the level of violence from the owner, which he thinks points to archaic ideas of judgment. In his estimation the *Gos. Thom.* version is the superior account. The owner of the vineyard in *Gos. Thom.* is a usurer, a negative figure, and his foolishness leads to loss. The parable is for him about the failure of avarice.[121]

Another recent trend sees the story as more realistic than people have thought and argues that Jesus intentionally borrows the language of Isaiah 5 to retell Israel's story with a new twist, one that confronts the Temple authorities and has implications for understanding Jesus' own mission.[122]

Decisions on the Issues

1. Does Matt 21:44 belong in the text? This is an important textual variant. If it is part of the Matthean text, it brings Matthew's account closer to Luke's and likely indicates they had non-Markan tradition for this parable. This verse is present in virtually all Greek manuscripts. It is omitted only by Codex Bezae (which is known for its aberrations), minuscule 33, and probably by P[104], but the latter is so fragmentary that its reading is uncertain.[123] The evidence of P[104] is important, but is no trump card. Despite the overwhelming textual evidence in its favor, this verse was printed in double brackets in the first three editions of the UBS Greek NT. The verse was felt to be an insertion from Luke 20:18. The fourth edition of the UBS text and the twenty-seventh edition of the Nestle-Aland Greek NT place the verse in single brackets to indicate that it is debated but probably belongs in the text.[124] The first part of v. 44 does not conform closely to Luke 20:18 (Matt 21:44a: *Kai ho pesōn epi ton lithon touton . . . ;* Luke 20:18a: *Pas ho pesōn ep' ekeinon ton lithon . . .*), and a better place for an insertion would be after 21:42, which would match Luke's order. A scribe's eyes could easily have passed from *autēs kai* at the end of v. 43 and beginning of v. 44 to *auton kai* at the end of v. 44 and beginning of v. 45. On both internal and external grounds, a strong case exists for considering v. 44 as part of the original text of Matthew, but certainty is not possible.

2. Does the parable belong in its present context? This parable is one of the few that is historically rooted in a particular time of Jesus' life. Other parables could have been told early or late, in Galilee or Judea, and were, no doubt, told several times, but this one is contextually tied in all three accounts to the question of Jesus' authority after the Temple "cleansing." It is not impossible that a version of this parable was told more than once and elsewhere, but that is unlikely. Every indication is that the parable was a veiled answer to the question of authority, and a juridical parable does not work a second time. This parable belongs toward the end of Jesus' ministry as part of the increasing conflict that led to his death. If the parable is directed against the Temple authorities, which I think is the case and will be discussed below, then the fit of the parable in this context is made even more certain.

3. What was the original form of the story? This question has engendered a detailed and thorny debate, leads to a parting of the ways, and creates a dilemma. Numerous attempts have been made to reconstruct a primitive version. Typically anything suspected of having allegorical significance or anything deemed theologically offensive has been removed.[125] Few controls exist for such efforts, and interpreters are increasingly uncomfortable with them. Parables cannot be reduced to the bland outlines NT scholars sometimes reconstruct. Rarely are parables told so poorly and without representational significance, especially parables functioning as analogies. At the same time, the Evangelists have shaped the parable redactionally, and such shaping can and should be identified, which is to say that any attempt to recover the history of transmission of a text is exceedingly difficult and involves a number of questions.

Without going into a detailed discussion or thinking that we can reconstruct *the* original form, several points about the parable can still be made. A crucial question concerns the allusion to Isa 5:1-7. If one excludes the allusion, then "the parable admits of a dazzling variety of interpretive possibilities."[126] In my estimation *the allusion to Isaiah 5 is part of the original.* Matthew and Mark both have several descriptions of the establishing of the vineyard that use language from Isaiah 5. The wording is close to the LXX, but there are significant differences in wording and order both between Matthew and Mark and between each and the LXX.[127] In the LXX someone speaks in the first person, but the Gospels use the third person singular. In the LXX the man plants a vine *(ampelon sōrēk)*; in the Gospels he plants a vineyard *(ampelōna)*. The word for "winepress" is different in all three (LXX *prolēnion*, Matthew *lēnon*, Mark *hypolēnion*). In the LXX the vineyard produces thorns, which play no role in the Gospels.[128] The wording of Matthew and Mark may have been partially assimilated to the LXX at some stage in the tradition.[129] Luke has only the words "he planted a vineyard" *(ephyteusen ampelōna, 20:9)*, but the claim that Luke does not allude to Isa 5:2 could be made only if his description neither reflects *ephyteusa ampelon* in Isa 5:2 nor is drawn from Matthew or Mark.[130] Even if the parable had only the words "he planted a vineyard," readers would probably have thought of Isaiah 5 anyway since that text is *the* classic vineyard text. Further, why a Christian would add the allusion later is not clear, especially since the parable goes a different direction than Isaiah 5 does. No one added an allusion to the other vineyard parables (Matt 20:1-16; 21:28-32; Luke 13:6-9).

Yet, if the parable goes a different direction from Isaiah 5, why is the allusion important? The allusion signals to readers that the parable has to do with the relation of God and his people. In all likelihood a story about a vineyard, even without other words from Isaiah 5, would establish that the story was about God and his people, as rabbinic parables often attest. There is another factor. Evidence from Jewish sources shows that Isaiah 5 was traditionally associated with the Temple,[131] so the allusions to Isaiah 5 root the concerns of the parable precisely in the Temple. The targum on Isa. 5:1-7 is even more striking in that it explicitly describes the Temple built in God's vineyard as coming under God's judgment, which would match the attitude in the parable, but the date of the targum is uncertain.[132] However, 4Q162, although fragmentary, interprets Isa 5:5-30 of the laying waste of the land in the last days because of the arrogance of the men of Jerusalem. If the anti-Temple polemic is associated with Isaiah 5, the case is even stronger, but at the very least the parable points to the Temple by its allusion to Isaiah 5.

The sending of the servants in Mark is clearly overloaded with three servants sent and mistreated and then many others, some to be beaten and some to be killed (12:5). Matthew has only two groups of servants, first three servants, one beaten, one killed, and one stoned. The language for mistreatment is a clear allusion to the mistreatment of the prophets, as is especially clear from Matt 23:37. Then a larger group is sent and treated the same way. Luke has a climactic three plus one formula and reserves killing for the son. Luke's allusion to the prophets is less obvious, but Matthew and Mark have emphasized the identification of the servants as the prophets. That identification was likely anyway with the very mention of a vineyard and servants. Servant language is, of course, used frequently of prophets in the OT.[133] Whether Matthew's two groups of servants or Luke's three individual servants is the original form and whether any of the servants were killed in the original story cannot be determined. Such differences reflect variations in oral performances of the parable.

The *description of the son* as "beloved" *(agapētos)*[134] in both Mark and Luke has been heightened to underscore his christological significance. Mark moves further in this direction with "last" *(eschatos)*. Matthew has neither word. "Beloved" is used by the heavenly voice in the baptism narratives of all three Evangelists and by Matthew and Mark in their transfiguration accounts (and also at Matt 12:18). I cannot imagine Matthew having dropped either "beloved" or "last" if he was aware of them. The christological heightening stems from a different tradition or oral performance than is represented by Matthew.

While interpreters debate the significance of the son, his presence in the story is an essential ingredient and a turning point in the narrative. In Matthew and Luke the son is cast out of the vineyard and then killed; in Mark he is killed and then cast out. This is frequently viewed as Matthew and Luke conforming the parable to Jesus' crucifixion outside the city. I find this unlikely. Neither Matthew nor Luke mentions that Jesus was crucified outside the city; that information comes from John 19:17-20 and Heb 13:12. Also, this would require the vineyard to be a symbol of *Jerusalem*. Would a reader be expected to discern this? Such an identification does not fit with the rest of the parable. Further, a logic exists for both descriptions. If the son is killed and then cast out, the desecration of the corpse heightens the offense. If the son is cast out and then killed, it would fit any purity concerns that might arise from having the vineyard rendered unclean by the murder. I do not think this variation in the accounts has any theological significance but may merely reflect different oral renditions.

Is the judgment statement included? While a few would suggest that the parable ends with the death of the son, a larger number would end the parable after the question of what the owner will do. That question, however, implies an answer, whether it comes from Jesus as in Mark and Luke or from the hearers as in Matthew. The concern of the parable is *not* about raising questions about violence, as important as such questions are. The deletion of the judgment saying seems motivated more by theological disdain for ideas of judgment[135] rather than by literary concerns about the parable. The focus of the parable is the tenants and what will happen to them, and the parable is incomplete without some indication of the outcome of their actions. If this is a juridical parable, by necessity the judgment must in some way be made clear. A decision about the exact wording of the judgment saying is impossible, but the story works the same way in all three accounts: the tenants are destroyed and the vineyard is given to others. Giving the vineyard to others is language that reflects the wording of lease agreements. The significance of the judgment saying and the degree to which the owner's action is realistic are treated below.

The question concerning *the fit of Ps 118:22-23 with the parable* is the most important question. Often the quotation is deleted as a later Christian insertion alluding to the resurrection of Jesus. Psalm 118:22 *is* important for the early church and is used of the resurrection in Acts 4:11 (see also 1 Pet 2:4, 7; *Barn.* 6:4). Whether the Evangelists expected readers to see a reference to the resurrection is another matter, but we must not forget that this psalm was important in Judaism as part of the great Hallel and for Jesus as well, as is evident in his use of it in the lament over Jerusalem (Matt 23:39/Luke 13:35) and in the

Markan and Lukan wording of the passion predictions (Mark 8:31; Luke 9:22; 17:25).[136] Moreover, the parable *needs* the quotation. Far from being an early church addition, the quotation is the key to understanding the parable. The problem, unnoticed by most, is that we read the parable and quotation with the knowledge of post-resurrection history, but how would the parable have been heard by Jesus' Jewish hearers? How do the hearers suddenly discern that the parable is about them, especially in the Matthean account, where they have just pronounced a verdict on the tenants? Even without the allusion to Isaiah 5 the listeners would know the parable was about God and his people, but no Jewish listener would identify himself or herself with the tenants.[137] Rather, the tenants would be evil people, possibly the Romans, who were violating God's vineyard, his people, or at least the purposes of God with his people. *Not until the stone quotation is the impact of the parable made clear,* and two features of the quotation are the revealing agents: the well-attested wordplay between *'eben* ("stone") and *ben* ("son")[138] and the use of "builders" to refer to the religious leaders.[139] The wordplay cannot be discounted by thinking it only works in Hebrew.[140] Some argue that the parable was given in Hebrew,[141] but if it was spoken in Aramaic, the wordplay would still have been understood. The wordplay is preserved *in Greek* by Josephus (see above, p. 277) in a document written first in *Aramaic* which describes the siege of Jerusalem. The residents of Jerusalem, where the parable in Josephus was told, were being bombarded by stones and certainly got the wordplay. Even someone who spoke only Aramaic would know the meaning of the Hebrew *ben,*[142] and certainly the wordplay would have been understood by *religious leaders in Jerusalem.* The quotation says explicitly and dramatically what the parable intends: the religious leaders have rejected the son, the climactic envoy from God, but this rejection will be reversed by God and the leaders will lose their role in God's purposes. The parable says essentially what the passion prediction in Mark 8:31 and the lament over Jerusalem say.[143] As N. T. Wright observes, the use of Psalm 118 is especially appropriate in connection with Jesus' Temple action, which had prompted the question of his authority, and indicates Jesus' intent in announcing judgment and restoration.[144]

It is difficult to determine if the remaining parts of the Gospels' presentation of the parable originally followed the quotation of Psalm 118 or were added for commentary. Matt 21:43 is usually considered redactional,[145] but only the introduction is clearly Matthean. "Kingdom of God" is not Matthew's normal language and may indicate that the verse was in Matthew's tradition.[146] In any case v. 43 does not add much to v. 41 other than to mark out that the hearers have judged themselves. More significant is the question concerning the second stone quotation in Matt 21:44/Luke 20:18. This quotation is a composite of Isa

8:14-15 and Dan 2:44-45 and is apparently proverbial.[147] Its intent is to emphasize the judgment pronouncement by alluding to the stone and enduring kingdom of Dan 2:44-45.[148]

While the differences in the accounts are considerable, they should not be
over-emphasized. The story is essentially the same in all three Synoptic accounts and is in the same context in all three. A man planted a vineyard, leased
it to tenants, and sent a servant or servants to collect his portion of the proceeds, but they were rejected and abused. He tried again with the same result
and then sent his son, thinking that the tenants would respect him. The tenants
killed the son to acquire possession of the vineyard for themselves. The parable
proper then ends with the question of what the owner will do and the judgment
that he will destroy the tenants and give the vineyard to other tenants. The quotation of Ps 118:22 (and probably 23) serves as the *nimshal*, the explanation, and
belonged to the parable from the outset.

4. Is this story realistic, and how realistic must it be? What landowner
would act as this one does, particularly in Mark's Gospel, in sending servants
repeatedly to be abused and then in sending his own son into such a situation?
We should remind ourselves first of J. Liebenburg's comment that "there is no *a
priori* law governing the genre 'parable' which requires that they adhere to 'realism.'"[149] Interpreters often use realism as a criterion of what Jesus could have
said or would have said in a parable, and if something is deemed unrealistic, it
is assigned to the early church. This procedure must be challenged. Jesus' teaching is not always realistic (e.g., Matt 5:22, 29-30; 16:24-25), and parables regularly have extravagant and hyperbolic features that shock and disorient (e.g.,
the parable of the Unforgiving Servant in Matt 18:23-35). On the other hand,
parables do have to make sense in the context of Jesus and first-century hearers;
they have to be stories that people could understand and by which they could
be persuaded.

Most of the features of this parable would have raised no questions in
first-century Palestine. The language used for leasing, development of the vineyard, conflict between owners and tenants, rejection of emissaries, and redress
of wrongs are paralleled in ancient contracts and parables.[150] Two or three missions to acquire the owner's share would not be surprising at all.[151] Some focus
on the fact that this is a newly planted vineyard and would not bear fruit for
four or five years and conclude that the conflict is over wages or that Mark's account is incoherent.[152] The parable has no concern for the number of years before the vineyard was productive. One does not know how many years passed
between the vineyard's creation and the owner's departure or whether he over-
saw those early years or made other arrangements. Parables rarely pay attention
to such details. The owner sends his servants when the time comes; that is all

that is needed. The sending of the son is an indication that legal action was being taken or at least that relations had moved to a different level. Servants or an agent could not lodge a formal protest.[153] No indication is given why the father cannot come, but a first-century audience would not see this feature as problematic. Parables do not usually provide motivation and, as David Flusser noted,[154] are not so much realistic as pseudo-realistic. The tenants do not think they will inherit the vineyard legally; they will take possession of it the way Ahab "inherited" Naboth's vineyard.[155]

Are things different with the reaction of the owner? John Kloppenborg views Mark 12:1-8 as largely realistic but finds v. 9 unrealistic because it assumes that the owner, as a normal course of action, would and could take the law into his own hands and could be confident that he would recover his property. For Kloppenborg these assumptions make sense only if the parable no longer intends to be realistic but is speaking of God's action. In other words, if the allusion to Isa 5:4-6 is granted (which Kloppenborg rejects), v. 9 makes sense but is not a realistic act in view of ancient attitudes toward self-help.[156]

The debate about realism is complex, and nothing is gained by overstating the case either way. Kloppenborg legitimately points to legal strictures to limit taking the law into one's own hands, but is it unrealistic to hear a story of people who did? Laws are laid down precisely because there is a problem. No one is suggesting that the parable narrates an everyday event; the question is whether it narrates something believable, and that is beyond question. Tenants and landowners had frequent conflicts, emissaries were mistreated and killed, and rabbinic parables have actions very much like those in this parable.[157] Further, we are dealing with a parable, not a courtroom, and accounts of punishment or someone exercising self-help to remedy a situation are common. The parable has been shaped to the reality depicted;[158] that is the way parables function. If we judge the ending of the story as improbable and unrealistic,[159] it is not so improbable that hearers would have been side-tracked. Is the parable a metaphorical narrative about God, his people, and God's judgment? Yes, and hearers would have assumed that and would not have thought the parable was incoherent.

5. Is this parable an allegory and, if so, do all the features in the story have some parallel in reality?[160] I do not think allegory is a genre; rather, it is a type of thinking.[161] But regardless of what language we use, this parable is allegorical. There are obvious correspondences that make it work. No Jew would need to be told that a story of an owner and his vineyard in some way had to do with God and his people. An assessment of these correspondences determines the meaning of the parable. This is no license to allegorize the individual features of the story. The focus in reading a story must be on the plot, the movements of the main characters, and the way the analogy functions. Details in the account set up resonances or add interest and move the story along; they are not to become the focus of speculation. I have repeatedly said that parable interpretation is not about finding correspondences, even where they exist, and that is still the case here. The correspondences are a *given,* either by the use of stock images or by something in the parable or its *nimshal* that discloses meaning. Both are at work with this parable. Stock features set up a frame for meaning, and the quotation of Ps 118:22 discloses the intent.

We can set aside those efforts that view the owner as a rich landowner who has confiscated peasant land. Such approaches are a misreading of the parable and give no viable meaning in Jesus' context.[162] Nothing in the parable gives any hint that the owner is a negative figure. We should not even assume that the tenants are poor peasants; they may be commercial farmers of some means.[163] Attempts to read the parable against the background of class conflict will not work, for nothing in the parable takes the reader in that direction. Nothing the owner does causes the tenants' action. This *is* a story about God and his people. The vine/vineyard language in the OT,[164] rabbinic vineyard parables, and Jesus' coming as a prophet all point in this direction.

Identification of the vineyard has always, at least since Origen,[165] been problematic. At the beginning of the parable the vineyard clearly points to God's relation to Israel, but at the end the vineyard is given to others. The vineyard cannot *be* Israel, for how could Israel be taken from Israel? The real intent with the vineyard is not known until the end of the parable. I do not think the targum on Isa 5:1-7 with its anti-Temple rhetoric is demonstrably early enough that we should conclude that the vineyard in Jesus' parable is the Temple, but the Temple is associated with Isaiah 5 and is probably symbolic of the parable's concerns. Stephen Bryan points out that the vineyard is both a positive and negative image, positive in pointing to God's election of Israel and negative as an image of judgment,[166] and both aspects are operative in the parable. What is taken from the tenants is the privilege of being engaged with the purposes of God, or in other words, election and the promises of God.

The identity of the tenants is unknown until the quotation of Ps 118:22. During the telling of the parable the hearers would only conclude that someone was interfering with God's purposes for his people. The servants, on the other hand, would surely have been recognized as an allusion to the prophets, messengers on God's behalf.[167]

The identity of the son requires more attention. The son is not merely part of the "machinery" of the story, for his coming and the tenants' treatment of him create a crisis. If the story were merely about the patience of God, continually sending servants would suffice. With the son's coming something more significant happens. But still the son is not the focus of the story; rather, the owner and the tenants are the focus. "Son" or "son of God" is not a stock metaphor and even the latter is *not necessarily* a messianic designation. In the rabbinic parables of a vineyard, the son is Jacob or Israel as a whole, neither of which works here. In Wis 2:10-20,[168] which has strong similarities to this parable, "son of God" (*huios theou*, 2:18) is used of a just man who is condemned to a shameful death but expects God to vindicate him. This passage from Wisdom may have influenced the shape of the parable.

A few suggest that the son is a reference to John the Baptist,[169] but this seems like a desperate attempt to avoid a self-reference on the part of Jesus. John the Baptist is the focus in the preceding context's question of authority, but it is hard to see how any hearer of the parable would think John was in mind.[170] John is never referred to as "son," and Herod Antipas was responsible for John's death, not the religious leaders.

While "son of God" is not specifically a messianic title, the claim that "son of God" had no messianic significance in pre-Christian Judaism has been proven erroneous, especially by the Qumran scrolls.[171] At least fifteen texts from early Judaism show Jews roughly contemporaneous with Jesus used "son" and "son of God" technically of "paradigmatic holy individuals, including the long-awaited Messiah."[172] Exactly what connotation the son would have carried for the original hearers of the parable is unclear. Some may have understood a reference to the messiah, but all hearers would at least have understood that reference was to a godly person who enjoyed intimacy with God.

The only conclusion that makes sense with this parable is that the son is an indirect self-reference to Jesus. "Son" here should not be understood with trinitarian ideas but within the contexts of first-century Judaism and of Jesus' ministry. The term has its origin in its use for Israel[173] and in Jesus' consciously taking on the task of Israel.[174] With that task he had a climactic role in God's purposes, purposes which were coming into effect in his own ministry and which created a crisis for the nation. That Jesus should make such a self-reference is plausible. He surely contemplated his own untimely death, given the opposition to him and what happened to John the Baptist. He enjoyed an intimacy with God which found expression in the family term "Abba," a sonship at least no less than that mentioned in Wis 2:13-20. Other texts in the Gospels point to his claim of being son of God, but equally important is the recognition that this parable is a claim to such a self-reference by Jesus. This parable may be the first public statement of such a relation with God and may be the basis for the high priest's question "Are you the Christ, the Son of the God/the Blessed?" (Matt 26:63/Mark 14:61).[175] This is the turning point of the parable and with it comes an implicit but significant christology.

Some in discussing the son point to *Targum Pss.* 118:22, which interprets the rejected stone as the boy *(ṭalyā')* David, who was rejected among the sons of Jesse but worthy to be appointed king and ruler.[176] This would have enormous significance if it were verifiable at the time the parable was told, but the targum is too late to instill confidence about the date of this tradition.

What is clear is that the stone quotation both reveals the meaning of the parable and moves beyond the parable. The narrative frame of the parable concludes with the vineyard given to others, but the quotation adds that the rejected stone/son will be vindicated.[177] The rejection-vindication paradigm is a frequent dynamic in the OT (e.g., the righteous sufferer, the servant) and elsewhere in Jesus' teaching.[178]

With regard to *the resultant meaning* of the parable, it is clear that the parable is a confrontation with the religious leaders, the builders of Israel, and especially the Temple authorities. As a prophet Jesus took a prophetic tool, the parable, and more precisely a specific parable theme, the vineyard of Isa 5:1-7, and recast the story to serve as a juridical parable, a self-indicting mirror, for the religious leaders. The parable turns on two directly related foci: the transfer of the kingdom and the special envoy of God. The kingdom is transferred because of failure to render what is due to God and at least partly because of the rejection of God's envoy. The parable may address quite specific injustices of the Temple authorities, specifically those associated with Ananias's withholding of tithes and forcibly seizing tithes meant for priests.[179] If this is the case, then the word "fruits" is not merely a metaphor for works but specifically refers to the way the finances of the Temple were misappropriated. If this is the specific context of the parable, it is a powerful accusation, and we can understand why the religious authorities might want to kill Jesus. The quotation of Ps 118:22 makes obvious Jesus' intent, which was not discerned until the quotation was placed beside the parable.

Like other passages in the Gospels, this parable attests to the crisis Jesus' ministry imposes on his hearers. While he refused to answer the question concerning the authority by which he performed his actions in the Temple, this parable shows not only that he had such authority but also that the religious leaders opposed God's work, for which they were to be punished and their privileges transferred to others.

The implied question the parable addresses is, Will people respond to God's climactic messenger before the crisis comes? Unlike the parable of the fig tree, it does not hold out much hope for the religious leaders. The message of the parable is the same as the lament over Jerusalem (Matt. 23:37-38//Luke 11:49-51). It is no accident that the eschatologically oriented Psalm 118 is used at the end of both. The parable says in story form what the lament says in narrative, but the parable is more polemical. In addition to the use of Psalm 118 both focus on the rejection of messengers from God, on Jesus' specific role, on judgment, and on restoration.

6. *Does the parable stem from Jesus or from the early church?* If this parable were judged to be from the church, at the very least it would have to stem from an early Semitic context. The numerous Semitisms,[180] the wordplay between "son" *(ben)* and "stone" *('eben)*, and the allusions to the Temple with Isaiah 5 verified by evidence from Qumran require at least that much. This precludes any thought that the parable's judgment saying should be seen in connection with the Jewish war of 70 A.D. Relatively few assign the whole parable to the early church, and justly so, but a truncated form without the quotation loses the parable's juridical effect. This parable fits admirably in the context of Jesus' conflict with the Temple leaders. Other than the incident with Stephen, little evidence exists that the church argued against the Temple. Further, the parable is too indirect to be the confession of the early church. From every indication we have the church did not compose parables, and nothing in this basic story points to an origin in the church. The artistry of this parable and its polemic against the Temple leaders points directly to Jesus as its author.

Still, we should recognize that this parable is unusual when compared to Jesus' other parables. He does not often attack the Temple establishment in parables or otherwise. The only parable that comes close is the Good Samaritan with its negative portrayal of the priest and the Levite. Also, Jesus makes a stronger self-reference in the parable of the Wicked Tenants than with any other. There is debate about how much the parables are christological. Some would say this is the only parable with a self-reference and others that virtually every parable is christological.[181] At least some other parables imply a self-reference, notably Luke's parable of the Feast and parable of the Talents. At least we must say that this is *the* most revealing parable about Jesus' own sense of his role in God's purposes and was a precipitating factor leading to his arrest.

7. *Does this parable, particularly in its Matthean form, teach that God has rejected Israel by giving the kingdom to Gentiles?*[182] This question must be answered quickly: No! God has not rejected Israel, and this parable does not teach that he has. The parable is directed against the leaders, and it is unfair to make it say something else. People read other parts of the Gospels into the story or assume that they know what the Evangelists thought.[183] The larger narratives of the Gospels, especially of Matthew, are polemical with regard to Judaism, but the texts should not be read more negatively than they are, and in particular this parable should not be read so negatively. A prophetic indictment, which is what this parable and much of the Gospel material are, is polemical, but not more so than OT prophets. In this parable there is no reference to the church or

to Gentiles. The "others" to whom the vineyard will be given is not specified other than that they will pay the fruits or will be a people who do the fruits of the kingdom (Matt 21:41 and 43 respectively).[184] The passage is quite vague. The time of the transfer is not indicated in any way. "People" in Matt 21:43 translates *ethnei,* the singular.[185] If Matthew had intended the Gentiles, the plural would have been used. The "you" in v. 43 must refer to the people speaking in v. 41, the religious leaders. We should notice as well that v. 43 is much milder than v. 41. In the latter the leaders pronounce a harsh sentence of destruction of the tenants, but Jesus' response in v. 43 omits destruction entirely.[186] Also of major importance is the fact that all three Evangelists say that the leaders knew the parable was against them but could do nothing because they feared the people (with Matthew adding that the people considered Jesus to be a prophet). Why would this positive comment about the people appear if rejecting the whole nation was in mind? The parable is a prophetic indictment of the leaders, especially the Temple leaders. The people would indeed have to decide whom they would follow, but this parable is not anti-Semitic and is not a rejection of the Jewish nation.

We are required to distinguish what a text does from what has been done to it, and we all are responsible for the way we treat texts.[187] We should grieve at the anti-Semitic reading that has been laid on this and other texts and combat such readings forcefully. People will read texts to justify their ideologies, but such readings must be challenged. If the parables are stories with intent, Jesus' intent, then his voice is the one we need to hear.

Adapting the Parable

Although the parable is historically rooted in Jesus' discussion with the Temple establishment, its themes are still relevant for a much broader audience. Like so many others, the parable is primarily about response. Will people respond to the claims God has on their lives or reject his messengers in favor of their own agenda? Will they live productively to "produce fruits" for God? The parable asserts (and offers) the privilege of living in covenant relation with God, but privilege always brings with it responsibility. Apart from living responsively in obedience to God, the privilege cannot be retained. No community — Christian or otherwise — may presume that gifts like grace and election are permanent possessions.[188] Rather, they are opportunities for life and response to God. The kingdom comes with limitless grace, but also with limitless demand.

The parable is relevant for all persons, but its relevance for those in leadership is prominent. Further, the parable is a judgment parable. It asserts that, contrary to appearances, God will judge and will achieve his purposes, and people will be held accountable. Judgment remains a central component of the teaching of Jesus.

If this parable is more christologically significant than any other, it is foundational for reflecting on Jesus' own mission and identity. He comes as one who is more than a prophet, one in intimate relation with God, and reaction to him determines involvement in God's kingdom. The stone quotation underscores the rejection-vindication motif and Jesus' importance in God's eternal building. The stone quotation also comes as a warning. The tendency to disparage people or events as insignificant needs to be countered. If we have eyes to see, we might see that God is doing something unexpected.

For Further Reading

Randall Buth and Brian Kvasnica, "Temple Authorities and Tithe-Evasion: The Linguistic Background and Impact of the Parable of the Vineyard, the Tenant and the Son," in *Jesus' Last Week: Jerusalem Studies in the Synoptic Gospels* (ed. R. Steven Notley, Mark Turange, and Brian Becker; Leiden: Brill, 2006), 1:53-80.

J. Duncan M. Derrett, "Fresh Light on the Parable of the Wicked Vinedressers," *Revue Internationale des Droits de l'Antiquité* 3/10 (1963): 11-42, although highly speculative. Also available in his *Law in the New Testament* (London: Darton, Longman & Todd, 1970), pp. 286-312.

C. H. Dodd, *The Parables of the Kingdom* (London: Nisbet, 1936), pp. 124-32.

Craig A. Evans, "God's Vineyard and Its Caretakers," in *Jesus and His Contemporaries: Comparative Studies* (AGJU 25; Leiden: Brill, 1995), pp. 381-406.

————. *Mark 8:27–16:20* (WBC 34B; Nashville: Thomas Nelson, 2001), pp. 210-40.

Martin Hengel, "Das Gleichnis von den Weingärtnern Mc 12,1-12 im Lichte der Zenonpapyri und der rabbinische Gleichnisse," *ZNW* 59 (1968): 1-39.

Michel Hubaut, *La parabole des vignerons homicides* (Paris: Gabalda, 1976).

J. Jeremias, *The Parables of Jesus* (2d ed., trans. S. H. Hooke; New York: Charles Scribner's Sons, 1963), pp. 70-77.

John S. Kloppenborg, *The Tenants in the Vineyard: Ideology, Economics, and Agrarian Conflict in Jewish Palestine* (WUNT 195; Tübingen: Mohr Siebeck, 2006).

Akira Ogawa, "Paraboles de l'Israel Véritable? Reconsideration Critique de Mt. XXI 28–XXII 14," *NovT* 21 (1979): 121-49.

Jean-Marie Sevrin, "Un groupement de trois paraboles contre les richesses dans

L'Évangile selon Thomas. EvTh 63, 64, 65," in *Les Paraboles Évangéliques. Perspective Nouvelles* (ed. Jean Delorme; Paris: Les Éditions du Cerf, 1989), pp. 425-39.

Klyne Snodgrass, *The Parable of the Wicked Tenants* (WUNT 27; Tübingen: Mohr-Siebeck, 1983).

—————. "Recent Research on the Parable of the Wicked Tenants: An Assessment," *BBR* 8 (1998): 187-215.

David Stern, "Jesus' Parables from the Perspective of Rabbinic Literature: The Example of the Wicked Husbandmen," in *Parable and Story in Judaism and Christianity*, ed. Clemens Thoma and Michael Wyschogrod (New York: Paulist, 1989), pp. 42-80.

Wolfgang Trilling, *Das wahre Israel* (3d ed.; Munich: Kösel, 1964).

N. T. Wright, *Jesus and the Victory of God*, vol. 2 of *Christian Origins and the Question of God* (Minneapolis: Fortress, 1996), pp. 178-79, 232, 497-501, 565-66.

THE WEDDING BANQUET AND THE FEAST
(Matt 22:1-14; Luke 14:15-24; *Gos. Thom.* 64)

Whether the accounts of this parable — Matthew on one hand and Luke/*Gos. Thom.* on the other — are two versions of the same parable or two separate parables is debatable, and, therefore, whether the two should even be treated together is questionable. Matthew's version is enough to make any interpreter go weak in the knees; I consider it among the most difficult parables of all. Both canonical parables deal with Israel, and the similarity of the accounts, their common background, cultural assumptions, and theological concerns makes it convenient to consider some aspects of these parables together. To anticipate discussion of the relation of the accounts, I do not think we have two versions of the same parable. After dealing with common themes, I will treat the two versions separately.

Parable Type

Luke's version is a double indirect narrative parable without an explicit *nimshal.* The story remains entirely on the narrative level, even though it has several resonances with the larger narrative of Luke's Gospel and virtually begs the reader to see through the parable to the intent. In its present form Matthew's version is a two-stage, double indirect narrative parable, but it may reflect two separate parables that have been joined. Unlike Luke's account, Matthew's story does not remain on the narrative level. It neither has nor needs a *nimshal*. It is almost diaphanous in that one sees through to the reality almost from the first. In fact, one sees more of the reality than the parable. The surface narrative is close to not being there at all. The final saying in Matt 22:14 appears to be an independent logion. It also appears as a textual variant at 20:16.

Issues Requiring Attention

1. What is the relation of the accounts (including *Gos. Thom.* 64)? Do Matthew and Luke record the same parable?
2. Against what background should these parables be read? Suggestions include exclusion of "blemished" persons from priestly roles (Lev 21:17-23) or from those who will participate in the eschatological war (1QSa 2.5-9 and 1QM 7.4-5; cf. *m. Soṭah* 8.7 and Deut 20:5-7; 24:5), the messianic banquet motif in Isa 25:6-12 and Matt 8:11-12/Luke 13:28-30, Wisdom's banquet (Prov 9:2-6), the story of the publican Bar Ma'yan (see below, pp. 303 and 311), ancient Hellenistic symposia, and, for Matthew, Zeph 1:7-18.
3. With regard to Luke:
   a. Is the focus of Luke's parable on the change in the host,[189] on attitudes toward the rich and the poor,[190] or on the rejection of the invitations?
   b. What is the significance of Luke's account for understanding election? Does Luke seek to correct a misunderstanding of the concept of election in Deuteronomy?[191]
   c. Are the persons addressed Pharisees, Jews in general, or some other group? If Pharisees, was Jesus challenging them to reconsider their exclusion of people they felt impure,[192] excluding them from the kingdom, or only warning them of their possible exclusion?
   d. What degree of allegorical correspondence is there in Luke's parable? Does Luke point to the missions to Israel and to the Gentiles — or possibly to the early and ongoing Gentile mission — with his two sendings to the substitute guests? Is Jesus or God represented by the host?
   e. What is the message and significance of Jesus' parable as rendered by Luke?
4. With regard to Matthew:
   a. Is Matthew's parable authentic or purely Matthean allegorizing?
   b. How do the two parts of Matthew's account fit together, if they do? Has Matthew joined two separate parables? Why is the man con-

demned for not having a proper garment when he was invited in off
the street?

   c. Does the proverb in v. 14 belong with the parable, and what is its intent?

5. Is either account anti-Semitic, and does either suggest that Israel is rejected by God?

Helpful Primary Source Material[193]

Canonical Material

- OT: Lev 21:17-23 (cf. 2 Sam 5:8); especially Isaiah 25; 62:4-5; 65:13-16; of debated relevance are Deut 20:5-7;[194] 24:5; and Zeph 1:7-16
- NT: Matt 8:11-12/Luke 13:28-30; Matt 25:1-13; Luke 22:28-30; Rev 19:9. The eucharistic texts in which Jesus anticipates eating in the kingdom of God are also relevant (Matt 26:26-29; Mark 14:22-25; Luke 22:15-18).

Early Jewish Writings

- 1QSa 2.3-9 within the context of 1:27–2:22 (describing those granted admission to the Qumran community and to the messianic banquet): "No man, defiled by any of the impurities of a man, shall enter the assembly of these; and no-one who is defiled by these should be established in his office amongst the congregation: everyone who is defiled in his flesh, paralysed in his feet or in his hands, lame, blind, deaf, dumb or defiled in his flesh with a blemish visible to the eyes, or the tottering old man who cannot keep upright in the midst of the assembly; these shall not en[ter] to take their place [a]mong the congregation of the men of renown, for the angels of holiness are among their [congre]gation."
- 1QM 7.4-5 (concerning those who go out in the eschatological battle): "And no lame, blind, paralysed person nor any man who has an indelible blemish on his flesh, nor any man suffering from uncleanness in his flesh, none of these will go out to war with them. All these shall be volunteers for war, perfect in spirit and in body, and ready for the day of vengeance."
- 11QTemple 45.12-18 prohibits the blind, lepers, and infected persons from entering the city of the Temple.
- *1 En.* 10:4: "Bind Azaz'el hand and foot (and) throw him into the darkness!" He is to remain in darkness until judgment day.
- *1 En.* 62:15-16: ". . . [the elect] shall eat and rest and rise with that Son of

Man forever and ever. . . . They shall wear the garments of glory. These garments of yours shall become the garments of life. . . ."

- *2 En.* 42:5 describes the rest prepared for the righteous as a banquet of joy.
- Philo, *Opif.* 78: "Just as givers of a banquet, then, do not send out the summonses to supper till they have put everything in readiness for the feast. . . ."
- Josephus, *Ant.* 9.264-67 recounts how Israelites mocked and finally killed ambassadors from Hezekiah who invited them to come to Jerusalem to observe the feast of Unleavened Bread.

Greco-Roman Writings

- Apuleius, *Metamorphoses* 3.12 recounts the custom of a double invitation to a dinner: "Just then a servant came running in. 'Your aunt Byrrhena,' he said, 'invites your presence, and reminds you that the party you promised last night to attend will soon be starting.'"
- A great deal more material dealing with symposia in the ancient world and critiques of such symposia could be included here.[195]

Early Christian Writings

- *4 Ezra* 2:38-40, 44-45:[196] "Rise, stand erect and see the number of those who have been sealed at the feast of the Lord. Those who have departed from the shadow of this age have received glorious garments from the Lord. Take again your full number, O Zion, and close the list of your people who are clothed in white, who have fulfilled the law of the Lord. . . . Then I asked an angel, 'Who are these, my lord?' He answered and said to me, 'These are they who have put off mortal clothing and have put on the immortal, and have confessed the name of God.'"
- *Gos. Thom.* 64: "Jesus said: A man had guests, and when he had prepared the banquet, he sent his servant to summon the guests. He went to the first (and) said to him, My master summons you. He said, Some merchants owe me some money; they will come to me this evening; I will go and give them orders. I pray to be excused from the dinner. He went to another (and) said to him, My master has summoned you. He said to him, I have bought a house, and they request me for a day; I will have no leisure. He came to another (and) said to him, My master summons you. He said to him, My friend will celebrate a wedding and I am to direct the banquet. I will not be able to come. I pray to be excused from the banquet. He went to another (and) said to him, My master summons you. He

302

said to him, I have bought a village; I go to collect the rent; I will not be able to come. I pray to be excused. The servant came (and) said to his master, Those whom you summoned to the banquet have excused themselves. The master said to his servant, Go out to the streets, bring those whom you will find, so that they may dine. The buyers and the merchants [shall] not [come] into the places of my Father."

Later Jewish Writings

- *m. Soṭah* 8.1 offers a midrash on Deut 20:2-3 and begins "When the Anointed for Battle speaks unto the people." What follows is a discussion of those not required to go to battle, but at 8.7 we find, "What has been said applies to a battle waged of free choice; but in a religious cause all go forth, even the bridegroom out of his chamber and the bride out of her bridechamber."
- *m. 'Abot* 4.16: "This world is like a vestibule before the world to come: prepare thyself in the vestibule that thou mayest enter into the banqueting hall."
- *t. Baba Qamma* 7.2 relates a parable of two men who planned a great wedding feast. One invited the inhabitants of the city, but not the king; the other invited neither the inhabitants of the city nor the king. The punishment of the former is worse.
- *y. Ḥagigah* 2.2 relates a parable of two men who died, a holy man and a tax collector named Bar Ma'yan. No one mourned the former, but the whole town mourned the latter. A dream reveals that the holy man did one sin; he put the head phylactery on before the hand phylactery. The tax collector did no meritorious deed. "But one time he made a banquet for the councillors of his town, but they did not come. He said, 'Let the poor come and eat the food, so that it not go to waste.'" Another dream reveals that the tax collector is tormented by being unable to reach water. Also at *y. Sanhedrin* 6.6.
- *b. Šabbat* 153a (commenting on Eccl 9:8 with regard to repentance): "This may be compared to a king who summoned his servants to a banquet without appointing a time. The wise ones adorned themselves and sat at the door of the palace. ['For,'] said they, 'is anything lacking in a royal palace?' The fools went about their work, saying, 'can there be a banquet without preparations?' Suddenly the king desired [the presence of] his servants: the wise entered adorned, while the fools entered soiled. The king rejoiced at the wise but was angry with the fools. 'Those who adorned themselves for the banquet,' ordered he, 'let them sit, eat and

drink. But those who did not adorn themselves for the banquet, let them stand and watch.'" Reference is then made to Isa 65:13. Very similar parables appear in *Eccl. Rab.* 9.8.1 and *Midr. Prov.* 16.11.

- *b. Pesaḥim* 119b, in dealing with Passover, describes God's great eschatological banquet after manifesting his love to the seed of Isaac. At this banquet heroes from Israel's past demur from saying grace because of their failures, but David then says grace and finds it fitting that he should.
- *Pesiqta Rabbati* 41.5 speaks of the banquet God prepares for the righteous in the time to come as the banquet of redemption. The words "O Israel, my called" in Isa 48:12 (LXX: *Israēl hon egō kalō*), are explained as "my invited guest." Jacob will rejoice, for he will be invited to the banquet.
- *Targum Zeph.* 1.7-18 describes God summoning guests to the destruction of Judah and Jerusalem and those who lie at ease upon their wealth. People will build houses, but not inhabit them, and will have vineyards, but not drink their wine.
- *Pesiqta de Rab Kahana* 12.19 tells a parable of God's giving the Torah even though Israel included people who were blind, lame, and deaf. The parable assumes that God healed the blemished before giving the Torah.
- *Gen. Rab.* 9.10: "Imagine a king who made a feast, invited the guests, and set a dish filled with all good things before them: 'Whoever will eat and bless the king,' said he, 'let him eat and enjoy it; but he who would eat and not bless the king, let him be decapitated with a sword.' Similarly, for him who lays up precepts and good deeds, lo! there is the angel of life; while for him who does not lay up precepts and good deeds, lo! there is the angel of death."
- *Lam. Rab.* 4.2, with reference to "the precious sons of Zion": "None of them would attend a banquet unless he was invited twice."[197]

Comparison of the Accounts

Excluding this parable, the narrative sequence of the Synoptics is close in reporting the passion story. Some differences exist, but the order of triumphal entry, Temple cleansing, question of authority, the parable of the Wicked Tenants, and entrapping questions from the religious leaders is shared by all three. As Matthew — or his tradition — placed the parable of the Two Sons before the Wicked Tenants, so now the parable of the Banquet is placed after the Wicked Tenants. Mark does not include this parable at all, and Luke uses his version of this story in an entirely different context, a collection of "feast" narratives and sayings in 14:1-24.

The Wedding Banquet and the Feast (Matt 22:1-14; Luke 14:15-24; Gos. Thom. 64)

Very little verbal correspondence exists between Matthew and Luke. Of the 223 words in Matt 22:1-14 only twelve are identical in Luke 14:15-24: *eipen* ("said"), *kai apesteilen* ("and sent"), *autou* ("his"), *tois keklēmenois* ("to the invited"), *hetoima* ("ready"), *agron* ("field"), *autou* ("his"), *eis tas hodous* ("into the ways"). Another seven Greek words are shared by the two accounts, but in different forms: *anthrōpos* ("man"), *poiein* ("make"), *doulos* ("servant," twice), *eipein* ("say"), *orgizein* ("be angry"), *exelthein* ("go out").

Both Matthew and Luke have three sendings of servants, but the narratives are framed differently. Matthew has two sendings of servants (plural) to the original guests, two excuses offered for the refusal, and one sending of servants to the substitute guests. Luke has only one sending of a servant (singular) to the original guests, three excuses as to why the guests cannot come, and two sendings to the substitute guests. Despite the differences in the two accounts both Luke 14 and Matthew 22 have an open invitation (14:15-24; 22:1-10) followed by demand (14:25-33; 22:11-14).

In Matthew the man is a king, and the banquet is a wedding feast for his son. On the second invitation one invited guest goes to his field, one to his business, and the rest seize the servants and beat and kill them. The king sends soldiers to destroy the murderers and burn their city. The servants are then sent to invite whomever they find, both evil and good. Matthew also appends the sayings about the king's inspection and the guest without a wedding garment and the generalizing conclusion "Many are called, but few are chosen."

In Luke the man is not a king and he gives not a wedding feast but a great dinner. (For what it is worth, 14:8 refers to a wedding and 14:31-32 is about a king going to war.) A son is not mentioned. One guest asks to be excused because he has bought a field and must see it, another because he has bought five yoke of oxen and must test them, and a third because he has married a wife. Luke specifies the substitute guests as the poor, crippled, blind, and lame. Luke also has the strong threat "None of those men invited will taste my dinner" (v. 24).

In *Gos. Thom.*, as in Luke, a man gives a banquet and sends his servant to summon the guests. The same summons is given to four different guests, and each gives an excuse for refusal. One is owed money and must meet his debtors, one has bought a house, one must direct a wedding, and one has bought a village and must go to collect the rent. The end of the parable is sparse. The owner does not get angry, nor is much description given of the orders to find substitute guests. Instead, focus is placed on the explanation of the parable: buyers and merchants will not come into the places of "my Father." This is similar to the ending of Luke, but clearly no longer within the plane of the narrative. Rather than being an independent tradition, the account in *Gos. Thom.* appears to be an expansion and refocusing of Luke's account to pronounce judgment on wealth (and marriage) as an impediment to salvation.[198]

Textual Features Worthy of Attention

If Thomas's sayings are arranged to deal with wealth, the canonical Evangelists have arranged their versions for theological purposes as well. Matthew has placed this parable as the third in a series of parables about Israel's leaders. For connections among the three parables in Matthew see above, pp. 269-83.

Luke's concern with Israel is not as direct, but no less real. His placement of the parable with several other pericopes dealing with eating and banqueting is obvious. The mention of reclining in the kingdom of God in 13:28-29 functions as an introduction to these banqueting sayings, and the lament over Jerusalem with its complaint that people refused to be gathered (13:34) anticipates the refusals in the parable by those who do not come to the banquet. In Luke, the Pharisees are not necessarily negative. In 13:31-33 certain Pharisees seek to warn Jesus of the danger from Herod. In 14:1-2 Jesus eats at the house of a Pharisee and, although he is watched to see if he will heal on the Sabbath, he instructs those present about humility (14:7-11) and his host about who should be invited to such meals (14:12-14).

The emphasis in the canonical Gospels is on the theme that all is ready (Matt 22:4 (twice), 8; Luke 14:17) and on election ("calling" or "inviting"). The verb *kaleō* ("call" or "invite") occurs five times in Matt 22:1-9 and the noun *eklektos* ("elect") appears in 22:14. The verb *kaleō* occurs twelve times in Luke 14:7-24.[199] For both Evangelists, the parable compels reconsideration of election in light of the ministry of Jesus.

The central section of Luke (9:51–19:48) may be chiastic.[200] On some arrangements the parable of the Banquet is set opposite 13:1-9, on others opposite 13:18-30, and in others as the climax and turning point of the structure.[201] Even though disagreement exists, one must grant that the central section of Luke is "largely chiastic."

Eating and meals are major themes in Luke's Gospel. Virtually every chapter contains something relevant to the subject. Already in 1:53 there are hints of the themes of this parable.

In Luke many are invited to the banquet, but the parable isolates only three rejected invitations. This illustrates both the rule of three and the economy of the parables. Further evidence of the economy of parables exists in the gap between vv. 21 and 22. The master gives a command to bring in the poor, but the parable assumes that action has taken place and moves to the response of the servant.

The excuses in Luke 14:18-20 are similar to the three dialogues on discipleship in 9:57-62, the three requirements of discipleship in 14:26-33,[202] and the comparison of the days of the Son of Man to the activities and judgment in the days of Noah and of Lot in 17:26-31. Family involvements, including wives (or husbands) (14:20 and 26), and possessions (14:18-19 and 33) are not to take precedence over discipleship.

The instruction of Luke 14:13 to invite the poor and afflicted is mirrored with slight modification in 14:21.

In Luke 14:24 the narrative shifts from the second person singular to the second person plural *(hymin)*. Whereas the host has been addressing his servant, here the host or Jesus addresses "you" — all those present (and those who read). V. 24 intentionally reverses v. 15.

In Luke 14:35 salt is thrown out *(exō ballousin)*, and in Matt 22:13 the man without a garment is thrown out *(ekbalete)*. The passages are quite different, but seem to suggest the same theological point.

Matthew's parable of the Wedding Feast is close to and apparently shaped by the parable of the Wicked Tenants. For details see above, p. 283.

As in Matt 13:24 and 18:23, Matt 22:2 introduces the parable with the aorist passive *hōmoiōthē* ("has become like"), which should be understood to indicate that the kingdom is present. It has broken on the scene.[203]

The servants are called *douloi* in Matt 22:3-10, but *diakonoi* in 22:13. Is this an indication that two parables have been joined or that a distinction is being made between human messengers and angels at the last judgment (cf. 13:41-43), or is the shift merely occasioned by the fact that *diakonoi* is more appropriate to waiting on tables?

Some similarity exists between the parables of the Wedding Feast/Banquet and other parables dealing with preparedness, especially that of the Ten Virgins in Matt 25:1-13. People do not realize the significance of what is happening, respond inappropriately, and are excluded.

The destruction of the rebellious in Matt 22:7 is similar to the destruction of the enemies in the parable of the Pounds (Luke 19:27).

Cultural Information[204]

Both parables assume a double invitation, and this practice is attested in various sources.[205] The first invitation tells of the event and seeks an initial acceptance, and the second is a reminder and tells the guests that all is ready and they should come.

As is still true, meals, especially banquets, were among the most important contexts for social relations. They were the primary context in which shame and honor were assigned.[206] Meals were and are a means for organizing society. Shame and honor were much more explicit in the ancient world than in our own, and — at least if one was in the race at all — people were more consciously preoccupied with shame and honor than is apparent in modern western societies. Cultural stratification, privilege, and indebtedness to reciprocate were strongly emphasized, as Luke 14:7-14 demonstrates.[207]

I do not think Greco-Roman symposia provide the context for understanding this parable, but they do provide insight into the role of meals in Mediterranean culture for acquiring honor and teaching wisdom. Several ancient writings from Plato on use the symposium as a means for teaching.[208]

Explanation of the Parable

Options for Interpretation

The church understood these parables as full-blown allegorical descriptions of salvation history and Christian living.[209] Origen understood the king as God, the marriage as the restoration of Christ's church to him, the servants as the rejected prophets, the banquet as the spiritual food of God's mysteries, "all things ready" as discourses concerning ultimate realities, the destruction of the city as the Jewish War, the command to invite all as the turning to the Gentiles, and the missing garment as ethical qualities like mercy and kindness. He also took the parable as referring to the marriage of the Logos and the individual.[210] Augustine even understood the five oxen as referring to the five senses, and he like others justified the use of force on heretics from Luke's "compel them to come in."[211]

Many scholars think these parables do indeed provide an allegorical representation of salvation history, but one that does not focus on minute details. A considerable amount of variation exists, but at a minimum the parables are assumed to depict the eschatological banquet, with God or Christ as the host and the messengers as emissaries from God, and the parable is understood to say that those who think they will be at the end-time banquet will not be. A common assumption is that Matthew has strongly allegorized his version so that the sending of the servants refers to the early and later prophets, the murder of the servants represents the murder of Jesus and the prophets, the burning of the city refers to the destruction of Jerusalem, and the third sending of servants is understood as the mission of the church.[212] Reconstructions of the parable often exclude Matt 22:6-7.[213] Some see the people addressed as all Israel, but others think only the Pharisees or religious leaders are addressed. Correspondingly, the substitute guests are either tax collectors and sinners or the poor. Most see both Matthew and Luke depicting the turn from Israel to the Gentiles even though they have arranged the sendings differently. Whereas some understand the three sendings to refer to the former and latter prophets and the invitation to the Gentiles, others understand the correspondences to be to the OT prophets, the disciples during Jesus' ministry, and missionaries after the resurrection or even to the pre-Easter disciples, the post-Easter disciples, and the ongoing mission of the church.[214]

Some see all of Matthew's account as his own creation, some see only vv. 11-14 as Matthean, and some see all of the pericope going back to Jesus, even though vv. 11-14 might be a separate parable. Most think vv. 11-14 are a message to Matthew's community that good conduct, not just being in the church, is necessary. The assumption is that Matthew's community is a *corpus permixtum*, a group containing both evil and good. The more an interpretation emphasizes the turn to the Gentiles, the easier it is to see the parable as anti-Semitic.

A few see the parables, especially Matthew's version, in connection to a call, not just to the eschatological banquet, but to the final eschatological battle. The basis for this approach lies in assumptions about the relation of the parable to OT texts. In connection with the hypothesis that Luke's travel narrative is framed on Deuteronomy, people find the connections between Luke 14:18-20 and Deut 20:5-7 and 24:5 (which concern exemptions from military service) sufficient to say that the parable is about the call to the final Holy War, a call that overrides every other obedience.[215] Others would emphasize Zeph 1:7-16, which discusses the day of the Lord in terms of battle, and with support from the targum would see Matthew's parable as a midrash on the Zephaniah passage.[216]

Especially for the Lukan version, rather than being a parable of Israel, some describe it as a fictional tale about the transformation/conversion of the host. This interpretation downplays the eschatological context and focuses on issues of honor and shame. The host gives a dinner in a quest for honor, but when he is snubbed, he rejects the whole system of valuation and transfers his social life to a different group. On this view the parable addresses wealthy people in Luke's church, who in the desire to maintain status in the society are refusing associations with poorer Christians.[217]

Decisions on the Issues

Many of the problems involved in discussion of this parable are caused by over-interpretation of the accounts (i.e., allegorizing), neglect of the context in Jesus' ministry, and a loss of how this analogy works. How does one know the parable in either account refers to the mission to the Gentiles? Is Augustine the only one guilty of allegorizing when Jeremias tells us that entry into the wedding hall is baptism or that, although Jesus could not have uttered the story as an allegory of the feast of salvation, he may well have had such in mind?[218] Especially if our concern is the intent of Jesus, we should at least *attempt* to hear his voice and not assume that the only situation addressed is that of the Evangelist's church.

1. What is the relation of the accounts (including Gos. Thom. *64)?* While the general structure is similar, there is very little correspondence in wording between Matthew and Luke. David Hill suggests that the divergences in the accounts are evidence of the freedom with which oral tradition transmitted and interpreted parables.[219] Obviously parables were shaped in various ways as they were transmitted, but I find it hard to accept that one account stands behind the two quite different accounts in Matthew and Luke. The situation with these parables is unique in that greater divergence exists here than with any other incidence of parallels.[220] Parables in the triple tradition witness to a much greater fidelity to the tradition than Hill's comments merit, and one has only to compare the accounts of the parable of the Wicked Tenants or the Sower to see that. Double tradition parables are either very close or, like here, not close at all. Why is this parable so different if both accounts are from the same source? Robert Funk asks an obvious question, which all would answer affirmatively, but the significance of which few do justice: Is it not likely that Jesus spoke a given parable on a number of occasions and in different contexts, adapting it each time, perhaps, to the circumstances?[221] A parable like that of the Banquet, especially if it was a challenge to Jesus' contemporaries, may have been told numerous times in various places and forms.[222] The more this is true the less one can reconstruct a primitive form. It is striking, however, how many scholars admit that an original form cannot be determined who then proceed to find one.

If only nineteen of 223 words are used in both accounts (see p. 305 above) and if the contexts and structures are different, I would argue that we have little reason to think these accounts have come from the same story. They should be analyzed separately. While Luke's context is rather definite, Matthew's is uncertain and the story could have been told almost anywhere.[223] In Matthew and Luke we have two similar stories, not two versions of the same story.[224]

The account in *Gos. Thom.* is neither superior nor simpler[225] and has been changed into an anti-wealth and anti-business saying.[226] Its extension of the invitations and excuses to four can hardly be early, and it seems to reflect portions of Luke especially.[227]

2. Against what background should these parables be read? The literary background for understanding this parable is crucial and intriguing, but also at points frustrating. I find little evidence to think the parable is based on Wisdom's invitation to the simple to feast at her table (Prov 9:2-6). The parallels are superficial, and a hearer/reader of the parable could be expected neither to make the connection nor to see its relevance.

J. Jeremias popularized the view that the parable is based on the story of the tax collector Bar Ma'yan.[228] This view has not found much reception, and rightly so. Even apart from questions of the date of the rabbinic account, no hint in the Gospel narratives suggests that the host is a tax collector or that a comparison is being made between the host and someone else. There is a similarity to the parable in that invited persons refuse to come to a banquet and the poor are brought in. However, in the talmudic story the poor are brought in only so that the food is not wasted. Further, no advantage in interpretation is gained by finding a background in this talmudic story.

Others suggest that ancient symposia and symposiastic writings provide the background for the parable.[229] Symposia were festive meals, often rather bawdy drinking parties, that provided a context for entertainment and philosophical discussion. I doubt that symposia have any relevance for understanding Jesus' meals. Writings on symposia have contributions from most people present at the meal and are long narratives; the Gospel accounts are brief and hardly anyone besides Jesus gives an opinion.[230] Other resonances may be set up by the meal context, such as honor-shame motifs or even an anti-symposium critique,[231] but they do not drive the story.

The crucial background is the evidence — both canonical and non-canonical — that God's fulfillment of his promises would be like a joyous banquet. Texts like Isaiah 25; 1QSa 2.5-22; 2 *En.* 42:5; *m. 'Abot* 4.16; and *Pesiqta Rabbati* 41.5 cannot be ignored, but just as important are Matt 8:11-12/Luke 13:28-30 and the meals in Jesus' ministry. By eating with toll collectors and sinners Jesus demonstrated the presence of the kingdom and the forgiveness made available.[232] The primary reason the story focuses on a banquet/wedding feast is to convey that the subject being addressed is the end-time banquet. Certainly both Evangelists point in that direction, especially Luke with the unnamed speaker in v. 15 explicitly saying how blessed the person will be who partakes of food in the kingdom of God. The Qumran texts listed above (1QSa 2.3-9; 1QM 7.4-5; and 11Q 45.12-18; see above, p. 301) draw on Lev 21:17-23 to exclude people with imperfections from the community and the eschatological events. Jesus' parable seems specifically to have been constructed to contradict such membership lists excluding the lame and blemished.[233]

The intriguing and frustrating part of the literary background is the possible parallels with Deut 20:5-7 (the exemptions for military duty) and the *Targum Zeph* 1.7-18. Paul Ballard emphasizes the former and J. Derrett adds the latter,[234] both to emphasize that the excuses come in a context of Holy War and that the issue is allegiance to the king who has summoned his troops for inspection. Even the destruction of the city in Matt 22:6-7 and the wedding garment from Matt 22:11-13 would make sense because the targum speaks of the slaughter that comes on the day of the Lord and Zeph 1:8 tells of the punishment of officials who dress in foreign attire (which is not mentioned in the targum, however). Especially if one is impressed with the argument that Luke's travel narrative is modeled on Deuteronomy, these parallels are attractive. However, real problems exist for this approach. At most the allusions, if they exist, are embedded deeply somewhere in the tradition, and hearers — even Jewish or Christian ones — could not be expected to catch them. Further, as H. Palmer pointed out, the excuses are in Luke, but the military language is in Matthew.[235] On closer analysis the parallels are not nearly as close as suggested. Deut 20:5-7 exempts those who have built a house but not dedicated it, planted a vineyard but not eaten from it, or become engaged but not yet married (Deut 24:5 exempts those newly married). The excuses in Luke 14:18-20 are that one purchased a field, one purchased five yoke of oxen, and one has recently married.[236] While the targum on Zephaniah is about judgment, especially on the wealthy, one looks in vain for any marker that would demonstrate that this is the background for either version of the parable. Attempts in this direction are a dead end. The background against which the parable must be understood is the vision of the kingdom of God or the day of the Lord as an eschatological banquet.

After consideration of these general questions, the analysis of each of the accounts should proceed separately. The parable in Luke will be treated first because it is easier.

3. According to Luke,[237] Jesus told the parable in response to a comment from a dinner guest in the house of a Pharisee: "Blessed is anyone who will eat bread in the kingdom of God!" (14:15). The arrangement of this section is clearly Lukan, and, while the parable could have been told in another context, it fits well in its present location. There is no reason the parable should not be seen as a reply to such thinking, but at the very least the parable assumes an understanding about the kingdom meal and its participants. Luke 14:14 records a blessing from Jesus which describes the reward at the resurrection for those who minister to the poor and disabled. The mention of the resurrection brings forth the blessing on those who will eat bread in the kingdom. Comparison with 11:27 is instructive, for there a woman blesses the womb that bore Jesus and the breasts that nourished him, to which he counters, "Rather, blessed are those who hear the word of God and keep it." Surely in 14:15 the man who gave the blessing expected an affirmation of his statement, possibly something like "May we be among the righteous who sit at that table" or "May that day come quickly."[238] As in 11:27 the blessing meets an unexpected response.

a. Is the focus of Luke's parable on the change in the host, on attitudes toward the rich and the poor, or on the rejection of the invitations? The interpretation of Luke's story as a narration of the conversion of the host and his rejection of prior social values cannot succeed. Certainly the social values of the kingdom are different, and this whole section seeks to promote a kingdom view of self and others. To focus on the conversion of the host, however, is a distortion for several reasons:

> This approach downplays the eschatological context too severely. It must set aside v. 15 with its yearning to eat bread in the kingdom, and it ignores the Jewish literary background and the parable's emphatic assertion that "all is now ready."
>
> It ignores the emphasis on election language in both accounts.[239]
>
> It assumes that the real focus is the situation of Luke's community, but the result of such "mirror reading" has to be laid on the parable, not drawn from it.
>
> Nothing suggests that the host gave his banquet as a quest for honor, and no conversion language is present either.[240]

Certainly this parable draws on the themes of wealth and concern for the poor evident in much of Jesus' teaching, themes that are of major redactional interest for Luke, but these subjects are not the primary focus of the parable; they are secondary factors. The third excuse is of one who has been married; poor people married too, which indicates that the issues are not about wealth and poverty. The parable has implications about attitudes toward the poor, but the main interest is elsewhere.

The focus of the parable is on the invitations spurned by one group and extended to others unexpectedly. This is what is given prominence by the structure. The question the parable addresses is not "What counts as shame and honor?" or "What should be one's attitude to the poor?" but "Who will be present at the banquet?" The excuses betray preoccupation with everyday business and relations. Indeed, the parable presumes people of some financial standing. The average farmer — to say nothing of the poor — does not buy five yoke of oxen: the man has at least 100 acres.[241] Whether the excuses are legitimate or paper-thin is debated,[242] but for Luke this question is irrelevant. His point is that no excuse is valid when one faces the kingdom. The excuses parallel themes in Jesus' teaching on discipleship, both in Luke and elsewhere, but especially in Luke 9:57-62 and 14:25-33. Luke, as indeed Jesus before him, is concerned that possessions and family do not prohibit discipleship.

b. What is the significance of Luke's account for understanding election? Regardless of whether one thinks Luke is directly countering abuses of the election teaching in Deuteronomy,[243] which may well be the case, at least the parable must be seen as a challenge to the predominant understanding of election among Jesus' contemporaries. The verb *kaleō* ("call") occurs twelve times in Luke 14:7-24. To ask "Who will be at the banquet?" is to ask "Who are the elect?" and the parable provides an unexpected answer. Like John the Baptist and the prophets before him, Jesus did not accept that election was established by birth from a Jewish mother. The intent of the parable in both Luke and Matthew is that those who assume that they are elect and will be present at the end-time banquet may not be. Attendance at the banquet is based on *response* to the invitation of God, not the title "invited one" or "elect one." The response intended is one that results in productive living.

This parable fits with Jesus' actions and teachings elsewhere. The idea that those who expect to be at the banquet ("the elect") will not be and that unexpected guests will be is paralleled in Matt 8:11-12/Luke 13:28-30 and resonates with several other texts.[244] Jesus' eating with toll collectors and sinners is a demonstration of the presence of the kingdom in his ministry and the forgiveness available to those who respond (Matt 9:10-13/Mark 2:15-17/Luke 5:29-32; Matt 11:19/Luke 7:34; cf. Luke 15:2; 19:5-10). The parable of the Prodigal in Luke 15 mirrors the celebration of the kingdom banquet to which the elder brother refuses to come. The point of these texts and of the parable of the Banquet can be summarized with a statement and a question: God is giving a party. Are you going to come?[245]

c. Are the persons addressed Pharisees, Jews in general, or some other group? Obviously neither Jesus nor Luke identifies explicitly who the original guests were. The Lukan context has the parable told in the house of a Pharisee, but we should not assume that all the guests were Pharisees or that the parable addresses them. The excuses of those who reject are not descriptive of Pharisees or religious leaders; they reflect general cares about life. Throughout the Lukan travel narrative Jesus seems to alternate addressing the religious leadership (lawyers, Pharisees, etc.), the crowd, and the disciples.[246] If the attempt is made to hear the parable within the context of Jesus' Jewish listeners, those who refuse the invitation can neither be limited to Pharisees nor broadened to include *all* Jews, for many Jews did follow Jesus' teaching. Those who refuse the invitation mirror hearers of any category who do not perceive the crisis Jesus' ministry brings. Yes, the parable is about Israel's response to Jesus, but it does not say that all Israel has refused and therefore is rejected. No specific group is pinpointed, even though in 15:1-2 and elsewhere Luke is especially concerned with Pharisees and scribes. The parable addresses failure to respond to God's eschatological activity and urges people to reconsider. All who take election for granted and are more concerned about mundane affairs than the kingdom are confronted by the parable.

d. What degree of allegorical correspondence is there in Luke's parable? The primary questions here have to do with determining the intent of the various sendings and whether Jesus is represented in the parable or not. Interpreters regularly argue that with the first sending Luke points to the mission to Israel and with the two later sendings either to an ongoing mission to Israel and one to the Gentiles or to the early and later Gentile mission.[247] Jesus is seen by some as the host, but others think God is the host with some concluding that Jesus is represented by the servant.[248]

It is worth reflecting on method before proceeding. How does one know to assign representational significance to some features of the parable and not others? No reasonable person would identify specifically the three people who reject the invitation or the elements in their excuses. No one assigns significance to the poor, lame, blind, and crippled; they are treated literally or at least understood as summarizing social outcasts. Why then do interpreters feel the various times the servant went out must have representational significance? On the other hand, there is clearly more than one point of contact between this parable and the reality it portrays, which even Jülicher had to admit.[249] The expectation of an eschatological banquet, the context, and the focus on all being ready require that the meal is understood as the end-time celebration, and surely the first thought is that the host of that meal is either God or the Messiah. The servant points to emissaries from God who bring the invitation, but only in very general terms. All that is needed in the analogy is people who reject and others to whom the invitation is extended. The parable does not invite speculation to identify any other feature.

In my opinion to argue that the three sendings refer to the mission to Israel during Jesus' life and two post-Easter mission efforts, at least one of which is to the Gentiles, is merciless allegorizing.[250] Despite the popularity of this understanding, it comes from preconceived ideas and not from the text. Nothing in Luke's narrative even hints at Gentiles.[251] Further, to worry over the fact that the parable depicts the host as inviting the wealthy and only later turning to the poor, as if God or Jesus became interested in the poor and outcasts only after other people rejected,[252] is allegorizing and assumes that every feature of the analogy must mirror reality. Such thinking also assumes that narrative time corresponds to real time, which is not true.[253] Parable chronology is not real-time chronology. A parable is a *partial* picture of reality, and it holds up part of reality to make a specific point or points, sometimes in an extreme fashion. Parables must be allowed to mirror the portion of reality they wish and not forced to picture a systematic theology or a chronology *in toto*.

Certainly Luke is concerned about a universal mission, and Jesus too may be suspected of a universal concern because of his understanding of Israel's task.[254] But this parable does not portray such concern. The substitute guests are explicitly the poor and disabled (cf. 14:13), the marginalized of society, not the Gentiles.[255] Because of Jesus' eating with toll collectors and sinners (note 15:1-2) and resonances between 14:21 and 7:22 (the description to the Baptist of the healing of the blind and lame and of the proclamation to the poor), we should probably think more generally of all those who have responded affirmatively to Jesus' ministry, the very people the religious leaders did not respect.[256] With "the poor, crippled, blind, and lame" the parabolic method is briefly dropped and reality intrudes. The second sending for substitute guests to fill the house has the purpose not of designating Gentiles but of excluding the original guests, as 14:24 shows.[257]

Is Jesus represented in the parable?[258] The most important verse for this question is v. 24, where the identity of the speaker is uncertain.[259] Is the host still speaking within the story world, has Jesus taken over and appended an explanation to the parable, or have the two voices merged at this point? At the very least, the host in the story takes the platform to address those outside the story, for the shift to the plural pronoun "you" *(hymin)* indicates this. Consequently, v. 24 becomes a personal warning to the hearers/readers. The words "For I say to you" look like a typical emphatic explanation from Jesus. Often this expression comes at the end of a parable,[260] but sometimes the expression is used by a person in a parable,[261] so we cannot exclude the possibility that v. 24 gives the words of the host in the parable. Probably the voice of Jesus and the host merge at this point, and if so, the christological implications are significant.[262] The eschatological meal is Jesus' meal, and he determines who is and who is not included. Doubtless, this is what Luke wants the reader to understand.

e. What is the message and significance of Jesus' parable as rendered by Luke? This parable as much as any emphasizes the presence of the kingdom in the ministry of Jesus. This parable fits with Jesus' enactment of the presence of the kingdom by eating with "sinners"; it asserts that the eschatological banquet is ready: "Come, because already it is ready" (v. 17). People should be responding eagerly. Instead, they are too busy with possessions and family and offer excuses as to why they cannot come.

The parable functions also as a challenge and warning. What possibly could be so important about mundane affairs that they keep one away from God's celebration? To reject the invitation is to exclude oneself from the eschatological meal.[263] The message of the parable is very close to 13:28, 34. Often God has sought to gather his people, but their refusal has left them outside with others taking their place at the table. The parable expresses an absolute exclusion, but the plane of the parable is not the plane of reality. People do not have to stay excluded. The hearers of Jesus' parable, like later readers, are confronted with a challenge to change course, to look past the superficial, and to respond to God's work taking place in Jesus' ministry. Many ancient Jews, particularly those who considered themselves pious, assumed that they as God's elect would be at the messianic banquet (or at least victorious and living with God) when evil was defeated.[264] The parable warns against such presumption.[265]

The parable also shows God's concern for outcasts and God's desire to "have a full house," that is, to obtain a people for himself, which is a theme throughout both Testaments.

Whether the host points analogically to God or Jesus is difficult to determine. In either case, though, it is fair to say Jesus processes his own experience with this parable.[266] All is ready because of what is taking place in his ministry. He has encountered refusals by the presumed elect and acceptance among the outcasts. V. 24, regardless of the identification of the host, is christologically significant. At least as God's agent Jesus is the one giving the meal.

4. With regard to Matthew, E. Haenchen remarked that going from the parable in Matthew to that in Luke is like going from a labyrinth to a park.[267] J. Lambrecht felt enough disquiet about the parable to confess a feeling that it should be ignored.[268] One can understand this because in retaliation for the murder of his servants the king sends soldiers to destroy the perpetrators and burn their city. After that, the meal is still ready, so people, both good and bad, are invited from the margins of the city. But someone who comes as an unexpected guest is bound hand and foot and cast to the outer darkness for not having on the right garment. This does not sound like what we know about Jesus. But then not all parables look like parks.

Presumably the parable in Matthew is addressed to the Jewish leaders because of the previous context. *Autois* in 22:1 could mean "about them" (the leaders) but more likely it means "to them." Matthew's placement of the parable illustrates and emphasizes the opposition of the religious leaders (21:45-46), opposition further evidenced by the confrontational questions in 22:15-46. The Pharisees are specifically in view, but they are not the only opponents.

a. Is Matthew's parable authentic or purely Matthean allegorizing? Answering this question presupposes decisions about the degree of allegorical correspondence in Matthew's account and in particular whether it depicts the post-Easter mission and the destruction of Jerusalem. Does Matthew point to the former and latter prophets with his two sendings to the original guests and to the destruction of Jerusalem in 70 A.D. with the soldiers destroying the murderers and burning their city? To answer these questions will also be to explain how Matthew sees Jesus' mission.

Our concern is the intent of Jesus with his parables. Could Jesus have told such a story, and, if he did, what could it possibly mean? Often NT scholars seem to try to protect Jesus from any description we do not like, particularly anything that has to do with judgment. However, which of Israel's prophets ever lacked a message of judgment? — and Jesus certainly came as a prophet. Further, in Matt 8:11-12/Luke 13:28-29 Jesus asserts that the sons of the kingdom will be cast out where there are weeping and gnashing of teeth, and others will recline at table with the patriarchs, very much as in this parable.

The parable is diaphanous — one can see through it from the first, but sometimes parables do that, particularly if the teller has no desire to camouflage the intent. Ezek 23:1-49 is the classic diaphanous parable.[269] For forty-nine verses the prophet describes the harlotry of two women, but already in v. 4 the two women are identified as Samaria and Jerusalem. Such directness could result from two different circumstances: the teller confronts his opponents with an intentionally sharp accusation, or the teller speaks to people he trusts about his opponents in their absence. In either case, the reality depicted dominates the story so that the story is a mixture of image and reality. That is precisely the case with Matt 22:1-14.

The question is whether the reality depicted is one that could come only from the church or whether it could derive from Jesus. At first glance, and because the theory is so often repeated, the parable looks like the church's description of the destruction of Jerusalem as retribution for the death of Christ. That could be, but closer analysis suggests otherwise. This parable is similar to that of the Wicked Tenants in the description of the twofold sendings of the servants, of their mistreatment in ways that remind of the prophets,[270] and of the destruction of the offenders. Unlike the previous parable, however, here the son plays virtually no role and *is not killed*. Would the church have presented the story like this, especially when for Matthew the son was killed in the previous parable? Why is the son so incidental and still alive if this is Matthean or early church allegorizing?[271] Also, in Josephus's description of the destruction of Jerusalem, it is the Temple that is burned, not the city. This parable does not depict any punishment of the Jews for the death of Christ.

Several studies have emphasized the importance of seeing the political emphases in Matthew's version. K. Rengstorf argued that the language of v. 7 is a literary "topos" for the destruction of a city.[272] Others, especially R. Bauckham, argue that the wedding of the king's son to which the great men of the kingdom are invited is a festal occasion of major political importance. Attendance is an expression of loyalty, and refusal is tantamount to insurrection. In such a context the war imagery in v. 7 makes sense and fits the narrative logic of the story.[273] The political overtones do not remove the harshness of the parable, but they do help in understanding how the narrative works.

But would Matthew or the early church so easily identify Rome's armies as God's soldiers?[274] In the OT God does use pagan nations to judge his people, but it is difficult to accept that this is the parable's intent. More plausibly, the parable uses language of Israel's *history* — the rejection of the prophets and the destruction of Jerusalem in 586 B.C. — to warn of the consequences of rejecting God's messengers.[275] This is a typical prophetic method of operation. Israel's past is the lens through which the parable announces a warning of urgency and judgment on all those who oppose God. If one seeks to lay out strict parallels and thinks the destruction of Jerusalem is in view, one would have to conclude that Matthew believed the gospel was only extended to the Gentiles after 70 A.D.[276] Surely such procedures are illegitimate. Nothing more is necessary than a warning to Jesus' hearers modeled on their own history.

Attempts to identify the messengers specifically with prophets or disciples quickly runs into difficulty. If the subject is the invitation to the eschatological feast, can the reference be to OT prophets, or does that invitation go out only after Jesus inaugurates the present kingdom?[277] Convinced of the latter, several have argued that the servants sent in vv. 3-6 are *Christian* messengers.[278] What prepares a reader to understand this or even hints that this is the intent? Is there a reference to the early and latter prophets of the OT, Christian missionaries before and/or after Easter, or some combination of both? The text gives no basis for any identification, and all attempts to specify the servants are misguided. The only important point is that the invited ones, the apparently elect, have repeatedly refused to come and have rebelled against the king/God.

The only thing in vv. 2-10 that suggests that the parable refers to Jesus' ministry — apart from the bare mention of the son, if even that does — is the emphasis on the fact that "all is ready." There are no allusions to Gentiles or apostles or various aspects of the Christian mission.[279] Left in the context of Jesus' own teaching, the story is a warning about the danger of presuming election and of ignoring the crisis of the kingdom present in his ministry.[280] The story is about the disaster of refusing a crucial invitation and provides an analogy to the failure to respond to the invitation to God's kingdom.

One of the main difficulties of the parable is its inattention to sequence. A military expedition takes place while the banquet is still ready to eat, or possibly the king merely sends his armies and proceeds with the feast. The parable focuses on all being ready and — as much as any parable so categorized — on the presence of the kingdom.[281] Yet at the same time vv. 11-13 focus on final judgment. Worth contemplating is the comment of G. R. Beasley-Murray that this parable is one of those utterances in which distinctions of time seem out of place.[282] Parables are pictures of reality, not histories, even if they pull on historical circumstances. The kingdom is like a prepared banquet, and to refuse its invitation is to encounter judgment. Yet, quite similar to the parable of the Net (13:47-50), the kingdom is a gathering process to be followed by judgment. Note the way that 22:10 prepares for the judgment scene by saying that the servants collected both evil and good, which in 5:45 is a way of referring to all humanity. I do not think Matthew is pointing to the mixed nature of the church.[283] He consistently describes the *kingdom* as a process of gathering to be followed by dividing at judgment (13:30, 41-43, 47-50; 25:31-33).

Matthew's parable is more blatant than Luke's in its confrontation with the religious leaders. It is not as christologically suggestive as Luke's account, but it has the same message concerning the presence of the kingdom and presumptions of election that Luke does. Matthew's account makes more sense coming from Jesus than from the church.[284]

b. How do the two parts of Matthew's account fit together, if they do? The most difficult question for me, one about which I remain ambivalent, is whether 22:11-14 belonged originally with this parable. If one were impressed with the parallels with Zeph 1:7-18 and its judgment of those in foreign apparel on the day of the Lord, the argument for the unity of vv. 2-13 would be easy,[285] but these connections are too tenuous to inspire confidence. In favor of seeing vv. 11-14 as originally a separate parable that has been joined to the Wedding Feast are the use of the plural "parables" in 22:1, the switch from *douloi* in vv. 3-10 to *diakanoi* in v. 13, and the fact that v. 10 seems like the conclusion of the parable.[286] Matthew was certainly free to splice his material as he saw fit. One could argue for two independent parables because two major teachings are presented about the kingdom: it is like a banquet to which some refuse to come and show themselves unworthy; it is like a gathering process followed by judgment. However, other parables have a double movement. The parable of the Compassionate Father with Two Sons (Luke 15:11-32) is an obvious example, and *douloi* could shift to *diakanoi* because the latter is the more appropriate word for those who wait on tables. Although ambivalent, I am inclined to think vv. 2-13 should be taken as a whole. As a unit these verses make the same point made in Matt 8:11-12/Luke 13:28-29: unexpected people are at the messianic banquet while the "sons of the kingdom" are cast into outer darkness. One problem with this, though, is that in 22:11-13 only one person is so harshly judged. The man is apparently to be understood as representative, but that is not explicit.

Regardless of the origin of vv. 11-13, the reason Matthew included them is clear. That both bad and good were "gathered" (cf. 13:30, 47) leads to the expectation that they will be separated. More than the other Gospels Matthew consistently reminds his readers that the unlimited grace of the kingdom always brings with it unlimited demand. The emphasis is on obedient response and an awareness of the reality of judgment. Here the narrative plane of the story is again broken by the reality being pictured. The punishment is no longer earthly, such as the destruction of cities, but final apocalyptic judgment.

That the man is expected to have a wedding garment is still troublesome. Apparently all that is intended is a clean garment.[287] To come with dirty clothes would show contempt for the king and his banquet.[288] Although the idea still circulates,[289] there is insufficient basis for the idea that garments were provided to guests at feasts.[290] Ideas from Luke's parable should not be imported; Matthew's parable does not say that the poor were invited or that people came straight in from the streets. The parable assumes that the man has had time to come appropriately attired. Efforts to identify the missing "garment" have usually focused on good works (see Rev 19:8), repentance, salvation (based on Isa 61:10), love, or more generally the eschatological garment awarded the righteous in the new age.[291] Precise identification is both impossible and inappropriate. What is important is that the man made no preparation to wear something fitting to the feast he chose to attend. If he is representative, he mirrors all the unrighteous who have made no preparation for God's judgment.[292] The parable then in its two parts contains three important themes: the refusal of the religious leaders, the gathering of the kingdom, and the separation that takes place at judgment. These themes are present both in other parables and in non-parabolic material.

c. Does the proverb in v. 14 belong with the parable, and what is its intent? The proverb is not integral to the parable and is likely a Matthean concluding statement. The intent in saying "Many are called, but few are chosen" is apparently "All are called, but not all are chosen."[293] Sometimes it is objected that the saying does not fit the parable, but it does summarize vv. 2-10 well.[294] Many (all) were invited, but not all showed themselves to be elect. The proverb demonstrates both divine grace and human responsibility.

5. Returning to a final question pertinent to both parables, *is either account anti-Semitic, and does either suggest that Israel is rejected by God?* If the parables are directed against the religious leaders, if they are a prophetic indictment, and if they envision other Jews — not Gentiles — among the substitute guests, neither parable can legitimately be described as anti-Semitic, and certainly neither suggests that God has rejected Israel. In both accounts little hope is held out for those who have refused the invitation, but both assume that others, other *Jews*, will respond. The tendency of both scholars and pastors to interpret these parables as showing God's rejection of Israel or her displacement by the church must itself be rejected. The problem of anti-Semitism has to be faced with other texts, but it should not be laid on these parables.

Adapting the Parable

The kingdom is still like a banquet. The invitation can still go out because all is ready and people may come and enjoy the feast now. The Lord's Supper is just such a celebration and anticipation. The kingdom is still — and will be — like a banquet at which those who were supposed to attend were too preoccupied to come and others not expected to attend come and enjoy the feast. The expected are absent and the unexpected are present. Repeatedly this theme sounds forth in Jesus' teaching in a discomforting way (Matt 7:21-23/Luke 13:25-27; Matt 8:11-12/Luke 13:28-30; Matt 11:25/Luke 10:21; Matt 21:28-32, 43; 25:1-12, 31-46). No one should take attendance at the messianic banquet for granted. Unfortunately, many people do: they have made a decision, they belong to the right group, they have the right schooling, and they have participated in numerous services and charitable efforts, so they can now get on with their lives. Proclamation of the kingdom is not about reassuring people, nor is the kingdom in keeping with the busyness and many of the values we presuppose. *Proclamation of the kingdom is a challenge to respond to the invitation of God.* These parables do not spell out what such a response looks like. Matt 22:11-14 underscores the moral expectation, and the previous parables emphasize the necessity of bearing fruit. In Luke the verses following the parable (14:25-33) point to the demands of discipleship.

Both parables teach that we cannot have the kingdom on our own terms. The invitation of grace brings with it demand. At stake is the issue of a person's identity. It is not enough to wear the right label ("the invited one"); rather, the kingdom must shape identity so that one has a whole different set of concerns. The warning of Luke must be heard: the biggest obstacles to discipleship are possessions and family, but they are also the biggest opportunities *for* discipleship.

Another note sounding in the parable is the sense of joy and urgency that attends the kingdom. The witness of the church should be characterized by the joy of inviting people to the banquet God has prepared, a banquet that is both present and future. Far too often the joy has been so muted that people are left with no pointers to the presence of the kingdom.

Quite possibly the key in appropriating this parable is a Christian understanding of time. We do not stand in the crisis Jesus' contemporaries stood in as he issued the invitation to God's kingdom. But if the kingdom was present in his ministry and continues as present through the work of the Holy Spirit, we live in a similar crisis with regard to the kingdom, and, furthermore, life has its own urgencies. Do we not have the responsibility to offer the invitation with the announcement that all is ready? Should not the joy of the celebration of the kingdom be so evident that the invitation becomes compelling? Do we not need to be alert enough to know that those who expect to be there — including ourselves — may not be and should be so warned about presumptions and pre-occupations? And should we not be alert enough to know that the invitation to those on the margins, whom we would not normally think of inviting, is essential? Having discovered from other parables that the kingdom comes with limitless grace but brings with it limitless demand, these same themes reverberate in the accounts of this parable in both Matthew and Luke. The invitation to God's table is sheer grace, but it is never cheap grace. The parable is not about mission, but it becomes a basis for reflection about mission.

There is an urgency especially with regard to Christian witness and preaching. Pastors sometimes preach with no sense of urgency, and when that is the case people find little compulsion to listen. Something about the kingdom brings with it a sense of urgency for life and for God's future activity.

Given the abuse in the church's history of the statement "Compel them to come in" (Luke 14:23),[295] we should make sure that no one misunderstands. This statement has nothing to do with physical force; the focus of the text is on the urgency of the invitation.

Finally, we must reflect again on judgment. This theme appears repeatedly in Jesus' teaching, and we are always uncomfortable with it. Couldn't God just be a nice God and not hold anyone accountable? We have already treated judgment before and will again later. At this point I respond to a question raised by U. Luz, "Does the concept of judgment negate the power of the promise of salvation?"[296] Without the concept of judgment one does not even need salvation, and any urgency about life and its importance, about justice, or even about God is, if not lost, at least greatly diminished. Grace is only grace if the outcome should have been otherwise, and the significance of life depends on accountability for life. We may not like judgment, but it is a central and necessary message of both Testaments and especially of Jesus' teaching.

For Further Reading

Kenneth Ewing Bailey, *Through Peasant Eyes: More Lucan Parables, Their Culture and Style* (Grand Rapids: Eerdmans, 1980), pp. 88-113.

Paul H. Ballard, "Reasons for Refusing the Great Supper," *JTS* 23 (1972): 341-50.

Francis W. Beare, "The Parable of the Guests at the Banquet: A Sketch of the History of Its Interpretation," in *The Joy of Study*, ed. S. E. Johnson (New York: Macmillan, 1951), 1-14.

Willi Braun, *Feasting and Social Rhetoric in Luke 14* (SNTSMS 85; Cambridge: Cambridge University Press, 1995).

W. D. Davies and Dale C. Allison, *A Critical and Exegetical Commentary on the*

Gospel According to Saint Matthew (3 vols.; ICC; Edinburgh: T. & T. Clark, 1988-97), 3:193-209.

J. Duncan M. Derrett, "The Parable of the Great Supper," in *Law in the New Testament* (London: Darton, Longman & Todd, 1970), 126-55.

Peter Dschulnigg, "Positionen des Gleichnisverständnisses im 20. Jahrhundert," *TZ* 45 (1989): 335-351.

Robert W. Funk, *Language, Hermeneutic, and Word of God* (New York: Harper & Row, 1966), pp. 163-98.

Eugene E. Lemcio, "The Parables of the Great Supper and the Wedding Feast: History, Redaction, and Canon," *HBT* 8 (1986): 1-26.

Humphrey Palmer, "Just Married, Cannot Come," *NovT* 18 (1976): 241-57.

J. A. Sanders, "The Ethic of Election in Luke's Great Banquet Parable," in *Essays in Old Testament Ethics*, ed. James L. Crenshaw and John T. Willis (New York: Ktav, 1974), pp. 245-71.

Klyne Snodgrass, "Common Life with Jesus: The Parable of the Banquet in Luke 14:16-24," in *Common Life in the Early Church: Essays Honoring Graydon F. Snyder*, ed. Julian V. Hills (Valley Forge: Trinity, 1998), pp. 186-201.

Anton Vögtle, *Gott und seine Gäste. Das Schicksal des Gleichnisses Jesu vom großen Gastmahl (Lukas 14,16b-24; Matthäus 22,2-14)* (Neukirchen-Vluyn: Neukirchener, 1996).

*   *   *

All five parables in this section deal with failure to produce or to respond appropriately. In fact, the majority of Jesus' parables have to do with response in some way. With these and other parables Jesus urged Israel to change course, to be what God had called her to be, and to enter into what God was currently doing as evidenced in Jesus' own work.

None of these parables should be considered anti-Semitic, certainly not as spoken by Jesus, but not as passed along by the Evangelists either. Anti-Semitism — or anti-any-other-ethnic-or-racial-group — has no place in the life of a Christian. The good news Jesus brought is first of all good news to and about Israel and has to do with God's keeping faith with his promises to Israel. These parables offer a prophetic critique of Israel, but only because God cares about his people. Of the five parables only the Fig Tree addresses the whole nation. Three parables (the Two Sons, the Wicked Tenants, and the Wedding Feast) are specifically addressed to the leaders of Israel. Luke's parable of the Banquet is less specific but still addressed to a segment of the nation. Obviously other hearers should apply the parables to themselves, but the concern is the

The Wedding Banquet and the Feast (Matt 22:1-14; Luke 14:15-24; Gos. Thom. 64)

path down which the leaders are taking the people. The warnings to Israel and the descriptions of her failure are sharp warnings for the church and as relevant for present-day Christians, especially leaders, as for ancient Jews.

Parables about Discipleship

In some respects any parable could be placed in this chapter, for all the parables are about discipleship to some degree. The Gospels were intended to create and enable disciples and, especially in Matthew, to enable disciples to create disciples. So it is not surprising that the parables have the same function. At the same time, some parables so specifically define and direct discipleship that they deserve to be treated together as especially appropriate to this topic. I place in this category the parables of the Two Builders, the Good Samaritan, and the Vineyard Workers and the twin parables of the Tower Builder and Warring King.

THE TWO BUILDERS
(Matt 7:24-27/Luke 6:47-49)

Parable Type

This is an antithetical double similitude which makes its point by the contrast between two men and their building efforts. Rhetorically such a form is labeled a "syncrisis," a comparison of opposites by juxtaposition. Twin parables such as those of the Treasure and the Pearl could each stand alone, but antithetical parables like this require both halves to make the point.[1]

Issues Requiring Attention

1. Is this parable from Jesus?
2. If it is authentic, is Matthew's account or Luke's closer to the words of Jesus?

3. What is the teaching of the parable? Does it teach about handling life's difficulties successfully or about security at eschatological judgment? Or is it about something less obvious such as the Temple or the roles of Peter and Paul?

4. Does the teaching of this parable fit with Christian salvation theology?

Helpful Primary Source Material

Canonical Material

- OT: Deuteronomy 28 (blessings and curses determined by obedience and disobedience); Prov 10:25; 12:7; 14:11; Ezek 13:10-16; 33:30-32
- NT: Matt 5:16-20, 48; 12:50/Mark 3:35/Luke 8:21; Matt 25:1-13; Luke 11:28; John 12:47-50; Rom 2:6-13; Jas 1:22-25; 1 John 3:17-18

Early Jewish Writings

- *Ahiqar* 168 (75): "[*The city*] of the wicked will be swept away in the day of storm, and its gates will fall into ruin. . . ."
- Sir 22:16-18:"A wooden beam firmly bonded into a building is not loosened by an earthquake; so the mind firmly resolved after due reflection will not be afraid in a crisis. . . . Fences set on a high place will not stand firm against the wind; so a timid mind with a fool's resolve will not stand firm against any fear."
- 1QH 14.22-32: "I [have become] like a sailor in a ship in the raging seas: their waves and all their breakers roar over me. . . . The deep thunders at my sigh, [my] so[ul nears] the gates of death. I have become like someone who enters a fortified city, and finds shelter on the high wall until salvation. My God, I le[an] on your truth, for you place the foundation upon rock, and beams to the correct size, and a t[rue] plumb line to [str]etch out, tested stones to build a fortress which will not shake. All those who enter there will not stagger, for a foreigner will not penetrate it; its [ga]tes are armoured doors which do not permit entry, with unbreakable strong bars. . . . Then the sword of God will pounce in the era of judgment, and all the sons of his t[ru]th will awaken, to destroy [the sons of] wickedness, and all the sons of guilt will no longer exist." See also 1QH 15.4, 8-9.
- Philo, *Praem.* 79-84: "If . . . you keep the divine commandments . . . not merely to hear them but to carry them out by your life and conduct, the first boon you will have is victory over your enemies. . . . For if our words

correspond with our thoughts and intentions and our actions with our words . . . happiness prevails. . . . Now while the commandments of the laws are only on our lips our acceptance of them is little or none, but when we add thereto deeds . . . shown in the whole conduct of our lives, the commandments will be as it were brought up out of the deep darkness into the light. . . ."

Greco-Roman Writings

- Epictetus, *Diatr.* 2.15.8-10 describes decisions as needing a good foundation while a rotten and crumbling foundation leads quickly to collapse.

Early Christian Writings

- Justin, *1 Apologia* 16: "And let those who are not found living as He taught, be understood to be no Christians, even though they profess with the lip the precepts of Christ; for not those who make profession, but those who do the works, shall be saved, according to His word: 'Not every one who saith to Me, Lord, Lord, shall enter into the kingdom of heaven, but he that doeth the will of My Father which is in heaven.' . . . And as to those who are not living pursuant to these His teachings, and are Christians only in name, we demand that all such be punished by you."
- *2 Clem* 3:4–4:3: "But how do we confess him? By doing what he says, and not disregarding his commandments, and honoring him not only with our lips, but with all our heart and all our mind. . . . So then, brethren, let us confess him with our deeds. . . ."

Later Jewish Writings

- *m. 'Abot* 1.17: "Simeon his son said: . . . not the expounding [of the Law] is the chief thing but the doing [of it]; and he that multiplies words occasions sin." Also in *'Abot de Rabbi Nathan* 22.
- *m. 'Abot* 3.18: "He [R. Eleazar b. Azariah] used to say: He whose wisdom is more abundant than his works, to what is he like? To a tree whose branches are abundant but whose roots are few; and the wind comes and uproots it and overturns it, as it is written, *He shall be like a tamarisk in the desert and shall not see when good cometh; but shall inhabit the parched places in the wilderness.* But he whose works are more abundant than his wisdom, to what is he like? To a tree whose branches are few but whose roots are many; so that even if all the winds in the world come and blow

329

against it, it cannot be stirred from its place, as it is written, *He shall be as a tree planted by the waters, and that spreadeth out his roots by the river, and shall not fear when heat cometh, and his leaf shall be green; and shall not be careful in the year of drought, neither shall cease from yielding fruit."* Also in *'Abot de Rabbi Nathan* 22 in reversed order, of one who has studied much Torah.

- *y. Yoma* 5.2, as part of the high priest's prayer on the Day of Atonement: "And for the people who live in the Sharon plain [where the poor built houses of mud and clay] he would say this prayer: May it be pleasing before you, Lord, our God and God of our fathers, that our houses not turn into our graves."
- *'Abot de Rabbi Nathan* 22 and 24 have several sayings stressing that good deeds and learning of Torah are both necessary, and 24 uses four parables to make the point. Of most significance is 24.1: "Elisha b. Abuyah says, One in whom there are good works, who has studied much Torah, to what may he be likened? To a person who builds first with stones and afterwards with bricks: even when much water comes and collects by their side, it does not dislodge them. But one in whom there are no good works, though he studied Torah, to what may he be likened? To a person who builds first with bricks and afterwards with stones: even when a little water gathers, it overthrows them immediately." Cf. *Pesiqta de Rab Kahana* 27.9.

Comparison of the Accounts

Matthew and Luke both place this parable at the end of the Sermon on the Mount/Plain, and in both it serves the same function: to underscore the significance of Jesus' teaching in the sermon and to urge obedience to his teaching by stressing that security stems from obedience but destruction comes from the failure to obey. Without question Matthew and Luke report the same parable, but the differences in their accounts are sufficient that some suggest the Evangelists had different versions of the parable.[2] This is probably not necessary since the differences are insignificant and could easily arise from the Evangelists' editing. For the differences (with no assumptions about priority intended with the word "adds"), see the table on page 331. Although a few think Luke preserves the earlier version,[3] most rightly think Matthew's parallelism and his more Palestinian description of the weather conditions indicate that his version is earlier.[4] Luke has both streamlined the text and apparently accommodated it to his non-Palestinian audience. Matthew is frequently viewed as responsible for the designations "wise" and "foolish," but they could as easily stem from Jesus.[5] Matthew

Matthew 7		Luke 6	
		v. 47	adds "coming to me"[6]
v. 24	present tense verbs: "hears," "does"		present tense participles: "coming," "hearing," "doing"
	adds "these" to "words of mine"		
	"will be likened *(homoiōthēsetai)*"		"I will show you what he is like *(estin homoios)*"
	adds "to a wise *(phronimos)* man"		
	aorist tense verb: "built his house"	v. 48	present tense participle: "building a house"
			adds "who dug and went deep and laid a foundation"
v. 25	describes the rain, rivers, and winds in detail and says the house did not fall because it was founded upon the rock		merely says a flood came and the river dashed against the house, but adds that the river was not able to shake the house because it was built well
v. 26	switches to present participles ("hearing . . . and not doing"); vv. 26-27 parallel vv. 24-25 exactly apart from the changes to "foolish" and "sand" and a different word for "beat against" *(prosekopsan* instead of *prosepesan)*	v. 49	switches to aorist participles ("having heard . . . and not having done . . . having built"), is much briefer, and says the house was built on the earth without a foundation; *proserēxen* used here and in v. 48 of the river striking the house
	ptōsis for the "fall" of the house		*rhēgma* for the "collapse" of the house

focuses on two different building sites and the description of the weather, whereas Luke focuses on two different building processes and the description of digging deeply. Matthew's future tense "he will be likened" points more clearly to eschatological judgment.[7] Since the parable functions in essentially the same way for both Evangelists, the differences should not be overemphasized.

Textual Features Worth Noting

This parable fits with OT contrasts of blessing and cursing (as in Deuteronomy 28 and Leviticus 26) and with contrasts of the righteous/wise and the unrighteous/foolish (as in Psalms 1 and 37; Prov 13:6). It also fits the pattern of hortatory material closing with such a contrast to urge people to obedience (Deut 30:1-20; Josh 24:14-24; *1 En.* 108; *Testament of Moses* 12:10-13).

Contrasts dominate the Sermon on the Mount/Plain, especially in Matthew (some Luke has here, some he omits, and some he has elsewhere). They include the correct and incorrect ways to give alms, pray, and fast (Matt 6:1-18), improper and proper treasure (6:19-21), sincere and evil eyes (6:22-23), God and money (6:24), anxiety and seeking the kingdom (6:25-34), the broad and narrow gates (7:13-14), good and worthless trees (7:15-20/Luke 6:43-44), and the two foundations (7:24-27/Luke 6:47-49). Such contrasts with their OT and Jewish parallels lead ultimately to the "two ways" teaching found in *Didache* 1–6.

Four of Matthew's discourses (or all five, depending on how one views 13:51-52) end with a focus on judgment, all but one by means of a parable (7:24-27; 13:37-50[-52]; 18:23-35; 25:31-46; not 10:40-42).

Note the focus on doing in the Sermon on the Mount/Plain (especially Matt 5:19-20; 7:12), the similarity of this parable to that of the Two Sons (21:28-32), and the complaint that the Pharisees "say and do not do" (23:3).

The changes in tenses in both versions are worthy of note, but the significance of these changes must be carefully weighed. Matthew makes no significant change in describing the two builders. Luke's present participles in 6:47-48 in all likelihood point to the ongoing process of discipleship, whereas the aorists in v. 49 view the man's failure as already accomplished.[8]

Phronimos ("wise" or "prudent") also appears in the parables of the Faithful or Unfaithful Servant, the Ten Virgins, and the Unjust Steward.

Language of storms and floods is often used as a metaphor for destruction and especially of God's judgment. As examples see 2 Sam 5:20; Job 22:16; Pss 69:2, 15; 88:7; 124:1-5; Isa 8:7-8; 28:2, 13-22; 30:30; Ezek 13:10-16; 38:22; Nah 1:7-8; Wis 5:22; Sir 40:13; 1QH 11.13-20, 27-41. Such imagery is used specifically of the end time in 1QH 14.21-38; Rev 8:5; 11:19; 16:18; *Sib. Or.* 3:685-95; 5:375-80; 2 *Bar.* 53:3-12.

Cultural Information

Building and foundation images are stock metaphors for learning and other human (and divine) efforts. In addition to the primary sources above note 2 Sam 7:13; Ps 89:14; Jer 22:13-14 (which refers to building a house both metaphorically and literally); 42:10; Mic 3:10; Hab 2:12; Matt 16:18; Mark 14:58; Rom 15:20; 1 Cor 3:10-11; 8:1; 14:4; Col 1:23, to mention only a few.[9]

Some houses were built with stone, especially in places where stones were easily available. Excavations indicate that houses often were one or two stories of rough masonry construction with foundations cut into rock. Most houses had a least a course or two of stone at their base even if mud brick was used for upper courses. Stone was less accessible in the Sharon Valley, and there the poor built houses of mud and clay.[10] Sand exists around the Sea of Galilee and especially along the Mediterranean coast, but also can be found inland at several places.[11]

The destructive force of water, floods, and tsunamis is too well known to all societies. Even in arid locales heavy rain can produce runoffs from mountains and hills that sweep away anything in their paths, and this is what happens in Palestine. The wet season there extends from mid-October to March with most of the rain coming in January. Jerusalem and London each receive about 22 inches of rain annually, but while London has 300 rainy days, Jerusalem has only 50. The high intensity of rainfall causes runoffs and flooding.[12] Luke seems to think more generally of a river flooding as a result of a storm.

Explanation of the Parable

Options for Interpretation

In both Matthew and Luke this is the first parable. Its intent is straightforward and clear, so much so that works on parables often do not even treat it.[13] Virtually everyone interpreting this parable focuses on the theme of doing and obedience to the will of God. There are a number of nuances suggested for the parable within this understanding, and they will be detailed below.

Decisions on the Issues

1. Is this parable from Jesus? Rather surprisingly, some reject the authenticity of this parable. The Jesus Seminar credits this parable to Q but prints both versions in black because "the image of the two foundations belongs to common Israelite, Judean, and rabbinic lore" and because "final judgment . . . is not characteristic of Jesus."[14] Neither claim merits consideration against the authenticity of the parable. The assumption that *all* Jesus' sayings were shocking, subversive, and counter to his culture is a gross exaggeration. Some of his teaching is shocking and subversive, but even there Jesus used imagery drawn from the OT and Jewish culture. Further, much of his teaching consciously adapts wisdom motifs, and this parable suits that genre.

To say that final judgment is not characteristic of Jesus is more a theological wish than an assessment of Jesus' teaching. By contrast, Marius Reiser argues Jesus could not preach the reign of God without speaking of judgment and points out that more than a *quarter* of the traditional discourse material is concerned with the theme of final judgment. Judgment is "the unavoidable precondition for the final salvation of the reign of God."[15] Much of Jesus' teaching on judgment speaks of judgment of the nation, but final judgment and judgment of individuals are also important themes. In fact, the final judgment, judgment of individuals, and the judgment of the nation are not always kept distinct. The focus on judgment is so strong in Jesus' teaching that, if final judgment is not characteristic of Jesus, can we know anything of him at all?[16]

Another issue related to authenticity is the question of the relation of this parable to the rabbinic parable in *'Abot de Rabbi Nathan* 24 (see above, p. 330). Did Jesus borrow this parable from rabbis,[17] or is the rabbinic parable dependent on Jesus' parable?[18] The rabbinic parable is in a document dating to about 500 A.D. and, for what it is worth, is attributed to a second-century rabbi. It could be dependent on earlier tradition, but from the evidence available it is difficult to argue that Jesus borrowed the parable. To argue for direct borrowing in either direction, however, is simplistic and unlikely. The two parables are not that close, and the logic in both cases is common sense enough that the two parables probably emerged independently.

2. Is Matthew's account or Luke's closer to the words of Jesus? See above, pp. 330-31, where this issue has been treated.

3. What is the teaching of the parable? Does the parable teach about handling life's difficulties successfully or about security at eschatological judgment? Or is it about something less obvious such as the Temple or the roles of Peter and Paul? We should first note how the parable functions. With the contrast Jesus sets up an absurd action to emphasize the foolishness of the second man. No one with any intelligence at all would build a house on sand or without adequate foundation (Luke's version). The point could have been made as easily if the second part of the parable had been introduced with *Tis ex hymōn:* "*Who from you* would build a house on the sand?" No one would be so foolish.[19] Regardless of what else is involved, the point of this analogy with wise and foolish builders is that security depends on hearing and doing Jesus' teachings and that mere hearing without doing leads to destruction.

The parable implies an astounding self-understanding on Jesus' part and emphasizes his authority.[20] Judaism knew the necessity of hearing and doing the Torah[21] but would have considered heretical any claim that Jesus' words were the norm for judgment.[22] Jesus was not saying that his teachings were authoritative without recourse to the Law,[23] which would not fit with Matt 5:17-20. Rather he viewed his teaching as showing what it meant to do the will of God expressed in the Law. Later, Jesus' words are said to endure beyond heaven and earth (Matt 24:35; Mark 13:31; Luke 21:33). Other texts, especially in Matthew, will focus on Jesus as eschatological judge (e.g., Matt 16:27; 25:31-32; Luke 9:26; 12:8-10). This parable is not so explicit, but it does fit with such an expectation.

The parable is not to be allegorized, even though it often has been. The rock is not God or Christ,[24] even though other texts make these metaphorical identifications on different grounds (e.g., Ps 18:2 and often for God; 1 Cor 10:4 for Christ), nor is the rock obedience to Christ[25] or Christ's teaching,[26] even though his teaching corresponds to the rock in the analogy. The parable is an *analogy,* not an allegory. The one who hears Jesus' teachings and does them is as wise as someone who provides a strong foundation on rock. The one who hears Jesus' teachings and does not do them is as foolish as someone building a house on the sand.

Metaphorical associations are created by the storm imagery, and to acknowledge the general significance of such associations is not allegorizing. Storm language is used in the OT both of life's difficulties (e.g., Ps 69:2) and of God's judgment (e.g., Isa 8:7-8; Ezek 38:22 and see above, p. 332). Which is intended here, and if reference is to God's judgment, is it to judgment in this life or to final judgment? Some have assumed that Jesus referred to the storms of this life,[27] but most modern commentators rightly conclude that the reference is to final judgment.[28] This is more obvious in Matthew with his future tense "will be likened to" *(homoiōthēsetai)* and his habit of ending other discourses with parables of final judgment, but it is valid for Luke as well. Earlier sayings in the Sermon suggest that final judgment is in view: "Your reward will be great in heaven" (Matt 5:12; Luke 6:23; cf. 6:21, 25, 35); "With what measure you measure it will be measured to you" (Matt 7:2/Luke 6:38). Hans-Dieter Betz suggests that the primary reference is to survival in this world but that eschatological meanings are involved.[29] It may be legitimate to apply the theological principle to life in this world, but Jesus' reference is to final judgment. This fits as well with the use of the word "wise" *(phronimos),* which elsewhere carries an eschatological nuance. The wise person is one who is aware of the eschatological hour and lives accordingly (cf. Matt 24:45/Luke 12:42; Luke 16:8).[30]

The imagery of the parable has invited several interpreters to read in nuances that are hard to justify. Betz suggests that the rock imagery in the parable should be connected to Peter, who is designated as the rock in Matt 16:13-19. Betz understands "sand" as a symbol of the multitude of nations and concludes that Matthew's text is a veiled polemic against the Gentile mission: "building on sand is what Paul and his churches are doing."[31] Although there is a tradition connecting the two Matthean texts (along with other passages mentioning a rock),[32] no basis exists for connecting them, and Betz's view is extreme allegorizing.

335

N. T. Wright reads the house built on the rock as a clear allusion to the Temple and sees this parable as "a dire warning that his [Jesus'] way of being Israel is the only way by which his followers may avoid ultimate disaster. . . . Unless Israel follows the way Jesus is leading, the greatest national institution of all is in mortal danger."[33] I do not think this parable makes any allusion to the Temple or that Matthew or Luke intended or could expect their readers to see such an allusion.

Kenneth E. Bailey also finds allusions to the Temple but on different grounds. He thinks that Luke's words "laid a foundation upon rock" (6:48) are an allusion to the rabbinic 'eben shetiyah ("stone of foundation") tradition based on Isa 28:16.[34] According to m. Yoma 5.2 stonemasons building the second Temple found a slightly raised stone in the Holy of Holies. Bailey thinks that Jesus claimed to be this foundation stone promised by Isaiah. Other NT texts do identify Jesus with the stone of Isa 28:16,[35] but there is no allusion to Isa 28:16 or the foundation stone tradition in the language of this parable. The parable speaks of a foundation (singular themelion) on a rock (petra). Isa 28:16 does not mention a rock at all, but refers to a cornerstone (akrogōniaios) set in the foundations (plural themelia). Both passages do use the idea of a secure foundation in a time of storm, but that is common language and there is no other connection between these texts. The 'eben shetiyah legend is connected with thoughts of the "navel of the earth" in Jewish tradition, and no basis exists for seeing any NT text pointing to this tradition. Certainly the parable does not allude to the legend. It focuses rather on the rock (petra), but the legend uses Hebrew 'eben, which corresponds to Greek lithos ("stone"). In Greek petra and lithos (and in Hebrew their counterparts ṣûr/selaʿ and 'eben) are consistently distinguished, with petra referring to rock that is part of a natural rock formation and lithos referring to stone that is separate from a natural rock formation (such as loose stones, stones in a building, etc.). The only time they are brought together is in the parallelism of Isa 8:14 and quotations of that text. The date of the 'eben shetiyah legend is questionable, but regardless of that, the parable is about digging into the solid rock to lay the foundation of a building and has no relation to a foundation stone.

4. *Does the teaching of this parable fit with Christian salvation theology?* It might be better to ask if today's salvation teaching fits with the teaching of Jesus. As Miroslav Volf complained, "*We may believe in Jesus, but we do not believe in his ideas. . . .*"[36] It is not the parable that is wrong but our understanding of the gospel. Christian salvation teaching often emphasizes faith apart from works, which is translated as belief in certain doctrines without any action. This is a distortion of Paul's theology, does not fit with NT teaching at all (which everywhere stresses behavior), and produces an abysmal result and an awful witness. Jesus stresses doing (as do Paul and every other NT writer), especially in

the Sermon. A glance at comments from scholars starts to do justice to Jesus' intent and sabotages the "no requirement" salvation teaching:

> Christ opens the way into life for those who *do* righteousness; he helps those, but only those. Christ gives his grace to the doers of the word. Any ethics of intention which is not willing to be measured by its fruit comes to ruin in view of this conclusion of the Sermon on the Mount. Praxis alone is important. . . . Standing or falling in the judgment depends on this praxis.[37]

> Thus it is not just that the hearing of Jesus' words is supposed to be followed up with appropriate action; rather, only in action does proper hearing take place.[38]

> The enormous frequency of this verb ["to do," *poiein*] in Luke 6:20-49 reveals the great importance given by Jesus to the practice of his teachings.[39]

> Everything depends on action . . . everything depends on obedience.[40]

The parable insists that we change our salvation theology so that it conforms to Jesus' teaching and focuses rightly on a relation with Jesus that produces action.

Adapting the Parable

The bottom line for this parable, stated in non-parabolic language, is this: *Anyone who hears Jesus' words and does not do them is a fool.* Many American Christians of all denominations mirror the foolish man. We have perverted faith in Jesus. Justin said those who are not found living as Jesus taught are not Christians (p. 329 above). When will modern Christians realize that affirmation of faith is not enough and that true faith leads to obedience? Scripture seeks most of all that people hear the Word of God, but valid hearing obeys. We should remember that the Hebrew word for hearing is often translated as "obey."[41] Obedience will not happen without choices, commitments, and the Spirit-energized exercise of will. Salvation is not attainable otherwise. Looking good is not good enough. Knowing right is not right enough. We must actually put into practice what we know is right.

Why does failing to do Jesus' teachings in the Sermon show one is foolish and doing them demonstrate that one is wise? Imagine a world — or community — where people do not abuse others verbally in anger, do not lust or violate marriage vows, always tell the truth, do not retaliate with violence, and love their enemies. All of us would want to live there. The failure to live this way is self-destructive and foolish. Living this way creates stability and peace. But this is to focus, validly enough, on the wisdom of following Jesus for life in this world. The parable is concerned primarily about final judgment. If God's judgment is taken seriously, failure to live according to his will really is foolish.

Do we have to have judgment? As little as we like the idea, judgment is an essential aspect of Christian teaching. If there is no judgment, we do not need salvation, and what we do does not really matter. Jesus teaches that life matters. Obedience to Jesus matters.

For Further Reading

Hans Dieter Betz, *The Sermon on the Mount* (Hermeneia; Minneapolis: Fortress, 1995), pp. 557-67 and 636-40.

W. D. Davies and Dale C. Allison, *A Critical and Exegetical Commentary on the Gospel According to Saint Matthew* (3 vols.; Edinburgh: T. & T. Clark, 1988-97), 1:719-24.

Ulrich Luz, *Matthew 1–7: A Commentary* (trans. Wilhelm C. Linss; Minneapolis: Augsburg, 1985), pp. 450-54.

Daniel Marguerat, *Le jugement dans L'Évangile de Matthieu* (2d ed.; Le Monde de la Bible 6; Geneva: Labor et Fides, 1995), pp. 203-11.

THE GOOD SAMARITAN
(Luke 10:25-37)

Parable Type

This is usually called an example story, at least in its present form, but this presupposes the answer to several questions. In my classification it is a single indirect narrative parable.[42] With its "Go and do likewise" ending it is the most explicit of the so-called example stories. Somewhat uncharacteristically for Jesus' parables, but very much like rabbinic parables, in its present context this is a parable explaining an OT text.

Issues Requiring Attention[43]

1. Does the story belong originally in its present context of the dialogue between Jesus and the lawyer concerning the way to eternal life and the love

commands? The story's omission from the other Gospels (even though they have similar discussions of the love command) and the disjunction between the lawyer's question ("Who is my neighbor?") and Jesus' counter-question ("Which of these proved neighbor?") lead many to separate the parable (vv. 30-35 or 36) from its context.

2. What relevance do other texts on the love command, especially the discussion with the scribe in Matt 22:34-40/Mark 12:28-34 (which Luke omits) have for understanding this parable?

3. Is this an "example story," or, better, a single indirect parable, or a double indirect parable, and if the latter, what is the metaphorical element?

4. Is there a trap in the lawyer's question about eternal life (v. 25)? Was the Pharisee merely testing Jesus' knowledge to determine his competence or seeking to trap him? If the latter, what is the trap? Is the Pharisee's first question (in 10:25) only a given and the real test "Why do you treat Samaritans with mercy and eat with sinners?" (cf. 9:52).

5. Is the story told from the perspective of the victim?

6. Is there a prophetic indictment of cult, racism, and superior attitudes or merely halakic discussion of which command takes precedence, the command to avoid corpse impurity or the love command?

7. Is Jesus' answer to the question about eternal life "right"? Is this works righteousness? What is the role of the OT law? What of the relation to the similar question of the Rich Young Ruler in Matt 19:16/Mark 10:17-22/Luke 18:18-23?

8. Does the parable have christological significance? Is Jesus the Good Samaritan?

9. Is the parable primarily eschatological or ethical in intent?

Helpful Primary Source Material

See also under Cultural Information below for sources dealing with Jewish and Samaritan relations.

Canonical Material

- OT: the love commands in Deut 6:5 and Lev 19:18, *both* of which are theocentric (19:18 ends with "I am Yahweh"); Lev 18:5; 21:1-15; and 22:1-9 (laws of cleanness for priests); Num 19:11-16; 2 Chron 28:1-15; Hos 6:1-11; 2 Kgs 17:24-34 (although caution should be used in equating the Samaritans in this text with later Samaritans). See also Isa 58:5-9 and Mic 6:8.[44]

- NT: Luke 9:51-56; 17:12-19; Matt 19:16-22/Mark 10:17-22/Luke 18:18-23; Matt 22:34-40/Mark 12:28-34; John 4:9; Jas 1:27

Early Jewish Writings

- Tob 4:17: "Place your bread on the grave of the righteous, but give none to sinners."
- Sir 12:1-7 cautions that one should know to whom one is doing good; vv. 4-5: "Give to the devout, but do not help the sinner. Do good to the humble, but do not give to the ungodly; hold back their bread, and do not give it to them . . ."; v. 7: "Give to the one who is good, but do not help the sinner."
- Sir 28:4: "If one has no mercy toward another like himself, can he then seek pardon for his own sins?"
- *Jub.* 20:2, 7: "And he commanded them that they should guard the way of the Lord so that they might do righteousness and each one might love his neighbor. . . . I exhort you, my sons, love the God of heaven, and be joined to all of his commands."
- *Jub* 36:4-8: ". . . be loving of your brothers as a man loves himself . . . and loving each other as themselves." The readers are urged not to love idols but to fear God and love their brothers with compassion and righteousness.
- 1QS 1.1-3, 9-10: "For [the Instructor] . . . in order to seek God [with all (one's) heart and with all (one's) soul; in order] to do what is good and just in his presence, as commanded by means of the hand of Moses and his servants the Prophets; in order to love everything which he selects and to hate everything that he rejects . . . in order to love all the sons of light, each one according to his lot in God's plan and to detest the sons of darkness. . . ."[45]
- 1QS 9.21-22 counsels hatred toward the "men of the pit."
- 1QS 10.19-21: "My anger I shall not remove from unjust men. . . . I shall have no mercy for all those who deviate from the path. I shall not comfort the oppressed until their path is perfect." However, see CD 6.20-21.
- Philo, *Spec. Leg.* 1.299-300: "God asks . . . something quite simple and easy. And this is just to love Him as a benefactor, or failing this to fear Him . . . as ruler and Lord . . . to serve Him . . . with thy whole soul. . . ."
- Philo, *Spec. Leg.* 2.63: "But among the vast number of particular truths and principles there studied, there stand out practically high above the others two main heads: one of duty to God as shown by piety and holiness, one of duty to men as shown by humanity and justice. . . ."

- Philo, *Hypothetica* 7.6-7: "What a man would hate to suffer he must not do himself to others. . . . If the poor or the cripple beg food of him he must give it as an offering of religion to God. He must not debar dead bodies from burial. . . ."
- Josephus, *Contra Apionem* 2.208: "He who refuses to a suppliant the aid which he has power to give is accountable to justice."
- *Jos. Asen.* 27-29 reports that Benjamin wounded the son of Pharaoh in the temple with a stone. While he was still on the ground, Benjamin started to kill him, but Levi stopped him, and the two of them took care of Pharaoh's son's wound, put him on a horse, and took him to his father. The passage emphasizes not doing evil to neighbors and enemies.
- *T. Iss.*[46] 5.2: "Love the Lord and your neighbor."
- *T. Iss.* 7.6: "I acted in piety and truth all my days. The Lord I loved with all my strength; likewise, I loved every human being as I love my children."
- *T. Dan* 5.3: "Throughout all your life love the Lord, and one another with a true heart."

Greco-Roman Writings

- Seneca, *De Vita Beata* 24.3-4 (discussing care with gifts to help people): "Nature bids me do good to all mankind — whether slaves or freemen, freeborn or freedmen. . . . Wherever there is a human being there is the opportunity for a kindness." He then refers to those who say, "You have no right to require me to live up to my own standard"!
- Diodorus Siculus 1.77.3: "Again, if a man, walking on a road in Egypt, saw a person being killed or, in a word, suffering any kind of violence and did not come to his aid if able to do so, he had to die; and if he was truly prevented from aiding the person because of inability, he was in any case required to lodge information against the bandits and to bring an action against their lawless act; and in case he failed to do this as the law required, it was required that he be scourged with a fixed number of stripes and be deprived of every kind of food for three days."

Early Christian Writings

- *Didache* 1:2: "The Way of Life is this: First, thou shalt love the God who made thee, secondly, thy neighbour as thyself. . . ."
- *Barn.* 19:2, 5: "Thou shalt love thy maker. . . . Thou shalt love thy neighbour more than thy own life."[47]

Later Jewish Writings

The *rabbinic evidence* pertinent to this parable is voluminous and confusing. Numerous passages debate relations between Samaritans and Jews, the relation of the law and life, issues of corpse defilement, how far the love command and obligations to help extend, and the effect of benevolence by Gentiles. The most important of these references will be included in the explanation of the parable. With these themes as much as anywhere, it is clear that we may *not* speak of *the* rabbinic position on many subjects. What one rabbi asserts is countermanded by another. *That is the character of rabbinic writings.* For some, Samaritans are true proselytes, considered under the Jewish umbrella;[48] for others (probably most), Samaritans are placed among the *minim,* the heretics.[49] Without doubt attitudes varied in different times as to how positively Samaritans were viewed.[50] From the evidence we have, relations in the first century were particularly poor, probably due to recent memories of Samaritans scattering bones in the Temple during Passover sometime just before 9 A.D.[51]

Some assertions about Jewish attitudes toward Samaritans are based on inadequate evidence and should not be followed. For example, some suggest that Jews believed accepting help from a foreigner would delay the redemption of Israel.[52] Others suggest that Jews cursed Samaritans publicly and prayed that they would have no share in the coming life.[53] Some may have done so, but such an assertion is based on a misappropriation of the twelfth of the Eighteen Benedictions, which is a curse against heretics.[54]

A few rabbinic texts should be included here:

- *m. Yebamot* 16.7 tells of Levites on the way to Jericho (Zoar) who left a sick companion at an inn.[55]
- *Tanḥuma Mishpatim* 6.1.1 tells a story of two donkey drivers who hated each other. The donkey of one lay down and the other man passed by, but then thought of Exod 23:5 (which says one must assist in such cases), returned, and shared the load. He began to think that his colleague actually loved him, and they entered an inn and ate and drank together.[56]
- *'Abot de Rabbi Nathan* 16: "no man should think of saying, 'Love the Sages but hate the disciples'; or 'Love the disciples but hate the *'am ha-'areṣ.*' On the contrary, love all these. But hate the sectarians, apostates, and informers." With regard to the application of love of neighbor (Lev. 19:18): "if he acts as thy people do, thou shalt love him; but if not, thou shalt not love him."
- *Eccl. Rab.* 11.1.1 tells of several incidents of a rabbi helping someone in distress. Bar Kappara aided a shipwrecked and naked Roman proconsul by

taking him home and by giving him food, drink, and money. Later Bar Kappara was honored by the proconsul. Almost the same story is told of Eleazar ben Shummua, but this time the victim is a descendent of Esau who asks help from pilgrims on the way to Jerusalem. Although he is a brother, they reject him with disdain, but Eleazar helps him and later the man becomes king and repays the kindness by saving the Jewish people from a decree of destruction. The similarity to Jesus' parable in contrasting the disdain of the "righteous" with true righteousness is obvious.

Comparison of the Accounts

Although the parable itself has no parallels in other Gospels, the preceding frame in vv. 25-28 is paralleled by Matt 22:34-40/Mark 12:28-34, both of which appear in the Temple debates just prior to Jesus' arrest. Luke does not have the corresponding question there even though he records the other debates. Some suggest there was a "Q" version of the discussion between Jesus and the scribe because Matthew and Luke agree at points against Mark. The dialogue here is similar to that of the Rich Young Ruler (Matt 19:16-22/Mark 10:17-22/Luke 18:18-23).

Whether Luke 10:25-28 is the same incident as that recorded in Matt 22:34-40/Mark 12:28-34 is debated. Luke could have adapted that material as the introduction for the parable, which would have originally stood alone, or these verses could record a similar but different incident, with Luke feeling that his inclusion of this incident rendered the later debate redundant. See the discussion below.

Matthew and Luke agree that it is a lawyer *(nomikos)* who tests Jesus, with Matthew specifying that he is a Pharisee. Mark calls the man a scribe *(grammateus)*. Matthew and Luke agree that the man is testing Jesus and that he calls Jesus a teacher. Other than these minor parallels between Matthew and Luke, the only real parallel is that all three texts use both love commands (with slightly different wording in each case).[57] In Matthew the lawyer asks which command is greatest, in Mark which command is first, but Luke has "What having done will I inherit eternal life?" (identical to Luke's account of the rich young ruler's question). Mark's account is much more positive toward the scribe than the others. Not only does he omit any idea of testing, but he has the scribe affirm what Jesus says and has Jesus inform the scribe that he is not far from the kingdom.

Textual Features Worthy of Attention

The dialogue and parable occur immediately after several sayings that emphasize the presence of the kingdom: the sending of the seventy (10:1-16, especially vv. 9 and 11), the return of the seventy and the announcement of Satan's fall (10:17-20), praise for God's revelation in the Son and the privilege the disciples have in witnessing this revelation (10:21-24). The lawyer's question in v. 25 in effect asks "What must I do to be ready for the kingdom?" echoing the last words of 9:62.

While the parable focuses on the command to love the neighbor, some suggest that the incident with Martha and Mary (10:38-42) demonstrates the first command, love for God, or possibly that parable and narrative show the necessity of both doing and hearing.[58]

The structure of vv. 25-28 is carefully paralleled in vv. 29-37. Each begins by revealing the motives of the lawyer. In each the lawyer asks a question, Jesus asks a counter-question, the lawyer answers Jesus' question, and then Jesus answers the original question:

Round one: the lawyer stands to test Jesus

1. Lawyer, Question 1   What must I do to inherit eternal life?
2. Jesus, Question 2   How do you read what is written in the Law?
3. Lawyer, Answer to 2   Love God and neighbor.
4. Jesus, Answer to 1   Do this and you will live.

Round two: the lawyer wishes to justify himself

5. Lawyer, Question 3   Who is my neighbor?
6. Jesus, Question 4   Who proved neighbor in the parable?
7. Lawyer, Answer 4   The one who showed mercy.
8. Jesus, Implicit answer to 3   Go and continue doing likewise.[59]

The emphasis throughout is on action and especially on "doing" (*poiein*, vv. 25, 28, 37 twice).

The parable itself focuses on the Samaritan. It has four movements: initial scene (v. 30, twenty words), the priest (v. 31, fourteen words), the Levite (v. 32, eleven words), the Samaritan (vv. 33-35, sixty words). The parable (and the whole of 9:31–10:42) suggests movement, particularly with forms of the verb *erchesthai*. Note the progression to the man: "a priest came down in that road," "a Levite came to that place," and "a Samaritan came to him."[60] All three travelers see the man, but for the priest and the Levite seeing is the impetus for caution and self-protection, while for the Samaritan seeing is the source of compassion which motivates his helping.

The parable conforms to Lukan style and concerns, especially with Luke's focus on Samaritans, the use of "and look" *(kai idou)* in v. 25, "a certain man" *(anthrōpos tis)* in v. 30, and other indications of Luke's hand.[61]

Several Semitic features appear as well, most notably the set phrases of Jewish scholarly debate ("In the Law what is written?" "How do you read?" and "You have answered correctly" in vv. 26 and 28; "Go and do likewise" in v. 37).

If Luke's travel narrative is chiastic, the counterpart to this parable may be found in the parable of the Pharisee and Toll Collector (18:9-14). Both depict the religious establishment negatively, both have an unlikely hero, and both use the verb "justify" *(dikaioun)*.[62] Others, however, find the counterpart in the account of the Rich Young Ruler (18:18-30), which also has impressive parallels.[63]

B. Van Elderen suggests that the account of Jesus stopping to heal blind Bartimaeus (Luke 18:35-43) is the message of this parable acted out.[64]

C. F. Evans's Deuteronomy hypothesis views this parable as parallel to Deuteronomy 7,[65] but no connection is obvious.

The parable has been influenced by 2 Chron 28:8-15 and possibly by Hos 6:1-11, although the contacts with the latter are less compelling.[66]

Cultural Information

The drop from Jerusalem, which lies 2700 feet above sea level, to Jericho, which lies 17 miles away about 800 feet below sea level, is more than 200 feet per mile. The terrain is barren, almost denuded of any vegetation, and hilly, with numerous hiding places for bandits along this notoriously treacherous road.

Jericho was such a popular residence for priests that estimates suggest that half of the twenty-four orders of priests (cf. 1 Chron 24:1-19) lived there, although this may be an exaggeration.[67] Each order would serve in the Temple for one week (cf. Luke 1:8).

Jews believed Samaritans to be people of doubtful descent and inadequate theology. They were thought to be descendants of people brought by the Assyrians (and other conquerors) to colonize the land.[68] They were monotheistic, accepted only the Torah, and argued that the true temple was on Mount Gerizim. They obviously shared some convictions with the Sadducees,[69] and in their rejection of the Jerusalem Temple were similar to the Qumran community.

Samaritans and Jews had notoriously bad relations. The following texts (by no means exhaustive) demonstrate the depth of the bad feelings.

- Sir 50:25-26: "Two nations my soul detests, and the third is not even a people: Those who live in Seir, and the Philistines, and the foolish people that live in Shechem."[70]

- *T. Levi* 7.2: "Shechem shall be called 'City of the Senseless,' because as one might scoff at a fool, so we scoffed at them."
- Josephus, *Ant.* 12.10: In the time of Alexander the Great Jews and Samaritans quarreled over whether sacrifices should be sent to the temple on Mount Gerizim or to the Temple in Jerusalem. Josephus reports (12.154-56) that the Samaritans did much mischief to the Jews, including laying waste to their land and carrying some off as slaves. At the time of Antiochus Epiphanes the Samaritans denied being kin to the Jews and renamed their temple a temple of Zeus to avoid persecution (see 12.257-64 and 2 Macc 6:2). According to *Ant.* 13.74-79, the conflict over the two temples was argued about 162 B.C. before Ptolemy Philometor.
- Josephus, *Ant.* 13.275-81: John Hyrcanus beseiged Samaria, for he hated the Samaritans, effaced their city entirely, dug beneath it so that it toppled in the river, and removed all signs of it having been a city (including the temple).
- Josephus, *Ant.* 18.29-30: Samaritans desecrated the Jerusalem Temple by scattering bones in it one night during Passover (shortly before 9 A.D.).
- Josephus, *Ant.* 20.118-36: About 50 A.D. hatred increased between Jews and Samaritans. Galileans at the time of festivals customarily went through Samaritan territory on their way to Jerusalem.[71] Samaritans from the village of Ginaë slew a number of them. The procurator Cumanus was bribed by Samaritans not to avenge the Jews. In response a Jewish vigilante group burned and sacked Samaritan villages. Quadratus, the governor of Syria, crucified both the Samaritans and the Jews who were involved. The dispute was taken all the way to the Emperor Claudius in Rome, who finally decided in favor of the Jews and had the Samaritan delegation killed (see *J.W.* 2.232-46). This is later than the time of Jesus, but it reveals the animosity between the groups.
- *Ascension of Isaiah* 2:12–5:16 tells of a Samaritan named Belkira who, it says, mistreated the prophets and seized Isaiah, which led to the prophet's execution.
- *m. Šeqalim* 1.5: The half-shekel temple tax is not accepted from a Samaritan. This probably means as well that a Samaritan would not have been permitted to enter the inner court of the Jerusalem Temple.
- *m. Roš Haššanah* 2.2: Jews had to change their custom of using signal fires to signal the new year because Samaritans lit fires to confuse them.
- *m. Giṭṭin* 1.5: No writ is valid which has a Samaritan as a witness except a writ of divorce or a writ of emancipation. See the debates in *b. Giṭṭin* 10a-b.
- *m. Niddah* 4.1: Daughters of Samaritans are viewed as menstruants from the cradle and therefore unclean, and Samaritans convey uncleanness to

anything beneath them or that they overshadow (cf. 7.1; *b. Niddah* 31b, 56b).

- *m. Šebi'it* 8.10: "R. Eliezer used to say: 'He that eats the bread of the Samaritans is like to one that eats the flesh of swine.'"
- *b. Sanhedrin* 57a: Different regulations are given for relations with Samaritans (and Gentiles) from those governing relations with other Jews. A Jew is not liable to the death penalty for killing a Samaritan and may withhold wages from a Samaritan. *Y. 'Abodah Zarah* 5.4 adds that interest may be charged Samaritans because they are not considered Israelites at all.
- *Gen. Rab.* 32.10; 81.3 and *Deut. Rab.* 3.6 attest to Samaritan and Jewish arguments over whether Mount Gerizim or the temple mount in Jerusalem is superior.

Still, the evidence is not totally negative. The extreme statement of Rabbi Eliezer in *m. Šebi'it* 8.10 is explicitly rejected by Rabbi Akiba in the same passage, and *t. 'Abodah Zarah* 3.1-19 shows that Gentiles were viewed much more negatively than Samaritans. Samaritan women could serve as midwives or wet nurses. Rabbinic regulations permit buying bread and wine from Samaritans and other business arrangements,[72] allow a Samaritan to be included in the number needed to say a common table grace,[73] to say a benediction,[74] and to pay tithes,[75] and a Samaritan to be a *ḥaber* (an associate).[76] Some rabbis considered Samaritans, in the commands they accepted, as more scrupulous than Jews.[77] That a Samaritan would be traveling in Judea is not improbable,[78] for the sources indicate commerce and contact between Jews and Samaritans were a normal part of life.

Inns were often viewed as dangerous places, but few other options existed for travelers needing lodging. There is much evidence that Jews (including scrupulous Jews) stayed in inns.[79] The two denarii given to the innkeeper would have provided room and board for about two weeks.[80]

Explanation of the Parable

Options for Interpretation

Five options merit mention.[81]

1. Patristic exegesis agreed unanimously that this parable is an allegory of salvation. Usually four primary themes were emphasized: the ruin of the human race, the devil's persecution, the inadequacy of the Law, and Christ's mercy. The Samaritan mirrored Christ's saving work and, as much as with any parable, virtually every detail was seen to represent some point in Christian

theology, as demonstrated above (p. 4) in Augustine's classic interpretation.[82] John Calvin is the first to reject this procedure, but some in the modern period still argue for christological allegory.[83]

2. B. Gerhardsson's study is the most serious modern attempt to argue for a christological intent with the Samaritan. He argues that "Who is my neighbor?" through a Hebrew wordplay between *rēaʿ* ("neighbor") and *roʿeh* ("shepherd") implies the deeper question "Who is the true shepherd?" which was the original concern of the parable. The victim is Israel, and the true Shepherd is the Son of Man, who tends the sheep and keeps the Law.[84] The emphasis was changed in the early church to a discussion of the neighbor.

3. The parable is most often interpreted as an example story intended to show that love does not allow limits on the definition of neighbor.

4. Some argue that the parable originally did not belong to the dialogue about the love commands and is not an example story. They reject the category of example story (for different reasons than I do) and see the parable as a metaphor for the reversal of values that the kingdom brings.[85]

5. The parable reflects halakhic debate over which command has precedence, the command to avoid corpse defilement or the love command (which could take the form of helping a victim or of fulfilling the obligation to bury a neglected corpse).[86]

Decisions on the Issues

1. Does the story belong originally in its present context of the dialogue between Jesus and the lawyer concerning the way to eternal life and the love commands? A decision here depends on assessments of the parallels with Matt 22:34-40 and Mark 12:28-34 and of the disjunction between the neighbor as object in the lawyer's question (v. 29) and the neighbor as subject in Jesus' question (v. 36). While one cannot exclude that Luke has joined two originally separate narratives, evidence for this is not convincing. Other than the use of the two love commands, the passages in Matthew and Mark have little in common with Luke, and if the love command is as central in Jesus' teaching as the Gospels suggest,[87] there is no surprise if he spoke of it more than once. Another indication that Luke 10:25-29 does not relate the same incident as Matt 22:34-40/Mark 12:28-34 is that the latter has Jesus quoting the love commands, whereas in Luke the lawyer quotes them. Luke, *if* he is dependent on Mark, would not likely take Jesus' words and place them in the mouth of the lawyer.[88]

The shift of perspective on how "neighbor" is understood fits Jesus' practice elsewhere of rearranging his questioner's world.[89] Further, for many the change in perspective on understanding "neighbor" is precisely the point of the parable.⁹⁰ Surprisingly, often the very people who see the context as secondary and limit the parable to vv. 30-35 still comment on how appropriately the parable and its context fit together.⁹¹ The parable would not have ended with v. 35 since some conclusion showing the significance of the story is necessary.⁹² At the very least one must say, as R. Funk does, that the context is not inappropriate and that the parable with or without its context treats the subject of the neighbor.⁹³ In fact, J. Nolland correctly says that the parable needs a narrative setting and that it is hard to think of a better one than the connection to the question of the neighbor.⁹⁴ Obviously the occurrence of "neighbor" in v. 36 presumes that the word has been mentioned before. Therefore, although the passage is certainly shaped by Luke, it is best to see vv. 25-37 as belonging together originally.

The case for the unity of context and parable is much stronger than many realize. Vv. 25-37 fit set phrases of Jewish scholarly debate, and both the narrative setting and the parable allude to Lev 18:5 (Luke 10:28, 37), a crucial verse in Jewish views of the Law, and may well reflect prior debates about that passage.⁹⁵ The occurrence of "having done" *(poiēsas)* in vv. 25, 37 forms an inclusio binding the passage together.⁹⁶

2. What relevance do other texts on the love command, especially the discussion with the scribe in Matt 22:34-40/Mark 12:28-34 (which Luke omits), have for understanding this parable? Other texts on the love commands (both in the Gospels and in Jewish writings) demonstrate the centrality of the love commands for Jesus and for much of Judaism and also demonstrate differences in the way the significance of the commands was assessed. We have already pointed to the centrality of the love commands for Jesus, but almost certainly Jesus was not the first to join the Shema (Deut 6:4-9; 11:13-21; Num 15:37-41), with its call for love of God, to the call in Lev 19:18 for the love of neighbor. Deut 6:5 and Lev 19:18 use the same Hebrew form *(wĕʾāhabĕtā)* to give the commands for love. This form occurs elsewhere in the OT only at Deut 11:1 and Lev 19:34. (The latter, which commands love of the alien, may well be in mind in the parable since the Samaritan fulfills this requirement.) In the mind of Jewish interpreters such identical forms drew each other like magnets. Several Jewish texts show the two love commands joined together and also attest efforts to encapsulate the Law.⁹⁷ In Luke the two commands have been fused into one.

The two love commands are the heart of Judaism and the foundation of Jesus' ministry, his creed from which all else stems.⁹⁸ The Shema, of course, was to be said twice a day by every Jewish male, and love for neighbor was central as well. Any disagreement between Jesus and his contemporaries was not over the significance of the love commands but over their application and extent. How far does love of neighbor reach? This parable is evidence of what is obvious elsewhere: Jesus will not allow boundaries to be set so that people may feel they have completed their obligation to God. Love does not have a boundary where we can say we have loved enough, nor does it permit us to choose those we will love, those who are "our kind." With the parable Jesus in effect says, "You should know already from Lev 19:34 that the love command extends to the stranger (or traveler) in your midst."

Recently it has become popular to interpret the command "love your neighbor as yourself" as a justification for self-love. As worthy as the efforts to undergird self-confidence may be, this understanding of the love command should be rejected. The intent with "as yourself" is equivalent to "as if your neighbor were yourself."[99] The other person is of equal value and should be treated as you would want to be treated. "The text does not urge a self-love, but a selfless love of the other. . . . The circle of self-love is not simply expanded; it is shattered."[100] Or, to put it differently, the only way to love oneself properly is by giving ultimate devotion to God.[101]

3. *Is this an "example story," or better, a single indirect parable, or a double indirect parable, and if the latter, what is the metaphorical element?* This is a decisive factor in interpretation, one that determines whether Jesus' concern with the parable was to teach about human relations and conduct or to provide a metaphor of the kingdom. I have already indicated in the introduction (pp. 13-15) that I do not think "example story" is a legitimate category for Jesus' parables, but a more detailed treatment is required here.[102]

Since Jülicher, four parables (the Good Samaritan, the Rich Fool, the Rich Man and Lazarus, and the Pharisee and the Tax Collector) have been labeled "example stories."[103] The label seems self-evident. The Good Samaritan is explicit in concluding with "Go and do likewise" (Luke 10:37) to indicate that the parable presents an example to be imitated. The other three stories are not so explicit, but at some level each implies that the hearer/reader should see the action of the character(s) as a model to imitate or avoid. However, this category is suspect at best, if not naive, and scholars reject example story as a legitimate category for one of four reasons or a combination thereof.

First, some reject this category because they insist that parables *must* be metaphorical and, since the so-called example stories are not, they either force these stories to be metaphorical or reject them — either rehabilitation or exclusion.[104] Those who rehabilitate them think they originally had different forms and purposes from what we see in Luke's Gospel. For example, J. D. Crossan grants that Luke's versions of these parables are example stories but argues that originally they were metaphorical. Their initial metaphorical character was stripped, and they have been turned into moral injunctions by the gospel tradition. With regard to the parable of the Samaritan, Crossan isolates Luke 10:30-36 as the original parable and argues that the literal level of the story causes the hearers' world to be turned upside-down and that the metaphorical point is that the kingdom breaks abruptly into one's consciousness and demands the overturn of values. For him all these stories were originally parables of reversal to demonstrate that the kingdom's in-breaking reorients expectations and values.[105]

However, the attempts to show these four stories were originally metaphorical are rather anemic. After reading a few analyses of parables concluding with a focus on reversal, one realizes that the theme is noticeably lacking in specificity and starts to sound hollow. The parable of the Samaritan does not mention the kingdom. Is there any reason to think an original version of this parable would enable hearers to see a reversal of values and conclude that *the kingdom* must have such a reversal?[106] I do not see how, and a nonmetaphorical story can effect a reversal of values as easily as a metaphorical story. To use my language, a single indirect parable can effect reversal as easily as a double indirect parable.

Second, rejection of example story as a category is also often based on a fear of simplistic and overly literal moralizing, such as taking the intent of the Good Samaritan to be that Christians should go and stand by the road to help people. Scholars sometimes recoil from any idea of moralism, as if a concern for morals were beneath Jesus.[107] Morals and eschatology are needlessly set in antithesis. I do not think example story is a legitimate category (for different reasons than those offered by people like Crossan), but morals and eschatology should not be opposed. Eschatology requires an ethic, and Jesus surely expected his vision of the kingdom to impinge on life in this world.[108] We would do well to ask ourselves why morals are so uninteresting to some when much of Jesus' teaching is precisely about morals, about, that is, how to live in obedience to God.

Third, people reject the category because these parables are not really different in form from others. J. Tucker in his important study shows that all the supposedly distinguishing features (that these stories provide moral examples, have religious language, name specific persons, groups, or places) can also be paralleled in other parables.[109] He is correct. No feature or trait allows us to identify these four parables as belonging to a category distinguished by form. *The so-called example stories are not different in form or in offering people as models to be imitated or avoided.* Even those who use the category "example story" see these parables as a subset of the larger category "narrative parables."[110] Certainly other parables provide people as models to imitate or avoid (e.g., the Unforgiving Servant, the Treasure in the Field, the Two Builders, the Two Sons).[111] Tucker suggests that we merely call the example stories what Luke called them: parables. But Luke also called the proverb "Physician, heal yourself" (4:23) a parable, and few will find that satisfactory. Tucker does not actually deal with the four stories in Luke; further, he confines his analysis to an investigation of the form of these stories without ever asking about their *function*. He and others grant that these stories do not effect a comparison.[112] They are not metaphors of some other arena. Yet they are also not literal. Jesus is not telling of historical incidents, even if the stories may be molded on incidents he knew. These stories point negatively or positively to something else, the life God intends. For some these four stories are similar to synecdoche, a naming of the part for the whole, in that they present a particular example to demonstrate a general principle.[113]

If indeed these stories function differently, as most seem to recognize, that should be determinative for how they are classified. And the fourth reason to reject the category of example story, the one I find determinative, is the different way these stories function. They do not focus on a comparative element in another realm. One does not look through one subject or narrative to see another reality. For example, in looking at the Rich Fool one is dealing directly with the subject of wealth, not some other subject. This is single indirect communication. Most parables are double indirect narratives, but these four stories are single indirect narratives,[114] and I add a fifth that functions the same way, the parable of the Unjust Steward. Direct communication speaks specifically about the hearer and about the subject at hand. Direct communication about the relation of God and Israel might say "Israel has failed to live as God intends and is in danger of judgment." Double indirect communication speaks specifically neither about the hearer nor the subject at hand. The parable of the Fig Tree is double indirect communication in that it does not speak directly about God and Israel. It uses another person, a certain man, and another subject, the man's unproductive fig tree, to address the hearer indirectly (even with the fig tree's metaphorical resonances). The five stories in question are different: they use *single* indirection. They address the reader indirectly by telling of another person, but directly by using the subject that is of concern. The parable of the Good Samaritan addresses the lawyer and the reader indirectly through the travelers, but the subject is the issue at hand, the love command and the definition of neighbor. Since these stories involve less indirection, their intent is more easily grasped.

The parable of the Good Samaritan is, then, a single indirect parable. The label "example story" is inadequate and inappropriate and should be dropped, no matter how entrenched it is in discussions of parables. The Good Samaritan is not a metaphorical story about some other reality. It is about a compassionate Samaritan and is intended to teach about the love command.

We must still ask about the presence of allusions or metaphorical nuances. Theoretically a single indirect parable could use features that allude to a larger reality or set off resonances in the hearers' minds as easily as double indirect parables (e.g., the Fig Tree). Is Jesus reflected in the Samaritan, as church tradition has often argued? Is Israel reflected in the Rich Fool?[115] While the theology in these stories may fit Jesus' actions or Israel's history, Jesus' concern seems to be much more the conduct and attitudes of individuals. The one indirect story that may have a larger concern is that of Lazarus and the Rich Man. The rich man's anxiety for his five brothers and their response to the Law and the Prophets mirror Israel's situation, but the parable is still directed toward actions and attitudes of individuals.

4. Is there a trap in the lawyer's question about eternal life (v. 25)? Was he merely testing Jesus' knowledge to determine his competence and where he stood on the issues, or was he hostile, seeking to trap Jesus into giving an unorthodox answer? If the latter, what is the trap and how might Jesus have failed the test? Opinion is divided,[116] and the text does not give much direction. The verb *ekpeirazein* appears infrequently and refers to testing in a negative sense except in LXX Deut 8:2, 16. But it appears to be synonymous with *peirazein*, which is used both positively and negatively.[117] Elsewhere in Luke "lawyer" *(nomikos)* is used of those who reject Jesus' message or do not understand what they should, but hostility to Jesus is not involved.[118] Even if hostility is implied, the question about eternal life need not be a trap. The rich young ruler asks the exact same question without intending a trap (18:18).

But a trap could be involved if the lawyer was anxious that Jesus' actions and teaching were unorthodox. Jesus' association with outcasts and sinners, his actions on the Sabbath, and his lack of concern for such "holiness" issues as touching the unclean (lepers, those with fevers, issues of blood, the dead, etc.) or eating with unwashed hands would obviously raise questions as to how he stood in relation to the Law (cf. Matt 5:17-20; 12:1-14/Mark 2:23–3:6/Luke 6:1-11; Matt 15:1-20/Mark 7:1-23). If the Law did not mark out boundaries between the righteous and the unrighteous, as Jews assumed, then what was its purpose, was it even useful, and what determined whether one would actually participate in the kingdom?[119] What did the lawyer expect Jesus to say in response to his question about eternal life?[120] Had he heard what the implied reader knows, that Jesus taught his disciples to follow him and to gain life by losing it? Such a statement or any other answer not doing justice to the Law could lead to a charge of heresy. Jesus' deft turning of the conversation so that the lawyer must focus on the intent of the Law avoided the charge and created an opportunity for instruction.

Some suggest that the question about eternal life is a setup for the real test, which comes in the second question, the one about the boundaries of the word "neighbor."[121] This may be correct, but at least it seems fair to think that Jesus' association with the wrong people led to the lawyer's question, and if so, the question is not innocent, especially in view of the lawyer's attempt to justify himself (v. 29). From a narrative standpoint Jesus' tolerance of Samaritans, even when they rejected him (9:52-56) prepares for the lawyer's question and the parable.

PARABLES ABOUT DISCIPLESHIP

5. Is the story told from the perspective of the victim? Robert Funk's helpful treatments have persuaded many interpreters that the hearer/reader is forced to identify with the victim since the victim is the only one present in every scene. There are problems with this approach. The victim is not present in v. 35 (or at least not mentioned) when the Samaritan addresses the innkeeper.[122] Also, Funk assumes that the victim is conscious and observes the other three travelers, something about which the text gives no clue, but which is essential for Funk's conclusion that "the future which the parable discloses is the future of every hearer who grasps and is grasped by his position in the ditch."[123] The issues raised from the victim's perspective are helpful: Will one allow oneself to be ministered to by an enemy? And when one understands being a victim, might one have a chance to understand the kingdom? But all this is meditation on the parable, legitimate theologizing spawned by the parable, but not Jesus' intent in telling the story. The story is not told from the perspective of the victim, but from the standpoint of the narrator. The hearer stands with the narrator outside the story watching its development and is required by the narrator to pass judgment on the events that take place.

6. Is there a prophetic indictment of cult, racism, and superior attitudes or merely halakic discussion of which command takes precedence, the command to avoid corpse impurity or the love command? With this question we come to the heart of the matter. A number of scholars assume that the parable is an attack on the Temple and the priesthood and would have drawn on anticlerical attitudes among the hearers.[124] Sometimes this is associated with the assumption that the priest and Levite belonged to the upper classes, but many priests and Levites did not. Some were poor. Further, no evidence of anticlerical attitudes exists in first-century Judaism except for that directed against the priestly aristocracy who ran the Temple.[125]

Other than the cleansing of the Temple, little evidence indicates that Jesus targeted priests and Temple functionaries with his teaching. He did deemphasize the Temple (e.g., Matt 12:6-7) and point to its coming destruction (Matt 24:1-2/Mark 13:1-2/Luke 21:5-6, etc.). Luke has a positive view of the Temple and priestly activities, especially at the beginning of both the Gospel and Acts. In Luke 5:14 (paralleled in Matt 8:4/Mark 1:44) and 17:14 Jesus tells cleansed lepers to show themselves to the priests.

The Temple is not under attack in the parable, but the shadow of the Temple is clearly present. The priest is going down from Jerusalem to Jericho, probably returning home after his Temple service. Also, the key source of conflict between Jews and Samaritans was the disagreement over the Temple. Prophetic indictment of the Temple cult may be present, but it is not the main concern. It serves more as the context in which the Samaritan's actions are emphasized.

Every society and segment of society draws barriers between itself and others. Racism and such barriers are of major concern in the parable, but again they are more the means by which the parable teaches than the focus of the teaching. As often noted, Jewish hearers may have expected the sequence priest, Levite, Israelite, a sequence evident in rabbinic texts that demonstrate a hierarchy of value, but some texts use this sequence to argue that greater knowledge of Torah gives a Gentile or a proselyte greater value than even a high priest.[126] The appearance of the Samaritan upsets the expectations to make a similar point about what is really important.

Is the parable then merely about a halakhic debate, as R. Bauckham argues,[127] about, that is, which has priority, the prohibition of defilement by a corpse or the love command? Contact with a corpse caused defilement for seven days and required set purification measures with financial costs (Num 19:11-22). Priests were prohibited from having contact with corpses except those of close relatives (Lev 21:1-4; 22:4-7; Ezek 44:25-27), and this exception was not allowed to the high priest (Lev 21:11) or a Nazarite (Num 6:6-12).[128] Jews believed that corpse defilement was conveyed not only by touching a corpse but also by touching what a corpse had touched or even through the air, by the shadow of a coffin or by one's shadow falling on a grave. Rabbinic texts instruct one to keep at least four cubits (about six feet) from a corpse.[129] Such thinking could lie behind the choice of the priest and the Levite to pass by on the other side.

At the same time, two other strongly held beliefs are relevant. First, Jews were required on religious grounds to bury a neglected corpse. Even though a high priest or a Nazarite was not to contract uncleanness from the body of a dead relative, they could do so — or were expected to do so — from a neglected corpse. In fact, texts debate which of them should contract defilement first to bury a neglected corpse.[130] Second, at least for most Jews, nothing — not even purity laws — legitimately stood in the way of saving a life. Laws were suspended when life was endangered.[131]

The victim in the parable is described as half-dead. That is, he is near death and in desperate need of help.[132] Whether the priest and the Levite thought he was dead or alive is unclear, but in either case they had the obligation to help, either to bury the corpse despite defilement or to assist the man in need. Jesus' hearers would assume the victim was a Jew, but whether he was is not an issue and would not be evident to anyone since his clothes were stripped off.[133] Further, the parable pays no attention to the motives of the priest and the Levite in passing by, whether fear for their own safety or fear of defilement. As interesting as Bauckham's proposal is, it does not satisfactorily explain the dynamics of the parable; most notably, it virtually ignores the Levite.[134] More is going on than corpse defilement and halakhic debate.[135]

7. Is Jesus' answer to the question about eternal life "right"? Is this works righteousness? What is the role of the OT Law? What of the relation to the similar question of the rich young ruler in Matt 19:16/Mark 10:17-22/Luke 18:18-23? Jesus' response to the lawyer about the avenue to eternal life and his similar response to the rich young ruler or the response of John the Baptist in Luke 3:10-14 are not the responses that Christians usually give, neither in the early church (cf. Acts 16:30-31) nor today.[136] Does Jesus' focus on doing in vv. 28 and 37 sound like "works righteousness"? Should he not have said "Make a decision for me"[137] or at least "Have faith and follow me"?

We always want Jesus to say words that fit our systems, but he neither fits our systems nor addresses Paul's problem of works righteousness (to say nothing of the fact that Paul has been severely misunderstood). Our systems need to be reorganized to do justice to Jesus' teaching and that of the early church. This parable does not advocate "earning one's salvation";[138] it advocates living out one's covenant relation with God, which is what Christian faith and the whole Bible seek. To love God with all one's being and the neighbor as oneself is not something *less* than faith. As was evident with the parable of the Two Debtors, one cannot love God apart from trust and obedience. The answer given by the lawyer and clarified by Jesus is not wrong. We may want to add more — as Luke certainly does — about how the covenant God has revealed himself in Christ, particularly in Christ's death and resurrection. But life, both now and eternally, is in knowing and loving the God revealed in Christ, the same God who worked throughout Israel's history, and in living in conformity with his character. Any claim of faith that does not do that is not biblical faith.

8. Does the parable have christological significance? Is Jesus the Good Samaritan? Despite the frequent assertion that Jesus is the Samaritan and that the parable reflects his coming to help humanity, I see no justification in the parable for any such identification. Gerhardsson's argument that the parable is about the true Shepherd is too speculative and unconvincing, particularly in arguing that both "Samaritan" and "neighbor" in their Hebrew forms point to a shepherd. No trace of any of this can be substantiated from the text.[139] Some suggest that Jesus told the parable to defend his own actions and mission,[140] but even if this is correct, it does not make the parable christological in the usual sense. Others make the identification more on theological grounds, but it is unfair to inject Jesus (and the rest of a salvation scheme) allegorically into the parable. It is one thing to say that the theology of the parable is also the theology that drives much of Jesus' actions but quite another to say that he intended a self-representation with the story.[141] Nor is he to be identified with the victim.[142] All attempts to find Jesus (or Israel) mirrored in the parable are illegitimate allegorizing.

9. Is the parable primarily eschatological or ethical in intent? Some scholars (and obviously those who think the parable is a metaphor of the kingdom) argue that the parable is eschatological.[143] Typical is Sandra Perpich, who claims that the parable jars the reader into a new eschatological awareness,[144] but such language is an exaggeration. The framing questions (vv. 25-28) are obviously eschatological, but even there the dialogue does not depend on the message of the kingdom. Theoretically the dialogue and the telling of the parable could both have taken place long before Jesus. That one would answer the question about eternal life by recourse to the love commands and Lev 18:5 is no surprise, and the command to love the foreigner as oneself is already in Lev 19:34. Being able to say "Good Samaritan" does not effect the experience of the kingdom, and a good act by a despised alien does not constitute the presence of the kingdom.[145] One would expect the kingdom to effect such acts, but such acts have, at times, taken place throughout human history and do not in themselves constitute the kingdom. The only things that make this parable eschatological are the one telling it and the context of his mission. Without denying in any way the eschatological basis of Jesus' ethical teaching, this parable is concerned not directly with eschatology but with ethics. Jesus' ethic is eschatologically heightened and conditioned by the presence of the kingdom, but it is grounded first in the OT.

We conclude then that this parable is intended to show that love does not allow limits on the definition of neighbor. How the lawyer expected Jesus to define "neighbor" is not obvious. Did he expect a boundary defined by those in the covenant,[146] those who are righteous,[147] or even some abstract and useless answer like "everyone"? What he received was a concrete and forceful image that destroyed any thought of boundaries for mercy and love.

The most helpful approaches to the parable are those that emphasize that the disjunction between the lawyer's question and Jesus' answer, between, that is, neighbor as object and neighbor as subject is the point of the parable. Jesus' answer to the lawyer's question turns out to be a negation of the question's premise that there are boundaries to the definition of neighbor.[148] The question "Who is my neighbor?" ought not be asked. No thought is allowed that a human can be a non-neighbor. Franz Leenhardt's often used statement is compelling: One cannot define one's neighbor; one can only be a neighbor.[149] We cannot say in advance who the neighbor is; rather, nearness and need define "neighbor." As T. W. Manson commented, "love does not begin by defining its objects: it discovers them" and "while mere neighborhood does not create love, love does create neighborliness."[150] S. Kierkegaard captured the goal by saying, "To love one's neighbor means, while remaining within the earthly distinctions allotted to one, essentially to will to exist equally for every human being without exception."[151] In other words, the parable addresses its hearers about their own identity. Does a sense of neighbor rooted in the two love commands — love of God and love of neighbor — define one's being? Such an identity excludes the possibility of asking about the boundaries of neighbor. Boundaries are an important means by which we establish our identities, but an identity growing out of Jesus' sense of being a neighbor obliterates boundaries that close off compassion or that permit racism and attitudes of superiority.

The parable underscores that compassion (the turning point of the parable, v. 33), mercy, and love are the key factors in living for God (and therefore in discipleship to Jesus). While Bauckham's approach is too limited in its focus on halakhic debate, he is correct to emphasize that this parable teaches the principle that the love command overrides all others, which is without parallel in Judaism.[152] The imagery of the parable and the implied indictment of the Temple officials evoke the antithesis between sacrifice and mercy common in the prophetic writings.[153] The parable is one more example of Jesus substituting the mercy code for the holiness code.[154]

The parable is almost certainly molded on 2 Chron 28:8-15, an earlier account of Samaritans helping Jews in a desperate situation. By using a Samaritan instead of the expected Israelite layperson, Jesus sets up an embarrassing scenario for his questioner. The Samaritan knows to show compassion and understands love for the stranger (Lev 19:34); how can you ask about the boundaries of "neighbor"?[155] If priests and Levites, like every Jewish male, repeat the Shema twice a day, why is it a Samaritan who shows what the love command means? Luke 17:16 has a parallel embarrassing contrast between a Samaritan who shows gratitude and nine others (presumably Jews) who do not.

With its underlying theme of racial hostility the parable is very close to Jesus' emphasis on loving one's enemies. We may not limit boundaries of care and obligation to our own group and have different or hostile standards for others.[156] The lawyer sought a boundary for his obligation of loving the neighbor, but Jesus by example obliterated any concept of boundary. We cannot say to God, "I met my obligation; I can quit now." Peter's request for a boundary for forgiveness (Matt 18:21-22) was met with the same kind of response.

We cannot do justice to this parable without emphasizing that it seeks action, that people must put love of neighbor into action.[157] Joel Green's comment that for Luke hearing is authenticated in doing[158] is true not only for Luke but for Jesus and the whole of Scripture, as a glance at the parable of the Two Builders (Matt 7:24-27/Luke 6:47-49) or numerous other texts shows. P. Jones is correct in saying that the parable exposes any religion with a mania for creeds and an anemia for deeds.[159]

The idea that action is the way to life[160] worries many that the parable suggests salvation by works. K. Bailey argues that the parable announces the failure of self-justification and that one may not earn eternal life,[161] but this is to read in concerns the parable does not have. Our fear of earning salvation has led to the idea that Christianity is a religion concerned only with what one believes/thinks, not what one is, but this is a shallow understanding of belief. The parable, like most of Scripture, is concerned with identity. In effect, when people asked Jesus "What do I have to do?" he asked in return "What kind of person are you?"[162] The answer to the second question also answers the first (as in the incident with the rich young ruler). The fear of works righteousness is far too exaggerated in most churches. Would that there were an equal fear of being found inactive! We would do better to realize that people who do not work cannot be righteous. The question of identity is never merely a question of what we believe as fact, but what we *are,* particularly what we are in relation to God and what motivates us and controls our being. We have torn thinking from being and being from doing, but what we are cannot be torn from what we do. What counts as life with God — and gives hope of future life with God — is a relation of love with God that gives us our identity and reflects that love to others (cf. John 17:3; 1 John 4:10-11). The idea of knowing God and yet not being conformed to God is a source of scandal, one that Scripture always combats and that modern Christians must combat as well. In the parable Jesus seeks to make a man of knowledge into a man of practice,[163] for anything less is not sufficient for eternal life. This is not a question of earning salvation; it is a question of being and identity that determine actions. It is not a question of whether we should work. We will work. The question is from what identity will we work.

Adapting the Parable

Adapting some parables, and certainly this one, is obvious: Just do it! Yet, some scholars and preachers shy away from any thought of morals, fearful that a concern for morals leads to "do-goodism," hypocrisy, and an attempt to earn salvation, all obvious failures to follow Jesus. Moralism and telling people to be good are not the answer, but if we do not intend to tell people how to live, why bother with teaching or preaching? Jesus (and all the NT writers) certainly did not hesitate to instruct people about how they should live. We are doomed to failure as long as the church refuses to take seriously what Jesus actually said about lifestyle issues, keeping the commands, loving one's enemies, helping the poor, and doing the will of the Father. Parables do not spell out every aspect of their theologies, but the presupposition of this one is of life in covenant relation with God, not just being good on one's own.

The parable forces us to realize the importance of one's neighbor. Christianity is a relational religion. We do not relate to God on our own, as much as we might try; our relation with God is expressed through our relation with the people around us, and it is God who enables our relations with our neighbor.[164]

This parable has been applied to virtually every aspect of ethics. If compassion is the issue, this parable is applied most notably with regard to medical services and relief of hunger. Allen Verhey uses the parable as the means to discuss the scarcity of medical resources.[165] Richard Hays applies it to abortion in relation to both mother and fetus: *"Jesus, by answering the lawyer's question with this parable, rejects casuistic attempts to circumscribe our moral concern by defining the other as belonging to a category outside the scope of our obligation."*[166] In a world torn by war and genocide this parable will not allow us to be passive. A journalist commenting on the genocide in Dafur asked, "Where is the piety in reading the Bible and averting our eyes from genocide?"[167] This parable is annoying, for it will not let us avert our eyes.

As several have argued, this parable challenges the hearer to put together two contradictory words in reference to the same person: "Samaritan" and "neighbor." In doing so it removes any limit on our obligation to help someone in need. The Samaritan was truly present to the victim, whereas the others were absent, and he truly saw, whereas they saw superficially.[168] Actually being present with people and actually seeing them is expected of followers of Jesus.[169]

Like the parable of the Unforgiving Servant, the parable of the Good Samaritan also insists "Is it not *necessary* for you also to show mercy to your fellow servant as I have shown mercy to you?" (Matt 18:33). The teaching of the parable of the Sheep and the Goats (Matt 25:31-46) likewise sounds the same theme. Mercy is a requirement for disciples of the kingdom; mercy must be demonstrated.

Yet, is the thinking of this parable realistic at all? Sigmund Freud argued that loving our neighbors as ourselves is neither desirable nor possible.[170] Is this parable idealistic, contrary to common sense, and destined to exhaust us and our resources?[171] The problem is that we want every parable to do the whole of theology, when instead they are intended to make us think — *and act.* Parables are compelling vignettes, sometimes even exaggerations to make a point, not whole theologies. This is not the only text, and its issues are not the only ones involved in deciding how assistance is to be given. Other questions exist or are spawned by the parable. What is the risk in helping? Any attempt to love is a risk. What action would the Samaritan have taken had he come while the robbery and beating were in process? Are there any limits? David Flusser, a Jewish NT scholar, asserted that "Christianity surpasses Judaism, at least theoretically, in its approach of love to all men, but its only genuine answer to the powerful wicked forces of this world is, as it seems, martyrdom."[172] Is martyrdom the only result?

Knowing how to implement this parable is a much harder task than we realize, and it certainly is not about moralism. Neither it nor any other section of the NT gives any indication of *how* to love neighbor as self or what the limits are — if any — before martyrdom. The NT is more an identity book than a guide book; it tells what Christian character is, not what actions must be done in each case. Disciples of Jesus are those who refuse boundaries for the identification of neighbor and instead love even their enemies. With that identity in place each person must determine what path of wisdom best expresses that identity. Further, we should not think merely in individualistic terms. We can operate much more effectively communally than individually. On the other hand, many times we must act individually as the occasion arises, and we cannot absolve ourselves from responsibility by waiting for the community to act. This parable may not tell us how to love our neighbor as ourselves, but it creates a reality that challenges our passivity and self-interest. Loving the neighbor as oneself is difficult, but no alternative is allowed for followers of Jesus.

We cannot leave this parable without making explicit that it confronts the sin of racism. Christians are as guilty as any of allowing illegitimate boundaries to exist. We must not be quiet about or tolerant of the sin of racism, whether in the United States or Western Europe or that which exists between Palestinians and Israelis. To be silent is to give permission. On the basis of this parable we must deal with our own racism but must also seek justice for, and offer assistance to, those in need, regardless of the group to which they belong.

For Further Reading

Kenneth Ewing Bailey, *Through Peasant Eyes: More Lucan Parables, Their Culture and Style* (Grand Rapids: Eerdmans, 1980), pp. 33-56.

Richard Bauckham, "The Scrupulous Priest and the Good Samaritan: Jesus' Parabolic Interpretation of the Law of Moses," *NTS* 44 (1998): 475-89.

Georges Crespy, "The Parable of the Good Samaritan: An Essay in Structural Research," *Semeia* 2 (1980): 27-50.

Robert W. Funk, "The Old Testament in Parable: The Good Samaritan," in *Language, Hermeneutic, and Word of God* (New York: Harper & Row, 1966), pp. 199-223.

Birger Gerhardsson, *The Good Samaritan — the Good Shepherd?* (Lund: Gleerup, 1958).

Helmut Gollwitzer, *Das Gleichnis vom barmherzigen Samariter* (Neukirchen: Neukirchener, 1962).

Peter Rhea Jones, *Studying the Parables of Jesus* (Macon: Smyth & Helwys, 1999), pp. 294-324.

F. J. Leenhardt, "La Parabole du Samaritain," in *Aux sources de la tradition chrétienne* (Neuchâtel: Delachaux & Niestlé, 1950), pp. 132-38.

T. W. Manson, *The Sayings of Jesus as Recorded in the Gospels According to St. Matthew and St. Luke Arranged with Introduction and Commentary* (London: SCM, 1949), pp. 259-63.

I. Howard Marshall, *The Gospel of Luke* (NIGTC; Grand Rapids: Eerdmans, 1978), pp. 439-50.

Llewellyn Welile Mazamisa, *Beatific Comradeship: An Exegetical-Hermeneutical Study on Lk 10:25-37* (Kampen: Kok, 1987).

Werner Monselewski, *Der barmherzige Samariter. Eine auslegungsgeschichtliche Untersuchung zu Lukas 10,25-37* (Tübingen: Mohr-Siebeck, 1967).[173]

THE WORKERS IN THE VINEYARD
(Matt 20:1-16)

Thematically this parable could have easily been placed elsewhere (e.g., with parables of the present kingdom or with parables about judgment). Since Matthew viewed this parable as dealing with discipleship, this is at least one obvious place for analysis.

For some, this is a marvelous parable about the grace of God. Hultgren placed it in his section on parables revealing God's extraordinary forgiveness and grace. Jülicher said it presents the gospel in a nutshell, Montefiore thought it one of the greatest parables of all, and Fuchs and Jüngel considered it the climax of Matthew.[174] I think all this is hyperbole and consider this one of the three most difficult parables (along with the Unjust Steward and Matthew's account of the Banquet).[175] This parable appears only loosely connected to its context, and most interpreters want it to say more theologically than it does. It is not that it presents numerous difficult issues; the problems are relatively easy, except for two: the identity of the original audience and the meaning of the parable.

Parable Type

This is a double indirect narrative parable with an introduction indicating that the kingdom is the point of reference and with a proverb as a concluding statement (v. 16) that seems only loosely related to the parable. The same proverb with minor variations in wording also precedes the parable to form an inclusio.

362

Issues Requiring Attention[176]

1. Was v. 16 (the proverb about the first being last, etc.) originally connected with the parable and does it fit the parable's intent?[177]
2. Is the parable intended to confront exploitation of workers? This implies another question: Is the owner a positive or a negative figure?
3. Is the parable "allegorical" with some or all of the elements in the story corresponding to theological realities?
4. Who was originally addressed by the parable, Pharisees or the disciples of Jesus?
5. Are all the workers accepted as truly people of God or are some rejected?
6. What did Jesus mean with the parable and what did Matthew mean?
7. What theological insight can be gained, especially with regard to christology, economic practice, or the nature of reward?

Helpful Primary Source Material

The relevance of some of the primary sources may not be obvious, if one is working with modern translations. In Matt 20:15 the owner of the vineyard asks, "Is your eye evil because I am good?" which the NRSV and NIV render "Are you envious because I am generous?" An "evil eye" in texts below is an expression for envy or stinginess.

Canonical Material

- OT: Lev 19:13; Deut 24:14-15; 1 Sam 30:21-25; Prov 22:9; 23:6; 28:22, 27
- NT: Matt 6:22-23/Luke 11:34-36; Matt 9:37-38; Mark 10:31/Luke 13:30

Early Jewish Writings

- 4Q424 frag. 1, 10: "Do not entrust [your] weal[th] to a man with an evil eye. . . ."
- *4 Ezra* 5:42: When Ezra is concerned that earlier or later generations may be at a disadvantage at the final judgment, he is told, "I shall liken my judgment to a circle; just as for those who are last there is no slowness, so for those who are first there is no haste."
- *2 Bar.* 30:2: After the resurrection of the righteous the multitude of souls will appear together. "And the first ones will enjoy themselves and the last ones will not be sad. . . . But the souls of the wicked will the more waste away." Here neither "the first" nor "the last" is a negative term.

- Josephus, *Ant.* 20.219-20: During the time of Agrippa, after the Temple construction was completed, 18,000 workmen were unemployed. Their need and the desire not to have money on deposit in the Temple because of fear of the Romans led to their being paid a day's wage for little work. "Hence, out of regard for the workmen and choosing to expend their treasures upon them — for if anyone worked for but one hour of the day, he at once received his pay for this. . . ."

Later Jewish Writings

Some of the rabbinic parables listed below are so close to Jesus' parables that scholars debate who is borrowing from whom.[178]

- *m. Baba Meṣi'a* 7.1-11 gives regulations governing the hiring of workers and whether they may eat of the produce where they are working. The regulations follow local custom about the time of work.
- *m. Baba Meṣi'a* 9.12: "The laws *In his day thou shalt give him his hire* [Deut 24:15], and *The wages of a hired servant shall not abide with thee all night until the morning* [Lev 19:13] apply alike to the hire of a man or of a beast or of utensils. . . . The law *In his day thou shalt give him his hire* applies also to the resident alien, but not the law *The wages of a hired servant shall not abide with thee all night until the morning.*" See the similar regulations insuring prompt payment in 9.11.
- *m. 'Abot* 1.3: "Antigonus of Soko . . . used to say: Be not like slaves that minister to the master for the sake of receiving a bounty, but be like slaves that minister to the master not for the sake of receiving a bounty; and let the fear of Heaven be upon you."
- *m. 'Abot* 2.9: "He said to them: Go forth and see which is the good way to which a man should cleave. R. Eliezer said, A good eye [other rabbis list other options]. . . . Go forth and see which is the evil way which a man should shun. R. Eliezer said, An evil eye."
- *m. 'Abot* 2.11: R. Joshua said: The evil eye and the evil nature and hatred of mankind put a man out of the world."
- *m. 'Abot* 2.14: "R. Eleazar said: Be alert to study the Law and know how to make answer to an unbeliever; and know before whom thou toilest and who is thy taskmaster who shall pay thee the reward of thy labour." Similar words appear in 2.16.
- *m. 'Abot* 2.15: "R. Tarfon said: The day is short, and the task is great and the laborers are idle and the wage is abundant and the master of the house is urgent."

- *m. 'Abot* 5.23: "Ben He-He said: According to the suffering so is the reward." This is a proverb applied to laboring at study of the Torah.
- *y. Berakot* 2.7: "When R. Bun bar Hiyya died [at a young age], R. Zeira came up and eulogized him [by expounding Eccl 5:12]. . . . To what [story] may [the life of] R. Bun bar R. Hiyya be compared? [To this story.] A king hired many workers. One worker excelled in his work. What did the king do? He took him and walked with him back and forth [through the rows of crops and did not let him finish his day's work.] Toward evening, when all the workers came to be paid, he gave him a full day's wages along with [the rest of] them. The workers complained and said, 'We toiled all day, and this one toiled only two hours, and he gave him a full day's wages!' The king said to them, 'This one worked [and accomplished] more in two hours than you did in a whole day.' So R. Bun toiled in the study of the Torah for twenty-eight years, [and he learned] more than an aged student could learn in a hundred years." This account with slight variation is also in *Eccl. Rab.* 5.17 and *Song Rab.* 6.13 and is reflected in *Midr. Tanhuma Ki Tissa* 110.
- *b. Berakot* 7a, in response to the assertion that God prays: "What does He pray? — R. Zutra b. Tobi said in the name of Rab: 'May it be My will that My mercy may suppress My anger, and that My mercy may prevail over My [other] attributes, so that I may deal with My children in the attribute of mercy and, on their behalf, stop short of the limit of strict justice.'"
- *b. 'Abodah Zarah* 17a: "One may acquire eternal life after many years, another in one hour! Rabbi also said: Repentants are not alone accepted, they are even called 'Rabbi'!" This is said about a rabbi who was granted life in the world to come despite visiting prostitutes but after much seeking of mercy.
- *Sifra Behuqotai* 262 (on Lev 26:9): "To what is the matter comparable? It is to be compared to the case of a king who hired a large work force, and there was there a certain worker, who did work for him over a long period of time. The workers came to collect their wages, and that worker came with them. The king said to him, 'My son, I shall turn to you [and pay you special attention]. These young workers who have worked for me have done a fair amount of work, so I shall give them a modest wage, but to you I am going to make a substantial settlement.' So the Israelites are in this world: They seek their reward before the Omnipresent, and the nations of the world seek their reward before the Omnipresent. The Omnipresent says to the Israelites, 'My children, I shall pay attention to you. The nations of the world who have worked for me have done a fair amount of work, so I shall give them a modest wage, but to you I am going to make a substantial settlement.'"

- *Deut. Rab.* 6.2: "It is as if a king hired for himself labourers and brought them straight into his garden without disclosing what he intended to pay for the various kinds of work in the garden, lest they should neglect the work for which the pay was little for work for which the pay was high. In the evening he called each one in turn and asked him: 'At which tree have you worked?' He replied: 'At this one.' Thereupon the king said to him: 'This is a pepper tree and the pay for working at it is one golden piece.' He then called another and asked him: 'At which tree have you worked?' And he replied: 'Under this tree.' The king thereupon said: 'This is a white-blossom tree and the pay for working at it is a half a golden piece.' He then called yet another, and asked him: 'At which tree have you worked?' And he replied: 'At this one.' Whereupon the king exclaimed: 'This is an olive tree and the pay for working at it is two hundred *zuz*.' Said the labourers to the king: 'You should have informed us from the outset which tree had the greater pay attached to it, so that we might have worked at it.' There-upon the king replied: 'Had I done this, how would the whole of my gar-den have been worked?' So God did not reveal the reward of the precepts, except of two, the weightiest and the least weighty" (honoring of parents is the weightiest and sparing a mother bird is the least weighty). *Pesiqta Rabbati* 23/24.2 and *Midr. Pss.* 9.3 are similar.
- *Midr. Pss.* 4.7: "If we have merit, deal with us accordingly; but if we have not, then show us righteousness and mercy."
- *Midr. Pss.* 26.3: "And so too, Solomon said to the Holy One, blessed be He: Master of the universe! When a king hires diligent workmen, and they do their work well, and he gives them their pay, should the king be praised? When is he to be praised? When he hires slothful workers, but gives them their pay in full. And Solomon went on to say: Our fathers worked dili-gently and received good pay. What kindness of Thine was in this, that they worked and were paid? Slothful workers, we! Yet give us good pay, and that would be Thy great kindness! Hence Solomon said: *The Lord our God be with us, as he was with our fathers* (1 Kgs 8:57)." Also in *Pirqe Rabbi Eliezer* 53; cf. *Midr. Pss.* 3.3; 105.13.
- *Midr. Pss.* 37.3: "With whom may David be compared? With a laborer who worked all his days for the king. When the king did not give him his hire, the laborer was troubled and said: 'Am I to go forth with nothing in my hands?' Then the king hired another laborer who worked for the king but one day, and the king laid meat before him, gave him drink, and gave him his hire in full. The laborer who had worked all his days for the king said: 'Such reward for this one who did no more than work but one day for the king? For me who have been working for the king all the days of my life,

how much more and more my reward!' The other laborer went away, and now the one who had been working all his days for the king was glad in his heart. So David said, *Thou hast put gladness in my heart, from the time their corn and their wine increased* (Ps 4:8). . . . From the prosperity of the wicked in this world, you can tell the reward of the righteous in the world-to-come."[179]

Textual Features Worth Noting

This parable is unusual in that it contains information and characters that are not really necessary to the plot (the workers hired in the middle hours and the steward). Similarly, the parable of the Unforgiving Servant has servants who report to their master but are not really necessary either.

The formulaic introduction "the kingdom of heaven is like" appears frequently in Matthew (13:31, 33, 44, 45, 47), but similar constructions also occur in Luke (see 13:18-21 and 6:47-49; 7:31-32).

While some suggest that the parable consists of two acts (vv. 1-7 and 8-15)[180] and some three (vv. 1-7, 8-11, and 12-15),[181] there is an advantage in noticing four movements within the brackets of the introduction and the concluding proverb:

> v. 1a: formulaic kingdom introduction
>> vv. 1b-7: the sequence of hirings
>> vv. 8-10: the payment
>> vv. 11-12: the complaint of injustice
>> vv. 13-15: the defense of goodness
> v. 16: concluding proverb

The hirings are structurally parallel.[182] In all five the owner goes out, the time is specified, and workers are sent to the vineyard. In the second and fifth the workers are found standing in the market.[183] In the first, second, and fifth dialogue is reported, but only in the last do those being hired speak.

The proverbs in Matt 19:30 and 20:16 are similar; the words "first" [*prōtoi*] and "last" [*eschatoi*] are plural:

> 19:30: And many first [people] will be last [people] and the last [people] first [people].
> 20:16: Thus the last [people] will be first [people] and the first [people] last [people].

Mark 10:31 has the identical proverb at the same point in the narrative as Matt 19:30, but Luke 13:30 has the proverb in a context unrelated to either Matthew or Mark and in the reversed order as in Matt 20:16.[184] Those convinced of the existence of Q often conclude that Matthew and Luke point to a Q version of the saying. Compare also Mark 9:35 and Luke 14:9.

The parable has Mattheanisms, which should occasion neither alarm nor surprise. Note *misthos* ("reward," ten Matthean occurrences, one in Mark, three in Luke), *apo . . . heōs* ("from . . . until," eight, three, and two respectively), *agathos/ ponēros* ("good"/"evil," eight, none, and two). *Oikodespotēs* ("Master of the house") occurs only in the Synoptics and is most frequent in Matthew (seven, one and four in Mark and Luke). But the claim for a high number of Mattheanisms is exaggerated.[185] Can *apodidōmi* ("pay") be listed as a Mattheanism (eighteen occurrences, one and eight in Mark and Luke) when seven of Matthew's occurrences appear in the parable of the Unforgiving Servant? Since Luke uses *homoios* ("like") with the verb "to be" as much as Matthew (eight each, none in Mark), is it fair to say that *homoia estin* ("is like") is Matthean?

The context is carefully framed by Matthew at least in 19:13–20:34 to deal with issues of status, wealth, greed, and discipleship. The underlying message in this section is the reversal of this world's values.[186]

> 19:13-15: The disciples are corrected for trying to keep children away; of such is the kingdom.
>
> 19:16-22: The rich man is instructed about his failure to keep the Law by loving his neighbors, the poor, with his wealth and is called to deny himself, take his cross, and follow Jesus.
>
> 19:23-26: The disciples are instructed on the deceit of money, perhaps the most obvious reversal of values.
>
> 19:27-30: Peter asks what the Twelve (presumably the intent of the first person pronoun) will receive for leaving everything and following Jesus and is told of their participation with the exalted Son of Man in leading a reconstituted Israel. The disciples are assured that all who have left family and possessions will receive one hundred times as much and will inherit eternal life. V. 30 is a summary proverb verifying that those who appear to have forfeited all (the last) will be richly rewarded (be first).
>
> 20:1-16: The parable of the Workers with the summary proverb repeated.
>
> 20:17-19: Jerusalem will not be the place of exaltation but of betrayal and death, but resurrection will follow.
>
> 20:20-28: The request of the mother of the sons of Zebedee for the chief seats for her sons when Jesus is exalted (cf. 19:28) becomes an occasion

for instruction in the reversal of values. Jesus' followers are not to view greatness the way this world does. Being first means being a servant (being last), and Jesus himself is the prime example. The parable and the summary proverb are an anticipation of this section, especially vv. 24-27.

20:29-34: The healing of the two blind men portrays the attitudes required of disciples. Whereas the sons of Zebedee sought status in reply to the question "What do you want?" (v. 21), in reply to the same question (v. 32) the blind men asked that their eyes be opened, and as a result of opened eyes they follow Jesus.

The identification of the master as "good" (v. 15) links back to 19:17, which identifies only one as good — God. All that is intended with this link is not clear, but at least it underscores within the narrative the character of God and makes clear that God is the referent with the owner of the vineyard.[187]

Parallels exist between this parable and that of the Prodigal Son.[188] Both have an authority figure expressing unexpected generosity, a complaint against the generosity, and a justification of the generosity. This assumes, however, that the focus of the parable is generosity, an assumption that must be validated.

Cultural Information

The picture the parable presents uses realistic but exaggerated features. The owner is probably reasonably well-off, but not so wealthy that he leaves oversight of his vineyard to agents. The picture of someone hiring day laborers from the market at a time of need is realistic,[189] as is the wage paid. Two items are exaggerations. The number of hirings is excessive and hardly conceivable because of the time involved in going back and forth from the vineyard, unless the vineyard was immediately adjacent to the market. Why were the last hired not seen earlier and why could the owner not calculate his needs better? Such questions are pertinent only if one thinks parables are always true to life. They are not. The repeated hirings are a setup to enable the parable to make its point. Also unrealistic is the equal pay of all the laborers, the very point of the parable.[190] Once again we see that parables use everyday materials but do not relate everyday occurrences.

The life of a day laborer in the ancient world was difficult by any estimation. Unemployment was a continual problem, and many slaves had an easier life because their owners had a financial investment that required protection and adequate care. Day laborers involved no such investment and could be hired for short periods and overworked or even abused.[191] But that does not tell us specifically about this parable and this owner. They are the "world" that forms the backdrop of the parable.

The workday was about twelve hours — from sunrise to sunset (Ps 104:22-23), and the complaints of those first hired that they have borne the burden and heat of the day (v. 12) are pointers to the difficulty of the work and the Palestinian sun.

The poverty of day laborers was so obvious that the Torah required that they be paid each day at sunset because they needed the money to survive (Lev 19:13; Deut 24:14-15). The rabbinic writings expect the same (*m. Baba Meṣi'a* 9.12; *b. Baba Meṣi'a* 83a, 110b).[192] The Tosefta mentions deceit from owners who promised higher pay and from workers who did not deliver, workers who suffered from heat prostration, and specific instructions to pay in proportion to work actually done if a worker works only part of the day (*t. Baba Meṣi'a* 7.1, 3).

A denarius was usually considered the average daily wage for a day laborer. It was subsistence pay at best. Usual estimates are that an adult in ancient Palestine needed about half a denarius a day to live and that an income of 200 denarii per year marked the poverty line.[193] Still, 200 denarii per year would hardly do more than keep a small family from going under. As always, though, not everyone was poor. The rich "fared sumptuously," and the disparity between rich and poor was great and offensive, as it still is.

"Friend" (v. 13) as used in this Gospel carries a negative connotation indicating something wrong in the relation (cf. 22:12 and 26:50).

Explanation of the Parable

Options for Interpretation

Seven options should be mentioned, but a myriad of nuances exist (especially on the relation of justice, work, and reward), including some "unusual" approaches.[194]

1. As might be expected, the church has allegorized this parable throughout its history. The allegorizing went in two directions. Most often the story was understood as referring to the successive ages of the world with the five hirings representing the periods from Adam to Noah, Noah to Abraham, Abraham to Moses, Moses to Christ, and Christ to the present. Alternatively the story was understood to represent the stages in life at which people experience conversion: childhood, adolescence, the prime of life, old age, and the point of death.[195] This reading confirmed the full validity of late conversion. Both readings viewed the denarius as eternal life or resurrection.

2. Many think the parable portrays God's gracious generosity, the grace of God in salvation, and argues against salvation by works.[196]

3. Often in combination with the previous option, many think the parable is Jesus' defense against the criticisms of his opponents for his accepting sinners.[197]

4. Some take the parable (or at least Matthew's understanding of it) as teaching the rejection of the Jews and the acceptance of the Gentiles.[198]

5. A few take the parable as demonstrating the abuse of peasants by wealthy landowners.[199] If this is the case, God's grace is contrasted with the generosity of the owner.

6. Some think the parable is directed against envy, greed, boasting, or any kind of reckoning among Jesus' disciples.[200]

7. A few argue that the parable teaches about human solidarity.[201]

These options are not mutually exclusive, and in fact one will often find two or more merged. In my opinion 1., 4., and 5. have little to commend them for serious consideration and 6. has the most in its favor, but all this must be demonstrated.

Decisions on the Issues

1. Was v. 16 (the proverb about the first being last, etc.) originally connected with the parable and does it fit the parable's intent? Both of these questions are usually answered in the negative,[202] and understandably so. The lack of fit was noticed at least as early as Chrysostom in the fourth century.[203] The only obvious connection between the parable and the proverb is that the last hired are paid first (v. 8). The proverb appears to have been a floating logion. Its relation to its context is direct and clear in Luke 13:30 but less direct in Mark 10:31/Matt 19:30, where "the first" by implication refers to the rich of several verses earlier. Matthew inserted the proverb after the parable in keeping with the focus on the reversal of values in this whole section.

More important is the question what the proverb accomplishes and whether Matthew thought the proverb was the *nimshal,* the explanation, of the parable. Since Jülicher at least, it has been argued that with this addition Matthew has turned a parable of grace into a parable of judgment.[204] George Beasley-Murray, on the other hand, thinks the proverb fits what Matthew is doing in the context.[205] Although v. 16 begins with *houtōs* ("thus"), I do not think it is intended to be the *nimshal* of the parable. It is, rather, placed here as a reminder of the point that dominates 19:13–20:34. *Gar* ("for") in 20:1 shows that Matthew saw the parable as in some way an example of the proverb, which indicates that human perceptions on ranking are without significance and will be stood on their heads in the kingdom, which is indeed the message of the parable.

2. *Is the parable intended to confront exploitation of workers? This implies another question: Is the owner a positive or a negative figure?* The view that the parable confronts exploitation of workers and that the owner is a negative figure has no basis. Because of the difficulty of this parable, W. Herzog argues that we should ignore as from Matthew v. 1a with its reference to the kingdom and that we should understand the parable as depicting the oppression of poor day laborers by a landowner. Several interpreters have followed Herzog. In his mind, the parable originally was not about the goodness of God but about the unfairness of the owner, who represents not God but oppressive landowners, with whom God would be contrasted. For Herzog, Matthew has distorted Jesus' original parable by creating a "theologory," investing it with theological values so that the vineyard owner is God, the vineyard is Israel or the church, the workers hired first are the Jews or Jesus' original disciples, the workers hired last are Gentiles or recent converts, etc. Herzog thinks the frequent trips of the owner originally underscored his unilateral power; the owner presents a "take it or leave it" proposition to the first workers and takes advantage of the other workers by offering them work without a wage agreement. The reversal of the order of payment is viewed as an affront to the first hired workers, a deliberate attempt to keep them subjugated. The owner's defense (vv. 13-15) is viewed as a demeaning insult. Further, his attitude of doing what he wants with his property is blasphemous in view of the Torah's insistence that the land belongs to God.[206]

If this were the meaning of the parable, then most people would have to give up any hope of understanding Jesus' parables, for nothing provides a bridge from the text to any of the conclusions Herzog draws.

We might wish that Jesus had confronted oppression of the poor more fully — though his parable of Lazarus and the Rich Man may be more than we can handle! — but Herzog's proposal illegitimately foists an ideology on the text. No one questions that day laborers had a difficult life in the ancient world, but for all of Herzog's interesting discussion of day laborers, his approach takes the parable out of its world. A vineyard, an owner, and workers in a Jewish context virtually requires that one understand the story as referring to God and the responsibility people have to God, at least unless there is some indication to the contrary. That God is in mind here is verified by "good" in 20:15, which harks back to 19:17, the statement that only God is good. The vineyard does not necessarily stand for Israel,[207] as we have seen with other parables, but it does represent responsibility and obedience to God. Jesus' other vineyard parables and the rabbinic parables above (pp. 364-67) verify that the subject is the work of God. Other rabbinic texts portray God as an employer,[208] and if rabbinic parables contrast a human with God, they make the contrast explicit. Nothing suggests that the owner was taking advantage in the wage agreement or the subsequent hirings. Nor is it blasphemy for the man to reserve the right to do what he wants with his property, even though God is the ultimate owner. Otherwise, he could not even give his possessions to the poor, which is what he is doing. On Herzog's view the payment of the workers hired last makes no sense. If the owner were as exploitive and cutthroat as suggested, why would he have paid the last workers so much?[209] Nothing encourages us to accept Herzog's argument. I find it telling that Herzog omits parables like that of the Prodigal Son which will not fit his scheme,[210] that is, parables in which the authority figure is a positive character and not negative in any way. Herzog's approach is an example of one laying the culture over the text, rather than letting the text lie in its culture, and then bending the text to one's own ideology.

3. Is the parable "allegorical" with some or all of the elements in the story corresponding to theological realities? This is an unavoidable question. Parables are analogies, and analogies have correspondences or they cannot work. The symbolic world of the parable points to God and those seeking to serve him, as already indicated. However, correspondences that make analogies work are a far cry from turning a story that was not allegory into allegory, which both the church and biblical scholars have often done. The attempt to see Jews represented in the first hired and Gentiles in the last hired — even in the mind of Matthew — requires a divining rod that the text does not give. None of the workers may legitimately be identified further than as people who seek to serve God or think they do. Jesus' audience was Jewish, but he was not contrasting Jews and Gentiles. Matthew's audience is Christian, largely Jewish Christian, but nothing in his description suggests Jews and Gentiles.

The frequent assumption that for Jesus the first hired represent Pharisees and the last hired represent tax collectors and sinners creates serious difficulty. Who was intended by the first and last hired — if indeed specific groups — is uncertain and one of the most difficult questions.[211] We will have to ask about these groups later, but to specify them without evidence is as much an error as assuming that the five stages of hiring represent various ages of history, times of human life, or the five senses, none of which has any legitimacy. The burden and heat of the day do not refer to the Law, the steward (v. 8) does not represent Christ, and the denarius does not stand for eternal life.[212] None of these details is to be taken as having allegorical significance.

4. Were the original addressees the Pharisees or the disciples? and *5. Are all the workers accepted as truly people of God or are some rejected?* These two questions are closely related and can be considered together. This parable is J. Jeremias's "poster child" for the church or the Evangelists having altered Jesus' parabolic message by changing the audience. Matthew's context is considered an obstacle to interpretation. Jeremias *assumes* that the parable was originally intended to be Jesus' defense against his critics.[213] Jeremias's position is often accepted, but how does he know that the parable was directed against Jesus' critics? The parable gives no hint of this. One could point to Luke 15:1-2, which explicitly mentions the scribes and Pharisees grumbling about Jesus' reception of tax collectors and sinners, and the parallels with the parable of the Prodigal Son. The workers hired first still receive their pay, and the elder brother is still addressed as "child" *(teknon)*. Do these parables reflect the period envisioned in the parable of the Fig Tree (Luke 13:6-9) when Jesus sought the repentance of Israel and its leaders? Or does Jesus merely suggest with this parable that Pharisees and sinners are treated the same?

Matthew indicates that the parable was addressed to the disciples and to the problem of envy,[214] which makes good sense, especially in light of the disciples' frequent discussion about who among them was the greatest (Matt 18:1/ Mark 9:34/Luke 9:46; Matt 20:20-28/Mark 10:35-45/Luke 22:24-27; Matt 23:11). That all the workers receive payment could exclude the idea that Jesus' opponents are addressed, but that is not certain.[215] D. Via sought to avoid the conclusion that all the workers are true workers by saying that the vineyard owner's order to "take what is yours and go" (v. 14) is a dismissal, an exclusion from the vineyard.[216] Few have followed him in this, especially since, as he admits, the workers were about to go home anyway.[217] A few assume that the Pharisees are intended and that they receive their payment, which indicates that they are not excluded from the kingdom.[218]

Other than the parallel with Luke 15 there is little to suggest that Pharisees were the original audience, and a good case exists for seeing the disciples as those addressed, but possibly the question is too narrowly framed. Had Jesus so divided his Jewish hearers from his disciples that he taught two different curricula? Or were parables like this told repeatedly and applied to different audiences — the crowds, opponents, and close followers? If so, the same parable or parabolic thought could have been directed both to disciples and to a broader audience. People assume on the basis of Mark 4:11/Luke 8:10 and Matt 13:34/Mark 4:34 that parables were not Jesus' method of teaching the disciples, but the parables were obvious topics of discussion with the disciples, and Matthew and Luke both — legitimately — have several parables addressed to the disciples.[219]

While the parable could have had a broader audience, it seems more likely it was addressed to the disciples. If the wages of the first hired would refer to inclusion in the kingdom, it does fit well with what Jesus says about the Pharisees elsewhere (cf. Matt 8:11-12/Luke 13:27-30, the latter containing Luke's version of the first-last proverb). Further, this parable is not like that of the Prodigal. As Pheme

Perkins points out, this parable does not give the disaffected much motivation to change their assessment of the owner.[220] Whereas the father goes out to urge *(parakalein)* the elder brother to join the celebration (Luke 15:28), the owner's response in this parable is more an indictment of a wrong attitude. Also, the focus on envy in v. 15 ("the evil eye") does not fit the Pharisees, but fits well with the disciples, not only in the context of Peter's question about reward (19:27), but also with the frequent discussions about which of them was the greatest.

On the other hand, the attempt to decide if all the workers were true workers in God's kingdom and whether the first hired inherit the kingdom looks like allegorizing. It pushes the parable well beyond what it seeks to do. No parable should be expected to present a detailed theological picture about the eternal state of all its characters. Parable interpretation is about how the analogy works, not deciding how each element fits with theology or Jesus' relation to his contemporaries.

To be explicit with regard to the two questions being addressed, the parable addresses the disciples, but it does not seek to delineate who truly are the people of God.

6. What did Jesus mean with the parable and what did Matthew mean? Determining the meaning of the parable is difficult and is impacted by the decision about the original addressees. If Jesus' opponents are the intended audience, the parable may emphasize the acceptance of tax collectors and sinners. If the disciples are those addressed, which I think is the case, it is intended to exclude arrogance, ideas of superiority over others in the kingdom, and any idea that God's assessment is to be understood by some kind of reckoning.

The most common view is that the parable is a picture of the grace of God to sinners, often with rather extravagant descriptions of God being extremely generous.[221] Often this is associated with a contrast between law and gospel, between a Jewish world of merit and a world of grace, or between works and grace.[222] But, while the parable is about the goodness of God at some level, it is not contrasting works and grace and is not about God's extreme generosity. B. Scott with justice complains that interpretations focusing on grace and generosity involve curious interpretive gymnastics.[223] No one in the parable receives a gift of grace. All the workers work and all receive their wage, albeit some more than anyone expected. The wage given is not especially generous (although those hired later might view it as such). If generosity were the focus, the wage for all the workers would not be set at one denarius, barely a subsistence wage; rather, we would expect an exaggerated amount — if not something parallel to the magnificent mercy of the king in the parable of the Unforgiving Servant, at least parallel to the debts cancelled in the parable of the Two Debtors. The owner's actions are more charitable than generous.

Nor can we say that grace is shown in the call to work in the vineyard or that the workers hired later expressed trust and a relationship with the owner, which mirrors faith in the theological realm.[224] All this is reading into the parable theological assumptions that are just not there. Nor is the parable's focus on an existence not based on merit. It is not about the equality of all people or the needed solidarity of humans.[225] It is not showing the equal value of those converted late in life or of those who become Christians in later stages in Christian history.[226] All such suggestions, true though they may be, obfuscate what this parable seeks to express. The parable focuses on the goodness of the owner and the complaint, *the envy,* of those who thought they should get more for their work. *The parable instructs us that God's treatment of people, his judgment, is not based on human reckoning and human standards of justice.*

The principle of equal pay for equal work is a virtual presupposition of our sense of justice.[227] Those who worked less should be paid less, but the owner gives all the same wage because without it those hired later would not have enough to live on. Humans, then and now, are continually comparing themselves with others, trying to assess fairness and level of accomplishment, which is exactly what the disciples were doing. The only fact that causes the first hired workers to complain is the comparison of their wage with that of those hired later. As with most humans, justice is in their eyes that which gives no one else — not even the poor — an advantage; it is defined from a self-centered perspective. Some prominence is given in the parable to the idea of what is right/just (*dikaion* in v. 4; *adikō,* "do wrong" in v. 13). To the complaint of injustice the owner defends his actions as just because he paid those hired first the agreed amount and because he can do as he wishes with his own property. For most of us injustice is what happens to our disadvantage, while what happens to our advantage is good luck.

The rule of end stress focuses attention on two facts: the "evil eye" of the complainers and the goodness of the owner. The expression "an evil eye" is descriptive of envy, jealousy, and lack of generosity.[228] Prov 28:22 links an evil eye with greed and Prov 22:9 says that the person with a good eye gives his bread to the poor. This is not sufficient to demonstrate that the parable alludes to these texts, but at least they illustrate the concerns of the parable. The owner is good because he gives to the poor, and the workers complain because they are jealous. With this, the statement that One is good in 19:17 takes on a new light: God is good because — unlike the rich young ruler — he gives to the poor.

Jesus' proclamation of the kingdom included metaphors for judgment and discussion of reward. Reward is *not* a bad motive; it is a way to talk about what pleases God and assures that following Christ is not a fruitless endeavor. The disciples, like most humans, were into calculating reward and seeking privilege. Peter's question was "What do we get for following?" (19:27), and he was assured that the reward is great. But does the promise of reward create status and ranking? The request of the sons of Zebedee is for a higher ranking, but Jesus rejects presumptions about status (20:20-28). Whether originally in the context of Peter's question or not, the parable addresses speculation about reward in comparison to others. Key in interpreting the parable is v. 10: those hired first *thought* they would receive more.[229] The parable breaks any chain of logic connecting reward, work, and human perceptions of what is right. God's judging is not regulated by human perceptions of justice,[230] and lurking behind that statement is a whole theology of mercy. The parable is not attempting to say anything about human effort and salvation. Rather, *just as no one should begrudge a good man who goes beyond justice and gives to the poor, so no one should begrudge God's goodness and mercy as if God's rewards were limited to strict calculation.*[231] Implicit is the assumption that God's judgment will be contrary to human expectations. Implicit as well is that envy — displeasure at someone else's success — is contrary to the kingdom. Jealousy and all thoughts of ranking or privilege must be jettisoned. If this is the message of Jesus, Matthew is correct to place the parable with other texts expressing similar ideas (see pp. 368-69 above).[232]

7. What theological insight can be gained, especially with regard to christology, economic practice, or the nature of reward? First, theological gain should not be sought from the picture of the hirings. Some urgency may be assumed from the owner's repeated trips, but the parable is not about urgency. Similarly, the call to the vineyard is not the point; it is the backdrop of the parable. Nothing negative is expressed by the owner's question why some workers were standing idle the whole day (v. 6).[233] The multiple hirings are a literary tool to heighten the contrast and create suspense, just as the reversal of the order of payment is a literary tool that allows the first hired to witness the payment to those hired last and creates the expectation that they deserve more. We should set aside as well any notion that the parable is about faith and works.

I do not think christological implications are present. The owner is a symbol for God, not Jesus,[234] and the steward serves only to create distance and allow narrative space for the grumbling to take place.[235] Possibly christological implications are present if one decides that the parable is told by Jesus to defend his acceptance of sinners. E. Linnemann and a few others point to such implications if Jesus defends *his* actions by telling a parable about how God acts.[236]

Economic practice is not to be derived from the parable either, as if the concern of the parable was to teach equal wages for all. On the other hand, by implication the parable does call for imitation of the owner. If the owner/God is good and gives to the poor without grudging, should not those who profess allegiance to God do the same?[237]

More difficult is the discussion about what we should conclude about a theology of reward. Does this parable have final judgment in view, or is it more concerned with present judgment?[238] Final judgment may be lurking in the background, but we must say, I think, that the parable has little concern to describe what it is like[239] and should not be used to derive a theology of reward. C. Blomberg does just this when he concludes that, while there are degrees of punishment (based on Luke 12:47-48), there are not degrees of reward, something that in his estimation does not fit the idea of the perfection of the life to come. All in the kingdom receive the same reward.[240] Obviously the Lukan version of the parable of the Talents (19:11-27) has no difficulty thinking of degrees of rewards, but is either parable intended to allow one to draw conclusions about final judgment?

This is not to say the parable is irrelevant for thinking about judgment. At least the parable warns that we should expect to be surprised at God's judgment; it will not occur along the lines of human calculations. As several interpreters have noted, the parable assures that no one will get less than promised or be treated unfairly and that many will get much more than they deserve.[241] The parable also assumes the sovereignty and mercy of God.[242]

Adapting the Parable

The obvious place where our thinking must engage the parable is with issues of envy, justice, and goodness done to others, not with the call to the vineyard. Why is goodness often the occasion for anger?[243] Why do we find it so difficult to rejoice over the good that enters other people's lives, and why do we spend our time calculating how we have been cheated?[244] Kierkegaard's focus on the sin of comparison fits well with this parable.[245] The life of God's kingdom with its focus on communal love cannot be experienced as long as we are comparing ourselves with others and calculating what is due us or being envious of what others receive. Even while we speak of justice, none of us is satisfied with average. We always think we deserve a little more.

Justice is terribly important and must not be sacrificed, but it should be redefined. Justice is not some cold standard by which the poor are kept poor. We worry about justice, but too often we dress up as justice what is in reality jealousy, or we use justice as a weapon to limit generosity.[246] Nor is justice a passive idea waiting to be violated, and it certainly is not to be defined by self-centered interests. Justice requires positive action seeking the good for all persons, especially the poor. True justice — at least God's justice — seeks mercy and ways to express love.[247] If the parable is about the goodness of God, then it asks that we give up envy and calculation of reward and, rather, both embrace and imitate God's goodness. That will mean that we give up the quest to be first, knowing that God's standards are different, that what appears to be first will be last.

We cannot ignore the relevance of the parable for speaking of reward, but its teaching is mostly preventive. It will not allow us to construct a scheme for calculating hierarchies, assigning relative values to people or work, and thinking some deserve more. God in his sovereignty will judge as God sees fit.

For Further Reading

Ingo Broer, "Die Gleichnisexegese und die neuere Literaturwissenschaft. Ein Diskussionsbeitrag zur Exegese von Mt 20,1-16," *BN* 5 (1978): 13-27.

W. D. Davies and D. C. Allison, *A Critical and Exegetical Commentary on the Gospel According to Saint Matthew* (ICC; Edinburgh: T. & T. Clark, 1997), 3:66-78.

Christian Dietzfelbinger, "Das Gleichnis von den Arbeitern im Weinberg," *EvT* 43 (1983): 126-37.

John R. Donahue, *The Gospels in Parable: Metaphor, Narrative, and Theology in the Synoptic Gospels* (Philadelphia: Fortress, 1988), pp. 79-85.

William R. Herzog, II, *Parables as Subversive Speech: Jesus as Pedagogue of the Oppressed* (Louisville: Westminster/John Knox, 1994), pp. 79-97.

Catherine Hezser, *Lohnmetaphorik und Arbeitswelt in Mt 20,1-16* (NTOA 15; Göttingen: Vandenhoeck & Ruprecht, 1990).

Arland J. Hultgren, *The Parables of Jesus: A Commentary* (Grand Rapids: Eerdmans, 2000), pp. 33-46.

Joachim Jeremias, *The Parables of Jesus* (2nd ed.; New York: Scribner's, 1972), 33-38, 136-39.

Pheme Perkins, *Hearing the Parables of Jesus* (New York: Paulist, 1981), pp. 137-46.

Bernard Brandon Scott, *Hear Then the Parable: A Commentary on the Parables of Jesus* (Minneapolis: Fortress, 1989), pp. 281-98.

THE TOWER BUILDER AND THE WARRING KING
(Luke 14:28-32)

Parable Type

The Tower Builder is an interrogative parable in the form of a "Who from you?" question.[248] The Warring King is also an interrogative parable, but here the question is impersonal ("What king . . . ?"). Both questions expect negative answers: no builder and no king would think of undertaking action without determining first that they have the capacity to fulfill the plan. Both questions are followed by reasons the builder or the king would make such calculations.

Issues Requiring Attention

1. Did these parables originally belong in this context?
2. Are these parables authentic parables from Jesus or are they later compositions of the church?
3. What is the meaning of each parable? Are they calls for serious reflection for would-be disciples, assurances that *God* does not begin enterprises he cannot complete, or are they statements that *Jesus* is the one who counted the cost and proceeded with faith?[249]
4. Is discipleship possible for all people?

Helpful Primary Source Material

Canonical Material

- OT: 1 Kgs 22:1-40 is an example of kings seeking wisdom whether to go to war or ways to deal with a superior opponent. Cf. 1 Sam 17:1-58; Prov 24:3, 6; 2 Sam 8:10.[250]
- NT: Matt 8:19-22/Luke 9:57-62; Matt 16:24-27/Mark 8:34-38/Luke 9:23-26/ John 12:24-25; Matt 10:38-39; Luke 17:33 (all statements on discipleship)

Early Jewish Writings

- 11Q Temple Scroll (11Q19) 68.1-21 gives instructions for the king concerning how many soldiers should be sent out in various circumstances when Israel is attacked. However, (line 18) soldiers are not to go forth to battle until the king has entered the presence of the high priest and the high priest has consulted for him the decision of the Urim and Thummin.
- Philo, *On Abraham* 105: When vice and virtue conflict "virtue's nature is most peaceable, and she is careful, so they say, to test her own strength before the conflict, so that if she is able to contend to the end she may take the field, but if she finds her strength too weak she may shrink from entering the contest at all" to avoid the reproach of defeat.
- *Testament of Judah* 9.7: "Then they asked us for peace terms, and follow-

ing consultation with our father we took them as subjects under tribute." This work may have been influenced by Christians.

Greco-Roman Writings

- Cicero, *De Officiis* 1.21 counsels anyone entering public life not to think only of the honor but to consider whether he has the ability to succeed and avoid discouragement and over-confidence. "In a word, before undertaking any enterprise, careful preparation must be made."
- Juvenal, *Satirae* 11.35: "If you are preparing to defend a great and difficult cause, take counsel of yourself and tell yourself what you are — are you a great orator, or just a spouter like Curtius and Matho? Let a man take his own measure and have regard to it in things great or small. . . ."
- Epictetus, *Diatr.* 3.15.1-13: "In each separate thing that you do consider the matters which come first, and those which follow after, and only then approach the thing itself. Otherwise, at the start you will come to it enthusiastically because you have never reflected upon any of the subsequent steps, but later on, when some of them appear, you will give up disgracefully." He discusses what is required to be an Olympic athlete or a philosopher. 9: "Man, consider first what the business is, and then your own natural ability, what you can bear *(dynasai bastasai)*."
- Epictetus, *Diatr.* 3.22.9-12 counsels consideration before one becomes a Cynic: "So do you also think about the matter carefully; it is not what you think it is. 'I wear a rough cloak even as it is, and I shall have one then; I have a hard bed even now, and so I shall then. . . .' If you fancy the affair to be something like this, give it a wide berth; don't come near it, it is nothing for you. But if your impression of it is correct, and you do not think too meanly of yourself, consider the magnitude of the enterprise that you are taking in hand."

Early Christian Writings

- *Gos. Thom.* 98: "Jesus said: The kingdom of the Father is like a man who wanted to kill a powerful man. He drew the sword within his house (and) ran it through the wall, so that he might know whether his hand would be strong (enough). Then he killed the powerful (man)."

Later Jewish Writings

- *Pesiqta de Rab Kahana* 17.2 tells of a mighty man the people trusted would chase off any hostile invaders, but when the invaders came he said, "I feel a weakness in my right hand." The point of the parable is that God would never speak this way.

- *Pesiqta de Rab Kahana* 24.11 tells a parable of a city which rebelled against its king. The king sent a general to destroy the city, but the general was experienced and coolheaded and advised the rebels, "Take time to consider what you are doing lest the king lay waste your city as he laid waste such-and-such a city. . . ." So too Hosea warned Israel to repent so that God would not do to them what he did to Samaria.
- *Pesiqta de Rab Kahana* Supplement 7.3 tells a parable of a king who, because of his anger against his city, removed himself ten miles. A man warned the city that the king might attack and advised them to go out and appease the king. The parable illustrates Isa 55:6: "Seek the Lord while he may be found."

Textual Features Worth Noting

Other occurrences of "Who from you?" *(tis ex hymōn),* not all of them parables, show that the expected answer in each case is "No one." See Matt 6:27; 7:9; 12:11; Luke 11:5, 11; 12:25; 14:28; 15:4; 17:7; and John 8:46.

Luke 14:25-27 repeats the classic statement of Jesus on discipleship, part of which appears at seven places in the Gospels. Luke is particularly concerned with discipleship throughout his travel narrative (9:51–19:44); see especially 9:57-62 and 19:11-27, which bracket this section. The open invitation of the preceding parable of the Feast (Luke 14:15-24) is followed by a focus on the demands of discipleship, a movement that is paralleled in Matthew's parable of the Banquet and the pericope that follows of the improperly attired guest (Matt 22:1-10 and 11-14).

There are verbal and conceptual links, especially regarding wisdom, in the parables of Two Builders (Luke 6:47-49) and the Ten Virgins (Matt 25:1-13).

The two parables here are parallel but not identical. Both ask about a hypothetical enterprise, analyze the adequacy of resources for the task, and focus on the consequences if the resources are not sufficient.[251] The first engages the hearer/reader directly; the second is less personal, but the stakes are higher. If a builder fails, he alone bears the brunt of the failure. If a king fails in planning for war, many will die or be subjugated.

Prominence is given in this whole section to the idea of being able *(dynamai,* 14:20, 26, 27, 33; *dynatos,* v. 31; *ischysen,* v. 30). The question implied is what makes one able to be a disciple. With the Tower Builder prominence is placed on the idea of completion.

In 19:42 Jesus, as he approaches Jerusalem and weeps, uses an expression from 14:32, "the things leading to peace" *(ta pros eirēnēn):* "If you, even you, knew this day the things leading to peace — but now it has been hidden from your eyes."

Cultural Information

The first parable especially is evidence of the strong emphasis on honor and shame in first-century Mediterranean culture. While mocking is degrading in any culture, it is particularly offensive in a culture driven by shame and honor.

Towers were used for a variety of agricultural and military purposes. Farmers built towers to guard property, especially vineyards (cf. Isa 5:2), and to store equipment and the harvest. Others built towers as lookouts and signal points and for protection.[252] The kind of building presupposed in v. 28 does not appear to be important.

The second parable uses language typical in descriptions of battles and negotiations for peace.[253] Several events may be imaginable sources for the second parable, but no specific event appears to be the source of Jesus' thinking.[254]

Explanation of the Parable

Options for Interpretation

1. The church allegorized the two parables in different directions. Building the tower was understood of spiritual perfection, the resources of which were spiritual capacities or good works. The weaker of the warring kings was understood as the Christian, with the stronger king being either God/Christ (Gregory) or Satan (Augustine). Gregory understood the powerful king as the coming of Christ to judge us, against which we cannot stand, and therefore we should engage in compassionate works to gain the peace of mercy.[255]

2. A few modern scholars have also suggested that God is the one who builds the tower and goes to war. The parables are then a call to certainty: God has begun his work and no one should doubt that he will complete it.[256] Similarly a few think Jesus is the one who calculates the cost.[257]

3. By far the preponderant view is that these two parables are a warning to disciples to calculate the cost of discipleship.[258]

Decisions on the Issues

1. Did these parables originally belong in this context? While it is possible that these parables were told in connection with the surrounding verses, this is not particularly likely. The context itself is unspecified, and the arrangement of this whole section is Lukan and has been framed to emphasize the theme of discipleship. If the invitation to the poor and outcasts is universal and free (14:21-23), the expectations accompanying the acceptance of the invitation are stringent. As is implied in the preceding parable of the Feast, the primary obstacles to discipleship (and the primary opportunities for discipleship) are possessions and family, points already made in 9:57-62 (cf. 12:22-34, 49-53). Cf. Matt 22:1-14 with its open invitation followed by demand.

The structure of this subsection of Luke is as follows:

14:25: narrative introduction
vv. 26-27: requirements of discipleship
vv. 28-32: twin parables of assessment
v. 33: further requirement of discipleship
vv. 34-35: sayings about salt, like Matt 5:13, understood as referring to discipleship, followed by the challenge to hear

This whole passage is arranged to promote discipleship, and clearly the statement "is not able to be my disciple" at the end of vv. 26, 27, and 33 has prominence. The unity of the sayings is not obvious, and, as several have noted, if the parables are omitted, the text that remains (vv. 26-27, 33) reads smoothly.[259] Some contrast the fact that vv. 26-27 and 33 are about renunciation or self-denial while the twin parables are about self-testing.[260] While the connection of the parables to this specific context is probably Lukan, the fit of the parables with the surrounding sayings is better than some suggest. They are not so much about self-testing as about assessment of capacity. The key word in vv. 26, 27, and 33 is "able" (*dynatai*, cf. v. 20), and what one is able to accomplish is the theme in the parables as well. The connection is implicit in v. 30 with "able to finish" (*ischysen*) and explicit in v. 31 with "if he is able" (*dynatos*).[261] The sayings about salt cohere but are understandable only through the parallel of Matt 5:13 and through the connection with the discipleship sayings here.

2. Are these parables authentic parables from Jesus or are they later compositions of the church? Apart from the efforts of the Jesus Seminar and a few others, the question of authenticity would not arise. Why anyone would want to pick on these two small parables is not obvious. Two reasons are given as a basis for rejecting them: such thinking is not distinctive of Jesus but is derived from a fund of proverbial wisdom,[262] and the parables have a high degree of Lukan vocabulary.[263]

These parables are common sense wisdom,[264] but the argument that they are from a fund of proverbial wisdom suggests that someone borrowed explicit sayings, but close parallels to these parables do not exist. The supposition that we can accept from Jesus only what is distinctive of him is a holdover from the abuses of the criterion of dissimilarity and leaves a very small amount of material as authentic.[265] It would be amazing if Jesus did not offer common sense wisdom as part of his teaching. Not everything he said was shocking and subversive, as simple analogies such as God providing for ravens and lilies (Matt 6:26, 28-29 par.) attest.[266] That the parables evidence Lukan stylistic traits is to be expected, although the Lukan characteristics are not particularly impressive.[267] And Lukan shaping certainly is no proof of Lukan creation. With Jülicher and most others there is no reason to doubt that these two parables are genuine words of Jesus.[268]

3. What is the meaning of the parable? In their present context the parables are clearly intended to warn against a premature and unaware acceptance of discipleship. Several interpreters suggest that the parables were not originally about discipleship and do not belong in this context. They argue that Jesus does not elsewhere advise caution or ask for calculation but, rather, asks people to follow him, and immediately they leave all and follow (e.g., Matt 4:18-22/Mark 1:16-20).[269] C. Hunzinger notes as well that parables beginning with the "Who from you?" formula usually compare human behavior with God's behavior. That is, if a human would do such and such, surely God will. From this he concludes that these parables originally were not about discipleship but provided assurance that God had considered the cost and had the resources to complete the tasks God had started.[270] C. Quarles argued that the parable of the Warring King portrays Jesus himself. With the parable of the Tower Builder Jesus was urging that people consider the cost of discipleship, but with the Warring King he urged people to consider the cost of refusing to follow him.[271]

As interesting as these suggestions are, they do not convince that the parables were originally about God or Jesus rather than discipleship. Did anyone really doubt that God had the ability to complete his plans? Introductory "Who from you?" questions do indeed often compare human behavior with God's behavior, but not always, and there is little reason to think it does so here. Matt 12:11 contains such a question but clearly does not refer to God with it.[272]

Jesus does urge reflection on what discipleship means. In Matt 8:18-22/Luke 9:57-62 he cautions would-be disciples,[273] and in Matt 16:26/Mark 8:36/Luke 9:25 he asks what profit a person has who gains the world and loses life, a question that presupposes the necessity of serious reflection. In the narrative of

James and John desiring to reign with Jesus (Matt 20:20-23) he challenges their ignorance and asks "Are you able?"[274] The dramatic story in Matt 4:18-22/Mark 1:16-20 of the calling of fishermen as disciples is impressive, but a glance at Luke 5:1-11 and John 1:35-42 suggests that the story has been trimmed to its bare essentials.[275] Discipleship is no light matter, and the urgency of the call does not diminish the seriousness of the commitment. With these parables Jesus does not seek to deter discipleship,[276] but his goal is not merely to gain as large a following as possible. It may well be that these parables were addressed to a smaller group of followers or at a late stage in Jesus' ministry,[277] but that they were about discipleship seems required.

The point of the parables is clear. Who would begin to build a tower without analyzing whether he or she had resources to accomplish the task? No one. What king would think of going out to defeat an attacking king without analyzing whether resources were sufficient for victory or whether submission is more advisable? No king would. Just as foolish would be any thought of being a disciple without assessing the impact on one's life. Discipleship changes allegiances with family, requires the willingness to die, shifts the focus off self-centeredness, places one at the disposal of another, and changes the way one handles financial resources. T. W. Manson reportedly commented, "Salvation may be free, but it is not cheap."[278] Protestants often stumble at the parable's focus on human effort and the implication that insufficient power negates discipleship,[279] but offensive or not, this is the assumption of these parables.

A couple of other proposals require comment. Some see an allusion to the tower of Babel (Gen 11:1-9), which those building could not complete,[280] but this is unlikely. The problem there was not that they started something with insufficient resources; rather, their efforts were prevented. Tom Wright suggests that the reference is to Israel, which was engaged in the greatest building program of the day and was headed for the greatest war she would fight. She was building a tower she could not complete and was about to engage in a war she could not win.[281] Some basis for reflecting on this possibility exists in Luke 19:42 with Jesus' repetition of "the things leading to peace" *(ta pros eirēnēn)* from 14:32 as he weeps over Jerusalem and announces its destruction. The wording is similar, but Wright's suggestion is more a co-opting of Jesus' words to describe Israel, not what Jesus originally had in mind. The parables are about discipleship. Several have suggested that the two parables function to warn in two different directions: against a too easy choice to follow and a choice not to follow. In A. M. Hunter's words, "In the first parable Jesus says, 'Sit down and reckon whether you can afford to follow me.' In the second he says: 'Sit down and reckon whether you can afford to refuse my demands.'"[282]

4. Is discipleship possible for all people? This question may seem strange, but A. Hultgren without explanation says, "Discipleship is not for everyone, and certainly not possible for everyone."[283] Possibly he assumes with C. G. Montefiore that Jesus distinguishes between the full disciple and the good person who can enter the kingdom although not a disciple.[284] That not all people will be disciples is a given; but no basis exists to argue that discipleship is not possible for all. The church implicitly or explicitly has often tried to establish two levels of Christianity, one for the really committed and one for those more engaged with other aspects of life. This "practical" idea has no basis. One is either a follower of Christ or one is not. Jesus' invitation is universal: all may and should become disciples. Finding life is dependent on following him, which also means taking one's identity from him. The shape discipleship takes will vary, but there is no lower standard than following Christ — and yes, it is possible for all.

Adapting the Parable

These parables differ greatly from the easy believism that marks so much of American Christianity. Churches urge everyone to believe, to accept Jesus, but make no demands on people's lives; the more adherents the better, even if the message is curtailed for "marketing" purposes. Such shallow ideas about conversion create enormous problems for individuals, churches, and societies. We need to do a much better job helping people understand what Christianity really is about. The concern is not going to heaven, as important as heaven is, but living now in accordance with Jesus' own life.

Counting the cost of discipleship is difficult since none of us on coming to faith has or can have any idea of the future or what sacrifices commitment to Christ will involve. To say "Jesus is Lord," though, does not mean "Jesus is Lord unless. . . ." Faith in Christ worth the name *by necessity* means discipleship with all its consequences. We are given over to another who shapes our lives. The parables are about more than considering the cost of discipleship. Presupposed and more significant is the fact that discipleship requires intent, choice, determination, and effort. It is not some light-hearted affair, and it does not just happen. The fear we have of focus on human effort must be jettisoned, for no discipleship occurs without human effort *or merely because of human effort*. Discipleship is not about humans straining on their own; it is the necessary result and consequence of faith in and following after Jesus (Luke 14:26-27). Relation to Christ activates and empowers the whole of life, but if humans do not choose to act and actually act, nothing happens.

The questions of honor and shame that underlie these parables also deserve reflection. Honor and shame are more implicit than explicit in our culture, but we have huge expectations of what gives or denies respectability, be it academic, ecclesial, familial, or peer respectability, just to mention a few. What our society finds respectable and where status originates is often misguided and even reprehensible. Discipleship means defining respectability in terms of Jesus' instruction and person. Various texts speak of eschatological shame (e.g., Mark 8:38/Luke 9:26; Rom 5:2-5; 9:33; 1 Thess 2:19); concern for honor and shame should be guided by a sense of eschatological honor and shame.

For Further Reading

Craig L. Blomberg, *Interpreting the Parables* (Downers Grove: InterVarsity, 1990), pp. 281-84.

J. Duncan M. Derrett, "Nisi Dominus Aedificaverit Domum: Towers and Wars (Lk XIV 28-32)," *NovT* 19 (1977): 241-61.

Bernhard Heininger, *Metaphorik, Erzählstruktur und szenisch-dramatische Gestaltung in den Sondergutgleichnissen bei Lukas* (Münster: Aschendorff, 1991).

Claus-Hunno Hunzinger, "Unbekannte Gleichnisse Jesu aus dem Thomas-Evangelium," in *Judentum-Urchristentum-Kirche*, ed. W. Eltester (BZNW 26; Berlin: Töpelmann, 1964), pp. 209-20.

Arland J. Hultgren, *The Parables of Jesus: A Commentary* (Grand Rapids: Eerdmans, 2000), pp. 137-45.

Charles Leland Quarles, "The Authenticity of the Parable of the Warring King: A Response to the Jesus Seminar," in *Authenticating the Words of Jesus*, ed. Bruce D. Chilton and Craig A. Evans (Leiden: Brill, 1999), 409-29.

Parables about Money

Three parables, all in Luke, focus on wealth: the Rich Fool, the Unjust Steward, and the Rich Man and Lazarus. Some would group the story of the Rich Man and Lazarus with parables of future eschatology, but, while this parable is relevant to eschatological concerns, addressing them is not its purpose. Both Luke's arrangement of the section and the parable itself suggest that the use of wealth is the primary interest. These parables are parables of discipleship, but more narrowly focused, for the first question regarding discipleship is what one does with money.

Luke, of course, has a major concern for how wealth and resources are used. Almost every chapter of both his Gospel and Acts has some reference to money and material resources. His concerns for the poor, denunciations of the rich, and discussions of attitudes toward wealth and its use repeatedly emphasize that discipleship in the kingdom of God requires a major redirection of how one thinks about and uses material possessions.[1] This is not surprising since use of possessions is a revelation of one's true self.[2]

The Rich Fool
(Luke 12:16-21)

Parable Type

This is a single indirect parable with an explicit *nimshal* (v. 21), but that decision presumes conclusions to questions discussed below.

389

Issues Requiring Attention

1. The textual variant in v. 21.
2. The relation of vv. 13-15 and 21 to the parable.
3. Is this parable a single indirect narrative parable or a metaphor for the kingdom?
4. What is the relation of the parable to other literature, especially Sir 11:18-19; *1 En.* 97:8-10; and *Gos. Thom.* 63 and 72?
5. Is the parable based on an assumption either that the rich man wanted to withhold grain and drive up market prices or that he had no friends?
6. What is the teaching of the parable? Is this parable about the death of the individual or is it a warning about future eschatology, as Jeremias suggested?[3] If about death, is it about the inevitable death awaiting all, or does it speak specifically of God's judgment on those who trust in wealth? What is intended with "*they* will ask your soul from you" (NRSV and other versions paraphrase: "your life is being demanded of you")? What does the parable teach about wealth? Does it condemn wealth, promote almsgiving, or what? What is the rich man's error?

Helpful Primary Source Material

The subject of wealth and denunciations of its misuse are *frequent* in the ancient world. Only the most relevant are included here.

Canonical Material

- OT: Job 31:24-32; Pss 14/53; 39:6; 49 (especially vv. 6 and 10); Prov 3:9-10; Eccl 2:1-26; 5:10-20; 8:15; Isa 22:13; Jer 9:23; Hos 12:8-10
- NT: Matt 6:19-21/Luke 12:33-34; Matt 16:24-26/Mark 8:34-37/Luke 9:23-25; Matt 19:16-30/Mark 10:17-31/Luke 18:18-30; Luke 12:29-34; 16:1-31, especially vv. 10-13; 1 Cor 15:32; 1 Tim 6:17-19; Jas 1:9-11; 2:2-7; 4:1-5; 5:1-6

Early Jewish Writings[4]

- CD-A 4.14 says that wealth is one of three nets by which Belial catches Israel.
- CD-A 6.14 urges people to abstain from wicked wealth, which defiles.[5]
- *Ahiqar* 13.207: "Let not the rich man say, 'In my riches I am glorious.'" See also 9.137.

- Wis 15:8: ". . . these mortals who were made of earth a short time before and after a little while go to the earth from which all mortals are taken, when the time comes to return the souls that were borrowed."
- Sir 5:1, 3: "Do not rely on your wealth, or say, 'I have enough,' . . . for the Lord will surely punish you."
- Sir 11:14-20, especially 18-19: "One becomes rich through diligence and self-denial, and the reward allotted to him is this: when he says, 'I have found rest, and now I shall feast on my goods!' he does not know how long it will be until he leaves them to others and dies."
- Sir 29:11: "Lay up your treasure according to the commandments of the Most High, and it will profit you more than gold." See also 31:8-9.
- *1 En.* 97:8-10: "Woe unto you who gain silver and gold by unjust means; you will then say, 'We have grown rich and accumulated goods, we have acquired everything that we have desired. So now let us do whatever we like; for we have gathered silver, we have filled our treasuries (with money) like water. And many are the laborers in our houses.' Your lies flow like water. For your wealth shall not endure but it shall take off from you quickly for you have acquired it all unjustly, and you shall be given over to a great curse." See also 94:7-10; 96:4-8; 98:1-3.
- *Pss. Sol.* 5:16-17: "Happy is (the person) whom God remembers with a moderate sufficiency; for if one is excessively rich, he sins. Moderate (wealth) is adequate — with righteousness; for with this comes the Lord's blessing: to be (more than) satisfied with righteousness."
- Pseudo-Phocylides 42: "The love of money is the mother of all evil." See also *Sib. Or.* 2.109-18.

Greco-Roman Writings

- P. Cair. Zen. 59.509, a tomb inscription from Aphrodisia (*Monumenta Asiae Minoris Antiqua* [London: Longmans, Gree, 1928-93], 8:569; see *Hellenistic Commentary to the New Testament*, ed. M. Eugene Boring, Klaus Berger, and Carsten Colpe [Nashville: Abingdon, 1995], pp. 439-40): "As long as you live, be happy, eat, drink, live high, embrace others. For this was the End."
- Seneca, *De Brevitate Vitae* 13.7: "O, what blindness does great prosperity cast upon our minds!"[6]
- Seneca, *Ad Helviam* 10.6, 10: "Why do you pile riches on riches? You really should remember how small your bodies are! . . . What folly then to think that it is the amount of money and not the state of mind that matters!"
- Seneca, *Epistulae Morales* 101.4-5, after telling of a successful businessman

who was snatched from the world: "But how foolish it is to set out one's life, when one is not even owner of the morrow! O what madness it is to plot out far-reaching hopes! To say: 'I will buy and build, loan and call in money, win titles of honour, and then, old and full of years, I will surrender myself to a life of ease.' Believe me when I say that everything is doubtful, even for those who are prosperous. No one has any right to draw for himself upon the future. The very thing that we grasp slips through our hands, and chance cuts into the actual hour which we are crowding so full."

Early Christian Writings

- *Sentences of Sextus* 21: "Consider that your soul is a trust from God."
- *Gos. Thom.* 63: "Jesus said: There was a rich man who had many possessions. He said, I will use my possessions that I may sow and reap and plant and fill my storehouses with fruit, so that I may lack nothing. These were his thoughts in his heart. And in that night he died. He who has ears, let him hear."
- *Gos. Thom.* 72: "[A man said] to him: Speak to my brothers that they divide my father's possessions with me. He said to him: O man, who made me a divider? He turned to his disciples (and) said to them: I am not a divider, am I?"

Later Jewish Writings

- *Pesiqta de Rab Kahana* 10.3: "[Give heed to] the story of a man who kept adding to his store of wine and oil, but never once paid the tithes due from him. What did the Holy One do? He caused a spirit of madness to enter into the man, so that he took a stick and began breaking his jars of wine and oil."
- *b. Ta'anit* 11a: "When the community is in trouble let not a man say, 'I will go to my house and I will eat and drink and all will be well with me'. For of him who does so Scripture says, And behold joy and gladness, slaying oxen and killing sheep, eating flesh and drinking wine — 'Let us eat and drink, for tomorrow we shall die.' What follows after this [verse]? — And the Lord of Hosts revealed Himself in mine ears; surely this iniquity shall not be expiated by you till ye die."
- *Lev. Rab.* 22.1: "A king that maketh himself servant to the field (Eccl 5:8). Even though he is a king and holds sway from one end of the world to the other, he is a 'Servant to the field'; if the earth yields produce he can ac-

complish something, if the earth does not yield he is of no use whatever. Accordingly, He that loveth silver shall not be satisfied with silver (Eccl 5:9), that is to say, he who loves money will not be satisfied with money, nor he that loveth abundance *(hamon)* with increase; this also is vanity, for he who is covetous *(homeh)* and greedy *(mehammeh)* for money but has no land, what benefit has he?" The same text appears at *Eccl. Rab.* 5:6.

Comparison of the Accounts

The sayings in Luke 12:13-14 appear in *Gos. Thom.* 72, Luke 12:15 has no parallel in *Gos. Thom.*, and the parable in *Gos. Thom.* appears earlier at saying 63. The story in *Gos. Thom.* is not about a good harvest and the man's contentment with himself but about a man who plans so that he lacks nothing. The version in *Gos. Thom.* is brief and rather bland. From a comparison of this one parable a case for dependence is not obvious, but the facts that sayings 63-65 are arranged as a denunciation of wealth and that saying 65 seems dependent on the Synoptics[7] make it difficult to argue *Gos. Thom.* contains an earlier account. The case is stronger that saying 72 is dependent on Luke 12:14, especially in the use of the vocative "O man" *(anthrōpe),* which elsewhere in the Gospels occurs only at Luke 5:20; 22:58, 60.[8]

Textual Features Worthy of Attention

The whole section from 12:4-59 is artfully arranged to deal with issues of fear, anxiety, and security. From 12:35 on these subjects are heightened by concerns of eschatology and judgment. Several "hooks," ideas, and connections tie this section together and would have helped a listening audience follow the flow and stay interested. (Most of Luke's audience would *hear* the Gospel being read to them.)

In 12:4-5 people are told both whom not to fear and whom to fear (God), but in v. 7 people are told not to fear, for they are worth much more than sparrows — a point underscored in v. 24. In v. 32 they are told again not to fear because their Father desires to give them the kingdom. In 12:11 people are told not to worry *(merimnaō)* what they will say when put to the test, and this same word is used in vv. 22, 25, and 26 to urge hearers not to worry about basic necessities. (V. 29 uses a different word for the same idea.) Further, in vv. 13-14 Jesus is asked to persuade a brother to "divide" *(merizō)* the inheritance, but Jesus rejects the role of "divider" *(meristēs)* and judge. Yet in vv. 51-53 division (*diamerismos, diamerizō*) is what he brings, and in v. 58 people are warned of facing the judge. (Similar "hooks" continue with the section that follows.) In fact, it seems that Luke has consciously used words with the letter combination *meri* to tie this section together.

Other "hooks" appear as well: repetition of the word *psychē* ("soul," "life") in vv. 19, 20, 22, and 23; cf. *zōē* ("life") in v. 15; "possessions" *(hyparchonta)* in vv. 15, 33, and 44; five sparrows in v. 6 and five in a house in v. 52; "thief" *(kleptēs)* in vv. 33 and 39; and "barns" *(apothēkē)* in vv. 18 and 24. Such rhetorical art teaches by repetition, but also advances new ideas or sets items in opposition that require reflection.

In Luke's narrative vv. 13-14 present the occasion, v. 15 Jesus' response, vv. 16-20 the parable, and v. 21 the *nimshal*. The story itself has four movements: the flourishing of the field (v. 16b), the problem (v. 17), the solution (vv. 18-19), and the interrupting judgment of God (v. 20).

The parable emphasizes that *the field* prospered, not the man, which makes the prosperity almost an accident or at least distances the man from the reason for his prosperity.

A wordplay exists between *euphorēsen* (v. 16) describing the prosperity of the field and *euphrainou* (v. 19) describing the man's intent to celebrate. K. Bailey suggests an implied wordplay in v. 14 between *meristēs* ("divider") and *mesitēs* ("reconciler").[9]

This is the only NT parable in which God appears as an actor in the narrative.[10]

Luke has a stylistic preference for soliloquy; see 5:21-22; 7:39; 15:17-19; 16:3; 18:4; 20:13.

Note especially the framing of the parable with vv. 15 and 23.

Cultural Information[11]

In 12:13-14 Jesus is asked to settle a dispute. Since disputes were often over how the Hebrew Scriptures should be interpreted, rabbis and other respected teachers were asked to adjudicate.[12]

Inheritance laws indicated that the eldest son should receive a double portion (Deut 21:15-17; see *m. Baba Batra* 8.1–9.10). That brothers should live together without dividing the inheritance was optimal and praiseworthy.[13] Some suggest that vv. 13-14 assume an elder brother who does not want to divide the inheritance and a younger brother who does. Others suggest that the elder brother is withholding an inheritance that should go to the younger. In either case the younger assumes that justice is on his side. However, when people approach Jesus for decision on some issue, he often redirects the focus, as if to say "Look to yourself first."[14]

Greed (*pleonexia,* the desire to have more) was considered a mark of depravity and the origin of other sins among both Jews and non-Jews.[15] Greed was a common subject in moral instruction in the Greco-Roman world and Luke seems to show awareness of this tradition in the way he has shaped his material.[16]

The trilogy "eat, drink, and celebrate" is conventional language, though not always with the exact wording. See Eccl 2:24; 3:13; 5:18; 8:15; Judg 19:4-9; Tob 7:10; Isa 22:13; 1 Cor 15:32.[17]

Explanation of the Parable

Options for Interpretation

1. The church usually focused on the dangers of greed and the necessity of giving alms. Only occasionally was this parable allegorized, and no thorough allegory of this parable exists in the patristic and medieval sources.[18]

2. Most frequently the story has been viewed as a negative example story showing the foolishness of basing one's life on possessions.[19]

3. A few, especially those who reject example story as a viable category, argue that this is a metaphorical parable about the kingdom. For Crossan the point is the necessity of making a proper decision when confronted with the urgency of Jesus' kingdom message.[20] For Scott the harvest points to the kingdom and the good life intended for the community, which requires the right use of wealth.[21]

4. A few suggest that the sudden judgment on the Rich Fool is a metaphor for judgment on Israel.[22]

5. A few suggest that the man is withholding grain from the market to drive the price of grain higher. Charles Hedrick thinks the man is a fool because he tore down his barns instead of harvesting his grain and that the parable raises questions about the meaning of life.[23] Strangely, Mary Ann Beavis thinks the parable shows the self-defeating nature of revenge and violence.[24]

Decisions on the Issuses[25]

1. *The textual variant in v. 21.* V. 21 is omitted only by Codex Bezae (D) and a few of the old Latin translations, making it an example of a "Western Non-Interpolation," but the external evidence (the manuscript evidence) for includ-

ing the verse is virtually unassailable (p^{45}, p^{75}, the major uncials, and almost all witnesses).[26] With regard to internal evidence, Luke is not likely to have moved directly from "God said" in v. 20 to "He [Jesus] said" in v. 22. A few later manuscripts add at the end of v. 21 "And saying these things he cried out, 'Let the one having ears to hear hear,'" which is also in *Gos. Thom.* 63.[27] The same words appear in Luke 8:8. As J. N. Birdsall points out, the origin of this addition does not have anything to do with *Gos. Thom.* but derives from lectionary usage and worship needs.[28] V. 21 without the additional words about hearing belongs to the text of Luke.

2. *The relation of vv. 13-15 and 21 to the parable.* The relation of the parable to its context is difficult to determine. This section could be made up of several originally independent sayings, for each saying begins with "he said" (*eipen*, vv. 13, 14, 15, 16, and 22, but also vv. 18 and 20 within the story). Vv. 13-14 obviously are a unit showing a question to Jesus and his response to the petitioner, a certain person from the crowd. However, v. 15 and the parable address "them," presumably the crowd. From v. 22 on the addressees are the disciples. Jeremias argued that vv. 13-15 did not belong originally with the parable because the two were not linked in *Gos. Thom.*, yet he thought the situation depicted in vv. 13-15 is necessary to understand the parable.[29] I think *Gos. Thom.* 63 is clearly secondary, but even if it is not it does not prove anything about the original connection in Luke.[30] Not a great deal is at stake with vv. 13-15. These sayings could originally have been independent units that Luke or the tradition has brought together, but specific options are difficult to prove. (The language is not particularly Lukan.) On the other hand, even though *Gos. Thom.* has preserved sayings 63 (the parable) and 72 (v. 21) separately, I find it unlikely that vv. 13-14 would have been remembered as an isolated saying. What purpose would they serve, especially since the early church thought Jesus *did* have a judging function and was a cause of division?[31] The parable presupposes some context like that of 12:13-15, and I find the connection between the parable and at least v. 15 likely. Both provide a warning against finding life in possessions, and the parable is a demonstration of v. 15b.

With v. 21 we have a saying that fits the parable, but which also is similar to Matt 6:19-21. Such sayings may have been used often by Jesus, and one can neither prove nor disprove whether Jesus used such a *nimshal* here or whether the context in which the story was originally told rendered a *nimshal* superfluous. It is sufficient to say that v. 21 is an appropriate, and in Luke's narrative necessary, explanation of the parable.[32] While this is often overlooked, v. 21 is a repetition of v. 20b. The act of treasuring for oneself is equivalent to preparing for oneself, so v. 21 does not alter the intent. Those who store up for themselves instead of storing up in relation to God are like prosperous fools who have no opportunity to enjoy their prosperity.[33]

3. Is this parable a single indirect narrative parable or a metaphor for the kingdom? J. D. Crossan argues this was originally a metaphorical parable about the kingdom that the church changed into an example story. His view is based on his conviction that *Gos. Thom.* 63 is more original,[34] but the arrangement of sayings 63-65 shows that saying 63 is part of *Gos. Thom.*'s denunciation of wealth, which militates both against interpreting the parable as one of the kingdom and an argument that the *Gos. Thom.* version is earlier. Crossan thinks the parable is about making a decision when confronted with the urgency of Jesus' kingdom message, but how he reaches this conviction is by no means clear. Nothing in the parable suggests that the kingdom is in view.

B. B. Scott's argument fails as well. He finds an implicit metaphorical reference to the kingdom in the harvest idea,[35] but the word "harvest" does not occur. How Scott's view really relates to the kingdom is not clear, especially since he rejects any idea of apocalyptic and assumes that "reality will continue."[36] This is not a metaphorical parable about the kingdom and it pertains to the kingdom only in its implications of what kingdom living might mean with regard to the use of resources.

While the rich man is a negative example, as discussed above, "example story" is inadequate and inappropriate as a category for parables.[37] The parable of the Rich Fool is a single indirect parable. It is not metaphorical. That is, it does not require transfer to some other arena, which also excludes Wright's suggestion that the parable is a picture of Israel. Jesus was not using the rich farmer as a lens on some other subject but as a negative example of a man who foolishly trusts in his possessions, someone who misses life by presuming possessions are life.

4. What is the relation of the parable to other literature, especially Sir 11:18-19; 1 En. 97:8-10? The similarity of Sir 11:18-19 and *1 En.* 97:8-10 is striking, but significant differences occur. In Sirach wealth is gained through diligence and self-denial, whereas in the parable it is *the land* that prospers. In *1 Enoch* the wealth is obtained unjustly, which is not an issue in the parable, unless at most by implication. No direct dependence on these passages is likely,[38] although Jesus' familiarity with literature such as Sirach and *1 Enoch* is a given (or at least the content of such literature) and demonstrable from other parables.[39] The shared attitudes toward wealth and toward the suddenness of death are common themes in the wisdom tradition, a tradition which clearly influenced Jesus, and in the writings of Greco-Roman moralists.[40] The parable shares a common moral view with various writings but is not directly related to any of them, as far as can be known.

5. Is the parable based on an assumption either that the rich man wanted to withhold grain and drive up market prices or that he had no friends? Neither of these options is evident in the parable. We can paint a scenario of an absentee landlord, a network of clients and patrons, and exploitation of peasants in the hoarding of grain[41] — all factors in first-century Palestine, but that would be reading into this parable assumptions that are not there. The only motive that can be discerned from the parable is the man's desire to protect and enjoy his good fortune. Once again the principle is operative that all attempts to understand a story from elements not present in the text are almost certainly wrong. As far as the parable is concerned, the man does not anticipate selling his goods at all; he plans only to take care of his own needs.

C. Hedrick views the rich man as foolish because he plans to tear down his barns when he should be harvesting crops,[42] but I see no evidence for such an interpretation. The parable only says that the land of the rich man flourished — not that it is time for harvest. Obviously the man thinks he still has time to prepare.[43]

The suggestion that the man has no friends is based on his use of soliloquy,[44] but such a conclusion is an unjustified deduction from the use of a rhetorical device. Soliloquy has nothing to do with whether one has friends. Some argue further that the man's use of the first person "I" proves he is self-centered, but first person pronouns are typical of soliloquy and prove nothing in themselves.[45] It is true that Luke uses soliloquy to depict negative characters, and the man is self-centered, but this is shown by his plans in v. 19, not merely by the fact that he uses soliloquy. The parable give no basis for discerning the man's social relations.

6. *What is the teaching of the parable?* A number of questions must be addressed. For the third person plural in v. 20 ("They will ask your soul [*psychē*] from you") several possibilities have been suggested: angels, the possessions, the man's mistreated neighbors, or a circumlocution for God.[46] In view of the similar construction at Luke 6:38 ("a good measure . . . *they* will give into your lap"; NRSV "will be put into your lap"), this is most likely a circumlocution for God,[47] but M. Reiser's point that such constructions are intended to suppress focus on the acting agent should be given its due.[48]

Whether this parable is about the death of the individual or a warning about eschatological judgment is debated,[49] but I see nothing to support the idea the parable was originally about the approaching eschatological catastrophe. The parable is about the death of an individual, and judgment is implicit at best, other than God's verdict that the man is a fool. The consequences of God's judgment are not specified, nor is death itself viewed as the judgment.[50] The parable points to the uncertainty and fragility of life, but it is concerned most with God's verdict on those who trust in wealth. Certainly in Luke's context the concern is the death of the individual, but this should not be written off as his moralizing agenda since many of the sayings here are paralleled in Matthew. Much of the concern from 12:4 on is security, often for life itself, and whom one should fear. 12:5-7 (and most of the chapter) teaches that people should fear the One who cares so much that fear is unnecessary! That means trusting in God and not material possessions. The parable of the Rich Man and Lazarus also focuses on the death of the individual, as does the saying in 23:43 concerning the repentant thief on the cross. The intervention of death aborts the man's plans and shows how foolish they were. His possessions are no basis for life and security.

The parable emphasizes how little control the man actually has over his life, despite what he thinks. His prosperity does not result from his effort; *the land* prospers (v. 16), not his work. Even what he thinks is most intimately his own — his soul — is only on loan and can be demanded at any time.[51]

At least until the intervention of God in v. 20 we are tempted to react positively to the man and say "Good for you!" What did the man do wrong that brings the negative verdict? Suggestions include that he ignored God, that he failed to plan for life beyond death, and that he was self-centered and inattentive to the needs of others. These options are not necessarily mutually exclusive. C. Hedrick is correct in saying the story raises in a dramatic way the question of the meaning of life.[52] The parable then functions as a commentary on the second half of 12:15 (life does not consist in abundance of possessions).[53]

Like the fool in Ps 14:1 the man left God out of the picture.[54] He sought security in possessions; but possessions do not give security, and life does not consist in "stuff." The man is the antithesis of Jesus' teaching that a disciple is to deny self and that the one who wishes to save life (*psychē*, as in 12:19) loses it (9:23-24). The real issue is the focus of life. The fool's focus was on preparing things for himself (vv. 20b-21). Foolishness consists in thinking that responsibilities end with securing one's own economic future.[55] Life should not be focused on self, but on God and his purposes ("being rich toward God"; cf. 16:13).

Is there any hint that the parable is about giving alms? Certainly within the broader context of Luke one knows that being rich toward God includes care for the poor and giving alms (e.g., 11:41; 12:33; 16:9). Tob 4:7-11 uses language similar to v. 21 to encourage almsgiving as a way to lay up a good treasure against the "day of necessity." Thus, one can understand that an emphasis on almsgiving is often associated with this parable.[56] Some scholars suggest that the rich fool's storing grain for himself is an allusion to Joseph storing Pharaoh's grain to provide food during the time of the famine.[57] If this were true, then the implication of abundance being used to assist the poor might be increased, but the Joseph story is about Joseph's business acumen on behalf of Pharaoh (Gen. 47:13-26), not about giving alms. Little reason exists to see an allusion to the Joseph story. The parable does not teach about wealth but warns against thinking that possessions are life. The explanation in v. 21 extends the parable to make clear that focus on possessions for oneself leads to impoverishment with God. The parable has no direct implication about almsgiving, but any Jew, and certainly Jesus, would know being rich toward God included the obligation to use material resources to assist those in need.

The parable is a brief but poignant demonstration that life is not about plans for our own security and that satisfaction from possessions is an illusion.

Adapting the Parable

Parables like this strike a tender nerve, especially when we admit to ourselves — as we must — that we want to be like the rich fool. We want to say to ourselves, "I have many good things (or a lot of money) laid up for many years; eat, drink, and celebrate." Jesus' comment in Matt 19:23/Mark 10:23/Luke 18:24 that the rich with difficulty enter the kingdom gives us little pause. We are more like Tevye in "Fiddler on the Roof" who sings "If I Were a Rich Man" or, when told that money is the world's curse, he responds "May the Lord smite me with it, and may I never recover!"

The message of this parable is as antithetical to our thinking as any Jesus told. I know of no more difficult topic to apply personally or to the lives of modern Western Christians. Our primary pursuits are our own security and pleasure, both, we think, achieved by possessions. However, one could in fact say — at least as far as Jesus and Luke are concerned — that possessions are one of the chief obstacles to salvation and life with God. Certainly resources are needed for life and ministry, as, for example, the women supporting Jesus' ministry knew (Luke 8:3). Further, resources are needed to make resources grow. The fault is not in the possessions themselves, but in how tightly we cling to them or the use we make of them (or refuse to make of them). The issue is the focus of our lives and the way that focus determines the use of our possessions. At the same time, any attempt to relieve the parable's accusation by thinking it is not wealth but only our attitude that is at fault will necessarily fail.

The parable underscores that life is fragile and uncertain and that one needs more than possessions. All of us know this truism, but often it has no impact on our lives. Few in Western society live as if possessions and security are not the most important aspects of life. This chapter of Luke opposes the idolatry of security and urges a profound trust in God, not money.

It is worth making explicit that parables like this are not merely for the wealthy. A person does not have to be wealthy to be like the rich fool. It may be easier for the wealthy to "treasure up for themselves," but those without resources can be just as driven by greed and just as wrongly focused on things instead of God.[58]

The most obvious arena where this parable deserves a voice is our view of retirement, which looks very much like the rich fool's soliloquy. We are not content to make a living; we want to make a killing or at least enough to retire early. But life is not about taking our ease and taking care of ourselves. To be "rich toward God" means to live productively, reflecting the character of God in all our relations.

Other areas where this parable has pertinence involve the choices we make with our resources, most notably in weddings and funerals. In modern society both have become pictures of fantasy and occasions for inordinate expense. Christians should rethink what it means to be rich toward God in our public displays.

Neither Luke nor Jesus is against celebrating, especially when celebration is a central theme in Jesus' gospel. Interestingly, while celebrating is negative in this parable, the same word *(euphrainein)* is used positively in Luke 15:24 and 32 of the necessity of celebrating at the return of the prodigal.

For Further Reading

Kenneth Ewing Bailey, *Through Peasant Eyes: More Lucan Parables, Their Culture and Style* (Grand Rapids: Eerdmans, 1980), pp. 57-73.

J. Duncan M. Derrett, "The Rich Fool: A Parable of Jesus Concerning Inheritance," in *Studies in the New Testament* (Leiden: Brill, 1978), 2:99-120.

Herman Hendrickx, *The Parables of Jesus* (San Francisco: Harper & Row, 1986), pp. 96-107.

Peter Rhea Jones, *Studying the Parables of Jesus* (Macon: Smyth & Helwys, 1999), pp. 142-62.

John Nolland, *Luke 9:21–18:34* (WBC 35B; Dallas: Word, 1993), 682-88.

THE UNJUST STEWARD
(Luke 16:1-13)

This parable is notoriously difficult, so difficult that hardly anyone suspects it could come from the early church.[59] Already Richard Trench in 1864 complained of the manifold and curious interpretations of this parable, stating that "very many interpreters . . . had 'overrun their game.'"[60] A bewildering number of explanations exist, many of which are still guilty of overrunning their game.

In fact, one feels that the lack of knowledge available to interpret this parable is inversely proportional to the amount written about it. This is a parable where one must fill in the blanks, and therefore, psychologizing is easier here than anywhere. The parable suggests numerous connections, nuances, and possibilities — most of them dead ends.

Parable Type

To label the parable is to assume its interpretation. This is a single indirect narrative parable that is also a "how much more" parable. It has a concluding explanation in v. 8b and an application in v. 9. Although several interpreters think the story presents an example,[61] only a few categorize it as an example story,[62] which is surprising. The description I have given is based on decisions made about the ending of the parable at v. 9. Appended after the parable are four sayings (vv. 10-13) that use key words from vv. 8-9.

Issues Requiring Attention

1. How are the legal/cultural circumstances of the parable to be understood? Who considers the steward unrighteous (the master? the debtors? the narrator?), and is his unrighteousness (v. 8) the squandering of possessions (v. 1) or the actions reducing debts (vv. 5-7)? Were his reductions legal/honest or illegal/dishonest? Did the steward give up his own profit or those of his master? Was he merely removing the interest-bearing portion of the contract, which should have been illegal for Jews anyway?

2. Where does the parable end? With v. 7, v. 8a, v. 8b, or v. 9? Are the explanation in v. 8b and the explanation and *nimshal* in vv. 8b-9 original and do they adequately explain the parable? What is the relation of vv. 10-13 to the parable? Are vv. 8b-13 or some part thereof later attempts to explain the parable, as Jeremias and many suggest?[63]

3. To whom does *kyrios* ("master" or "Lord") refer in v. 8a? The master in the narrative world of the parable or, as Jeremias suggests on analogy with 18:6,[64] Jesus in Luke's narrative?

4. Who is the focus of the parable, the steward or the master? Is the description of the master as rich intended to depict him negatively?

5. Why does the master (and why would Jesus) praise the servant for what appears to be a dishonest act?

6. What is the intent of vv. 8b-9? Specifically what is the intent in v. 9 of

"making friends," "*mammon* of unrighteousness," "it fails" (NRSV "when it is gone"), and "they will receive you into eternal tabernacles"? Is this a parable about the use of money, the crisis facing Israel, or Jesus' actions?

7. To whom is the parable addressed, the disciples, as Luke indicates, Israel generally, or the Jewish leaders, in particular, the Pharisees?
8. How does this parable function and what is its intent?

Helpful Primary Source Material

Whereas for most parables several helpful parallels can be listed, with this difficult parable relatively little exists in primary sources that is truly parallel and helpful.[65] Some primary source material is included below in the section on culture.

Canonical Material

- OT: Ezra 7:22, which lists up to 100 *kors* of wheat and 100 *baths* of oil among the supplies made available to Ezra; see also Prov 18:16
- NT: Matt 6:24; 25:21, 23/Luke 19:17, 19; Luke 12:42 are pertinent for the sayings in Luke 16:10-13, but they have little direct bearing on the parable.

Early Jewish Writings

- Pseudo-Phocylides 158: "And if someone has not learned a craft, he must dig with a hoe."

Greco-Roman Writings

- BGU 1.300, a second-century contract granting authority to conduct business as an agent: "I have empowered you by this document to administer my estate . . . to arrange new leases . . . to give receipts in my name, and to transact any business connected with stewardship, just as I can transact it when I am present, and to distribute the plots in Karamis, restoring to me what remains over, as to which matter I rely on your good faith, and I confirm whatever you decide about them."[66]
- Dio Cassius, *Historia Romanorum* 52.37.5-6 advises one to keep freedmen and all others rigorously under discipline so as not to be brought into discredit by them. Everything they do will be set to the patron's account. He will be considered of the same character as any conduct of theirs to which he does not object.

- Seneca, *De Beneficiis* 4.27.5 speaks of the foolishness of entrusting the care of one's patrimony to a person condemned for bad management.
- Seneca, *Epistulae Morales* 18.13: "For he alone is in kinship with God who has scorned wealth. . . ."
- Quintilian *Inst.* 6.3.93: "Again when his steward, being unable to account for certain sums of money, kept saying, 'I have not eaten it: I live on bread and water,' he replied, 'Master sparrow, pay what you owe.'"
- *Select Papyri* (LCL) 2:571 (no. 419) presents a first-century letter from Apollonius, a strategos, to Akous, a toparch, demanding an immediate accounting to determine whether he will be allowed to remain on duty or sent to the prefect for neglect of the collecting.
- *Select Papyri* (LCL) 2:571 (no. 420) is a first-century letter from another strategos named Paniscus to a royal scribe explaining that, since the tax "farmers" refused to bid for the jobs for fear of incurring losses, he had reduced the amounts in the tax leases.
- Dio Chrysostom, *Oratio* 66.13 speaks of the difficulty facing a slave having two masters.

Later Jewish Writings[67]

- *Exod. Rab.* 31.2 uses an analogy of a man in trouble with the king whose good friends plead for him to show that when one fulfills the commands, studies Torah, and practices charity, while Satan accuses him before God, his good friends point out his good deeds. Prov 18:16 is added for verification.
- *Pesiqta de Rab Kahana* 14.5 tells of a king who deposited all he possessed with a steward before going on a journey. When the king returned and asked for his possessions, the steward denied being the king's servant and that the king had deposited anything with him. The king had him suspended on a torturer's scaffold until he admitted the truth. The parable explains Pharaoh's denial of God and his being brought to confession of God in Exod 9:27.
- *Pesiqta de Rab Kahana* 19.2 uses a parable to explain the hostility of Israel's neighbors. A king did not allow his wife to talk, borrow, or lend to her neighbors. When she was deposed and expelled from the palace and sought shelter from the neighbors, none would take her in. A similar account concerning Adam appears at 20.6.
- Various contracts exist for debts of wheat and oil, and the rabbis attempted to define what is and is not usury with such debts.[68]

Textual Features Worthy of Attention

Several other parable introductions in this section are identical. Luke 10:30; 14:16; 15:11; 16:1; 16:19; and 19:12 all begin with "A certain man" (*anthrōpos tis*; cf. 13:6 and 18:2).[69]

Most of Luke 16 is thematically arranged and concerns money, which, of course, is one of Luke's strongest redactional interests in both his Gospel and Acts. Vv. 10-13 are sayings on money appended to the parable. Money is still the subject in v. 14 and at least partly in v. 15 and the main concern in the parable of the Rich Man and Lazarus. Vv. 16-18 fit somewhat awkwardly in this section, but vv. 16-17 anticipate the discussion in the parable of the Rich Man and Lazarus.

Luke 12:33, 42 and 19:17 parallel ideas in the parable and its accompanying sayings.

Several connections exist between this parable and the parable of the Prodigal. Both begin with "A certain man" and use *diaskorpizein* ("squander"). Both the prodigal and the steward betray a trust, use soliloquy, seek relief from a crisis, and receive an unexpected response, a forgiveness that seems unfair.

Debtor parables are a common framework for Jesus. In some the debt is forgiven (the Two Debtors, Luke 7:40-48, and the Unforgiving Servant, Matt 18:23-35), but in others the failure to pay is a cause for judgment (e.g., the Wicked Tenants, Matt 21:33-45/Mark 12:1-12/Luke 20:9-19, the Talents, Matt 25:14-30, and the Pounds, Luke 19:11-27). The subject of debts appears in Matt 5:25-26/Luke 12:58 and forgiveness of debts in the Lord's Prayer (Matt 6:12/Luke 11:4 with the appended statement in Matt 6:14-15), and release (forgiveness: *aphesis*) is the focus in Luke 4:18.

The audience in Luke's travel section alternates between disciples, crowds, and opponents, usually the Pharisees. In 16:1 Luke indicates that this parable was directed to the disciples, but 16:14 indicates that Pharisees heard what was said. This alternation is a literary device which keeps both the teaching of Jesus and his conflict with (and differences from) his opponents in view. It also requires the reader to keep asking, like Peter in 12:41, "Is this for us?"

Prominence is given to doing *(poiein)* in vv. 3, 4, 8 (NRSV "acted"), and 9 (NRSV "make").

Vv. 4 and 9 are purposely similar: "so that when *(hina hotan)*," "they may receive me/you into . . . *(dexōntai me/hymas eis . . .)*."

Key words from vv. 8-9 are repeated in vv. 10-13: "unrighteous" (*adikia* in v. 8, *adikos* in vv. 10 and 11), "*mammon*" in vv. 9, 11, and 13, and "master/Lord" in vv. 3, 5, 8, and 13.

Among the Gospel writers only Luke uses *oikonomos* ("steward") and *oikonomia* ("stewardship"), and all the occurrences are in this parable except for *oikonomos* in 12:42.

Cultural Information

The amount of the debts is very large, although suggestions of the exact figures vary. One hundred *baths* of oil (a bath is a unit of measurement) would be equivalent to about 800 or 900 gallons, the yield of possibly 150 olive trees and equivalent to the wages of about three years for the average worker. One hundred *kor* of wheat would be almost 1100 bushels, probably enough to feed 150 people for a year, the produce of 100 acres, and equivalent to seven and one-half years of labor for the average worker.[70] In each case the steward reduced the bill by the same amount, about 500 denarii or the wages of more than two years for a day laborer. The parable tells of fairly large business dealings. None of the people involved are poverty-stricken peasants or even people with average incomes. Most likely the parable assumes that the debtors have contracted to farm the master's land and give him a portion of the produce. Alternatively, the debtors could be wholesalers,[71] but this seems less likely. The man is almost certainly an agent rather than a slave. A slave would not be simply dismissed from service but would receive some form of punishment and assignment to unpleasant work.

As indicated in the contract recorded above (p. 403), this parable assumes the custom of the day that a man's agent is as himself. Derrett points to the three great maxims of Jewish laws on agency: a man's agent is like himself, there is no agency for wrongdoing, and it is a legal presumption that an agent carries out his mission.[72] What the agent does is as if the master did it himself.[73]

The other assumption of the parable is an ethic of reciprocity, which was a fixed element in the Mediterranean world. Generous or benevolent acts brought with them an expectation they would be repaid, as Luke 14:12-14 shows.

Explanation of the Parable

Options for Interpretation

The number of options is bewildering, but the most important for gaining perspective and an overview are the following.[74]

1. With early interpreters this parable most often was taken as an argu-

ment for giving alms. The parable was allegorized less than other parables, but in later interpretations allegorizing became more common.[75]

2. The traditional view of this parable, represented early and frequently, is that the steward's wisdom is praised, particularly his wisdom in using money, not his dishonesty. His radical action within his sphere serves as an analogy for radical action in another sphere. This position is most attractive when it combines wisdom with regard to wealth with an emphasis on the eschatological character of the kingdom. Jesus emphasizes that the coming of his kingdom alters one's decisions about the use of financial resources.[76]

3. A. Jülicher argued that the parable (which he limited to vv. 1-7) is not about the right use of riches but about the purposeful use of the present as the condition for an enjoyable future.[77]

4. J. Jeremias limits the parable to vv. 1-8a but argues that initially the parable was addressed to the hesitant in the crowd to warn them of the imminent crisis. The early church applied the parable to the right use of wealth, but this shift Jeremias regards as more an actualization of the parable than a misinterpretation.[78]

5. J. D. M. Derrett argued that the actions of the steward were not dishonest: he merely his canceled the interest hidden in the contract, which was not permissible for Jews anyway. Although both the owner and the steward were deprived by the reductions, it was money to which they were not entitled. The steward's action makes the master look like a righteous man in the eyes of the community. If the master repudiates the steward's action, he reveals his own ungraciousness and his lack of righteousness. By accepting the action he gained a reputation for piety. The parable teaches about right use of resources and the validity of God's standards.[79] Aspects of Derrett's approach have been incorporated in several other studies.

6. J. A. Fitzmyer differs only slightly from Derrett in arguing that the manager has foregone his own (usurious) commission to win favor.[80] The point of comparison is the prudent use of material wealth in view of the present eschatological crisis.

7. Kenneth Bailey rejected the approaches of Derrett and Fitzmyer, arguing on the basis of *m. Baba Batra* 10:4 that the contracts would be public and known to the master. The steward experienced mercy when first found out and with his reductions risked everything on the master's continuing mercy. Again, the owner can reject the reductions and make the debtors angry or accept them and the praise that would follow. The parable (vv. 1-8) is an eschatological warning to sinners to entrust everything to God's mercy. Vv. 9-13 are a unity playing on the *'amen* root and are to be read separately from the parable.[81]

8. Stanley Porter is a recent advocate of the position that the parable with

its commendatory statements in vv. 8-9 should be read as irony. He sees any accommodation to the standards of the world (as in vv. 8-9) as a contradiction of Jesus' message. The sons of this age *think* their wise behavior can influence the age to come, but nothing could be further from the truth. He argues also for the inclusion of the whole of vv. 1-13 and sees v. 13 as an ironical question expecting a negative answer.[82]

9. D. Flusser argued that with "sons of light" Jesus was not referring to his followers, but was referring ironically to the Essenes, who tried to avoid contamination from the wealth of wickedness, the wealth of the surrounding world. Jesus viewed this economic separatism as dangerous (i.e., the sons of this age are wiser than the Essenes in that they keep economic contact with others) and called for a sharing of property with all. Vv. 10-12 must be included with the parable.[83]

10. For John Kloppenborg the master — not the steward — is on trial. The very label "rich" would convey something negative to peasant hearers. The steward's squandering is fraudulent and places the master's honor in question, but the master does not seek to regain his honor. The parable celebrates the master's conversion from the myopia of ascribed honor.[84]

11. As he does with many of the parables, N. T. Wright understands this one as an eschatological warning to Israel. As with the steward, judgment is hanging over Israel's head.[85]

12. A few scholars see Jesus himself depicted by the actions of the steward; the parable is his own biography. On this view the parable is addressed to the scribes and Pharisees and shows their reaction to Jesus, whom they view as one squandering the religious tradition. Jesus as God's agent remits the debts people owe to God, and the parable is a defense of Jesus' rogue ministry of grace.[86]

13. Dan Via argues that the parable is addressed to Jesus' critics. The parable (16:1-8a) is a picaresque comedy which tells of a successful rogue who makes conventional society look foolish, but without establishing any positive alternative. Both he and the rich man are negative characters. The parable says that the present is a crisis because the future is threatening, but the appeal to overcome this danger is configured as a picaresque mode of a moral holiday. It is comic relief from dead seriousness and shows that our well-being does not rest ultimately on our dead seriousness.[87]

14. A few scholars suggest that the parable reorients values. B. Scott argues the steward is a rogue, but that the rich man is a negative figure too and gets what he deserves. By a powerful questioning and juxtaposition of images, the parable breaks the bond between power and justice. It equates justice and vulnerability and forces the hearer in the world of the kingdom to establish new coordinates for power, justice, and vulnerability.[88]

John Donahue thinks the story is about the foolish master, who is blithely unconcerned about his steward's dishonesty. It evokes a world where God does not exact punishment but gives time and cancels debts even in the midst of human machinations. While Luke may have used the parable to counter fear and anxiety in Christian leaders, Christians are summoned by the story to be freed from slavery to wealth *and* from servile fear of God.[89]

15. Somewhat similar is the suggestion that the steward's release of debts is a symbolic act rejecting the provision of the *prosbul,* legislation to avoid the requirement of forgiving debts in the seventh year (Deut 15:1-2),[90] and asserting the priority of religious law over secular economic law.[91]

16. Some interpretations seek a grammatical or linguistic solution. Douglas Parrott concluded that something is wrong with the end of the parable and suggested it originally ended with a question expecting a negative answer such as, "And would the master have commended the dishonest steward for his cleverness?"[92]

A few scholars have suggested that *ek* in v. 9 does not mean "make friends *from* unrighteous *mammon,*" but, in keeping with the Aramaic word *min,* "make friends *apart from* (or *without*) unrighteous *mammon.*"[93]

Some of these suggestions are hardly believable. Via's suggestion that the parable is comic relief from dead seriousness — assumedly not made in jest — is an act of desperation. Flusser's suggestion that Jesus was arguing against Essene separation has little to commend it in that "sons of light" does not necessarily point to Essenes. Several studies, like that of Scott, while giving helpful information, become unclear and fail to show how the parable works to express the meaning they suggest. A parable with such an unclear and uncompelling message would not have been remembered, much less given a prominent place in the Gospel narative. Whatever else we say, we must remember that Luke thought this parable was of major and compelling significance.

Several of the suggestions are temporarily attractive — most scholars can make their case seem reasonable, but on reflection and after rereading the text, the arguments are often far less enticing. Often suggestions fit one feature of the parable, but do not deal with the whole story and do not show how the parable functions. In fact, it is relatively easy to raise objections to most of the solutions offered. J. Kloppenborg's suggestion that the parable is about the master's conversion to a new understanding of honor founders because no hint in the text suggests that the issue is the master's honor, and without some indication in this direction no reader could draw this conclusion. The same is true for the suggestion of irony; without some textual clue that irony is involved no reader will understand this.

N. T. Wright, in arguing that the steward's crisis is a figure of Israel's crisis, paints with too broad a brush. He can point to nothing in the parable to support his suggestion. That some parables involving masters and servants point to God and Israel does not mean that every such parable does.

Similarly the view that the parable is a biography of Jesus' own actions in forgiving sins cannot be accepted because it does not deal with all the parable. We could understand that Jesus might be accused of squandering forgiveness, but v. 2 would make no sense. What would it mean for Jesus to be put out of his stewardship by the master? If an accusation of squandering forgiveness were the point, would not the parable have the master defend the steward against the charge? Further, if forgiveness were the concern, would not the steward have forgiven the debts entirely?[94] Nothing in the parable encourages us to accept this view.

It is clear from this parable that interpreting parables does not mean assigning correspondences to the elements. The manager who praises wrongdoing hardly "represents" God, nor does the steward stand for anyone. The parable is an analogical argument, not an allegorical representation.

Is there a way forward, given the difficulty of the parable and the numerous suggestions?

Decisions on the Issues

1. *How are the legal/cultural circumstances of the parable to be understood?* The case for understanding the steward's actions as an honest reduction of his own profit or the removal of illegitimate interest (as suggested by Derrett and Fitzmyer) does not stand up to investigation,[95] nor is there any basis for seeing a symbolic act against the *prosbul*. That the man is called "the steward of unrighteousness"[96] in v. 8 suggests that it is his actions in vv. 5-7 that qualify him for this label, not his squandering of goods in v. 1. Given the very large amounts of the reductions (three years' wages), if the steward had been taking in such amounts as his own, he would hardly be in an immediate crisis, and further, in v. 5 the amounts are clearly owed to the master. Kloppenborg points out that standard interest rates do not match the amounts of reductions, so readers could not be expected to assume that the interest was being removed.[97] Most importantly, nothing in the text prepares the reader for such an assumption. From a literary standpoint no parable proceeds with information necessary for interpretation only implied. As du Plessis notes, "the reader can never be left in ignorance without paying the price of ending up with a warped interpretation. . . . Without any other information from the text the reader has to accept that the manager acted dishonestly. . . ."[98] His comment is a verification of the principle that an interpretation based on what is not there is almost certainly

wrong. That the debtors are told to act quickly (v. 6) adds to the conviction of dishonesty. We have a manager of an estate who cheats his master in order to ingratiate himself with his clients, and everyone — the master, the narrator, and the hearers — would consider him unrighteous.[99]

2. Where does the parable end and how do vv. 8b-13 relate to the parable? Suggestions for the end of the parable include v. 7, v. 8a, v. 8b, and v. 9. Some think v. 9 is the key to the parable's meaning and some that it distorts the parable's intent. Jeremias viewed vv. 8b-13 as several attempts to explain the parable, some view vv. 10-13 as sayings not directly related to the parable, and some view these same verses as originally belonging with vv. 1-9.

With regard to the end of the parable, possibly the issue is what one means with "end." If one means the end of the story, then v. 8a with its report of the master's response is the end, but if one includes the explanation of the parable, then vv. 8b-9 should be included. The suggestion that the parable concludes with v. 7 is unconvincing.[100] Without the response in v. 8a the parable has no resolution, and one does not know whether the steward's action was successful or abortive. Further, the parable began with a reference to a rich man who had a steward, and it would be strange if no further mention of the master were made. Probably the majority position is that the parable ends with v. 8a, but this too leaves the narrative incomplete, for one has no idea why this story was told or why anyone bothered to remember it. Both v. 8b and v. 9 are necessary to make the story work and are from Jesus. V. 8b is an explanatory comment showing the arena of the parable's relevance,[101] and v. 9 is the explanation that makes the application specific.

Decision at this point — for or against the inclusion of v. 9 — is crucial, for if this verse is included, the direction and intent of the parable are set. If only vv. 1-8a are included, most will argue that the parable is about wisdom in the eschatological crisis. If vv. 1-9 are accepted, most will accept that the parable has something to do with the wise use of material resources in view of the eschatological crisis. It is difficult to think that v. 9 ever circulated as an independent saying, given the ease with which it would be misunderstood *and* the way it has been formulated on vv. 4 and 8, the verses that give the steward's plan and the master's commendation.[102] Even if enigmatic, these words fit with the parable and nowhere else. If they are not original, they are Luke's explanation of the parable. Rather than being an anomaly, however, as several scholars argue, *v. 9 is the key to the parable.*[103] The words "And I tell you" at the beginning of v. 9 also are an argument for the inclusion of the verse. These words are a typical introduction for important sayings of Jesus and appear (with slight variations) particularly at the conclusions of parables in Matt 18:13; 21:43; 24:47/Luke 12:44; Luke 11:8; 14:24; 15:7, 10; 18:8. Further, v. 9 provides the elements to which the following verses connect.

The relation of vv. 10-13 to the parable is not as crucial for the under-standing of the parable, but certainly Luke did not view these sayings as at-tempts to counter or explain an embarrassing parable.[104] They are additional teachings on the same topic. Some argue that vv. 10-13 were originally attached to the parable,[105] which can neither be proven nor disproven, but three facts are evident. First, v. 13 uses "slave" *(oiketēs)*, not "steward" *(oikonomos)* as in the parable. Second, v. 13 is paralleled in Matt 6:24 without the accompanying para-ble and sayings in Luke 16:10-12. Therefore, v. 13 circulated independently in some contexts. Third, the sayings in vv. 10-13 are joined to v. 9 and each other through repetition of key words: "unrighteous," *"mammon,"* and "master." What is not obvious in Greek or English is that "faithful" *(pistos),* "entrust" *(pisteusei)* and "true" *(alēthinon)* in Hebrew and Aramaic all derive from the same root as *"mammon"* — assuming *mammon* means "that in which one places trust" and is derived from *'amen.* Bailey suggests a skillful play on words resonating through the whole section and expressed succinctly in v. 11:

> if therefore in the unrighteous *mammon*
> *'amen* you are not
> the *'emunah*
> who will *yeyminken?*[106]

Vv. 10-12 could be sayings joined together because of similar words, or they could have been a unit from the beginning. While one cannot be certain, it is likely that this unit and v. 13 were attached to the parable because of the words "unrighteous" and *"mammon."* (The latter occurs only in this context and in Matt 6:24.)

To summarize, the parable extends through v. 8a, and vv. 8b-9 are Jesus' explanation of the parable. The other sayings, because of shared terms, have been attached as commentary on the use of wealth.

3. *To whom does* kyrios *("master" or "Lord") refer in v. 8a?* Jeremias, fol-lowed by a few others, thought "master" in v. 8a should be understood of Jesus. He pointed to 18:6, where *kyrios* at the end of a parable clearly points to Jesus, and to the fact that seventeen other occurrences of *kyrios* in Luke's narrative re-fer to Jesus.[107] But what looks like a valid argument fades on closer inspection. "The Lord said" in 18:6 clearly stands outside the parable of the Unjust Judge, which is not the case with 16:8a, so it is no parallel. *Kyrios* is used with surpris-ing flexibility in Luke: of God, of Jesus, in the vocative with a range of mean-ings, and of human masters. In one verse (12:42) it is used in the narrative of Je-sus and in a parable of a human master. It is used of a human master in parabolic material twenty-two times, of which seven are in the vocative.[108] Of

the five other times *kyrios* occurs in a parable section without any qualifier (such as a genitive or a pronoun), three times it is of a master (12:37, 42b; 14:23) and two times of Jesus (12:42; 18:6). Most importantly, unlike 18:1-8, *kyrios* occurs twice of the master in this parable (vv. 3 and 5), and the hearer/reader has no indication of a shift in subject and would not hear it as a comment from Jesus. The description of the rich man and his comments in vv. 1-2 set up the expectation that he will reappear and give a judgment on the steward's actions.[109] Even if we have difficulty knowing why the master praises the steward, *kyrios* in v. 8a must refer to the master.

4. *Who is the focus of the parable, the steward or the master? Is the description of the master as rich intended to depict him negatively?* A few who see the master as the focus see him as gracious and kind,[110] but most who see the master as the focus view him negatively, at least until his "conversion" to a new sense of honor at the end. He is rich, which is understood to say he has defrauded others, and his judgment of the steward without trial is an indication of his caprice and injustice.[111] Issues of shame and honor were of paramount significance in the ancient world, and it is true that Luke is not sympathetic with the rich, to say the least. A glance at the parable of the Rich Man and Lazarus (16:19-31) shows what Luke wants to say to the rich — to say nothing of the woes to the rich in 6:24-26. Still, to argue that the parable is about the rich man, his insensitivity, and his resulting conversion or graciousness is to contort the parable in directions it was not intended to go. Not all rich people in Luke are condemned merely for being rich. One has only to think of the women who supported Jesus (8:3), the returning master (12:36-46), the banquet giver (14:16), the father of the prodigal (15:11-32), Zacchaeus, who is specifically called rich (19:1-10), and the nobleman who gives money to invest (19:11-27).[112] Nothing in the story suggests that the rich man should be viewed negatively or that he is the focus or that he is concerned with regaining honor.[113] If the issue were gaining honor by reducing debts, one wonders why the master was not smart enough to give away his money earlier! From space alone it is clear that the steward and his actions are the primary focus. The focus of the story must be seen in the steward, his actions, *and* the master's response to those actions.

5. *Why does the master (and why would Jesus) praise the servant for what appears to be a dishonest act?* This is by far the most difficult question. The text gives us no clues. Only two options exist: the steward is praised because he did something either just and effective or unjust *but* effective. We saw that theories which say the steward was reducing his own profit or the usurious amounts of the contracts are unjustified. His reduction of the debts was unjust but effective.

We would expect that he would be condemned. Caught in squandering, the steward's recourse is calculated fraud. There is nothing magnanimous or just about his action.[114] The master lost money from the events leading to the original charge,[115] and then lost more with the reductions. In the real world the steward more likely would have been indicted and punished, but parables are pseudo-realistic and stories like this *do* fit a pattern. At least part of the background against which the steward's shrewdness and the master's praise are to be understood is the parables, fables, and comedies of the ancient world. One has to think only of the shrewdness of Ahiqar, who escapes a death sentence and solves the riddles of the king of Egypt with subterfuge (subterfuge that would *not* be accepted in the real world). Mary Ann Beavis points to three stories in which Aesop is in trouble with a master or mistress and takes action to get the best of his superior.[116] More striking are the similarities to Greco-Roman comedies highlighted by B. Heininger, even though the comedies are much longer.[117] Here one finds stories with crisis situations, people wondering aloud what to do, solutions expressed via soliloquy, servants winning out over masters, and masters affirming their shrewdness. This is not to suggest any dependence on these writings but to point to a backdrop of popular stories and common motifs against which our parable may be understood. If so, the master praised the steward for his quick thinking, his shrewdness or wisdom, to insure his own future. No more is intended than that. If this is the case, we should not think the steward is throwing himself on the mercy of the master.

6. *What is the intent of vv. 8b-9?* I have argued, as others do, that the relevance of the story and the master's praise can only be understood with vv. 8b-9. V. 9 is difficult, but v. 8b is clear and shows the significance of the parable. With v. 8b Jesus marks off two arenas that operate in two different ways: this age and the generation of the children of light. Clearly the steward, a child of this age, and his actions belong in a different arena than the children of light. The words "with their own age" (NRSV "generation," *genea*) assume that another age exists. This implies an eschatological understanding of this age and the age to come. Since the children of light already exist and should be living according to their "generation," also implied is the presence of the coming age.[118] This fits with Jesus' eschatological teaching.[119] The praise of the children of this age, however, is an accusation against the children of light. The steward, as a child of this age, knew how to handle the system to his best advantage, but the children of light do not know how to live wisely within *their* "system." That is, they do not know how to live in keeping with the kingdom already present.

The language of v. 9 is unexpected and disorienting. Apart from its connection to the parable, the saying would be unintelligible. Three questions must be resolved: the intent of "make friends for yourselves by means of dishonest wealth [literally '*mammon* of unrighteousness']," "when it is gone [literally 'when it fails']," and "they may welcome you into eternal tabernacles."

Mammon can be a neutral word for money or property and is synonymous with the word for "property" *(ta hyparchonta)* in v. 1,[120] but often *mammon* carries a negative connotation.[121] But is "*mammon* of unrighteousness" money obtained by unrighteous means, merely money that belongs to this world (to the sphere of unrighteousness), or money that tends toward unrighteousness, that is, money that tends to corrupt? While a case can be made for all three options,[122] the last two have most in their favor and should be employed to yield what is intended, "money of this world, which tends to corrupt."[123] This is the assumed meaning in the verses that follow. In v. 11 "unrighteous *mammon*" is contrasted with "the true," that is, true wealth, which obviously points to eternal possessions not belonging to this world, but in v. 13 *mammon* is set up as a potential idol, hence its corrupting tendency. "Make friends for yourselves by means of the *mammon* of unrighteousness" then can only mean "make friends by your use of money, which is so easily put to wrong use."

With "when it is gone" three options exist: when the money is gone,[124] when life is gone (at death),[125] and when this age is gone (at the parousia). If the intent is when the money is gone, it would not be intended literally. Giving away money would not be the way to prepare for when the money is gone. "When the money is gone" would have to be a figurative way of referring to death or to the end of the age, that is, when worldly wealth is gone, when the possessions of this world come to an end.[126] The choice beween death and the end of the age makes little practical difference, for one has no options in either case. Given Luke's concern for what happens at the death of two rich men (12:20; 16:22), a reference to death cannot be excluded, but more likely the reference is to the end of the age.

As in Luke 12:20, the impersonal *"they"* in "they may welcome you" could refer to the poor or to angels[127] or could be a circumlocution for God. In one sense all three options point to the same thing. If the poor receive anyone into eternal tabernacles, they do so only as ones already received by God, and if the angels are intended, they are only representatives of God. As in 12:20 the likelihood is that we have a reference to God.[128]

The expression "eternal homes" or "eternal tents" *(aiōnious skēnas)* has little precedent and is odd enough to be suspected of being irony,[129] but that seems unlikely. The reference is to an eternal home with God. A few texts show similar ideas, especially Ps 61:4: "Let me abide in your tent forever."[130] In *T. Ab.* 20:14 Abraham is reported as taken into paradise, "where there are the tents of my righteous ones."[131]

By way of summary then, v. 9 may be paraphrased "Put yourself in a good position through your use of money, which so easily leads you astray, so that when this age is over God will receive you into his eternal dwelling."

7. *To whom is the parable addressed, the disciples as Luke indicates, Israel generally, or the Jewish leaders, in particular, the Pharisees?* To whom the parable is addressed is determined by decisions made about the extent of the parable. If the end is at v. 7 or v. 8a, the intent is enigmatic, and Luke's designation of the disciples as the addressees could be a result of his redaction. If one accepts only vv. 1-7 or 1-8a and interprets the parable generally in terms of the eschatological crisis, one could argue that Israel is addressed. The suggestion that the leaders of the people or specifically the Pharisees are addressed has little in its favor.[132] If vv. 1-9 comprise the parable, as I accept, then Luke's indication that the disciples are addressed makes good sense. They are the less wise children of light instructed about reception into eternal dwellings. However, we should not think that with "disciples" merely the twelve are in mind. Luke tells us that large crowds were traveling with Jesus (14:25) and that the tax collectors and sinners were coming to hear him (15:1). The rest of the Gospel tradition shows how important teaching about possessions was for Jesus, and it would be incredulous that he did not teach the broader group of disciples on this topic.

8. *How does this parable function and what is its intent?* Any attempt to treat the parable as if it were an allegory with the rich man representing God and the steward representing the disciples or some other group fails. While there are correspondences, this is an analogy, not an allegory. The decision and actions in one arena are analogous to those in another arena.

Most agree that this is a crisis parable. Jesus' eschatological preaching presented a crisis to his hearers generally and to his disciples in particular. Like the parables of the Friend at Midnight and the Unjust Judge this is a "how much more" parable that makes its point *by a contrast.* Just as the steward acted in his world to safeguard his well-being, how much more in this eschatological crisis should Jesus' hearers act to safeguard their own eternal well-being. Dishonesty is no more endorsed than is rudeness with the Friend at Midnight or lack of respect for God and people with the Unjust Judge. What is commended is action born of wisdom in view of the crisis, similar to the parable of the Treasure in the Field. While some think the parable speaks generally of wisdom in the time of crisis and that it has been adapted to the issue of money,[133] these concerns do not have to be and should not be separated. The point is indeed the ability of the steward to deal with a crisis,[134] but specifically ability in dealing with money. The parable is about the wise use of possessions *in view of the eschatological crisis.* As is often noted, wisdom language in the Gospels most often connotes eschatological awareness,[135] but eschatological awareness impacts how one views material possessions. Wisdom calls for using wealth astutely in view of the presence of the kingdom and of coming judgment. In other words, money is to be used wisely, given kingdom economics, rather than for self-centered purposes. Giving alms is not the explicit concern,[136] and in fact the expression "giving alms" is too weak to convey what Jesus intends. However we express it, showing mercy with money is an obvious application of the parable, and this idea is buttressed both by the placement of the parable near that of the Rich Man and Lazarus and by the similarity of v. 9 to 12:33 ("Sell your possessions and give to the poor; make purses for yourselves that do not wear out, inexhaustible treasure in heaven . . .").

The complaint has been made that v. 9 sounds like life insurance and that philanthropy motivated by self-interest hardly fits with Jesus' teaching,[137] but the complaint is illegitimate. "Self-interest" deserves reflection. Nothing happens without self-interest. The question is whether the self-interest is short-sighted and self-centered or true self-interest from an eternal perspective. Jesus calls for radical self-renunciation, but only because in denying self one truly finds self (Matt 16:25-26/Mark 8:35-37/Luke 9:24-25). Without reading the parable in a crass way, like the rest of Scripture it assumes that positive and negative judgment by God are determined by obedience to the will of the Father.

The parable seeks to motivate action. The word "do" *(poieō)* has prominence throughout: vv. 3, 4, 8, and 9 (English "make"). Like the steward, the hearer should ask, "What shall I do?" and then plan and act wisely in using possessions in a way consonant with the kingdom.

Several secondary overtones exist that should not be ignored. The release from debts and the master's praise contain an implicit message that forgiving debts is a good thing and that one should not be so tied to money that this is impossible (cf. Luke 4:18-21 with its allusions to Jubilee). Also, something negative is said about money as that which has only temporary value. A day will come when it has no value, so one should use it wisely now.[138]

Adapting the Parable

The accusation is still painfully true that the people of this age are wiser in their arena than the "children of light" are in theirs. Is it because with one eye on this age and one eye on the kingdom — a necessary split vision — we allow ourselves to be determined more by our age than Christ's kingdom? Christians are dominated by the same concerns as the rest of society, but Jesus' teaching is intended to give us a different set of concerns.

This parable cannot be implemented without an eschatological awareness, the wisdom that the parable seeks to elicit. If the kingdom is in some sense present and if judgment is a reality, both implicit in the parable, then actions and life stances must be determined by the kingdom and an awareness of the necessity of giving account of our stewardship of all of life and especially of our possessions.

The parable conveys the urgency that was present in Jesus' ministry. The sense of urgency was different even in the early church, to say nothing of today, but that a sense of urgency accompanies life and discipleship is still true. The parable gives no easy answers about what to do with money; it compels reflection concerning what wise, kingdom-conditioned use of possessions means. Sermons often address stewardship and giving, as indeed they should. A pastor who begs off preaching on stewardship emaciates Jesus' teaching. But churches and individuals rarely actually *discuss* or hold the community accountable for responsible, kingdom-driven decisions regarding possessions. Such discussions would lead to the reduction of hoarding and consumerism, change how we view and attain security, enable various ministries, and relieve the plight of the poor. Economic decisions are not easy, but the church should not only lead the way but demonstrate by its use of money the reality of its gospel.

Once again the subject of works-righteousness may suggest itself, but only because we have distorted the subjects of faith and obedience. In Jesus' teaching obedience to the will of the Father determines eternal destiny and earns approval. The idea of faith without such obedience is nonsense.

For Further Reading

Kenneth Ewing Bailey, *Poet and Peasant: A Literary Cultural Approach to the Parables in Luke* (Grand Rapids: Eerdmans, 1976), pp. 86-118.

C.-S. Abraham Cheong, *A Dialogic Reading of The Steward Parable (Luke 16:1-9)* (Studies in Biblical Literature 28; New York: Peter Lang, 2001).

J. Duncan M. Derrett, "The Parable of the Unjust Steward," *Law in the New Testament* (London: Darton, Longman & Todd, 1970), pp. 48-77.

Joseph A. Fitzmyer, "The Story of the Dishonest Manager," in *Essays on the Semitic Background of the New Testament* (Missoula: Scholars, 1974), pp. 161-84.

Herman Hendrickx, *The Parables of Jesus* (San Francisco: Harper & Row, 1986), pp. 170-97.

Richard H. Hiers, "Friends by Unrighteous Mammon: The Eschatological Proletariat (Luke 16:9)," *JAAR* 38 (1970): 30-36.

Dennis J. Ireland, *Stewardship and the Kingdom of God: An Historical, Exegetical, and Contextual Study of the Parable of the Unjust Steward in Luke 16:1-13* (NovTSup 70; Leiden: Brill, 1992).

Michael Krämer, *Das Rätsel der Parabel vom ungerechten Verwalter, Lk 16,1-13: Auslegungsgeschichte — Umfang — Sinn. Eine Diskussion der Probleme und Lösungsvorschläge der Verwaltereparabel von den Vätern bis heute* (BiblScRel 5; Zurich: PAS, 1972).

Stanley E. Porter, "The Parable of the Unjust Steward (Luke 16:1-13): Irony *is* the Key," in *The Bible in Three Dimensions,* ed. David J. A. Clines, et al. (Sheffield: JSOT, 1990), 127-53.

THE RICH MAN AND LAZARUS
(Luke 16:19-31)

The uniqueness of this parable is self-evident. Only here do characters within the parable have names, and only here does a parable from Jesus transcend everyday reality to focus on the afterlife.[139]

Parable Type

This is a single indirect, two-stage narrative parable that serves as a warning. No transfer to some other subject is required. This is one of the four stories traditionally labeled an "example story," but the inappropriateness of the label is evident. We are not told enough about the actions of either the rich man or Lazarus for either actually to be an example. By implication the rich man is a negative example, but that has to be deduced. The story merely begins and ends; there is no application or explanation and no transition from the previous or to the following sayings.[140]

Issues Requiring Attention[141]

1. Is this a parable?
2. What is the origin of this story, and what relevance does the story's origin have for interpretation?
3. Is there any relation to John 11?
4. How is the structure of the original parable to be understood? Was the original story only vv. 19-26 with vv. 27-31 being a later Christian addition pointing to the resurrection of Jesus and the failure of Jews to believe? Are the textual variants in v. 31 significant?
5. What is the primary focus?
6. What significance does Lazarus have?

7. What is the basis for the judgment that sends the rich man to Hades and Lazarus to Abraham's bosom?
8. What is the parable's teaching — if anything — about life after death, the "intermediate state," and judgment? What can be known about beliefs in first-century Judaism concerning the afterlife? Specifically, what does *ḥadēs* really mean?
9. What is the parable's teaching about attitudes and actions concerning wealth and poverty?

Helpful Primary Source Material

Canonical Material (in addition to the texts listed under the two previous parables)

- OT: Deut 30:11-13; 1 Sam 28:7-19; Pss 49; 73; Isa 58:6-7; Ezek 32:21-30
- NT: Matt 3:8-10/Luke 3:8-9; Luke 1:51-53; 6:20-25; 11:41; 12:29-33; 1 Tim 6:6-10, 17-19; Jas 1:9-11; 2:5-7; 5:1-6

Early Jewish Writings

- Beginning in Wisdom 2 and extending for several chapters is a contrast between the judgment of the unrighteous and the righteous; the souls of the latter are in the hand of God (3:1).
- *1 En.* 22:1-14 reports that Enoch was taken to a place with four corners[142] where the souls of the dead *await* judgment. The righteous are separated by a spring of water with light from three categories of sinners: those on whom judgment was not enacted during their lives, those with accusations to bring concerning their deaths, and those who collaborated with the lawless.[143]
- *1 En.* 103:5–104:6 warns wealthy sinners who are unpunished in life that they will experience evil, tribulation, darkness, and burning flame in Sheol. The righteous who have been afflicted in life are told not to focus on their plight but on their hope, for the windows of heaven will be opened for them. Cf. 98:1-3.
- 1QS 4.11-14: "And the visitation of those who walk in it [the paths of darkness] will be for a glut of punishments at the hands of all the angels of destruction, for eternal damnation, for the scorching wrath of the God of revenge, for permanent error and shame without end with the humiliation of destruction by the fire of the dark regions. And all the ages of their

generations they shall spend in bitter weeping and harsh evils in the abysses of darkness until their destruction, without there being a remnant or a survivor among them." Cf. 2.4-8, which refers to the gloom of everlasting fire; for other passages on judgment see 5.12-13; 1QpHab 10.12-13; 4Q542 2.8.

- Tob 4:10: "For almsgiving delivers from death and keeps you from going into the Darkness."
- *4 Ezra* 7:36: "Then the pit of torment shall appear, and opposite it shall be the place of rest; and the furnace of Hell shall be disclosed, and opposite it the Paradise of delight. Then the Most High will say to the nations that have been raised from the dead. . . . Look on this side and on that; here are delight and rest, and there are fire and torments! Thus he will speak to them on the day of judgment. . . ."
- *4 Ezra* 7:75-99: In response to his question whether rest and torment occur immediately at death, Ezra is told that the spirits of the unrighteous do not enter "habitations" but wander in torments and confusion. The righteous receive rest and are gathered into chambers waiting the glory of the last days. Part of the torment of the unrighteous is that they can see the reward of those who trusted the covenant, and part of the rest of the righteous is that they can see the perplexity of the ungodly and their future torment. Cf. 8:59 and *4 Macc* 13:17.
- *Testament of Judah* 18:2–19:1 says that sexual promiscuity and love of money — among other things — distance one from God's Law, blind the soul, and do not permit a person to show mercy to his neighbor. Love of money leads to idolatry. Money makes anyone who has it go out of his mind.[144]
- *Pss. of Sol.* 14:6-10 says that the enjoyment of sinners is brief, but their inheritance is Hades and darkness and destruction. The devout inherit life in happiness. See also 15:10.
- *T. Ab.* tells of Abraham's refusal to surrender his soul to Michael the angel until he is given a tour of the inhabited world (9:1-8). On seeing the sin in the world he calls down death on people, but out of compassion God stops the tour (10:1-15). Abraham is then shown the future joy of the righteous and the judgment that awaits the sinful so that he will repent of his harshness. With this knowledge Abraham intercedes for those he has caused to die, and they are restored. At his death Abraham is conducted to heaven by angels (chs. 11–20).
- *L.A.B.* 33 reports Deborah's deathbed warning that repentance after death is not possible, her plea for reform in the light of the Law, and the rejection of the idea that the fathers are a source of hope unless one has lived like them.

- *Jannes and Jambres* 24afp reports that Jannes' "shade" (his death existence) returned from Hades to warn Jambres of the burning and darkness and to do good.

Greco-Roman Writings

- An Egyptian story from the mid-first century tells of Setme, who observes the elaborate funeral procession of a rich man and the absence of any procession for a poor man being carried to the graveyard. He thinks the rich are much better off, but his son Si-Osire (a reincarnated deliverer) expresses the desire that Setme at his death will experience what the poor man did. Setme's grief at this statement is set aside when Si-Osire takes him on a tour of the realm of the dead. Setme sees an elegantly dressed man seated close by the god Osiris; it is the poor man dressed in the rich man's clothes, and he is so honored because his good deeds were more numerous than his sins and he was not compensated on earth. The rich man, however, had more sins than good deeds and is punished by having a hinge-pin from the gate to the realm of the dead left in his right eye. Whoever is good on earth, to that person the underworld is also good, and for whoever is evil on earth, it goes badly there.[145]
- Plato, *Republic* 10.614B-616A tells of a soldier named Er who was killed but after twelve days revived, saying he was sent back to tell people about the world beyond. He saw two openings[146] in the earth and two in heaven, between which judges sit and direct the righteous to the right and up to heaven and the unjust to the left and down to punishments below the earth. (These assignments are not permanent.)
- Plutarch, *Divine Vengeance* 563D-568 similarly tells of one Aridaeus who died and was revived after three days. While he saw some joyful souls, most of the description is of those who are being punished, especially those who suffered no punishment during life.[147] In Plutarch's *Sign of Socrates* 590C-591C Timarchus's soul departs and sees islands, a sea, and two openings receiving rivers of fire. He also sees a great abyss[148] filled with darkness, wailings, and lamentations.
- In several works Lucian describes journeys to Hades either in dreams or by someone later resuscitated. Most relevant is *Cataplus,* which tells of Charon ferrying the dead to Hades and contrasts the fates of Megapenthes, a rich tyrant, and Micyllus, a poor cobbler. Micyllus lived next door to Megapenthes and observed his purple clothing, his luxury, and his feasting. Micyllus is not punished, but Megapenthes, rather than being thrown in the burning river, like Tantalus is chained and not allowed

to drink the water that all the dead drink.[149] *Dialogues of the Dead* 1.328-35 tells of Pollux returning from the dead to invite the philosopher Menippus to come down to observe the humiliation and punishment of the rich and assure the poor that all are equal after death.[150] *Menippus* tells of a philosopher by this name who while alive descended to Hades through a chasm and observed "the Lake, the River of Burning Fire, and the palace of Pluto" (10). He saw the rich singled out for harsh punishment (11-12), but the poor deserving punishment received half as much punishment (14). The dead pass a resolution condemning the rich, punishing their bodies, and consigning their souls to enter into donkeys for 250,000 years (20).

Later Jewish Writings

- *y. Sanhedrin* 6.6 (23c)/*y. Ḥagigah* 2.2 (77d) see above, p. 303: These parallel accounts are one of seven Jewish versions of the story of a scholar and Bar Ma'yan the tax collector and their fates after death.[151]
- *Exod. Rab.* 31.5 tells of the reversal of the rich and the poor in the world to come. In this world the wicked are rich and prosperous and secure, while the righteous are poor. In the world to come God will open the treasures of paradise for the righteous, but the wicked who have profited from interest and usury will bite their own flesh.
- *Ruth Rab.* 3.3 describes two wicked men, one of whom repented before death and ends in the company of the righteous. The other ends in woe in the company of the unrighteous and can see his friend but cannot change his fate.
- *Midr. Ps.* 46.1 says that those who trusted in their wealth are punished, that Abraham cannot deliver the wicked, and that the righteous see the wicked in torment.

Textual Features Worthy of Attention

This parable is one of four two-stage parables (the others are the Wedding Feast in Matthew, the Prodigal Son, and the parable of the Pounds in Luke).

The contrasts and spatial imagery in the parable are striking. The pictures of the two men and their fates are carefully balanced. The gate at which Lazarus was laid deserves emphasis and reflection.[152] The rich man lives luxuriously and in honor on one side of the gate and Lazarus miserably on the other, a gate that could have been an opening to help Lazarus and that mirrors the chasm between the men after death.[153] In the reversal the rich man is miserable on one side of the chasm and Lazarus is in a place of comfort and honor, but the chasm cannot be crossed. Formerly the rich man banqueted every day; after death Lazarus presumably is at the eschatological banquet. Lazarus's misery is paralleled by the rich man's misery after the reversal. Both futilely desire merely a small thing to alleviate pain, and both endure physical pain and torment. The rich man and Abraham both make three remarks; by coincidence each speaks a total of sixty-nine words. Abraham's responses to the rich man are rather dismissive.

A reversal of fortunes appears earlier in Luke 1:52-53. The advice in 3:11 and 14:13-14 to share with the poor and the blessings on the poor and woes on the rich in 6:20-21, 24-25 anticipate the concerns of the parable.

Luke 13:28-30, with its focus on the patriarchs, the eschatological banquet, and the reversal of fortunes, is almost a presupposition of the parable.

Several "hooks" exist between this parable and that of the Prodigal Son.[154] Both Lazarus and the prodigal in distress desire to be filled (15:16: *epithymei chortasthēnai;* 16:21: *epithymōn chortasthēnai*). Both have contact with impure animals. A celebration (*euphrainesthai* in 15:23, 24, 29, 32) occurs at the return of the prodigal, while with a quite different intent the rich man celebrates luxuriously every day (*euphrainesthai* in 16:19). Such "hooks" do not mean that the phrases or the parables mean the same thing, but they assist hearers. Some people suggest that Abraham parallels the father in the story of the prodigal and that the five brothers parallel the elder brother of the prodigal. Some draw parallels with the parable of the Good Samaritan, which also has a person in need and the negative example of those who do not help. In neither case does the suggestion have merit.

Those who accept C. F. Evans's theory about the structure of Deuteronomy shaping Luke's travel narrative would place Luke 16:19–18:8 opposite Deut 24:6–25:3, which partly deals with relations to the poor (cf. Deut 15:1-11).[154]

Those who accept that Luke's travel narrative is a chiasmus drawn from an earlier parables source place this parable in relation to 12:13-21 (the teaching on greed and the parable of the Rich Fool).[155]

Vv. 14-18 sit rather awkwardly between two parables about money. They appear to be random sayings with no close relation to the two parables. A closer look shows that the only verse without direct relation is v. 18, which deals with divorce. The story of the Rich Man and Lazarus demonstrates the validity of both vv. 14-15 and vv. 16-17. What humans value so highly — money and luxurious living — is abominable to God (vv. 14-15), and the Law and the prophets are still valid for the rich man's brothers, even though the kingdom has arrived.[156]

The two parables in Luke 16 are closely related. The behavior of the rich man is the opposite of that of the unjust steward.[157] Compare 16:9 and 26: the rich man failed to "make friends with unrighteous mammon" and cannot be received in the eternal dwellings.

Cultural Information

Numerous texts attest to linen and purple clothing as marks of luxurious living, particularly fitting for royalty and those proud of their wealth.[158] Purple was rare and expensive because of the difficult process of obtaining the best dye from marine snails.

The food that fell from the rich man's table is not food that fell accidentally, but pieces of bread used to wipe the hands that were then thrown under the table.[159]

Both Lazarus's running sores and the dogs licking his sores would have rendered him ritually impure. The dogs were not household pets helping him, but scavengers seeking nourishment.

Many Jews would assume that the rich man was blessed by God and that the poor man was cursed (cf. John 9:2 and Job). Burial was extremely important in the ancient world,[160] and not being buried was viewed as a sign of God's curse. Lazarus's burial is not mentioned, but his reception in Abraham's bosom subverts any thought that he is cursed.[161] His name, which means "God helps," would as well, if readers knew of the name's significance.[162] It is a shortened form of the name Eliezer (or Eleazar), the name of Abraham's servant in Gen 15:2.

The bosom of Abraham is clearly an image of honor and may also point to intimacy (as in John 1:18), but most likely Luke intends his reader to think of the eschatological banquet (13:28-30) and of Lazarus having the place of honor at the table next to Abraham (cf. John 13:23).[163]

Explanation of the Parable

Options for Interpretation

1. This parable was allegorized less than most other parables. Augustine and Gregory the Great, as might be expected, were the chief allegorizers. The most significant points in the allegorizing are finding in the relation between the rich man and Lazarus the relation between Jews and Gentiles (with the five brothers mirroring the five books of the Law) and in seeing the sores as confession. In another allegory Augustine views Lazarus as a Christ figure. Perhaps the strangest allegorical identification is Ambrose's interpretation of Lazarus as Paul.[164]

2. From the earliest days interpreters have focused on the parable's moral impact with its denunciation of the wealthy who neglect the poor. Other options are minority opinions. Possibly the most vigorous use of the parable is by John Chrysostom, who preached seven sermons on it within a relatively brief period.[165] In modern critical studies most interpreters still see the parable as denouncing the misuse of resources and the neglect of the poor.

3. A few argue that the parable is about what is happening in Jesus' ministry. The welcome of the poor into Abraham's bosom was taking place in Jesus' welcome of sinners and was a sign that the return from exile, resurrection, was taking place. The parable is a warning then for Pharisees (or Israel more generally) to repent.[166]

4. J. Crossan removes the parable from its context, accepts only vv. 19-26, and says that Jesus was not interested in moral instruction about riches. For him the parable is about the reversal that comes with the kingdom's advent.[167]

It is hard to imagine any approach other than the second doing justice to the parable.[168]

Decisions on the Issues

1. *Is this a parable?* Preachers and certain people throughout church history sometimes have asserted that this story is not a parable but depicts real people and the consequences of their lives.[169] I am not aware of any modern scholar who would agree.[170] Certainly Luke viewed this as a parable. It appears in a collection of parables, possibly stands chiastically parallel to the parable of the Rich Fool,[171] and uses the exact same introductory words *(anthrōpos tis)* which Luke uses to introduce several other parables.[172] This is without question a parable.[173]

The identification of the persons addressed with this parable is not as crucial as elsewhere. Luke may have had the Pharisees in mind (v. 14), but that is not certain. We should probably think of a double audience of both disciples and Pharisees,[174] but the absence of any indication of the audience may be intentional to make the parable universal in application.[175]

2. *What is the origin of this story and what relevance does the story's origin have for interpretation?* Joachim Jeremias made popular Hugo Gressmann's suggestion that this parable has its origin in the Egyptian story of Setme,[176] but when one looks at all the data, this is unlikely. There were dozens of stories in various cultures over thousands of years that tell of trips to the realm of the dead, often castigating the rich.[177] Stories like the *Gilgamesh Epic,* the *Odyssey,* and *1 Enoch* had broad influence, and numerous Greek and Jewish stories tell of the experiences of various heroes and average people who visit the realm of the

dead.[178] One cannot preclude that the Egyptian story made its way to Palestine and that Jesus adapted and modified it. Such usage of preexisting materials is evident in other parables and would not be surprising. In this case, though, such a theory is unlikely and unnecessary, especially when the Gospel story is so different from the Egyptian and Jewish accounts.[179] The Gospel story uses common folkloric motifs shared by several cultures: descent to the underworld, reversal of circumstances, and denunciation of the rich for their neglect of the poor.[180] Lucian's use of these themes in a variety of works, although from the second century A.D., shows how futile it is to think of even indirect dependence on a specific account. As several recent studies have concluded, it is neither convincing, helpful, nor necessary to argue for the dependence of the Gospel parable on some other account.[181] This decision will have impact on other issues, particularly that of the unity of the story.

3. Is there any relation to John 11? Several studies have suggested that the parable emerges from the account of the raising of Lazarus in John 11 or that the raising of Lazarus is a historicizing of the parable.[182] Such theories are not surprising given that both accounts tell of a man named Lazarus who died and both have to do with resurrection and belief, but such arguments are forced. The similarities are superficial, and Lazarus was a very common name. Further, the account in John 11 reports the very incident — resurrection — that the parable precludes. Neither account should be explained on the basis of the other.[183]

4. How is the structure of the original parable to be understood? Was the original story only vv. 19-26 with vv. 27-31 being a later Christian addition pointing to the resurrection of Jesus and the failure of Jews to believe? Are the textual variants in v. 31 significant?

Quite common among critical studies is the assumption that the structure of the original story included only vv. 19-26 and that vv. 27-31 are either Jesus' addition to a traditional story or a later Christian addition pointing to the resurrection of Jesus. This division derives partly from the assumption that the origin of the parable is found in the Egyptian account of Setme discussed above and partly from R. Bultmann's argument that the two halves of the parable stand in conflict with each other.[184] The problem of the Jews not believing in the resurrection of Jesus and similarities between vv. 27-31 and the resurrection story in Luke 24 are seen as further evidence that this latter section is a Christian addition.[185] We should add that Bultmann thought the *whole* story was too Jewish and had been placed in Jesus' mouth, whereas a few others would see either the first half as too Jewish or the second half as too Christian.[186]

Even apart from the strangeness of the argument that the parable is too Jewish, the attempt to separate vv. 19-26 from vv. 27-31 is misguided. The parable is not dependent on the story of Setme (or any other earlier account) and cannot be conformed to it. The two halves of the parable do not conflict, and the similarities with Luke 24 are superficial.[187] Recent studies tend to argue for the unity of the parable because of comparison with other descent stories and especially because of literary analyses, none of which divide the story merely into two sections separated at v. 26, for *that is in the middle of the dialogue* between the rich man and Abraham.

The theme of vv. 27-31, the revelation of the fate of the dead to the living, is found in many stories, including the story of Setme and its Jewish counterpart, *Jannes and Jambres,* and several Greek accounts.[188] One would expect such a continuation of the story. If the narrative ended at v. 26, the story would be left incomplete.

Recent literary analyses divide the parable into *three* parts, not two: vv. 19-21, vv. 22-23, and vv. 24-31. The parable provides two snapshots (before and after) and a dialogue. This approach preserves the unity of the dialogue, a unity which is evidenced by the parallels between v. 24 and v. 27.[189]

Both the reversal of fortunes of rich and poor and the motif of the revelation of the fate of the dead, sometimes even by resuscitation, fit the genre of stories of travel to the realm of the dead. Therefore, the mention of resurrection and disbelief do not automatically point to Jesus' resurrection or show that vv. 27-31 are secondary any more than the description of the prodigal as dead and living again (*anazēsen,* 15:24) is secondary. Also relevant to the discussion of the resurrection is the textual variant in v. 31, which is often ignored (including by the UBS Greek text). The Freer manuscript (W) has "go *(apelthē)* from the dead," not "rise *(anastē)* from the dead," and a similar reading is evidenced in old Latin and old Syriac manuscripts. This reading parallels *poreuthē* ("go") in v. 30, and some argue that it is original.[190] "Go from the dead" is not Christian resurrection language, and, if this is the correct reading, the mention of the resurrection in some manuscripts of v. 31 is a secondary christological enhancement. However, I do not think the originality of the Freer reading can be proven or, if it is not, that the mention of rising from the dead discounts vv. 27-31 as a later reference to Jesus' resurrection.[191] The idea of return from the dead fits the story pattern well, even though the parable actually rejects the possibility of a return from the dead (v. 26).[192] A secondary allusion to Christ's resurrection seems to be intended by Luke, however, given Acts 28:23-24, which tells of Paul trying to convince Jews in Rome concerning Jesus from Moses and the prophets, with some persuaded but some disbelieving.

5. What is the primary focus? The discussion about the primary focus of the parable is somewhat pedantic, for all the components are necessary. Jeremias argued that as in all two-pronged parables the second part of the parable (vv. 27-31) is the primary focus,[193] but surely this is an abuse of the rule of end stress. Must we not say that at least two themes of the parable — judgment for the use of wealth and the sufficiency of the Scriptures — are equally important? So much attention is given by the story to the descriptions of the rich man and Lazarus and their reversals that the first part of the parable cannot be accorded secondary status.

The question of focus appears in a different way with those who isolate either the rich man or Lazarus as the chief character. Certainly the story is told from the perspective of the rich man. He is mentioned first, has a major speaking role, and his concerns initiate both halves of the dialogue. With good reason some call this the parable of the Six Brothers.[194] Lazarus neither acts nor speaks; other than desiring something to eat, he is a passive character. Still, he is not secondary, and more attention is given to describing him and his death than to the rich man and his death.[195] The truth is that all the characters are important, and none should be pushed to the background.

6. What significance does Lazarus have? Just what significance should be accorded Lazarus and the fact that he and Abraham are the only persons named in all Jesus' parables?[196] The name Lazarus may have been desirable to facilitate the dialogue (although other parabolic dialogues occur without names), may have been inherent in the genre of "descents,"[197] or may have been necessary to prevent the reversal pattern being applied to all poor people.[198] While these options merit consideration, the name probably has, if not a different purpose, at least an additional purpose. "Lazarus" is a shortened version of ʾEliʿezer or ʾElʿāzār, both of which mean "God helps." If we can presume that this meaning was understood by the hearers of the parable, then it signifies God's identification with the poor and does not permit the hearer to think Lazarus is cursed because of his condition. He is poor and miserable, but God is still on his side.[199]

7. What is the basis for the judgment that sends the rich man to Hades and Lazarus to Abraham's bosom? One of the most bothersome aspects of this parable is that the basis for the judgment of the two men is not made explicit. We expect some justification for the fate of the two men, but this "neglect" is intentional and increases the confrontational power of the story, particularly when many hearers might have assumed that the rich man was blessed and that Lazarus's misery was some form of punishment. On the other hand, an implied censure of the rich man would exist for some in the description that he is rich and banquets luxuriously every day,[200] but one must resist the idea that the parable presupposes that Lazarus has faith or any moral advantage. That is just not the concern of the parable, and we must remember that parables are vignettes, not systems, and certainly not systematic theologies. This is not a literal description of how judgment will take place. No reason is given for Lazarus's positive fate, a narrative move that engages the reader. At least though, the parable must be understood as expressing God's identification with the poor.[201]

The reversal of the conditions of the two men fits with the reversals in so many other parables of Jesus, and some see the explanation of the reversal in v. 25 as the basis for judgment.[202] More, however, needs to be said, at least for the rich man. The fact that he wants his brothers to repent (v. 30) shows that he recognizes his own error. Surely his judgment is based on the *injustice of the juxtaposition* of his wealth and Lazarus's poverty and his *neglect* to do anything about it.[203] The rich man's error is precisely that of those on the left in the parable of the Sheep and the Goats: neglect of the poor and those in need. Only in *hạdēs* does the rich man raise his eyes to see, but even there his concern is only for his own kind, his brothers. The parable forces the understanding that Lazarus, the child of Abraham, was also his brother and should have been the object of his concern.[204] An *intent* to allude to Cain's question "Am I my brother's keeper?" (Gen 4:9) is probably not justified,[205] but the parable *does* answer the question.

The parable also attacks another error. Certainly lurking behind the story are a false sense of election and the conviction that no descendant of Abraham could be lost.[206] That the rich man calls Abraham "father" and Abraham calls him "child" creates an oxymoron: a child of Abraham is in the place of torment. In this way the parable reinforces the warning in Matt 3:8-10/Luke 3:8-9 that no one should presume to say "We have Abraham as father." Rather, the children of Abraham are those who obey Moses and the prophets and share their wealth with the poor.[207]

8. What is the parable's teaching — if anything — about life after death, the "intermediate state," and judgment? What can be known about beliefs in first-century Judaism concerning the afterlife? Specifically, what does hạdēs really mean? When we turn our attention to what the parable teaches about life after death, in most scholarly treatments we find the caution that the parable is not intended to give a description of life after death. This caution is both necessary and true and must be emphasized, but how do we know the parable does not teach about the future life?[208] It would be as foolish to ignore the parable's relevance for future eschatology as it would be to think it presented a picture of the actual state of affairs. The use of folkloric themes and the fact that this is a parable with an intent other than teaching about the future life should warn against taking the picture too literally, and conformity with the rest of Luke's teaching (and the NT) on the future life would seem required for any conclusions.

The problem of understanding the biblical material on life after death is much more problematic than most Christians are aware. We know far less, and Scripture is far less clear, than most think. Conclusions have been based on very little evidence, and it is only fair to say we have been influenced more by Greco-Roman and medieval ideas than by Scripture. The English word "hell" has much more substance than Greek *geenna* or *hadēs,* to say nothing of Hebrew *šĕ'ôl.* Part of the problem is that words are taken over from the OT, Judaism, and the Greco-Roman world, but a variety of meanings was present for those words. Further, the words occur infrequently enough that no clear ideas emerge. What content do we pour into these words to understand the biblical texts and from where did we get that content?

Hebrew *šĕ'ôl* refers to the place of the dead, but most times does not appear to mean anything more than "the grave" or "death."[209] Israel's neighbors did not use this word to describe life after death, and the OT gives almost no information about *šĕ'ôl* other than that it is down, dark, and silent. *Hadēs,* the word the LXX typically uses to translate *šĕ'ôl,* referred in Greek thought first to the god of the underworld and then to the place. Various descriptions of the place of the dead appear in Greek writings, and especially in Judaism a variety of eschatological conceptions is attested from *1 Enoch* on.[210] Sometimes the places of both punishment and reward are in the heavens, and sometimes both the wicked and the righteous are in *hadēs* — note that Jesus is assumed to be in *hadēs* in Acts 2:27.[211] Should we, like some, assume that "Abraham's bosom" is in *hadēs* or merely that the rich man is in *hadēs* while Abraham and Lazarus are in paradise and that people can see from one side to the other? Early on, *hadēs* was not so much a place of punishment as a place where people are detained until judgment day. Later, as in this parable, it is a place where punishment is already taking place. The NT uses *hadēs* infrequently and without description — other than in the present text — but, much like *šĕ'ôl* in the OT, of both the grave (Acts 2:27, 31) and the place of the dead.

The other word for the place of judgment is *geenna,* a word adapted from Hebrew *gē hinnom,* the valley of Hinnom outside Jerusalem, which had been a site of child sacrifice (2 Kgs 23:10) and was made a pit for burning garbage. Jeremias assures us that the NT distinguishes between *hadēs* as one's location during the intermediate state and *geenna* as the place of punishment after the final judgment,[212] but this distinction is not verifiable. In the NT *hadēs* only occurs ten times and *geenna* only twelve, with virtually no details to explain the reference in any case.[213] Further, occasionally in later writings *geenna* and *šĕ'ôl* are used synonymously.[214]

Further caution against taking the details about *hadēs* in this parable literally is evident in the character of texts talking about tours of hell. Especially for the Jewish writings many function as theodicies that warn of future judgment. The frequent assumption that the righteous and the evil can see the bliss or punishment of each other is necessary to demonstrate to each that justice has prevailed but is a terrible reality if taken literally.[215] Often precisely the documents making this point realize how awful such a reality would be and have a righteous person offer prayers for mercy to end the punishment.[216] In the parable no plea for mercy appears, and the ability to see across the divide is necessary for the story to emphasize the judgment and its finality and to allow the rich man to ask that Lazarus be allowed to warn his brothers. The nature of the story does not allow it to be taken as an actual description of the future life.[217]

Another fact is relevant. The parable asserts that no one in *hạdēs* is allowed to return to earth, a conviction often repeated,[218] but this rejects the whole idea of information being brought back to those still alive. For Bauckham this means that the parable uses the motif of a return in order to reject it and subverts its own revelation of the places of the dead.[219] This could be countered only by saying that Jesus with divine knowledge intended to convey such information with the parable, but that is not the parable's intent. Rather, the parable uses these folkloric motifs to make its point concerning the use of wealth.

Another question that arises is whether the parable depicts the intermediate state or final judgment. Those who are impressed by Jeremias's distinction between *hạdēs* and *geenna,* by the parallels between the parable and *1 Enoch* 22, and by the fact that the rich man's brothers are still alive while he is in *hạdēs* will be convinced the parable is about the intermediate state.[220] Those who emphasize the parable's finality about the fates of the rich man and Lazarus will argue that it is not.[221] Luke has an unparalleled interest in the death of individuals,[222] but he does not sacrifice a more collective and general eschatology for an individual one. Rather both eschatologies run parallel with no explanation of their relation.[223] Luke clearly believes in a conscious life after death and in future judgment, making a reference to the intermediate state more likely, but he does not give enough information for a firm conclusion. The parable is not intended to provide a schedule or details about precisely what happens after death. The "bosom of Abraham" is not literal, but points to a place of honor and celebration. If this detail is not literal, then caution must be applied to the other details as well.

Are any conclusions about the afterlife possible? Although the caution about reading the details too literally is needed, the parable's eschatological relevance cannot be wiped away. The themes of reversal and judgment must be given their due. The parable is a warning to the rich and emphasizes the importance of what humans do with the present, and it still teaches that humans will be judged for the way they lived and that the consequences will be serious.

9. *What is the parable's teaching about attitudes and actions concerning wealth and poverty?* The parable's primary teaching is not about wealth and poverty generally, nor is it a general warning to Israel as a whole.[224] It is specifi-

cally a warning to the wealthy for their neglect of the poor. As the reference to Moses and the prophets indicates, the message of the parable was not limited to the time of the in-breaking of the kingdom. On the other hand, the proclamation of the presence of the kingdom would heighten the need for repentance, similar to the response to John the Baptist's eschatological preaching in 3:10-14. Repentance in view of the kingdom means the right use of wealth and the repudiation of exploitation and injustice.[225]

Claims of ignorance about responsibility for the poor are rejected. In effect, the rich man's plea that someone be sent to his brothers implies that he himself has been deprived of sufficient knowledge. By implication he blames God for his predicament.[226] Vv. 27-31 thwart the complaint. Moses and the prophets are fully clear about issues of justice and assistance for the poor. The actions required at the coming of the kingdom are the actions God always wanted from humans. Also obvious here is the rejection of any request for a sign, which fits with Jesus' refusal to give signs elsewhere.[227]

The parable is left open-ended. Will the five brothers repent? The reader must answer this question for him- or herself before it is too late.

Adapting the Parable

People have often wondered why Albert Schweitzer, given his theology, left his status as a professor, gave up his organ playing, and went to Africa as a missionary doctor. He answered this question directly by pointing to this parable. In his mind the parable seemed spoken directly to Europeans: "We are Dives. . . . Out there in the colonies, however, sits wretched Lazarus."[228] The situation has not changed, but it is not limited to Africa. For much of the Western world *we are still Dives* living luxuriously.

As early as Ambrose we are cautioned against sanctifying all poverty and vilifying all wealth,[229] which is fair enough. Poverty is not a gift from God, but a problem — often the result of sin by numerous people — that needs relieving.[230] Wealth may indeed be a blessing of God and the result of hard work, but also "Property is a veil for many evils."[231] What the parable attacks is a particular kind of wealth, wealth that does not *see* poverty and suffering. It attacks the idea that possessions are for one's own use and that they are owned without responsibility to God and other people. This is not, as some have feared, an opiate for the poor which will keep them satisfied with a handout. The parable does not tell us how the wealthy are to assist the poor, but it insists that the poor are brothers and sisters of the wealthy and that *the injustice of the juxtaposition of wealth and poverty cannot be tolerated.*

Increasingly our societies are divided into the haves and the have-nots, especially as the stock market has skyrocketed and technology has flourished. In many countries the disparity is obscene. In urban areas (like Chicago) the "Gold Coast" frequently overshadows poverty-stricken neighborhoods. Lazarus is still at the gate. Parables like this one insist that Christians must not be like the rich man who cares only for his own kind and cannot see the poor until too late. We dare not have a gospel with an evangelistic emphasis and no concern for the poor. Any gospel that is not good news to the poor is not the gospel of Jesus (see Luke 4:18-22).

As in the parables of the Good Samaritan, the Two Debtors, and the Sheep and the Goats, even though it is not explicit, the issue here is the willingness and ability to see a person in need and respond. The rich man's wealth and self-centeredness do not allow him to see Lazarus. If Jesus asked Simon, "Do you see this woman?" (Luke 7:44), he could as well have asked the rich man, "Do you see Lazarus?" The ability to see is the mark of Christian discipleship.

Other obvious lessons lie on the surface of this parable. It reminds us that special signs are not required to know the will of God, nor will they convince those who do not wish to obey. It underscores that the Hebrew Scriptures — not merely the Law, but the Law and the prophets read together — already mark out the will of God.

Numerous questions exist about how individuals and churches should help poor people — to say nothing of dealing with more systemic poverty or poor countries. Let us have our discussions about how we should act and the problems to avoid. But God forbid that we not see, not care, and not act to alleviate the plight of the poor. Open your eyes to see Lazarus at the gate.

For Further Reading

Richard Bauckham, "The Rich Man and Lazarus: The Parable and the Parallels," in *The Fate of the Dead: Studies on the Jewish and Christian Apocalypses* (NovTSup 93; Leiden: Brill, 1998), pp. 97-118.

Johannes Hintzen, *Verkündigung und Wahrnehmung. Über das Verhältnis von Evangelium und Leser am Beispiel Lk 16,19-31 im Rahmen des lukanischen Doppelwerkes* (BBB 81; Frankfurt: Hain, 1991).

Ronald F. Hock, "Lazarus and Micyllus: Greco-Roman Backgrounds to Luke 16:19-31," *JBL* 106 (1987): 447-63.

Joachim Jeremias, *The Parables of Jesus* (2d ed.; trans. S. H. Hooke; New York: Charles Scribner's Sons, 1963), pp. 182-87.

Peter Rhea Jones, *Studying the Parables of Jesus* (Macon: Smyth & Helwys, 1999), pp. 163-95.

Outi Lehtipuu, "Characterization and Persuasion: The Rich Man and the Poor Man in Luke 16.19-31," in *Characterization in the Gospels: Reconceiving Narrative Criticism,* ed. David Rhoads and Kari Syreeni (Sheffield: Sheffield Academic, 1999), pp. 73-105.

Richard L. Rohrbaugh, *The Biblical Interpreter: An Agrarian Bible in an Industrial Age* (Philadelphia: Fortress, 1978), pp. 69-85.

F. Schnider and W. Stenger, "Die Offene Tür und die unüberschreitbare Kluft," *NTS* 25 (1979): 273-83.

Parables concerning God and Prayer

Three parables address the subject of prayer, all in Luke: the Friend at Midnight, the Unjust Judge, and the Pharisee and the Tax Collector. As we will see, they are less about how to pray and more about attitudes to have when praying.

THE FRIEND AT MIDNIGHT
(Luke 11:5-8)

Parable Type

This is an interrogative "how much more" parable. Vv. 5-7 is one long question and v. 8 provides an assurance. No *nimshal* is provided, so the hearer must provide an interpretation that says "Likewise . . ." or "So much more . . ." and explains the relevance of the parable. I argue the latter.

Issues Requiring Attention[1]

1. Where does the "Who from you" question beginning in 11:5 end, and what is its correct answer?
2. What is the meaning of the Greek word *anaideia*, which occurs nowhere else in the NT and only once in the LXX (Sir 25:22)?[2] The word signifies "shamelessness," but is it negative or positive? If negative, it means one has either no understanding of what is shameful or no hesitation in committing shameful acts. The shameless person has no proper sense of shame to guide conduct. If positive, it means one has a proper sense of shame and seeks to act in ways that will not bring shame.

437

3. In v. 8 how should the four occurrences of the third person masculine pronoun "him/his" *(autou)* be understood? Does "his" shamelessness refer to the petitioner who comes in the middle of the night, or does it refer to the man inside who gets up and provides food? If the reference is to the petitioner, the shamelessness could be either negative (he has no sense of shame that prevents his coming in the middle of the night) or positive (he asks for food to avoid bringing shame on himself and his community by being inhospitable). If the reference is to the sleeping man, the shamelessness would almost certainly be positive, referring to the man's desire to avoid the shame of being inhospitable.

4. Does *anaideia* have any connotation of persistence?

5. What does this text teach about God and prayer?

Helpful Primary Source Material

Canonical Material

- NT: Matt 6:26-34, especially 27-30 with its "Who from you" *(tis ex hymōn)* form; Matt 7:7-11/Luke 11:9-13; Luke 18:1-8

Early Jewish Writings

- Sir 25:22: "There is wrath and impudence [no sense of shame, *anaideia*] and great disgrace when a wife supports her husband."[3]
- Josephus, *J.W.* 1.84: "How long, most shameless body *(sōma anaidestaton)*, wilt thou detain the soul. . . ." The same expression occurs in the close parallel at *Ant.* 13.317.
- *J.W.* 6.199: Josephus describes people during the famine (caused by the Roman seige of Jerusalem) eating leather and withered grass and then says, "But why tell of the shameless resort to inanimate articles of food induced by the famine, seeing that I am here about to describe an act unparalleled in the history whether of Greeks or barbarians. . . ?"[4] He then tells of a woman who roasts and eats her nursing child.

Greco-Roman Writings

- Aristotle, *Topica* 150b: "Shamelessness" *(anaideia)* is defined as "made up of courage and false opinion."
- Plato, *Laws* 647a: "Does not, then, the lawgiver, and every man who is worth anything, hold this kind of fear in the highest honour, and name it

'modesty' *(aidōs)*; and to the confidence which is opposed to it does he not give the name 'immodesty' *(anaideia)*, and pronounce it to be for all, both publicly and privately, a very great evil?"

- Demosthenes, *Oration* 21 *(Against Meidias)* 62: "No one has ever been so lost to shame *(anaideia)* as to venture on such conduct as this."
- Demosthenes, *Oration* 24 *(Against Timocrates)* 65: "It seems to me that, so far as effrontery *(anaideia)* goes, such a man is ready to do anything."
- Menander Comicus, *Fragmenta* 1090.1-2: ". . . who knows neither blushing nor fear, he has the first things of every shamelessness."[5]
- Plutarch, *Moralia* fragments 31.2: "This is the extremity of evil. For when shamelessness *(anaideia)* and jealousy rule men, shame *(aidōs)* and indignation leave our race altogether, since shamelessness and jealousy are the negation of these things . . . whereas shamelessness *(anaideia)* is not a counterfeit of shame, but its extreme opposite, masquerading as frankness of speech."
- Plutarch, *Isis and Osiris* 363F-364A: "God hates *anaideia*."[6]
- Dio Cassius, *Roman History* 45.16.1. describes the Romans of a particular period as hating those who act with insolence *(anaideia)* even in the smallest matters.

Early Christian Writings

- Hermas, *Vis.* 3.3.2: "Yet you will not cease asking for revelations, for you are shameless *(anaidēs)*."
- Hermas, *Vis.* 3.7.5: "I was still unabashed *(anaideusamenos)* and asked her whether really all these stones which have been cast away. . . ."
- Hermas, *Mand.* 11.12: ". . . that man who seems to have a spirit exalts himself and wishes to have the first place, and he is instantly impudent and shameless *(anaidēs)* and talkative, and lives in great luxury and in many other deceits. . . ."
- Basil, *On the Renunciation of the World* 31.648.21: "Humility is the imitation of Christ, but high-mindedness, boldness, and shamelessness *(anaideia)* are the imitation of the devil."

Later Jewish Writings[7]

- *b. Berakot* 31b: "To what is this matter like? To a king who made a feast for his servants, and a poor man came and stood by the door and said to them, Give me a bite, and no one took any notice of him, so he forced his way into the presence of the king and said to him, Your Majesty, out of all the feast which thou hast made, is it so hard in thine eyes to give me one bite?" This parable is told in describing Hannah's praying for a son in 1 Samuel 2.

- *Midr. Pss.* 28.6: "R. Simon told a parable of a king who had a single pearl. When his son came and said to him: 'Give it to me,' the king answered: 'It is not thine.' But when the son wearied him with begging, the king gave it to his son. Just so, Israel singing . . . to the Holy One . . . entreated Him to give them the Torah. Thereupon, God said to them: 'It is not yours. It belongs to those above.' But when they wearied him with begging, He gave it to them, as is said The Lord gave strength unto His people."

Textual Features Worthy of Attention

The central section of Luke, the "travel narrative," is largely chiastic (see p. 306 above), and this parable intentionally corresponds to the parable of the Widow and the Unjust Judge (Luke 18:1-8). Note the parallel between "Do not cause me trouble" in 11:7 *(mē moi kopous pareche)* and "Because this widow causes me trouble" in 18:5 *(dia ge to parechein moi kopon).*[8]

The parable of the Friend at Midnight is not in the other Gospels, but the rest of the material in Luke 11:1-13 is in Matthew at two different places. Matthew has the Lord's Prayer at 6:9-15 and has parallels to most of Luke 11:9-13 at 7:7-11. Matt 7:9 includes a saying Luke does not have: "What man from you whose son asks for bread would give him a stone?" Luke probably omitted this saying because he already had the parable about a friend asking for bread. Luke has an additional saying in 11:12 that Matthew does not have: "Or will he ask for an egg and he [a father] will give him a scorpion?"

Luke has a redactional emphasis on prayer and has arranged the material in 11:1-13 around this theme. Elsewhere Luke emphasizes the prayer life of Jesus by including seven references not present in Matthew and Mark: at his baptism, 3:21; after the cleansing of the leper and before the conflict with authorities, 5:16; before choosing the Twelve, 6:12; before Peter's confession and the passion prediction, 9:18; at the transfiguration, 9:28; the Lord's Prayer 11:1; and on the cross at 23:34 (omitted in several manuscripts), 46 (see also 22:41, which does have parallels, and 44, which also is omitted in several manuscripts). The parables in 18:1-14 also deal with prayer.

The Lord's Prayer and the parable are connected by the request for bread in both.

The difficulties of this parable may be partly due to the impact of Aramaic or Hebrew.[9]

Cultural Information

A foundational assumption is the strong sense of responsibility for hospitality in the ancient world, which was part of the virulent shame and honor system of the ancient world. Inns were not numerous and, though used, often were places of corruption, so travelers depended on hospitality. The host had a responsibility to care for his guest, and the sleeping man had obligations to help his neighbor. The parable seems to assume that the house of the sleeping man was small (but not necessarily just one room).

Baking was often done in an oven in a courtyard and might involve the whole family (cf. Jer 7:18), so a neighbor might know who had baked bread recently. There were professional bakers in cities,[10] but such matters make no contribution to understanding the parable. Several details are debated: the size of the loaves, how many were needed for a meal, how frequently bread was baked,[11] and whether a late arriving guest was unusual or common as a result of people traveling at night to avoid the heat of the day. The understanding of the parable does not depend on such questions, nor can they be satisfactorily answered.

Explanation of the Parable

Options for Interpretation

1. The church understood that the parable was about prayer and allegorized it so that the bread represents some form of spiritual benefit, the friend represents Christ, and the petitioner represents a believer. Several more detailed explanations appear as well.[12]

2. Several quite different approaches emphasize that this is a "how much more" parable, that is, that its logic is from the lesser to the greater, or, as the rabbinic expression states it, *qal waḥomer,* "light and heavy." If a conclusion applies in an easy case, it also applies in a more important one. If humans will respond to a request, how much more will God respond?

2a. Early and often the parable has been understood to urge persistence in praying.[13] If a human will respond to persistent asking, how much more will God?

2b. A significant number think the parable is about the avoidance of shame by the one inside. If a human will respond to avoid shame, how much more will God?[14]

2c. Others think the focus is on the shamelessness of the one outside asking. If a human will respond, even if because someone has no sense of shame, how much more will God respond to one's legitimate request?[15]

3. Herman C. Waetjen thinks *anaideia* is used positively here for the first time and that the parable subverts one's view of the world.[16]

4. The suggestion has been made that the parable teaches that humans should help others.[17]

5. A few focus on honor codes in the ancient world and on hospitality and urge that the parable focuses on friendship as one of the values of the kingdom.[18]

Decisions on the Issues

1. Where does the "Who from you" question beginning in 11:5 end, and what is its correct answer? Translations often change the question to a statement such as "Suppose one of you . . . ," which is misleading. This is an interrogative parable; it consists of a long question and Jesus' answer to his own question. The question extends from v. 5 through v. 7: "Who from you will have a friend and he will go to him in the middle of the night and say to him, 'Friend, lend me three loaves since my friend came to me from the road and I have nothing which I may place before him,' and that one inside would answer, 'Don't bother me, already the door has been closed and my children are with me in bed; I am not able having risen to give you [anything]?'"[19] The whole point is no one would say such a thing and refuse to get up and give his friend what he needs. Such a refusal is unthinkable. The question "Who from you *(Tis ex hymōn)*" appears eleven times in the Gospels.[20] In all of them the question asks if anyone would do some hypothetical action, and in each case the implied answer is "No one." For example, in Luke 14:28 the words "Who from you wishing to build a tower will not first sit down and calculate the cost?" means "Obviously no one would build without first calculating the cost." Framing questions in this way forces hearers to obvious conclusions on the level of everyday life that must then be transferred to the level of Jesus' teaching.

Commentators *regularly* assume that the sleeping friend initially refused the request but then relented or that the petitioner knocks repeatedly or asks repeatedly.[21] *The parable has no refusal and does not mention knocking at all, nor does it mention any repetition of the request.* The parable is merely a straightforward question describing circumstances of a request that no one would refuse. The ideas of continued knocking and asking come from vv. 9-10, but they are *not* part of the parable, and it is important not to read them into the parable.

2. What is the meaning of the Greek word anaideia? If "shamelessness" is a negative quality, it means one has either no understanding of what is shameful or no hesitation in committing shameful acts. The shameless person has no proper sense of shame to guide conduct. If positive, it means that one has a proper sense of shame and seeks to act in ways that will not bring shame. This question has caused much uncertainty in interpretation of the parable. Translations frequently make the problem worse by rendering *anaideia* as "importunity" (KJV, RSV) or "persistence" (NIV 1978, NRSV). "Importunity" is hardly a serviceable word any more, but conveys the idea of asking persistently. The NLT audaciously and without any basis adds in v. 8 the words "if you keep knocking long enough" and translates *anaideia* as "shameless persistence." The NIV of 1984 backed off from "persistence" and substituted for it "boldness," but this still is misleading. Of major translations, only the NEB gives a clear and viable translation by retaining "shamelessness."[22]

Using the end of the fourth century A.D. as a reasonable range for analysis, the *Thesaurus Linguae Graecae* database includes at least 258 occurrences of *anaideia,*[23] all of which are demonstrably negative, except where Christian writers have assigned a positive use in dependence on Luke 11:8. This word refers to people who have no proper sense of shame and willingly engage in improper conduct, as the primary source material above (pp. 438-40) and numerous other examples show. No positive use of this word — referring to a good sense of what is shameful and a desire to avoid it — occurs except where Christians have adapted it after the beginning of the second century in dependence on Luke 11:8.

Most NT scholars know that this word is a negative word, but some, because they cannot make the parable yield a sufficiently significant teaching on prayer from the negative meaning, argue that *anaideia* is a positive term, applied to the man *inside* who rises to *avoid shame.*[24] When joined with a focus on Middle Eastern attitudes about hospitality,[25] this position is deceptively attractive, one I thought initially was correct, but it is untenable in light of the thoroughly negative use of *anaideia,* which is used in association with a host of other terms for outrageous and offensive behavior such as rashness, insolence, disorder, coarse behavior, and recklessness. Rather than representing the avoidance of shame, the word expresses an ignorance about or disregard of what is shameful and the absence of any sense of proper behavior.[26] Especially with such statements as "God hates *anaideia,*"[27] it is very hard to make the word positive.

The obvious question is whether Luke 11:8 is the first occurrence of a positive use or merely a negative use that becomes the catalyst for a later positive use by Christians. Only the latter is feasible. No bridge exists by which a hearer or reader could understand either avoidance of shame or good shamelessness as in later Christian usage. In Luke 11:8 *anaideia* refers to the insensitivity, the rudeness, of the man who comes asking in the middle of the night, as it is understood in the NEB translation.[28] It is how the petitioned man evaluates the conduct of the petitioner.[29]

Still, NT scholars have strained mightily to make *anaideia* positive. J. Jeremias followed A. Fridrichsen, who argued that the shamelessness was a quality the sleeper wanted to avoid,[30] but without offering substantiation shifted the negative quality to be avoided to a positive quality to be preserved. In effect, he turned shamelessness into honor.[31] J. Derrett suggested that the word had become neutral by Luke's time, but his whole discussion is vitiated by the fact that he treats only related words or cognates. For example, he finds Sir 4:21 demonstrative: "There is a shame that leads to sin, and there is a shame that is glory and favor." But, the word twice translated "shame" there is *aischynē*, not *anaideia*.[32] K. Bailey, despite knowing that all previous occurrences are negative, still interpreted *anaideia* as referring to the sleeper's avoidance of shame. He offered the possibilities that *anaideia* was originally *anaitios* ("blamelessness") or that *aidōs* (used of shame as a negative quality) plus an *alpha* privative yields "avoidance of shame," on the basis that two negatives make a positive.[33] This is not algebra, and neither suggestion is likely. B. Scott with some difficulty retained the negative meaning "shamelessness," but assigned its reference to the shame of the man inside, who does not act out of honor (friendship), but out of shamelessness to avoid dishonor. "He has done out of shamelessness what he ought to have done out of honor."[34] This attempt requires far too much of a reader and does not do justice to what "shamelessness" intends, namely, that a person does not know or care about shame.[35]

Herman Waetjen acknowledges my earlier work demonstrating that *anaideia* is thoroughly negative, but still argues that Jesus' use in this parable is the first positive use. He complains that I must reach outside the parable to v. 13 for the "how much more" contrast, which is true, but no matter what approach one takes, one must reach outside vv. 5-8 for the solution. Delaying explicit mention of the "how much more" argument until v. 13 seems to be a Lukan rhetorical strategy to elicit reflection and build to a climax.[36] We should note as well that the chiastic parallel of this parable, the parable of the Unjust Judge in 18:1-8, also functions with a "how much more" argument. What Waetjen assumes is *not* in the parable, namely, that the petitioner repeatedly knocks on the door, that the man inside initially refuses to get up and give bread, that the petitioner's *anaideia* is "some kind of emotional response to the neighbor's outrageous refusal to help," and that the man inside decides to help only after the emotional outburst.[37] The parable says nothing about knocking; that is from vv. 9-10, which are not part of the parable, and their parallel in Matt 7:7-8 is not connected to the Lord's Prayer. The parable says nothing about the man inside refusing to get up. Vv. 5-7 present one long question which expects the answer "No one,"[38] and if so, there is no refusal.[39]

Waetjen presupposes that all parables must subvert our view of the world and that this one does as well, but not all parables do so. Some are straightforward and simple (e.g., Mark 13:28-29). His conclusion is that God, as the metaphorical referent of the sleeper, does not respond on the basis of the reciprocity of friendship. Rather, God is free and responds to all human petitions. Waetjen also argues for a good shamelessness, impudence or dishonorable conduct that is divinely legitimated in pursuit of justice. I have no doubt that God is free and does not respond on the basis of reciprocity, but if that is the point of this parable, how is one supposed to arrive at this conclusion? This is a conclusion that must be brought not only from outside the parable, but from outside the Lukan context, and that does not fit easily with Jesus' context. The parable is not focused on friendship; the meaning suggested is not paralleled in non-parabolic material, and it is difficult to imagine Jesus being concerned to convey such a meaning.

"Shamelessness" cannot have a positive meaning in this passage. It is a negative term describing the rudeness of the man outside asking for bread.

3. In v. 8 how should the four occurrences of the third person masculine pronoun "him/his" (autō/autou) *be understood?* Obviously decisions here are impacted by one's determination of the meaning of *anaideia*. Those who have understood *anaideia* as avoidance of shame could understand "his" of *either* the petitioner or the sleeper. Both would be seeking to maintain honor and show hospitality. But if, as I think I have demonstrated, it is a thoroughly negative word, then "his *(autou)* shamelessness" refers to the petitioner who comes in the middle of the night.

On any reading the references to people in the parable are confusing. "Friend" occurs four times: in v. 5a and 5b, both of the sleeper, in v. 6 of the traveler, and in v. 8 of the sleeper. "Him" refers to the sleeper in v. 5 and to the traveler in v. 6. In v. 8 all four occurrences of "him" or "his" refer to the petitioner. Clearly both occurrences of "him" refer to the petitioner in the phrase "give to him." The first occurrence of "his" does as well, for "friend" refers to the sleeper.[40] Even if this were not the case, *anaideia* is so negative that the second "his" would still have to refer to the man asking. V. 8 then should be understood this way:

> I say to you, even if he [the sleeper] having arisen will not give to him [the petitioner] because of being his [the petitioner's] friend, because of his [the petitioner's] shamelessness, having gotten up, he will give him [the petitioner] whatever he needs.

4. Does anaideia *have any connotation of persistence?* Not surprisingly, this parable is usually interpreted as encouraging persistence in prayer, since this theme follows in 11:9-10. Luke *is* concerned to promote faithfulness in prayer, but the translation of *anaideia* as "persistence" or "importunity" in five of the seven translations mentioned above is startling. Commentaries surprisingly keep saying that *anaideia* means persistence, when little or no evidence exists for such a conclusion. The connection of the parable with the emphasis on knocking and asking in 11:9-10 and the parallels with 18:1-8 have contributed to this interpretation, but the word *anaideia* and this parable do not. *The man in the parable neither knocks nor repeats his request.*[41]

Two suggestions seek to substantiate a connotation of persistence with *anaideia*. K. Bailey argued that the LXX use of the cognate expression *apostrophēn anaidē* ("shameless turning away") to translate *mĕšubâh niṣṣaḥat* ("enduring apostasy") in Jer 8:5 gives one clear reference of *anaidēs* meaning "continual." Possibly this is relevant, but one does not know if the translator of the LXX was attempting to express the idea of persistence or to mark the shamelessness of the apostasy.[42]

David Catchpole assumed that some of the references from Josephus express persistence,[43] but an examination of the texts cited shows this is not true. No doubt, shamelessness can often express itself in stubborn or persistent conduct, but that does not mean that *anaideia* carries the connotation of persistence. In *J.W.* 1.84/*Ant.* 13.317, we find "How long, most shameless body *(sōma anaidestaton),* wilt thou detain the soul. . . ." That "shameless" occurs in the same sentence with "how long" does not prove that "shamelessness" carries the connotation of persistence. This statement is merely the guilt-ridden complaint of one who wants to die. In *J.W.* 6.199 Josephus describes people who during the Roman siege of Jerusalem ate leather and withered grass and then says, "But why tell of the shameless resort *(anaideia)* to inanimate articles of food induced by the famine . . ." and goes on to speak of the ultimate tragedy of a woman eating her own child. Famines by nature are persistent, but the use of *anaideia* here refers to the rashness and disorderliness to which people were driven by the famine, not the persistence of the famine. The occurrence of *anaideia* in *Ant.* 17.119 ("Have you indeed so much confidence in your shamelessness that you ask to be put to the torture . . .") also fails to show that this word means "persistence." Rather, the word conveys brazen recklessness.

Two other texts exist where one could more plausibly argue that persistence is inherent in the word. In Hermas, *Vis.* 3.3.2 the "lady" who reveals everything to Hermas asks him not to trouble her about revelation because these revelations are fulfilled. Then she tells him, "Yet you will not cease asking for revelations, for you are shameless *(anaidēs)."* *Anaidēs* here does not mean persistent; it still means shameless, but what is shameless is Hermas's continual asking. This text cannot be used to find the meaning of Luke 11:8 because it has been influenced by the Lukan text. Note that the request not to be troubled any more *(kai mēketi moi kopous pareche)* is derived from Luke 11:7.

The only really relevant text to suggest that *anaideia* connotes persistence is one in which Plutarch describes the error of compliancy and speaks of "loathing and resenting the *brazen importunity (anaideia)* that overthrows and masters our reason."[44] Whether "brazen importunity" is the correct translation or "shamelessness" would be adequate is debatable, but the following context shows that persistence is present in this context. The next sentence refers to "those who wring concessions from us by their importunity," but the Greek translated "importunity" here is *tous dysōpountas.* A few lines later Plutarch adds, "For being too weak to refuse we promise persistent suitors *(tois liparousin)* many things beyond our power. . . ." Is persistence inherent here in *anaideia,* or does it derive from the other words used in the context? The latter is more likely: the shamelessness here only takes on a particular character. Even if *anaideia* implies persistence here, that is slim evidence for an argument that it means persistence and should be translated so in Luke 11:8.[45] Praying continually and faithfully is a good thing, but persistence, especially persistence as repetitious prayer, should not be imported into this parable.[46]

5. What does this text teach about God and prayer? Problems have arisen with this parable because interpreters have wanted a more direct application to a theology of prayer than the parable seems to offer. We assume that it should be a comparison dealing with prayer, but many parables are not comparisons. We want to know in what way God is like the sleeper and how people who pray are like the petitioner. In fact, it appears that the desire to ward off wrong perceptions about prayer have led to the attempts to understand the parable of the sleeper's avoidance of shame. The whole point of the parable, however, is that God is *not* like the sleeper. It is a parable contrasting God with the sleeper.[47]

The parable is made more difficult by the fact that it has no *nimshal,* no explicit statement showing its purpose and intent. As most interpreters agree, it is an argument from the weaker to the stronger. It is a "how much more" argument, a procedure common in Jewish hermeneutics, but the reader must supply the "stronger" element that makes explicit the intent of the parable.[48] A second "how much more" argument is explicit in 11:13 and shows how the parable in 11:5-8 is to be interpreted. Luke apparently felt it more powerful to include the "how much more" statement only after the sayings in vv. 9-12 and thus to avoid the redundancy of placing it in both places. The parable says in effect: "If a human will obviously get up in the middle of the night to grant the request even of a rude friend, will not God much more answer your requests?" The primary concern appears to be the request for bread in the Lord's Prayer (11:3). If a human will respond to the request of a rude friend for bread, how much more will God provide bread in response to the requests of his people?[49] The parable expresses with reference to prayer precisely the point of Matt 6:26-34/Luke 12:22-34: freedom from anxiety. Note especially Matt 6:27 with its "Who from you?" *(tis ex hymōn)* form. If God cares about birds and flowers, will he not care about you? If a friend will get up and give a person bread because he needs it, will not your heavenly Father?

The parable does not invite rudeness in praying any more than it suggests that God is asleep. The parable does not teach that God is a friend,[50] nor that a hearing is certain if we weary God through continual prayer.[51] This parable is *not* like *Midr. Pss.* 28.6, which suggests that God gets weary of repeated begging and gives in. The parable addresses the implied question "Will God respond to prayer?" and argues as follows: "If among humans a request is granted even when or because it is rude, how much more will your heavenly Father respond to your requests?"[52] Indirectly the parable does encourage boldness in praying. If one is assured of being heard receptively, and particularly if one thinks of God as a Father to his children as in v. 11, praying boldly is much easier. One may legitimately say that Luke 11:9-10 and the structural relation between the parable of the Friend at Midnight and that of the Unjust Judge (Luke 18:1-8)[53] encourage perseverance in praying, and one can understand why the church adapted the parable in this direction. Yet, nothing in the parable of the Friend at Midnight teaches persistence in prayer. Rather the parable teaches the certainty of a God who hears prayer and responds.

Adapting the Parable

We must not change the focus of this parable and speak of persistence. The parable has no continual asking or knocking and no initial refusal. We would do well to remember Jesus' caution against repetitious praying, thinking we will be heard for our many words (Matt 6:7). If a matter of concern continues, of course we should continue praying, but discussions of persistence usually carry the implication that if we speak long enough and passionately enough, God will change his mind. What kind of God is implied with such a theology, and what do we say when the formula does not work? Faith would suggest something different, and faith is an underlying assumption of the parable, as is the character of God. Is God of such a character that he responds to prayers? The parable answers, "Of course!" Well beyond what a human might do, God will respond. Jesus' conviction is that God is a God who eagerly hears the prayers of his people, is biased in their favor, and can be trusted to respond. The parable affirms the importance of prayer and is an invitation to pray. Should a person of faith pray faithfully as part of a continual walk with God? Of course! Surely if you would ask for and expect help from a neighbor, how much more should you seek and expect the help of God?

For Further Reading

Kenneth Ewing Bailey, *Poet and Peasant: A Literary Cultural Approach to the Parables in Luke* (Grand Rapids: Eerdmans, 1976), pp. 125-33.

David Crump, *Knocking on Heaven's Door: A New Testament Theology of Petitionary Prayer* (Grand Rapids: Baker, 2006), pp. 60-76.

J. Duncan M. Derrett, "The Friend at Midnight: Asian Ideas in the Gospel of St. Luke," in *Donum Gentilicum: New Testament Studies in Honour of David Daube*, ed. E. Bammel, C. K. Barrett, and W. D. Davies, (Oxford: Clarendon, 1978), pp. 78-87.

Joachim Jeremias, *The Parables of Jesus* (2d ed.; trans. S. H. Hooke; New York: Charles Scribner's Sons, 1963), pp. 157-60.

Alan F. Johnson, "Assurance for Man: The Fallacy of Translating *Anaideia* by 'Persistence' in Luke 11:5-8," *JETS* 22 (1979): 123-31.

Klyne Snodgrass, "*Anaideia* and the Friend at Midnight (Luke 11:8)," *JBL* 116 (1997): 505-13.

Herman C. Waetjen, "The Subversion of 'World' by the Parable of the Friend at Midnight," *JBL* 120 (2001): 703-21.

THE UNJUST JUDGE
(Luke 18:1-8)

I consider this one of the more difficult parables. If the introduction of any parable seems misplaced, it would be here. The parable itself (vv. 2-5) is brief, and without its explanation (vv. 6-8) there is little indication of its intent.

Parable Type

Indications of the category into which this parable should be placed are not as clear as elsewhere, but especially because the parable is about two specific people in a specific locale (something not true of similitudes) this is a double indirect narrative parable functioning as a *contrast*. It has a "how much more" logic and is accompanied by a call for discernment (v. 6), three assurances of God's gracious vindication (a strong affirmation in the form of a question, v. 7a; a statement or possibly a question in v. 7b; and a further statement in v. 8a), and a question whether faith will exist when vindication comes (v. 8b).

Issues Requiring Attention

1. Do vv. 2-8 belong together as a unit, or are vv. 6-8 later additions to the parable?
2. Is the introduction in v. 1, which specifies the intent of the parable as promoting unwearying prayer, in keeping with the parable itself, and is it at odds with the focus on the vindication of the elect in vv. 6-8?
3. To what degree is the interpretation of this parable determined by 11:5-8 or other parallels such as Sir 35:12-20?
4. Is the intent with *ekdikein* (vv. 3 and 5) and its cognate *ekdikēsis* (vv. 7-8) "avenge" or "vindicate/grant justice"?
5. How should the judge's motive for action be understood? Did he fear physical violence from the woman? Should *hypōpiazein* be understood literally of physical violence (cf. 1 Cor 9:27, its only other NT occurrence) or metaphorically so that the judge fears the woman will wear him out (annoy him) or possibly that she will shame him? Does *eis telos* (literally: "unto the end") in v. 5 connect to the participle *erchomenē* ("coming") or to the main verb *hypōpiazein* (NIV and NRSV: "wear me out")? That is, is the judge's concern that she will come continually, that she will completely annoy him, or that she will finally strike him (depending on how *hypōpiazein* is taken)?
6. How should v. 7 be understood? Translations cover over the difficulties in this complex verse, for which nine different options have been suggested.[54]
7. Does *en tachei* in v. 8a mean "quickly/soon" or "suddenly" as several argue?[55]
8. What is the meaning of the parable?

Helpful Primary Source Material

Canonical Material

For passages describing the plight of widows in the OT and God's bias toward them see Exod 22:22; Deut 24:17; 27:19; Jer 22:3; and Zech 7:10. God is their helper and refuge in Deut 10:18; Pss 68:5; 146:9; Prov 15:25. Care for widows is expected from God's people (Isa 10:2; Jer 7:6), especially judges and leaders, and God witnesses against oppressors of widows (Mal 3:5). The trilogy of widows, orphans, and strangers is a standard description of those who are vulnerable.

- Other OT texts: Exod 34:6; Prov 25:15
- NT: Matt 15:22-28/Mark 7:24-30; Luke 12:45-46; 21:36; 22:44; 1 Cor 9:27; 2 Pet 3:4-12

Early Jewish Writings[56]

- Sirach 35:14-25(11-23): "Do not offer him a bribe, for he will not accept it; and do not rely on a dishonest sacrifice; for the Lord is the judge, and with him there is no partiality. He will not show partiality to the poor; but he will listen to the prayer of one who is wronged. He will not ignore the supplication of the orphan, or the widow when she pours out her complaint. Do not the tears of the widow run down her cheek as she cries out against the one who causes them to fall? The one whose service is pleasing to the Lord will be accepted, and his prayer will reach to the clouds. The prayer of the humble pierces the clouds, and it will not rest until it reaches its goal; it will not desist until the Most High responds and does justice for the righteous, and executes judgment. Indeed, the Lord will not delay *(ou mē bradynein)*, and like a warrior will not be patient *(oude mē makrothymēsei ep' autois)* until he crushes the loins of the unmerciful and repays vengeance *(ekdikēsin)* on the nations; until he destroys the multitude of the insolent, and breaks the scepters of the unrighteous; until he repays mortals according to their deeds, and the works of all according to their thoughts; until he judges the case of his people and makes them rejoice in his mercy."
- Bar 4:21-25: "Take courage, my children, cry to God, and he will deliver you from the power and hand of the enemy. . . . joy has come to me from the Holy One, because of the mercy that will soon *(en tachei)* come to you from your everlasting savior. . . . For as the neighbors of Zion have now seen your capture, so they soon *(en tachei)* will see your salvation by God. . . . My children, endure with patience *(makrothymēsate)* the wrath that has come upon you from God. Your enemy has overtaken you, but you will soon *(en tachei)* see their destruction and will tread upon their necks."
- Philo, *Moses* 1.47 describes Moses in Arabia praying for God to save the oppressed and punish the oppressors. God listened to Moses' prayers but

while divine judgment was still waiting Moses disciplined himself to be fit for life.

- *Corpus Inscriptionum Iudaicarum* 725 is a plea for God to avenge innocent blood, the murder of a young girl, very quickly.[57]

Greco-Roman Writings

- Plutarch, *Mor.* 179C-D (Sayings of Kings and Commanders, Philip the Father of Alexander 31): "When a poor old woman insisted that her case should be heard before him, and often caused him annoyance, he said he had no time to spare, whereupon she burst out, 'Then give up being king.' Philip, amazed at her words, proceeded at once to hear not only her case but those of the others."[58] The same account is mentioned in *Life of Demetrius* 42 as a contrast to the lack of reception people found with Demetrius.
- P. Mich. 29 is a letter from a widow asking for help in retrieving a stolen donkey.[59]
- *Select Papyri* (LCL) 2:271 (P. Tebt. 776), a petition in which a woman seeks restitution for a dowry given to a tax farmer to exclude her from her rights: "I therefore, being a defenceless woman, beg and request you not to suffer me to be deprived of what is pledged for my dowry through the misbehaviour of the accused. . . ."

Early Christian Writings

- *1 Clem* 23:1–24:1 emphasizes the compassion of God on those who come to him and that quickly and suddenly his will shall be accomplished. See especially 23:5.

Later Jewish Writings

- *m. 'Abot* 4.8: "He [Rabbi Ishmael] used to say: Judge not alone, for none may judge alone save One." 4:22 expresses belief that God will hold all to account and will be the Judge, Witness, and Complainant.
- See *Midr. Pss.* 28:6, p. 440 above.

Textual Features Worthy of Attention

In addition to the information on Luke's focus on prayer above (p. 440), the themes in the parable are reflected in 12:35-46 (especially vv. 45-46); 21:36; and 22:40-46.

This parable also shares themes with both the preceding and following sections. With the preceding section it shares the theme of eschatology, and the parable serves as the conclusion for the eschatological discourse, which extends from 17:20 to 18:8. Parables provide the conclusion to other major discourses or sections in Luke (see 6:46-49; 19:11-27).[60] The concern for faith in 18:8 is already the subject in 17:5-6, 19.

This parable shares with the parable of the Pharisee and the Tax Collector, which follows, the theme of prayer and the prominence given to words in the *dikaios* ("righteous, just") word group, from which this parable has *antidikos* ("the opponent," v. 3), *adikia* ("unjust," v. 6), *ekdikein* ("vindicate," vv. 3, 5), and *ekdikēsis* ("vindication," vv. 7, 8).[61] Those two parables and Luke's parable of the Talents (19:11-27) are the only ones for which an explanation precedes the parable.

Repetition gives prominence to the description of the judge (vv. 2 and 4) as a central feature for understanding.[62] That he neither fears God nor respects humans is a violation of the double love command.[63]

Widows receive special focus in Luke-Acts: Anna in 2:36-38; the widow of Zarephath in 4:25-26; the widow of Nain in 7:11-17; the denunciation of scribes who devour widows' houses in 20:47; the widow's offering in 21:1-4; the distribution of food to widows in Acts 6:1-6; and the widows mourning at the death of Dorcas in Acts 9:39-41.

Cultural Information

Widows were easily recognized by their distinctive attire, which indicated their status (see Gen 38:14, 19; Jdt 8:5; 10:3; 16:8). Since women married in their early teens, widows were numerous but not necessarily old.

Widows were often left with no means of support. If her husband left an estate, she did not inherit it, although provision for her upkeep would be made. If she remained in her husband's family, she had an inferior, almost servile, position. If she returned to her family, the money exchanged at the wedding had to be given back. Widows were so victimized that they were often sold as slaves for debt.[64] Note the parallelism in Lam 1:1-2.

Various commentators discuss the judicial structure of ancient Judaism. J. Derrett argues there were two court systems, Jewish and Gentile, and understands the parable's judge as a Gentile judge.[65] The Mishnah (*m. Sanhedrin* 1.1) states that three judges are to decide cases concerning property, whereas the Talmud (*b. Sanhedrin* 4b-5a) later allows one authorized judge to decide money matters. Josephus claims to have appointed local courts with seven judges in

Galilee (*J.W.* 2.569-71). Information about how the judicial system functioned in first-century Palestine is, however, sketchy at best.[66] The saying in Matt 5:25-26/Luke 12:57-59 assumes a court with one judge, and it could be that only one judge is mentioned here in keeping with the brevity of parables.[67] The interpretation of the parable does not turn on specific knowledge about the kind of court. One need only know the desperate situation of many widows and the possibility of unsympathetic and/or corrupt judges.[68]

Explanation of the Parable

Options for Interpretation

1. Already Augustine recognized that this parable, with vv. 6-8, provided a negative comparison and a "how much more" argument: if the wicked judge could be swayed by persistent entreaty, how much more certain may we be that God hears our prayers. Augustine went on to allegorize the woman as the church and the vengeance as either the death or conversion of the evil or the devil's final defeat.[69]

2. Many scholars today follow in seeing the parable as a negative comparison and a "how much more" argument which emphasizes the need for faithful prayer, but if they identify the woman, the correspondence is with the individual believer.[70] A variety of views exists for deciding the meaning of v. 7 and for understanding the nature of the vindication. The focus of the parable may be seen as the necessity of prayer, the certainty of God's hearing prayer, or both.

3. In addition to the "how much more" argument emphasis is sometimes placed on perseverance during oppression and an assertion of the value of prayer, not the repetition of the same prayers. The issue is being found faithful rather than giving up.[71]

4. Particularly when the parable is limited to vv. 2-5, several suggest that the parable has something to do with seeking justice, although interpreters get to this option by quite different paths. H. Hendrickx applies the parable to the red tape and bureaucracy of today's society and the bribery and venality of judges, as a result of which Christians should seek justice.[72] W. Herzog interprets the scene as a clear violation of Jewish legal practice, since only one judge is present. The widow refuses to be silent and by shameless behavior achieves a just verdict. He concludes that the oppressed must collude in their oppression for the system to work and by implication suggests a refusal to accommodate to the system.[73] Wendy Cotter thinks the parable is a burlesque of the whole justice system and offers prophetic insight about the power for justice available for those who remain independent of the social codes.[74]

5. Several novel solutions are "singular" readings; they do not find support from other scholars. Dan Via takes a Jungian approach and views the parable as presenting a problem in male psychology. The male ego refuses to respond to the *anima,* the archetype of a woman in a man's unconscious.[75] B. Scott focuses on the widow's continued wearing down of the judge as a metaphor for the kingdom. The kingdom keeps coming, keeps battering down regardless of honor or justice and may even come under the guise of shamelessness.[76] C. Hedrick argues that the parable presents the judge as a thoroughly honest man who in the end compromises his integrity for his own comfort, which should lead readers to reflect on the integrity of their own compromises.[77]

Decisions on the Issues

As will be evident, I do not find much basis for the suggestions that the parable is generally about seeking justice or about what is found by any of the "novel" approaches, but all that depends on decisions on the issues. Although the problems in v. 7b cause consternation, the intent of the parable is clear. Regardless of how decisions are made on the issues, Jesus addressed this parable to his disciples,[78] and it is a "how much more" parable using the standard reasoning "from light to heavy."[79] If even an unjust judge will vindicate a widow who keeps coming to him, how much more will God answer the cries for vindication from his people? With this picture of the elect crying to God for vindication, one should compare Rev 6:10.

1. Do vv. 2-8 belong together as a unit, or are vv. 6-8 later additions to the parable? The coherence of the material in these eight verses is debated, and a decision about the inclusion of vv. 6-8 is determinative. If they are included, the parable has to do with prayer in some way; if they are removed, little direction remains for the interpretation of the parable. Since v. 1 is clearly a Lukan introduction[80] and vv. 6-8 are an explanation, scholars often isolate vv. 2-5 as the parable, to which vv. 6-7, 8a, and 8b were added at a pre-Lukan stage. Various suggestions are made,[81] including a few who argue that the parable is from an early Christian prophet or from Luke,[82] but other scholars argue forcefully that vv. 2-8[83] or at least 2-8a belonged together from the first and derive from Jesus.

Vv. 1 and 6a ("The Lord said") are clearly from Luke. The rest of v. 6 is nothing more than an attention-getter, a call for discernment similar to "Let the one who has ears to hear hear," which is an obvious feature of Jesus' teaching.[84] The wording of vv. 6-8 is not Lukan and has Semitic features. The possibility exists that vv. 2-5 are the original parable, to which the other sayings were later joined, but the problem is that vv. 2-5 by themselves are enigmatic and give no hint as to the referent(s) of the parable. The parable needs some explanation,[85] and vv. 7-8a provide an explanation that is not forced. They make explicit that to which the parable points.

Another reason to think vv. 7-8 (or at least 8a) belong with the parable is the parallel with Sir 35:14-25(11-23). The more that text is seen as providing the building blocks for the parable, the less one can separate the parable from the words that follow it. The parallels between the two show that the parable has borrowed from and adapted the features of the earlier text.

The Parable	Sir 35:12-20
A widow continually asks an unrighteous judge for vindication from her opponent until she gets it (vv. 2-5).	A widow pours out her complaint to God, the righteous judge, and her cries accuse the man who caused her tears (vv. 14-15).
God vindicates his elect who cry to him day and night (v. 7a).	God hears the appeal of the orphan, the widow, and the pious who do not stop praying until justice is done (v. 17).
God has patience on them (*makrothymei ep' autois*, v. 7b).	God will *not* be patient with the wicked (*mē makrothymēsei ep' autois*, v. 18).
God will bring their vindication (*ekdikēsin*) quickly (v. 8a).	God will send retribution (*ekdikēsin*) on the heathen ("nations") (v. 18).

Although the two accounts have different understandings of "patience" and "vindication," the similarities are too close to be accidental.[86] *Makrothymein* ("have patience") is not a frequently used word, and its presence underscores the relationship of these two texts.

Since parallels exist in both vv. 2-5 and vv. 7-8, the parable and its explanation were likely together from the first. Some argue that the presence of an unjust judge made an interpretation indispensable,[87] but in any case, the interpretation fits the parable well.[88] At least vv. 7-8a belonged with the parable originally. One could view v. 8b as a floating logion that Luke has attached here because of similar concerns in the preceding eschatological discourse (17:20-37). Son of Man sayings appear in 17:22, 24, 26, and 30, and faith/faithfulness[89] is emphasized in 17:5-6 and 19.

On the other hand, D. Catchpole has presented a strong case for 18:2-5 and 7-8, including 8b, being a unity from the beginning. He argues that a pattern is present in passages discussing *makrothymia* ("patience") with the result that patience and judgment coexist and patience mitigates the intensity of judgment.[90] A further reason that v. 8b belongs with the parable is that, if *pistis* is understood as faithfulness, as I think it should be, rather than faith (either the act of believing or the content of belief), then this saying fits the parable and its eschatological context. Jesus asks if the Son of Man will find that people have been *faithful* and are thus ready for his coming.[91]

If vv. 7-8 belong with the parable, it is not about humans seeking justice, as important as that subject is.

2. Is the introduction in v. 1, which specifies the intent of the parable as promoting unwearying prayer, in keeping with the parable itself, and is it at odds with the focus on the vindication of the elect in vv. 6-8? Determinative here is the question of the relation of the parable to the eschatological discourse in 17:20-37.

At first glance 18:1 seems like an obvious misappropriation of the parable, but this is not the case. Luke's introductory comment is not an encouragement to persistent prayer *in general,* an assumption often made because of the influence of 11:5-8, though the Unjust Judge must not be forced to conform to the earlier parable. Luke's concern in 18:1 is not prayer in general, but praying and not becoming weary (or giving up, *enkakein*)[92] *with respect to the eschaton,* the time when deliverance comes. The injunction to pray and not give up derives its significance from the context of the whole eschatological discourse, which began in 17:20. The disciples will long to see one of the days of the Son of Man, but will not (17:22), and people will go about their lives and be caught unprepared as in former instances of judgment. The opposite of becoming weary is steadfastness, faithfulness, and readiness.

Part of the problem is that interpreters center on either the judge or the widow, but surely the parable is about the *process* involving both parties, even if the judge is given more weight.[93] The contrast drawn between the judge and God is *with respect to the hearing* each gives the petitioner. For the analogical contrast to work, the parable presupposes that people praying are in a much more advantageous relation to a righteous God who loves and hears his elect than the widow is to the unrighteous and uncaring judge.[94] Luke's concern is that believers not give up while they are waiting for their vindication, which in this context is tied closely to the coming of the Son of Man. For Luke faith/ faithfulness and praying are necessary ingredients of readiness for eschatological deliverance.[95] Charles Talbert's comments are appropriate: disciples should go on praying "thy kingdom come," and the maintenance of faith depends on persistence in prayer.[96] If this is the case, then Luke's introduction to the parable is not inappropriate.

3. To what degree is the interpretation of this parable determined by 11:5-8 or other parallels such as Sir 35:14-25? Luke 11:5-8 is an obvious parallel to this parable as the verbal similarities and the chiastic structure of Luke's travel narrative show.[97] Neither parable is about persistence in general.[98] Their main similarity is use of a "how much more" argument in relation to God hearing prayer. Still, the parable in 18:1-8 provides a greater contrast (God is not like the judge), and the structure of 11:5-8 with its "Who from you" question makes it an entirely different kind of parable. The parable in 11:5-8 should *not* be used as a grid to which 18:1-8 must conform.[99]

I have already shown how Sir 35:14-25(11-23) provides the materials from which the parable was framed. Jesus' parable uses the themes of Sirach but subverts them. Whereas Sirach says God will not have patience toward the nations and focuses on retribution on them, Jesus says that God will have patience toward the elect and focuses on their vindication.

4. *Is the intent with* ekdikein *(vv. 3 and 5) and its cognate* ekdikēsis *(vv. 7-8) "avenge" or "vindicate/grant justice"?* This issue may be dealt with quickly. Surely the intent with *ekdikein* and *ekdikēsis* in this legal context is "vindicate/ grant justice," rather than "avenge."[100] The woman wants justice done for her, almost certainly the return of property taken illegally from her. More difficult and more important is the meaning of *ekdikēsis* in v. 7, which speaks of God's vindicating his elect. What act of God is in mind? This will be treated below.

5. *How should the judge's motive for action be understood? What did he fear that the woman would do?* Even if *hypōpiazein* connotes physical violence, its use here is surely metaphorical or sarcastic.[101] The judge fears not that the woman will strike him but that she will annoy him to death.[102] Whether *eis telos* ("unto the end") in v. 5 connects to the participle "coming" or to *hypōpiazein* is less clear. In either case, however, the judge fears there will be no end to this widow's coming and annoying him.[103]

6. *How should v. 7 be understood?* Compare the following translations:

> KJV: And shall not God avenge his own elect, which cry day and night unto him, though he bear long with them?
>
> NIV: And will not God bring about justice for his chosen ones, who cry out to him day and night? Will he keep putting them off?
>
> NRSV: And will not God grant justice to his chosen ones, who cry to him day and night? Will he delay long in helping them?
>
> NEB: . . . and will not God vindicate his chosen, who cry out to him day and night, while he listens patiently to them?
>
> A *literal translation:* Will not God surely acquire justice (aorist subjunctive) for his elect who cry to him day and night? And he is having patience (present indicative) over them.

The problem is in the second sentence.[104] Should it be understood as a question, like the first clause (as in NIV and NRSV), a statement (as in my literal translation), a concessive clause (as in KJV), or a relative clause ("the elect . . . *whom* he hears graciously")?[105] Further, does *makrothymein* mean "have patience" (and if so, in what sense), "delay," or "be gracious"?[106] How does this verse, with its suggestion of some length of time,[107] fit with the next verse, which affirms that God will achieve justice for the elect quickly?

The suggestions that the second sentence should be interpreted as concessive or as if it were a relative clause are neither convincing nor viable.[108] Whether it should be punctuated as an affirmation or a question is unclear, but in the end does not change the intent. If it is a question, it connects with the previous question and likewise expects an emphatic affirmative answer ("Of course he will have patience over them"), which is verified by v. 8a. If it is a statement, it is grammatically independent of the previous clause and asserts that God will indeed have patience. The change of tense from aorist subjunctive *poiēsē* to present indicative *makrothymei* suggests that it is an affirmation, even though this makes the connection with v. 8a less smooth.

With regard to the meaning of *makrothymei,* the evidence for "delay" is not strong.[109] LXX use of the *makrothymos* word group in reference to God's actions with his people shows convincingly that these words convey that God mercifully restrains his wrath in dealing with them.[110]

This statement in Luke 18:7 is, then, embedded in the question as a means of heightening the contrast with the unjust judge. The intent is "Will not God surely vindicate his elect who cry to him day and night [given that] he is mercifully patient with them?" Whereas the judge does not care, this clause emphasizes that God does care for his people. Without this patience they could not expect a favorable judgment. As several people suggest, the implication is that God's people need to examine themselves as they await the vindication of God.[111] While the vindication is still future (vv. 7a and 8a), God's patience is at work in the present (v. 7b, which explains the switch to the present tense).

7. Does en tachei *in v. 8a mean "quickly/soon" or "suddenly" as several argue?*[112] Perhaps the intent of *en tachei* is the most difficult problem in the text. Without doubt the overwhelming intent with this expression is that something is to happen quickly or soon, even if just how soon may not be clear.[113] The evidence for the meaning "suddenly" is less convincing.[114] The problem is, however, that Luke seems to have "suddenly" in mind. In 17:26-37 the message is that the coming of the Son of Man will be as it was with Noah and Lot. People were going about their daily routines, and suddenly destruction came. Similarly, when the Son of Man comes, one on the roof is not to go down into the house to get things, nor is the one in the field to return home. Two people are together working, and suddenly one is taken and one left. Also in 21:34-36, which is closely related to the thought of the parable, believers are to watch lest carousing and the concerns of this life weigh them down and "that day" come upon them "suddenly" *(aiphnidios)*. Of course, "suddenly" and "quickly" are not that far removed, as is evidenced by *1 Clem.* 23:5, which uses both together in reference to God's coming.

Still, the emphasis on both length of time and quick vindication seems at odds. We should not conclude that God is testing the elect by not answering immediately[115] or that prayer or good works shorten the time till the parousia.[116] Rather, delay and quick vindication frequently stand as parallel themes in biblical and Jewish eschatology. Possibly Hab 2:3 is most instructive: "For there is still a vision for the appointed time; it speaks of the end, and does not lie. If it seems to tarry, wait for it; it will surely come, it will not delay." The Qumran interpretation is just as striking: "The final age will be extended and go beyond all that the prophets say, because the mysteries of God are wonderful. Though it might tarry, wait for it; it definitely has to come and will not delay" (1QpHab 7.7-10). The use of *en tachei* and *makrothymein* in Bar 4:24-25 is also instructive.[117] People are to endure in patience despite the fact that deliverance comes soon. Like our parable Baruch seeks to provide assurance that God will vindicate his people despite the lengthy time without vindication. This seems to be conventional language to express the certainty of God's inbreaking into human affairs to vindicate his people.[118] Similarly Jas 5:7-9 evidences the call for patience from believers and at the same time an assertion that the Lord's coming is near.

Waiting and quickness are thus held in tension, but "quickly" *(en tachei)* does not make any statement about the time of the parousia.[119] Certainly Luke does not remove the idea of near expectation in this text, but he is less concerned with the timing of the parousia than with its impact because he knows that an interval exists before the coming of the Son of Man (17:22-23). His main concern is the reality of the Son of Man's appearance, which will bring vindication and will be a sudden intrusion into human affairs.

8. What is the meaning of the parable, particularly with regard to vindication (ekdikēsis)? Two problems concerning eschatology are addressed by the parable: an overly realized eschatology and doubt that deliverance will come.[120] Vindication will certainly come, but that is no cause for laxity. This parable, like 17:22-37, warns that vindication is far enough removed that people will long for it to come. Deliverance will not come immediately, and readiness and faithfulness are required. Such readiness is enabled and accompanied by prayer.

To what does the soon vindication refer? We may fairly say that the question concerning Jesus' intent with his teaching about the timing of future vindication is the most difficult part of his message. Was he merely mistaken? Did he point primarily to the resurrection or to the destruction of Jerusalem? Did he anticipate the coming of the Son of Man at some unspecified date? Spencer and Spencer suggest that this parable points to the end of the Roman persecution.[121] Bailey argues that the vindication is also in the present in Jesus' death and resurrection.[122] John Nolland suggests that for Luke the time of one's death, the time of the destruction of Jerusalem, and the time of the final judgment and vindication are closely related.[123] The only other Lukan occurrence of *ekdikēsis* refers to the destruction of Jerusalem (21:22), but this does not help much in interpreting 18:8 since it speaks of Jerusalem's destruction, not vindication. It implicitly warns that the *ekdikēsis* may not be what people expect it to be.

Nolland may be correct to connect the various threads, but surely the primary emphasis is final judgment and ultimate vindication. We may suspect that the tension between now and not yet which is so much a part of NT eschatology is present here, but the parable itself is not explicit. The parable assures that God will vindicate his people. The concern is not the timing of the event — despite *en tachei* — but the patience of God toward his people, the certainty of his acting on their behalf, and the necessity for them to live in readiness and faithfulness. The parable then addresses the implied question "Will God respond to pleas for deliverance from his people?" to which the answer is "Certainly," but a second question is appended: "Will his people remain faithful?"[124]

Adapting the Parable

Repeated requests appear at two other places that merit reflection. Jesus heard the Syro-Phoenician woman's repeated requests, did not respond initially, and then granted her request (Matt 15:22-28 par.). He would himself make repeated prayers in Gethsemane (Matt 26:36-46/Mark 14:32-42/Luke 22:39-46), but, although he was strengthened by a divine messenger, his request was not granted. Isa 64:7-12 also deserves reflection in connection with this parable. In v. 7 the prophet recognizes that — in effect — no one remains faithful. As a consequence the people are in a desperate situation (vv. 9-11). V. 12 asks if God will restrain himself, keep silent, and punish the people so severely. Here and elsewhere the question of God's delay in bringing justice is a major factor of life. This parable offers no answer as to why God moves slowly in bringing final vindication and justice, but it urges prayerful and faithful living in the confidence that God will act.

The parable is *not* about persistence in praying or badgering God until we get our desires. Communicating the parable should concentrate on two primary areas: the character of God, who is *not* like the uncaring, unrighteous judge, but is merciful, patient, and eager to assist his people, and the necessity of staying alert and ready for God's vindication and judgment. Vindication has begun with the kingdom and the resurrection of Jesus, but it awaits God's future eschatological action. The evidence of faithfulness and a primary path to alertness and faithfulness is prayer, constant involvement with God as we interpret and deal with the world in which we live.[125]

For Further Reading

Kenneth Ewing Bailey, *Poet and Peasant: A Literary Cultural Approach to the Parables in Luke* (Grand Rapids: Eerdmans, 1976), pp. 127-41.

George Beasley-Murray, *Jesus and the Kingdom of God* (Grand Rapids: Eerdmans, 1986), pp. 203-9.

David R. Catchpole, "The Son of Man's Search for Faith (Luke XVIII 8b)," *NovT* 19 (1977): 81-104.

Gerhard Delling, "Das Gleichnis vom gottlosen Richter," *ZNW* 53 (1962): 1-25.

John Mark Hicks, "The Parable of the Persistent Widow (Luke 18:1-8)," *ResQ* 33 (1991): 209-23.

Joachim Jeremias, *The Parables of Jesus* (2d ed.; trans. S. H. Hooke; New York: Charles Scribner's Sons, 1972), pp. 153-56.

I. Howard Marshall, *Commentary on Luke* (NIGTC; Grand Rapids: Eerdmans, 1978), pp. 669-77.

John Nolland, *Luke 9:21–18:34* (WBC 35B; Dallas: Word, 1993), pp. 864-71.

Wilhelm Ott, *Gebet und Heil. Die Bedeutung der Gebetsparänese in der lukanischen Theologie* (Munich: Kösel, 1965), pp. 13-72.

Susan M. Praeder, *The Word in Women's Worlds: Four Parables* (Wilmington: Michael Glazier, 1988), pp. 51-71.

William David Spencer and Aida Besançon Spencer, *The Prayer Life of Jesus: Shout of Agony, Revelation of Love: A Commentary* (Lanham: University Press of America, 1990), pp. 39-64.

THE PHARISEE AND THE TAX COLLECTOR
(Luke 18:9-14)

Parable Type

This is a single indirect narrative parable. Technically it is a "syncrisis," a comparison of opposites by juxtaposition.[126]

Issues Requiring Attention[127]

1. Is this a single indirect narrative parable or a metaphorical story of the reversal in the kingdom?
2. Should the word order be *statheis tauta pros heauton proseucheto* ("having stood, these things he prayed to himself," that is, silently, or possibly "he prayed about himself") or *statheis pros heauton tauta proseucheto* ("Having stood to himself, these things he was praying")?
3. Was the parable originally addressed to the disciples, the Pharisees, or a larger general audience?
4. How much of this passage belonged to the parable originally? Do vv. 9 and 14a belong? Does v. 14b belong, or is this a floating logion that has been added as commentary?
5. Is the Pharisee depicted as self-righteous and arrogant, or, because of the similarity with Deuteronomy 26, is he presented as sincere, doing what was required by the Torah? Similarly, are Luke's descriptions of the Pharisee and the tax collector caricatures or straightforward assessments?
6. Why is acquittal assigned to the tax collector and not the Pharisee? What is the Pharisee's error?
7. Does the fact that the prayers take place in the Temple mean that the tax collector's prayer meant "Let the sacrifice taking place be for me"?[128]
8. Is the parable either anti-Torah or anti-Semitic?
9. What is the teaching of the parable?

Helpful Primary Source Material[129]

Canonical Material

- OT: Deut 26:1-19; Ps 79:9 (LXX 78:9c: *hilasthēti tais hamartiais hēmōn*, "forgive us our sins," which is close to *hilasthēti moi tō hamartōlō*, "be merciful to me, the sinner," in Luke 18:13); Ezra 9:6. See also Pss 51:1-4;[130] 78:38; Prov 3:34; 27:2; 29:23; LXX Ezek 21:26(31); 33:13; and the "Psalms of Innocence": 5, 7, 17, and 26.
- NT: Matt 5:3; 23:1-36; Luke 1:51-52; 16:14-15; 1 Cor 4:7; 8:1-3; 2 Cor 1:9; Phil 3:3-11; Rev 3:17

Early Jewish Writings

- 1QH 15.34-35: "[I give you thanks], Lord, because you did not make my lot fall in the congregation of falsehood, nor have you placed my regulation in the counsel of hypocrites, [but you have led me] to your favour and your forgiveness. . . ."

- *1 En.* 13:5 describes fallen angels as unable to raise their eyes to heaven as a result of their sins.
- *4 Ezra* 8:47-50: "For you come far short of being able to love my creation more than I love it. But you have often compared yourself to the unrighteous. Never do so! But even in this respect you will be praiseworthy before the Most High, because you have humbled yourself, as is becoming for you, and have not considered yourself to be among the righteous. You will receive the greatest glory, for many miseries will affect those who inhabit the world in the last times, because they have walked in great pride."
- *Prayer of Manasseh* 1:8-9: "Therefore you, O Lord, God of the righteous, have not appointed repentance for the righteous, for Abraham and Isaac and Jacob, who did not sin against you, but you have appointed repentance for me, who am a sinner. For the sins I have committed are more in number than the sand of the sea; my transgressions are multiplied, O Lord, they are multiplied! I am not worthy to look up and see the height of heaven because of the multitude of my iniquities."
- *Jos. Asen.* 10:2–13:15 (first century B.C. or A.D.) describes Aseneth several times as striking her breast, bowing her head, and having no confidence in approaching God when she seeks forgiveness for her sin.
- Josephus, *Ant.* 11.143 describes Ezra as ashamed to look up at heaven because of the sins committed by the people (see Ezra 9:6).
- *As. Mos.* 7:9-10, speaking of impious rulers: "And though their hands and minds touch unclean things, yet their mouth shall speak great things, and they shall say furthermore: 'Do not touch me lest thou shouldst pollute me in the place (where I stand). . . .'"[131]

Greco-Roman Writings

- *Aesop's Fables* 666 (in Perry's appendix, LCL, p. 575) contains a story about a man who prays, "Lord God, look thou with favor upon me and my wife and my children and upon no one else." Another man overhears and prays: "Lord, Lord, Almighty God, confound that fellow and his wife and his children, and nobody else."
- Plato, *Alcibiades* 2.148-49 tells of Athenians inquiring of the god Amnon why they were always defeated by the Spartans even though they sacrificed diligently and the Spartans did not. Amnon's reply was, "I would rather have the reverent reserve of the Spartans than all the ritual of the Greeks."

Early Christian Writings

- *1 Clem.* 38:2: "Let him who is humble-minded not testify to his own humility, but let him leave it to others to bear witness; let not him who is pure in the flesh be boastful, knowing that it is another who bestows on him his continence."
- *Didache* 8:1: "Let not your fasts be with the hypocrites, for they fast on Mondays and Thursdays, but you fast on Wednesdays and Fridays."

Later Jewish Writings

- *m. 'Abot* 2.5: "Hillel said: Keep not aloof from the congregation and trust not in thyself until the day of thy death, and judge not thy fellow until thou art come to his place. . . ." Obviously not all Jewish views were legalistic or condescending.
- *b. Berakot* 28b: "I give thanks to Thee, O Lord my God, that Thou hast set my portion with those who sit in the Beth ha-Midrash and Thou hast not set my portion with those who sit in [street] corners, for I rise early and they rise early, but I rise early for words of Torah and they rise early for frivolous talk; I labour and they labour, but I labour and receive a reward and they labour and do not receive a reward; I run and they run, but I run to the life of the future world and they run to the pit of destruction." Note the parallel in *y. Berakot* 4.2, but also note the different attitude in *b. Berakot* 17a, in which rabbis express their awareness of sin and human finitude and a reluctance to judge.
- *b. 'Erubin* 13b: "This teaches you that him who humbles himself, the Holy One, blessed be He, raises up, and him who exalts himself, the Holy One, blessed be He, humbles; from him who seeks greatness, greatness flees, but him who flees from greatness, greatness follows. . . ."[132]
- *b. Menaḥot* 43b: "R. Judah used to say, A man is bound to say the following three blessings daily: [Blessed art thou . . .] who hast not made me a heathen, . . . who hast not made me a woman, and . . . who hast not made me a brutish man." The same prayer is recorded in *y. Berakot* 9.1 and *t. Berakot* 6.18.

Textual Features Worthy of Attention

The structure of the passage is clear; it consists of:

a narrative introduction explaining the intent (v. 9),

the story (vv. 10-13), including descriptions of the Pharisee's prayer (vv. 11-12) and the tax collector's prayer (v. 13),

the storyteller's pronouncement of judgment on the two individuals (v. 14a), and

an explanation of the basis of the judgment (v. 14b).

Both prayers start the same way with an address to God. The Pharisee's posture is described briefly while his prayer is long; the tax collector's prayer is brief, but his posture is described at length. The description of the tax collector is poignant. He stands far off and does not lift his eyes toward heaven, surely because he feels he does not deserve to be in the midst of God's people and in conversation with God. He repeatedly beats (*etypten*, imperfect tense) his chest and uses the definite article in describing himself as *the* sinner, possibly picking up a slanderous taunt by which others had addressed him.

This parable is bound to the preceding parable by subject matter (prayer and judgment) and by several occurrences of the *dikaios* ("righteous") word group: *ekdikeō/ekdikēsis* ("vindicate"/"vindication") in 18:3, 5, 7, and 8; *antidikou* ("opponent") in 18:3; *adikia* ("unrighteousness") in 18:6; *dikaios* ("righteous") in 18:9; *adikos* ("unrighteous") in 18:11; and *dikaioō* ("acquit, declare righteous") in 18:14. The material that follows in 18:15-17 also stresses the importance of humility, especially when compared to Matt 18:1-5; 19:13-15. Much of Luke's material emphasizes the acceptance of inferior and excluded people into the kingdom.

This parable, the previous parable of the Unjust Judge, and that of the Pounds in 19:11-27 are the only ones for which the purpose of the parable is stated before the parable.[133]

The contrast in this parable mirrors the contrast in the parable of the Prodigal Son (Luke 15:11-32) between the desperate and humble confession of the prodigal and the distancing and disdain of the elder brother. The attitude of the Pharisee is reflected as well in 7:36-50 with Simon the Pharisee's disdain for the woman who washes Jesus' feet. The parable of the Good Samaritan is similar with its contrast of the Samaritan to the priest and Levite (10:25-37).[134] Other contrasts worthy of reflection include those between the unforgiving servant and the king in Matt 18:23-35, the two sons in Matt 21:28-32, and the privileged guests who refuse to come and outcasts who do in Luke 14:15-24.

Luke's Gospel has several narratives involving tax collectors or Pharisees. The Pharisees are often depicted as grumbling, unreceptive, or hesitant about Jesus and his message,[135] but not always. In 13:31 they seek to help Jesus by warning him of Herod. Tax collectors are depicted as receptive and as finding salvation. The treatment of Zacchaeus in 19:1-10 mirrors the acquittal of the tax collector in the parable.

The language of the parable is strongly Semitic. Note the occurrences of asyndeton[136] in vv. 11, 12, and 14, *heis . . . heteros* ("the one . . . the other") in v. 10, and *par' ekeinon* ("instead of that one," apparently translating Aramaic *min,* "from").[137]

Cultural Information

Pharisees were highly respected among most Jews and would have been considered righteous, scrupulous in their efforts to obey God. Their directions for worship, prayer, and righteous living had heavy influence on Jewish religious culture.[138] The Pharisee in this parable goes beyond all requirements of the Law. Fasting was required of Jews only on the Day of Atonement. As the Bible attests, people facing crises would also fast, and particularly godly people would fast more frequently.[139] In fasting twice a week, apparently on Monday and Thursday,[140] the Pharisee probably viewed himself as fasting to make atonement for all of Israel. In tithing all he acquired, he tithed items he purchased that other people should have already tithed. *M. Demai* discusses regulations for tithing produce when one is uncertain whether it has already been tithed.

If Pharisees were respected, attitudes toward tax collectors were close to the opposite end of the spectrum. Tax collectors bid for and purchased the right to collect taxes for a specific region, and various kinds of taxes were levied: poll taxes, land taxes, toll charges on travel and the transportation of goods from one region to another, sales taxes, and inheritance taxes. What tax collectors and toll collectors raised beyond their contracts was sheer profit. At least in Judea, Jewish tax collectors — and the tax collector in the parable is certainly Jewish — were considered traitors because they had contracted with the ruling powers to collect taxes and tolls or were underlings hired by such people to make the actual collections.[141] The civil tax burden was onerous, on top of which the Temple tax would have been added. The status of the man in the parable is uncertain; he may have been fairly well off or possibly a lower level toll collector.[142] Attitudes toward tax collectors and especially toll collectors were quite negative.[143] Such people were notorious for dishonesty and in the Mishnah are classified with murderers and robbers, people to whom one does not have to tell the truth. At least later they were deprived of civic rights and were not allowed to be judges or witnesses in court.[144]

Some suggest that no one would have heard of a tax collector going to the Temple to pray,[145] but this is an exaggeration. People are often forced into actions they would rather not do and still seek communion with God. Tax collectors did not fear public recognition when they approached John the Baptist for baptism and direction for living (Luke 3:12-13).

Modern readers must grasp how surprising and stunning for Jesus' hearers it would have been that the tax collector was the one declared to be in the right. That would contravene everything they knew.

The words "went up"/"went down" are used because of the elevation of the Temple Mount. Note the Psalms of Ascent, especially Psalms 122, 134, and 135. Although people certainly prayed at other times, the customary hours for prayer were 9:00 a.m. and 3:00 p.m. at the morning and afternoon sacrifices (cf. Acts 2:15; 3:1). After the sacrifice and during the burning of incense, the congregation gathered to observe the proceedings and to offer prayers (*m. Tamid* 5.1; cf. Sir 50:5-18; Jdt 9:1).[146] "The unclean" were made to stand in the Eastern Gate (*m. Tamid* 5.6). Whom the Mishnah intends by "the unclean" is uncertain, but even if it refers only to those who were temporarily ritually unclean, it betrays an attitude that explains why the tax collector stood at a distance.[147]

Various postures are described for prayer, but standing is common (see 1 Sam 1:26; 1 Kgs 8:14, 22; Matt 6:5; Mark 11:25). Lifting one's eyes is common in prayer; note that Jesus lifts his eyes to pray in Matt 14:19/Mark 6:41/Luke 9:16; Mark 7:34; John 11:41; 17:1.

Restitution of money gained by extortion required an additional fifth be added (Lev 6:1-5). The tax collector's situation would be hopeless, for he could never know everyone he had wronged.[148]

Explanation of the Parable

Options for Interpretation

1. Most often the church did not allegorize this parable but interpreted it in terms of its teaching on pride and humility. Augustine, followed by a number of others, interpreted the Pharisee and tax collector as representing Jews and Gentiles.[149]

2. The parable is frequently interpreted as a contrast between self-righteousness and spiritual poverty or humility.[150] At times the self-righteousness is framed as Jewish legalism.[151]

3. J. D. Crossan, having stripped vv. 9 and 14b and having rejected example story as a category, views the parable as a reversal, the metaphorical point of which is the reversal of accepted human judgment whereby the kingdom forces its way into human awareness.[152]

4. A few see the parable as calling for reform of the Temple. The presup-

position here is that the oppressive Temple taxes are in view with the Pharisee being seen as a retainer of the Temple system.[153]

5. A few view one or both characters as a caricature. With this approach the tax collector may be a positive figure, or both men are viewed as unacceptable alternatives.[154]

6. A few think the Pharisee is described as doing exactly what Deuteronomy 26 prescribes for one bringing his tithes and affirming his obedience to the covenant.[155]

7. A significant number think the problem of the Pharisee is in the disdain he shows for others and specifically for the tax collector.[156]

While aspects of several of these options may be true, I will argue that a combination of options two and seven provides the best understanding of the parable.

Decisions on the Issues

1. Is this a single indirect narrative parable or a metaphorical story of the reversal in the kingdom? I have argued that "example story" is inappropriate as a category,[157] and that is especially true with this parable. The two men do function partly as negative and positive examples, but, as we have seen, numerous parables offer people as examples. Exactly what should be imitated or avoided here with either man is not clear, and even with the tax collector we could not say, "Go and do likewise."[158] Also, "example story" is too limiting to embrace what the parable has to teach about God.

On the other hand, the argument that the parable is a metaphor of the reversal of judgment effected by the kingdom is not convincing either. The parable has a reversal of expectations, but it is not metaphorical. We are not to see through the two characters to some other reality; rather, we are to see them. The parable is a single indirect narrative framed as a syncrisis (a comparison of opposites by juxtaposition). It tells about the prayers of a particular Pharisee and a particular tax collector and what may be learned from them.

2. Should the word order be statheis tauta pros heauton proseucheto *("having stood, these things he prayed to himself")* or statheis pros heauton tauta proseucheto *("Having stood to himself, these things he was praying")?* The former is sometimes taken to mean that the Pharisee prayed silently, but it could also mean "he prayed *about* himself."[159] The second reading would indicate that the Pharisee stood by himself, indicating either that he took a prominent position or that he separated himself from others to avoid contact. A decision about this textual variant is difficult because either reading makes sense and the textual evidence is rather balanced.[160] The manuscript evidence for *statheis tauta pros heauton proseucheto* ("having stood, he was praying these things with/about himself") includes P[75],[161] but *statheis pros heauton tauta proseucheto* ("having stood to himself, he was praying these things")[162] seems to be the more difficult reading and the one that can account for the emergence of the others. And if the focus is on the Pharisee's standing alone, then the parable speaks of both men as praying apart from other people.

Furthermore, the proposed meanings of *statheis tauta pros heauton proseucheto* have little in their favor. Some have suggested that the Pharisee is praying *to* himself, but that can hardly be the intent since both prayers begin with an address to God. People in antiquity usually prayed aloud, so it is unlikely the intent is that the Pharisee prays silently. The third suggested meaning, a supposed *pros* ("toward") of reference meaning that the Pharisee prayed "about" himself, is shaky at best.[163] *Proseuchesthai pros* never has that meaning in the LXX or the NT. The *pros* refers instead to the person addressed.[164] Since the proposed meanings for this alternate reading do not seem to fit, we should conclude that the correct reading is *statheis pros heauton* and that it describes the man as standing by himself.[165]

3. *Was the parable originally addressed to the disciples, the Pharisees, or a larger general audience?* The arrangement of the context is from Luke, and we do not have information on the context in which the parable was told. It could have been told on more than one occasion and in any Jewish context, whether to Jesus' disciples, Jews in general, or specifically Pharisees. It would have been most forceful if told in Jerusalem, which seems likely. Luke has placed the parable in his travel narrative, and while not many geographical indicators are given about this journey nor much progress recorded, the shadow of Jerusalem falls over the whole narrative (9:51; 13:4, 22, 34-35; 17:11; 18:31; 19:11). Throughout the travel narrative Jesus' teaching is addressed at different times to his disciples, to the crowds, or to Pharisees, enough that Peter must ask in 12:41 for whom a parable was intended. In Luke the Pharisees seem to hear even when material is addressed to the disciples (e.g., 16:14).[166] It seems to me more likely that this parable was addressed to the crowds in general or to the disciples. If it were addressed to the Pharisees, we would expect some reaction on their part. Luke has intentionally kept the audience general: "certain ones who trusted in themselves."[167] Even if the parable was originally addressed to Pharisees, Luke wanted his Christian readers to know that they were equally in danger of the failure it depicts.

4. *How much of this passage belonged to the parable originally? Do vv. 9 and 14a belong?* V. 9 is clearly a Lukan introduction that provides the intent of the parable in advance and that was shaped from v. 14a. By giving the intent first the narrative focuses more attention on the Pharisee as a negative figure and lessens the suspense and shock that the original parable would have had with-

out the introduction. Some suggest that the parable ended with v. 13, especially those who think both men are negative figures,[168] but nothing in the parable makes the tax collector a negative figure. With regard to both logic and form v. 14a must be considered the original conclusion to the parable.[169] Without it the parable has no meaning. With regard to form, the parallels between "went up" (*anebēsan*, v. 10) and "went down" (*katebē*, v. 14a) and between "this tax collector" in the Pharisee's disdainful remark (v. 11) and "this one" in the verdict (v. 14a) show that v. 14a is an inherent part of the account. The contrast here is close to the contrast between the sinful woman and the Pharisee in 7:36-50, and as is often noted, the contrast in v. 14a is exclusive: "This man went down to his house acquitted and not that one."[170]

Did v. 14b belong, or is it a floating logion that has been added as a commentary? V. 14b could be either an explanatory statement originally used by Jesus with the parable or a floating logion attached to the parable by tradition or re-used here by Luke as an explanatory statement.[171] Nothing is really at stake with any of these options, for such a general principle was no doubt spoken by Jesus on various occasions, as its presence in Matt 23:12 and Luke 14:11 attests. Interestingly, both these other occurrences appear in contexts dealing with Pharisees. Some think Luke is responsible for v. 14b because it uses the future tense and points to an eschatological reversal, whereas in v. 14a the tax collector has already been acquitted.[172] A. Feuillet argues that v. 14b is original because he thinks Isaiah 53, the only other text with the combination of justification, humiliation, and exaltation (*dikaioun, tapeinoun,* and *hypsoun*), stands behind the parable.[173] I do not think we can prove that v. 14b originally belonged with the parable or that it did not. We can say that it is a suitable conclusion that provides a general principle reflected in the parable.

5. Is the Pharisee depicted as self-righteous and arrogant, or, because of the similarity with Deuteronomy 26, is he presented as sincere, doing what was required by the Torah? Usually the Pharisee's prayer is understood to be pretentious, prideful, and self-righteous, particularly with its fivefold reference to "I." This is understandable for Christians who have become accustomed to negative descriptions of Pharisees, and it is not difficult to find evidence of pretentiousness, self-righteousness, or disdain for the ʿam ha-areṣ among Pharisees or in other groups (including Christians in later writings).[174] Centuries of interpretation have led us to see the Pharisee as a negative character, but Jews listening to Jesus would have assumed that the Pharisee was a righteous man.

The parallels between Deuteronomy 26 and the parable tempt us to think that he is not pretentious.[175] In Deut 26:12-15 individuals are to come with their tithes, affirm their obedience to God, and pray for his blessing. However, the Pharisee of the parable does not bring tithes, does not pray for a blessing, and does not affirm that he has kept the commandments. Instead, he thanks God he is not like others and points to his going beyond the commandments. In the end the connection to Deuteronomy 26 is not that strong.

Regardless of any connection to Deuteronomy 26,[176] the error is not that the Pharisee is obedient or that he says he is obedient. The "Psalms of Innocence" show petitioners affirming that they have done what God has commanded.[177] At the very least the Pharisee's prayer is self-centered. Unlike Deuteronomy 26, there is no focus on God as the one to whom allegiance is owed and from whom blessing comes, and there is no focus on the poor to whom tithes should be given.

Are Luke's descriptions of the Pharisee and the tax collector caricatures or straightforward assessments?[178] The two men are presented as polar opposites, which is the nature of syncrisis, but neither description is a caricature. The attitude of the Pharisee is evident in primary sources,[179] and nothing in the text gives any hint that he is a caricature. Even less reason exists to see the tax collector as a caricature.

6. Why is acquittal assigned to the tax collector and not the Pharisee? What is the Pharisee's error? The error of the Pharisee, which some surprisingly struggle to find,[180] is surely that he thinks he can be obedient to God and still have disdain for people like the tax collector — that is, that he can fulfill what the Torah demands with no attention to the love command.[181] He is certain that his acts put him in good standing with God and that his pious acts make him better than his contemporaries. What may have started as legitimate affirmation that he has kept the covenant has detoured into disdain and self-congratulation. Jesus frequently emphasized that one cannot be obedient to God's Law without loving one's neighbor as oneself,[182] and he repeatedly challenged those who were certain of their good standing with God to reconsider.[183] This parable expresses both themes.

The basis of the acquittal of the tax collector is not expressed unless one takes v. 14b as original with the parable. Luke's introduction shows that his concern is primarily with the Pharisee. The lack of any further basis for the verdict heightens the shock that the wrong person is given the verdict of righteousness. By implication, the basis of the acquittal is the tax collector's sense of his need, his throwing himself on the mercy of God, and the compassion of God who forgives sinners, again recurring themes in Luke's portrayal of Jesus' message.

7. Does the fact that the prayers take place in the Temple mean that the tax collector's prayer means "Let the sacrifice taking place be for me"? For some, that the two men go up to the Temple at the same time indicates that we should think of the prayers in relation to either the morning or evening sacrifice.[184] Others think assigning a time for the prayers is unnecessary speculation because between the sacrifices people went to the Temple for private prayer.[185]

One cannot be certain, but the evidence strongly suggests that most Jewish hearers would have thought of prayers at the time of sacrifice. Luke mentions the daily sacrifice in several other contexts. Luke 1:5-23 describes Zechariah offering the afternoon sacrifice, and Acts 3:1 says that Peter and John went up to the Temple at the hour of prayer, the ninth hour, the time of the afternoon sacrifice. An allusion to the daily sacrifice is present in Luke 24:50-53 and possibly other texts.[186] Further, the expression *hilastheti moi* in the tax collector's prayer has sacrificial overtones, even if it should be translated "Be merciful to me" rather than "Be propitiated to me."[187] Even if one decides that the time of prayer is irrelevant, the context of praying in the Temple, the place of God's presence and forgiveness, would still be determinative for understanding the intent of the prayer. The tax collector's prayer is a poignant plea that the sacrifice will be effective enough to enable God to have mercy on him.

This makes the views that the parable is a critique of the Temple or the Temple tax system unlikely. There is no indictment of the Temple in the parable, or evidence of any negative attitude toward the Temple, and if these views were correct we would expect the contrasting figure to be a priest or at least a Levite rather than a Pharisee. Once again the principle is affirmed: any interpretation based on what is not in the parable is almost certainly wrong. Parables do not always spell out their functions, but they do give the necessary information to designate the arena for interpretation.

8. Is the parable anti-Torah or anti-Semitic? Anti-Semitism is a major problem, but this parable is neither anti-Torah nor anti-Semitic.[188] It does not set Law and grace against each other, nor is it a condemnation of Judaism or even Pharisaism, even though Jesus in Luke often complains about the Pharisees. This is a parable about a particular Pharisee, not all Pharisees. It sets a misunderstanding of Torah, as fulfilled in obedience to ritual apart from love of neighbor, over against mercy and love, which God requires and which display God's character. Like the elder brother in Luke 15:25-32, who had not transgressed the commands but still had disdain for his brother,[189] the Pharisee thinks he is true to the Torah's stipulations but does not see the Torah's intent of love for neighbor (cf. Matt 23:23). Luke 17:7-10 already indicates the proper attitude when affirming one's own obedience. One should say, "We are unworthy servants; we have done what we were supposed to do."

9. What is the teaching of the parable? The parable addresses the implied question "What counts as righteousness before God?" Righteous acts without compassion and love are not considered righteous by God. Jesus' decision as to which man was righteous must have sounded paradoxical, surprising, and maybe even unacceptable to his hearers. This parable, like some others, is a verbal slap in the face. Jesus called a man righteous who was known to be unrighteous and refused this description for a man whom everyone would recognize as a righteous person, one who had done good things, even beyond what the law expected — that is, unless Jesus' hearers were keyed in to the importance of the love command. Modern readers must make the effort to realize the shock of Jesus' statement to his first-century Jewish hearers. By implication, this parable also serves as a defense of Jesus' eating with tax collectors and sinners and instructs against disdain for the so-called unrighteous.[190] M. Hengel points out that the person proud of his or her orthodoxy and orthopraxy is in the most danger and, by use of a wordplay, summarizes the parable as saying that those who are written off elsewhere are written in by God in the gospel.[191] "A proud prayer is . . . a self-contradictory endeavor."[192] Conversely, humility is an essential aspect of true prayer.

That the tax collector is justified because he pleads for mercy is in accord with Jesus' focus on forgiveness and mercy elsewhere, most obviously in the parable of the Unforgiving Servant (Matt 18:21-35, especially vv. 27, 32), but also in other texts (Matt 5:3-7; Luke 6:20-21; 7:36-50). "Justified" (from the verb *dikaioō*) is legal language which means "shown to be in the right," "acquitted." The word appears infrequently in the Gospels but should not be filled too quickly with Pauline connotations.[193] The Gospels do not contrast Law and grace as Paul does. On the other hand, it is legitimate to say that Paul's justification teaching has its origin in and is an extension of the teaching of Jesus in texts such as this.[194] The passive verbs in v. 14 ("justified," "humbled," "exalted") are divine passives; they point to God as the one doing the act.

This parable has christological implications. Jesus had the confidence to declare the mind of God with regard to judgment. That does not prove he fits some transcendent category, but it certainly is an unexpected claim to authority.[195] A. Feuillet finds even stronger christological implications because he thinks the parable is based on Isaiah 53, the only other biblical text combining justification, humiliation, and exaltation *(dikaioun, tapeinoun,* and *hypsoun).*[196] The connections he finds are intriguing, but I do not think he has proved his case.

The implications the parable has about God are even stronger in that it contains a revelation of God. In fact, the attitudes of the two men reveal two images of God, one presupposed by the Pharisee, which is false, and one hoped for but not presumed by the tax collector, which is right.[197] God is not a God impressed with pious acts and feelings of superiority. He is, rather, a God of mercy who responds to the needs and honest prayers of people. On the other hand, God is not a God whose mercy can be taken for granted. Within the parable the tax collector does not even know the outcome of his prayer. The verdict of acquittal stands outside the parable. There is no basis for him to congratulate himself.

This parable is less about prayer than it is about attitudes toward self and neighbor, nor is this the only teaching about prayer that is necessary. No mention is made of repentance or restitution, nor should we expect it. Parables make no attempt to cover everything related to their topics.

Adapting the Parable

Martin Luther gave at least thirteen different sermons on this text,[198] and it still merits repeated attention in today's churches. Christians are as easily guilty of self-satisfaction as the Pharisee, as the denunciation of the church at Laodicea (Rev 3:17) already shows. The temptation lies at hand to pray, "I thank God I am not like this Pharisee or like unbelievers." Søren Kierkegaard's sermon on this parable highlights three points about penitence: *being alone with God,* for when we are alone with God we realize how far from God we are; *looking downward,* for when we see God's holiness we realize our own wretchedness; *awareness of being in danger* before God, for if we feel safe like the Pharisee we really are in peril.[199] H. Thielicke, among others, argued that it is wrong to assume "publican's pride," to make oneself out as utterly vile with constant babblings about sin as if God is pleased with self-abasement, and warned that grace can easily go bad in our hands and lead to pharisaic pride.[200] J. S. Glen rightly asserted that the modern-day counterpart of the Pharisee would be welcomed into any respectable community, religious or social, and given a responsible position. It is surprising how much egotism and rigorous devotion will be tolerated if a person is just and clean-living and gives of her or his substance.[201]

The parable raises the question of how our assessment of people squares with God's assessment. All too frequently, like Simon the Pharisee (Luke 7:39-40), we secretly judge people as less than ourselves. In doing so are guilty of the sin of comparison, against which Kierkegaard warns, and we reveal how far we are from the mind of God. In excluding people we are in danger of excluding ourselves from God. The parable, therefore, raises the question of the separation of God's people from sinful people. How do we both deal with separation and demonstrate grace? How do we implement both the attitude in Psalm 1 of not choosing the way of sinners and yet display the humility this text calls for? The parable does not answer that question, but it excludes every thought that would elevate one above other people or that would view others with disdain.

For Further Reading

Kenneth Ewing Bailey, *Poet and Peasant: A Literary Cultural Approach to the Parables in Luke* (Grand Rapids: Eerdmans, 1976), pp. 142-56.

Craig A. Evans, "The Pharisee and the Publican: Luke 18:9-14 and Deuteronomy 26," in *The Gospels and the Scriptures of Israel,* ed. Craig A. Evans and W. Richard Stegner (Sheffield: Sheffield Academic, 1994), pp. 342-55.

Charles W. Hedrick, *Parables as Poetic Fictions: The Creative Voice of Jesus* (Peabody: Hendrickson, 1994), pp. 208-35.

Joachim Jeremias, *The Parables of Jesus* (2d ed.; trans. S. H. Hooke; New York: Charles Scribner's Sons, 1963), pp. 139-44.

John Nolland, *Luke 9:21–18:34* (WBC 35B; Dallas: Word, 1993), pp. 872-79.

Franz Schnider, "Ausschließen und ausgeschlossen werden. Beobachtungen zur Struktur des Gleichnisses vom Pharisäer und Zöllner, Lk 18,10-14a," *BZ* 24 (1980): 42-56.

Luise Schottroff, "Die Erzählung vom Pharisäer und Zöllner als Beispiel für die theologische Kunst des Überredens," in *Neues Testament und christliche Existenz,* ed. Hans Dieter Betz and Luise Schottroff (Tübingen: Mohr-Siebeck, 1973), pp. 439-61.

*　　*　　*

The parables in this chapter are not so much about prayer as about the God to whom we pray and the attitudes we should have in praying. The focus in prayer is on the character of the God to whom we pray. These parables emphasize that God is merciful and eager to hear prayer, but also a God of justice. The people in the parables pray seeking assistance, justice, and forgiveness. These parables teach that God is eager to assist and forgive; they are parables of encouragement. On the other hand, Luke is not teaching that one may bend God's will by first bending his ear.[202] Nor is there a conflict between Luke's focus on praying without giving up and the warning against repetitive prayer in Matt 6:7. Luke is not merely calling for repetitive prayer, but for a faithful lifestyle that stays alert and ready by being in conversation with God. Prayer is itself the defense against weariness and giving up.[203] It is not the means to acquire what one wishes but the means by which one's wishes are made known to God and then brought into conformity with God's will, regardless of the circumstances.

The two parables in Luke 18 also teach that God is concerned with justice and will bring it into reality. But with their focus on justice they also become warnings for the one praying to examine himself or herself. Prayer always borders on being a dangerous activity and is particularly so for the unreflective.

476

Parables of Future Eschatology

Again we start with the disclaimer that our groupings of the parables lay a scheme on them that does not do full justice. The parables dealing with Israel are of obvious relevance to eschatological parables, and parables grouped in other categories easily could be placed here instead. Most obviously, the parables of the Wheat and the Weeds, the Unforgiving Servant, the Unjust Judge, and Lazarus and the Rich Man, which I placed elsewhere, should be included in any understanding of Jesus' parabolic teaching on future eschatology.

Even with an undeniable focus on the presence of the kingdom, Jesus still taught his disciples to pray, "Your kingdom come."[1] The central feature of Jesus' preaching was not yet fully achieved. The kingdom in its fullness was still a future hope for Jesus, and parables of future eschatology help us understand part of what that hope involved. As we will see though, most of the focus is not on the character of the future kingdom but on the character of those awaiting its arrival.

Jesus' teaching with regard to the future is one of the most crucial and most debated topics in NT studies. Adequate treatment would divert our attention from the parables, but some issues must be addressed. Scholars, both past and present — from Adolf Harnack to Marcus Borg, have attempted to remove the eschatological focus from the message of Jesus. For example, Borg argues that Jesus did not preach the end of the world, that the coming Son of Man sayings are not authentic, and that, while Jesus did believe in final judgment, the kingdom language was a symbol to evoke the whole story of God's relation to Israel and humanity.[2] N. T. Wright also argues against the idea that Jesus was proclaiming the end of the world, but the last thing he would do is think of a non-eschatological Jesus. Whereas Borg ends up with an understanding of the kingdom that spans from the beginning of time to the end, Wright argues that the kingdom is understood as the fulfillment in Jesus' actions of the OT promises that God would return as king to restore his promises. The focus is not the end of the world but new creation. He understands the coming Son of Man texts to be Jesus' reference to the coming destruction of Jerusalem at the hand of the Roman armies.[3] A third alternative is offered by Dale Allison. He argues that Jesus came as a millenarian prophet focused on the restoration of Israel, that he did preach — erroneously — the end of the world within the lifetime of his generation and that his references to the coming Son of Man were meant literally.[4]

These are but three alternatives in a bewildering discussion, and they reveal the assumptions and issues. But I find myself unconvinced that any of the three does justice to the Gospel passages. What can we say to guide our investigation of the parables about the future?

No message about the kingdom of God could make sense that did not express at least the hope of the fulfillment of God's universal rule. It would have to include fulfillment of the promises to Israel. Kingdom preaching could mean nothing less. We have seen the focus on the present kingdom and on the warnings and hopes for Israel in earlier chapters, but even with those themes the message is incomplete. Jesus' story is an unfinished story, not merely from the standpoint of the early church, not only in terms of what Judaism expected, but also from the perspective of Jesus' own message.[5] Jesus, rightly or wrongly, did not think his story was over with his arrival in Jerusalem. If we can know anything about Jesus, his message gave prominent attention to the crisis of judgment, the destruction of Jerusalem, the fulfillment of the promises to Israel, and the coming of the Son of Man in glory. But how do these themes relate? Some texts clearly point to judgment on Jesus' contemporaries,[6] while others point to the final judgment.[7] Some texts point to the presence of the kingdom and the promises being fulfilled in Jesus' ministry.[8] Others point to future fulfillment.[9]

As is obvious with the views of Borg, Wright, and Allison, NT scholars disagree mightily over how Jesus' language about the coming of the Son of Man should be understood and whether such language is even from Jesus. To what was Jesus referring with the coming Son of Man and with "this generation" language, and when did he think it would happen? Did Jesus think either the end of the world or the new creation would happen within the lifetime of his disciples? How does "the coming" relate to Jesus' warning of the destruction of Jerusalem? The difficulty is increased because the eschatological discourses in Matthew 24-25/Mark 13/Luke 21 interlace questions about the destruction of Jerusalem and the coming of Jesus/the Son of Man (see Matt 24:3 in particular).

Most today would agree that Jesus expected to die; the death of John the Baptist and the prophets made such an expectation easy. Most would agree as well that Jesus expected to be vindicated, but just how is not often specified. How does his future expectation fit with his anticipation of his own death?

Justice cannot be done to these questions, but certain options are excluded in my estimation. First, Jesus did not proclaim a timeless kingdom as a symbol to evoke the whole story of God's relation to Israel and humanity. That does no justice to the fulfillment motif and the focus on the kingdom having drawn near or having arrived. If the Gospels point to anything, it is not a timeless kingdom but something new taking place with Jesus to fulfill the promises of God. Second, the coming of the Son of Man in glory cannot be equated with the destruction of Jerusalem as N. T. Wright suggests.[10] Jerusalem had been destroyed in 586 B.C. and would be again in 135 A.D. What makes the destruction in 70 A.D. so crucial that it would be described as the coming of the Son of Man, and why was that destruction so *un*important to the early church that it is never mentioned? The destruction of Jerusalem is not sufficient, in my estimation, to be labeled the vindication of Jesus or the victory of God. The early church saw the vindication and victory in the resurrection, the pouring out of the Holy Spirit, and in the expected parousia.[11] Third, Jesus did not predict the end of the world or the new creation within the lifetime of his generation. The most obvious referent of texts focusing on what happens to that generation is the destruction of Jerusalem. That seems certain for Matt 23:36/Luke 11:51, and most likely for Matt 24:34/Mark 13:30/Luke 21:32, but the latter saying is heavily debated[12] and rendered difficult by the interlacing of the destruction of Jerusalem and the coming of the Son of Man. The assertion in the same context[13] that no one knows "that day and hour," not even the Son, receives far too little attention,[14] but at least it should prevent an assumption that "the end" would happen within the lifetime of Jesus' generation.

These issues land us in the center of the hermeneutical circle, for the parables on the future are *a resource for understanding Jesus' expectation,* and yet we need to know his expectation in order to interpret the parables. Granted that the relevant parables must be inserted into the larger picture of Jesus' teaching, they also must be studied in their own right, even if they do not answer our questions directly. They are first-hand evidence of what Jesus believed would happen, not merely passive vessels to be filled with the content of reconstructed theories of his teaching. As elsewhere, we must correlate what Jesus taught in parables with what he taught in non-parabolic material. Further, we must have a bipolar focus in interpreting the parables. We must ask what and how extensive the expectation of Jesus was in his confrontation with the nation Israel, but we must also ask how that expectation was reframed after the resurrection and the coming of the Holy Spirit as the early church continued to teach this material.

Before analyzing the parables dealing with future eschatology, some minimal sketch of Jesus' expectation is necessary. Of most importance are the facts that Jesus expected judgment on his contemporaries, his own death, a subsequent vindication/resurrection, and the coming of the Son of Man in glory to bring salvation and final judgment. While some doubt that Jesus spoke of his own coming (parousia), the eschatological parables are evidence that he did,[15] but what was he claiming? I understand that with the coming Son of Man Jesus was referring to himself[16] and that his allusion to Dan 7:13 at least partly expressed his certainty of vindication. He cannot have thought that he would die and that was it, that the kingdom would fail. No one accepts martyrdom with such an expectation. Like other Jews, surely Jesus believed in resurrection, and like the mother and her seven sons in 2 Macc 7:1-42 went to death confident of resurrection and restoration in God's kingdom, in which he still would have a crucial role.[17] It seems the only solution possible is that Jesus expected an interval of unknown duration between the immediate events pertaining to his death and the vindication referred to with the coming of the Son of Man. Several texts point in this direction and cannot be set aside.[18] For example:

> The sons of the bridegroom are not able to mourn as long as the bridegroom is with them, are they? But the days will come when the bridegroom will be taken away from them, and then they will fast (Matt 9:15/Mark 2:19-20/Luke 5:34-35).

> A time of persecution will arise (Matt 5:10-12/Luke 6:22-23; cf. Matt 10:16-23; 23:34-36; Matt 24:9-14/Mark 13:9-13/Luke 21:12-19).

> Wars and famines and earthquakes will take place, but they do not mark the end (Matt 24:6-8/Mark 13:7-8/Luke 21:9-11)

> Behold your house is left desolate to you, for I say to you, you will in no way see me from now until you say, "Blessed is the one coming in the name of the Lord" (Matt 23:38-39/Luke 13:35).

> I say to you, from now I will in no way drink from this fruit of the vine until that day when I drink it new with you in the kingdom of my Father. (Matt 26:29/Mark 14:25; cf. Luke 22:16, 18).[19]

> The days will come when you will desire to see one of the days of the Son of Man, and you will not (Luke 17:22).

Will not God surely vindicate his elect who cry to him day and night and have mercy on them? I tell you he will vindicate them quickly. But, when the Son of Man comes will he find faith in the earth? (Luke 18:7-8).

Several of Jesus' parables are also evidence of an interval in Jesus' portrayal of future expectation. The parables of the Growing Seed, the Mustard Seed, the Leaven, the Faithful and Unfaithful Stewards, the Wheat and the Tares, the Barren Fig Tree, the Unjust Judge, the Ten Virgins, the Talents, and especially the Minas all point at least to some length of time. Therefore, a minimal sketch of Jesus' expectation includes his own death and subsequent vindication, an interval of unknown length, judgment on Israel/Jerusalem, and the coming of the Son of Man to gather the elect and to judge.[20]

I have already indicated that the destruction of Jerusalem is not what Jesus had in mind when he spoke of vindication or the coming of the Son of Man. The coming of the Son of Man is a time of crisis and will bring both blessing and judgment, but the many warnings Jesus gives point to various crises: the crisis of his own ministry, his impending death, the destruction of Jerusalem, the death of the individual, and final judgment. These various warnings cannot be collapsed onto one referent, especially not the destruction of Jerusalem,[21] even though I would emphasize the central role the restoration of Israel has in Jesus' ministry. However, judgment is only part of the picture, for the fullness of the kingdom brings both judgment and blessing/salvation. Jesus proclaimed judgment on the nation Israel, but also on all humans individually.[22] He also promised reward and the messianic banquet for the faithful and merciful. The restoration of Israel will not be complete until the kingdom comes in its fullness. The parables in this chapter point to the anticipated fullness of the kingdom.

Several theories exist to account for the variety of expectations in the eschatological sayings,[23] but the argument of G. B. Caird is most helpful in explaining that Jesus' various sayings are very much like those of OT prophets, who were able to see one picture of the impending future coalesce with another of the ultimate future. With this double vision the historical crisis facing Israel is linked to and is a lens for the crisis of final judgment (and vice versa).[24] This is why the disciples' question about the destruction of Jerusalem is answered by sayings dealing with the end and why portions of the eschatological discourse must be understood as referring to two different events, the destruction of Jerusalem and the end time.[25] Both the imminence of the crisis and the uncertainty of the time must be kept together,[26] something that many scholars find themselves unable to do.

Despite the popularity of the assumption, I do not think the delay of the parousia caused a rewriting of the church's eschatology.[27] In the NT, rather than the problem of a delay, more evidence exists for the problem of an overly realized eschatology, the assumption that the parousia is very near or that the resurrection has already taken place. (See 2 Thess 2:2; 2 Tim 2:17-18.)[28]

Whether this provisional sketch is adequate depends on the degree to which it is supported by investigation of the parables themselves without coercing the parables into a system.

THE NET
(Matt 13:47-50)

Whether this parable is primarily about future eschatology and should be treated here or is also about present eschatology and should be treated in that chapter is a matter of debate. Its similarity to the parable of the Wheat and Weeds suggests it should be discussed with the other parables in Matthew 13, but it seems to me that this one is so heavily oriented to future eschatology that it should be treated here, even if its separation from Matthew 13 is awkward. The parables in Matthew 13 are all about the present kingdom and, except for the Wheat and Weeds and especially its interpretation, at most only hint of the future kingdom. The language used for the Net is close to the judgment language in the interpretation of the Wheat and Weeds, but there are differences.

Treatment of this simple parable involves more questions than one would expect, but some of them are a result of interpreters reading their theology into the parable.

Parable Type

This is a similitude,[29] but unlike many other similitudes (such as the Mustard Seed, the Leaven, the Treasure, and the Pearl in Matthew 13) it has an explanatory *nimshal*.[30] There is no developed plot.

Issues Requiring Attention

1. Are the parable and its interpretation authentic teachings from Jesus?
2. What OT texts, if any, form the background of the parable and with what significance?
3. To what degree does this parable reflect Matthew's community? Is this a parable about the mixed state of the church?

4. To what degree do the features of this parable have allegorical significance? Is there christological significance?
5. What is the teaching of the parable?

Helpful Primary Source Material

Canonical Material

- OT: Eccl 9:12; Ezek 47:10; Dan 3:6; Hab 1:14-17
- NT: Matt 3:12/Luke 3:17; Matt 7:17-18/Luke 6:43; Matt 12:33; 13:39-42; 22:9-10; 25:31-32[31]

Early Jewish Writings

- 1QH 13.7-9: "You made my lodging with many fishermen, those who spread the net upon the surface of the water, those who go hunting the sons of injustice. And there you established me for the judgment, and strengthened in my heart the foundation of truth."
- *1 En.* 56:1: "Then I saw there an army of the angels of punishment marching, holding nets of iron and bronze."

Greco-Roman Writings

- Aesop *Fables,* Babrius 4, has an account of a fisherman who draws in the net with small and large fish. The small ones escape through the net, but the large ones are caught. The explanation is that being small prevents trouble, but being one of great reputation has many risks. The relevance for Jesus' parable is minimal.

Early Christian Writings[32]

- *Gos. Thom.* 8: "And he said: Man is like a wise fisherman who cast his net into the sea; he drew it out of the sea when it was full of little fishes. Among them the wise fisherman found a large good fish. The wise fisherman cast all the little fishes down into the sea (and) chose the large fish without difficulty. He who has ears to hear, let him hear."

Later Jewish Writings[33]

- *m. 'Abot* 3.17: "All is given against a pledge, and the net is cast over all the living; the shop stands open and the storekeeper gives credit, but the account-book lies open and the hand writes and every one that wishes to borrow let him come and borrow; but the collectors go round continually every day and exact payment of men with their consent or without their consent, and they have that on which they can rely; and the judgment is a judgment of truth; and all is made ready for the banquet."
- *'Abot de Rabbi Nathan* A 40 describes four kinds of fish (an unclean fish, a clean fish, one from the Jordan, and one from the "Great Sea"). The unclean is interpreted as a poor youth who studies and is without understanding; the next three are all clean and refer to different levels of understanding.

Comparison of the Accounts

Neither Mark nor Luke has this parable, but *Gos. Thom.* 8 has a similar parable, though some think it is unrelated to the one in Matthew.[34] There are significant differences, but they are not unlike the differences between the Matthean and *Gos. Thom.* versions of the parable of the Treasure.[35]

Matthew compares the kingdom to a net cast into the sea, but *Gos. Thom.* compares "man" to a wise fisherman who casts his net into the sea. *Gos. Thom.* has nothing parallel to Matthew's "caught from every kind." Both have the net drawn out when it is full, but while Matthew designates the place "upon the shore," *Gos. Thom.* describes the content of the net full "of little fishes." *Gos. Thom.* has nothing paralleling Matthew's description of the fishermen (literally "they") sitting down and dividing the good fish from the worthless ones, nor is there any parallel to vv. 49-50 with its description of judgment. Instead, in *Gos. Thom.* the wise fisherman finds one large, good fish, casts all the little fishes into the sea, and chooses the one large fish without difficulty. This is followed with the injunction for the one with ears to hear.

The *Gos. Thom.* version bears some similarities to the fable in Babrius 4 (see above, p. 483) but goes in an entirely different direction. The change from kingdom to "man" is often viewed as an adaptation to Gnosticism, as is the focus on one large fish to the exclusion of the others, an idea paralleled in *Gos. Thom.* 107, in which the lost sheep is the largest and the one the shepherd loves more than the others he has left behind. A few have argued that the *Gos. Thom.* version of the Net is independent and preferable.[36] More likely it is secondary,

484

even if not directly dependent on Matthew, but it seems to have been influenced by Matthew's parable of the Pearl (13:45-46).[37] Its similarity to the parable of the Pearl is acknowledged by both sides of the debate.[38]

Textual Features Worth Noting

All the discourses in Matthew close with a saying on judgment, four of which sayings are parables of judgment, and the Net fills this role for the parables discourse. In *Gos. Thom.* the Net is the first parable in the Gospel.

A decision has to be made about the significance of "again" *(palin)* in v. 47. The exact same introduction occurs for the parable of the Pearl in v. 45. Does "again" tie the Net to the parables of the Treasure and the Pearl in some constitutive way so that the previous two parables partly determine interpretation,[39] or is "again" merely a connector, as if to say "Here is another similitude"? I think it is merely a connector, not a determiner of meaning.

The arrangement of the parables in Matthew 13 is artistically designed to provide implicit commentary. The parable of the Wheat and the Weeds and its interpretation bracket the parables of the Mustard Seed and Leaven, all communicating the presence of the kingdom despite appearances. The interpretation of the Wheat and Weeds and the Net bracket the Treasure and the Pearl, emphasizing that neglect of this priceless kingdom and its ethical implications leads to severe judgment.[40]

Parallels exist between this parable and Matt 13:2. Both have a form of "gather" *(synagō)*, a form of the words for "sit" *(kathēmai* in v. 2, *kathizō* in v. 48), and the word "shore" *(aigialos)*, which occurs nowhere else in Matthew. Is this an intended inclusio so that the reader is to equate the fish being sorted with the people before Jesus, an inclusio without interpretive significance (i.e., merely indicating the end of the section), or is this merely a coincidence resulting from the subject matter? In my opinion at most the connections only indicate the close of the section and are not clues to meaning.[41]

Of most significance are the parallels between Matt 13:38-43 (the interpretation of the Wheat and the Weeds) and vv. 48-50. Both focus on the good *(kalon,* vv. 38 and 48) and on the righteous *(dikaioi,* vv. 43 and 49) as designations of the children of the kingdom, both use identical language to refer to the consummation of the age *(synteleia aiōnos,* vv. 39-40 and 49),[42] both use "gather" *(syllegō,* vv. 40-41 and 48) for the separation process, both refer to angels doing the separation, vv. 42 and 50 are identical in describing the rejected being thrown into a furnace of fire where there are weeping and gnashing of teeth *(kai balousin autous eis tēn kaminon tou pyros; ekei estai ho klauthmos kai ho brygmos tōn odontōn).*

The differences ought not be overlooked. An enemy or the devil does not appear in the Net and its interpretation. In the Wheat and the Weeds the rejected element is introduced later, but in the Net the "good" and the "bad" are caught at the same time. With the Net the division takes place immediately, not after a time of waiting. The interpretation of the Wheat and Weeds has a balanced focus on both good and bad in the judgment; the Net focuses almost entirely on the judgment of the bad. The Son of Man sends the angels in the interpretation of the Wheat and Weeds but is not mentioned in the Net. Still, whatever else is said, Matthew has shaped the interpretation of the Net to repeat and parallel much that is found in the interpretation of the Wheat and the Weeds.

Several Matthean expressions are present in the parable and its interpretation: "kingdom of heaven"; "consummation of the age"(13:39, 40, 49; 24:3; 28:20; elsewhere in only Heb 9:26), the contrast of evil and good (*ponēros* and *agathos*, 5:45; 12:34-35; 22:10),[43] angels as agents of final judgment (13:39, 41, 49; 16:27; 24:31; 25:31), and possibly "weeping and gnashing of teeth" (which occurs six times in Matthew and elsewhere only at Luke 13:28).[44] The judgment theme occurs frequently in Matthew; note 3:10-12; 5:21-26, 29-30; 7:13-14, 19, 23, 24-27; 8:11-12; 10:15, 28, 32-33; 11:20-24; 12:31, 34-37; 13:39-43, 49-50; 16:27; 18:6-9, 34-35; 22:13; 24:51; 25:30, 31-46.

Dan 3:6 may be behind the furnace of fire imagery, but fire and furnace language for judgment is common.[45]

Sometimes the passive verbs *blētheisę* and *eplērōthē* (vv. 47-48) are viewed as divine passives, but this is unlikely. Both are perfectly natural in the telling of the parable.

Cultural Information

Several different words for fishing nets exist with some fluidity among them. The word here, *sagēnē*, is a seine or dragnet. Such a net could be quite long with cork floats along the top and lead weights along the bottom. It could be stretched between two boats or laid out from one and then pulled to shore by ropes. Everything in its path would be caught as it was pulled in.[46] Herodotus (*Histories* 6.31.1-2) uses the related verb form metaphorically to describe a long line of soldiers linking arms and marching across an island to "net" all the people.

There are as many as twenty-four species of fish in the Sea of Galilee.[47] While any fisherman would sort his catch to exclude inedible fish or undesirable creatures, Jewish law necessitated sorting, for it allowed only fish with scales and fins to be eaten.[48] The "bad" *(sapra)* fish would be fish without scales or fins — "unclean" for Jews, not fish that had become spoiled.[49]

Explanation of the Parable

Options for Interpretation

We know that parables beginning like this one do not mean merely that the kingdom is like the first item mentioned. A simile would have sufficed if that were the intent. Rather, such beginnings mean the kingdom is like the whole process described. But is the whole process equally in focus? By focusing on one aspect of the process the meaning is changed. The options for interpreting this parable result from people emphasizing one aspect more than the others and are not mutually exclusive. They include:

1. Some say that the parable is about the ministry of the church. The net is the church, the sea is the world, and people from all nations are brought in. The church is a *corpus permixtum* of good and evil, which will one day be separated at judgment. With some variation this is the traditional allegorizing interpretation from the third century until the modern period.[50]

2. Some ignore Matthew's interpretation in vv. 49-50, focus on the expression "of every kind," and say the parable points to the universality of Jesus' ministry and his association with all kinds of people.[51]

3. Others focus on the spreading of the net and view the parable as teaching about present eschatology as well.[52]

4. Some view the parable as reflecting the mixed character of Matthew's church and a warning of judgment to false disciples.[53]

5. Finally, some focus primarily on the separation and view the parable as a warning about judgment generally.[54]

Decisions on the Issues

1. Are the parable and its interpretation authentic teachings from Jesus? Despite the Jesus Seminar's rejection of this parable,[55] most treatments accept that at least part of it is from Jesus. Some accept that only v. 47 is from Jesus, and some vv. 47-48, but scholars regularly dismiss the interpretation in vv. 49-50 because it is so heavily Matthean in language and thought and identical to v. 42. The difference between the parable and the interpretation is thought to be significant with Jesus' parable focusing primarily on gathering while Matthew's interpretation focuses entirely on judgment.[56] The parable focuses on gathering if one limits it to v. 47, but direction for interpretation is then implicit at best. Some say that even with v. 48 the parable is ambiguous.[57] There is no question that vv. 49-50 are Matthean in word and thought and are taken over from the end of the interpretation of the Wheat and Weeds. The question is whether the interpretation is in line with the parable's intent. J. Liebenburg suggests vv. 49-50 are not so much an explanation as an elaboration which assumes the metaphorical intent of the parable and explains in apocalyptic-eschatological language the judgment to which the separation refers.[58] The parable itself stops with the worthless fish thrown away; the interpretation goes well beyond that and changes the imagery entirely. We are no longer dealing with fish in the interpretation. If the separation in Jesus' similitude points to final judgment, Matthew has underlined and made specific the intent to provide a warning, as he has at the end of Jesus' other discourses. In doing so he has eliminated the metaphorical distance of the parable and made its concern so obvious that one cannot miss the message. Judgment is very much part of Jesus' message, and vv. 49-50 cohere with that emphasis, but this may be a parable that had a broader intent which has been narrowed by the *nimshal* provided by, or at least shaped by, the Evangelist. In other words, vv. 49-50 fit with aspects of Jesus' teaching, but could be from the Evangelist.

2. *What OT texts, if any, form the background of the parable, and with what significance?* The OT background of this parable's imagery has been strangely ignored by many. By ignoring this background and viewing the parable independently of the Matthean interpretation one can claim that there is no reason to see this as a judgment parable.[59] But the net and fishing imagery has a long OT history of representing hardship, captivity, and judgment from God. For example, Hab 1:14-17 views God as having made people like fish and Babylon as being allowed to catch them in nets and then sacrifice to his nets.[60] Ezek 32:3 says God will throw his net over Pharaoh and haul him up in his dragnet.[61] The psalmist of 1QH 13.8-9 uses a fishing net to describe the instrument for the task of judgment God has given him.[62] Then in *m. 'Abot* 3.17 a net is used as a symbol for judgment even though it does not fit the imagery of credit and ledgers, the real subject of the saying.[63] Clearly a net could be expected to evoke thoughts of judgment for Jewish hearers. If so, three results emerge: it is less likely that anyone would think the parable was positive and focused only on the gathering process, it is not surprising that Matthew's interpretive comment focuses on negative judgment to the neglect of the "good" fish, and Matthew's interpretive comment, even if exaggerated, is in the direction of the parable itself.

The net is not only an image of negative judgment. In Ezek 47:10 fishing with nets along the river that proceeds from the eschatological temple is a sign of blessing. The origin of the parable's "of every kind" could be this verse. This is not certain, but if there is a joining of the negative metaphor and this text, it would account for the positive aspects of the parable.[64]

3. *To what degree does this parable reflect Matthew's community? Is this a parable about the mixed state of the church?* Hopefully we have moved past

thinking every detail in the Gospels is a reflection of a situation in the Evangelists' churches, but the argument is often made that the separation of good and bad in the parable reflects the mixed Matthean community. No one has argued this case more than J. Kingsbury. He distinguishes between this parable, which he sees as treating the problem of "bad and good" within the church, and the Wheat and the Weeds, which he sees as dealing with the problem of "believing Israel" (the church) opposed to "unbelieving Israel" (Pharisaic Judaism). In his estimation the two parables are not companions. The evil (or worthless) in the Net are understood to be those in the church guilty of moral laxity. The expression "from the midst of the righteous" is taken as proof that the reference is to false Christians. He concludes from this, as some do with the Weeds, that no effort should be made to establish a pure community. Separation comes only at the end.[65]

That Matthew has a different focus with the Net from that in the Wheat and Weeds and its interpretation is difficult to accept, especially given the identical language in the Net and the interpretation of the Wheat and Weeds. The question of the mixed state of Matthew's church was dealt with in connection with the parable of the Wheat and the Weeds.[66] With that option for the Wheat and Weed rejected, nothing justifies reinstating it here. Nor is there any basis in this parable for saying that Matthew advised against seeking a pure community. That just does not fit with the rest of the Gospel (especially 18:15-18). The separation of the evil "from the midst of the righteous" (v. 49) is not their removal from the church but their exclusion from the kingdom. Matthew knows about false prophets and lax Christians (7:15-23), but nothing indicates that this is his concern with the parable of the Net.

"From every kind" is sometimes interpreted as expressing Matthew's universal concerns and as an anticipation of the Great Commission in 28:19-20, especially since "kind" *(genos)* is used of races or nations.[67] This is possible, but difficult to verify. It is easy to hypothesize what Matthew may have had in the back of his mind, but would a reader be expected to discern this? More importantly, if we seek to hear the voice of Jesus,[68] what would his intent have been? The word "kind" is perfectly natural in talking about kinds of fish — Josephus uses it this way.[69] If there is a universal emphasis here, it is because the *kingdom* is universal and not merely because of the expression "from every kind." I see no basis for detecting anything specific about Matthew's community from the wording of the parable and its interpretation.

4. To what degree do the features of the parable have allegorical significance? Is there christological significance? We are not surprised that any parable was allegorized by the church, but similar allegorizing still takes place among scholars, particularly where emphasis on redaction criticism is strong. J. Kingsbury's explanation looks surprisingly like the church's allegorical approach. For him the sea is a Jewish metaphor for the nations and the catching of fish prefigures the Christian mission. Jesus Kyrios calls men of all nations ("of every kind") into God's kingly rule through the medium of his earthly ambassadors, so for practical purposes the net becomes a picture of the church. "When it was full" *(hote eplērōthē)* refers to the end of the age and the coming of the Son of Man with the angels to do final judgment.[70] U. Luz finds the sitting of the fishermen reminiscent of the sitting of the Son of Man, the world judge (19:28; 25:31; 26:64), and suggests that the parable has an underlying christological meaning.[71] I have no objection to finding correspondences, as treacherous as the task at times is, but I find all this a bit much. Matthew stated in 13:41-43 that the Son of Man will judge, but that is not repeated here. Those sitting *(plural)* in the parable correspond to the angels in the interpretation, so it is difficult to think Matthew was alluding to the sitting of the Son of Man. This parable makes no christological statement, as far as I can see.

Further, I do not think the net is the church or the gospel or that there is an allusion to the Gentile mission in the parable. Even Matthew's exaggerated interpretation pays no attention to this possibility. Questions of method remain front and center. How much correspondence between picture and reality should we seek? Whose reality do we presuppose is being pictured — that of Jesus, of Matthew, of the church, or even our own? We read stereoscopically both for the *Sitz im Leben* of Jesus and that of Matthew, as difficult as it may be, but the first level has to be the reality of Jesus' own kingdom proclamation. If Matthew's larger theology or situation becomes evident, that is a bonus, but Matthew thinks he is telling us about Jesus' teaching.

Again we must remember that the kingdom is not like the net or any particular feature of the parable; the kingdom is like the whole process. Neither the net, the sea, the shore, the fishermen, or the vessels stand for anything. The kingdom is like the process of seine fishing, which at the end requires separation so that one keeps the valuable and discards the worthless. That is all. The interpretation gives much more explicit, additional information about the nature of the separation and especially the discarding, with no attention to keeping what is valuable. We do not need to seek for allegorical significance in any of the features, although obvious correspondences exist between the good and the righteous, the worthless and the evil, the fishermen's separating and the angels' separating, and the casting out and the casting into the furnace of fire. Analogies by necessity have correspondences, but that does not make them allegories.[72] Long ago Origen, who could allegorize with the best, still recognized that ". . . in the case of the similitudes in the Gospel, when the kingdom of heaven is likened unto anything, the comparison does not extend to all the features of that to which the kingdom is compared, but only to those features which are required by the argument in hand."[73] Would that he and all of us remembered that.

5. What is the teaching of the parable? If we ask to what question the parable is an answer, I would suggest that question is: "If the kingdom is present, why is evil still here?" The parable of the Wheat and the Weeds shows that evil exists alongside the kingdom and that the time of Jesus' ministry is not the time for judgment. This parable is different in that it stresses that separation and judgment will indeed occur. The parable of the Wheat and the Weeds focuses on the presence of the kingdom; the Net does not. Rather, it assumes the presence of the kingdom with the aorist passive *blētheisē* (literally "having been cast") and the present *synagagousē* ("gathering"); the kingdom is at work, but there is little description of how the kingdom is present. A focus on gathering would suggest that every person is caught up in the kingdom's net, but this parable is not teaching universalism. The concern with "gathering" is not about making people "fishers of humans" (4:19) or about calling people into the kingdom. It is about gathering them for judgment.[74] The kingdom is like a process of gathering and separation.[75] The rule of end stress requires that the concern of the parable is not the gathering process or Jesus' implied association with sinners but the separation process (v. 48b).

The primary concern of the parable is that separation will occur,[76] that at the end the evil will be excluded from God's kingdom. This was not a new revelation, for any Jew hoping for the kingdom would believe that, but it was a confirmation from Jesus that his present kingdom would indeed lead to the time when evil would be obliterated. The sorting does not take place until the net is full and dragged on shore, until the end of the age. Neither the time of Jesus nor that of Matthew is the time for sorting, but it will take place. This is both a promise and a warning. The wording of Matthew reflects the warning in 8:11-12/Luke 13:28-29 that the children of the kingdom will be cast into outer darkness, where there are weeping and gnashing of teeth. The basis of the sorting is not ritual cleanness, as it is with fish, or any other external feature like ethnicity. The basis of the judgment is ethical, whether one is judged good/righteous or worthless/evil.[77]

On judgment consisting of being thrown into a furnace where there are weeping and gnashing of teeth, see p. 210, n. 153.

Adapting the Parable

Judgment in our time may well be the despised doctrine. We cringe at the exaggerated language about judgment, and we lament that the church has often misused judgment language to bash and scare sinners. We do not need that, but we do need to recover a healthy understanding of judgment, which undeniably was a central feature of Jesus' message both with regard to Israel and as part of his kingdom preaching. Judgment is an essential part of the Christian message.[78] We should never forget that without judgment there is no need for salvation. Without judgment life is cheapened, for what we do does not matter. With Jesus and his kingdom what we do matters. How can the modern church find the balance to do justice to the grace and magnanimous love of God and at the same time treat fairly the warnings of judgment, metaphorical as indeed they are? Whatever else we do, we fail if we do not provide the warning that how we live really matters to God and that we will be held accountable. The sorting and accountability are part of the kingdom and its future. I refer, of course, to God's judgment at the end of the age, not to humans condemning one another.

For Further Reading

Arland J. Hultgren, *The Parables of Jesus: A Commentary* (Grand Rapids: Eerdmans, 2000), pp. 303-9.

Jack Dean Kingsbury, *The Parables of Jesus in Matthew 13: A Study in Redaction-Criticism* (Richmond: John Knox, 1969), pp. 117-25.

Jacobus Liebenberg, *The Language of the Kingdom: Parable, Aphorism, and Metaphor in the Sayings Material Common to the Synoptic Tradition and the Gospel of Thomas* (BZNW 102; Berlin: Walter de Gruyter, 2001), pp. 258-75.

Ulrich Luz, *Matthew 8–20* (trans. James E. Crouch; Minneapolis: Fortress, 2001), pp. 281-84.

The Eschatological Discourse

Attention must be given to the literary context in which the Evangelists have placed the eschatological parables. I will treat only the longer narrative parables (the Faithful or Unfaithful Servant, the Ten Virgins, the Talents/Minas, and the Sheep and the Goats) and give only passing attention to shorter metaphorical sayings (such as the Doorkeeper).

David Wenham suggests that the Gospel writers knew a preexisting eschatological discourse which concluded with several parables.[79] Although the suggestion is not crucial or determinative for treating the parables, I find that a comparison of the Synoptic evidence and the use of these images elsewhere seems to bear this out. The Evangelists follow essentially the same order through Matt 24:36/Mark 13:32/Luke 21:33, but then both the differences and similarities are noteworthy.

	Mark 13:33-37 contains warnings and the brief analogy of the Door-keeper.	Luke 12:35-38 has a similar analogy of waiting servants.[80]
Matt 24:37-44 uses the days of Noah as analogous to the coming of the Son of Man to serve as a warning and also uses the analogy of the thief.		Luke 17:26-36 uses both the days of Noah and of Lot as analogous to the coming to serve as a warning. 12:39-40 contains the analogy of the thief.
24:45-51 — the Parable of the Faithful or Unfaithful Servant		12:42-46 — the Parable of the Faithful or Unfaithful Servant
25:1-13 — the Parable of the Ten Virgins		
25:14-30 — the Parable of the Talents		19:11-27 — the Parable of the Minas
25:31-46 — the Parable of the Sheep and the Goats		

The beginning of Mark's Doorkeeper parable is sufficiently close to the beginning of Matthew's parable of the Talents that Wenham suggests Mark started to include this parable, but then abandoned it.[81] Luke has obviously distributed the materials of the "Olivet Discourse" throughout chs. 12, 17, 19, and 21 of his travel narrative, but the similarity of wording between Matthew and Luke is very close for the analogy of the thief and the parable of the Faithful or Unfaithful Servant, and to a lesser degree with the analogy of the days of Noah. That Paul, the author of Revelation, and the author of 2 Peter have sayings using the thief image, watching, and that Revelation also uses knocking at the door suggests an eschatological source (or at least a collection of sayings) that were well known (see 1 Thess 5:2, 4; 2 Pet 3:10; Rev 3:3, 20; 16:15).[82]

The purpose of the eschatological discourse is not to give a detailed sequence of events but to provide parenetic instruction in view of the catastrophe coming on Jerusalem, in view of God's ultimate victory, and in view of the distractions that keep people from living as they should. The focus is on deception, difficulties, persecution, tribulation, the coming of the Son of Man, the uncertainty of the time of his coming, and exhortations to watch, which is a metaphor for active and diligent service.[83] Matthew has five sayings underscoring that no one knows the time of the coming (24:36, 42, 44, 50; 25:13).

The parables in Matthew's discourse are not haphazardly arranged (and Luke's arrangement is certainly not haphazard either).[84] The parable of the Faithful/Unfaithful Servant is given pride of place in Matthew as an introductory statement or a summary of the material that follows.[85] The parables of the Virgins and the Talents are both commentary on the parable of the Faithful or Unfaithful Servant (and the exhortations preceding it in 24:43-44) and have words in common that connect back to this parable. The parable of the Virgins develops the themes of wisdom, readiness, and watching and connects with the ideas of delay (*chronizō*, 24:48; 25:5) and not knowing the time (24:50; 25:13). The parable of the Talents develops the theme of faithfulness (24:45; 25:21, 23) and connects with the ideas of possessions (24:47; 25:14) and of exclusion and weeping and gnashing of teeth (24:51; 25:30). The parables of the Faithful or Unfaithful Servant and of the Ten Virgins deal with the theme of preparedness, but with different emphases. The parables of the Talents and the Sheep and the Goats will demonstrate what it means to be prepared.

In dealing with each of the following parables, pertinent information should be gleaned from the other parables in this chapter.

THE FAITHFUL OR UNFAITHFUL SERVANT
(Matt 24:45-51; Luke 12:42-46)

Despite the importance that Matthew places on this parable, not many commentaries and works on parables give it much attention.

Parable Type

This parable, commonly classified as a parable of crisis, is a double antithetical similitude, a syncrisis.[86] It is an *implied* analogy of contrasting examples, expressed as a metaphorical question with a brief positive answer and promise of reward followed by a negative example and the threat of warning. There is no *nimshal*.

Issues Requiring Attention

1. Does "My master is delayed" presuppose the delay of the parousia and the theological anxiety of the church over the delay? If so, does this indicate

that the parable was created by the early church in response to a crisis caused by the delay of the parousia?

2. Does the master have a referent, and if so, is he a "God" figure or a "Christ" figure?

3. To whom is the parable addressed? Does the servant correspond to the disciples or to faithful and faithless Jews? Is there a focus on church leaders?

4. Is there reference to the parousia?

5. What does *dichotomēsei* (NRSV "cut in pieces," Matt 24:51/Luke 12:46) mean? Why bother assigning someone a place with the hypocrites/unbelievers if that person has been cut into pieces?

6. What is the teaching of the parable?

Helpful Primary Source Material

Canonical Material

- OT: Psalm 37, especially vv. 9-13 and 34-40
- NT: Matt 26:40-41/Mark 14:37-38/Luke 22:45-46; Luke 12:35-38; 1 Cor 4:1-2; 1 Thess 5:6-8; 2 Pet 3:10; Rev 3:3, 20; 16:15

Early Jewish Writings

- Susanna 1:55, 59 (the punishment of two elders for their false accusation of Susanna): "And Daniel said, 'Very well! This lie has cost you your head, for the angel of God has received the sentence from God and will immediately cut you in two.' . . . Daniel said to him, 'Very well! This lie has cost you also your head, for the angel of God is waiting with his sword to split you in two, so as to destroy you both.'"
- 1QS 2.16-17: "May God separate him for evil, and may he be cut off from the midst of all the sons of light because of his straying from following God on account of all his idols and the obstacle of his iniquity. May he assign his lot with the cursed ones for ever."
- 4Q171 (4QPs37) 2.1-2 says that the wicked will die by the sword and will be cut off. Hypocrisy is specifically targeted. That the wicked will be cut off is repeated in 3.11-13 ("cut off and exterminated forever") and 4.1, 18 ("perish and be cut off").

Early Christian Writings

- *Didache* 16:1: "'Watch' over your life: 'let your lamps' be not quenched 'and your loins' be not ungirded, but be 'ready,' for ye know not 'the hour in which our Lord cometh.'"
- *Sib. Or.* 2.177-86 has been framed on Jesus' parable of the Faithful or Unfaithful Servant. It describes as blessed those whom the master finds awake when he comes.

Later Jewish Writings

- In the Syriac, Arabic, and Armenian versions of *Ahiqar* 3:2; 4:15; and 8:38 Nathan, Ahiqar's wicked nephew, is described as eating and drinking with the gluttonous and beating the male and female slaves. At the end he swells up, bursts open, dies, and in the Arabic version also goes to hell.
- *b. Šabbat* 153a/*Eccl. Rab.* 9.8.1 have a parable about guests invited to a king's banquet but without the time designated. The wise prepare themselves and are ready; the foolish who do not prepare are not allowed to participate. (See above, pp. 303-4 and p. 508 below.)

Comparison of the Accounts

The accounts in Matt 24:45-51 and Luke 12:42-46 are extremely close and provide a good example of reasons to argue for a "Q" source. For the bulk of the parable the two accounts not only have the same words,[87] even *dichotomēsei* which occurs nowhere else in the NT and only once in the LXX (Exod 29:17), they also rarely deviate in the order of the words. The variations are minor, primarily stylistic, and with little consequence for interpretation. Most scholars argue that Matthew has preserved "Q" better (if "Q" exists!), except for a few words. The differences meriting mention are:

> Whereas Matthew uses "servant" *(doulos)* throughout, Luke 12:42 uses "steward" *(oikonomos),* but then reverts to "servant." The only other occurrences of *oikonomos* in the Gospels are in Luke 16:1-8.
> Matthew labels the servant "evil" *(kakos)* in 24:48, which is not present in Luke.
> Matthew assigns the lot of the evil servant with the "hypocrites," whereas Luke has "unbelievers," which may be more suitable for his Gentile audience, particularly in view of 1QS 2.16-17.[88]

Matthew has "There will be the weeping and the gnashing of teeth," which Luke does not have. Elsewhere in the NT this expression occurs only in Matt 8:12; 13:42, 50; 22:13; 25:30; Luke 13:28. Is this an expression Matthew has emphasized or one that the other Evangelists have deemphasized (or omitted)? The language comes from the OT.[89]

Textual Features Worthy of Attention

Other triadic parables have an authority figure judging between two subordinates or groups: the Two Sons, the Talents/Minas,[90] the Ten Virgins, the Sheep and the Goats, and the Prodigal Son. Sometimes the authority figure stands outside the narrative of the parable or is implied as with the Two Builders, the Two Debtors, the Rich Man and Lazarus, and the Pharisee and the Tax Collector.

Five parables involve a master's departure and return: this one, the Doorkeeper (Mark 13:34-36), the talents (Matt 25:14-30), the Minas (Luke 19:11-27), and the Wicked Tenants (Matt 21:33-44; Mark 12:1-12; Luke 20:9-19). There are also rabbinic parables with this theme.[91]

See above (p. 494) for the connections between Matthew's parable and its immediate context. Note the repetition of eating (although using different Greek words) and drinking from 24:38 in v. 49.

For Luke's account focus throughout ch. 12 is on eschatological ideas and the warnings against being dominated by the mundane affairs of life. The context of treasure in heaven, security, and the meaning of life prepares for the themes of watchfulness and faithfulness. A symmetry exists between 12:37 and vv. 43-44 in the use of a blessing followed by a reward introduced by "Amen, I say to you."

Luke has a corresponding emphasis on faithfulness and wisdom in 16:8-12 and on faithfulness in 19:17.

The idea of being placed over all the master's possessions (Matt 24:47/ Luke 12:44) is mirrored in Matt 25:21, 23/Luke 19:17-19 where servants are placed over many things or cities.

Cultural Information

With *doulos* in this parable we are probably dealing with a slave, although the word is used for servants as well. That a slave is placed in charge is not unusual. The best biblical example and with wording similar to the parable is the account of Joseph being given authority both in the home of Potiphar and by Pharaoh. See LXX Gen 39:4-8; 41:39-43; and Ps 104(105):21. Imagine how powerful the slave in charge of food supplies would be. He or she literally controlled the health and welfare of the other slaves.

Drunkenness and beating slaves are both traditional descriptions of an uncontrolled life. See *Ahiqar* 3:2; 4:15 (above, p. 496); Luke 21:34; Eph 5:18; 1 Thess 5:7.

On the meaning of the word *dichotomeō*, see below, but that people, slaves and martyrs especially, were — regretfully still are — cut in two (or into pieces) is a fact of life and the ancient world. See 1 Sam 15:33; Heb 11:37; *Martyrdom of Isaiah* 5:1-14; *Lives of the Prophets* 1:1; *3 Bar.* 16:3; *b. Sanhedrin* 52b.

Explanation of the Parable

Options for Interpretation[92]

1. The church understood the parable to depict the relation of Christ as master to his disciples, the leaders entrusted with the care of the church. Occasionally the parable was applied to the giving of alms to the poor.[93]

2. A number of interpreters deny that this is a parable of Jesus because of the mention of a delay and because of allegorical correspondences. It is understood as an early Christian creation addressed to Christian leaders to urge attention to pastoral duties.[94]

3. Some interpret this parable as Jesus' warning to Jewish leaders that a day of accounting is at hand or an accusation of their unfaithfulness. The only crisis is the one Jesus' coming brings. When that situation had passed, the church applied the parable to its own situation.[95]

4. Often the parable is viewed as Jesus' instruction to his disciples to remain faithful in his absence before the coming of the final kingdom or of the Son of Man, both of which would entail judgment.[96] In this case the correspondences stem from Jesus.

Decisions on the Issues

This parable does not stay within its narrative plane. It is an *implied* analogy, and we discern quickly that it is not speaking about literal servants because of its context in the teaching of Jesus, its hyperbole, and the fact that the intended reference starts to show through in the choice of such words as "blessed," "hypocrites"/"unbelievers" and "weeping and gnashing of teeth." That parables do not stay entirely within the metaphorical plane is not that unusual, particularly if there is no need to "deceive into the truth,"[97] and is particularly true of eschatological parables.

The parable begins with a question: "Who is the faithful and wise servant. . . ?" An introductory question in a Semitic language can function as the equivalent of the protasis of a conditional sentence (e.g., Matt 12:11/Luke 14:5; cf. Luke 6:9),[98] which would be equivalent to "If a faithful and wise servant. . . ." That is probably the intent here, but at the very least the question format engages the reader in considering what faithful and wise service means.[99] Only one servant is in mind with two possible courses of action,[100] and both from the rule of end stress and from the amount of words used the emphasis falls on the negative example.

1. Does "My master is delayed" presuppose the delay of the parousia and the theological anxiety of the church over the delay? If so, does this indicate that the parable was created by the early church in response to a crisis caused by the delay of the parousia? Some think the mention of delay is proof that the church either created the parable or rewrote it extensively,[101] but the delay is required by the plot. In the second scene the servant is tempted to shirk his responsibility only because of the delay.[102] *Chronizein* ("stay away," "linger") is *not* technical or customary language for the delay[103] and outside this parable occurs only in the parable of the Ten Virgins (Matt 25:5), for Zechariah's slowness in emerging from the Temple (Luke 1:21), and in Heb 10:37, a quotation of Hab 2:3 promising that there will not be a delay. As we have seen, delay and imminence stand together in OT prophecy and Jewish apocalyptic writings.[104] Even more decisive, this parable is *not* about delay but unpreparedness when a master returns *sooner* than expected.

Joseph Fitzmyer argues — correctly in my estimation — that it is an oversimplification of the NT data to ascribe sayings on watchfulness solely to church creation. Watchfulness and expectation are frequently urged in connection with the eschatological day of Yahweh in the OT.[105] In fact, it would be strange if Jesus promised a future coming of the kingdom and/or the Son of Man and did not warn of readiness in view of that coming. This parable fits with other parables from Jesus with the similar themes of departure and return. Given that and with no grounds for saying that the servant's wrong expectation that his master will linger points to the delay of the parousia, there is little reason to think the parable has its origin in the church.[106]

2. Does the master have a referent, and if so, is he a "God" figure or a "Christ" figure? The attempts cannot succeed that deny any eschatological significance to the parable, as if it were originally only about stewardship with no meaningful content assigned to the master, his coming, or the servants.[107] The more complex a parable is the more correspondences are necessary to convey the point, and this parable is fairly complex. But, who should we understand is going away and returning? Some sayings indicate that Jesus taught that he would go away,[108] and some that he anticipated his death, but in other texts and in Jewish parables a "God" figure goes away.[109] Does the parable refer to the crisis present in the ministry of Jesus (as the parables of Israel),[110] God coming at the time of the future kingdom, or to the coming of the Son of Man at the time of the future kingdom? Obviously both Evangelists situate the parable in relation to the coming of the Son of Man, but decision here is partly dependent on the question of the persons addressed. The same ambiguity concerning the identity of a person returning will face us in the parables of the Ten Virgins and of the Talents/Minas. Conceivably Jesus could have warned hearers to be alert and faithful in view of the crisis of his own ministry to Israel, and then the early church could reasonably have adapted the warnings to their expectation of the parousia. More likely, since Jesus anticipated an interval, the warnings apply to the end-time and full appearance of the kingdom, whether the thought is of God coming or of the Son of Man. It is inconceivable to me that Jesus expected an interval but neither gave directions for life during that interval nor pointed to the time of fulfillment. The more this parable is grouped with other parables emphasizing watchfulness, as the Evangelists have arranged it, the less likely it refers to the crisis Jesus offers the nation. Why emphasize watching for something that has already occurred?[111] This parable, however, is more concerned with the time during the interval than it is with the return.[112]

If this is the case, the parable is further evidence that Jesus spoke of an uncertain interval before the coming of the Son of Man.[113] There will be a time of fulfillment when he will have completed the task God has given him, or at least when his task will have been completed. Anything less does not result in the defeat of evil and the vindication of Jesus' followers. An interval does not lessen the focus on the suddenness of the coming. This parable focuses on the unexpectedness of the coming, and the servant is caught unprepared. Conversely the next parable in Matthew, the Ten Virgins, focuses on the foolishness of those who do not anticipate a delay. In both cases the emphasis is on readiness and watching, regardless of whether the time is short or long.

In the end, whether the parable refers to the coming of God or the coming of the Son of Man is relatively unimportant. Both images point to the final kingdom coming with power and glory.

3. *To whom is the parable addressed? Does the servant correspond to the disciples or to faithful and faithless Jews? Is there a focus on church leaders?* In both Matthew and Luke the parable is explicitly addressed to Jesus' disciples (Matt 24:3; Luke 12:22).[114] Luke forces the reader to consider the relevance of the para-

bles in 12:35-40 for disciples by having Peter ask whether this parable was for them or for everyone (12:41). The question is not answered, which heightens the reader's engagement with the relevance and applicability of that material and what follows.[115]

Jeremias granted that the disciples could be the addressees but argued we should disregard the context in the Gospels, and following Dodd, concluded that the persons originally warned to watch and fulfill their task were the Jewish leaders, especially the scribes who possess the keys to the kingdom.[116] One can appreciate the attempt to hear Jesus addressing the Jewish people, but it is hard to imagine that Jesus with this parable is targeting Jewish leaders. Would Jesus have described the religious leaders by the image of a gluttonous and drunk servant who beats his helpers?[117] Even more, if he did, would the leaders, the people, or even his disciples have recognized his intent?

The parable does not address the crowd generally but those in a servant relation, that is, those who have professed commitment. The parable could be addressed to the disciples charging them with the responsibility of caring for Israel by proclaiming the kingdom, healing, and exorcism, for which they will be held accountable.[118] That seems like allegorizing to me, and I think the parable more likely addresses the broader group of Jesus' followers, not merely leaders or the Twelve. In interpreting the parables Jeremias gives little attention to Jesus' teaching to disciples. With his approach only three parables are clearly directed to the disciples (the Budding Fig Tree, the Friend at Midnight, and the Unjust Judge).[119] Jesus surely attempted to prepare his followers for the events following his death (e.g., Luke 22:31-32), and if he did, it is hard to imagine that parables did not enter into the conversation.

This parable is easily applied to church leaders, and Luke especially may have leaders in view, but the description of the wicked slave fits there no more easily than in the claim it describes Jewish leaders.[120] The description is hyperbole, but it is probably better that this antithetical portrayal of faithfulness be understood as addressed to all Jesus' followers, not just leaders.[121]

4. Is there reference to the parousia? We cannot preclude the possibility that this parable is about Jesus' proclamation of the coming of God to establish the kingdom, not the parousia of the Son of Man. Nothing in the parable itself is explicit concerning the identity of the servant's master (*kyrios*, "master" or "lord"). It is the context of both Matthew and Luke that specifies that the reference is to the Son of Man. There is a real hesitancy from some to believe that Jesus could have spoken of *his own* future coming,[122] but that doubt should be challenged. If Jesus did not speak of his own coming, why and how did the early church develop such a belief so quickly — quickly enough to be attested in the fundamental Aramaic prayer *Marana tha?*[123] Jesus expected vindication from

God. With this question, we are at a crossroads. If Jesus believed in *a* resurrection and if he believed God's kingdom would come, regardless of what happened to him, it is difficult to think he anticipated the fullness of God's kingdom and his not being involved with it. His story *needs* an end.[124] If he proclaimed the eschatological restoration of Israel and viewed himself as having a fundamental role in that restoration,[125] his departure could not be the end. By necessity he also is restored. Dale C. Allison asks fairly, "And . . . are the odds really so staggeringly high against the thought that Jesus, as Joachim Jeremias argued, anticipated eschatological vindication, which he sometimes associated with resurrection and other times with the imagery of Dan 7:14, and that the post-Easter church introduced the necessary adjustments in the light of its faith in the resurrection?"[126] The exact words Jesus used cannot be determined, but that he anticipated being restored to his disciples after his departure seems to me a given. The only other option is that he died in disappointment with the cry of dereliction being the only clue to the real circumstance. If Jesus did anticipate restoration, this parable should be understood as encouragement and warning for disciples during his absence. In our language, it is talking about the parousia.

5. *What does* dichotomēsei *(NRSV "cut in pieces," Matt 24:51/Luke 12:46) mean? Why bother assigning someone a place with the hypocrites/unbelievers if that person has been cut into pieces?* This rare word means "cut in two" or "cut into pieces," and although often softened, shows both the cruelty of the ancient world[127] and the shock of some of Jesus' parables. Since being placed with the hypocrites/unbelievers after being cut in two seems anticlimactic, some suggest that *dichotomēsei* refers to physical death and being placed with the hypocrites/unbelievers to eternal punishment. Some follow O. Betz's suggestion that *dichotomēsei* is a more literal and dramatized rendering of a Hebrew expression meaning "cut off *from* the midst of." The close parallels in 1QS 2.16-17 to both parts of the judgment saying of the parable (see above, p. 495) are offered as evidence for Betz's view.[128] The most intriguing part of Betz's suggestion, however, has been ignored. He pointed to the importance of Psalm 37 as the ground of Qumran's concept of God cutting off (see 4QPs37) and suggested that Jesus' parable is an eschatological version of the psalm. The parallels between the parable and the psalm are striking: the righteous wait patiently for the Lord (Ps 37:7, 9, 34), give generously (vv. 21, 26), and shall inherit the land (vv. 9, 11, 22, 29, 34); the wicked abuse others (vv. 12, 14, 32), shall perish (vv. 15, 20, 38), are cut off (vv. 9, 22, 28, 34, 38), and gnash their teeth (v. 12). *Jesus' parable looks like an eschatological version of Psalm 37 applied to disciples* through use of the servant imagery. Qumran verifies the importance of the psalm and that it was interpreted eschatologically. This same psalm, of course, is the basis of the third be-

atitude (Matt 5:5, drawn from Ps 37:11). If this psalm does stand behind Jesus' parable, it is another example of the influence of the OT on the formation of the parables.

Betz's argument that *dichotomēsei* should be understood as "cut off from the midst of" is not convincing,[129] as helpful as the rest of his argument is. Given that the word means "cut in two" or "cut in pieces," is this meant literally or metaphorically? Within the context of the parable the word is meant literally,[130] but what does it mean really to say the word is literal in an analogy? The word is a gripping hyperbole to underscore the punishment of the unfaithful servant, the polar opposite of the blessing to the faithful servant. One other factor may have led to the use of this word. For some the punishment of being cut in two mirrors the divided loyalty that already exists in the unfaithful servant.[131]

"Weeping and gnashing of teeth" denotes extreme sorrow and emotion.[132] This expression occurs only seven times in the NT, six of which are in Matthew (Matt 8:12/Luke 13:28; Matt 13:42, 50; 22:13; 24:51; 25:30), all of them denoting end-time exclusion from the blessings of God. Five of these occurrences are in concluding statements of Matthean parables.[133]

6. What is the teaching of the parable? Jesus' use of this parable to instruct disciples fits his focus elsewhere on faithfulness (e.g., Matt 25:21-23; Luke 16:10-13; 19:17). The servant-master/Lord relation, which is established imagery from the OT for God and his people, is frequent in the parabolic and non-parabolic sayings of Jesus.[134] Obviously if the parable points to Jesus, a christology is implied, but in any case he who comes in the parable is responsible for judgment.[135] The antithesis of the faithful and unfaithful options and their results both woos the hearer toward faithfulness and warns against unfaithfulness. The faithfulness in question, both in the parable and elsewhere, is not faithfulness in general but faithfulness in view of the eschaton. Christianity is at its core an eschatological religion, and to be a Christian means having an awareness of living between the times, an awareness that the kingdom has come right in the midst of the old age but has not yet reached consummation. It also means being faithful, not merely believing certain ideas. This faithfulness, born of conviction and faced with uncertainty, was needed by Jesus' disciples as they faced the time when he would not be present. It is still needed with all its conviction and uncertainty for the time after Pentecost. The parable is an impulse to right and wise living. The wise servant is the one who understands the significance of the end — whether soon or late — and lives accordingly. Wisdom is an eschatological virtue.

Adapting the Parable

The church cannot afford to neglect the eschatological aspect of its message. An understanding of the gospel that does not include the future is not the Christian gospel and is insufficient for dealing with the problem of evil. Richard Bauckham goes so far as to say that apart from the parousia Jesus could not be called the Christ in the NT meaning of the word.[136] He is right. At the same time Christians must avoid any fascination with and speculation about the end. The nature of the documents does not encourage or allow drawing of charts and schedules to plot out the sequence of events. Any attempt to do so founders on the NT evidence itself, and that was not the purpose of the eschatological teaching. Its purpose was to give warning, to give hope, and to teach people how to live in the present.

The violent language of "cutting in two" is offensive and would yield a terrible view of God if taken literally, but it is not intended as a literal picture of judgment. Jesus often used hyperbole, and such language is used for its shock value. Judgment is serious in the teaching of Jesus, but what we say theologically about judgment must be much more nuanced without lessening its seriousness.[137]

Christian ethics are eschatologically driven. The attitudes and behavior expected of Christians (such as self-giving love) are grounded in a theology of the kingdom present and coming. Without such grounding in the future, the ethic is truly irrational.

At the same time, life over the long haul poses an acute challenge to Christian faith. How can the church acknowledge both its own long history and its lively hope without looking silly? Both patience and impatience are legitimate and necessary responses. Given the NT emphasis that no one knows the time and the length of time that has passed, patience is required, for God's timing and purposes never fit our agenda. Patience undergirds the faithful living which is the primary concern of this parable. The wise and faithful Christian is the one who understands the significance of the end and actively serves, whether the time is long or short. Impatience is called for as well. We should be impatient with those who assert they do know the time and draw eschatological charts. We should be as impatient with those who deny the importance of Jesus' future vindication. Further, we should be impatient for the End to come, weary of evil and longing for that time when evil is set aside and righteousness is established. Christian faith is always faith on tiptoe, looking to that day, and because of that day, living in accord with such anticipation.[138]

The focus on faithfulness reminds us again that Christian faith is not about believing certain ideas but about living out convictions over the long

504

haul. The church is often impressed with claims to faith. Claims and short-lived faith suffice for nothing. What counts is faithfulness to the end.

For Further Reading

Otto Betz, "The Dichotomized Servant and the End of Judas Iscariot," *RevQ* 5 (1964): 43-58.

Ulrich Luz, *Matthew 21–28: A Commentary* (trans. James E. Crouch; Minneapolis: Fortress, 2005), pp. 222-25.

I. Howard Marshall, *Commentary on Luke* (NIGTC; Grand Rapids: Eerdmans, 1978), pp. 532-45.

Neotestamentica 22/2 (1988) is comprised of articles which use Luke 12:35-48 as a test case to explain various interpretive methodologies. Although helpful, the focus is more on the methodologies than the passage in Luke.

John Nolland, *Luke 9:21–18:34* (WBC 35B; Dallas: Word, 1993), pp. 697-705.

A. Weiser, *Die Knechtsgleichnisse der synoptischen Evangelien* (SANT 29; Munich: Kösel, 1971), pp. 131-225.

THE TEN VIRGINS
(Matt 25:1-13)

Clearly some scholars do not care for this parable, and often it is omitted or treated briefly.[139] D. Flusser, on the other hand, thinks this is a beautiful parable, only lightly edited, and an excellent example of Jesus' accomplished skill as a teller of parables.[140] As with the previous parable, not many really helpful discussions exist. More than with any other parable, what one thinks about Jesus' eschatological teaching is determinative. However, the parable deserves to be heard in its own right as possible *evidence* of Jesus' eschatology.

Parable Type

This double indirect narrative parable is also a syncrisis,[141] an *implied* analogy of contrasting examples. It compares readiness to participate in the celebration of a wedding to readiness to participate in the coming kingdom.[142] There is no interpretive *nimshal*, but v. 13 is an appended application.

Issues Requiring Attention

1. How should the wedding circumstance be understood? To whose house (or to what place) is the bridegroom coming?
2. Is the reference to the coming of God or the coming of Jesus? An answer involves deciding whether Jesus used the bridegroom as a messianic image.
3. Do the elements in the parable, especially the bridegroom, the virgins, and the oil have allegorical significance?
4. To whom is the parable addressed? Jesus' Jewish contemporaries? Jesus' disciples? Would-be disciples?
5. Is "delay" an essential element of the parable, or does it refer to the church's experience of the problem of the delay of the parousia and demonstrate an origin in the church rather than from Jesus?
6. Does "sleep" carry any negative connotations in this parable?
7. Are the wise virgins ethically culpable for not sharing?
8. Does v. 13 with its exhortation to watch fit the parable since all ten virgins slept?
9. What is the teaching of the parable?

Helpful Primary Source Material

Canonical Material

- OT: Psalm 45, especially vv. 14-17; Song 3:4-11; 5:2; Isa 22:22; 61:10; 62:4-5
- NT: Matt 7:22; Mark 13:32-33; Luke 12:35-40; 13:25-27; 21:34-36; 1 Thess 4:15–5:11; Rev 3:2-3, 7

Early Jewish Writings

- 1 Macc 9:37-42 describes a slaughter that takes place during a wedding celebration. The bride was being conducted from her home in a tumultuous procession with a large escort and much baggage. V. 39 indicates that the bridegroom came out to meet the entourage with his friends and brothers with tambourines, musicians, and many weapons. After the groom's arrival the entourage was ambushed.
- *4 Ezra* 10:1 tells of a groom who fell and died on entering his wedding chamber, as a result of which all the participants in the marriage feast put out their lamps.

Greco-Roman Writings

▪ Plutarch, *Mor.* 798B (*Precepts of Statecraft* 1), as an analogy of uselessness, refers to those who trim their lamps but fail to pour in oil.

Early Christian Writings

▪ *Didache* 16:1: "'Watch' over your life: 'let your lamps' be not quenched 'and your loins' be not ungirded, but be 'ready,' for ye know not 'the hour in which our Lord cometh.'"
▪ *Epistula Apostolorum* 43-45 allegorizes parts of this parable to define those who will be in the kingdom and accordingly how people should live in the present.[143] Of most significance in this supposed discussion of Jesus with his disciples is that the disciples are sad and troubled for those who are shut out. They even ask if the wise did not open the door or pray to the bridegroom to open the door. To which the Lord answers "Whoever is shut out is shut out."

Later Jewish Writings

▪ *m. Soṭah* 9.14: "During the war of Vespasian [69-79 A.D.] they forbade the crowns of the bridegrooms and the [wedding] drum. During the war of Titus they forbade the crowns of the brides and that a man should teach his son Greek. In the last war [132-135 A.D.] they forbade the bride to go forth in a litter inside the city; but our Rabbis permitted the bride to go forth in a litter inside the city."
▪ *t. Berakot* 4.9 tells of a custom in Jerusalem pertaining to guests invited to meals: "They spread out a cloth in the doorway. As long as the cloth is spread out, guests may enter. Once the cloth has been removed, guests are not allowed to enter."
▪ *Mekilta Baḥodesh* 3:115-19 interprets Exod 19:17 (which tells of Moses bringing the people to meet God at Mount Sinai) of the Lord coming to receive Israel as a bridegroom comes forth to meet his bride. With regard to this same text *Pirqe de Rabbi Eliezer* 41 describes Moses rousing the Israelites from sleep to receive the Torah: "Arise ye from your sleep, for behold your God desires to give the Torah to you. Already the bridegroom wishes to lead the bride and to enter the bridal chamber. The hour has come for giving you the Torah, as it is said 'And Moses brought forth the people out of the camp to meet God' (Exod 19:17)."[144]
▪ *Sifra Shemini* 99.2.5 (on Leviticus 9) applies Song 3:11 to the consecration

of the tabernacle. This verse urges the daughters of Jerusalem to come out and welcome King Solomon who wears a crown on his wedding day, and *Sifra* understands this wedding to represent the coming of God's presence to the tabernacle.

- *b. Šabbat* 153a relates a parable which contrasts the wise and foolish guests whom a king summoned to a banquet without appointing a time. The parable is interpreted of the world to come. See above, pp. 303-3. *Eccl. Rab.* 9.8.1 uses this parable to interpret the statement "Let your garments be always white" and also includes a parable about the wife of a sailor who kept herself adorned so as to be prepared if he should appear suddenly.[145]
- *Pesiqta de Rab Kahana* 19.4 records a parable of a king who, desiring to wed a noblewoman, pledged various treasures to her and then went to a far country and remained for many years. People mocked her for waiting for him, but she comforted herself by reading the marriage settlement. After many years the king returned and marveled that she had waited. The parable is interpreted as the nations' mocking Israel for waiting for God, Israel's reading in the synagogues of God's pledges to her, and the coming time of redemption.
- *Pesiqta de Rab Kahana* Supplement 6.5: "The splendor of the garment He puts on the Messiah will stream forth from world's end to world's end, as implied by the words 'As a bridegroom putteth on a priestly diadem'" (Isa 61:10). *Pesiqta Rabbati* 37.2-3 interprets the bridegroom and bride of Isa 61:10 of the Messiah and Israel and has the same interpretation of Isa 61:10 as referring to God's clothing the Messiah.
- *Midr. Pss.* 10.2 tells a parable of a traveler who turned down an offer of refuge in a military post. At midnight he returned and asked admittance but was told the doors could not be opened. The parable is of God's refusal to hear Israel since Israel refused to hear God.
- *Exod. Rab.* 15.31 views this world as a time of betrothal of Israel and God and the actual marriage as occurring in the Messianic time.

Textual Features Worthy of Attention

Several themes are given prominence in this section: the fivefold repetition that no one knows the day or the hour (24:36, 42, 44, 50; 25:13), "watch" (*grēgoreō*, 24:42-43; 25:13 — note the similarity of 24:42 and 25:13), "wise" (*phronimos*, 24:45; 25:2, 4, 8, 9), prepared (*hetoimos*, 24:44; 25:10), and delay (*chronizō*, 24:48; 25:5).

Language concerning weddings, bridegrooms, and brides is not frequent.

"Wedding" *(gamos)* occurs eight times in Matt 22:2-12 and in Matt 25:10; Luke 12:36; 14:8; John 2:1-2; Heb 13:4 (of the state of being married); Rev 19:7, 9. Outside the four occurrences in this parable (vv. 1, 5, 6, 10) "bridegroom" *(nymphios)* occurs only in Matt 9:15/Mark 2:19-20/Luke 5:34-35; Matt 22:1-14; John 2:9; 3:29; Rev 18:23. "Bride" *(nymphē)* occurs only in Matt 10:35/Luke 12:53; John 3:29; Rev 18:23; 21:2, 9; 22:17.

The contrast between two persons or groups, one in the right and one not, appears elsewhere in Jesus' teaching: Matt 7:13-20/Luke 13:24; 6:43-45; Matt 7:24-27/Luke 6:47-49; Matt 12:33, 35; 21:28-32; 24:45-51; 25:31-46; Luke 7:41-43; 12:51-53; 15:11-32; 16:19-31; 18:9-14. In this context the contrast between wise and foolish mirrors the emphasis on one taken and one left in Matt 24:40-41.

The similar wording in Luke 12:35-38; 13:25 leads some to conclude that Luke knew this parable but did not use it. At least it shows the focus on the theme of preparedness in the teaching of Jesus.

This is the only parable to begin with *tote* ("then"). This word is so frequent with Matthew that it could be a mere connective, but more likely it refers to the coming of the future kingdom, which was alluded to in 24:50-51.

The future *homoiōthēsetai* ("will be like") in the NT occurs only here and in Matt 7:24, 26, where again the contrast is between the wise and the foolish. As elsewhere, the coming of the kingdom is likened to the whole course of events in the parable, not just to ten virgins.

V. 1 functions as a heading for the whole parable,[146] which precludes any idea that the virgins went out twice (vv. 1 and 6).

In vv. 11-12 with the closed door, the address "Lord, Lord," and the language of rejection we are no longer confined to the story world. We have moved past the parable into the reality which it portrays. The veil of the parable has become diaphanous, revealing the eschatological judgment it mirrors. All parables are to some degree created on the frame of the reality they mirror, and with some parables that reality shows through more than with others. Particularly at the ends of parables the reality is more likely to show through as an author seeks to emphasize the point. The result is a mixing of parabolic and nonparabolic language.[147] The reality shows through most often in two circumstances: prophetic denunciation of opponents[148] and conversation with friends where one does not need to be guarded. The language is surely shaped by Matthew (see 7:21-23), but the only question is whether Jesus gave such warnings and challenged his followers, which I think is almost beyond doubt.[149]

Cultural Information

Young women of marriageable age could be anywhere from age twelve on up. The groom typically would have been eighteen to twenty years old.

To the frustration of all interpreters of this parable, information about wedding customs in the ancient world is relatively sparse, and practices may have differed from place to place. Typically the betrothal took place in the bride's father's house and was a festive occasion with blessings, candles, and celebration. During the period between betrothal and marriage, which could extend several years — the young woman remained in her father's house. When the wedding day came, after the bride was suitably adorned and perfumed, she would be taken in a festive procession to the groom's home (or that of his parents, if the couple were to live there). About nightfall the procession would begin and the bride would be escorted to the groom's house by an entourage with torches or lanterns.[150] The groom would go out to receive the bride and bring her into his home where blessings and celebration would last as long as seven days.[151] In some texts bride and groom are both accompanied by an entourage through the streets on the way to where the festivities will be held. It was a religious duty of those observing to join in the celebration.[152] If Greco-Roman sources are used and if Palestinian customs are assumed to be similar, which is not unreasonable, the groom is understood as bringing his bride back to his (or his parents') house *after* obsesrving a banquet at the home of the bride. The virgins then wait in the home of the groom.[153] This is an attractive explanation and would make good sense of the text, but certainty does not exist about where they are and exactly what is described.

Considerable debate exists over whether the ten girls carried torches or lamps,[154] and even whether the problem with the oil is with regard to oil in reserve or whether the foolish girls did not bring oil at all.[155] Since they say "our lamps are going out," it is likely that the foolish girls did not bring extra oil.

Shops would not have been open at midnight, but is midnight the intent or just "well into the night"?[156] In *Semaḥot* 8.10 a parable tells of people who left a king's banquet at various times. Some left in the second and third hours of the night when some shops were still open.[157] In any locale people know whom to contact for emergency needs, especially if a major banquet is occurring.[158] Parables are not always realistic and do not need to be. The parable assumes the girls were successful in finding oil.

The words "I do not know you" in v. 12 may reflect a ban formula by which a disciple is forbidden access to a teacher.[159]

Explanation of the Parable

Options for Interpretation

1. As expected, in the history of the church this parable has been understood as an allegory of final judgment with most of the features being taken up in the allegory. Although considerable variety exists, typically the groom is Christ, the virgins are those who have accepted the faith of Christianity, the oil is good works or love, and the sleep is death, but several options exist for interpreting the number ten and the vendors. Such explanations are still in use by both pastors and scholars.[160]

2. Some like G. Bornkamm often assume that Matthew intended an allegory of judgment quite similar to the way the church has taken it. However, since he views the events narrated as conflicting with first-century wedding customs, he understands the parable to be an artificial creation by Matthew that is dominated by his eschatological intent. The parable is not from Jesus but is part of the process by which the church dealt with the delay of the parousia.[161] J. Lambrecht is uncertain about the parable's origin, but, because of its harshness, goes so far as to ask whether the parable should be dropped from the church's lectionary.[162]

3. The position made popular by C. H. Dodd and Joachim Jeremias is that the parable was originally Jesus' warning of the crisis inherent at the coming of God for judgment on Israel. The bridegroom's coming is representative of God's coming. Only later after the resurrection was the parable adapted by the church as a parousia parable with the necessary alterations and with the foolish virgins understood as Israel while the wise are understood as the Gentiles.[163] Often scholars following this approach strip the parable of any feature that could have allegorical significance (such as much or all of vv. 5 and 11-13) and end up with a truncated version.[164] However, others, like Craig Blomberg,[165] accept the parable pretty much as is, but still see it as addressed originally to Israel and adapted later by the church to the parousia.

4. Others, such as W. G. Kümmel and I. H. Marshall,[166] urge that the parable is about Jesus' own coming in the future. They accept that it is from Jesus, that it anticipates an interval, and that it warns hearers to be ready for the coming parousia.

5. Feminist readings of the parable sometimes rewrite it so that no one is excluded.[167]

Several other options exist but have little in their favor, such as that the parable is about pastoral problems caused by the death of Christians or about the judgment of Israelites when the millennium begins, or that it is an allegory about the hypocrisy of Torah scholars.[168]

Decisions on the Issues

1. How should the wedding circumstance be understood? To whose house (or to what place) is the bridegroom coming? Because of the paucity of good evidence, this is one of the more difficult decisions. Implicit in the question is a determination of the *realism* of the wedding. For some, if the description does not fit what is known of Palestinian weddings, the lack of realism means the church created the parable. The primary sources above show some variety. Explanations usually assume the bride is to be escorted to the home of the groom (or his parents), where the wedding takes place, but even that is not certain. Several options have been suggested:

> The virgins are at the bride's house and the wedding will take place there, which is less common but possible.[169]
> The virgins are at the bride's house, and the groom arrives there to find his bride and take her back to his house in a celebrative procession.
> The virgins have left the bride's house and have stopped somewhere on the way to await the groom,[170] for which I know of no evidence. This view seems to have emerged from a misunderstanding of 25:1, which should be seen as a title for the whole parable, not evidence that the virgins went out twice.
> The virgins and the bride are already at the groom's house awaiting his arrival, which is not the usual pattern.
> The virgins are at the groom's house and await his return *with* his bride.[171]

Except for an inferior textual variant in 25:1,[172] the bride is never mentioned, as is true of all other Synoptic texts mentioning a bridegroom or wedding festivities,[173] so no clues are offered. A decision will be determined by how one assesses the necessity of realism in parables, how the meager evidence is understood, and how one reads 25:10b. Those who think the parable is unrealistic assume that v. 10b shows the groom entering the house where he has come and the festivities take place there, not that the groom takes the bride back to his house, but that assumption may itself be faulty.[174] Several possibilities exist, for evidence can be garnered for weddings in the house of either bride or groom. Song of Songs 3:4-11 appears to have a wedding taking place at the bride's home, but that does not tell us what is assumed for this parable. The virgins could be waiting with the bride at the groom's house,[175] but that seems unlikely to me.

It is hard to speak of realism when there is insufficient information about first-century Palestinian weddings, and it will not do to point to Arabic or Indian weddings of later times, as interesting as they may be.[176] No doubt, practices varied in different locales and in different circumstances, such as when either the bride or groom lived some distance away.[177] The early texts attest a bridegroom going out to meet his bride as she is brought to him and to the celebration of the coming of the bridegroom.[178] If the virgins wait at the groom's house, they are part of his clan, and he is probably escorting his bride to his home *after* a banquet at the bride's home.[179] If they are at the bride's house, they are her friends and wait with her for the coming of the groom. They will go out to meet him when his approach has been announced and escort him to the house. Either option is possible, but the former seems more likely. The most important thing is that the bridegroom's appearance is a sign for the festivities to begin. The parable is not unrealistic. It is sufficiently within the bounds of what is known that, even if it presents unusual circumstances, it works, and its warning to be ready is clear.[180]

Questions are raised about the realism of other features as well: (1) Would shops be open in the middle of the night? (2) Would the groom tarry until midnight? (3) Do not vv. 11-12 exceed any reasonable conversation among the participants? The first was treated above (see p. 510), and, unless interpreted literalistically, is not a disorienting factor. If the groom was at a banquet at the bride's house, the delay in coming is understandable. The third question will be treated below. In any case, questions of realism cannot be the determining factor in interpretation. Some parables are realistic (like the Good Samaritan), while others are pseudo-realistic and may contain unusual features (like the Wicked Tenants). The primary question is whether the parable functions as a narrative development with sufficient plot and resolution that hearers would be carried along. That is the case here.

2. Is the reference to the coming of God or to the coming of Jesus? An answer involves deciding whether Jesus used the bridegroom as a messianic image. To ask the question another way, should the hearers locate themselves at the beginning of the parable before the young women sleep or toward the end of the parable just before the groom's coming?[181] The former would assume a parable of Jesus' future return and the latter the crisis of God's coming in the kingdom in the ministry of Jesus.

J. Jeremias, among others, argued that the metaphor of the Messiah as a bridegroom is foreign to the OT and the literature of late Judasim. This is taken as evidence that the parable is about God's coming, not the parousia, and for some, evidence that the parable's origin is in the church. Jeremias argued that Jesus told a story of an actual wedding and that his hearers would not have thought of the Messiah with the image of the bridegroom. As elsewhere, what

Jeremias takes away with one hand he grants with the other, since he suggests that the parable at most contains a Messianic reference which only the disciples would understand.[182] Of course, if the messianic reference was understood by the disciples, then Jesus' intent and what others may have understood are open questions.

In the OT God is compared to a bridegroom in relation to Israel,[183] and it would make perfectly good sense if Jesus were referring to the coming of God. A significant number of scholars understand this to be the intent of Jesus' parable. It fits with Jesus' preaching of the coming kingdom, and the parable would express the joy of the salvation present with Jesus and warn people not to miss this time of joy.[184] One qualification is needed. The reference must still be to something future, not to what has already occurred. The kingdom was present with Jesus, but its fullness and a final intervention of God are still expected. The kingdom still has a future. The command to be prepared or awake makes no sense if the event is already past.[185]

Others argue instead that Jesus referred to himself with the bridegroom image,[186] which must be given considerable weight because of the use of the term as a self-reference in Matt 9:15/Mark 2:19-20/Luke 5:34-35 (cf. John 3:29).[187]

Usually the evidence for the bridegroom being an image for the Messiah is thought to be late,[188] but two texts from Qumran suggest rethinking this conclusion. The reading of Isa 61:10 in 1QIs^a suggests this chapter was understood of the Messiah of Aaron, as argued by William Brownlee long ago. Instead of the words repesented by the Masoretic text "As a bridegroom decks himself"[189] 1QIs^a has "as a priest."[190] More compelling, if it is properly restored, is 4Q434a fragments 1 and 2, 6-7, which, even if referring to God, at least describes messianic times when nations and the evil are eliminated, all the earth is filled with his glory, and sins are atoned. Then we are told, "As someone whose mother consoles him, so will he console them in Jerusal[em. . . . Like a bridegroom] with his bride he will liv[e] for[ev]er [. . .] his throne is for ever and ever. . . ." The association of a bridegroom with messianic ideas is not late.

Further, if the application of the bridegroom image to Jesus was made by the church, one would have expected the bride to be included.[191] Other images or prerogatives of God (like "shepherd," "king," and the one who forgives) are applied to the Messiah or taken over by Jesus,[192] and it would be no surprise if the bridegroom image were as well. I would argue that the bridegroom is a self-reference by Jesus.

However, the way the question is posed with its contrast of God's coming or Jesus' coming should be challenged. Would Jesus have made such a distinction? Do not events like the Triumphal Entry fit with Jesus' sayings (such as Luke 4:18-21; Matt 11:4-6/Luke 7:22-23) to suggest that in *his* ministry God is coming to establish his kingdom?[193] The rabbinic passages focusing on a bridegroom, late as they may be, have no difficulty using the image of both God and the Messiah *in the same context.*[194] We are still left with the question whether the parable refers to God coming in Jesus' ministry or to the parousia in the future, which will be addressed below. Hearers cannot know from the parable whether they stand at its opening or its closing but only that they should be prepared, which fits with Matthew's fivefold repetition that the hour cannot be known.

   3. Do the elements in the parable, especially the bridegroom, the virgins, and the oil have allegorical significance? As always, the intent of the introduction to the parable is to say that the kingdom is like the whole process narrated in the story, not merely the virgins. In the analogy there is correspondence between the coming kingdom (and by implication the King) and the coming of the bridegroom and between those prepared or not prepared and the two groups of young women. Many other associations have been suggested, but it is doubtful that any are valid. The virgins are not the bride or the church, the two classes of virgins do not stand for Gentiles and Jews, the number ten has no particular significance, sleep does not suggest lack of vigilance, sleep and rising from sleep do not refer to death and resurrection, the middle of the night does not refer to the expectation that the parousia comes in the night, and the oil does not refer to good works or to the Holy Spirit.[195] All such ideas are projections on Jesus (and Matthew), are not demonstrable from the text, and do not further the analogy, which is concerned to promote preparedness.

   4. To whom is the parable addressed? Jesus' Jewish contemporaries? Jesus' disciples? Would-be disciples? The answer to this question is tied to the identification of the bridegroom image. If one thinks the bridegroom is a reference to God, then the original audience will be seen as Jesus' Jewish contemporaries. If the bridegroom is a self-reference by Jesus, then the audience could be either Jesus' contemporaries or his disciples.[196] As with the parable of the Faithful or Unfaithful Servant, neither option may be excluded.[197] Conceivably and without difficulty a warning to Israel concerning readiness for God's coming could have been adapted by the church for readiness at Jesus' coming. Matthew obviously has the parable directed at Jesus' disciples, and this is more likely in the end. The similar language at 7:21-23 addresses those who think they are followers of Jesus. Even if the similarity here is a result of Matthew's shaping, Luke also uses similar language at 12:35 in addressing the disciples. If one accepts that Jesus anticipated an interval between his death and final vindication, then the disciples would be addressed with teaching regarding readiness for the parousia.[198] I suggest that is the case.

   5. Is "delay" an essential element of the parable, or does it refer to the church's experience of the problem of the delay of the parousia and demonstrate an origin in the church rather than from Jesus?[199] The issue of the significance of the delay is a crucial question. One cannot delete the delay as a secondary or unimportant feature. The parable is framed on the fact of the delay, and without the delay there is no parable. A delay is required for the lamps to go out and for time for the young women to go to sleep. It is the delay that demonstrates the wisdom or foolishness of the participants.[200] But is the delay only a necessary feature of the parable or an indication of the experience of the delay in the early church? Jeremias's argument that the delay was caused by negotiations in the marriage contract does not inspire confidence.[201] Similarly, the claim that delay was a standard feature of Jewish weddings is not adequately demonstrated.[202] If, however, the reason for the delay is the banquet in the bride's house,[203] nothing artificial is involved.

Nor does the parable or Matthew betray any anxiety about the delay of the parousia.[204] Matthew emphasizes only that no one knows the time of the coming and that one should be prepared, themes belonging to the teaching of Jesus. *Chronizō* (the verb for "delay" in v. 5) is not technical language for the delay of the parousia. In the parable of the Faithful or Unfaithful Servant *chronizō* is used (24:48) to depict a coming *sooner* than expected, but in the parable of the Ten Virgins it is used (25:5) to depict a coming *later* than expected. Matthew is concerned about readiness, not the delay of the parousia.[205] Bornkamm and others without justification have imposed a concern for the delay on this parable and compared it to the situation in 2 Thessalonians.[206]

Several facts bear repetition: Jesus declared that he did not know the time of "that day" (Matt 24:36/Mark 13:32; Luke 12:40), he anticipated an interval of some duration,[207] and he warned his disciples in both parabolic and non-parabolic language to be prepared (Matt 24:37-51; Mark 13:34-37; Luke 12:35-40; 21:34-36). This parable coheres with these facts and is further evidence of Jesus' expectation of an interval prior to his vindication.[208] The parable deserves to be interpreted in the context of Jesus and not encumbered with allegorical nuance nor read as an expression of the church's experience of the delay of the parousia. The problem of the end of the parable (vv. 11-13) still remains to be considered.

6. Does "sleep" carry any negative connotations in this parable? There is no reason to think sleep carries any negative connotation, for both the wise and the foolish virgins sleep. Sleep is used negatively in texts like Matt 26:38-46/Mark 14:34-42/Luke 22:45-46, but no negative evaluation of sleep arises from the text of the parable.

7. Are the wise virgins ethically culpable for not sharing? Several people object that this parable is antithetical to Jesus' teaching, for it expresses oppression, the bridegroom is ungracious, and the wise young women do not share or practice solidarity.[209] Such charges betray an insensitivity both to the situation depicted and to how stories function. If the oil the wise brought for their lamps was divided with the foolish, all the lamps would go out, and the celebration could not proceed in the dark. More to the point, these complaints show a dismal failure to understand how parables work. Parable and reality are not connected with equal signs. Parables are not direct pictures of reality and do not claim to portray life as it should be. They only partially map the realities they seek to reveal.[210] Further, this is a syncrisis, which by its very nature contrasts positive and negative processes or entities. This parable is not about ethics but about wisdom and foolishness with regard to being prepared. We will never understand the parables unless we are willing to focus on the function of the analogy,[211] and doing so will prevent such complaints.

8. *Does v. 13 with its exhortation to watch fit the parable since all ten virgins slept?* On the surface the warning to watch *(grēgoreō)* does not fit the parable since even the wise slept. *Grēgoreō* literally means "be or stay awake" but is used metaphorically with the sense "be alert." Watching is not a passive activity, merely watching for an event to occur, but a metaphor for readiness and faithful fulfillment of the Christian calling.[212] In that sense it is a fitting description of the goal of the parable and has nothing to do with the sleeping and rising in the parable.[213] David Flusser argued that Jesus used this concluding sentence as the original ending of the parable, even though the saying is older than the parable.[214] More likely this was a repeated theme of Jesus' teaching to his disciples that Matthew placed here as a fitting conclusion. The similarity of the wording in 24:42-43 points to Matthean shaping.

9. *What is the teaching of the parable?* This is not a parable merely about wisdom but specifically the wisdom needed in view of the eschaton. As with the previous parable the focus is on the negative part of the contrast, as is evident in vv. 10-12. With these verses no longer are we tied to the metaphorical world. The image of a bridegroom is not very suitable for a warning of impending judgment,[215] and here at the end the parable reflects more the reality it depicts, is more revealing about the identity of the bridegroom ("Lord, Lord") and the consequences of being unprepared, and reverts back to the focus on the kingdom from v. 1. The language is shaped to Matthean themes, as is evident by comparison with 7:22-23, but the themes of renunciation and a closed door are not merely Matthean (cf. Luke 13:25).[216] Such language points to final judgment and the future parousia. As elsewhere, the teaching is that the kingdom will be a time of separation.[217]

The parable underscores that wisdom means understanding the eschatological outlook of Jesus' teaching and then living in a way that fits with the expectation of vindication and the full coming of God's kingdom. I think this parable should be understood as Jesus' urging his disciples to live with such wisdom. If the original concern was for his Jewish contemporaries to have a similar wisdom about his own ministry, the practical effect is not much different, and the church has only extended the message. The important point is that wisdom is eschatologically defined. Wisdom and readiness are virtual synonyms.

The parable urges readiness, preparedness, in view of the coming of the kingdom. The previous parable warned that the kingdom may come sooner than expected, this one that it may come later than expected. The time is not known; the certainty and import of the coming are taken for granted. The parable does not say in what readiness consists; that will be spelled out in the next two parables, but for Matthew and his readers this is already obvious from what has been said about discipleship throughout the Gospel.

In urging both wisdom and readiness, this parable is close to the parable of the Unjust Judge (Luke 18:1-8): it, too, asserts the certainty of the coming of the kingdom — despite appearances — and in effect asks if the Son of Man will find faith on the earth when he comes. The parables of the Tower Builder and the Warring King have a similar focus on wisdom.

Adapting the Parable

The eschatological focus of this parable should not be lost. Suggestions that the parable be applied to death, loss of opportunity, or responsibility[218] may not be totally inappropriate, but they render the parable bland and without force. At the heart of the Christian faith is the expectation that one day God will set things right — that the kingdom will come and that Jesus will be vindicated and his dream put into effect.[219] Living as a wise human means being prepared for God's reign. Readiness is an attitude, a commitment, and a lifestyle. It means living in ways that comport with the character of the kingdom and being faithful at all times.

The parable is not about the delay of the parousia, but the delay is a factor for us. We cannot — and should not — live in eschatological excitement and anxiety, something the NT never suggests. The unknown length of time is not really the issue. The determining factors are the character of God and our response to it. Evil and injustice are still plaguing problems. The teaching of Jesus and the Christian view of God insist that they do not get the last word. That is a stance of faith, but it calls for faithfulness and mission fulfilling the purposes of God for creation. Or, as Richard Bauckham puts it, "The delay of the parousia is filled with the mission of the church."[220]

For Further Reading

W. D. Davies and Dale C. Allison, *A Critical and Exegetical Commentary on the Gospel According to Saint Matthew* (3 vols.; ICC; Edinburgh: T. & T. Clark, 1988-97), 3:374-77, 391-401.

David Flusser, *Die rabbinischen Gleichnisse und der Gleichniserzähler Jesus* 1: *Das Wesen der Gleichnisse* (Bern: Peter Lang, 1981), pp. 177-92.

Joachim Jeremias, *The Parables of Jesus* (2d ed.; trans. S. H. Hooke; New York: Charles Scribner's Sons, 1963), pp. 51-53, 171-75.

Evald Lövestam, *Spiritual Wakefulness in the New Testament* (trans. W. F. Salisbury; LUÅ 55; Lund: Gleerup, 1963), pp. 108-22.

Susan Marie Praeder, *The Word in Women's Worlds: Four Parables* (Wilmington: Michael Glazier, 1988), pp. 72-98.

Armand Puig i Tarrech, *La Parabole des Dix Vierges. Mt 25,1-13* (AnBib 102; Rome: Biblical Institute, 1983).

Ruben Zimmermann, "Das Hochzeitsritual im Jungfrauengleichnis. Sozialgeschichtliche Hintergründe zu Mt. 25:1-3," *NTS* 48 (2002): 48-70.

THE TALENTS AND THE MINAS
(Matt 25:14-30; Luke 19:11-27)

These two parables have been strangely neglected, not even discussed by several books on parables, even though they are among the longer narrative parables and are clearly important for the Evangelists. Further, the primary source material is less helpful for these parables, and none of the explanations by scholars is fully satisfactory — to say nothing of the fact that many people do not like these parables.

Parable Type

Matthew's version is a fairly straightforward double indirect narrative parable without a *nimshal*. The *nimshal* is unnecessary because the reality depicted is allowed to shine through in the telling of the story and because of the context in which it appears. Luke's version is a double indirect narrative parable with two interwoven plots and also without a *nimshal*. As in Matthew, the context allows the reality to shine through so that a *nimshal* is unnecessary.

Issues Requiring Attention[221]

1. What is the relation of the parables in Matthew and Luke? Can the earliest version be determined?
2. Has the original intent of the parables been changed by allegorical additions (e.g., in Matthew: "after a long time" in v. 19, "enter into the joy of your master" in vv. 21 and 23, casting into the outer darkness in v. 30; in Luke: the direct order to "do business" in v. 13, the throne claimant elements, and authority over cities in vv. 17 and 19)?
3. To whom is each parable addressed?
4. What is the failure of the third servant? Would Jesus' hearers have identified with the third servant in Matthew as taking a commendable safe course, with Luke adding the explicit command to "do business" to establish the man's guilt?[222]
5. Does Luke's account allude to the events surrounding Archelaus after the death of Herod the Great?
6. Do these parables point to the return of *Jesus* after an interval or to his announcement of the soon coming of *God* for judgment? That is, is the master a "God" figure, a "Christ" figure, or neither? Do the hearers/readers stand near the beginning of the narrative when the master is leaving or at the end when he returns?
7. What is the meaning of Luke 19:11? Did Jesus tell this parable to prevent eschatological excitement among his followers or to *announce* the imminence of the kingdom?
8. What is the teaching of each parable?
9. Does the harsh language in Matt 25:29-30 and Luke 19:26-27 belong to the original versions? How should this harshness be handled?
10. Is either parable anti-Semitic?

Helpful Primary Source Material

Canonical Material

- NT: Matt 13:12/Mark 4:25/Luke 8:18; Matt 24:45-51; Mark 13:33-37; Luke 12:35-40, 41-46; 16:10-12; 19:43-44; 22:29; Rev 2:26

Early Jewish Writings

- *Ahiqar* 192: "If your master entrusts you with water to keep [and you are not trustworthy with it, how can he] leave gold in your hand?"

- Tob 1:14; 4:20-21; 5:3: Tobit leaves ten talents of silver in trust with a certain Gabriel/Gabael in Media and twenty years later tells his son Tobias about the money in trust. The rest of the book is about the journey of Tobias to retrieve the money. The money is returned *with the seals intact* (9:5). Obviously this was money left for safe-keeping, not money left to invest.
- Josephus, *J.W.* 2.1-38, 80-111; *Ant.* 17.208-49, 299-320: These passages tell of the events following the death of Herod the Great. Archelaus and his entourage went to Rome to persuade Caesar to confer on him the authority to succeed Herod as king. (Antipas also made the trip as a throne claimant.) In addition a delegation of fifty Jews from Israel, joined by 8000 Jews in Rome,[223] appeared before Caesar to argue against Archelaus being made king. While these texts tell of Archelaus killing 3000 troublesome Jews *before* going to Rome, no details of revenge on the Jewish delegation in Rome opposing him are given. Josephus does say, "Archelaus, on taking possession of his ethnarchy, did not forget old feuds, but treated not only the Jews but even the Samaritans with great brutality" (*J.W.* 2.111).[224]
- *3 Bar.* 12–16 (which was possibly later and reworked by Christians) tells of three groups of angels carrying baskets of flowers representing the virtues of the righteous. The angels with full baskets are to reward a hundredfold "our friends" who have laboriously done good works. Those with half full baskets are to reward accordingly, and the angels with empty baskets are to cause the humans responsible to be provoked and afflicted with plagues and punished with the sword and death, and their children with demons. In the Slavonic version Baruch asks to cry on their behalf and is permitted to do so.

Early Christian Writings

- *Gos. Thom.* 41: "He who has (something) in his hand, to him will be given (more); and he who has nothing, from him will be taken even the little which he has."
- The Gospel of the Nazarenes (as recorded by Eusebius, *Theophania* 4.22):[225] "But since the Gospel [written] in Hebrew characters which has come into our hands enters the threat not against the man who had hid [the talent], but against him who had lived dissolutely — for he [the master] had three servants: one who squandered his master's substance with harlots and flute-girls, one who multiplied the gain, and one who hid the talent; and accordingly one was accepted (with joy), another merely rebuked, and another cast into prison — I wonder whether in Matthew the

threat which is uttered after the word against the man who did nothing may refer not to him, but by epanalepsis[226] to the first who had feasted and drunk with the drunken."

Later Jewish Writings

- *m. 'Abot* 3.1: "Consider three things and thou wilt not fall into the hands of transgression. Know whence thou art come and whither thou art going and before whom thou art about to give account and reckoning. 'Whence thou art come' — from a putrid drop; 'and whither thou art going' — to the place of dust, worm, and maggot; 'and before whom thou art about to give account and reckoning' — before the King of kings of kings, the Holy One, blessed is he."
- *m. 'Abot* 3.17 refers to judgment as rendering account. See above, p. 484.
- *m. 'Abot* 4.2: "Run to fulfil the lightest duty even as the weightiest, and flee from transgression; for one duty draws another duty in its train, and one transgression draws another transgression in its train; for the reward of a duty [done] is a duty [to be done], and the reward of one transgression is [another] transgression." Cf. Matt 25:29/Luke 19:26.
- *b. B. Meṣi'a* 42a: "Samuel said: Money can only be guarded [by placing it] in the earth." The corresponding section of the Mishnah, *m. Baba Meṣi'a* 3.10-12 discusses liability for money left for safekeeping. According to 3.10 "If a man left money in his fellow's keeping, and his fellow bound it up and hung it over his back, . . . he is liable." However, money left in trust is different from money left to invest.[227]
- *'Abot de Rabbi Nathan* 14: When Rabban Yohanan ben Zakkai's son died, his disciples came to comfort him. Four rabbis attempted to console him by pointing to Adam, Job, Aaron, and David, all of whom had children who died and all accepted comfort, but these rabbis only added to the father's distress. R. Eleazar b. Arakh said, "I shall tell thee a parable: to what may this be likened? To a man with whom the king deposited some object. Every single day the man would weep and cry out, saying: 'Woe unto me, when shall I be quit of this trust in peace?' Thou too, master, thou hadst a son: he studied the Torah, the Prophets, the Holy Writings, he studied Mishnah, Halakha, Agada, and he departed from the world without sin. And thou shouldst be comforted when thou hast returned thy trust unimpaired." The rabbi accepted this as proper comfort.[228] Again, however, this parable treats something valuable given for safekeeping, not money given to invest.

Comparison of the Accounts

Mark 13:34 has a one-verse analogy about a man who departs and entrusts his servants with authority to work. Although the context in the eschatological discourse and the initial wording are similar to Matthew, Mark's comparison lacks any narrative plot or development. It is more the use of similar imagery than a parallel. As indicated above (pp. 492-93), I find compelling Wenham's argument that there was a pre-Synoptic eschatological discourse concluding with several parables, one of which was the Talents/Minas.[229]

Matthew places his parable of the Talents in his eschatological discourse, *after* Jesus' triumphal entrance into Jerusalem, the Temple incident, and questions of entrapment put to Jesus. The passion events follow immediately after the close of this discourse. Luke places his parable of the Minas just after the Zacchaeus incident in Jericho and just *before* Jesus' entrance into Jerusalem.

Of 301 words in Matthew's version and 281 in Luke's only fifty are identical, and only ten more are the same word in different forms or a cognate. Much greater similarity exists in parables of the triple tradition than in parables common to Matthew and Luke. Whereas the former tend to be very close, the dissimilarity in some of the double tradition parables is sufficient to question whether one is dealing with the same account. (See the parables of the Lost Sheep and the Wedding Feast/Banquet.)

Matthew's account is more coherent and divides easily into three sections, each with three movements corresponding to the three servants: the distribution of money (vv. 14-15); the action of the servants (vv. 16-18); the reckoning (vv. 19-30). Luke's account is less balanced because of the introduction and the interweaving of two plots, that of the servants and that of the throne claimant: introduction (v. 11), the distribution of money (vv. 12-13), hatred and embassy of the citizens (v. 14), the reckoning of the three servants (vv. 15-26), and slaughter of the rebellious citizens (v. 27).

The major differences between the accounts are:

Matthew	Luke
	Introduction concerning expectations near Jerusalem (v. 11).
A man going on a journey distributes five, two, and one talents to his servants according to their ability (vv. 14-15).	A *nobleman* going to a *far country specifically to obtain a kingdom* distributes to *ten* servants *one mina each* (vv. 12-13).

In Luke the servants are specifically told to "do business" until he returns, but no description of their efforts is given (v. 13).

The servants do not need to be told what to do with the money, but their efforts are detailed: the first two servants doubled their amount, while the third servant buried the money in the ground (vv. 16-18).

Rebellious citizens and an embassy reject this king (v. 14).

The reckoning occurs after a long time, and the same words are said to the first two servants: "Well done, good and faithful servant. You have been faithful over a few things; I will set you over many things. Enter into the joy of your master" (vv. 19-23).

The reckoning occurs after the nobleman has received a kingdom and so that he may know what his servants have gained. *Only three of the ten servants appear.* The first gained ten minas and the second five. The first servant is told, "Well done, good servant; because you were faithful in a small thing, have authority over ten cities." The second is merely told, "You will be over five cities" (vv. 15-19).

The third servant says he knew the man was hard *(sklēros)*, reaping where he did not sow and gathering where he did not scatter, and being afraid he buried the money which he now returns (vv. 24-25).

The third servant hid his mina in a cloth. He was afraid because he knew the man to be harsh *(austēros)*, taking where he did not deposit and reaping where he did not sow (vv. 20-21).

The master calls the third servant evil and hesitant (or possibly lazy) and asserts, given the man's knowledge, that he should have put the money in the bank so that he could have gained interest (vv. 26-27).

The master asks the servant, given his opinion, why he did not put the money in the bank (vv. 22-23).

524

Command is given to take the talent from him and give it to the servant who has ten (v. 28).	Bystanders are directed to give this servant's mina to the one with ten (v. 24) and the bystanders respond (v. 25, but some texts omit this verse). No other punishment is mentioned for the third servant.
The proverb: "To everyone who has will be given *and he will have abundance,* but to the one who does not have even what he has will be taken *from him*" (v. 29).	The proverb "To everyone who has will be given, but from the one who does not have even what he has will be taken" (v. 26).
	The command to slaughter the rebellious citizens (v. 27).
Command is given to cast the useless servant into the outer darkness, where there will be weeping and gnashing of teeth (v. 30).	

If these two parables derive from the same original, then the traditions on which Matthew and Luke depend must have diverged very early. Serious consideration must be given to the fact that these are two similar but independent parables. See below, pp. 529-31.

Textual Features Worthy of Attention

Both Matthew and Luke

The responsibility assigned the servants gives them an obligation, and these parables then are close to those in which debtors appear. Obligation/debt is a major theme in Jesus' parables. In addition to these two parables, compare the parables of the Unforgiving Servant (Matt 18:23-35), the Two Sons (Matt 21:28-32), the Wicked Tenants (Matt 21:33-45/Mark 12:1-12/Luke 20:9-18), the Two Debtors (Luke 7:41-43), the Dishonest Steward (Luke 16:1-13), the Faithful and Unfaithful Steward (Matt 24:45-51; Luke 12:42-46), and the Man Going on a Journey (Mark 13:34-36).

The device of dialogue between a master and a subordinate (or subordinates) in the wrong appears also in the parables of the Unforgiving Servant

PARABLES OF FUTURE ESCHATOLOGY

(Matt 18:23-35), the Workers in the Vineyard (Matt 20:11-15), the Marriage Garment (Matt 22:11-13), the Ten Virgins (Matt 25:1-13), the Sheep and the Goats (Matt 25:31-46), the Prodigal Son (Luke 15:11-32), and the Rich Man and Lazarus (Luke 16:19-31).

The master in these parables is addressed with the Greek word *kyrios,* which is the right word to use of a human master, but is also used with reference to God, or later in the church, the exalted Christ. What nuance should we assign to this flexible word, particularly when the Son of Man as Judge is addressed as *Kyrie* in Matt 25:37 and 44, but no other word is suitable for a servant/slave to use of a master? Compare in Luke 19:33-34 the use of *kyrioi* for the owners of the colt Jesus will ride and the use of *kyrios* of Jesus, the colt's true master/Lord.

Specific to Matthew

As indicated earlier, Matthew has a fivefold emphasis on no one knowing the date of the coming of the Son of Man (24:36, 42, 44, 50; 25:13), and he gives prominence to themes such as watching, wisdom, and faithfulness.[230] Here note additionally the praise of faithful servants (24:45-46; 25:21, 23; 25:34), the focus on possessions (24:47; 25:14), and the exclusions from the presence of the returning master/Lord (24:51; 25:10, 30, 46, with weeping and gnashing of teeth in 24:51; 25:30).

The parable of the Faithful or Unfaithful Servant (Matt 24:45-51) is quite similar to that of the Talents. In both a master gives a servant/servants responsibility in his absence and rewards the faithful with additional responsibility and punishes the unfaithful harshly in a place where there is weeping and gnashing of teeth.

Hōsper gar ("For it is just like," v. 14) should not be understood so that the parable is seen merely as an explanation of v. 13 and the idea of being alert. More likely it illustrates the broader themes of the whole section, as its parallels with 24:45-51 attest.

The structure of the parable is clear: vv. 14-15 introduce the circumstances, vv. 16-18 detail the activity of the servants, v. 19 sets the stage of the master's return to settle accounts, vv. 20-23 use identical language to describe the reports of the first two servants and the responses of the master, and vv. 24-30, the largest section of the parable, describe the report of the third servant and the master's response, with vv. 28-30 telling of the punishment rendered.

Specific to Luke

Luke's placement of the parable after the Zacchaeus incident and before the triumphal entry deserves close attention. The statement to Zacchaeus, "Today salvation has come to this house" (19:9), provides the reason within the narrative why some thought the kingdom was immediately to appear. Several features of Luke's narrative of the last days in Jerusalem connect to features of the parable: in the accounts of the triumphal entry Luke alone has Jesus acclaimed as "king" (19:38), the rebellious citizens and their destruction in the parable are mirrored in the lament over Jerusalem (19:41-44), and the attitude of the rebellious citizens is mirrored in that of the chief priests, the teachers of the law, and the leaders of the people (19:47).[231]

This section of Luke is dramatic in the way it describes Jesus' approach to Jerusalem. Jesus was near *(engys)* Jerusalem (19:11), going ahead *(emprosthen,* also in v. 27) and ascending to the city, drew near *(ēngisen)* to Bethphage (v. 28), drew near *(engizontos)* to the descent down the Mount of Olives (v. 37), and came near *(ēngisen),* saw the city, and wept. Two different spellings of Jerusalem are used: *Ierousalēm* (v. 11) and *Hierosolyma* (v. 28).[232]

Compare Luke's ten slaves, only three of which are treated, to the parable of the Workers in the Vineyard (Matt 20:1-16), which has five groups hired, only two of which are treated.

The idea of the righteous being set over cities (or nations, 19:17, 19) is paralleled in the rewards to the righteous described in Rev 2:26-27 and Wis 3:8.

V. 25 is not present in a few manuscripts: Codices Bezae and Washington, eight minuscules (not listed by UBS[4]), and some lectionary and versional evidence. Usually it is accepted as part of the text, but the transition from the "D" level of confidence for placing the verse in single brackets in UBS[1] to the "A" for inclusion without brackets in UBS[4] is startling. Whereas this verse says the first servant has ten minas, he actually has eleven. The verse does not contribute much, which may have led to its omission.

Cultural Information

It is no surprise that economic arrangements between those with resources and workers were common in the ancient world, as attested by several of Jesus' parables and various other sources.[233] Whether the persons in the parable entrusted with money were slaves or servants is debated. *Doulos* can mean either. Derrett argued that they were servants because slaves would not have had the powers an agent needed for commercial enterprise.[234] Others insist the men are managerial slaves,[235] which may be more likely, but certainty is not possible. The distinction makes little difference in the parable, for the master has absolute control over their futures, whether because they are slaves or because the reality represented by the parable shows through.

OT law prohibited Israelites charging interest *to other Israelites* (Exod 22:25; Lev 25:35-37; Deut 23:19-20), a law that was often broken (cf. Ps 15:5; Jer 15:10; Ezek 18:8, 13, 17; 22:12), but interest could be charged to non-Israelites (Deut 23:20). Further, the discussion of interest in ancient Palestine is complicated, and it may be that no prohibition on *business* loans was in effect in the first century.[236] In the rabbinic material considerable effort was made to distinguish interest from legitimate increase.[237]

The definition we know of "talent" referring to human ability was derived from this parable, and, even though people interpreted "talent" in connection with ability much earlier, this use of the word did not emerge until the fifteenth century. For modern readers this meaning is at least distracting and potentially misleading. A talent in the ancient world was a monetary weight of approximately 60 to 90 pounds. (There was significant variation in different times and locales.) Depending on the metal in question, the value of a talent was equivalent to 6000 days' wages for a day laborer (roughly twenty years' work), so the man given five talents was given an enormous sum. Obviously the "one talent" man still had an enormous amount.[238] The values are so large that some think the amounts in Matthew are a result of his redactional changes, as is also alleged for the enormous sum in his parable of the Unforgiving Servant. Since parables often have hyperbole though, the basis of such a decision is shaky at best.

Luke's figures are much smaller but still involve a significant amount. Each servant was given one mina, the equivalent of about 100 days' wages for a common laborer.

Hiding money in the ground was a common security measure. The Qumran Copper Scroll (3Q15) is a list of hidden treasures. See above, p. 241.

Explanation of the Parable

Options for Interpretation

1. The allegorical interpretation of the church viewed the man departing as Christ ascending to heaven, his return as the parousia, and the rewards and punishment as what will be rendered to the saved and unsaved. The parable was understood more specifically about the reception of the gospel. With some variations the first servant represented the conversion of Jews, the second the conversion of the Gentiles, and the third the unconverted. Some viewed the servants as referring to teachers, the first sent to the Jews, the second to the Gentiles, and the third being negligent ministers who did not do their work. That the Lord reaps where he did not sow was sometimes understood as point-

ing to those saved through natural law, sometimes as referring only to punishment, and sometimes just as an untruth.[239]

2. Popular among preachers and some scholars is the interpretation of this parable primarily in terms of stewardship with little or no focus on eschatological themes. The parable then teaches that reward is gained only through effort, faithfulness leads to success, and lack of faithfulness leads to loss.[240]

3. The parable depicts the time from Jesus' death and resurrection to the parousia and is directed toward the disciples to encourage kingdom living. This is the traditional and most obvious understanding of the present form of the parable.[241]

4. What is now a parousia parable originally was a parable against Jewish leaders, who built a fence around the Law and created a barren religion, or especially against scribes, who were entrusted with the Word of God.[242] Later the parable was given ethical and eschatological features by the early church.

5. The parable in Luke is not pointing to the delay but is *announcing* the manifestation of the kingdom *immediately*. Luke Johnson argued for this approach and has been followed by several, especially N. T. Wright, who views Jesus' entry into Jerusalem as a symbolic enactment of Yahweh's coming to Zion to judge and to save. He sees the parable as the key explanatory riddle showing the significance of Jesus' arrival. Rather than being at the beginning of the story, the hearers stand near the end of the story when the master is about to return.[243] Somewhat related is the approach that interprets the parable of Jesus' preaching of the kingdom and the reception by his hearers.[244]

6. The master in the parable is not a positive figure, but a negative one, and the action of the third servant is commendable. For a peasant this is a text of terror; the parable functions as a warning to those who mistreat the poor. R. Rohrbaugh initiated this approach, and his view has been expanded by several others, especially W. Herzog, who suggested that the first two servants dealt in "honest graft" and that the master thought exploitation and wasteful living were honorable.[245]

Decisions on the Issues

1. What is the relation of the parables in Matthew and Luke? Can the earliest version be determined? Parables as divergent as the accounts of entrusted money in Matthew and Luke generate numerous theories about their tradition history. The typical scholarly approach to these parables argues:

> that the two versions are divergent accounts of a single original, though it
> is difficult to trace the relation of the accounts to Q,

> that Matthew's account is closer to the original, but Matthew has shaped
the parable allegorically to reflect a concern for eschatology and the
delay of the parousia by placing it in his eschatological discourse, by
several additions some of which may be due to the tradition ("after a
long time" in v. 19, "enter into the joy of your master" in vv. 21 and 23,
the proverb in v. 29, casting into the outer darkness in v. 30), and by
the change from *minas* to *talents,* and

> that Luke has somewhat ineffectively joined two parables (that of the
minas and that of the throne claimant) and has also shaped the resulting parable eschatologically by placing it just before the entry to Jerusalem, by his introduction in v. 11, and by the direct order to "do business" in v. 13.

Undoubtedly, both accounts have been shaped and have anomalies, especially Luke's, and one can understand how such scholarly reconstructions
arise. At the same time I am increasingly suspicious of both the methods and
the results. Almost invariably the methods and assumptions of scholars are
mechanistically applied, and the reconstructions are short, unattractive ren-
derings. Can we really separate tradition and redaction as easily as some suggest? Awareness of the uncertainty does not stop people from offering reconstructions. J. Lambrecht assumes that the original text must be free from all
Matthean or Lukan additions and rewriting,[246] and Alfons Weiser assumes
that he can distinguish what comes from Matthew's special source, from Matthew's redaction, and from Q, even though he recognizes that the special
source and Matthean redaction are very close in wording and substance.[247]
Word statistics and redactional tendencies, as helpful as they are, do not demonstrate origin. The ideas or accounts an Evangelist received were *both preserved and reshaped* in his own style. Further, one must grant that the Evangelist's language and thought not only shape the tradition, but equally *were
shaped by the tradition he valued.* To exclude all material showing redactional
tendencies, as Lambrecht and others do, will invariably exclude authentic material. When one takes seriously what everyone admits — that most of the stories of Jesus were told on numerous occasions — any thought of moving back
to some pristine original must be given up.

Some scholars acknowledge that we cannot go back to an original form,
although often these same people still offer shortened reconstructions of Jesus'
parables. B. Scott and others argue for an originating structure, but the reconstructions here are not different and are no more convincing or helpful.[248]

Dale Allison comments in a denunciation of the standard attempts to reconstruct original sayings, "It should trouble us that none of our speculative

tradition-histories can ever be falsified."[249] The subjectivity that shapes Jesus to fit our criteria vitiates our so-called critical methods. If Jesus was as eschatologically focused as Allison argues, the presuppositions on which this parable has been reconstructed must be jettisoned. Others, notably — as different as they are — N. T. Wright and Luise Schottroff, also lack confidence in the old methods and are bypassing them.[250] What is required of all scholars is more caution and humility.[251]

Given the significant differences between the two accounts, three options are possible:

> We have two independent parables developing the same plot with the throne claimant being original to Luke's parable.
> We have two independent parables, but Luke (or his tradition) added the throne claimant elements.
> We have a common original which developed in two directions and which Luke (or his tradition) altered by merging the throne claimant elements.

None of these options can be excluded. At least three parables besides these two deal with the same themes of entrusted possessions, a master's absence, and a later reckoning: the Faithful or Unfaithful Servant (Matt 24:45-51), the Man Going on a Journey (Mark 13:34-36), and the Wicked Tenants (Matt 21:33-45/Mark 12:1-12/Luke 20:9-18). Other parables are closely related, and rabbinic parables use the same themes.[252] Given that such stories were told often and given the lack of common language between Matthew and Luke, I do not think the two accounts render the same parable or have any genetic relation. One of the first two options is more likely.

3. To whom is each parable addressed? This is a crucial question. The explanation from C. H. Dodd and J. Jeremias that Jesus originally told these parables against Jewish leaders or scribes has been influential,[253] but it has little in its favor. If the third servant mirrors the Jewish leaders who were entrusted with the Law, whom do the first two servants reflect? While the emphasis is placed on the third servant, the parables are about both faithfulness/reward and unfaithfulness/punishment. If Jewish leaders had been in view, this could have been a parable about only one servant or one group of unfaithful servants. Also, the Jewish leaders and scribes cannot be accused of "burying" their deposit or of being lazy. They were continually and assiduously engaged with teaching the Law and extending its influence, as Matt 23:15 attests. Nor is the parable addressed to Jews in general. It is much more likely that both versions were originally addressed to disciples of Jesus or at least to those who had responded positively to his preaching of the kingdom.[254] To hear the message of the kingdom is not only a privilege but also a responsibility, and people will be held accountable for what they do with the message.

4. *What is the failure of the third servant?* Attempts to suggest that Jesus' hearers would have identified with the third servant or seen him as taking a commendable safe course[255] will not work. Nor is it likely that Luke changed the intent of the parable by adding the command to do business to make the third servant more culpable. The rabbinic passages referred to in arguments that the third servant's action was commendable (*m. Baba Meṣiʿa* 3.10 and *b. Baba Meṣiʿa* 42a — see above, p. 522) discuss money *left for safekeeping.* In that case, burying the money is appropriate, but the money in the parable is not left for safekeeping. The assumption, which all would recognize, is that the servants are to use the money to create profit, or "to each according to his ability" in Matt 25:15 would make no sense. Other options with regard to the third servant will be treated below. Luke 19:13b only makes explicit what everyone would assume.

Unlike the procedure with other parables whereby the issues could be treated in sequence, the accounts of Matthew and Luke are so different that from this point it is necessary to treat them separately. The issues for each parable will be dealt with as appropriate.

Remaining Issues Specifically regarding Matthew. 2. Has the original intent of the parable been changed by allegorical additions? In Matthew at question are: "after a long time" in v. 19, "enter into the joy of your master" in vv. 21 and 23, and the casting into the outer darkness in v. 30. Such expressions break the boundaries of the story so that the intended reality shows through. This is not necessarily evidence of redactional interpretation. We have seen before that a strict separation of image and fact in parables is not always maintained by Jesus or the OT prophets. Parables most likely to stay completely within the story are those addressed to opponents from whom the truth is concealed until they are "deceived into the truth" but who are being urged to change. Parables most likely to allow the fact side to show through are those addressed to followers or those intended to be direct confrontations with opponents.[256] The words "after a long time" (v. 19, literally "after much time") are assumed by some to point to the delay of the parousia,[257] but some length of time was required for the servants to carry out their responsibilities, and this may be all that is meant. If Matthew added this statement, he did not gain much from it. A decision about such words as "enter into the joy of your master" will depend on other decisions about the parable and on broader views about Jesus and the tradition of the Gospels. They could be the result of the tradition or Matthew underlining what is at stake, but if Jesus addressed the parable to his disciples, the language could just as well stem from him, as suggested by his promise that the twelve will sit on twelve thrones judging Israel (19:28) or comments that brought forth the request of James and John to sit on his right and left (20:21). Once again we have a diaphanous parable.

Decisions about the end of the parable are more involved and are treated below.

The question whether Matthew changed *minas* to *talents* to exaggerate the amount of money is relatively unimportant, but whether changed by Matthew or original, how can the master say to the servant who received five talents (one hundred years' wages!) and the one who received two (forty years' wages) that they had been faithful over a *few* things (vv. 21 and 23)? Other texts have equally large sums,[258] and we should not just assume Matthew made the change. While not entirely satisfactory, it is more likely that money itself is viewed as insignificant in contrast to the larger eschatological gift being granted.

6. Do these parables point to the return of Jesus after an interval or to Jesus' announcement of the soon coming of God for judgment? Do the hearers/readers stand near the beginning of the narrative when the master is leaving or at the end when he returns? N. T. Wright argues that the parables in Matthew 25 are not about Jesus' return but the judgment coming soon on Jerusalem and her leaders. For him the hearers stand near the end of the account.[259] Matthew, I think it is safe to say, understood the parable to refer to the time between Jesus' departure and his return, but I will suggest that Luke's parable goes a different way. For Matthew we are left with the same options as with the two previous parables. It is possible that Jesus told a parable about the coming of the kingdom of God and that the church reapplied the parable to its situation after Jesus' death and resurrection. However, it is less clear just how *this* parable would fit with a focus on the present kingdom or on the judgment of Israel's leaders. If either were the purpose of the parable, why so much focus on the activities of the two faithful servants? The parable is a call to faithfulness and a warning against unfaithfulness. It anticipates passage of time when faithfulness is necessary. Also, at least in its present form the parable thinks of final judgment, not the destruction of Jerusalem. In Matthew's version there is nothing to suggest the destruction of Jerusalem.

8. What is the teaching of Matthew's parable? Three questions must be addressed in interpreting the parable of the Talents:

> Did Jesus tell this story to emphasize stewardship and without eschatological concerns?
> Was Jesus' original parable a warning about mistreatment of the poor?

What does the parable teach with regard to Jesus' expectation of the coming kingdom?

To support the emphasis on stewardship *rather* than eschatology David Flusser can argue legitimately that the departure of the master in rabbinic parables was a technical means to describe how human beings would behave if they believed that God was not present.[260] The parable is about stewardship, but is the issue stewardship in general or specifically stewardship *in relation to the kingdom?* If the parable is placed within the whole context of Jesus' teaching, which is quite different from that of rabbis,[261] it is difficult to deny the eschatological intent of the parable. Jesus' teaching consistently points to a crisis and judgment for his hearers. The stewardship themes are important, but they derive their significance within the context of Jesus' teaching about the kingdom and the future.

The argument that this parable is a warning about mistreating the poor is based on the approaches that argue the master and first two servants are negative figures and the third servant is a positive figure whose actions would have been viewed as commendable.[262] This approach avoids viewing the harshness and judgment of the master as speaking of God, but it is more a usurpation of the parable than an interpretation. If this is a warning about mistreating the poor, it is cryptic in the extreme. The servant's description of the master as harsh is not supported by the master's actions with the first two servants and is not affirmed in the narrative.[263] The third servant's own words are merely the basis on which he is judged. Hearers would hardly identify with the third servant and his fear,[264] which leads him to hide the money, and his actions are hardly defiance of an oppressive system.[265] As indicated above, burying the money (as in Matthew) is not a commendable action which Luke's account renders more culpable by having the servant hide the money in a napkin. The money was not left for safekeeping but for investment, even without the direct command to do business in Luke 19:13b, as the actions of the first two servants show. The presumption of the parable is that failure to invest the money was a dereliction of duty. Further, the rule of end stress places the emphasis on the master's verdict, not on the actions of the third servant.[266] The third servant is a thoroughly negative example, and this parable has nothing to do with warning against mistreating the poor.

The accusation of harshness in effect places the master on trial, but the charge is given no focus. It is not answered explicitly, but the master's treatment of the first two servants suggests that the charge is unfounded.[267]

Matthew's intent with the parable is clear. He understood the parable as an exhortation for followers of Jesus to be faithful in their obedience until his return. Little evidence exists that *this* parable addresses the issue of the delay of the parousia, but it should be considered as evidence for an expected interval when Jesus would no longer be with his disciples. Unless the minimal sketch of Jesus' future expectation given above is wrong,[268] then the master mirrors Jesus himself rather than God. Certainly this is Matthew's intent. If Jesus anticipated an interval of unknown duration, then a parable to his disciples about faithfulness to the kingdom during that interval is perfectly logical. We should expect Jesus to prepare his disciples for the absence caused by his death. The concern is not to set an agenda for the future. In fact, Jesus consistently avoids such apocalyptic speculation.[269] The parable more assumes eschatology than teaches it. It certainly should not be allegorized so that the departure is the ascension and every detail is accounted for, but the parable anticipates Jesus' absence and return and both reward (probably the messianic banquet) and punishment, like most other texts speaking of judgment.[270] We do not need to allegorize the talents or other aspects of the parable to know how the analogy works. The talents do not stand for anything other than the great value of the kingdom and the significant responsibility it brings.[271] As a master rewards or punishes his servants for their productivity during his absence, so Jesus will hold his followers accountable for their productivity in the kingdom during his absence.

9. Does the harsh language in Matt 25:29-30 belong to the original version? How should this harshness be handled? V. 28 is not a satisfactory conclusion to the parable, for hearers expect something more negative for the third servant than the loss of something he did not want anyway.[272] The proverb in v. 29 is paralleled in Luke's parable (19:26) but also appears in Matt 13:12 and Mark 4:25/Luke 8:18, all three in close proximity to the parable of the Sower. In these three occurrences the proverb is applied to how one responds to the message of the kingdom, which is not far from its use in the parables under consideration. To the one who responds more is given; to the one who does not respond even what he or she has is lost. Whether the first use of the proverb was in connection with the proclamation of the kingdom or the parables here cannot be determined,[273] but it is more likely that the proverb originated elsewhere, was used often, and has been joined to this parable either by Jesus or in the tradition. It seems as well that some form of the punishment saying was always present at the end of the story. Otherwise the failure of the third servant has no negative result.

Dealing with the harshness of the language is more of an issue with Luke's text than Matthew's, but some comment is necessary here.[274] Judgment is not an attractive topic for most of us, and often scholars not only avoid ideas of judgment but also deemphasize moral responsibility, as if moral lessons were somehow inferior. In doing so life is cheapened, for one's actions mean nothing. Several interpreters even argue that this parable is about grace,[275] partly because the money was made available by the master. H. Weder goes so far as to deny that Jesus says anything of judgment with this parable, and A. Puig i Tarrech asserts that Jesus does not threaten hearers.[276] Such efforts appear to be attempts to bring Jesus' teaching into line with ideas of justification by grace and to avoid moralism. Jesus' parables — and certainly this one — do emphasize moral responsibility and carry an unavoidable threat of judgment. Prophets use strong language, and this language functions to shock, arrest, and force consideration. If the kingdom is about anything, it is about accountability to the will of the Father.

Casting into outer darkness is mentioned elsewhere only in Matt 8:12 and 22:13 and means separation from everything good, specifically God. All three occurrences are followed by "There will be the weeping and gnashing of teeth," on which see above, pp. 497 and 503. The use of "cast into a furnace of fire" in 13:42 and 50 verifies that Matthew thought of Gehenna. This fits with Jesus' warning about punishment in Gehenna in other texts.[277] We cannot avoid the focus on judgment in Jesus' teaching, but our concern must be with the *function* of the language to arrest, warn, and force consideration, not to give a description of the judgment.

10. Is this parable anti-Semitic? This parable does not attack the Jewish people, and obviously if Matthew's parable is addressed to disciples, the parable is not anti-Semitic. It is concerned that disciples may fail to be disciples.

Remaining Issues Specifically Regarding Luke. Some of the decisions made in analyzing Matthew's version will apply here as well. *2. Has the original intent of the parable been changed by allegorical additions?* In Luke at question are the direct order to "do business" in v. 13 (which was dealt with above, p. 532), the throne claimant elements (vv. 12a, 14, and 27), and the authority over cities in vv. 17 and 19.

Both versions of this parable have anomalies, but Luke's version of the parable is much more difficult. The throne claimant elements shift the focus of the parable and weave a second plot that causes some loss. No mention is made of the punishment of Luke's third servant, a feature lost in the announcement of punishment on the rebellious citizens. Ten servants are given a mina but only three are met in the reckoning, which leaves some sense of incompleteness. In Matthew servants entrusted with huge sums were told they have been faithful over a *few* things. A similar anomaly occurs here. Why question giving a mina (about three months' wages for a day laborer) to a man who has not just ten minas, but ten cities? The reward of cities stems directly from the throne claimant imagery. Other "double plot" parables exist — the Prodigal Son, the Rich Man and Lazarus, and Matthew's version of the Wedding Banquet, but the plots are usually kept separate.[278] Also, with regard to incompleteness, the parable of the Workers in the Vineyard has five groups hired but only treats the first and last in the reckoning.[279]

Most scholars accept that the throne claimant elements were added later, although some argue that Luke's account preserves an original parable essentially as told by Jesus.[280] Certainty cannot be obtained, and not a great deal is at stake. More important is understanding what Luke meant to convey by telling the story as he has and what Jesus might have meant with these two plots. While Jesus could have told a story this complicated, the anomalies favor the view that Luke or his tradition joined two parables dealing with a master who departs and returns to settle accounts.[281]

5. Does Luke's account allude to the events surrounding Archelaus after the death of Herod the Great? No one served as a vassal king without Rome's permission, and people petitioned the emperor for the right to rule. Herod the Great did so, and both his sons Antipas and Archelaus, among others, also went to Rome to seek the right to be king. What Josephus records concerning Archelaus's attempt sounds surprisingly like the events of the parable. After Herod died, Archelaus went to Rome to obtain the right to be king. A Jewish embassy followed to lobby Caesar to reject Archelaus's request, and although no explicit report of Archelaus's vengeance exists, Josephus refers to "old feuds" and Archelaus's brutality.[282] Archelaus's palace was in Jericho,[283] the city that Jesus had just left in Luke's narrative. Although some find it difficult to think Jesus would allude to Archelaus in a positive way,[284] the parallels are so striking that it is difficult to think otherwise or to think hearers would not have thought of Archelaus. In effect the parable charges that some Jews were resisting the reign of the Messiah as if he were Archelaus. This is a good example of a parable being used as a weapon and gives Luke's parable a different emphasis from Matthew's, even though the second plot concerning faithfulness is still present.

6. Do these parables point to the return of Jesus after an interval or Jesus' announcement of the soon coming of God? That is, is the master a "God" figure, a "Christ" figure, or neither? Do the hearers/readers stand near the beginning of the narrative when the master is leaving or at the end when he returns? 7. What is the meaning of Luke 19:11? Did Jesus tell this parable to prevent eschatological excitement among his followers or to announce the imminence of the kingdom? If the former, which is the traditional understanding, the parable points to an interval when Jesus would not be with his followers and to a later time when he would return. If the latter, he was enacting the promised return of Yahweh to Zion. The intent of 19:11 has become a deciding factor for interpretation. Because of the number of Lukanisms, this narrative seam is almost certainly from Luke. But why did Luke make this comment when his post-resurrection readers already knew that the kingdom did not appear when Jesus entered Jerusalem? Was he attempting to correct some early Christian misunderstanding about eschatology, perhaps that the resurrection (or the ascension) was the parousia?[285] That is possible, but it would be hard to discern this from this specific text.

Recently, partly because of the influence of Luke Johnson, some have argued that the traditional understanding of this text is wrong. Instead of refuting expectations that the kingdom would come as Jesus entered Jerusalem, Johnson argues Jesus told the parable to *confirm* such expectations. The parable is not about the second coming, then, but about the imminent coming of the kingdom as Jesus enters Jerusalem and is acclaimed as king.[286] To support this view Johnson argued regarding 19:11 that, although *anaphainō* usually means "appear," here it means "go to be declared" and is not technical language for the parousia.[287] Instead of dampening expectations, Jesus is understood as confirming an immediate manifestation of God's kingdom. Johnson's argument concerning *anaphainō* is not borne out by the evidence, and other problems exist with his theory, not the least of which are that the kingdom is not fully realized and the slaughter of the rebellious must be interpreted symbolically as the rejection of the Jewish leaders.[288]

Similarly N. T. Wright argues that the third servant represents Israel and its leaders and that the parable expands Mal 3:1-3 to depict the soon coming of Yahweh in judgment on Israel.[289] Aspects of this approach are attractive, but it has serious difficulties. If Yahweh is represented by a nobleman going to a far country to receive a kingdom, from whom would he receive it? Further, the judgment focus does not work. Can we interpret the parable as a warning of imminent judgment if judgment does not occur for forty more years? Even more, I have difficulty thinking that the imminent appearance of the kingdom is to be found in the Roman destruction of Jerusalem.[290] Yet, Johnson and Wright raise issues that force a better understanding of this parable. Why, if Luke 19:11 explains the concern to dampen enthusiasm, does the rest of the entrance narrative heighten it? What is the relation of the (present) kingdom of Jesus and the kingdom of God? How can it be that the kingdom has both come (11:20) and is still to come (11:2)?

There is every reason to believe that Luke has correctly reported the excited mood of the disciples as they approached Jerusalem.[291] Passages like Matt 20:20-21/Mark 10:35-37 and Luke 9:54 presuppose such excitement. But Luke's concern is not merely historical, and his text takes a surprising twist. The ultimate kingdom of God, as Luke and his readers know, is still future (Luke 22:16, 18, 28-30). At least three other times in Luke-Acts someone asks Jesus when the kingdom will come (17:20; 21:7; Acts 1:6), and in each case Jesus discourages any thought of a soon appearing of the kingdom. The intent of 19:11 is to *refute* ideas that the kingdom would appear when Jesus got to Jerusalem. At the same time, the relation of the parable to its context is striking, for while the parable fends off any idea the kingdom is to appear immediately, the narrative shows that Jesus appears as king (19:38, in which the word *basileus* — "king" — has been redactionally added to the psalm quotation) and is crucified as King (23:2-3, 37-38). Further, the parable must not be read in isolation from the material that follows. While the parable does not equate the coming of the kingdom and the destruction of Jerusalem, the parable and the following narrative do see the rebellion of the citizens against the king and their slaughter mirrored in Jesus' weeping over Jerusalem because Jerusalem does not know the things that lead to peace or the time of her visitation from God and because she will be destroyed (19:41-44). The parable and its context deal with both the presence and the futurity of the kingdom.[292] One could say that the kingdom will not come immediately, but the king has.[293] That may underplay the presence of the kingdom too severely, but the parable holds off expectation, affirms the king's role, calls for faithfulness, and warns against both unfaithfulness and the refusal to acknowledge the king. There is still an interval before the kingdom arrives fully.

For Luke, too, the nobleman corresponds to Jesus, not the coming of God, but again, the coming of Jesus and the coming of God should not be set against each other.[294] Decision about the point of time at which the hearers stand is more difficult. Neither departure nor return seems right. In Luke's estimation Jesus does not need to depart to acquire the kingdom, for it has already been granted to him, as the entrance narrative and 22:29-30 show. This last text asserts that Jesus has already been given — aorist *dietheto* — the kingdom by the Father and gives the disciples the kingdom that they may sit on twelve thrones judging the tribes of Israel, language for the reconstitution of Israel. The parable assumes that the kingship has been granted but the reckoning has not yet taken place. It gives no further information about the time of the reckoning, and therefore should not be thought of as a parable of the parousia, even if it could be applied in that way. Whatever else it does, the parable assumes a time when people will need to be faithful before the kingdom arrives. That fits not only with the parables in this chapter but also with the focus on faithfulness in Luke 16:10-12 and with the question whether the Son of Man will find faith/faithfulness on the earth in Luke 18:8. Whether we think Luke has joined two parables or that Jesus told such a complex parable originally, the ideas and themes are fully consonant with Jesus' teaching elsewhere.

8. What is the teaching of each parable? See above, pp. 533-35 concerning the teaching of Matthew's parable, for many of the same points apply to Luke's. Here as well the eschatological focus should be kept in view. The issue is faithfulness in view of the present and future kingdom.

Many interpreters attempt to read the parable as if it were an allegory in which every event corresponded to some reality in the history of Jesus and the church. At first glance this seems to fit: Jesus is the nobleman, the far country is heaven, the journey is the ascension, the return and reckoning are the parousia and the final judgment, the servants are faithful and unfaithful disciples, the rebellious citizens are Jews, and their slaughter is the destruction of Jerusalem. But parables are analogies, and such allegorizing does not work. No one hearing Jesus would have or could have interpreted the story this way. We have seen already that Jesus does not need to depart to get the kingdom. He appears in Jerusalem as king. The ascension and parousia are not in view. In the parable the slaughter of the rebellious follows the return and reckoning, but Luke and his readers know the parousia and final judgment did not precede the destruction of Jerusalem.

Rather than allegorizing this parable, we need once again to understand how the analogy works. Given the assumption of an interval necessitated by the coming death of Jesus, the analogy works easily. In its present double plot form the analogy states: Like some Jews who resisted the reign of Archelaus, so some now resist the reign of the Messiah, but they will encounter judgment;[295] further, the adherents of the Messiah will also be judged regarding their faithfulness. Both themes fit well in the last days of Jesus' ministry. The parable serves as a warning to Jesus' Jewish contemporaries — both those who followed him and those who did not.

9. *Does the harsh language in Luke 19:26-27 belong to the original parable? How should this harshness be handled?* The language of 19:27 is startlingly harsh, something we do not often associate with Jesus' teaching. For this reason people often assign this verse to Luke or the tradition. This escapist route solves the problem only briefly and shifts the blame to the Evangelist or the tradition, whose thinking is always inferior to our own. Reconsideration of this language is merited.

Jesus does not need to be protected from harshness, but several points are worth remembering. The uncomfortable language occurs *at the parabolic level* and is a warning of judgment, not a realistic portrayal of the judgment. It is the words of the parable king and not the direct teaching of Jesus. Again the principle is important that teaching not validated by, and conformable with, non-parabolic material cannot be taken as describing Jesus' "theology." This does not mean the language is irrelevant. It *is* part of Jesus' teaching and has a purpose. Parables are prophetic instruments, and this is prophetic language used for shock and to force thought and is not to be brought straight across unchanged to reality. The violence of the story, of course, fits the ancient world — *and the modern,* but prophets often used such harsh language to describe the judgment of God, sometimes reporting the harsh language as the very words of God. People forget the harshness and shock of prophetic language, but page after page in the prophetic writings details the judgment God brings on Israel and the surrounding nations. Sometimes the punishment comes at the hands of invading armies, but sometimes it is by the hand of God. For example:

> See, the day of the Lord comes, cruel, with wrath and fierce anger. . . . I will punish the world for its evil. . . . Whoever is found will be thrust through, and whoever is caught will fall by the sword. Their infants will be dashed to pieces before their eyes (Isa 13:9, 11, 15-16).

> The Lord is about to hurl you away violently, my fellow. He will seize firm hold on you, whirl you round and round, and throw you like a ball into a wide land (Isa 22:17-18a).

> For the Lord is enraged against all the nations, . . . he has doomed them, has given them over to slaughter (Isa 34:2).

> Therefore, the days are surely coming, says the Lord, when it will no more be called Topheth, . . . but the valley of slaughter (Jer 7:32).

> I, I myself will bring a sword upon you. . . . I will lay the corpses of the people of Israel in front of their idols (Ezek 6:3b, 5a).

Dozens of such texts could be cited. We would like only to hear of the God who saves, but the prophets and Jesus both underscore that God's coming always involves both salvation and judgment. Jesus' harsh language is intended to shock so that people take the warning seriously.

Another fact must be mentioned. As Luke and his readers knew, rather than doing the slaughtering, Jesus is the one slaughtered. He is caught up in the judgment he announces, but there is still a day of reckoning.

10. Is either parable anti-Semitic? Luke is no more anti-Semitic than Matthew or the prophets who, like Jesus, announced judgment through tears.[296] With its two-pronged plot the parable is directed at both disciples and the Jewish nation, particularly the leadership. The parable seeks to solicit, not renounce, Jesus' contemporaries and Luke's readers, regardless of the ethnic identity of those readers.

Adapting the Parable

With 2000 years of church history behind us, the eschatological teaching of the NT causes difficulty for those attempting to adapt the text to modern life. Christians today seem no more ready to deal with the eschatology of Jesus than were Jülicher and Harnack. Consequently, sermons on these parables often deal only with themes pertaining to stewardship. Some focus on the "law of increase," a form of positive thinking — thoughts and attitudes based on abundance and success attract and produce more abundance and success.[297] Failure to use a gift/talent results in its loss. Such statements may be true, but this parable is not about positive thinking and use of abilities. The "law of increase" with which the proverb (Matt 25:29 and Luke 19:26) is concerned is the use that one makes of the message of the kingdom.

The theme of faithfulness must be brought directly into relation with Jesus' teaching about the present and future kingdom. Knowledge of God's reign and salvation brings with it added responsibility. To accept the kingdom and its salvation is to accept a trust.[298] It enlists one as an agent on behalf of the kingdom, and all those so enlisted will be rewarded or judged in terms of their faithfulness to their task. Once again the theme of responsibility for action is emphasized. It is important to note in Matthew that the same words are said to the second servant as were said to the first. Even though the first servant had greater ability, his reward was not greater. The servants were judged on the basis of their faithfulness.

The fact of the delay of the parousia does not negate eschatological faith; instead it raises the question of faithfulness.[299] We still live in the "now and not yet" of all NT eschatology (e.g., 1 John 3:2). We know that God has acted decisively in Jesus' life, death, and resurrection, and we still believe that one day God will attain ultimate victory. One day evil will be set aside. The issue is how we live in the in-between time.

Sometimes eschatological expectations get overheated so that people are sure the end of time is about to occur, but parables about the future are not intended to set a sequence of events. Rather, "One speaks of the future judgment for the sake of the present."[300] The concern is for right living. We need to keep reminding ourselves that no one knows the time of the end. The time of the church could still be quite long. Luke 19:11 concerns people accompanying Jesus, but it provides ground for a caution to us as well. Similarly, the shock language of the parable should not be overplayed but taken for what it is — an extreme statement to force thought.

The second plot of the parable in Luke's version is also still pertinent. Just as really as first-century Jewish leaders, we too can in our own way resist the Messiah as if he were Archelaus. The human ego can find limitless reasons why no one should reign over us (Luke 19:14). The parable is not telling us how to obtain salvation, but it is calling us to commitment to the one who truly is king and to faithfulness to his purposes.

For Further Reading

George Beasley-Murray, *Jesus and the Kingdom of God* (Grand Rapids: Eerdmans, 1986), pp. 215-18.

W. D. Davies and Dale C. Allison, *A Critical and Exegetical Commentary on the Gospel According to Saint Matthew* (3 vols.; ICC; Edinburgh: T. & T. Clark, 1988-1997), 3:374-77 and 401-12.

Werner Foerster, "Das Gleichnis von den anvertrauten Pfunden," in *Verbum Dei Manet in Aeternum. Eine Festschrift für D. Otto Schmitz,* ed. Werner Foerster (Witten: Luther, 1953), pp. 37-56.

V. Fusco, "'Point of View' and 'Implicit Reader' in Two Eschatological Texts (Lk 19,11-28; Acts 1,6-8)," in *The Four Gospels 1992: Festschrift Frans Neirynck,* ed. F. Van Segbroeck, et al. (Leuven: Leuven University Press, 1992), pp. 1677-96.

Luke Timothy Johnson, "The Lukan Kingship Parable (Lk. 19:11-27), *NovT* 24 (1982): 139-59.

John Nolland, *Luke 18:35–24:53* (WBC 35C; Dallas: Word, 1993), pp. 908-19.

Richard L. Rohrbaugh, "A Peasant Reading of the Parable of the Talents/Pounds: A Text of Terror?" *BTB* 23 (1993): 32-39.

N. T. Wright, *Jesus and the Victory of God,* vol. 2 of *Christian Origins and the Question of God* (Minneapolis: Fortress, 1996), pp. 631-39.

M. Zerwick, "Die Parabel vom Thronanwärter," *Biblica* 40 (1959): 654-74.

THE SHEEP AND THE GOATS
(Matt 25:31-46)

Parable Type

This is not really a parable. At most we have a parabolic saying about the separation of sheep and goats in vv. 32-33 which provides an analogy, an implied similitude, to the separation which will take place at the final judgment. This is followed by a detailed explanation of the reason for and the significance of this separation in vv. 34-46. One could say that we have a two-verse analogy and that the rest is explanation.

Issues Requiring Attention

1. Is this account from Jesus, or does it derive from Matthew or some other early Christian?
2. To whom is this material addressed?
3. Does "all the nations" refer to all people universally, all people except Christians, or all people except Jews? Who is gathered for judgment?
4. Does "these least brothers of mine" refer to all the poor and needy, Jews, Christian missionaries, or all Christians? Are these least ones included in the judgment, or are they exempt?
5. How does the picture of judgment on the basis of acts of love expressed in this passage fit with salvation based on faith and confession of Jesus? What is the relation between the salvation granted in v. 34 and the acts listed in vv. 35-36? Does this passage teach "works righteousness," that is, that one can earn salvation by doing good deeds?
6. What does this passage teach, especially with regard to eternal judgment?

Helpful Primary Source Material

Canonical Material

- OT: Job 31:16-23, 31; Ps 41:1; Prov 14:31; 19:17; Isa 58:7; 66:18; Ezek 18:7, 16; 34:15-24; Dan 7:13-14, 22; 12:2; Joel 3:1-21; Zeph 3:8
- NT: Matt 7:21-23; 10:32-33/Luke 12:8-9; Matt 10:40-42/Mark 9:41/Luke 10:16/John 13:20; Matt 13:36-43, 47-50; 16:27 (cf. Mark 8:38/Luke 9:26); Matt 24:30-31/Mark 13:26-27/Luke 21:27-28; Matt 18:5/Mark 9:37/Luke 9:48; Matt 19:28; 28:19; Luke 21:36; John 5:27-29; 13:20; Heb 13:2-3; Jas 1:27

Ancient Near Eastern Texts

- *Egyptian Book of the Dead* 125: A deceased person is to confess in the hall of Osiris a long list of sins he or she has not done and a shorter list of good deeds he or she has performed: giving bread to the hungry, water to the thirsty, clothes to the naked, and a ferry to those without ships.[301]

Early Jewish Writings

- Sir 7:32-36: "Stretch out your hand to the poor, so that your blessing may be complete. Give graciously to all the living; do not withhold kindness even from the dead. Do not avoid those who weep, but mourn with those who mourn. Do not hesitate to visit the sick, because for such deeds you will be loved. In all you do, remember the end of your life, and then you will never sin."

- Tob 1:16-17: Tobit lists acts of charity he has done: giving food to the hungry and clothing to the naked and burying abandoned corpses.
- Tob 4:7: "Give alms from your possessions, and do not let your eye begrudge the gift when you make it. Do not turn your face away from anyone who is poor, and the face of God will not be turned away from you."
- Tob 4:16: Part of the ethical advice Tobit gives to his son is that he should give some of his food to the hungry and some of his clothing to the naked.
- *1 En.* 90:17-42 is significant both because it is pre-Christian and because it forms the conclusion to a history under the guise of a vision of animals and their treatment of Israel, the latter being designated "the sheep." In this section the Lord of the sheep strikes the earth to punish the other animals and birds and then has the books opened for judgment of guilty shepherds and sheep who are thrown into an abyss full of fire and flame. A new house is built and the sheep and other animals left are gathered. Chs. 94–108 tell of woes that await sinners, angels gathering people for a fiery judgment, and blessings for the righteous.

The date of the central section of *1 Enoch,* the so-called *Similitudes of Enoch* (chs. 37–71), is debated, especially since none of these chapters has been found at Qumran and all the other chapters have. Some would suggest that they stem from the first century, but some would argue for a date in the third century A.D. Several chapters describe the Elect One or the Son of Man sitting on a throne of glory judging the just and the unjust. Although these chapters cannot be used to determine the origin of these ideas, the assumptions concerning judgment by the Son of Man are similar to Matthew's and deserve attention.

- *1 En.* 45:3-6: "On that day, my Elect One shall sit on the seat of glory and make a selection of their deeds. . . . But sinners have come before me so that by judgment I shall destroy them from before the face of the earth." In ch. 46 this Elect One is referred to as the Son of Man.
- *1 En.* 61:8: "He placed the Elect One on the throne of glory; and he shall judge all the works of the holy ones in heaven above, weighing in the balance their deeds."
- *1 En.* 62:2, 6, 11: The Lord of the Spirits has sat down on the throne of his glory, and the spirit of righteousness has been poured out upon him. The word of his mouth will do the sinners in; and all the oppressors shall be

eliminated from before his face . . . and pain shall seize them when they see that Son of Man sitting on the throne of his glory. . . . So he will deliver them to the angels for punishments in order that vengeance shall be executed. . . ."

- *1 En.* 69:29: "Thenceforth nothing that is corruptible shall be found; for that Son of Man has appeared and has seated himself upon the throne of his glory; and all evil shall disappear from before his face. . . ."
- *2 En.* 9:1: Paradise is the place prepared for the righteous, those ". . . who carry out righteous judgment, to give bread to the hungry, and to cover the naked with clothing, and to lift up the fallen, and who help the injured and orphans. . . ." In 10:2-6 Enoch is shown a place of torment, black fire, and ice for those who abuse the hungry and naked, and in 42:8 and 63:1 happiness and reward are awarded to those who clothe the naked and feed the hungry.
- *2 En.* 44:2: "He who treats with contempt the face of any person treats the face of the Lord with contempt."
- *2 Bar.* 72:2: ". . . when . . . the time of my Anointed One comes, he will call all nations, and some of them he will spare, and others he will kill." Cf. *4 Ezra* 7:37-38.
- *T. Zeb.* 5:3: "Have mercy in your inner being, my children, because whatever anyone does to his neighbor, the Lord will do to him."
- *T. Zeb.* 6:6: ". . . for whoever shares with his neighbor receives multifold from the Lord."
- *T. Zeb.* 7:1–8:6 relates an incident of providing clothing to a man in distress and urges compassion with mercy to every person "in order that the Lord may be compassionate and merciful to you."
- *T. Jos.* 1:5-7: Joseph was hungry, weak, in prison, etc., and God ministered to him in each regard.
- *T. Benj.* 10:6: When God's salvation is revealed to all the Gentiles, you will then see Enoch, Noah, Shem, Abraham, Isaac, and Jacob raised up at the right hand in great joy. Christian influence in this section is possible.
- *T. Ab.* 12:1–14:15 describes a wondrous man, Abel, sitting on a terrifying throne with an angel on his right recording righteous deeds and another on his left recording sins. This judgment is followed by judgment by the twelve tribes of Israel and final judgment by God.

Greco-Roman Writings

- Homer, *Odyssey* 11.568-71 describes Minos, the son of Zeus, judging the dead from his seat.

- Virgil, *Aeneid* 6.540-43: "Here is the place, where the road parts in twain: there to the right . . . is our way to Elysium, but the left wreaks the punishment of the wicked; and sends them on to pitiless Tartarus." 6:548-751 describes both the torture of Tartarus and the bliss of Elysium.
- Plutarch, *Mor.* 167A points to popular belief in punishment by fire and torture.
- Plato, *Phaedo* 113D-114A describes people being judged according to their merits, with the truly wicked being sent to Tarturus, from which they will not emerge.
- Plato, *Republic* 10:614C-615D tells of a journey to the world of the dead where there are two openings in the earth and two in heaven, with judges sitting between them. The righteous go to the right and up to heaven, and the unjust to the left and down.
- Lucian, *Menippus* 10-15 describes the place of the dead with its river of fire, its tormentors, and its punishments for wrongdoers. See also his *On Funerals* 7-9, which similarly describes judgment of the good and the wicked.

Early Christian Writings

- *4 Ezra* 2:20-21: "Guard the rights of the widow, secure justice for the fatherless, give to the needy, defend the orphan, clothe the naked, care for the injured and the weak, do not ridicule a lame man, protect the maimed, and let the blind man have a vision of my glory." This and the following section are part of a later addition and are dependent on Matthew.
- *4 Ezra* 2:34-41: "Therefore I say to you, O nations that hear and understand, 'Wait for your shepherd; he will give you everlasting rest, because he who will come at the end of the age is close at hand. Be ready for the rewards of the kingdom. . . .'" The rest of the passage is primarily about the joy awaiting those who fulfill the law.
- *Sentences of Sextus* 378: "If when you can you do not give to the needy, you will not receive from God when you are in need."
- *Vision of Ezra* 27–32 describes angels submerging sinners in a fiery stream, partly because they did not receive strangers and did not give alms.
- *2 Clem.* 17:4 comments on Isa 66:24 to describe the last judgment according to works and the torture in unquenchable fire awaiting the unrighteous.
- *Testament of Isaac* 6:21: Those who have shown mercy by giving a cup of cold water are granted a lifetime in the kingdom. This document may be a Jewish writing redacted by Christians.

- *Testament of Jacob* 2:23: "Blessed be the one who will perform acts of mercy in honor of your several names, and will give someone a cup of water to drink, . . . or will take in strangers, or visit the sick and console their children, or will clothe a naked one. . . ."
- *Testament of Jacob* 7:23-25: ". . . do for the poor what will increase compassion for them here and now, so that God will give you the bread of life forever in the kingdom of God. For to the one who has given a poor person bread in this world God will give a portion from the tree of life. Clothe the poor person who is naked on the earth, so that God may clothe you with the apparel of glory in the kingdom of heaven. . . ."

Later Jewish Writings

- *'Abot de Rabbi Nathan* 7 tells of the poor talking of what they ate and drank at Job's house and of his clothing the naked, all drawn from Job 31:16-23.
- *Mekilta Pisḥa* 14.99-100 (on Exod 12:41): "Likewise you find that whithersoever Israel was exiled, the Shekinah, as it were, went into exile with them."
- *Mekilta Amalek* 3.245-246 (on Exod 18:12): ". . . when one welcomes his fellow man, it is considered as if he had welcomed the Divine Presence."
- *Sib. Or.* 2.78-94 lists clothing the naked, feeding the hungry, and receiving the homeless among acts of charity assessed at judgment. 2.80: "Whoever gives alms knows that he is lending to God." Cf. the similar text in *Pseudo-Phocylides* 22-29.
- *b. Soṭa* 14a (on the meaning of "You shall walk after the Lord your God," Deut 13:5): "But [the meaning is] to walk after the attributes of the Holy One, blessed be He. As He clothes the naked, for it is written, *And the Lord God made for Adam and for his wife coats of skin, and clothed them,* so do thou also clothe the naked. The Holy One, blessed be He, visited the sick, for it is written, *And the Lord appeared unto him by the oaks of Mamre,* so do thou also visit the sick. The Holy One, blessed be He, comforted mourners, for it is written, *And it came to pass after the death of Abraham, that God blessed Isaac his son,* so do thou also comfort mourners. The Holy one, blessed be He, buried the dead, for it is written, *And He buried him in the valley,* so do thou also bury the dead." See the similar text in *Targum Pseudo-Jonathan* on Deut 34:6.
- *b. Šabbat* 127a: "Hospitality to wayfarers is as 'great' as early attendance at the Beth Hamidrash. . . . Hospitality to wayfarers is greater than welcoming the presence of the Shechinah. . . . There are six things, the fruit of

which man eats in this world, while the principal remains for him for the world to come, viz.: Hospitality to wayfarers, visiting the sick, meditation in prayer, early attendance at the Beth Hamidrash, rearing one's sons to the study of the Torah, and judging one's neighbour in the scale of merit."

- *b. Nedarim* 40a: "He who does not visit the sick is like a shedder of blood. . . . He who visits the sick will be delivered from the punishments of Gehenna, for it is written, Blessed is he that considereth the poor: the Lord will deliver him in the day of evil."
- *Ruth Rab.* 5.9: "The poor man stands at your door, and the Holy One, blessed be He, stands at his right hand. If you give unto him, He who stands at his right hand will bless you, but if not, He will exact punishment from you, as it is said, Because He standeth at the right hand of the needy [Ps 109:31]." Virtually the same text appears in *Lev. Rab.* 34:9.
- *Derek Ereṣ Rab.* 2.21: "Concerning them who are merciful, who feed the hungry, give drink to the thirsty, clothe the naked and distribute alms Scripture declares, 'Say ye of the righteous that it shall be well with him' [Isa 3:10]."
- *Midr. Tannaim* on Deut 15:9: "And so the Holy One, blessed be He, said to Israel, 'My children, whenever you gave food to the poor I counted it as though you had given it to me.'" Cf. Prov. 19:17.
- *Midr. Pss.* 90.12 (on Ps 90:3): The Garden of Eden and Gehenna are two of the seven things preceding the creation of the world by 2000 years. "The Garden of Eden was at the right of the Holy One, blessed be He, and Gehenna was at His left."
- *Midr. Pss.* 118.17 (on Ps 118:19): In the world to come people will be asked what they have done. To those who answer that they fed the hungry, gave drink to the thirsty, clothed the naked, brought up the fatherless, gave alms, or performed deeds of kindness will be said, "This is the gate of the Lord. Enter into it." Compare *Egyptian Book of the Dead* 125 above.
- Accounts of judgment and of judgment based on good deeds appear in a variety of texts, of course including many biblical texts. Cf. *Midr. Pss.* 1.22; 31.5-6; *Pesiqta Rabbati* 35.

Textual Features Worthy of Attention

Matt 16:27 and 19:28, like 25:31-46, link the throne of the Son of Man and judgment. All three texts are drawn from Dan 7:13-14 (and are paralleled by passages in *1 Enoch*). Cf. John 5:27-29 and Matt 26:64/Mark 14:62/Luke 22:69.

All five of Matthew's major discourses end with a focus on judgment, which is only one feature of Matthew's focus on judgment throughout his Gospel. Judgment is announced already in 3:7-12. The judgment saying in this fifth discourse occupies a crucial role for Matthew, and the judgment of "all the nations" *(panta ta ethnē)* anticipates the use of the same phrase in the Great Commission (28:19-20). This passage may justly be viewed as the climax of Jesus' teaching in the Gospel.

In the infancy narrative (2:6), Jesus is already announced to be the shepherd of Israel on the basis of the prophecy from Mic 5:2. Matthew emphasizes the love command (5:43-48; 19:19; 22:34-40; cf. 7:12) and mercy (5:7; 6:2-4; 9:13; 12:7; 18:33; 23:23). Concern for the afflicted is expressed in the Beatitudes and in Jesus' direction to the rich young man to sell his possessions and give the proceeds to the poor (Matt 19:21/Mark 10:21/Luke 18:22).

The fourfold repetition of the acts of mercy gives them an unavoidable prominence. There is a gradual shortening of the description.

The two *amēn* sayings ("Truly I say to you") in vv. 40 and 45 agree except that the latter omits "brothers" and inserts "not" twice, as required by the logic.

Neither Mark nor Luke has a parallel to Matt 26:1-2, which records Jesus' announcement of the crucifixion of the Son of Man. The juxtaposition of these verses with 25:31-46 is striking. The Son of Man who will come in glory and judge the nations will himself be crucified. His judgment, based on the treatment of the oppressed, stems from his own solidarity with the oppressed.[302]

Cultural Information

"Sheep" is a frequent designation for Israel as the people of God in the OT and Jewish writings (e.g., Ezekiel 34; *1 En.* 89-90), but "goats" is not.

Some suggest that sheep and goats were separated each night because goats were more vulnerable to the cold and would need more protection.[303] This explanation has been repeated often because of Jeremias's influence, but is without basis. Klaus Wengst shows that this theory is based on a misunderstanding of a comment from G. Dalman and is not supportable from early Palestine. He suggests that the division took place to separate young males for slaughter.[304] Others suggest that it is the separation of the ewes for milking. It is not even certain that "goats" are in view, for the word so translated, *eriphos*, refers to a young male kid.[305] In the end, no reason is given for the separation, and the text does not say that such a separation takes place each night. The reason for the separation does not impact interpretation.

Goats, if that is the right translation, do not carry a negative connotation in ancient Palestine; both sheep and goats were valued and were pastured together. The analogy is built on the separation of right and left, not on the character or valuation of goats, even if sheep would have been valued more highly.[306] Nothing cultural prepares the reader for the strong condemnation of the goats.

Right and left are traditionally, but not necessarily (cf. 20:21, 23), associated with positive and negative respectively. According to later rabbinic tradition both Gehenna and the Garden of Eden existed long before the world, the former on the left of God's throne and the latter on the right.[307]

Explanation of the Passage

Options for Interpretation

This story, which seems so straightforward, has always been problematic and in recent years has become the source of serious disagreement among interpreters.[308] Early on, Origen worried that people would conclude that salvation could be obtained by charitable acts, and he and others gave spiritual significance to these acts (e.g., receiving strangers signified taking Christ into our hearts).[309] The primary points of contention are the meaning of the expressions "these least brothers of mine" and "all the nations." Four primary options for interpretation exist:

1. The *universal/non-restrictive approach* interprets this passage as describing the final judgment of all persons including Jews, Christians, and non-Christians. The "least brothers" are all needy persons, and the criterion of judgment is love and compassion shown to the needy.[310]

2. The *ecclesiastical/restrictive approach*, which was the most prevalent interpretation throughout the church's history until the twentieth century, interprets the passage as referring to the judgment of Christians. Non-Christians and Jews are often not even considered, and the "least brothers" are needy Christians.[311]

3. The *exclusive/missionary or particularist approach*, which apparently is first attested in the eighteenth century,[312] interprets the passage as referring to the judgment of non-Christian nations for their reception of Jesus' least brothers, the disciples/missionaries who are propagating the faith. By their reception of the messengers these nations show their attitude toward the message, but the narrative is viewed as a word of comfort to an oppressed church as much as it is a statement about the judgment of non-Christians. This view assumes that Matthew implies two judgments, a judgment of Christians and a judgment of the nations.[313]

4. The *dispensational* approach, which emerged only in the twentieth century, interprets the passage as referring not to final judgment but to the judgment of nations or individuals for their treatment of Jews (Jesus' "least brothers") during the tribulation. Those who were compassionate to Jews during the tribulation will be granted access to the millennial kingdom.[314]

According to Gray's analysis, throughout all periods of church history about 59% of interpreters understood "all the nations" in v. 32 to refer to the judgment of all humanity. Interpretation of the "least brothers" has been less clear because so many interpreters do not reveal whether they take it as "the least" among all people or restrict it in some way. If the "neutral" witnesses are excluded, about 39% of interpreters have restricted the reference to Christians (or Christian missionaries), and about 21% have understood the expression to refer to anyone. The universal/non-restrictive position is represented most strongly in the twentieth century.[315] Caution should be used in assessing the history of interpretation, for, as Luz points out, Christian discussions of this passage in the post-Constantinian era often ignored the existence of non-Christians.[316] Writings intended to motivate Christian compassion in the Christian community do not always reveal what is believed about the necessity of broader compassion or universal judgment.

Variations on the four options exist.[317] J. Jeremias understood the passage to refer to the judgment of the "heathen," those who have never known Christ. Christians are judged on the basis of a faith that is lived out, but non-Christians are judged on the basis of acts of love.[318] T. Preiss saw in this text the basis of a juridical mysticism in which the Son of Man makes himself one with those needing help. Christ was mysteriously present in the wretched, in his brethren who are hungry, naked, sick, and in prison.[319] Also, several interpreters argue that Jesus spoke of *God's* universal judgment based on deeds of compassion but Matthew changed the narrative so that it speaks of *Jesus'* judgment of the nations for their reception of missionaries.[320]

Decisions on the Issues

Some of the options for interpretation can be set aside rather quickly. Nothing in the passage or its context justifies or prepares a reader to think along the lines of the dispensational interpretation. How is a reader to know that this judgment is not the final judgment but a judgment of those living during the great tribulation which assesses their care of Jews during the tribulation to determine their qualification to enter the millennial kingdom? No reader of Matthew could discern this. It is evidence of a system laid on the text rather than an interpretation emerging from the text.

Also unjustified is Jeremias's attempt to restrict the subject of this passage to judgment on the "heathen," those who have not heard of Christ. The context in Matthew does not indicate or prepare one for such a shift. Here and with many interpretations of this narrative theological systems and presuppositions are more in control than a reading of the text.

1. Is this an account from Jesus, or does it derive from Matthew or some other early Christian? A few interpreters attribute this passage entirely to Matthew.[321] Others see it as containing Matthean allegorizing of a simpler parable of the Last Judgment,[322] and some are suspicious of the transition from the Son of Man in v. 31 to the king in v. 34. Certainly the material has been edited by Matthew, as expected; Matthean traits include "then" *(tote)* in v. 31, "gather" *(synagō)* in v. 32 (but with the sense "show hospitality" in vv. 35, 38, and 43), "my Father" *(patēr mou)* in v. 34, and the emphasis on judgment. The Mattheanisms are mostly confined to vv. 31-32a and not so evident in vv. 32b-46.[323] I find the frequent suspicion of the transition from "Son of Man" to "king" surprising. Matthew could be responsible for the transition, but a king is already implied in v. 31, which says the Son of Man sits on a glorious throne, and this imagery has its origin in Dan 7:13-14, where the Son of Man receives dominion, glory, and an enduring kingdom.[324] If "Son of Man" was a self-designation for Jesus, granted Matthean shaping and interests, little reason exists to question the authenticity of this teaching as from Jesus.

Some maintain the authenticity of the parabolic saying and its accompanying explanation only by arguing that Jesus' original teaching was about *God's* judgment (either on Israel or more frequently on all humanity) and that Matthew has narrowed it to a focus on the disciples and shifted the meaning of "least brothers" so that now the passage is about the judgment of the nations for their reception of the disciples.[325] It is true that "king" is regularly used in Jewish writings in reference to God, but such a reorientation of the passage is neither convincing nor helpful. This issue will be dealt with below in connection with the question of the identification of the "least ones."

2. To whom is this material addressed? One can imagine Jesus using such material with a Jewish audience as part of his teaching on the kingdom and as a warning of the coming judgment, but the effect would not be different if this material was addressed to the disciples.[326] We must remind ourselves, though, that Jesus' concern typically was not the world at large but those in Israel who heard his words about the kingdom. Even if the focus here is universal judgment in keeping with apocalyptic concerns elsewhere, the warning is for Jesus' contemporaries. The themes of compassion and judgment were regular features of Jesus' teaching both generally and to the disciples. While a decision about the addressees does not change things, Matthew has these sayings addressed to the disciples with Jesus reminding them — and later Christians — of the criteria for judgment and encouraging them to show mercy and love. As Luz comments, *"The entire parenesis of 24:32–25:30 has no purpose if it does not end with a judgment scene that includes the church."*[327] In the context of his eschatological discourse, Matthew's four parables in 24:45–25:46 are all intended to encourage alert, wise, and faithful living in anticipation of the coming parousia.[328]

3. *Does "all the nations" (panta ta ethnē) refer to all people universally, all people except Christians, or all people except Jews? Who is gathered for judgment?* The identifications of "all the nations" and "these least brothers" determine virtually everything else. *Ethnē* (the plural of *ethnos*) can be translated as "nations" or "Gentiles" and can refer to Christians or non-Christians (e.g., Eph 3:1; 4:17). "All the nations" is used in the LXX most frequently of all nations other than Israel (e.g., Exod 33:16; Deut 7:7), but occasionally of all nations, including Israel (e.g., LXX Ps 48:2; Isa 25:6-7). Significantly, in view of the fact that Matt 25:31-32 alludes to Dan 7:13-14, "all the nations" occurs in LXX Dan 7:14 in the declaration that all nations will serve the Son of Man. In the NT "nations" is used of Gentiles as opposed to Jews (Rom 1:5) and of non-Christians, including Jews (Luke 24:47). As always, meaning can only be determined in context. In Matthew *ethnē* is used of Gentile nations (e.g., 10:5) and presumably of all nations, including the Jews (20:25). The expression "all the nations" appears three times in Matthew outside this passage (24:9, 14; 28:19), and all three appear to include both Gentiles and Jews, although this is debated. In 24:14 and 28:19 the expression indicates the arena for the proclamation of the gospel.

This language stems from several OT texts (Joel 3:2 [Hebrew 4:2]; Isa 66:18; Zeph 3:8; Zech 14:2) which speak of all the nations being gathered for judgment, for which the LXX uses the same Greek words or compounds as Matt 25:32 *(panta ta ethnē* and *synagein)*. Isa 66:18-24 with its language of undying worms and unquenchable fire was especially influential for subsequent descriptions of judgment. Later Jewish texts also anticipate all the nations being gathered for judgment (e.g., 11QMelchizedek 2.7-25; *1 En.* 90–91; *Pss. Sol.* 17:21-35; *2 Bar.* 72:2; *4 Ezra* 7:37-38). Here the nations are judged instead of Israel, and the judgment includes subjugation to Israel.

Just as important for understanding "all the nations" is the understanding of judgment in Jesus' teaching and in Matthew. Apart from Matt 25:31-46 Jesus' teaching on judgment focuses on Israel, not the nations or Gentiles, except to make the point that some Gentiles will fare better than Israel at judgment.[329] Is it likely that Jesus at this point leaves Israel out of the judgment? No, rather his picture of judgment subverts the usual picture by placing Israel with the other nations. With regard to Matthew, no evidence exists that he restricts judgment to non-Christians or that he has two judgments, one for Christians and one for non-Christians.[330] On the contrary, this Gospel warns repeatedly of a time of separation of the righteous from the unrighteous and that Jesus' followers are also liable to this judgment (7:21-23; 13:30, 36-43, 47-50; 16:27; 18:23-35; 22:10-14).[331] With "all the nations" it is more likely that the passage depicts the eschatological judgment of all persons. This will need to be verified by examination of the rest of the narrative.

4. Does "these least brothers of mine" refer to all the poor and needy, Jews, Christian missionaries, or all Christians? Are these least ones included in the judgment, or are they exempt? Related is the question whether the hardships listed are those of the poor and afflicted or those that Christian missionaries encounter.

The identity of the "least brothers" is the determinative issue in interpreting the passage. At first glance the reference seems obviously to be any needy person, but in recent years the view that the "least brothers" are Jesus' own disciples has gained increasing acceptance among some NT scholars (not among Christians in general). This position deserves serious consideration and has gained support for three reasons: it is easier to handle theologically in that it does not suggest salvation by works; more importantly, analysis of Matthew's language shows he uses "brothers" and "little ones" elsewhere of disciples; and sayings in Matthew and the other Gospels record Jesus teaching that receiving his disciples is the same as receiving him. The most pertinent parallel is Matt 10:40-42:

> The one receiving you receives me, and the one receiving me receives the one who sent me. The one who receives a prophet in the name of a prophet will receive a prophet's reward, and the one who receives a righteous person in the name of a righteous person will receive the reward of a righteous person. And whoever gives one of these little ones a cup of cold water only in the name of a disciple, truly I tell you, that person will in no way lose his reward.

The idea of having encountered Jesus in someone else and the mention of giving someone a drink are striking parallels. The frequency of passages treating the theme of encountering Jesus in his disciples (Mark 9:41; Matt 18:5/Mark 9:37/Luke 9:48; Luke 10:16/John 13:20; *Didache* 11:2) underscores the importance of these ideas. The argument then is that with this material Jesus reassures his disciples that all the nations will be judged on the basis of their treatment of them, similar to the way some Jews expected the nations to be judged for their treatment of Jews (e.g., *1 En.* 62:9-13; 90:17-42; 103:7-104:5; *2 Bar.* 72:2-6).

There are two alternatives with this view. For some the issue is treatment of Christians in general, God's oppressed people who will be vindicated at Judgment Day.[332] For others the issue is treatment specifically of Christian missionaries, those who proclaim the word. By showing how they respond to the messengers, the nations show their response to the message.[333]

Despite the recent popularity of this approach, closer analysis suggests that the parallels are more misleading than convincing. Matthew uses *adelphos* ("brothers" or "brothers and sisters") thirty-eight times, of which twenty refer to literal brothers. At least eight of the eighteen metaphorical occurrences do not have the sense "disciple" but are used generically in the sense of one's neighbor (e.g., 5:22: ". . . everyone angry at his brother or sister . . .").[334] The most important occurrences that suggest that "brothers" does refer to the disciples are 12:46-50; 23:8; and especially 28:10. Are these occurrences sufficient by themselves to elevate "brothers" to the level of a title for the disciples so that the mere appearance of the word in 25:40 indicates that the issue is the reception of Christians or more specifically of Christian missionaries? Does "brother" have in view only Christian brothers and sisters? Metaphorical uses such as 5:22 surely argue against such constriction of the word.

The argument that the addition of "least" (*elachistos,* the superlative of *mikros)*[335] to "brothers" also points to the disciples has cogency at first, but here, too, examination of the evidence suggests otherwise. The disciples of Jesus are referred to as "little ones" *(mikroi)* at least four times (Matt 10:42; 18:6, 10, 14),[336] but not as *elachistoi* unless here in 25:40. In fact, the word is used with a negative connotation for disciples in 5:19.[337] The evidence does not exclude a reference to Christians or Christian evangelists, but neither is it strong support for such an interpretation.

Some of the parallel sayings are impressive, but others are not. Mark 9:41, which is parallel to Matt 10:42, speaks explicitly of cold water given to disciples "because you bear the name of Christ,"[338] but in Matt 25:35-37 a drink is given with no awareness that Christ is being served. Matt 18:5/Mark 9:37/Luke 9:48 states that those who receive one little child (a literal child) in the name of Christ receives Christ. This would favor taking 25:40 as saying that those who minister to the needy — not Christian messengers — minister to Christ. The language for the acts of benevolence is of little help in making a decision. The acts are traditional descriptions of helping the needy, but a case can be made that they parallel the difficulties in which Christian missionaries find themselves, as for example in 2 Cor 11:23-29.[339] It must be admitted, though, that such an interpretation expects a lot from readers.

While identifying the brothers as Christians or missionaries alleviates concern about a salvation based on deeds, it creates larger interpretive and theological problems. Is there evidence elsewhere that Matthew thought judgment would be determined by one's acts of benevolence to Christians in general?[340] I find this hard to imagine, and without parallel sayings to reinforce such an idea it is difficult to accept this interpretation. Is there evidence elsewhere that Matthew or Jesus thought entrance to the kingdom could be obtained merely by being nice to missionaries, regardless of theology and conduct? The support from 10:40-42 for this view is superficial, and this approach places demands on the reader so severe that it is difficult to think this is Matthew's intent or the original intent of the teaching. The saying in 10:40-42 was fifteen chapters earlier. There the context is about mission, but here it is not. Can a reader be expected to remember and make the connection when nothing in the text points that way? Further, is it even clear in 10:42 that the "little ones" were missionaries?[341] What is argued as well with this position is that the real concern is not response to the missionaries as such, but response to their message. What helps a reader make this leap? Even more, if either of these alternatives is Matthew's view, one must say this is a very narrow theology, and the complaints leveled against it are justified.[342]

At issue is the purpose of the parabolic saying and its explanation. Are they and their placement in Matthew intended to console threatened Christians, as Stanton argues, or to motivate faithful discipleship marked by mercy and love?[343] The latter is the purpose, both because of the context and the concerns of Jesus and Matthew. Jesus' teaching and this Gospel both focus on mercy and love, and, in fact, on judgment based on mercy and love.[344] Of primary importance is the focus on judgment in 7:21-23. Entrance into the kingdom is based on doing the will of the Father, and the Judge addresses those who have done lawlessness — and for both Jesus and Matthew the Law is encapsulated in the love commands — and tells them "depart from me," very similar to 25:41. Unless the standard of judgment changed somewhere in the Gospel — for which there is no basis — this passage is a paraphrase of 7:21-23. The discourse in chs. 24–25 is intended to increase faithfulness, not provide consolation. Rather than interpret 25:31-46 in light of 10:40-42, we would do better to interpret 10:40-42 in light of the judgment pronouncements at the end of the other four discourses (chs. 7, 13, 18, and 25). This would allow us to see 10:40-42 as a specific application to mission of broader concerns about judgment. And no basis exists for thinking "the least" refers only to Jews. "These least brothers of mine" must be understood generally of those in need.[345]

I find it interesting that those who argue for the particularist view (the "least" as either Christians or missionaries) often argue that this is Matthew's view and that Jesus originally told a passage about God's universal judgment,[346] or at least that we should understand the parable to speak of universal judgment, even if Matthew meant something else.[347] If people find themselves

PARABLES OF FUTURE ESCHATOLOGY

drawn to the more universal understanding, why is it necessary to think Matthew had some more restricted view, particularly when it does not work well?

The particularlist view usually sees the least brothers as exempt from judgment. They stand with the Son of Man and are on neither the left nor the right, but neither Matthew nor Jesus has a group that is exempt from judgment.[348] *This is a parabolic saying and an explanation,* not a realistic portrayal of judgment. The dialogues between the Judge and the two groups have the purpose only of establishing the basis of judgment. The least brothers are needed to make this case and are not a basis for an exempt group.

Regarding whether the passage was originally about *God's* judgment, interpreters choose this because of Jewish use of "king" as a metaphor for God and the assumption that Jesus would not refer to himself as king. But "king" fits with the Son of Man language, and the latter cannot easily — and should not — be excised from the text.[349] And it is not unimaginable that Jesus used "king" language of himself. As God's agent Jesus claimed to embody the reign of God and acted in ways that led to his being crucified as king of the Jews. What would it mean other than king to say Jesus took on the task of reconstituting Israel under his own leadership?[350] Any thought on his part of taking on a messianic role involved ideas of being king. One of E. P. Sanders's "highly probable" results regarding Jesus is that his disciples thought of him as "king" and that Jesus either explicitly or implicitly accepted that role.[351] The Son of Man/king in the passage does not displace God but is an agent of God. An attempted reconstruction of this narrative with God at the center not only suffers from lack of methodological controls but also does not do justice to the fluidity of views in Judaism and the NT about how judgment will take place. In Judaism judgment is administered by angels, Abel, the Messiah, Melchizedek, the Elect One, Elijah, the Son of Man, and God.[352] If sayings exist that grant the disciples the privilege of sitting on thrones and judging Israel (Matt 19:28/Luke 22:30), it is not unthinkable that Jesus guardedly and among his disciples used king language of himself. The parabolic saying and its explanation point to the time of vindication when all will be judged.

5. How does the picture of judgment on the basis of acts of love expressed in this passage fit with salvation based on faith and confession of Jesus? What is the relation between the salvation granted in v. 34 and the acts listed in vv. 35-36? Does this passage teach "works righteousness," that is, that one can earn salvation by doing good deeds? These questions reflect a debate over the meaning of "for" or "because" *(gar)* at the beginning of vv. 35 and 42. Catholic exegetes historically have argued that "for" points to the basis of the decision, while Protestants have argued that it indicates the result, the evidence of redemption.

The worry about "works righteousness" stems from our deficient views of the gospel. Some outlet is sought because our systems, especially systems shaped by Reformation conflicts, are suspicious of any text that connects salvation and good deeds. Knowing that salvation is through faith and that no one can earn salvation, we force texts to comply. The problem is that neither Jesus nor Matthew set faith over against works. Further, we have often misunderstood Paul and have reduced faith to such banal notions that it bears little resemblance to the kind of life Jesus, Paul, and other early Christians had in mind with the word. Here, too, we must remember that parables are not whole systems of theology. They are limited analogies, and we interpret them correctly only when we stay within the analogies they propose.

This picture of judgment was intended to urge the disciples to know that only faithful obedience to the will of the Father — obedience marked by love and mercy — would suffice at judgment. This truism for Matthew creates difficulty for modern interpreters who fear that this passage compromises christological confession (cf. 10:32-33) or teaches works righteousness.[353] Consequently, some interpreters assume or seek to show that faith and/or grace are presupposed in this text,[354] but this narrative is not intended to be a complete statement of Matthew's view of discipleship or of the way to salvation.[355] The narrative is a piece of the Gospel, not its whole theology in miniature. To debate the implication of "for" for the theory of salvation taught here is to push the passage beyond its intent. It warns that judgment will be determined by acts of mercy, but does not address whether this mercy is the result of redemption or its cause.

This anxiety about salvation earned by good deeds is foreign to Matthew. Although neither Jesus in the Gospels nor Matthew speaks of grace *(charis)*,[356] both emphasize that forgiveness and the kingdom are gifts of God's favor and love.[357] Faith plays an important role in the Gospel (however, not faith in the sense it has in Paul's letters), but it does not need to be brought into this passage. In keeping with Jesus' rejection of the hypocrisy of the Pharisees, this Gospel is more concerned about the lack of authentic obedience than about anyone trying to earn salvation by works. To raise the problem of works righteousness is to foist on Jesus and Matthew a concern that is not theirs. Their concern is a discipleship that is evidenced in love and mercy. The judgment evidenced in this narrative does not ask if a person has accumulated x number of merciful acts but asks "What kind of person are you?" Identity is always the issue. Are you a person characterized by the love and mercy evidenced in Jesus' kingdom — which is what faith is all about, or are you one characterized by no concern for those in need? Salvation requires such acts.[358] The point is that a person cannot claim the identity without evidencing it in acts of mercy. Sins of omission are judged as harshly as overt sinful acts.

559

6. What does this passage teach, especially with regard to eternal judgment? As much as the judgment language captures our attention, that is not the most important teaching in this material. The emphasis is first on the responsibility for compassion and the warning that people will give account of their treatment of the oppressed. The foundational idea is that relation to God is by necessity lived out in relation to humans. It is not necessary to think the surprise of the righteous points to "anonymous Christians."[359] The surprise is a literary device indicating that the service rendered was not done for a reward.[360] Nor should we think of a juridical mysticism in which Christ is present in the oppressed.[361] A focus on anonymous Christians or juridical mysticism takes the narrative out of its context in the ministry of Jesus to Israel and makes it answer questions it was not designed to answer.[362] At the same time there is an assumption that in dealing with someone in the image of God we have to do with God, which is reflected in Jewish writings as well.

This material also emphasizes Jesus' identification with the poor and oppressed, which is evidenced partly in his baptism and his eating with tax collectors and sinners. God's identification with the poor is more explicitly expressed in the OT and Jewish writings,[363] but the juxtaposition of 25:31-46 with its portrayal of the Son of Man in glory identifying with the oppressed and with 26:2, which announces the Son of Man soon to be crucified, is striking. The king who identifies with the poor and oppressed does so out of his own experience. Other NT writers also know that Jesus is the real recipient of treatment directed at other persons (see Acts 9:4; Rom 14:15, 18; 1 Cor 8:12; Eph 6:5, 7).

Regarding judgment, we need to be cautious about conclusions drawn from this material. Its purpose is to promote compassion and warn of a responsibility for which one will be held accountable. Here and elsewhere Matthew gives *limited and evocative pictures*[364] of the final judgment of all persons to motivate discipleship. He does not give a unified portrayal so that judgment can be literally described. He uses conventional language for judgment,[365] derived no doubt from texts like Joel 3:1-21 and Dan 7:13-14 and from common Jewish conceptions, as is evident in the parallels from *1 Enoch*.[366] Still, as is evident with other parables and sayings, the judgment language is strong, even harsh, and creates discomfort. Prophets announce judgment; they *want* us to be uncomfortable. Jesus as a prophet emphasized judgment sufficiently that at least a quarter of the traditional sayings material is estimated to be concerned with judgment.[367] Judgment itself is merely truth-telling, but the consequences of judgment are more serious. Unlike the OT prophets, with Jesus the issues are heightened, for he speaks of eternal judgment, which could be interpreted as lasting for eternity or as having eternal consequences.[368] The point, of course, is that people should change course and live compassionately as part of discipleship to Jesus.

Repeatedly we have seen that the kingdom comes with limitless grace in the midst of an evil world, but with it comes limitless demand. This passage represents the second half of this statement. C. Leslie Mitton pointed out long ago that the teaching of Jesus and Paul presents us with a dilemma: our acceptance with God is entirely a gift from God bestowed through Jesus Christ, but only those who love their neighbors and show compassion to the distressed are acceptable to God.[369] The church, especially the Reformation branch, has often stressed the first to the neglect of the second. So much is this the case that Ulrich Luz finds judgment according to works a *theo*logical impossibility, which may, however, be *anthropo*logically necessary. That is, as humans we need the idea of judgment, even if it does not fit with the God revealed in Jesus.[370] But is not this a skewing of the biblical message? Neither the OT, the teaching of Jesus, nor any part of the NT finds the idea of judgment according to works difficult. In fact, it is the thoroughly consistent teaching of both Testaments.[371] Must we go back and fix the judgment teaching of the OT prophets too, or does the character of God require holding humans responsible in such a way that what they do has consequences? Judgment is not merely one element of Jewish eschatology but the most important element, and Jesus could not preach the reign of God without speaking of judgment.[372] Further, judgment is not some inferior theological conception, but a necessary ingredient for speaking of the righteousness of God and the importance of human life. What humans do or do not do matters. The present is not banal and unimportant, but the arena that determines eternal destiny.[373] Neither point of Mitton's dilemma can be slighted. The obvious truth is that the NT writers cannot imagine a person being brought into association with Jesus without having love evident in his or her life.

This passage is not about christology, but its christological implications should be noticed. Jesus as Son of Man has the authority to summon all the nations and to pass judgment. The angels accompany him, and he is the one who performs the desires of the Father.

Adapting the Narrative

Why, if the NT, Jewish writings, Greco-Roman sources, and the Egyptian *Book of the Dead* can agree that judgment is based on mercy and compassion, do so many of all faiths fail just at this point? No matter what our disagreements, compassion and mercy make more sense than any rival agenda. Granted that this narrative does not say everything that should be said, we should at least let it have its say. A person cannot be a follower of Jesus and be void of compassion, which is at the heart of his gospel. Why have so many Christians thought we could have the grace without the demand?

This has always been among the most influential parabolic texts, and Christians have used it frequently for preaching and ethical thinking. Possibly no one made more effective use of it than John Chrysostom, in whose works are no less than 170 quotations and 220 allusions to this passage. It was the basis of his emphasis on social justice and a motivating factor for his ministry,[374] and justly so. Other aspects of Christian thought need to be included, but the theology inherent in this text is both essential and formative. A person is not a disciple of Christ on the basis of ancestry, ritual act, or liturgical confession. One is a disciple in actually following Jesus' compassion and obedience to the will of the Father.

This is not works-righteousness; acts of mercy are not done as a means to an end, but are expressions of knowledge of God's love. Some have suggested that the narrative holds up an inferior ethic that is not specifically Christian, but there is no higher ethic than the love command. Christianity does not bring a new ethic that other humans do not know. It brings a new motivation, enabling, and understanding of the extent to which love is willing to go (cf. 1 John 2:7-11).

The passage focuses on "the least" for good reason. If people had known the identity of the king, they would have acted differently. Kings we treat nicely; the little people we ignore, which only shows that we act from selfish motives. But compassion has no other motive than meeting a need. It springs from an identity shaped by its Creator.

To adapt this text is to heed its warning and to know that all persons, and especially Christians, will be held accountable for their response to the will of God, especially in acts of compassion. The reminder that judgment is an assessment not only of what we have done but also of what we have failed to do — sins of omission — makes us uncomfortable, but this passage does not seek our comfort. Our churches (and our society) do not give much attention to judgment and explain faith in such a way that little is necessary from individual Christians. Jesus' teaching is different on both accounts. Either judgment is part of Christian preaching or no one even needs good news. We should not pretend to know what judgment will entail and should avoid sensationalism. Judgment is not the only motivation for living lives of mercy and compassion, but it is a necessary one. The strongest witness to the gospel will be lives of mercy and compassion.

We cannot separate our relation with God from our relation with people. To experience the compassion of God makes one a medium of compassion, and in the needs of others we encounter our own relation to God. For those in Christ the origin and recipient of every act is Christ himself.[375]

This passage does not address whether salvation is possible apart from Christ.[376] On the basis of Romans 2 I have argued that judgment is according to works on the basis of light received,[377] which is not only thoroughly defensible, but relieves much of the strain in traditional explanations of judgment. The judgment scene in this text would easily cohere with such an explanation, but it does not demand such a conclusion.

For Further Reading[378]

George Beasley-Murray, *Jesus and the Kingdom of God* (Grand Rapids: Eerdmans, 1986), pp. 307-12.

W. D. Davies and Dale C. Allison, *A Critical and Exegetical Commentary on the Gospel According to Saint Matthew* (3 vols.; ICC; Edinburgh: T. & T. Clark, 1988-97), 3:416-35.

David A. De Silva, "Renewing the Ethic of the Eschatological Community: The Vision of Judgment in Matthew 25," *Koinonia* 3 (1991): 168-94.

John R. Donahue, "The 'Parable' of the Sheep and the Goats: A Challenge to Christian Ethics," *TS* 47 (1986): 3-31; see also his *The Gospel in Parable* (Philadelphia: Fortress, 1988), pp. 109-25.

Sherman W. Gray, *The Least of My Brothers: Matthew 25:31-46, a History of Interpretation* (SBLDS 114; Atlanta: Scholars, 1989).

Ulrich Luz, "The Final Judgment (Matt 25:31-46): An Exercise in 'History of Influence' Exegesis," in *Treasures New and Old: Recent Contributions to Matthean Studies,* ed. David R. Bauer and Mark Allan Powell (Atlanta: Scholars, 1996), 271-310.

―――. *Matthew 21–28* (trans. James E. Crouch; Hermeneia; Minneapolis: Fortress, 2005), pp. 263-96.

J. Ramsey Michaels, "Apostolic Hardships and Righteous Gentiles," *JBL* 84 (1965): 27-37.

Theo Preiss, *Life in Christ* (trans. Harold Knight; Chicago: Allenson, 1954), pp. 43-60.

Graham N. Stanton, "Once More: Matthew 25.31-46," in *A Gospel for a New People: Studies in Matthew* (Edinburgh: T. & T. Clark, 1992), pp. 207-31.

*   *   *

If we reflect on these five parables on future eschatology, they tell us relatively little about the future kingdom. Brief references appear about the privilege, honor, and joy of the kingdom, but the goodness of the kingdom is more presupposed than described. Not a great deal more is detailed about the character of judgment, even though more graphic language is used, language used traditionally by both Jews and Gentiles to describe judgment. The descriptions are evocative, hyperboles to arrest and command attention. Clearly the descriptions of the future are not intended to give a theologically precise portrayal of the kingdom or of judgment.

Nor do these parables give much focus to christology. They assume Jesus' authority as *the* agent of God to separate evil from God's world. They are first-level witnesses to Jesus' expectation of an interval in which his disciples need to live out the identity to which he has called them, but they also express a conviction and hope with regard to the future. Even with the cross looming before Jesus, God's future and the defeat of evil were still certain.

More than anything, however, the parables of the future are not about the future. They are about life in the present. Each of the five parables in this chapter holds up two ways, one leading to life and one leading to death. The parables summon people to wise and faithful living. Their sole purpose is to persuade people — in view of God's future — to do the will of the Father and to show his compassion. All else is ancillary.

Epilogue

I have sought Jesus' intent with the parables, knowing full well that every retelling of a story, even by the same person, is a new communication. Matthew's telling of the parable of the Sower is not identical in meaning to Jesus' or Mark's or Luke's telling, but the interpretation of all four takes place in the field of the relations of Jesus and his mission, not in the field of patristic theology, modern psychology, or any other field of our choosing. Parables are a means of communication intended to persuade. Other nuances are important, but what really counts is what *Jesus* intended to communicate. Parables have numerous implications and significances within that intent. Meaning is contextual because it is the value assigned to a set of relations. If you change the context, you change the story. My concern has been as much as possible to keep people in the context of Jesus. If we seek to hear parables in the context of Jesus' telling, that will be plurisignificant enough, but that is quite different from retelling his story in another context. Everyone admits that the parables are the surest source we have of Jesus' teaching. If we place them in some other context, we will not hear Jesus or understand who he was. The parables need to be heard in terms of his purpose with Israel in the first century.

If OT, Greco-Roman, and rabbinic parables teach us anything, it is that analogies have correspondences, but what counts is understanding the purpose and limits of an analogy. Analogies regularly have contextual features and explanations. That is just the way parables work.

The parables inform, but their primary purpose is to elicit a response. The response will be to move positively toward Jesus and his message or negatively away from him and his concerns. In seeking a response, parables appeal to the emotions. The descriptions of the extravagant love and grace of God and of grievous judgment, the antitheses of wisdom and foolishness, and the common features of everyday life and relations are framed to urge people to understand that God's kingdom is already at work and to woo them to decide to be involved in that kingdom. The response parables require is action; it is not enough to study the parables, admire them, and reflect on them.

Like much of Scripture, parables are primarily concerned with identity, even if they more directly deal with some other subject, such as the present kingdom. What identity results for the ideal readers of the parables? Identities formed by the parables lead to people who understand grace and its demands and take it seriously enough to respond, who know the joy of the kingdom and are willing to celebrate, who are changed and enabled to see people — not just look at them, who love their neighbors and take care of the poor and troubled, and who are wise and faithful in view of God's future defeat of evil at the coming of the Son of Man.

In addition, parables give us the language with which to think and theologize. They open imagistic worlds that compel thought, and they possess master metaphors that become handles for theology, as is evidenced in expressions such as "Lazarus is still at the gate" or "the willingness to embrace." They deserve all the attention we will give them.

Appendices

Occurrences of παραβολή *(parabolē)* in the NT

Matt 13:3   parables (with reference to the parable of the Sower and the parables that follow)

     13:10   parables (with reference to the parable of the Sower)

     13:13   parables (with reference to the parable of the Sower)

     13:18   parable (with reference to the parable of the Sower)

     13:24   parable (with reference to the parable of the Wheat and the Weeds)

     13:31   parable (with reference to the parable of the Mustard Seed)

     13:33   parable (with reference to the parable of the Leaven)

     13:34   parable [two occurrences]

     13:35   parables

     13:36   parable (with reference to the parable of the Wheat and the Weeds

     13:53   parables

     15:15   analogy (What goes into the mouth does not defile but what comes out.)

     21:33   parable (with reference to the parable of the Wicked Tenants)

     21:45   parables (with reference to the parables of the Two Sons and the Wicked Tenants)

     22:1   parables (with reference to the parable of the Banquet)

	24:32	parable (with reference to the parable of the Fig Tree and Its Leaves)
Mark	3:23	riddles (or analogies) ("How can Satan cast out Satan?")
	4:2	parables (with reference to the parable of the Sower and the parables that follow)
	4:10	parables (with reference to the parable of the Sower)
	4:11	parables
	4:13	parable (two occurrences)
	4:30	parable (with reference to the parable of the Mustard Seed)
	4:33	parables (with reference to the parables in ch. 4 and others)
	4:34	parables
	7:17	analogy (What goes into the mouth does not defile but what comes out.)
	12:1	parables (with reference to the parable of the Wicked Tenants)
	12:12	parable (with reference to the parable of the Wicked Tenants)
	13:28	parable (with reference to the parable of the Fig Tree and Its Leaves)
Luke	4:23	proverb ("Doctor, cure yourself.")
	5:36	analogy ("No one tears a piece from a new garment and sews it on an old garment.")
	6:39	analogical question ("Can a blind person guide a blind person?")
	8:4	parable (with reference to the parable of the Sower)
	8:9	parable (with reference to the parable of the Sower)
	8:10	parables (with reference to the parable of the Sower)
	8:11	parable (with reference to the parable of the Sower)
	12:16	parable (with reference to the parable of the Rich Fool)
	12:41	parable (with reference to the parable of the Waiting Servants)
	13:6	parable (with reference to the parable of the Fig Tree)
	14:7	analogy (or instruction) (Instruction not to choose the chief seats)
	15:3	parable (with reference to the parable of the Lost Sheep)
	18:1	parable (with reference to the parable of the Unjust Judge)
	18:9	parable (with reference to the parable of the Toll Collector and the Pharisee)

Occurrences of παραβολή (parabolē) *in the NT*

19:11 parable (with reference to the parable of the Pounds)

20:9 parable (with reference to the parable of the Wicked Tenants)

20:19 parable (with reference to the parable of the Wicked Tenants)

21:29 parable (with reference to the parable of the Fig Tree and Its Leaves)

Heb 9:9 symbol (or analogy): the high priest's yearly entrance in the Holy of Holies is an analogy for the present time

11:19 figure (referring to Abraham's receiving Isaac back from the dead in a figurative sense)

Occurrences of the Verb מָשַׁל *(māšal)* in the OT

Num	21:27	ballad singers, poets (participle)
Job	17:6	byword
	30:19	become like
Pss	28:1	be like
	49:12	be like
	49:20[21]	be like
	143:7	be like
Isa	14:10	become like
	46:5	compare
Ezek	12:23	use a proverb
	16:44	use a proverb (twice)
	17:2	tell a parable
	18:2	use a proverb
	18:3	use a proverb
	20:49 (21:5)	speak a parable
	24:3	tell a parable

Occurrences of the Noun מָשָׁל *(māšāl)* in the OT

Items in bold print are translated in the LXX by παραβολή *(parabolē)*.

Num	23:7	oracle
	23:18	oracle
	24:3	oracle
	24:15	oracle
	24:20	oracle
	24:21	oracle
	24:23	oracle
Deut	28:37	a proverb (parallel to an object of horror and a byword)
1 Sam	10:12	proverb
	24:13	proverb
1 Kgs	4:32 (5:12)	proverb
	9:7	proverb (parallel to taunt)
2 Chron	7:20	proverb (parallel to a byword)
Job	13:12	proverb
	27:1	discourse
	29:1	discourse
	41:33	equal
Pss	44:14 (15)	byword
	49:4 (5)	proverb
	69:11 (12)	a byword
	78:2	parable
Prov	1:1	proverb
	1:6	proverb
	10:1	proverb
	25:1	proverb
	26:7	proverb
	26:9	proverb
Eccl	12:9	proverb
Isa	14:4	taunt

Jer	24:9	a byword
Ezek	12:22	proverb
	12:23	proverb
	14:8	a byword
	17:2	allegory
	18:2	proverb
	18:3	proverb
	20:49 (21:5)	allegory
	24:3	allegory
Joel	2:17	a byword
Mic	2:4	taunt song
Hab	2:6	taunt

Occurrences of **παραβολή** *(parabolē)* in the LXX

Num	23:7	oracle
	23:18	oracle
	24:3	oracle
	24:15	oracle
	24:20	oracle
	24:21	oracle
	24:23	oracle
Deut	28:37	a proverb, parallel to an object of horror and a taunt
1 Kgdms (1 Sam)	10:12	a proverb ("Is Saul also among the prophets?")
	24:14 (13)	a proverb ("Out of the wicked comes forth wickedness.")
2 Kgdms (2 Sam)	23:3	a comparison ("One who rules over people justly . . . is like the light of morning.")
3 Kgdms (1 Kgs)	4:32 (5:12)	proverbs (presumably: "Solomon spoke three thousand proverbs.")
2 Chron	7:20	proverb (parallel to *diēgēma,* an account, possibly in the sense "a spectacle")
Pss	43:15 (44:14[15])	a proverb (parallel to a shaking of the head, i.e., an object of disbelief or ridicule)
	48:5 (49:4[5])	a proverb (parallel to riddle)
	68:12 (69:11[12])	a taunt (an object of derision)
	77:2 (78:2)	parable or proverb (parallel to riddle, enigmatic saying)
Prov	1:6	a proverb (parallel to a dark saying)
Eccl	1:17	proverbs (or parables)
	12:9	proverbs
Jer	24:9	a proverb (parallel to *oneidismos,* a disgrace, and *misos,* an object of hatred, and *katara,* a curse)
Ezek	12:22	proverb ("The days are prolonged, and every vision comes to nothing.")

	12:23 (2×)	proverb
	16:44	proverb ("Like mother, like daughter.")
	17:2	parable (or allegory) (parallel to *diēgēma*, "account"; a narrative of the eagles, the tree, and the vine follows, with reference to the king of Babylon, the king of Jerusalem and the latter's seeking the help of Egypt)
	18:2	proverb ("The parents have eaten sour grapes, and the children's teeth are set on edge.")
	18:3	proverb
	19:14	proverb of lamentation
	21:5 (20:49)	parable (or proverb or allegory)
	24:3	parable (or allegory; the image of the boiling cauldron follows)
Dan	12:8	parables (or images?)
Mic	2:4	a taunt (parallel to *thrēnos*, lamentation)
Hab	2:6	a taunt
Tob	3:4	object of ridicule
Wis	5:4	object of derision (parallel to laughter)
Sir	1:25	sayings of understanding
	3:29	a proverb (or parable)
	13:26	proverbs (or comparisons)
	20:20	a proverb
	21:16	textual variant: a proverb?
	38:33 (34)	proverbs
	39:2	parables (or proverbs)
	39:3	parables (or proverbs) (parallel to *paroimiai*, proverbs)
	43:8	as an inferior variant
	47:15	proverbs
	47:17	proverbs (or parables) (parallel to *ōdai*, songs, and *paroimiai*, proverbs)

Occurrences of **παραβολή** *(parabolē)* in the Apostolic Fathers

Barn.	6:10	parable (or allegory)
	17:2	parable (or dark saying)
Hermas, *Vis.*	3.3.2	parable (allegory of the tower)
	3.12.1	parable (analogy)
	5:5	parable (twice, in reference to allegorical descriptions)
	5:6	parable (in reference to allegorical descriptions)
Hermas, *Mand.*	10.1.3	parables (of things not understood)
	10.1.4	parables (of the Godhead, i.e., deep things of God)
	11:18	riddle
Hermas, *Sim.*		Plural as a title at the beginning of *Sim.* and singular as a title in *Sim.* 2, 3, 4, 5, 6, 7, 8, and 9.
	2.4	analogy (of the Vine and the Elm)
	5.2.1	parable (of the Field)
	5.3.1	parable (dark sayings not understood)
	5.4.1	parable (of the Field, twice)
	5.4.2	parable (dark sayings not understood)
	5.4.3	parable (dark sayings not understood, twice)
	5.5.1	parable (dark sayings not understood)
	5.5.1	parable (dark sayings not understood)
	5.5.5	parable (with reference to the parable of the Field)
	5.6.8	parable (with reference to the parable of the Field)
	9.1.1	parable
	9.5.5	parable
	9.29.4	parable (of the Mountains)

Classification of Parables

Similitudes

  The Sower: a fourfold similitude

  The Growing Seed

  The Mustard Seed

  The Leaven

  The Treasure in the Field

  The Pearl of Great Price

  The Two Builders: an antithetical double similitude

  The Net

  The Faithful and Unfaithful Steward: an antithetical double similitude, close to being a mixed type with its introductory question

  The Children in the Market Place

  The Good and Worthless Trees

  The Budding Fig Tree

Implied Similitudes

  The Man Going on a Journey

  The Sheep and the Goats (vv. 32-33 only)

Interrogative parables

  The Lost Sheep (both versions)

  The Lost Coin

  The Tower Builder

  The Warring King

  The Sheep in the Pit

  The Friend at Midnight

Double indirect narrative parables

  The Unforgiving Servant: two-stage double indirect narrative

  Prodigal Son: two-stage double indirect narrative

  The Wheat and the Weeds

  The Barren Fig Tree

The Feast

The Banquet: two-stage double indirect narrative

The Workers in the Vineyard

The Unjust Judge

The Ten Virgins

The Talents

The Pounds: a double indirect narrative parable with two interwoven plots

Juridical parables

The Two Debtors

The Two Sons

The Wicked Tenants in Matthew; in Mark and Luke the juridical character is implicit

Single indirect narrative parables

The Good Samaritan

The Rich Fool

The Unjust Steward

The Rich Man and Lazarus: a two-stage single indirect narrative parable

The Pharisee and the Toll Collector

"How much more" parables

The Friend at Midnight

The Lost Sheep

The Lost Coin

The Unjust Steward

The Unjust Judge

Notes

Notes to "Introduction to the Parables of Jesus"

1. See especially John W. Sider, "Proportional Analogy in the Gospel Parables," *NTS* 31 (1985): 1-23; and *Interpreting the Parables: A Hermeneutical Guide to Their Meaning* (Grand Rapids: Zondervan, 1995); and also Ernst Fuchs, *Hermeneutik* (2d ed.; 2 vols.; Bad Cannstatt: R. Mullerschön, 1958), 1:211-20. In ancient rhetoric one of the steps in elaborating a chreia (a witty or wise saying from a famous person) was analogy (*ek tou parabolēs* [sic]). See *The Chreia and Ancient Rhetoric: Classroom Exercises* (trans. and ed. Ronald F. Hock and Edward N. O'Neil; Atlanta: Society of Biblical Literature, 2002), pp. 83-84 *et passim*. Wolfgang Harnisch denies that Jesus' parables are analogical, even though he grants that other parables are. (See his "Language of the Possible: The Parables of Jesus in the Conflict between Rhetoric and Poetry," *ST* 46 [1992]: 41-54, esp. p. 52 and the apparent contradiction on pp. 50-51 where he denies that a parable is aimed at something outside itself and yet says the parable points to something beyond itself.) In his "Die Spachkraft der Analogie," *ST* 28 (1974): 1-20, he assumed parables are analogies. As we will see, Greco-Roman, OT, and rabbinic parables are all analogical, and there are no grounds for saying Jesus' parables are not.

2. Cf. Aristotle, *Rhet.* 2.20.1-8. See also Klaus Berger, "Hellenistische Gattungen im Neuen Testament," *ANRW* 25.2 (ed. Wolfgang Haase; Berlin: Walter de Gruyter, 1984), pp. 1114-15. Harnisch ("Die Sprachkraft der Analogie") disputed the argumentative character of Jesus' parables in favor of their opening existentially a new attitude toward life, even though he viewed them as promoting a decision (p. 20). Parables do open a new attitude toward life, but in doing so they present a case and are a means of proof.

3. Some seek to deny that Jesus' parables reference the kingdom, but this is a very difficult argument with virtually nothing in its favor. See e.g., Charles W. Hedrick, *Parables as Poetic Fictions: The Creative Voice of Jesus* (Peabody, Mass.: Hendrickson, 1994), esp. pp. 25-35, 76-78, and 86-87, who, not surprisingly, concludes that Jesus' parables were banal. (Adolf Jülicher similarly concluded that Jesus' parables were about trivial matters; see his "Parables," *Encyclopaedia Biblica* [New York: Macmillan, 1902], 3:3563-67, here p. 3566.) Or see William R. Herzog II, *Parables as Subversive Speech: Jesus as Pedagogue of the Oppressed* (Louisville: Westminster/John

Knox, 1994), p. 7, who thinks the parables address systems of oppression. Without reference to Jesus' own mission and his proclamation of the kingdom to Israel the parables have little meaning that can be recovered by us.

4. This is in accord with Ben F. Meyer's focus on critical realism. See his *Critical Realism and the New Testament* (Allison Park, Pa.: Pickwick Publications, 1989).

5. The attempt to answer this question does not suggest hermeneutical naïveté or make one guilty of the "intentional fallacy," a simplistic understanding of intentionality that assumes it can get into the other's head. Rather, it seeks the communicative intent of discourse and assumes that the discourse indeed had a purpose. For more detailed treatment of these issues, see my "Reading to Hear: A Hermeneutics of Hearing," *HBT* 24 (2002): 1-32.

6. Two recent exceptions are Arland J. Hultgren, *The Parables of Jesus: A Commentary* (Grand Rapids: Eerdmans, 2000); and Peter Rhea Jones, *Studying the Parables of Jesus* (Macon, Ga.: Smyth & Helwys, 1999), although Jones's preaching suggestions are sometimes not as convincing as his scholarship.

7. See especially Warren S. Kissinger, *The Parables of Jesus: A History of Interpretation and Bibliography* (Metuchen, N.J.: Scarecrow, 1979), pp. 1-230; Norman Perrin, *Jesus and the Language of the Kingdom* (Philadelphia: Fortress, 1976), pp. 89-193; Craig L. Blomberg, *Interpreting the Parables* (Downers Grove, Ill.: InterVarsity, 1990), pp. 29-167; and his "The Parables of Jesus: Current Trends and Needs in Research," in *Studying the Historical Jesus: Evaluations of the State of Current Research* (ed. Bruce Chilton and Craig A. Evans; Leiden: Brill, 1994), pp. 231-54; and two articles of my own, "From Allegorizing to Allegorizing: A History of the Interpretation of the Parables of Jesus," in *The Challenge of Jesus' Parables* (ed. Richard N. Longenecker; Grand Rapids: Eerdmans, 2000), pp. 3-29; and "Modern Approaches to the Parables," in *The Face of New Testament Studies: A Survey of Recent Research* (ed. Scot McKnight and Grant Osborne; Grand Rapids: Baker, 2004), pp. 177-90.

8. There were exceptions, such as Tertullian, John Chrysostom and the School of Antioch, and John Calvin, but most of the church followed the allegorizing methods of the School of Alexandria. See Chrysostom's advice regarding the parable of the Vineyard Workers: "The saying is a parable, wherefore neither is it right to inquire curiously into all things in parables word by word, but when we have learnt the object for which it was composed, to reap this, and not to busy one's self about anything further" (*The Gospel of Matthew,* Homily 44.3). Note that G. B. Caird (*The Language and Imagery of the Bible* [Philadelphia: Westminster, 1980], pp. 167-71) distinguishes five types of allegorizing: rationalist (to remove offensive material), moralist, atomistic, exegetical, and polemical.

9. *Quaest. Ev.* 2.19.

10. Gregory the Great, *Forty Gospel Homilies* 31.

11. E.g., "Let there be light" taken literally could refer to creation, allegorically could mean "Let Christ be born in the church," ethically could mean "May we be illumined in mind and inflamed in heart through Christ," and with regard to heaven could mean "May we be conducted to glory through Christ" (Thomas Aquinas, *Commentary on the Epistle to the Galatians* 4.7).

12. See Irenaeus, *Haer.* 2:27 on the "Proper Mode of Interpreting Parables and Obscure Passages of Scripture."

13. See David Steinmetz, "Calvin and the Irrepressible Spirit," *Ex Auditu* 12 (1996): 94-107, here p. 97.

14. *Die Gleichnisreden Jesu* (Freiburg i. B.: Akademische Verlagsbuchhandlung von J. C. B. Mohr, vol. 1, 1888; vol. 2, 1889). This work was reprinted in one volume by Wissenschaft-

liche Buchgesellschaft (Darmstadt: 1963). Others had protested allegorizing before Jülicher, but no one made such a hard-hitting case as he.

15. *Die Gleichnisreden Jesu* 1:44-70 and 80-81. Paradoxically Jülicher retained confidence generally about the genuineness of the parable tradition, and he knew that parables in "Hellenistic scribal learning" sometimes were enigmatic (1:42). Eta Linnemann (*Parables of Jesus: Introduction and Exposition* [London: SPCK, 1966], p. 24) followed Jülicher in saying parables do not need interpretation.

16. How Jülicher intended the German word *uneigentlich* to be understood is debated. It could mean "figurative," as John Sider argues (*Interpreting the Parables*, pp. 247-50), or it could mean "inauthentic," which is how it is understood by Dan Otto Via, Jr. (*The Parables: Their Literary and Existential Dimension* [Philadelphia: Fortress, 1967], p. 8) and is so translated in Wolfgang Harnisch's "The Metaphorical Process in Matthew 20:1-15" (in *Society of Biblical Literature 1977 Seminar Papers* [ed. Paul J. Achtemeier; Missoula, Mont.: Scholars Press, 1977], pp. 231-50, here p. 232). Jülicher certainly meant "figurative" with some uses (e.g., 2:265), but his view of *uneigentliche* forms was so negative that the translation may not matter. It is possible that Jülicher intended a double entendre. See Roger Lundin, Clarence Wahlout, and Anthony C. Thiselton, *The Promise of Hermeneutics* (Grand Rapids: Eerdmans, 1999), p. 159.

17. See *Die Gleichnisreden Jesu* 2:431-32 for his reconstruction of the parable of the Banquet in Matt 22:1-14 and Luke 14:15-24.

18. *Altjüdische Gleichnisse und die Gleichnisse Jesu* (Tübingen: Mohr-Siebeck, 1904); and *Die Gleichnisreden Jesu im Lichte der rabbinischen Gleichnisse des neutestamentlichen Zeitalters* (Tübingen: Mohr-Siebeck, 1912).

19. The classic discussion is that of Hans-Josef Klauck, *Allegorie und Allegorese in synoptischen Gleichnistexten* (Münster: Aschendorff, 1978); see esp. pp. 354-56 where in summarizing he distinguishes *Allegorie* (a rhetorical and poetic process related to various forms), *Allegorese* (an exegetical method which neglects the texture of a document and inserts elements anachronistically from a philosophical or theological preunderstanding), and *Allegorisierung* (subsequent revision of a text in the direction of an allegorical understanding).

20. Madeleine Boucher, *The Mysterious Parable* (Washington: The Catholic Biblical Association of America, 1977); and Sider, *Interpreting the Parables*. Jülicher's reaction against allegory is part of a nineteenth-century distaste for allegories written from the sixteenth to the eighteenth centuries. (See, e.g., Mary Ford, "Towards the Restoration of Allegory: Christology, Epistemology and Narrative Structure," *St. Vladimir's Theological Quarterly* 34 [1990]: 161-95, here pp. 162-63.) Others attacking Jülicher's position include Matthew Black ("The Parables as Allegory," *BJRL* 42 [1959-60]: 273-87), Raymond Brown ("Parable and Allegory Reconsidered," in *New Testament Essays* [Garden City, N.Y.: Doubleday, 1968], pp. 321-33), Maxime Hermaniuk (*La Parabole Évangélique* [Louvain: Bibliotheca Alfonsiana, 1947]), David Flusser, *Die rabbinischen Gleichnisse und der Gleichniserzähler Jesus*, Teil 1: *Das Wesen der Gleichnisse* [Bern: Peter Lang, 1981]), David Stern (*Parables in Midrash* [Cambridge, Mass.: Harvard University Press, 1991]), and Craig Blomberg (*Interpreting the Parables*).

21. E.g., Jülicher, *Die Gleichnisreden Jesu* 2:352 and 432. Craig Blomberg comments, ". . . few interpreters who claim to abide by the nonallegorical, one-main-point approach ever succeed for long in following their own rules." ("Interpreting the Parables of Jesus: Where Are We and Where Do We Go from Here?" *CBQ* 53 [1991]: 50-78, here p. 52.)

22. E.g., Robert W. Funk's chapter "The Parable as Metaphor," in *Language, Hermeneutic, and Word of God: The Problem of Language in the New Testament and Contemporary Theology*

(New York: Harper & Row, 1966), pp. 133-62; and Hans Weder's book *Die Gleichnisse Jesu als Metaphern* (Göttingen: Vandenhoeck & Ruprecht, 1978).

23. E.g., Jan Lambrecht, *Once More Astonished* (New York: Crossroad, 1981), p. 40.

24. *The Teaching of Jesus* (Cambridge: Cambridge University Press, 1939), p. 65.

25. *The Parables of the Kingdom* (London: Nisbet, 1936), pp. 15-16.

26. *The Parables of the Kingdom*, p. 16.

27. "Biblical Hermeneutics," *Semeia* 4 (1975): 29-148; see pp. 30, 75, 88-89.

28. *Progymnasmata* 1.21; 4.2 *(mythos esti logos pseudēs eikonizōn alētheian).*

29. This definition is derived from Marianne Moore's description of poetry. See her poem "Poetry," *Twentieth Century American Poetry* (ed. Conrad Aiken; New York: Random House, 1944), pp. 176-77.

30. H. J. Rackham, *The Fable as Literature* (London: Athlone Press, 1985), pp. xi and 245. He adds (p. 238) that a fable has unmistakable meaning or else it fails miserably.

31. David Stern, "Jesus' Parables from the Perspective of Rabbinic Literature: The Example of the Wicked Husbandmen," in *Parable and Story in Judaism and Christianity* (ed. Clemens Thoma and Michael Wyschogrod; New York: Paulist, 1989), p. 58.

32. *Søren Kierkegaard's Journals and Papers,* 6 vols. (ed. and trans. Howard V. Hong and Edna H. Hong; Bloomington, Ind.: Indiana University Press, 1967), 1:288. Kierkegaard offered a detailed explanation of indirect communication. See also Thomas C. Oden (ed.), *Parables of Kierkegaard* (Princeton: Princeton University Press, 1978), p. xiii; and Fred B. Craddock, *Overhearing the Gospel* (Nashville: Abingdon, 1978), pp. 79-100. On parables as indirect communication, see also Charles E. Carlston, *The Parables of the Triple Tradition* (Philadelphia: Fortress, 1975), pp. 98-99.

33. See *Song Rab.* 1.1.8. See the discussion of Bernard Brandon Scott, *Hear Then the Parable: A Commentary on the Parables of Jesus* (Minneapolis: Fortress, 1989), pp. 52-62.

34. *Søren Kierkegaard's Journals and Papers,* 1:273, 282. Worth consideration is his comment that all communication of knowledge is direct communication, whereas all communication of capability is indirect communication.

35. Boucher, *The Mysterious Parable,* p. 22.

36. See Appendix 4 on parables in the Apostolic Fathers; Robert M. Johnston in his survey of early Christian Greek writings shows how little exists in the church's literature that even approximates the parable form. See his "Greek Patristic Parables," in *Society of Biblical Literature 1977 Seminar Papers* (ed. Paul J. Achtemeier; Missoula, Mont.: Scholars, 1977), pp. 215-29.

37. Birger Gerhardsson ("The Narrative Meshalim in the Synoptic Gospels: A Comparison with the Narrative Meshalim in the Old Testament," *NTS* 34 [1988]: 339-63, here pp. 358-61) with some justification says that parables are not in themselves proclamatory. They illuminate. He argues that Jesus did not speak initially in parables, but that parables appear when he explains himself more closely on specific questions. The parables were created to illuminate different aspects of the kingdom.

38. Joachim Jeremias rightly says, "Every one of them [Jesus' parables] calls for an answer on the spot" (*The Parables of Jesus,* 2d rev. ed., trans. S. H. Hooke; New York: Charles Scribner's Sons, 1972, p. 21). On Jesus as a prophet see N. T. Wright, *Jesus and the Victory of God,* vol. 2 of *Christian Origins and the Question of God* (Minneapolis: Fortress, 1996), pp. 147-97. Throughout the book Wright emphasizes the role of the parables in Jesus' ministry; note esp. his insightful summary on pp. 181-82.

39. William Herzog's suggestion that Jesus' parables were discussion starters does no justice to their power and pointedness. See his *Parables as Subversive Speech,* pp. 78, 259-61.

40. See above, p. 2, n. 1.

41. See the discussion by John Sider, *Interpreting the Parables,* pp. 29-75. Some object to the division of *Sache* and *Bild,* but one does not have to buy into their division to accept the reality of the two in analogies.

42. *Interpreting the Parables,* p. 84. He argues that analogies may have two or more points of resemblance (pp. 58-62), and points out that Jeremias in his *The Parables of Jesus* claims that parables have only one point of comparison but actually finds eight in the parable of the Growing Seed and nine in the parable of the Unforgiving Servant (see Sider, *Interpreting the Parables,* pp. 60-61 and 67-69 respectively).

43. Despite Quintilian's complaint (*Inst.* 5.11.30) against those who show pedantic zeal in making a minute classification of similes. The material in this section was presented as part of a lecture to be printed as "Prophets, Parables, and Theologians," in *BBR.*

44. E.g., note the distinction J. Jeremias makes between nominative and dative forms of parables, i.e., those that begin with a noun in the nominative case (Mark 4:3) and those that begin with a dative case (Mark 4:30-31). See his *The Parables of Jesus,* pp. 100-103. C. Blomberg *(Interpreting the Parables)* classifies parables as triadic, dyadic, and monadic based on the number of main characters. See also G. Sellin, "Lukas as Gleichniserzähler: die Erzählung vom barmherzigen Samariter (Lk 10:25-37)," *ZNW* 65 (1974): 166-89, who classifies parables according to their introductions (*tis ex hymōn* ["Who from you?"], *anthrōpos tis* ["A certain man"], and *anthrōpos* ["A man"]). See the discussion of Jeffrey T. Tucker, *Example Stories: Perspectives on Four Parables in the Gospel of Luke* (JSNTSup 162; Sheffield: Sheffield Academic Press, 1998), pp. 209-19.

45. The Hebrew title of the book of Proverbs is *mishlê,* the plural construct form of *mashal,* the word also used for "parable." The Aramaic word for parable is *mĕtal* and is used in the Cave 4 versions of *1 En.* 1:2 and 3 to refer to the whole work, either in the sense of "discourse" or "oracle." It is used similarly at 93:1 and 3. In the *Similitudes of Enoch,* preserved only in Ethiopic, the corresponding Ethiopic word is used at 37:5; 38:1; 45:1; and 58:1 of visions, and 43:4 uses it of an interpretation.

46. "The Secret of the Transmission of the Unwritten Jesus Tradition," *NTS* 51 (2005): 1-18, here p. 11; and "The Narrative Meshalim," 341-42. He counts a total of fifty-five narrative *meshalim* in the Synoptics.

47. Hultgren, *The Parables of Jesus,* p. 3. Detlev Dormeyer, partly in dependence on Quintilian, has only two subgenres for parables: parables in the narrow sense (essentially similitudes) and parables (stories in the past tense telling of "one-off cases"). See his *The New Testament among the Writings of Antiquity* (trans. Rosemarie Kossov; Sheffield: Sheffield Academic, 1998), pp. 156-73. The distinction between similitudes and parables was already recognized and discussed by Origen. See his treatment of Matt 13:44 in his *Commentary on Matthew* 10.4, 16 (*ANF* 9:415-16 and 423-24), in which he says that similitudes are generic while parables are specific and that parables were told to the multitudes while similitudes were told to the disciples. Cf. Quintilian, *Inst.* 5.11.1-2, 22-23. Jan Lambrecht's attempt to distinguish similitude and parable is exaggerated. He argues that the listener is passive in a similitude but active in a parable and that "a similitude *in-*forms, a parable *re-*forms." He also says that a parable is image alone and does not need an introduction or have explicit application. See his *Out of the Treasure: The Parables in the Gospel of Matthew* (Grand Rapids: Eerdmans, 1991), pp. 77-79. A listener is just as active in a similitude, and a similitude can also reform. Parables often do need introductions and explanations, as a glance at OT and rabbinic parables shows.

48. Which is explicitly labeled a *parabolē* in Luke.

49. Jülicher labeled several passages as parables *(Parabeln)* which most now call similitudes (e.g., the parables of the Lost Sheep and Lost Coin, the Mustard Seed, the Leaven, the Treasure, and the Pearl). Note that Bultmann, although following Jülicher, treats all these as similitudes *(Gleichnisse)*. See his *The History of the Synoptic Tradition* (rev. ed.; trans. John Marsh; New York: Harper and Row, 1976), pp. 170-73.

50. Note J. Dominic Crossan's division of parables into aphoristic, extended, and narrative parables ("Parable," *ABD*, 5:148-49).

51. See above, p. 8.

52. The Mustard Seed in Mark has the present tense and the aorist subjunctive. For the same parable Luke has the aorist, and Matthew has both present and aorist. This causes some to label Matthew and Luke's version a parable instead of a similitude. See among others Harry Fleddermann, "Mustard Seed and Leaven in Q, the Synoptics, and Thomas," *Society of Biblical Literature 1989 Seminary Papers 1989* (ed. David J. Lull; Atlanta: Scholars Press, 1989), pp. 216-36, here p. 216. W. D. Davies and Dale C. Allison (*A Critical and Exegetical Commentary on the Gospel According to Saint Matthew*, 3 vols. [ICC; Edinburgh: T. & T. Clark, 1988-97], 2:416), following N. A. Huffman, label the Q version (represented by Luke) a "true parable" about a particular mustard seed, and, since it is in the past tense, as less influenced by the church. Drawing the opposite conclusion, Peter Rhea Jones (*Studying the Parables of Jesus* [Macon, Ga.: Smyth & Helwys, 1999], p. 85) sets Matthew's and Luke's past tense parable against Mark's present tense similitude and concludes that Mark's version fits better with Jesus' time, whereas the past tenses of Matthew and Luke fit the time of the church. Tenses are dubious support for such conclusions about the influence of the church. *Tense is no ultimate guide* to the distinction between similitudes and parables, as a glance at the different tenses in the parables of the Treasure in the Field and of the Pearl shows. The parable of the Treasure uses the aorist for "hid" *(ekrypsen)* and then uses the present tense. The parable of the Pearl uses the perfect tense for "sold" *(pepraken)*, the imperfect for "had" *(eichen)*, and the aorist for "bought" *(ēgorasen)*. However, the aorist active indicative of *pipraskō* seems to have fallen out of use. See S. M. B. Wilmshurst, "The Historic Present in Matthew's Gospel: A Survey and Analysis Focused on Matthew 13:44," *JSNT* 25 (2003): 269-87, here p. 281.

53. Cf. Georg Baudler (*Jesus im Spiegel seiner Gleichnisse* [Stuttgart: Calwer, 1986], pp. 58-79) who distinguishes between "procedure parables" *(Vorgangsgleichnissen)* and "parables with a plot" *(Handlungsgleichnissen)* and Eckhard Rau (*Reden in Vollmacht: Hintergrund, Form, und Anliegen der Gleichnisse Jesu* [FRLANT 149; Göttingen: Vandenhoeck & Ruprecht, 1990], 30), who distinguishes between descriptive parables and narrative parables *(besprechenden und erzählenden Gleichnissen)*.

54. B. T. D. Smith (*The Parables of the Synoptic Gospels* [Cambridge: Cambridge University Press, 1937], pp. 30-32) points out that similes and similitudes can take the form of a statement, a question, or a command. Luke 12:36 is one of a few examples of an imperatival similitude. Parables with plot development by their very nature do not take the form of an imperative.

55. This is the case for every NT occurrence. It holds true as well for Greco-Roman writers. See Epictetus, *Diatr.* 1.27.19-20 (*Tis hymōn eis balaneion apelthein thelōn eis mylōna apēlthen* — "Who among you when he wishes to go to a bath goes to a mill instead?"); see also 1.4.31; 3.5.17; Josephus, *J.W.* 2.376: *Tis hymōn ouk akoē pareilēphen to Germanōn plēthos* ("Which of you has not heard tell of the horde of Germans?"); Dio Chrysostom, *Oratio* 64 *(De Fortuna)* 13.2; Arrian, *Anabasis* 7.10.1.3; Plutarch *Mor.* 320F. *(Fortuna Romanorum* 7); Dionysius of Halicarnassus, *Ant. Rom.* 7.42.2.1, all of which use *tis hymōn* and expect a negative answer. Contra Jeremias (*The Parables of Jesus*, p. 103) and Heinrich Greeven ("Wer unter Euch . . . ?" *WD* 3

[1952]: 86-101, here p. 100), who say this question does not have contemporary parallels. See Klaus Berger, "Materialien zu Form und Überlieferungsgeschichte neutestamentlicher Gleichnisse," *NovT* 15 (1973): 1-37, here pp. 32-33.

56. Cf. Smith, *The Parables of the Synoptic Gospels*, p. 34.

57. E.g., Jülicher, *Die Gleichnisreden Jesu*, 2:2; and Bultmann, *History of the Synoptic Tradition*, p. 174, but this opinion results from the confusion over the word "similitude" itself.

58. For discussions of this genre, see Uriel Simon, "The Poor Man's Ewe-Lamb: An Example of a Juridical Parable," *Bib* 48 (1967): 207-42; Adrian Graffy, "The Literary Genre of Isaiah 5,1-7," *Bib* 60 (1979): 400-409; Gale Yee, "A Form Critical Study of Isaiah 5:1-7 as a Song and a Juridical Parable," *CBQ* 43 (1981): 30-40; and Ulrich Mell, *Die "anderen" Winzer. Eine exegetische Studie zur Vollmacht Jesu Christi nach Markus 11,27–12,34* (Tübingen: Mohr-Siebeck, 1994), pp. 82-85. *4 Ezra* 4:13-21 is a juridical parable about the forest and the sea told after Ezra complains that it would be better not to have lived. The plans of forest and sea to subdue each other is deemed foolish by Ezra. If he could judge that correctly, why did he not discern that those who inhabit the earth can understand only what is on earth and those in heaven can understand what is above the height of the heavens?

59. Edward Albee: "The purpose of serious theater has always been to hold a mirror up to people and say, 'This is you; if you don't like what you see, why don't you change?' That is always the function of all the arts . . ." (The News Hour with Jim Lehrer, Friday, June 3, 2005).

60. See, e.g., *Søren Kierkegaard's Journals and Papers*, 1:266-76.

61. Three other juridical parables also occur in the OT: the parable of the Widow and the Avengers which Joab arranges for a wise woman from Tekoa to tell David (2 Sam 14:1-20); the parable of the Fake Injury, by which an unnamed prophet confronts Ahab (1 Kgs 20:35-42); and the parable of the Vineyard (Isa 5:1-7), which expresses judgment on the house of Israel and the people of Judah for being so unproductive. The self-condemnation in Isaiah 5 is implied.

62. The parable of the Pharisee and the Toll-Collector (Luke 18:9-14) is also very close to being a juridical parable.

63. Bultmann viewed other accounts also as example stories, such as Luke 14:7-11 and 12-14. See his *History of the Synoptic Tradition*, p. 179. The most important treatments of example stories are Tucker, *Example Stories*, even though in the end I do not think his solution is satisfactory; and Ernst Baasland, "Zum Beispiel der Beispielerzählungen. Zur Formenlehre der Gleichnisse und zur methodik der Gleichnisauslegung," *NovT* 28 (1986): 193-219.

64. "Parable and Example Story: A Literary-Structuralist Approach," *Semeia* 1 (1974): 105-33, esp. 119. He says the narrative of the Good Samaritan is a metaphor which gives new meaning to neighborliness but not a metaphor of the kingdom and, therefore, not a parable. How does such a statement square with the breadth of the term *mashal*?

65. John Dominic Crossan, "Parable and Example in the Teaching of Jesus," *NTS* 18 (1972): 285-307.

66. Tucker, *Example Stories*, pp. 264-74. See also Wolfgang Harnisch, *Die Gleichniserzählungen Jesu. Eine hermeneutische Einführung* (3d ed.; Göttingen: Vandenhoeck & Ruprecht, 1995), pp. 84-92.

67. Baasland, "Zum Beispiel der Beispielerzählungen," 218-19. Note Tucker's legitimate conclusion (*Example Stories: Perspectives on Four Parables in the Gospel of Luke*, p. 399) that if there is a difference between example story and parable, it is a difference of degree, not kind.

68. These stories are similar to synecdoche, a naming of the part for the whole, in that they present a particular example to demonstrate a general principle. See Boucher, *The Mysterious Parable*, p. 22. She calls the example stories "extended synecdoches."

69. Jesus' double and single indirect narrative parables have superficial parallels to Aristotle's historical and invented examples *(paradeigmata)* and to two kinds of rabbinic proofs, the *ma'aseh* (a precedent) and the *mashal* (an analogy/parable), but Jesus was not offering proofs by historical precedent nor precedents for halakhic rulings. Rather, he was presenting human behavior as a way to confront people with decisions about life. The single indirect stories are neither historical examples nor *ma'asim.* See p. 55 herein.

70. See pp. 350-51 herein.

71. *A fortiori* parables is an alternative label.

72. Talia Thorion-Vardi discusses a related but different kind of contrast parable in rabbinic literature. With these parables usually a person or king "of flesh and blood" or the ways of the world are contrasted with God and God's ways. That the parable is a contrast is usually explicit. See her *Das Kontrastgleichnis in der rabbinischen Literatur* (Judentum und Umwelt 16; Frankfurt am Main: Peter Lang, 1986).

73. Birger Gerhardsson divides Jesus' parables into four groups depending on how strongly they involve contrasts within the parable. Of his fifty-five parables he lists eleven with highly stylized contrasts (such as the Two Builders) and ten with the contrast clear and important but not as dominant or clear-cut as the first group. See his "Illuminating the Kingdom: Narrative Meshalim in the Synoptic Gospels," in *Jesus and the Oral Gospel Tradition* (ed. Henry Wansbrough; JSNTSup 64; Sheffield: Sheffield Academic Press, 1991), pp. 266-309, here pp. 273-74.

74. As Sider (*Interpreting the Parables,* p. 45) notes, "We can hardly make analogies about God without some sense of "how much more."

75. This definition is not wholly satisfactory in that one could have a story that was allegorical over its whole meaning and not in the various parts. As a result, the points in the story may not conform to points being illustrated. See Boucher, *The Mysterious Parable,* p. 20. She defines allegory as the extension of metaphor over a whole story. Cf. Heinrich Lausberg, *Handbook of Literary Rhetoric: A Foundation for Literary Study* (trans. Matthew T. Bliss, Annemiek Jansen, and David Orton; ed. David Orton and R. Dean Anderson; Leiden: Brill, 1998), pp. 398-99: "The allegory is to an idea what the metaphor is to a single word. . . . The relation of allegory to metaphor is quantitative; an allegory is a metaphor sustained for the length of a whole sentence (and beyond)."

76. *Interpretation Theory: Discourse and the Surplus of Meaning* (Fort Worth: Texas Christian University Press, 1976), pp. 52-56. Cf. John Dominic Crossan, *In Parables* (New York: Harper & Row, 1973), p. 11. At the same time Ricoeur does say that different modes of discourse (parables, eschatological sayings, proverbial sayings) may be translated into one another. See his "Biblical Hermeneutics," 101-2.

77. Via, *The Parables,* pp. 24-25. Cf. James R. Edwards, *The Gospel According to Mark* (Grand Rapids: Eerdmans, 2002), p. 127, who says "An allegory can be understood from the 'outside,' but parables can be understood only from within, by allowing oneself to be taken into the story and hearing who God is and what humans may become. Parables are like stained glass windows in a cathedral, dull and lifeless from the outside but brilliant and radiant from within."

78. Among those questioning that parables are untranslatable are Boucher, *The Mysterious Parable,* p. 30; Gerhardsson, "The Narrative Meshalim," pp. 355-56; Blomberg, "Interpreting the Parables of Jesus," 54; William A. Beardslee, "Listening to the Parables of Jesus: An Exploration of the Uses of Process Theology in Biblical Interpretation," in *Texts and Testaments: Critical Essays on the Bible and Early Church Fathers* (ed. W. Eugene March; San Antonio, Tex.: Trinity

University Press, 1980), pp. 201-18, here p. 214; and Klaus Berger, *Formen und Gattungen im Neuen Testament* (Tübingen: A. Francke, 2005), pp. 89-90.

79. Bultmann (*History of the Synoptic Tradition*, p. 198) argued parables and similitudes involve a transference of judgment from one sphere to another, but that allegory does not and instead seeks to disguise some situation in secret or fantastic forms to serve prophetic and other purposes. W. O. E. Oesterley (*The Gospel Parables in the Light of Their Jewish Background* [New York: Macmillan, 1936], pp. 14-15) found the difference between parable and allegory to be the difference between "to be like" and "to mean," between "to place side by side" and "to identify," between "to compare" and "to indicate," and said that a parable is explained, whereas an allegory is interpreted. H. D. A. Major, T. W. Manson, and C. J. Wright (*The Mission and Message of Jesus* [New York: Dutton, 1938], p. 327) said, ". . . the parable is meant to create trust in God and love to man by an appeal to conscience and insight, while the allegory is meant to convey information, stimulating interest by an appeal to the imagination." Linnemann (*The Parables of Jesus*, pp. 6-7) asserted that an allegory says something other than what it means, whereas a parable means what it says, and she claims that a parable speaks to opponents, whereas an allegory addresses the initiated. John R. Donahue (*The Gospel in Parable* [Philadelphia: Fortress, 1988], p. 102) suggested, "The test of whether a text is an allegory is twofold: (a) whether the details are unrealistic; and (b) whether some of these details admit of other explanations," neither of which is a valid test. Harnisch (*Die Gleichniserzählungen Jesu*, p. 64) distinguished parable and allegory by saying a parable is autonomous, does not need an outside frame of reference, and is self-evident, whereas an allegory is dependent on references to outside stories. He also said (pp. 154-55) that a parable adds a new story to an old one in a way that disturbs the old story and expresses a new one, whereas in allegory one story replaces the other through a chain of substitutions. Peter Rhea Jones (*Studying the Parables of Jesus*, p. 24) suggested that parable drives toward participation rather than information, that it creates participation and in doing so is never expendable, whereas allegory presumes participation and is expendable. Andrew Parker (*Painfully Clear: The Parables of Jesus* [Sheffield: Sheffield Academic Press, 1996], p. 37) asserted that a parable is designed to open the hearers' eyes, but an allegory puts forward a given ideological interpretation on a take-it-or-leave-it basis; i.e., allegories are extended assertions.

In my estimation none of these arguments has *any* validity. Note that R. M. Johnston (*Parabolic Interpretations Attributed to Tannaim* [Ph.D. Dissertation, Hartford Seminary Foundation, 1978], pp. 513 and 600-12) from studying over 300 rabbinic parables says the distinction is unusable. See also M. D. Goulder's comments (*Midrash and Lection in Matthew* [London: SPCK, 1974], p. 56), "I have argued elsewhere ["Characteristics of the Parables in the Several Gospels," *JTS* 19 (1968): 58-62] that few distinctions have been more ill-starred for the criticism of the Gospels than that between parable and allegory, which are often seen as two different *genres* of literature."

80. Numerous scholars could be listed here, not least of whom would be M. Boucher, C. Blomberg, D. Flusser, and D. Stern, but see the trenchant comments of Robert W. Funk ("Beyond Criticism in Quest of Literacy: The Parable of the Leaven," *Int* 25 [1971]: 149-70, here p. 154). He accuses C. H. Dodd and J. Jeremias of being trapped by Jülicher and having been thrown into anarchy and then says, "Jülicher's legacy is a trap because he was never able to escape from the allegory he so fervently rejected. . . . Parable interpretation is at an impasse. The way forward is away-from-here."

81. I find it amazing how frequently people, Jülicher included, find multiple correspondences between image and reality in a parable but then deny the form is an allegory. See Bultmann, *History of the Synoptic Tradition*, pp. 198-99; Robert H. Stein, *An Introduction to the*

Parables of Jesus (Philadelphia: Westminster, 1981), pp. 117-18; Kenneth Bailey, *Poet and Peasant: A Literary Cultural Approach to the Parables in Luke* (Grand Rapids: Eerdmans, 1976), pp. 158-59; and Via, *The Parables*, p. 164, all of whom see in the parable of the Prodigal that the elder brother represents the scribes and Pharisees, the prodigal represents the publicans and sinners, and the father is a symbol of God and then explicitly deny this is allegory.

82. Blomberg, *Interpreting the Parables*, pp. 29-69; John Dominic Crossan, *Cliffs of Fall* (New York: Seabury, 1980), esp. 96-97; "Parable, Allegory, and Paradox," *Semiology and the Parables* (ed. Daniel Patte; Pittsburgh: Pickwick, 1976), pp. 247-81, esp. pp. 271-78.

83. See Boucher, *The Mysterious Parable*, pp. 17-25; Sider, *Interpreting the Parables*, pp. 19-23; and Ford, "Towards the Restoration of Allegory: Christology, Epistemology and Narrative Structure," esp. 167-68.

84. See the well-known article by Graham Hough, "The Allegorical Circle," *The Critical Quarterly* 3 (1961): 199-209. Note David Stern's comment: "My purpose in mentioning this scholarly consensus [the disdain for allegory] is not only to dispute its exclusion of allegory from the literary form of the parable, but to suggest that the terms allegory and parable, as they have figured in past scholarship, are simply not relevant to understanding the mashal and its tradition. If the term allegory is taken in its largest possible sense, there is no question that the rabbinic mashal — not to speak of Jesus' parables — contain authentic allegorical characteristics . . ." ("Rhetoric and Midrash: The Case of the Mashal," *Prooftexts* 1 [1981]: 261-91, quoting p. 264).

85. "Illuminating the Kingdom," 272.

86. Which German scholars call *szenische Zweiheit*, usually referred to in English as "the law of stage duality."

87. Paul Ricoeur, "Listening to the Parables of Jesus," in *The Philosophy of Paul Ricoeur: An Anthology of His Work* (ed. Charles E. Reagan and David Stewart; Boston: Beacon, 1978), pp. 239-45, here p. 239.

88. Jacobus Liebenburg (*The Language of the Kingdom and Jesus: Parable, Aphorism, and Metaphor in the Sayings Material Common to the Synoptic Tradition and the Gospel of Thomas* [BZNW 102; Berlin: Walter de Gruyter, 2001], p. 355, n. 253) comments, ". . . there is no *a priori* law governing the genre 'parable' which requires that they adhere to 'realism'. . . ."

89. Flusser, *Die rabbinischen Gleichnisse und der Gleichniserzähler Jesus*, pp. 34 and 125. Ricoeur ("Biblical Hermeneutics," 32, 99, 114-18) justly points to the extravagance of the parables, but at the same time some parables do not have such elements. See also his "Listening to the Parables of Jesus," p. 244: "Like paradox, hyperbole is intended to jolt the hearer from the project of making his life something continuous." He speaks of reorientation by disorientation.

90. This claim gets old quickly. Not all parables shock and shatter worlds, and such an assumption cannot be used as a critical tool for determining authenticity. Note the comment of Harvey K. McArthur and Robert M. Johnston (*They Also Taught in Parables* [Grand Rapids: Zondervan, 1990], pp. 173-74): "The element of surprise is not inherent to parables. It is a confusion of form and content to assume surprise is of the essence of a parable. A parable is a parable whether it opens up a brand new world or whether it simply illlustrates, clarifies, or adorns a world long known."

91. Cf. Isa 40:18, which has a double question similar to Mark 4:30; the introductions of rabbinic parables frequently use questions.

92. For a good example of such theologizing with a parable see Miroslav Volf, *Exclusion and Embrace: A Theological Exploration of Identity, Otherness, and Reconciliation* (Nashville: Abingdon, 1996), pp. 156-65.

93. See esp. Crossan, *In Parables,* pp. 53-78, but I think he overplays his hand with this dynamic.

94. E.g., Jotham's fable to Abimelech at his coronation starts as a coronation in the world of trees (Judg 9:1-21); or Nathan's parable to David (2 Sam 12:1-10), just to mention two obvious cases.

95. See Birger Gerhardsson, "If We Do Not Cut the Parables Out of Their Frames," *NTS* 37 (1991): 321-35, who comments (p. 328), "The subject is lord, the mashal just a servant."

96. Cf. the comments of Ricoeur, "Biblical Heremeneutics," 100-101; and Berger, *Formen und Gattungen,* p. 110. See also Wright, *Jesus and the Victory of God,* p. 181.

97. Hans Weder focuses regularly on christological readings. See his *Die Gleichnisse Jesu als Metaphern: Traditions- und redaktionsgeschichtliche Analysen und Interpretationen* (4th ed.; Göttingen: Vandenhoeck & Ruprecht, 1978).

98. Herzog, *Parables as Subversive Speech,* pp. 7, 73, 84-97 and *passim;* Luise Schottroff, *The Parables of Jesus* (trans. Linda M. Maloney; Minneapolis: Fortress, 2005), p. 3.

99. See the discussions herein of the parables of the Good Samaritan, the Pharisee and the Toll Collector, the Seed Growing Secretly, the Sower, the Lost Sheep, and the Wicked Tenants.

100. Goulder (*Midrash and Lection in Matthew,* pp. 50 and 64). He also overstates several other distinctions between the parables in each Gospel.

101. See Jeremias, *The Parables of Jesus,* pp. 70-77, on the Wicked Tenants; or Goulder, *Midrash and Lection in Matthew,* p. 410, on the Workers in the Vineyard.

102. Luke specifically connects the kingdom only to the parables of the Sower, the Mustard Seed, the Leaven, the Wedding Feast, and the Pounds.

103. This statement is not original, but I can no longer find its source.

104. This is also the case with philosophical discussions, e.g., Epictetus, *Diatr.* 2.23.36-41; 4.1.78-80, 86-90; 4.8.36-40; *Ench.* 7.

105. In Hos 2:1-13 the subject has apparently been Gomer, but at least in vv. 8-13 it is Israel who has been serving Baal. See also *m. 'Abot* 3:17; 4:16.

106. T. W. Manson (*The Teaching of Jesus,* pp. 66-69) lists sixty-five, not counting doublets. Jeremias (*The Parables of Jesus,* pp. 247-48) lists forty-one in his index, Crossan (*In Parables,* pp. 138-39) thirty-seven, and Hultgren (*The Parables of Jesus,* pp. vii-ix) thirty-eight. Gerhardsson ("The Narrative Meshalim," 344) counts fifty-five narrative *meshalim,* but that number is reduced to forty-three when parallels are excluded.

107. Such as the parable of the Slave at Duty in Luke 17:7-10.

108. See the discussion in Bailey, *Poet and Peasant,* pp. 79-85; and the critique of Craig L. Blomberg, "Midrash, Chiasmus, and the Outline of Luke's Central Section," in *Gospel Perspectives III: Studies in Midrash and Historiography* (ed. R. T. France and David Wenham; Sheffield: JSOT, 1983), pp. 217-61.

109. The Little Children in a Field: "Mary said to Jesus: What are your disciples like? He said: They are like little children who dwell in a field which does not belong to them. When the owners of the field come, they will say, Leave our field to us! They are naked in their presence, as they leave it to them (and) give back their field to them." A saying similar to Matt 24:43/Luke 12:39 follows, somewhat as an explanation.

A Woman Carrying a Jar of Meal: "Jesus said: The kingdom of the [Father] is like a woman who was carrying a jar full of meal. While she was walking [a] long way, the handle of the jar broke (and) the meal spilled out behind her on the road. She did not know (it); she did not perceive the accident. After she came into her house, she put the jar down (and) found it empty."

A Killer's Test: "Jesus said: The kingdom of the Father is like a man who wanted to kill a powerful man. He drew the sword within his house (and) ran it through the wall, so that he might know whether his hand would be strong (enough). Then he killed the powerful (man)."

110. The Shepherds (the Lost Sheep?), the Seed, the Building, the Lamps of the Virgins, the Wage of the Workmen, the Didrachma, and the Woman. Conceivably the last two could be taken as one parable. Note the reference to parables in 7:1-10, which echoes the language of John 16:25. On the noncanonical parables see Johnston, "Greek Patristic Parables," pp. 215-29; and William D. Stroker, "Extracanonical Parables and the Historical Jesus," *Semeia* 44 (1988): 95-120, but not necessarily accepting his conclusions about the antiquity of this material.

111. For the following texts see *The Nag Hammadi Library in English* (ed. James M. Robinson; New York: Harper & Row, 1977), pp. 32-34.

The Date Palm: "Do not allow the kingdom of heaven to wither; for it is like a palm shoot whose fruit has dropped down around it. It put forth leaves, and after they had sprouted they caused the pith to dry up. So it is also with the fruit which had grown from this single root; when it had been picked (?), fruit was borne by many (?). It (the root) was certainly good, (and) if it were possible to produce the new plants now, you (sing.) would find it (?)."

The Grain of Wheat: "For the word is like a grain of wheat: when someone had sown it, he had faith in it; and when it had sprouted, he loved it because he had seen many grains in place of one. And when he had worked, he was saved because he had prepared it for food, (and) again he left (some) to sow. So also can you yourselves receive the kingdom of heaven; unless you receive this through knowledge, you will not be able to find it."

The Ear of Grain: "For the kingdom of heaven is like an ear of grain after it had sprouted in a field. And when it had ripened, it scattered its fruit and again filled the field with ears for another year. You also: hasten to reap an ear of life for yourselves that you may be filled with the kingdom!"

112. For a brief discussion of these views, see Robert H. Stein, "The Genre of the Parables," in *The Challenge of Jesus' Parables* (ed. Richard N. Longenecker; Grand Rapids: Eerdmans, 2000), pp. 30-50, here pp. 32-38.

113. *Eigentlich*, if that is the way the word should be translated. See n. 15 above and see Jülicher, *Die Gleichnisreden Jesu*, 1:49, 52, etc. On similes and parables not needing interpretation, see 1:56-57, 66-68, 76, 81, 106.

114. For understanding "language event" see Robert W. Funk, *Language, Hermeneutic, and Word of God*, pp. 20-71; Ernst Fuchs, *Studies of the Historical Jesus* (trans. Andrew Scobie; SBT 42; Naperville, Ill.: Allenson, 1964), pp. 207-28; Anthony Thiselton, "The Parables as Language-Event: Some Comments on Fuchs's Hermeneutics in the Light of Linguistic Philosophy," *SJT* 23 (1970): 437-68.

115. "The Genre of the Parables," pp. 36-37.

116. Quite a number of scholars rightly insist that parables must be interpreted. See, e.g., Scott, *Hear Then the Parable*, p. 177; Boucher, *The Mysterious Parable*, p. 17; and Gerhardsson, "The Narrative Meshalim," 356.

117. See James D. G. Dunn, "Altering the Default Setting: Re-Envisaging the Early Transmission of the Jesus Tradition," *NTS* 49 (2003): 139-75; and his *Jesus Remembered*, vol. 1 of *Christianity in the Making* (Grand Rapids: Eerdmans, 2003), esp. pp. 210-54. Dunn has sought to change the default so that justice is done to the oral character of Jesus' teaching, but in analyzing

individual texts he too frequently operates with a literary model. See also Terence C. Mournet, *Oral Tradition and Literary Dependency* (WUNT 2, 195; Tübingen: Mohr-Siebeck, 2005).

118. A point underscored especially by Linnemann (*Parables of Jesus*, pp. 33-35), even though she rejected any validity of the specific contexts of parables, pp. 43-44.

119. See Stephen I. Wright, *The Voice of Jesus: Studies in the Interpretation of Six Gospel Parables* (Cumbria, U.K.: Paternoster, 2000), pp. 31-32. Because of this, Wright sees Jesus' parables as metonymies, with each parable focusing on an aspect of the Gospel. The interaction between parable and narrative is a given, but I do not find metonymy a satisfactory description of parables.

120. Removing the parables from their specific contexts and their general context with Jesus is the foundation for the polyvalent approach of Mary Ann Tolbert. See her *Perspectives on the Parables: An Approach to Multiple Interpretations* (Philadelphia: Fortress, 1979). Her discussion of context (pp. 51-62) is revealing. She grants that the more context one has the less flexibility there is in interpretation, but she finds the Gospels' contexts often ambiguous or inappropriate. That, of course, depends on how one reads the text. For an insistence on the Gospels' contexts, see Gerhardsson, "If We Do Not Cut the Parables Out of Their Frames."

The term "polyvalent" is itself ambiguous. Some, like Tolbert, use it to refer to ways modern interpreters may "exploit" the polyvalency of parables so as to find ways ancient Scriptures address contemporary concerns. This is akin to a return to the allegorizing of the early church. See my "From Allegorizing to Allegorizing," pp. 3-29. Others, such as C. Blomberg, use the word "polyvalent" to refer to multiple perspectives *within* the story, not to finding new meanings by putting the parables in new contexts. See his "Poetic Fiction, Subversive Speech, and Proportional Analogy in the Parables," *HBT* 18 (1996): 115-32, here p. 123.

121. See my "Reading to Hear: A Hermeneutics of Hearing."

122. Linnemann argues for one point and then says numerous correspondences exist (*Parables of Jesus*, pp. 24 and 26). Sider complains (*Interpreting the Parables*, pp. 60-62) about Jeremias finding eight points in the parable of the Seed Growing Secretly, even though Jeremias suggests that he argues for only one.

123. Morton Smith argued the rich man is Satan and the steward is every human! See his *Tannaitic Parallels to the Gospels* (JBLMS 6; Philadelphia: Society of Biblical Literature, 1951), p. 140.

124. E.g., *Midrash Tanḥuma ki Tissa* 9:15 has a story about a matron and an orphan girl corresponding in reality to Moses and Joshua!

125. Analogies are not exact because metaphors often are not exact or "correct." Isa 60:16 promises that people will suck the breasts of the nations and of kings (!), and vv. 19-20 say both that the sun will no longer be the light by day and that the sun will not go down.

126. Sider, *Interpreting the Parables*, pp. 238-41.

127. *Interpreting the Parables*, p. 163. The Levite and the priest are not two different points in the parable of the Good Samaritan, and, to be fair, Blomberg does not argue that they are two separate main characters. In the Unforgiving Servant there are three main characters but more than three points, and some lesser characters in this parable have no significance at all.

128. *Life Is a Miracle: An Essay against Modern Superstition* (Washington, D.C.: Counterpoint, 2000), p. 46. This is not a new discussion. See Origen, *Commentary on Matthew* 10.11: ". . . so conceive with me also that, in the case of the similitudes in the Gospel, when the kingdom of heaven is likened unto anything, the comparison does not extend to all the features of that to which the kingdom is compared, but only to those features which are required by the argument in hand."

129. Liebenberg (*The Language of the Kingdom and Jesus,* p. 158) is very helpful on this. He points out that parables are rarely simple metaphors and often are quite elaborate metaphors and that one must come to grips both with the novel metaphors they create and the conventional metaphors evoked by them. In making this point he rejects the distinction between one point of comparison and allegorizing and notes that some parables may map only one aspect of the kingdom, while others may map quite a few aspects of the kingdom, and still others may have "kingdom" merely as a heading to indicate the story should be interpreted metaphorically without there being specific reference to the kingdom.

Often exaggerated claims are made for metaphor. Among many treatments of metaphor see Liebenburg, *The Language of the Kingdom and Jesus,* pp. 48-166; Paul Ricoeur, *The Rule of Metaphor: Multi-Disciplinary Studies of the Creation of Meaning in Language* (Toronto: University of Toronto Press, 1977); Janet Martin Soskice, *Metaphor and Religious Language* (Oxford: Clarendon Press, 1985); Mogens Stiller Kjargaard, *Metaphor and Parable: A Systematic Analysis of the Specific Structure and Cognitive Function of the Synoptic Similes and Parables Qua Metaphors* (Acta theologica Danica 20; Leiden: Brill, 1986); Peter W. Macky, *The Centrality of Metaphors to Biblical Thought* (Lewiston, N.Y.: Mellen, 1990).

130. See Ricoeur, "Biblical Hermeneutics," 97-98.

131. See pp. 313-15 herein.

132. See pp. 245 and 251 herein.

133. On the principle of verification from nonparabolic teaching see Dodd, *The Parables of the Kingdom,* p. 32; and George Eldon Ladd, *The Presence of the Future* (Grand Rapids: Eerdmans, 1974), p. 190. This principle alone renders several books on parables suspect.

134. Except for the interpretation of the parable of the Sower.

135. M. L. Scharlemann (*Proclaiming the Parables* [St. Louis: Concordia, 1963], p. 30) asserted: "Finally, we must be aware of the fact that parables cannot be used to develop theological arguments" and referred to the statement *Theologia parabolica non est theologia argumentativa.* This statement has a long history. See Richard Chenevix Trench, *Notes on the Parables of Our Lord* (9th ed.; London: Macmillan, 1864), pp. 39-46, who says that parables may not be the first sources and seats of doctrine and that they may be the outer ornamental fringe but not the main texture of proof.

This curtails the significance of parables unnecessarily. Parables may well be the impetus for *establishing* a theological idea, even if we still say that the teaching of parables must be confirmed by nonparabolic material.

136. Among many, see Jülicher, *Die Gleichnisreden Jesu,* 1:24; Jeremias, *The Parables of Jesus,* p. 11. Dormeyer (*The New Testament among the Writings of Antiquity,* pp. 165-66) traces thirty-one of the thirty-six parables he lists back to the pre-Easter Jesus. The Jesus Seminar printed twenty-one of thirty-three parables in red or pink. See Robert W. Funk, Bernard Brandon Scott, and James R. Butts, *The Parables of Jesus: Red Letter Edition* (Sonoma, Calif.: Polebridge, 1988), p. 74.

137. See p. 24 herein. E. P. Sanders (*Jesus and Judaism* [Philadelphia: Fortress, 1985], p. 320) writes, "There may have been great tellers of parables in the early Christian movement," but one is hard pressed to name one or to find evidence this was the case.

138. *Matthew 8–20: A Commentary* (trans. James E. Crouch; Minneapolis: Fortress, 2001), p. 282.

139. Wright, *Jesus and the Victory of God,* p. 87; Schottroff, *The Parables of Jesus,* pp. 99, 106-7, and 112; Dale C. Allison, *Jesus of Nazareth: Millenarian Prophet* (Minneapolis: Fortress, 1998), pp. 35-36, 45-46.

140. Lambrecht (*Once More Astonished*, p. 218) argues, "Whoever wishes to reconstruct Matthew's source must remove all Matthean elements," but that suggests an evangelist cannot convey authentic material in his own words.

141. As Scott (*Hear Then the Parable*, p. 18) suggests.

142. See Matthew Black's accusation ("The Parables as Allegory," *BJRL* 42 [1959-60]: 273-87, here p. 283) that C. H. Dodd both ran with the allegorical hare and hunted with the Jülicher hounds. J. Jeremias is frequently guilty of rejecting allegory but reinserting it in interpretation.

143. *The Tendencies of the Synoptic Tradition* (SNTSMS 9; Cambridge: Cambridge University Press, 1969).

144. See *The Parables of Jesus*, pp. 23-114. His ten principles of transformation of the parables are: (1) the translation of the parables into Greek, (2) representational changes (to communicate with Hellenists), (3) embellishment, (4) influence of OT and folk-story themes, (5) change of audience, (6) change to a hortatory purpose, (7) influence of the church's situation (with regard to the parousia or the church's mission), (8) allegorization, (9) collection and conflation of the parables, and (10) change of settings (esp. introductions and conclusions).

145. See Richard Bauckham, "For Whom Were Gospels Written?" in *The Gospels for All Christians: Rethinking the Gospel Audiences* (Grand Rapids: Eerdmans, 1998), pp. 9-48. All the essays in this volume argue this point.

146. See, for example, B. Scott's suggestion (*Hear Then the Parable*, p. 362) that the parable of the Sower teaches that in failure and everydayness lies the miracle of God's activity.

147. Notice the comment of Christopher F. Evans, "Uncomfortable Words — V," *ExpTim* 81 (1969-70): 228-31, here p. 228: "Without its concluding words a parable is, of course, ineffective. . . . A parable is a fragile thing, and is in danger of turning out to be an inefficient instrument for its purpose. For it is first conceived in the mind of the teller, the end already foreseen in the beginning." Later he adds that a parable is not yet a parable until its concluding sentence.

148. See Priscilla Patten, "The Form and Function of Parables in Select Apocalyptic Literature and Their Significance for Parables in the Gospel of Mark," *NTS* 29 (1983): 246-58. Apocalyptic parables are not revelatory by themselves, for the meaning comes with interpretation. Wright (*Jesus and the Victory of God*, p. 181) sees apocalyptic as the most immediate background of Jesus' parables, but the OT seems a better candidate for that role.

149. See Daniel Boyarin, "History Becomes Parable: A Reading of the Midrashic *Mashal*," in *Mapping of the Biblical Terrain: The Bible as Text* (ed. Vincent L. Tollers and John Maier; Lewisburg, N.Y.: Bucknell University Press, 1990), pp. 54-71. Boyarin, in discussing midrashic parables, says (p. 56), "Finally, the *mashal* as an interpretive structure is anything but indeterminate. There is indeed hardly any room for interpretation at all of the *mashal*. Its meaning is rigidly controlled by its textual form. . . . The *mashal* is a closed text — not an open one — at least insofar as any text can be closed." Jesus' parables are not identical to midrashic parables, but they are not indeterminate.

150. *Jesus Remembered*, pp. 126-32.

151. *The So-Called Historical Jesus and the Historic Biblical Christ* (trans. Carl E. Braaten; Philadelphia: Fortress, 1964).

152. See David Aune, "Oral Tradition and the Aphorisms of Jesus," in *Jesus and the Oral Gospel Tradition* (ed. Henry Wansbrough; JSNTSup 64; Sheffield: Sheffield Academic Press, 1991), 211-65, here p. 223: "While I accept the basic validity of the two-source theory (Mark and Q were used as sources by Matthew and Luke), rather than the priority of Matthew (Luke is dependent on Matthew, while Mark combined and conflated portions of both), it has become increasingly clear that different versions of both Mark (Mark^{Mt} and Mark^{Lk}) and Q (Q^{Mt} and Q^{Lk})

were used by Matthew and Luke . . . and that frequently the differences between the Matthaean and Lukan versions of the double tradition may reflect the impact of oral transmission upon the written version of Q with which each evangelist was familiar."

153. See John P. Meier, *A Marginal Jew: Rethinking the Historical Jesus* (3 vols.; New York: Doubleday, 1991-2001), 1:124-29; Hultgren, *The Parables of Jesus,* pp. 430-40; Christopher M. Tuckett, "Thomas and the Synoptics," *NovT* 30 (1988): 132-57; "Q and Thomas: Evidence of a Primitive 'Wisdom Gospel'?" *ETL* 67 (1991): 346-60; Craig L. Blomberg, "Tradition and Redaction in the Parables of the Gospel of Thomas," *The Jesus Tradition Outside the Gospels* (vol. 5 of *Gospel Perspectives;* ed. David Wenham; Sheffield: JSOT Press, 1985), pp. 177-205; Risto Uro, "'Secondary Orality' in the Gospel of Thomas?" *FFF* 9 (1993): 305-29; and my "The Gospel of Thomas: A Secondary Gospel," *SecCent* 7 (1990): 19-38. Nicholas Perrin argues that *Gos. Thom.* is dependent on Tatian's *Diatessaron.* See Perrin's *Thomas and Tatian: The Relationship between the Gospel of Thomas and the Diatessaron* (Academia Biblica 5; Atlanta: Society of Biblical Literature, 2002).

Notes to "Parables in the Ancient World"

1. Despite Joachim Jeremias's claim that Jesus' parables are something entirely new in his *The Parables of Jesus* (2d ed.; trans. S. H. Hooke; London: SCM, 1972), p. 12.

2. The dispute between the date palm and the tamarisk, reproduced in *ANET,* pp. 410-11. Several other items should be mentioned from *The Context of Scripture* (3 vols.; ed. William W. Hallo and K. Lawson Younger, Jr.; Leiden: Brill, 2003): analogies of destruction in "The First Soldier's Oath" for those who break oaths (1:165-67); a Hurro-Hittite Bilingual Wisdom Text with several parable-like stories, mostly of animals, but in each case an interpretation explicitly stating that the story is not about the animal or an object but a human (1:216-17) — these are the most obvious examples of parables from so early; a fable of the Heron and the Turtle (1:571-73); and disputation stories where two entities argue over which is greater (e.g., wheat vs. a ewe) (1:575-88).

3. *Die Gleichnisreden Jesu,* 2 vols. (Freiburg i. B.: J. C. B. Mohr, vol. 1, 1888; vol. 2, 1889), 1:94-100. See also Mary Ann Beavis, "Parable and Fable," *CBQ* 52 (1990): 473-98; George W. Coats, "Parable, Fable, and Anecdote," *Int* 35 (1981): 368-82. For a broader discussion of Hellenistic forms, see Klaus Berger, "Hellenistische Gattungen im Neuen Testament," *ANRW* 25.2 (ed. Wolfgang Haase; Berlin: Walter de Gruyter, 1984), pp. 1031-1432.

4. See the beginning of part two of the collection of Aesop's fables in *Babrius* (*Babrius and Phaedrus,* LCL, p. 139) and also pp. xxvii-xxxiv. See Ronald J. Williams, "The Fable in the Ancient Near East," in *A Stubborn Faith: Papers on Old Testament and Related Subjects Presented to Honor William Andrew Irwin* (ed. Edward C. Hobbs; Dallas: Southern University Press, 1956), pp. 3-26.

5. Joseph Jacobs, "Aesop's Fables among the Jews," *The Jewish Encyclopedia* (ed. Isidore Singer; New York: Funk & Wagnalls, 1906), 1:221-22.

6. In focusing on parables as prophetic tools I do not diminish their use and even their probable origin in wisdom literature. Prophets used the tools of wisdom thinking to shape their own message.

7. David Flusser (*Die rabbinischen Gleichnisse und der Gleichniserzähler Jesus I: Das Wesen der Gleichnisse* [Bern: Peter Lang, 1981], esp. pp. 17-19 and 146-48) even argues that one will not make much progress in understanding the parables by looking at the OT. He mentions

only the story of Nathan to David in 2 Sam 12:1-7, which he says is not a parable in the actual sense. Flusser is content to see Jesus' parables as derived from the broad sphere of rabbinic parables. Bernard Brandon Scott (*Hear Then the Parable: A Commentary on the Parables of Jesus* [Minneapolis: Fortress, 1989], pp. 7 and 63-64), although he views the Hebrew word *mashal* as a background against which to understand NT parables, argues that the parable genre is not found in the Hebrew Bible. Contrast this with someone like John Drury (*The Parables in the Gospels* [New York: Crossroad, 1985], p. 8), who says the OT is full of parables, or Claus Westermann (*The Parables of Jesus in the Light of the Old Testament* [trans. and ed. by Friedemann W. Golka and Alastair H. B. Logan; Minneapolis: Fortress, 1990]), who identifies numerous OT texts as parables. Part of the problem is, of course, definition; if like Scott we draw a narrow circle defining "parable," not many examples will be found. He defines a parable as "a *mashal* that employs a short narrative fiction to reference a symbol" (p. 35). Many *meshalim* (the plural of *mashal*) occur in the OT, but Scott does not find any short narrative fictions that reference *symbols* such as the kingdom or the Torah. But why should a parable have to reference a symbol? In fact, Westermann argues that OT parables compare a *process* or an *event* in one arena with that in another (pp. 11, 85, 152-54). If, contrary to Scott's definition, "parable" is defined as a *mashal* that employs a short narrative fiction to reference reality or one's relation to God, then the OT certainly has parables.

8. See his *Rabbinic Literature and the New Testament: What We Cannot Show, We Do Not Know* (Valley Forge, Pa.: Trinity Press International, 1994), esp. pp. 185-90.

9. This same breadth is present in Sumerian proverb collections. See Edmund I. Gordon, "Sumerian Animal Proverbs and Fables: 'Collection Five,'" *JCS* 12 (1958): 1-75, 3-4. See also his "A New Look at the Wisdom of Sumer and Akkad," *BO* 17 (1960): 122-52.

10. Francis Brown, S. R. Driver, and Charles A. Briggs, eds., *A Hebrew and English Lexicon of the Old Testament* (Oxford: Clarendon, 1962), p. 605. The editors may have been influenced by Otto Eissfeldt's *Der Maschal im Alten Testament* (Gießen: Alfred Töpelmann, 1913). See also the discussions by Bernard Brandon Scott, *Hear Then the Parable*, pp. 8-19; A. S. Herbert, "The 'Parable' (Māšāl) in the Old Testament," *SJT* 7 (1954): 180-96; John Drury, "Origins of Mark's Parables," in *Ways of Reading the Bible* (ed. Michael Wadsworth; Totowa, N.J.: Barnes & Noble, 1981), pp. 171-89, here pp. 174-77; Timothy Polk, "Paradigms, Parables, and *Měšālîm*: On Reading the *Māšāl* in Scripture," *CBQ* 45 (1983): 564-83.

11. See, for example, Ludwig Koehler and Walter Baumgartner, *The Hebrew and Aramaic Lexicon of the Old Testament* (Leiden: E. J. Brill, 1995), 2:647-48.

12. Whether the word is pointed correctly as an infinitive is debatable.

13. Cf. the similar thought in Sir 39:2-3, which uses *parabolē* twice in connection with enigmatic sayings. For other texts in the Hebrew Bible using *mashal* with the sense of "proverb" see Deut 28:37; 1 Kgs 4:32 [5:12]; 9:7; 2 Chron 7:20; Job 13:12; Prov 10:1; 25:1; 26:7, 9; Eccl 12:9; Ezek 12:22, 23; 18:2, 3.

14. See also Pss 44:14 [15] and 69:11 [12].

15. See also 23:18; 24:3, 15, 20, 21, and 23.

16. Other words used in the Septuagint to translate *mashal* include *aphanismon* ("byword" [literally, "something lost"]), *prooimion* ("preamble"), *paroimia* ("proverb"), *isos* ("equal"), and *thrēnos* ("lament").

17. "The Narrative Meshalim in the Old Testament Books and in the Synoptic Gospels," in *To Touch the Text: Biblical and Related Studies in Honor of Joseph A. Fitzmyer* (ed. Maurya P. Horgan and Paul J. Kobelski; New York: Crossroad, 1989), p. 291; or his "The Narrative Meshalim in the Synoptic Gospels: A Comparison with the Narrative Meshalim in the Old Tes-

tament," *NTS* 34 (1988): 339-63, here p. 343. His five are Judg 9:7-15; 2 Sam 12:1-4; 2 Kgs 14:9; Isa 5:1-6; Ezek 17:3-10, and the ten borderline cases are 2 Sam 14:5-7; Prov 9:1-6, 13-18; Isa 28:23-29; Ezek 15:1-8; 16:1-58; 19:2-9, 10-14; 23:1-29; and 24:3-14.

1 Kgs 4:32 [5:12] indicates that Solomon authored 3000 proverbs/parables [*mashal*]. Cf. Josephus, *Ant.* 8.44: "[Solomon] . . . composed a thousand and five books of odes and songs, and three thousand books of parables and similitudes [*parabolōn kai eikonōn*], for he spoke a parable about every kind of tree from the hyssop to the cedar, and in like manner about birds and all kinds of terrestrial creatures and those that swim and those that fly."

18. *The Teaching of Jesus* (Cambridge: Cambridge University Press, 1939), pp. 62-63. The two fables he lists are Judg 9:7-15 and 2 Kgs 14:9, and the nine parables are 2 Sam 12:1-14; 14:1-11; 1 Kgs 20:35-40; Isa 5:1-7; Ezek 17:3-10; 19:2-9, 10-14; 21:1-5; 24:3-5.

19. Westermann, *The Parables of Jesus in the Light of the Old Testament*, pp. 5-151; see p. 3.

20. Westermann, *The Parables of Jesus in the Light of the Old Testament*, pp. 2, 20-112.

21. The self-condemnation in Isaiah 5 is implied.

22. Surely one of the most powerful parables ever told, esp. with its theology of God as one who brings back the banished (2 Sam 14:14).

23. E.g., Westermann, *The Parables of Jesus in the Light of the Old Testament*, p. 81.

24. Cf. also 15:1-8, which is close to being a parable about the vine.

25. Sometimes the explanations contain a mixture of literal and metaphorical speech, as in Ezek 17:22-24.

26. This imagery appears often; other obvious examples are Psalm 23; Isa 40:11; and Mic 7:14.

27. See John Sider's listing of OT texts with parabolic forms in his *Interpreting the Parables: A Hermeneutical Guide to Their Meaning* (Grand Rapids: Zondervan, 1995), pp. 251-52.

28. See also the potter (18:1-11), the broken pot (19:1-13), and the yoke of bonds and bars (27:1–28:17).

29. Isaiah walked about naked and barefoot for three years as a sign against Egypt and Ethiopia (20:2-6). Several times Ezekiel acted out the siege and plight of the city of Jerusalem and the exiled people (4:1–5:4; 12:1-20; and 24:15-27). Ezekiel was himself a sign to the people (24:24, 27). Nehemiah stood and shook out the folds of his garment and said, "So may God shake out everyone from house and from property who does not perform this promise" (Neh 5:13).

30. In Jer 24:1-10 two baskets of figs, one good and one bad, mirror those taken captive to the land of the Chaldeans and those who stay in Judah or go to Egypt. Amos is well-known for his series of visions from God: locusts, fire, plumb-line, and summer fruit (7:1-9 and 8:1-3). Zech 1:7–6:8 is primarily a series of visions and interpretations. The dreams and interpretations in Daniel 2 and 7 depict the succession of human kingdoms and the ultimate kingdom of God.

31. Note also Hos 12:10[11] and the difference between the NIV ("I spoke to the prophets . . . and told parables through them") and the NRSV ("Through the prophets I will bring destruction"). This results from choices between two different words with the same letters (*dāmāh*), one meaning "be like" and the other meaning "cease" or "cause to cease."

32. As Neusner and others have argued repeatedly, the attributions of parables to specific rabbis cannot be accepted uncritically. An attribution to an early rabbi found in a late document does not necessarily mean that we have an early parable. See Jacob Neusner, *Rabbinic Literature and the New Testament*, esp. pp. 13-40.

33. See sayings 125 (". . . a man who chops wood in the dark when he cannot see is like a thief who breaks into a house and is caught") and 159 ("A man of fine character and a happy dis-

position is like a mighty city which is built on a hill") (*OTP* 2:502, 505). This story stems from at least the sixth century B.C. and probably from a Mesopotamian context. It is referred to in Tobit 1:21-22 and 14:10.

34. Including Aesop's fables; see *Babrius and Phaedrus* (LCL), p. 139.

35. See pp. 257-58 and 496 herein for possible influence on Jesus' parables of the Faithful and Unfaithful Servants and of the Fig Tree. Some speak confidently of Jesus' awareness of and dependence on *Ahiqar*. See F. C. Conybeare, J. Rendel Harris, and Agnes Smith Lewis, *The Story of Aḥiḳar from the Aramaic, Syriac, Arabic, Armenian, Ethiopic, Old Turkish, Greek and Slavonic Versions* (2d ed.; Cambridge: Cambridge University Press, 1913), pp. lxii-lxviii; R. H. Charles, ed., *Apocrypha and Pseudepigrapha of the Old Testament* (Oxford: Clarendon, 1913), 2:719. However, the closest parallels come from later versions of this work which are apparently from the Christian era. See *OTP* 2:480, 488.

36. It is used parallel to "riddle" and in the sense "byword"; see 4Q300, frag. 1.2.1; 4Q301 frag. 1.2; frag. 2.2; and 11Q19 59.2. 1QpHab 8.6 uses the verb form with the sense "to chant verses."

37. See, e.g., 1QH 14.22-35, 15.20-22, 16.4-36.

38. See Erling Hammershaimb, "Om lignelser og billedtaler i de gammeltestamentlige Pseudepigrafer," *SEÅ* 40 (1975): 36-65.

39. See the discussion of David Winston Suter, "*Māšāl* in the Similitudes of Enoch," *JBL* 100 (1981): 193-212, in which he understands the similitudes as cosmological and eschatological comparisons. See also Priscilla Patten, "The Form and Function of Parable in Select Apocalyptic Literature and Their Significance for Parables in the Gospel of Mark," *NTS* 29 (1983): 246-58.

40. *The Books of Enoch* (Oxford: Clarendon, 1976), p. 43.

41. See C. Burchard's comments, *OTP* 2:189.

42. Note also the analogical dreams in *Testament of Naphtali* 5-6 and *Testament of Joseph* 19:1-10.

43. For discussion of this text see Klaus Berger, "Materialen zu Form und Über-lieferungsgeschichte neutestamentlicher Gleichnissse," *NovT* 15 (1973): 1-37, here pp. 2-9.

44. Chs. 1–2 and 15–16 are usually understood to be later Christian additions. Christian influence in other sections cannot be excluded.

45. Among other analogies see also 5:46-49, 51-55; and 7:3-16. Note also the visions and their allegorical interpretations in chs. 11-13.

46. Patten, "The Form and Function of Parable in Select Apocalyptic Literature," 247.

47. *Traditions of the Rabbis From the Era of the New Testament* I: *Prayer and Agriculture* (Grand Rapids: Eerdmans, 2004), pp. 151-52.

48. Flusser, *Die rabbinischen Gleichnisse und der Gleichniserzähler Jesus*, p. 31.

49. *Str-B* 1:654 lists this as the only parable from the pre-Christian rabbinic literature.

50. Jeremias (*The Parables of Jesus*, p. 12) asserts that not a single parable has come to us from the time before Jesus. For a helpful list of rabbinic parables pertinent for Gospels study (with dates for the rabbi to whom the parable is attributed) see Craig A. Evans, "Jesus and Rabbinic Parables, Proverbs, and Prayers," in *Jesus and His Contemporaries: Comparative Studies* (ed. Craig A. Evans; Leiden: Brill, 1995), pp. 251-97, here pp. 252-57. The same information is available in his *Ancient Texts for New Testament Studies: A Guide to the Background Literature* (Peabody, Mass.: Hendrickson, 2005), pp. 418-23.

51. E.g., comparison: Plato, *Philebus* 33b; Isocrates, *Panathenaicus* 227; Philo, *Conf.* 1.99; Plutarch, *De Recta Ratione Audienda* 40E. Of more developed forms: Aristotle, *Rhet.* 2.20.4; Quintilian *Inst.* 5.11.23. Among other uses, the word can be used of an objection to an argument, of ships broadside to each other, or of the conjunction of stars. See LSJ, p. 1305.

52. On this subject see Berger, "Hellenistische Gattungen im Neuen Testament," pp. 1031-1432, esp. 1074-75 and 1110-48; Detlev Dormeyer, *The New Testament among the Writings of Antiquity* (trans. Rosemarie Kossov; Sheffield: Sheffield Academic Press, 1998), pp. 156-73; Michael Ernst, "Hellenistischen Analogien zu ntl. Gleichnissen. Eine Sammlung von Vergleichstexten sowie Thesen über die sich aus der parabolischen Redeweise ergebenden gesellschafts-politischen Konsequenzen," in *Ein Gott, Eine Offenbarung. Beiträge zur biblische Exegese, Theologie und Spiritualität.* Festschrift für Notker Füglister (ed. Friedrich V. Reiterer; Würzburg: Echter Verlag, 1991), pp. 461-80; François Vouga, "Formgeschichtliche Überlegungen zu den Gleichnissen und zu den Fabeln der Jesus-Tradition auf dem Hintergrund der hellenistischen Literaturgeschichte," in *The Four Gospels 1992: Festschrift Frans Neirynck* (ed. F. Van Segbroeck, C. M. Tuckett, G. Van Belle, and J. Verheyden; Leuven: Leuven University Press, 1992), pp. 173-87; Mary Ann Beavis, "Parable and Fable," 473-98; and Marsh H. McCall, Jr., *Ancient Rhetorical Theories of Simile and Comparison* (Cambridge, Mass.: Harvard University Press, 1969).

53. See also the accounts of Tantalus (*Odyssey* 11.582-93) and Sisyphus (*Odyssey* 11.594-600). See the treatment of Hermann Fränkel, *Die Homerischen Gleichnisse* (Göttingen: Vandenhoeck & Ruprecht, 1921).

54. See, e.g., Homer, *Odyssey*, 23.232-40; *Iliad* 9.13-16; 12.299-308; 21.361-63. See also Virgil, *Aeneid* 1.148-54.

55. Which Theon refers to as a *mythos* (a fable). See his *Progymnasmata* 2.14.

56. The application is that one must work for what one desires.

57. Among other examples from Seneca, see "On Anger" 2.23.1-2; 3.31.3; 3.39.4; 3.43.1-2; "On Mercy" 1.3.5; 1.19.2-3; 2.2.1-2; 2.7.4-5.

58. Among other examples from Plutarch's *Moralia* see 39D; 41F; 42C; 42D; 42F; 43B; 43C-D; 46 E-F; 143C; 157A-B; 168E-F; 610C; 610F; 611F; and also see *Lives: Alexander* 65.

59. Other Greco-Roman "Who from you" parables appear as well. See p. 46, n. 54.

60. For additional parabolic material, among other passages, see *Diatr.* 1.15.6-8; 1.19.4-6; 1.24.3-5; 1.24.11-16; 1.24.20; 1.25.18-20; 1.26.16-17; 1.27.15-21; 2.3.2-5; 2.4.4-7; 2.5.10-14; 2.12.17-25; 2.14.23-29; 2.15.13-20; 3.22.96-99; 3.23.30-32; 4.1.86-90; 4.3.4-8; 4.7.5; 4.7.22-24; 4.13.11-16; *Ench.* 14.

61. See Theon, *Progymnasmata* 4.6-13.

62. Lane C. McGaughy says of Babrius's fables that seventeen percent are about humans, thirty-four percent are about both animals and humans, and another fourteen percent deal at least partly with supernatural characters. See his "Pagan Hellenistic Literature: The Babrian Fables" in *Society of Biblical Literature 1977 Seminar Papers* (ed. Paul J. Achtemeier; Missoula, Mont.: Scholars, 1977), pp. 205-14, here p. 206. Beavis ("Parable and Fable," 479) adds that about thirty percent of Phaedrus's fables and sixteen percent of ancient fables preserved elsewhere (there are over 500) deal with human actions or the relations of humans and the gods.

63. *Phaedrus* 1.2 is a mild exception. *Phaedrus* 2.5 claims to be a true story. The collectors of both *Babrius* and *Phaedrus* express concern for how critics will evaluate their work, as is evidenced by the prologues and by *Phaedrus* 4.22.

64. See the prologues of all five books of *Phaedrus*.

65. Vouga's claim ("Formgeschichtliche Überlegungen zu den Gleichnissen und zu den Fabeln," pp. 183-84) that the relation of Jesus and the Evangelists is exactly like that of Aesop and Phaedrus is a gratuitous assumption and does no justice to the differences between Jesus' parables and Aesop's fables. The chronological distance of Phaedrus from Aesop — 500 years or so — hardly parallels the relation of the Evangelists and Jesus, and Phaedrus's "discipleship" has nothing to do with the discipleship of the Gospel writers.

On the relation of fables and parables see also H. J. Rackham, *The Fable as Literature* (London: Athlone, 1985), pp. xiii and 186-87.

66. Section 4 of Theon's *Progymnasmata* is devoted to a discussion of fables, including the recognition of various Greek words to designate them *(mythoi, logoi,* and *ainoi).* See *Progymnasmata: Greek Textbooks of Prose Composition and Rhetoric* (trans. George A. Kennedy; Atlanta: Society of Biblical Literature, 2003), pp. 23-28. See also Quintilian, *Inst.* 1.9.2-6.

67. See *The Chreia and Ancient Rhetoric: Classroom Exercises* (trans. and ed. Ronald F. Hock and Edward N. O'Neil; Atlanta: Society of Biblical Literature, 2002), pp. 83-84. Cf. *Rhetorica ad Alexandrum* 1422a.28-36.

68. See Aristotle, *Rhet.* 3.19.5; *Rhet. Her.* 4.43.56–4.44.58; 4.45.59; and the discussion by Hock and O'Neil, *The Chreia and Ancient Rhetoric,* pp. 84-90.

69. John of Sardis, a ninth-century commentator on Aphthonius's *Progymnasmata,* distinguished *parabolē* from *paradeigma* by saying that the former is made up of unspecified persons and the latter of specific persons (and events). See Hock and O'Neil, *The Chreia and Ancient Rhetoric,* p. 109; and also Tryphon (first century B.C.), *Peri Tropōn* 200.31–201.2. Of note is that the parable of the Rich Man and Lazarus is the only parable of Jesus to name specific people (Lazarus and Abraham).

70. See also Xenophon, *Memorabilia* 1.2.9, where the same example is used.

71. *Rhet.* 2.20.1-8. He mentions two examples of fables: the horse and the stag, told by Phalaris to warn against his own dictatorship, and the fox and the hedgehog, told by Aesop to defend a demagogue on trial. The distinction between comparisons and fables is that the former are realistic and the latter are improbable and therefore less effective. Specific examples seem to be preferred to general analogies by Libanius (A.D. 314-93), *Progymnasmata* 3:29: "But why is it necessary for us to spend time on these analogies when we have useful examples which attest more clearly Isocrates' saying?" See Hock and O'Neil, *The Chreia and Ancient Rhetoric,* pp. 180-81.

72. See *Rhet. Her.* 4.45.59–4.48-61. The four aims are to embellish, prove, clarify, or vivify; the corresponding forms of presentation are contrast, negation, detailed parallel, and abridged comparison. Examples of these include contrasting a runner in a relay to a new general taking over from a previous (the runner handing over the baton is exhausted and needs to be relieved, whereas the new general is inexperienced and therefore inferior); the argument that as an untrained horse, even if well-built, is not fit for service, so an untrained person, no matter how well endowed, cannot attain to virtue; and a detailed parallel noting that as a player on a lyre who, though magnificent in clothing and appearance, cannot sing and is rude is scorned and derided, so a person of high station and opulent resources, if he lacks virtue, will be scorned and cast from association with good people. See also 4.44.57, which compares the contempt deserved by one who in a voyage prefers his own to his vessel's security to the contempt of one seeking his own safety instead of the society's; and 4.48.61, which compares swallows fleeing at the appearance of frost to false friends who flee in the "winter of our fortune."

73. *Rhet. Her.* 4.47.60; 4.48.61.

74. This noun does not occur in the NT but the verb *paradeigmatizō* appears in Heb 6:6 and as a variant in Matt 1:19.

75. *Inst.* 5.11.6, 9, 23. He points out that Cicero, on whom he depends significantly, translates *parabolē* as *collatio,* and he includes an example from Cicero's writings: sailors coming in from sea warning others about specific dangers are like Cicero's attitude in warning another man. See Cicero, *Pro Murena* 2.4.

76. Some have thought he depreciates parables with his comments, but he is explicit in his reference to *fables*.

77. For additional parable-like examples see Plato, *Republic* 488A-489A, an extended comparison (called an *eikōn*) of philosophers and cities to sailors and ships; 514A-520A (the parable of the cave, called an *eikōn* at 517B). *Phaedrus* 276a-277a uses seeds and planting to discuss writing and learning (and disparages the written word). Cicero, *de Finibus* 4.27.75-76 refutes the analogy that all the strings of a lyre being out of tune shows that all sins are equal (also listing other false analogies). Dio Chrysostom, *De Avaritia* (*Or.* 17) 3-4, compares people with ophthalmia rubbing their eyes to the majority who know something is not advantageous but still do it. Xenophon, *Memorabilia* 2.1.19-33 (cf. Philo *Sacr.* 19-34) relates a fable of Heracles at a crossroads where two women (virtue and vice) try to persuade him about which road to take. In *Memorabilia* 2.7.12-14, when women complain that Aristarchus is the only one in the household who eats the bread of idleness, Socrates relates the story of the sheep dog against whom the sheep complain that the dog gives nothing to the master, the dog replying that he keeps the sheep from being stolen. Xenophon, *Oeconomicus* 8.10-20 argues for the order of a household from the careful order of a ship. In *Oeconomicus* 10.2-8 Ischomachus convinces his wife to abandon makeup by asking if he would appear more worthy of her love by exaggerating the account of his belongings or if he were smeared with red. Hesiod, *Works and Days* 200-214 relates the fable of a hawk who has captured a nightingale and can do as he wishes with her, but Hesiod urges his brother to abandon violence.

78. In *Vis.* 5.5-6 Hermas is commanded to write "the commands and parables," apparently a summary description of all that had been revealed to him.

79. *Mand.* 10.1.3-4 also uses *parabolai* of items not understood.

80. *Mand.* 10.1.3; *Sim.* 5.3.1; 5.4.2-3; *Barnabas* 17:2.

81. E.g., "Whoever puts his hand to the plow and looks backwards, is his furrow well set?" The questions are a rebuke of Philip for being unmerciful. For discussion of this text see Berger, "Materialen zu Form und Überlieferungsgeschichte neutestamentlicher Gleichnisse," 25-30.

82. On this subject see Asher Feldman, *The Parables and Similes of the Rabbis* (Cambridge: Cambridge University Press, 1904); Paul Fiebig, *Altjüdische Gleichnisse und die Gleichnisse Jesu* (Tübingen: Mohr-Siebeck, 1904); *Die Gleichnisreden Jesus in Lichte der rabbinischen Gleichnisse des neutestamentlichen Zeitalters* (Tübingen: Mohr-Siebeck, 1912); Ignaz Ziegler, *Die Königsgleichnisse des Midrasch beleuchtet durch die romische Kaiserzeit* (Breslau: Schottlaender, 1903); Robert M. Johnston, "Parabolic Interpretations Attributed to Tannaim" (Ph.D. Dissertation, Hartford Seminary Foundation, 1978); Flusser, *Die rabbinischen Gleichnisse und der Gleichniserzähler Jesus;* Clemens Thoma and S. Lauer, *Die Gleichnisse der Rabbinen* (4 vols.; Bern: Peter Lang, 1986-); Peter Dschulnigg, *Rabbinische Gleichnisse und das Neue Testament. Die Gleichnisse der PesK im Vergleich mit den Gleichnissen Jesu und dem Neuen Testament* (Bern: Peter Lang, 1988); Harvey K. McArthur and Robert M. Johnston, *They Also Taught in Parables* (Grand Rapids: Zondervan, 1990); David Stern, *Parables in Midrash: Narrative and Exegesis in Rabbinic Literature* (Cambridge, Mass.: Harvard University Press, 1991); Philip L. Culbertson, *A Word Fitly Spoken: Context, Transmission, and Adoption of the Parables of Jesus* (Albany: SUNY, 1995); Jacob Neusner, *Rabbinic Narrative: A Documentary Perspective* (4 vols.; The Brill Reference Library of Judaism; Leiden: Brill, 2003); Brad H. Young, *Jesus and His Jewish Parables: Rediscovering the Roots of Jesus' Teaching* (New York: Paulist, 1989); *The Parables: Jewish Tradition and Christian Interpretation* (Peabody, Mass.: Hendrickson, 1998).

83. Such as "to what is the matter like?" "to what may this be compared?" "this may be

likened to," and "a certain man." See Johnston, "Parabolic Interpretations Attributed to Tannaim," pp. 161-64; or Stern, *Parables in Midrash,* pp. 21-22.

84. Such as "thus" or "so." See Johnston, "Parabolic Interpretations Attributed to Tannaim," pp. 161-64; or Stern, *Parables in Midrash,* p. 8.

85. At the same time the dependence of Jesus' parables on the OT is sometimes undervalued. They are not exegetical tools like the rabbinic parables, *except* for the parable of the Good Samaritan, which at least in its present context explains Lev 19:18, and they do not quote OT texts, *except* for the parable of the Wicked Tenants, which alludes clearly to Isa 5:1-2 and quotes Ps 118:22-23. The OT is important for other parables of Jesus as well. The Pharisee and the Toll Collector may depend on Deut 26:1-15; the Good Samaritan may allude to 2 Chron 28:8-15; the Lost Sheep may allude to Ezekiel 34; the Mustard Seed may depend on Ezek 17:23; and the Sower seems framed on Isa 6:9-13.

86. Johnston, "Parabolic Interpretations Attributed to Tannaim," pp. 633-35.

87. Flusser, *Die rabbinischen Gleichnisse und der Gleichniserzähler Jesus,* p. 18; see also *Str-B* 1:654, where the same point is made about the Palestinian origin of most parables. See also Shmuel Safrai, "Spoken and Literary Languages in the Time of Jesus," in *Jesus' Last Week: Jerusalem Studies in the Synoptic Gospels* (ed. R. Steven Notley, Marc Turnage, and Brian Becker; Leiden: Brill, 2006), 1:225-44, here p. 238.

88. Flusser, *Die rabbinischen Gleichnisse und der Gleichniserzähler Jesus,* p. 18. See also Randall Buth and Brian Kvasnica, "Temple Authorities and Tithe Evasion: The Linguistic Background and Impact of the Parable of *the Vineyard, the Tenants and the Son,*" in *Jesus' Last Week: Jerusalem Studies in the Synoptic Gospels* (ed. R. Steven Notley, Marc Turnage, and Brian Becker (Leiden: Brill, 2006), 1:53-80, here pp. 57-58.

89. *Pesiqta de Rab Kahana* 9.5; 27.6; 24.14.

90. Clemens Thoma and Simon Lauer, *Die Gleichnisse der Rabbinen,* pp. 56-57. The renaissance of Hebrew resulted, in their opinion, from the confrontation with the world. See also *Lev. Rab.* 34:3, which gives two analogies attributed to Hillel the Elder, one in Hebrew and the other in Aramaic. Cf. Johnston, *Parabolic Interpretations Attributed to Tannaim,* p. 144, who indicates that later Amoraim used Hebrew more consistently than earlier ones.

91. In private correspondence Randall Buth expressed doubts about Thoma and Lauer's explanation and suggested that the habit of introducing parables with the word *mashal* might have triggered the use of Hebrew. If this procedure became fixed, Hebrew would be used for parables even where *mashal* was not used as an introduction. This is an important topic begging for further research, but it is beyond my expertise.

92. Joseph Fitzmyer, "The Languages of Palestine in the First Century A.D.," *CBQ* 32 (1970): 501-31; and see the most recent discussion by Safrai ("Spoken and Literary Languages in the Time of Jesus"), which argues that Hebrew was the dominant language of all of Palestine, including Galilee.

93. One place where dependence of a rabbi on Jesus' teaching no matter how encountered is *b. 'Arakin* 16b, which reports R. Tarphon (ca. A.D. 120) as saying, "I wonder whether there is any one in this generation who accepts reproof, for if one says to him: Remove the mote from between your eyes, he would answer: Remove the beam from between your eyes!"

94. As examples see *m. Berakot* 1.1; *m. Šabbat* 16.8; *m. Sukkah* 2.8; *m. Ta'anit* 3.9-10; and see Jacob Neusner, *Rabbinic Narrative: A Documentary Perspective* 4:7-107, for a full discussion and examples from several rabbinic documents, mostly the Mishnah and Tosefta. For more extended examples, see *Lev. Rab.* 6:3 and *y. Šebu'ot* 6.5.

95. *Rabbinic Narrative: A Documentary Perspective,* 4:109-14 and 220-25.

96. *Rabbinic Narrative: A Documentary Perspective*, 4:109-10. This is paralleled in the Greco-Roman context by the distinction some made between *paradeigma* and *parabolē*.

97. *Rabbinic Narrative: A Documentary Perspective*, 4:107.

98. *Rabbinic Narrative: A Documentary Perspective*, 4:221, 185.

99. "They propounded a parable: To what can it be compared? — to a slave who came to fill the cup for his master and he poured the pitcher over his [the slave's] face."

100. "The Sages spoke in a parable about woman: [There are in her] a chamber, an antechamber, and an upper-room: blood in the chamber is unclean; if it is found in the antechamber, its condition of doubt is deemed unclean, since it is presumed to be from the fountain."

101. "The Sages spoke in a parable about woman: [She is like] an unripe fig, or a ripening fig, or a fully ripe fig; 'an unripe fig' — while she is yet a child; and a 'ripening fig' — these are the days of her girlhood . . . and 'a fully ripe fig' — after she is past her girlhood. . . ."

102. Cf. Neusner, *Rabbinic Narrative: A Documentary Perspective*, 4:116: "I do not know what kind of writing is claimed to have ceased." Is the reference to narrative parables, as is often assumed, or is it to more simple analogies?

103. Neusner, *Rabbinic Narrative: A Documentary Perspective*, 4:220.

104. Johnston, *Parabolic Interpretations Attributed to Tannaim*, pp. 164-65; or McArthur and Johnston, *They Also Taught in Parables*, p. 99.

Notes to "Grace and Responsibility"

1. *Die Gleichnisreden Jesu* (Freiburg i. B.: Akademische Verlagsbuchhandlung von J. C. B. Mohr, vol. 1, 1888; vol. 2, 1889), 2:305.

2. See the comment of Peter Rhea Jones, *Studying the Parables of Jesus* (Macon, Ga.: Smyth & Helwys, 1999), p. 282.

3. See above, pp. 11-13.

4. John Dominic Crossan, *In Parables: The Challenge of the Historical Jesus* (New York: Harper & Row, 1973), p. 106.

5. The authenticity of this parable is not usually questioned. One of the few to do so is R. Gundry, who thinks Matthew composed the parable based on the similar parable of the Two Debtors in Luke 7:41-47. See his *Matthew: A Commentary on His Literary and Theological Art* (Grand Rapids: Eerdmans, 1982), p. 371. I find nothing to commend the suggestion. The Jesus Seminar printed the parable as pink (meaning Jesus probably said something like this), except for v. 35 which is black (he did not say it). See Robert W. Funk, Bernard Brandon Scott, and James R. Butts, *The Parables of Jesus: Red Letter Edition* (Sonoma, Calif.: Polebridge, 1988), p. 49; see also Jones, *Studying the Parables of Jesus*, pp. 267-68.

6. For a list of redactional features in this parable see Ulrich Luz, *Matthew 8–20: A Commentary* (trans. James E. Crouch; Minneapolis: Fortress, 2001), pp. 468-69.

7. Luz, *Matthew 8–20*, p. 469; Arland J. Hultgren, *The Parables of Jesus: A Commentary* (Grand Rapids: Eerdmans, 2000), p. 29.

8. Which is striking given that the word does not occur in the NT outside the Synoptics and in the LXX only at 2 Macc 6:8, but there with the meaning of eating the internal organs of a sacrifice.

9. See my "The Gospel of Jesus," in *The Written Gospel* (ed. Markus Bockmuehl and

Donald A. Hagner; Cambridge: Cambridge University Press, 2005), pp. 31-44. The other three are celebration, Israel, and the kingdom.

10. For information on slaves in the ancient world, see James A. Harrill, *Slaves in the New Testament* (Minneapolis: Fortress, 2006); Jennifer A. Glancy, *Slavery in Early Christianity* (Oxford: Oxford University Press, 2002), esp. pp. 102-29, the latter emphasizing how central the imagery of slavery and the brutality directed at slaves are, but showing less interest in the theological reasons Jesus used the imagery.

11. Eta Linnemann, *Parables of Jesus* (trans. John Sturdy; London: SPCK, 1966), p. 109.

12. E.g., Josephus, *Ant.* 15.289-90 (including torture of women); 16.232.

13. *ABD*, 6:907-8 (i.e., about 225 tons).

14. Jones (*Studying the Parables of Jesus*, pp. 270-71) estimates that one talent would be the wages of about 24 years for an average worker, but this calculation does not include weekends. Hultgren (*The Parables of Jesus*, p. 23) raises the estimate to 200,000 years, and Craig S. Keener (*A Commentary on the Gospel of Matthew* [Grand Rapids: Eerdmans, 1999], p. 459) to 250,000 years. Joachim Jeremias (*The Parables of Jesus* [2d ed., trans. S. H. Hooke; New York: Charles Scribner's Sons, 1963], p. 210) indicates that one talent was equal to 10,000 denarii, which he concludes from a comparison of Josephus, *Ant.* 17.323 and 17.190. This would make the servant's debt 100,000,000 denarii. Ten thousand was the highest number *used for calculating,* not the highest number known. Tob 5:15 also reports a wage of one drachma a day. A drachma and a denarius were apparently equivalent.

15. See Joachim Jeremias, *Jerusalem in the Time of Jesus* (Philadelphia: Fortress, 1969), pp. 346-47.

16. See Stephen L. Wailes, *Medieval Allegories of Jesus' Parables* (Berkeley, Calif.: University of California Press, 1987), pp. 132-37.

17. Bernard Brandon Scott, *Hear Then the Parable: A Commentary on the Parables of Jesus* (Minneapolis: Fortress, 1989), pp. 267-80.

18. William Herzog, *Parables as Subversive Speech: Jesus as Pedagogue of the Oppressed* (Louisville: Westminster/John Knox, 1994), pp. 131-49; among others see Warren Carter, "Resisting and Imitating the Empire: Imperial Paradigms in Two Matthean Parables," *Int* 56 (2002): 260-72; Sharon H. Ringe, "Solidarity and Contextuality: Readings of Matthew 18:21-35," in *Reading from This Place* (ed. Fernando F. Segovia and Mary Ann Tolbert; Minneapolis: Fortress, 1995), 1:199-212; Luise Schottroff, *The Parables of Jesus* (trans. Linda M. Maloney; Minneapolis: Fortress, 2006), pp. 196-203.

19. John R. Donahue, *The Gospel in Parable: Metaphor, Narrative, and Theology in the Synoptic Gospels* (Philadelphia: Fortress, 1988), p. 73.

20. Contra Linnemann, *Parables of Jesus,* p. 178.

21. E.g., Jeremias, *The Parables of Jesus,* p. 97.

22. W. D. Davies and Dale C. Allison, *A Critical and Exegetical Commentary on the Gospel According to Saint Matthew* (3 vols.; ICC; Edinburgh: T. & T. Clark, 1988-97), 2:791-94.

23. See Davies and Allison, *Matthew,* 2:792: "Is not the effect of the juxtaposition to inculcate an attitude of forgiveness in the midst of the necessary but unpleasant proceedings just described?"

24. Other passages using the phrase where there is no direct causal connection to what precedes are 6:25; 12:31; 13:13, 52; 23:34; and 24:44. (The remaining occurrences are 12:27; 14:2; and 21:43.) As a translation of *dia touto* Davies and Allison (*Matthew,* 2:796) suggest "So then," and John Nolland (*The Gospel of Matthew: A Commentary on the Greek Text* [Grand Rapids: Eerdmans, 2005], p. 255) suggests "In this connection."

25. E.g., Martinus DeBoer, "Ten Thousand Talents? Matthew's Interpretation and Redaction of the Parable of the Unforgiving Servant (Matt 18:23-35)," *CBQ* 50 (1988): 214-32. On the other hand, the Jesus Seminar viewed such exaggeration as typical of Jesus' stories. See Funk, Scott, and Butts, *The Parables of Jesus: Red Letter Edition*, p. 49.

26. See *Ant.* 14.78 and also 14.39 (someone escaping punishment by paying 1000 talents), 14.72, and 14.105 (which report 2000 talents in the temple treasury). *Ant.* 12.175-76 reports a tax farmer offering to collect 16,000 talents, and 12.203, 208 report 1000 talents being given to a youth. 17.323 reports that Caesar gave 1500 talents to the children of Herod. 1 Chron 29:4-9 reports that David provided 3000 talents of gold and 7000 talents of silver for overlaying the temple. The Copper Scroll from Qumran (3Q15 1.8) indicates that 900 talents are hidden in a cistern. According to 2 Macc 5:21 Antiochus carried off 1800 talents from the temple, and in 8:10 Nicanor raises 2000 talents due to Rome. In *4 Maccabees* 4:17 Jason promises to pay Antiochus 3660 talents annually. *Sifre Deut.* 355 tells of a man buying 10,000 talents worth of oil and then 18,000 talents more. In Plutarch, *Mor.* 180B, Darius offers Alexander *myria talanta*, the same expression as in Matthew. Davies and Allison (*Matthew*, 2:790, n. 48) list other similarly high numbers, but unexpectedly attribute the amount to Matthew.

27. As mentioned in the previous note, a tax farmer offered to collect 16,000 talents (Josephus, *Ant.* 12.175-76). See the discussion by J. Duncan M. Derrett, "The Parable of the Unmerciful Servant," in *Law in the New Testament* (London: Dartman, Longman & Todd, 1970), pp. 32-47; S. R. Llewelyn, "Tax Collection and the τελῶναι of the New Testament," *NewDocs* 8:47-76; 9:39-44, esp. 8:54-55 and 74, which indicate that the tax farmer was subject to state control and could not seize property or proceed directly against a taxpayer.

28. See 1 Sam 29:3 (David as a "slave" of Saul); 2 Kgs 5:6 (Naaman as a "slave" of the king of Syria); Josephus, *Ant.* 16.296 (Sylleus, governor of Arabia, described as a wicked "slave"). See also *TDNT*, 2:266-67.

29. Among those who insist that the man was a slave is Jennifer A. Glancy, "Slaves and Slavery in the Matthean Parables," *JBL* 119 (2000): 67-90, here pp. 86-87.

30. As Derrett argued, "The Parable of the Unmerciful Servant," pp. 39-40.

31. Against Herzog, *Parables as Subversive Speech*, p. 142, who views the threat to sell the man and his family as seeking to put the bureaucrat in his place and the plea for patience as re-establishment of allegiance and an indication that some of the debt can be paid.

32. E.g., *m. 'Abot* 3.17; *t. Qiddušin* 1.14. See *TDNT* 5:561-65 and also pp. 69 and 79 herein.

33. Esp. Scott, *Hear Then the Parable*, p. 271; but also others such as Keener, *A Commentary on the Gospel of Matthew*, p. 457; Luz, *Matthew 8–20*, p. 472.

34. Scott, *Hear Then the Parable*, 267-80. Scott's approach is followed by Daniel Patte for one reading of the parable, the point of which is supposedly what the kingdom is not. It is not the refusal to forgive, for demanding punishment upon the wicked turns God into a cruel God comparable to a Gentile king. He argues further in light of 18:15-20 that one of the fellow servants should have gone privately to the first servant to confront him with his fault. Surely, however, if the story developed along these lines, everyone would have blamed Matthew for manipulating the text. See Patte, "Bringing Out of the Gospel-Treasure What Is New and What Is Old: Two Parables in Matthew 18–23," *Quarterly Review* 10 (1990): 79-108.

35. Cf. Herzog, *Parables as Subversive Speech*, p. 138. See also W. O. E. Oesterley, *The Gospel Parables in Light of Their Jewish Background* (London: SPCK, 1936), pp. 95-97.

36. See LXX 1 Kgs 20:41 (David's obeisance to Jonathan); 24:9 (David to Saul); 25:23 (Abigail to David); 28:14 (Saul to Samuel); 2 Kgs 14:33 (Absalom to David); 4 Kgs 2:15 (prophets to Elisha). See *LSJ*, p. 1518.

37. Cf. 1 Macc 1:29-32, which relates a tax collector plundering Jerusalem, burning the city, and taking captive women and children. Confiscation of women, children, and goods was routine business for victors. See 1 Macc 5:13 in reference to Gentiles, 5:23 on the recovery of Jewish captives, and 5:28, 35, 51: the Jewish victors kill all the males and seize the spoils in various towns. In 1 Macc 10:43 the offer is made to forgive the debt of those who have sought refuge in the temple and to restore their property, and in 2 Macc 5:24 Antiochus orders women and boys sold as slaves. See also Adolf Deissmann, *Light from the Ancient East* (trans. Lionel R. M. Strachan; Grand Rapids: Baker, 1965 repr. of the 4th ed.), p. 270. Philo (*Spec. Leg.* 3.159-63) tells of a collector of taxes in his own district who, when debtors defaulted and fled, subjected their women, children, parents, and other relatives to torture to find where the fugitives had fled or to get them to pay the debt. Josephus, *J. W.* 1.97 reports that Alexander Jannaeus crucified 800 captives and butchered their wives and children before their eyes. *J. W.* 7.415-19 describes torture of Jews and of their children to force them to acknowledge Caesar. *Basanos* and related words for torture were used for checking calculations and the testing of metal coins. It was apparently adapted to the testing of people in the attempt to get information from them about resources. A fourth-century Christian letter tells of a man's children and clothing being sold to pay a debt (*Select Papyri II*, LCL, pp. 378-81). See *TDNT* 1:561-62.

38. See 1 Macc 2:46; 3:5, 8; 10:85. Of course, Jews were often the victims of torture too, as the famous accounts of Eleazar and the mother and her seven sons attests; see 2 Macc 6:10–7:42; *4 Maccabees* 5:3–18:24.

39. A king appears elsewhere in Jesus' parables only at Matt 22:1-14; 25:31-46; Luke 14:31-32; and by implication in Luke 19:11-27. See also Alfons Weiser, *Die Knechtsgleichnisse der synoptischen Evangelien* (SANT 29; Munich: Kösel, 1971), p. 75.

40. E.g., Exod 15:18; 1 Sam 8:7; 12:12; Pss 93:1-4; 96:10; 103:19; Isa 6:1, 5; 24:23; Obad 21; Jdt 9:12; Tob 13:6; *1 En.* 25.3, 5; 91.13; Philo, *Opif.* 1.88; *Cher.* 1.29, 99; *Plant.* 1.51, etc.

41. See the long list of such parables provided by Keener, *A Commentary on the Gospel of Matthew*, p. 457, n. 34; and see the treatment of king parables by David Stern, *Parables in Midrash: Narrative and Exegesis in Rabbinic Literature* (Cambridge, Mass.: Harvard University Press, 1991), pp. 19-34 (including examples of God punishing) and 93-97. Such parables, even though modeled on the Roman royal court, reflect a Jewish defense against imperial Rome. See Ignaz Ziegler, *Die Königsgleichnisse des Midrash beleuchtet durch die römische Kaiserzeit* (Breslau: Schlesische Verlags-Anstalt, 1903). Note too that *b. Sanhedrin* 91a-b has a parable of a king but later in the parable he is called the owner of the orchard, the same kind of shift as in Matthew's parable.

42. Wolfgang Harnisch (*Die Gleichniserzählungen Jesu. Eine hermeneutische Einführung* [3d ed.; Göttingen: Vandenhoeck & Ruprecht, 1995], pp. 259-62) limits the parable to vv. 23b-33. See also Ernst Fuchs, *Studies of the Historical Jesus* (trans. Andrew Scobie; SBT; Naperville, Ill.: Allenson, 1964), p. 153, who thinks vv. 32-34 overstep the limits of the image. Hans Weder (*Die Gleichnisse Jesu als Metapher* [Göttingen: Vandenhoeck & Ruprecht, 1990], pp. 211-18) suggests that the original parable consisted only of vv. 23-30 and that v. 35 returns to the question of v. 21. Neither argument has validity. Weder fears unnecessarily that the latter part of the parable relativizes the focus on the mercy of God, which must come first. He admits, however (p. 215, n. 28), that no parallels exist for the kind of abrupt conclusion resulting from his suggestion. See also Jan Lambrecht, *Out of the Treasure: The Parables in the Gospel of Matthew* (LTPM 10; Louvain: Peeters, 1991), p. 62, who wrongly argues that the first and second stages of the parable carry the main point. Clearly the main character is the unforgiving servant, the only character in all three scenes. Lambrecht's suggestion hardly does justice to the rule of end stress.

43. See above, pp. 61-72. Crossan (*In Parables,* p. 107) even says that apart from v. 35 the dramatic unity of the story is flawless.

44. Marius Reiser, *Jesus and Judgment: The Eschatological Proclamation in Its Jewish Context* (trans. Linda M. Maloney; Minneapolis: Fortress, 1997), p. 278; see also Weiser, *Die Knechtsgleichnisse der synoptischen Evangelien,* pp. 90-93.

45. As Ulrich Luz notes, *Matthew 8–20,* p. 470.

46. See the history of interpretation U. Luz provides (*Matthew 8–20,* pp. 476-77). He points out that John Calvin and Martin Luther both viewed loss of forgiveness as a possibility.

47. Schottroff, *The Parables of Jesus,* pp. 196-203.

48. See above, p. 64, for the parable found in *Midr. Tanḥuma Emor* 8.30.

49. She says that God does not come with military power to destroy those unable to pay (as does the king in the parable), as if all parts of the parable should mirror reality.

50. Herzog, *Parables of Subversive Speech,* pp. 146-47. He suggests that the servant has in some way violated his master's sense of honor.

51. This is what Schottroff argues against, but what she allows for the rabbinic parable she does not allow for Jesus' parable, i.e., that not everything in the story depicts theological realities. See her *The Parables of Jesus,* pp. 87, 98, 200.

52. Barbara E. Reid, "Violent Endings in Matthew's Parables and Christian Nonviolence," *CBQ* 66 (2004): 237-55, here p. 254.

53. See Wendell Berry's comment to this effect, p. 28 above.

54. Douglas E. Oakman argues such parables would have sounded subversive to heavily-taxed Palestinians, but this parable is not offered as an attack on the taxation system. See his *Jesus and the Economic Questions of His Day* (Lewiston, N.Y.: Mellen, 1986), p. 169. Birger Gerhardsson ("If We Do Not Cut the Parables Out of Their Frames," *NTS* 37 [1991]: 321-35, here p. 334) argues that all the authority figures in Jesus' parables are viewed as fully justified in their actions.

55. If Otto Betz is correct in saying Psalm 103 stands behind the parable — note the focus on compassion, forgiveness, and God's kingdom in the psalm, then any doubt that the king points to God is removed. See his "Jesu Lieblingspsalm. Die Bedeutung von Psalm 103 für das Werk Jesu," *TBei* 15 (1984): 253-69, here pp. 259-61.

56. Among others see James A. Sanders, "Sins, Debts, and Jubilee Release," in *Luke and Scripture: The Function of Sacred Tradition in Luke-Acts* (ed. Craig A. Evans and James A. Sanders; Minneapolis: Fortress, 1993), pp. 84-92. Whether the Jubilee was ever observed is debated, but it is discussed in ancient sources. At least the Jubilee was an ideal and of significant metaphorical value.

57. D. A. Carson, "The ΟΜΟΙΟΣ Word-Group as Introduction to Some Matthean Parables," *NTS* 31 (1985): 277-82, here p. 279.

58. See Linnemann, *Parables of Jesus,* p. 111.

59. See Patte, "Bringing Out of the Gospel-Treasure What Is New and What Is Old," 83; Ernst Fuchs, "The Parable of the Unmerciful Servant (Matt. 18,23-35)," in *Studia Evangelica* (ed. Kurt Aland; Berlin: Akademie-Verlag, 1959), pp. 487-94, here pp. 487-89.

60. E.g., see the covenant language of Leviticus 19, Jesus' teaching in Matt 5:48/Luke 6:36, and 1 Cor 11:1; Eph 5:1.

61. The holiness code being that part of the law (drawn especially from Leviticus 17–20) which emphasized not only the contamination of sin and uncleanness, but also separation from the sinner. See Marcus J. Borg, *Conflict, Holiness, and Politics in the Teachings of Jesus* (Studies in

the Bible and Early Christianity 5; New York: Mellen, 1984), pp. 123-34. See also my "Matthew and the Law," in *SBL Seminar Papers, 1988* (ed. David J. Lull; Atlanta: Scholars, 1988), pp. 536-54.

62. In the OT only Gen 50:17; Exod 10:17; 1 Sam 25:28; and Prov 17:9 focus on this theme.

63. On the subject of violence see Warren Carter, "Construction of Violence and Identities in Matthew's Gospel," in *Violence in the New Testament* (ed. Shelly Matthews and E. Leigh Gibson; London: T. & T. Clark, 2005), pp. 81-108. Carter argues that violence is a theological construct for Matthew, present in texts where the kingdom is asserted. Violence is reserved for God's future activity, not disciples in the present. It is a way of assuring the oppressed of God's future vindication.

64. Although a few Jewish texts speak of God torturing, e.g., Wis 11:9; 12:23; 2 Macc 7:17; *T. Ab.* 12.18 (above, p. 63).

65. See above, p. 30.

66. See Gerhardsson, "If We Do Not Cut the Parables Out of Their Frames," 329. See also his "The Narrative Meshalim in the Synoptic Gospels," *NTS* 34 (1988): 339-63, esp. 354. Gerhardsson argues that Jesus' parables were not intrinsically kerygmatic; rather, they are for illumination. Note that Hultgren (*The Parables of Jesus*, p. 20) lists only five parables as "predominantly theological," but instead of including the parable of the Two Debtors, he places the parable of the Workers in the Vineyard in this category. However, the parables of the Friend at Midnight and of the Unjust Judge also focus on the character of God.

67. John W. Sider says that Jeremias, while claiming to find only one point, actually finds nine points in this parable. See his *Interpreting the Parables: A Hermeneutical Guide to Their Meaning* (Grand Rapids: Zondervan, 1995), pp. 67-69.

68. As Ernst Käsemann emphasized; see "'The Righteousness of God' in Paul," *New Testament Questions of Today* (NTL; trans. W. J. Montague; London: SCM, 1969), pp. 168-82, esp. 174-75.

69. See *TDNT* 1:569; Weder, *Die Gleichnisse Jesu als Metapher*, p. 216.

70. The word appears only twelve times, all in the Synoptics, and apart from one request for compassion from Jesus (Mark 9:22) and three occurrences in parables (Matt 18:27; Luke 10:33; and 15:20), is used only of Jesus having compassion.

71. "The Parable of the Unmerciful Servant (Matt. 18.23-35)," p. 493.

72. The statement here is worded slightly differently from that of Jeremias, *The Parables of Jesus*, p. 213.

73. As does Sharon Ringe, "Solidarity and Contextuality," pp. 199-212. She seems to confuse reading the parable and applying it, and her suggestion that this parable perpetuates domestic violence because it requires forgiven women to forgive reflects a misappropriation. Anyone who uses this parable to justify or tolerate oppression really does not understand anything.

74. C. G. Montefiore, *The Synoptic Gospels* (2 vols.; 2d ed.; London: Macmillan, 1927), 2:437. Surprisingly, he adds that if Judaism does not come to terms with the Gospels it must always be a creed in a corner with little influence and no expansive power.

75. The Jesus Seminar's report does not even list this parable. See Funk, Scott, and Butts, *The Parables of Jesus: Red Letter Edition.*

76. *Mekilta Baḥodesh* 6.112-15 has a parable whose question form and simplicity are parallel to the parable in Luke 7:41-43: "To what is this comparable? To the conduct of a king of flesh and blood when he goes out to war. Against whom does he wage war, against the living or against the dead? The philosopher then said, 'Indeed, only against the living.'"

77. The NRSV translation of John 12:1 ("the home of Lazarus") is misleading; the Greek text has only *Bēthanian, hopou ēn Lazaros* ("Bethany, where Lazarus was").

78. François Bovon, *Luke 1: A Commentary on the Gospel of Luke 1:1–9:50* (trans. Christine M. Thomas; Minneapolis: Fortress, 2002), pp. 291-92. His arguments that this passage is a polemic against the synagogue and that the woman's love is a reference to the calling of the Gentiles are excessive and allegorizings of the narrative. Other attempts to find a *Sitz im Leben* in judgmental attitudes in the early church have little attraction. See John Nolland, *Luke 1–9:20* (WBC 35A; Dallas: Word, 1989), p. 352. Also arguing that the four accounts point to the same event is Robert Holst, "The One Anointing of Jesus: Another Application of the Form-critical Method," *JBL* 95 (1976): 435-46.

79. Sanders, "Sins, Debts, and Jubilee Release," pp. 84-85. Sanders at least wants this option on the table.

80. Craig L. Blomberg, *Interpreting the Parables* (Downers Grove, Ill.: InterVarsity, 1990), p. 185.

81. Jülicher, *Die Gleichnisreden Jesu*, 2:301; Hultgren, *The Parables of Jesus*, p. 213. Hultgren and some others think the anointing itself is secondary.

82. Thomas L. Brodie, "Luke 7,36-50 as an Internalization of 2 Kings 4,1-37: A Study of Luke's Rhetorical Imitation," *Bib* 64 (1983): 457-85, here pp. 457-59.

83. Joseph A. Fitzmyer, *The Gospel According to Luke (I–IX): Introduction, Translation, and Notes* (AB 28; Garden City, N.Y.: Doubleday, 1983), p. 686. A variant in the text at 7:46 does not mention the anointing of the feet. Even though this variant is not strongly attested and anointing of the feet is already present in 7:38, K. Weiss argued unconvincingly that the woman never anointed Jesus' feet; rather she anointed his head or his person. On his view the reference to feet was added later from John. See his "Der westliche Text von Lc 7:46 und sein Wert," *ZNW* 46 (1955): 241-45.

84. Quite possibly with the later anointing being an intentional imitation of the earlier one.

85. Bovon, *Luke 1*, p. 291.

86. But "sinners" is not always used positively: e.g., 6:32-34 and 24:7.

87. Lukan concerns are clearly present throughout; on proposed Lukanisms see Bovon, *Luke 1*, p. 293, n. 13; and Nolland, *Luke 1–9:20*, p. 355.

88. Reinhard von Bendemann ("Liebe und Sündenvergebung. Eine narrativ-traditionsgeschichtliche Analyse von Lk 7, 36-50," *BZ* 44 [2000]: 161-82, here p. 164) groups these texts and 7:36-50 with 5:29-39 and argues that a similar structure exists in all four: a meal setting, various acts, the reaction, Jesus' answer, another objection, and Jesus' concluding answer. B. Heininger (*Metaphorik, Erzählstruktur und szenisch-dramatische Gestaltung in den Sondergutgleichnissen bei Lukas* [Münster: Aschendorff, 1991], p. 86) argues that a Lukan pattern of conflict, dispute, and parable appears in Luke 5:29-39; 11:37-54; 14:1-24; 15:1-32; and 19:1-27. Although these passages have similarities and parables frequently are used in contexts of dispute, neither of these arguments is fully persuasive. The form and arrangement of these passages are not as uniform as the arguments suggest.

89. E.g., 4:24; 7:3-17; 13:33; and 24:19 among others; see Sanders, "Sins, Debts, and Jubilee Release," p. 85.

90. D. A. S. Ravens ("The Setting of Luke's Account of the Anointing: Luke 7.2–8.3," *NTS* 34 [1988]: 282-92) thinks Luke was still presenting Jesus as *the* prophet, partly because he thinks Luke had Isa 52:7 in mind and understood the woman's action as "beautifying" preparation for announcing the good news. I see no basis for this.

91. See Gen 27:26; 2 Sam 15:5; and the instances of such a greeting being turned to treach-

ery by Joab (2 Sam 20:9) and Judas (Matt 26:48). Note the frequent instructions for Christians to greet each other with a holy kiss (Rom 16:16, etc.).

92. See e.g., Ps 2:12; *b. Ketubot* 49b-50a tells of a man kissing a rabbi's feet because the rabbi had ruled that his sons, to whom he had assigned his estate, must provide for his support; *b. Ketubot* 63a tells of a rabbi's betrothed wife and her father both kissing his feet; *b. Sanhedrin* 27b tells of a man who kissed a rabbi's feet for his exposition of Scripture; and *b. Baba Batra* 16a reports that even Satan kissed the feet of a rabbi for his exposition of Scripture.

93. See Esth LXX 4:17 (13:13): "I would have been willing to kiss the soles of his feet to save Israel!" The same at *Midr. Esther* 8.7. Epictetus (*Diatr.* 4.1.17) complains that people kiss the feet of a pet slave even though they would regard being forced to kiss Caesar's feet as insolence and extravagant tyranny.

94. In Mark 14:3-5 and John 12:3-5 the value of the *myron* is estimated to be 300 denarii, roughly a year's wages for a day laborer. The only occurrences of *alabastros* in the NT are in Matt 26:7/Mark 14:3 and Luke 7:37, and alabaster containers were used for effective storage of perfumed ointments. See Pliny the Elder, *Naturalis Historia* 13.3.19: "Ointments keep best in alabaster."

95. In Xenophon, *Symposium* 2.3, the suggestion is made that perfumes be brought to the banquet so people may dine amid pleasant odors, a suggestion which Socrates rejects as inappropriate for men.

96. 11QT^a 22.14-16 (= 11QT^b 6.7-8) does speak of people eating and anointing themselves with oil and olives as part of a festival of oils. In a parable about the end-time banquet in *Eccl. Rab.* 9.7 a king instructs people to prepare for the banquet by washing and anointing themselves with oil.

97. *b. Menaḥot* 85b (also in *Sifre Deut.* 355.15, on Deut 33:24) tells only of a man's handmaiden who brings water for him to wash his feet and then oil for him to dip his hands and feet. See also the shameful act reported by Petronius (see p. 79 above).

98. Nearly all commentators assume that she is a prostitute because of the expression "in the city a sinner" (7:37). Jeremias (*The Parables of Jesus*, p. 126) viewed the woman as either a prostitute or the wife of a man engaged in a dishonorable occupation. She could be an adulteress or someone in regular contact with Gentiles or even someone disabled. See Barabara E. Reid, "'Do You See This Woman?' Luke 7:36-50 as a Paradigm for Feminist Hermeneutics," *BR* 40 (1995): 37-49. Ceslaus Spicq (*Agape in the New Testament* [trans. Marie Aquinas McNamara and Mary Honoria Richter; St. Louis: Herder, 1963], 1:97), following P. Lagrange, thinks the servants would not have allowed a prostitute to enter and that the woman was a person of good society who lived loosely, affair after affair. John J. Kilgallen ("Forgiveness of Sins, Luke 7:36-50," *NovT* 40 [1998]: 105-16) argues that the order of the words means not that Luke considered her a sinner but that she was considered by the city to be a sinner. Neither Spicq nor Kilgallen is convincing.

99. Judith anointed herself with perfume when she prepared to seduce Holofernes (Jdt 10:3; 16:8). J. D. M. Derrett ("The Anointing at Bethany and the Story of Zacchaeus," in *Law in the New Testament* [London: Darton, Longman & Todd, 1970], pp. 266-85) suggested that, since prostitutes and former prostitutes could not pay tithes and offerings in the normal way (Deut 23:18), the woman made her offering to the temple of Jesus' body. No evidence supports this suggestion.

100. *M. Ketubot* 7.6: a woman is not to go outdoors with her head uncovered. See also *m. Soṭah* 3.8; *b. Giṭṭin* 90a; *b. Baba Qamma* 90a-91a; *Gen. Rab.* 17.8; and *Num. Rab.* 2.26. This last text tells of a woman with seven sons, all of whom served as high priest, who attributed this good fortune to the fact that in all her life the rafters of her house had never looked upon the

hair of her head. *T. Soṭah* 5.9 says that it is a command to divorce a woman who goes around with her hair a mess or shoulders uncovered or is guilty of other shameless acts. See also *Acts of Thomas* 56 and Valerius Maximus, *Memorable Deeds and Sayings* 6.3.10, which also prohibits women going out with their heads uncovered.

101. The imperfect *katephilei* is used in v. 38, and that she kept kissing his feet is verified by v. 45.

102. Fitzmyer, *The Gospel According to Luke (I–IX)*, p. 688; see also Bovon, *Luke 1*, p. 295.

103. See Charles H. Cosgrove, "A Woman's Unbound Hair in the Greco-Roman World, with Special Reference to the Story of the 'Sinful Woman' in Luke 7:36-50," *JBL* 124 (2005): 675-92. Cosgrove admits that unbound hair could be sexually suggestive in the ancient world but rejects this connotation for Luke 7. He argues for two possible interpretations: the woman has been forgiven and expresses her gratitude and devotion; she comes weighed down by guilt seeking forgiveness. He seems too quickly to have dismissed the sexual connotations.

104. E.g., Plato's *Symposium*, Plutarch's *Quaestiones Conviviales*, and Xenophon's *Symposium*.

105. E.g., R. F. Collins, "The Man Who Came to Dinner" in *Luke and His Readers* (ed. R. Bieringer, G. Van Belle, and J. Verheyden; Leuven: Leuven University Press, 2005), pp. 151-72.

106. See Craig L. Blomberg, *Contagious Holiness: Jesus' Meals with Sinners* (NSBT 19; Downers Grove, Ill.: InterVarsity, 2005), pp. 86-96.

107. See the documents named in n. 104 above and also Petronius's *Satyricon*.

108. J. Neusner argues that Pharisees applied rules for temple ritual purity to non-cultic meals as well. For a summary of his argument and his debate with E. P. Sanders see his "Sanders's Pharisees and Mine: Jewish Law from Jesus to the Mishnah," in *Judaic Law from Jesus to the Mishnah: A Systematic Reply to Professor E. P. Sanders* (Atlanta: Scholars, 1993), pp. 247-73.

109. Luke 10:38-42 depicts a meal scene with Martha serving and Mary seated by the feet of Jesus, very much like the position of the sinful woman in 7:36-50. *Hypodechesthai* in 10:38 means "entertain as a guest." If it was not a meal, what serving was Martha doing?

110. Kenneth E. Bailey, *Through Peasant Eyes: More Lucan Parables, Their Culture and Style* (Grand Rapids: Eerdmans, 1980), p. 5.

111. See Jospehus, *J.W.* 2.427. For examples of contracts of indebtedness see Heininger, *Metaphorik, Erzählstruktur und szenisch-dramatische Gestaltung*, p. 92; or *Select Papyri* (LCL), 1:185-207.

112. This parable was not allegorized much by the church, not even by Augustine, but from Ambrose on the debtors who owed less and more respectively were understood as Jews and Gentiles. See Wailes, *Medieval Allegories of Jesus' Parables*, p. 208.

113. See Georg Braumann, "Die Schuldner und die Sünderin. Luk. VII. 36-50," *NTS* 10 (1964): 487-93, here p. 488. Braumann thinks v. 47 was probably added after the story and the parable had been combined, but he suggests that the story only became a parable when inserted into the narrative and that the original meaning of the story cannot be known, which does not instill much confidence in his argument. Others who regard the parable and the narrative as originally independent include Heininger, *Metaphorik, Erzählstruktur und szenisch-dramatische Gestaltung*, pp. 83-84; Fitzmyer, *The Gospel According to Luke (I–IX)*, pp. 684, 687; and Bovon, *Luke 1*, p. 297. However, earlier (p. 295) Bovon viewed the parable as opening a new reality to Simon, which assumes that they belonged together from the first.

114. See Hultgren, *The Parables of Jesus*, p. 215; Nolland, *Luke 1–9:20*, pp. 351, 356; Hans Drexler, "Die große Sünderin Lucas 7:36-50," *ZNW* 59 (1968): 159-73, here p. 165.

115. In addition to arguing that the anointing and the parable were originally indepen-

dent, Braumann ("Die Schuldner und die Sünderin," 489, 493) argues that vv. 47 and 50 are secondary. B. Heininger (*Metaphorik, Erzählstruktur und szenisch-dramatische Gestaltung*, pp. 83-89) argues that Luke joined several pieces of tradition (an anointing story, the parable, and a wisdom saying reflected in vv. 43 and 47b) but that the frame and dialogue form are from Luke himself (esp. vv. 39 and 48-50). J. Fitzmyer (*The Gospel According to Luke, I–IX*, p. 684) thinks the pronouncement story (vv. 36-40, 44-47a-b) and the parable (vv. 41-43) were conflated prior to Luke, that v. 47c ("But the one to whom . . .") is an editorial addition, and that vv. 48-50 are from Luke. I. Howard Marshall (*The Gospel of Luke: A Commentary on the Greek Text* [NIGTC; Grand Rapids: Eerdmans, 1978], pp. 306-7) thinks only vv. 46 and v. 50 may be secondary. Hultgren (*The Parables of Jesus*, p. 213) removes all the elements related to an anointing (vv. 37c, 38c, 46, and 48-50) and the three occurrences of the name "Simon." Nolland (*Luke 1–9:20*, pp. 351-52) grants that the attempts to identify later additions are unsuccessful but suggests that vv. 48-49 are a Lukan expansion. I see no basis for Bovon's suggestion (*Luke 1*, p. 292) that the parable was created from Jesus' parables of the Unforgiving Servant and the Unjust Steward.

116. Mark 5:34/Luke 8:48; "Your faith has saved you" also appears in Luke at the conclusion of miracle stories in 17:19 and 18:42.

117. John J. Kilgallen, "A Proposal for Interpreting Luke 7:36-50," *Bib* 72 (1991): 305-30, here p. 329; elsewhere ("Forgiveness of Sins," 108-9) he argues that the woman's faith is in view from the beginning of the story.

118. The healing of the paralytic (Matt 9:1-8/Mark 2:1-12/Luke 5:17-26) does bring together faith and forgiveness. Matt 9:22/Mark 5:34/Luke 8:48; Mark 10:52/Luke 18:42; Luke 8:12, 50; 17:19 connect belief and salvation.

119. Bendemann ("Liebe und Sündenvergebung," 161) sees vv. 36-50 as a short summary and interpretation of related narratives which began in 5:1-11.

120. Nolland *Luke 1–9:20*, p. 353. K. Bailey (*Through Peasant Eyes*, pp. 1-2) suggests a chiasmus with the parable at the center: introduction (vv. 36-37a), outpouring of the woman's love (vv. 37b-38), a dialogue (v. 39), the parable (vv. 40-42), a dialogue (v. 43), the outpouring of the woman's love in retrospect (vv. 44-47), conclusion (vv. 48-50). Brodie's attempt ("Luke 7,36-50 as an Internalization of 2 Kings 4,1-37") to connect to 2 Kings 4 has little to commend it.

121. C. Spicq (*Agape in the New Testament*, 1:96) views Simon as more curious than friendly and thinks the imperfect tense ērōta ("invited") shows that the Pharisee insisted Jesus dine with him. K. Bailey (*Through Peasant Eyes*, p. 11) deduces from the soliloquy in v. 39 that the real intent in inviting Jesus was to test the claim that he is a prophet. F. Bovon (*Luke 1*, pp. 296-97) sees in the Pharisee a hidden contempt for Jesus or a doubt about his greatness. All such efforts are unfair.

122. That "Pharisee" is not to be understood as "one who opposes God"; see Joel B. Green, *The Gospel of Luke* (NICNT; Grand Rapids: Eerdmans, 1997), pp. 307-8.

123. Bailey (*Through Peasant Eyes*, pp. 5, 8) describes the Pharisee's actions as an insult equivalent to a declaration of war. On the other hand, L. Schottroff's charge that this passage has an incipient anti-Judaism is unjust. Her inability to imagine that the Pharisees of Jesus' day would recognize themselves in Simon does not stem from objectivity. See her *Let the Oppressed Go Free: Feminist Perspectives on the New Testament* (trans. Annemarie S. Kidder; Louisville: Westminster /John Knox, 1993), pp. 141-42.

124. Matthew Black, *An Aramaic Approach to the Gospels and Acts* (3d ed.; Oxford: Clarendon, 1967), pp. 181-82; Bailey, *Through Peasant Eyes*, pp. 12-13.

125. Schottroff (*Let the Oppressed Go Free*, p. 154) thinks her tears are not tears of repentance or gratitude but an expression of her distress before God and people. Spicq (*Agape in the*

New Testament, 1:98, n. 6) thinks they are tears of repentance and shame, and Drexler ("Die große Sünderin Lucas 7:36-50," 164) that they are tears of repentance and despair.

126. Jeremias, *The Parables of Jesus,* p. 126.

127. See above, p. 82.

128. Cf. Borg, *Conflict, Holiness, and Politics in the Teachings of Jesus,* pp. 134-36.

129. Evelyn R. Thibeaux, "'Known to Be a Sinner': The Narrative Rhetoric of Luke 7:36-50," *BTB* 23 (1993): 151-60, here pp. 152-53.

130. Cf. Heininger, *Metaphorik, Erzählstruktur und szenisch-dramatische Gestaltung,* p. 94; contra Fitzmyer, *The Gospel According to Luke I–IX,* p. 690.

131. John Sider (*Interpreting the Parables,* p. 67) rightly comments that one-point explanations simply fail to do the text justice.

132. See above, pp. 64, 68-69, and 78.

133. So Thibeaux, "'Known to Be a Sinner,'" 155.

134. 11QMelch; 4Q235; and see among many James Sanders, "From Isaiah 61 to Luke 4," in *Christianity, Judaism, and Other Cults* (ed. Jacob Neusner; Leiden: Brill, 1975), 1:75-106.

135. Frederick W. Danker, *Jesus and the New Age: A Commentary on St. Luke's Gospel* (Philadelphia: Fortress, 1988), p. 171; Sharon H. Ringe, *Jesus, Liberation, and the Biblical Jubilee* (Philadelphia: Fortress, 1985), p. 71; Sanders, "Sins, Debts, and Jubilee Release," 86-91.

136. See pseudo-Aeschines, *Epistles* 12.14; and Philo, *Spec. Leg.* 2.39. Josephus, *Ant.* 6.144 also uses the word for forgiveness of sins.

137. Bendemann, "Liebe und Sündenvergebung," 174-75; Blomberg, *Interpreting the Parables,* p. 184; Heininger, *Metaphorik, Erzählstruktur und szenisch-dramatische Gestaltung,* pp. 94, 97. Jülicher (*Die Gleichnisreden Jesu,* 2:298) granted that the woman is the one forgiven most and that the parable teaches that the greater love will be from the one who is forgiven more, but sought to avoid the identification of God with the creditor. If one grants that the parable is about the woman and forgiveness, how does one avoid seeing the correspondences between the creditor and God and the person who owed less and Simon? Kilgallen ("A Proposal for Interpreting Luke 7:36-50," 309-10) argued against the identification of the lesser debtor and Simon since there is no indication that Simon was forgiven anything, but later ("Forgiveness of Sins," 111-12) he argued that it is difficult to believe that Simon should not apply the principle of the parable to himself and that Simon is the figure forgiven little, if at all.

138. Jeremias, *The Parables of Jesus,* p. 127. See also H. G. Wood, "The Use of ἀγαπάω in Luke vii.42, 47," *ExpTim* 66 (1954-55): 319-20.

139. Fitzmyer, *The Gospel According to Luke I–IX,* p. 690.

140. For this meaning of *hoti* see Maximilian Zerwick, *Biblical Greek* (Rome: Scripta Pontificii Instituti Biblici, 1963), §§422, 427; Nigel Turner, *Grammatical Insights into the New Testament* (Edinburgh: T. & T. Clark, 1965), pp. 37-40, who sees *hoti* in the sense of proof as a feature of Lukan style. See also Marshall, *The Gospel of Luke,* pp. 313-14; Fitzmyer, *The Gospel According to Luke I–IX,* pp. 686-87, 692 for discussion.

141. Jülicher, *Die Gleichnisreden Jesu,* 2:297. Bailey (*Through Peasant Eyes,* p. 17) argues that Jesus does not actually forgive her sins on the spot; rather he announces a forgiveness that has already taken place and is *misquoted* by the hostile guests in the following verse. This is overly defensive against salvation by works.

142. Bovon, *Luke 1,* p. 297.

143. Cf. Nolland, *Luke 1–9:20,* pp. 354, 358, who connects her response to forgiveness experienced under John the Baptist.

144. Schottroff's claim (*Let the Oppressed Go Free,* pp. 145, 151, 153, 155) that Jesus did not

expect prostitutes to give up their lives as prostitutes as the consequence of God's forgiveness is surely wrong.

145. John A. Mackay, *God's Order: The Ephesian Letter and This Present Time* (New York: Macmillan, 1953), p. 177.

146. Arrogance also leads to insensitivity and to defensiveness.

147. Cf. Blomberg, *Contagious Holiness,* esp. pp. 136-37, 164-80.

Notes to "Parables of Lostness"

1. Some suggest that singular *parabolēn* should be translated "a parabolic discourse." See the brief treatment by Joseph A. Fitzmyer, *The Gospel According to Luke X–XXIV* (AB 28B; Garden City, N.Y.: Doubleday, 1985), p. 1076. Kenneth Bailey (*Jacob and the Prodigal: A Study of the Parable of the Prodigal Son in the Light of the Saga of Jacob* [Downers Grove, Ill.: InterVarsity, 2003], p. 60) thinks the singular signifies that all three parables function as a unit, as does Jacobus Liebenberg (*The Language of the Kingdom and Jesus: Parable, Aphorism, and Metaphor in the Sayings Material Common to the Synoptic Tradition and the Gospel of Thomas* [BZNW 102; Berlin: Walter de Gruyter, 2001], p. 416). Luke 5:36 also uses the singular but gives two parables, and Mark 12:1 uses the plural but has only one parable.

2. Hans Weder (*Die Gleichnisse Jesu als Metaphern. Traditions- und redaktionsgeschichtliche Analysen und Interpretationen* [4th ed.; Göttingen: Vandenhoeck & Ruprecht, 1990], p. 170) thinks Luke found the first two together and added the third. Bailey (*Jacob and the Prodigal,* p. 60) thinks all three were originally told together. Fitzmyer (*The Gospel According to Luke X–XXIV,* p. 1073) is sure the first two were not told on the same occasion and not found together in Luke's tradition. John Nolland (*Luke 9:21–18:34* [WBC 35B; Dallas: Word, 1993], p. 769) thinks it likely that the three parables were connected in the tradition prior to Luke. Other nuanced theories abound.

H. B. Kossen ("Quelques Remarques sur l'Ordre des Paraboles dans Luc XV et sur la Structure de Matthieu XVIII 8-14," *NovT* 1 [1956]: 75-80) argues that the structure of the chapter came from Christian scribes who linked specific OT texts with testimonies about Jesus and made notes in the margins as rabbis did. He thinks Jer 31:10-20 accounts for the order of ch. 15 with the Lost Sheep paralleling 31:10-14, the Lost Coin 31:15-17, and the Prodigal 31:18-20. His case is not very convincing because other texts are more likely for the Lost Sheep and Jer 31:15-17 does not fit the Lost Coin at all.

3. See Ernst Wendland, "Finding Some Lost Aspects of Meaning in Christ's Parable of the Lost — and Found (Luke 15)," *TJ* 17 (1996): 19-65, here pp. 22-23; H. D. A. Major, T. W. Manson, and C. J. Wright, *The Mission and Message of Jesus* (New York: Dutton, 1938), p. 574; Fitzmyer, *The Gospel According to Luke X–XXIV,* pp. 1071-72.

4. For rabbinic triplet parables see *Pesiqta de Rab Kahana* 2.7; 6.3; 11.7; 12.11; 14.5. For an example of Greek *chreiai* see *The Chreia and Ancient Rhetoric: Classroom Exercises* (trans. and ed. Ronald F. Hock and Edward N. O'Neil; Atlanta: Society of Biblical Literature, 2002), pp. 178-81. Cf. Herman Hendrickx, *The Parables of Jesus* (San Francisco: Harper & Row, 1986), p. 141.

5. Hendrickx, *The Parables of Jesus,* p. 140.

6. Note Matt 9:9-13/Mark 2:13-17/Luke 5:27-32; Matt 11:19/Luke 7:34; Matt 21:31-32; Luke 7:29; 15:1-2; 18:9-14; 19:1-10.

7. Although I do not think the Vineyard Workers is addressed to Pharisees; rather, it addresses grumbling among the disciples. See pp. 373-75 herein.

8. Greg W. Forbes, *The God of Old: The Role of the Lukan Parables in the Purpose of Luke's Gospel* (JSNTSup 198; Sheffield: Sheffield Academic Press, 2000), p. 118.

9. In vv. 6 and 9 we find "calls friends and neighbors, saying" (*synkalei tous philous kai tous geitonas legōn* and *synkalei tas philas kai geitonas legousa,* with only appropriate changes of gender, esp. to indicate that the man calls his male associates and the woman her female associates) and "rejoice with me because I found" *(syncharēte moi hoti heuron)* and in vv. 7 and 10 "I say . . . thus joy . . . over one sinner repenting" (*legō hymin . . . houtōs chara . . . epi heni hamartōlǭ metanoounti,* with slight changes in word order).

10. "The Gospel of Jesus," in *The Written Gospel* (ed. Markus Bockmuehl and Donald A. Hagner; Cambridge: Cambridge University Press, 2005), pp. 31-44.

11. Francis H. Agnew ("The Parables of Divine Compassion," *The Bible Today* 27 [1989]: 35-40, here p. 36) thinks both the Lost Sheep and the Lost Coin are paradoxical similitudes. Also labeling the Lost Sheep as a similitude are Madeleine Boucher (*The Mysterious Parable: A Literary Study* [CBQMS 6; Washington, D.C.: The Catholic Biblical Association of America, 1977], p. 3) and Jan Lambrecht (*Out of the Treasure: The Parables in the Gospel of Matthew* [LTPM 10; Louvain: Peeters, 1991], pp. 45-48). Peter Rhea Jones (*Studying the Parables of Jesus* [Macon, Ga.: Smyth & Helwys, 1999], p. 201) thinks Matthew's account is a similitude while Luke's is a little narrative parable.

12. Is this due to dependence on Jesus' parable or the use of traditional material, as Klaus Berger suggests ("Materialien zu Form und Überlieferungsgeschichte neutestamentlicher Gleichnisse," *NovT* 15 [1973]: 1-37, here pp. 19-20)?

13. Cf. *Gen. Rab.* 86.4, a story of a drover with twelve cows laden with wine. When one entered a shop belonging to a Gentile, he left the eleven and followed the one for fear of the wine becoming unclean.

14. An exception is William Petersen, who argues that *Gos. Thom.* is the earliest and, rather than being Gnostic, reflects Jewish tradition in which God loves Israel more than any other nation. See his "The Parable of the Lost Sheep in the Gospel of Thomas and the Synoptics," *NovT* 23 (1981): 128-47. His argument has found little acceptance, partly because it fits with little else known about *Gos. Thom.* and its concerns. Elsewhere in *Gos. Thom.* little respect is accorded the Jews; see sayings 43, 52, and 53. See the critique of Liebenberg (*The Language of the Kingdom and Jesus,* p. 426), who, like Petersen, does not think *Gos. Thom.* is Gnostic.

15. W. G. Thompson (*Matthew's Advice to a Divided Community* [AnBib 44; Rome: Biblical Institute Press, 1970], pp. 168-69, n. 59) thinks *Gos. Thom.* depends on Luke. Liebenberg (*The Language of the Kingdom and Jesus,* p. 430) thinks it is a reaction against the understanding in the Synoptics. See also Norman Perrin, *Rediscovering the Teaching of Jesus* (London: SCM, 1967), pp. 98-99; W. D. Davies and Dale C. Allison, *A Critical and Exegetical Commentary on the Gospel According to Saint Matthew* (3 vols.; ICC; Edinburgh: T. & T. Clark, 1988-97), 2:776.

16. Gnostics made frequent use of this parable, as is evidenced by *Gospel of Truth* 31-32 and Irenaeus, *Haer.* 1.8.4; 1.16.1; 1.23.2; 2.24.6. For the understanding of this parable in the early centuries of the church see Robert C. Gregg, "Early Christian Variations on the Parable of the Lost Sheep," *Duke Divinity School Review* 41 (1976): 85-104.

17. Davies and Allison, *Matthew,* 2:768; John Nolland, *The Gospel of Matthew: A Commentary on the Greek Text* (Grand Rapids: Eerdmans, 2005), p. 740.

18. See Bailey, *Jacob and the Prodigal,* p. 65.

19. See also Luke 12:51; 13:2, 4; 22:24.

20. E.g., *Gen. Rab.* 20.8; 70.13; *b.* ʿ*Erubin* 52a; *b.* ʿ*Arakin* 25b. David Flusser (*Die rab-*

binischen Gleichnisse und der Gleichniserzähler Jesus 1: Das Wesen der Gleichnisse [Bern: Peter Lang, 1981], p. 55) argues that the question in Matthew is original.

21. Cf. "Who among you?" *(tis en hymin)* in Isa 42:23; 50:10; Hag 2:3. The use of *tis* and *anthrōpos* to frame a question is frequent, e.g., Pss 24:10; 33:12.

22. Cf. the similar question and logic in *m. Qiddušin* 4:14.

23. In addition to the passages mentioned on pp. 94-95 above, see Matt 9:9-13/Mark 2:15-17/Luke 5:27-32; Matt 11:16-19/Luke 7:31-34.

24. Among a number of texts on "sinners" see Sir 13:17 ("What does a wolf have in common with a lamb? No more has a sinner with the devout."). Among rabbinic texts see *m. Demai* 2.3: "He that undertakes to be an Associate may not sell to an *Am-haaretz* [literally, "people of the land," i.e., common people] [foodstuff that is] wet or dry, or buy from him [foodstuff that is] wet; and he may not be the guest of an *Am-haaretz* nor may he receive him as a guest in his own raiment"; *m. Ḥagigah* 2.7: "For Pharisees the clothes of an *Am-haaretz* count as suffering *midras*-uncleanness"; *b. Pesaḥim* 49b: after a list of desired wives the warning ". . . but let him not marry the daughter of an *'am ha-arez*, because they are detestable and their wives are vermin, and of their daughters it is said, 'Cursed be he that lieth with any manner of beast.' . . . 'An *'am ha-arez*, it is permitted to stab him [even] on the Day of Atonement which falls on the Sabbath. . . . One must not join company with an *'am ha-arez* on the road.' . . . 'One may tear an *'am ha-arez* like a fish!' . . . 'Whoever marries his daughter to an *'am ha-arez* is as though he bound and laid her before a lion: just as a lion tears [his prey] and devours it and has no shame, so an *'am ha-arez* strikes and cohabits and has no shame.' . . . 'Whoever studies the Torah in front of an *'am ha-arez* is as though he cohabited with his betrothed in his presence.' . . . Six things were said of the *'am ha-arez*: We do not commit testimony to them; we do not accept testimony from them; we do not reveal a secret to them; we do not appoint them as guardians for orphans; we do not appoint them stewards over charity funds; and we must not join their company on the road." No doubt, there were variations in attitudes.

25. Of course, meals are important boundary markers in every culture.

26. E.g., see 1QSa 2.2-21 which lists those present at the messianic banquet and those excluded. See Jerome Neyrey, "Ceremonies in Luke-Acts: The Case of Meals and Table-Fellowship," in *The Social World of Luke-Acts: Models for Interpretation* (ed. Jerome H. Neyrey; Peabody, Mass.: Hendrickson, 1991), pp. 361-87. See also the discussion of Pharisaic *ḥaburah* ("fellowship"), which often focused on meals, in *m. Demai* 2.2-3 or the parable in *Lam. Rab.* 4.3-4. See also the excursus "Ein altjüdisches Gastmahl," *Str-B* 4:611-39; Philip Francis Esler, *Community and Gospel in Luke-Acts* (SNTSMS 57; Cambridge: Cambridge University Press, 1987), pp. 71-109.

27. See also *m. Qiddušin* 4.14: "A man should not teach his son to be an ass-driver or a camel-driver, or a barber or a sailor, or a herdsman or a shopkeeper, for their craft is the craft of robbers"; cf. *b. Qiddušin* 82a; *b. Sanhedrin* 25b: "A Tanna taught: They further added to the list [of those ineligible to be witnesses and judges] herdsmen, tax collectors and publicans"; 26a is evidence of the low status of shepherds, virtually using the word as a derogatory term, and 57a states, "A Cuthean and a [Jewish] shepherd of small cattle [sheep, goats, etc.] need neither be rescued [from a pit] nor may they be thrown [therein]!"; *b. Baba Qamma* 94b: "Come and hear: 'For shepherds, tax collectors, and revenue farmers it is difficult to make repentance, yet they must make restitution [of the articles in question] to all those whom they know [they have robbed].'"

28. Kenneth E. Bailey, *Poet and Peasant: A Literary Cultural Approach to the Parables in*

Luke (Grand Rapids: Eerdmans, 1976), p. 147; *Finding the Lost: Cultural Keys to Luke 15* (St. Louis: Concordia, 1992), pp. 64-65.

29. For this and the next note see the primary sources above (pp. 96-98) and Pss 28:9; 80:1; Jer 31:10; Ezek 34:15, 31; Mic 7:14.

30. Various leaders are described as shepherds: David (2 Sam 5:2; 7:7; 1 Chron 11:2; 17:6; Ps 78:71-72; cf. 11Q5), Cyrus (Isa 44:28), Jeremiah (Jer 17:16), Zechariah (Zech 11:4, 7, 9), unspecified rulers (Ezek 34:1-22; Mic 5:4; Zech 11:3, 5), failed leaders (Jer 23:2; Zech 11:16-17; 13:7), good leaders (Jer 23:4), a Davidic shepherd (Ezek 34:23; 37:24; and see 4Q504, 4.4-8: "For you loved Israel more than all the peoples. And you chose the tribe of Judah, and established your covenant with David so that he would be like a shepherd, a prince over your people, and would sit in front of you on the throne of Israel for ever"). The specific application of the shepherd image to the Messiah is evident in Matt 2:6 (from Mic 5:2); *4 Ezra* 2:34; *Pss. Sol.* 17:40 (referring to the Lord Messiah, "Faithfully and righteously shepherding the Lord's flock, he will not let any of them stumble in their pasture"). The metaphorical use of "sheep" and "shepherd" for rulers and people is common in both Semitic and Greco-Roman cultures, on which see Arland J. Hultgren, *The Parables of Jesus: A Commentary* (Grand Rapids: Eerdmans, 2000), p. 52.

31. Num 27:17; 1 Kgs 22:17; 2 Chron 18:16; Ezek 34:5, 8; Zech 10:2; 13:7; Matt 9:36; 26:31; Mark 6:34; 14:27; Jdt 11:19.

32. Joachim Jeremias, *The Parables of Jesus* (2d ed.; trans. S. H. Hooke; New York: Charles Scribner's Sons, 1972), p. 134.

33. For details see Fitzmyer, *The Gospel According to Luke X–XXIV,* p. 1077.

34. See George Foot Moore, *Judaism in the First Centuries of the Christian Era: The Age of the Tannaim* (Cambridge, Mass.: Harvard University Press, 1950), 1:507-34 (p. 520: "Repentance is the sole, but inexorable, condition of God's forgiveness and restoration of his favor, and the divine forgiveness and favor are never refused to genuine repentance").

35. Several scholars note this unrealistic feature, e.g., Liebenberg, *The Language of the Kingdom and Jesus,* p. 417. Adolf Jülicher (*Die Gleichnisreden Jesu* [2 vols.; Freiburg i. B.: Akademische Verlagsbuchhandlung von J. C. B. Mohr, 1888-89], 2:324) and W. O. E. Oesterley (*The Gospel Parables in the Light of Their Jewish Background* [New York: Macmillan, 1936], p. 182) both comment on the "Oriental" proclivity for public demonstrations.

36. See Stephen L. Wailes, *Medieval Allegories of Jesus' Parables* (Berkeley, Calif.: University of California Press, 1987), pp. 128-30.

37. Norman Perrin, *Rediscovering the Teaching of Jesus* (London: SCM, 1967), p. 101; John Dominic Crossan, *In Parables: The Challenge of the Historical Jesus* (New York: Harper & Row, 1973), pp. 38-39, 74.

38. The Jesus Seminar voted to use pink print ("Jesus probably said something like this") for Matt 18:12-13 and Luke 15:4-6, black (Jesus did not say it) for Matt 18:14 and Luke 15:7, and gray (the ideas are close to those of Jesus) for *Gos. Thom.* 107. See Robert W. Funk, Bernard Brandon Scott, and James R. Butts, *The Parables of Jesus: Red Letter Edition* (Sonoma, Calif.: Polebridge, 1988), p. 38.

39. See Eta Linnemann, *Parables of Jesus* (trans. John Sturdy; London: SPCK, 1966), pp. 65-69; Thompson, *Matthew's Advice to a Divided Community,* pp. 164-73; Fitzmyer, *The Gospel According to Luke X–XXIV,* pp. 1073-75. Those taking this view usually are following Rudolf Bultmann (*History of the Synoptic Tradition* [trans. John Marsh; New York: Harper & Row, 1963], p. 171). Those who think Luke presents the earlier account include K. Bailey (*Poet and Peasant,* pp. 151-53), J. Duncan M. Derrett ("Fresh Light on the Lost Sheep and the Lost Coin," *NTS* 26 [1979]: 36-60, here pp. 46 and 59), both of whom think Luke is more Jewish, and

W. Tooley ("The Shepherd and Sheep Image in the Teaching of Jesus," *NovT* 7 [1964-65]: 15-25, here p. 22). I. Howard Marshall (*Commentary on Luke* [NIGTC; Grand Rapids: Eerdmans, 1978], pp. 600-601) thinks it more likely that Luke has preserved the original ending of the parable and that Matthew has abbreviated it, but that there are no grounds for seeing one form as more original than the other.

40. See further, e.g., Lambrecht, *Out of the Treasure*, pp. 39-52; Jeremias, *The Parables of Jesus*, pp. 38-40; Jacques Dupont, "Les implications christologiques de la parabole de la brebis perdue," in *Jesus aux Origines de la Christologie* (BETL 40; Leuven: Leuven University Press, 1975), pp. 331-50, here pp. 332-36; and Perrin, *Rediscovering the Teaching of Jesus*, p. 99.

41. Lambrecht (*Out of the Treasure*, pp. 44 and 47) reconstructs both a Q version and Jesus' original. See among several others Weder, *Die Gleichnisse Jesu als Metaphern*, p. 173; David Catchpole, "Eine Schaf, eine Drachme und ein Israelit: Die Botschaft Jesu in Q," in *Die Freude an God. Unsere Kraft* (ed. Johannes J. Degenhardt; Stuttgart: Verlag Katholisches Bibelwerk, 1991), pp. 89-101, here p. 94; Bernhard Heininger, *Metaphorik, Erzählstruktur und szenisch-dramatische Gestaltung in den Sondergutgleichnissen bei Lukas* (NTAbh 24; Münster: Aschendorff, 1991), p. 142. In Heininger's reconstruction the parable of the Lost Sheep is shorter than that of the Lost Coin.

42. Among several see Hultgren, *The Parables of Jesus*, p. 49; Marshall, *Commentary on Luke*, p. 600.

43. Dupont, "Les implications christologiques de la parabole de la brebis perdue," p. 332.

44. Many assume that Matt 18:14 is an addition (e.g., Davies and Allison, *Matthew*, 2:776). Jülicher (*Die Gleichnisreden Jesu*, 2:331) thought it could be an authentic logion placed here. Paul Fiebig thought v. 14 fit well and was original to the parable (*Die Gleichnisreden Jesus in Lichte der rabbinischen Gleichnisse des neutestamentlichen Zeitalters* [Tübingen: Mohr-Siebeck, 1912], p. 195).

45. U. Luz, *Matthew 8–20* (trans. James E. Crouch; Minneapolis: Fortress, 2001), p. 443.

46. Liebenberg (*The Language of the Kingdom and Jesus*, p. 423) argues similarly that Matt 18:14 makes an addition to the parable in that context. Some find tension between the seemingly passive sheep/coin and the sinner's more active repentance, yet some suggest that this is the understandable tension between divine sovereignty and human response. See the discussions of Lambrecht (*Out of the Treasure*, p. 46) and Craig Blomberg (*Interpreting the Parables* [Downers Grove, Ill.: InterVarsity, 1990], p. 181), both of whom downplay the tension. Is the parable concerned with either of these issues?

47. Cf. the parables of the Wheat and Tares (Matt 13:24-30, 36-43), the Wicked Tenants (Matt 21:33-46/Mark 12:1-12/Luke 20:9-19), esp. the Matthean and Lukan forms, the Unjust Judge (Luke 18:1-8), depending on how one sees the ending, which is also true for other parables, and *Pesiqta de Rab Kahana* 17.2.

48. Note E. P. Sanders's comment (*Jesus and Judaism* [Philadelphia: Fortress, 1985], p. 179): "I do not wish to allegorize the parables, but it is hard not to see the Lost Coin and the Lost Sheep as corresponding to the tax collectors and sinners. . . . Luke's setting in 15:1f. . . . is of course his own contribution, as are the concluding summaries to the first two parables. . . . But Luke seems to have been on the right track. Jesus was concerned with the 'lost'." See also Jones, *Studying the Parables of Jesus*, p. 201; C. H. Dodd, *The Parables of the Kingdom* (London: Nisbet, 1935), p. 120.

49. Nolland (*The Gospel of Matthew*, p. 742) argues that a full passive force ("be led astray") should be given to *planēthē*, even though he is aware that the passive of this word often means merely "go astray."

50. David Buttrick, *Speaking Parables: A Homiletic Guide* (Louisville: Westminster John Knox, 2000), p. 219.

51. Agnew, "The Parables of Divine Compassion," 37-38.

52. Bernard Brandon Scott, *Hear Then the Parable: A Commentary on the Parables of Jesus* (Minneapolis: Fortress, 1989), pp. 415-17; Charles W. Hedrick, *Many Things in Parables: Jesus and His Modern Critics* (Louisville: Westminster John Knox, 2004), pp. 14 and 49.

53. Hedrick, *Many Things in Parables,* p. 50. Daniel Patte (*The Gospel According to Matthew: A Structural Commentary on Matthew's Faith* [Philadelphia: Fortress, 1987], p. 251) takes the abandonment of the ninety-nine as an image of self-denial!

54. See *m. Baba Qamma* 6.2 and *b. Baba Qamma* 55b, 56b above, p. 98. See also among many Jeremias, *The Parables of Jesus,* pp. 133-34 (who, like several, mentions the goatherder who discovered the Qumran scrolls, leaving his flock with two companions when he went to search for a lost goat); Bailey, *Finding the Lost,* pp. 72-73 (who suggests that a herd of one hundred sheep would have at least two shepherds); E. F. F. Bishop, "The Parable of the Lost or Wandering Sheep," *ATR* 44 (1962): 44-57, here p. 45; F. Bussby, "Did a Shepherd Leave Sheep upon the Mountains or in the Desert?" *ATR* 45 (1963): 93-94.

55. See Perrin, *Rediscovering the Teaching of Jesus,* p. 99; Nolland, *Luke 9:21–18:34,* p. 772. Luise Schottroff (*The Parables of Jesus* [trans. Linda M. Maloney; Minneapolis: Fortress, 2006], p. 152) assumes that the shepherd took the sheep into the house.

56. Luke's question expects a negative answer. No shepherd would allow a lost sheep to stay lost. See above, pp. 12-13 and 101 on the expected answer for "Who from you?" questions, the form in Luke. In Matt 18:12, a form of *ou* is used, which in questions anticipates an affirmative answer. Of course a shepherd would leave the ninety-nine and search for the lost.

57. In Luke 15:31 the father says to the elder son, "You are always with me, and all my things are yours."

58. See esp. Jer 23:1-6; Zech 11:3-17. See p. 102, nn. 29 and 30 above.

59. Hultgren (*The Parables of Jesus,* p. 53) is one of several who have no doubt that the parable was framed on Ezekiel 34. Davies and Allison (*Matthew,* 2:769) believe the parable was associated with Ezekiel 34 in the course of transmission, which is difficult to validate. Explicit verbal contacts with the LXX of Ezekiel 34 other than v. 16 are not strong.

60. "Psalm 23 and Luke 15: A Vision Expanded," *IBS* 12 (1990): 54-71, in which eight parallels are found between Psalm 23 and Luke 15; *Finding the Lost,* pp. 11, 67-92, 194-212, in which Bailey finds thirteen parallels between the two chapters. See also *Jacob and the Prodigal,* p. 85.

61. *Finding the Lost,* pp. 75, 91-92; *Poet and Peasant,* p. 154.

62. *Jacob and the Prodigal,* pp. 121-218; "Jacob and the Prodigal: A New Identity Story," *Theological Review* 18 (1997): 54-72.

63. Ruth 4:15; 1 Kgs 17:22; Job 33:30; Pss 19:7 [8]; 116:7; Lam 1:11, 16.

64. John Albert Bengel, *Gnomon of the New Testament* (3 vols.; trans. Andrew R. Fausset; Edinburgh: T. & T. Clark, 1873), 2:137. He suggested that the three parables in Luke 15 refer to the stupid sinner, the sinner altogether ignorant of himself, and the knowing and willful sinner (2:136).

65. Contra Bailey, who does not hesitate to say that Jesus is the good shepherd and the good woman. See *Finding the Lost,* pp. 93-108, esp. 106; and *Jacob and the Prodigal,* pp. 86-94, esp. 92. Carol Schersten LaHurd ("Rediscovering the Lost Women in Luke 15," *BTB* 24 [1994]: 66-76, here p. 72) points to the constraints that prohibit such an easy identification.

66. Contra Crossan, *In Parables,* pp. 38-39; Perrin, *Rediscovering the Teaching of Jesus,* pp.

100-101. Equally unfounded is Derrett's suggestion ("Fresh Light on the Lost Sheep and the Lost Coin," 43-46) that both the shepherd and the woman in these two parables reenact the Passover.

67. Forbes (*The God of Old*, pp. 121-22) correctly sees that God is the ultimate referent and that it is Jesus through whom God acts. Liebenberg (*The Language of the Kingdom and Jesus*, p. 419) argues instead that the shepherd is Jesus.

68. Jer 23:4-5; Ezek 34:23-24; 37:24; Mic 5:2-4; see also *Pss. Sol.* 17:40; 4Q 504 iv, 4-8; *4 Ezra* 2:34.

69. Among many see Dupont, "Les implications christologiques de la parabole de la brebis perdue," pp. 346-48; Hendrickx, *The Parables of Jesus*, p. 161; Nolland, *Luke 9:21–18:34*, pp. 771, 773; and Weder, *Die Gleichnisse Jesu als Metaphern*, pp. 174-75.

70. Note the other uses of the shepherd imagery in Jesus' teaching: Matt 26:31/Mark 14:27; Matt 15:24; John 10:1-18.

71. *Once More Astonished* (New York: Crossroad, 1981), p. 45.

72. Bailey, *Finding the Lost*, pp. 68-70, 91; *Jacob and the Prodigal*, pp. 66-67, 79-82. Bailey is correct to point out that repentance with Jesus is de-Zionized and de-nationalized. Weder (*Die Gleichnisse Jesu als Metaphern*, p. 251, cf. 175) also and for similar reasons describes repentance as the willingness to be found; Linnemann (*Parables of Jesus*, p. 72) takes the same view and is anxious that repentance not be viewed as a human act.

73. There are five occurrences of the verb "repent" *(metanoein)* in Matthew, two in Mark, nine in Luke, none in John, and five in Acts. Matthew also has three occurrences of the related verb *metamelesthai.*

74. See esp. Matt 4:17/Mark 1:15; Matt 11:20-21/Luke 10:13; Matt 12:41/Luke 11:32.

75. Bailey, *Finding the Lost*, pp. 88-91; Forbes, *The God of Old*, p. 120; and Hultgren, *The Parables of Jesus*, p. 60, respectively.

76. Such as Abraham, Isaac, Jacob, and Jeremiah. See Pr. Man. 8; *T. Ab.* 10.13 (but see 9.3); *2 Bar.* 9.1.

77. See Jean Cantinat, "Les Parables de la Misericorde," *TD* 4 (1956): 120-23, here p. 121; Blomberg, *Interpreting the Parables*, pp. 182-83, who says that "righteous" does not refer to the sinless but to those who place their hope in God and that Jesus had a wider group of Jews in mind than those he elsewhere denounces as hypocrites.

78. See Marshall, *Commentary on Luke*, p. 602; *BDAG*, p. 433.

79. Hendrickx, *The Parables of Jesus*, p. 160. Schottroff (*The Parables of Jesus*, pp. 152, 154) with justification says that the statement is more for rhetorical than theological reasons.

80. Jesus uses "I say to you" (either singular or plural) to introduce a solemn or important saying fifty-nine times in Matthew, nineteen in Mark, and forty-seven in Luke. In Matthew thirty-one of these introductions are preceded by "amen," in Mark thirteen, and in Luke only six. "Amen" serves to emphasize the validity of the statement and is a mark of the authority with which Jesus taught. No one else precedes sayings with "amen" in Judaism or Christianity. The only exception is Rev 7:12, which uses "amen" both at the beginning and the end of a statement.

81. See Thompson, *Matthew's Advice to a Divided Community*, pp. 154-55.

82. This is acknowledged by nearly all, e.g., Liebenberg, *The Language of the Kingdom and Jesus*, pp. 418-19. D. Catchpole ("Eine Schaf, eine Drachme und ein Israelit," pp. 97, 99) seeks to broaden the parable so that it is an appeal to all Israel.

83. Forbes, *The God of Old*, p. 122.

84. C. G. Montefiore, *The Synoptic Gospels* (2 vols.; 2d ed.; London: Macmillan, 1927), 2:520.

85. Cf. the Pauline summary of the gospel as God for us and his statements that God demonstrated his love for us even when we were sinners (Rom 8:31-38; 5:6-8).

86. Points made by Heininger, *Metaphorik, Erzählstruktur und szenisch-dramatische Gestaltung in den Sondergutgleichnissen bei Lukas,* pp. 144-45.

87. Whether the time of the joy anticipated with the future "will be" (15:7, *estai*) is a reference to the final judgment or not is debated. Jeremias (*The Parables of Jesus,* pp. 135-36) and Fitzmyer (*The Gospel According to Luke X–XXIV,* p. 1077) think final judgment is in view, while Hultgren (*The Parables of Jesus,* p. 60), Forbes (*The God of Old,* p. 117), and Jülicher (*Die Gleichnisreden Jesu,* 2:322) do not limit the reference to final judgment. Forbes and Jülicher see the future tense as pointing to a logical consequence rather than a reference to final judgment. It seems to me the focus is on the present.

88. Count Nicholas von Zinzendorf wrote, "The essence of Christianity does not consist in being pious but in being joyous," as quoted by Karl A. Olsson, *By One Spirit* (Chicago: Covenant, 1962), p. 17.

89. C. G. Montefiore, *The Synoptic Gospels,* 2:522, but having said that this parable is one of the homeliest, quaintest, and most telling, he says nothing else about it!

90. Hultgren (*The Parables of Jesus,* p. 65) classifies the Lost Coin as a parable because it speaks of the specificity of a particular woman's actions, which is not true. This is a question about what any woman with ten coins would do, not an account of what a particular woman did. See also Heininger's summary of the discussion (*Metaphorik, Erzählstruktur und szenisch-dramatische Gestaltung in den Sondergutgleichnissen bei Lukas,* p. 143 and n. 16).

91. Two different coins.

92. Bailey lists 27 examples, some questionable. See *Finding the Lost,* pp. 97-99. See also *Jacob and the Prodigal,* pp. 88-91.

93. Contra Susan Marie Praeder, *The Word in Women's Worlds: Four Parables* (Wilmington: Michael Glazier, 1988), p. 44; Susan Durber, "The Female Reader of the Parables of the Lost," *JSNT* 45 (1992): 59-78, here pp. 70-71.

94. As Joel Green argues; see his *The Gospel of Luke* (Grand Rapids: Eerdmans, 1997), p. 576, following Jeremias, *The Parables of Jesus,* p. 134.

95. The article *tas* governs both *philas* and *geitonas* (which functions for both masculine and feminine), so the latter refers to female neighbors in this case.

96. Cf. Praeder, *The Word in Women's Worlds,* p. 46.

97. The Jesus Seminar prints vv. 8-9 pink and v. 10 black; see Funk, Scott, and Butts, *The Parables of Jesus: Red Letter Edition,* p. 36.

98. Nolland (*Luke 9:21–18:34,* p. 775) thinks some form of v. 10 is needed.

99. Contra Jülicher, *Die Gleichnisreden Jesu,* 2:320.

100. Gen 24:22; Exod 39:2; Tob 5:14; 2 Macc 4:19; 10:20; 12:43; 3 Maccabees 3:28. See Praeder's discussion of the drachma (*The Word in Women's Worlds,* pp. 37-39).

101. According to Marshall (*Commentary on Luke,* p. 603) about 300 B.C. a drachma equaled the value of a sheep but by the first century had been considerably devalued.

102. Schottroff, *The Parables of Jesus,* p. 154.

103. Jülicher (*Die Gleichnisreden Jesu,* pp. 316-17) says that she is not poor but belongs to the middle class.

104. See Praeder, *The Word in Women's Worlds,* p. 41. See also Peter Richardson, *Building Jewish in the Roman East* (Waco, Tex.: Baylor University Press, 2004), pp. 76-81.

105. Jeremias (*The Parables of Jesus,* p. 134) and Bailey (*Poet and Peasant,* p. 157) have popularized this assumption, but Bailey apparently changed his mind (see *Finding the Lost,* p. 102).

106. To which Scott points (*Hear Then the Parable*, p. 311).

107. See Praeder, *The Word in Women's Worlds*, p. 39; and Hultgren, *The Parables of Jesus*, p. 66.

108. See Augustine, *Exposition of the Psalms 121–150*, III/20 of *The Works of Saint Augustine: A Translation for the 21st Century* (translation and notes, Maria Boulding; ed. Boniface Ramsey; Hyde Park, N.Y.: New City, 2004); Wailes, *Medieval Allegories of Jesus' Parables*, pp. 234-35.

109. Barbara E. Reid, "Beyond Petty Pursuits and Wearisome Widows: Three Lukan Parables," *Int* 56 (2002): 284-94, here p. 289. She points to Prov 1:20-23; 8:1-5; and 9:1-11, texts describing Wisdom's seeking the simple and inviting them to her banquet. I see no connection between these texts and Luke 15.

110. Crossan, *In Parables*, pp. 73-74; Heininger, *Metaphorik, Erzählstruktur und szenisch-dramatische Gestaltung in den Sondergutgleichnissen bei Lukas*, p. 145 (who suggests that it could point to the experience of Jesus). Cf. Perrin, *Rediscovering the Teaching of Jesus*, pp. 101-2.

111. Contra Bailey, *Finding the Lost*, p. 103, and others. LaHurd ("Rediscovering the Lost Women in Luke 15") examined modern Arabic female attitudes to the parables in Luke 15. Among other things she found (pp. 66-67) that these women did not focus on the woman. Alfred Plummer (*A Critical and Exegetical Commentary on the Gospel According to Luke* [4th ed.; ICC; Edinburgh: T. & T. Clark, 1901], p. 370) thought the woman, if anything, represents the church rather than divine wisdom.

112. E.g., Luke 7:36-50; 8:1-3; 10:38-42.

113. Catchpole, "Eine Schaf, eine Drachme und ein Israelit," pp. 91-92.

114. Durber, "The Female Reader of the Parables of the Lost," 59-78; Mary Ann Beavis, "Joy in Heaven, Sorrow on Earth: Luke 15.10," in *The Lost Coin: Parables of Women, Work and Wisdom* (ed. Mary Ann Beavis; Sheffield: Sheffield Academic Press, 2002), pp. 39-45. Beavis finds 15:10 an offense to victims of abuse and suggests a new ending: "Likewise, I tell you, the angels of Godde [sic] rejoice more over one innocent person who is vindicated than over the repentance of the sinners who have abused them!"

115. The text does not explicitly deal with spouse abuse, but should the subject of forgiveness of sinners be seen as a violation of women because it suggests that even abusers can be forgiven? (See the previous note.) Must we not deal both with justice and forgiveness, even though that is no easy task?

116. Contra Bailey, *Finding the Lost*, p. 106.

117. Contra Robert Menzies, "The Lost Coin," *ExpTim* 64 (1953): 274-76, here p. 276.

118. Contra Scott, *Hear Then the Parable*, pp. 312-13, 326, 362.

119. The Greek word translated "carefully," *epimelōs*, appears only here in the NT and infrequently in the LXX. It is used especially in contexts of diligently carrying out a king's commands. Josephus (*Ant.* 12.318) uses it of the care Judas Maccabeus took in sanctifying the temple.

120. Cf. Fitzmyer, *The Gospel According to Luke X–XXIV*, p. 1080.

121. See also Praeder, *The Word in Women's Worlds*, p. 48.

122. As both Forbes (*The God of Old*, pp. 122, 124) and Weder (*Die Gleichnisse Jesu als Metaphern*, p. 251) recognize.

123. Plummer's suggestion (*The Gospel According to Luke*, p. 371) that "in the presence of angels" means "in the judgment of the angels" misses the circumlocution used to refer to God's rejoicing.

124. Despite Weder (*Die Gleichnisse Jesu als Metaphern*, p. 251) and Bailey (*Finding the Lost*, p. 106).

125. For the remarkable influence of this parable on art, literature, and film see Mikeal C. Parsons, "The Prodigal's Elder Brother: The History and Ethics of Reading Luke 15:25-32," *PRSt* 23 (1996): 147-74; Manfred Siebald and Leland Ryken, "Prodigal Son," *A Dictionary of Biblical Tradition in English Literature* (ed. David Lyle Jeffrey; Grand Rapids: Eerdmans, 1992), pp. 640-44; Fitzmyer, *The Gospel According to Luke X–XXIV*, pp. 1083-84. Henri J. M. Nouwen's work *The Return of the Prodigal Son* (New York: Doubleday, 1992) is a meditation on Rembrandt's painting of the return of the prodigal. The meditation is interesting and helpful but at times "over the top" in psychologizing and theologizing.

126. Kenneth E. Bailey (*Finding the Lost*, p. 193 n. 2) suggests that the omission resulted from Marcion's identification of the father with the God of the OT (since the prodigal starts in the house and returns to the same house).

127. The title of the English translation of Helmut Thielicke's book on the parables (*The Waiting Father* [trans. John W. Doberstein; New York: Harper & Row, 1959]) and that suggested by Jeremias (*The Parables of Jesus*, p. 128), respectively.

128. Brad Young, *Jesus the Jewish Theologian* (Peabody, Mass: Hendrickson, 1995), p. 143. The title "the parable of the Two Sons" is as old as Irenaeus (*Haer.* 4.36.7). Cf. P. R. Jones's suggestion "the parable of the Compassionate Father and the Angry Brother" (*Studying the Parables of Jesus*, p. 215).

129. Flusser (*Die rabbinischen Gleichnisse und der Gleichniserzähler Jesus*, pp. 57 and 71) labels this parable *"ein Exemplum,"* but, while the prodigal's repentance is instructive, neither son is held up as an example to follow.

130. The Jesus Seminar printed this parable in pink with the vast majority of the fellows voting either red or pink. See Funk, Scott, and Butts, *The Parables of Jesus: Red Letter Edition*, pp. 26 and 40. Among those who think the parable is Luke's creation are Luise Schottroff, "Das Gleichnis vom verlorenen Sohn," *ZTK* 68 (1971): 27-52; John Drury, *The Parables in the Gospels* (New York: Crossroad, 1985), pp. 141-47; Heikki Räisänen, "The Prodigal Gentile and His Jewish Christian Brother, Lk 15,11-32," in *The Four Gospels 1992: Festschrift Frans Neirynck* (ed. F. Van Sebbroeck, C. M. Tuckett, G. Van Belle, J. Verheyden; Leuven: University Press, 1992), 2:1617-36; Michael D. Goulder, *Luke: A New Paradigm* (2 vols.; JSNTSup 20; Sheffield: JSOT Press, 1989), 2:609-18. Their reasons for doubt include awareness of Lukan style and the fear that the parable fits too easily with Luke's soteriology. Again, stylistic factors do not *necessarily* indicate origin but often only the Evangelists' influence and shaping, which are to be expected. Concern that the parable reflects too much Luke's own soteriology presupposes that Luke was not influenced by the Jesus tradition and that one can ferret out those places where he is not, both very unlikely.

131. However, I do not think the parable of the Workers in the Vineyard is a true parallel.

132. Joachim Jeremias, "Tradition und Redaktion in Lukas 15," *ZNW* 62 (1971): 172-89; Ingo Broer, "Das Gleichnis vom verlorenen Sohn und die Theologie des Lukas," *NTS* 20 (1974): 453-62; Herman Hendrickx, *The Parables of Jesus*, p. 150.

133. On stoning of rebellious sons see also Josephus *Ant.* 4.264; *Against Apion* 2.206 (which adds that the Law ranks honor to parents second only to honor to God); *m. Sanhedrin* 7.4; 8.4.

134. F. H. Colson, the translator of the Loeb edition, says that Philo's words here come nearer to the spirit of the Prodigal than anything he has seen elsewhere in ancient philosophy (vol. 9, p. 542). Cf. *Every Good Man Is Free* 57.

135. The editor considers this guideline as probably fictitious, created to establish the situation to be debated.

136. Also in *Inst.* 7.6.5; 7.1.55; Seneca the elder, *Controversiae* 1.7.

137. See also *In Timarchum* 75, 94-106, 153-54.

138. No. 846 of *Aegyptische Urkunden aus den Koeniglichen Museen zu Berlin* (III). Text and translation available also in Adolph Deissmann's *Light from the Ancient East* (trans. Lionel R. M. Strachan; Grand Rapids: Baker, reprint of Harper & Row edition), pp. 187-88.

139. See George Milligan, *Selections from the Greek Papyri* (Cambridge: Cambridge University Press, 1912), pp. 71-72.

140. *Exod. Rab.* 46.4 tells of a son of an eminent physician who addressed a quack as father until he became sick and then called for his real father. The father went to him without delay but said, "Now, however, that you are in trouble, you call me father." *Lev. Rab.* 32:2 tells of a king who was angry with his son and decreed that he should not enter the palace. But then the king tore down the palace and built another into which his son could come. This is seen as an analogy of God's actions.

141. Two textual variants merit mention. In v. 16 "to fill his belly from" *(gemisai tēn koilian autou apo)* is preferred by some commentators (e.g. David A. Holgate, *Prodigality, Liberality and Meanness in the Parable of the Prodigal Son: A Greco-Roman Perspective on Luke 15:11-32* [JSNTSup 187; Sheffield: Sheffield Academic, 1999], pp. 41-43; Nolland, *Luke 9:21–18:34*, p. 780) as more likely to be original than the more refined "to be satisfied from" *(chortasthēnai ek)*, but the latter has much stronger textual support. In v. 21 some manuscripts include "make me as one of your hired hands" just as in v. 19. Most commentators (e.g., Fitzmyer, *The Gospel According to Luke X–XXIV*, pp. 1089-90) accept the shorter text because it has stronger textual support and because the longer text is viewed as an assimilation to v. 19. Holgate (*Prodigality, Liberality and Meanness in the Parable of the Prodigal Son*, pp. 43-44) argues for the longer reading, but his text-critical decisions seem to be driven by what is most helpful to his larger argument.

142. W. Harnisch, *Die Gleichniserzählungen Jesu* (Göttingen: Vandenhoeck & Ruprecht, 2001), pp. 73-84. C. Blomberg calls them "Three Point Parables" (*Interpreting the Parables*, pp. 171-251).

143. Michael R. Austin ("The Hypocritical Son," *EvQ* 57 [1985]: 307-15) and J. F. Kilgallen ("Luke 15 and 16: A Connection," *Bib* 78 [1997], 369-76) argue that the parable of the Prodigal should be read with the parables in ch. 16 rather than with the two earlier parables in ch. 15, an unnecessary conclusion.

144. Bailey's suggestion (*Poet and Peasant*, pp. 159-60 and 191), however, of a twin chiastic structure for 15:11-24 and 15:24[sic]-32 is forced and arbitrary:

<pre>
1   A son is lost — "Give me my share"
  2   Goods wasted in extravagant living
    3   Everything lost
      4   The great sin (feeding pigs for gentiles)
        5   Total rejection — no one gave him anything
          6   A change of mind — he came to himself
          6' An initial repentance — make me a servant
        5' Total acceptance — the father ran and kissed him
      4' The great repentance — I am no more worthy to be called your son
    3' Everything gained — restored to sonship
  2' Goods used in joyful celebration
1' A son is found
</pre>

and

1   He comes
    2   Your brother — safe, a feast
      3   A father comes to reconcile
        4   Complaint I — how you treat me
        4′   Complaint II — how you treat him
      3′   A father tries to reconcile
    2′   Your brother — safe, a feast
1′   [Missing]

Some actions are omitted in Bailey's layout (such as the refusal of the elder son to come in). In the first chiasmus neither of the separations of repentance into two stages at 6, 6′, and 4′ is warranted. Nor in the second chiasmus is there justification for dividing the elder son's complaints into two stages.

Mary Ann Tolbert (*Perspectives on the Parables,* Philadelphia: Fortress, 1979, p. 98) suggests alternating narrated discourse and direct discourse in both halves of the parable:

Narrated Discourse	Direct Discourse
introduction (v. 11)	the request (v. 12)
the journey away (vv. 12b-16)	the decision to return (vv. 17-19)
the father's reception (v. 20)	confession and the father's response (vv. 21-24a)
the elder son's return (v. 24b[?]-26)	the servant's explanation (v. 27)
the father's reception of the elder son (v. 28)	the elder son's accusation and the father's response (vv. 29-32).

It is arbitrary, however, to put the statements of the younger son and the father or of the elder son and the father as one discourse (vv. 21-24a, 29-32).

145. The Entrevenes Group (*Signs and Parables: Semiotics and Gospel Texts* [trans. Gary Phillips; Pittsburgh: Pickwick, 1978], pp. 141-42) suggests that vv. 11-16 show degradation, vv. 17-24 reintegration, and vv. 25-32 the resulting debate. Joost Smit Sibinga ("Zur Kompositationstechnik des Lukas in Lk. 15,11-32," in *Tradition and Re-Interpretation in Jewish and Early Christian Literature* [ed. J. W. Van Henten, et al., Leiden: Brill, 1986], p. 113) is similar but places v. 24c with vv. 25-32. Hultgren (*The Parables of Jesus,* p. 73) says vv. 11-19 show departure, vv. 20-24 return and welcome, and vv. 25-32 the elder son. Geraint Vaughn Jones (*The Art and Truth of the Parables* [London: SPCK, 1964], pp. 121-22) focuses on three stages of action in vv. 11-20a, 20b-27, and 28-32.

146. See Holgate, *Prodigality, Liberality and Meanness in the Parable of the Prodigal Son,* p. 46, who also divides the last section into two parts (vv. 25a-28b and 28c-32d).

147. See Fitzmyer, *The Gospel According to Luke X–XXIV,* p. 1084.

148. Bailey (*Finding the Lost,* p. 152) thinks the servants have followed the father, which is required in his reconstruction so that there will be witnesses to the father's welcome.

149. See Holgate, *Prodigality, Liberality and Meanness in the Parable of the Prodigal Son,* p. 144, who presents a variety of ancient texts expressing the commonly held view that all prodigals were sexually immoral.

150. *The God of Old,* p. 305. With this parable it is a loss of emphasis on the mercy and love of God.

151. "The Central Section of St. Luke's Gospel," in *Studies in the Gospels* (ed. D. E. Nineham; Oxford: Blackwell, 1955), pp. 37-53, esp. 43.

152. See 11QTemple 64.2-6 and p. 120, n. 133 above. On attitudes toward parents, see already Ahiqar (Aramaic) 6.6; 9.49.

153. In addition to the texts above, note Hesiod's *Works and Days,* 376-78: one should have an only son to feed his father's house, but if he has another son he should die old!

154. Note in Gen 37:29–42:38 that Reuben, the eldest son, takes the role as leader.

155. Lucian, *Abdicatus* 21. In addition to the primary sources above, see Aristotle, *Nichomachean Ethics* 4.1.4, which says that prodigality is extremely wicked because it is a combination of vices. See also Aesop, *Babrius* 131, a parable about a prodigal who suffers misfortune and death, and Horace, *Satirae* 1.2.1-24 on Tigellius, a glutton who feared being called a prodigal.

156. Joachim Jeremias lists ten disasters that hit Jerusalem between 169 B.C. and A.D. 70. Eight of them were famines or crop disasters because of water shortage or storms (*Jerusalem in the Time of Jesus* [Philadelphia: Fortress, 1969], pp. 140-44).

157. See Lev 11:7-8; Deut 14:8; Isa 65:4; 66:17. 1 Macc 1:47 relates that Antiochus Epiphanes ordered swine to be sacrificed as part of the desecration of Israel. 2 Macc 6:18 and 7:1 tell of Jews under torture choosing death rather than eating the flesh of swine. Most notable among Greco-Roman writers is Dio Chrysostom, *Oratio* 30.33, which compares prodigals (*asōtous*) to pigs in a sty.

158. Cf. Robert H. Stein, *An Introduction to the Parables of Jesus* (Philadelphia: Westminster, 1981), p. 120.

159. Irene Jacob and Walter Jacob, "Flora," *ABD* 2:809; *Flora and Fauna of the Bible* (2d ed.; London: United Bible Societies, 1980), pp. 103-4. Bailey (*Poet and Peasant,* pp. 172-73) argues instead that the reference is to wild carobs for which pigs grub and which are bitter and without nourishment. Texts referring to carobs as fodder suggest that the usual identification is correct. See *m. Ma'aśerot* 3.4; *b. Šabbat* 155a. Carobs are attested much earlier as the food of the impoverished in an Akkadian text; see Pritchard, *ANET,* p. 603. Sometimes carob pods are referred to as St. John's bread because John the Baptist supposedly ate them.

160. See Sir 19:30: "A person's attire and hearty laughter and the way he walks show what he is"; Aristotle, *Nichomachean Ethics* 4.3.34: "Other traits generally attributed to the great-souled man are a slow gait, a deep voice, and a deliberate utterance."

161. Note *b. Šabbat* 152a: "Now, he [the Sadducee] saw that he [R. Joshua] was not wearing shoes, [whereupon] he remarked, 'He [who rides] on a horse is a king, upon an ass, is a free man, and he who has shoes on his feet is a human being; but he who has none of these, one who is dead and buried is better off.'" The importance of shoes is evident in *b. Šabbat* 129a; *b. Pesaḥim* 112a and 113b. Jewish mourners were forbidden to wear shoes (*b. Pesaḥim* 4a and *b. Mo'ed Qaṭan*).

162. See *b. Qiddušin* 22b and *b. Baba Batra* 33b.

163. Bailey estimates that the fatted calf would feed 100 people, but later suggests it would feed 200 people (*Poet and Peasant,* p. 187; *Finding the Lost,* pp. 120, 155). Both estimates seem high and presuppose that the whole calf was eaten immediately. In 1 Sam 28:24-25 a fatted calf is killed for Saul and his two servants (cf. 28:8).

164. *The Parables of Jesus,* p. 81.

165. Wailes, *Medieval Allegories of Jesus' Parables,* pp. 236-45; Yves Tissot, "Patristic Allegories of the Lukan Parable of the Two Sons (Luke 15:11-32)," in *Exegesis: Problems of Method and Exercises in Reading (Genesis 22 and Luke 15)* (ed. François Bovon and Grégoire Rouiller; trans. Donald G. Miller; Pittsburgh: Pickwick, 1978), pp. 362-409; Parsons, "The Prodigal's Elder Brother," 150-54.

166. G. Jones, *The Art and Truth of the Parables,* pp. 167-205.

167. James Breech, *The Silence of Jesus: The Authentic Voice of the Historical Man* (Philadelphia: Fortress, 1983), pp. 184-212. Breech argues further that the father had forgotten the elder son and took him for granted and that the elder sought not things but only a sign of the father's love. He fears that the father's love and forgiveness amount primarily to indulging the parasitical and decadent. He ends up seeing the father as a rather pathetic figure. If Breech were correct, Luke's tour de force would be a masterpiece in creativity! Richard Q. Ford (*The Parables of Jesus: Recovering the Art of Listening* [Minneapolis: Fortress, 1997], pp. 90-114) is virtually alone in following Breech, but he focuses more on the prodigal and views the father even more negatively as one who prevents his sons' development!

168. *Perspectives on the Parables,* pp. 101-14. See also the attempted psychological readings by Dan O. Via, Jr. "The Prodigal Son: A Jungian Reading," *Semeia* 9: *Polyvalent Narration: Practice Case Study on the Parable of the Prodigal Son* (1977): 21-43; and Louis Beirnaert, "The Parable of the Prodigal Son, Luke 15:11-32, Read by an Analyst," in *Exegesis: Problems of Method and Exercises in Reading (Genesis 22 and Luke 15)* (ed. François Bovon and Grégoire Rouiller; trans. Donald G. Miller; Pittsburgh: Pickwick, 1978), pp. 197-210.

169. Richard L. Rohrbaugh, "A Dysfunctional Family and Its Neighbors (Luke 15:11b-32)," in *Jesus and his Parables* (ed. V. George Shillington; Edinburgh: T. & T. Clark, 1997), pp. 141-64.

170. Wolfgang Pöhlmann, "Die Abschichtung des Verlorenen Sohnes (Lk 15:12f.) und die erzählte Welt der Parabel," *ZNW* 70 (1979): 194-213; *Der verlorene Sohn und das Haus. Studien zu Lukas 15,11-32 im Horizont der antiken Lehre von Haus, Erziehung und Ackerbau* (WUNT 68; Tübingen: Mohr-Siebeck, 1993). Herman Hendrickx ("A Man Had Two Sons: Lk 15:11-32 in Light of the Ancient Mediterranean Values of Farming and Household," *East Asian Pastoral Institute* 31 [1994]: 46-66) renders Pöhlmann's view into English.

171. N. T. Wright, *Jesus and the Victory of God,* vol. 2 of *Christian Origins and the Question of God* (Minneapolis: Fortress, 1996), pp. 125-31, 242, 254-55.

172. See, e.g., Lambrecht, *Once More Astonished,* pp. 24-56; Green, *The Gospel of Luke,* pp. 577-86; Hultgren, *The Parables of Jesus,* pp. 70-91.

173. Jack T. Sanders, "Tradition and Redaction in Luke XV.11-32," *NTS* 15 (1969): 433-38; Petr Pokorný, "Lukas 15, 11-32 und die lukanische Soteriologie," in *Christus Bezeugen. Festschrift für Wolfgang Trilling zum 65 Geburtstag* (ed. Karl Kertelge, et al.; Leipzig: St. Benno, 1989), pp. 179-92, here p. 180; Bernhard Heininger, *Metaphorik, Erzählstruktur und szenisch-dramatische Gestaltung in den Sondergutgleichnissen bei Lukas,* pp. 147-56. Heininger is one of the few who offers a reconstruction, and he suggests that the parable originally included only vv. 11-17, 20, 22-23, and 24c. But, clearly Heininger's critical theory is theologically motivated by his fear that repentance will be seen as the condition for receiving forgiveness (p. 165). The prodigal's confession of being unworthy to be a son is an integral piece, and there is no basis for omitting it. Cf. Weder (*Die Gleichnisse Jesu als Metaphern,* p. 252), who says that though Luke has edited the parable, no feature could be excluded without destroying it.

174. Jeremias, "Tradition und Redaktion in Lukas 15"; John J. O'Rourke, "Some Notes on Luke XV.11-32," *NTS* 18 (1972): 431-33.

175. Especially if they accept the structural analyses of either Tolbert or Bailey. See above, p. 124, n. 144.

176. E.g., Goulder, *Luke: A New Paradigm,* 2:609-14.

177. Matthew uses *tekna* in 21:28, whereas Luke uses *huious* in 15:11.

178. One has only to think of Cain and Abel, Isaac and Ishmael, and Jacob and Esau. An Akkadian text, "The Babylonian Theodicy," contrasts two sons, the elder destitute and the younger living luxuriously (Pritchard, *ANET,* p. 603). For Jewish materials with stories of two sons,

some beginning explicitly with "A man had two sons," see Philo, *Prov.* 2.2-6; *QG* 4.198; *Sifré Deut.* 48; *Gen Rab.* 30.10; *Lev. Rab.* 37.2; *Num. Rab.* 17.3; *Lam. Rab.* prologue 2; *Eccl. Rab.* 3.15; *Midr. Pss.* 9.1; *Pesiqta de Rab Kahana* 15.4. Among Greco-Roman materials see Terence, *The Brothers;* Seneca the elder, *Controversiae* 2.4; Teles, *Autark.* 95-96; Hesiod, *Works and Days,* 27-41; Horace, *Satirae* 2.3.168-86. It is striking how many texts in the ancient world, especially the *Controversiae* of the elder Seneca, treat the themes of this parable: a father and a prodigal son, a father and two sons contrasted, and inheritance or disinheritance issues.

179. Hultgren, *The Parables of Jesus,* p. 224.

180. Kenneth E. Bailey, "Jacob and the Prodigal Son: A New Identity Story: A Comparison Between the Parable of the Prodigal Son and Gen. 27–35," *Theological Review* 18 (1997): 54-72; *Jacob and the Prodigal;* Nolland, *Luke 9:21–18:34,* p. 784.

181. Heininger, *Metaphorik, Erzählstruktur und szenisch-dramatische Gestaltung in den Sondergutgleichnissen bei Lukas,* p. 159; Drury, *The Parables in the Gospels,* p. 144. See also Roger David Aus, *Weihnachtsgeschichte, Barmherziger Samariter, Verlorener Sohn. Studien zu ihrem jüdischen Hintergrund* (Berlin: Institut Kirche und Judentum, 1988), pp. 126-73, who emphasizes Jewish traditions about Joseph.

182. Colin Brown, "The Parable of the Rebellious Son(s)," *SJT* 51 (1998): 391-405; Craig A. Evans, "Luke 16:1-18 and the Deuteronomy Hypothesis," in *Luke and Scripture* (ed. Craig A. Evans and James Sanders; Minneapolis: Augsburg/Fortress, 1993), pp. 121-39, here pp. 132-33. J. Duncan M. Derrett ("The Parable of the Prodigal Son," in *Law in the New Testament* [London: Darton, Longman, and Todd, 1976], pp. 100-125, here p. 100, n. 2) suggests that the parable may plausibly be read as a sermon on Deut 32:6-26 and elaborated with the aid of Deuteronomy 21–22.

183. Bailey, *Finding the Lost,* pp. 194-212; "Psalm 23 and Luke 15: A Vision Expanded," *IBS* 12 (1990): 54-71; Wendland, "Finding Some Lost Aspects of Meaning in Christ's Parable of the Lost — and Found (Luke 15)," 19-65.

184. Otto Betz, "Jesu Lieblingspsalm. Die Bedeutung von Psalm 103 für das Werk Jesu," *TBei* 15 (1984): 253-69.

185. N. T. Wright, *Jesus and the Victory of God,* p. 127; Kossen, "Quelques Remarques sur l'Ordre des Paraboles dans Luc XV et sur la Structure de Matthieu XVIII 8-14," 75-80.

186. Otfried Hofius, "Alttestamentliche Motive im Gleichnis vom verlorenen Sohn," *NTS* 24 (1977): 240-48.

187. Bailey, *Finding the Lost,* pp. 11, 194-212.

188. "Jacob and the Prodigal Son."

189. *Jacob and the Prodigal.*

190. Aus, *Weihnachtsgeschichte, Barmherziger Samariter, Verlorener Sohn,* pp. 172-73. Earlier Aus argued that Jesus used traditions that were also applied to Rabbi Eliezer. See Aus, "Luke 15:11-32 and R. Eliezer Ben Hyrcanus's Rise to Fame," *JBL* 104 (1985): 443-69.

191. Karl Heinrich Rengstorf, *Die Re-Investitur des Verlorenen Sohnes in der Gleichniserzählung Jesu Luk. 15,11-32* (AFLNW 137; Köln: Westdeutscher, 1967). See the critique by Christoph Dempke, "Rengstorf, Karl Heinrich. Die Re-Investitur des Verlorenen Sohnes in der Gleichniserzälung Jesu Luk. 15,11-32," *TLZ* 94 (1969): 762-63.

192. Holgate, *Prodigality, Liberality and Meanness in the Parable of the Prodigal Son,* esp. pp. 132-251.

193. *Der verlorene Sohn und das Haus,* esp. pp. 183-89. Pöhlmann can take his approach only by assuming that the original situation of the parable is lost and that the kingdom is the hermeneutical key (pp. 158-59).

194. John Nolland downplays the focus on money and possessions in this parable. See his "The Role of Money and Possessions in the Parable of the Prodigal Son (Luke 15:11-32): A Test Case," in *Reading Luke: Interpretation, Reflection, Formation* (ed. Craig G. Bartholomew, Joel B. Green, and Anthony Thiselton; Scripture and Hermeneutics Series 6; Grand Rapids: Zondervan, 2005), pp. 178-209.

195. Fitzmyer, *The Gospel According to Luke X–XXIV,* p. 1086.

196. See esp. 11QMelch and 4Q521.

197. John R. Donahue, *The Gospel in Parable* (Philadelphia: Fortress, 1988), p. 153; Nolland, *Luke 9:21–18:34,* p. 782; Linnemann, *Parables of Jesus,* pp. 73-74.

198. See above, p. 122, and see also Diogenes Laertius, *Lives* 9.35-36, which tells of Democritus, a third son, who divided the family property (*ousia,* as in Luke 15:12), which is understood to mean that he chose a smaller portion in money in order to finance his travels. Abraham divides his possessions during his life, but it is clearly near the end of his life (Gen 25:5-6), and Tobit receives half of his father-in-law's possessions while he is still living (Tob 8:21).

199. Note esp. *T. Iss.* 6.1-4; *Apocalypse of Sedrach* 6.4; Aeschines, *In Timarchum* 30-47. Wasting his inheritance with luxurious living would have heightened the shame, as Prov 28:7 and a host of other texts show.

200. Sir. 3:12; *T. Iss.* 3.1-8; Quintilian, *Declamatio* 5; Plutarch, *On Brotherly Love* 479F-480A.

201. Bailey, *Finding the Lost,* pp. 109-13; *Poet and Peasant,* pp. 161-62.

202. Holgate, *Prodigality, Liberality and Meanness in the Parable of the Prodigal Son,* p. 208.

203. Hendrickx, "A Man Had Two Sons," 61.

204. François Bovon, "The Parable of the Prodigal Son (Luke 15:11-32): First Reading," in *Exegesis: Problems of Method and Exercises in Reading (Genesis 22 and Luke 15)* (ed. François Bovon and Grégoire Rouiller; trans. Donald G. Miller; Pittsburgh: Pickwick, 1978), pp. 43-73, see p. 53; Donahue, *The Gospel in Parable,* p. 154.

205. Wilfrid Harrington, "The Prodigal Son," *Furrow* 25 (1974): 432-37, see p. 432; Linnemann, *Parables of Jesus,* p. 75.

206. Derrett, "The Parable of the Prodigal Son," p. 111; Forbes, *The God of Old,* p. 137; Hultgren, *The Parables of Jesus,* p. 77.

207. Also *m. Baba Batra* 8.4-5.

208. Despite a number of scholars who assume that he received and sold part of the family farm, a notion rightly rejected by Derrett, "The Parable of the Prodigal Son," p. 107; and Oesterley, *The Gospel Parables in the Light of Their Jewish Background,* p. 184.

209. Derrett, "The Parable of the Prodigal Son," p. 107.

210. David Daube, "Inheritance in Two Lukan Pericopes," *Zeitschrift der Savigny-Stiftung für Rechtsgeschichte* 72 (1955): 326-34, see 329-33; Derrett, "The Parable of the Prodigal Son," p. 108.

211. Cf. Hultgren, *The Parables of Jesus,* p. 73.

212. *b. Yebamot* 40a in reference to the firstborn in a Levirate marriage.

213. Schottroff (*The Parables of Jesus,* pp. 141, 143) assumes that the father promises the younger son a share in the inheritance.

214. Especially for Plutarch, *On Brotherly Love* 482E-483A. See Bailey, *Finding the Lost,* p. 122.

215. Bailey, *Finding the Lost,* pp. 121-22; *Jacob and the Prodigal,* pp. 102, 153, 171-72. Bailey

follows Rengstorf in thinking the *qetsatsah* is in mind. On this ceremony see *Ruth Rab.* 7.11 on 4:7; *y. Ketubot* 2.10; *y. Qiddušin* 1.5.

216. Cf. LaHurd, "Rediscovering the Lost Women in Luke 15," 66-76. Arabic women with whom LaHurd discussed the parable did not even hint at the idea of the father protecting the prodigal. Again, though, modern Arabic attitudes do not reflect first-century Jewish attitudes.

217. "A Dysfunctional Family and Its Neighbors (Luke 15:11b-32)." Against this see Ronald F. Hock, "Romancing the Parables of Jesus," *PRSt* 29 (2002): 11-37, who finds the language and assumptions of the parable reflected in Greek romances.

218. Note *T. Iss.* 6.1-4; Philo, *Prov.* 2.2-6; *Mekilta Beshallaḥ* 4.35-41; *Deut. Rab.* 2.24.

219. *Jesus and the Victory of God,* pp. 126-31, 179. Bailey adopts Wright's stance in his "Jacob and the Prodigal Son" but is more nuanced in *Jacob and the Prodigal.* For an assessment of Wright's approach see my "Reading and Overreading the Parables in *Jesus and the Victory of God,*" in *Jesus and the Restoration of Israel: A Critical Assessment of N. T. Wright's "Jesus and the Victory of God"* (ed. Carey Newman; Downers Grove, Ill.: InterVarsity, 1999, pp. 61-76.

220. Wright, *Jesus and the Victory of God,* pp. 9, 15, 17, 662.

221. Forbes (*The God of Old,* p. 111) with justice says it is difficult to think of a more appropriate setting than the one Luke provides. Wright (*Jesus and the Victory of God,* p. 129) accepts that Luke's context is correct, even though he interprets the parable as reflecting Israel's exile and return. Linnemann (*Parables of Jesus,* p. 69) and E. P. Sanders (*Jesus and Judaism* [Philadelphia: Fortress, 1985], p. 179) think vv. 1-2 are redactional but that Luke has correctly hit on the right historical situation.

222. Although Nolland (*Luke 9:21–18:34,* p. 780) argues that the three parables were combined before Luke.

223. See pp. 94-95 above.

224. See Crossan, *In Parables,* p. 74; Pöhlmann, *Der verlorene Sohn und das Haus,* p. 158. Derrett ("The Parable of the Prodigal Son," pp. 102, 122) rejects the idea that the parable has anything to do with eating with sinners but still sees the Pharisees represented in the elder brother. Jülicher (*Die Gleichnisreden Jesu,* 2:361, 363) rejects the idea that the parable was occasioned by the circumstances of vv. 1-2, yet he thinks the parable teaches that God does not allow the righteous to complain when he accepts sinners.

225. Cf. the story of the rich young ruler who also claims to have kept the Law and is not explicitly challenged.

226. Scott, *Hear Then the Parable,* esp. pp. 105, 123-25; Parsons, "The Prodigal's Elder Brother," 171-72.

227. Most obvious are the Matthean judgment parables (the Ten Virgins, the Sheep and the Goats, etc.) but also many Lukan parables as well (e.g., the Banquet and Lazarus and the Rich Man). Nonparabolic sayings pointing to such division include Matt 7:13-14, 21-23; 8:11-12/ Luke 13:23-30.

228. Forbes, *The God of Old,* p. 142. Is there a progression in the three parables of ch. 15? The first speaks of those who do not need repentance, the second does not mention repentance, and the third implies the need of repentance.

229. Cf. Hultgren, *The Parables of Jesus,* p. 82.

230. Cf. Forbes, *The God of Old,* p. 145; Austin, "The Hypocritical Son," 308.

231. Jülicher, *Die Gleichnisreden Jesu,* 2:352, 361. See also his interpretation of the Banquet in Luke. Stein (*An Introduction to the Parables of Jesus,* pp. 117-18) finds several correspondences between image and reality with the Prodigal but denies that this makes the story an allegory. If one takes such a stance, what constitutes allegory? D. Via (*The Parables* [Philadelphia: Fortress,

1967], p. 164) admits the correspondences but denies that the story is allegorical because the connections are internal and centripetal rather than external. See the discussion of parable and allegory, pp. 15-17 above.

232. Schottroff, *The Parables of Jesus*, pp. 144-49.

233. E.g., Harrington, "The Prodigal Son," 434-35; Stein, *An Introduction to the Parables of Jesus*, pp. 117-18 (both of whom like Jülicher still must deny that the story is an allegory); see also Eckhart Rau, "Jesu Auseinandersetzung mit Pharisäern über seine Zuwendung zu Sünderinnen und Sündern. Lk 15,11-32 und Lk 18,10-14a als Worte des historischen Jesus," *ZNW* 89 (1998): 5-29, here p. 10; Nolland, *Luke 9:21–18:34*, p. 780.

234. Various meanings have been assigned especially to the robe and ring, most notably for both, the Holy Spirit.

235. Bailey, *Finding the Lost*, pp. 148-49; Weder, *Die Gleichnisse Jesu als Metaphern*, pp. 260-61.

236. Karl Barth, *Church Dogmatics* (trans. G. W. Bromiley; Edinburgh: T. & T. Clark, 1958) 4/2:21-25; Carl L. Taylor, "Jesus, the Prodigal Son," *Covenant Quarterly* 57 (February, 1999): 36-48.

237. Durber, "The Female Reader of the Parables of the Lost," 70. She argues women cannot read these texts at all. Even more egregious is the distortion of this parable by Mary Ann Beavis, "'Making Up Stories': A Feminist Reading of the Parable of the Prodigal Son (Lk. 15.11b-32)," in *The Lost Coin: Parables of Women, Work and Wisdom* (ed. Mary Ann Beavis; Sheffield: Sheffield Academic Press, 2002), pp. 98-122. She recasts the story as if it told of a dysfunctional family (following Rohrbaugh) in which both sons had been sexually molested by the father, which was why the prodigal left. She acknowledges that her interpretation does not recover Jesus' meaning.

238. Scott, *Hear Then the Parable*, pp. 115, 117. Alicia Batten ("Dishonor, Gender, and the Parable of the Prodigal Son," *TJT* 13 [1997]: 187-200, here p. 196) finds a "feminine" concern in the parable's focus on reconciliation within the family.

239. Note LaHurd ("Rediscovering the Lost Women in Luke 15," 68), who reports that the Arabic women she interviewed were unimpressed that the mother was not mentioned and that they assumed her presence.

240. The Entrevenes Group, *Signs and Parables*, pp. 153-54.

241. Both points argued by Scott, *Hear Then the Parable*, pp. 115, 117. He thinks the father is a failure as a father but a success as a mother. Bailey, *Finding the Lost*, p. 203, also thinks the kiss is more appropriate for a mother.

242. Bailey, *Finding the Lost*, p. 150; *Jacob and the Prodigal*, pp. 117, 175; Robert G. Crawford, "A Parable of the Atonement," *EvQ* 50 (1978): 2-7; Robert Farrar Capon, *The Parables of Grace* (Grand Rapids: Eerdmans, 1988), p. 141.

243. Jülicher, *Die Gleichnisreden Jesu*, 2:364-65.

244. See Jülicher, *Die Gleichnisreden Jesu*, 2:334.

245. E.g., Jeremias, *The Parables of Jesus*, p. 132; Lambrecht, *Once More Astonished*, pp. 47-48; Forbes, *The God of Old*, p. 148, among others.

246. Breech, *The Silence of Jesus*, pp. 195-96; see Rohrbaugh, "A Dysfunctional Family and Its Neighbors (Luke 15:11b-32)," p. 143; and the caustic comments of Buttrick, *Speaking Parables: A Homiletic Guide*, p. 284.

247. Bailey, *Finding the Lost*, p. 133. Surely, however, v. 19 shows remorse. Pharaoh's confession ("I have sinned against the LORD your God, and against you") is the same as Luke 15:21 in thought but not wording ("I have sinned against heaven and before you").

248. See among others 2 Sam 12:13; 24:10, 17; Pss 41:4; 51:4; Mic 7:9. See also Matt 27:4.

249. *Finding the Lost,* pp. 85, 130. He thinks the prodigal's plan is to work and pay back his father. See also *Poet and Peasant,* pp. 173-80. Bailey's desire to avoid seeing repentance as a work humans do is implicit in several of his discussions but explicit in "Psalm 23 and Luke 15," 60. He argues ("Jacob and the Prodigal Son," p. 67) that the son is still lost at the edge of the village until the father finds him.

250. Jeremias, *The Parables of Jesus,* p. 130, following Str.-B. 2:215, 1:261; Brad Young, *The Parables: Jewish Tradition and Christian Interpretation* (Peabody, Mass.: Hendrickson, 1998), p. 146; see the critique by Bailey, *Poet and Peasant,* pp. 173-75.

251. See *BDAG,* p. 395; and the discussions of Green, *The Gospel of Luke,* pp. 581-82; and Hultgren, *The Parables of Jesus,* p. 76. "Come to one's senses" is the meaning in *T. Jos.* 3.9; *3 Bar.* 17.3; Diodorus Siculus 13.95.2; Epictetus, *Discourses* 3.1.15 (cf. 3.23.16). This same expression occurs as a variant in D at Luke 18:4 with reference to the unjust judge who does not repent. Cf. Acts 12:11 "came to himself" *(en heautō genomenos),* which has nothing to do with repentance, and "recovering his senses" *(par' autō genomenos)* in Plutarch, *Mor.* 563B-E.

252. See Fitzmyer, *The Gospel According to Luke X–XXIV,* p. 1088; Hultgren, *The Parables of Jesus,* p. 76; Green, *The Gospel of Luke,* p. 581. Holgate (*Prodigality, Liberality and Meanness in the Parable of the Prodigal Son,* p. 201) would go further and argue from the passages in Epictetus that the expression means "a true understanding of one's moral condition."

253. See e.g., Forbes, *The God of Old,* p. 136; Green, *The Gospel of Luke,* pp. 581-82.

254. Miroslav Volf, *Exclusion and Embrace: A Theological Exploration of Identity, Otherness, and Reconciliation* (Nashville: Abingdon Press, 1996), pp. 159-60; Hultgren, *The Parables of Jesus,* p. 86.

255. As Forbes, *The God of Old,* pp. 136-37, 147.

256. See the concern that Hultgren (*The Parables of Jesus,* pp. 86-87) expresses.

257. See Räisänen, "The Prodigal Gentile and His Jewish Christian Brother, Lk 15,11-32," pp. 1624-27, although he admits that the identification does not work well. See also Pokorný, "Lukas 15, 11-32 und die lukanische Soteriologie," p. 189. F. C. Baur thought the younger and elder sons represented the Gentile Christian and Jewish Christian churches. See Christophe Senft, "Ferdinand Christian Baur, Methodological Approach and Interpretation of Luke 15:11-32," in *Exegesis: Problems of Method and Exercises in Reading (Genesis 22 and Luke 15)* (ed. François Bovon and Grégoire Rouiller, trans. Donald G. Miller; Pittsburgh: Pickwick, 1978), pp. 77-96.

258. People who take this approach often deny that the parable is from Jesus.

259. Bailey, *Finding the Lost,* p. 181; Hultgren, *The Parables of Jesus,* p. 184.

260. François Bovon, "The Parable of the Prodigal Son: Second Reading," in *Exegesis: Problems of Method and Exercises in Reading (Genesis 22 and Luke 15)* (ed. François Bovon and Grégoire Rouiller, trans. Donald G. Miller; Pittsburgh: Pickwick, 1978), pp. 441-66; Lambrecht, *Once More Astonished,* p. 52; Pokorný, "Lukas 15, 11-32 und die lukanische Soteriologie," p. 191; Räisänen, "The Prodigal Gentile and His Jewish Christian Brother, Lk 15,11-32," pp. 1626-27. Holgate (*Prodigality, Liberality and Meanness in the Parable of the Prodigal Son,* pp. 235, 247-51) thinks Luke is addressing reluctance to share possessions.

261. Each of the three has its advocates: e.g., for the father, the most prevalent view, Donahue (*The Gospel in Parable,* p. 157); Fitzmyer, *The Gospel According to Luke X–XXIV,* p. 1085; for the prodigal, Green, *The Gospel of Luke,* p. 578; for the elder at least being the climax, Lambrecht, *Once More Astonished,* p. 32.

262. Compassion is a major theme in Jesus' ministry. Note Matt 9:36; 14:14/Mark 6:34; Matt 15:32/Mark 8:2; Matt 18:27; 20:34; Mark 1:41; 9:22; Luke 7:13; 10:33; 15:20.

263. Cf. among others G. Jones, *The Art and Truth of the Parables*, p. 169; and Heininger, *Metaphorik, Erzählstruktur und szenisch-dramatische Gestaltung in den Sondergutgleichnissen bei Lukas*, p. 165. One is bewildered that Buttrick (*Speaking Parables*, pp. 289-93) finds it necessary to undercut traditional interpretation (because it is too familiar) and finds the merciful God mirrored in the parable to be a naked laughable God.

264. Hultgren (*The Parables of Jesus*, p. 79) erroneously thinks the younger son has in effect supplanted the elder.

265. Räisänen's attempt ("The Prodigal Gentile and His Jewish Christian Brother, Lk 15,11-32," p. 1622) to view the elder son's use of *douleuein* ("serve," "serve as a slave") as a term of respectful service does not fit the context of the complaint. On both sons being servants, see among others Donahue, *The Gospel in Parable*, p. 157; Green, *The Gospel of Luke*, p. 579.

266. Cf. Bovon, "The Parable of the Prodigal Son (Luke 15:11-32): First Reading," p. 61.

267. Some worry that vv. 24 and 32 are theological interpretations provided by Luke, for the words "was dead and lives again" and "was lost and has been found" do not fit the parable. See esp. Georg Braumann, "Tot — lebendig, verloren — gefunden (Lk 15,24 und 32)," in *Wort in der Zeit. Festschrift für K. H. Rengstorf* (ed. W. Haubeck und M. Bachmann; Leiden: Brill, 1980), 156-64, here p. 158; Raisanen, "The Prodigal Gentile and His Jewish Christian Brother, Lk 15,11-32," p. 1618; Bovon, "The Parable of the Prodigal Son (Luke 15:11-32): First Reading," p. 58; Rohrbaugh, "A Dysfunctional Family and Its Neighbors (Luke 15:11b-32)," p. 162. Yet Bovon (p. 63) thinks these words are the epitome of the message, and Rohrbaugh says that they summarize the parable beautifully. Ronald F. Hock demonstrates from Greek romances that the language of vv. 22-24 is conventional and expected. See "Romancing the Parables of Jesus," 11-37. The language of death and resurrection is metaphorical. The prodigal could have been considered dead either because he was not a part of the household, because he was feared dead, or because he was considered morally dead. See Fitzmyer, *The Gospel According to Luke X–XXIV*, p. 1090; Forbes, *The God of Old*, p. 140. Philo, *Flight* 55, 58, uses "death" and "life" metaphorically to refer to an evil life and a virtuous life. *Gen. Rab.* 71.6 (on 30:1) reports R. Samuel as saying "Four are regarded as dead: the leper, the blind, he who is childless, and he who has become impoverished." Nolland (*Luke 9:21–18:34*, p. 786) rightly says that there are no adequate reasons to view vv. 24 and 32 as additions.

268. See Lambrecht, *Once More Astonished*, p. 50; Sibinga, "Zur Kompositationstechnik des Lukas in Lk. 15,11-32," 110-11; Broer, "Das Gleichnis vom verlorenen Sohn und die Theologie des Lukas," 462; and Rau, "Jesu Auseinandersetzung mit Pharisäern über seine Zuwendung zu Sünderinnen und Sündern," esp. p. 10.

269. Linnemann, *Parables of Jesus*, p. 80.

270. As a host of scholars conclude. See, e.g., Heininger, *Metaphorik, Erzählstruktur und szenisch-dramatische Gestaltung in den Sondergutgleichnissen bei Lukas*, p. 165; Hultgren, *The Parables of Jesus*, pp. 84-85; Jeremias, *The Parables of Jesus*, p. 131; Nolland, *Luke 9:21–18:34*, p. 791. Crossan (*In Parables*, p. 74) is one of the few who objects, saying that this is to confuse cause and effect. He thinks this parable (as many others) is about the reversal of the human condition, an argument that is difficult to sustain.

271. J. Green, *The Gospel of Luke*, p. 586.

272. Hendrickx, *The Parables of Jesus*, p. 166; P. Jones, *Studying the Parables of Jesus*, p. 230; Lambrecht, *Once More Astonished*, p. 48.

273. Cf. Henry David Thoreau: "Not until we are lost do we begin to understand ourselves."

274. *The Waiting Father*, p. 40.

275. Volf, *Exclusion and Embrace.*

276. See Christopher A. Hall, "Rejecting the Prodigal," *Christianity Today* (Oct. 26, 1998): 73-76, without citation, but the passage in question is Tertullian, *On Modesty* 9 (*ANF* 4:82-83).

Notes to "The Parable of the Sower and the Purpose of Parables"

1. Prior to ch. 13 Matthew has only the parable of the Two Builders (7:24-27) and parabolic sayings such as the log in the eye (7:3-5), the narrow gate, trees known by their fruits (7:13-20), the bridegroom, a patch on a garment, wineskins (9:15-17), and the sayings about a divided kingdom and about breaking into a strong man's house. Matthew does not use the word *parabolē* prior to 13:3. Mark and Luke have parabolic sayings parallel to Matthew, but Mark uses the word *parabolē* in 3:23 of the sayings concerning the divided kingdom and the strong man's house. Prior to ch. 8 Luke uses the word *parabolē* at 4:23 of a proverb, at 5:36 of the patch on a garment, and at 6:39 of the blind leading the blind. Luke also has the parable of the Two Builders at 6:47-49.

2. In addition to the parable of the Sower Matthew includes the parables of the Mustard Seed, the Leaven, the Wheat and the Weeds (and its interpretation), the Treasure in the Field, the Pearl of Great Price, the Fish Net, and, if it is a parable, the householder who takes from his treasure things new and old.

3. Even though sometimes the reasons given for assuming authenticity are questionable. H.-J. Klauck (*Allegorie und Allegorese in synoptischen Gleichnistexten* [NTAbh 13; Münster: Aschendorff, 1978], p. 197) argues that the eschatological slant of the parable fits only with Jesus, assuming that the focus of the parable is eschatological. J. Marcus (*Mark 1–8: A New Translation with Introduction and Commentary* [AB 27; New York: Doubleday, 2000], pp. 293-94) thinks the agricultural motif and the obscurity of the parable point to authenticity, that the parable is intentionally obscure, and that Mark wants the reader to be as confused as the disciples, which is difficult to imagine. The Jesus Seminar printed the parable in pink but gave more credence to the shortened *Gos. Thom.* version. On the authenticity of the parable see Philip Barton Payne, "The Authenticity of the Parable of the Sower and Its Interpretation," in *Studies of History and Tradition in the Four Gospels,* vol. 1 of *Gospel Perspectives* (ed. R. T. France and David Wenham; Sheffield: JSOT Press, 1980), pp. 163-207. C. Carlston (*The Parables of the Triple Tradition* [Philadelphia: Fortress, 1975], pp. 146-48) is one of the few to raise doubts about the authenticity of this parable, partly by saying there is little evidence Jesus was concerned about his hearers' hearts!

4. E.g., Arland J. Hultgren, *The Parables of Jesus: A Commentary* (Grand Rapids: Eerdmans, 2000), pp. 190, 193.

5. Rudolf Bultmann, *The History of the Synoptic Tradition* (trans. John Marsh; New York: Harper & Row, 1963), pp. 199-200; Eta Linnemann, *Parables of Jesus: Introduction and Exposition* (trans. John Sturdy; London: SPCK, 1966), p. 117.

6. Joel Marcus, *The Mystery of the Kingdom of God* (SBLDS 90; Atlanta: Scholars, 1986), pp. 41, 43.

7. John Nolland, *Luke 1–9:20* (WBC 35A; Dallas: Word, 1989), pp. 372-73; Petra von Gemünden, *Vegetationsmetaphorik im Neuen Testament und seiner Umwelt* (NTOA 18; Göttingen: Vandenhoeck & Ruprecht, 1993), p. 209.

8. Madeleine Boucher, *The Mysterious Parable* (Washington, D.C.: The Catholic Biblical

Association of America, 1977), p. 45; Jack Dean Kingsbury, *The Parables of Jesus in Matthew 13* (Richmond: John Knox, 1969), p. 33.

9. Ulrich Luz, *Matthew 8–20: A Commentary* (trans. James E. Crouch; Minneapolis: Fortress, 2001), p. 242; C. F. D. Moule, "Mark 4:1-20 Yet Once More," in *Neotestamentica et Semitica: Studies in Honor of Matthew Black* (ed. E. E. Ellis and Max Wilcox; Edinburgh: T. & T. Clark, 1969), pp. 95-113, here p. 109; David Flusser, *Die rabbinischen Gleichnisse und der Gleichniserzähler Jesus* 1: *Das Wesen der Gleichnisse* (Bern: Peter Lang, 1981), p. 122.

10. See p. 149 herein.

11. Joachim Jeremias, *The Parables of Jesus* (2d ed.; trans. S. H. Hooke; New York: Charles Scribner's Sons, 1963), pp. 77-79.

12. Also Hermas, *Sim.* 9.20.1-2 appears to be dependent on Matt 13:22 par.

13. Luz, *Matthew 8–20*, p. 237. David Wenham argues for a pre-Markan text to which all three Evangelists had access; see his "The Interpretation of the Parable of the Sower," *NTS* 20 (1974): 299-319, esp. 305.

14. Nolland, *Luke 1–9:20*, pp. 377, 382.

15. Some make the unlikely suggestion that this is a later insertion into Matthew's Gospel because the LXX text is used; e.g. Krister Stendahl, *The School of St. Matthew and Its Use of the Old Testament* (2d ed.; Lund: Gleerup, 1968), pp. 131-32. Quotations would easily have been assimilated to the LXX by the tradition.

16. Mary Ann Tolbert, *Sowing the Gospel: Mark's Gospel in Literary-Historical Perspective* (Minneapolis: Fortress, 1989), pp. 121-22. Marcus (*The Mystery of the Kingdom*, p. 230) argues that ch. 4 is Mark's most sustained meditation on the subject of God's word. Boucher (*The Mysterious Parable*, p. 43) says essentially the same.

17. Tolbert (*Sowing the Gospel*, pp. 123-24), among others, argues this for Mark, but it is true of Matthew and Luke as well. John Drury is probably overly detailed in arguing that each occurrence in the parable of the Sower in Mark has an exact equivalent in the narrative (*The Parables in the Gospels* [New York: Crossroad, 1985], pp. 51-52).

18. In 2 Kgs 19:29-30 we find both literal and figurative uses within two verses: "This year you shall eat what grows of itself . . . then in the third year sow, reap . . . and eat their fruit. The surviving remnant . . . shall again take root downward, and bear fruit upward." Isa 27:6 and Amos 9:13-15 look forward to an eschatological harvest. See also Pss 1:3; 80:8-19; Isa 40:24; Jer 4:3; 17:8; Hos 10:12-13, and many others. In the NT among many uses of this imagery see Matt 3:8-10/ Luke 3:8-10; Matt 7:16-20/Luke 6:43-45; Matt 12:33-35; John 4:36; 12:24; 15:1-17; Rom 1:13; 6:22-23; 7:4-5; 11:17-24; Gal 5:22; 6:8; Eph 5:9; Col 1:6, 10; Heb 6:7-8. See also 4Q213 frag. 5 1.8-9; Sir 1:20; 37:17-18; *Jub.* 1.16; 7.34-37; *Pss. Sol.* 14:3-4; *T. Levi* 13.6; *4 Ezra* 8:6; *2 Bar.* 70.2; Philo, *Det.* 111 and *Leg.* 3.248-53; Hippocrates, *Lex* 3; Antiphon, frag. 60; Plato, *Phaedrus* 276E-77A; Plutarch, *De Pythiae Oraculis* 394E; Seneca, *Epistulae* 38.2; Quintilian, *Inst.* 5.11.24; Hermas, *Sim.* 9.1.6; 9.20.1; 9.21.1-3.

19. E.g., Jeremias, *The Parables of Jesus*, p. 150; Gemünden, *Vegetationsmetaphorik im Neuen Testament und seiner Umwelt*, p. 218; and many others think the reference is to an eschatological harvest. Ferdinand Hahn finds the figures unimaginable; see his "Das Gleichnis von der ausgestreuten Saat und seine Deutung (Mk iv.3-8, 14-20)," in *Text and Interpretation* (ed. Ernest Best and R. Wilson; Cambridge: Cambridge University Press, 1979), pp. 133-42, here p. 135.

20. E.g., K. D. White, "The Parable of the Sower," *JTS* 15 (1964): 300-307, here pp. 301-2; R. T. France, *The Gospel of Mark: A Commentary on the Greek Text* (NIGTC; Grand Rapids: Eerdmans, 2002), p. 192.

21. E.g., Gemünden (*Vegetationsmetaphorik im Neuen Testament und seiner Umwelt*, p. 218), although admitting the reference could be to individual seeds.

22. Or up to twelvefold if barley was the crop. Cf. Sir 7:3. See Douglas Oakman, *Jesus and the Economic Questions of His Day* (Lewiston, N.Y.: Edwin Mellen, 1986), pp. 63-64; Robert K. McIver, "One Hundred-Fold Yield — Miraculous or Mundane? Matthew 13.8, 23; Mark 4:8, 20; Luke 8:8," *NTS* 40 (1994): 606-8.

23. Jeremias (*The Parables of Jesus*, p. 150, n. 84) follows G. Dalman in concluding that a yield of 7.5 is an average yield. Linnemann (*Parables of Jesus*, p. 117) also follows Dalman to argue that each ear yields thirty-five seeds on average and occasionally even one hundred. See Dalman's *Arbeit und Sitte in Palästina* (Hildesheim: Georg Olms, 1964), 3:153-65. Dalman himself (p. 163) interprets the one hundredfold of Gen 26:12 as a result of godly blessing, the highest thinkable. Further, for the numbers in the parable he argues that Jesus stays with what is conceivable, contrary to what Jeremias would have one think. *B. Baba Meṣi'a* 105b indicates a yield of a field at 7.5 as the least amount with which a tenant must be satisfied (and therefore is not evidence for Jeremias's position). The following texts evidence numbers in keeping with the parable: *Sib. Or.* 3:264 ("For these alone the fertile soil yields fruit from one- to a hundredfold, and the measures of God are produced"); Herodotus, *Hist.* 1.193 (corn yields in Babylon of 200-fold and even 300-fold, which is disbelieved by those who have not visited there); Pliny the Elder, *Hist. nat.* 18.21.94-95 (who cites examples of great fertility as high as 150-fold and later speaks of 400 shoots from a single seed, which he finds almost incredible); also 18.40.141 and 18.40.162 (one hundredfold); Varro, *Rerum rusticarum* 1.44.2 (who speaks of one hundredfold but with reservations); and Theophrastus, *Enquiry into Plants* 8.7.4 ("And, if the ground is ill-cultivated, it produces fifty fold, if it is carefully cultivated, a hundred fold"); Strabo, *Geogr.* 15.3.11 (one hundredfold and even two hundredfold); also 16.1.14 (three hundredfold according to a report). McIver ("One Hundred-Fold Yield — Miraculous or Mundane?" 606-8) argues that such numbers are exaggerations but is not convincing, especially given Gen 26:12 and *Sib. Or.* 3.264. See the discussion of Payne, "The Authenticity of the Parable of the Sower and Its Interpretation," pp. 181-86.

24. *1 En.* 10.18-19: "And in those days . . . one measure will yield a thousand"; *2 Bar.* 29.5: ten thousandfold; *b. Ketubot* 111b-112a: 50,000 *kōr* from one *se'â*, which is 1.5 millionfold (this passage has several other exaggerated figures); see also Irenaeus *Haer.* 5.33.3. Cf. Amos 9:13.

25. Since the canonical interpretation already explained the parable in some detail other than clarifying that the sower is Jesus, the early church focused its allegorizing tendencies primarily on assigning theological ideas or ethical accomplishments to the various levels of successful growth. E.g., the levels thirty, sixty, and one hundred were understood as pointing to the married, the widowed and continent, and to virgins, with some taking the highest level as referring to martyrdom. See Stephen L. Wailes, *Medieval Allegories of Jesus' Parables* (Berkeley, Calif.: University of California Press, 1987), pp. 97-103.

26. One of the most unusual and distorted readings is that of William R. Herzog (*Jesus, Justice, and the Reign of God: A Ministry of Liberation* [Louisville: Westminster John Knox, 2000], pp. 193-95) who reads the parable of the Sower as a system of coded symbols. He thinks the "predators" in the parable (the birds, the sun, and the thorns) are Herodian aristocrats who exploit people. For him the problem is not the land; it produces abundantly, even without peasant tithes to support the temple. He finds from this an implication that the temple may not be the key that unlocks the abundance of the good land.

27. Jeremias, *The Parables of Jesus*, pp. 13-18, 77-79, 149-50. John Dominic Crossan (*In Par-*

ables [New York: Harper and Row, 1973], pp. 50-51) concludes that the kingdom is surprise and gift, but his explanation is surprisingly truncated and minimal.

28. Hultgren, *The Parables of Jesus*, p. 188; Peter Rhea Jones, *Studying the Parables of Jesus* (Macon, Ga.: Smyth & Helwys, 1999), pp. 71-78; James R. Edwards, *The Gospel According to Mark* (Grand Rapids: Eerdmans, 2002), p. 138.

29. David E. Garland, *Reading Matthew: A Literary and Theological Commentary on the First Gospel* (New York: Crossroad, 1993), p. 144.

30. John R. Donahue, *The Gospel in Parable: Metaphor, Narrative, and Theology in the Synoptic Gospels* (Philadelphia: Fortress, 1988), pp. 38-39, 46; Christian Dietzfelbinger, "Das Gleichnis vom ausgestreuten Samen," in *Der Ruf Jesu und die Antwort der Gemeinde* (ed. E. Lohse; Göttingen: Vandenhoeck & Ruprecht, 1970), pp. 80-93, esp. 85, 91-93; cf. Jacobus Liebenburg, *The Language of the Kingdom and Jesus: Parable, Aphorism, and Metaphor in the Sayings Material Common to the Synoptic Tradition and the Gospel of Thomas* (BZNW 102; Berlin: Walter de Gruyter, 2001), pp. 390-91.

31. Hans Weder, *Die Gleichnisse Jesu als Metaphern. Traditions- und redaktionsgeschichtliche Analysen und Interpretationen* (4th ed.; Göttingen: Vandenhoeck & Ruprecht, 1990), pp. 109-11, who also emphasizes the responsibility to listen and sees the parable reflecting Jesus' experience. The emphasis is placed on the seed.

32. N. T. Wright, *Jesus and the Victory of God*, vol. 2 of *Christian Origins and the Question of God* (Minneapolis: Fortress, 1996), pp. 230-39; Paul Garnet, "The Parable of the Sower: How the Multitudes Understood It," in *Spirit Within Structure* (ed. Edward J. Furcha; Allison Park, Pa.: Pickwick, 1983), pp. 39-54; Gerhard Lohfink, "Die Metaphorik des Aussaat im Gleichnis vom Sämann (Mk 4,3-9)," in *A Cause de L'Évangile. Études sur les Synoptiques et les Actes* (Lectio Divina 123; Paris: Cerf, 1985), pp. 211-28.

33. John W. Bowker, "Mystery and Parable: Mark 4:1-20," *JTS* 25 (1974): 300-317; see also Craig Evans, *To See and Not Perceive: Isaiah 6.9-10 in Early Jewish and Christian Interpretation* (JSOTSup 64; Sheffield: Sheffield Academic Press, 1989), pp. 99-106; "A Note on the Function of VI,9-10 in Mark IV." *RB* 88 (1981): 234-35; "On the Isaianic Background of the Sower Parable," *CBQ* 47 (1985): 464-68; Wright, *Jesus and the Victory of God*, pp. 236-38.

34. John Painter, *Mark's Gospel: Worlds in Conflict* (New Testament Readings; London: Routledge, 1997), pp. 78-81; Flusser, *Die rabbinischen Gleichnisse und der Gleichniserzähler Jesus*, p. 63; cf. Liebenburg, *The Language of the Kingdom and Jesus*, p. 385.

35. E.g., Jan Lambrecht, *Once More Astonished: The Parables of Jesus* (New York: Crossroad, 1981), pp. 86-87; Joanna Dewey, *Markan Public Debate: Literary Technique, Concentric Structure, and Theology in Mark 2:1–3:6* (SBLDS 48; Chico, Calif.: Scholars, 1980), p. 150, who divides the text as A = vv. 1-2a, B = vv. 2b-20, C = vv. 21-25, B′ = vv. 26-32, A′ = vv. 33-34.

36. See Greg Fay, "Introduction to Incomprehension: The Literary Structure of Mark 4:1-34," *CBQ* 51 (1989): 65-81, esp. 69; Donahue, *The Gospel in Parable*, p. 31 (who finds the parallels in the chiasmus to have virtually the identical number of lines); Marcus, *The Mystery of the Kingdom of God*, p. 221 (following J. Dupont). Boucher (*The Mysterious Parable*, p. 42) comes very close to this organization, although she does not view the passage as a chiasmus.

37. Contra Bernard Brandon Scott (*Hear Then the Parable: A Commentary on the Parables of Jesus* [Minneapolis: Fortress, 1989], p. 346) I do not think the description of Jesus in the boat carries an allusion to Ps 29:10.

38. No indications of time, location, or addressees are given for the parables of the Growing Seed and the Mustard Seed.

39. For obvious examples note how 8:14-21 (the disciples' seeing and not seeing) and 27-

33 (Peter's half-understood confession) are illumined by 8:22-26 (the blind man whose sight is partially restored to see people like trees walking and then fully restored). The disciples' faith and Peter's confession are the equivalent of such poorly formed vision. Similarly, 11:12-14 and 11:20-25 (the cursing of the fig tree and its withering) bracket 11:15-19 (the temple "cleansing") to portray the temple as a fruitless fig tree.

40. This simplistic view of parables is rooted in A. Jülicher's *Die Gleichnisreden Jesu* (Freiburg i. B.: Akademische Verlagsbuchhandlung von J. C. B. Mohr, vol. 1, 1888; vol. 2, 1889), 1:135-48. For Jülicher, we are left with an either-or situation, either the Evangelists or Jesus (p. 148).

41. *The Parables: Their Literary and Existential Dimension* (Philadelphia: Fortress, 1967), p. 8. He says the same about Matthew ("Matthew on the Understandability of the Parables," *JBL* 84 [1965]: 430-32).

42. Taking *en parabolais* as "in riddles" in keeping with the breadth of the Hebrew term *mashal*.

43. Mark and the Targum agree against the Hebrew and LXX in using participles and third person verbs instead of the imperatives and second person verbs in Isa 6:9 and in using "forgive" instead of "heal" in v. 10.

44. Jeremias, *The Parables of Jesus*, pp. 13-18. Both Greek *mēpote* and Aramaic *dilma'* can mean "lest" or less frequently "perhaps." In Matt 25:9; Luke 3:15; John 7:26; and 2 Tim 2:25 *mēpote* means "perhaps." Note, however, that J. F. Stenning's translation of *The Targum of Isaiah* (Oxford: Clarendon, 1949) uses "lest" in the translation of Isa 6:10. For others who, like Jeremias, turn the statement into an expression of hope, see Peter Lampe, "Die markinische Deutung des Gleichnisses vom Sämann, Markus 4:10-12," *ZNW* 65 (1974): 140-50; W. Manson, "The Purpose of the Parables: A Re-Examination of St. Mark in iv.10-12," *ExpTim* 68 (1956-57): 132-35, esp. 134, where Manson translates the debated words as "that they may indeed see, *though* they do not perceive . . . *in case* they yet turn and are forgiven" (italics his).

Jeremias (*The Parables of Jesus*, p. 14, n. 11) thinks the distinctions between Jesus, the tradition, and Mark are nowhere so clear as in Mark 4.

Others seek to reconstruct the original parable — almost always in a truncated form — and to explain the growth of the tradition. See Crossan, *In Parables*, pp. 39-44; or Weder, *Die Gleichnisse Jesu als Metaphern*, pp. 99-117. Although the material has obviously been shaped in the course of transmission, I have no confidence in such efforts, subjective and simplistic as they always are, and they yield little help in understanding the parable. See the comments of U. Luz, *Matthew 8–20*, p. 243.

45. *The Teaching of Jesus* (Oxford: Clarendon, 1939), pp. 75-80.

46. Bastiaan Van Elderen, "The Purpose of the Parables According to Matthew 13:10-17," in *New Dimensions in New Testament Study* (ed. Richard N. Longenecker and Merrill C. Tenney; Grand Rapids: Zondervan, 1974), pp. 180-90, see 188.

47. Carl Heinz Peisker, "Konsekutives ἵνα in Markus 4:12," *ZNW* 59 (1968): 126-27. See the overview of options given by Evans, *To See and Not Perceive*, pp. 91-99.

48. *Mark — Traditions in Conflict* (Philadelphia: Fortress, 1971), pp. 139-49, esp. 147. Weeden assigned 4:3-9, 11-12, 14-20, and 26-34 all to Mark's opponents.

49. Which C. F. D. Moule ("Mark 4:1-20 Yet Once More," 99) calls "a pitiful literalism."

50. *Homilies on Matthew* 45.

51. See above, pp. 38-42; Claus Westermann, *The Parables of Jesus in the Light of the Old Testament* (trans. and ed. Friedemann W. Golka and Alastair H. B. Logan; Minneapolis: Fortress, 1990), pp. 2, 20-30, 150-60; and my "Parables and the Hebrew Scriptures," in *To Hear and*

Obey: Essays in Honor of Fredrick Carlson Holmgren (ed. Bradley J. Bergfalk and Paul E. Koptak; Chicago: Covenant Publications, 1997 [*Covenant Quarterly* 55/2-3]), pp. 164-77.

52. *Jesus and the Victory of God,* pp. 147-97, esp. 164-65. See also Scot McKnight, "Jesus and Prophetic Actions," *BBR* 10 (2000): 197-232.

53. Note the connection of this quotation to the parable of the Treasure *Hidden* in the Field in Matt 13:44.

54. Cf. e.g., E. P. Sanders, *Jesus and Judaism* (Philadelphia: Fortress, 1985), pp. 319-26.

55. As suggested by Morna D. Hooker, *The Gospel According to Saint Mark* (BNTC; Peabody, Mass.: Hendrickson, 1991), p. 127; see also Frank E. Eakin, Jr. "Spiritual Obduracy and Parable Purpose," in *The Use of the Old Testament in the New and Other Essays* (ed. James M. Efird; Durham, N.C.: Duke University Press, 1972), p. 90.

56. "Mark 4:1-20 Yet Once More," p. 100.

57. Note Isa 1:2-31; 2:6–4:1; 5:1-30. Rikki Watts (*Isaiah's New Exodus and Mark* [Tübingen: Mohr Siebeck, 1997], pp. 183-210) argues that the blindness and deafness imagery reflects a complaint against idolatry, with people becoming blind, deaf, and without understanding just like their idols.

58. E.g., among many texts see Jer 1:10-19; 5:21 (which uses words straight from Isa 6:9); 7:16 (where Jeremiah is told not to pray for the people, for God will not hear); Ezek 2:2-7 (where Ezekiel is sent to a nation of rebels who will oppose him); 3:7-11 (where Ezekiel is told that the house of Israel will not listen for they "have a hard forehead and a stubborn heart"); 12:2 (again taken straight from Isa 6:9); and Zech 7:11-12 (which describes the people as refusing to listen, turning a stubborn shoulder, stopping their ears, and making their hearts adamant in order not to hear the words sent by God's Spirit through the former prophets).

59. Isa 1:16-20, 27; 7:13; 8:9-22; 12:1-6; 26:20–27:5; 28:14-29; 30:9-30; 31:6; 32:1-20; 33:13-24.

60. Bruce Hollenbach, "Lest They Should Turn and Be Forgiven: Irony," *Bible Translator* 34 (1983): 312-21. Jerry Camery-Hoggatt argues that Mark 4:10-11 is not irony; see his *Irony in Mark's Gospel: Text and Subtext* (SNTSMS 72; Cambridge: Cambridge University Press, 1992), pp. 126-30.

61. Which Volker A. Lehnert calls *paradoxe Intervention.* See his *Die Provokation Israels. Die paradoxe Funktion von Jes 6,9-10 bei Markus und Lukas* (Neukirchener Theologische Dissertationen und Habilitationen 25; Neukirchen-Vluyn: Neukirchener, 1999), pp. 152-63. Cf. Eakin, "Spiritual Obduracy and Parable Purpose," pp. 89-99, who describes the commission of Isaiah as "a masterful study in contradiction" (p. 89).

62. Isa 10:20-23; 28:5-6; 37:31-32.

63. Jer 5:21; Ezek 12:2; John 9:39; 12:39-40; Acts 28:26-27.

64. Our problem is that we read pericopes, not documents, and in the process do not see the sets of relations the various authors weave.

65. See Evans, *To See and Not Perceive,* pp. 101-6; and Watts, *Isaiah's New Exodus and Mark,* pp. 184-210. This is clear in Mark 7:6-7 and esp. texts drawing on Isaiah 61 such as Luke 4:18-19; Matt 11:5-10/Luke 7:22-27; and the Beatitudes; also Matt 21:33/Mark 12:1; Matt 24:29/Mark 13:24-25/Luke 21:25; and at least at some level the use of suffering servant ideas.

66. On correspondence in history as an interpretive device see my "The Use of the Old Testament in the New Testament," in *Interpreting the New Testament: Essays on Methods and Issues* (ed. David Alan Black and David S. Dockery; Nashville: Broadman and Holman, 2001), pp. 215, 224.

67. Boucher (*The Mysterious Parable,* p. 45) rejects the idea that 4:10-12 contradicts other parts of this chapter which call for right hearing and says, "It would be more correct to say that

the whole chapter is properly understood only when the statement on the purpose of parables is taken together with these other units."

68. See also Isa 1:9; 10:20-22; 11:11, 16; 37:31-32; Jer 23:3; 31:7; Ezek 11:13; Mic 5:7-8, etc. The LXX does not include at Isa 6:13 the words about the holy seed, but they are present in 1QIsaᵃ.

69. Stenning's translation of the Targum of Isa 6:13b is: ". . . like a terebinth and like an oak, which appear to be dried up when their leaves fall, though they still retain their moisture to preserve a seed from them: so the exiles of Israel shall be gathered together, and shall return to their land; for a holy seed is their plant." The interpretation is significant regardless of the date of the Targum.

70. "Mystery and Parable: Mark iv.1-20," 300-317; see esp. 311. See also Evans, *To See and Not Perceive*, p. 100; P. Jones, *Studying the Parables of Jesus*, p. 73.

71. *Jesus and the Victory of God*, pp. 230-39. Cf. Matt 15:13. See also Gerhard Lohfink, "Die Metaphorik der Aussaat im Gleichnis vom Sämann," pp. 211-28.

72. See my "Reading and Overreading the Parables in *Jesus and the Victory of God*," in *Jesus and the Restoration of Israel: A Critical Assessment of N. T. Wright's* Jesus and the Victory of God (ed. Carey Newman; Downers Grove, Ill.: InterVarsity, 1999), pp. 61-76.

73. Contra W. D. Davies and Dale C. Allison, Jr., *A Critical and Exegetical Commentary on the Gospel According to Saint Matthew* (3 vols.; Edinburgh: T&T Clark, 1991), 2:377. See Moule ("Mark 4:1-20 Yet Once More," p. 113), who sees vv. 1-20 as an intelligible whole, "composed by the Evangelist but with a historically sensitive use of genuinely traditional material."

74. Eugene Lemcio, "External Evidence for the Structure and Function of Mark 4:1-20, 6:14-23 and 8:14-21," *JTS* 29 (1978): 324-38; Davies and Allison, *Matthew*, 2:387. Cf. Priscilla Patten, "The Form and Function of Parables in Select Apocalyptic Literature and Their Significance for Parables in the Gospel of Mark," *NTS* 29 (1983): 246-58. See, e.g., Ezek 12:2-7, 8-9, 10-16; 17:2-10, 11-12a, 12b-24; Zech 4:1-3, 4-5, 6-14; *1 En.* 24.1-6 (vision), 25:1-2 (surprise and request), 3-6 (explanation); *4 Ezra* 9:38–10:26 (vision), 10:27-37 (intervening material), 10:38-54 (explanation); 11:1–12:3a (vision), 12:3b-9 (request for interpretation), 12:10-39 (interpretation); 13:1-13 (vision), 13:14-20 (request for interpretation), 13:21-56 (interpretation); *2 Bar.* 13.1-12 (vision); 14.1-19 (question and erroneous interpretation); 15.1-8 (correct interpretation); 36.1–37.1 (vision); 38.1-4 (request for explanation); 39.1–40.4 (interpretation); 53.1-12 (vision); 54.1-22 (request for explanation); 55.1–74.4 (interpretation); Hermas, *Sim.* 5.2.1-11 (parable); 5.3.1–5.5.1 (requests for explanation); 5.5.2–5.6.8 (interpretation). According to *Sim.* 5.4.3 only to those who seek understanding is explanation given; the weak and idle in prayer hesitate to ask for help in understanding, which is similar to the picture in Mark 4:10.

75. See also 54:4-16 and *1 En.* 48:7; 82:2-3; 104:12. In *4 Ezra* 14:26, 45-48 Ezra is told to make some things public and to deliver some things in secret to the wise.

76. See Luz, *Matthew 8–20*, p. 247.

77. See Lehnert, *Die Provokation Israels*, pp. 152-63; and Robert M. Fowler, *Let the Reader Understand: Reader-Response Criticism and the Gospel of Mark* (Minneapolis: Fortress, 1991), pp. 168-70.

78. If *hoi par' autou* in 3:21 is to be understood of Jesus' family. On the crowds see 1:5, 22, 28, 32-33, 37, 45; 2:2, 12-15; 3:7-8, 20; 5:21, etc. On the religious leadership and Jesus' family see also 2:6-8, 24; 3:2, 6; 6:1-6, etc.

79. R. P. Meye ("Mark 4,10: 'Those about Him with the Twelve,'" in *Studia Evangelica II* [ed. F. L. Cross, Berlin: Akademie-Verlag, 1964], pp. 211-18) thinks Mark's expression refers to a smaller group within the Twelve, but this is unlikely. Moule's description of this group ("Mark

4:1-20 Yet Once More," p. 98) as a chance gathering is inappropriate. See Bowker, "Mystery and Parable: Mark iv.1-20," 309.

80. L. Schottroff takes "those outside" as an eschatological concept and as referring to those who refuse to hear, whom God will judge, and concludes therefore that no human may label another as an outsider. See her *The Parables of Jesus* (trans. Linda M. Maloney; Minneapolis: Fortress, 2006), p. 70.

81. See Marcus, *Mark 1–8*, p. 306. R. Watts correctly points out that there are five groups designated in 3:20–4:33, not just insiders and outsiders, and that the sifting of Israel is still in process (*Isaiah's New Exodus and Mark,* pp. 201-7).

82. Cf. Paul Ricoeur, who discusses pre-ethical obedience and the importance of "hearkening," listening. See *The Conflict of Interpretations: Essays in Hermeneutics* (ed. Don Ihde; Evanston: Northwestern University Press, 1974), pp. 449-55.

83. Bowker, "Mystery and Parable: Mark iv.1-20," 313 (italics his) and 315.

84. The expression occurs at 3:23; 4:2, 11; 12:1.

85. As Boucher (*The Mysterious Parable,* p. 56) points out, Mark did not invent the mysterious character of parables. See also Moule, "Mark 4:1-20 Yet Once More," p. 106.

86. It is fair to say there is an ambiguous relation between the work of God and the response of people, for the Spirit is the one who enables hearing. Cf. Deut 29:4 (3); Ps 143:8; Isa 50:4-5; see also Deut 30:12-20; and 1QH 1.21: "You have unstopped my ears to marvelous mysteries." Both divine causation and human responsibility are kept in tension, and, as M. Boucher (*The Mysterious Parable,* pp. 60-63) points out, God assists people in the choices they make. Cf. Rom 1:24-28. However, these are not the concerns of Mark 4:10-12 par.

87. In addition to Raymond Brown's *The Semitic Background of the Term "Mystery" in the New Testament* (Philadelphia: Fortress, 1968), see Bowker, "Mystery and Parable," 305-9, who views "mystery" as referring "to something which can be well known, but only to those to whom God chooses to give that knowledge" (p. 305), and lists references in rabbinic literature to that which constitutes or identifies Israel in its special relation to God (p. 307).

88. Several passages in the Dead Sea Scrolls speak of God revealing his mysteries to his servants or of his opening their ears. See 1QpHab 7.4-5, 8 (the interpretation of Hab 2:2 concerns the Teacher of Righteousness, to whom God has disclosed all the wonderful mysteries of the words of his servants, the prophets); 1QM 10.10-11 (Israel is a nation of hearers of the glorious voice, those with opened ears hearing profound things); 1QH 5.3-6 (the simple will understand the mysteries); 6.17 (thanks to the abundance of God's goodness, the psalmist knows); 9.21 (the psalmist knows because God opened his ears to wondrous mysteries); 12.26c-27 (through the psalmist God has enlightened the face of the many for God showed him wondrous mysteries). Cf. Wis 2:22 (evil people persecute the righteous one because they do not know the secret purposes of God) and 1QS 3.21-24 (because of the Angel of Darkness even the sons of justice stray, and their mutinous deeds are under his dominion in compliance with the mysteries of God).

89. Although Luke has a different context for this saying, like Matthew he has placed it in a context dealing with revelation.

90. *The Mysterious Parable,* p. 83. She adds (p. 84), ". . . those who do not understand are those who will not allow its lesson to impinge on their own existence." Liebenburg (*The Language of the Kingdom and Jesus,* p. 377) makes the point that being given the mystery is not the same as understanding it.

91. See Davies and Allison, *Matthew,* 2:389; Aloysius M. Ambrozic, *The Hidden Kingdom: A Redaction-Critical Study of the References to the Kingdom of God in Mark's Gospel* (CBQMS 2;

Washington, D.C.: The Catholic Biblical Association of America, 1972), pp. 91-92; and Wright, *Jesus and the Victory of God*, pp. 230-39, to mention only a few.

92. Davies and Allison, *Matthew*, 2:396-99 (with a fair amount of caution); Luz, *Matthew 8–20*, pp. 238-44; Donald A. Hagner, *Matthew 1–13* (WBC 33a; Dallas: Word, 1993), p. 377; Craig Keener, *A Commentary on the Gospel of Matthew* (Grand Rapids: Eerdmans, 1999), pp. 381-85. On other Gospels see Robert H. Gundry, *Mark: A Commentary on His Apology for the Cross* (Grand Rapids: Eerdmans, 1993), pp. 209-11; France, *The Gospel of Mark*, pp. 202-3; and Nolland, *Luke 1–9:20*, p. 383 (cautiously). Among others who accept the interpretation see Boucher, *The Mysterious Parable*, pp. 49-50 (who says it fits the parable perfectly); C. E. B. Cranfield, "St. Mark 4:1-34," *SJT* 4 (1951): 398-414 and 5 (1952): 49-66; R. Brown, "Parable and Allegory Reconsidered," in *New Testament Essays* (Garden City, N.Y.: Doubleday, 1968), pp. 321-33; Flusser, *Die rabbinischen Gleichnisse und der Gleichniserzähler Jesus*, p. 63 (who says that rabbinic parallels show unavoidably that the interpretation always belonged to this parable); Birger Gerhardsson, "The Parable of the Sower and Its Interpretation," *NTS* 14 (1968): 165-93, esp. 187 (". . . the parable and the interpretation fit each other as hand to glove") and 191-92; Moule, "Mark 4:1-20 Yet Once More," pp. 109-13; Payne, "The Authenticity of the Parable of the Sower and Its Interpretation," pp. 163-207; Schottroff, *The Parables of Jesus*, p. 71. Liebenburg (*The Language of the Kingdom and Jesus*, pp. 350-51) argues that the basic metaphor is "preaching is sowing," which the hearers would have thought on their own, and that the interpretations of the Evangelists presuppose and use the interpretations of hearers for greater nuance.

Among the many rejecting the interpretation are Charles E. Carlston, *The Parables of the Triple Tradition*, p. 148; Crossan, *In Parables*, pp. 41-42; Linnemann, *Parables of Jesus*, pp. 117-19; Hahn, "Das Gleichnis von der ausgestreuten Saat und seine Deutung (Mk iv.3-8, 14-20)," pp. 133-42 (but admitting that the interpretation is closer to the parable than most accept); Barry W. Henaut, *Oral Tradition and the Gospels: The Problem of Mark 4* (JSNTSup 82; Sheffield: Sheffield Academic, 1993), p. 195; Hultgren, *The Parables of Jesus*, pp. 189-90 (but his own interpretation is quite close to the interpretation in the Gospels); Klauck, *Allegorie und Allegorese in synoptischen Gleichnistexten*, pp. 200-206; Peter Lampe, "Die markinische Deutung des Gleichnisses vom Sämann, Markus 4:10-12," *ZNW* 65 (1974): 140-50, esp. 148-50; Marcus, *The Mystery of the Kingdom*, pp. 31, 69; Weder, *Die Gleichnisse Jesu als Metaphern*, pp. 103-13; Ulrich Mell, *Die Zeit der Gottesherrschaft. Zur Allegorie und zum Gleichnis von Markus 4:1-9* (Stuttgart: Kohlhammer, 1998), pp. 41, 55-65. Jülicher (*Die Gleichnisreden Jesu*, 2:531-38) was surprisingly cautious in his comments on the interpretation.

93. *Matthew 8–20*, p. 244 (italics his); cf. 251: "None of the attempts . . . to interpret our text in terms of grace in any way come as close to it as did its classical parenetic interpretation." Luz also says (p. 244) that if we assume the interpretation was formulated by the church it may still be accurate, and he grants that the parable and the interpretation may both originate from the church.

94. See above, pp. 6 and 15-17.

95. The efforts to distinguish parable and allegory invariably fail. See above, pp. 15-17 for discussion of allegory. J. D. Crossan went through a change so that in his recent work he even embraces allegory. See his *Cliffs of Fall* (New York: Seabury, 1980), esp. pp. 96-97; and "Parable, Allegory, and Paradox," in *Semiology and the Parables* (ed. Daniel Patte; Pittsburgh: Pickwick, 1976), pp. 247-81, esp. 271-78.

96. The omission of the interpretation fits with the goal of *Gos. Thom.* to present the *secret* words of Jesus so that those who find the explanation will not taste death (see *Gos. Thom.* introduction and 1). No interpretive help will be given to the unenlightened. Any thought that

this document has an earlier version is vitiated by the additions of the worm, of the idea of seed growing up to heaven, and of the yield being set at 60 and 120. See Klauck, *Allegorie und Allegorese in synoptischen Gleichnistexten*, pp. 209 and 199-200, who rejects the idea that *Gos. Thom.* has any claim to originality; Marcus, *The Mystery of the Kingdom of God*, pp. 33-34, who suggests *Gos. Thom.* may be a reworking of Mark. See also Henaut, *Oral Tradition and the Gospels: The Problem of Mark 4*, pp. 222-32, who concludes that neither *1 Clement* nor *Gos. Thom.* represents an independent version and that the latter displays some type of textual relation to Markan tradition.

97. If the parable is at all about the word being sown in people, the fluidity is inherent in the logic of the metaphor — we speak of both seed and ground being sown. In Col 1:6, 10 both the gospel and the people are described as bearing fruit and increasing. Cf. *4 Ezra* 8:41; 9:31. Gundry comments (*Mark*, p. 207), "It is difficult to imagine how the parable as explained would make sense unless the seed represents both the word and the hearers. See also Nolland, *Luke 1– 9:20*, p. 383. Luz, *Matthew 8–20*, p. 248, follows Jülicher, *Die Gleichnisreden Jesu*, 2:533, in thinking the double reference is due to popular carelessness. Joel Marcus ("Blanks and Gaps in the Markan Parable of the Sower," *BibInt* 5 [1997]: 247-62, here p. 251) suggests that the double referent may be due to the complexity of ideas. P. Payne may be correct that Mark probably meant *speiromenoi* to mean *soil* being sown *with seed* ("The Seeming Inconsistency of the Interpretation of the Parable of the Sower," *NTS* 26 [1979-80]: 564-68).

98. E.g., Joseph A. Fitzmyer, *The Gospel According to Luke I–IX* (AB 28; Garden City, N.Y.: Doubleday, 1981), p. 711; but see Nolland, *Luke 1–9:20*, p. 383.

99. *Die Gleichnisreden Jesu*, 2:534-38.

100. Marcus, *The Mystery of the Kingdom*, pp. 70-71; W. O. E. Oesterley, *The Gospel Parables in the Light of Their Jewish Background* (London: SPCK, 1936), p. 41.

101. E.g., Hahn, "Das Gleichnis von der ausgestreuten Saat und seine Deutung (Mk iv.3-8, 14-20)," p. 138.

102. See pp. 38-59 above.

103. Flusser is particularly strong in arguing that interpretations often accompany parables, that the interpretations of the Evangelists are usually correct, and specifically that the interpretation of the parable of the Sower is authentic (*Die rabbinischen Gleichnisse und der Gleichniserzähler Jesus*, esp. pp. 63, 119, 122, 133, 137). A. Ambrozic, who is primarily concerned with Mark's understanding, points out (*The Hidden Kingdom*, p. 82) that in *1 Enoch mashal* is used of both visions of the end and their interpretations, concluding that "Interpretation thus shares in the nature of *māšāl*" (cf. *1 En.* 38.1; 43.4). He thinks the interpretation and the parable came to Mark as a unit. M. D. Goulder, *Midrash and Lection in Matthew* (London: SPCK, 1974), pp. 56-60, esp. 60: "It was . . . normal for parables to be interpreted. All five OT parables receive interpretations on the spot, and 97 of our hundred rabbinic parables move on at their conclusion with such a comment as 'Even so will the Holy One. . . .'" However, it is unclear whether he thinks the interpretation of the Sower is from Mark. See also Yves Tissot, "Patristic Allegories of the Lukan Parable of the Two Sons (Luke 15:11-32)," in François Bovon and Grégoire Rouiller, *Exegesis: Problems of Method and Exercises in Reading (Genesis 22 and Luke 15)* (trans. Donald G. Miller; Pittsburgh: Pickwick, 1978), pp. 362-409, here p. 363: "Indeed, by its nature a parable requires an allegorical interpretation, for it *speaks of another thing*" (italics his).

104. E.g., see the detailed identifications esp. of *Sipre Deut.* 312; *Midr. Tanḥuma Beshallaḥ* 4.7; *Exod. Rab.* 30.17 (p. 279 herein).

105. ". . . Lebanon is the Council of the Community and the animals are the simple folk

of Judah. . . . the city is Jerusalem. . . . The violence (done to) the country are the cities of Judah which he plundered of the possessions of the poor."

106. *L.A.B.* 37.1-5 interprets the trees in Jotham's parable (Judg 9:8-20) by saying, ". . . the apple tree signifies the chastisers, and the fig tree signifies the people, and the vine signifies those who were before us. And now the bramblebush will be . . . like Abimelech. . . ." Cf. *Midr. Tanḥuma Wayyera* 4.29, which also interprets Jotham's parable in detail. The trees are Israel, the olive tree is Othniel ben Kenaz, the fig tree is Deborah, etc. See also *L.A.B.* 47.1-9; *4 Ezra* 4:13-21, 47-51; 9:38–10:59; 12:10-35; *2 Bar.* 39-40; 56.1-16; *m. 'Abot* 3.18; 5.15 and the examples named above, pp. 57-58. *Exod. Rab.* 15.19; 20.1, tells a parable about a swineherder who will not restore a ewe-lamb to its rightful owner, a king, and in the interpretation we find, "This king . . . is God — the King of kings; the ewe-lamb is Israel; the swineherd is Pharaoh." Such identifications are attested frequently. Other texts with such explicit identifications include *Mekilta Beshallaḥ* 4.35-41; *Mekilta Baḥodesh* 9.2-41 (which interprets Gen 15:17 item for item); *Midr. Tanḥuma Shemot* 1.10; *Midr. Tanḥuma Ki Tissa* 9.15; *Midr. Tanḥuma Emor* 8.30; *Lev. Rab.* 1.14-15; 4.5; 13.5; *Num. Rab.* 16.3; *Deut. Rab.* 2.24; *Eccl. Rab.* 5.11-13; *Pesiqta Rabbati* 10.4. *Mekilta Beshallaḥ* 2.104-18 and *b. 'Abodah Zarah* 54b are examples of allegorical parables with obvious correspondences that are not explicitly interpreted. Such examples are numerous. Hermas, *Sim.* 5.5.1-3 gives a detailed explanation of each element of the parable of the vineyard (5.2.1-11), which is true of other extended parables in this work. See also Ignatius, *Ephesians* 9.1.

107. Similar to *m. 'Abot* 5.15 above, p. 149. Schottroff (*The Parables of Jesus*, p. 72) underscores that only two types of hearing are depicted, not four.

108. Which by itself is reason enough to reject Edwards's suggestion (*The Gospel According to Mark*, p. 136) that the parable explains christology and the interpretation explains discipleship. The parable obviously has implications for both subjects, but neither is the focus of the parable or of the interpretation.

109. Excess can run in either direction: either rejecting any identification of features or finding reference that does not exist. I see no basis for Ulrich Mell's suggestion (*Die Zeit der Gottesherrschaft*, pp. 56-63) that the farmer is the early church missionary who sows the word, the birds are a threat of extinction to disobedient Christians, the thorns are people who cannot control their desires, and the rocky ground is a reference to Peter. This is allegorizing.

110. Note the following texts with *ho logos* not referring to the gospel: Matt 15:12; 19:11 (a saying of Jesus but with variants); 19:22 (with variants)/Mark 10:22; Mark 1:45 (the man was spreading the news about Jesus' miracle, not preaching the gospel); 5:36; 8:32 (teaching about Jesus' rejection, death, and resurrection); 9:10; Luke 1:29; 5:15; 16:2 (a saying of Jesus); and John 4:37 (a saying of Jesus).

111. Cf. e.g. Matt 7:24-26; 15:6; 24:35. Luke uses "the word of God" in 5:1 to refer to Jesus' teaching; when he identifies the seed as the word of God in 8:11, surely he refers to Jesus' teaching, not the church's gospel, which is called "word of God" in Acts 4:31.

112. See among many texts Jdg 3:19-20; 2 Sam 23:2; 24:11; 2 Kgs 9:5; Isa 2:1; 31:2; 55:11; Jer 11:1; 15:16; 18:18; Ezek 12:23; Hos 1:1; Jon 1:1; 3:1; Luke 4:32; 10:39; John 4:41; Acts 15:32; cf. *BDAG*, p. 599, which offers as the first definition of *logos* "communication whereby the mind finds expression."

Jeremias also finds indication of an origin in the church because the word causes persecution, grows, or bears fruit. But such ideas are common in the OT and elsewhere. The prophets, especially Jeremiah, were persecuted because of the word (e.g., Jer 20:8), and the wording of the texts Jeremias views as parallels (1 Thess 1:6; 2 Tim 1:8; 2:9; 1 Pet 2:8) is quite different from the parable. Deut 8:3 refers to the word of the Lord as nourishment, and Jeremiah ate God's words and found joy in them (Jer 15:16). Deut 29:18 refers to people turning from the Lord as roots producing bitter poison. Prov 12:12 says the root of the righteous will bear fruit. Hosea urges people to sow righteousness, reap the fruit of unfailing love, and break up their unplowed ground, but laments that they planted wickedness, reaped evil, and ate the fruit of deception (cf. Jer 4:3). *4 Ezra* 9:30-31 speaks of the Law being sown and bearing fruit and of people perishing for not keeping what was sown. *T. Levi* 13.6 tells people to sow good things in their souls so that they will find them in their lives (cf. 4Q213). In *Odes of Solomon* 17:14 the speaker says, "And I sowed my fruits in hearts, and transformed them through myself." Quintilian speaks of the mind requiring cultivation; if neglected it produces thorns but if cultivated it will bear fruit (*Inst.* 5.11.24). Seneca speaks of words being scattered like seed which on favorable ground unfolds its strength and grows (*Epistulae Morales* 38.2). See also p. 155, n. 18 above.

113. See *The Parables of Jesus,* pp. 77-78.

114. The idea of receiving the word (or instruction, correction, etc.) is a perfectly natural expression. "Receiving the word" appears also in 1 Thess 2:13; Acts 11:1; 17:11; 2 Cor 11:4; and Jas 1:21, but similar expressions occur in John 12:48 (Jesus referring to those not receiving his words [*rēmata*]); Acts 7:38 (of Moses receiving living oracles), 53 (of receiving the law); 17:15 (a command); Col 4:10 (a command); Heb 10:26 (knowledge of the truth); 11:13 (the promises, but with a variant). Note in the LXX Deut 33:3; Job 4:12; Prov 1:3; 2:1; 4:10; 9:9; 10:8; 16:7; 30:1; Jer 2:30; 5:3; 7:27; 9:19; 17:23; Zeph 3:2, 7; Zech 1:6; Jdt 11:5; Sir 51:6.

115. Job 15:29; Prov 12:3; cf. Isa 40:24. Sir 23:25 says with regard to a promiscuous woman: "Her children will not take root, and her branches will not bear fruit"; 40:15 is similar: "The children of the ungodly put out few branches; they are unhealthy roots on sheer rock." Wis 4:3-4 says that the root of the ungodly has no depth. *m. 'Abot.* 3.18 compares those who have more wisdom than works to trees with branches and few roots. *Pss. Sol.* 14:3-4 refers to the devout as trees of life whose planting is firmly rooted forever.

116. See the critiques of Jeremias by Moule ("Mark 4:1-20 Yet Once More," pp. 111-12) and Bowker ("Mystery and Parable," 316). Bowker argues that much of the language results almost inevitably if the passage is related to Isaiah 6. See also Cranfield, "St. Mark 4.1-34, Part I," 408-11; Payne, "The Authenticity of the Parable of the Sower and Its Interpretation," pp. 177-80.

117. Jeremias, *The Parables of Jesus,* pp. 11-12.

118. "The Parable of the Sower," *JTS* 15 (1964): 300-307. See Isa 28:24; Hos 10:11; Jer 4:3. J. Fitzmyer (*The Gospel According to Luke I–IX,* p. 703) judged White's evidence as inconclusive, esp. for Palestine. Other texts not mentioned by White but also presupposing that plowing comes first include Job 4:8; *Gos. Thom.* 20; Sir 6:19; 20:28 (apparently); 38:26.

119. J. Jeremias, "Palästinakundliches zum Gleichnis vom Sämann (Mark IV.3-8 par)," *NTS* 13 (1966-67): 48-53.

120. Some pictures from the ancient world show the plow preceding the sower, and others show it following right behind the sower. See von Gemünden, *Vegetationsmetaphorik im Neuen Testament und seiner Umwelt,* pp. 212-14; *b. Šabbat* 73b attests to both practices but indicates that in Palestine sowing preceded plowing.

121. P. B. Payne, "The Order of Sowing and Ploughing in the Parable of the Sower," *NTS* 25 (1979): 123-29; von Gemünden, *Vegetationsmetaphorik im Neuen Testament und seiner Umwelt,* p. 213.

122. Contra von Gemünden, *Vegetationsmetaphorik im Neuen Testament und seiner Umwelt,* p. 217; Nolland, *Luke 1–9:20,* p. 372. If the idea were that the sower sows with joyous abandon or is embracing risks, it would have been stated more explicitly.

123. Luz, *Matthew 8–20,* p. 241; Liebenburg, *The Language of the Kingdom and Jesus,* p. 356. Nor is there any basis for J. Marcus's seeing a disparity between a realistic sowing method

in the parable and an unrealistic method in the interpretation, where seed is intentionally sown where it will not flourish. (See his "Blanks and Gaps in the Markan Parable of the Sower," 258.)

124. Luz, *Matthew 8–20*, p. 241.

125. *Jub.* 11.11-24 speaks of birds as agents of "Prince Mastema" (a name for Satan) who devour seed being sown in order to rob humankind of their labor. Abraham was born and scared all the crows off. Then he taught those making implements how to plant so that the seeds would drop onto the point of the plow and be hidden in the earth, so they were not afraid of the crows any more.

126. Wright, *Jesus and the Victory of God*, p. 235; see also Scott, *Hear Then the Parable*, p. 353.

127. But the singulars should be understood as collective nouns ("some seeds") rather than a single seed in each case.

128. Charles W. Hedrick (*Parables as Poetic Fictions: The Creative Voice of Jesus* [Peabody, Mass.: Hendrickson, 1994] pp. 164-86) argues that the parable is about farming. From the fact that there is a good yield with no effort by the farmer (no plowing at all) or intervention by God, he concludes that the story subverts a religious view of the natural processes, a view that sacramentalizes the cosmos. Once again the principle is demonstrated that any interpretation based on what is not in the story is almost certainly wrong. If the point had been that the farmer did nothing, the parable would have stated this explicitly.

129. E.g., Marcus, *The Mystery of the Kingdom of God*, p. 50. Cf. Liebenburg, who thinks that the audience would have understood and that the interpretation builds on what the audience would have concluded already, but it is not clear how he sees the interpretation as an advance on what they were to conclude.

130. E.g., Boucher, *The Mysterious Parable*, pp. 47-48.

131. See p. 155 and p. 155, n. 18 above.

132. Prov 11:18; Hos 10:12; Zech 8:12; Hippocrates 3; Quintilian, *Inst.* 5.11.24; *4 Ezra* 9:31-37; cf. Isa 55:10-11. Burton L. Mack points to these and other texts and argues with reference to Hellenistic hearers that cultivation is the foundational analogy for culture in general. See his "Teaching in Parables: Elaboration in Mark 4:1-34," in *Patterns of Persuasion in the Gospels* (Sonoma, Calif.: Polebridge, 1989), pp. 143-60, here pp. 155-56. See also the discussion and texts listed by G. Lohfink, "Die Metaphorik der Aussaat im Gleichnis vom Sämann," pp. 211-28, who suggests that the metaphor "seed" for the word appears to be Greek (p. 223).

133. Job 4:8; *4 Ezra* 4:28-32. Cf. Hos 8:7: "sow the wind" as a metaphor for foolish living. See Ignatius, *Ephesians* 9.1 for reference to Christians who stop their ears so as not to receive false teaching being sown among them.

134. This is a natural development of referring to children as seed (e.g., the seed of Abraham). Other texts use the metaphor of God *scattering* his people to punish them.

135. A point made by Garnet ("The Parable of the Sower: How the Multitudes Understood It," pp. 39-54, esp. 41) and Michael P. Knowles, who suggested that *Jub.* 11:10-24 provides a background for the parable of the Sower ("Abram and the Birds in *Jubilees* 11: A Subtext for the Parable of the Sower," *NTS* 41 [1995]: 145-51). Numerous texts describe Israel, and especially her restoration, as God's plant. See Exod 15:17; 2 Sam 7:10; 1 Chron 17:9; Pss 1:3; 44:3; 80:8-19; Isa 5:1-7; 40:24; 60:21; 61:3 (is there a connection of the terebinth in this text with the terebinth in 6:13?); Jer 18:9; 24:6; 31:27; 32:41; 42:10; Ezek 17:22-24; 31:8-11; Hos 2:22-23; Amos 9:15; Zech 10:8-9; *Pss. Sol.* 14:3-4; *Jub.* 1.16; 7.34; *1 En.* 10.16; 62.8; 93.10; 1QS 8.5; 1QH 6.15-17.

136. "Die Metaphorik des Aussaat im Gleichnis vom Sämann," pp. 211-28.

137. As Lohfink ("Die Metaphorik des Aussaat im Gleichnis vom Sämann," p. 217) points out, Hos 2:21-23 corresponds to 1:10–2:1 (2:1-3), where the name "Jezreel" occurs again.

138. Liebenberg, *The Language of the Kingdom and Jesus*, pp. 362-76. Other evidence for sowing as a metaphor for preaching includes 1 Cor 9:11; Jas 1:21; John 4:36-38 and *4 Ezra* 9:30-35.

139. As Wright (*Jesus and the Victory of God*, pp. 230-39) argued. See above, p. 161. Craig Evans (*To See and Not Perceive*, pp. 57-58) and others have argued on the basis of 1QIsaᵃ 6.13 that the Qumran community saw themselves as the holy seed.

140. Although Hagner (*Matthew 1–13*, p. 379) thinks Jesus is probably the sower, he correctly notes that the title does not point to the main subject but to the opening words of the parable, which is the usual way of identifying passages in the ancient world. Even Matthew does not focus on christology (contra Painter, *Mark's Gospel: Worlds in Conflict*, p. 78). Some think *exēlthen* ("went out") in 4:3 points to Jesus as the sower because of its use in Mark 1:38 and 2:13 of Jesus' going out, but the word is too general and is used of other people as well.

141. Cf. Liebenberg (*The Language of the Kingdom and Jesus*, pp. 358, 361), who speaks of the innate dependency of the seed on the soil into which it is sown.

142. See Luz, *Matthew 8–20*, pp. 238-44, 251.

143. The kingdom is not mentioned explicitly in the parable, and Luz (*Matthew 8–20*, p. 244) denies that the parable is about the kingdom. However, Matthew refers explicitly to the kingdom in the interpretation and all the Evangelists place the parable in that context.

144. Among a number taking this approach see Lambrecht, *Once More Astonished*, pp. 103-4; Nolland, *Luke 1–9:20*, p. 376; Wright, *Jesus and the Victory of God*, p. 230 (but not accepting that the three failures point to the rejection of the prophets as he suggests on p. 236).

145. There are at least eight levels of hearing represented by the verb *shāmaʿ*: hearing sound, understanding a language, understanding the intent, recognizing, summoning (hiphil form, causing to hear), paying attention, agreeing with or believing, and obeying. See my "A Hermeneutics of Hearing Informed by the Parables with Special Reference to Mark 4," *BBR* 14 (2004): 59-79.

146. Luz, *Matthew 8–20*, p. 244.

147. See Donald H. Juel, "Encountering the Sower: Mark 4:1-20," *Int* 56 (2002): 273-83. For Juel — astonishingly — the parable teaches that the coming of the kingdom is not something over which we have any control, the parable promises nothing, and Mark's whole Gospel awaits a speaking that occurs beyond the confines of the narrative. Juel focuses on the agency of preachers, the sacraments in the church, and God's mercy, even though the truthfulness of the parable for him is still an open question. J. Marcus (*Mark 1–8*, p. 311) also thinks soil is chosen for its passivity, but the challenge to hear is anything but passive.

148. The passage is about the hardness of hearts, not the wholesale rejection of Israel. Contra Joachim Gnilka, *Die Verstockung Israels. Isaias 6,9-10 in der Theologie der Synoptiker* (Munich: Kösel, 1961), pp. 83-86.

149. See Moule, "Mark 4:1-20 Yet Once More," pp. 101-2.

150. *Gar* in Mark 4:22 and 25 indicates that these verses are to be regarded as commentary on the logia preceding them, and vv. 14-20 should be regarded as commentary on vv. 3-9. See Willem S. Vorster, "Meaning and Reference: The Parables of Jesus in Mark 4," in *Speaking of Jesus* (ed. J. Eugene Booths; Leiden: Brill, 1979), pp. 161-97, esp. 176.

151. As any number have argued. See Boucher, *The Mysterious Parable*, p. 53; Hooker, *The Gospel According to Saint Mark*, p. 120; Wright, *Jesus and the Victory of God*, pp. 174-82; Patten, "The Form and Function of Parable in Select Apocalyptic Literature and Their Significance for Parables in the Gospel of Mark," 246-58, esp. 249-52.

152. *Søren Kierkegaard's Journals and Papers* (6 vols.; ed. and trans. Howard V. Hong and Edna H. Hong; Bloomington, Ind.: Indiana University Press, 1967), 1:288.

153. For parallels to this idea see *b. Berakot* 40a; 55a; *b. Soṭah* 9a-b; *b. Sukkah* 46a-b; *t. Soṭah* 4.17-19; *Gen. Rab.* 20.5; *Eccl. Rab.* 1.17.

154. Contra Carlston (*The Parables of the Triple Tradition*, pp. 97-98), Ambrozic (*The Hidden Kingdom*, pp. 73-74), and others, I do not accept that 4:33 and 4:34 represent different stages of the tradition with v. 34 correcting v. 33. Attempts to explain these two verses by redaction explain the difficulties but not why an editor should have put them in this order. See Ivor Harold Jones, *The Matthean Parables: A Literary and Historical Commentary* (NovTSup 80; Leiden: Brill, 1995), p. 287. Both verses come from Mark; see Henaut, *Oral Tradition and the Gospels: The Problem of Mark 4*, pp. 148-67. V. 34 cannot be taken absolutely; clearly Jesus earlier in Mark (and certainly in Matthew and Luke) taught without using parables.

155. Why Luz (*Matthew 8–20*, p. 242) downplays the parable's connection to the kingdom is unclear. If the parable is about reception of the message, what else could be the focus with Jesus? All three Evangelists place the parable in a context discussing the kingdom, especially Matt 13:11/Mark 4:11/Luke 8:10, but only Matt 13:19 makes explicit the connection of either the parable or its interpretation to the kingdom.

156. Boucher (*The Mysterious Parable*, p. 43): "The entire Markan passage (4:1-34) is a lesson on how to hear the word about the kingdom spoken in parables"; see also J. Marcus, *The Mystery of the Kingdom of God*, p. 230.

157. For instance, Davies and Allison's suggestion (*Matthew*, 2:402) that Matthew changed the order of the increase because of the failure of preaching. Some see the synagogue mirrored by the crowds and the church mirrored by the disciples, but this is an imposition on the text, as J. Dupont indicates. See his "Le point de vue de Matthieu dans le chapitre des paraboles," in *L'Évangile selon Matthieu. Rédaction et théologie* (ed. M. Didier; Gembloux: J. Duculot, 1972), pp. 221-59; see pp. 230 and 237-50.

158. So Hagner, *Matthew 1–13*, p. 371.

159. Contra Marcus, *Mark 1–8*, p. 311.

160. This is true as well for Matt 11:25-27. There is a reason that the message is hidden from the wise and understanding and revealed to infants, and it has to do with arrogance and pride. As R. France (*The Gospel of Mark*, p. 195) comments with regard to Mark, revelation is not restricted to a predetermined circle but is given to those who ask. The group is self-selected rather than predestined. See also Watts, *Isaiah's New Exodus and Mark*, pp. 208-9; Luz, *Matthew 8–20*, p. 247.

161. See Lambrecht, *Out of the Treasure*, pp. 155-62. He and others think Matthew avoids *didaskein* because it was more suited for the Law than parables. This is a severe overreading of the material and presupposes that Matthew considered parables unintelligible for the people, which is not the case, and that Jesus had not yet spoken in parables in Matthew, despite 7:24-27; 9:16-17, 37-38; 12:25-30, 33-37. It also does not do justice to the use of *didaskein* throughout Matthew.

162. Luz, *Matthew 8–20*, p. 246.

163. See Luz, *Matthew 8–20*, pp. 229-30. Sometimes vv. 1-35 are seen as addressed to the crowds and vv. 36-52 to the disciples, but this will not work. Vv. 10-23 are addressed to the disciples. D. Wenham ("The Structure of Matthew XIII," *NTS* 25 [1979]: 516-22) accepts these two divisions and argues that the eight parables form a chiasmus. The Wheat and the Weeds and the Net obviously correspond to each other, but it is difficult to see the Sower corresponding to the Scribe Trained for the Kingdom in vv. 51-52. J. Dupont ("Le point de vue de Matthieu dans le

chapitre des paraboles," p. 231) suggests a different twofold division (vv. 1-23 and vv. 24-52), but this does not do justice to the complexity of the second section.

Some count only seven parables (ignoring v. 52). J. A. Bengel, among others, interpreted Matthew's seven parables as depicting seven distinct periods of the church's history up to the eschaton. See his *Gnomon of the New Testament* (trans. James Bandinel; Edinburgh: T. & T. Clark, 1877), 1:282-83.

164. Davies and Allison, *Matthew*, 2:370-71. B. Gerhardsson argues for only seven parables with the other six explaining the four parts of the Sower. The Wheat and the Weeds interprets those who reject the word, the Mustard Seed and Leaven those on rocky ground, the Treasure and Pearl those among the thorns, and the Net those on good ground. He argues further that the whole discourse is based on the *Shema* with the parables explaining what it means to love God with all one's heart (the Wheat and the Weeds), soul (the Mustard Seed and the Leaven), and might (the Treasure and the Pearl). See his "The Seven Parables in Matthew XIII," *NTS* 19 (1972): 16-37. I do not see the connections he finds between the parables and with the Shema.

165. J. Kingsbury (*The Parables of Jesus in Matthew 13*, pp. 16 and 130) and John Drury (*The Parables in the Gospels* [New York: Crossroad, 1985], pp. 82-83) both argue that ch. 13 is the turning point of Matthew, but this is an overstatement. Kingsbury esp. is aware that judgment was already the theme in 11:16-24 and 12:22-45 and that a number of passages point to the lack of response to Jesus' message (e.g., 8:10-12). Cf. Luz, *Matthew 8–20*, p. 229.

166. Garland, *Reading Matthew: A Literary and Theological Commentary on the First Gospel*, pp. 143-44. Note the similarity of 1QS 3.21-24, which refers to the Angel of Darkness leading the sons of justice astray, and 4.9-11, which says ". . . to the spirit of deceit belong greed, . . . blindness of eyes, hardness of hearing, stiffness of neck, hardness of heart in order to walk in all the paths of darkness and evil cunning."

167. Cf. the similar statement in *Pss. Sol.* 17:44.

168. Luke 5:3 parallels Mark's earlier reference to Jesus teaching from a boat at Mark 3:9.

169. In fact, Abraham Malherbe ("The Christianization of a *Topos*, Luke 12:13-34," *NovT* 38 [1996]: 123-35, see pp. 131 and 135) suggests that Luke 12 is almost a commentary on 8:9-18, esp. with regard to covetousness.

170. Cf. Rom 10:17.

171. Keener, *A Commentary on the Gospel of Matthew*, p. 38.

172. Cf. Luz, *Matthew 8–20*, p. 250, but his attempt to make the parable address the question of the certainty of salvation (p. 251) seeks to make the parable do the whole of theology. It does not address this question. Luz is right to assert that the parable is understood correctly only when understood self-critically.

173. The suggestions respectively of P. Jones, *Studying the Parables of Jesus*, pp. 75-78; and B. Scott, *Hear Then the Parable*, pp. 361-62.

Notes to "Parables of the Present Kingdom in Matthew 13, Mark 4, and Luke 13"

1. The Mustard Seed and the Leaven, 13:18-20.

2. The others are 1:1; 2:27; 3:20-21; 7:3-4, 32-37; 8:22-26; 9:29, 39b, 48-49; 11:11a; 13:33-37 (which is similar to Matt 24:42; 25:13-15); 14:51-52. See Burnett Hillman Streeter, *The Four Gospels: A Study of Origins* (New York: Macmillan, 1964), p. 195.

3. José O'Callaghan ("New Testament Papyri in Qumrān Cave 7?" *Supplement to JBL* 91.2

[1972]: 1-14, 10-11) argued that 7Q6 1 preserves a few letters from Mark 4:28. There is little basis for the suggestion and even less acceptance of it.

4. T. W. Manson, *The Sayings of Jesus as Recorded in the Gospels According to St. Matthew and St. Luke Arranged with Introduction and Commentary* (London: SCM, 1949), p. 192; H.-J. Klauck, *Allegorie und Allegorese in synoptischen Gleichnistexten* (NTAbh 13; Münster: Aschendorff, 1978), pp. 226-27.

5. Heinrich Baltensweiler even suggests that Mark added this parable after Matthew and Luke had already used his material — again an unlikely option. See his "Das Gleichnis der selbstwachsenden Saat (Markus 4,26-29) und die theologische Konzeption des Markus-evangelisten," in *Oikonomia. Heilsgeschichte als Thema der Theologie. Festschrift für Oscar Cullmann* (ed. Felix Christed; Hamburg-Bergstadt: Reich, 1967), pp. 69-75, here p. 69.

6. After the use of the aorist in v. 26 for the act of sowing and except for the perfect used of the arrival of the harvest in v. 29c.

7. C. H. Dodd, *The Parables of the Kingdom* (London: Nisbet, 1936), pp. 179-80; Robert H. Gundry, *Mark: A Commentary on His Apology for the Cross* (Grand Rapids: Eerdmans, 1993), pp. 221-23, respectively.

8. Some view this introduction as awkward, but Bernard Brandon Scott (*Hear Then the Parable: A Commentary on the Parables of Jesus* [Minneapolis: Fortress, 1989], p. 365) remarks that clumsiness in parable introductions is common. *Houtos . . . ōs* ("Thus . . . as") does occur elsewhere in figurative, nonparabolic material. See among others Sir 39:23; 1 Cor 3:15; 4:1; 9:26; Josephus, *Ant.* 12.304; Justin, *1 Apologia* 12.10. Eph 5:28, 33 and Jas 2:12 use this construction but with a different function.

9. Matt 7:17; 13:40, 49; 18;14, 35; 20:16; Luke 12:21; 15:7, 10.

10. *BDAG*, p. 742. A. Jülicher (*Die Gleichnisreden Jesu* [Freiburg i. B.: Akademische Verlagsbuchhandlung von J. C. B. Mohr, vol. 1, 1888; vol. 2, 1889], 2:539) suggests that the expression means the same as *homoia estin* ("It is like") or *hōmoiōthē* ("It is likened to").

11. Additional explicit parabolic connections to the kingdom occur in Luke only with the parables of the Leaven (13:18-21), the Feast (14:15-24), and the Pounds (19:11-27). Matthew explicitly connects parables and the kingdom much more frequently: the Sower (13:11 and 19), the Wheat and the Tares (13:24-30 and 36-42), the Mustard Seed and the Leaven (13:31-33), the Treasure, Pearl, and Net (13:44-50), the Scribe (13:52), the Unforgiving Servant (18:23-35), the Vineyard Workers (20:1-16), the Two Sons (21:28-32), the Wicked Tenants (21:33-44, see v. 43), the Wedding Banquet (22:1-14), the Ten Virgins (25:1-13), and the Sheep and the Goats (25:31-46). How David Flusser can say that only five parables (the Growing Seed, the Mustard Seed, the Leaven, the Treasure, and the Pearl) were kingdom parables is a mystery. See his *Die rabbinischen Gleichnisse und der Gleichniserzähler Jesus* 1: *Das Wesen der Gleichnisse* (Bern: Peter Lang, 1981), pp. 65-66.

12. Klauck (*Allegorie und Allegorese in synoptischen Gleichnistexten*, p. 225) would not even attribute *euthys* to Mark. Aloysius M. Ambrozic thinks only the allusion to Joel may show Markan redaction. See his *The Hidden Kingdom: A Redaction-Critical Study of the References to the Kingdom of God in Mark's Gospel* (CBQMS 2; Washington, D.C.: The Catholic Biblical Association of America, 1972), p. 108.

13. Scott (*Hear Then the Parable*, p. 366) suggests that the parable has a stairstep pattern: man, seed, ground, seed, ground, fruit, fruit.

14. John R. Donahue, *The Gospel in Parable* (Philadelphia: Fortress, 1988), p. 35; George Beasley-Murray, *Jesus and the Kingdom of God* (Grand Rapids: Eerdmans, 1986), p. 195.

15. Herman Hendrickx, *The Parables of Jesus* (San Francisco: Harper & Row, 1986), pp. 21-

24; Jacques Dupont, "Encore la parabole de la Semence qui pousse toute seule (Mc 4,26-29)," in *Jesus und Paulus. Festschrift für Werner Georg Kümmel zum 70. Geburtstag* (ed. E. Earle Ellis and Erich Gräßer; Göttingen: Vandenhoeck & Ruprecht, 1975), pp. 96-108, here p. 99. Even less likely is a contrast of the incomprehensible growth of the seed and its enormous end, as Rainer Stuhlmann suggests ("Beobachtungen und Überlegungen zu Markus IV.26-29," *NTS* 19 [1972]: 153-62, here p. 157).

16. Peter Rhea Jones is correct — naming a parable is tantamount to interpreting it. See his *Studying the Parables of Jesus* (Macon, Ga.: Smyth & Helwys, 1999), p. 100.

17. Joachim Jeremias, *The Parables of Jesus* (2d ed.; trans. S. H. Hooke; New York: Charles Scribner's Sons, 1963), p. 151.

18. Mary Ann Tolbert, *Sowing the Gospel: Mark's Gospel in Literary-Historical Perspective* (Minneapolis: Fortress, 1989), p. 161.

19. Richard Eckstein, "Die von selbst wachsende Saat, Matthäus 4:26-29 [sic]," in *Gleichnisse aus Altem und Neuem Testament* (Stuttgart: Klotz, 1971), pp. 139-45, here p. 142. He also suggests the Harvest Will Come for Sure.

20. Baltensweiler, "Das Gleichnis der selbstwachsenden Saat (Markus 4, 26-29) und die theologische Konzeption des Markusevangelisten," p. 72. Other suggestions include the Blade, the Ear, and the Full Corn (A. B. Bruce, *The Parabolic Teaching of Christ: A Systematic and Critical Study of the Parables of Our Lord* [3d ed.; New York: A. C. Armstrong and Son, 1887], p. 120), the Reaper (John Dominic Crossan, *In Parables* [New York: Harper & Row, 1973], p. 85), and the Confident Investor (J. Duncan M. Derrett, "Ambivalence: Sowing and Reaping at Mark 4,26-29," *Estudios bíblicos* 48 [1990]: 489-510, here p. 489).

21. Flusser (*Die rabbinischen Gleichnisse und der Gleichniserzähler Jesus*, p. 57) is virtually alone in saying Mark created it.

22. Robert A. Guelich, *Mark 1–8:26* (WBC; Dallas: Word, 1989), pp. 238-39; Joel Marcus, *Mark 1–8: A New Translation with Introduction and Commentary* (AB 27; New York: Doubleday, 2000), p. 325.

23. E.g., Rudolf Bultmann, *The History of the Synoptic Tradition* (trans. John Marsh; New York: Harper & Row, 1963), p. 173. He did so because he did not find it easy to relate this similitude to the kingdom.

24. Jülicher, *Die Gleichnisreden Jesu*, 2:543-45; Klauck (*Allegorie und Allegorese in synoptischen Gleichnistexten*, p. 220) argued that the reference to the harvest is original and necessary but that the allusion to Joel was added later. Heinz-Wolfgang Kuhn would eliminate vv. 27-28a (*Ältere Sammlungen im Markusevangelium* [SUNT 8; Göttingen: Vandenhoeck & Ruprecht, 1971], pp. 104-12), and D. Crossan ("The Seed Parables of Jesus," *JBL* 92 [1973]: 244-66, here pp. 251-53) would eliminate v. 28 and the allusion to Joel in v. 29. None of these suggestions has merit or has received much acceptance.

25. Ambrozic, *The Hidden Kingdom*, p. 108; Klauck, *Allegorie und Allegorese in synoptischen Gleichnistexten*, p. 225.

26. For histories of interpretation of this parable see Ambrozic, *The Hidden Kingdom*, pp. 108-20; Gerd Theißen, "Der Bauer und die von selbst Frucht bringende Erde. Naiver Synergismus in Mk 4:26-29?" *ZNW* 85 (1994): 167-82, esp. 169-73; Eckhard Rau, *Reden in Vollmacht. Hintergrund, Form, und Anliegen der Gleichnisse Jesu* (FRLANT 149; Göttingen: Vandenhoeck & Ruprecht, 1990), pp. 120-31; Stephen L. Wailes, *Medieval Allegories of Jesus' Parables* (Berkeley, Calif.: University of California Press, 1987), pp. 200-202.

27. Wailes, *Medieval Allegories of Jesus' Parables*, pp. 200-202. The man's sleep was under-

stood to refer to Jesus' death and his not knowing to Christ's not letting people know which works result in salvation.

28. Jülicher is often mentioned in this connection; see *Die Gleichnisreden Jesu,* 2:543-46; see also Bruce, *The Parabolic Teaching of Christ,* pp. 118-27.

29. The harvest is readily associated with the end time. One thinking the parable deals with delay is Ernst Fuchs, *Studies of the Historical Jesus* (SBT 42; trans. Andrew Scobie; Naperville, Ill.: Allenson, 1964), pp. 134, 180.

30. Dodd, *The Parables of the Kingdom,* pp. 175-80.

31. E.g., Jeremias, *The Parables of Jesus,* p. 152.

32. Among many arguing this is R. Bultmann, *Theology of the New Testament* (trans. Kendrick Grobel; New York: Charles Scribner's Sons, 1951), p. 8.

33. Fuchs, *Studies of the Historical Jesus,* pp. 134, 180-81.

34. Heinrich Kahlefeld, *Parables and Instructions in the Gospels* (trans. Arlene Swidler; New York: Herder and Herder, 1966), pp. 23-24; see also Craig L. Blomberg, *Interpreting the Parables* (Downers Grove, Ill.: InterVarsity, 1990), pp. 263-64; Fuchs, *Studies of the Historical Jesus,* p. 181; Gundry, *Mark,* pp. 219-26.

35. See Jülicher, *Die Gleichnisreden Jesu,* 2:539; Jones, *Studying the Parables,* p. 106.

36. Herman Hendrickx, *The Parables of Jesus* (San Francisco: Harper & Row, 1986), pp. 16-18; Morna D. Hooker, "Mark's Parables of the Kingdom (Mark 4:1-34)," in *The Challenge of Jesus' Parables* (ed. Richard N. Longenecker; Grand Rapids, Eerdmans, 2000), pp. 79-101, here p. 97.

37. *New Testament Theology* (ed. L. D. Hurst; Oxford: Clarendon, 1994), p. 124. See the discussion herein concerning the intent of the allusion to Joel.

38. Gundry, *Mark,* pp. 219-26; R. T. France, *The Gospel of Mark* (NIGTC; Grand Rapids: Eerdmans, 2002), p. 212.

39. For such ideas see Scott, *Hear Then the Parable,* pp. 367-71; Bruce, *The Parabolic Teaching of Christ,* pp. 118-26; Fuchs, *Studies of the Historical Jesus,* pp. 180-81; Jones, *Studying the Parables of Jesus,* pp. 112-13; Blomberg, *Interpreting the Parables,* p. 264; Raymond F. Collins, "The Story of the Seed Growing by Itself: A Parable for Our Times," *Emmanuel* 94 (1998): 446-52, here p. 452; Tolbert, *Sowing the Gospel,* p. 168.

40. See Peter Dschulnigg, *Rabbinische Gleichnisse und das Neue Testament* (Judaica et Christiana 12; Bern: Lang, 1988), pp. 90 and 92, n. 10; Rudolf Pesch, *Markusevangelium* (HTKNT, 2d ed.; Freiburg: Herder, 1977), 1:256, n. 5; Stuhlmann, "Beobachtungen und Überlegungen zu Markus IV.26-29," 157.

41. Cf. Guelich, *Mark 1–8:26,* p. 238.

42. On the first see Joel Marcus, *The Mystery of the Kingdom of God* (SBLDS 90; Atlanta: Scholars, 1986), p. 184; on the second see, e.g., Baltensweiler, "Das Gleichnis der selbstwachsenden Saat (Markus 4, 26-29) und die theologische Konzeption des Markusevangelisten," pp. 72-76. His understanding that the man's not knowing is an expression of unbelief, willful not knowing, and reflects disciples who have left Jesus (as in John 6:66) has no basis.

43. See also Josh 6:5; 2 Kgs 19:29; Job 24:24; Wis 17:6; Philo, *Fug.* 170-72; *Mut.* 260; *Opif.* 80-81; Josephus, *Ant.* 1.46; 12.317.

44. Because of the use of this word in Lev 25:5, 11; 4 Kgdms 19:29, Scott (*Hear Then the Parable,* pp. 368-71) understands that the land is on sabbatical, which he sees as verified in the non-action and ignorance of the man. The parable is understood as a sign of grace. The harvest is not apocalyptic war but a harvest of sabbatical aftergrowth planted by an ignorant farmer and evidence of God's grace. For Scott this offers the reader a chance to define the kingdom from the

Joel quotation or to reframe the Joel quotation on the basis of the parable. This seems very unlikely to me.

45. Contra Stuhlmann, "Beobachtungen und Überlegungen zu Markus IV.26-29," 153-57.

46. George Eldon Ladd, *The Presence of the Future: The Eschatology of Biblical Realism* (Grand Rapids: Eerdmans, 1974), p. 191.

47. Among others Jülicher, *Die Gleichnisreden Jesus,* 2:543-45; Crossan, "The Seed Parables of Jesus," 251-53; Hans Weder, *Die Gleichnisse Jesu als Metaphern. Traditions- und redaktionsgeschichtliche Analysen und Interpretationen* (4th ed.; Göttingen: Vandenhoeck & Ruprecht, 1990), pp. 104-5, 117.

48. See e.g., Dupont, "Encore la parabole de la Semence qui pousse toute seule (Mc 4,26-29)," 102; Gundry, *Mark,* p. 226. It is not necessary to think as J. Marcus does (*Mark 1–8,* p. 323) that a deliberate reversal of Joel's rejection of the Gentiles is intended.

49. Dupont ("Encore la parabole de la Semence qui pousse toute seule, Mc 4,26-29," 102-3) thinks the allusion is to a Greek text; Peter Stuhlmacher (*Biblische Theologie des Neuen Testaments. Grundlegung von Jesus zu Paulus* [Göttingen: Vandenhoeck & Ruprecht, 1992], p. 123) thinks the allusion is to the Hebrew.

50. For other uses of the sickle as a metaphor of judgment see Jer 50(27):16; *T. Ab.* (A) 4.11; *b. Sanhedrin* 95b; *Midr. Ps.* 8.1, 8; *Song Rab.* 8.19. These last three texts use both the sickle and the harvest image and quote Joel 3(4):13. Cf. also Hermas, *Sim.* 8.1.2, which uses *drepanon* of an instrument used in a judging process. On harvest as a metaphor for judgment see also Matt 13:30, 39; Gal 6:8-9; *4 Ezra* 4:24-39; *2 Bar.* 70.2.

51. *The Parables of the Kingdom,* pp. 179-80.

52. Jones, *Studying the Parables of Jesus,* p. 107; Marcus, *Mark 1–8,* p. 322.

53. Arland J. Hultgren (*The Parables of Jesus: A Commentary* [Grand Rapids: Eerdmans, 2000], p. 389) also adds that for Mark the present is a time of waiting.

54. Dodd, *The Parables of the Kingdom,* pp. 178-80.

55. See Vincent Taylor, *The Gospel According to St. Mark* (London: Macmillan, 1957), p. 266. France (*The Gospel of Mark,* pp. 212-15) and Gundry (*Mark,* pp. 219-26) also see the seed as the word.

56. Among many, see Marcus, *The Mystery of the Kingdom of God,* pp. 177-99; Stuhlmacher, *Biblische Theologie des Neuen Testaments,* p. 123; M. Gourges, "Faire confiance à la grâce de Dieu. La parabole du blé qui pousse tout seul (Mc 4,25-29)," *NRTh* 117 (1995): 364-75, here pp. 372-74. N. T. Wright also sees overtones of resurrection (*Jesus and the Victory of God,* vol. 2 of *Christian Origins and the Question of God* [Minneapolis: Fortress, 1996], p. 241). The suggestion that the seed planted is a reference to the crucifixion is from James G. Williams, *Gospel against Parable: Mark's Language of Mystery* (Sheffield: JSOT, 1985), pp. 96, 172, 184.

57. Hendrickx (*The Parables of Jesus,* pp. 21-24) takes the sower as God, as does Jacques Dupont ("La parabole de la semence qui pousse toute seule," *RSR* 55 [1967]: 367-92, here p. 382). Theißen ("Der Bauer und die von selbst Frucht bringende Erde," 179-80) seems to suggest that the sower could refer to both God and the disciples. John Paul Heil points to both Jesus and the disciples ("Reader-Response and the Narrative Context of the Parables about Growing Seed in Mark 4:1-34," *CBQ* 54 [1992]: 271-86, here pp. 274, 278, 282). He also takes the seed as both the word and the people (p. 282).

58. Respectively Marcus, *The Mystery of the Kingdom of God,* p. 184; Claude Pavur, "The Grain Is Ripe," *BTB* 17 (1987): 21-23, here p. 22.

59. Respectively Heil, "Reader-Response and the Narrative Context of the Parables about Growing Seed in Mark 4:1-34," 283; Marcus, *The Mystery of the Kingdom of God,* p. 195.

60. As Weder (*Die Gleichnisse Jesu als Metaphern*, p. 118), Dschulnigg (*Rabbinische Gleichnisse und das Neue Testament*, p. 91), and Dupont ("La parabole de la semence qui pousse toute seule," p. 389) suggest for Jesus. C. Blomberg (*Interpreting the Parables*, pp. 77, 263-64) concludes that the sower is first God and then derivatively Jesus and all who preach the word but says that while sleeping and ignorance apply to Christians, we cannot press the parable with regard to God's sleeping or ignorance.

61. Guelich, *Mark 1–8:26*, p. 240; see Wailes, *Medieval Allegories of Jesus' Parables*, p. 202.

62. Gundry, *Mark*, p. 226; France, *The Gospel of Mark*, p. 214; W. G. Kümmel, *Promise and Fulfilment: The Eschatological Message of Jesus* (SBT 23; trans. Dorthea M. Barton; Naperville, Ill.: Allenson, 1957), p. 128.

63. Among many see Nils Dahl, "The Parables of Growth," in *Jesus in the Memory of the Early Church* (Minneapolis: Augsburg, 1976), pp. 147 and 156-66; Hultgren, *The Parables of Jesus*, p. 389; Rau, *Reden in Vollmacht*, pp. 155-56; Eckstein, "Die von selbst wachsende Saat," pp. 142-43.

64. Notably Jeremias, *The Parables of Jesus*, p. 152; Beasley-Murray, *Jesus and the Kingdom of God*, p. 196.

65. See Rau, *Reden in Vollmacht*, pp. 132, 155.

66. See Dahl, "The Parables of Growth," pp. 164-65. In his words, the kingdom has a "history."

67. I do not think a fixed apocalyptic schedule is presupposed by this parable as some do. See Dahl, "The Parables of Growth," pp. 151-54; Marcus, *Mark 1–8*, pp. 322-23.

68. Among many see Ambrozic, *The Hidden Kingdom*, pp. 119-20; Dupont, "La parabole de la semence qui pousse toute seule (Marc 4,26-29)," 385-92; Wright, *Jesus and the Victory of God*, pp. 240-41; Baltensweiler, "Das Gleichnis der selbstwachsenden Saat (Markus 4,26-29) und die theologische Konzeption des Markusevangelisten," pp. 71-75; Klauck, *Allegorie und Allegorese in synoptischen Gleichnistexten*, pp. 224-25; and Beasley-Murray, *Jesus and the Kingdom of God*, pp. 126-27, 196.

69. Ladd, *The Presence of the Future*, pp. 189-90.

70. Cf. W. O. E. Oesterley, *The Gospel Parables in the Light of Their Jewish Background* (New York: Macmillan, 1936), pp. 70-71.

71. I see little to support Theißen's thought ("Der Bauer und die von selbst Frucht bringende Erde," 179-80) that the parable promotes a naive synergism.

72. Several other interpretations of the parable have little possibility of being correct. B. Scott (*Hear Then the Parable*, pp. 370-71) says that it forces the reader to choose between patient growth or bloody harvest. D. Derrett ("Ambivalence: Sowing and Reaping at Mark 4,26-29," 503) sees the parable as indicating that good deeds and intentions are meritorious. Crossan ("The Seed Parables of Jesus," 266) takes it as an image of resolute and prudent action since the farmer knows how and when to move. William R. Herzog (*Jesus, Justice, and the Reign of God: A Ministry of Liberation* [Louisville: Westminster John Knox, 2000], pp. 196-97) argues that it is about the disjuncture between the land and the temple. The land does not require the sacrificial system and elaborate purity injunctions to ensure its fertility, and Jesus saw the fertility of the land as a symbol of the continuing covenant of God with the people. There is no evidence of an allusion to the temple, which vitiates this interpretation.

73. Contra Jones, *Studying the Parables of Jesus*, pp. 112-13.

74. Cf. Ambrozic, *The Hidden Kingdom*, p. 113; Kümmel, *Promise and Fulfilment*, p. 129.

75. See Matt 11:15; 13:9; Mark 4:9, 23; 7:16 (which some manuscripts omit); Luke 8:8; 14:35; Rev 2:7; 13:9.

76. *Gen. Rab.* 61.6 relates a parable of a good tree and a bad tree that were intertwined.

Should the caretaker water them or not? His decision was to water them and leave the decision to God.

77. D. A. Carson, "The ΟΜΟΙΟΣ Word-Group as Introduction to Some Matthean Parables," *NTS* 31 (1985): 277-82, here p. 279.

78. The word *synteleia* occurs also in 13:49; 24:3; 28:20, but outside Matthew only in Heb 9:26.

79. 5:45; 13:48; 22:10. The contrast between good and bad is, of course, more frequent.

80. "Weeping and gnashing of teeth" appears also in 8:12; 13:50; 22:13; 24:51; 25:30. Outside Matthew the expression occurs only in Luke 13:28.

81. Although the Net lacks explicit identifications such as "This is" or "The field is."

82. Irene and Walter Jacob, "Flora," *ABD*, 2:816.

83. *Arbeit und Sitte in Palästina* 2: *Der Ackerbau* (Hildesheim: Georg Olms, 1964), p. 325.

84. A helpful overview of this role is provided by Roland Bainton, "Religious Liberty and the Parable of the Tares," in *The Collected Papers in Church History* (Boston: Beacon, 1962), 1:95-121. He calls this parable "the proof passage of religious liberty" (p. 95). See also Bruce, *The Parabolic Teaching of Christ*, pp. 49-54; Wailes, *Medieval Allegories of Jesus' Parables*, pp. 103-8.

85. *The Refutation of All Heresies* 9.7 (*ANF* 5:131).

86. See his *Answer to the Letters of Petilian the Donatist*, 2.26, 39, 79; 3:2 (*NPNF1* 4:545, 555, 570, 597-98); *Sermons on Selected Lessons of the New Testament* 23 (*NPNF1* 6:334-35); *Ad Donatistas post Collationem* 8; and *Contra Epistolam Parmeniani* 3.2.11-14; *To the Donatists*, Letters 76 and 105.

87. See John Chrysostom, *Homilies on Matthew* 46 (*NPNF1* 10:288-89); Martin Luther, *Church Postil* on Matt 13:24-30, *Sermons on the Gospels*, vol. 11 of *Luther's Works* (ed. John Nicholas Lenker; Minneapolis: Lutherans in All Lands, 1906), p. 102; Thomas Aquinas, *Summa Theologiae* 2a2ae 10.8; and the discussion by Bainton, "Religious Liberty and the Parable of the Tares."

88. F. W. Beare, *The Gospel According to Matthew* (San Francisco: Harper & Row, 1981), p. 289; Ulrich Luz, "Vom Taumellolch im Weizenfeld," in *Vom Urchristentum zu Jesus* (ed. Hubert Frankemölle and Karl Kertelge; Freiburg im Breisgau: Herder, 1989), pp. 154-71, here pp. 155, 163; *Matthew 8–20* (trans. James E. Crouch; Minneapolis: Fortress, 2001), pp. 254, 270, n. 36. Luz uses this uncertainty as grounds to justify creating new meanings. Luz's discussion of hermeneutics (pp. 162-71 and 270-72 in the respective works) is strange in that he denies the original meaning or the canonical text any regulative control. Rather the Risen Christ may create new meanings in new situations. Yet, this Risen Christ is none other than the earthly Jesus, and how is this Risen Christ/earthly Jesus to be known other than through the Gospels themselves? Do we use one method in determining the character of the earthly Jesus and then another in the production (Luz's word) of new meanings? Cf. Robert Farrar Capon, *Parables of the Kingdom* (Grand Rapids: Zondervan, 1985), p. 129, who says his commitment to Scripture as the whole deck of cards does not prevent his *playing* with Scripture (italics his).

89. Excluding the unbridled psychologizing of Robert Winterhalter and George W. Fisk (*Jesus' Parables: Finding Our God Within* [New York: Paulist, 1993], pp. 45-48), who see the sower as the conscious mind, the field as the subconscious mind, the good seed as thoughts in harmony with the indwelling Christ, the tares as negative thoughts and beliefs, the enemy as collective belief in evil and limitation, and sleep as a careless and indifferent attitude. Also without merit is Douglas E. Oakman's suggestion (*Jesus and the Economic Questions of His Day* [Lewiston, N.Y.: Edwin Mellen, 1986], pp. 119-23) that the landowner is a negative model of wis-

dom and that "the parable exposes the arrogance of human decisions made self-centeredly without adequate assessment of the forces of contingency."

90. Weder, *Die Gleichnisse Jesu als Metaphern,* pp. 123-25; see also Eduard Schweizer, *The Good News According to Matthew* (trans. David E. Green; Atlanta: John Knox, 1975), pp. 303-4, who sees the original as vv. 24, 26, and 29-30a; Jack Dean Kingsbury, *The Parables of Jesus in Matthew 13* (Richmond: John Knox, 1969), p. 65, who sees vv. 24b-26 as the original core; and David R. Catchpole, "John the Baptist, Jesus and the Parable of the Tares," *SJT* 31 (1978): 557-70, who limits the original to vv. 24b, 26b and 30b. U. Luz (*Matthew 8–20,* 255-56; "Vom Taumellolch im Weizenfeld," 158) and H. Hendrickx (*The Parables of Jesus,* 57-71) also suggest theories on the movement of the tradition and the forces causing changes.

91. Cf. the comments of W. D. Davies and Dale C. Allison, Jr., *Matthew,* 2:410.

92. E.g., Jülicher, *Die Gleichnisreden Jesu,* 2:562; Robert H. Gundry, *Matthew: A Commentary on His Handbook for a Mixed Church Under Persecution* (2d ed.; Grand Rapids: Eerdmans, 1994), pp. 261-62; Luz, *Matthew 8–20,* p. 254.

93. B. H. Streeter offered this as one possibility (*The Four Gospels,* 171). Baltensweiler suggested that Mark added it after his gospel had been used by Matthew and Luke. See p. 179, n. 5 above.

94. The suggestion of Gundry, *Matthew,* pp. 261-62; Ivor Harold Jones, *The Matthean Parables: A Literary and Historical Commentary* (NovTSup 80; Leiden: Brill, 1995), p. 312.

95. See Hultgren, *The Parables of Jesus,* pp. 294-95; Kingsbury, *The Parables of Jesus in Matthew 13,* p. 64.

96. Robert W. Funk, Bernard Brandon Scott, and James R. Butts, *The Parables of Jesus: Red Letter Edition, the Jesus Seminar* (Sonoma, Calif.: Polebridge, 1988), p. 65; Gerhard Barth, "Auseinandersetzungen um die Kirchenzucht im Umkreis des Matthäusevangelium," *ZNW* 69 (1978): 158-77, see 163.

97. Crossan, "The Seed Parables of Jesus," 261.

98. See the treatments by Davies and Allison, *Matthew,* 2:409, 415; Hultgren, *The Parables of Jesus,* p. 295; Weder, *Die Gleichnisse Jesu als Metaphern,* pp. 124-25; Wolfgang Schrage, *Das Verhältnis des Thomas-Evangeliums zur synoptischen Tradition und zu den koptischen Evangelienübersetzungen* (BZNW 29; Berlin: Töpelmann, 1964), pp. 124-26. Obviously those like Gundry (*Matthew,* p. 265) who think Matthew composed the parable will argue that the account in *Gos. Thom.* is dependent. Jacobus Liebenberg (*The Language of the Kingdom and Jesus: Parable, Aphorism, and Metaphor in the Sayings Material Common to the Synoptic Tradition and the Gospel of Thomas* [BZNW 102; Berlin: Walter de Gruyter, 2001], pp. 208-24) argues against using the abbreviated nature of *Gos. Thom.* to argue for dependence on Matthew, but admits that *Gos. Thom.* could presuppose Matthew.

99. For these objections see Jülicher, *Die Gleichnisreden Jesu,* 2:548-57; Manson, *The Sayings of Jesus,* pp. 193-94; Luz, "Vom Taumellolch im Weizenfeld," pp. 154-58; *Matthew 8–20,* pp. 252-56; and Capon, *Parables of the Kingdom,* pp. 97-98, who suggests that Jesus was not a good gardener!

A different kind of problem exists with later rabbinic law which might view leaving the weeds in the field as a violation of the commands concerning diverse kinds. See *b. Makkot* 21b; *b. 'Abodah Zarah* 63b.

100. See the discussions by A. J. Kerr ("Matthew 13:25, Sowing Zizania among Another's Wheat: Realistic or Artificial?" *JTS* 48 [1997]: 108-9) and Oesterley (*The Gospel Parables in the Light of Their Jewish Background,* pp. 60-61). Modern examples are reported by David H. Tripp ("Zizania, Matthew 13:25: Realistic, If Also Figurative," *JTS* 50 [1999]: 628) and Dalman, *Arbeit*

und Sitte in Palästina, 2:308-9. Luz (*Matthew 8–20,* p. 255, n. 29) dismisses Dalman's story as mere evidence of Middle Eastern storytelling, but he ignores *Sib. Or.* 1.396 and the data discussed by Kerr.

101. *Satire* 14.145-50.

102. Dalman, *Arbeit und Sitte in Palästina,* 2:324-25.

103. As several point out, e.g., Jeremias, *The Parables of Jesus,* p. 225.

104. See *Fauna and Flora of the Bible* (2d ed.; London: United Bible Societies, 1980), p. 194; Oakman, *Jesus and the Economic Questions of His Day,* pp. 117-18.

105. Note that Dalman (*Arbeit und Sitte in Palästina,* 2:325), on whose information Luz bases his objections to the parable, did not think the problems were so great as to make the parable difficult.

106. For a good overviews of the general debate on the church as a mixed community in Matthew see Petri Luomanen, "Corpus Mixtum — An Appropriate Description of Matthew's Community?" *JBL* 117 (1998): 469-80; Robert H. Gundry, "In Defense of the Church in Matthew as a Corpus Mixtum," *ZNW* 91 (2000): 153-65.

107. "Das Kirchenverständnis des Matthäus im Spiegel seiner Gleichnisse," *NTS* 38 (1992): 337-56, esp. 337-39. See also Barth, "Auseinandersetzungen um die Kirchenzucht im Umkreis des Matthäusevangelium," 158-77.

108. *The Gospel According to Matthew* (Philadelphia: Fortress, 1987), p. 194. He views vv. 1-35 as explaining the hidden existence and origin of evil.

109. E.g., Liebenberg, *The Language of the Kingdom and Jesus,* pp. 201-5. Often this understanding is associated with seeing "sleep" as a metaphor for neglect, but Liebenberg does not make this move.

110. Luz, *Matthew 8–20,* pp. 272-74; "Vom Taumellolch im Weizenfeld," 167-71; Hendrickx, *The Parables of Jesus,* pp. 72-73. See also Franz-Josef Steinmetz, "'Unkraut unter dem Weizen' (Mt 13,24-30). Ein aktuelles, aber nichtssagendes Gleichnis?" *Geist und Leben* 66 (1993): 1-9; Wolfgang Bittner, "Lasset beides miteinander wachsen bis zur Ernte . . ." in *Basileia* (ed. Hans Dürr and Christoph Ramstein; Basel: Mitenand, 1993), pp. 15-35. Bittner (pp. 29-34) distinguishes between judgment in the sense of weeding, which is reserved for God and angels, and judgment in sense of identifying evil. He is compelled to argue against being passive toward evil in one's life or the church if one can make changes.

111. Cf. Luomanen, "Corpus Mixtum — An Appropriate Description of Matthew's Community?" 475. Identifications of Matthew's supposedly mixed community vary greatly and are speculative at best. From ch. 18 Roloff ("Das Kirchenverständnis des Matthäus im Spiegel seiner Gleichnisse," 342-44) concludes there was a fundamental problem in Matthew's church caused by the prejudices and tensions between two groups. The "small" in Matthew refer to the local community who are not able to satisfy the rigorous demands of radical discipleship. The other group is wandering Jewish-Christian charismatics who practiced a radical discipleship ethic. Matthew belonged to the latter and addressed this group. David C. Sim (*Apocalyptic Eschatology in the Gospel of Matthew* [SNTSMS 88; Cambridge: Cambridge University Press, 1996], pp. 210-14, 230) thinks Matthew's community was an isolated group that had two groups of opponents, Jews and the Satan-induced law-free Christians, both of whom Matthew consigns to hell. C. W. F. Smith ("The Mixed State of the Church in Matthew's Gospel," *JBL* 82 [1963]: 149-68) argued that the opponents are former members of the Qumran community.

112. Liebenberg (*The Language of the Kingdom and Jesus,* p. 186, n. 72) asserts, "Regardless of the 'interpretation' which specifies the field as the world, there is no doubt that the reference in the parable as it stands is to the Matthean Christian community." He attempts to justify this

by the fact that the possessive pronouns in vv. 25 and 27 are not taken up in the interpretation, which has no bearing. Smith ("The Mixed State of the Church in Matthew's Gospel," 153) argued that "world" is a temporal rather than spatial term.

113. Davies and Allison, *Matthew,* 2:408-9, quotation on 409. See also J. DuPont, "Le point de vue de Matthieu dans le chapitre des paraboles," in *L'Évangile selon Matthieu. Rédaction et théologie* (ed. M. Didier; Gembloux: J. Duculot, 1972), pp. 221-59.

114. DuPont, "Le point de vue de Matthieu dans le chapitre des paraboles," esp. p. 229.

115. Despite Luz ("Vom Taumellolch im Weizenfeld," 170; *Matthew 8–20,* pp. 271, 274) and various psychologizing approaches.

116. Kingsbury, *The Parables of Jesus in Matthew 13,* pp. 63-77. Cf. the similar views of Luz (*Matthew 8–20,* p. 255, with regard to an earlier stage of the tradition) and Luomanen ("Corpus Mixtum — An Appropriate Description of Matthew's Community?" 479-80; *Entering the Kingdom of Heaven* [Tübingen: Mohr-Siebeck, 1998], pp. 138-42), who suggests that the impossibility of uprooting refers to the incapability of Matthew's community to take action against synagogue Judaism or to the fear that action might bring down the Gentiles on both Jews and Christians. Surely this is allegorizing.

117. See pp. 192-95 above. Judaism knew that it too combined both good and evil. See *Exod. Rab.* 2.5: "Also, just as the thorn-bush produces thorns and roses, so among Israel are there righteous and wicked" (cf. *Song Rab.* 1.1.6).

118. Deut 29:28; 1 Kgs 14:15; Ps 52:5; Jer 1:10; Zeph 2:4; Wis 4:4; Jude 12.

119. Kingsbury gives sparse attention to 15:12-14. See the discussion by Dupont, "Le point de vue de Matthieu dans le chapitre des paraboles," pp. 221-59.

120. Pheme Perkins, *Hearing the Parables of Jesus* (New York: Paulist, 1981), p. 85.

121. Madeleine I. Boucher, *The Parables* (Wilmington, Del.: Michael Glazier, 1981), pp. 81-84; Hendrickx, *The Parables of Jesus,* pp. 59-62; Weder, *Die Gleichnisse Jesu als Metaphern,* pp. 125-26, among others.

122. Hendrickx's language (*The Parables of Jesus,* p. 59), summarizing those who see the parable directed against Jewish ideas. He argues (p. 60) that the criticism comes rather from Jesus' Galilean disciples.

123. Cf. Matt 11:12 (possibly); Mark 9:38-40; Luke 9:52-56.

124. Cf. John Drury, *The Parables in the Gospels* (New York: Crossroad, 1985), p. 86; Donald A. Hagner, *Matthew 1–13* (WBC 33a; Dallas: Word, 1993), p. 392, who says that placement of two parables between this one and its interpretation suggests that all three parables belong together and address the same reality, the mystery of the kingdom.

125. Hagner, *Matthew 1–13,* p. 382.

126. See among others C. H. Dodd, *The Parables of the Kingdom* (London: Nisbet, 1936), p. 185; Dahl, "The Parables of Growth," pp. 147, 159-66; Beasley-Murray, *Jesus and the Kingdom of God,* pp. 133-34; Davies and Allison, *Matthew,* 2:410-11; cf. Boucher, *The Parables,* pp. 81-82.

127. E.g., Davies and Allison, *Matthew,* 2:413; Gundry, *Matthew: A Commentary on His Handbook for a Mixed Church Under Persecution,* p. 264; Luz, *Matthew 8–20,* p. 256.

128. *The Parables of Jesus in Matthew 13,* p. 72; cf. p. 109.

129. Even Kingsbury ("The Title 'Kyrios' in Matthew's Gospel," *JBL* 94 [1975]: 246-55) argues that *kyrios* is an auxiliary christological title for Matthew and that Son of Man is much more important. If one takes a closer look at the evidence, thirty-one of Matthew's seventy-three uses of *kyrios* are in the vocative, and eighteen of the seventy-three refer to God.

130. Cf. Hultgren, *The Parables of Jesus,* p. 296. Twenty-five of Matthew's seventy-three

occurrences of *kyrios* are in parables about masters and slaves, and seven of the twenty-five are in the vocative.

131. Cf. R. T. France, *Matthew: Evangelist and Teacher* (Grand Rapids: Zondervan, 1989), pp. 287-91.

132. Importing all possible meanings into a given context.

133. Jülicher (*Die Gleichnisreden Jesu*, 2:563) thought this parable should hardly be called a parable of Jesus. B. Scott (*Hear Then the Parable*) omits any serious discussion of this parable. The "Jesus Seminar" (Funk, Scott, and Butts, *The Parables of Jesus: Red Letter Edition*, p. 65) printed the parable in gray (for both Matthew and *Gos. Thom.*) and the interpretation in black.

134. E.g., Jeremias, *The Parables of Jesus*, pp. 81-85 and 224; Davies and Allison, *Matthew*, 2:408-11, 426-32. Davies and Allison seem to argue for authenticity of the parable, but in the end leave the question of its origin open.

135. Jülicher (*Die Gleichnisreden Jesu*, 2:555-59) thought the parable is as allegorical as the interpretation. Barth ("Auseinandersetzungen um die Kirchenzucht im Umkreis des Matthäusevangelium," 158-77), among other things, objects that the theme of patience does not fit in Jesus' ministry and that the parable presupposes the delay of the parousia. Beare (*The Gospel According to Matthew*, p. 304) asks rhetorically if the crowds were dreaming of conducting a purge of Israel. See also Manson, *The Sayings of Jesus*, pp. 192-96; Gundry, *Matthew: A Commentary on His Handbook for a Mixed Church Under Persecution*, pp. 261-65.

136. The shadow of Jülicher; see above, pp. 5-7 and 15-17.

137. *The Parables of Jesus*, pp. 81-85.

138. Dodd (*The Parables of the Kingdom*, p. 184) asserts that the picture of judgment is the developed eschatology of the church, a picture we shall do well to forget as completely as possible. Beare (*The Gospel According to Matthew*, pp. 311-13) wonders if Matthew really thought in these terms or borrowed some "alien myth." Capon (*Parables of the Kingdom*, pp. 127-30) views the judgment focus as a "dog biscuit" — a condescension — that Jesus throws to his disciples but does not really believe.

139. Manson, *The Sayings of Jesus*, p. 194.

140. See above, p. 165, and esp. n. 107.

141. *The Words of Jesus* (trans. D. M. Kay; Edinburgh: T. & T. Clark, 1902), pp. 166-69. But if the expression is allowed in 16:26 par., why not elsewhere?

142. In fact, this is more likely and would leave the expression ambivalent as to whether the reference were to the earth or to the land of Israel.

143. Most of the "absolute" uses of "the kingdom" appear in composite expressions such as "the gospel of the kingdom." "Kingdom" appears with some regularity qualified only by possessive pronouns such as "your kingdom" (Matt 6:10/Luke 11:2, etc.), which is not far removed from an absolute use. Cf. also Luke 12:32; 22:29.

144. *The Parables of Jesus*, pp. 81-85.

145. Michel de Goedt, "L'Explication de la Parabole de L'Ivraie (Mt. XIII, 36-43)," *RB* 66 (1959): 32-54. Only nine of Jeremias's items are mentioned in John C. Hawkins, *Horae Synopticae* (Oxford: Clarendon, 1899), pp. 4-7.

146. *The Matthean Parables*, p. 332.

147. *The Parables of Jesus*, p. 82.

148. That Matthew likes introductory participles is a given, but that does not make the word here a Matthean characteristic.

149. As with *phrason* ("explain," v. 36), elsewhere only at 15:15. Why Jeremias would say *eis tēn oikian* ("into the house," v. 36) occurs elsewhere only at 9:28 and 17:25 with this meaning is

unclear. The expression occurs also at 9:23; 10:12; 12:29; Mark 1:29; 3:27; 10:10; Luke 4:38; 7:44; 8:51; 10:38; 22:10, 54. Why is *hoi huioi tēs basileias* ("the sons of the kingdom," v. 38) used of Christians, which occurs nowhere else, to be regarded as characteristic of Matthew?

150. On the consummation of the age see *1 En.* 10.12; 16.1; *T. Job* 4.6; *T. Levi* 10.2; *T. Benj.* 11.3; *As. Mos.* 12.4; cf. Dan 9:27; 12:4, 13; *4 Ezra* 7:113; *2 Bar.* 13.3; 19.5; 21.8; 27.15; 29.8; 30.3; 54.21; 69.4; 83.7. For partial parallels to "weeping and gnashing of teeth" see *1 En.* 108.15; *2 En.* 40.12; *Sib. Or.* 2.203; cf. Luke 6:25; *4 Ezra* 7:80-87.

151. *L.A.E.* 17; *T. Job* 47:10 (cf. 7:11); *T. Dan* 6:1-4; *3 Bar.* (Greek) 13.2; cf. *Mekilta Amalek* 1.1-9 (on Exod 17:8), which interprets "then came Amalek" allegorically to argue that when Israel separated from the Torah the enemy came.

152. Jer 27:16 LXX; 51:33; Hos 6:11; Joel 3(4):13; Rev 14:14-20; *4 Ezra* 4:28, 35, 39; *Sib. Or.* 2.164-65; *Midr. Ps.* 8.1.

153. Numerous passages could be listed. On fire as judgment see Isa 47:14; Obad 18; Mal 4:1 (3:19); *1 En.* 10.6, 13 (cf. 18.13-15); 21.7-10; 54.1, 6; 90.24-27; 100.9; 102.1; 103.7-8; *2 En.* 10.1-4; *Jub.* 9.15; CD 2.5-6; *Sib. Or.* 2.196-220; *4 Ezra* 7:61; *Vision of Ezra* 48-58; *2 Bar.* 44.18; *Apoc. Zeph.* 6.1-3; *b. 'Abodah Zarah* 4a; *Midr. Ps.* 21.5. The furnace language is derived from Dan 3:6. Passages explicitly focusing on a furnace at judgment include Rev 9:2; *1 En.* 54.6; *4 Ezra* 7:36; *Mekilta Baḥodesh* 9.25-26 (on Exod. 20:18); *b. 'Erubin* 19a; *Song Rab.* 7.3.3; *Eccl. Rab.* 1.11/*Gen. Rab.* 6.6.

154. Angels as ones gathering sinners for judgment: Matt 24:31/Mark 13:27; Rev 14:15-19; *1 En.* 54.6; 63.1; 99.3; 100.4; CD 2.5-6; *Apoc. Zeph.* B 4.1-7; *Midr. Ps.* 8.1; cf. Luke 16:22.

155. Dan 12:3; cf. Mal 4:2 (3:20); *1 En.* 38.4; 58.3; 104.2; 108.12; *4 Ezra* 7:97 (cf. 7:125); *b. Sanhedrin* 100a; *Eccl. Rab.* 1.4; *Sipre Deut.* 10.

156. See Dale C. Allison, *Jesus of Nazareth: Millenarian Prophet* (Minneapolis: Fortress, 1998), esp. pp. 129-71.

157. See Marius Reiser, *Jesus and Judgment: The Eschatological Proclamation in Its Jewish Context* (trans. Linda M. Maloney; Minneapolis: Fortress, 1997); Wright, *Jesus and the Victory of God,* esp. pp. 320-83.

158. See Manson, *The Sayings of Jesus,* p. 194; de Goedt, "L'Explication de la Parabole de L'Ivraie (Mt. XIII, 36-43)," 45-49.

159. See above, p. 208.

160. A point made long ago by Paul Fiebig (*Altjüdische Gleichnisse und die Gleichnisse Jesu* [Tübingen: Mohr-Siebeck, 1904], p. 160). See also Oesterley, *The Gospel Parables in the Light of Their Jewish Background,* p. 64.

161. See above, p. 161.

162. See above, p. 190, n. 74.

163. Since the quotation is described as a word of "the prophet," Jan Lambrecht (*Out of the Treasure: The Parables in the Gospel of Matthew* [LTPM 10; Grand Rapids: Eerdmans, 1992], p. 168) assumes that Matthew attributed the saying to Isaiah, but "prophet" is used loosely merely to refer to the psalmist. See Acts 2:30.

164. *Die Gleichnisreden,* 2:555. Cf. Liebenberg (*The Language of the Kingdom and Jesus,* pp. 206-7), who thinks the explanation is superfluous and only confirms the metaphorical understanding which a competent reader would reach anyway. Schweizer (*The Good News According to Matthew,* p. 309) thinks the interpretation is totally unlike Jesus because it is allegorical, yet says it is obvious that Jesus is the sower and the enemy is the devil. Note how much Davies and Allison (*Matthew,* 2:431) use the interpretation, even though they view it as secondary.

165. "Die Deutung des Gleichnisses vom Unkraut unter dem Weizen," in *Abba* (Göt-

tingen: Vandenhoeck & Ruprecht, 1966), pp. 261-65, see 264. Cf. Boucher (*The Parables*, p. 85) who finds the interpretation appropriate even if it is from Matthew.

166. Contra Kingsbury, *The Parables of Jesus in Matthew 13*, p. 66. Lambrecht (*Out of the Treasure*, p. 170) explains the separation of parable and interpretation as a result of the desire to warn the disciples, which has no merit.

167. Liebenberg (*The Language of the Kingdom and Jesus*, pp. 206-8 and 350-51) thinks hearers would have interpreted the parables and that the interpretations both confirmed their assumptions and gave further nuances than the parable alone could give.

168. Hendrickx (*The Parables of Jesus*, p. 71) and de Goedt ("L'Explication de la Parabole de L'Ivraie (Mt. XIII, 36-43)," 49) even argued that there must have been an original allegorical interpretation that explained all the elements.

169. Jülicher, *Die Gleichnisreden Jesu*, 2:555; Fiebig, *Altjüdische Gleichnisse und die Gleichnisse Jesu*, p. 158.

170. Hagner (*Matthew 1–13*, p. 394) notes the similarity between 13:43 and the description of the transfiguration (17:2).

171. See also Mark L. Bailey, "The Parable of the Tares," *BSac* 115 (1998): 266-79, esp. 278.

172. Günther Bornkamm, Gerhard Barth, and Heinz Joachim Held, *Tradition and Interpretation in Matthew* (NTL; trans. Percy Scott; Philadelphia: Westminster, 1963), p. 44.

173. See above, pp. 202-4.

174. Contra Lambrecht, who says the kingdom of the Son of Man refers to territory, a domain, and is equivalent to the world, whereas the kingdom of heaven apparently is understood as a reign (*Out of the Treasure*, p. 170).

175. Note Gundry (*Matthew: A Commentary on His Handbook for a Mixed Church Under Persecution*, p. 270) who suggests that the kingdom of the Son of Man emphasizes the judgment motif, whereas the kingdom of the Father emphasizes the Father's care. See also George Eldon Ladd, *A Theology of the New Testament* (rev. ed., ed. Don Hagner; Grand Rapids: Eerdmans, 1993), p. 94.

176. Kingsbury, *The Parables of Jesus in Matthew 13*, p. 98; Luz, *Matthew 8–20*, p. 270.

177. See Kingsbury, *The Parables of Jesus in Matthew 13*, pp. 97-98. The only other passage explicitly bringing the kingdom and the Father together is Luke 12:31-32. The designation of the kingdom as the kingdom of the Son of Man or the kingdom belonging to Jesus is also infrequent. See Matt 16:28; 20:21; Luke 22:30.

178. See e.g., Ladd, *A Theology of the New Testament*, pp. 94-95; Craig S. Keener, *A Commentary on the Gospel of Matthew* (Grand Rapids: Eerdmans, 1999), p. 385; and Dahl ("The Parables of Growth," pp. 159-60), who comments, "Even if Jesus did not create the pure community, the powers of the age to come were already at work and the events of the final age already occurring. . . ." I would not say as Robert K. McIver ("The Parable of the Weeds among the Wheat [Matt 13:24-30, 36-43] and the Relationship between the Kingdom and the Church as Portrayed in the Gospel of Matthew," *JBL* 114 [1995]: 643-59, here pp. 658-59) does that the kingdom is present in the present community of believers. The kingdom is God's activity in the ministry of Jesus and the Spirit *reflected* in the community.

179. Note the following texts where God plants (or does not plant) people: Isa 5:7; 6:13; 40:24-26; 43:5; 44:3-4; 60:21; 61:3; Jer 2:21; 24:6; 31:27-28; 32:41; 42:10; 45:4; Ezek 34:29; Hos 2:23; Amos 9:15 (the italicized texts are eschatological). Cf. Isa 1:4, which refers to people as an evil seed, and 57:4, which refers to children of transgression as a seed of falsehood.

Note too that the "harvest" metaphor is not used with the same reference in all its occurrences. In Matt 9:37-38 it refers to the harvest taking place during Jesus' ministry, whereas in this parable it obviously refers to the eschaton, as it does often in Jewish writings.

180. Dodd, *The Parables of the Kingdom*, p. 185; Kümmel, *Promise and Fulfillment*, p. 135.

181. This may be the reason the quotation of Isaiah 61 in Luke 4:18-19 omits 61:2b ("and the day of vengeance of our God"). Cf. Beasley-Murray, *Jesus and the Kingdom of God*, p. 134. Unlike the parable of the Fig Tree, the parable of the Wheat and the Weeds does not focus on repentance or time to make amends (contra I. Jones, *The Matthean Parables*, p. 341).

182. Hultgren (*The Parables of Jesus*, p. 292) sees judgment as the dominant theme in this parable.

183. Cf. Fiebig, *Altjüdische Gleichnisse und die Gleichnisse Jesu*, p. 159. McIver ("The Parable of the Weeds among the Wheat," 646-47) argues against the universalist interpretation of the parable (that the field is the world) because this would mean merely that good and evil exist side by side until judgment, a bland point. But the parable is not about good and evil in the world, but good and evil *in the kingdom*, which is hardly a bland point in Jesus' context, when expectations of the obliteration of evil were high.

184. Kingsbury, *The Parables of Jesus in Matthew 13*, pp. 68-69; and Liebenberg, *The Language of the Kingdom and Jesus*, pp. 201-2, respectively.

185. As often in church tradition; see Wailes, *Medieval Allegories of Jesus' Parables*, p. 105; more recently, Hendrickx, *The Parables of Jesus*, p. 60; I. Jones, *The Matthean Parables*, p. 320. Sleep is not a negative image in the parable of the Ten Virgins (Matt 25:1-13). Nor does the parable suggest that the disciples had the power to uproot evil but not the permission, contra Charles Edwin Carlston, "A *Positive* Criterion of Authenticity," *BR* 7 (1962): 33-44, see 42.

186. See pp. 310, n. 218, and 314-16.

187. See Russell Pregeant (*Christology beyond Dogma: Matthew's Christ in Process Hermeneutic* [Philadelphia: Fortress, 1978], pp. 111-12) who says the sowing of the Son of Man refers to Christian preaching, but that the sowing of Satan is more difficult to pin down. To do so, however, is to push the parable beyond its purpose.

188. Note in addition to the temptation narratives Matt 12:22-30/Mark 3:22-27/Luke 11:14-23; Matt 16:23/Mark 8:33; Luke 10:18; 13:16; 22:3, 31. See Beasley-Murray, *Jesus and the Kingdom of God*, p. 133.

189. Davies and Allison, *Matthew*, 2:408.

190. Contra Patte, *The Gospel According to Matthew*, p. 194; and Perkins, *Hearing the Parables of Jesus*, p. 85, respectively. Completely unacceptable is Capon's (*Parables of the Kingdom*, pp. 105-9) illegitimate totality transfer by which he uses the meaning "forgive" for *aphiēmi* ("let" in the parable or "leave") to say the parable teaches that we are not to attack evil but to forgive it. *Aphiēmi* can mean "forgive," but the context of v. 30 requires the meaning "let." By analogy, if Capon were right, we would have to understand that v. 36 meant that Jesus forgave (*aphiēmi*) the crowds and went in the house!

191. Crossan, "The Seed Parables of Jesus," 259-61, sees the man in the parable outwitting his enemy by using the weeds as fuel, thus turning the problem to his advantage. For him the parable is an example of prudent and resolute action pointing to the kind of action demanded by the kingdom's advent. This view has little in its favor.

192. Harry Fleddermann, "Mustard Seed and Leaven in Q, the Synoptics, and Thomas," *Society of Biblical Literature 1989 Seminary Papers 1989* (ed. David J. Lull; Atlanta: Scholars, 1989), pp. 216-36, here p. 216; Luz, *Matthew 8–20*, p. 258; Guelich, *Mark 1–8:26*, p. 247 (but he thinks this shows how immaterial the distinctions between similitudes and parables can be). Some analogies use the present tense, some the past tenses. Cf. Dodd (*The Parables of the King-*

dom, p. 18), who suggests as a *rough* guideline that figurative sayings have no more than one verb, similitudes have more than one verb in the present tense, and parables have a series of verbs in the historic tense. But he also says that precise lines between the classes cannot be drawn and that one class melts into another. See above, p. 12.

193. The authenticity of this parable is rarely questioned. The Jesus Seminar prints the *Gos. Thom.* version in red and the Synoptic versions in pink. See Funk, Scott, and Butts, *The Parables of Jesus: Red Letter Edition,* p. 34.

194. Other than the Jesus Seminar (see n. 193 above) virtually all commentators view the account in *Gos. Thom.* as inferior and as influenced by the Synoptic tradition. E.g., Davies and Allison, *Matthew,* 2:421; Fleddermann, "Mustard Seed and Leaven in Q, the Synoptics, and Thomas," p. 229.

195. Of the minor textual variants in these texts, two deserve mention. In Mark 4:31 the dative *kokkō* is preferable to the accusative *kokkon.* It is conceivable that the dative is an assimilation to Matthew and Luke, but the accusative probably was introduced to fit better with *thōmen* ("may we place") in v. 30 and with the neuter participle *on* ("which being") in v. 31b. Further, the dative represents the Hebrew/Aramaic *lĕ* which appears in parabolic introductions: "To what may it be compared? To . . ." (e.g., *m. Sukkah* 2.9). In Luke 13:19 a number of manuscripts have added *mega* ("great") to *dendron* ("tree") to heighten the contrast.

196. E.g., *m. Sukkah* 2.9; *b. Sukkah* 29a; *b. Berakot* 7b, 11a.

197. E.g., Klauck (*Allegorie und Allegorese in synoptischen Gleichnistexten,* p. 211) discounts the relevance of this OT text, but Hans-Werner Bartsch ("Eine bisher übersehene Zitierung der LXX in Mark 4,30," *TZ* 15 [1959]: 126-28) argues that it is alluded to specifically.

198. See the parables of the Treasure and the Pearl, the Wheat and the Weeds and the Net, and the Tower Builder and the Warring King. For rabbinic examples see *Pesiqta de Rab Kahana* 5.11; 10.7; Supplement 3. An example of a triplet is the collection of the parables of the Lost Sheep, the Lost Coin, and the Lost Two Sons in Luke 15; see *Pesiqta de Rab Kahana* 2.7; 6.3; 21.3. Even longer groupings occur as well in *Pesiqta de Rab Kahana.*

199. Liebenberg, *The Language of the Kingdom and Jesus,* p. 306.

200. See Matt 17:20/Luke 17:6; *m. Niddah* 5.2 ("[A man's discharge] renders him unclean whatsoever its bulk, even though it be like to a grain of mustard, or less than this"); *b. Berakot* 31a ("R. Zera said: The daughters of Israel have undertaken to be so strict with themselves that if they see a drop of blood no bigger than a mustard seed they wait seven [clean] days after it"); see also *m. Teharot* 8.8; *m. Nazir* 1.5; *Lev. Rab.* 31.9 (although lost in the Soncino translation). Antigonus of Carystus 91 and Diodorus Siculus 1.35.2 with identical statements have the least-greatest contrast but not with reference to mustard seeds.

201. See P. Jones, *Studying the Parables of Jesus,* p. 86; Claus-Hunno Hunzinger, "σίναπι," *TDNT* 7:287-91, here p. 289.

202. E.g., those who debate the inerrancy of Scripture over such an issue. See John A. Sproule, "The Problem of the Mustard Seed," *Grace Theological Journal* 1 (1980): 37-42. Like others, he argues that mustard is the smallest *garden* variety seed.

203. W. Harold Mare ("The Smallest Mustard Seed — Matthew 13:32," *Grace Theological Journal* 9 [1968]: 3-11) is one who argues for the comparative sense.

204. Michael Zohary, *Plants of the Bible* (Cambridge: Cambridge University Press, 1982), p. 93.

205. A few texts describe mustard plants as if they were trees, but they are exaggerations in an attempt to describe the fertility of Israel prior to the destruction of the temple. See *y. Pe'ah* 7.4; *b. Ketubot* 111b.

206. Theophrastus is often cited as evidence for loose use of language. In his *Enquiry into Plants* 1.3.1-4 he classifies all plants as trees, shrubs, undershrubs, and herbs but cautions that "These definitions however must be taken and accepted as applying generally and on the whole. For in the case of some plants it might seem that our definitions overlap; and some under cultivation appear to become different and depart from their essential nature, for instance, mallow when it grows tall and becomes tree-like." Jülicher (*Die Gleichnisreden Jesu* 2:575) comments that a Middle Eastern person who does not teach botany could easily call a bush a tree if he wanted to compare its height with the smallness of the mustard seed.

207. *Natural History* 20.87.236-38.

208. Jülicher, *Die Gleichnisreden Jesu*, 2:576.

209. The regulation reads, "A garden-bed six handbreadths by six may be sown with five kinds of seeds. . . . Not every kind of seed may be sown in a garden-bed, but any kind of vegetable may be sown therein. Mustard and small beans are deemed a kind of seed and large beans a kind of vegetable." Restrictions about sowing in fields appears in *m. Kil'ayim* 2.8: "They may not flank a field of grain with mustard or seed of safflower, but they may flank a field of vegetables with mustard or seed of safflower." The concern is that a stranger will assume that mustard, which was harmful to grain would not have been sown by a neighbor and must have been sown by the person who sowed the grain and, therefore, that that person had violated Lev 19:19.

210. I. Howard Marshall, *The Gospel of Luke* (NIGTC; Grand Rapids: Eerdmans, 1978), p. 561; Rudolf Laufen, "ΒΑΣΙΛΕΙΑ und ΕΚΚΛΗΣΙΑ. Eine traditions- und redaktionsgeschichtliche Untersuchung des Gleichnisses vom Senfkorn," in *Begegnung mit dem Wort. Festschrift für Heinrich Zimmermann* (ed. Josef Zmijewski and Ernst Nellessen; BBB 53; Bonn: Peter Hanstein, 1979), pp. 105-40, here p. 112.

211. Scott, *Hear Then the Parable*, pp. 382-87.

212. See Liebenberg, *The Language of the Kingdom and Jesus*, pp. 318-20; Brad H. Young, *Jesus and His Jewish Parables: Rediscovering the Roots of Jesus' Teaching* (New York: Paulist, 1989), p. 207.

213. Possibly the word for "seed" (*kokkos*) may be a collective, as the related word *sperma* is (cf. Matt 13:24, 27).

214. See Wailes, *Medieval Allegories of Jesus' Parables*, pp. 108-13; Luz, *Matthew 8–20*, pp. 258-61. Luz rightly complains about the inappropriateness of triumphalist readings and the narrowness of individual and eschatological readings. Bernard Schultze allegorized the details of the parable to focus on the expansion and exclusive legitimacy of the Roman Catholic church. See his "Die ekklesiologische Bedeutung des Gleichnisses vom Senfkorn (Matth. 13,31-32; Mk. 4,30-32; Lk. 13,18-19)," *Orientalia Christiana Periodica* 27 (1961): 362-86.

215. For overviews of these options see Mark L. Bailey, "The Parable of the Mustard Seed," *BSac* 155 (1998): 449-59, here pp. 455-59; Martin H. Scharlemann, "The Parables of the Leaven and the Mustard Seed: A Suggested Methodological Model," in *Studies in Lutheran Hermeneutics* (ed. John Reumann; Philadelphia: Fortress, 1979), pp. 335-54, here pp. 348-49.

216. Dodd, *The Parables of the Kingdom*, pp. 190-91.

217. Robert W. Funk, "The Looking-Glass Tree Is for the Birds," *Int* 27 (1973): 3-9.

218. See among many Kümmel, *Promise and Fulfillment*, pp. 130-31; France, *The Gospel of Mark*, p. 216; Franz Mussner, "1Q Hodajoth und das Gleichnis vom Senfkorn (Mk 4:30-32 Par.)," *BZ* 4 (1960): 128-30.

219. See Dahl, "The Parables of Growth," p. 155; Davies and Allison, *Matthew*, 2:417; Beasley-Murray, *Jesus and the Kingdom of God*, pp. 123-25.

220. And despite the fact that Bultmann thought the original point of both the Mustard Seed and the Leaven is irrecoverable (*The History of the Synoptic Tradition,* p. 200).

221. E.g., P. Jones, *Studying the Parables of Jesus,* pp. 84-85; Jacques Dupont, "Le couple parabolique du sénevé et du levain, Mt 13,31-33; Lc 13,18-21," in *Jesus Christ in Historie und Theologie. Neutestamentliche Festschrift für Hans Conzelmann zum 60. Geburtstag* (ed. Georg Strecker; Tübingen: Mohr-Siebeck, 1975), pp. 331-45, here p. 333; Klauck, *Allegorie und Allegorese in synoptischen Gleichnistexten,* p. 210.

222. E.g., Jülicher, *Die Gleichnisreden Jesu,* 2:571; Fleddermann, "Mustard Seed and Leaven in Q, the Synoptics, and Thomas," p. 226; Luz, *Matthew 8–20,* p. 258. Franz Kogler rejects Q and argues that the only source for Matthew and Luke was a deutero-Markan recension, which is difficult to demonstrate. See his *Das Doppelgleichnis vom Senfkorn und vom Sauerteig in seiner traditionsgeschichtlichen Entwicklung. Zur Reich-Gottes-Vorstellung Jesu und ihren Aktualisierungen in der Kirche* (FB; Würzburg: Echter, 1988).

223. E.g., Laufen, "ΒΑΣΙΛΕΙΑ und ΕΚΚΛΗΣΙΑ," pp. 107-14; Hultgren, *The Parables of Jesus,* pp. 397-98; Fleddermann, "Mustard Seed and Leaven in Q, the Synoptics, and Thomas," pp. 217-24. Several attempt to trace different stages and theologies in each of the Synoptics, but the differences are either minimal or not demonstrable. See e.g., Weder, *Die Gleichnisse Jesu als Metaphern,* pp. 104-6 and 128-33; and Liebenberg, *The Language of the Kingdom and Jesus,* pp. 277-335.

224. See the discussion of Zeba Antonin Crook, "The Synoptic Parables of the Mustard Seed and the Leaven: A Test Case for the Two-Document, Two-Gospel, and Farrer-Goulder Hypotheses," *JSNT* 78 (2000): 23-48, who as much as anything shows the difficulty of establishing any particular theory.

225. See p. 25 above and esp. p. 24, n. 116.

226. E.g., Kümmel (*Promise and Fulfillment,* p. 132) and Fleddermann ("Mustard Seed and Leaven in Q, the Synoptics, and Thomas," p. 230) think they were, Davies and Allison (*Matthew,* 2:421) that they were not.

227. The compiler of *Gos. Thom.* may be responsible for the separation, for he has placed the Mustard Seed parable with sayings about the kingdom and discipleship and the Leaven parable with another parable about a woman.

228. E.g., Heil, "Reader-Response and the Narrative Context of the Parables about Growing Seed in Mark 4:1-34," 283-85; Marcus, *The Mystery of the Kingdom of God,* pp. 213-16. Marcus sees the sowing of the seed as the proclamation of the word by both Jesus and the early church and the final stage of the parable pointing to the time of the church, the parousia, and the death and resurrection of Jesus. In his commentary (*Mark 1–8,* pp. 331, 329) he takes the mature plant as referring to both the Christian mission and the parousia and thinks Mark's "smaller than all the other seeds on earth" indicates the beleaguered self-image of Mark's community. M. Scharlemann ("The Parables of the Leaven and the Mustard Seed," p. 346) goes so far as to say "'The man' of any parable is a symbol for God."

229. Marcus, *The Mystery of the Kingdom of God,* p. 214. The identification of the birds as Gentiles occurs frequently.

230. Gundry, *Mark,* p. 230, and Marcus, *Mark 1–8,* p. 133, respectively.

231. Wendy J. Cotter, "The Parables of the Mustard Seed and the Leaven: Their Function in the Earliest Stratum of Q," *TJT* 8 (1992): 37-51, here pp. 45-48.

232. In addition to the OT texts mentioned see Jdg 9:15; 1QH 14.14-16; 16.4-9 (p. 217 above); and the Targum on Ezek 17:22-23, which interprets the tree messianically: "Thus says the Lord God, 'I Myself will bring near *a child from the kingdom of the house of David which is lik-*

ened to the lofty cedar, *and I will establish him from among his children's children; I will anoint and establish him by My Memra* on a high and exalted mountain. On the *holy* mountain of Israel will I *establish him, and he shall gather together armies and build fortresses and become a mighty king;* and *all the righteous shall rely upon him, and all the humble* shall dwell in the shade *of his kingdom'* " (see H. Levey Samson, *The Targum of Ezekiel Translated, with a Critical Introduction, Apparatus, and Notes* [The Aramaic Bible 13; Wilmington, Del.: Michael Glazier, 1987]). The date of this targum, however, is late. See also the language of Lam 4:20 and Bar 1:12.

233. E.g., among many see Dodd, *The Parables of the Kingdom,* pp. 190-91; Davies and Allison, *Matthew,* 2:420; Hendrickx, *The Parables of Jesus,* pp. 36-37; Hultgren, *The Parables of Jesus,* pp. 396-98; Kingsbury, *The Parables of Jesus in Matthew 13,* pp. 81-82. Some (e.g., Ambrozic, *The Hidden Kingdom,* p. 133; Hagner, *Matthew 1–13,* p. 387) accept the allusion to a kingdom but balk at the idea of inclusion of the Gentiles.

234. *The Parables of Jesus,* p. 147. He bases his view on *Jos. Asen.* 15.7 (which does not refer to a tree): "And your name shall no longer be called Aseneth, but your name shall be City of Refuge, because in you many nations will take refuge with the Lord God, the Most High, and under your wings many peoples trusting in the Lord God will be sheltered *(kataskēnoun)*. . . ."

235. Notably Liebenberg, *The Language of the Kingdom and Jesus,* pp. 289-300; Crossan, *In Parables,* pp. 47-48.

236. Liebenberg, *The Language of the Kingdom and Jesus,* pp. 291-300. He points to other occurrences of "the birds of heaven" (Matt 6:26; 8:20/Luke 9:58; Luke 8:5) and the impossibility of taking these passages as OT allusions, but the parable accounts also have the image of a tree/plant and branches/shadow, which gives more reason to see an allusion. Laufen ("ΒΑΣΙΛΕΙΑ und ΕΚΚΛΗΣΙΑ," pp. 119-20) suggests that the language was used merely to show the large size of the plant and was later made into an allusion to the OT.

237. Marcus, *The Mystery of the Kingdom of God,* pp. 203-4; Hultgren, *The Parables of Jesus,* p. 396; Davies and Allison, *Matthew,* 2:420. Hultgren (p. 396) and Guelich (*Mark,* p. 251) both argue against the allusion being a later addition. Among other things, the imagery belongs to the basic structure of the parable and some statement of the significance of the result is needed.

238. Cf. France, *The Gospel of Mark,* pp. 216-17.

239. Cf. among others, Joseph A. Fitzmyer, *The Gospel According to Luke X–XXIV* (AB 28A; Garden City, N.Y.: Doubleday, 1985), p. 1017; Hagner, *Matthew 1–13,* p. 387. Some point to *1 En.* 90.30, 33, 37, but both animals and birds are mentioned there, and to *Midr. Ps.* 104.10 (on Ps 104:12), which interprets birds as Gentiles, but in 104.9 the birds are understood literally and in 104.14 (on Ps 104:17) the birds are interpreted as the Levites.

240. Funk, "The Looking-Glass Tree Is for the Birds."

241. Note, however, that *2 Bar.* 36:1–39:8 has a vine (interpreted messianically) replace the whole forest and the "reigning" cedar.

242. See especially Dahl, "The Parables of Growth," 156-66; Jeremias, *The Parables of Jesus,* p. 149. J. Marcus (*The Mystery of the Kingdom of God,* p. 218) reads the parable as addressing the problems of persecution and despair in the Markan church and thinks the question addressed is "Is there hope for the world?"

243. For a summary discussion of Jewish expectation see N. T. Wright, *The New Testament and the People of God,* vol. 1 of *Christian Origins and the Question of God* (Minneapolis: Fortress, 1992), pp. 280-338.

244. E.g., Kümmel, *Promise and Fulfillment,* pp. 128-31.

245. E.g., Laufen, "ΒΑΣΙΛΕΙΑ und ΕΚΚΛΗΣΙΑ," pp. 115-17; Hagner, *Matthew 1–13,*

p. 387; and Kingsbury's reading of Mark and Matthew (*The Parables of Jesus in Matthew 13*, p. 77).

246. E.g., Beasley-Murray, *Jesus and the Kingdom of God*, pp. 123-24; Otto Kuss ("Zum Sinngehalt des Doppelgleichnisses vom Senfkorn und Sauerteig," *Bib* 40 [1959]: 641-53, here pp. 651-53) focuses on contrast and the process of growth.

247. Dahl, "The Parables of Growth," pp. 154-55 (who includes contrast, growth, and organic unity); Davies and Allison, *Matthew*, 2:415-16 (contrast and organic unity); Fitzmyer, *The Gospel According to Luke X–XXIV*, pp. 1015-16 (growth, power, and organic unity). Of course, organic unity of beginning and end assumes growth.

248. Some, especially Jeremias (*The Parables of Jesus*, pp. 148-49) and Crossan (*In Parables*, pp. 50-51), seeking to avoid the idea of process or growth, argue that the parable emphasizes the miraculous (and for Jeremias the resurrection). Jeremias does so on the assumption that people of the Bible viewed growth as a miracle. Nothing justifies a focus on miracle. Kuss ("Zum Sinngehalt des Doppelgleichnisses vom Senfkorn und Sauerteig," 650) and Dahl ("The Parables of Growth," pp. 148-50) show that ancients did not view growth as a miracle.

249. Parable interpretation is often implicitly an answer to the question of what time it is in the parable. C. H. Dodd thought this similitude was about the time of the full-grown plant. Rather, it assumes that this is the time when things seem small, the time of planting a mustard seed.

250. Davies and Allison, *The Gospel According to Saint Matthew*, 2:416.

251. Jülicher (*Die Gleichnisreden Jesu*, 2:580); Erich Grässer (*Das Problem der Parusieverzögerung in den synoptischen Evangelien und in der Apostelgeschichte* [2d ed; BZNW 22; Berlin: Töpelmann, 1960], p. 61), and Harvey K. McArthur ("The Parable of the Mustard Seed," *CBQ* 33 [1971]: 198-210, here p. 209) all focus on certainty.

252. Hultgren, *The Parables of Jesus*, p. 401; B. T. D. Smith, *The Parables of the Synoptic Gospels* (Cambridge: Cambridge University Press, 1937), p. 120.

253. E.g., A. B. Bruce's interpretations of the Mustard Seed and Leaven. The first is thought to teach about the kingdom's "increase in outward bulk as a visible society," and the second about the kingdom's "spiritual power exercising a progressive moral influence." (See *The Parabolic Teaching of Jesus*, p. 90.) Grässer is so opposed to the idea of growth that its presence in these parables is assigned to later tradition (*Das Problem der Parusieverzögerung in den synoptischen Evangelien und in der Apostelgeschichte*, p. 63).

254. Fleddermann, "Mustard Seed and Leaven in Q, the Synoptics, and Thomas," pp. 233-34; Grässer, *Das Problem der Parusieverzögerung in den synoptischen Evangelien und in der Apostelgeschichte*, pp. 141-43.

255. See Anna Wierzbicka, *What Did Jesus Mean? Explaining the Sermon on the Mount and the Parables in Simple and Universal Human Concepts* (Oxford: Oxford University Press, 2001), pp. 278-87; Capon, *Parables of the Kingdom*, pp. 98-112. The possibility was already raised and rejected by A. B. Bruce (*The Parabolic Teaching of Jesus*, p. 111).

256. Capon (*Parables of the Kingdom*, pp. 101-2) goes so far as to argue that the kingdom began at the beginning of creation and that the world has always been the kingdom. Cf. John W. Sider, *Interpreting the Parables: A Hermeneutical Guide to Their Meaning* (Grand Rapids: Zondervan, 1995), pp. 36-39.

257. Which is precisely what Wierzbicka does. See *What Did Jesus Mean?* p. 281.

258. Note that N. T. Wright (*Jesus and the Victory of God*, pp. 241-42) says that the leaven of Jesus' message is hidden within Israel so that it may work its way through the whole people.

259. Kingsbury, *The Parables of Jesus in Matthew 13*, p. 84.

260. Unless one accepts the textual variant *ekrypsen* ("hid") in Luke 13:21. The better attested reading is *enekrypsen* like Matthew, although that could be due to assimilation to Matthew. There is no difference in meaning.

261. The word *palin* occurs only two other times in the Gospel and only five times in Acts.

262. Including those in the Jesus Seminar who print the canonical versions in red and the *Gos. Thom.* version in pink. See Funk, Scott, and Butts, *The Parables of Jesus: Red Letter Edition*, p. 29. Elizabeth Waller ("The Parable of the Leaven: A Sectarian Teaching and the Inclusion of Women," *USQR* 35 [1979-80]: 99-109, here pp. 102-3) is one of the few who argues that *Gos. Thom.* is earlier, but she seems to do so because that version is more amenable to feminist concerns.

263. While *enekrypsen* is used in 13:33, the simpler *kryptein* occurs in the other verses: *kekrymmena* in v. 35 and *kekrymmenō* and *ekrypsen* in v. 44.

264. Robert W. Funk ("Beyond Criticism in Quest of Literacy: The Parable of the Leaven," *Int* 25 [1971]: 149-70, here p. 159) says appropriately that the word "hidden" was chosen to vibrate in its context and attract attention.

265. Hendrickx (*The Parables of Jesus*, pp. 46-47) was sure that the original parable mentioned the small amount of leaven, and, since Matthew and Luke do not have this or mention a contrast, their versions do not preserve the original form.

266. Calling it rotten dough and loathsome as Denis Campbell does ("The Leaven," *ExpTim* 104 [1993]: 307-8, here p. 307) is overly pejorative.

267. See S. Safrai and M. Stern, *The Jewish People in the First Century* (CRINT; Assen: Van Gorcum, 1974), 2:730; Susan Marie Praeder, *The Word in Women's Worlds: Four Parables* (Wilmington, Del.: Michael Glazier, 1988), pp. 11-19; Holly Hearon and Antoinette Clark Wire, "Women's Work in the Realm of God (Mt. 13.33; Lk. 13.20, 21; Gos. Thom. 96; Mt. 6.28-30; Lk. 12.27-28; Gos. Thom. 36)," in *The Lost Coin: Parables of Women, Work and Wisdom* (ed. Mary Ann Beavis; London: Sheffield Academic, 2002), pp. 136-57, here pp. 137-42.

268. See Josephus *Ant.* 9.85: "Now the saton is equal to one and a half Italian *modii*." The *modius* was a little under two gallons. For discussion of these issues see Kingsbury, *The Parables of Jesus in Matthew 13*, p. 85; Praeder, *The Word in Women's Worlds: Four Parables*, p. 23; Luz, *Matthew 8–20*, p. 262.

269. Wailes, *Medieval Allegories of Jesus' Parables*, pp. 113-17.

270. See the overview by Waller ("The Parable of the Leaven: A Sectarian Teaching and the Inclusion of Women," 99-100) for some of these options.

271. Dodd, *The Parables of the Kingdom*, pp. 191-93, quotation on p. 193.

272. E.g., Hendrickx, *The Parables of Jesus*, p. 47.

273. Praeder, *The Word in Women's Worlds: Four Parables*, pp. 26-35, but she is content with other polyvalent readings. See the discussion of B. Scott's view under the question whether leaven is a negative symbol, and also see Barbara E. Reid, "Beyond Petty Pursuits and Wearisome Widows: Three Lukan Parables," *Int* 56 (2002): 284-94, here p. 286.

274. Kingsbury, *The Parables of Jesus in Matthew 13*, pp. 86-87; Keener, *A Commentary on the Gospel of Matthew*, p. 388; and Luz, *Matthew 8–20*, p. 263.

275. E.g., Funk, "Beyond Criticism in Quest of Literacy," 160-66.

276. Hearon and Wire, "Women's Work in the Realm of God," pp. 146-56.

277. Waller, "The Parable of the Leaven: A Sectarian Teaching and the Inclusion of Women," 107.

278. E.g., Oesterley, *The Gospel Parables in the Light of Their Jewish Background,* p. 79; Simon J. Kistemaker, *The Parables of Jesus* (Grand Rapids: Baker, 1980), p. 44.

279. As Jülicher (*Die Gleichnisreden Jesu,* 2:579) already noted.

280. Rau, *Reden in Vollmacht,* pp. 114, 117-18.

281. Scott, *Hear Then the Parable,* pp. 321-29. He mistakenly says that only negative references appear in ancient literature. He unjustly views the woman and the word "hide" as negative terms as well and views Hos 7:4 as background to conclude that all will be corrupted. This does not fit with the message of Jesus elsewhere.

282. The LXX has *metra* while Matthew has *sata.*

283. Waller, "The Parable of the Leaven: A Sectarian Teaching and the Inclusion of Women," 102-5; Praeder, *The Word in Women's Worlds: Four Parables,* pp. 28-31.

284. Funk, "Beyond Criticism in Quest of Literacy," 162-63, following Ernst Lohmeyer, *Das Evangelium des Matthäus* (ed. Werner Schmauch; 2d ed.; KEK; Göttingen: Vandenhoeck & Ruprecht, 1958), pp. 220-21. Lohmeyer suggests that leaven as an image for the eschatological kingdom is set over against the emphasis on unleavened bread in the temple, the symbol of God's kingdom on earth. Any connection to the temple is a real stretch. See also Waller ("The Parable of the Leaven: A Sectarian Teaching and the Inclusion of Women," 102-5), who argues for the allusion to Gen 18:6 and the notion of epiphany but does not connect this to the temple.

285. Davies and Allison (*Matthew,* 2:423) suggest this.

286. See John Nolland, *Luke 9:21–18:34* (WBC 35B; Dallas: Word, 1993), p. 730; Fleddermann, "Mustard Seed and Leaven in Q, the Synoptics, and Thomas," p. 233. Sarah surely did not bake bread for 100 people to feed three, and Gideon and the witch at Endor surely did not bake bread for 100 people to feed one. In the last two cases the bread was not leavened, and Sarah's probably was not either, which would make a significant difference in the number of people the bread would feed.

287. Specifically Isaiah 61; see my "The Gospel of Jesus," in *The Written Gospel* (*Festschrift* for Graham Stanton, ed. Markus Bockmuehl and Donald A. Hagner; Cambridge: Cambridge University Press, 2005), pp. 31-44.

288. I see no basis (contra Hearon and Wire, "Women's Work in the Realm of God," pp. 146-47) for the suggestion the parable is about God's providential care and a challenge to those tied to their work to represent God from town to town.

289. But the aorist active indicative of this word seems to have fallen out of use. See S. M. B. Wilmshurst, "The Historic Present in Matthew's Gospel: A Survey and Analysis Focused on Matthew 13:44," *JSNT* 25 (2003): 269-87, here p. 281.

290. The authenticity of this parable is rarely questioned. For what it is worth, the Jesus Seminar printed both the Matthean and *Gos. Thom.* versions in pink (Funk, Scott, and Butts, *The Parables of Jesus: Red Letter Edition,* p. 37).

291. Despite the suggestion of a few, I do not think Prov 2:4-5 bears any relation to this parable.

292. See the treatment of Klaus Berger, "Materialien zu Form und Überlieferungsgeschichte neutestamentlicher Gleichnisse," *NovT* 15 (1973): 1-37, here pp. 2-9.

293. Text from *Aesop's Fables,* trans. Laura Gibbs (Oxford: Oxford University Press, 2002), p. 228.

294. Jeremias (*The Parables of Jesus,* p. 32) views the *Gos. Thom.* version as "utterly degenerated" and Matthew as "certainly original." Crossan (*Finding Is the First Act: Trove Folktales and Jesus' Treasure Parable* [Philadelphia: Fortress, 1979], pp. 105-6) argues that *Gos. Thom.* has

adapted the Jewish story possibly to avoid the immorality of the finder's actions in the canonical account.

295. See saying 95. Liebenberg (*The Language of the Kingdom and Jesus*, pp. 236-42) argues that saying 109 is positive, despite saying 95.

296. See Luz, *Matthew 8–20*, p. 275; Davies and Allison, *Matthew*, 2:437; Weder, *Die Gleichnisse Jesu als Metaphern*, p. 139, among others. Charles W. Hedrick ("The Treasure Parable in Matthew and Thomas," *FFF* 2/2 [1986]: 41-56, and *Parables as Poetic Fictions: The Creative Voice of Jesus* [Peabody, Mass.: Hendrickson, 1994], pp. 132-41) and Scott (*Hear Then the Parable*, pp. 392-93) are among the few arguing that the *Gos. Thom.* version is independent and to be preferred. Is saying 110 in *Gos. Thom.* an interpretation of saying 109?

297. Hagner (*Matthew 1–13*, p. 396) thinks it certain that *Gos. Thom.* is dependent on Matthew for this parable and that of the Pearl. This is one of four parables unique to Matthew among the Synoptics that are paralleled in *Gos. Thom.*, the other three being the Wheat and the Weeds (saying 57), the Pearl (saying 76), and the Net (saying 8).

298. John C. Fenton, "Expounding the Parables: IV. The Parables of the Treasure and the Pearl (Mt. 13:44-46)," *ExpTim* 77 (1966): 178-80, here p. 178.

299. "Again" *(palin)* is inserted in some manuscripts.

300. On these and a few other supposed Mattheanisms see Luz, *Matthew 8–20*, p. 275; Hultgren, *The Parables of Jesus*, p. 414.

301. *J.W.* 7.113-15: "Of the vast wealth of the city no small portion was still being discovered among the ruins. Much of this the Romans dug up, but the greater part they became possessed of through the information of the prisoners, gold and silver and other most precious articles, which the owners in view of the uncertain fortunes of war had stored underground." See also Deut 33:19 and Virgil, *Aeneid* 1.358-59, which refers to "treasures long hidden underground, a mass of gold and silver known to none."

302. Ephraim Stern, "Buried Treasure: The Silver Hoard from Dor," *BAR* 24 (1998): 46-51, 62. *Select Papyri* 278 (LCL) contains a complaint of robbery when a person hired to demolish some walls steals a treasure hidden in a wall. This case is not like the Gospel account, for both the owner (the householder's mother) and the exact amounts were known. Also the thief admitted to throwing away the box in which the treasure was kept.

303. In addition to Sir 40:18 (p. 236 above), see Plotinus, *Enneades* 2.3.14, which says that with success from a treasure trove something from the All has entered into action.

304. Irenaeus (*Haer.* 4.26) saw Christ as the treasure hid both in the Scriptures and in the world. Origen interprets similarly; see his *Commentary on Matthew* 10.5-6. Jerome (*On Matthew* 1.288) saw the treasure as Christ hid in the flesh. Cf. *Acts of Peter* 20; *Acts of John* 109.

305. See Wailes, *Medieval Allegories of Jesus' Parables*, pp. 117-20.

306. Flusser suggests (*Die rabbinischen Gleichnisse und der Gleichniserzähler Jesus*, p. 131) that similar rabbinic parables are indicative to show the love of God for Israel, while Jesus' parables of the Treasure and the Pearl are imperative, urging the hearer to sell all.

307. *The Parables of Jesus*, pp. 200-201.

308. Jeffrey A. Gibbs, "Parables of Atonement and Assurance: Matthew 13:44-46," *CTQ* 51 (1987): 19-43; J. Dwight Pentecost, *The Parables of Jesus* (Grand Rapids: Zondervan, 1982), pp. 60-61.

309. See Wilmshurst, "The Historic Present in Matthew's Gospel," esp. 283-85. However, his argument needlessly reduces the parable of the Pearl to a subordinate role, and the idea of "hidden" in the parable of the Treasure is viewed as peripheral as well because it is expressed in the aorist tense *(ekrypsen)*. This seems to conclude too much.

310. *Finding Is the First Act,* p. 3.

311. *Finding Is the First Act,* pp. 93-94, 113, 120. Others who think the act is illegal include Jülicher, *Die Gleichnisreden Jesu,* 2:583; Oesterley, *The Gospel Parables in the Light of Their Jewish Background,* p. 81; Peter S. Hawkins, "Parable as Metaphor," *CSR* 12 (1983): 226-36; I. Jones, *The Matthean Parables,* pp. 347-48.

312. *Hear Then the Parable,* pp. 398-402.

313. A mistake also made by Ernst Lohmeyer, *Das Evangelium des Matthäus,* p. 227.

314. J. Duncan M. Derrett, "The Treasure in the Field," in *Law in the New Testament* (London: Darton, Longman, and Todd, 1976), pp. 1-16. Contrary to what Derrett suggests, I do not think Lev 6:2-3 has any relevance since it concerns lost property, not unknown property. Nor is his suggestion valid that Matt 13:36-51 is an elaborate sermon based on Mal 3:16–4:3.

315. See *m. Baba Batra* 4.8; *y. Baba Meṣiʿa* 2.8; *b. Meṣiʿa* 10a, 10b, 12b, 25a-b, 118a, some of which are quoted above, pp. 238-40. It cannot be assumed the man was a day laborer.

316. Among others, see, e.g., Davies and Allison, *Matthew,* 2:436; Hultgren, *The Parables of Jesus,* p. 412.

317. See among others Sider, "Interpreting the Hid Treasure," 369.

318. Warren Carter and John Paul Heil, *Matthew's Parables: Audience-Oriented Perspectives* (Washington, D.C.: Catholic Biblical Association of America, 1998), p. 87. Note the difficulty that Capon (*Kingdom, Grace, Judgment,* pp. 114-17) gets into with this identification.

319. See Gibbs, "Parables of Atonement and Assurance," 19-43; Pentecost, *The Parables of Jesus,* pp. 60-61.

320. The disciples are brought back into the context in 13:51-52, but with the redactional arrangement of this section by Matthew we cannot presume that the parables of the Treasure and the Pearl were directed only to disciples.

321. Cf. the similarity of Jesus' directions to the young man in 19:21 and note the contrast between the joy of this parable and the sorrow of the young man. To think this parable is addressed only to believers is to forget the context of Jesus' message to Israel.

322. See among many Davies and Allison, *Matthew,* 2:435; Hagner, *Matthew 1–13,* pp. 396-97; Kingsbury, *The Parables of Jesus in Matthew 13,* pp. 115-17. Kingsbury argues from the rule of end stress that the focus is especially on sacrifice and total investment. The rule of end stress is less significant in similitudes and very short analogies.

323. *The Parables of Jesus,* p. 100.

324. Flusser, *Die rabbinischen Gleichnisse und der Gleichniserzähler Jesus,* pp. 129, 131.

325. Cf. also *b. Pesaḥim* 49a: "Let a man always sell all he has and marry the daughter of a scholar, for if he dies or goes into exile, he is assured that his children will be scholars." In his analysis of treasure stories Crossan found no parallels that went so far as someone selling everything (*Finding Is the First Act,* p. 79).

326. Contra Hultgren, *The Parables of Jesus,* p. 413. Sider ("Interpreting the Hid Treasure," 371) also suggests that as the price of the field is less than the value of the treasure, so all a human can do is less than the riches of grace, but the parable is not about grace. Just as little basis exists for the opposite conclusion drawn by I. Jones (*The Matthean Parables,* p. 351) that words like "treasure," "find," and "hidden" evoke the strenuous exertions required to win the kingdom.

327. Cf. Jeremias, *The Parables of Jesus,* p. 200. Contra Hedrick ("The Treasure Parable in Matthew and Thomas," 53-54) who thinks that finding is the significant act. His claim (p. 52) that there is an anti-Torah motif has no basis. Neither does Matt 6:33 tell how to find the kingdom; it, too, in effect is about the value of the kingdom.

328. Contra Fenton, "Expounding the Parables: IV. The Parables of the Treasure and the Pearl," 178-79.

329. "The Gospel of Jesus," 31-44.

330. As with the Treasure, the authenticity of this parable is rarely questioned.

331. See also *Gen. Rab.* 39.10, in which "The king has found his pearl" is interpreted as referring to Abraham and David (also at *Ruth Rab.* 8.1); *Exod. Rab.* 42.3: "Does a man exchange a good thing for a bad one? Does he choose the piece of coal and disdain the pearl when both are placed before him for choice?"; *Song Rab.* 1.1.9: "Said Solomon to himself: If I ask for silver and gold and precious stones and pearls. . . ."

332. Which is the meaning of *polytimon,* not "of great price."

333. Davies and Allison, *Matthew,* 2:440; Luz, *Matthew 8–20,* p. 275; Weder, *Die Gleichnisse Jesu als Metaphern,* p. 139; R. Schippers, "The Mashal-Character of the Parable of the Pearl," *SE* 2 (= *TU* 87) (1964): 236-41. Among the few arguing that *Gos. Thom.* is closer to the original are Scott, *Hear Then the Parable,* p. 318 (except for the description that the merchant is prudent), and C. Hunzinger, "Unbekannte Gleichnisse Jesu aus dem Thomas-Evangelium," in *Judentum-Urchristentum-Kirche* (BZNW 26; ed. W. Eltester; Berlin: Töpelmann, 1964), pp. 209-20, here pp. 219-20. Hunzinger thinks Matthew's account of the man selling all is an exaggeration going far beyond what an intelligent merchant would do. Exaggeration is, however, common in parables, a point Schippers makes in his refutation of Hunzinger.

334. A pearl is used of a beloved child. See *TDNT* 4:472; Michael Ernst, "'. . . verkaufte alles, was er besass, und kaufte die Perle' (Mt 13,46). Der ἔμπορος im Neuen Testament und in dokumentarischen Papyri," *Protokolle zur Bibel* 6 (1997): 31-46.

335. See Ernst, ". . . verkaufte alles, was er besass, und kaufte die Perle," 31-46.

336. Origen, *Commentary on Matthew* 10.8-10. Cf. *Acts of Peter* 20; *Acts of John* 109.

337. Jerome, *On Matthew* 1.290.

338. See Wailes, *Medieval Allegories of Jesus' Parables,* pp. 120-24.

339. Otto Glombitza, "Der Perlenkaufmann. Eine exegetische Studie zur Matth. XIII.45-6," *NTS* 7 (1960-61): 153-61, here pp. 158-59.

340. Scott's idea (*Hear Then the Parable,* p. 319) that the pearl has no value and that the kingdom's corrupting power is the desire to possess it finds no fit with Jesus' parable.

341. Contra Hultgren, *The Parables of Jesus,* p. 422. The parable of the Sower underscores that joy is not enough, but that thought is foreign to this parable.

342. As an example of anxiety about kingdom language, see Luise Schottroff, *The Parables of Jesus* (trans. Linda M. Maloney; Minneapolis: Fortress, 2006), pp. 120-22.

Notes to "Parables Specifically about Israel"

1. N. T. Wright, *Jesus and the Victory of God,* vol. 2 of *Christian Origins and the Question of God* (Minneapolis: Fortress, 1996), especially pp. 181-84, 229-43, 253-57, and 331-32. Parables may be addressed to Israel without mirroring Israel's national history or present situation.

2. In v. 9 a significant number of manuscripts place the words *eis to mellon* (literally "unto the coming"; NRSV: "next year") after *ei de mē ge* ("if not") so that the verse says "If not, next year you will cut it down." The alternative places *eis to mellon* after *karpon* ("fruit") so that the meaning is "If it bears fruit next year. . . ." Most editions and translations rightly choose the latter, following the manuscript tradition of P[75], ℵ, B, and several other manuscripts.

The authenticity of this parable is questioned by relatively few, even though it is singly attested, and usually is not even discussed. The members of the Jesus Seminar expressed their doubts about the parable because it uses material common in Judaism — why is this a cause for doubt? — but ultimately decided that the exaggerated effort of the gardener's request pointed to an origin with Jesus. Sixty-nine seminar fellows voted either red or pink with thirty-one voting gray or black, with the result that the parable is printed in pink. See Robert W. Funk, Bernard Brandon Scott, and James R. Butts, *The Parables of Jesus: Red Letter Edition* (Sonoma: Polebridge, 1988), pp. 60, 74.

3. The *Apocalypse of Peter* dates to the middle of the second century, but the words quoted here are from the Ethiopic translation, which is later. See the discussion of this text by Richard Bauckham, "The Two Fig Tree Parables in the Apocalypse of Peter," *JBL* 104 (1985): 269-87. Bauckham suggests that the version in the *Apocalypse of Peter* may be independent of Luke's account, but that is not certain.

4. *Pistis Sophia: A Gnostic Miscellany* (trans. G. R. S. Mead; 2nd ed.; London: John M. Watkins, 1955).

5. Joachim Jeremias, *The Parables of Jesus* (2d ed.; trans. S. H. Hooke; New York: Charles Scribner's Sons, 1963), p. 170. He says the story is older than the fifth century B.C. While the *Story of Ahiqar* is that old, the Arabic version which he quotes is certainly not. The fragmentary Elephantine manuscript, the earliest known version, does not preserve this parable. See the discussion of J. M. Lindenberger, "Ahiqar," *OTP*, 2:479-93; and Bernhard Heininger, *Metaphorik, Erzählstruktur und szenisch-dramatische Gestaltung in den Sondergutgleichnissen bei Lukas* (NTAbh 24; Münster: Aschendorff, 1991), p. 129 n. 36. Similar parables exist in other versions (Syriac 8.35 and Armenian 25), but the tree in these accounts is not fruitless. Rather, the fruit falls into the river.

6. Cf. *'Abot de Rabbi Nathan* 16, which has a parable of a field that yielded little despite being fertilized and watered.

7. Or "cut it out." Kenneth Ewing Bailey (*Through Peasant Eyes: More Lucan Parables, Their Culture and Style* [Grand Rapids: Eerdmans, 1980], p. 83) argues this should be the meaning of the verb *katargeō* in v. 7, but surely his argument is in reference to the verb *ekkoptō*. The future "you will cut it down" may be a polite form of permission.

8. In the Greek text of v. 9 the apodosis is implied; the text reads literally "And if it bears fruit unto the coming, if not, you will cut it down."

9. E.g., Matt 13:30; 20:15; Luke 14:24; 15:32; 16:31; see David Flusser, *Die rabbinischen Gleichnisse und der Gleichniserzähler Jesus*, 1: *Das Wesen der Gleichnisse* (Bern: Peter Lang, 1981), pp. 300-301.

10. Flusser, *Die rabbinischen Gleichnisse und der Gleichniserzähler Jesus*, p. 82.

11. Michel Gourges, "Regroupement Littéraire et Équilibrage Théologique. Le Cas de Lc 13,1-9," in *The Four Gospels 1992: Festschrift Frans Neirynck*, ed. F. Van Segbroeck, C. M. Tuckett, G. Van Belle, and J. Verheyden (3 vols.; Leuven: Leuven University Press, 1992), pp. 1591-1602, here p. 1599.

12. See William R. Telford, *The Barren Temple and the Withered Tree: A Redaction-Critical Analysis of the Cursing of the Fig-tree Pericope in Mark's Gospel and Its Relation to the Cleansing of the Temple Tradition* (JSNTSup 1; Sheffield: JSOT, 1980), pp. 132-63 and 176-96. Cf. J. Duncan M. Derrett, "Figtrees in the New Testament," in *Midrash in Action and as a Literary Device*, vol. 2 of *Studies in the New Testament* (Leiden: Brill, 1978), pp. 148-64.

13. The regulation against mixed sowing in a vineyard does not apply to fig trees and vines. On the basis of Josephus, *Ant.* 4:228, the issue is plants that would require plowing.

14. The whole section from 3.74c to 3.80e is a detailed discussion of figs.

15. It is no surprise that this event is not reported in secular sources. I. Howard Marshall (*The Gospel of Luke: A Commentary on the Greek Text* [NIGTC; Grand Rapids: Eerdmans, 1978], p. 553) provides a summary of attempts to identify the event. One of the possibilities most often mentioned is the killings in connection with Pilate's use of temple funds to build an aqueduct (See Josephus, *J.W.* 2.175-77 and *Ant.* 18.60-62.) Pilate's cruelty and vindictiveness are attested in a letter of Agrippa I reproduced by Philo (*Embassy to Gaius* 299-305). See also Emil Schürer, *The History of the Jewish People in the Age of Jesus Christ (175 B.C.–A.D. 135)*, rev. ed. by Geza Vermes, Fergus Millar, and Matthew Black (4 vols.; Edinburgh: T. & T. Clark, 1973-87), 1:383-87.

16. See Stephen L. Wailes, *Medieval Allegories of Jesus' Parables* (Berkeley: University of California Press, 1987), pp. 220-25; Ambrose, *Traité sur l'Évangile de S. Luc*, ed. Gabriel Tissot (2 vols.; Sources Chrétiennes 45, 52; Paris: Cerf, 1956-58), 2:67-72; Augustine, *Sermon 110 (PL* 38, cols. 638-39). Sometimes the three stages were understood as the times of the Law, the prophets, and the gospel. See also Adolf Jülicher, *Die Gleichnisreden Jesu* (2 vols.; Freiburg: Mohr, 1888, 1889), 2:440-41.

17. Charles W. Hedrick ("An Unfinished Story about a Fig Tree in a Vineyard, Luke 13:6-9," *PRSt* 26 [1999]: 169-92) suggests that the story is about a fig tree neglected by two men, neither of whom knows much about fig trees. It could be about unrepentant and arrogant hearers or about the decisive action of one obeying Lev 19:23-25, regulations prohibiting use of fruit from trees until the fifth year. He concludes that there is still a message of hope. Bernard Brandon Scott (*Hear Then the Parable: A Commentary on the Parables of Jesus* [Minneapolis: Fortress, 1989], p. 338) concludes that the ellipsis in v. 9 is the kingdom, which leaves the question whether hope is possible. His conclusion — that we must keep on fertilizing since there is nothing else to do — sounds fatalistic. Mary Ann Beavis suggests that Aesop's fable (p. 256 above) is instructive for understanding Jesus' parable and that the parable may have addressed the impatience of Jesus' followers at the fruitlessness of the preaching to Israel and that the early church may have reflected on whether the mission to the Jews should be abandoned. See her "Parable and Fable," *CBQ* 52 (1990): 473-98, here pp. 484-88. Telford suggests something similar if the parable is a community product (*The Barren Temple and the Withered Tree*, p. 225).

18. For the latter see Michael D. Goulder, *Luke: A New Paradigm* (2 vols.; JSNTSup 20; Sheffield: JSOT, 1989), 2:561-62. For a discussion of the issues see Telford, *The Barren Temple and the Withered Tree*, pp. 233-37; H.-Konrad Harmansa, *Die Zeit der Entscheidung. Lk 13,1-9 als Beispiel für das lukanische Verständnis der Gerichtspredigt Jesu an Israel* (Erfurter Theologische Studien 69; Leipzig: Benno, 1995), pp. 146-48.

19. Richard A. Cantrell ("The Cursed Fig Tree," *The Bible Today* 29 [1991]: 105-8) suggests that Luke omitted the cursing of the fig tree because he did not expect his readers to make sense of it because it alludes to Jer 8:10-13, of which vv. 11-12 are omitted from the LXX, which would hinder Greek readers from making the connection to this OT text.

20. See Brent Kinman, "Lucan Eschatology and the Missing Fig Tree," *JBL* 113 (1994): 669-78, who argues that Mark's theology was incompatible with Luke's more positive view of Israel's future.

21. *Through Peasant Eyes*, pp. 81-82, 87.

22. Gourges, "Regroupement Littéraire et Équilibrage Théologique," pp. 1598-99. See also John Nolland, *Luke 9:21–18:34* (WBC 35B; Dallas: Word, 1993), p. 719. Joseph A. Fitzmyer thinks Jesus addressed his contemporaries but that at a later stage the parable addresses the Christian individual facing the end of life. See his *The Gospel According to Luke X–XXIV* (AB 28B; Garden City: Doubleday, 1985), p. 1005. This is not explicit in the text but is instead an application of the parable.

23. Cf. Luke 10:25-38; 12:13-21, 41-48; 14:15-24; 15:1-7.

24. Note Job 4:7-8; 8:20; 22:4-30; John 9:1-2; Acts 12:19b-23.

25. E.g., Luke 11:27-28; 12:13-15; John 21:21-22.

26. Jeremias (*The Parables of Jesus*, pp. 182-83) suggests that the historic present "he says" *(legei)* in v. 8 may point to the use of traditional material. All six occurrences of the historic present in Luke's parables are understood as evidence of traditional material. Usually Luke avoids the historic present.

27. See Josef Blinzler, "Die letzte Gnadenfrist. Lk 13,6-9," *BL* 37 (1963-64): 155-69, here p. 167; cf. Greg W. Forbes, *The God of Old: The Role of the Lukan Parables in the Purpose of Luke's Gospel* (JSNTSup 198; Sheffield: Sheffield Academic, 2000), pp. 91-92.

28. Gourges ("Regroupement Littéraire et Équilibrage Théologique," p. 1594) points out that Luke uses the formula "he was saying this parable" in other contexts to tie a parable to what precedes (5:36; 6:39; 12:16; 20:9; 21:29).

29. Jülicher, *Die Gleichnisreden Jesu*, 2:442-44.

30. *Metaphorik, Erzählstruktur und szenisch-dramatische Gestaltung in den Sondergut-gleichnissen bei Lukas*, pp. 128-29.

31. Jacobus Liebenburg, *The Language of the Kingdom and Jesus: Parable, Aphorism, and Metaphor in the Sayings Material Common to the Synoptic Tradition and the Gospel of Thomas* (BZNW 102; Berlin: Walter de Gruyter, 2001), pp. 104-11. He is describing Luke's narrative and makes no claim that the parable goes back to Jesus.

32. See above, pp. 256-58.

33. Those who think Jesus is represented by the gardener include François Bovon, *Das Evangelium nach Lukas* (EKKNT; Zurich: Benziger, 1996), 2:388; Jeremias, *The Parables of Jesus*, pp. 170-71 (at least for the disciples); Forbes, *The God of Old*, p. 92; and Harmansa (*Die Zeit der Entscheidung*, p. 120). Steven M. Bryan argues that the vineyard keeper has no referent outside the parable. See his *Jesus and Israel's Traditions of Judgement and Restoration* (SNTSMS 117; Cambridge: Cambridge University Press, 2002), p. 75.

34. Bailey (*Through Peasant Eyes*, p. 82) reads Lev 19:23 so that the fruit of the fourth year is actually the seventh year of the tree's life, and since the owner has been seeking the fruit three years, the parable assumes it has been nine years since the planting of the tree. Jeremias (*The Parables of Jesus*, p. 170) assumes six years have passed since planting. See the summary of these issues offered by Arland J. Hultgren, *The Parables of Jesus: A Commentary* (Grand Rapids: Eerdmans, 2000), pp. 243-44.

35. Like *b. Tamid* 29a, *b. Baba Batra* 26a views cutting down even marginally productive trees as a violation, one which a rabbi refuses to commit because cutting down a tree led to death for another person. His refusal is reminiscent of the end of Jesus' parable: "You, Sir, can cut them down if you like." A similar attitude toward cutting down trees is evident in Deut 20:19 and in the parable from Aesop, p. 256 above.

36. As Bovon (*Das Evangelium nach Lukas*, 2:388) seems to do. Several suggest that the parable reflects a tension between mercy and judgment; see Forbes, *The God of Old*, p. 93; Hultgren, *The Parables of Jesus*, p. 245; and Bailey, *Through Peasant Eyes*, p. 85. This seems like an overstatement. The parable is about delay, not mercy. Bailey further notes (p. 86) that the word translated "Let it alone" *(aphes)* can also mean "forgive" and concludes that Jesus is saying that forgiveness can be offered again, but he is guilty here of "illegitimate totality transfer" and reading in a theology not in the text.

37. Jülicher, *Die Gleichnisreden Jesu*, 2:443.

38. Cf. Matt 7:16-20.

39. Gourges, "Regroupement Littéraire et Équilibrage Théologique," p. 1600. See 3:3-8; 5:32; Acts 26:20.

40. Forbes (*The God of Old,* p. 93) correctly points out that this parable cannot be used to support the idea of the delay of the parousia.

41. Heininger, *Metaphorik, Erzählstruktur und szenisch-dramatische Gestaltung in den Sondergutgleichnissen bei Lukas,* p. 131. The laments should not be seen as the rejection of Israel, for they hold out the possibility of salvation. See Dale C. Allison, Jr., "Matthew 23.39 = Luke 13:35B as a Conditional Prophecy," *JSNT* 18 (1983): 75-84.

42. Luise Schottroff, *The Parables of Jesus* (trans. Linda M. Maloney; Minneapolis: Fortress, 2006), p. 63.

43. Franklin W. Young, "Luke 13:1-9," *Int* 31 (1977): 59-63, here p. 62.

44. Unlike the parable of the Prodigal, this parable does not begin with "A certain man had two sons *(huioi)*" but with "A man had two children *(tekna)*." It may well be that the audience would have imagined two sons, but by rights this parable should be entitled the parable of the Two Children. Given the strength of the traditional title, however, this would only create confusion. For treatment of this issue see Edwin K. Broadhead, "An Example of Gender Bias in the UBS³," *BT* 40 (1989): 336-38.

45. For a treatment of this genre see above, p. 13.

46. Or five, if one accepts the variant reading at 6:33. The other two are in 12:28 and 19:24.

47. Sarah calls Abraham *kyrios* (Gen 18:12; 1 Pet 3:6), and other texts also have fathers addressed as *kyrios* (Gen 31:35; *Jos. Asen.* 4.6; *T. Job* 46.2). *Kyrios* is the right word for an owner of animals, vineyards, etc. Cf. Matt 20:8; 21:3/Mark 11:3/Luke 19:31; Gal 4:1.

48. For lists see Helmut Merkel, "Das Gleichnis von den 'ungleichen Söhnen' (Matth. XXI.28-32)," *NTS* 20 (1974): 254-61, here pp. 255-56; Robert H. Gundry, *Matthew: A Commentary on His Literary and Theological Art* (Grand Rapids: Eerdmans, 1982), p. 422; and Ron Cameron, "Matthew's Parable of the Two Sons," *FFF* 8 (1992): 191-209, here pp. 200-201.

49. The other occurrences of *ti hymin dokei* (literally "What does it seem to you?") are in 18:12 (the only other occurrence in a parable); 22:42; and 26:66. In 17:25 and 22:17 the question occurs with the singular pronoun *(ti soi dokei).* The form of the questions in Luke 10:36 *(tis toutōn tōn triōn plēsion dokei soi,* "Which of these three seems to you a neighbor?") and 22:24 *(tis autōn dokei,* "Which of them seems . . .") are similar. In Jewish writings see *Gen. Rab.* 20.8; 70.13; *Ruth Rab.* Prologue 4; *Lam. Rab.* Prologue 22; *b. ʿErubin* 52a; *b. ʿArakin* 25b.

50. See J. Gibson, "Hoi Telōnai kai hai Pornai," *JTS* 32 (1981): 429-33. On prostitutes, see Craig S. Keener, *A Commentary on the Gospel of Matthew* (Grand Rapids: Eerdmans, 1999), pp. 508-9. On tax collectors, see pp. 462-76 herein on the parable of the Toll Collector and the Pharisee.

51. Wailes, *Medieval Allegories of Jesus' Parables,* p. 145.

52. Wailes, *Medieval Allegories of Jesus' Parables,* p. 146.

53. Jülicher, *Die Gleichnisreden Jesu,* 2:385.

54. Jan Lambrecht, *Out of the Treasure: The Parables in the Gospel of Matthew* (LTPM 10; Louvain: Peeters, 1992), pp. 99-100. Hans Weder also interprets the parable christologically; see his *Die Gleichnisse Jesu als Metaphern. Traditions- und redaktionsgeschichtliche Analysen und Interpretationen* (4th ed.; Göttingen: Vandenhoeck und Ruprecht, 1990), pp. 237-38.

55. Scott, *Hear Then the Parable,* p. 84.

56. Hultgren, *The Parables of Jesus,* pp. 220-23.

57. Codex Bezae does have an anti-Semitic bias, but whether that accounts for the reading is unclear. J. Ramsey Michaels ("The Parable of the Regretful Son," *HTR* 61 [1968]: 15-26) ar-

gues that this reading is the origin of the other two, but he has an unusual reconstruction of the text's history. He understands *metamelesthai* ("changed his mind") as less than *metanoein*, the more customary word for repentance, *hysteron* not as "finally" but as "too late," and *apēlthen* not as "he went" to the vineyard but as "he went away" in disobedience — all of which is questionable. He labels the story "the Parable of the Regretful Son" and reconstructs it in a form admittedly unattested by any Greek manuscript.

58. See the treatment by Bruce M. Metzger, *A Textual Commentary on the Greek New Testament* (2d ed.; New York: United Bible Societies, 1994), pp. 44-46. Among those opting for the first reading are Hultgren (*The Parables of Jesus*, p. 219); Donald A. Hagner (*Matthew 14–28* [WBC 33B; Dallas: Word, 1995], pp. 611-12); Ulrich Luz (*Matthew 21–28* [trans. James E. Crouch; Minneapolis: Fortress, 2005], pp. 25-26); and Petri Luomanen (*Entering the Kingdom of Heaven: A Study on the Structure of Matthew's View of Salvation* [WUNT 2/101; Tübingen: Mohr-Siebeck, 1998], p. 157). Among those arguing for the third reading (with the first son initially agreeing to go) are Wesley G. Olmstead (*Matthew's Trilogy of Parables: The Nation, the Nations, and the Reader in Matthew 21:28–22:14* [SNTSMS 127; Cambridge: Cambridge University Press, 2003], pp. 167-76), who provides a good summary discussion, Cameron ("Matthew's Parable of the Two Sons," 193-96), and Weder (*Die Gleichnisse Jesu als Metaphern*, pp. 233-34). Paul Foster argues that the first reading was the original pre-Matthean sequence, which later reemerged in the textual tradition, and that Matthew himself changed the order to that of the third reading. See his "A Tale of Two Sons: But Which One Did the Far, Far Better Thing? A Study of Matt 21.28-32," *NTS* 47 (2001): 26-37.

Codex Bezae's omission of the negative in the last clause of v. 32 creates another nonsensical reading.

59. Merkel, "Das Gleichnis von den 'ungleichen Söhnen,'" 254-61; Gundry, *Matthew*, pp. 422-24; Cameron, "Matthew's Parable of the Two Sons," 197-204. For some reason this parable is not treated in Funk, Scott, and Butts, *The Parables of Jesus: Red Letter Edition*. It is printed in gray in *The Five Gospels: The Search for the Authentic Words of Jesus* (ed. Robert W. Funk, Roy W. Hoover, and the Jesus Seminar; New York: Macmillan, 1993), p. 231, although fifty-eight percent of the fellows voted red or pink for the parable and fifty-three percent for the saying in v. 31b (see p. 232).

60. E.g., Jeremias, *The Parables of Jesus*, pp. 80-81; Lambrecht, *Out of the Treasure*, pp. 95-97. Weder (*Die Gleichnisse Jesu als Metaphern*, p. 233) and Luomanen (*Entering the Kingdom of Heaven*, p. 161) argue that the parable ends with the question in v. 31a.

61. E.g., Rudolf Bultmann, *History of the Synoptic Tradition* (rev. ed. trans. John Marsh; New York: Harper & Row, 1963), p. 177; Jülicher, *Die Gleichnisreden Jesu*, 2:381-82; and Allan W. Martens, "'Produce Fruit Worthy of Repentance': Parables of Judgment against the Jewish Religious Leaders and the Nation (Matt 21:28–22:14, par.; Luke 13:6-9)," in *The Challenge of Jesus' Parables* (ed. Richard N. Longenecker; Grand Rapids: Eerdmans, 2000), pp. 151-76, here pp. 156-57. Martens does not include the question in v. 28a.

62. Hagner, *Matthew 14–28*, pp. 612-15; Craig L. Blomberg, *Interpreting the Parables* (Downers Grove: InterVarsity, 1990), pp. 187-88; J. Duncan M. Derrett, "The Parable of the Two Sons," *ST* 25 (1971): 109-16; Hultgren, *The Parables of Jesus*, pp. 223-24. Hultgren thinks that the question in v. 28a may be redactional, and with regard to vv. 31c-32 that the verses are at least pre-Matthean and reflect the attitude of Jesus.

63. For these arguments, among others, see Jülicher, *Die Gleichnisreden Jesu*, 2:382; Jeremias, *The Parables of Jesus*, p. 80; Luz, *Matthew 21–28*, p. 28; and Luomanen, *Entering the Kingdom of Heaven*, p. 159.

64. E.g., Jülicher, *Die Gleichnisreden Jesu,* 2:383; Luz, *Matthew 21–28,* p. 27.

65. Flusser (*Die rabbinischen Gleichnisse und der Gleichniserzähler Jesus,* p. 74) viewed Luke 7:29 as evidence that Luke knew the parable, but did not use it. Some think 21:32 was shaped in line with 11:18, but the connections are superficial at best.

66. Note the role of the Baptist in other passages of the Gospels. In addition to the accounts of John's ministry and of the baptism of Jesus, see Matt 11:2-19/Luke 7:18-35; Matt 14:1-12/Mark 6:14-29/(Luke 9:7-9); Matt 17:10-13; Matt 21:23-27/Mark 11:27-33/Luke 20:1-8; John 3:22-30; 5:33-36.

67. *Out of the Treasure,* p. 100. He comments, "At a certain moment the original hearers will have realized that, in fact, Jesus has pointed to a decisive choice for or against him," but he gives no indication how the hearers could move to that certain moment.

68. Some point to "kingdom of God" in 21:43 as evidence of Matthew's redactional use of the phrase, but that is to assume the redactional origin of the expression there, which is by no means certain. Gundry's suggestion (*Matthew,* p. 423) that there is a contextual need for the personal emphasis on God's name is not convincing at all.

69. See Hultgren, *The Parables of Jesus,* p. 223.

70. Cf. Flusser, *Die rabbinischen Gleichnisse und der Gleichniserzähler Jesus,* pp. 74, 128.

71. Contra Jülicher, *Die Gleichnisreden Jesu,* 2:383.

72. E.g., see Jeremias, *The Parables of Jesus,* p. 125, n. 48 (arguing from a supposed Aramaic original), and Hultgren, *The Parables of Jesus,* pp. 221-22, respectively). Origen did not read the parable as excluding the Jews; see Wailes, *Medieval Allegories of Jesus' Parables,* p. 146.

73. Luomanen (*Entering the Kingdom of Heaven,* p. 163) suggests that Matthew has a tendency to use "kingdom of God" when referring to the present kingdom and "kingdom of heaven" when referring to the future, but there are not enough examples of the former to justify the claim.

74. Lambrecht, *Out of the Treasure,* pp. 98-104; Weder, *Die Gleichnisse Jesu als Metaphern,* p. 237. Lambrecht views the parable as a challenge to all to choose Jesus and accept his message. He suggests that Matthew's application to John the Baptist is an unfortunate degradation of the parable and that the tax collectors and prostitutes prefigure Christians who will replace unwilling Jews. Surely this is to allegorize the parable.

75. Which would not necessarily be messianic if it were used.

76. For representatives of the alternatives see respectively Benno Przybylski, *Righteousness in Matthew and His World of Thought* (SNTSMS 41; Cambridge: Cambridge University Press, 1980), especially pp. 94-96; and Donald A. Hagner, "Righteousness in Matthew's Theology," in *Worship, Theology and Ministry in the Early Church: Essays in Honor of Ralph P. Martin,* ed. Michael J. Wilkins and Terence Paige (JSNTSup 87; Sheffield: Sheffield Academic, 1992), pp. 101-20.

77. See Matt 6:2-4, 16-18; 12:1-14; 15:1-20; 21:18-22; 23:1-36.

78. A point made strongly by Weder, *Die Gleichnisse Jesu als Metaphern,* pp. 235-38.

79. See above, pp. 13 and 266.

80. A voluminous amount of primary source material, especially contracts for land leases, sheds light on this parable, too much to include here. For further information see Martin Hengel, "Das Gleichnis von den Weingärtnern Mc 12,1-12 im Lichte der Zenonpapyri und der rabbinische Gleichnisse," *ZNW* 59 (1968): 1-39; my *The Parable of the Wicked Tenants* (WUNT 27; Tübingen: Mohr-Siebeck, 1983), pp. 31-40; S. R. Llewelyn, "Self-Help and Legal Redress: The Parable of the Wicked Tenants," *NewDocs* 6:86-105; Craig A. Evans, "God's Vineyard and Its Caretakers," in *Jesus and His Contemporaries: Comparative Studies* (AGJU 25; Leiden: E. J. Brill,

1995), pp. 381-406; and especially John Kloppenborg, *The Tenants in the Vineyard: Ideology, Economics, and Agrarian Conflict in Jewish Palestine* (WUNT 195; Tübingen: Mohr Siebeck, 2006), pp. 355-549.

81. The LCL translation is adapted but altered, especially for the clause "The son is coming," which LCL translates rather loosely as "Sonny's coming." Behind Josephus's statement is the well-known Semitic wordplay between *'eben* ("stone") and *ben* ("son"). The hurried warning "the stone is coming" sounded like "the son is coming." On this wordplay see Matt 3:9 and my *The Parable of the Wicked Tenants*, pp. 113-18. See p. 290 herein.

82. Only the first three letters and the last letter are preserved in the text. See p. 281 herein.

83. Logion 67 — "He who knows the All but fails (to know) himself has missed everything" — may be an attempt to explain Ps 118:22.

84. See the chapter on viticulture in A. Feldman, *The Parables and Similes of the Rabbis: Agricultural and Pastoral* (2d ed.; Cambridge: Cambridge University Press, 1927), pp. 125-49; Philip Culbertson, "Reclaiming the Matthean Vineyard Parables," *Enc* 49 (1988): 257-83; and my *The Parable of the Wicked Tenants*, especially pp. 23-24 and 31-40.

85. The correspondences are detailed in the following sentences.

86. See p. 35 above. Regarding this parable see Wolfgang Schrage, *Das Verhältnis des Thomas-Evangelium zur synoptischen Tradition und zu den koptischen Evangelienübersetzungen* (BZNW 29; Berlin: Töpelmann, 1964), p. 140; and three of my contributions: *The Parable of the Wicked Tenants*, pp. 52-54; "The Gospel of Thomas: A Secondary Gospel," *Second Century* 7 (1989-90), especially pp. 28-31; and "Recent Research on the Parable of the Wicked Tenants: An Assessment," *BBR* 8 (1998): 187-216. Kloppenborg (*The Tenants in the Vineyard*, pp. 242-77) is one who still argues for the independence and originality of the *Gos. Thom.*

87. Kloppenborg's attempt (*The Tenants in the Vineyard*, pp. 259-60) to sidestep this evidence seems like special pleading.

88. Not directly on the old Syriac Gospels.

89. Jean-Marie Sevrin, "Un groupement de trois paraboles contre les richesses dans L'Évangile selon Thomas. EvTh 63, 64, 65," in *Les Paraboles Évangéliques. Perspective Nouvelles*, ed. Jean Delorme (Lectio Divina 135; Paris: Les Éditions du Cerf, 1989), pp. 425-39. See also the discussion by Stephen J. Patterson (*The Gospel of Thomas and Jesus* [Sonoma: Polebridge, 1993], pp. 142-43), who accepted that *chrēstēs* is the probable reading.

90. See pp. 302-3 herein.

91. Kloppenborg (*The Tenants in the Vineyard*, pp. 43-45, 242-77) knows that the Coptic *Gos. Thom.* shows traces of the Synoptic Gospels but thinks this is due to later assimilation (pp. 243-48), something he will not allow when talking about the allusion to the LXX version of Isaiah 5 (pp. 171 and 351), but he thinks the Greek version of *Gos. Thom.* was less like the Synoptics than the Coptic version we possess (p. 243). This argument is based on rather fragmentary and uncertain evidence. He interprets logion 66 as referring to the knowledge of the owner of the vineyard, which makes little sense and does not explain why the psalm quotation was placed here. Are we to believe that a stone saying was placed next to the parable accidentally, even though it is tied to the parable by wordplay and by the word "builders"? The quotation makes sense in the Synoptics if one understands the Semitic background; it makes no sense in *Gos. Thom.* See pp. 286 and 289-90 herein.

92. Matthew has "the chief priests and Pharisees," Mark has "they," and Luke has "the scribes and chief priests." All three Synoptics refer to the chief priests in the context preceding the parable. See Matt 21:23/Mark 11:27/Luke 20:1.

93. J. A. T. Robinson, "The Parable of the Wicked Husbandmen: A Test of Synoptic Relations," *NTS* 21 (1975): 443-61 (although he resorted to an *Ur-Markus* theory); Luz, *Matthew 21–28*, p. 35.

94. Randall Buth and Brian Kvasnica, "Temple Authorities and Tithe-Evasion: The Linguistic Background and Impact of the Parable of *the Vineyard, the Tenant and the Son*" in *Jesus' Last Week: Jerusalem Studies in the Synoptic Gospels,* ed. R. Steven Notley, Mark Turange, and Brian Becker (Leiden: Brill, 2006), 1:53-80; Flusser, *Die rabbinischen Gleichnisse und der Gleichniserzähler Jesus,* pp. 195-98. Even some who assume Markan priority think Luke has edited the parable back close to its original form. E.g., John Nolland, *Luke 18:35–24:53* (WBC 35C; Dallas: Word, 1993), p. 948.

95. The focus on the people in 20:9, *prosetheto pempsai* ("he added to send," i.e., he sent another) in 20:11 and 12, the use of soliloquy in 20:13, and the streamlining of the account.

96. They agree that the son is cast out and then killed, that the listeners respond to Jesus' question, and in the addition of a second stone saying, if Matt 21:44 is original. See W. D. Davies and Dale C. Allison, *A Critical and Exegetical Commenatry on the Gospel According to Saint Matthew* (3 vols.; ICC; Edinburgh: T. & T. Clark, 1988-97), 3:175. They do not think v. 44 is original to the texts but say that if it is "one would be required to postulate either a literary relationship between Matthew and Luke or common use of some third source."

97. See among many Jeremias, *The Parables of Jesus,* pp. 72, 76-77. Why is Matthew's use of *exedeto* an allusion to the covenant at Sinai, when Mark and Luke have the same word, apparently without any such allusion?

98. Cf. Robinson, "The Parable of the Wicked Husbandmen: A Test of Synoptic Relations," 449; Aaron A. Milavec, "Mark's Parable of the Wicked Husbandmen as Reaffirming God's Predilection for Israel," *JES* 26 (1989): 289-312, here pp. 303-4.

99. On Matthew's account being preferable, see among others my *The Parable of the Wicked Tenants,* pp. 56-62; Heinrich Kahlefeld, *Gleichnisse und Lehrstücke im Evangelium* (Frankfurt: Josef Knecht, 1964), pp. 89-90; Xavier Léon-Dufour, "La parabole des vignerons homicides," *ScEccl* 17 (1965): 392-93. To argue that Matthew's account is the earliest and least allegorical is not to argue for the priority of Matthew as a whole. We should remember that for a given pericope any of the Gospels may preserve the earliest account, even if that Gospel was the last to be written down. Kloppenborg (*The Tenants in the Vineyard,* p. 80, n. 31) objects to my arguing for a more primitive version of the parable in Matthew without arguing for the priority of Matthew as a whole, but he does the same thing for other Synoptic sayings and for *Gos. Thom.* (see his p. 247).

100. See n. 80. For examples, see *Midr. Tanḥuma Qedoshim* 7.6; *m. Baba Batra* 3.2; *P. Oxy.* 1631; *P. Columbia* 270, col. 1; *P. Oxy.* 1628 (available in the LCL *Select Papyri* 1:54-59, 118-21, and 122-25 respectively). *P. Oxy.* 1631 is still pertinent, even if it is in part a labor agreement for wages. Rents are stipulated in the latter portion of the contract. See the complaint against its relevance by Llewelyn, "Self-Help and Legal Redress," p. 95. See the rules for leasing fields in *m. Baba Meṣiʿa* 9.1-10; *t. Baba Meṣiʿa* 9.1-33; *b. Baba Meṣiʿa* 103b-110a; *m. Baba Batra* 10.4; and *Exod. Rab.* 41.1. Columella, *De Re Rustica* 1.2.1-2 and 1.7.1-3 gives advice on setting up a farm and on collecting payment from workers. For information on tenants see David Fiensy, *The Social History of Palestine in the Herodian Period* (Lewiston: Mellen, 1991), pp. 80-85.

101. *b. Berakot* 5b; see the rules controlling disputes over land ownership in *m. Baba Batra* 3.1-6; *b. Baba Batra* 28a-59b. Cf. *P. Tebt.* 39 (114 B.C., *Select Papyri* 2:252-55), which reports violence directed at one attempting to collect payment, and *P. Rylands* 119 (mid-first century A.D., *Select Papyri*, 2:260-65), which reports a creditor wrongly confiscating rents from a farm

and repeatedly ignoring requests and perverting justice. Interestingly, this petition complains that the summons was against the man and his sons, but that his sons made light of the case and did not appear before the court. See also the discussions in Evans, "God's Vineyard and Its Caretakers," pp. 384-90, and my *The Parable of the Wicked Tenants*, pp. 34-36. William Herzog (*Parables as Subversive Speech: Jesus as Pedagogue of the Oppressed* [Louisville: Westminster/John Knox, 1994], pp. 102-4) unjustifiably uses class conflict in the ancient world to depict the owner in the parable as a rich man who usurps land from peasants. For general information on land ownership in Galilee, see Seán Freyne, *Galilee from Alexander the Great to Hadrian, 323 B.C.E. to 135 C.E.: A Study of Second Temple Judaism* (Wilmington: Glazier, 1980), pp. 156-70.

102. Hengel, "Das Gleichnis von den Weingärtnern Mc 12,1-12 im Lichte der Zenonpapyri und der rabbinische Gleichnisse," especially 11-16 and 20-31. Evans ("God's Vineyard and Its Caretakers," 384-90) has made much of this material available in English.

103. Nor that he went to "another country" (NRSV). *Apodēmeō* means only that he went on a journey some distance away, that he was absent.

104. Hengel, "Das Gleichnis von den Weingärtnern Mc 12,1-12 im Lichte der Zenonpapyri und der rabbinische Gleichnisse," 25-31; Evans, "God's Vineyard and Its Caretakers," pp. 384-90. See also the information provided by Pheme Perkins, *Hearing the Parables of Jesus* (New York: Paulist, 1981), pp. 188-90. According to *b. Baba Batra* 27b, the law may be taken into one's own hands to protect from irreparable loss, and *b. Baba Qamma* 34b says that when there are two claimants to property but no evidence, the stronger can take possession. 2 Macc 4:27-28 reports that Menelaus withheld money owed the king and that Sostratus, the captain of the citadel, kept requesting payment.

105. E.g., *m. Baba Batra* 3.3. In *P. Strasbourg* 22 11.10-24 (207 A.D., *Select Papyri* 2:206-9) the period is ten years for people who "live in the provinces."

106. *J.W.* 8.359-60. See also Sir 24:20 and 1 Macc 6:24. Kloppenborg (*The Tenants in the Vineyard*, p. 330, n. 193) rejects the relevance of these texts by saying that 3 Kgdms 20:3 speaks of the vineyard as Naboth's inheritance from his fathers. His argument has no force, for Jezebel still says "Get up and take possession (LXX *klēronomei*) of the vineyard of Naboth" and the text reports that Ahab went down to take possession (LXX *klēronomēsai*) of it (3 Kgdms 20:15-16).

107. For a more detailed treatment of options see Snodgrass, "Recent Research on the Parable of the Wicked Tenants: An Assessment," 187-216.

108. Wailes, *Medieval Allegories of Jesus' Parables*, pp. 147-53.

109. Jülicher, *Die Gleichnisreden Jesu*, 2:385-406.

110. W. G. Kümmel, "Das Gleichnis von den bösen Weingärtnern (Mark 12,1-9)," in *Aux sources de la tradition chrétienne. Mélanges offerts à M. Maurice Goguel* (Neuchâtel: Delachaux & Niestle, 1950), pp. 120-31. Others who assign the parable to the early church include Charles E. Carlston, *The Parables of the Triple Tradition* (Philadelphia: Fortress, 1975), pp. 178-90; and Ulrich Mell, *Die "anderen" Winzer. Eine exegetische Studie zur Vollmacht Jesu Christi nach Markus 11,27–12,34* (WUNT 77; Tübingen: Mohr-Siebeck, 1994), pp. 114-64.

111. C. H. Dodd, *The Parables of the Kingdom* (London: Nisbet, 1936), pp. 124-32; Jeremias, *The Parables of Jesus*, pp. 70-77.

112. E.g., Joel Marcus, *The Way of the Lord: Christological Exegesis of the Old Testament in the Gospel of Mark* (Louisville: Westminster/John Knox, 1992), pp. 111-16; Michel Hubaut, *La parabole des vignerons homicides* (CahRB 16; Paris: Gabalda, 1976), p. 131.

113. The Jesus Seminar uses pink ink for *Gos. Thom.* 65 (the parable) and black for logion 66 (the psalm quotation). Gray ink is used for Matt 21:33-39/Mark 12:1b-8/Luke 20:9b-15a and

black for Matt 21:40-43 (with v. 44 omitted)/Mark 12:9-11/Luke 20:15b-18. See Funk, Scott, and Butts, *The Parables of Jesus: Red Letter Edition,* pp. 50-51.

114. See the complaint of Matthew Black, "The Parables as Allegory," *BJRL* 42 (1959-60): 273-87, here p. 283.

115. Malcolm Lowe, "From the Parable of the Vineyard to a Pre-Synoptic Source," *NTS* 28 (1982): 257-63; David Stern, "Jesus' Parables from the Perspective of Rabbinic Literature: The Example of the Wicked Husbandmen," in *Parable and Story in Judaism and Christianity,* ed. Clemens Thoma and Michael Wyschogrod (New York: Paulist, 1989), pp. 42-80, here pp. 65-68; Thomas Schmeller, "Der Erbe des Weinbergs. Zu den Gerichtsgleichnissen Mk 12,1-12 und Jes 5,1-7," *MTZ* 46 (1995): 183-201. This hypothesis was proposed much earlier by A. Gray ("The Parable of the Wicked Husbandmen," *HibJ* 19 [1920-21]: 42-52), but has found relatively little support.

116. John Dominic Crossan, *In Parables* (New York: Harper & Row, 1973), pp. 86-96, 111; see also Marcus, *The Way of the Lord,* p. 112.

117. John Dominic Crossan, "Structuralist Analysis and the Parables of Jesus," *Semeia* 1 (1974): 192-221, here pp. 208-9.

118. *Hearing the Parables of Jesus,* pp. 191-94. Similarly, Jane E. and Raymond R. Newell ("The Parable of the Wicked Tenants," *NovT* 14 [1972]: 226-37) argued that Jesus was teaching his audience of Zealot sympathizers that violence leads to self-destruction.

119. Herzog, *Parables as Subversive Speech,* pp. 98-113; see also J. D. Hester, "Socio-Rhetorical Criticism and the Parable of the Wicked Tenants," *JSNT* 45 (1992): 27-57; and William E. Arnal, "The Parable of the Tenants and the Class Consciousness of the Peasantry," in *Text and Artifact in the Religions of Mediterranean Antiquity* (Waterloo: Wilfrid Laurier University Press, 2000), pp. 135-57. L. Schottroff (*The Parables of Jesus,* 15-28) also thinks that the owner has exploited peasants, that the parable shows how indebtedness leads to violence and hatred, and that the rejected stone is a metaphor for the suffering of the people. I find little basis for any of these approaches.

120. Scott, *Hear Then the Parable,* especially p. 253.

121. Kloppenborg, *The Tenants in the Vineyard,* especially pp. 43-48, 108, 251-57, 271-72, 347-49.

122. Among several, see Wright, *Jesus and the Victory of God,* pp. 178-79, 497-501, 565-66; Craig A. Evans, *Mark 8:27–16:20* (WBC 34B; Nashville: Thomas Nelson, 2001), pp. 210-40.

123. Peter M. Head discusses P[104] and judges with some caution that there is not room in the fragment for v. 44. See his "Some Recently Published NT Papyri from Oxyrhynchus: An Overview and Prelimiary Assessment," *TynBul* 51 (2000): 1-16, 9. See the textual commentary by Wieland Welker at http://www-user.uni-bremen.de/~wie/TCG/index.html. A photograph of this papyrus is available at http://www.papyrology.ox.ac.uk/POxy/index.html (P. Oxy. 64 4404).

124. However, they do not reference P[104]. The explanation by Bruce M. Metzger (*A Textual Commentary on the Greek New Testament* [2d ed.; United Bible Societies, 1994]) seems at odds with the introduction to the fourth edition of the UBS text, p. 2.

125. For examples of reconstructions see Jeremias, *The Parables of Jesus,* pp. 70-77; B. M. F. van Iersel, *"Der Sohn" in den synoptischen Jesusworten* (Leiden: Brill, 1961), pp. 124-45; Lambrecht, *Out of the Treasure,* p. 113; Weder, *Die Gleichnisse Jesu als Metaphern,* pp. 153-54; Wolfgang Harnisch, "Der bezwingende Vorsprung des Guten. Zur Parabel von den bösen Winzern," in *Die Sprache der Bilder. Gleichnis und Metapher in Literatur und Theologie,* ed. Hans Weder (Gütersloh: Gerd Mohn, 1989), pp. 22-38, here p. 27; and Kloppenborg, *The Tenants in the Vineyard,* p. 276.

126. Kloppenborg, *The Tenants in the Vineyard,* p. 108. He excludes the allusion.

127. The reasons for the variations are not clear. Whether the wording is taken from the LXX and, therefore, from the Hellenistic church is debated. Craig Evans argues for the non-LXX character of parts of the allusion, whereas John Kloppenborg views the allusion as entirely from the LXX. The debate is important because, by arguing that the LXX is used, Kloppenborg rejects that the parable, if from Jesus, alludes to Isaiah 5 as Mark 12:1 and 9 do, which allows him to exclude the judgment saying at the end of the parable. See Evans, *Mark 8:27–16:20*, pp. 224-26; "How Septuagintal Is Isa 5:1-7 in Mark 12:1-9?" *NovT* 45 (2003): 105-10; John S. Kloppenborg Verbin, "Egyptian Viticultural Practices and the Citation of Isa 5:1-7 in Mark 12:1-9," *NovT* 44 (2002): 134-59; "Isa 5:1-7 and Mark 12:1, 9 Again," *NovT* 46 (2004): 12-19; *The Tenants in the Vineyard*, pp. 149-72. The LXX of Isa 5:2 has *kai phragmon periethēka . . . kai ephyteusa ampelon sōrēk kai ǭkodomēsa pyrgon . . . kai prolēnion ōryxa . . . epoiēsen de akanthas.* Matt 21:33 has *anthrōpos ēn oikodespotēs hostis ephyteusen ampelōna kai phragmon autǭ periethēken kai ōryxen en autǭ lēnon kai ǭkodomēsen pyrgon,* while Mark has *ampelōna anthrōpos ephyteusen kai periethēken phragmon kai ōryxen hypolēnion kai ǭkodomēsen pyrgon.*

128. Kloppenborg Verbin ("Egyptian Viticultural Practices and the Citation of Isa 5:1-7 in Mark 12:1-9," 155, 159; and *The Tenants in the Vineyard*, p. 167) concludes unjustifiably that the thorns show the LXX has inserted the idea of neglect by caretakers, which he thinks is then picked up by Mark.

129. To which Kloppenborg objects, even though he uses a similar argument when discussing the relation of *Gos. Thom.* and the Synoptics (*The Tenants in the Vineyard*, pp. 171, 243-48).

130. Luke 20:15 may allude to Isa 5:4. The claim that *Gos. Thom.* does not allude to Isaiah 5 is valid only if this document is independent of the Synoptic tradition and if the words "A man had a vineyard" would not call Isa 5:1-2 to mind.

131. 4Q500 is fragmentary but uses language from Isa 5:1-7 in a description of the temple. See Joseph M. Baumgarten, "4Q500 and the Ancient Conception of the Lord's Vineyard," *JJS* 4 (1989): 1-6; George J. Brooke, "4Q500 1 and the Use of Scripture in the Parable of the Vineyard," *DSD* 2 (1995): 268-94. The connection is verifed by *t. Me'ilah* 1.16; *t. Sukkah* 3.15; and *1 En.* 89:56, 66-67. The tower is already a symbol for the Temple in Mic 4:8. See the discussion in Evans, "God's Vineyard and Its Caretakers," pp. 397-406; *Mark 8:27–16:20*, pp. 226-27.

132. Kloppenborg ("Isa 5:1-7 LXX and Mark 12:1, 9, Again," 18; *The Tenants in the Vineyard*, pp. 94-96) thinks this targum is at least post-70 A.D., whereas Evans thinks Jesus' parable presupposes such an Aramaic interpretive tradition (*Mark 8:27–16:20*, pp. 226-27, 231; "God's Vineyard and Its Caretakers," pp. 397-99). Johannes C. De Moor also argues the targumic tradition of Isa 5:1-7 is from before 70 A.D. ("The Targumic Background of Mark 12:1-12: The Parable of the Wicked Tenants," *JSJ* 29 [1998]: 63-80).

133. See among many texts 2 Kgs 9:7; 17:13; Jer 7:25; 26:5; 29:19; 35:15; 44:4; Ezek 38:17; Zech 1:6; 4 Ezra 1:32; 2:1. See also Alfons Weiser, *Die Knechtsgleichnisse der synoptischen Evangelien* (SANT 29; Munich: Kösel, 1971), pp. 49-57.

134. This word may derive from reflection on Isa 5:1.

135. E.g., note John S. Kloppenborg's assertion that ". . . the framer of v. 9 . . . reaches back to archaic representations of God . . . and to archaic codes of human behavior . . ." ("Self-Help or *Deus ex Machina* in Mark 12:9?" *NTS* 50 [2004]: 495-518, here p. 517; *The Tenants in the Vineyard*, p. 347).

136. Ps 118:26 was also sung (probably antiphonally) by the crowds during the triumphal entry (Matt 21:9/Mark 11:9/Luke 19:38/John 12:13).

137. Note the rabbinic examples above (p. 279) in which the tenants are interpreted in

one parable as Abraham and Isaac, in whom something objectionable was found, and in the other as the Canaanites.

138. The wordplay is most obvious in Matt 3:9/Luke 3:8, but for further evidence see my *The Parable of the Wicked Tenants*, pp. 113-18; Buth and Kvasnica, "Temple Authorities and Tithe-Evasion," p. 76.

139. 1QIsaᵃ 54.13; CD 4.19; 8.12; Acts 4:11; *b. Šabbat* 114a; *b. Berakot* 64a; *Song Rab.* 1.5.3; *Exod. Rab.* 33.10; *Targum Pss.* 118:22-29. See also Stern, "Jesus' Parables from the Perspective of Rabbinic Literature," p. 67.

140. Hultgren argues (*The Parables of Jesus*, p. 363), followed by Kloppenborg (*The Tenants in the Vineyard*, pp. 85-86), against the originality of the quotation on the grounds that the wordplay is too subtle and that the Aramaic *bar* ("son") would not suggest *'eben* ("stone"). The wordplay is attested in both languages and would not be missed by anyone. Nor should the switch from agricultural to architectural imagery cause any concern. That transition is already in Isa 5:1-7; 1QS 8.5 and is also present in 1 Cor 3:9; Eph 2:21; 4:16.

141. See Buth and Kvasnica, "Temple Authorities and Tithe-Evasion," pp. 53, 57-58. That is possible but has not been proven. At the very least the quotation stems from a Semitic context.

142. The Aramaic *bar*, "son," in the plural forms is very close to the Hebrew counterpart.

143. The bridge between the Son of Man and Ps 118:22 in the passion prediction may be the stone of Daniel 2, which is parallel to the Son of Man in Daniel 7.

144. *Jesus and the Victory of God*, pp. 498-99.

145. See Luz, *Matthew 21–28*, pp. 35-36; and Wolfgang Trilling, *Das wahre Israel. Studien zur Theologie des Matthäus Evangeliums* (SANT 10; 3rd ed.; Munich: Kösel, 1964), pp. 58-65.

146. See above, pp. 269 and 273.

147. A similar rabbinic proverb is preserved in *Esth. Rab.* 7:10.

148. See R. Swaeles, "L'Arrière-fond scripturaire de Matt. XXI.43 et son lien avec Matt. XXI.44," *NTS* 6 (1959-60): 310-13.

149. Jacobus Liebenburg, *The Language of the Kingdom and Jesus: Parable, Aphorism, and Metaphor in the Sayings Material Common to the Synoptic Tradition and the Gospel of Thomas* (BZNW 102; Berlin: Walter de Gruyter, 2001), p. 355, n. 253. Note also that lack of verisimilitude is not the same as lack of narrative integrity and that lack of verisimilitude is fully compatible with narrative integrity, points emphasized by Richard Bauckham, "The Parable of the Royal Wedding Feast (Matthew 22:1-14) and the Parable of the Lame Man and the Blind Man (Apocryphon of Ezekiel)," *JBL* 115 (1996): 471-88, here pp. 482-83.

150. See Hengel, "Das Gleichnis von den Weingärtnern Mc 12,1-12 im Lichte der Zenonpapyri und der rabbinische Gleichnisse," 9-31; Snodgrass, *The Parable of the Wicked Tenants*, pp. 31-40; Evans, "God's Vineyard and Its Caretakers," pp. 382-94; Evans, *Mark 8:27–16:20*, pp. 220-22; Kloppenborg, *The Tenants in the Vineyard*, pp. 106-48, 278-349. For Kloppenborg certain features of the Synoptic versions are unrealistic, most notably the owner's recourse to self-help and violence.

151. We should not think literally of fruits; the word is a metaphor for the owner's share agreed on in the lease contract.

152. For the former see J. Duncan M. Derrett, "Fresh Light on the Parable of the Wicked Vinedressers," in *Law in the New Testament* (London: Darton, Longman & Todd, 1970), pp. 286-312; for the latter see John S. Kloppenborg, "Isaiah 5:1-7, The Parable of the Tenants and Vineyard Leases on Papyrus," in *Text and Artifact in the Religions of Mediterranean Antiquity* (Waterloo: Wilfrid Laurier University Press, 2000), pp. 111-34, especially 129-31; *The Tenants in the Vineyard*, pp. 326-30.

153. See *m. Shebu'ot* 4.12; cf. 5.1 and *m. Roš Haššanah* 1.7; *b. Baba Qamma* 70a; P. Oxy. 2110 (*Select Papyri* 2:148-55). The last reports a senator's son representing him, but it may be too far removed contextually to be relevant. Kloppenborg (*The Tenants in the Vineyard*, pp. 322-26) thinks the sending of the son is a social trump card, an appeal to the difference in social status between the owner and the servants.

154. Flusser, *Die rabbinischen Gleichnisse und der Gleichniserzähler Jesus*, p. 34.

155. See above, p. 284. Unprotested possession of land for three years conveyed ownership, but the Mishnah explicitly states that tenants may not acquire land by this means. See *m. Baba Batra* 3.1-6. I do not think that with "Come, let us kill him" in Matt 21:38/Mark 12:7 there is an allusion to Gen 37:20.

156. "Self-Help or *Deus ex Machina* in Mark 12:9?" especially 507-17; *The Tenants in the Vineyard*, pp. 335-47.

157. See the primary source material above, pp. 279-80, including the punishment expected from Xerxes, and *Gen. Rab.* 9.10, p. 304 herein. A discussion about taking the law into one's own hands to protect one's interests in *b. Baba Qamma* 27b shows that rabbis disagreed on the topic, with one saying a person may break another's teeth and tell him he is taking possession of what is his. In *b. Baba Batra* 34b we are told that in a conflict between claimants who cannot produce evidence, the stronger can take possession of the property. Among other rabbinic parables showing someone exercising self-help see *Pesiqta de Rab Kahana* 5.11 (a king "wearing a cloak of vengeance" forcibly frees his captured son — an analogy of God's freeing Israel from Egypt) and 14.5 (a steward who denied being entrusted with all the property of a king was seized by the king and suspended from a torturer's scaffold until he confessed and returned the property — an analogy of Pharaoh's attitude toward God). See also the punitive measures Cicero took in collecting debts (*Epistulae ad Atticum* 5.21; 6.1) and the discussion in David Stern, *Parables in Midrash: Narrative and Exegesis in Rabbinic Literature* (Cambridge: Harvard University Press, 1991), pp. 22-34, which has a collection of rabbinic parables with examples of God punishing.

158. As Evans comments ("God's Vineyard and Its Caretakers," p. 394), the parable has been made to fit biblical history, not common sense.

159. As Llewelyn does ("Self-Help and Legal Redress," 86-105, here p. 105), but he goes on to say that this does not mean that the parable lacks a historical core or could not have been told by Jesus.

160. For more complete discussion of the allegorical features of this parable, see my *The Parable of the Wicked Tenants*, pp. 73-110, and "Recent Research on the Parable of the Wicked Tenants: An Assessment," 199-209.

161. See above, pp. 15-17.

162. Craig Evans's comment (*Mark 8:27–16:20*, p. 224) is just: "Having taken the parable out of its Markan/synoptic context, these interpreters have no idea what the parable originally meant."

163. Craig A. Evans, "Jesus' Parable of the Tenant Farmers in Light of Lease Agreements in Antiquity," *JSP* 14 (1996): 65-83.

164. See Ps 80:9-20; Isa 3:14; 5:1-7; 27:2-6; Jer 2:21; 6:9; 12:7-17; Ezek 19:9-14; Hos 10:1; 14:6-9.

165. See Wailes, *Medieval Allegories of Jesus' Parables*, pp. 149-50.

166. Steven M. Bryan, *Jesus and Israel's Traditions of Judgment and Restoration* (SNTSMS 117; Cambridge: Cambridge University Press, 2002), p. 52. He points also to *L.A.B.* 28.4.

167. See above, p. 288.

168. See above, p. 277.

169. See p. 285, n. 115.

170. *Ekephaliōsan* ("strike on the head") in Mark 12:4 is a far cry from decapitation and is no allusion to John.

171. See 1QSa 2:11-22; 4QFlor (4Q174); 4Q246; 4Q369. See Craig A. Evans, "The Recently Published Dead Sea Scrolls and the Historical Jesus," in *Studying the Historical Jesus*, ed. Bruce Chilton and Craig A. Evans (Leiden: Brill, 1994), pp. 549-51.

172. James H. Charlesworth, "Jesus' Concept of God and His Self-Understanding," in *Jesus within Judaism: New Light from Exciting Archaeological Discoveries* (New York: Doubleday, 1988), pp. 131-64, here pp. 149-52. See also his "Jesus as 'Son' and the Righteous Teacher as 'Gardener,'" in *Jesus and the Dead Sea Scrolls*, ed. James H. Charlesworth (New York: Doubleday, 1992), pp. 140-75. Cf. J. C. O'Neill, "The Source of the Parables of the Bridegroom and the Wicked Husbandmen," *JTS* 39 (1988): 485-89. Convinced that "son" is a messianic title but that the parable is not from Jesus (because Jesus did not refer to himself) or the church, O'Neill suggests that the parable was told by John the Baptist!

173. E.g., Exod 4:22-23; Ps 80:15 (Hebrew 80:16); Hos 11:1; Wis 18:13.

174. Wright, *Jesus and the Victory of God*, pp. 485-86, 648-53.

175. This is argued by Jack Dean Kingsbury, "The Parable of the Wicked Husbandmen and the Secret of Jesus' Divine Sonship in Matthew: Some Literary-Critical Observations," *JBL* 105 (1986): 643-55; Lambrecht, *Out of the Treasure*, p. 121.

176. See Evans, *Mark 8:27–16:20*, p. 229; De Moor, "The Targumic Background of Mark 12:1-12," 77-79. De Moor points to *Song of David* A18 from the Cairo Genizah (unavailable to me), dating to the Second Temple period and argues that Ps 118:22 is interpreted eschatologically in Davidic terms. If substantiated, that would be of enormous significance.

177. Often the stone is assumed to be a capstone, the crowning stone at the top of a building. See especially Michael Cahill, "Not a Cornerstone! Translating Ps 118,22 in the Jewish and Christian Scriptures," *RB* 106 (1999): 345-57. The position of the stone is of no importance in understanding the quotation and the parable. The only thing that matters is that the rejected stone becomes the most important stone in the building. However, I think "stone of the corner" *(kephalē gōnias)* refers not to a capstone but to a foundational cornerstone just as *akrogōniaios* unquestionably does. Ps 118:22 appears to allude to the foundation stone laying ceremony in Ezra 3:8-13.

178. See the classic treatment by C. F. D. Moule, *The Phenomenon of the New Testament* (London: SCM, 1967), pp. 82-99.

179. See the important article by Buth and Kvasnica, "Temple Authorities and Tithe-Evasion," especially pp. 65-73; and De Moor, "The Targumic Background of Mark 12:1-12," 71. See Josephus, *Ant.* 20.180-81, 205-7; *b. Pesaḥim* 57a; *Sipre Deut.* 105 (on Deut 14:22-23).

180. For lists of Semitisms see Evans, *Mark 8:27–16:20*, p. 224; Hengel, "Das Gleichnis von den Weingärtnern Mc 12,1-12 im Lichte der Zenonpapyri und der rabbinische Gleichnisse," 7-8.

181. Luz, *Matthew 21–28*, p. 38, and Philip B. Payne, "Jesus' Implicit Claim to Deity in His Parables," *TJ* 2 (1981): 3-23, respectively. Cf. Birger Gerhardsson, "The Earthly Jesus in the Synoptic Parables," in *Christology, Controversy and Community: New Testament Essays in Honour of David R. Catchpole*, ed. David G. Horrell and Christopher M. Tuckett (Leiden: Brill, 2000), pp. 49-62, who argues that Jesus makes self-pronouncements in aphoristic *meshalim* but that narrative *meshalim* are not used to "elucidate" who he is.

182. Joel Marcus places Mark's version in the context of the destruction of Jerusalem and accuses it of distorting Isaiah 5 in order to argue against God's eternal covenant with Israel ("The Intertextual Polemic of the Markan Vineyard Parable," in *Tolerance and Intolerance in*

NOTES TO PAGES 296-306

Early Judaism and Christianity, ed. Graham N. Stanton and Guy G. Strousma [Cambridge: Cambridge University Press, 1998], pp. 211-27). Tania Oldenhage (*Parables for Our Time: Rereading New Testament Scholarship after the Holocaust* [Oxford: Oxford University Press, 2002], pp. 60-69 and 139-51, especially 149) refers to this parable as a tainted text which reminds her of Nazi atrocities. She has little interest in the historical meaning of the parable.

Esth. Rab. 1.13 does say that Ahasuerus sat on the throne of his kingdom because Israel's possession of the kingdom was removed as a result of their sin and given to the nations.

183. Bryan (*Jesus and Israel's Traditions of Judgment and Restoration,* p. 55) and Luz (*Matthew 21–28,* p. 42) both grant that the leaders are in view but think the entire nation is implicated.

184. As David L. Turner argues ("Matthew 21:43 and the Future of Israel," *BSac* 159 [2002]: 46-61, 58), the issue is ethics, not ethnicity.

185. Similar to 1 Pet 2:9, pointing to the true people of God. Matthew uses *ethnos* fifteen times, all plural except here and in 24:7 ("nation shall rise against nation").

186. The seriousness of the issue is underscored by v. 44, if it is part of the Matthean text, but it is a proverbial warning, not a sentence of destruction, like v. 41.

187. Luz (*Matthew 21–28,* p. 44) rightly emphasizes this.

188. Some branches of the church have focused on eternal security ("the perseverance of the saints") to such an extent that the biblical connection between election and obedience is totally lost.

189. Willi Braun, *Feasting and Social Rhetoric in Luke 14* (SNTSMS 85; Cambridge: Cambridge University Press, 1995), especially pp. 98-131.

190. Luise Schottroff, "Das Gleichnis vom großen Gastmahl in der Logienquelle," *EvT* 47 (1987): 192-211.

191. J. A. Sanders, "The Ethic of Election in Luke's Great Banquet Parable," *Essays in Old Testament Ethics,* ed. James L. Crenshaw and John T. Willis (New York: Ktav, 1974), pp. 245-71, especially 255-66.

192. Edmund Arens, "Ein Tischgespräch über Essen und (Ex)Kommunikation. Das Gleichnis vom Festmahl (Lk. 14,16-24)," *Katechetisches Blätter* 111 (1986): 449-52. He can take this position only by excluding v. 24.

193. See the discussion by J. Priest, "A Note on the Messianic Banquet," in *The Messiah: Developments in Earliest Judaism and Christianity,* ed. James H. Charlesworth (Minneapolis: Fortress, 1992), pp. 222-38.

194. 1 Macc 3:56 reports that Judas Maccabeus followed this text in exempting certain people from military duty.

195. For discussion of such material, see above, pp. 79 and 82-83; Braun, *Feasting and Social Rhetoric in Luke 14.*

196. This section of *4 Ezra* is considered to be a later Christian addition, dating perhaps to the end of the second century. It is often labeled *5 Ezra* for that reason. Priest ("A Note on the Messianic Banquet," p. 225) asks if the author of this passage has attempted to deal with Matt 22:11-13.

197. The reason for this required double invitation seems to be different from the usual custom, for which see herein under cultural information. Here it is to make sure the invitation was not a mistake. *Midr. Lam.* 4.3 relates a disaster when the wrong person was invited to a banquet. This story is also interesting for what it reveals about attitudes of shame and honor.

198. Contra Fitzmyer, *The Gospel According to Luke,* 2:1050-52. See Sevrin, "Un

groupement de trois paraboles contre les richesses dans L'Évangile selon Thomas. EvTh 63, 64, 65," pp. 425-39. Note the attitude toward women in *Gos. Thom.* 114.

199. Including in v. 12 *antikaleō*, "invite in return."

200. See, e.g., Kenneth Ewing Bailey, *Poet and Peasant: A Literary Cultural Approach to the Parables in Luke* (Grand Rapids: Eerdmans, 1976), pp. 80-82, and for a broader discussion see Craig L. Blomberg, "Midrash, Chiasmus, and the Outline of Luke's Central Section," in *Gospel Perspectives III: Studies in Midrash and Historiography,* ed. R. T. France and David Wenham (Sheffield: JSOT, 1983), pp. 217-61.

201. The last is the argument of Blomberg, who also suggests a chiastic parable source used by Luke.

202. See W. Gregory Carey, "Excuses, Excuses: The Parable of the Banquet (Luke 14:15-24) within the Larger Context of Luke," *IBS* 17 (1995): 177-87.

203. See above, pp. 71-72.

204. See also "Ein altjüdisches Gastmahl," *Str-B* 4:611-39.

205. In addition to Philo, *Opif.* 78; *Lam. Rab.* 4.2; and Apuleius, *Metamorphoses* 3.12 above, note Esth 5:8; 6:14; Sir 13:9; Plutarch, *Mor.* 511D-E. For discussion of ancient wedding invitations see *NewDocs* 9:62-66. Noteworthy is the fact that the time *is* usually designated on the invitation. Crossan assumes without justification that in the original parable, as in *Gos. Thom.,* the banquet was planned suddenly and imprudently and people invited without warning. See his *In Parables,* pp. 72-73.

206. *Lam. Rab.* 4.2.3 illustrates this with a story of a man's enemy who was erroneously invited to his banquet. The man pleads not to be forced to leave, even offering to pay for the whole banquet, if he is not shamed into leaving. *Lam. Rab.* 4.2.4, commenting on why Jews are precious (Lam 4:2), says none of them would attend a dinner without knowing who the fellow diners would be.

207. See Braun, *Feasting and Social Rhetoric in Luke 14,* pp. 100-131; Jerome Neyrey, "Ceremonies in Luke-Acts: The Case of Meals and Table-Fellowship," in *The Social World of Luke-Acts: Models for Interpretation,* ed. Jerome H. Neyrey (Peabody: Hendrickson, 1991), pp. 361-87.

208. E.g., in addition to Plato, others using the symposium format include Xenophon, Plutarch, and Lucian of Samosota.

209. For discussion of the history of interpretation see Wailes, *Medieval Allegories of Jesus' Parables,* pp. 153-66; Francis W. Beare, "The Parable of the Guests at the Banquet: A Sketch of the History of Its Interpretation," in *The Joy of Study: Papers on the New Testament and Related Subjects,* ed. S. E. Johnson (New York: Macmillan, 1951), pp. 1-14; Luz, *Matthew 21–28,* pp. 57-59.

210. *Commentary on Matthew* 17.

211. See *Sermon 62 (NPNF1* 6:447); *The Correction of the Donatists (Epistle* 185) 6.23-24 (*NPNF1* 4:642).

212. Davies and Allison, *Matthew,* 3:197. As he often does, Jeremias (*The Parables of Jesus,* pp. 63) thinks the original message concerned Jesus' defense of his offering the gospel to the poor.

213. E.g., Jülicher, *Die Gleichnisreden Jesu,* 2:422; Crossan, *In Parables,* p. 71.

214. See the discussions by Lambrecht, *Out of the Treasure,* pp. 133, 139; Anton Vögtle, *Gott und seine Gäste. Das Schicksal des Gleichnisses Jesu vom großen Gastmahl* (Biblische-theologische Studien 29; Neukirchen-Vluyn: Neukirchener, 1996), pp. 37-39, 54-55, and 78-79; Luz, *Matthew 21–28,* pp. 53-54; Hultgren, *The Parables of Jesus,* pp. 344-45; and cf. Weiser, *Die Knechtsgleichnisse der synoptischen Evangelien,* pp. 66-69.

215. See Paul Ballard, "Reasons for Refusing the Great Supper," *JTS* 23 (1972): 341-50, who calls the parable a midrash on Deut 20:5-7.

216. J. Duncan M. Derrett, "The Parable of the Great Supper," in *Law in the New Testament* (London: Darton, Longman and Todd, 1970), pp. 126-55; Daniel C. Olson, "Matthew 22:1-14 as Midrash," *CBQ* 67 (2005): 435-53.

217. Braun *(Feasting and Social Rhetoric in Luke 14),* who will not admit that the story is a parable (p. 64), provides the most detailed presentation of this thesis. He also downplays the Jewish context of the parable. His view is an expansion of Richard L. Rohrbaugh, "The Pre-Industrial City in Luke-Acts: Urban Social Relations," in *The Social World of Luke-Acts,* ed. Jerome H. Neyrey (Peabody: Hendrickson, 1991), pp. 137-47; and Detlev Dormeyer, "Literarische und theologische Analyse der Parabel Lukas 14,15-24," *BibLeb* 15 (1974): 206-19. Scott (*Hear Then the Parable,* p. 173) and Schottroff (*The Parables of Jesus;* "Das Gleichnis vom großen Gastmahl in der Logienquelle," especially 204-9) have a similar understanding. Joel B. Green (*The Gospel of Luke* [NICNT; Grand Rapids: Eerdmans, 1997], pp. 554-63) has accepted this interpretation because he feels the eschatological banquet view gives an unflattering portrait of God as one who extends invitations originally in a way consistent with the social elite of Luke's world and only turns to the poor when rebuffed by the rich (p. 556). Robert C. Tannehill also adopts Rohrbaugh's reading, but advocates a polyvalent approach that accepts as well the eschatological meal interpretation and a third reading based on Luke 10:1-24, which sees the experience of early Christian missionaries reflected in the parable. See his "The Lukan Discourse on Invitations (Luke 14, 7-24)," in *The Four Gospels: Festschrift Frans Neirynck,* ed. F. Van Segbroeck, C. M. Tuckett, G. Van Belle, and J. Verheyden [Leuven: Leuven University Press, 1992], 2:1603-16). This is to confuse meditation on the parable with hearing it in its original context.

218. Jeremias, *The Parables of Jesus,* p. 69.

219. David Hill, *The Gospel of Matthew* (London: Oliphants, 1972), p. 301. Luz (*Matthew 21–28,* p. 60) argues from this parable that the bearers of the tradition freely projected their own experience into the parable, and therefore we should feel free to change the tradition as well.

220. Two other parables showing similar measures of variation between Matthew and Luke are those of the Lost Sheep and of the Talents/Pounds.

221. Robert W. Funk, *Language, Hermeneutic, and Word of God* (New York: Harper & Row, 1966), p. 163, n. 1.

222. This does not render Jesus impoverished nor present a caricature of Jesus imitating himself, as Jülicher (*Die Gleichnissenreden Jesu,* 2:407) charged.

223. Matthew is responsible for the arrangement of the three parables in 21:28–22:14. Note the similarity of 22:1-2 to 13:24, 45, 47; 18:23. See above, pp. 268-69 and 283.

224. Cf. Eta Linnemann, *Parables of Jesus: Introduction and Exposition* (London: SPCK, 1966), p. 166; Luz, *Matthew 21–28,* p. 47.

225. Contra Funk, *Language, Hermeneutic, and Word of God,* pp. 166-67 (among others), who also thinks it noteworthy that Thomas records the parable without setting, but then Thomas does not provide settings for any of his sayings and has arranged this parable with two others dealing with money.

226. See especially Sevrin, "Un groupement de trois paraboles contre les richesses dans L'Évangile selon Thomas. EvTh 63, 64, 65," pp. 425-39.

227. See E. Haenchen, "Das Gleichnis vom großen Mahl," *Die Bibel und Wir. Gesammelte Aufsätze* (Tübingen: Mohr-Siebeck, 1968), pp. 135-55, here pp. 148-50; Weder, *Die Gleichnisse Jesu als Metaphern,* p. 185.

228. Jeremias, *The Parables of Jesus,* pp. 178-80. See *y. Ḥagigah* 2.2 and *y. Sanhedrin* 6.6 above, p. 303.

229. See especially Plato's *Symposium* and in Plutarch's *Moralia, Septem Sapientium Convivium* ("The Dinner of the Seven Wise Men") and his nine books of *Quaestiones Conviviales* ("Table Talk"). For discussion of Luke 14 and symposia, see Craig L. Blomberg, *Contagious Holiness: Jesus' Meals with Sinners* (NSBT 19; Downers Grove: InterVarsity, 2005), pp. 86-96; Braun, *Feasting and Social Rhetoric in Luke 14,* pp. 136-44; E. Springs Steele, "Luke 11:37-54 — a Modified Hellenistic Symposium?" *JBL* 103 (1984): 379-94; X. de Meeûs, "Composition de Lc., XIV et genre symposiaque, *ETL* 37 (1961): 847-70; Josef Ernst, "Gastmahlgespräche. Lk 14,1-24," in *Die Kirche des Anfangs. Für Heinz Schürmann,* ed. Rudolf Schnackenburg, Josef Ernst, and Joachim Wanke (Freiburg: Herder, 1978), pp. 57-78.

230. See above, pp. 82-83.

231. See Braun, *Feasting and Social Rhetoric in Luke 14,* especially pp. 98-131; "Symposium or Anti-Symposium? Reflections on Luke 14:1-24," *TJT* 8 (1992): 70-84.

232. See especially Matt 9:10-13/Mark 2:15-17/Luke 5:29-32 and the relevance of the last verse in this pericope to the wording of the parable. John Dominic Crossan (*The Historical Jesus: The Life of a Mediterranean Jewish Peasant* [San Francisco: Harper, 1991], pp. 261-62) emphasizes that the parable teaches an open or egalitarian commensality. The parable may teach that, but to limit the parable to it is to downplay the eschatological focus.

233. Sanders, "The Ethic of Election in Luke's Great Banquet Parable," especially pp. 255-66. See also James D. G. Dunn, "Jesus, Table-Fellowship, and Qumran," in *Jesus and the Dead Sea Scrolls,* ed. James H. Charlesworth (New York: Doubleday, 1992), pp. 254-72. Cf. Matt 21:14. In addition to the passages listed above, see Sir 9:16 and 1QS 6.3-7.

234. Ballard, "Reasons for Refusing the Great Supper," 341-50; Derrett, "The Parable of the Great Supper," especially pp. 127-28.

235. Humphrey Palmer, "Just Married, Cannot Come," *NovT* 18 (1976): 241-57. Palmer accepts the allusions to Deuteronomy as valid, but thinks they were meant to be humorous.

236. It will not do to suggest as Willard M. Swartley does that the oxen in Luke tilled the vineyard referred to in Deuteronomy ("Unexpected Banquet People [Luke 14:16-24]," in *Jesus and His Parables,* ed. V. George Shillington [Edinburgh: T. & T. Clark, 1997], p. 185).

237. The authenticity of Luke's parable is rarely questioned. Over seventy percent of the fellows of the Jesus Seminar voted to print Luke's version in either red or pink. Over ninety percent did the same for the version in *Gos. Thom.* See Funk, Scott, and Butts, *The Parables of Jesus: Red Letter Edition,* pp. 42-43, 98.

238. See Bailey, *Through Peasant Eyes,* p. 92. Scott (*Hear Then the Parable,* p. 164) follows Erich Grässer (*Das Problem der Parusieverzögerung in den synoptischen Evangelien und in der Apostelgeschichte* [BZNW 22; 2d ed.; Berlin: Töpelmann, 1960], p. 196) in seeing in 14:15 an allusion to the delay of the parousia, but I see no basis for this.

239. Note that Braun (*Feasting and Social Rhetoric in Luke 14,* pp. 84-85) will not grant that the people in the story are Jews. If the story was told by Jesus in Palestine (and obviously if in the house of a Pharisee), on what grounds should we assume that some other ethnic group is in mind, particularly with the election language? Nor do I find his argument convincing that 14:1-24 is an eight-step structure of a chreia argument (pp. 162-64).

240. A point Braun (*Feasting and Social Rhetoric in Luke 14,* pp. 127-28) admits. No doubt parables like this one fit well theologically with Luke's later concerns in the Book of Acts, but that they are to be interpreted allegorically in light of Acts is procedurally unacceptable. *Contra* Thomas J. Lane, *Luke and the Gentile Mission* (Frankfurt: Peter Lang, 1994), p. 149.

241. See Jeremias, *The Parables of Jesus*, p. 177.

242. At least the first two are not very impressive. No urgency exists with either excuse, and one is unlikely to have bought a field or oxen without examining them first.

243. As Sanders suggests ("The Ethic of Election in Luke's Great Banquet Parable," p. 255).

244. See also Matt 7:21-23/Luke 13:25-27; Matt 25:31-46.

245. Cf. Linnemann, *Parables of Jesus*, p. 80.

246. Cf. 12:41, where Peter has to ask if a parable is for the disciples or for everyone.

247. Fitzmyer (*The Gospel According to Luke*, 2:1053) and Bovon (*Das Evangelium nach Lukas*, 2:506) say that Luke refers to the time of Jesus (vv. 17-20) and to the church's mission to Israel (v. 21) and to the nations (v. 23). Vögtle (*Gott und seine Gäste*, pp. 78-79) suggests the early and later Gentile mission. See above, pp. 308-9 and n. 214.

248. E.g., Ferdinand Hahn ("Das Gleichnis von der Einladung zum Festmahl," in *Verborum Veritas. Festschrift für Gustav Stahlin*, ed. Otto Bocher and Klaus Haaker [Wuppertal: Brockhaus, 1970], pp. 51-82, 72-73) thinks Jesus is the host, whereas Marius Reiser (*Jesus and Judgment: The Eschatological Proclamation in Its Jewish Context* [trans. Linda M. Maloney; Minneapolis: Fortress, 1997], p. 242) thinks God is the host. Jülicher (*Die Gleichnisreden Jesu*, 2:416) and Forbes (*The God of Old*, p. 98) think Jesus is the servant.

249. See *Die Gleichnisreden Jesu*, 2:432. He takes elements from each account to create a shorter original, but even then admits that the image of the meal strongly tempts one to a more spiritual understanding and that correspondences existed between God and the host, those invited and entrance into the kingdom, and the servants and God's messengers, of whom Jesus himself was the most important. He offers no explanation for the correspondences but only reasserts that allegorical elements were added later. The inability to avoid or to explain the correspondences reveals how untenable his position is.

250. Weder's attempt to see the first and second groups as depicting two sides in the hearer (his old attitude on the future of the eschatological meal and his new insight into what is at hand now) has even less to commend it (see Weder, *Die Gleichnisse Jesu als Metaphern*, p. 189).

251. See among others Eugene E. Lemcio, "The Parables of the Great Supper and the Wedding Feast: History, Redaction, and Canon," *HBT* 8 (1986): 1-26, 12-13; Braun, *Feasting and Social Rhetoric in Luke 14*, p. 89; Green, *The Gospel of Luke*, p. 561.

252. As Haenchen ("Das Gleichnis vom grossen Mahl," pp. 153-55), who, because he seeks such strict correspondence, decides the parable could not be from Jesus; see also Green, *The Gospel of Luke*, p. 556.

253. See Dschulnigg, "Positionen des Gleichnisverständnisses im 20. Jahrhundert," 350.

254. See Matt 8:11-12/Luke 13:28-30; Matt 10:18; Mark 11:17; Matt 24:9, 14/Mark 13:10; Matt 25:32. See Stephen G. Wilson, *The Gentiles and the Gentile Misssion in Luke-Acts* (SNTSMS 23; Cambridge: Cambridge University Press, 1973), pp. 1-28.

255. See the discussion of the social stratification of ancient cities by Rohrbaugh, "The Pre-Industrial City in Luke-Acts: Urban Social Realities," pp. 125-49. The elite lived in the inner city, which was walled off from the outer precincts of the non-elite, where one found beggars, traders, and ethnic minorities. Social regulations limited access by lower classes. "Compel them to come in" should probably be seen in this light, rather than, with Bailey, *Through Peasant Eyes*, p. 108, as indicating that in the Middle East an unexpected invitation must be refused, at least initially for reasons of etiquette. Note the similarity of Tob 2:2, which tells of an invitation to a poor person to eat with Tobit at the festival of Pentecost.

256. Cf. also Isa 35:5-6.

257. Linnemann (*Parables of Jesus,* p. 89) argues that the original guests intended to come late, which requires her to see v. 20 as a later insertion. Nothing supports her contention.

258. The suggestion that Jesus is the servant has no basis in my estimation.

259. I see no reason to think v. 24 did not originally belong to the parable. The verse states the consequences for those who have rejected the invitation. Derrett ("The Parable of the Great Supper," p. 141) and a number of others argue that v. 24 expresses a refusal of the host to send portions of his meal to the absent guests. I see no evidence to commend the suggestion.

260. E.g., Luke 11:8; 15:7, 10; 18:8, 14.

261. E.g., Matt 25:12, 40, and 45. It is also used by John the Baptist in Matt 3:9/Luke 3:8.

262. Ernst R. Wendland sees Jesus represented in the servant but suggests that v. 24 may be a rhetorical device whereby Jesus identifies himself, the story-teller, with the banquet-giver, namely God. "'Blessed Is the Man Who Will Eat at the Feast in the Kingdom of God' (Lk 14:15): Internal and External Intertextual Influence on the Interpretation of Christ's Parable of the Great Banquet," *Neot* 31 (1997): 159-94, here p. 164.

263. Hultgren (*The Parables of Jesus,* pp. 339 and 349) thinks that for both versions of the parable any idea of exclusion is too negative, but exclusion is precisely what is intended, as 13:28 shows. There are consequences for rejecting the invitation from God; to continue to reject is to exclude oneself.

264. E.g., *1 En.* 1:1-9; 5:7-10; 58:1-4; 62:1-10; *2 Bar.* 13:8-12.

265. Cf. the warning of John the Baptist that God is able to raise children for Abraham from the stones (Matt 3:9/Luke 3:8).

266. Dschulnigg, "Positionen des Gleichnisverständnisse im 20. Jahrhundert," 350.

267. "Das Gleichnis vom grossen Mahl," 143.

268. Lambrecht, *Out of the Treasure,* p. 128. Similarly Vögtle (*Gott und seine Gäste,* p. 81) expresses the hope that Matthew's account will be dropped from the lectionary.

269. Parables do not necessarily stay imagistic but may be a mixture of image and the fact to which they refer. For example, in the parable of the Lion and her cubs in Ezek 19:2-9, the second lion cub becomes a man-eater who devastates cities (vv. 5-9), but lions do not devastate cities. In Luke 14:21 the poor, lame, crippled, and blind are not an image but the reality to which reference is made. This mixture of parabolic image *(Bild)* and reality *(Sache)* demonstrates that there should be no thought of separating the two.

270. But not necessarily of the former and latter prophets. The twofold sending is determined more by the conventions of storytelling than the divisions of the Jewish canon.

271. Luz (*Matthew 21-28,* p. 59) complains of the christological shortcoming of this parable, but that is to presume that christology is and should be part of every parable.

272. And not therefore specifically about Jerusalem. See Karl Heinrich Rengstorf, "Die Stadt der Mörder," in *Judentum, Urchristentum, Kirche,* ed. W. Eltester (Berlin: Töpelmann, 1960), pp. 106-29.

273. "The Parable of the Royal Wedding Feast (Matthew 22:1-14) and the Parable of the Lame Man and the Blind Man (Apocryphon of Ezekiel)," *JBL* 115 (1996): 471-88. He also points out that people too frequently read elements of Luke into Matthew's account. Matthew says neither that the people invited lived in the city where the wedding feast was held nor that the people invited from the streets were poor. He suggests that Matthew's account allows time for people to go home and change their clothes.

In connection with the political theme see Diodorus Siculus (33.4.2), who reports how

Demetrius punished the people of Antioch. He killed those who did not surrender their arms, and when riots broke out he burned the greater part of the city.

274. See Bo Reicke, "Synoptic Prophecies on the Destruction of Jerusalem," in *Studies in New Testament and Early Christian Literature*, ed. David Aune (Leiden: E. J. Brill, 1972), pp. 121-34, here p. 123.

275. See the similar comments by John Nolland, *The Gospel of Matthew: A Commentary on the Greek Text* (NIGTC; Grand Rapids: Eerdmans, 2005), pp. 887-88; and Schottroff, "Das Gleichnis vom großen Gastmahl in der Logienquelle," 207.

276. As pointed out by Gundry, *Matthew: A Commentary on His Literary and Theological Art*, pp. 436-37. Gundry sees an allusion to Isa 5:24-25 in Matthew's words about the destruction of the city, but I do not find this convincing, nor do I think "their city" in v. 7 refers to the separation of the church and Judaism.

277. A point made by Hahn, "Das Gleichnis von der Einladung zum Festmahl," p. 79.

278. E.g., Hahn, "Das Gleichnis von der Einladung zum Festmahl," p. 79; Olmstead, *Matthew's Trilogy of Parables*, p. 122 (at least with v. 4); Hultgren, *The Parables of Jesus*, p. 344 (who sees both OT prophets and the killing of Jesus and the disciples reflected in vv. 3-6).

Lambrecht's assumptions of allegory lead him to suggest (*Out of the Treasure*, p. 135) that vv. 2-7 deal with unfaithful Jews, whereas vv. 8-14 deal with Christians. Such a move has no basis.

279. The assumption that Matthew has allegorized the parable with Christian history faces the difficulty that he has not done this with any other parable.

280. See Wright, *Jesus and the Victory of God*, pp. 182-83, 234, 328.

281. As the aorist passive *hōmoiōthē* ("has become like") in 22:2 underscores.

282. *Jesus and the Kingdom of God* (Grand Rapids: Eerdmans, 1986), p. 122.

283. *Contra* Gundry, *Matthew*, p. 438, and many others.

284. Just for the record, the fellows of the Jesus Seminar decided to print Matthew's parable with gray print, with seventy-eight voting either gray or black and twenty-two voting red or pink. See Funk, Scott, and Butts, *The Parables of Jesus: Red Letter Edition*, pp. 42-43, 99.

285. Note that Daniel Patte, *The Gospel According to Matthew* (Philadelphia: Fortress, 1987), p. 301, argued 22:11-14 is an integral part of the parable and expresses its main point, but apparently he implies in n. 27 that the parable is from Matthew.

286. Weiser (*Die Knechtgleichnisse der synoptischen Evangelien*, p. 71) concludes that the *diakonoi* had no special significance for Matthew.

287. Jeremias, *The Parables of Jesus*, p. 187; Derrett, "The Parable of the Great Supper," pp. 128-29, 142-43.

288. See Bauckham, "The Parable of the Royal Wedding Feast (Matthew 22:1-14) and the Parable of the Lame Man and the Blind Man (Apocryphon of Ezekiel)," 485-87.

289. See Simon Kistemaker, *The Parables of Jesus* (Grand Rapids: Baker, 1980), p. 101; Robert Farrar Capon, *The Parables of Judgment* (Grand Rapids: Eerdmans, 1989), p. 123. For evidence that is remote from the first century, see Klaus Haacker, "Das hochzeitliche Kleid von Mt. 22,11-13 und ein palästinisches Märchen," *ZDPV* 87 (1971): 95-97.

290. 2 Kgs 10:22 provides no basis.

291. See e.g., *1 En.* 62:16; Bar 5:1-2. See also David C. Sim, "Matthew 22:13a and 1 Enoch 10:4a: A Case of Literary Dependence," *JSNT* 47 (1992): 3-19, especially 15-18, but not accepting the arguments that 22:11-13 are a Matthean creation. The allusion to *1 En.* 10:4 is likely. Possibly there is allusion to the prohibition of the ḥaberim (a subset of the Pharisees) receiving an ʿam hāʾareṣ as a guest in his own garment. See *m. Demai* 2.2-3 and the discussion by Jacob Neusner,

Fellowship in Judaism: The First Century and Today (London: Vallentine, Mitchell, 1963), pp. 22-40. Such an allusion would make the parable a strong indictment.

292. I do not see how David C. Sim's argument that the man represents both the wicked of v. 10 and the Jewish leaders can be correct. See "The Man without a Wedding Garment (Matthew 22:11-13)," *HeyJ* (1990): 165-78.

293. Ben F. Meyer, "Many (= All) Are Called, But Few (= Not All) Are Chosen," *NTS* 36 (1990): 89-97. Note the similarity of Matt 7:13-14/Luke 13:23-24. Cf. *4 Ezra* 8:3; 9:15; *Barn.* 4:14.

294. Hagner, *Matthew 14–28*, p. 632.

295. See Frederick A. Norwood, "'Compel Them to Come In': The History of Luke 14:23," *Religion in Life* 23 (1954): 516-27.

296. *Matthew 21–28*, p. 59.

Notes to "Parables about Discipleship"

1. Cf. the parables of the Two Sons (Matt 21:28-32), the Faithful and Unfaithful Servants (Matt 24:45-51/Luke 12:41-48), the Ten Virgins (Matt 25:1-13), the Sheep and the Goats (Matt 25:31-46), the Two Debtors (Luke 7:41-42), the Rich Man and Lazarus (Luke 16:19-31), and the Pharisee and the Toll Collector (Luke 18:9-14). See Adolf Jülicher, *Die Gleichnisreden Jesu* (2 vols.; Freiburg i. B.: J. C. B. Mohr, 1888, 1889), 2:260; W. D. Davies and Dale C. Allison, *A Critical and Exegetical Commentary on the Gospel According to Saint Matthew* (3 vols; ICC; Edinburgh: T. & T. Clark, 1988-97), 1:719.

2. E.g., Ulrich Luz, *Matthew 1–7: A Commentary* (trans. Wilhelm C. Linss; Minneapolis: Augsburg, 1985), p. 451.

3. E.g., Jülicher (*Die Gleichnisreden*, 2:260, 265) because he fears Matthew is too easily understood christologically; Kamal Abou-Chaar ("The Two Builders: A Study of the Parable in Luke 6:47-49," *Theological Review* 5 [1982]: 44-58, here p. 48) who thinks Luke's account is more personal and therefore genuine and is more realistic with regard to the digging process.

4. E.g., Luz, *Matthew 1–7*, pp. 451-52.

5. The argument that "wise" and "foolish" are from Matthew goes back to Jülicher (*Die Gleichnisreden Jesu*, 2:261), who felt a parable should not force an interpretation on the hearer prematurely but should allow the hearer to come to an understanding independently. Not all parables function the same way, and the whole point of this parable is the foolishness of hearing Jesus' words and not doing them. Wisdom and foolishness appear elsewhere in Jesus' teaching. For "wise" (*phronimos* and related words) see Matt 10:16; 24:45/Luke 12:42; Matt 25:1-13; Luke 16:8. For "fool" (*mōros*) see Matt 23:17, 19; 25:1-13; Luke uses a synonym, *aphrōn*, at 11:40; 12:20.

6. Commentators often see this phrase as derived from 6:18, but this connection is tenuous at best. Robert H. Gundry (*Matthew: A Commentary on His Literary and Theological Art* [Grand Rapids: Eerdmans, 1982], p. 133) thinks "coming to me" is omitted in Matt 7:24 because Matthew regarded "the one coming" as a sacrosanct messianic title. The latter is not so obvious, and the suggestion unjustly presumes a great deal about the tradition before Matthew.

7. Daniel Marguerat, *Le jugement dans L'Évangile de Matthieu* (2d ed.; Le Monde de la Bible 6; Geneva: Labor et Fides, 1995), pp. 203-11, here p. 204.

8. Hans Dieter Betz (*The Sermon on the Mount* [Hermeneia; Minneapolis: Fortress, 1995], p. 637) says the aorist points to interruption; Arland Hultgren (*The Parables of Jesus: A Commentary* [Grand Rapids: Eerdmans, 2000], p. 136) says it points to judgment.

9. For nonbiblical references see Betz, *The Sermon on the Mount*, p. 558.

10. For information on houses in ancient Palestine see S. Safrai and M. Stern, *The Jewish People in the First Century* (CRINT; Assen: Van Gorcum, 1976), 2:730-35; John S. Holladay, Jr., "House, Israelite," *ABD* 3:308-18; Peter Richardson, *Building Jewish in the Roman East* (Waco: Baylor University Press, 2004), pp. 73-90; Yizhar Hirschfeld, *The Palestinian Dwelling in the Roman-Byzantine Period* (Studium Biblicum Franciscanum, Collection Minor 34; Jerusalem: Franciscan, 1995).

11. Gordon Franz argues that the houses in both versions are built on alluvial sand near Bethsaida and that the issue is not where they were built but how, i.e., whether a foundation down to bedrock was provided ("Text and Tell: The Parable of the Two Builders," *Archaeology in the Biblical World* 3 [1995]: 6-11). This does not seem to fit Matthew's description of two different building places.

12. Frank S. Frick, "Palestine, Climate of," *ABD* 5:119-26, here pp. 122, 124.

13. Even Stephen Wailes, *Medieval Allegories of Jesus' Parables* (Berkeley: University of California Press, 1987) omits this one.

14. Robert W. Funk, Roy W. Hoover, and the Jesus Seminar, *The Five Gospels: The Search for the Authentic Words of Jesus* (New York: Polebridge, 1993), pp. 158, 159; see also p. 299. These parables are not treated in the earlier report of Robert W. Funk, Bernard Brandon Scott, and James R. Butts, *The Parables of Jesus: Red Letter Edition* (Sonoma: Polebridge, 1988).

15. Marius Reiser, *Jesus and Judgment: The Eschatological Proclamation in Its Jewish Context* (trans. Linda M. Maloney; Minneapolis: Fortress, 1997), pp. 302, 304, 316.

16. Richard Jeske argues that Jesus' teaching did not conform to traditional hopes and end-time speculation but was concerned more with God's rule in the present, while at the same time being marked by a confidence about God's future. In his description Jesus' preaching was characterized by an eschatological reserve which was formed from joining wisdom and apocalyptic. See his "Wisdom and the Future in the Teaching of Jesus," *Dialog* 11 (1972): 108-17.

17. As David Flusser seems to suggest (*Die rabbinischen Gleichnisse und der Gleichniserzähler Jesus.* 1: *Das Wesen der Gleichnisse* [Bern: Peter Lang, 1981], p. 98), although on p. 103 he acknowledges that Jesus could be the creator of the parable.

18. Jülicher, *Die Gleichnisreden Jesu*, 2:267.

19. See A. Puig Tarrech, "Une parable à l'image antithétique," in *The Sayings Source Q and the Historical Jesus*, ed. Andreas Lindemann (Leuven: University Press, 2001), pp. 681-93, here p. 690.

20. See especially Craig S. Keener, *A Commentary on the Gospel of Matthew* (Grand Rapids: Eerdmans, 1999), pp. 255-57. See also François Bovon, *Luke 1: A Commentary on the Gospel of Luke 1:1–9:50* (trans. Christine M. Thomas; Minneapolis: Fortress, 2002), p. 255.

21. For other references besides the ones listed under primary sources see Keener, *A Commentary on the Gospel of Matthew*, pp. 254-55.

22. Flusser (*Die rabbinischen Gleichnisse und der Gleichniserzähler Jesus*, pp. 99-100) found it necessary to deny that Jesus referred to his own words and asserted without justification that Jesus referred to the words of the Torah or of God.

23. Contra Tàrrech, "Une parable à l'image antithétique," p. 686.

24. Augustine (*Sermon on the Mount* 2.25.87), among others, thought the rock was Christ. Martin Luther (*Luther's Works*, ed. J. Pelikan, H. C. Oswald, and H. T. Lehmann [Saint Louis: Concordia, 1955-86], 21:281-84) saw Christ as the foundation and doctrine about Christ as the rock.

25. Abou-Chaar ("The Two Builders," 55) said the rock was obedience to Christ and

allegorized the rest of the parable so that the house was one's self, the flood was the crisis of the coming kingdom, and the collapse of the house was being kept out of the kingdom.

26. As suggested by John Chrysostom (*Homilies on Matthew* 24.3) and Davies and Allison, *Matthew*, 1:721.

27. So, e.g., Augustine, *Sermon on the Mount* 2.25.87; Chrysostom, *Homilies on Matthew* 24.3.

28. E.g., Davies and Allison, *Matthew*, 1:720; Luz, *Matthew 1–7*, p. 452.

29. Betz, *The Sermon on the Mount*, pp. 558, 566.

30. A point made frequently; see Joachim Jeremias, *The Parables of Jesus* (trans. S. H. Hooke; New York: Charles Scribner's Sons, 1963), p. 194; Marguerat, *Le jugement dans L'Évangile de Matthieu*, p. 208; Luz, *Matthew 1–7*, p. 453.

31. Betz, *The Sermon on the Mount*, pp. 563-66, quoting p. 566.

32. Evidenced in the longer version of Ignatius, *Philadelphians* 1.1 (*ANF* 1:79).

33. N. T. Wright, *Jesus and the Victory of God*, vol. 2 of *Christian Origins and the Question of God* (Minneapolis: Fortress, 1996), p. 292, see also 334.

34. Kenneth E. Bailey, "'Inverted Parallelisms' and 'Encased Parables' in Isaiah and Their Significance for Old and New Testament Translation and Interpretation," in *Literary Structure and Rhetorical Strategies in the Hebrew Bible*, ed. L. J. de Regt, J. de Waard, and J. P. Fokkelman (Assen: Van Gorcum, 1996), pp. 14-30, here pp. 18-19. Jeremias (*The Parables of Jesus*, p. 194) also connects this parable to Isa 28:15-16. Earlier Jeremias provided the classic discussion of the *'eben shetiyah* legend. See his *Golgotha* (Leipzig: Pfeiffer, 1926), 1:51-77.

35. Rom 9:32-33; Eph 2:20; 1 Pet 2:4-6.

36. Miroslav Volf, *Exclusion and Embrace* (Nashville: Abingdon, 1996), p. 276 (italics added).

37. Luz, *Matthew 1–7*, p. 454.

38. Georg Strecker, *The Sermon on the Mount: An Exegetical Commentary* (trans. O. C. Dean, Jr.; Nashville: Abingdon, 1988), p. 171; see also Marguerat, *Le jugement dans L'Évangile de Matthieu*, p. 210.

39. M. A. Garcia, "Committed Discipleship and Jesus' Lordship: Exegesis of Luke 6:46-49 in the Context of Jesus' Discourse in the Plain," *African Christian Studies* 9 (1993): 3-10, here p. 9.

40. Jeremias, *The Parables of Jesus*, p. 194.

41. See my "Reading to Hear: A Hermeneutics of Hearing," *HBT* 24 (2002): 1-32.

42. See above, pp. 13-15, and pp. 350-52 herein.

43. The authenticity of this parable is rarely questioned. It is one of only five that the Jesus Seminar printed in red (vv. 30-35; see Funk, Scott, Butts, *The Parables of Jesus: Red Letter Edition*, p. 26). Among the few to view the parable as a Lukan creation are Gerhard Sellin ("Lukas als Gleichniserzähler. Die Erzählung vom barmherzigen Samariter, Lk 10:25-37," *ZNW* 66 [1975]: 19-60) and Michael D. Goulder (*Luke: A New Paradigm* [JSNTSup 20; Sheffield: Sheffield Academic, 1989], 2:488-91). For a critique of their approaches see John Nolland, *Luke 9:21–18:34* (WBC 35B; Dallas: Word, 1993), pp. 588-90.

44. Some point to LXX Job 6:13-23, where Job complains that his near relations have ignored him, but I do not think there is any direct connection to the parable. For this suggestion see Roger Aus, *Weihnachtsgeschichte, Barmherziger Samariter, Verlorener Sohn. Studien zu ihrem jüdischen Hintergrund* (Berlin: Institut Kirche und Judentum, 1988), pp. 76-78.

45. Although significant words relative to Deut 6:5 have been restored, the restoration is doubtlessly correct. Compare 4Q255.

46. The *Testaments of the Twelve Patriarchs* have Christian interpolations, so this and the next item may not be witnesses of early Jewish writings.

47. See also Justin, *Dialogue* 93.

48. See *m. Niddah* 7.3; *b. Niddah* 56b. Cf. *y. Demai* 3.4. Josephus apparently considered Samaritans to be heterodox Jews. See his description of Palestine in *J.W.* 3.35-53 and the discussion in Emil Schürer's *The History of the Jewish People in the Age of Jesus Christ* (rev. and ed. Geza Vermes, et al.; Edinburgh: T. & T. Clark, 1979), 2:6-7, n. 11, and pp. 17-19); contrast the description of Palestine in *m. Šebi'it* 9.2, which leaves Samaria out of consideration.

49. In the same text (*b. Niddah* 56b) other rabbis consider them "lion proselytes," i.e., proselytes as a result of conversion based on fear (see 2 Kgs 17:25-26). Other negative assessments are seen in 4Q371 (Samaritans are enemies and not sons of Joseph); *y. 'Abodah Zarah* 5.4; *m. Šeqalim* 1.5; *b. Soṭah* 33b; *b. Giṭṭin* 45b. Cf. *b. Ḥullin* 13b.

50. See *b. Mo'ed Qaṭan* 12a and the editor's comment in the Soncino edition.

51. See below, p. 346 herein.

52. This assertion is based on the misuse of a late tradition in *b. Baba Batra* 10b and comments in *Str-B* 4/1, pp. 538 and 544. The explicit interpretation is based on Rashi. Of possible (but late) relevance is *b. 'Abodah Zarah* 27b, which prohibits dealings with *minim*, including refusing to be healed by them, but this passage is concerned more with Christians.

53. See Walter Wink, "The Parable of the Compassionate Samaritan: A Communal Exegesis Approach," *RevExp* 76 (1979): 210.

54. See *b. Berakot* 28b-29a and the discussions of Reuven Kimelman, "*Birkat Ha-Minim* and the Lack of Evidence for an Anti-Christian Prayer in Late Antiquity," in *Aspects of Judaism in the Greco-Roman Period*, vol. 2 of *Jewish and Christian Self-Definition*, ed. E. P. Sanders with A. I. Baumgarten and Alan Mendelson (Philadelphia: Fortress, 1981), pp. 226-44; Steven T. Katz, "Issues in the Separation of Judaism and Christianity after 70 c.e.: A Reconsideration," *JBL* 103 (1984): 43-76; and David Instone-Brewer, "The Eighteen Benedictions and the Minim before 70 ce," *JTS* 54 (2003): 25-44. The curse may have been added toward the end of the first century and, if so, is too late for our purposes. Instone-Brewer argues that a form of the Benedictions with the curse appeared before the destruction of the Temple but that it was directed against the Sadducees. Others argue that it was directed generally against all "heretics," not against Jewish Christians.

55. Aus, *Weihnachtsgeschichte, Barmherziger Samariter, Verlorener Sohn*, pp. 62-75, thinks an oral form of this tradition has influenced Jesus' parable. This seems unlikely to me, and an early date for this material cannot be demonstrated.

56. Has the parable of the Good Samaritan influenced this story?

57. Luke's version of the quotation conforms at first to Mark's wording, but then switches to Matthew's. The command in Deut 6:5 is to love God with all one's heart, soul, and strength. Matthew has heart, soul, and mind, while Mark and Luke have in different orders heart, soul, strength, and mind.

58. For the view that the two narratives demonstrate the two love commands, see Nolland, *Luke 9:21–18:34*, pp. 579-80; Robert W. Wall, "Martha and Mary (Luke 10:38-42) in the Context of a Christian Deuteronomy," *JSNT* 35 (1989): 19-35; for the focus on hearing and doing see Herman Hendrickx, *The Parables of Jesus* (San Francisco: Harper & Row, 1986), p. 75.

59. Your neighbor is the one you see in need. See Kenneth E. Bailey, *Through Peasant Eyes: More Lucan Parables, Their Culture and Style* (Grand Rapids: Eerdmans, 1980), pp. 34-35; Georges Crespy, "The Parable of the Good Samaritan: An Essay in Structural Research," *Semeia* 2 (1980): 27-50, here pp. 37-38.

60. See Crespy, "The Parable of the Good Samaritan," pp. 28-29; Bailey, *Through Peasant Eyes*, p. 48.

61. *Plēgas epithentes* ("beat him," v. 30) reappears at Acts 16:23 (but also in Rev 22:18); *peripiptein* ("fall among," v. 30) appears elsewhere only in Acts 27:41 and Jas 1:2; *epibibazein* ("put someone on," v. 34) appears elsewhere only in Luke 19:35 and Acts 23:24; *agein* ("lead," v. 34) occurs four times in Matthew and three in Mark, but thirteen times in Luke and twenty-six in Acts; *epanerchersthai* ("return," v. 35) occurs elsewhere only in Luke 19:15. See Sellin, "Lukas als Gleichniserzähler. Die Erzählung vom barmherzigen Samariter, Lk 10:25-37," 35-36.

62. Mikeal C. Parsons, "Landmarks along the Way: The Function of the 'L' Parables in the Lukan Travel Narrative," *SwJT* 40 (1997): 33-47.

63. See Kenneth Ewing Bailey, *Poet and Peasant* (Grand Rapids: Eerdmans, 1976), pp. 80-82; and Charles H. Talbert, *Reading Luke* (New York: Crossroad, 1982), pp. 111-12.

64. "Another Look at the Parable of the Good Samaritan," in *Saved By Hope*, ed. James I. Cook (Grand Rapids: Eerdmans, 1978), pp. 109-19.

65. "The Central Section of St. Luke's Gospel," in *Studies in the Gospels*, ed. D. E. Nineham (Oxford: Blackwell, 1955), pp. 37-53, especially 43; see also Wall, "Martha and Mary (Luke 10:38-42) in the Context of a Christian Deuteronomy," pp. 19-35. For a critique see Craig L. Blomberg, "Midrash, Chiasmus, and the Outline of Luke's Central Section," in *Gospel Perspectives III: Studies in Midrash and Historiography*, ed. R. T. France and David Wenham (Sheffield: JSOT, 1983), pp. 217-61.

66. On the influence of 2 Chron 28:8-15 see especially F. Scott Spencer, "2 Chronicles 28:5-15 and the Parable of the Good Samaritan," *WTJ* 46 (1984): 317-49; Aus, *Weihnachtsgeschichte, Barmherziger Samariter, Verlorener Sohn*, pp. 79-80. On the influence of Hos 6:1-11 see J. Duncan M. Derrett, "The Parable of the Good Samaritan," in *Law in the New Testament* (London: Dartman, Longman, & Todd, 1970), pp. 208-27, who sees the parable as a midrash on Hosea 6 or at least a sermon based on this text; and Bailey, *Through Peasant Eyes*, p. 49, who finds twelve echoes of Hosea 6 in the parable.

67. See *b. Ta'anit* 27a; cf. *m. Ta'anit* 4.2; Josephus, *Ant.* 7.365.

68. See 2 Kgs 17:24-33; Josephus, *Ant.* 9.277-91. Samaritans saw themselves as true descendents of the northern tribes and as keepers of the Law *(šāmērîm)*. See Robert T. Anderson, "Samaritans," *ABD* 5:940-47; John P. Meier, *A Marginal Jew: Rethinking the Historical Jesus 3: Companions and Competitors* (New York: Doubleday, 2001), pp. 532-42.

69. Daughters of Sadducees were regarded as Samaritan women. See *m. Niddah* 4.2; *b. Niddah* 33b.

70. I.e., Edomites, pagans (or Hellenists), and Samaritans, Shechem being the major Samaritan city near Mount Gerizim.

71. Cf. *Vita* 269, where Josephus tells of writing to friends asking them to provide safe conduct through Samaria for some soldiers and says that rapid travel to Jerusalem required going through Samaria. From Galilee one could reach Jerusalem in three days going through Samaria. See also *m. Nedarim* 3.10; *b. Nedarim* 31a on benefiting from Samaritans when going up to Jerusalem for festivals. I have found no evidence other than implication for the frequent assumption that Jews went around Samaria. On the subject of pilgrimages see S. Safrai, "Pilgrimage to Jerusalem at the End of the Second Temple Period" in *Studies on the Jewish Background of the New Testament*, ed. O. Michel, et al. (Assen: Van Gorcum, 1969), pp. 12-21.

72. *m. Demai* 3.4; 5.9; 7.4; *b. 'Erubin* 36b; *b. Yoma* 55b; *b. Gittin* 28a; *b. 'Abodah Zarah* 15b; *y. 'Abodah Zarah* 5.4.

73. *m. Berakot* 5.8.

74. *m. Berakot* 8.8.

75. *m. Terumot* 3.9.

76. *b. Niddah* 33b.

77. *b. Giṭṭin* 10a.

78. Contra Joseph A. Fitzmyer, *The Gospel According to Luke* (AB 28B; Garden City: Doubleday, 1985), 2:883.

79. See among other texts *m. Yebamot* 16.7; *m. Giṭṭin* 8.9; *m. Qiddušin* 4.12; *b. Soṭah* 47a; *b. Baba Meṣi'a* 86a; *Tanḥuma Mishpatim* 6.1.1.

80. Nolland, *Luke 9:21–18:34*, p. 596; Hultgren, *The Parables of Jesus*, p. 99.

81. Some other interpretations strain credulity: (1) that the story addresses the problem of evil and the possibility of death by a meaningless accident or motiveless murder and presents the Samaritan as a symbol of superabundant vitality (James Breech, *The Silence of Jesus* [Philadelphia: Fortress, 1983], pp. 158-83); (2) that the story is Luke's apologetic for a mission to the Gentiles (A. J. Mattill, Jr., "The Good Samaritan and the Purpose of Luke-Acts: Halévy Reconsidered," *Enc* 33 [1972]: 359-76; cf. Sellin, "Lukas als Gleichniserzähler," 44-45); (3) that the story is a satire, a parody of the ideal of a righteous person since one can live by neither the outlandish benevolence of the Samaritan nor the callous indifference of those who pass by (Charles W. Hedrick, *Parables as Poetic Fictions* [Peabody: Hendrickson, 1994], pp. 93-116).

82. Rarely did an interpreter deviate from the general picture, but isolated examples exist of Christ being represented in the animal, the innkeeper, or the traveler (with Jews being the robbers). See Wailes, *Medieval Allegories of Jesus' Parables*, pp. 210-14; Robert H. Stein, "The Interpretation of the Parable of the Good Samaritan," in *Scripture, Tradition, and Interpretation*, ed. W. Ward Gasque and William Sanford LaSor (Grand Rapids: Eerdmans, 1978), pp. 278-95.

83. See Jean Daniélou, "Le Bon Samaritain," in *Mélanges bibliques rédigés en l'honneur de André Robert* (Paris: Bloud & Gay, 1956), pp. 457-65, who draws connections to the Good Shepherd in John 10; also J. Ian H. McDonald, "Alien Grace (Luke 10:30-36): The Parable of the Good Samaritan," in *Jesus and His Parables*, ed. V. George Shillington (Edinburgh: T. & T. Clark, 1997), pp. 35-51, who at the same time views the compassion in the parable as the compassion of God. Allegorical interpretations are presented also by Robert Farrar Capon, *The Parables of Grace* (Grand Rapids: Eerdmans, 1988), pp. 58-65, who sees Christ as the victim and says that we are to imitate his passion; Mike Graves, "Luke 10:25-37: The Moral of the 'Good Samaritan' Story?" *RevExp* 94 (1997): 269-75; and Robert Winterhalter with George W. Fisk, *Jesus' Parables: Finding Our God Within* (New York: Paulist, 1993), pp. 148-51, for whom the robbers are negative thoughts, the Samaritan is the indwelling Christ, and the priest and Levite are formal religion.

84. Birger Gerhardsson, *The Good Samaritan, the Good Shepherd?* (ConBNT 16; Lund: Gleerup, 1958), pp. 12-31.

85. Robert W. Funk, "The Old Testament in Parable: The Good Samaritan," in *Language, Hermeneutic, and Word of God* (New York: Harper & Row, 1966), pp. 199-223; John Dominic Crossan, *In Parables* (New York: Harper & Row, 1973), pp. 57-66.

86. Richard Bauckham, "The Scrupulous Priest and the Good Samaritan: Jesus' Parabolic Interpretation of the Law of Moses," *NTS* 44 (1998): 475-89.

87. In addition to passages already mentioned see Matt 5:43-48/Luke 6:27-36; Matt 19:19. Love, of course, undergirds Jesus' whole ministry.

88. Brad H. Young, *The Parables: Jewish Tradition and Christian Interpretation* (Peabody: Hendrickson, 1998), p. 104.

89. In Luke 7:36-50 a similar shift takes place since in the parable the person forgiven

more loves more, but the woman is forgiven because she loves. Cf. Luke 12:13-15; 17:20-21; Matt 19:16-22/Mark 10:17-22/Luke 18:18-23.

90. See pp. 357-59 herein.

91. Crossan (*In Parables*, p. 61) says that despite the divergent use of neighbor the passage is a "a beautifully constructed double controversy dialogue"; Jan Lambrecht (*Once More Astonished* [New York: Crossroad, 1981], p. 79) sees the tension between vv. 29 and 36 as a result of Luke's inattentiveness, but then admits that the shift "does not function all that badly"; McDonald ("Alien Grace [Luke 10:30-36]," 45) says there is no necessary connection between the parable and the debate over the love commands, but that the connection is appropriate enough; Bernard Brandon Scott (*Hear Then the Parable: A Commentary on the Parables of Jesus* [Minneapolis: Fortress, 1989], pp. 190-91) views the parable and its context as originally separate, but still finds a strong internal consistency between the lawyer's question and the parable. Cf. C. G. Montefiore (*The Synoptic Gospels* [2 vols.; London: Macmillan, 1927], 2:465), who thinks v. 29 is editorial, yet finds it very odd that the verse is so badly constructed.

92. See Nolland, *Luke 9:21–18:34*, pp. 579, 596; Charles W. F. Smith, *The Jesus of the Parables* (Philadelphia: Pilgrim, 1975), p. 107, who also adds that the parable is unduly involved and of needless artifice unless preceded by some situation as in v. 29.

93. "The Old Testament in Parable: The Good Samaritan," p. 211. In a later article ("The Good Samaritan as Metaphor," *Semeia* 2 [1974]: 74-81) Funk downplays the focus on neighbor because of his attempt to view the parable from the victim's perspective and because he thinks the parable is metaphorical.

94. Nolland, *Luke 9:21–18:34*, p. 580.

95. See especially William Richard Stegner, "The Parable of the Good Samaritan and Leviticus 18:5," in *The Living Text*, ed. Dennis E. Groh and Robert Jewett (Lanham: University Press of America, 1985), pp. 27-38. As Stegner points out, a popular Jewish interpretation of Lev 18:5 (attested in at least four texts) has striking similarities to Luke 10:25-37:

> R. Meir used to say: "Whence do we know that even an idolater who studies the Torah is equal to a High Priest? From the following verse: *Ye shall therefore keep My statutes and My ordinances which, if a man do, he shall live by them.* It does not say 'If a Priest, Levite, or Israelite do, he shall live by them,' but 'a man'; here, then, you can learn that even a heathen who studies the Torah is equal to a High Priest!" (*b. 'Abodah Zarah* 3a; see also *b. Sanhedrin* 59a; *b. Baba Qamma* 38a; *Num. Rab.* 13.15-16).

See also Eduard Verhoef, "(Eternal) Life and Following the Commandments: Lev 18,5 and Luke 10,28," in *The Scriptures in the Gospels*, ed. C. M. Tuckett (Leuven: Leuven University Press, 1997), pp. 571-77. With regard to the significance of Lev 18:5 in Judaism see Ezek 20:11, 13, 21; CD 3.12-16, 20; *Pss. Sol.* 14:5; Philo, *Congr.* 86-87; *b. Makkot* 23b; *Num. Rab.* 13.15-16; *Midr. Ps.* 1.18; *Sifra Aharé Mot* 193 (on Leviticus 18); and possibly *m. 'Abot* 6.7. Note too that Paul quotes Lev 18:5 in his debates with opponents (Gal 3:12; Rom 10:5) in a way that suggests that they used Lev 18:5 against him. E. Earle Ellis ("How the New Testament Uses the Old," in *New Testament Interpretation*, ed. I. Howard Marshall [Grand Rapids: Eerdmans, 1977], pp. 205-6) argues that 10:25-37 is a *yelammedenu rabbenu* ("let our master teach us") structure, which apart from its interrogative opening follows the proem midrash: vv. 25-27 gives the dialogue including the question and initial texts; v. 28 offers a second text (Lev. 18:5); vv. 29-36 provide exposition linked to the original texts by "neighbor" *(plēsion)* and "do" *(poiein)*; and v. 37 concludes with an allusion to the second text. This is possible, but I do not find the case convincing that this explains the structure or the intent of either Jesus or Luke.

96. Others who argue for keeping context and parable together include Bauckham, "The Scrupulous Priest and the Good Samaritan"; Gerhardsson, *The Good Samaritan, the Good Shepherd?* pp. 23-29; Peter Rhea Jones, *Studying the Parables of Jesus* (Macon: Smyth & Helwys, 1999), p. 296; I. Howard Marshall, *The Gospel of Luke* (NIGTC; Grand Rapids: Eerdmans, 1978), pp. 440-46; cf. Kristján Búason, "The Good Samaritan, Luke 10:25-37: One Text, Three Methods," in *Luke-Acts: Scandinavian Perspectives,* ed. P. Luomanen (Göttingen: Vandenhoeck & Ruprecht, 1991), pp. 1-35, especially 25-26, but not accepting that the parable presupposes a Christian mission in dialogue with Jews.

97. *Jub.* 36:4-8; 1QS 1.1-3, 9-10; *T. Iss.* 5:2; 7:6; *T. Dan* 5:3; Philo, *Spec. Leg.* 1.299-300; 2.63 — all quoted or summarized above (pp. 340-41). See also Philo, *De Decalogo* 106-10, which reveals how duties to God and humanity are summarily characterized as love. The first five commands relate to lovers of God; the second five to lovers of humans. Cf. *m. 'Abot* 6.6 and the focus given to love of neighbor in CD 6.20-21. In *Sifra Qedoshim* 200 (on Lev 19:17-18) and *Gen. Rab.* 24.7 R. Aqiba states that Lev 19:18 is the encompassing principle of the Torah. The two love commands are also joined in later Christian writings. See *Didache* 1:2; *Barn.* 19:2, 5; Justin, *Dialogue* 93 (above, p. 341). See also Dale C. Allison, Jr., "Mark 12:28-31 and the Decalogue," in *The Gospels and the Scriptures of Israel,* ed. Craig A. Evans and W. Richard Stegner (Sheffield: Sheffield Academic, 1994), pp. 270-78; Serge Ruzer, "The Double Love Precept in the New Testament and the Community Rule," in *Jesus' Last Week: Jerusalem Studies in the Synoptic Gospels,* ed. R. Steven Notley, Marc Turnage, and Brian Becker (Leiden: Brill, 2006), 1:81-106. Why Hendrickx (*The Parables of Jesus,* p. 82) should think it difficult that a Jewish lawyer would combine these two commands is bewildering.

Several texts in the OT and Jewish writings are summaries of the Law: Deut 10:12-13; Psalms 15 and 24; Isa 58:6-7; 66:2b; Jer 22:3-4; Mic 6:8; Zech 8:16-17; *b. Šabbat* 31a; *b. Berakot* 63a; *b. Makširin* 23b-24a; *Mekilta Vayassa* 1.158-60 (on Exod 15:26).

98. See Scot McKnight's popular book *The Jesus Creed: Loving God, Loving Others* (Brewster: Paraclete, 2004).

99. See J. Duncan M. Derrett, "'Love Thy Neighbor as a Man like Thyself'?" *ExpTim* 83 (1971): 55-56; cf. Nolland, *Luke 9:21–18:34,* p. 585.

100. Norman H. Young, "The Commandment to Love Your Neighbor as Yourself and the Parable of the Good Samaritan (Luke 10:25-37)," *AUSS* 21 (1983): 265-72, especially 267-68, who is dependent partly on Karl Barth, *Church Dogmatics,* 1/2 (trans. G. Thomson and Harold Knight; Edinburgh: T. & T. Clark, 1956), p. 450. See the discussion by Klaus Berger, *Identity and Experience in the NT* (trans. Charles Muenchow; Minneapolis: Fortress, 2003), pp. 226-27.

101. Robert L. Short, *The Parables of Peanuts* (San Francisco: HarperSanFrancisco, 1968), p. 68, following Søren Kierkegaard, *Works of Love* (ed. and trans. Howard V. Hong and Edna H. Hong; Princeton: Princeton University Press, 1946), p. 22, who says that loving the neighbor as oneself properly understood means "You shall love yourself in the right way."

102. The most important treatments of "example stories" are Jeffrey Tucker's *Example Stories: Perspectives on Four Parables in the Gospel of Luke* (JSNTSup 162; Sheffield: Sheffield Academic, 1998), even though in the end I do not think his solution is satisfactory; and Ernst Baasland, "Zum Beispiel der Beispielerzählungen. Zur Formenlehre der Gleichnisse und zur Methodik der Gleichnisauslegung," *NovT* 28 (1986): 193-219.

103. Some would also include Luke 14:7-11 or even 15:11-32.

104. The description is from Tucker, *Example Stories: Perspectives on Four Parables in the Gospel of Luke,* p. 170.

105. John Dominic Crossan, "Parable and Example in the Teaching of Jesus," *NTS* 18

(1972): 285-307. Funk's approach is similar. See his "The Good Samaritan as Metaphor," pp. 74-81, where he argues the parable is a metaphor of the kingdom's mercy always coming as a surprise to those who do not deserve it.

106. In addition to Crossan and Funk, others who attempt a metaphorical understanding include Llewellyn Welile Mazamisa, *Beatific Comradeship: An Exegetical-Hermeneutical Study on Lk 10:25-37* (Kampen: Kok, 1987), pp. 106, 140; McDonald, "Alien Grace: (Luke 10:30-36)," 44-47; Sandra Wackman Perpich, *A Critique of Structuralist Exegesis with Specific Reference to Lk 10.29-37* (Lanham: University Press of America, 1984), pp. 196-200; and Scott, *Hear Then the Parable,* pp. 200-201. In a related vein Douglas E. Oakman ("Was Jesus a Peasant? Implications for Reading the Samaritan Story, Luke 10:30-35," *BTB* 22 [1992]: 117-25) argues that the bandits would be viewed as the heroes and the Samaritan trading in oil and wine as an oppressor who foolishly left the man in a dangerous inn (which the cultural evidence above disproves) and that the kingdom is like this foolish action. For critiques of the attempt to see the parable as metaphor, see Via, "Parable and Example Story," 105-33; Hendrickx, *The Parables of Jesus,* p. 92.

107. Most blatantly Capon (*The Parables of Grace,* pp. 61-65), who wants to "skewer the idea" that the parable offers an example to imitate; and Wink, "The Parable of the Compassionate Samaritan: A Communal Exegesis Approach," especially 203, who asserts for some unknown reason that the desire to be a good Samaritan chokes the roots of compassion. How does the desire to put love into action choke compassion?

108. Tucker, *Example Stories: Perspectives on Four Parables in the Gospel of Luke,* pp. 402-12.

109. Tucker, *Example Stories: Perspectives on Four Parables in the Gospel of Luke,* pp. 264-74.

110. E.g., Adolf Jülicher, "Parables," *Encyclopaedia Biblica* (New York: Macmillan, 1902), 3:3563-67, here p. 3566.

111. Flusser (*Die rabbinischen Gleichnisse und der Gleichniserzähler Jesus,* pp. 57, 71) labels the Prodigal an *"ein Exemplum,"* but, while the prodigal's repentance is instructive, neither son is held up as an example to follow.

112. *Example Stories: Perspectives on Four Parables in the Gospel of Luke,* p. 184.

113. See Madeleine Boucher, *The Mysterious Parable* (Washington: The Catholic Biblical Association of America, 1977), p. 22. She calls the example stories "extended synecdoches."

114. See above, pp. 11-15.

115. As Wright (*Jesus and the Victory of God,* p. 331) suggests.

116. E.g., Joel B. Green, *The Gospel of Luke* (NICNT; Grand Rapids: Eerdmans, 1997), p. 428; Jones, *Studying the Parables of Jesus,* p. 297; and Mazamisa, *Beatific Comradeship: An Exegetical-Hermeneutical Study on Lk 10:25-37,* pp. 144-45, view the scribe as hostile. Eta Linnemann, *Parables of Jesus* (trans. John Sturdy; London: SPCK, 1966), p. 57; Marshall, *The Gospel of Luke,* p. 439; and Luise Schottroff, *The Parables of Jesus* (trans. Linda M. Maloney; Minneapolis: Fortress, 2006), p. 132, do not.

117. *Ekpeirazein* occurs only nine times in biblical Greek: LXX Deut 6:16 (twice); 8:2, 16; Ps 77:18; Matt 4:7; Luke 4:12; 10:25; and 1 Cor 10:9 (where it is used in parallelism with *peirazein*). As examples of the positive use of *peirazein* see John 6:6; 2 Cor 13:5; Rev 2:2.

118. The word occurs of people only at 7:30; 10:25; 11:45, 46, 52; 14:3; and outside Luke only in Matt 22:35 and Tit 3:13. Note the assumption of decent relations in 11:45 and 14:3.

119. Cf. Wright, *Jesus and the Victory of God,* pp. 305-7.

120. Note the similar question asked by disciples of Rabbi Eliezer in *b. Berakot* 28b. Cf. *m. 'Abot* 6.7.

121. See especially John J. Kilgallen, "The Plan of the 'ΝΟΜΙΚΟΣ' (Luke 10.25-37)," *NTS* 42 (1996): 615-19. In effect, the real question is "Why do you treat Samaritans with mercy and eat with sinners?"

122. Jones, *Studying the Parables of Jesus*, pp. 310-12. Jones views v. 35 as the Achilles' heel of Funk's argument. Scott (*Hear Then the Parable*, pp. 191-92) argues that the concluding question was not originally part of the parable, even though he sees the parable as breaking down barriers, but such a reduction of the parable results in an abrupt and unfinished ending.

123. "The Old Testament in Parable: The Good Samaritan," pp. 212-14, quotation from p. 214. See also his "The Good Samaritan as Metaphor," 74, 77-79; on p. 79 he assumes that the victim would not want the help of a Samaritan, which not only requires that the victim be conscious but also does not square with the evidence. The sources show Samaritans as "associates," trading with Jews, helping Jews on pilgrimage (*m. Nedarim* 3.10), Samaritan women serving as wet nurses, and many other kinds of interchange between the two groups. Scott (*Hear Then the Parable*, pp. 199-201) also emphasizes that the reader must identify with the victim in the ditch.

124. Funk, "The Good Samaritan as Metaphor," 78; Jeremias, *The Parables of Jesus*, p. 204. Several take the Samaritan's oil and wine as mirroring the use of oil and wine in the Temple sacrifices (Lev 23:13): Derrett, "The Parable of the Good Samaritan," p. 220; Bailey, *Through Peasant Eyes*, p. 50; and John R. Donahue, *The Gospel in Parable* (Philadelphia: Fortress, 1988), p. 132. This is possible, but probably at most ironical (Hultgren, *The Parables of Jesus*, p. 99). Oil and wine were commonly used in healing. See Isa 1:6; Mark 6:13; 1 Tim 5:23; Jas 5:14. They were also mixed and used on those just circumcised; see *b. Šabbat* 133a-134a.

125. See Bauckham, "The Scrupulous Priest and the Good Samaritan," 479, who points to Josephus, *Ant.* 20.181, 207.

126. *m. Giṭṭin* 5.8: "A priest reads first, and after him a levite, and after him an Israelite — in the interests of peace"; *m. Horayot* 3.8: "A priest precedes a levite, a levite an Israelite, an Israelite a bastard. . . . This applies when they all are [otherwise] equal; but if a bastard is learned in the Law and a High Priest is ignorant of the Law, the bastard . . . precedes the High Priest. . . ." On the study of Torah giving greater value see above, p. 349 and n. 95 and the four rabbinic texts listed there.

The attempt by A. J. Mattill ("The Good Samaritan and the Purpose of Luke-Acts: Halévy Reconsidered," *Encounter* 33 [1972]: 359-76) to resurrect J. Halévy's view that an Israelite stood originally as the third person in the parable and that Luke substituted the Samaritan to prefigure the Samaritan mission has little support or acceptance. The claim that it is unlikely that Samaritans traveled about as in the parable ignores the frequent discussions of contacts between Jews and Samaritans when traveling and when meeting in various cities.

127. Bauckham, "The Scrupulous Priest and the Good Samaritan," 475-89. See also Jacob Mann, "Jesus and the Sadducean Priests: Luke 10:25-37," *JQR* 6 (1915-16): 415-22.

128. See 11QTemple (11Q19) 45.17: one defiled by corpse contact may not enter the city of the Temple.

129. See *b. Soṭah* 44a and also 18a, 22b, and 43b. Four cubits seems to have been a determinative measure for many issues. No one who has contracted corpse defilement may mount the Temple rampart (*m. Kelim* 1.7). A priest who has suffered uncleanness from the dead is unqualified to serve in the Temple until he pledges not to suffer uncleanness from the dead any more (*m. Bekorot* 7.7). The priest in the parable is leaving Jerusalem, but defilement would still have consequences for eating priestly food. On uncleanness see *m. Kelim* 1.1, 6-9; and Appendix 4, "The Rules of Uncleanness," in *The Mishnah*, trans. Herbert Danby (Oxford: Clarendon, 1933), pp. 800-804. See also CD 12.15-18; Josephus, *Ant.* 18.36-38. Note the practice reflected in Matt

23:27 of marking tombs so that people may avoid defilement, attested also in *m. Ma'aser Šeni* 5.1. On corpse defilement see Byron R. McCane, "Is a Corpse Contagious? Early Jewish and Christian Attitudes toward the Dead," *Society of Biblical Literature 1992 Seminar Papers,* ed. Eugene H. Lovering, Jr. (Atlanta: Scholars, 1992), pp. 378-88; E. P. Sanders, *Jewish Law from Jesus to the Mishnah* (Philadelphia: Trinity, 1990), pp. 33-35, 41-42, 137-38, 184-92.

130. *m. Nazir* 7.1; *b. Nazir* 42b-43b, 48a-48b; *Mekilta Neziqin* 4.82-109 (on Exod 21:14), which indicates that the conduct of the Temple cult is set aside for burial of a neglected corpse and debates whether Sabbath laws are; cf. Tob 1:17-19; Philo, *Hypothetica* 7.6. According to Jacob Mann ("Jesus and the Sadducean Priests," p. 419) Sadducees did not accept any grounds for corpse defilement.

131. 1 Macc 2:39-41; Josephus, *J.W.* 1.146; *m. Yoma* 8.6; *m. Šabbat* 18.3; *Mekilta Neziqin* 4.105-9; *b. Yoma* 82a, 84b-85a. CD 11.16-17 apparently prohibits work on the Sabbath to save a life, but this text is debated. Further, according to *Semaḥot* (Tractate Mourning) 1.1 a dying person was to be treated in all respects as living.

132. Ulrich Mell thinks this means that the man, even with help, would die. See his "Der barmherzige Samaritaner und Gottes Gerechtigkeit. Eine Auslegung von Lk 10:30-35 in Anknüpfung an Adolf Jülicher," in *Die Gleichnisreden Jesu 1899-1999. Beiträge zum dialog mit Adolf Jülicher,* ed. Ulrich Mell (BZNW 103; Berlin: Walter de Gruyter, 1999), pp. 113-48, here pp. 129-32.

133. Philip F. Esler ("Jesus and the Reduction of Intergroup Conflict: The Parable of the Good Samaritan in the Light of Social Identity Theory," *BibInt* 8 [2000]: 325-57, here p. 338) thinks that since the man was stripped the travelers could see whether he was circumcised, but this presumes too much about the victim's position and is not a concern of the parable.

134. Bauckham ("The Scrupulous Priest and the Good Samaritan," 486) admits that we do not know if Levites in Jesus' day were bound by the same purity laws as priests. His claim that Samaritans were viewed as least likely to keep the Law is valid with respect to the Temple, but some viewed Samaritans in the commands they did accept as more particular than Jews (e.g., *b. Giṭṭin* 10a).

135. *Str-B* (2:183) and Green (*The Gospel of Luke,* p. 430) are among those rejecting any idea of corpse defilement.

136. Craig A. Evans ("Do This and You Will Live": Targumic Coherence in Luke 10:25-28," in Bruce Chilton and Craig A. Evans, *Jesus in Context* [Leiden: Brill, 1997], pp. 377-93, especially 391) argues that this "wrong answer" is evidence for the authenticity of the question and the answer.

137. As Gerhardsson (*The Good Samaritan — the Good Shepherd?* p. 9) suggests.

138. Note the muddle that J. Dwight Pentecost (*The Parables of Jesus* [Grand Rapids: Zondervan, 1982], pp. 71-75) gets into because he fears that the parable teaches salvation by works. Cf. the equally distorted discussions by Mike Graves ("Luke 10:25-37: The Moral of the 'Good Samaritan' Story?" 269-75), who interprets the parable christologically because he thinks a moral message makes the parable law and not grace, and Eduard Verhoef ("[Eternal] Life and Following the Commandments: Lev 18,5 and Luke 10,28," pp. 571-77), who drives an unnecessary wedge between the views of Jesus and Paul, even granted that the issues here are complex. Van Elderen ("Another Look at the Parable of the Good Samaritan," pp. 109-11) attempted to solve the problem of reward for a good deed by saying that the scribe's use of the aorist "having done" (v. 25, *poiēsas*) implies a focus on one single good deed, whereas Jesus employed the present tense "keep on doing" (v. 28, *poiei*). The change is tense is noteworthy, but I doubt that the scribe's question can be interpreted in such a restricted fashion.

139. For critique of Gerhardsson, see Funk, "The Old Testament in Parable: The Good Samaritan," pp. 199-223.

140. Lambrecht, *Once More Astonished*, pp. 72-74, but on p. 77 he concedes that the christological dimension has almost disappeared in Luke.

141. Note that Funk ("The Old Testament in Parable: The Good Samaritan," p. 215) suggested that Jesus hovers behind the parable. In an earlier version of this article (*Encounter* 26 [1965]: 251-67) he added that "while Jesus (or God) does not 'appear' he is the off-stage qualifier of the situation, a decisive factor in the penumbral field" (p. 266). Mazamisa (*Beatific Comradeship: An Exegetical-Hermeneutical Study on Lk 10:25-37*, pp. 169-71) says first that the story is pregnant with its Narrator, but then that Jesus speaks about himself in the parable.

142. Contra Capon (*The Parables of Grace*, pp. 61-65) and Hans Binder ("Das Gleichnis vom barmherzigen Samariter," *TZ* 15 [1959]: 176-94).

143. Crossan, *In Parables*, pp. 65-66; Funk, "The Good Samaritan as Metaphor," pp. 74-81; Lambrecht, *Once More Astonished*, p. 72; and Mazamisa, *Beatific Comradeship: An Exegetical-Hermeneutical Study on Lk 10:25-37*, pp. 140, who claims that Jesus gives an eschatological interpretation of the Law and that "Do this" is an eschatological pointer.

144. Perpich, *A Critique of Structuralist Exegesis, With Specific Reference to Lk 10.29-37*, p. 200, see also 210.

145. Contra Crossan, "Parable and Example in the Teaching of Jesus," 295-96; and Perpich, *A Critique of Structuralist Exegesis, With Specific Reference to Lk 10.29-37*, p. 200.

146. Which was the intent with Lev 19:18.

147. As Sir 12:1-7; see above, p. 340.

148. This view is quite popular; e.g., Nolland, *Luke 9:21–18:24*, p. 596; Jones, *Studying the Parables of Jesus*, pp. 306-7; Funk, "The Old Testament in Parable: The Good Samaritan," pp. 210, 221. Several point out that the question is about the periphery of neighborliness, how far "neighbor" extends, while the parable is about the center from which one acts, which eliminates questions of limit. See Hendrickx, *The Parables of Jesus*, pp. 84, 89. The idea stems from Ernst Fuchs, "Was heißt: 'Du sollst deinen Nächtsen lieben wie dich selbst'?" in *Gesammelte Aufsätze II. Zur Frage nach dem historischen Jesus* (Tübingen: Mohr-Siebeck, 1960), pp. 1-20, here p. 5.

149. F. J. Leenhardt, "La Parabole du Samaritain," in *Aux sources de la tradition chrétienne* (Neuchâtel: Delachaux & Niestlé, 1950), pp. 132-38, here p. 136; see also H. Greeven, *"plēsion,"* *TDNT* 6:317.

150. *The Sayings of Jesus as Recorded in the Gospels According to St. Matthew and St. Luke Arranged with Introduction and Commentary* (London: SCM, 1949), pp. 261, 263.

151. *Works of Love*, pp. 83-84.

152. Bauckham, "The Scrupulous Priest and the Good Samaritan," 475, 484-85, 488-89.

153. The Entrevernes Group, "'Go and Do Likewise': Narrative and Dialogue (Luke 10:25-37)," in *Signs and Parables* (trans. Gary Phillips; Pittsburgh: Pickwick, 1978), pp. 13-64, see p. 32; see also *b. Sukkah* 49b.

154. See above, p. 72.

155. This is even more the case if any memory exists of the attempt to rename the temple of Gerizim as a temple of Zeus, the friend of strangers. See 2 Macc 6:2.

156. Judaism and groups within Judaism often had different regulations for those inside and those outside the group. In addition to Sir 12:1-7; 1QS 1.10; 9.21-22; 10.19-21, listed above, see *m. Baba Qamma* 4.3; *b. Baba Qamma* 38a; *b. ʿAbodah Zarah* 26a; *b. Sanhedrin* 57a; *ʾAbot de Rabbi Nathan* 16.6; *Lev. Rab.* 13.2.

157. Jones (*Studying the Parables of Jesus*, p. 299) sees the Samaritan as a model, but fears

that "example story" lacks dynamism. I reject the category "example story," but the fault lies more in *our* lack of dynamism than anything inherent in a parable category.

158. Green (*The Gospel of Luke*, p. 426); why he (p. 425) says that Jesus' words "Go and do" (v. 37) do not present a moral obligation to act in a particular way is beyond understanding.

159. *Studying the Parables of Jesus*, p. 314.

160. The expression is from Jeremias, *The Parables of Jesus*, p. 202.

161. Bailey, *Through Peasant Eyes*, p. 55.

162. As Glanville Downey points out, the question "Who is my neighbor?" implies the further question "What am I?" ("Who Is My Neighbor? The Greek and Roman Answer," *ATR* 47 [1965]: 3-15, here p. 4). Downey provides evidence of the limits Greeks and Romans put on the definition of "neighbor."

163. See the Entrevenes Group, "'Go and Do Likewise': Narrative and Dialogue (Luke 10:25-37)," 45.

164. Note the comment of Joachim Jeremias (*New Testament Theology* 1: *The Proclamation of Jesus* [trans. John Bowden; London: SCM, 1971], p. 193): "The way to God goes through a man's neighbour." Note Dietrich Bonhoeffer's comment (*The Cost of Discipleship* [New York: Touchstone, 1995], p. 98): "Christ stands between us, and we can only get into touch with our neighbors through him."

165. *Reading the Bible in the Strange World of Medicine* (Grand Rapids: Eerdmans, 2003), pp. 359-93.

166. Richard B. Hays, *The Moral Vision of the New Testament: Community, Cross, New Creation: A Contemporary Introduction to New Testament Ethics* (San Francisco: HarperSanFrancisco, 1996), p. 451 (italics original).

167. *The NewsHour with Jim Lehrer*, April 20, 2006.

168. See Leenhardt, "La Parabole du Samaritain," pp. 132-38.

169. Cf. the parable of the Two Debtors above, pp. 88, 90.

170. Sigmund Freud, *Civilization and Its Discontents* (trans. and ed. James Strachey; New York: Norton, 1962), pp. 49, 56-59, 89-90. He attributes such thinking to the unpsychological proceedings of the cultural superego. On the other hand, Wendell Berry ("Property, Patriotism, and National Defense," *Home Economics* [San Francisco: North Point, 1987], pp. 98-111) argues that civilization needs the love command, especially now: "It may be that the only possibly effective defense against the ultimate weapon is no weapon at all. It may be that the presence of nuclear weapons in the world serves notice that the command to love one another is an absolute practical necessity, such as we never dreamed it to be before, and that our choice is not to win or lose, but to love our enemies or die" (p. 111).

171. As Hedrick (*Parables as Poetic Fictions*, pp. 112-16) argued, leading him to think the story is a parody of the ideal of a righteous person.

172. David Flusser, "A New Sensitivity in Judaism and the Christian Message," in *Judaism and the Origins of Christianity* (Jerusalem: Magnes, 1988), pp. 469-92, quotation from p. 492.

173. See also Hans Gunther Klemm, *Das Gleichnis vom barmherzigen Samariter. Grundzüge der Auslegung im 16./17. Jahrhundert* (Stuttgart: Kohlhammer, 1973).

174. Hultgren, *The Parables of Jesus*, pp. 33-46; Jülicher, *Die Gleichnisreden Jesu*, 2:471; Montefiore, *The Synoptic Gospels*, 2:272; E. Fuchs, "Das Zeitverständnis Jesu," in *Gesammelte Aufsätze II. Zur Frage nach dem historischen Jesus* (Tübingen: Mohr-Siebeck, 1960), 304-76, here p. 362; Eberhard Jüngel, *Paulus und Jesus* (Tübingen: Mohr-Siebeck, 1962), p. 164 (following Fuchs).

175. See the critique of the usual explanations by Karen Lebacqz, "Justice, Economics,

and the Uncomfortable Kingdom," *ASCE* 3 (1983): 27-53, although her own interpretation does not take us very far.

176. The authenticity of this parable is rarely questioned; this is one of five parables printed entirely in red by the Jesus Seminar (See Funk, Scott, and Butts, *The Parables of Jesus: Red Letter Edition*, p. 33). Among the few who assign the parable to Matthew are M. D. Goulder, *Midrash and Lection in Matthew* (London: SPCK, 1974), pp. 409-11; and Gundry, *Matthew: A Commentary on His Literary and Theological Art*, pp. 395-99. Can one take seriously Gundry's argument that the financial dimensions of the parable tally with Matthew's occupation as a tax collector? The method behind his stylistic analysis is no more convincing. Catherine Hezser (*Lohnmetaphorik und Arbeitswelt in Mt 20,1-16* [NTOA 15; Göttingen: Vandenhoeck & Ruprecht, 1990], p. 249) argues that the parable cannot be from Matthew because the critique of those hired first is not formulated sharply enough.

177. There is a textual variant in v. 16 that adds "Many are called but few are chosen," for which considerable manuscript evidence exists despite its absence in ℵ, B, L, Z, and a few minuscules. Most rightly accept that these words have been added under the influence of 22:14, where they also occur at the end of a parable. The editors of the UBS fourth edition rate the certainty of the omission as "A." Nothing in these words displays a logical connection to this parable or this section of Matthew. For a cautious dissenting opinion see Edmund F. Sutcliffe, "Many Are Called but Few Are Chosen," *ITQ* 28 (1961): 126-31.

178. Jeremias (*The Parables of Jesus*, p. 138) and John Drury (*The Parables in the Gospels* [New York: Crossroad, 1985], p. 95) both suggest rabbinic dependence on Jesus. Jülicher (*Die Gleichnisreden Jesu*, 2:467-68) suggested that Jesus may have known a rabbinic parable like this one. The influence of Jesus' parables on the later rabbinic parables is likely, but the influence could go in both directions. Jesus may have drawn upon Jewish traditional stories in composing the parables, but this cannot be demonstrated.

179. See also *Eccl. Rab.* 5.11; *Song Rab.* 6.8 (on 6:2).

180. E.g., Davies and Allison, *A Critical and Exegetical Commentary on the Gospel According to Saint Matthew*, 3:66; V. George Shillington, "Saving Life and Keeping Sabbath (Matt 20:1b-15)," in *Jesus and His Parables: Interpreting the Parables of Jesus Today*, ed. V. George Shillington (Edinburgh: T. & T. Clark, 1997), pp. 87-101 (see p. 96 — his suggestion of a chiastic structure has little in its favor).

181. Wolfgang Harnisch, "The Metaphorical Process in Matthew 20:1-15," in *Society of Biblical Literature Seminar Papers 1977*, ed. Paul J. Achtemeier (Missoula: Scholars, 1977), pp. 231-50, here p. 239; Donahue, *The Gospel in Parable*, p. 79.

182. Donald A. Hagner, *Matthew 14–28* (WBC 33B; Dallas: Word, 1995), p. 570.

183. The focus is not on their posture but on their presence in the market as they wait.

184. *Gos. Thom.* 4 has an altered form of the proverb: "For many of the first will be last, and they will become a single one."

185. Goulder (*Midrash and Lection in Matthew*, p. 410) lists these Mattheanisms and other semi-Matthean words and suggests that of 239 words in the parable sixty-two are characteristic of Matthew. But are words like "vineyard," "came," "take," "agree," and many more in his list really semi-Matthean? His method is unacceptable. Despite thinking the parable is Matthean in origin, he grants that it does not bear what he thinks is the usual Matthean stamp. See the discussion by Ivor Harold Jones (*The Matthean Parables: A Literary and Historical Commentary* [NovTSup 80; Leiden: Brill, 1995], pp. 414-18) who concludes from Goulder's list that statistical analysis suggests a strong traditional element (p. 417).

186. B. Rod Doyle, "The Place of the Parable of the Labourers in the Vineyard in Matthew 20:1-16," *AusBR* 42 (1994): 39-58, especially 45-50.

187. Which some reject. See pp. 371-73 herein.

188. See Rudolf Hoppe, "Gleichnis und Situation. Zu den Gleichnissen von guten Vater (Lk 15,11-32) und gütigen Hausherrn (Mt 20,1-15)," *BZ* 28 (1984): 1-21; Davies and Allison, *Matthew*, 3:69.

189. For a discussion of realism see Norman Huffman, "Atypical Features in the Parables of Jesus," *JBL* 97 (1978): 207-10.

190. Luise Schottroff, "Human Solidarity and the Goodness of God: The Parable of the Workers in the Vineyard," in *God of the Lowly*, ed. Willy Schottroff and Wolfgang Stegemann (trans. Matthew J. O'Connell; Maryknoll: Orbis, 1984), pp. 129-47. Contra J. Duncan M. Derrett, who argued from rabbinic evidence (*m. Baba Meṣi'a* 2.9; 5.4; *m. Bekorot* 4.6; *b. Baba Meṣi'a* 31b, 76b-77b; *b. Bekorot* 29a-b) that an employer was obligated to pay a minimum wage *(po'el baṭel)* to workers. See his "Workers in the Vineyard: A Parable of Jesus," in *Studies in the New Testament* (Leiden: Brill, 1977), 1:48-75, especially 59-60. Derrett's suggestion has not found much acceptance. The evidence is late and not directly related; he assumes facts the parable does not mention (such as it being harvest time), and clearly the parable assumes this wage is unexpected. That is the basis of the complaint against the owner. See Scott, *Hear Then the Parable*, p. 274. Johannes B. Bauer ("Gnadenlohn oder Tageslohn [Mt 20,8-16]?" *Bib* 42 [1961]: 224-28) argued that the owner was obligated to pay workers for the full day even if they worked only a part, but as with Derrett's argument, this runs counter to the expectation of the complainers.

191. For evidence on day laborers see David A. Fiensy, *The Social History of Palestine in the Herodian Period* (Lewiston: Mellen, 1991), pp. 85-90; and for information specifically treating the plight of workers, see Felix Gryglewicz, "The Gospel of the Overworked Workers," *CBQ* 19 (1957): 190-98; Schottroff, "Human Solidarity and the Goodness of God," pp. 131-32; William Herzog, *Parables as Subversive Speech: Jesus as Pedagogue of the Oppressed* (Louisville: Westminster/John Knox, 1994), pp. 88-90; Hezser, *Lohnmetaphorik und Arbeitswelt in Mt 20,1-16*, pp. 95-96, 296.

192. *m. Baba Meṣi'a* 7:1-8 even lays down regulations governing what day laborers may eat while working with crops.

193. See Fiensy, *The Social History of Palestine in the Herodian Period*, pp. 86-90; F. M. Heichelheim, "Roman Syria," in *An Economic Survey of Ancient Rome* (Paterson: Pageant, 1959), 4:178-82; Ekkehard W. Stegemann and Wolfgang Stegemann, *The Jesus Movement: A Social History of Its First Century* (trans. O. C. Dean, Jr.; Minneapolis: Fortress, 1999), pp. 81-93; and the discussion in Scott, *Hear Then the Parable*, pp. 290-91. For evidence from primary sources see Tob 5:15, where an unrecognized angel is paid a denarius for his day's work; *b. Baba Batra* 86b-87a; *b. 'Abodah Zarah* 62a; and *b. Yoma* 35b, which view Hillel as poor since he worked each day for half a denarius. R. Meir as a scribe was paid two denarii a day because of the value of his trade (*Eccl. Rab.* 2.24 [on 2:18]). People who earned more than 200 denarii per year were not allowed to glean with the poor (see *m. Peah* 8:8). See also Tacitus, *Annals* 1.17, where payment contracted for soldiers is a denarius a day.

194. For an overview of treatments see Joachim Gnilka, *Jesus of Nazareth: Message and History* (trans. Siegfried S. Schatzmann; Peabody: Hendrickson, 1997), pp. 82-93. Among the "unusual" several works should be mentioned. K. Lebacqz ("Justice, Economics, and the Uncomfortable Kingdom," pp. 27-53) thinks the parable addresses what we should do when the kingdom is less than expected and finds the solution to the parable in expectation that the Jubilee will restore equilibrium. As important as the Jubilee is, nothing in this parable justifies such

a suggestion. G. Shillington ("Saving Life and Keeping Sabbath," pp. 87-101) suggests that Jewish ideas of work and rest are addressed and that Sabbath observance is critiqued. In his view the Sabbath, which anticipates the kingdom and was to have an equalizing effect, cannot be observed by the poor. As important as the Sabbath is, the parable gives no hint that any reference to it is involved. Philip Culbertson ("Reclaiming the Matthean Vineyard Parables," *Encounter* 49 [1988]: 257-83) for some reason thinks this parable is an amplification of Isa 45:9-13 and is about Jewish responsibilities in God's vineyard. Gryglewicz ("The Gospel of the Overworked Workers," 190-98) thinks Jesus was drawing attention to workers being overworked and was seeking rest for them.

195. For discussion of these and other less popular allegorizing approaches see Wailes, *Medieval Allegories of Jesus' Parables,* pp. 137-44; Hezser, *Lohnmetaphorik und Arbeitswelt in Mt 20,1-16,* pp. 1-44; and J. M. Tevel, "The Labourers in the Vineyard: The Exegesis of Matthew 20:1-7 in the Early Church," *VC* 46 (1992): 356-80. Blomberg's interpretation (*Interpreting the Parables,* p. 224) is not far from the "stages in life" approach since he thinks the parable shows that God's people come to repentance in different ways and times and with varying levels of commitment, but is this parable about repentance and commitment?

196. Jülicher, *Die Gleichnisreden Jesu,* 2:465-67; Dan Otto Via, *The Parables* (Philadelphia: Fortress, 1967), pp. 149-54; Wilfrid Haubeck, "Zum Verständnis der Parabel von den Arbeitern im Weinberg (Mt 20,1-15)," in *Wort in der Zeit,* ed. Wilfrid Haubeck and Michael Bachmann (Leiden: Brill, 1980), pp. 95-107; Jan Lambrecht, *Out of the Treasure: The Parables in the Gospel of Matthew* (LTPM 10; Louvain: Peeters, 1992), pp. 81, 85-86; Brad H. Young, *The Parables: Jewish Tradition and Christian Interpretation,* pp. 69-81, who sees the focus on grace as an expression of Jewish theology; and Hultgren, *The Parables of Jesus,* pp. 41-43. Gnilka (*Jesus of Nazareth,* pp. 91-92) also takes such an approach and asserts that with the parable Jesus establishes a new order, which is a lot to read from this one enigmatic parable.

197. Among many see Jülicher, *Die Gleichnisreden Jesu,* 2:466-67; Jeremias, *The Parables of Jesus,* p. 38; Linnemann, *Parables of Jesus,* pp. 86-87 and 155-58; G. De Ru, "The Conception of Reward in the Teaching of Jesus," *NovT* 8 (1966): 202-22, here pp. 208-9.

198. See Hagner, *Matthew 14-28,* 2:574; Doyle, "The Place of the Parable of the Labourers in the Vineyard in Matthew 20:1-16," 49-53; Daniel Patte, "Bringing Out of the Gospel-Treasure What Is New and What Is Old: Two Parables in Matthew 18-23," *Quarterly Review* 10 (1990): 79-108, here pp. 95-96; Lambrecht, *Out of the Treasure,* p. 84.

199. Notably Herzog, *Parables as Subversive Speech,* pp. 79-97; Schottroff, *The Parables of Jesus,* pp. 209-17.

200. Davies and Allison, *Matthew,* 3:67-68; Ingo Broer, "Die Gleichnisexegese und die neuere Literaturwissenschaft. Ein Diskussionsbeitrag zur Exegese von Mt 20,1-16," *BN* 5 (1978): 13-27, here pp. 20-21; John H. Elliott, "Matthew 20:1-15: A Parable of Invidious Comparison and Evil Eye Accusation," *BTB* 22 (1992): 52-65.

201. Schottroff, "Human Solidarity and the Goodness of God," pp. 137-47; Robert Fortna, "You Have Made Them Equal to Us," *JTSA* 72 (1990): 66-72; Patte, "Bringing Out of the Gospel-Treasure What Is New and What Is Old," 93, 98.

202. E.g., Jeremias, *The Parables of Jesus,* pp. 36-37; Lambrecht, *Out of the Treasure,* p. 70. Most accept that the parable encompasses vv. 1-15, and J. Crossan (*In Parables,* pp. 112-14) is virtually alone in limiting it to vv. 1-13. Hans Weder (*Die Gleichnisse Jesu als Metaphern. Traditions- und redaktionsgeschichtliche Analysen und Interpretationen* [4th ed.; Göttingen: Vandenhoeck & Ruprecht, 1990], p. 219) thinks vv. 1-15 are unaffected by editorial intervention.

203. See his *Homilies on Matthew* 64.3, 4 (*NPNF1* 10:393-95).

204. Jülicher, *Die Gleichnisreden Jesu,* 2:469; several others take this approach, especially Weder (*Die Gleichnisse Jesu als Metaphern,* pp. 229-30). Ulrich Luz (*Matthew 8–20: A Commentary* [trans. James E. Crouch; Minneapolis: Fortress, 2001], p. 537) thinks the warning is to members of Matthew's community.

205. *Jesus and the Kingdom of God* (Grand Rapids: Eerdmans, 1986), p. 117. He suggests that Matthew may have been anticipating the parable of the Two Sons in 21:28-32. For a treatment of how the parable fits in its context see also Warren Carter and John Paul Heil, *Matthew's Parables: Audience-Oriented Perspectives* (CBQMS 30; Washington: The Catholic Biblical Association of America, 1998), pp. 125-34.

206. Herzog, *Parables as Subversive Speech,* pp. 79-97, followed by Schottroff, *The Parables of Jesus,* pp. 209-17.

207. Culbertson ("Reclaiming the Matthean Vineyard Parables," 263) thinks it is virtually impossible to imagine Jesus using the vineyard to refer to anything other than the people of Israel. While the image does emerge from Isa 5:1-7, where the vineyard is a symbol for the house of Israel, the focus is not on the nation as an entity but on God's people living out their covenant obligations.

208. As do the parables above; see *m. 'Abot* 1.3; 2.14-16; *y. Berakot* 2.7; *Sifra Behuqotai* 262 (on Lev 26:9); *Deut. Rab.* 6.2; *Midr. Pss.* 26.3 (all listed above on pp. 364-66); cf. Schottroff, "Human Solidarity and the Goodness of God," pp. 135-36.

209. Note that Schottroff (*The Parables of Jesus,* p. 212), who follows Herzog's approach, concludes that the parable is unsatisfying and that hearers can only go on discussing it.

210. Although some do indeed make the father in the Prodigal a negative character.

211. Cf. Harnisch, "The Metaphorical Process in Matthew 20:1-15," p. 243; Luz, *Matthew 8–20,* pp. 532 n. 75, 536-37.

212. Contra among others Goulder, *Midrash and Lection in Matthew,* pp. 410-11, but he does not see the steward as a christological reference.

213. *The Parables of Jesus,* pp. 33-38. This was suggested already by Jülicher, *Die Gleichnisreden Jesu,* 2:466. See also Linnemann, *Parables of Jesus,* pp. 86, 154-55; Christian Dietzfelbinger, "Das Gleichnis von den Arbeitern im Weinberg," *EvT* 43 (1983): 126-37; Fortna, "You Have Made Them Equal to Us," 66.

214. Blomberg, *Interpreting the Parables,* p. 222. Simon J. Kistemaker (*The Parables of Jesus* [Grand Rapids: Baker, 1980], pp. 80-81) thinks the disciples were the original audience but that the Pharisees were present. Hagner (*Matthew 14–28,* 572-73) thinks the disciples identified themselves with the first hired but that Matthew's church possibly identified the first hired with Israel. I see no basis for either conclusion.

215. As argued by Blomberg, *Interpreting the Parables,* p. 222.

216. *The Parables,* p. 154.

217. See Broer ("Die Gleichnisexegese und die neuere Literaturwissenschaft," 19), who points out that "go" is also used in vv. 4 and 7, that its use in v. 14 is not as negative as Via suggests, and that the owner with his questions seeks understanding, not exclusion.

218. Patte, "Bringing Out of the Gospel-Treasure What Is New and What Is Old," 99; W. Sanday, "The Parable of the Labourers in the Vineyard," *Expositor* 1st series 3 (1876): 81-101, see 99; cf. Donahue, *The Gospel in Parable,* p. 83; and Goulder, *Midrash and Lection in Matthew,* p. 409. Schottroff ("Human Solidarity and the Goodness of God," p. 147) thinks the parable is an invitation to the Pharisees, not a critique of them. On the other hand, Montefiore (*The Synoptic Gospels,* 2:276) thought that the first who become last are excluded.

219. Jeremias has only three parables addressed to the disciples (the Budding Fig Tree,

Matt 24:32-33/Mark 13:28-29/Luke 21:29-31; the Friend at Midnight, Luke 11:5-8; and the Unjust Judge, Luke 18:1-8), but surely other parables were also addressed to disciples; e.g., the Two Builders, the Unforgiving Servant, and the parables of future eschatology, if not also the present kingdom parables.

220. *Hearing the Parables of Jesus* (New York: Paulist, 1981), pp. 142-43. Contra Schottroff, "Human Solidarity and the Goodness of God," pp. 138, 147.

221. Lambrecht (*Out of the Treasure,* p. 81) speaks of "God's immense goodness," Hultgren (*The Parables of Jesus,* p. 35) of the owner's "extreme generosity," Anna Wierzbicka (*What Did Jesus Mean? Explaining the Sermon on the Mount and the Parables in Simple and Universal Human Concepts* [New York: Oxford University Press, 2001], p. 330) of God's grace being open to all, and Young (*The Parables,* p. 81) of God's unlimited grace for each person. Montefiore (*The Synoptic Gospels,* 2:273) asserts that the original intention of the parable was to teach that eternal life is the result of grace rather than work.

222. See especially Hultgren, *The Parables of Jesus,* pp. 42-43; Jeremias, *The Parables of Jesus,* p. 139; Via, *The Parables,* pp. 152-55; and W. O. E. Oesterley, *The Gospel Parables in the Light of Their Jewish Background* (London: SPCK, 1938), pp. 104-5, who sees the parable as directed against a Jewish doctrine of works, although he knows some rabbinic texts reject ideas of weighing good and evil deeds.

223. *Hear Then the Parable,* p. 282.

224. Scott (*Hear Then the Parable,* p. 297), Kistemaker (*The Parables of Jesus,* p. 73), and Oesterley (*The Gospel Parables in the Light of Their Jewish Background,* pp. 107, 109) all view the hiring as an act of grace. F. C. Glover ("Workers for the Vineyard," *ExpTim* 86 [1975]: 310-11); Kistemaker (*The Parables of Jesus,* pp. 74-75); and *Str-B* ("Das Gleichnis von den Arbeitern im Weinberg Mt 20,1-16 u. die altsynagogale Lohnlehre," 4:484-500, here pp. 486-87) think a relation of trust was established. Several think the workers hired first were privileged to be employed all day. This may be true given the harsh economic realities, but the hearers would not have perceived them as the privileged ones.

225. Culbertson ("Reclaiming the Matthean Vineyard Parables," 265), Young (*The Parables: Jewish Tradition and Christian Interpretation,* p. 80), and Patte ("Bringing Out of the Gospel-Treasure What Is New and What Is Old," 98), among others, say the parable is about equality. Schottroff ("Human Solidarity and the Goodness of God," pp. 137-38), Fortna ("You Have Made Them Equal to Us," 70), and Patte ("Bringing Out of the Gospel-Treasure What Is New and What Is Old," 93, 98) say it is about solidarity.

226. Manson (*The Sayings of Jesus,* p. 218) suggested that the disciples will receive the same reward as the patriarchs! Davies and Allison (*Matthew,* 3:76) say those converted late in life will not suffer disadvantage. Cf. Brad Young, *Jesus and His Jewish Parables: Rediscovering the Roots of Jesus' Teaching* (Mahwah: Paulist Press, 1989), p. 265.

227. And presupposed by *t. Baba Meṣiʿa* 7.1-3.

228. John H. Elliott, "Matthew 20:1-15: A Parable of Invidious Comparison and Evil Eye Accusation," *BTB* 22 (1992): 52-65. Elliott (p. 58) describes envy as displeasure at the assets and success of another. See also Henry J. Cadbury, "The Single Eye," *HTR* 47 (1954): 69-74. Note Mark 7:22; Matt 6:22-23/Luke 11:34. See Sir 14:8: "Evil is the eye of the envious person who turns away and disregards people" (my translation); 14:10: "The evil eye [NRSV 'miser'] begrudges bread"; cf. 31:13. See also Tob 4:7: "Do not let not your eye begrudge the gift when you make it."

229. Broer, "Die Gleichnisexegese und die neuere Literaturwissenschaft," 20; cf. Crossan, *In Parables,* p. 114.

230. Anders Nygren, *Agape and Eros* (trans. Philip S. Watson; London: SPCK, 1954), p. 86.

Cf. Scott (*Hear Then the Parable,* pp. 292, 297-98) who underscores that justice involves charity and means doing what is right in community but also that justice as humanly conceived cannot organize the kingdom.

231. Cf. Luz, *Matthew 8–20,* 2:534; Perkins, *Hearing the Parables of Jesus,* p. 237; Davies and Allison, *Matthew,* 3:70, 76.

232. Schottroff ("Human Solidarity and the Goodness of God," p. 145) with some justice suggests that Matthew had in mind Christians who claimed privileges because they do more. Hezser (*Lohnmetaphorik und Arbeitswelt in Mt 20,1-16,* especially pp. 290-98) argues that Matthew must combat wandering charismatics. She thinks he describes two kinds of discipleship, that of the charismatics (represented in the narrative by Peter) and that of the residents in the community (represented by the rich young ruler), but that with this parable he argues against two kinds of reward. I see no basis for such a theory.

233. They are not at fault for not being hired and the question is not a reproach (contra Jeremias, *The Parables of Jesus,* pp. 37, 136-37; Jülicher, *Die Gleichnisreden Jesu,* 2:460), nor did other employers view them as unworthy (contra Hagner, *Matthew 14–28,* 2:571).

234. Contra Via, *The Parables,* p. 150; Doyle, "The Place of the Parable of the Labourers in the Vineyard in Matthew 20:1-16," 52.

235. Dietzfelbinger, "Das Gleichnis von den Arbeitern im Weinberg," 130.

236. Linnemann, *Parables of Jesus,* pp. 87, 156-57.

237. Cf. Hezser, *Lohnmetaphorik und Arbeitswelt in Mt 20,1-16,* p. 97; Lambrecht, *Out of the Treasure,* p. 85.

238. Jeremias (*The Parables of Jesus,* p. 35) and Lambrecht (*Out of the Treasure,* p. 82) both reject the idea that the parable is about final judgment.

239. The more one sees Jesus' opponents as the target and being made last as exclusion from the kingdom, the more one will see a focus on final judgment. Cf. Jülicher, *Die Gleichnisreden Jesu,* 2:470.

240. Blomberg, *Interpreting the Parables,* pp. 222-25.

241. At least this can be derived from the parable. From a broader perspective we would need to say that *all* will get much more than they deserve.

242. Jüngel, *Paulus und Jesus,* p. 165.

243. Cf. Dietzfelbinger, "Das Gleichnis von den Arbeitern im Weinberg," 133.

244. Several commentators point to the welfare debate as a context similar to that of the parable.

245. Søren Kierkegaard, *Purity of Heart Is to Will One Thing* (trans. Douglas V. Steere; New York: Harper & Row, 1938), pp. 208, 216.

246. See C. L. Mitton, "Expounding the Parables: The Workers in the Vineyard (Matthew 20:1-16)," *ExpTim* 77 (1965-66): 307-11, specifically 309; and Schottroff, "Human Solidarity and the Goodness of God," p. 137.

247. Manson (*The Sayings of Jesus,* p. 220), after explaining that a twelfth part of a denarius was a pondion, rightly says there is no such thing as a twelfth part of God's love.

248. Rudolf Bultmann (*History of the Synoptic Tradition* [trans. John Marsh; New York: Harper & Row, 1963], pp. 170-71) classifies both the Tower Builder and the Warring King as *Gleichnisse* (similitudes; see p. 184 of the German original), but this does not do justice to the question form. At best they are similitudes only by implication.

249. J. Duncan M. Derrett ("Nisi Dominus Aedificaverit Domum: Towers and Wars [Lk XIV 28-32]," *NovT* 19 [1977]: 241-61, here pp. 244-46) accepts that the parable is about both God and Jesus.

250. J. Drury suggests (*The Parables in the Gospels,* p. 138) that 2 Sam 8:10 may have influenced the parable or that there may be an allusion to the events of 70 A.D. and the failure of Jewish nationalists to come to terms with Rome. The relation to the parable is not so direct in either case. In 2 Sam 8:10 Toi may be seeking peace (LXX "to ask the things of peace"; cf. Luke 14:32) but sends gifts because David has defeated an enemy he himself has been fighting. The relation to the destruction of Jerusalem is treated below.

251. Green, *The Gospel of Luke,* p. 566.

252. See E. B. Banning, "Towers," *ABD,* 6:622-24.

253. See Hultgren, *The Parables of Jesus,* pp. 142-43; Jülicher, *Die Gleichnisreden Jesu,* 2:204-5.

254. Charles Leland Quarles ("The Authenticity of the Parable of the Warring King: A Response to the Jesus Seminar," in *Authenticating the Words of Jesus,* ed. Bruce D. Chilton and Craig A. Evans [Leiden: Brill, 1999], pp. 409-29, here pp. 422-23) suggests that the event that calls forth the parable is Aretas's war with Herod Antipas for putting away his wife, who was Aretas's daughter (Josephus, *Ant.* 18.109-15), but no evidence supports this connection. Jülicher (*Die Gleichnisreden Jesu,* 2:209) made the same suggestion earlier.

255. See Wailes, *Medieval Allegories of Jesus' Parables,* pp. 230-33.

256. Derrett, "Nisi Dominus Aedificaverit Domum," 241-61; Claus-Hunno Hunzinger, "Unbekannte Gleichnisse Jesu aus dem Thomas-Evangelium," in *Judentum-Urchristentum-Kirche,* ed. W. Eltester (Berlin: Töpelmann, 1964), pp. 209-20; Peter G. Jarvis, "Expounding the Parables V: The Tower-Builder and the King Going to War (Luke 14:25-33)," *ExpTim* 77 (1966): 196-98. Derrett argues for a midrash on Prov 24:3, 6, sees allusions to the story of the Tower of Babel in Genesis 11, deletes 14:30, and thinks Luke constructed the Warring King parable from "something easier" that did not refer to a king.

257. J. Louw ("The Parables of the Tower-Builder and the King Going to War," *ExpTim* 48 [1936-37]: 478) thinks the parables refer to Jesus' own sitting down and calculating the cost just after his baptism.

258. E.g., Joseph A. Fitzmyer, *The Gospel According to Luke X–XXIV: Introduction, Translation, and Notes* (AB 28A; Garden City: Doubleday, 1983), p. 1062.

259. E.g., Derrett, "Nisi Dominus Aedificaverit Domum," 242; Hultgren, *The Parables of Jesus,* p. 138. Jülicher (*Die Gleichnisreden Jesu,* 2:208-9) was well aware of the formal unevenness between the parables and the context but still thought the parables fit in very well. Paul Fiebig argued that such unevenness and the omission of transitional thoughts are typical in rabbinic parables; see *Die Gleichnisreden Jesu im Lichte der rabbinischen Gleichnisse des Neutestamentlichen Zeitalters* (Tübingen: Mohr-Siebeck, 1912), pp. 174-75.

260. Bernhard Heininger, *Metaphorik, Erzählstruktur und szenisch-dramatische Gestaltung in den Sondergutgleichnissen bei Lukas* (NTAbh 24; Münster: Aschendorff, 1991), p. 132.

261. Heininger (*Metaphorik, Erzählstruktur und szenisch-dramatische Gestaltung in den Sondergutgleichnissen bei Lukas,* p. 133) and Derrett ("Nisi Dominus Aedificaverit Domum," 260) argue that Luke is responsible for v. 30, but this seems neither likely nor necessary.

262. Funk, Scott, and Butts, *The Parables of Jesus: Red Letter Edition* pp. 68-69 and 105; Funk, Hoover, and the Jesus Seminar, *The Five Gospels,* p. 354. Both print these parables with black ink.

263. Drury, *The Parables in the Gospels,* p. 139.

264. A point recognized already by A. B. Bruce (*The Parabolic Teaching of Christ* [3d ed.;

New York: Armstrong and Son, 1887], p. 9), who does not even treat these parables and thinks they are of no independent didactic importance, although certainly from Jesus.

265. See the discussion by James D. G. Dunn, *Jesus Remembered*, vol. 1 of *Christianity in the Making* (Grand Rapids: Eerdmans, 2003), pp. 81-83.

266. Which the Jesus Seminar accepts as authentic. Cf. also the simple analogies of a new patch on an old cloth (Matt 9:16/Mark 2:21/Luke 5:36), of the budding fig tree (Matt 24:32-33/ Mark 13:28-29/Luke 21:29-30), and of the ability people have to discern the weather but not the nature of the time (Matt 16:2-3/Luke 12:54-56), none of which the Jesus Seminar accepts.

267. Drury (*The Parables in the Gospels*, p. 139) points only to *ei de mē ge* ("if not," which occurs five times in Luke, twice in Matthew, and once in Paul), *symballein* ("meet," "consider," which occurs only in Luke-Acts but only six or seven times, depending on the reading at 11:53), and *bouleuomai* ("deliberate," which occurs three times in Luke-Acts, twice in John, and once in 1 Corinthians).

268. Jülicher, *Die Gleichnisreden Jesu*, 2:206; see also Norman Perrin, *Rediscovering the Teaching of Jesus* (London: SCM, 1967), p. 127; Hultgren, *The Parables of Jesus*, p. 142. See the discussion by Quarles, "The Authenticity of the Parable of the Warring King," pp. 409-29, but with reservations about some of his arguments.

269. Derrett, "Nisi Dominus Aedificaverit Domum," 246-49; Peter G. Jarvis, "Expounding the Parables V"; Hunzinger, "Unbekannte Gleichnisse Jesu aus dem Thomas-Evangelium," pp. 213-14.

270. Hunzinger, "Unbekannte Gleichnisse Jesu aus dem Thomas-Evangelium," pp. 214-17.

271. Quarles, "The Authenticity of the Parable of the Warring King," especially pp. 413, 415. See also Louw, "The Parables of the Tower-Builder and the King Going to War," 478.

272. "Who from you will have one sheep, and if it falls in a pit on the Sabbath, will not take hold of it and raise it?" Matt 6:27/Luke 12:25 and John 8:46 also do not refer to God, but these passages do not contain parables. Cf. also Luke 14:5.

273. Despite Hunzinger's attempt to set these verses aside. He attributes the application of these parables to discipleship to the missionary church in the context of candidates for baptism ("Unbekannte Gleichnisse Jesu aus dem Thomas-Evangelium," p. 214).

274. See also the account of the rich young ruler (Matt 19:16-22/Mark 10:17-22/Luke 18:18-23).

275. Heininger (*Metaphorik, Erzählstruktur und szenisch-dramatische Gestaltung in den Sondergutgleichnissen bei Lukas*, p. 138) suggests that they are an ideal picture which hides the realities.

276. Hultgren, *The Parables of Jesus*, p. 140; see also G. B. Caird, *The Gospel of St. Luke* (New York: Seabury, 1968), p. 179.

277. Suggested by both Heininger (*Metaphorik, Erzählstruktur und szenisch-dramatische Gestaltung in den Sondergutgleichnissen bei Lukas*, pp. 138-39) and Jülicher (*Die Gleichnisreden Jesu*, 2:211-12).

278. Perrin, *Rediscovering the Teaching of Jesus*, p. 128.

279. A point recognized by Jülicher (*Die Gleichnisreden Jesu*, 2:211).

280. E.g., Derrett, "Nisi Dominus Aedificaverit Domum," 252.

281. *Jesus and the Victory of God*, p. 405.

282. *Interpreting the Parables* (Philadelphia: Westminster, 1960), p. 65.

283. Hultgren, *The Parables of Jesus*, p. 140. He may be influenced by Christophe Singer, "La difficulté d'être disciple: Luc 14/25-35," *ETR* (1998): 21-36, who argues that the parables urge

readers to take account of the insufficiency of their lives and the impossibility of being a disciple. The parables then open a new system from this defeat.

284. *The Synoptic Gospels,* 2:515.

Notes to "Parables about Money"

1. Most obviously in his version of the Beatitudes in 6:20-26 and in 12:33-34 and 14:33. For discussion of Luke's economic concerns see Robert J. Karris, "Poor and Rich: The Lukan *Sitz im Leben,*" in *Perspectives on Luke-Acts,* ed. Charles H. Talbert (Danville: Association of Baptist Professors of Religion, 1978), pp. 112-25. He argues that Luke is more concerned with those who have money than with the poor. For example, he argues that the parable of the Rich Fool is addressed to the rich in Luke's community who neglect the Christian poor. But must we think that every text in Luke is targeted at a need in his community?

2. Note Luke T. Johnson's comment (*The Literary Function of Possessions in Luke-Acts* [SBLDS 39; Missoula: Scholars, 1977], p. 221) that "Luke sees possessions as a primary symbol of human existence, an immediate exteriorization of and manifestation of the self."

3. Joachim Jeremias, *The Parables of Jesus* (trans. S. H. Hooke; New York: Charles Scribner's Sons, 1963), p. 165.

4. See also Philo, *Leg.* 3.227; Josephus, *Ant.* 1.227.

5. 1QH 18.29-30 seems to equate, or at least associate, wealth and robbery. See also the warnings against wealth in 4Q416, 417, and 418 (which are copies of the same document).

6. Seneca's moral essays and letters deserve to be read. From his *Epistulae Morales* see especially 17 ("On Philosophy and Riches"), 110 ("On True and False Riches"), and 115 ("On the Superficial Blessings").

7. See above, pp. 280-81.

8. For a detailed study arguing that *Gos. Thom.* 72 is dependent on Luke, see Tjitze Baarda, "Luke 12, 13-14: Text and Transmission from Marcion to Augustine," in *Christianity, Judaism and Other Greco-Roman Cults,* ed. Jacob Neusner (Leiden: Brill, 1975), 1:107-62, esp. 149-55.

9. Kenneth Ewing Bailey, *Through Peasant Eyes: More Lucan Parables, Their Culture and Style* (Grand Rapids: Eerdmans, 1980) p. 61. The suggestion is difficult to verify.

10. The unjust judge is described as not fearing God (Luke 18:2, 4) and the Pharisee and tax collector pray to God (Luke 18:11, 13).

11. Charles W. Hedrick (*Parables as Poetic Fictions: The Creative Voice of Jesus* [Peabody: Hendrickson, 1994]. pp. 147-48, 155-57) focuses on ancient practices in storing grain, but I do not find this helpful for interpreting the parable.

12. With the words "judge or divider" *(kritēn ē meristēn)* in v. 14 some see an allusion to Exod 2:14 where similar words are used of Moses. Acts 7:27 and 35 quote Exod 2:14 in a Septuagintal form, which has "ruler and judge" *(archonta kai dikastēn).* Whether Luke 12:14 intends to allude to this OT verse, but using a different textual tradition, is doubtful. (There are textual variants in manuscripts of Luke that are closer to the LXX.) Those who see an allusion to Exod 2:14 interpret the statement in terms of a second-Moses christology, which Jesus either rejects or modifies. See J. Duncan M. Derrett, "The Rich Fool: A Parable of Jesus Concerning Inheritance," in *Studies in the New Testament* (Leiden: Brill, 1978), 2:99-120, 101-2; Gerhard Maier, "Verteilt Jesus die Güter dieser Erde?" *TBei* 5 (1974): 149-58. Because of the second Moses allusions, Maier views the request in 12:13 as a messianic temptation, and T. Gorringe more explic-

itly views the request as a temptation stemming from Zealots who want Jesus to divide to Jewish brothers the inheritance of the restored Israel ("A Zealot Option Rejected? Luke 12:13-14," *ExpTim* 98 [1987]: 267-70).

13. See Ps 133:1, but note the attendant difficulties in Gen 13:3-7 and apparently Matt 6:24/ Luke 16:13.

14. The language is from Bailey, *Through Peasant Eyes*, p. 60.

15. E.g., *Letter of Aristeas* 277; Josephus, *Ant.* 7.37; Diodorus Siculus (21.1.4) called it "the metropolis of all evil deeds," and Dio Chrysostom (*Oratio* 17 ["On Covetousness"]:6) called it "the cause of the greatest evils." See also Eph 5:5 and Col 3:5.

16. Abraham Malherbe, "The Christianization of a *Topos* (Luke 12:13-34)," *NovT* 38 (1996): 123-35.

17. For other Jewish and non-Jewish parallels see Joseph A. Fitzmyer, *The Gospel According to Luke X–XXIV* (AB 28B; Garden City: Doubleday, 1985), 2:973, and Bernard Brandon Scott, *Hear Then the Parable: A Commentary on the Parables of Jesus* (Minneapolis: Fortress, 1989), pp. 135-36.

18. See Stephen L. Wailes, *Medieval Allegories of Jesus' Parables* (Berkeley: University of California Press, 1987), pp. 219-20.

19. E.g., Herman Hendrickx, *The Parables of Jesus* (San Francisco: Harper & Row, 1986), pp. 96-107; Fitzmyer, *The Gospel According to Luke X–XXIV*, 2:971.

20. John Dominic Crossan, "Parable and Example in the Teaching of Jesus," *NTS* 18 (1971-72): 285-307, here pp. 296-97.

21. B. Scott, *Hear Then the Parable*, pp. 138-40.

22. N. T. Wright, *Jesus and the Victory of God*, vol. 2 of *Christian Origins and the Question of God* (Minneapolis: Fortress, 1996), p. 331.

23. *Parables as Poetic Fictions*, pp. 142-63.

24. Mary Ann Beavis, "The Foolish Landowner (Luke 12:16b-20)" in *Jesus and His Parables*, ed. V. George Shillington (Edinburgh: T. & T. Clark, 1997), pp. 55-68. She draws this conclusion because she rewrites the story and suggests that the man was killed in a peasant uprising. She does this to avoid the idea of God taking the man's life.

25. The authenticity of this parable is not usually questioned. The decision of the Jesus Seminar was to print both Luke 12:16-20 and *Gos. Thom.* 63 with pink ink. See Robert W. Funk, Bernard Brandon Scott, and James R. Butts, *The Parables of Jesus: Red Letter Edition* (Sonoma: Polebridge, 1988), p. 52. A few scholars reject the authenticity of the parable and its context. Michael D. Goulder (*Luke, A New Paradigm* [Sheffield: Sheffield Academic, 1989], pp. 534-39) does so because of his view of the way Luke used Matthew and because of Lukan stylistic traits. Bernhard Heininger (*Metaphorik, Erzählstruktur und szenisch-dramatische Gestaltung in den Sondergutgleichnissen bei Lukas* [NTAbh 24; Münster: Aschendorff, 1991], pp. 110 and 117-21) does so because these verses do not critique wealth per se (such as Matt 19:24/Mark 10:25/Luke 18:25) but only trusting in wealth. Neither scholar has received much acceptance, and rightly so.

26. Minor variations also exist in v. 20 concerning the word order and whether the verb "ask" is the simple *aitousin* or the compound *apaitousin*.

27. A few manuscripts have only "Let the one having ears to hear hear."

28. "Luke XII.16ff. and the Gospel of Thomas," *JTS* 13 (1962): 332-36.

29. Jeremias, *The Parables of Jesus*, pp. 164-65.

30. Contra Fitzmyer (*The Gospel According to Luke X–XXIV*, 2:971) who knows *Gos. Thom.* is secondary, yet uses it to demonstrate that these sayings were originally independent. See above, p. 393.

31. E.g., 12:42-46, 53. Hendrickx (*The Parables of Jesus,* p. 98) suggests that the saying was retained to show that Jesus did not want his disciples and the leaders of the community mixed up in disputes about possessions, but would vv. 13-14 by themselves make that point?

32. On a text-pragmatic plane v. 21 is only a repetition of v. 15 as an instruction to the disciples. It signals the need to apply the text to life. See Walter Magass, "Zur Semiotik der Hausfrömmigkeit (Lk 12, 16-21). Die Beispielerzählung 'Vom reichen Kornbauer,'" *LB* 4 (1971): 2-5, here p. 4.

33. Verse 21 is ethical instruction based on an implied eschatology. See Greg W. Forbes, *The God of Old: the Role of the Lukan Parables in the Purpose of Luke's Gospel* (JSNTSup 198; Sheffield: Sheffield Academic, 2000), p. 86.

34. "Parable and Example in the Teaching of Jesus," 296-97. Crossan presumes that *Gos. Thom.* 63 is earlier, which few would accept for this parable, even though he grants that Luke is more original and effective if this is an example story.

35. *Hear Then the Parable,* pp. 134, 138-40. He thinks the bountiful harvest can only point to a miracle from God and is a metaphor for the kingdom. He entitles the parable "How to Mismanage a Miracle."

36. *Hear Then the Parable,* p. 139.

37. See above, pp. 13-15 and 350-52.

38. Contra S. Aalen, "St. Luke's Gospel and the Last Chapters of 1 Enoch," *NTS* 13 (1967): 1-13; and Heininger, *Metaphorik, Erzählstruktur und szenisch-dramatische Gestaltung in den Sondergutgleichnissen bei Lukas,* p. 114. See especially George W. E. Nickelsburg, "Riches, The Rich, and God's Judgment in 1 Enoch 92–105 and the Gospel According to Luke," *NTS* 25 (1978): 324-44.

39. E.g., see the parable of the Unjust Judge, p. 456 herein.

40. See above, pp. 390-93 and especially Psalm 49.

41. As Mary Ann Beavis does. See her "The Foolish Landowner," pp. 55-68.

42. Hedrick, *Parables as Poetic Fictions,* pp. 158-61. He argues that the parable is nihilistic and offers no hope, future, meaning, or theology, but only despair, death, and absurdity. He is left with such a negative picture because he deleted the intrusion of the divine voice in v. 20 from his "originating core" and viewed v. 21 as Luke's moralizing application (pp. 143 and 151).

43. Even if this were not the case, chronological features of parables should not be pushed unless the story itself gives grounds for doing so. Parable chronology is often collapsed and curtailed.

44. Bailey, *Through Peasant Eyes,* p. 65.

45. Cf. Hedrick, *Parables as Poetic Fictions,* p. 159. On soliloquy see Philip Sellew, "Interior Monologue as a Narrative Device in the Parables of Luke," *JBL* 111 (1992): 239-53.

46. The suggestion that the possessions are meant derives from Frank Stagg (*Studies in Luke's Gospel* [Nashville: Convention, 1965], pp. 90-91); that mistreated neighbors are meant is a result of Beavis's attempt ("The Foolish Landowner," pp. 65-66) to protect God from being involved in the man's death. Neither of these suggestions has merit.

47. Note also Luke 12:48 where a divine passive ("much will be required") stands parallel to the use of the third person plural ("they will ask him more"; NRSV "even more will be demanded").

48. Marius Reiser, *Jesus and Judgment: The Eschatological Proclamation in Its Jewish Context* (trans. Linda M. Maloney; Minneapolis: Fortress, 1997), pp. 270-73. As he points out, the agent is not to be mentioned because the reader or hearer knows who the subject is.

49. Jeremias (*The Parables of Jesus,* p. 165) argues that the reference is to future eschato-

logical judgment and is followed by several, such as David Peter Seccombe, *Possessions and the Poor in Luke-Acts* (Linz: Fuchs, 1983), p. 143; and Madeleine I. Boucher, *The Parables* (Wilmington: Michael Glazier, 1981), p. 127. Against this approach see Egbert W. Seng, "Der Reiche Tor," *NovT* 20 (1978): 136-55; and Fitzmyer, *The Gospel According to Luke X–XXIV*, 2:971.

50. Mary Ann Beavis ("The Foolish Landowner," pp. 55-68) worries that Luke's version of this parable presents a negative view of God, for it presents God as a cruel patriarch who kills humans. She sees the involvement of God in the man's death as a "poisonous pedagogy" (p. 67), which led her to suggest that the man's mistreated neighbors were responsible for his death. The parable is much more nuanced than her portrayal. It describes the man's death, not his executioner. Jesus and the NT writers are not squeamish about judgment, but this parable neither focuses on death as judgment nor is explicit that God takes the man's life. However, this could be implied and would fit with Acts 5:1-11; 12:20-23. Death and its capacity to intrude at any time are presupposed realities, realities the man did not consider.

51. For the idea of the soul on loan see especially Wis 15:8.

52. Hedrick, *Parables as Poetic Fictions*, p. 161, although he thinks the original version was ultimately nihilistic.

53. Although sometimes debated, "life" *(zōē)* in this verse refers to life on this earth as God intended it, not merely salvation or spiritual life.

54. *If* one could be sure of C. F. Evans's hypothesis that Luke's travel narrative coheres thematically with Deut 1–26 ("The Central Section of Luke's Gospel," in *Jesus and the Gospels*, ed. D. E. Nineham [Oxford: Blackwell, 1955], pp. 37-53), interpretation of this parable would be set parallel to Deut 12:17-27 (concerning where tithes may be eaten). The parallels are superficial at best. Actually Deut 12:6-12 would be more helpful since it directs people to eat their tithes before God with their families, their servants, and the Levites, rejoicing in their work in which God has blessed them, not doing what is right in their own eyes.

55. John Nolland, *Luke 9:21–18:34* (WBC 35B; Dallas: Word, 1993), p. 687.

56. Ambrose poignantly commented that the rich man has storage plenty in the mouths of the needy (*De Nabuthe* 7). Such a comment might be expected from a bishop, but one should note that before becoming a bishop Ambrose was the wealthy governor of northern Italy. At the death of the bishop of Milan there was a political-theological struggle for a successor. Ambrose went to the cathedral to quiet the crowd, but they started chanting "Ambrose bishop." Though still unbaptized, he was elected bishop. He gave his wealth to the poor and to the church.

57. Derrett, "The Rich Fool: A Parable of Jesus Concerning Inheritance," p. 111; Nolland, *Luke 9:21–18:34*, pp. 687-88; and Scott, *Hear Then the Parable*, pp. 134-38, who suggests that the bounteous harvest implies a lean future.

58. For a practical discussion of adapting this parable, see Ronald E. Vallet, *Stepping Stones of the Steward* (Grand Rapids: Eerdmans, 1994), pp. 78-89.

59. This is one of only five parables that the Jesus Seminar grants red status to indicate that it is undoubtedly from Jesus. See Funk, Scott, and Butts, *The Parables of Jesus: Red Letter Edition*, p. 32. (The other four are the Leaven, the Good Samaritan, the Vineyard Laborers, and the *Gos. Thom.* version of the Mustard Seed.) James Breech (*The Silence of Jesus* [Philadelphia: Fortress, 1983], p. 101) even says that the wording of the Unjust Steward has been preserved perfectly intact, except for the ending.

60. *Notes on the Parables of Our Lord* (9th ed.; London: Macmillan, 1864), p. 405.

61. Stephen Irwin Wright, *The Voice of Jesus: Studies in the Interpretation of Six Gospel Parables* (Carlisle: Paternoster, 2000), pp. 190, 202-3, 206-7; Bruce D. Chilton, *A Galilean Rabbi*

and His Bible (Wilmington: Glazier, 1984), p. 122; and I. J. Du Plessis, "Philanthropy or Sarcasm? Another Look at the Parable of the Dishonest Manager," *Neot* 24 (1990): 1-20, here p. 10.

62. Such as Claus Westermann, *The Parables of Jesus in the Light of the Old Testament* (trans. Friedemann W. Golka and Alastair H. B. Logan; Minneapolis: Fortress, 1990), p. 189.

63. *The Parables of Jesus,* pp. 46-48, but unlike some Jeremias thought the exhortation on money that various people added in vv. 8b-13 was already implicit in the parable. In his view the additions actualize the parable.

64. *The Parables of Jesus,* pp. 45-46.

65. *The Hellenistic Commentary to the New Testament,* ed. M. Eugene Boring, Klaus Berger, and Carlsten Colpe (Nashville: Abingdon, 1995), pp. 226-27, lists the "Teaching of the mayor and vizier of Ptahhotep," in several versions from the sixteenth to the tenth century B.C., but the date is problematic, the translation debated, and the relevance questionable. It does apparently speak of using money to acquire standing with friends and to be welcomed by them. The text is available as well in *ANET,* p. 413. Hultgren (*The Parables of Jesus,* p. 147) points to a passage in Herodotus (2.121) which relates an old Egyptian tale (from the twelfth century B.C.) of a shrewd man who outwits a king and is praised and rewarded for his shrewdness.

66. Quoted in full by David Daube, "Neglected Nuances of Exposition in Luke-Acts," in *ANRW* 25.3, ed. Wolfgang Haase (Berlin: Walter de Gruyter, 1985), pp. 2329-56, here p. 2335.

67. Bernd Kollmann ("Jesus als jüdischer Gleichnisdicter," *NTS* 50 [2004]: 457-75, here pp. 471-72) suggests that *Mekilta Baḥodesh* 5.81-92 is a significant parallel, but it only mentions an agent under suspicion and has little relevance for this parable.

68. See *b. Baba Meṣiʿa* 62b, 65a-b, 75a and the discussion of J. Duncan M. Derrett, "The Parable of the Unjust Steward," in *Law in New Testament* (London: Darton, Longman, and Todd, 1976), pp. 48-77, 65-66; and his "'Take Thy Bond . . . and Write Fifty' (Luke XVI.6): The Nature of the Bond," in *Studies in the NT I* (Leiden: Brill, 1977), pp. 1-3, for examples of contracts with interest included but not stipulated. The attempt to avoid usury is obvious in *m. Baba Meṣiʿa* 5.9, which prohibits borrowing of wheat on the promise of repaying at threshing time for fear that the price would increase. A person must have a prospect of repaying at the current cost. A woman may not borrow bread without attempting to determine the value in money in case the price goes up. However, Josephus (*Ant.* 4.266-70) seems only to prohibit lending food and drink on usury, and Jewish contracts exist with interest included. See DJD 2:100-104 and 240-43.

69. In Greek other parables in this section beginning with a question look similar; cf. *tis anthrōpos* in 15:4 and *tis gynē* in 15:8.

70. See Douglas E. Oakman, "Jesus and Agrarian Palestine: The Factor of Debt," in *Society of Biblical Literature 1985 Seminar Papers,* ed. Kent Harold Richards (Atlanta: Scholars, 1985), p. 71; James Breech, *The Silence of Jesus* (Philadelphia: Fortress, 1983), pp. 107-8; and Jeremias, *The Parables of Jesus,* p. 181. Nolland (*Luke 9:21–18:34,* p. 799) suggests that the size of the wheat debt is the yield of 200 acres. Josephus gives two different valuations of the *kor* in *Ant.* 3.321 and 15.314.

71. See Jeremias, *The Parables of Jesus,* p. 181; Herzog, *Parables as Subversive Speech,* pp. 249-51.

72. Derrett, "The Parable of the Unjust Steward," p. 52. See *b. Giṭṭin* 77b: "The hand of a slave is as the hand of his master" and the same or similar sayings in *b. Baba Meṣiʿa* 96a; *b. Qiddušin* 43a; and *b. Baba Qamma* 113b. Regarding no agency for wrong doing, see *b. B. Qam.* 51a, 79a; and *b. Qiddušin* 42b. That it is "a legal presumption that an agent carries out his mission," see *b. ʿErubin* 31b.

73. Several letters and contracts from the ancient world provide parallels to the parable: a

loan of wheat to be paid back at 150 percent, exhortations to report on accounts, suspicions concerning accounts, contracts with directions and penalties, and corn collectors using wrong measures. See *Select Papyri I* (LCL), pp. 202-3, 330-31, 350-53 and *Select Papyri II*, pp. 10-35 (especially 20-23) and 59-75 (especially 64-65).

74. See the summary of recent interpretation of this parable by Dennis J. Ireland, *Stewardship and the Kingdom of God: An Historical, Exegetical, and Contextual Study of the Parable of the Unjust Steward in Luke 16:1-13* (NovTSup 70; Leiden: Brill, 1992), pp. 5-47; Michael Krämer, *Das Rätsel der Parabel vom ungerechten Verwalter, Lk 16,1-13. Auslegungsgeschichte — Umfang — Sinn. Eine Diskussion der Probleme und Lösungsvorschläge der Verwalterparabel von den Vätern bis heute* (BiblScRel 5; Zurich: PAS, 1972).

75. See Wailes, *Medieval Allegories of Jesus' Parables,* pp. 247-53. Augustine (*Quaestiones Evangeliorum* 2.34) commented that not all things about the steward were to be imitated and that this parable, as some others, teaches by contraries.

76. See especially Ireland, *Stewardship and the Kingdom of God;* Seccombe, *Possessions and the Poor in Luke-Acts,* pp. 160-72.

77. *Die Gleichnisreden Jesu* (2 vols.; Freiburg i. B.: J. C. B. Mohr, 1888-89), 2:495-514, especially 510-11.

78. *The Parables of Jesus,* pp. 45-48 and 181-82.

79. "The Parable of the Unjust Steward," pp. 48-77.

80. Joseph A. Fitzmyer, "The Story of the Dishonest Manager (Lk 16:1-13)," in *Essays on the Semitic Background of the New Testament* (Missoula: Scholars, 1974), pp. 161-84. He and others point to Josephus, *Ant.* 18.157, which reports a contract written at 20,000 drachmas, but the borrower was forced to take 2500 less. This was an attempt by the one making the loan to recover money of which he had been defrauded. Several earlier explanations that the steward reduced his own commission have been offered. See especially Paul Gächter, "The Parable of the Dishonest Steward after Oriental Conceptions," *CBQ* 12 (1950): 121-31.

Note that Kierkegaard reflected on the steward's actions as if the money owed was his own, even though Kierkegaard knew it was not. He encouraged people to follow the steward's example but to use their own money. See *Søren Kierkegaard's Journals and Papers* (6 vols., ed. and trans. Howard V. Hong and Edna H. Hong; Bloomington: Indiana University Press, 1967), 1:185.

81. *Poet and Peasant: A Literary Cultural Approach to the Parables in Luke* (Grand Rapids: Eerdmans, 1976), pp. 86-118.

82. "The Parable of the Unjust Steward (Luke 16:1-13): Irony *Is* the Key," in *The Bible in Three Dimensions,* ed. David J. A. Clines, et al. (Sheffield: JSOT, 1990), pp. 127-53. See also Du Plessis, "Philanthropy or Sarcasm? Another Look at the Parable of the Dishonest Manager," 1-20; and Donald R. Fletcher, "The Riddle of the Unjust Steward: Is Irony the Key?" *JBL* 82 (1963): 15-30. See also n. 93 below and Paul Trudinger's suggestion of sarcasm.

83. "Jesus' Opinion about the Essenes," in his *Judaism and the Origins of Christianity* (Jerusalem: Magnes, 1988), pp. 150-68; see also "The Parable of the Unjust Steward: Jesus' Criticism of the Essenes," in *Jesus and the Dead Sea Scrolls,* ed. James H. Charlesworth (New York: Doubleday, 1992), pp. 176-97. Brad H. Young (*The Parables: Jewish Tradition and Christian Interpretation* [Peabody: Hendrickson, 1998], pp. 232-48), Flusser's student, combines Flusser's approach and Bailey's and concludes the parable both ridicules the Essenes and teaches that God's grace is unlimited (because the master in the story is gracious and loves the people). C-S Abraham Cheong (*A Dialogic Reading of the Steward Parable [Luke 16:1-9]* [Studies in Biblical Litera-

ture 28; New York: Peter Lang, 2001], p. 109) thinks the "sons of light" is a pejorative title for the Pharisees.

84. "The Dishonoured Master (Luke 16,1-8a)," *Bib* 70 (1989): 474-95. See also David Landry and Ben May, "Honor Restored: New Light on the Parable of the Prudent Steward (Luke 16:1-8a)," *JBL* 119 (2000): 287-309.

85. *Jesus and the Victory of God*, pp. 332 and 638.

86. Ehrhard Kamlah, "Die Parabel vom ungerechten Verwalter (Luk. 16, 1ff.) im Rahmen der Knechtsgleichnisse," in *Abraham Unser Vater*, ed. Otto Betz, et al. (Leiden: Brill, 1963), pp. 276-94; G. Baudler, "Das Gleichnis vom 'betrügerischen Verwalter' (Lk 16, 1-8a) als Ausdruck der 'inneren Biographie' Jesu," *TGW* 28 (1985): 65-76; William Loader, "Jesus and the Rogue in Luke 16,1-8a, the Parable of the Unjust Steward," *RB* (1989): 518-32; Colin Brown, "The Unjust Steward: A New Twist?" in *Worship, Theology and Ministry in the Early Church*, ed. Michael J. Wilkins and Terence Paige (Sheffield: JSOT, 1992), pp. 121-45. Brown thinks the parable is both an indictment of usury and about the burden of sin. By way of contrast Hans-Joachim Degenhardt (*Lukas: Evangelist der Armen* [Stuttgart: Katholisches Bibelwerk, 1965], p. 118) sees the parable as addressed to the religious leaders, who are about to be put out of office, but whom Jesus calls to act wisely and relieve the burden of the people. In his view the parable was not originally about the right use of possessions.

87. *The Parables* (Philadelphia: Fortress, 1967), pp. 155-62. Via (p. 160), Breech (*The Silence of Jesus*, pp. 106-9), and John Dominic Crossan (*In Parables: The Challenge of the Historical Jesus* [New York: Harper & Row, 1973], pp. 109-10), all paint the steward in negative terms. Crossan says one gets the picture of laziness organizing itself under crisis.

88. *Hear Then the Parable*, pp. 255-66.

89. *The Gospel in Parable* (Philadelphia: Fortress, 1988), pp. 162-69.

90. See *m. Šebi'it* 10.3-4.

91. Thomas Hoeren, "Das Gleichnis vom Ungerechten Verwalter (Lukas 16:1-8a). Zugleich ein Beitrag zur Geschichte der Restschuldbefreiung," *NTS* 41 (1995): 620-29.

92. "The Dishonest Steward (Luke 16.1-8a) and Luke's Special Parable Collection," *NTS* 37 (1991): 499-515, here p. 513.

93. J. C. Wansey, "The Parable of the Unjust Steward: An Interpretation," *ExpTim* 47 (1935-36): 39-40; R. B. Y. Scott, "The Parable of the Unjust Steward (Luke xvi.1ff.)," *ExpTim* 49 (1937-38): 284-85; and Mary Ann Beavis, "Ancient Slavery as an Interpretive Context for the New Testament Servant Parables with Special Reference to the Unjust Steward (Luke 16:1-8)," *JBL* 111 (1992): 37-54, here p. 52.

Many other interpretations could be listed, but some are of questionable viability. Mary Ann Tolbert (*Perspectives on the Parables* [Philadelphia: Fortress, 1979], p. 88) finds the parable to be the basis for a stewardship of injustice when traditional morality conflicts with the well-being of an individual: ". . . the Unjust Steward makes a complicated decision to secure his own happiness and well-being at the expense of traditional ethics, and in so doing he displays a wise stewardship of injustice. . . ." Similarly Andrew Parker (*Painfully Clear: The Parables of Jesus* [Sheffield: Sheffield Academic, 1996], pp. 155-56) argues the thrust of the story is that *"since it is seeking life that counts, giving up and dying because that is what morality dictates would be plain stupid"* (italics original). Therefore, is it not right that people champion their lives rather than become slaves of the community's precepts? One shudders to think of the implications of these arguments.

William Herzog (*Parables as Subversive Speech* [Lousiville: Westminster/John Knox, 1994], pp. 233-58) cannot make the parable work and only suggests that it shows how weapons of the weak can produce results. He views the entire economic system in the story as exploitive and predatory and the rich man as guilty of an endless pursuit of power and prestige. The moral content of the charge is irrelevant because no single morality governs the village. His explanation goes nowhere. For similar approaches see Justin S. Ukpong, "The Parable of the Shrewd Manager (Luke 16:1-13): An Essay in Inculturation Biblical Hermeneutic," *Semeia* 73 (1996): 189-210; and Stephen I. Wright, "Parables on Poverty and Riches (Luke 12:13-21; 16:1-13; 16:19-31)," in *The Challenge of Jesus' Parables,* ed. Richard N. Longenecker (Grand Rapids: Eerdmans, 2000), pp. 217-39.

Paul Trudinger even wonders whether Jesus had a specific meaning in mind or only intended to engage his hearers in discussion. He suggests that v. 9 is oxymoronic sarcasm, an exhortation to retain a good sense of humor. Because of a commitment to polyvalence (which is not really polyvalence, for he thinks interpretation must be tied to the historical situation), following Herzog, he suggests that Jesus told the story in anger to expose the depth of oppression. See his "Exposing the Depth of Oppression (Luke 16:1b-8a): The Parable of the Unjust Steward," in *Jesus and His Parables,* ed. V. George Shillington (Edinburgh: T. & T. Clark, 1997), pp. 121-37, and his "Ire or Irony? The Enigmatical Character of the Parable of the Dishonest Steward (Luke 16:1-13)," *The Downside Review* 116 (1998): 85-102, which offers both an ironical reading and one with Jesus angry at oppression.

94. Dave L. Mathewson, "The Parable of the Unjust Steward (Luke 16:1-13): A Reexamination of the Traditional View in Light of Recent Challenges," *JETS* 38 (1995): 29-39, here p. 31.

95. See especially the arguments of Bailey, *Poet and Peasant,* pp. 87-94; Kloppenborg, "The Dishonoured Master," 479-86; and Ireland, *Stewardship and the Kingdom of God,* pp. 79-82. As several point out, if the steward were overcharging, he would hardly be accepted into the homes of the debtors.

96. A Hebraic genitive meaning a steward characterized by unrighteousness. Although debated, Hans Kosmala's suggestion ("The Parable of the Unjust Steward in the Light of Qumran," *ASTI* 3 [1964]: 114-21) that nothing is intended about the steward's character other than that he is a person of this world in which unrighteousness is the ruling principle is unacceptable.

97. "The Dishonoured Master," 483-84. One point in favor of thinking interest might be in mind is C. F. Evans's Deuteronomy hypothesis concerning Luke's travel narrative. *If* this theory is valid, Luke 16:1-18 is parallel to Deut 23:15–24:4, which includes instructions for Israelites to take in runaway slaves (receive into their houses?) and instructions concerning usury. See above, p. 345, n. 65 and also Craig A. Evans, "Luke 16:1-18 and the Deuteronomy Hypothesis," in *Luke and Scripture,* ed. Craig A. Evans and James Sanders (Minneapolis: Augsburg/Fortress, 1993), pp. 121-39, especially 134. One should not draw conclusions about the cultural issues on such a questionable basis, and I do not think interest is a factor in the parable at all.

98. "Philanthropy or Sarcasm? Another Look at the Parable of the Dishonest Manager," 8. Cf. Richard Bauckham, "The Rich Man and Lazarus: The Parable and the Parallels," in *The Fate of the Dead* (NovTSup 93; Leiden: Brill, 1998), pp. 97-118, here p. 104 (with regard to a different parable): "What is not stated is not relevant."

99. I do not see any basis for the suggestion of a few (e.g., Hultgren, *The Parables of Jesus,* p. 150) that the steward's actions are an attempt to get even.

100. One who sees v. 7 as the end is Hans Weder, *Die Gleichnisse Jesu als Metaphern. Traditions- und redaktionsgeschichtliche Analysen und Interpretationen* (4th ed.; Göttingen: Vandenhoeck & Ruprecht, 1990), pp. 262-63.

101. Nolland's comment (*Luke 9:21–18:34,* p. 800) that Jesus does not elsewhere in an ap-

plication comment on a character in a parable does not have force, for this parable is not like other parables. Further, while all parables have at least an implicit evaluation of the characters, Jesus does comment explicitly on characters in some parables. See the Friend at Midnight (Luke 11:8), the Banquet (14:24), the Unjust Judge (18:6), and the Pharisee and the Tax Collector (18:14).

102. See especially Richard H. Hiers, "Friends by Unrighteous Mammon: The Eschatological Proletariat (Luke 16:9)," *JAAR* 38 (1970): 30-36, here pp. 32-33. Fletcher ("The Riddle of the Unjust Steward: Is Irony the Key?" 20) attributes much of the implausible exegesis of this parable to the attempt to remove v. 9. He argues further that v. 9 is not self-contained, but rather "leans on the parable." Heininger (*Metaphorik, Erzählstruktur und szenisch-dramatische Gestaltung in den Sondergutgleichnissen bei Lukas*, p. 169) is alone in arguing that v. 4 was framed on v. 9 rather than the reverse. This results from his attempt to see the soliloquy in this parable as a Lukan creation.

103. Hiers, "Friends by Unrighteous Mammon: The Eschatological Proletariat (Luke 16:9)," 36; Krämer, *Das Rätsel der Parabel vom ungerechten Verwalter, Lk 16,1-13*, pp. 236-38; Ireland, *Stewardship and the Kingdom of God*, pp. 91-105; Seccombe, *Possessions and the Poor in Luke-Acts*, pp. 161-63; and Chilton, *A Galilean Rabbi and His Bible*, pp. 119-21.

104. As Markus Barth points out ("The Dishonest Steward and His Lord, Reflections on Luke 16:1-13," in *From Faith to Faith*, ed. Dikran Y. Hadidian [Pittsburgh: Pickwick, 1979], pp. 65-74, here p. 66), if Luke thought the parable needed correcting he could more easily have omitted it, like the other Evangelists.

105. Ireland, *Stewardship and the Kingdom of God*, pp. 105-15; and possibly Porter, "The Parable of the Unjust Steward (Luke 16:1-13): Irony *Is* the Key," p. 130. Hendrickx (*The Parables of Jesus*, p. 191) says that we may accept without doubt that v. 13 and the parable belong to the same *Sitz im Leben* and may have originated on the same occasion. Some who do not take v. 9 with the parable see vv. 9-13 as a unit. See Bailey, *Poet and Peasant*, pp. 110-17, who argues that vv. 9-13 are a poem.

106. *Poet and Peasant*, p. 114. See also Fitzmyer, "The Story of the Dishonest Manager," pp. 169-70; and the wordplay on *mammon* at *Num. Rab.* 22.8.

107. *The Parables of Jesus*, pp. 45-46; also Luise Schottroff, *The Parables of Jesus* (trans. Linda M. Maloney; Minneapolis: Fortress, 2006), pp. 157 and 160. The word *kyrios* occurs more frequently than Jeremias suggests and more frequently of Jesus. Occurrences in the vocative cannot be ignored. *Kyrios* occurs frequently for masters in parables, often with a qualifier such as a personal pronoun.

108. 12:36, 37, 42, 43, 45, 46, 47; 14:21, 23; 16:3, 5(2), 13; 20:13, 15 and in the vocative at 13:8, 25; 14:22; 19:16, 18, 20, 25.

109. Goulder (*Luke: A New Paradigm*, p. 625) argues that Jeremias's position on v. 8a is "multiply forced," and he points out that every other Lukan parable that starts with "A certain man" keeps the man in the story to the end. Kamlah ("Die Parabel vom ungerechten Verwalter (Luk. 16, 1ff.) im Rahmen der Knechtsgleichnisse," p. 286) says that the judgment of a master over a servant's activity is the common point of departure of all servant parables.

110. On the latter see both Barth, "The Dishonest Steward and His Lord," p. 72; and Young, *The Parables*, pp. 237, 242, and 247. Young even says that the master loves the people; he takes the parable as a parable of God's grace.

111. Kloppenborg, "The Dishonoured Master," pp. 487-88. Daube ("Neglected Nuances of Exposition in Luke-Acts," p. 2235) goes so far as to say that "the tycoon, embodiment of mam-

mon, is the villain of the plot." See also Hans J. B. Combrink, "A Social-Scientific Perspective on the Parable of the Unjust Steward," *Neot* 30 (1996): 281-306.

112. The rich man is presented negatively in the description of his life and his ignoring Lazarus, not merely in the word "rich." Note that *euphrainō* ("enjoy," "celebrate") is used negatively in 12:19 and 16:19 of the excesses of the rich but positively in 15:23, 24, 29, and 32 of the return of the prodigal.

113. See Hendrickx, *The Parables of Jesus*, p. 174; and Bailey, *Poet and Peasant*, p. 88. As Ronald A. Piper points out ("Social Background and Thematic Structure in Luke 16," in *The Four Gospels: Festschrift Frans Neirynck*, ed. F. Van Segbroeck, et al. [Leuven: University Press, 1992], 2.1637-62, see p. 1640), if the honor issues were clearly understood by Mediterranean readers, why did Luke not recognize this and use the parable more effectively? On the other hand, I see no basis for Piper's seeing an intra-church problem that Luke addresses with this parable.

114. *Contra* Jeremias, *The Parables of Jesus*, p. 47; and Nolland, *Luke 9:21–18:34*, p. 800, who say the steward acted for the benefit of others rather than for himself. From every indication in the parable he acts to save his own hide.

115. Was the original charge true or false? The parable presumes that the charges were valid, especially in light of any lack of protest on the steward's part. Contra Mary Ann Beavis who argues ("Ancient Slavery as an Interpretive Context for the New Testament Servant Parables with Special Reference to the Unjust Steward," 48) that *diaballō* (16:1) usually means "accuse falsely." The word could be used of accusations without malice or falsehood or of giving hostile information without any implication of falsehood. See LSJ, p. 390. Certainly the word is not necessarily about false charges since a compound of it *(endiaballein)* can be used of the confrontation of Balaam by the angel of the Lord (LXX Num 22:22).

116. "Ancient Slavery as an Interpretive Context for the New Testament Servant Parables with Special Reference to the Unjust Steward," 46-47. The stories are found in *Life of Aesop* 3,50a and Perotti's index to *Phaedrus* 17.

117. *Metaphorik, Erzählstruktur und szenisch-dramatische Gestaltung in den Sondergutgleichnissen bei Lukas*, p. 168. See, e.g., the comedies of Plautus (who died about 184 B.C.), *Amphitruo, Pseudolus, Epidicus, and Bacchides*, much of which draw on Greek stories.

118. See Matt 12:32; Mark 10:30/Luke 18:30. See also Robert H. Stein, *Luke* (NAC 24; Nashville: Broadman, 1992), pp. 414-15.

119. Nolland, *Luke 9:21–18:34*, p. 801 (following Kloppenborg), argues that the contrast between the sons of this age and the sons of light is difficult to attribute to Jesus, but if indeed Jesus distinguished this age and the coming one, such a contrast would be easy. It is worth remembering that the expressions "sons of light" and "children of light" are not frequently used of Christians, the former appearing elsewhere only at John 12:36 and 1 Thess 5:5, the latter only at Eph 5:8. "Sons of light," of course, occurs frequently in the Qumran Scrolls. See 1QS 1.9; 2.16; 3.13; 1QM 1.3, 9, 11, 13, et al.

120. See 1QS 6.2, 19; CD 14.20; m. 'Abot 2.12; m. Ketubot 2.9; 3.2; Exod. Rab. 31.5; Pirqe Rabbi Eliezer 26. See also Hans Peter Rüger, "Μαμωνᾶς," *ZNW* 64 (1973): 127-31, who provides numerous references.

121. Especially in the targums where one finds *mammon dišqar* ("mammon of falsehood," i.e., unjust gain): *Targum Neofiti* and *Targum Pseudo-Jonathan Exod.* 18:21; *Targum 1 Sam.* 12:3; *Targum 2 Sam* 14:14; *Targum Isa.* 5:23; 33:15; *Targum Ezek.* 22:27; *Targum Hos.* 5:11.

122. Flusser ("The Parable of the Unjust Steward," pp. 178-80) and Kosmala ("The Parable of the Unjust Steward in the Light of Qumran," 116) point to similar phrases from Qumran to

argue for money that is part of this world, which especially for Kosmala makes money an evil thing. "Wealth of evil" (*hon harish'ah*) appears at CD 6.15; 8.5; 4Q183 5 and "wealth of violence" (*hon hamas*) at 1QS 10.19. Chilton (*A Galilean Rabbi and His Bible*, pp. 117-22) points to *Targum Isa.* 5:23 and 33:15 as verification that the expression conveys the idea of bribery (see the previous note). Fitzmyer ("The Story of the Dishonest Manager," p. 183) argues that money tends to lead to dishonesty.

123. Cf. 1 Tim 6:10.

124. Apparently the intent of the NRSV. See also 1 Macc 3:29.

125. A few inferior manuscripts have *eklipēte* ("when you are gone"), a change that makes the reference to death obvious.

126. Stein, *Luke*, p. 416.

127. Cf. *T. Ab.* 20:10, 12, where angels carry Abraham's soul away at death.

128. See pp. 398-99; and Thomas E. Schmidt, *Hostility to Wealth in the Synoptic Gospels* (JSNTSup 15; Sheffield: Sheffield Academic, 1987), p. 153.

129. See J. F. McFadyen, "The Parable of the Unjust Steward," *ExpTim* 37 (1925-26): 535-39, especially 536. The only parallel to Luke's expression is *4 Ezra* 2:11, but that could be dependent on Luke. Eccl 12:5 has "eternal home."

130. LXX: *Paroikēsō en tō skēnōmati sou eis tous aiōnas*. See also Heb 8:2; 9:11; Rev 21:3.

131. *b. Baba Batra* 75a says "the Holy One . . . will in time to come make a tabernacle for the righteous from the skin of Leviathan." See also 2 Cor 5:1; *1 En.* 39:4.

132. Unless one thinks the parable is a biography of Jesus' own actions and that he is accused by the Pharisees of squandering Israel's religious resources. Some have suggested that the Pharisees are accused of squandering their tradition, but the parable is not about squandering and it is difficult to see what the parable would intend for them.

133. See especially Hendrickx, *The Parables of Jesus*, pp. 192-94; Nolland, *Luke 9:21–18:34*, pp. 802 and 808. The parable is not merely about relations with God as Hultgren (*The Parables of Jesus*, p. 154) and Heininger (*Metaphorik, Erzählstruktur und szenisch-dramatische Gestaltung in den Sondergutgleichnissen bei Lukas*, p. 174) suggest.

134. Hendrickx, *The Parables of Jesus*, pp. 192-93.

135. See Ireland, *Stewardship and the Kingdom of God*, pp. 82-83. Of nine NT occurrences of the adjective *phronimos* eight are in parables and carry eschatological connotations: Matt 7:24; 24:45; 25:2, 4, 8, 9; Luke 12:42; 16:8. The remaining occurrence is in Matt 10:16. Ireland argues correctly (p. 156) that eschatology is the fundamental theological context for the teaching on possessions in Luke-Acts.

136. Schmidt (*Hostility to Wealth in the Synoptic Gospels*, p. 154) argues that the parable is more about dispossession of wealth than charity.

137. Du Plessis, "Philanthropy or Sarcasm? Another Look at the Parable of the Dishonest Manager," 14-15.

138. See Seccombe, *Possessions and the Poor in Luke-Acts*, p. 167, who points out that while money belongs to this evil age, it can be converted and used appropriately for the kingdom.

139. In the parable of the Sheep and the Goats the parabolic element is limited to the analogy of a shepherd dividing his flock (Matt 25:32-33). The depiction of judgment drops the parabolic form.

140. The story fits G. Sellin's category of "dramatic triangle" parables, which have two persons of equal status but different function and a third person that functions as an authority figure. See his "Lukas as Gleichniserzähler. Die Erzählung vom barmherzigen Samariter (Lk 10:25-37)," *ZNW* 65 (1974): 166-89, here p. 180. This pattern reappears in other "A certain man"

parables in Luke. These dramatic triangle parables emphasize a reversal of expectations. See also Craig Blomberg, *Interpreting the Parables* (Downers Grove: InterVarsity, 1990), pp. 171-253.

141. The authenticity of the parable, especially the second part (vv. 27-31), is also an issue for some, but this is not discussed frequently. The arguments against authenticity are not strong. The Jesus Seminar was divided on vv. 19-26 and used gray print, but rejected vv. 27-31 entirely. See Funk, Scott, and Butts, *The Parables of Jesus: Red Letter Edition*, p. 64. Rudolf Bultmann (*The History of the Synoptic Tradition* [trans. John Marsh; rev. ed.; New York: Harper & Row, 1963], p. 203) considered it a Jewish story put in the mouth of Jesus. The place of vv. 27-31 will be discussed below. See pp. 427-28 herein.

142. Or "hollow places" as Greek manuscripts have it.

143. This fourfold division is unique; elsewhere only two compartments are mentioned. See Richard Bauckham, "Visiting the Places of the Dead in the Extra-Canonical Apocalypses," in *The Fate of the Dead*, pp. 86-87.

144. In effect, sexual promiscuity and love of money make one deaf to God's word, blind to one's neighbor, and crazy.

145. The story is on the back of two business documents, one dated the seventh year of Claudius (46-47 A.D.). See *Hellenistic Commentary to the New Testament*, pp. 227-28. For a more complete account see Hugo Gressmann, *Vom reichen Mann und armen Lazarus. Eine literargeschichtliche Studie* (Abhandlungen der königlich preussischen Akademie der Wissenschaften: Philosophisch-historische Klasse, 1918, no. 7), pp. 3-89.

146. *Chasmata*, the plural of the word translated "chasm" in Luke 16:26, but the word has a different reference. Cf. *1 En.* 18:11.

147. Plutarch uses Luke's expression "great chasm" (*chasma mega*) in 565E, although with a different referent. Note his assumption of reincarnation in 564C and 567E-F. In his *Consolation to His Wife* 611C-612B he comforts his wife on the death of their two-year-old daughter by assuring her that the child has passed to a place of no pain and to a better and more divine region.

148. Again *chasma mega* (590F), but again different from Luke's usage. See also Lucian, *Dialogues of the Dead* 4.421.

149. On Tantalus, see Lucian, *Dialogues of the Dead*, 7:406-8.

150. *Dialogues of the Dead* 28:426-29 tells of a man restored to life for one day to allow him to convince his recent bride to join him in death. Mention is made of the story of Orpheus who went to Hades to retrieve Eurydice. See also *Demonax* 25 and *The Dead Come to Life* for other expressions of the dead returning to life.

151. The other six are late, preserved only in medieval sources. The text of all seven versions is provided by Gressmann, who, like Jeremias and others, assumed that the Jewish versions are derived from the Egyptian. Richard Bauckham, however, argues that the Jewish versions arose independently ("Rich Man and Lazarus: The Parable and the Parallels," pp. 97-101). The story is also in *Hellenistic Commentary on the New Testament*, pp. 228-29, and is viewed by some as the background of the parable of the Feast in Luke 14:15-24. See above, pp. 303 and 311.

152. F. Schnider and W. Stenger, "Die Offene Tür und die unüberschreitbare Kluft," *NTS* 25 (1979): 273-83. If taken literally, the text says Lazarus was "thrown" (*ebebléto*) at the gate. Was he a cripple or just too weak to walk? This word is used elsewhere in connection with the sick. See Matt 8:6, 14; 9:2; Mark 7:30.

153. How does Scott (*Hear Then the Parable*, p. 159) decide that grace is the gate?

154. See Evans, "The Central Section of St. Luke's Gospel," pp. 37-53, especially 49.

155. See Craig L. Blomberg, "Midrash, Chiasmus, and the Outline of Luke's Central Sec-

tion," in *Gospel Perspectives III: Studies in Midrash and Historiography*, ed. R. T. France and David Wenham (Sheffield: JSOT, 1983), pp. 217-61, especially pp. 241-43, 247; Nolland, *Luke 9:21–18:34*, p. 825.

156. See Charles H. Talbert, *Reading Luke* (New York: Crossroad, 1982), pp. 156-59.

157. Among others, Michael Ball, "The Parables of the Unjust Steward and the Rich Man and Lazarus," *ExpTim* 106 (1994-95): 329-30; A. Feuillet, "La parabole du mauvais riche et du pauvre Lazare (Lc 16,19-31) antithèse de la parabole de l'intendant astucieux (Lc 16, 1-9)," *NRTh* 101 (1979): 212-23.

158. See Judg 8:26; Esth 8:15; Prov 31:22; Dan 5:7; Acts 16:14; Rev 18:12. The bride and the armies of the Lamb in Rev 19:7, 14 wear fine linen. Lucian, *Demonax* 41 describes a man proud of the breadth of the purple band on his clothes (cf. 1 Macc 8:14), and *Menippus* 12 during his view of the underworld describes those proud of wealth being punished harshly and reminded of their garments of purple or gold.

159. C. G. Montefiore, *The Synoptic Gospels* (2 vols.; London: Macmillan, 1927), 2:538.

160. Funeral societies were formed to insure proper burial. See Joel B. Green, *The Gospel of Luke* (NICNT; Grand Rapids: Eerdmans, 1997), p. 607.

161. Why Nolland (*Luke 9:21–18:34*, p. 829) suggests that Lazarus was translated to heaven like Enoch and Elijah is a mystery.

162. Luke does not explain the name as he sometimes does, e.g., Acts 4:36; 13:8.

163. In *Pesiqta Rabbati* 43.4 the bosom of Abraham is the place of martyrs who refuse to bow to an idol and is contrasted with the bosom of Esau for those who acquiesce and bow down. The word for "bosom" *(kolpos)* is singular in Luke 16:22 but plural in v. 23, apparently with no difference in meaning. Ronald F. Hock ("Lazarus and Micyllus: Greco-Roman Backgrounds to Luke 16:19-31," *JBL* 106 [1987]: 447-63, here p. 456) points to Greek parallels for a similar use of "bosom," particularly on epitaphs. In *4 Macc.* 13:14-17 Abraham, Isaac, and Jacob receive the righteous at death.

164. See Wailes, *Medieval Allegories of Jesus' Parables*, pp. 255-60.

165. See *St. John Chrysostom on Wealth and Poverty* (trans. and introduced by Catharine P. Roth; Crestwood: St. Vladimir's Seminary Press, 1984); and Edward Mathews, Jr., "The Rich Man and Lazarus: Almsgiving and Repentance in Early Syriac Tradition," *Diakonia* 22 (1988-89): 89-104.

166. C. H. Cave, "Lazarus and the Lukan Deuteronomy," *NTS* 15 (1969): 319-25, who thinks the description of Lazarus is based on Isa 1:5-6 and that the Gentiles are putting Israel to shame; and Wright, *Jesus and the Victory of God*, pp. 255-56.

167. *In Parables*, pp. 67-68. In effect, he wants to force the parable to be a double indirect parable.

168. Herzog (*Parables as Subversive Speech*, pp. 114-30) is none too clear about the message of the parable but thinks it codifies the relation of rich and poor and the appeals to the afterlife that justify present social arrangements. Following J. L. Segundo he suggests that wealth is not a sign of blessing and that Lazarus participates in the eschatological banquet just because he was poor. Frank W. Hughes ("The Parable of the Rich Man and Lazarus [Luke 16.19-31] and Graeco-Roman Rhetoric," in *Rhetoric and the New Testament: Essays from the 1992 Heidelberg Conference*, ed. Stanley E. Porter and Thomas H. Olbricht [Sheffield: Sheffield Academic, 1993], pp. 29-41) thinks this parable gives Luke's reason why Christian evangelization of Jews failed so miserably.

169. Unfortunately, the more a preacher says "I believe" the less evidence he or she is likely to have. The conviction that this story was historical was common among early interpret-

ers. See Wailes, *Medieval Allegories of Jesus' Parables,* p. 255. John Calvin thought it was a true story. See his *Commentary on a Harmony of the Evangelists: Matthew, Mark, and Luke* (trans. William Pringle; Grand Rapids: Eerdmans, 1949), 2:184.

170. Jeffrey Khoo ("The Reality and Eternality of Hell: Luke 16:19-31 as Proof," *STJ* 6 [1998]: 67-76) comes close. He grants that the account is a parable but still regards the story as factual.

171. Especially if Luke used a chiastic parable source; see Blomberg, "Midrash, Chiasmus, and the Outline of Luke's Central Section," pp. 240-43.

172. See p. 405 above. The identification of this narrative as a parable is explicit in the reading of Codex Bezae: "And he told them another parable."

173. Claus Westermann (*The Parables of Jesus in the Light of the Old Testament* [trans. Friedemann W. Golka and Alastair H. B. Logan; Minneapolis: Fortress, 1990], p. 188) says this passage is not a parable, but he gives no explanation or alternative. Does he mean that it is not metaphorical?

174. See Outi Lehtipuu, "Characterization and Persuasion: The Rich Man and the Poor Man in Luke 16.19-31," in *Characterization in the Gospels: Reconceiving Narrative Criticism,* ed. David Rhoads and Kari Syreeni (Sheffield: Sheffield Academic, 1999), pp. 73-105, here pp. 101-2. Luke describes the Pharisees in v. 14 as lovers of money *(philargyroi).* Is there an intentional wordplay with making friends *(philous)* in v. 9? The description of the Pharisees as "lovers of money" does not mesh easily with Josephus's statement that "the Pharisees simplify their standard of living, making no concession to luxury" (*Ant.* 18.12). Josephus was himself a Pharisee and no doubt attempted to show them in a good light, but Green (*The Gospel of Luke,* p. 601) argues that "lovers of money" was often used with descriptions of self-glorying as an accusation against false teachers. To be fair, most humans inappropriately allow themselves to be impressed with wealth.

175. Several people suggest that the rich man is a Sadducee, but that does not have much in its favor. Would Sadducees be impressed with talk of angels and torment after death? See Jones, *Studying the Parables of Jesus,* p. 170.

176. Jeremias, *The Parables of Jesus,* p. 183. See Gressmann, *Vom reichen Mann und armen Lazarus,* and above, pp. 303 and 422.

177. Only some of the relevant material is included with the primary sources above. For more complete discussions see Richard Bauckham, "Descent to the Underworld," *ABD,* 2:145-59; reprinted (along with several other pertinent articles) in *The Fate of the Dead,* pp. 9-48. See also R. Ganschinietz, "Katabasis," *PW* 10/2 (1919): 2359-2449; Martha Himmelfarb, *Tours of Hell* (Philadelphia: University of Pennsylvania Press, 1983).

178. People like Orpheus, Heracles, Persephone, Pythagoras, Elijah, and Isaiah — to name just a few.

179. The Gospel parable does not focus on the burials as the motivating factor, does not reveal the real facts to someone still alive, and does not focus on works as the cause of the reversal. See Bauckham, "The Rich Man and Lazarus: The Parable and the Parallels," pp. 99-100.

180. The conflict between the rich and the poor is a frequent subject of rhetorical declamations. See Hughes, "The Parable of the Rich Man and Lazarus (Luke 16.19-31) and Graeco-Roman Rhetoric," pp. 29-41. The denunciation of the rich for neglect of the poor is also present in Jewish works, most obviously in *1 Enoch* and Wisdom of Solomon.

181. See the several articles by Bauckham in *The Fate of the Dead,* especially "The Rich Man and Lazarus"; Hock, "Lazarus and Micyllus: Greco-Roman Backgrounds to Luke 16:19-31";

Hughes, "The Parable of the Rich Man and Lazarus (Luke 16.19-31) and Graeco-Roman Rhetoric."

182. R. Dunkerley ("Lazarus," *NTS* 5 [1959]: 321-27) and Donald J. Bretherton ("Lazarus of Bethany: Resurrection or Resuscitation?" *ExpTim* 104 [1993]: 169-73) argue that the parable was based on the actual raising of Lazarus. Keith Pearce ("The Lucan Origins of the Raising of Lazarus," *ExpTim* 96 [1985]: 359-61) and Charles F. W. Smith (*The Jesus of the Parables* [Philadelphia: United Church Press, 1975], p. 166) argue the reverse, although Pearce suggests that John presupposes stories rather than uses them. P. Trudinger ("A 'Lazarus Motif' in Primitive Christian Preaching?" *Andover Newton Quarterly* 7 [1966]: 29-32) argues that a Lazarus theme in Christian preaching shows that belief in resurrection alone (without the cross) was not sufficient.

183. For more detailed treatment see John P. Meier, *A Marginal Jew: Rethinking the Historical Jesus* 2: *Mentor, Message, and Miracles* (New York: Doubleday, 1994), pp. 822-31.

184. *History of the Synoptic Tradition,* p. 178.

185. See Crossan, *In Parables,* pp. 66-67, who lists four links between the parable and Luke 24 and the Book of Acts: disbelief, the double mention of Moses and the prophets, a resurrected person, and "they will repent" in Acts 2:38. See also Scott (*Hear Then the Parable,* pp. 142-45), who grants that Crossan's presentation of the evidence is "lean," but tries to strengthen the case; Heininger, *Metaphorik, Erzählstruktur und szenisch-dramatische Gestaltung in den Sondergutgleichnissen bei Lukas,* pp. 179-80.

186. Bultmann (*History of the Synoptic Tradition,* p. 203) thought the second half, like Deut 30:11-14, rejected the validity of asking for a confirming miracle; see also Donahue, *The Gospel in Parable,* p. 170; John Drury, *The Parables in the Gospels* (New York: Crossroad, 1985), pp. 150-51. Vincent Tanghe argues ("Abraham, son fils et son envoyé," *RB* 91 [1984]: 557-77) that the parable points to a polemic between Jews and Christians and that the assertions of the parable that no one returns from the dead and that the Law and prophets suffice are *Jewish* views, not the views of Luke or Christians.

187. The disbelief in Luke 24 is of disciples who have not encountered the risen Christ (vv. 11, 25) or who disbelieve from joy (v. 41). The two references to Moses and the prophets in Luke 24 are in two different contexts (vv. 27, 44). Both texts do assume the sufficiency of the Hebrew Scriptures and speak of resurrection.

188. See Bauckham, "The Rich Man and Lazarus: The Parable and the Parallels," pp. 101-2, 108-16. Among other examples see Plato, *Republic* 10:614B-616A; Lucian, *Dialogues of the Dead* 1.328-35, above, pp. 422-23.

189. F. Schnider and W. Stenger, "Die Offene Tür und die unüberschreitbare Kluft," 275-76, 282. Walter Vogels ("Having or Longing: A Semiotic Analysis of Luke 16:19-31," *EgT* 20 [1989]: 27-46, 29) and Heininger (*Metaphorik, Erzählstruktur und szenisch-dramatische Gestaltung in den Sondergutgleichnissen bei Lukas,* pp. 178-79) suggest the division be vv. 19-21, v. 22, vv. 23-31, but Heininger still views vv. 27-31 as from Luke. Cf. Karel Hanhart, *The Intermediate State in the New Testament* (Groningen: V. R. B., 1966), p. 197.

190. Tanghe, "Abraham, son fils et son envoyé," 560-63; Bauckham, "The Rich Man and Lazarus: The Parable and the Parallels," p. 115. Other readings are attested besides the two mentioned here, and the same confusion of verbs is present in v. 30.

191. Bauckham ("The Rich Man and Lazarus: The Parable and the Parallels," p. 115) points out that Jesus did not appear to unbelieving Jews to reveal their future fate. See also Richard L. Rohrbaugh, *The Biblical Interpreter: An Agrarian Bible in an Industrial Age* (Philadelphia:

Fortress, 1978), p. 75. Herzog (*Parables as Subversive Speech*, p. 125) argues that the rich man's request is not for Lazarus's resurrection, but only that his spirit convey a message.

192. Luke's readers, of course, already know of one such return in the narrative, that of the son of the widow of Nain (7:11-17).

193. *The Parables of Jesus*, p. 186.

194. See Jones, *Studying the Parables of Jesus*, p. 163.

195. Jones, *Studying the Parables of Jesus*, p. 163. Heininger (*Metaphorik, Erzählstruktur und szenisch-dramatische Gestaltung in den Sondergutgleichnissen bei Lukas*, pp. 183-84, 189) goes too far in making Lazarus the central figure and the example with whom one should identify. As Hans Kvalbein ("Jesus and the Poor: Two Texts and a Tentative Conclusion," *Themelios* 12 [1987]: 80-87, especially 84 and 86) points out, the parable does not tell the poor how to be saved, nor is Lazarus an ideal to follow.

196. Typically people are not named in Jewish or Greco-Roman parables either, but occasionally are, e.g., *Gen. Rab.* 65.11; Plato, *Phaedrus* 2.5. The rich man is named Neyēs in p^{75} and the Sahidic Coptic and Ethiopic versions and Dives in tradition because of the Vulgate ("Dives" is Latin for "rich"). K. Grobel (". . . Whose Name Was Neves," *NTS* 10 [1964]: 373-82, especially 381) argues that the reading in p^{75} originated from the Coptic tradition and meant "Nothing." Other names for the rich man also appear in tradition.

197. According to Bauckham ("The Rich Man and Lazarus: The Parable and the Parallels," p. 116), people are almost always named in descent stories.

198. Nolland, *Luke 9:21–18:34*, p. 828.

199. Others have attempted to draw more from the name Lazarus. J. D. M. Derrett ("Fresh Light on St. Luke XVI: II. Dives and Lazarus and the Preceding Sayings," *NTS* 7 [1961]: 364-80, especially 371) points to Gen 15:2, which mentions Abraham's servant Eliezer, whose name is essentially the same as Eleazar. Derrett assumes that Lazarus is Abraham's servant sent to see how his descendants are dealing with his property. The similar name is intriguing, but the story does not depend on this connection and Derrett's proposal has little to commend it. Others have seen Lazarus as a Christ figure, the one in whom God's help is made available, but this is not the intent of the parable. See Otto Glombitza, "Der reiche Mann und der arme Lazarus," *NovT* 12 (1970): 166-80, especially 178; Tanghe, "Abraham, son fils et son envoyé," 577; Robert Farrar Capon, *The Parables of Grace* (Grand Rapids: Eerdmans, 1988), p. 159.

200. See Hock, "Lazarus and Micyllus: Greco-Roman Backgrounds to Luke 16:19-31," 461-62.

201. The reminder that the word "poor" is not merely, or essentially, an economic term but also a term for God's people is pertinent. See Kvalbein, "Jesus and the Poor: Two Texts and a Tentative Conclusion." On the other hand, in this parable the concern *is* economic.

202. E.g., Lehtipuu, "Characterization and Persuasion: The Rich Man and the Poor Man in Luke 16.19-31," pp. 94-95.

203. Bauckham, "The Rich Man and Lazarus: The Parable and the Parallels," pp. 104-7; Rohrbaugh, *The Biblical Interpreter: An Agrarian Bible in an Industrial Age*, pp. 78-85.

204. Lehtipuu, "Characterization and Persuasion: The Rich Man and the Poor Man in Luke 16.19-31," pp. 98-99. Is it fair, however, to say that the rich man, even in *hạdēs*, views Lazarus as his inferior because he wants to send him to his brothers? This seems to be going too far.

205. Larry Kreitzer ("Luke 16:19-31 and 1 Enoch 22," *ExpTim* 103 [1992]: 139-42, especially 141) argues for the allusion because *1 En.* 22:5-7 refers to Cain and Abel, and he views *1 En.* 22 as the background of the parable, following L. W. Grensted ("The Use of Enoch in St. Luke xvi.19-31," *ExpTim* 26 [1915]: 333-34).

206. See *m. Sanhedrin* 10.1: "All Israelites have a share in the world to come"; and *b. 'Erubin* 19a, which states that the fire of Gehenna has no power over transgressors of Israel because Abraham rescues them; cf. *4 Macc.* 13:17. See Jones, *Studying the Parables of Jesus*, p. 176; Thorwald Lorenzen, "A Biblical Meditation on Luke 16:19-31," *ExpTim* 87 (1976): 39-43, especially 42.

207. Nickelsburg, "Riches, the Rich, and God's Judgment in 1 Enoch 92–105 and the Gospel According to Luke," 338. In rabbinic writings Abraham is especially known for his hospitality. See Scott, *Hear Then the Parable*, pp. 153-54.

208. The question is asked by Christopher F. Evans, "Uncomfortable Words — V," *ExpTim* 81 (1969-70): 228-31.

209. See, e.g., Job 17:13-16; Pss 30:3; 88:3-5; Prov 7:27; Isa 14:11; and Ps 49:14; Isa 28:15, 18; Hos 13:14; Hab 2:5.

210. On *šě'ôl*, *hadēs*, and *geenna* see the discussions by Theodore J. Lewis, "Dead, Abode of the," *ABD*, 2:101-5; Duane F. Watson, "Gehenna," *ABD*, 2:927-28; and Richard Bauckham, "Hades, Hell," *ABD*, 3:14-15; and several articles from Bauckham's *The Fate of the Dead*: "Descents to the Underworld," pp. 9-48; "Early Jewish Visions of Hell," pp. 49-80; and "Visiting the Places of the Dead in the Extra-Canonical Apocalypses," pp. 81-96.

211. Does *hadēs* here mean merely "grave," similar to Sheol in the OT? Note the parallel with "corruption."

212. *The Parables of Jesus*, p. 185.

213. The texts indicate only that *geenna* is a place of fire and destruction and that *hadēs* (other than in Luke 16) is downward and is closely associated with death.

214. See *1 En.* 63:10; *b. Baba Batra* 79a; *b. 'Erubin* 19a; *Midr. Ps.* 31:3, but Rev 20:14 indicates that death and *hadēs*, assumedly synonymous at this point, will be thrown into the lake of fire.

215. See *1 En.* 108:14-15; *4 Ezra* 7:36-38, 83; *Apocalypse of Elijah* 5:27-28; also Luke 13:28-29.

216. E.g., *T. Ab.* 14:10-15. See the discussion of such texts by Richard Bauckham, "The Conflict of Justice and Mercy: Attitudes to the Damned in Apocalyptic Literature," in *The Fate of the Dead*, pp. 132-48.

217. One who still would argue that the parable is factual and should be taken literally and is a powerful support of a theory of conscious, eternal punishment is Khoo ("The Reality and Eternality of Hell: Luke 16:19-31 as Proof").

218. Job 7:9: "Those who go down to Sheol do not come up"; cf. 10:21; 16:22; 2 Sam 12:23. The return of Samuel to the witch at Endor (1 Sam 28:8-25) is the obvious exception. In Wis 2:1 the ungodly say "No one has been known to return from Hades," which is a denial of resurrection and future life to justify their lifestyle.

219. "Visiting the Places of the Dead in the Extra-Canonical Apocalypses," p. 96; "The Rich Man and Lazarus: The Parable and the Parallels," p. 117: "But in that case the parable's own account of the fates of the rich man and Lazarus (vv. 22-26) is deprived of the status of such a revelation. . . . The story in effect deprives itself of any claim to offer an apocalyptic glimpse of the secrets of the world beyond the grave. . . . It has only the status of parable."

220. *1 En.* 22 is clearly about the intermediate state, and although it has several parallels with this parable, the punishment in *1 Enoch* is not yet occurring, at least for most. See e.g., J. Osei-Bonsu, "The Intermediate State in Luke-Acts," *IBS* 9 (1987): 115-31; A. J. Mattill, Jr., *Luke and the Last Things* (Dillsboro: Western North Carolina, 1979), p. 27. Both Osei-Bonsu (p. 122) and Mattill (p. 27) think the rich man's request for a tiny bit of water is actually a request for the water of life referred to in *1 En.* 17:4, which is possible.

221. E.g., Hanhart, *The Intermediate State in the New Testament*, pp. 198-99.

222. In addition to this parable see 12:20; 23:43; Acts 5:5, 10; 7:55-60; 12:23.

223. See John T. Carroll, *Response to the End of History* (Atlanta: Scholars, 1988), p. 60, and his discussion of "individual eschatology" in Luke-Acts, pp. 60-71.

224. Contra Cave, "Lazarus and the Lukan Deuteronomy"; Wright, *Jesus and the Victory of God*, pp. 255-56.

225. Cf. 19:8 and see Lehtipuu, "Characterization and Persuasion: The Rich Man and the Poor Man in Luke 16.19-31," p. 94.

226. See among others Herzog, *Parables as Subversive Speech*, p. 125.

227. See Matt 12:38-40; Matt 16:1-4/Mark 8:11-12/Luke 11:29-32; Luke 11:16; John 2:18; 6:30.

228. *On the Edge of the Primeval Forest* (trans. C. T. Campion; New York: Macmillan, 1931), p. 1.

229. See Stephen Wright, *The Voice of Jesus*, pp. 90-91. The reference is to Ambrose's *Expositio Evangelii Secundum Lucam* 8.137-38.

230. See Kvalbein, "Jesus and the Poor: Two Texts and a Tentative Conclusion," 85.

231. Menander, fragments from unidentified plays 90K.

Notes to "Parables Concerning God and Prayer"

1. The authenticity of this parable is not frequently questioned. No treatment of this parable occurs in the report of the Jesus Seminar (see Robert W. Funk, Bernard Brandon Scott, and James R. Butts, *The Parables of Jesus: Red Letter Edition* [Sonoma: Polebridge, 1988]), but in *The Five Gospels: The Search for the Authentic Words of Jesus* (Robert W. Funk, Roy W. Hoover, and the Jesus Seminar [New York: Macmillan, 1993], pp. 327-28) this parable is printed in pink on the assumption that it was originally about the sleeper avoiding shame. What the purpose of such a parable would be on their explanation is not clear. One who rejects the authenticity of the parable is H. T. Fleddermann, "Three Friends at Midnight (Luke 11,5-8)," in *Luke and His Readers*, ed. R. Bieringer, G. Van Belle, and J. Verheyden (Leuven: Leuven University Press, 2005), pp. 265-82, here p. 269.

2. For many other references to texts using the word *anaideia* ("shamelessness") see my article *"Anaideia* and the Friend at Midnight (Luke 11:8)," *JBL* 116 (1997): 505-13.

3. "Impudence" is unsatisfactory as a translation. As the parallel words show, the man has no sense of shame.

4. *Kai ti dei tēn ep' apsychois anaideian tou limou legein?*

5. Also at *Fragmenta* FIF. 173.1-2 and 528.2-3.

6. Clement of Alexandria offers a slightly different version of the imagery (*Stromateis* 5.7). John Chrysostom likewise speaks of God hating shamelessness (see *De Poenitentia* 49.285). See also Aesop, *Fables* 183.3.18 (TLG), which has another story about God (or a god) hating shamelessness; several accounts of this story exist.

7. *y. Ta'anit* 3.4 tells of a poor woman lighting a fire (as if she were baking bread) to avoid the shame of her neighbors knowing she had nothing. A miracle provides bread for her, but this account has little relevance for our parable. Cf. *b. Ta'anit* 25a.

8. Compare the similar wording at Matt 26:10 and Gal 6:17.

9. François Bovon, *Das Evangelium nach Lukas* (EKKNT; Zurich: Benziger, 1996), 2:146; Adolf Jülicher, *Die Gleichnisreden Jesu* (2 vols.; Freiburg i. B.: J. C. B. Mohr, 1888-89), 2:268.

10. For cultural information on family life, houses, and baking, see S. Safrai, "Home and Family," *JPFC*, 2:728-40.

11. See William Herzog, *Parables as Subversive Speech: Jesus as Pedagogue of the Oppressed* (Louisville: Westminster/John Knox, 1994), pp. 199-200. Some argue that three loaves were necessary for a meal, while others argue that one loaf was sufficient. Herzog's assumption (p. 200) that the host or his wife would go to other houses for other parts of the meal and to borrow the best crockery to lay out an extravagant meal is apparently drawn from Kenneth Ewing Bailey (*Poet and Peasant: A Literary Cultural Approach to the Parables in Luke* [Grand Rapids: Eerdmans, 1976], pp. 122-23), but both go far beyond the evidence of the parable.

12. See Stephen L. Wailes, *Medieval Allegories of Jesus' Parables* (Berkeley: University of California Press, 1987), pp. 214-19.

13. E.g., Joseph A. Fitzmyer, *The Gospel According to Luke X–XXIV* (AB 28B; Garden City: Doubleday, 1985), p. 910; Arland J. Hultgren, *The Parables of Jesus: A Commentary* (Grand Rapids: Eerdmans, 2000), pp. 227, 232-33; Luise Schottroff, *The Parables of Jesus* (trans. Linda M. Maloney; Minneapolis: Fortress, 2006), pp. 189-90. Craig L. Blomberg (*Interpreting the Parables* [Downers Grove: InterVarsity, 1990], p. 276) says the parable teaches that one should practice bold, unabashed forthrightness in prayer.

14. E.g., Joachim Jeremias, *The Parables of Jesus* (2d ed.; trans. S. H. Hooke; New York: Charles Scribner's Sons, 1972), pp. 158-59; Bailey, *Poet and Peasant,* pp. 120, 128-33; John Nolland, *Luke 9:21–18:34* (WBC 35B; Dallas: Word, 1993), pp. 624-27.

15. I have advocated this approach in "*Anaideia* and the Friend at Midnight," and it is close to the view of Walter L. Liefeld ("Parables on Prayer [Luke 11:5-13; 18:1-14]," in *The Challenge of Jesus' Parables,* ed. Richard N. Longenecker [Grand Rapids: Eerdmans, 2000], pp. 240-62, here pp. 247-52), but he thinks the shamelessness would also have rested on the sleeper if he had not gotten up and that accordingly we may approach God in a shameless way.

16. "The Subversion of 'World' by the Parable of the Friend at Midnight," *JBL* 120 (2001): 703-21.

17. Fleddermann, "Three Friends at Midnight (Luke 11,5-8)," especially pp. 279-82, who finds parallels binding this parable to that of the Good Samaritan. He concludes that the obligation to respond to human need is so great that the Christian (represented by the host in the parable) must be prepared to violate all social norms to achieve the goal (p. 281).

18. Herzog, *Parables as Subversive Speech,* pp. 207-14. He thinks that the parable depicts a sympathetic village's reception of an itinerant disciple and that the adjective *anaidēs* sometimes refers to greed, but even then it refers to unacceptable behavior. It does not mean greed. He suggests that the hospitality of the villagers was shameless to the elites, i.e., that it was foolish, and that v. 8 is intended ironically. With some difficulty he has forced the parable to address issues of oppression. Another focusing on friendship and hospitality is Bernard Brandon Scott, *Hear Then the Parable: A Commentary on the Parables of Jesus* (Minneapolis: Fortress, 1989), pp. 87-92. He views the kingdom metaphorically as a village in which the approved way of attaining the goal is subverted. Shamelessness, not honor, has brought the desired loaves.

19. The interrogative sense with which the parable begins is not lost, contra Fleddermann, "Three Friends at Midnight (Luke 11,5-8)," p. 267.

20. Matt 6:27; 7:9; 12:11; Luke 11:5, 11; 14:5, 28; 15:4, 8; 17:7; John 8:46. See also Isa 42:23; 50:10; Hag 2:3 and above, pp. 12-13.

21. E.g., David R. Catchpole, "Q and 'the Friend at Midnight' (Luke xi.5-8/9)," *JTS* 34 (1983): 407-24, here p. 411. This leads him unnecessarily to assign v. 8a to Luke or a redactor, which leaves him, as he admits, with a parable that is trivial. Among others assuming an original refusal are Herzog (*Parables as Subversive Speech,* p. 195) and Bailey (*Poet and Peasant,* pp. 127-28).

22. "I tell you that even if he will not provide for him out of friendship, the very *shame-lessness* of the request will make him get up and give him all he needs."

23. Depending on how one counts; some texts are repeated. The Duke Papyri (from the Packard Humanities Institute CD-ROM) have five more occurrences, all showing the same understanding as those in the TLG data base. See my article "*Anaideia* and the Friend at Midnight." The cognates of *anaideia* carry the same negative connotation. See *anaidēs* in Deut 28:50; 1 Sam 2:29; Prov 7:13; 25:23; Eccl 8:1; Sir 23:6; 26:11; 40:30; Isa 56:11; Jer 8:5; Bar 4:15; Dan LXX 8:23; Dan Th 2:15; 8:23, and *anaidōs* in Prov 21:29.

24. See Jeremias, *The Parables of Jesus*, pp. 158-59; Bailey, *Poet and Peasant*, pp. 119-20 and 128-33; Scott, *Hear Then the Parable*, pp. 89-91; Alan Johnson, "Assurance for Man: The Fallacy of Translating *Anaideia* by 'Persistence' in Luke 11:5-8," *JETS* 22 (1979): 123-31; and Nolland, *Luke 9:21–18:34*, p. 626. Note Nolland's translation (p. 622): ". . . because of the prospect of him being shamed, he will get up. . . ."

25. Too often demonstrated by recourse to modern Arab culture, as with Bailey, *Poet and Peasant*, pp. 119-33; see also J. Duncan M. Derrett, "The Friend at Midnight: Asian Ideas in the Gospel of St. Luke," in *Donum Gentilicum: New Testament Studies in Honour of David Daube*, ed. E. Bammel, C. K. Barrett, and W. D. Davies (Oxford: Clarendon, 1978), pp. 78-87, here pp. 79-81; and Evertt W. Huffard, "The Parable of the Friend at Midnight: God's Honor or Man's Persistence?" *ResQ* 21 (1978): 154-60.

26. Later Christian writers knew that *anaideia* was a thoroughly negative word and often used it that way, but they also spoke of a "good shamelessness," which is an oxymoron. By this they refer to a boldness or even desperation that enables people to approach God or Christ to find help for life. Explicitly, John Chrysostom, *De Caeco et Zaechaeo* 59.601.42-46: ". . . knowing that shamelessness is good for godliness, for if for property many are shameless, for salvation of the soul is it not best to put on the good shamelessness?"

27. See above, p. 439.

28. Cf. Libanius, *Oration* 1.121, who considered it rude *(anaideia)* to accompany the emperor at sacrifice unless invited. That the petitioner is the shameless one is confirmed by Hermas, *Vis.* 3:2, as Klaus Berger points out ("Materialien zu Form und Überlieferungs-geschichte neutestamentlicher Gleichnisse," *NovT* 15 [1973]: 1-37, here pp. 33-36).

29. Catchpole, "Q and the 'Friend at Midnight,'" 411.

30. "Exegetisches zum Neuen Testament," *SO* 13 (1934): 38-46, here p. 42, even though the text has "*his* shamelessness."

31. Bailey (*Poet and Peasant*, p. 130) draws attention to Jeremias's subtle move. See Jeremias, *The Parables of Jesus*, pp. 158-59. Jeremias points to *b. Taʿanit* 25a as an example of a woman who seeks to avoid shame, when in reality she is ashamed of her circumstance and seeks to hide it. See n. 7 above.

32. Derrett, "The Friend at Midnight," pp. 82-85. The same argument is offered by Klaus Haacker, "Mut zum Bitten. Eine Auslegung von Lukas 11,5-8," *TBei* 17 (1986): 1-6, here p. 4.

33. Bailey, *Poet and Peasant*, pp. 125-33. See also Nolland, *Luke 9:21–18:34*, pp. 624-26; Johnson, "Assurance for Man," 130-31; Herzog, *Parables as Subversive Speech*, pp. 203, 213-14, who follow Bailey's argument.

34. Scott, *Hear Then the Parable*, pp. 88-91. The quotation is from p. 91.

35. B. Heininger (*Metaphorik, Erzählstruktur und szenisch-dramatische Gestaltung in den Sondergutgleichnissen bei Lukas* [Münster: Aschendorff, 1991], pp. 106-7) attempted to argue that in the NT period *anaideia* was no longer thoroughly negative by pointing to Prov 7:13 and Sir 40:30, neither of which makes his point. The use of *anaidēs* in Prov 7:13 will not support a

positive use, for it reports the shameless request of a prostitute. Sir 40:30 only says that in the mouth of the shameless begging will be sweet, which certainly is no positive use of shamelessness when in 40:28 one finds, "It is better to die than to beg." Heininger followed Wilhelm Ott (*Gebet und Heil. Die Bedeutung der Gebetsparänese in der lukanischen Theologie* [Munich: Kösel, 1965], p. 27) in seeing 11:8 as a disruptive, redactional insertion related to Luke 11:2-4. David Catchpole, "Q and 'the Friend at Midnight,'" 413 also removed 11:8a (through *anaideia autou*, "his shamelessness") as redactional. David Michael Crump (*Jesus the Intercessor: Prayer and Christology in Luke-Acts* [WUNT 2; Tübingen: Mohr-Siebeck, 1992], pp. 27-30) also views v. 8 as secondary and as devaluing the theme of friendship, which, of course, erroneously assumes that the parable is about friendship. That the words of v. 8 cause difficulty for modern interpreters is no reason to excise them as unimportant redactional material.

36. Cf. Bovon, *Das Evangelium nach Lukas,* 2:151.

37. Waetjen, "The Subversion of 'World' by the Parable of the Friend at Midnight," 703-20. For the quotation see p. 715.

38. Why the UBS Greek text does not use the symbol for a question at the end of v. 7 is unclear; they should have and did in 11:11; 14:5, 28, 31; 15:4, 8; and 17:7-8.

39. David Crump, *Knocking on Heaven's Door: A New Testament Theology of Petitionary Prayer* (Grand Rapids: Baker, 2006), p. 70.

40. See Blomberg, *Interpreting the Parables,* p. 276, following Jülicher, *Die Gleichnisreden Jesu,* 2:273. Blomberg points out that in Luke's usage of *dia to einai* the subject of the infinitive is usually the subject of the sentence (see Luke 2:4; 19:11; Acts 18:3). But Blomberg also notes that Acts 27:4 does not follow this practice. See as well Fitzmyer, *The Gospel According to Luke X–XXIV,* 2:912. Note the textual variants showing scribal attempts to clarify the reference.

41. Contra Catchpole, "Q and 'the Friend at Midnight,'" 411, who argues that v. 8 implies a persistent repetition of the request.

42. On p. 126 Bailey *(Poet and Peasant)* recognizes that the meaning could be merely "shameless apostasy."

43. *J.W.* 1.84 (= *Ant.* 13.317); 6.199; *Ant.* 17.119. See Catchpole, "Q and 'the Friend at Midnight,'" 409-10.

44. The LCL translation of *Moralia* 533D ("On Compliancy"). At 528E Plutarch defines compliancy as excess of shame on the part of good people, which allows the shameless to act.

45. See also Johnson, "Assurance for Man," 123-31, who rejects the meaning "persistence."

46. Crump (*Knocking on Heaven's Door,* p. 61) rightly distinguishes between persistence as continual prayer and persistence as repetitious prayer. See his whole discussion (pp. 60-76) and rejection of the wrong kind of persistence.

47. For examples of parables of contrast see *Pesiqta de Rab Kahana* 3e; 4.2; 12.22; 17.2; 24.8, 10. Often these parables have specific indicators, such as "the way of the world," "the way of flesh and blood" or "not so with the Holy One." The NT examples are more implicit.

48. Whether the original form had a *nimshal* cannot be determined. David Catchpole ("Q and 'the Friend at Midnight,'" 407-24) argued that the parable was originally in a Q collection that consisted of Matt 6:7-8; Matt 6:9-13/Luke 11:2-4; Matt 7:7/Luke 11:5-9 (with v. 8a deriving from Luke); Matt 7:8/Luke 11:10; Matt 7:9-11/Luke 11:11-13; and Matt 6:25-33/Luke 12:22-31, but I do not find his argument convincing or even enticing. If this material was originally a unified teaching on prayer, what was the impetus for both Matthew and Luke to divide it up? See the critique by C. M. Tuckett, "Q, Prayer, and the Kingdom," *JTS* 40 (1989): 367-76, and the reply by Catchpole, "Q, Prayer, and the Kingdom: A Rejoinder," *JTS* 40 (1989): 377-88.

49. This fits well with the focus of 12:22-34 and helps explain why Luke omitted the state-

ment in Matt 7:9 (assuming that the shorter reading in 11:11 is correct). Robert Farrar Capon (*The Parables of Grace* [Grand Rapids: Eerdmans, 1988], pp. 70-74) reads death and resurrection into this passage by viewing shamelessness as death to self: "then precisely because of his shamelessness, his total lack of a self-regarding life, he would be raised out of death by his rising friend." Cf. p. 74: "a shameless acceptance of your death." He justifies this by the fact that words used elsewhere of the resurrection appear in the parable (*anistanai* in v. 7 and *egeirein* in v. 8). This is fanciful eisegesis. Derrett ("The Friend at Midnight," pp. 86-87) also saw a reference to the resurrection.

50. Contra Haacker, "Mut zum Bitten. Eine Auslegung von Lukas 11,5-8," 6, and Heininger, *Metaphorik, Erzählstruktur und szenisch-dramatische Gestaltung in den Sondergutgleichnissen bei Lukas,* p. 106. If the argument is "how much more," then the point is not that God is a friend. The man does not *stand* for God, contra David Daube, "Shame Culture in Luke," in *Paul and Paulinism: Essays in Honour of C. K. Barrett,* ed. M. D. Hooker and S. G. Wilson (London: SPCK, 1982), pp. 355-72, here p. 358.

51. As Heininger (*Metaphorik, Erzählstruktur und szenisch-dramatische Gestaltung in den Sondergutgleichnissen bei Lukas,* p. 107) accuses Luke of believing.

52. Cf. David Daube's comment ("Neglected Nuances of Exposition in Luke-Acts," *ANRW* 25/3, p. 2332): "The primary message of the simile of the Helper at Midnight is that, since even our human neighbor will undergo considerable inconvenience for our sakes if we press him in an emergency, surely God is always ready to hear the needy." Daube's use of "if we press him," however, still points needlessly to persistence.

53. See Bailey, *Poet and Peasant,* pp. 80-82.

54. See I. Howard Marshall, *Commentary on Luke* (NIGTC; Grand Rapids: Eerdmans, 1978), pp. 674-75.

55. E.g., Jeremias, *The Parables of Jesus,* pp. 155 ("before they realize it"), 157; John Mark Hicks, "The Parable of the Persistent Widow (Luke 18:1-8)," *ResQ* 33 (1991): 209-23, here p. 220.

56. In addition to the items listed here Steven L. Bridge (*"Where the Eagles Are Gathered": The Deliverance of the Elect in Lukan Eschatology* [JSNTSup 240; Sheffield: Sheffield Academic, 2003], pp. 104-6) finds affinities between Luke 18:1-8 and *1 En.* 47:1-4; 97:3, 5; 99:3; 103:14-15; 104:1-5. He finds further affinities between *1 Enoch* and Luke 18:9-14 and suggests that Luke's reliance on *1 Enoch* explains why these two parables appear together. The affinities in neither case are sufficient to show reliance, especially those regarding 18:9-14.

57. *Corpus inscriptionum iudaicarum,* ed. Jean-Baptiste Frey (2 vols.; Rome: Pontificio Istituto di Archeologia Cristiana, 1936), 1:523-25.

58. In addition to the items listed here, see *Select Papyri* (LCL) 2, selection 293 (P. Ryl. 114, from about 280 A.D.), a petition of a widow to a prefect for justice after someone has seized her flocks at her husband's death.

59. C. C. Edgar, ed., *Michigan Papyri* 1: *Zenon Papyri* (Ann Arbor: University of Michigan Press, 1931), pp. 90-91.

60. See A. J. Mattill, Jr., *Luke and the Last Things: A Perspective for the Understanding of Lukan Thought* (Dillsboro: Western North Carolina, 1979), p. 89.

61. These last two words appear only three more times each in the rest of the NT. Note the occurrence of the noun in 21:22 with reference to the destruction of Jerusalem.

62. Several parallels exist to the description of the judge. See Dionysius of Halicarnassus, *Roman Antiquities* 10.10.7 (denouncing conspirators who intend to carry out wicked plans): "without either fearing the anger of the gods or heeding the indignation of men"; Cicero, *Pro Cluentio* 6.15 (quoted by Quintilian, *Inst.* 4.2.105) speaks of a wicked woman who "had no re-

gard for the vengeance of heaven and the opinion of man"; Josephus, *Ant.* 10.83: King Jehoiakim "was neither reverent toward God nor kind to man" (cf. *Ant.* 1.72); Homer, *Odyssey* 22.39. See Susan M. Praeder, *The Word in Women's Worlds: Four Parables* (Wilmington: Michael Glazier, 1988), pp. 58-60. These parallels exclude the suggestion by Charles W. Hedrick that the judge is a thoroughly honest man (based on resonances with texts like Deut 1:16-17). See his *Parables as Poetic Fictions: The Creative Voice of Jesus* (Peabody: Hendrickson, 1994), pp. 194-97. Of course, the conventional images of a widow and a judge presume that she is innocent and he is questionable, to say nothing of the description of him as a judge "of unrighteousness" *(tēs adikias)* in 18:6. This is a Semitic expression meaning he is characterized as being unrighteous or as belonging to the realm of the unrighteous.

63. François Bovon, *Das Evangelium nach Lukas (Lk 15,1–19,27)* (EKKNT 3/3; Düsseldorf: Benziger, 2001), p. 190.

64. See G. Stählin, "χήρα," *TDNT,* 9:441-48.

65. J. Duncan M. Derrett, "Law in the New Testament: The Parable of the Unjust Judge," *NTS* 18 (1971-72): 178-91.

66. See Scott, *Hear Then the Parable,* p. 184.

67. See Praeder, *The Word in Women's Worlds,* pp. 56-57.

68. Several interpreters (e.g., W. O. E. Oesterley, *The Gospel Parables in the Light of Their Jewish Background* [New York: Macmillan, 1936], p. 223; and Scott, *Hear Then the Parable,* p. 183) blame the widow for not being more polite with the judge, but surely manners are not expected from the widow in her exasperation, and to make such a feature a matter of interpretation is misguided. Oesterley (p. 226) and Alfred Plummer (*A Critical and Exegetical Commentary on the Gospel According to Luke* [4th ed.; ICC; Edinburgh: T. & T. Clark, 1901], p. 411) emphasize Judaism's devaluing of continued prayer, but I do not find this relevant for interpreting this parable.

69. Wailes, *Medieval Allegories of Jesus' Parables,* p. 263.

70. Among many see Kenneth Bailey, *Through Peasant Eyes: More Lucan Parables, Their Culture and Style* (Grand Rapids: Eerdmans, 1980), pp. 128, 136-41; Hultgren, *The Parables of Jesus,* pp. 258-60.

71. Crump, *Jesus the Intercessor,* pp. 131-32; see also his *Knocking on Heaven's Door,* pp. 77-89.

72. Herman Hendrickx, *The Parables of Jesus* (San Francisco: Harper & Row, 1986), pp. 231-32. Similarly, Barbara E. Reid ("Beyond Petty Pursuits and Wearisome Widows: Three Lukan Parables," *Interpretation* 56 [2002]: 284-94) takes the widow as a God figure and argues that one is like God when doggedly resisting injustice. See also Mary W. Matthews, Carter Shelley, and Barbara Scheele, "Proclaiming the Parable of the Persistent Widow (Lk. 18.2-5)," *The Lost Coin: Parables of Women, Work and Wisdom,* ed. Mary Ann Beavis (London: Sheffield Academic, 2002), pp. 46-70.

73. *Parables as Subversive Speech,* pp. 215-32.

74. Wendy Cotter, "The Parable of the Feisty Widow and the Threatened Judge (Luke 18:1-8)," *NTS* 51 (2005): 328-43. See also Stephen Curkpatrick, "Dissonance in Luke 18:1-8," *JBL* 121 (2002): 107-21, who thinks 18:2-5 is wrongly framed and fits better with the theme in the Magnificat concerning justice.

75. "The Parable of the Unjust Judge: A Metaphor of the Unrealized Self," in *Semiology and Parables,* ed. Daniel Patte (Pittsburgh: Pickwick, 1976), pp. 1-32.

76. *Hear Then the Parable,* pp. 175-87.

77. *Parables as Poetic Fictions,* pp. 187-207. Additionally, Robert M. Price argued that this

parable was originally an exemplary story which has been adulterated by Luke to keep women in submission. The parable in his view attests the bitterness of widows mistreated by church officials. The unjust judge is the pastor, and the parable advises widows to get justice by the terrorism of nuisance. See his *The Widow Traditions in Luke-Acts: A Feminist-Critical Scrutiny* (SBLDS 155; Atlanta: Scholars, 1997), pp. 191-201, here p. 195. Hermann Binder, *Das Gleichnis vom dem Richter und der Witwe, Lk 18,1-8* (Neukirchen-Vluyn: Neukirchener, 1988) thinks the judge and the widow are an ironic depiction of Jesus and his disciples.

78. The reasons offered by Eta Linnemann (*Parables of Jesus* [London: SPCK, 1966], pp. 121-22, 187-88) for tracing the parable to a Christian prophet instead of Jesus are not convincing. One cannot merely assert that applications are frequently secondary, and her rejection of the use of "the elect" in v. 7 as inappropriate for Jesus has no basis. The OT uses "the elect" in reference to the people of God, and Jesus was quite consciously gathering a community around himself as he reconstituted Israel under his leadership. See David R. Catchpole, "The Son of Man's Search for Faith (Luke XVIII 8b)," *NovT* 19 (1977): 81-104, here pp. 90-92, 103.

79. The rabbinic *qal waḥomer*. See, e.g., Bailey, *Through Peasant Eyes*, pp. 128, 136.

80. Note especially the use of *elegen de* and *pros to dein*.

81. Including Fitzmyer's (*The Gospel According to Luke X–XXIV,* 1176) that the parable originally consisted of vv. 2-6.

82. E.g., Linnemann, *Parables of Jesus,* pp. 121-22 and 187-88, although in her recent work she rejects entirely the method and procedure in her work on parables; see her *Historical Criticism of the Bible: Methodology or Ideology?* (trans. Robert W. Yarbrough; Grand Rapids: Baker, 1990), p. 20. Bovon (*Das Evangelium nach Lukas,* 3:194-96) thinks v. 7a is from a Christian prophet and that v. 7b is from Luke and corrects v. 7a.

83. See Catchpole, "The Son of Man's Search for Faith," 81-104; Hicks, "The Parable of the Persistent Widow," 209-23.

84. Jesus is reported as calling for sensitive listening at least eleven other times. See Matt 11:15; 13:9, 18, 43; 15:10; Mark 4:3, 9, 23; 7:14; Luke 8:8; 14:35. See also Matt 17:5; 21:33; Mark 9:7; Luke 9:35; 16:29.

85. Among several see Hultgren, *The Parables of Jesus,* p. 258; Hicks, "The Parable of the Persistent Widow," and Gerhard Delling, "Das Gleichnis vom gottlosen Richter," *ZNW* 53 (1962): 1-25, here pp. 1-4.

86. The wording in Luke's account is not drawn from the Greek text of Sirach, but may be influenced by it. Jesus' framing of the parable would assumedly be based on knowledge of the Hebrew version of Sirach. See also Sir 18:11; 2 Macc 6:14. Catchpole ("The Son of Man's Search for Faith," 87-88) points to similar motifs in Wisdom 1–5.

87. E.g., Jeremias, *The Parables of Jesus,* p. 156.

88. Catchpole, "The Son of Man's Search for Faith (Luke XVIII 8b)," 90.

89. The word translated "faith" *(pistis)* can mean either.

90. Catchpole, "The Son of Man's Search for Faith," 92-104. The pattern, which is at least partly present in Luke 18:2-8, includes:

A. a special relationship between God and certain persons,

B. the sinful failure of God's people,

C. the experience of suffering interpreted as judgment,

D. repentance and the reestablishment of the intended God-human relationship,

E. a prayerful appeal to God by the sufferer,

F. a time note setting a limit on the period before God intervenes, and

G. the intervention itself, depicted as mercy or by means of the "righteousness" *(dikaios)* word group and seen as judgment on the third party.

Element D is present with the focus on faith in 18:8b. See also Hicks, "The Parable of the Persistent Widow," 212-13.

91. Since the article is used with *pistis* (faith/faithfulness), the intent could be either such faithfulness as evidenced by the widow or the faithfulness called for in 18:1, more likely the latter. Faithfulness is a theme, of course, of other parables and sayings. See e.g., Matt 24:43-50; 25:1-13; Luke 12:35-48.

92. Note the other occurrences of *enkakein* in the NT: 2 Cor 4:1, 16; Gal 6:9; Eph 3:13; 2 Thess 3:13. In Eph 3:12-13 Paul refers to God's faithfulness (so I would understand the genitive *pisteōs*) and prays that he (or his addressees) will not lose heart because of his afflictions.

93. See Hicks, "The Parable of the Persistent Widow," 222; Blomberg, *Interpreting the Parables*, p. 271.

94. Ott, *Gebet und Heil*, p. 43.

95. Cf. 21:36 and, without the focus on eschatology, 22:32.

96. Charles H. Talbert, *Reading Luke: A Literary and Theological Commentary on the Third Gospel* (New York: Crossroad, 1982), p. 169.

97. See above, p. 440.

98. On 11:5-8 see above, pp. 446-47.

99. Ott (*Gebet und Heil*, pp. 23-27, 59-60) is guilty of forcing 18:1-8 and 11:5-8 into too close an association.

100. One should note that the only other Lukan usage of these words is in reference to the destruction of Jerusalem (21:22). Of course, any legal judgment in one person's favor is at some expense to the adversary, and God's coming throughout Scripture always includes both salvation and judgment.

101. Cf. 1 Cor. 9:27, the only other NT occurrence. Plutarch (*Mor.* 921-22), like others, uses the word of blackening the eye.

102. Bovon, *Das Evangelium nach Lukas*, 3:193. Plutarch *Mor.* 921-22 would support taking *hypōpiazein* as causing the judge shame, but this is not likely the intent since the narrative asserts twice that the judge does not fear God or respect humans. Therefore, he would not care about shame.

103. Note the Greek imperfect *ērcheto* in v. 3 emphasizing her repeated coming.

104. Marshall lays out nine possible options for understanding this clause (*Commentary on Luke*, pp. 674-75).

105. Jeremias (*The Parable of Jesus*, pp. 154-55) argues for the concessive sense, and Hendrickx (*The Parables of Jesus*, p. 225) for understanding the expression as equivalent to a relative clause.

106. Some suggest that *ep' autois* ("over them") refers not to the elect, but to their enemies, but there is no basis for this in this text.

107. The elect cry out day and night.

108. See H. Ljungvik, "Zur Erklärung einer Lukas-Stelle," *NTS* 10 (1963): 289-94. Ljungvik suggests taking *kai* as adversative and translates "but will have mercy on them." However, if this clause is seen as a continuation of the first question, it is also an emphatic question: "and will he not surely have mercy on them?"

109. J. Horst, *TDNT*, 4:374-87, especially 381, n. 56. Despite the suggestion of parallelism

in Sir 35:18, *makrothymein* and *bradynein* are not merely synonyms. See Ott, *Gebet und Heil,* p. 57.

110. Catchpole, "The Son of Man's Search for Faith," 92-104; Horst, *TDNT,* 4:376-81. Ott (*Gebet und Heil,* p. 44) points out that eighteen of thirty-four occurrences of *makrothymeō* and related words in the LXX have to do with God's patience with his people. Thirteen of those eighteen are used in connection with *polyeleos* ("very merciful") or some other word for mercy.

111. Delling ("Das Gleichnis vom gottlosen Richter," 24-25) says that participation in salvation is not obvious even for those who know they are the elect. The community asks if God will stand by his word; God asks if the community will stand by and with the Son of Man.

112. E.g., Jeremias, *The Parables of Jesus,* p. 155 ("before they realize it"), 157; Hicks, "The Parable of the Persistent Widow," 220.

113. Note, e.g., in Acts 12:7 *en tachei* means immediately, but in Acts 25:4, 6 it means after eight or ten days.

114. The occurrence in LXX Ps 2:12 is one of the few that provide evidence for "suddenly." See also LXX Ezek 29:5. For other NT occurrences of the phrase see Acts 12:7; 22:18; 25:4; Rom 16:20; Rev 1:1; 22:6. The meaning of the first three is clearly "quickly" or "soon," whereas the meaning of the last three is more open to discussion.

115. Contra Marshall, *Commentary on Luke,* p. 675.

116. Contra Blomberg, *Interpreting the Parables,* p. 274.

117. See p. 451 above.

118. Dionysius of Halicarnassus (*Roman Antiquities* 5.59.3) reports that aid was repeatedly promised soon *(en tachei)* for a besieged city, but did not come. The opposite of *tachos* is *bradytēs;* see Plutarch, *Lives, Lucullus* 28.9.4; Josephus *Ant.* 17.83; *J.W.* 2.45.

119. See C. E. B. Cranfield, "The Parable of the Unjust Judge and the Eschatology of Luke-Acts," *SJT* 16 (1903): 297-301; Delling, "Das Gleichnis vom gottlosen Richter," 20; Nolland, *Luke 9:21–18:34,* p. 871. Nolland argues that "quickly" is a statement about the character of God, that 18:8b makes clear that "quickly" is not immediately, and that one needs to hang on to this "quickly." That the parable is not about the delay of the parousia, see Catchpole, "The Son of Man's Search for Faith," 89; Praeder, *The Word in Women's Worlds,* p. 68; Delling, "Das Gleichnis vom gottlosen Richter," 20, n. 86.

120. Cf. Talbert, *Reading Luke,* p. 166. On doubt about the parousia, see 12:45-46; 2 Pet 3:4-12; *1 Clem.* 23:3–24:1; *2 Clem.* 11:1-7.

121. William David Spencer and Aida Besançon Spencer, *The Prayer Life of Jesus: Shout of Agony, Revelation of Love: A Commentary* (Lanham: University Press of America, 1990), p. 62. Others also point to persecution and oppression as the context in which the parable emerged or was used, but this is certainly not a main focus in Luke-Acts.

122. *Through Peasant Eyes,* p. 140.

123. *Luke 9:21–18:34,* p. 871. The parable of the Rich Fool gives some credence to these connections.

124. See Delling, "Das Gleichnis vom gottlosen Richter," 24-25.

125. Interesting "tandem" readings are offered by Barbara Green (*Like a Tree Planted* [Collegeville: Liturgical, 1997], pp. 72-88) and Don C. Benjamin ("The Persistent Widow," *The Bible Today* [1990]: 213-19). The former links the parable with Psalm 18 as a meditative exercise, while the latter connects the parable to the Book of Ruth.

126. As are several other parables; see above, p. 327; Bovon, *Das Evangelium nach Lukas,* 3:205.

127. The authenticity of this parable is not usually questioned. The prevailing decision of

the Jesus Seminar was to print it in pink. See Funk, Scott, and Butts, *The Parables of Jesus: Red Letter Edition*, p. 56. E. P. Sanders (*Jesus and Judaism* [Philadelphia: Fortress, 1985], 175, 281) is one who doubts the parable's authenticity, but his primary reason for doing so seems to be to defend the Pharisees. His contention that Jesus gave no attention to "the interior religious attitudes of the righteous" (281) is incredible. Michael Goulder is one who rejects authenticity. See his *Luke: A New Paradigm* (2 vols.; JSNTSup 20; Sheffield: Sheffield Academic, 1989), pp. 667-70. Luise Schottroff suggests the contrast of the parable is harder to imagine as a debate within Judaism than at a distance from Judaism. See her "Die Erzählung vom Pharisäer und Zöllner als Beispiel für die theologische Kunst des Überredens," in *Neues Testament und christliche Existenz*, ed. H. Betz and L. Schrottroff (Tübingen: Mohr-Siebeck, 1973), pp. 439-61, here p. 454.

128. Bailey, *Through Peasant Eyes*, p. 154.

129. For parallels close to the saying in Luke 18:14 concerning those exalting themselves being humbled and vice versa, see *Ahiqar* 60 (Aramaic); *b. 'Erubin* 13b; Diogenes Laertius, *Lives of the Philosophers* 1.69.

130. Jeremias (*The Parables of Jesus*, p. 144), among others, argues that the tax collector's prayer is a quotation of the opening words of Psalm 51, but this is not so certain, even if there are common themes. Whereas LXX Ps 78:9 (English and Hebrew 79:9) uses *hilasthēti* ("be propitiated" or "be merciful"), the same word that is used in Luke 18:13, to translate Hebrew *kapēr* ("cover", "atone"), these are not the words used in the LXX and the Hebrew in Ps 51:1 (LXX Ps 50:3; Hebrew 51:3). The Hebrew has *ḥānnēnî* ("be gracious to me"), which the LXX translates as *eleēson* ("have mercy"). *Hilaskesthai* is not used in the LXX to translate *ḥānan*.

131. Who is described with these words is unclear. R. H. Charles suggested the priestly aristocracy of the Sadducees (see R. H. Charles, ed., *The Assumption of Moses* [London: Black, 1897], pp. 23-26). Cf. Bailey, *Through Peasant Eyes*, pp. 148-49, and note the use of "the place" in John 11:48 and Acts 6:14 to refer to the Temple. On the idea of standing aloof, see *m. 'Abot* 2.5.

132. See also *'Abot de Rabbi Nathan* 11; *Midr. Tanḥuma Wayyiqra* 1.4.

133. Note that Ezek 23:4 provides an explanation at the beginning for the long metaphorical story in 23:1-49.

134. Only the parables of the Pharisee and the Tax Collector and of the Good Samaritan are described as taking place at specific locations. Both accounts also use "acquit" (or "justify," *dikaioō*). Craig L. Blomberg ("Midrash, Chiasmus, and the Outline of Luke's Central Section," in *Gospel Perspectives III: Studies in Midrash and Historiography*, ed. R. T. France and David Wenham [Sheffield: JSOT, 1983], pp. 240-44) thinks the two parables are linked in a chiastic arrangement.

135. 5:21, 30, 33; 6:2, 7; 7:30, 36-50; 11:38-54; 14:3; 15:1-2; 16:14-15.

136. Omission of Greek connective particles.

137. See Matthew Black, *An Aramaic Approach to the Gospels and Acts* (3d ed.; Oxford: Clarendon, 1967), pp. 59, 108, 117; Jeremias, *The Parables of Jesus*, pp. 140-42.

138. At least if Josephus's description is to be trusted (*J. W.* 1.110-12; *Ant.* 13.289, 298; 18.15). See Anthony J. Saldarini, "Pharisees," *ABD* 5:289-303.

139. E.g., 1 Sam 7:6; Ps 35:13; Zech 7:5; Matt 6:16-18; Mark 2:18-20; Luke 2:36-38; Acts 13:2-3; 2 Cor 11:27. Fasting later was seen as a means of overcoming temptation, especially in the *Testament of the Twelve Patriarchs*. On fasting generally, see Joseph F. Wimmer, *Fasting in the New Testament* (New York: Paulist, 1982).

140. See *m. Ta'anit* 1.6; *b. Ta'anit* 12a; *Didache* 8:1; and also S. Safrai, "Religion in Everyday Life," *JPFC* 2:814-16.

141. The degree to which tax collectors were viewed as traitors would have been some-

what different in Judea under Roman rule than in Galilee under Herod Antipas, but attitudes in Galilee could not have been that much more positive.

142. See Fritz Herrenbrück, *Jesus und die Zöllner. Historische und neutestamentlich-exegetische Untersuchungen* (WUNT 2/41; Tübingen: Mohr-Siebeck), 1990; John R. Donahue, "Tax Collectors and Sinners: An Attempt at Identification," *CBQ* 33 (1977): 39-61; "Tax Collector," *ABD* 6:337-38. Donahue would prefer the term "toll collector" for *telōnēs*, i.e., those who collected tolls at toll stations. On taxation in Galilee, see Seán Freyne, *Galilee from Alexander the Great to Hadrian: 323 B.C.E. to 135 C.E.* (Wilmington: Michael Glazier, 1980), pp. 183-94. See also Josephus, *Ant.* 12.154-59, 175-86; *Select Papyri* (LCL) 2, selections 286, 358, 381, 382, and 420.

143. This is true both for Jews and for the Greco-Roman world as well. On the latter see Donahue, "Tax Collector," 337-38; for the former see Joachim Jeremias, *Jerusalem in the Time of Jesus: An Investigation into the Economic and Social Conditions During the New Testament Period* (trans. F. H. and C. H. Cave; Philadelphia: Fortress, 1969), pp. 310-11.

144. See *m. Nedarim* 3.4; *m. Baba Qamma* 10.1-2; *b. Sanhedrin* 25b. Cf. *m. 'Abot* 3.17, apparently drawing on the image of tax collectors, which speaks of collectors exacting payment with or without people's consent. 4Q424 also assumes a negative view of tax collectors. *M. Teharot* 7.6 reports that tax gatherers entering a house render the house unclean; cf. *m. Hagigah* 3.6. Hyam Maccoby ("How Unclean Were Tax-Collectors?" *BTB* 31 [2002]: 60-63) argues — fairly, it seems — that tax collectors were viewed as sinners morally and not de facto ritually unclean.

145. E.g., Hultgren, *The Parables of Jesus,* p. 121.

146. S. Safrai, "The Temple," *JPFC* 2:885-90.

147. Note the attitude expressed in *As. Mos.* 7:9-10 above.

148. On the difficulty of tax collectors making restitution, see *t. Baba Meṣiʿa* 8.26; *b. Baba Qamma* 94b.

149. Wailes, *Medieval Allegories of Jesus' Parables,* p. 265. See *NPNF1* 8:353-54 on Psalm 75, section 11. Augustine also frequently interprets the parable with regard to pride and humility. E.g., *NPNF1* 8:126 on Psalm 40, section 19.

150. Hultgren, *The Parables of Jesus,* p. 126; Martin Hengel, "Die ganz andere Gerechtigkeit," *TBei* 5 (1974): 1-13; Hans Joachim Eckstein, "Pharisäer und Zöllner. Jesu Zuwendung zu den Sündern nach Lukas 18,9-14," in *Der aus Glauben Gerechte wird leben. Beiträge zur Theologie des Neuen Testaments* (BVB 5; Münster: Lit, 2003), pp. 143-51; Betty O. S. Tan, "The Parable of the Pharisee and the Tax-Collector in Luke 18:9-14: A Study on the Practice of Prayer," *AJT* 14 (2000): 286-303.

151. J. Stanley Glen, *The Parables of Conflict in Luke* (Philadelphia: Fortress, 1962), pp. 54-63.

152. John Dominic Crossan, "Parable and Example in the Teaching of Jesus," *NTS* 18 (1972): 285-307, here p. 300.

153. Herzog, *Parables as Subversive Speech,* pp. 173-93. The claim is that Jesus' pedagogy of the oppressed was designed to demystify the Temple, the role of the redemptive media, and the name-calling of the Pharisaic rule-enforcers so that peasants could name oppression as a prelude to renaming their world (p. 193). See also Michael Farris, "A Tale of Two Taxations (Luke 18:10-14b): The Parable of the Pharisee and the Toll Collector," in *Jesus and His Parables: Interpreting the Parables of Jesus Today,* ed. V. George Shillington (Edinburgh: T. & T. Clark, 1997), pp. 23-33.

154. Schottroff, "Die Erzählung vom Pharisäer und Zöllner," pp. 439-61. Whereas Schottroff views the tax collector as a figure with whom one should identify (pp. 453-55), F. Ger-

ald Downing thinks both characters are caricatures of self-absorption and warnings to the hearers, with the tax collector betraying a despairing lack of confidence in God. See his "The Ambiguity of 'The Pharisee and the Toll-Collector' (Luke 18:9-14) in the Greco-Roman World of Late Antiquity," *CBQ* 54 (1992): 80-99, especially 89. Similarly Hedrick (*Parables as Poetic Fictions*, pp. 227-35) thinks both are negative characters and that the tax collector wants mercy without repentance or restitution. For him the parable is left with two unacceptable alternatives and no resolution so that one must ponder one's own relation to God.

155. See Craig A. Evans, "The Pharisee and the Publican: Luke 18:9-14 and Deuteronomy 26," in *The Gospels and the Scriptures of Israel*, ed. Craig A. Evans and W. Richard Stegner (Sheffield: Sheffield Academic, 1994), pp. 342-55. Evans bases his conclusion partly on the hypothesis that Luke shaped his travel narrative to Deuteronomy. He points to verbal and thematic coherences between the two texts, but he is not convincing in showing how the parallel really helps in interpreting the parable. See also Fred Holmgren, "The Pharisee and the Tax Collector: Luke 18:9-14 and Deuteronomy 26:1-15," *Int* 48 (1994): 252-61. John Lightfoot (*Horae Hebraicae et Talmudicae* [reprint, Oxford: Oxford University Press, 1859], 3:185) pointed to the relevance of Deuteronomy 26 for this parable in the seventeenth century.

In an informative article Timothy A. Friedrichsen takes the Pharisee's role in a much more positive, but in my estimation impossible, light. Having deleted vv. 9 and 14b (and part of 14a) from the parable and reading the Pharisee's prayer positively, he suggests that the Pharisee tithed more than required on behalf of those who could not fulfill their duty and that the tax collector was justified because he had benefited from the vicarious virtue of the Pharisee's fasting and tithing. See his "The Temple, a Pharisee, a Tax Collector, and the Kingdom of God: Rereading a Jesus Parable (Luke 18:10-14a)," *JBL* 124 (2005): 89-119.

156. E.g., Jacques Schlosser, "Le Pharisien et le Publicain (Lc 18, 9-14)," in *Les Paraboles Évangélique. Perspectives nouvelles,* ed. Jean Delormé (Paris: Cerf, 1989), pp. 271-88, here p. 288; Greg W. Forbes, *The God of Old: The Role of the Lukan Parables in the Purpose of Luke's Gospel* (JSNTSup 198; Sheffield: Sheffield Academic, 2000), p. 216.

157. See above, pp. 13-15 and 350-52.

158. See especially the arguments of Schottroff, "Die Erzählung vom Pharisäer und Zöllner," pp. 441-46.

159. Hultgren (*The Parables of Jesus*, pp. 119, 122) and Fitzmyer (*The Gospel According to Luke X–XXIV*, 2:1186) argue for the latter.

160. Codex Bezae and limited versional witnesses read *statheis kath' heauton tauta,* which is a scribal attempt to make clear that the Pharisee stands alone. Other readings omit *pros heauton* or *tauta* or both, but are not well attested.

161. This is the choice of KJV, RSV, and NIV.

162. The choice of the UBS[4] Greek text, the Nestle-Aland[27] Greek text, and NRSV.

163. Hultgren (*The Parables of Jesus*, p. 119) offers Luke 12:41; 14:6; 20:19; and Acts 24:16 as evidence, but none of these is a close parallel to Luke 18:11.

164. E.g., Gen 20:17; Exod 10:17; 1 Sam 1:10; Ps 5:3; and frequently.

165. Bovon (*Das Evangelium nach Lukas,* 3:209) would prefer not to choose between the readings; he thinks this is a typical Lukan ambiguity.

166. Joel Green points out that the borders between Jesus' followers and others is porous in this section of Luke. See *The Gospel of Luke* (NICNT; Grand Rapids: Eerdmans, 1997), p. 644.

167. For the words "trusted in themselves," see 2 Cor 1:9, and more generally for the words "trusted in" *(peithein epi)* see LXX Ezek 33:13; Matt 27:43; Mark 10:23; Luke 11:22; 2 Cor 2:3; Heb 2:13.

168. E.g., Downing, "The Ambiguity of 'The Pharisee and the Toll-Collector,'" 86, 96-97; and Hedrick, *Parables as Poetic Fictions*, pp. 211, 234-35. A conclusion at v. 13 allows them to see both characters as rejected and the parable as without resolution.

169. Nolland, *Luke 9:21–18:34*, p. 874; Schlosser, "Le Pharisien et le Publicain," 278-80; Franz Schnider, "Ausschließen und ausgeschlossen werden. Beobachtungen zur Struktur des Gleichnisses vom Pharisäer und Zöllner," *BZ* 24 (1980): 42-56, here pp. 46 and 50.

170. A textual question exists in v. 14a (which is not included in the UBS text) about the words translated "rather than the other." See Juan B. Cortés, "The Greek Text of Luke 18:14a: A Contribution to the Method of Reasoned Eclecticism," *CBQ* 46 (1984): 255-73. He argues for the reading *ē gar ekeinos,* which he also takes as exclusive. He suggests the possibility of a question expecting a negative answer, such as "Did you think the other?"

171. Cf. the similar sayings at Jas 4:6, 10; 1 Pet 5:5-6, both quoting Prov 3:34.

172. See especially Heininger, *Metaphorik, Erzählstruktur und szenisch-dramatische Gestaltung in den Sondergutgleichnissen bei Lukas,* p. 210; Hultgren, *The Parables of Jesus,* p. 125.

173. André Feuillet, "La signification christologique de Luc 18, 14 et les références des Evangiles au Serviteur souffrant," *Nova et Vetera* 15 (1980): 188-229, here pp. 199-200. Schottroff ("Die Erzählung vom Pharisäer und Zöllner") thinks the frame suits the narration. Evans ("The Pharisee and the Publican: Luke 18:9-14 and Deuteronomy 26," p. 351) thinks v. 14b is secondary, but as part of his theory of a parallel between the parable and Deuteronomy 26 he still finds a connection between this verse and the humiliation/exaltation theme in Deut 26:6-8.

174. Even *m. Soṭa* 3.4 says that the (self-inflicted) wounds of a Pharisee wear out the world. See *b. Soṭa* 22b, which in explaining the expression "plague of the Pharisees," describes seven types of Pharisees, most of whom are guilty of false humility or ostentation. See similar accounts in *'Abot de Rabbi Nathan* 37; *y. Berakot* 9.5 and the discussion in George Foot Moore, *Judaism in the First Centuries of the Christian Era* (Cambridge: Harvard University Press, 1927), 2:192-94. See also *b. Sukkot* 45b for descriptions of arrogance. On the avoidance of dealings with the *'am ha-areṣ* (the common people, literally "people of the land"), see *m. Demai* 2.3; *m. Ḥagigah* 2.7; *m. Ṭoharot* 7.4-6; 8.3. Cf. John 7:49.

175. Evans ("The Pharisee and the Publican: Luke 18:9-14 and Deuteronomy 26," pp. 346-51) points to verbal, thematic, and exegetical coherence between the two texts. With regard to verbal parallels, the reference to "tithes" with a relatively rare word (*apodekatoun,* which appears only six times in the LXX and three times in the Gospels) and to the humiliation-exaltation language in v. 14b and Deut 26:6-8 are among the most important. Particularly striking are Josephus's comments on Deuteronomy 26, which use three words that are in the parable: "stand," "give thanks," and "mercy." See *Ant.* 4.242-43.

176. Blomberg ("Midrash, Chiasmus, and the Outline of Luke's Central Section," pp. 217-59) argues against the hypothesis that the central section of Luke is framed on Deuteronomy.

177. See Psalms 5, 7, 17, and 26.

178. See n. 154 above.

179. See above, pp. 463-65, especially 1QH 15.34-35; *As. Mos.* 7:9-10; and of course Matt 23:23/Luke 11:42.

180. Schottroff, "Die Erzählung vom Pharisäer und Zöllner," pp. 451-52. She thinks that if the prayer is sincere the parable must lead to the rejection of Judaism. This is what leads her to see the prayer of the Pharisee as a caricature. Scott (*Hear Then the Parable,* p. 97) also has trouble finding fault in the Pharisee or merit in the tax collector.

181. Forbes, *The God of Old,* p. 216; Hedrick, *Parables as Poetic Fictions,* p. 232; Schnider, "Ausschließen und ausgeschlossen werden," 46-47, 49.

182. For the most obvious, Luke 10:25-37; Matt 19:16-22; 22:34-39.

183. E.g., Matt 7:21-23/Luke 13:25-27; Luke 14:16-24.

184. E.g., Bailey, *Through Peasant Eyes*, p. 154.

185. E.g., Hedrick, *Parables as Poetic Fictions*, p. 214; M. Hengel ("Die ganz andere Gerechtigkeit," 1) assumes that the two went up for private prayer between the sacrifices.

186. See the discussion by Dennis Hamm, "The Tamid Service in Luke-Acts: The Cultic Background behind Luke's Theology of Worship (Luke 1:5-25; 18:9-14; 24:50-53; Acts 3:1, 10:3, 30)," *CBQ* 65 (2003): 215-31.

187. See David Hill, *Greek Words and Hebrew Meanings* (Cambridge: Cambridge University Press, 1967), p. 36. The proximity to other cultic words of the same root cannot be ignored. See *hilastērion* in Rom 3:25; Heb 9:5 and *hilasmos* in 1 John 2:2; 4:10. *Hilaskomai* occurs in the NT outside this parable only in Heb 2:17.

188. Contra Scott, *Hear Then the Parable*, p. 93. Nor is the parable an instruction in the futility of religion, contra Capon, *The Parables of Grace*, p. 178.

189. Note the similarity between the elder brother's description of the Prodigal ("this [*houtos*] son of yours") and the Pharisee's description of the tax collector ("as this [*houtos*] tax collector").

190. Schottroff, "Die Erzählung vom Pharisäer und Zöllner," 455; see also Henry Mottu, "The Pharisee and the Tax Collector: Sartrian Notions as Applied to the Reading of Scripture," *USQR* 29 (1974): 195-213, here p. 201.

191. Hengel, "Die ganz andere Gerechtigkeit," 6, 8.

192. Peter Rhea Jones, *Studying the Parables of Jesus* (Macon: Smyth & Helwys, 1999), p. 254.

193. Elsewhere in the Gospels only in Matt 11:19; 12:37; Luke 7:29, 35; 10:29; 16:15. The last two approximate the meaning "acquit" as in 18:14.

194. Jeremias, *The Parables of Jesus*, p. 141; F. F. Bruce, "Justification by Faith in the Non-Pauline Writings of the New Testament," *EvQ* 24 (1952): 66-69.

195. See Forbes, *The God of Old*, p. 221.

196. "La signification christologique de Luc 18, 14 et les références des Évangiles au Serviteur souffrant," 190, 194, 196-205, 222-29.

197. See Schnider, "Ausschließen und ausgeschlossen werden," 51-52; Hendrickx, *The Parables of Jesus*, pp. 244-46.

198. See Lowell C. Green, "Justification in Luther's Preaching on Luke 18:9-14," *Currents in Theology and Mission* 43 (1972): 732-47, especially 734.

199. Søren Kierkegaard, *Christian Discourses* (trans. Walter Lowrie; New York: Oxford University Press, 1961), pp. 371-77.

200. Helmut Thielicke, *The Waiting Father* (trans. John W. Doberstein; New York: Harper & Row, 1959), pp. 128, 133.

201. Glen, *Parables of Conflict in Luke*, p. 59.

202. The words are from Crump, *Jesus the Intercessor*, p. 131.

203. Note Eph 3:13 and *2 Clem.* 2:2.

Notes to "Parables of Future Eschatology"

1. The eschatological nature of the Lord's Prayer deserves more emphasis than it receives, even if the ethical and present focus does not need to be diminished.

2. Marcus Borg, "A Temperate Case for a Non-Eschatological Jesus," *FFF* 2 (1986): 81-102.

3. N. T. Wright, *Jesus and the Victory of God,* vol. 2 of *Christian Origins and the Question of God* (Minneapolis: Fortress, 1996), pp. 202-43, 510-19, 638 and for discussion of the larger questions pp. 13-82.

4. Dale Allison, *Jesus of Nazareth: Millenarian Prophet* (Minneapolis: Fortress, 1998), pp. 95-171. For Allison, whether Jesus' use of the coming Son of Man was a self-reference is not clear. See pp. 111 and 159-62. In his commentary on Matthew (W. D. Davies and Dale C. Allison, *A Critical and Exegetical Commentary on the Gospel According to Saint Matthew* [3 vols.; ICC; Edinburgh: T. & T. Clark, 1988-97], 2:50) he concludes that Jesus used Son of Man in reference to Daniel 7 as a prophecy of his own person and fate.

5. James D. G. Dunn (*Jesus Remembered,* vol. 1 of *Christianity in the Making* [Grand Rapids: Eerdmans, 2003], pp. 393-96) lists fourteen items that — with variations — were regularly part of Jewish expectation: (1) the scattered of Israel regathered and the unity of the twelve tribes reestablished, (2) renewed and abundant prosperity, removal of disabilities and defects, and restoration of paradise, (3) the messianic age/banquet, sometimes with reference to a particular messianic figure or divine agent, (4) for some, a renewed covenant, turning from transgression, and outpouring of the Spirit, (5) building of a new temple, (6) Yahweh's return to Zion, (7) destruction of other nations or, more commonly, a pilgrimage of other nations to Zion to pay tribute or to worship, (8) sometimes, a focus not just on the land of Israel but on the whole earth, (9) a climactic period of tribulation, (10) cosmic disturbances, even the destruction of creation and a new creation, (11) destruction of evil and of Satan, (12) final judgment, (13) resurrection, and (14) Sheol/Hades. Even with a focus on the presence of the kingdom, none of these expectations was fully met and some not at all.

While Jesus' preaching embraced much of this expectation, there are notable differences. He has no opposition to the other nations and, remarkably, does not focus on Israel's national interests or the land of Israel. Also, a major new feature is his emphasis on eschatological reversal (the poor, mourning, and meek being blessed, etc.).

6. E.g., Matt 23:35-39/Luke 11:47-51; Matt 24:34/Mark 13:30/Luke 21:32; Luke 13:1-9.

7. E.g., Matt 11:20-24/Luke 10:12-15; Matt 13:36-50; Matt 16:27; Matt 19:28-29/Mark 10:29-30/Luke 18:29-30; Matt 25:31-46; and Luke 22:29-30.

8. E.g., Matt 11:2-6/Luke 7:18-23; Matt 11:12/Luke 16:16; Matt 12:28/Luke 11:20; Matt 13:16-17/Luke 10:23-24; Luke 4:18-21; 17:21.

9. E.g., Matt 6:20/Luke 12:33; Matt 7:21-22; Matt 8:11/Luke 13:28-29; 22:30.

10. *Jesus and the Victory of God,* vol. 2 of *Christian Origins and the Question of God* (Minneapolis: Fortress, 1996), pp. 360-67, 510-19; see also Scot McKnight, *A New Vision for Israel* (Grand Rapids: Eerdmans, 1999), pp. 134-35, 139, who argues that Jesus could not see past 70 A.D. Unlike Allison (*Jesus of Nazareth,* pp. 218-19) who thinks that Jesus was mistaken but that his dream is the only dream worth dreaming, McKnight does not think Jesus' shortness of sight means he was mistaken.

11. As others have pointed out, an essential unity exists in the various revelations of the glory of God in such acts. I cannot accept that the vindication of Jesus takes place through the Romans, contra McKnight, *A New Vision for Israel,* p. 143; and Wright, *Jesus and the Victory of God,* pp. 317, 636.

12. As are Matt 10:23 and Matt 16:28/Mark 9:1/Luke 9:27.

13. Matt 24:36/Mark 13:32.

14. Note George R. Beasley-Murray's reconsideration of this text and his change of mind in *Jesus and the Last Days: The Interpretation of the Olivet Discourse* (Peabody: Hendrickson,

1993), pp. 448-49, 453-68. C. H. Dodd (*The Parables of the Kingdom* [London: Nisbet, 1935], p. 146) suggested that the coming of the Son of Man was seen as relatively remote, but within the lifetime of the existing generation. If no one knows the time, can such boundaries be set?

15. If Jesus did not speak of his coming, how did the early church develop such a belief so quickly? Why would traditions such as Matt 20:20-28/Mark 10:35-45 or Matt 19:28/Luke 22:30 appear? If it is not *his* kingdom, the NT evidence is truly strange.

16. Some scholars think Jesus referred to someone other than himself with this title, and some still reject certain kinds of sayings as from Jesus. That Jesus referred to himself see James D. G. Dunn, *Jesus Remembered,* 724-62; Gerd Theissen and Annette Merz, *The Historical Jesus: A Comprehensive Guide* (trans. John Bowden; Minneapolis: Fortress, 1998), pp. 541-53; and Wright, *Jesus and the Victory of God,* pp. 512-19. The explanation of B. Chilton that Jesus used the term in two different ways — generically of himself and of the Danielic Son of Man in heaven — is not far from Dunn's approach. Chilton thinks Jesus and this second Son of Man were both agents of God's final intervention. See "(The) Son of (the) Man, and Jesus," in *Authenticating the Words of Jesus* (ed. Bruce D. Chilton and Craig A. Evans; Leiden: Brill, 1999), pp. 259-87. The evidence forces Dunn and Chilton to conclude that Jesus used the term of himself, even with allusion to Dan 7:13, but both react against the thought that Jesus laid claim to the title. Yet, both speak of Jesus' conviction of being God's eschatological agent at the climax of God's purposes for Israel. If Jesus saw himself as God's final agent, little difficulty remains in thinking he might describe himself with Son of Man language, recognizing, of course, that the title was first of all a corporate title, like most of the other christological titles.

17. See C. K. Barrett, *Jesus and the Gospel Tradition* (Philadelphia: Fortress, 1968), pp. 76-88, who points to the expectation that those who gave their lives for the nation would not lose their reward; see Dan 12:2; 2 Macc 7:14, 37.

18. See the treatment of this subject by W. G. Kümmel, *Promise and Fulfillment: The Eschatological Message of Jesus* (Naperville: Alec R. Allenson, 1957), pp. 64-83. See also Eduard Schweizer, "The Significance of Eschatology in the Teaching of Jesus," in *Eschatology and the New Testament,* ed. W. Hulitt Gloer (Peabody: Hendrickson, 1988), pp. 1-13.

19. The words of institution in Luke 22:19 and 1 Cor 11:24-25 anticipate some length of time observing the Lord's Supper until the parousia, as do passages teaching on subjects like divorce and taxes.

20. How do Jesus' expected vindication and the coming of the Son of Man relate to each other? A lot depends on how one views the passion predictions and sayings like John 2:19-22. If one accepts them as pointing to resurrection after three days, then vindication and the coming of the Son of Man are two different items. No saying mentions the two together. See the discussion of Ben F. Meyer, *The Aims of Jesus* (London: SCM, 1979), pp. 202-9.

21. As Dale Allison (*Jesus of Nazareth,* p. 160) points out, Paul did not interpret the tradition behind Mark 13:24-27 as referring to the destruction of Jerusalem.

22. Jesus often points, not to national judgment, but to judgment on individuals as to whether they are good or evil and whether they have been productive or useless.

23. For overviews of the theories, see David Aune, "The Significance of the Delay of the Parousia for Early Christianity," in *Current Issues in Biblical and Patristic Interpretation,* ed. Gerald F. Hawthorne (Grand Rapids: Eerdmans, 1975), pp. 87-95; George Eldon Ladd, *The Presence of the Future* (Grand Rapids: Eerdmans, 1974), pp. 3-42; and for extensions of the discussion into the present, Allison, *Jesus of Nazareth,* pp. 95-129.

24. G. B. Caird, *New Testament Theology* (compiled and ed. L. D. Hurst; Oxford: Claren-

don, 1994), pp. 247, 258-63. See also Ladd, *The Presence of the Future*, p. 315, who argues for a prophetic outlook that can hold the present and the future in a dynamic and unresolved tension.

25. See Davies and Allison, *Matthew*, 3:329 and the overview on pp. 328-33, but their own explanation on p. 331 is none too clear.

26. It will not do to suggest, as McKnight does (*A New Vision for Israel*, p. 132), that Jesus did not know the particular time but did know the general time, i.e., within his generation. See Caird, *New Testament Theology*, p. 255.

27. See the classic argument that the delay was a major factor in reshaping the church's thought by Erich Grässer, *Das Problem der Parusieverzögerung in den synoptischen Evangelien und in der Apostelgeschichte* (2d ed.; Berlin: Töpelmann, 1960), and for discussions of the issue, see Aune, "The Significance of the Delay of the Parousia for Early Christianity," pp. 87-109; and Richard J. Bauckham, "The Delay of the Parousia," *TynBul* 31 (1980): 3-36. V. Balabanski argues that the passing of time was an insignificant factor in the development of the church's eschatology (*Eschatology in the Making: Mark, Matthew and the Didache* [SNTSMS 97; Cambridge: Cambridge University Press, 1997], p. 23). Note also John T. Carroll's insistence that delay and imminent expectation go hand-in-hand for Luke and for other NT writers. See Carroll's *Response to the End of History: Eschatology and Situation in Luke-Acts* (SBLDS 92; Atlanta: Scholars, 1988), pp. 94, 165-67.

28. See Caird, *New Testament Theology*, p. 263.

29. Jack Dean Kingsbury (*The Parables of Jesus in Matthew 13: A Study in Redaction-Criticism* [Richmond: John Knox, 1969], pp. 119, 124) finds traits characteristic of both the similitude and the fable, partly because the past tense is used, and calls this parable a fable in a mixed form, i.e., an allegorical parable. But tense is no indicator of form. Delmar Jacobson ("An Exposition of Matthew 13:44-52," *Int* 29 [1975]: 277-82) calls this parable an allegory, but that presupposes both that allegory is a genre and that all the features have allegorical significance, neither of which is justified.

30. Other similitudes with an explanatory *nimshal* include the Children in the Market Place (Matt 11:16-19/Luke 7:31-35) and the Good and Worthless Trees (Matt 7:16-20/Luke 6:43-46).

31. I do not see any relevance of the "fishers of men" statement in Matt 4:19/Mark 1:17/Luke 5:10 to this parable.

32. Clement of Alexandria, *Stromateis* 6.95.3 (*ANF* 2:502 [VI.11]), quotes this parable but does nothing with it.

33. *b. 'Abodah Zarah* 3b-4a compares humans to fish and says that when "the day" comes it burns as a furnace and will set the wicked ablaze, but the passage is not really close to the text in Matthew.

34. E.g., Arland J. Hultgren, *The Parables of Jesus: A Commentary* (Grand Rapids: Eerdmans, 2000), p. 304; Jacobus Liebenberg, *The Language of the Kingdom: Parable, Aphorism, and Metaphor in the Sayings Material Common to the Synoptic Tradition and the Gospel of Thomas* (BZNW 102; Berlin: Walter de Gruyter, 2001), p. 275.

35. See above, p. 240.

36. E.g., Gilles Quispel, "Jewish-Christian Gospel Tradition," in *Gospel Studies in Honor of Sherman Elbridge Johnson*, ed. Massey H. Shepherd, Jr., and Edward C. Hobbs (AThRSS 3; Evanston: Anglican Theological Review, 1974), pp. 112-16; Claus-Hunno Hunzinger, "Unbekannte Gleichnisse Jesu aus dem Thomas-Evangelium," in *Judentum-Urchristentum-Kirche*, ed. W. Eltester (Berlin: Töpelmann, 1964), pp. 209-20, 217-20. Hunzinger thinks that this parable is closely related to the parable of the Pearl and that it assumes the large fish was not in

the net with the small ones and the small ones were released so the net could be thrown over the large one, which is doubtful.

37. See Ulrich Luz, *Matthew 8–20* (trans. James E. Crouch; Minneapolis: Fortress, 2001), p. 282; Davies and Allison, *Matthew*, 2:443; Hans Weder, *Die Gleichnisse als Metaphern. Traditions- und redaktionsgeschichtliche Analysen und Interpretationen* (4th ed.; Göttingen: Vandenhoeck & Ruprecht, 1990), pp. 143-44. Tjitze Baarda has four articles arguing against Quispel's thesis, the most important of which is "'Chose' or 'Collected': Concerning an Aramaism in Logion 8 of the Gospel of Thomas and the Question of Independence," *HTR* 84 (1991): 373-97. William G. Morrice also discusses the relation of the two versions of the parable in "The Parable of the Dragnet and the Gospel of Thomas," *ExpTim* 95 (1984): 269-73.

38. If the *Gos. Thom.* version of the Net was influenced by the parable of the Pearl, it would be strong indication that the author was aware of Matthew's order.

39. Liebenberg, *The Language of the Kingdom,* p. 259; Ivor Harold Jones, *The Matthean Parables: A Literary and Historical Commentary* (NovTSup 80; Leiden: Brill, 1995), p. 355.

40. Cf. John R. Donahue, *The Gospel in Parable* (Philadelphia: Fortress, 1988), p. 69; Morrice's argument for a chiastic arrangement of the chapter ("The Parable of the Dragnet and the Gospel of Thomas," 271) is not convincing.

41. For discussion of this issue see Warren Carter and John Paul Heil, *Matthew's Parables: Audience Oriented Perspectives* (Washington: Catholic Biblical Association of America, 1998), p. 90; and Luz, *Matthew 8–20,* 2:283, who find significance in the connection, and Davies and Allison, *Matthew,* 2:441, who do not.

42. Apparently drawn from Dan 12:13.

43. Or of the good and the worthless (or rotten, *agathos/kalos* and *sapros/ponēros,* 7:17-18; 13:48) or of the righteous and unrighteous (*dikaioi/adikaioi,* 5:45; cf. 25:37, 46).

44. On "consummation of the age" and "weeping and gnashing of teeth," see above pp. 209 and 503.

45. Fire is a sign of God's judgment or purification (e.g., Gen 19:24; Exod 9:24; Lev 10:2). It was understood that fire would announce the Day of the Lord, destroying God's enemies (e.g., Joel 2:30; Isa 66:15, 24; Ezek 38:22; 39:6; Mal 4:1). An oven or furnace is often used as a metaphor for punishment, particularly God's (e.g., Isa 48:10; Jer 11:4, Ezek 22:18-22). This same use of the images continues in Jewish writings.

46. Wilhelm H. Wuellner (*The Meaning of "Fishers of Men"* [Philadelphia: Westminster, 1967], pp. 18, 39) mentions evidence of ten different kinds of nets and of dragnets as large as seven hundred feet long and fifteen feet wide.

47. Joachim Jeremias, *The Parables of Jesus* (2d ed.; trans. S. H. Hooke; New York: Charles Scribner's Sons, 1963), p. 226, following G. Dalman. Edwin Firmage, "Zoology," *ABD* 6:1146 lists only nineteen.

48. Lev 11:9-12; Deut 14:9-10; cf. *m. Ḥullin* 3.7.

49. *b. Ḥullin* 63b indicates that there are 700 kinds of unclean fish.

50. See Stephen L. Wailes, *Medieval Allegories of Jesus' Parables* (Berkeley: University of California Press, 1987), pp. 125-26. Sometimes the net is understood as Scripture or as Christian truth. See e.g., Origen, *Commentary On Matthew,* 10.11-12.

51. E.g., B. T. D. Smith, *The Parables of the Synoptic Gospels* (Cambridge: Cambridge University Press, 1937), p. 201.

52. E.g., George Beasley-Murray, *Jesus and the Kingdom of God* (Grand Rapids: Eerdmans, 1986), pp. 136-37, 200-201.

53. Kingsbury, *The Parables of Jesus in Matthew 13,* pp. 117-24.

54. Jeremias, *The Parables of Jesus,* p. 226.

55. See Robert W. Funk, Bernard Brandon Scott, and James R. Butts, *The Parables of Jesus: Red Letter Edition* (Sonoma: Polebridge, 1988), pp. 27, 70, 75. They reject the parable because it is thought to reflect the church's desire to distinguish itself from the surrounding world.

56. See Hultgren, *The Parables of Jesus,* p. 307; Charles W. F. Smith, "The Mixed State of the Church in Matthew's Gospel," *JBL* 82 (1963): 149-68, here pp. 154-55; Luz, *Matthew 8–20,* 2:281-84; Morrice, "The Parable of the Dragnet and the Gospel of Thomas," 270-72; and Bernard Brandon Scott, *Hear Then the Parable: A Commentary on the Parables of Jesus* (Minneapolis: Fortress, 1989), p. 314.

57. See Luz, *Matthew 8–20,* 2:282; David Flusser, *Die rabbinischen Gleichnisse und der Gleichniserzähler Jesus.* 1: *Das Wesen der Gleichnisse* (Bern: Peter Lang, 1981), pp. 64-65. J. D. M. Derrett ("'ΗΣΑΝ ΓΑΡ ΆΛΙΕΙΣ [Mk. I:16]: Jesus's Fishermen and the Parable of the Net," *NovT* 22 [1980]: 108-37, here p. 128) questions whether vv. 49-50, although Matthean, can be simply torn off. I. Jones (*The Matthean Parables,* p. 357) claims that those who include v. 48 have a problem in that it "draws in" only to "reject," while those who restrict the parable to v. 47 have a parable that says virtually nothing.

58. Liebenburg, *The Language of the Kingdom,* pp. 265-66.

59. Note Weder, *Die Gleichnisse Jesu als Metaphern,* p. 144.

60. 1QpHab 5.12–6.1 interprets this passage of the Kittim, that is, the Romans, and their wealth and weapons.

61. With four different Hebrew words the image of a net (not always a fishing net) serves as a figure for God's judgment (see Job 19:6; Ps 66:11; Isa 51:20; Lam 1:13; Ezek 12:13; 17:20; Hos 7:12) or more generally for being caught and treated badly by the wicked, from which God can deliver (Job 18:8; Pss 9:15; 10:9; 25:15; 31:4; 35:7-8). Eccl 9:12 apparently uses a net as an image of death. Cf. *Eccl. Rab.* 9.14 and *Esth. Rab.* 3.14. The latter says, "The wicked man does not depart from the world before God shows him the net in which he is to be caught."

62. See above, p. 483. On the basis of Isa 24:17 CD 4.12 describes three nets of Belial: fornication, wealth, and defilement of the temple.

63. See above, p. 484.

64. Derrett ("'ΗΣΑΝ ΓΑΡ ΆΛΙΕΙΣ," 117-21, 125-31) goes so far as to suggest a midrash on Ezekiel, partly because of Ezek 29:2-10, which refers to fish thrown from the water onto a field to be eaten by birds.

65. Kingsbury, *The Parables of Jesus in Matthew 13,* pp. 117-25. D. Hagner (*Matthew* [WBC; Dallas: Word, 1993], 1:399-400) and Robert H. Gundry (*Matthew: A Commentary on His Literary and Theological Art* [Grand Rapids: Eerdmans, 1982], pp. 279-80) make similar arguments and also think the parable is about false Christians. Adolf Jülicher (*Die Gleichnisreden Jesu* [Darmstadt: Wissenschaftliche Buchgesellschaft, 1963, reprint], 2:568) forcefully rejects any idea of tolerating wrong.

66. See above, pp. 202-4.

67. E.g., Mark 7:26; Acts 18:2; Phil 3:5.

68. Luz (*Matthew 8–20,* 2:282) gives up on knowing what Jesus meant.

69. *J.W.* 3.508. The word is used with a wide variety of categories (e.g., kinds of tongues, spirits, plants, or animals).

70. Kingsbury, *The Parables of Jesus in Matthew 13,* pp. 120-21.

71. Luz, *Matthew 8–20,* 2:283.

72. Davies and Allison (*Matthew,* 2:442) assume the angels are also those who cast the net

and do the gathering, which Davies and Allison find mystifying. Surely, however, this is to lay a one-for-one correspondence on the parable that does not exist.

73. *Commentary on Matthew* 10.11.

74. Craig S. Keener, *A Commentary on the Gospel of Matthew* (Grand Rapids: Eerdmans, 1999), p. 393.

75. A description evident also in the metaphors of the good and bad trees and the division that follows (Matt 7:17-27/Luke 6:43-49) and the parables of the Wheat and the Weeds (Matt 13:24-30 and 36-43), the Wedding Banquet (Matt 22:1-14), and the Sheep and the Goats (Matt 25:31-46).

76. Liebenberg, *The Language of the Kingdom,* pp. 262-63, who also finds a second theme of the gathering from every nation; see also Paul Archbald, "Interpretation of the Parable of the Dragnet (Matthew 13:47-50)," *Vox Reformata* 48 (1987): 3-14, here pp. 8-9. C. H. Dodd (*The Parables of the Kingdom,* pp. 187-89) categorizes this parable as a parable of growth and is followed by Kingsbury (*The Parables of Jesus in Matthew* 13, p. 118), a choice for which I see no basis. Dodd rejects the idea that the parable is "an allegory of the Last Judgment" (p. 187) but then accepts that it is about selection and sifting, which is the divine judgment (pp. 188-89). This seems another instance of Dodd's "running with the allegorical hare and yet hunting with the Jülicher hounds," to quote Matthew Black ("Parable as Allegory," *BJRL* 42 [1959-60]: 273-87, here p. 283).

77. Liebenberg, *The Language of the Kingdom,* p. 263.

78. On the topic of judgment generally, see vol. 20 of *Ex Auditu* (2004).

79. David Wenham, *The Rediscovery of Jesus' Eschatological Discourse,* vol. 4 of *Gospel Perspectives* (Sheffield: JSOT, 1984), pp. 52, 101; also his comments on method on pp. 370-73; see also Jan Lambrecht, *Out of the Treasure: The Parables in the Gospel of Matthew* (LTPM 10; Louvain: Peeters; Grand Rapids: Eerdmans, 1992), p. 184.

80. Luke 12:35-38 and Mark 13:33-37 represent different parables with similar teaching, contra C. H. Dodd, *The Parables of the Kingdom,* pp. 160-62. See Craig Blomberg, "When Is a Parallel Really a Parallel? A Test Case: The Lukan Parables," *WTJ* 46 (1984): 78-103, especially 80-85.

81. Wenham, *The Rediscovery of Jesus' Eschatological Discourse,* pp. 18-28. The story does not develop, and what happens to the servants is not mentioned. In v. 34 the man goes on a journey, but the shift to the doorkeeper in vv. 34c-35 suggests that he is only out for an evening. H. Weder (*Die Gleichnisse als Metaphern,* p. 163) with others complains of the inconsistencies between vv. 34 and 35, but this is to assume that the two verses are a parabolic unit. Rather, v. 34 describes a setting where watching is necessary, and the analogy drawn in v. 35 is limited to the theme of watching. V. 35 merely specifies the purpose of the image and is the application of the parable, not a continuation of it.

82. Cf. Richard Bauckham, "Synoptic Parousia Parables and the Apocalypse," in *The Climax of Prophecy* (Edinburgh: T. & T. Clark, 1993), pp 92-117, especially 93-109. From these texts Bauckham argues for a process of deparabolization in the early church. M. Goulder's suggestion that Matthew was dependent on Paul is simplistic and unlikely (*Midrash and Lection in Matthew* [London: SPCK, 1974], p. 167). Note that *Gos. Thom.* 21 and 103 also have forms of the thief saying.

83. Lambrecht, *Out of the Treasure,* p. 190.

84. Whether there are seven parables in Matt 24:32–25:46, as Jeremias suggests (*The Parables of Jesus,* p. 93), depends on whether one is justified in starting with 24:32, whether one is convinced that Matthew intended seven parables, especially with the comparison to the days of Noah in 24:37-39, and whether one can ignore 24:40-41. The seven are the Fig Tree (24:32-36),

the Days of Noah (24:37-41), the Burglar (24:42-44), the Faithful Servant (24:45-51), the Ten Virgins (25:1-13), the Talents (25:14-30), and the Sheep and Goats (25:31-46).

85. Lambrecht (*Out of the Treasure*, p. 190) pairs the sayings in 24:36-44 with the parable of the Ten Virgins and the parable of the Faithful or Unfaithful Servant with the parable of the Talents, these last two further defining the first two. This does not take notice of the connections between the Ten Virgins and the Faithful or Unfaithful Servant.

86. See above, pp. 327 and 462.

87. Of 111 words in Matt, Luke has 85 words identical and 5 more that are different forms of the same word.

88. See Otto Betz, "The Dichotomized Servant and the End of Judas Iscariot," *RevQ* 5 (1964): 43-58, especially 45.

89. See especially LXX Ps 111:10; but also LXX Job 16:9; Pss 34:16; 36:12; Lam 2:16; and also Acts 7:54. Cf. Jdt 16:17.

90. The two positive servants are usually viewed as a unity.

91. See n. 228 herein.

92. Several unexpected and unacceptable interpretations should be mentioned: (1) J. Dwight Pentecost (*The Parables of Jesus* [Grand Rapids: Zondervan, 1982], pp. 149-51) suggests that the servants represent the people of the nation of Israel, who will be God's stewards during the tribulation; (2) Robert Winterhalter, with George W. Fisk (*Jesus' Parables: Finding Our God Within* [New York: Paulist, 1993], pp. 93 and also 84-88) thinks the parable is about each person being the steward over his or her own thoughts and words, with the beating of male and female servants being the entertaining of negative thoughts and emotions; and (3) B. Scott (*Hear Then the Parable*, p. 212) argues the parable unmasks the uselessness of an apocalyptic expectation that needs God's presence to right wrongs or to extract moral behavior.

93. Wailes, *Medieval Allegories of Jesus' Parables*, pp. 173-77. On the application to alms see John Chrysostom, *Homilies on Matthew* 77 (*NPNF1* 10:465-66). Cf. Hermas, *Sim.* 2, especially 2.7.

94. Erich Grässer, *Das Problem der Parusieverzögerung in den synoptischen Evangelien und in der Apostelgeschichte*, pp. 88-95; Lambrecht, *Out of the Treasure*, pp. 191-94. Funk, Scott, and Butts (*The Parables of Jesus: Red Letter Edition*) do not even consider this parable, but it is printed with black ink in the work by Robert W. Funk, Roy W. Hoover, and the Jesus Seminar, *The Five Gospels: The Search for the Authentic Words of Jesus* (New York: Macmillan, 1993), pp. 253-54.

95. Dodd, *The Parables of the Kingdom*, pp. 160, 165, 170-74; Jeremias, *The Parables of Jesus*, pp. 55-58; Jones, *The Matthean Parables*, pp. 433-42. D. Flusser (*Die rabbinischen Gleichnisse und der Gleichniserzähler Jesus*, p. 91) argued that the parable is about the responsibility of humans who leave God out of consideration. A. Hultgren (*The Parables of Jesus*, pp. 160-61) suggested that the parable might have been spoken to the disciples to press on them the necessity of caring for the people of Israel by proclaiming the kingdom, healing, and casting out demons, for which they would be held accountable to God later.

96. Kümmel, *Promise and Fulfilment*, pp. 54-59; Joseph A. Fitzmyer, *The Gospel According to Luke X–XXIV* (AB 28A; Garden City: Doubleday, 1985), p. 987. Cf. Ulrich Luz, *Matthew 21–28: A Commentary* (trans. James E. Crouch; Minneapolis: Fortress, 2005), pp. 222-23.

97. Note how image and reality are interlaced in Isa 50:1; Ezek 19:2-9; 23:1-21; Epictetus, *Enchiridion* 7. With religious language the literal and metaphorical planes are often intermingled. That parables have such intermingling is not essentially different from expressions like "all the house of Israel is uncircumcised in heart" (Jer 9:26).

98. See Matthew Black, *An Aramaic Approach to the Gospels and Acts* (3d ed.; Oxford: Clarendon, 1967), pp. 118-19; or I. Howard Marshall, *Commentary on Luke* (NIGTC; Grand Rapids: Eerdmans, 1978), p. 540.

99. This is the only parable that forms the introductory question with *tis ara* ("Who then?").

100. Contra Jones, *The Matthean Parables*, p. 436. The addition of "evil" in Matt 24:48 makes the logic of the condition more awkward and seems at first glance to suggest that two servants are in view.

101. In addition to those mentioned above in n. 95, see Harry Fleddermann, "The Householder and the Servant Left in Charge," in *Society of Biblical Literature 1986 Seminar Papers,* ed. Kent Harold Richards (Atlanta: Scholars, 1986), pp. 17-26. For the argument that the portion of the parable dealing with the unfaithful servant is a secondary accretion see Jones, *The Matthean Parables,* p. 441; and G. Schneider, *Parusiegleichnisse im Lukas-Evangelium* (Stuttgart: Katholisches Bibelwerk, 1975), pp. 27-28.

102. See John Nolland, *Luke 9:21–18:34* (WBC 35B; Dallas: Word, 1993), p. 704; John Dominic Crossan, *In Parables: The Challenge of the Historical Jesus* (New York: Harper and Row, 1973), p. 100. In Crossan's opinion the point in Matt 24:48/Luke 12:45 may fit the problem of the delay of the return of the Son of Man but did not derive from it.

103. See Alfons Weiser, *Die Knechtsgleichnisse der synoptischen Evangelien* (SANT 29; Munich: Kösel, 1971), pp. 158-60; Jones, *The Matthean Parables,* pp. 436-38.

104. See above, pp. 459-61; and see also Richard Bauckham, "The Delay of the Parousia," 3-19. 2 *Baruch* is especially revealing. See also *b. Sanhedrin* 97b-98a.

105. *The Gospel According to Luke X–XXIV,* p. 987. See Isa 13:6; Ezek 30:3; Joel 1:15; 2:1; Amos 5:18; Obad 15; Zeph 1:14-18; Mal 3:23-24 (4:5-6 in English versions); see also 1QS 6.7; 4QPs37. Of course, the idea of waiting on Yahweh is common.

106. As an additional argument for authenticity Scott (*Hear Then the Parable,* pp. 210-12) sees the shock of the severe punishment at the end of the parable as characteristic of Jesus' style.

107. Weiser (*Die Knechtsgleichnisse der synoptischen Evangelien,* p. 183) argued that Jesus gave no content to the master and servants.

108. See above, pp. 480-81. The most pointed text about Jesus' departure is John 14:1-3 and related sayings in the Johannine farewell discourses (chs. 13-17).

109. E.g., the parable of the Wicked Tenants and *Midr. Tanḥuma Beshallah* 4.7 (see above, p. 279). One thinks also of OT texts describing both God abandoning the Temple and promises of his return.

That a particular image may be used in various ways urges caution. Note that with the analogy of the thief (Matt 24:43-44/Luke 12:39-40) the householder is neither a "God" nor a "Christ" figure but corresponds to a disciple. The analogy urges that like a householder guarding against theft, disciples too should be vigilant and prepared. Whether the thief image is intended to convey anything negative is debated. Some argue that it only speaks of unexpectedness and stress the need for care in pushing metaphors. See Joel B. Green, *The Gospel of Luke* (NICNT; Grand Rapids: Eerdmans, 1997), p. 502. Evald Lövestam argues, however, that one cannot eliminate the destructive elements from the image. See his *Spiritual Wakefulness in the New Testament* (trans. W. F. Salisbury; LUÅ 55; Lund: Gleerup, 1963), pp. 98-99. He also points out (p. 96) that the absence of the thief simile in Jewish eschatological imagery points to Jesus as its origin. Nolland (*Luke 9:21–18:34,* p. 699) argues similarly that the bold use of the negative image of the thief more likely stems from Jesus.

110. C. H. Dodd, *The Parables of the Kingdom*, pp. 158-71; Jeremias, *The Parables of Jesus,* pp. 49, 55-58. Wright (*Jesus and the Victory of God,* p. 183) seems to take the same approach.

111. See Dunn, *Jesus Remembered,* p. 431.

112. Weiser, *Die Knechtsgleichnisse der synoptischen Evangelien,* p. 179.

113. I. H. Marshall, *Eschatology and the Parables* (London: Tyndale, 1963), p. 47.

114. In this section of Luke the audience alternates between disciples and the crowd.

115. See Green, *The Gospel of Luke,* p. 503.

116. *The Parables of Jesus,* p. 58; Dodd, *The Parables of the Kingdom,* pp. 159-60.

117. See Weiser, *Die Knechtsgleichnisse der synoptischen Evangelien,* pp. 146-50, 184, 208-10. Note that Jeremias ignores the negative servant in his analysis. See also Beasley-Murray's critique (*Jesus and the Kingdom of God,* pp. 209-10) of Jeremias's attempt to distinguish between the day of the Lord and the parousia. More generally, I. H. Marshall (*Commentary on Luke,* p. 534) points out the weakness of Jeremias's view in its failure to explain how Jesus produced parables so ideally suited for the church's later allegorical use.

118. Hultgren, *The Parables of Jesus,* pp. 158-68, especially 160-61. He suggests that the language about providing food alludes to Pss 104:27; 145:15, so that the slave is viewed as providing food on behalf of God. But the connection with the psalms is general at best. He also suggests (p. 166), unconvincingly, that Luke's future tense *katastēsei* ("will put in charge"), as opposed to Matthew's aorist *katestēsen,* points forward allegorically to leaders in the church.

119. Contrast Ernst Fuchs, who argued that the parables were intended to prepare the disciples for the future. See his *Hermeneutik* (2d ed., Bad Cannstatt: R. Müllerschön, 1958), p. 226. Even with their statements that Jesus taught the crowds with parables (Matt 13:10-11, 34/Mark 4:11, 33-34/Luke 8:10), the Evangelists clearly have other parables addressed to the disciples.

120. Lambrecht (*Out of the Treasure,* p. 195) thinks Matthew had in mind church leaders who were behaving like the wicked servant. That is possible but unlikely, and if Matthew's concern were to address such problems, I suspect he would have chosen another genre. P. van Staden's suggestion that Theophilus is explicitly addressed and may have been misbehaving is to be rejected ("A Sociological Reading of Luke 12:35-48," *Neot* 22 [1988]: 337-53, here p. 351).

121. The similarity of the positive reward (being placed over all the master's possessions) to the reward in Luke 19:17, 19 (being placed over cities), which is not merely for leaders, is further reason to think the reference here is more general.

122. See Richard Bauckham's treatment of "the strange absence of the parousia from christology" ("The Future of Jesus Christ," *SBET* 16 [1998]: 97-110, here pp. 97-100).

123. 1 Cor 16:22; *Didache* 10:6; cf. Rev 22:20.

124. See Bauckham, "The Future of Jesus Christ," and the comments of Davies and Allison, *Matthew,* 3:328 with regard to Matthew's intent. See above, pp. 477-82.

125. As argued, e.g., by E. P. Sanders, *Jesus and Judaism* (Philadelphia: Fortress, 1985), pp. 321-26, 333-34.

126. *Jesus of Nazareth,* pp. 111-12. Allison does not appear to think Jesus spoke of his own return as Son of Man.

127. See above, p. 498, and Mary Ann Beavis, "Ancient Slavery as an Interpretive Context for the New Testament Servant Parables with Special Reference to the Unjust Steward (Luke 16:1-8)," *JBL* 111 (1992): 37-54, especially 42-43.

128. Betz, "The Dichotomized Servant and the End of Judas Iscariot," especially 45-47.

129. See Kathleen Weber, "Is There a Qumran Parallel to Matthew 24,51//Luke 12,46?" *RevQ* 16 (1995): 657-63.

130. See David C. Sim, "The Dissection of the Wicked Servant in Matthew 24:51," *Harvard Theological Studies* 58 (2002): 172-84.

131. E.g., Blaine Charette, *The Theme of Recompense in Matthew's Gospel* (JSNTSup 79; Sheffield: Sheffield Academic, 1992), pp. 152. He suggests also that the word recalls the punishment of those who transgress the covenants established by passing through the two halves of a carcass. See Gen 15:9-17 and especially Jer 34:18-20.

132. On gnashing of teeth as a figure of extreme sorrow, see Ps 112:10; Amos 4:6; Sir 30:10; elsewhere it is an image of rage: Pss 35:16; 37:12; Job 16:9 (of God!); Lam 2:16; Acts 7:54.

133. Matt 24:51 and 25:30 conclude parables for which there are Lukan parallels (Luke 12:41-46; 19:11-27). In both cases Luke has a statement of punishment and exclusion much more graphic than Matthew's.

134. E.g., Matt 6:24/Luke 16:13; Matt 10:24-25/Luke 6:40/John 13:16; 15:20; Matt 18:23-35, to mention only representative passages.

135. Cf. Matt 16:27; 19:28; 25:31-46; Luke 17:30-37; 21:25-35.

136. "The Future of Jesus Christ," 101.

137. See the comments of I. Howard Marshall, *Beyond the Bible: Moving from Scripture to Theology* (Grand Rapids: Baker, 2004), pp. 66-67 and 85-86, the latter being Kevin Vanhoozer's response.

138. Lambrecht (*Out of the Treasure,* p. 196) applies the parable to a Christian's own personal future, but while a legitimate application of the theology of the parable, this places the accent in the wrong place. See the discussion of individual eschatology in Luke by Carroll, *Response to the End of History,* pp. 60-71.

139. E.g., Scott (*Hear Then the Parable,* pp. 68, 70-72) who after minimal discussion says that this parable could not stem from Jesus' teaching because it deals exclusively with the concerns of the church. He argues that the parable is concerned with who is in and who is out — community-building and maintenance — whereas Jesus was more concerned to eliminate boundaries than create them. He sees this parable as common wisdom and not exhibiting a distinctive voice. His first judgment is not valid, for Jesus often distinguishes between those in and those out, not least with Matt 8:11-12/Luke 13:28-29. His second judgment unfairly assumes that Jesus' teaching was *always* contrary to expectations. If that were the case, it is doubtful that Jesus would have gotten a hearing.

140. *Die rabbinischen Gleichnisse und der Gleichniserzähler Jesus,* p. 178.

141. See above, pp. 327 and 462.

142. Whether the crisis presented by Jesus' ministry or the parousia must be determined.

143. See the discussion by Julian Hills, *Tradition and Composition in the Epistula Apostolorum* (Minneapolis: Fortress, 1990), pp. 146-72.

144. See also *Pesiqta de Rab Kahana* 12.11; 22.4-5 (the latter listing ten texts in which Israel is called a bride); *Exod. Rab.* 20.8.

145. See also *Eccl. Rab.* 3.9.1.

146. Luz, *Matthew 21–28,* pp. 227, 233.

147. Sec Isa 5:7; Mark 13:35.

148. E.g., Ezek 23:1-49.

149. E.g., Matt 10:33/Luke 12:9; Matt 19:23-24/Mark 10:23-24/Luke 18:24; Luke 9:62; 13:24-30; 14:25-33; 21:34-36.

150. G. Lamsa (*Gospel Light* [Philadelphia: A. J. Holman, 1936], p. 137) argued that butter would be used as fuel instead of the more expensive olive oil. See *b. Šabbat* 23a, which argues that olive oil is superior for burning and other tasks.

151. *JPFC* 2:752-60; *Str-B* 1:500-17; Armand Puig i Tarrech, *La Parabole des Dix Vierges: Mt 25,1-13* (AnBib 102; Rome: Biblical Institute Press, 1983), pp. 203-9; Susan Marie Praeder, *The Word in Women's Worlds: Four Parables* (Wilmington: Michael Glazier, 1988), pp. 73-79.

152. See *'Abot de Rabbi Nathan* 4; *b. Berakot* 50b; 59b; *b. Pesahim* 49a; 101b; *b. Gittin* 57a; *b. Ketubot* 8a.

153. Ruben Zimmermann, "Das Hochzeitsritual im Jungfrauengleichnis. Sozialgeschichtliche Hintergruende zu Mt. 25:1-3," *NTS* 48 (2002): 48-70. This construal was suggested earlier by Evald Lövestam, *Spiritual Wakefulness in the New Testament* (Lund: Gleerup, 1963), p. 109. See, for example, Lucian, *Symposium* 5-9, 47.

154. "Torches" is the more common connotation of the *lampades,* but it could be used of lamps in a room (cf. John 18:3 and Acts 20:8). This debate has received more attention than it deserves. Jeremias argued for "torches" ("Lampades in Matthew 25:1-13," in *Sola Deo Gloria,* ed. J. McDowell Richards [Richmond: John Knox, 1968], pp. 83-88). See the discussions by Praeder, *The Word in Women's Worlds,* pp. 75-79 and 85; and Davies and Allison, *Matthew,* 3.395-96, who opt for "lamps." Praeder (p. 76) also quotes Rashi's description of ten pole lights carried in front of a bride in the bridal procession. Probably we should think of "container torches," vessels for oil and burning rags carried on top of poles. See Luz, *Matthew 21–28,* pp. 229-30.

155. See John Nolland, *The Gospel of Matthew: A Commentary on the Greek Text* (NIGTC; Grand Rapids: Eerdmans, 2005), pp. 1004-5.

156. See Nolland, *The Gospel of Matthew,* p. 1007; Weder, *Die Gleichnisse Jesu als Metaphern,* p. 241, n. 154.

157. Any traveler to the Middle East today, of course, knows that shops are open quite late.

158. See A. W. Argyle, "Wedding Customs at the Time of Jesus," *ExpTim* 86 (1975): 214-15.

159. See *b. Mo'ed Qatan* 16a; *Str-B* 1:469. In the case mentioned the ban is for thirty days.

160. For the allegorical interpretation of the church, see Wailes, *Medieval Allegories of Jesus' Parables,* pp. 177-84. For others who allegorize see A. Feuillet, "La parabole des vierges," *La Vie spirituelle* 75 (1946): 667-77; and his "Les épousailles messianiques et les références au Cantique dans les évangiles synoptiques," *Revue Thomiste* 84 (1984): 399-424.

161. Günther Bornkamm, "Die Verzögerung der Parusie," in *Geschichte und Glaube* (BEvT 48; Munich: Kaiser, 1968), pp. 46-55. See also Grässer, *Das Problem der Parusieverzögerung in den synoptischen Evangelien und in der Apostelgeschichte,* pp. 119-26; Karl Paul Donfried, "The Allegory of the Ten Virgins (Matt 25:1-13) as a Summary of Matthean Theology," *JBL* 93 (1974): 415-28. Donfried thinks oil represents good deeds, sleep represents death, and that vv. 5-7 refer to death and resurrection.

162. *Out of the Treasure,* p. 203.

163. Dodd, *The Parables of the Kingdom,* pp. 171-74; Jeremias, *The Parables of Jesus,* pp. 51-53, 171-75; somewhat differently, Ingrid Maisch, "Das Gleichnis von den klugen und torichten Jungfrauen," *BibLeb* 11 (1970): 247-59, here pp. 256-57.

164. E.g., Lambrecht, *Out of the Treasure,* pp. 202-11; Weder, *Die Gleichnisse Jesu als Metaphern,* pp. 239-42; Puig i Tarrech, *La Parabole des Dix Vierges. Mt 25,1-13,* pp. 189-92, 263-68.

165. *Interpreting the Parables* (Downers Grove: InterVarsity, 1990), pp. 193-97, 301-2.

166. Kümmel, *Promise and Fulfilment,* pp. 54-59; Marshall, *Eschatology and the Parables,* pp. 40-43.

167. See Vicky Balabanski, "Opening the Closed Door: A Feminist Rereading of the 'Wise and Foolish Virgins' (Mt. 25:1-13)," in *The Lost Coin: Parables of Women, Work and Wisdom,* ed. Mary Ann Beavis (Sheffield: Sheffield Academic, 2002), pp. 71-97. She offers three different

readings and in part argues that the groom is ungracious, that the binary opposition of wise and foolish perpetuates patriarchal power, that the foolish women were seeking compassion, and that the "kyriarch" of the story (the bridegroom) resolves the story in favor of justice rather than mercy. The bridegroom symbolizes, not Christ, but all kyriarchs who make their own rules and use them to exclude others. She finds the closed door of Jesus' tomb a hope for liberation.

Marianne Blickenstaff ('*While the Bridegroom is with Them*': *Marriage, Family, Gender and Violence in the Gospel of Matthew* [JSNTSup 292; London: T. & T. Clark, 2005], pp. 78-109) argues for a resisting reading because the bridegroom acts contrary to what Jesus advised. She concludes that this wedding is not a place one should want to be and that the wise virgins are negative characters because they do not share. Yet in the end she cannot avoid saying that the parable warns of final judgment when all will not get in (p. 109).

Luise Schottroff (*The Parables of Jesus* [trans. Linda M. Maloney; Minneapolis: Fortress, 2006]) argues that this is a story of violence and social oppression, that the young women are presenting themselves for marriage in a competitive situation, that the wise ones do not practice human solidarity, and that the door is not closed, for the foolish can reply, "But we know you, and we will receive you."

Luz (*Matthew 21–28*, p. 245) points to (and prefers) a similar rewriting by Nikos Kazantzakis.

168. See respectively Jones, *The Matthean Parables*, p. 459; Pentecost, *The Parables of Jesus*, pp. 152-54; and J. Massingberd Ford, "The Parable of the Foolish Scholars," *NovT* 9 (1967): 107-23.

169. See Beasley-Murray, *Jesus and the Kingdom of God*, p. 214. Judges 14 and Tobit 7–8 are evidence of such exceptions, but both took place under unusual circumstances. In *Jos. and Asen.* 21:8-9 the wedding festivities apparently take place in Pharaoh's house. Song of Songs 3:4-11 apparently describes a wedding in which the groom is received into the house of the bride, even taking over the bride's mother's bedroom. Cf. Gen 24:67.

170. Eta Linnemann, *Parables of Jesus* (trans. John Sturdy; London: SPCK, 1966), p. 124.

171. Zimmermann, "Das Hochzeitsritual im Jungfrauengleichnis."

172. The words "and the bride" are added in a few manuscripts and in some of the versional evidence, especially the old Latin.

173. Matt 9:15/Mark 2:19-20/Luke 5:34-35; Matt 22:1-14; see also John 2:1-10.

174. See Zimmermann, "Das Hochzeitsritual im Jungfrauengleichnis."

175. As Hultgren argues in *The Parables of Jesus*, p. 171.

176. Jeremias, *The Parables of Jesus*, pp. 173-74; W. O. E. Oesterley, *The Gospel Parables in the Light of Their Jewish Background* (New York: Macmillan, 1936), p. 141; J. Alexander Findlay, *Jesus and His Parables* (London: Epworth, 1957), pp. 111-12; Flusser, *Die rabbinischen Gleichnisse und der Gleichniserzähler Jesus*, pp. 179-80.

177. *Exod. Rab.* 20.8 compares Moses not entering the promised land to a *shoshbin*, one who escorts the bride to the bridegroom but does not enter the bridegroom's house.

178. Of primary relevance are Song 3:4-11; 1 Macc 9:37-42; *m. Soṭah* 9.14; *Mekilta Baḥodesh* 3.115-19; *Pirqe de Rabbi Eliezer* 41 on Exod 19:17; *Sifra* 99.2.5 on Leviticus 9. See above, pp. 507-8.

179. See Zimmermann, "Das Hochzeitsritual im Jungfrauengleichnis, 68, and above, p. 510.

180. Feuillet suggests ("Les épousailles messianiques et les références au Cantique dans les évangiles synoptiques," 414-15) that the parable was constructed with Song 3 and 5 in mind, which if true could help explain the shape of the parable, but that is by no means certain.

181. Dunn, *Jesus Remembered*, pp. 430-31.

182. *The Parables of Jesus,* pp. 52-53.

183. See Hos 2:16; Isa 54:5-6; 62:4-5; Jer 31:32; and Ezek 16:6-43. *Pesiqta de Rab Kahana* 22.1, 2, 3 (in association with Zech 9:9), 4, and 5 interpret Isa 61:10 of God's coming to bring joy to Jerusalem. In the last, Israel is ten times called a bride and ten times God clothes himself with a garment appropriate to the occasion. Supplement 6 of the same document is an extended interpretation of Isa 61:10. In Supplement 6.2 God rejoices over the rebuilding of Jerusalem as a bridegroom rejoices over a bride (Isa 62:5). In Supplement 6.5 God is again described as putting on ten appropriate garments. When the Messiah arrives, he puts on the sixth. Then we are told that God puts a garment on the Messiah, the splendor of which will stream forth from one end of the earth to the other, as implied by the words of Isa 61:10, "As a bridegroom puts on a priestly diadem." See also the very similar material in *Pesiqta Rabbati* 37.2-3.

184. Luz, *Matthew 21–28,* p. 232; Davies and Allison, *Matthew,* 3:393-95; Weder, *Die Gleichnisse Jesu als Metaphern,* pp. 244-46.

185. Dunn, *Jesus Remembered,* pp. 431, 436.

186. E.g., Lövestam, *Spiritual Wakefulness in the New Testament,* pp. 111-12; Richard T. France, "On Being Ready (Matthew 25:1-46)," in *The Challenge of Jesus' Parables,* ed. Richard N. Longenecker (Grand Rapids: Eerdmans, 2000), pp. 177-95, here p. 181; Simon Legasse, "La Parabole des Dix Vierges (Mt 25,1-13). Essai de synthèse historico-litteraire," in *Les Paraboles Evangeliques. Perspectives Nouvelles,* ed. Jean Delorme (Lectio Divina 135; Paris: Cerf, 1989), pp. 349-60, here p. 351; and Flusser, *Die rabbinischen Gleichnisse und der Gleichniserzähler Jesus,* pp. 182-86, who rejects the idea that the bridegroom refers to God because it would be uncomfortably anthropomorphic, but *Pesiqta de Rab Kahana* 22.1-5; Supplement 6.2, 5; and *Pesiqta Rabbati* 37.2-3 have no difficulty with the idea.

187. Jeremias's attempt (*The Parables of Jesus,* p. 52, n. 13) to say that "while the bridegroom is with them" *(en hǭ ho nymphios met' autōn)* in Mark 2:19 is a circumlocution for "during the wedding" is not the least convincing.

188. *Pesiqta de Rab Kahana* 22; Supplement 6.2; 5; *Pesiqta Rabbati* 37.2-3. See above, n. 178.

189. Literally "priests it" *(yĕkahēn).*

190. *kkwn;* See William H. Brownlee, "Messianic Motifs of Qumran and the New Testament," *NTS* 3 (1957): 195-210, 205-6.

191. Outside the Gospels texts mentioned, *nymphios* and *nymphē* appear in the NT only at Rev 18:23, which is not christological. This is not the church's christological language, even though one would expect such usage from texts like Eph 5:24-27 and Rev 19:7, 9; 21:2, 9; and 22:17. Linnemann (*Parables of Jesus,* p. 194) correctly says that if the bride is not mentioned, then the narrator did not have in mind the allegory of the bridegroom and the church.

192. See Lövestam, *Spiritual Wakefulness in the New Testament,* 111, and such obvious texts as *Pss. Sol.* 17 and Matt 9:1-8.

193. See esp. Wright, *Jesus and the Victory of God,* pp. 612-53.

194. *Pesiq. R. Kah.* 22 and S6:2 and 5; *Pesiq. Rab.* 37:2-3. See above, n. 178.

195. These views are all represented among scholars: Feuillet ("La parabole des vierges," 670, 672; "Les épousailles messianiques et les références au Cantique dans les évangiles synoptiques," 406, 408, 416) argues that the virgins are the bride and that sleep is a negative image. Jeremias (*The Parables of Jesus,* p. 51) argues that "at a very early date" the two sets of virgins were taken as Gentiles and Jews. Karl Donfried ("The Allegory of the Ten Virgins [Matt 25:1-13] as a Summary of Matthean Theology," *JBL* 93 [1974]: 415-28) took sleep and rising from sleep as referring to death and resurrection. Bornkamm ("Die Verzögerung der Parusie," pp. 51-52) thought the middle of the night refers to the expectation of the parousia at night; Lambrecht

(*Out of the Treasure,* p. 211) and many others that the oil stands for good works; and John F. Walvoord ("Christ's Olivet Discourse on the End of the Age: The Parable of the Virgins," *BSac* 129 [1972]: 99-105) that the oil stands for the Holy Spirit. With regard to Bornkamm, the passages listed supposedly showing that the parousia is expected at night do not demonstrate the case. See Linnemann, *Parables of Jesus,* p. 193; Legasse, "La Parabole des Dix Vierges," p. 358. Luke 17:31-34 and similar texts anticipate either day or night for "that day." Some evidence exists in Jewish literature that oil represents good works (especially *Num. Rab.* 13.15-16), but the moment one makes such an identification, one must ask whether the torches, shops, and dealers also represent something about works. Donfried must argue that it is absurd to buy good works and that the foolish virgins were unsuccessful, both of which are impositions on the parable. Note A. B. Bruce's comment that the oil is "anything you please" in *The Parabolic Teaching of Jesus* (London: Hodder & Stoughton, 1882), p. 502.

196. The argument of Puig i Tarrech (*La Parabole des Dix Vierges,* pp. 203-14, 263-68) that the audience was would-be disciples of Jesus who did not understand the radical call of the kingdom depends on his rewriting the parable so that both the delay and the sleep of the virgins are not original. In his reconstruction the events take place as the bride's entourage reaches the groom's house and he comes out to meet them. As with most reconstructions we are left with a rather insipid account. Note Flusser's caustic comments on scholarly reconstructions and fear of allegorical elements (*Die rabbinischen Gleichnisse und der Gleichniserzähler Jesus,* p. 188).

197. Cf. Blomberg, *Interpreting the Parables,* pp. 301-2.

198. See France, "On Being Ready," p. 179.

199. Vv. 1-12 are printed with gray ink and v. 13 with black by Funk, Scott, and Butts, *The Parables of Jesus: Red Letter Edition,* pp. 27 and 67. See above, pp. 499 and 505.

200. Some suggest that the designation of the virgins as either foolish or wise in 25:2 is a later addition, but the same designation at the beginning of a parable is evidenced by *b. Šabbat* 153a/*Eccl. Rab.* 9.8.1. See above, pp. 303-4.

201. See Philip L. Culbertson, *A Word Fitly Spoken: Context, Transmission, and Adoption of the Parables of Jesus* (Albany: State University of New York Press, 1995), p. 135, n. 25, who points out that such negotiations would usually have been agreed on at the betrothal.

202. See Blomberg, *Interpreting the Parables,* pp. 194-95, who offers as evidence only Findlay's recounting of his modern experiences in Palestine (*Jesus and His Parables,* pp. 111-12).

203. See above, pp. 510-13.

204. As most now grant; see, e.g., Davies and Allison, *Matthew,* 3:398-99; Luz, *Matthew 21–28,* pp. 233-34.

205. Legasse ("La Parabole des Dix Vierges," p. 355) points out four synonyms in this section: wise, ready, faithful, and watch. In his opinion Matthew envisages neither the proximity of the end nor its retreat to a distant horizon, and the delay of the parousia is not a problem for Matthew.

206. "Die Verzögerung der Parusie." Linnemann (*Parables of Jesus,* pp. 193-95) provides a critique of Bornkamm, even though she viewed the parable as an early church creation. See also Max Meinertz, "Die Tragweite des Gleichnisses von den zehn Jungfrauen," in *Synoptische Studien,* ed. Alfred Wikenhauser (Munich: Kösel, 1954), pp. 94-106, here pp. 103-6.

207. See above, pp. 479-82 and 500.

208. See Marshall, *Eschatology and the Parables,* pp. 40-43; Kümmel, *Promise and Fulfillment,* pp. 54-58; and note Stephen S. Smalley, "The Delay of the Parousia," *JBL* 83 (1964): 41-54, here pp. 43-47.

209. See above, p. 755, n. 167. In addition Geza Vermes (*Jesus and the World of Judaism*

[Philadelphia: Fortress, 1983], p. 51), viewed the wise virgins as cunning and selfish and charged that this parable is a travesty of Jesus' teaching.

210. A point made strongly by Jacobus Liebenburg, *The Language of the Kingdom and Jesus: Parable, Aphorism, and Metaphor in the Sayings Material Common to the Synoptic Tradition and the Gospel of Thomas* (BZNW 102; Berlin: Walter de Gruyter, 2001), especially pp. 155-59.

211. See my forthcoming article "Prophets, Parables, and Theologians," in *BBR*.

212. Note the parallel between watching in Luke 12:37 and doing in v. 43.

213. See Lövestam, *Spiritual Wakefulness in the New Testament*, pp. 121-22.

214. *Die rabbinischen Gleichnisse und der Gleichniserzähler Jesus*, pp. 178 and 180.

215. See Lövestam, *Spiritual Wakefulness in the New Testament*, p. 111, n. 1; Linnemann, *Parables of Jesus*, pp. 190-91.

216. Vv. 10-12 cannot be eliminated as if they do not cohere with Jesus' warnings elsewhere. The closed door, instead of referring to exclusion from the celebration, could refer to exclusion from the bridal chamber, at which a doorkeeper was posted. See Zimmermann, "Das Hochzeitsritual im Jungfrauengleichnis," 67.

217. I do not think Matthew with five wise and five foolish virgins indicates the mixed nature of the church.

218. Dan Otto Via, Jr. (*The Parables of Jesus* [Philadelphia: Fortress, 1967], p. 125) suggests that the meaning of the parable is that existence may be lost and that when a crisis is not met further opportunities may be cut off. Oesterley (*The Gospel Parables in the Light of Their Jewish Background*, pp. 137-38) emphasizes responsibility as the significance of the parable.

219. Note Dale Allison's comment (*Jesus of Nazareth*, p. 219): "his [Jesus'] dream is the only one worth dreaming."

220. "The Delay of the Parousia," *TynBul* 31 (1980): 3-36, here p. 33.

221. The authenticity of these parables is not usually questioned, even though certain statements in them may be viewed as later additions. The members of the Jesus Seminar departed from their normal procedure and chose to identify the suspected later additions. They printed both parables with pink ink but used black for the last portion of Matt 25:21 and 23 ("Enter into the joy of your master"), vv. 29-30; Luke 19:14, 15b ("having received the kingdom"), the last portion of vv. 17 and 19 (in each case the reference to cities), and vv. 25-27. See Funk, Scott, and Butts, *The Parables of Jesus: Red Letter Edition*, pp. 54-55.

222. As argued by Lane C. McGaughy, "The Fear of Yahweh and the Mission of Judaism: A Postexilic Maxim and Its Early Christian Expansion in the Parable of the Talents," *JBL* 94 (1975): 235-45; Scott, *Hear Then the Parable*, p. 228.

223. Josephus is sometimes, and possibly here, guilty of exaggeration.

224. See also *Ant.* 17.313, a comment from Josephus which assumes Archelaus's revenge. Josephus mentions frequently the similar cruelty of Herod the Great. For other accounts of attempts to derive kingship from Rome or with Rome's help, see *Ant.* 14.302; 16.295; 18.236-52.

225. See *New Testament Apocrypha* (ed. Edgar Hennecke and Wilhelm Schneemelcher; trans. R. McL. Wilson; Philadelphia: Westminster, 1963), 1:149.

226. Literally, a resumption or repetition.

227. See already the Code of Hammurabi for legislation on money lent for trading (*Laws*, 97-107, *ANET*, p. 170).

228. Several rabbinic parables tell of items entrusted and a reckoning later. *Song Rab.* 7.14.1 is a parable of a woman who invested successfully what her husband left her when he went on a trip. *Eliyyahu Rabbah* 26 (28) relates a parable about a king who returns from a long trip to two servants, both of whom had awe for the king, though one loved him and one did not. The

former planted orchards and presented to the king the produce, and the king was pleased. The other did nothing, presented some dried things to the king, and then trembled at the king's displeasure. *Eliyyahu Zuṭa* 2 records a parable of a king who gave wheat and flax to two servants. The clever one made bread and a table cloth, while the other did nothing. In the reckoning scene the clever servant is loved and the foolish is shamed. (For these last two parables see *Tanna děbe Eliyyahu: The Lore of the School of Elijah* [trans. William G. Braude and Israel Kapstein; Philadelphia: The Jewish Publication Society of America, 1981], pp. 347-48, 408.) To illustrate the return of the human spirit to God *b. Šabbat* 152b tells a parable of a king who distributed royal apparel to his servants. The wise preserved them, whereas the fools worked in them. When the king demanded his garments, he was pleased with the wise but angry with the fools, confining the latter to prison. By analogy God will cast out the souls of his enemies as from a sling. *Mekilta Baḥodesh* 5.81-92 (on Exod 20:2) has a parable of a king who sets one administrator over some straw and another over silver and gold. The former is suspected of thievery and complains because he was not set over silver and gold. He is judged a fool for thinking he would be placed over silver and gold when he is suspected of stealing straw. *Sifre* Deut 48.3 has a parable of a king entrusting a bird to a servant with the threat of death for its loss. *Sifre* Deut 357.11 records a parable about a reliable person with whom everyone left deposits for safekeeping. The parable is an illustration of God's taking the souls of the righteous.

229. David Wenham, *The Rediscovery of Jesus' Eschatological Discourse,* pp. 52, 101.

230. See above, pp. 493-94 and 508.

231. See among others Laurie Guy, "The Interplay of the Present and Future in the Kingdom of God: (Luke 19:11-44)," *TynBul* 48 (1997): 119-37.

232. The former is the more common spelling. Some attempt to view the two forms of the name in 19:11 and 28 as distinguishing between the holy city and the city which refuses to receive its king *(Hierosolyma).* See Adelbert Denaux, "The Parable of the King-Judge (Lk 19,12-28) and Its Relation to the Entry Story (Lk 19,29-44)," *ZNW* 93 (2002): 35-57, here p. 44; Ignace de la Potterie, "La Parabole du Prétendant à la Royauté (Lc 19,11-28)," in *À Cause de L'Évangile. Études sur les Synoptiques et les Actes* (Lectio Divina 123; Paris: Cerf, 1985), pp. 613-41, here p. 629. This does not seem to be borne out in the rest of Luke, where the spelling *Hierosolyma* only occurs three other times (2:22, which is hardly negative; 13:22; 23:7). *Hierosolyma* is also the spelling used in Matthew, Mark, and John, but while *Ierousalēm* is common in Luke, in the other Gospels it occurs only in Matt 23:37.

233. In addition to the evidence listed on p. 759, n. 228, see 1 Macc 13:15, which reports Jonathan being detained for a debt of 100 talents owed the royal treasury in connection with offices he held; *Gen. Rab.* 8.3, which tells of a king indignant over losses incurred in doing business through an agent; *m. Baba Meṣiʿa* and *m. Baba Batra,* which deal with problems arising from property and business deals; *b. Šabbat* 63a, which says "He who lends [money] is greater than he who performs charity; and he who forms a partnership is greater than all"; and *b. Beṣah* 32b, which decrees that the rich men of Babylon will go down to Gehenna for failing to provide a particular man with facilities for trading. Obviously from these last two references, business arrangements could be looked on as a way of showing mercy.

234. J. Duncan M. Derrett, "The Parable of the Talents and Two Logia," in *Law in the New Testament* (London: Darton, Longman, & Todd, 1970), pp. 17-31, see pp. 18-19. He argues as well (pp. 22-23) that half the money would often be considered a trust and half a loan. An agent's share of the profit might be one-third, but a servant's would be less. Cf. the unjust steward *(oikonomos)* in Luke 16:1-9, who is clearly an agent and not a slave.

235. E.g., Jennifer A. Glancy, "Slaves and Slavery in the Matthean Parables," *JBL* 119

(2000): 67-90, and her *Slavery in Early Christianity* (Oxford: Oxford University Press, 2002), pp. 112-29.

236. See Nolland, *Luke 9:21–18:34,* 2:798.

237. See *m. Baba Meṣi'a* 5.1, 4, 6 and the rabbinic commentaries on these passages.

238. For more on "talent" see above, pp. 66 and 68.

239. See Wailes, *Medieval Allegories of Jesus' Parables,* pp. 184-94.

240. See among others Jülicher, *Die Gleichnisreden Jesu,* 2:472-95; David Flusser, "Aesop's Miser and the Parable of the Talents," in *Parable and Story in Judaism and Christianity,* ed. Clemens Thoma and Michael Wyschogrod (New York: Paulist, 1989), pp. 9-25; Brad H. Young, *The Parables: Jewish Tradition and Christian Interpretation* (Peabody: Hendrickson, 1998), pp. 82-97. For an exposition using this approach, see J. M. Ross, "Talents," *ExpTim* 89 (1978): 307-9.

241. E.g., Beasley-Murray, *Jesus and the Kingdom of God,* pp. 215-18.

242. Dodd, *The Parables of the Kingdom,* pp. 151-52; Jeremias, *The Parables of Jesus,* pp. 61-62. Lane C. McGaughy ("The Fear of Yahweh and the Mission of Judaism," 235-45) argued that the third servant symbolized Israel's mission of guarding the sacred tradition, that hearers would have identified with *the third servant,* and that the complaint against the master reflects post-exilic complaints against Yahweh. See also Lambrecht, *Out of the Treasure,* pp. 234-36; Scott, *Hear Then the Parable,* pp. 233-35; Wright, *Jesus and the Victory of God,* pp. 632-39.

243. Luke Timothy Johnson, "The Lukan Kingship Parable (Lk. 19:11-27)," *NovT* 24 (1982): 139-59; Wright, *Jesus and the Victory of God,* pp. 631-39. See also I. de la Potterie, "La Parabole du Prétendant à la Royauté (Lc 19, 11-28)," pp. 613-41.

244. Alfons Weiser, *Die Knechtsgleichnisse der synoptischen Evangelien,* pp. 263-66.

245. Richard L. Rohrbaugh, "A Peasant Reading of the Parable of the Talents/Pounds: A Text of Terror?" *BTB* 23 (1993): 32-39; Herzog, *Parables as Subversive Speech,* pp. 150-68; Craig A. Evans, *Noncanonical Writings and New Testament Interpretation* (Peabody: Hendrickson, 1992), 179-82; Robert T. Fortna, "Reading Jesus' Parable of the Talents through Underclass Eyes, Matt 25:14-30," *Forum* 8 (1992): 211-27; Richard Q. Ford, *The Parables of Jesus: Recovering the Art of Listening* (Minneapolis: Fortress, 1997), pp. 32-46; Schottroff, *The Parables of Jesus,* pp. 181-87, 221-24.

246. *Out of the Treasure,* p. 222.

247. Weiser, *Die Knechtsgleichnisse der synoptischen Evangelien,* pp. 230-31, 237, 247.

248. *Hear Then the Parable,* pp. 218, 223-28; see also Weder, *Die Gleichnisse Jesu als Metaphern,* pp. 195, 202-3.

249. *Jesus of Nazareth,* p. 31. See also p. 7 and his whole discussion in pp. 1-77. As an example of reconstruction, see Wilhelm Resenhöfft ("Jesu Gleichnis von den Talenten, ergänzt durch die Lukas-Fassung," *NTS* 26 [1979-80]: 318-31) who combines Matthew's parable of the Talents and Luke's parable of the Pounds (minus the throne claimant elements) to achieve one complete account. Similarly, he combines Matthew's parable of the Wedding Feast (minus 22:6-7) and Luke's parable of the Banquet to make one complete account. He joins the throne claimant elements from Luke 19:11-27 with Matt 22:6-7 to make a third parable. The explanation cannot be falsified, but one cannot imagine how the originally combined elements of the three parables he recovers were separated as he suggests.

250. Wright, *Jesus and the Victory of God,* p. 87; Schottroff, *The Parables of Jesus,* pp. 99, 106-7, 112.

251. See Allison, *Jesus of Nazareth,* pp. 31-32.

252. See above, p. 525, and for similar rabbinic parables, p. 759, n. 228.

253. Christian Dietzfelbinger ("Das Gleichnis von den anvertrauten Geldern," *Berliner*

Theologische Zeitschrift 6 [1989]: 222-33, here pp. 229-32) suggests that the Pharisees are in view. Daniel J. Harrington ("Polemical Parables in Matthew 24–25," *USQR* 44 [1991]: 287-98) takes the parables in this section of Matthew as a polemic against "the synagogue across the street" and thinks Matthew's third servant is a symbol for his rabbinic rivals who bury the treasures of Judaism.

254. See Beasley-Murray, *Jesus and the Kingdom of God*, p. 217; Davies and Allison, *Matthew*, 3:403-4; Weiser, *Die Knechtsgleichnisse der synoptischen Evangelien*, pp. 260-63; Werner Foerster, "Das Gleichnis von den anvertrauten Pfunden," in *Verbum Dei Manet in Aeternum. Eine Festschrift für D. Otto Schmitz*, ed. Werner Foerster (Witten: Luther, 1953), pp. 37-56, here pp. 51-53.

A few scholars argue that the harsh description of the master points to post-exilic complaints by Jews against the hardness of Yahweh. Appeal is made by L. McGaughy ("The Fear of Yahweh and the Mission of Judaism," 243) to *'Abot de Rabbi Nathan* 14.4 (see p. 522 above) as showing that Israel's central calling was to guard the sacred tradition. However, the rabbinic parable does not focus on the Scriptures as a deposit from God (though they may be). The parable leaves the deposit unspecified, but on the plane of reality the deposit mirrors the rabbi's son, not the Scriptures. The Scriptures are mentioned only to show the virtue of the son. McGaughy argues for a post-exilic maxim that Jesus took up, the content of which was similar to sayings in Job. To say nothing of the question of the date of this rabbinic material (*'Abot de Rabbi Nathan* may be as late as 500 A.D.), the identification of a post-exilic maxim which Jesus used is highly speculative, and not many Jews would have sympathized with the charge that God was harsh. B. Scott (*Hear Then the Parable*, pp. 233-34) adapts McGaughy's approach to argue not that the parable is about the harshness of God but that it is about how one is to claim the future in freedom of action rather than in preserving the gift. I see little that suggests that the parable ever carried such a connotation.

255. As argued by McGaughy, "The Fear of Yahweh and the Mission of Judaism," 235-45; Scott, *Hear Then the Parable*, p. 228.

256. Ezekiel 23 is a direct accusation which allows the fact side to show through from the first.

257. Dietzfelbinger, "Das Gleichnis von den anvertrauten Geldern," 225.

258. Tob 1:14 indicates that Tobit left ten talents in trust. In *b. Yoma* 35b Potiphar's wife is reported to have offered Joseph 1000 talents of silver to yield to her! See the discussion of talents above, pp. 66-68.

259. Wright, *Jesus and the Victory of God*, pp. 632-39.

260. "Aesop's Miser and the Parable of the Talents," pp. 9-25, see p. 22.

261. Unless one is content to argue for a non-eschatological Jesus, which I find inconceivable.

262. See option 6 above, p. 529. Note that Rohrbaugh ("A Peasant Reading of the Parable of the Talents or Pounds," pp. 37-38) thinks the parable has a good deal of ambiguity and that its canonical forms are possibly not from Jesus but from affluent Christians seeking to justify their worldview.

263. Matt 25:26 and Luke 19:22 can be punctuated as questions or statements, but even if a statement, it does not necessarily agree with the assessment.

264. Luz (*Matthew 21–28*, pp. 252-62) focuses on a contrast between the fear in the parable and love and finds the parable deficient since "For Jesus the courage of love is that we need have no fear before God . . ." (p. 255). But this distorts the parable, which is not focused on love at all and does not need to present all of theology.

265. See Joel R. Wohlgemut, "Entrusted Money (Matthew 25:14-28): The Parable of the Talents/Pounds," in *Jesus and His Parables,* ed. V. George Shillington (Edinburgh: T. & T. Clark, 1997), pp. 103-20, especially 112-17.

266. Flusser ("Aesop's Miser and the Parable of the Talents," 10) argues that in all parables having human life as their theme, the proprietor symbolizes God.

267. Lambrecht (*Out of the Treasure,* p. 234) suggests that the accusation of harshness derives from the conviction of the scribes and Pharisees that the God Jesus proclaims is unjust. The parable is viewed as Jesus' self-defense. This seems to read a good deal into the parable.

268. Pp. 479-82.

269. Note Adolf Schlatter's comment: "People asked Jesus when his rule would be revealed. He resisted this question resolutely and persistently (Luke 17:20-37; 19:11; Matt 24:3; Lk. 13:23; Matt 20:22; Acts 1:6)" (*The History of the Christ: The Foundation of New Testament Theology* [trans. Andreas J. Köstenberger, Grand Rapids: Baker, 1997], p. 346). See also Schnackenburg, *God's Rule and Kingdom,* p. 209.

270. As Beasley-Murray comments, the parable has an essential concern with the parousia even apart from its redaction. See his *Jesus and the Kingdom of God,* p. 218. As he and others note, if reckoning alone were the point, the master's departure would be unnecessary, which is the case with the parables of the Unforgiving Servant and of the Dishonest Steward.

271. Contra Ben Chenowith ("Identifying the Talents: Contextual Clues for the Interpretation of the Parable of the Talents [Matthew 25:14-30]," *TynBul* 56 [2005]: 61-72) who argues that because of the similarity of Matt 13:12 and 25:29 the talents refer to knowledge of the secrets of the kingdom.

272. This criticism applies to most of the reconstructions scholars offer of the parable. See Foerster, "Das Gleichnis von den anvertrauten Pfunden," p. 50.

273. Foerster ("Das Gleichnis von den anvertrauten Pfunden," p. 50) argued that v. 29 was the original conclusion of the parable and summarized the entire account. Flusser ("Aesop's Miser and the Parable of the Talents," p. 23, n. 15) likewise argued that the proverb originated with the parable and that use of it in Matt 13:12 par. was taken from the parable.

274. Consideration of judgment in any parable needs to deal with the theme as it arises in other parables, which would include at least the parables of the Two Builders, the Wheat and Weeds, the Net, the Unforgiving Servant, the Wicked Tenants, the Wedding Banquet/Feast, the Faithful/Unfaithful Servant, the Ten Virgins, the Sheep and Goats, the Rich Fool, the Fig Tree, the Rich Man and Lazarus, and the Pharisee and Tax Collector.

275. Oesterley, *The Gospel Parables,* p. 145; Armand Puig i Tarrech, "La Parabole des Talents (Mt 25, 14-30) ou des Mines (Lc 19, 11-28)," in *À Cause de L'Évangile. Études sur les Synoptiques et les Actes* (Lectio Divina 123; Paris: Cerf, 1985), pp. 165-93, here pp. 187-88 (see also p. 180, where he suggests that speaking of the servant's responsibility places the parable on a too moralizing terrain); Robert Farrar Capon, *Kingdom, Grace, Judgment: Paradox, Outrage, and Vindication in the Parables of Jesus* (Grand Rapids: Eerdmans, 2002), pp. 417-25 and 502-4, who also allegorizes the parable in terms of death (the far country) and resurrection, says the parable is about the Lord's joy at throwing his money around, and assures us that God is not a bookkeeper looking for productive results.

276. Weder, *Die Gleichnisse Jesu als Metaphern,* p. 206; Puig i Tarrech, "La Parabole des Talents (Mt 25,14-30) ou des Mines (Lc 19,11-28)," p. 187.

277. The word *gehenna* occurs in Jesus' teaching only in Matt 5:22, 29, 30; 10:28; 18:9; 23:15, 33; Mark 9:43, 45, 47; Luke 12:5. Outside the teaching of Jesus it appears only in Jas 3:6.

278. The exception would be the Wedding Banquet, which possibly should be described as having three plots.

279. The charge that a mistake appears in 19:25 in that the first servant now has eleven minas instead of ten may be a misreading of *prosērgasato* in 19:16. Does the word mean "Your mina gained ten more minas" or is this typical business language for "Your mina produced ten minas"?

280. Wilhelm Pesch, *Der Lohngedanke in der Lehre Jesu. Vergleichen mit der religiösen Lohnlehre des Spätjudentums* (Munich: Karl Zink, 1955), pp. 30-32; Blomberg, *Interpreting the Parables,* pp. 218-21; Wright, *Jesus and the Victory of God,* p. 633. Wenham (*The Rediscovery of Jesus' Eschatological Discourse,* p. 73) argues that Luke merged two parables and notes that Luke is conservative in editing his material but sits lightly with regard to the original contexts.

281. The use of *heteros* ("the other") in 19:20 is particularly revealing, although Blomberg (*Interpreting the Parables,* p. 219) argues that it should be understood as "the next."

282. See above, p. 521.

283. Josephus, *Ant.* 17.340.

284. See Scott, *Hear Then the Parable,* p. 223; Marcel Didier, "La Parabole des Talents et des Mines," in *De Jesus aux Evangiles. Tradition et redaction dans les Evangiles synoptiques,* ed. I. de la Potterie (Gembloux: J. Duculot, 1967), pp. 248-71, here p. 261. Max Zerwick ("Die Parabel vom Thronanwärter," *Bib* 40 [1959]: 654-74, here p. 668) comments that the riskier the comparison the more certainly it goes back to Jesus.

285. Marshall, *The Gospel of Luke,* p. 702; see Charles H. Talbert, "The Redaction Critical Quest for Luke the Theologian," in *Jesus and Man's Hope,* ed. D. G. Buttrick (Pittsburgh: Pittsburgh Theological Seminary, 1970), pp. 171-222.

286. Johnson, "The Lukan Kingship Parable," 139-59; Wright, *Jesus and the Victory of God,* pp. 631-39; de la Potterie, "La Parabole du Prétendant à la Royauté (Lc 19, 11-28)," pp. 613-41.

287. Johnson, "The Lukan Kingship Parable," 149-50.

288. For a critique of this approach see V. Fusco, "'Point of View' and 'Implicit Reader' in Two Eschatological Texts (Lk 19,11-28; Acts 1,6-8)," in *The Four Gospels 1992: Festschrift Frans Neirynck,* ed. F. Van Segbroeck, et al. (Leuven: Leuven University Press, 1992), pp. 1677-96, here pp. 1688-90; Carroll, *Response to the End of History,* pp. 100-103; Laurie Guy, "The Interplay of the Present and Future in the Kingdom of God," 125-28. The arguments of de la Potterie ("La Parabole du Prétendant à la Royauté (Lc 19,11-28)," pp. 613-41) are no more convincing than Johnson's. He argues for an inclusio between 19:11 and 28, that the two different spellings of Jerusalem in the Greek text (*Ierousalēm* in 19:11 and *Hierosolyma* in 19:28) designate the city as guilty of not receiving its Lord, that the parable is an allegory of Jesus going to heaven (the far country) to receive the kingdom at his heavenly enthronement, that the enthronement of Jesus on the Mount of Olives is a symbolic prefiguration (19:37-38), but that the perspective is ecclesial, not eschatological, since the Christ comes continually for his own, and that the time of reward and judgment is situated at the beginning of the church and refers to participating in the government of the Christian community.

289. Wright, *Jesus and the Victory of God,* pp. 632-39.

290. See my assessment of Wright's treatment of the parables in "Reading and Overreading the Parables in *Jesus and the Victory of God,*" *Jesus and the Restoration of Israel: A Critical Assessment of N. T. Wright's Jesus and the Victory of God,* ed. Carey Newman (Downers Grove: InterVarsity, 1999), pp. 61-76.

291. A. J. Mattill, *Luke and the Last Things: A Perspective for the Understanding of Lukan Thought* (Dillsboro: Western North Carolina Press, 1979), p. 127. V. Fusco ("'Point of View' and

'Implicit Reader,'" 1683-84) reminds us that three points of view must be kept in mind with this narrative: the time in the life of Jesus when the events are still future, the narrator's point of view when some of the events have been fulfilled, and the setting of the author and readers, probably after the destruction of Jerusalem. For evidence of the importance of Jerusalem as the place the kingdom is revealed, see *Targum Isa.* 31:4-5.

292. Laurie Guy, "The Interplay of the Present and the Future in the Kingdom of God." She suggests that OT accounts of accession in 1 Kgs 1:28-30 and 2 Kgs 9:13 have influenced Luke's account.

293. See Jean-Noel Aletti, "Parabole des Mines et/ou Parabole du Roi, Lc 19,11-28. Remarques sur l'écriture parabolique de Luc," in *Les Paraboles Evangeliques. perspectives nouvelles* (Lectio Divina 135; Paris: Cerf, 1989), pp. 309-32, here pp. 318-22; Denaux, "The Parable of the King-Judge (Lk 19,12-28) and Its Relation to the Entry Story (Lk 19,29-44)," 36.

294. See Wright (*Jesus and the Victory of God,* pp. 632-39) who, rather than contrast the coming of God and the coming of Jesus, would say that Jesus was enacting the coming of God.

295. See Francis D. Weinert, "The Parable of the Throne Claimant (Luke 19:12, 14-15a, 27) Reconsidered," *CBQ* 39 (1977): 505-14, who views the parable as Jesus' warning to those opposing him.

296. Contra Jack T. Sanders, "The Parable of the Pounds and Lucan Anti-Semitism," *TS* 42 (1981): 660-68.

297. See Winterhalter and Fisk, *Jesus' Parables: Finding Our God Within,* pp. 97-98.

298. Beasley-Murray, *Jesus and the Kingdom of God,* p. 217.

299. See Carroll, *Response to the End of History,* p. 100.

300. Luz, *Matthew 21–28,* p. 258.

301. See the translation in Beasley-Murray, *Jesus and the Kingdom of God,* p. 308, or "The Protestation of Guiltlessness," *ANET,* pp. 34-36. See the similar text from *Left Ginza* 3.9 reprinted in *Hellenistic Commentary to the New Testament,* ed. M. Eugene Boring, Klaus Berger, and Carlsten Colpe (Nashville: Abingdon, 1995), pp. 143-44.

302. This juxtaposition is emphasized by Francis Watson, "Liberating the Reader: A Theological-Exegetical Study of the Parable of the Sheep and the Goats (Matt 25:31-46)," in *The Open Text: New Directions in Biblical Studies?* ed. Francis Watson (London: SCM, 1993), pp. 57-84, here pp. 76-77.

303. Jeremias, *The Parables of Jesus,* p. 206.

304. Klaus Wengst, "Wie aus Böcken Ziegen wurden (Mt 25,32f)," *EvT* 54 (1994): 491-500; see also Ulrich Luz, "The Final Judgment (Matt 25:31-46): An Exercise in 'History of Influence' Exegesis," in *Treasures New and Old: Recent Contributions to Matthean Studies,* ed. David R. Bauer and Mark Allan Powell (Atlanta: Scholars, 1996), pp. 271-310, here pp. 295-97, or *Matthew 21–28,* pp. 276-77, who follows Wengst, but admits that the thesis cannot be proven. The misunderstanding arose from a citation error in Gustaf Dalman's *Arbeite und Sitte in Palästina* (Gütersloh: Bertelsmann, 1939), 6:276.

305. See Luz, *Matthew 21–28,* p. 277.

306. See Kathleen Weber, "The Image of Sheep and Goats in Matthew 25:31-46," *CBQ* 59 (1997): 657-78. Some Greco-Romans associated goats with unbridled sexual behavior, but others attributed positive values to goats. John J. Pilch argued that goats were an image of shame associated with women ("Separating the Sheep from the Goats," *Professional Approaches for Christian Educators* 20 [1992]: 215-18), but evidence will not support such ideas in Palestine or Judaism.

307. See *Midr. Pss.* 90.12 (on 90:3) above and cf. *4 Ezra* 3:6; on right and left see also

b. Šabbat 88b; *Num. Rab.* 22.9; *T. Ab.* 12:12; Plato, *Republic* 10.614C; Hermas, *Vis.* 3.2.1. See also J. M. Court, "Right and Left: The Implications for Matthew 25.31-46," *NTS* 31 (1985): 223-33.

308. For histories of the interpretation of this parable see Sherman W. Gray, *The Least of My Brothers, Matthew 25:31-46: A History of Interpretation* (SBLDS 114; Atlanta: Scholars, 1989); Graham N. Stanton, "Once More: Matthew 25.31-46," in *A Gospel for a New People: Studies in Matthew* (Edinburgh: T. & T. Clark, 1992), pp. 207-31; and Luz, "The Final Judgment (Matt 25:31-46): An Exercise in 'History of Influence' Exegesis."

309. Wailes, *Medieval Allegories of Jesus' Parables*, pp. 196, 198; Gray, *The Least of My Brothers*, pp. 20-21.

310. E.g., Davies and Allison, *Matthew*, 3:422-23, 428-29.

311. E.g., Luz, *Matthew 21–28*, pp. 271-74, although he takes "all the nations" universally (p. 275). At points his intent is not clear. On p. 282 he describes the judgment as universal, with Matthew thinking primarily of the church.

312. So Luz, *Matthew 21–28*, p. 273, but ideas close to this position appear as early as Origen; see his Commentary on John 1:13 (*ANF* 9:304).

313. E.g., Stanton, "Once More: Matthew 25.31-46."

314. E.g., Pentecost, *The Parables of Jesus*, pp. 157-59, who restricts the brothers to 144,000 Jewish witnesses to Christ during the Tribulation (based on Rev 7:1-8); Eugene W. Pond, "The Background and Timing of the Judgment of the Sheep and Goats," *BSac* 159 (2002): 201-20, 288-301, 436-48.

315. Gray, *The Least of My Brothers*, especially pp. 348-51.

316. Luz, "The Final Judgment (Matt 25:31-46): An Exercise in 'History of Influence' Exegesis," 280, n. 37.

317. Gray (*The Least of My Brothers*, p. 255) counts thirty-two positions in the twentieth century on the meaning of "all the nations" and "these least brothers of mine." An unusual approach is that of Robert Maddox, who argued that while all the nations are gathered, this passage is only about the judgment of Christian leaders. See his "Who Are the 'Sheep' and the 'Goats'? A Study of the Purpose and Meaning of Matthew xxv:31-46," *AusBR* 13 (1965): 19-28. His approach founders on "all the nations" in v. 32, which he unconvincingly tries to separate from "divided them" in the second half of the verse.

318. Jeremias, *The Parables of Jesus*, p. 209.

319. Theo Preiss, *Life in Christ* (trans. Harold Knight; SBT 13; Chicago: Allenson, 1954), especially pp. 51-53.

320. See among others Nolland, *The Gospel of Matthew*, pp. 1023, 1035 (who thinks the passage speaks of God's judgment of Israel); Schuyler Brown, "Faith, the Poor and the Gentiles: A Tradition-Historical Reflection on Matthew 25:31-46," *TJT* 6 (1990): 171-81, here pp. 175-77; Ingo Broer, "Das Gericht des Menschensohnes über die Völker. Auslegung von Mt 25,31-46," *BibLeb* 11 (1970): 273-95; and Jan Lambrecht, *Once More Astonished: The Parables of Jesus* (New York: Crossroad, 1981), pp. 219-27, but in his *Out of the Treasure*, pp. 273-79, he concluded that the parable is a Matthean composition and about universal judgment. Ulrich Wilckens argued that Jesus' parable was focused more on missionaries and that Matthew reframed it to refer to universal judgment. See his "Gottes geringste Brüder — zu Mt 25,31-46," in *Jesus und Paulus*, ed. E. Earle Ellis and Erich Gräßer (Göttingen: Vandenhoeck & Ruprecht, 1975), pp. 363-83.

321. E.g., Lamar Cope ("Matthew XXV:31-46: 'The Sheep and the Goats' Reinterpreted," *NovT* 11 [1969]: 32-44) argued against the parable being from Jesus on the grounds that (1) it draws on Jewish motifs of agency, motifs evidenced elsewhere in Matthean redaction, (2) a judgment determined by acceptance or rejection of the disciples reflects the concerns of the

church, (3) it equates Jesus with the Son of Man (one of the surer signs of non-authenticity), and (4) there is no evidence of an Aramaic original and a Hebrew original is more likely. None of these arguments is valid to support his conclusion. Jewish motifs of agency should be expected and are in evidence in other Gospels (e.g., John 13:20). Whether the parable teaches that judgment is determined by acceptance or rejection of the disciples is itself debated, and I will argue against such an interpretation. The use of the title "Son of Man" cannot be denied to Jesus; in fact, it seems rather to be his preferred title. Aramaic backgrounds are significant, but in the end do not provide proof of origin. Further, we do not know in what language Jesus' parables were told. They may have been told in Aramaic, but in view of the fact that rabbinic parables are nearly always reported in Hebrew even if the document is in Aramaic, we should be cautious about drawing such a conclusion. See above, p. 54. Funk, Hoover, and the Jesus Seminar (*The Five Gospels,* pp. 257-58) print the whole passage using black ink. No justification is given for the decision other than that it fits Matthew's theological scheme.

322. See J. A. T. Robinson, "The Parable of the Sheep and the Goats," in *Twelve New Testament Studies* (Naperville: Allenson, 1962), pp. 76-93; reprinted from *NTS* 2 (1956): 225-37. He provides a shortened version of the parable, which removes v. 31 and any item referring to division, separation, or punishment.

323. As Luz (*Matthew 21–28,* p. 265) points out. For a slightly different assessment which emphasizes Matthean theological traits, not just stylistic traits, see Robinson, "The Parable of the Sheep and the Goats," p. 86. He too finds the dialogue section (vv. 35-40 and 42-45) free of editorial traits.

324. See David R. Catchpole, "The Poor on Earth and the Son of Man in Heaven: A Reappraisal of Matthew xxv.31-46," *BJRL* 61 (1979): 355-97, here pp. 383-87.

325. See above, p. 552.

326. Jesus obviously could have taught such material several times, both to Jews in general and to his disciples.

327. Luz, "The Final Judgment (Matt 25:31-46): An Exercise in 'History of Influence' Exegesis," p. 294 (italics added).

328. Weber ("The Image of Sheep and Goats in Matthew 25:31-46," 677) argues that at the story level the passage is universal in intent, but at the discourse level is strongly devoted to exhortation of Christians. This does not, however, make both views of *panta ta ethnē* correct on different levels. John Heil also argued for both views being operative. See his "The Double Meaning of the Narrative of Universal Judgment in Matthew 25.31-46," *JSNT* 69 (1998): 3-14.

329. See Matt 8:11-12/Luke 13:28-29; Matt 11:20-24/Luke 10:13-15; Matt 12:41-42/Luke 11:29-32.

330. Contra Stanton, "Once More: Matthew 25.31-46," p. 213, who suggests that Matthew implies two judgments. While nothing in Matthew implies two judgments, *T. Benj.* 10:9 (which may reflect Christian interpolation) has three judgments: a judgment of Israel and then of nations, then Israel by the chosen Gentiles. *T. Abr.* 13:1-8 has three judgments as well: in the first Abel is a wondrous judge seated on a throne to judge all creation. Here God disavows judgment so that man is judged by man, but at a second parousia they will be judged by the twelve tribes of Israel, and then by God. See also *1 En.* 90–91; *4 Ezra* 13:33-50, but neither of these so clearly anticipates two judgments.

331. See Luz, "The Final Judgment (Matt 25:31-46): An Exercise in 'History of Influence' Exegesis," 294; John R. Donahue, "The 'Parable' of the Sheep and the Goats: A Challenge to Christian Ethics," *TS* 47 (1986) 3-31, here pp. 12-13; Davies and Allison, *Matthew,* 3:422-23.

332. E.g., Stanton, "Once More: Matthew 25.31-46," pp. 214-30; and Jean-Claude Ingelaere, "La 'parabole' du jugement dernier (Matthieu 25/31-46)," *RHPR* 50 (1970): 23-60.

333. E.g., J. Ramsey Michaels, "Apostolic Hardships and Righteous Gentiles," *JBL* 84 (1965): 27-37. Michaels also thinks the issue includes the way *Christian* communities respond to their leaders. For him, it concerns not so much Christians and non-Christians, but those who teach and those who are taught. *Didache* 4:1-8 could be seen as supporting this interpretation.

334. See also the occurrences in 5:22-24, 47; 7:3-5. Whether other occurrences should be included in this category depends on how texts like 18:15, 21 are understood.

335. Which may carry an elative sense, i.e., "very small."

336. Whereas 10:42 could be understood of acts of love in general, the parallel in Mark 9:41 clearly shows that the acts are directed to the disciples. See also Mark 9:42; Luke 17:2.

337. Notice Lambrecht's anxiety over the fact that "little" is used for the disciples and for weak Christians (*Once More Astonished*, pp. 227-28).

338. NRSV; literally, "in the name because you are Christ's."

339. See especially Michaels, "Apostolic Hardships and Righteous Gentiles," 31-37, who points to 2 *Clem.* 17:3, which seems to allude to our parable, and *Acts of Thomas* 145; and Stanton, "Once More: Matthew 25.31-46," pp. 219-20, who admits that it is difficult to imagine non-Christian Gentiles visiting Christians in jail.

340. Similarly, it is hard to imagine Jesus saying to his disciples that judgment would be conditioned on the way people treated them.

341. The parallel at Mark 9:41 does concern disciples, but the identity of the "little ones" in Matt 10:42 is not obvious.

342. Schuyler Brown argued that "'the least' exhibit the megalomania characteristic of extreme sectarianism" and "Such a reading seems to confirm the self-righteousness of a closed, particularist community" ("Faith, the Poor and the Gentiles," 174, 178). David L. Bartlett asserted that this parable "was a story told by oppressed, poor, minority Christians. It was their assertive and even arrogant way of insisting that their cause was God's cause" ("An Exegesis of Matthew 25:31-46," *Foundations* 19 [1976]: 211-13, quoting p. 212).

343. C. E. B. Cranfield ("Who Are Christ's Brothers? Matthew 25.40," *Metanoia* 4 [1994]: 31-39) argued that Stanton's view yields an incredible anticlimax at this crucial point in the Gospel (p. 37).

344. On love see 5:43-48; 19:19; 22:34-40; cf. 7:12; on mercy see 5:7; 6:2-4; 9:13; 12:7; 18:33; 23:23; on judgment see especially 12:33-37; 13:36-43, 47-50; 16:27; 18:33-35. The concern for the downtrodden and the poor is evident in the Beatitudes, the miracle accounts, and elsewhere (especially 8:17; 9:35-36; 11:5 with its allusions to Isa 61:1; 11:28; 19:21).

345. See Hultgren, *The Parables of Jesus*, pp. 320-23, who lists twelve reasons for interpreting "the least" as all needy persons. Davies and Allison, *Matthew*, 3:429, argue that it is unlikely that Matthew thought all the nations would have opportunity to help needy Christians. Victor Paul Furnish (*The Love Command in the New Testament* [Nashville: Abingdon, 1972], p. 83) argued on the basis of 24:24 that Matthew thought all nations will be evangelized before judgment (24:14) and therefore that it is futile to debate whether "brothers" refers to Christians or the world at large since at that time all will be in the kingdom in the sense that they will have formally received the gospel. I do not think Matthew's expectation was that optimistic.

346. See above, p. 766, n. 320, and p. 552.

347. Luz, "The Final Judgment (Matt 25:31-46)," pp. 308-10; *Matthew 21–28*, pp. 283-84.

348. See David A. De Silva, "Renewing the Ethic of the Eschatological Community: The Vision of Judgment in Matthew 25," *Koinonia* 3 (1991): 168-94, here p. 181. De Silva also points

out that neither Jesus nor Matthew allows a boundary between a brother and a non-brother; see Matt 5:44-48 and Luke 10:25-37.

349. See Catchpole, "The Poor on Earth and the Son of Man in Heaven," 383-87.

350. Among others, see Wright, *Jesus and the Victory of God*, p. 131.

351. Sanders, *Jesus and Judaism*, p. 326. See also Wright, *Jesus and the Victory of God*, pp. 624-53, especially 624-29 on "Sharing the Throne of God."

352. Among a variety of references see respectively *1 En.* 91:15; *T. Ab.* 13:2-3; *2 Bar.* 72:2-6; 11QMelch 2.9-13; *1 En.* 49:2–50:5; *Lives of the Prophets* 21:3; Dan 7:13-14 (and John 5:27); and *1 En.* 1:3-9. The parallel in John 5:27-29 is especially important, for it also describes the Son of Man dispensing resurrection of life or resurrection of judgment on the basis of good acts or evil acts respectively. Most writings have several conceptions. See Marius Reiser, *Jesus and Judgment: The Eschatological Proclamation in Its Jewish Context* (trans. Linda M. Maloney; Minneapolis: Fortress, 1997), p. 161.

353. See Russell Pregeant, "The Matthean Undercurrent: Process Hermeneutic and 'The Parable of the Last Judgment,'" in *Society of Biblical Literature 1975 Seminar Papers*, ed. George MacRae (Missoula: Scholars, 1975), 2:143-59, who says that Matthew develops a standard of salvation that overextends his christology (p. 147), that he presents a soteriology grounded in a real theology of grace to which Jesus, despite his authority, is related only indirectly, and that it is Torah that actually functions salvifically (p. 151).

354. See Pentecost, *The Parables of Jesus*, p. 159; Brown, "Faith, the Poor and the Gentiles," pp. 171-72; Dan O. Via, "Ethical Responsibility and Human Wholeness in Matthew 25:31-46," *HTR* 80 (1987): 79-100, especially 95-96.

355. See Via, "Ethical Responsibility and Human Wholeness," 97, 100.

356. In the Gospels *charis* occurs only in Luke 1:30; 2:40, 52 (with the sense "favor"); 4:22 (words "of grace"); 6:32, 33, 34 (with the sense "benefit"); and 17:9 (with the sense "thanks") and in John 1:14 and 17 in the expression "grace and truth" and in 1:16 in "grace on top of grace."

357. Most obviously in 5:3-5; 7:11; 9:9-13; 10:8; 10:29-31; 11:28-30; 13:44; 18:10-14; 18:23-35; 20:28.

358. Alan P. Stanley goes so far as to say Jesus does teach salvation by works, if rightly understood. See his *Did Jesus Teach Salvation by Works: The Role of Salvation in the Synoptic Gospels* (Eugene: Wipf and Stock, 2006).

359. The expression coined by Karl Rahner; see his "Anonymous Christians," and "Anonymous Christianity and the Missionary Task of the Church," *Theological Investigations* (London: Darton, Longman, and Todd), 6:390-98, 12:161-78.

360. Luz, "The Final Judgment (Matt 25:31-46): An Exercise in 'History of Influence' Exegesis," pp. 300-301. The surprise is particularly difficult for the missionary approach since those receiving the cup of cold water would have made known that they represented Jesus in their preaching about him.

361. Preis, *Life in Christ*, pp. 43-60.

362. See Richard C. Oudersluys, "The Parable of the Sheep and Goats (Matthew 25:31-46): Eschatology and Mission, Then and Now," *Reformed Review* 26 (1973): 151-61, here p. 156. It is perfectly legitimate to reflect on other questions, but the text must not be squeezed for unintended meanings. There is a difference between interpreting texts and reflecting on them. Luz's suggestion ("The Final Judgment (Matt 25:31-46)," 308-10; and *Matthew 21–28*, pp. 283-84) that we can interpret a text against its original sense is unacceptable. Had he not interpreted the parable as consoling suffering disciples he would not have needed to think about interpreting it against its sense.

363. See especially Prov 19:17; and in addition to the primary sources listed above, see *Exod. Rab.* 31.13; *Ruth Rab.* 5.9.

364. Donahue, "The 'Parable' of the Sheep and the Goats," 11. See also Reiser, *Jesus and Judgment,* p. 310.

365. Davies and Allison, *Matthew,* 3:418.

366. I do not think Matthew is dependent on the *Similitudes of Enoch,* as some suggest. Catchpole ("The Poor on Earth and the Son of Man in Heaven," 379-80) thinks both the *Similitudes* and Matthew go back to earlier material. Ezek 34:17-22 is probably not the backdrop against which the parable should be seen. In this OT text God announces that he will judge between the strong and the weak, not between sheep and goats or sheep and rams. The Hebrew words *ṣō'n* and *śeh* used in this text can both refer to either sheep or goats. See above, pp. 550-51.

367. Reiser, *Jesus and Judgment,* p. 304.

368. Many Christians do not take seriously how extreme eternally enduring punishment is. Such language seems to me to be hyperbolic. See the discussion by Clark H. Pinnock, "What Is Hell?" *Ex Auditu* 20 (2004): 47-59.

369. "Present Justification and Final Judgment: A Discusion of the Parable of the Sheep and the Goats," *ExpTim* 68 (1957): 46-50; see p. 49.

370. *The Theology of the Gospel of Matthew* (Cambridge: Cambridge University Press, 1995), p. 132 (italics his). That is, judgment according to works does not fit the God who abides in Jesus. He suggests that the anthropological necessity may be the solution to the dilemma of judgment and grace.

371. See Job 34:11; Ps 9:7-20 (note esp. v. 18); 58:11; 62:9, 12; 96:10, 13; Prov 10:16; 24:12; Eccl 12:14; Isa 3:10-11; 59:18; Jer 17:10; 25:14; 32:19; Ezek 33:20; Lam 3:64; Hos 4:9; Matt 7:21; 12:36; 16:27; John 5:29; Rom 2:6-15; 14:10-12; 2 Cor 5:10; 11:15; Eph 6:8; Col 3:25; 2 Tim 4:14; Jas 1:25; 2:24; 1 Pet 1:17; Rev 2:23; 14:13; 20:12-13; 22:12.

372. Reiser, *Jesus and Judgment,* p. 302.

373. See C. E. B. Cranfield, "Diakonia," in *If God Be for Us* (Edinburgh: T. & T. Clark, 1985), pp. 97-111, specifically p. 102.

374. See Gray, *The Least of My Brothers,* p. 50.

375. See my discussion of Eph 6:5-9 in *Ephesians: The NIV Application Commentary* (Grand Rapids: Zondervan, 1996), pp. 323-24, 326-29, 331-33.

376. As Davies and Allison, *Matthew,* 3:423, think is possible.

377. See "Justification by Grace to the Doers: An Analysis of the Place of Romans 2 in the Theology of Paul," *NTS* 32 (1986): 72-93.

378. German scholarship has given more attention to this parable than English-speaking scholars. In addition to numerous articles, there are at least five German books on it: E. Brandenburger, *Das Recht des Weltenrichters. Untersuchung zu Matthäus 25,31-46* (Stuttgart: Katholisches Bibelwerk, 1980); R. Brändle, *Matth. 25.31-46 im Werk des Johannes Chrysostomos* (Tübingen: Mohr-Siebeck, 1979); P. Christian, *Jesus und seine geringsten Brüder. Mt. 25,31-46 redaktionsgeschichtlich untersucht* (Leipzig: St. Benno, 1975); J. Friedrich, *Gott im Bruder? Eine methodenkritische Untersuchung von Redaction, Überlieferung und Traditionen in Mt. 25,31-46* (Stuttgart: Calwer, 1977); M. Puzicha, *Christus Peregrinus. Die Fremdenaufnahme (Mt. 25,35) als Werk der privaten Wohltätigkeit im Urteil der Alten Kirche* (Münster: Aschendorff, 1980).

Bibliography

Primary Sources

Ancient Near Eastern Texts Relating to the Old Testament. 3d ed. Ed. James B. Pritchard. Princeton: Princeton University Press, 1969.

The Aramaic Bible. Ed. Martin McNamara, et al. Wilmington: M. Glazier, 1986-.

The Babylonian Talmud. Ed. I. Epstein. 35 vols. London: Soncino, 1960.

Charles, R. H., ed. *Apocrypha and Pseudepigrapha of the Old Testament.* Oxford: Clarendon, 1913.

————. *The Assumption of Moses.* London: Black, 1897.

Conybeare, F. C., Rendal J. Harris, and Agnes Smith Lewis. *The Story of Ahiqar from the Aramaic, Syriac, Arabic, Armenian, Ethiopic, Old Turkish, Greek, and Slavonic Versions.* 2d ed. Cambridge: Cambridge University Press, 1913.

The Dead Sea Scrolls: Study Edition. Ed. Florentino García Martínez and Eibert J. C. Tigchelaar. 2 vols. Leiden: Brill/Grand Rapids: Eerdmans, 1997.

The Fathers According to Rabbi Nathan. Trans. Judah Goldin. Yale Judaica Series 10. New Haven: Yale University Press, 1955.

Loeb Classical Library. Cambridge: Harvard University Press.

Mekhilta De-Rabbi Ishmael: A Critical Edition, Based on the Manuscripts and Early Editions, with an English Translation, Introduction, and Notes. Ed. Jacob Z. Lauterbach. 2 vols. Philadelphia: The Jewish Publication Society, 2004.

The Midrash on Psalms. Trans. William G. Braude. 2 vols. Yale Judaica Series 13. New Haven: Yale University Press, 1959.

Midrash Rabbah: Translated into English with Notes, Glossary and Indices. Ed. H. Freedman and Maurice Simon. 10 vols. London: Soncino, 1939.

Midrash Tanḥuma: Translated into English with Introduction, Indices, and Brief Notes. Trans. John T. Townsend. 2 vols. Hoboken: Ktav, 1989.

Milik, J. T. *The Books of Enoch.* Oxford: Clarendon, 1976.

Milligan, George. *Selections from the Greek Papyri*. Cambridge: Cambridge University Press, 1912.

The Mishnah: Translated from the Hebrew with Introduction and Brief Explanatory Notes. Trans. Herbert Danby. Oxford: Clarendon, 1933.

New Testament Apocrypha. Ed. Edgar Hennecke and Wilhelm Schneemelcher. Trans. and ed. R. McL. Wilson. 2 vols. Philadelphia: Westminster, 1965.

The Old Testament Pseudepigrapha. Ed. James H. Charlesworth. 2 vols. Garden City: Doubleday, 1983.

Pěsiḳta dĕ-Raḇ Kahăna: R. Kahana's Compilation of Discourses for Sabbaths and Festal Days. Trans. William G. (Gershon Zev) Braude and Israel J. Kapstein. Philadelphia: Jewish Publication Society of America, 1975.

Pesikta Rabbati: Discourses for Feasts, Fasts, and Special Sabbaths. Trans. William G. Braude. 2 vols. Yale Judaica Series 18. New Haven: Yale University Press, 1968.

Pirḳê De Rabbi Eliezer: The Chapters of Rabbi Eliezer the Great According to the Text of the Manuscript Belonging to Abraham Epstein of Vienna. Trans. Gerald Friedlander. Benjamin Blom, 1971.

Sifra: An Analytical Translation. Trans. Jacob Neusner. 3 vols. Brown Judaic Studies 138-40. Atlanta: Scholars, 1988.

Sifre: A Tannaitic Commentary on the Book of Deuteronomy. Trans. Reuven Hammer. Yale Judaica Series 24. New Haven: Yale University Press, 1986.

Synopsis Quattuor Evangeliorum. Locis parallelis evangeliorum apocryphorum et patrum adhibitis edidit. Ed. Kurt Aland. Stuttgart: Württembergische Bibelanstalt, 1976.

Tanna Dĕḇe Eliyyahu: The Lore of the School of Elijah. Trans. William G. (Gershon Zev) Braude and Israel J. Kapstein. Philadelphia: The Jewish Publication Society of America, 1981.

The Targum of Isaiah. Trans. J. F. Stenning. Oxford: Clarendon, 1949.

The Tosefta: Translated from the Hebrew with a New Introduction. Trans. Jacob Neusner. 2 vols. Peabody: Hendrickson, 2002.

Secondary Sources

Aalen, S. "St. Luke's Gospel and the Last Chapters of 1 Enoch." *NTS* 13 (1967): 1-13.

Abou-Chaar, Kamal. "The Two Builders: A Study of the Parable in Luke 6:47-49." *Theological Review* 5 (1982): 44-58.

Agnew, Francis H. "The Parables of Divine Compassion." *The Bible Today* 27 (1989): 35-40.

Allison, Dale C., Jr. *Jesus of Nazareth: Millenarian Prophet*. Minneapolis: Fortress, 1998.

———. "Mark 12:28-31 and the Decalogue." Pages 270-78 in *The Gospels and the Scriptures of Israel*. Ed. Craig A. Evans and W. Richard Stegner. Sheffield: Sheffield Academic, 1994.

———. "Matthew 23:39 = Luke 13:35b as a Conditional Prophecy." *JSNT* 18 (1983): 75-84.

Ambrozic, Aloysius M. *The Hidden Kingdom: A Redaction-Critical Study of the References to the Kingdom of God in Mark's Gospel*. CBQMS 2. Washington: The Catholic Bible Association of America, 1972.

Anderson, Robert T. "Samaritans." *ABD* 5:940-47.

Archbald, Paul. "Interpretation of the Parable of the Dragnet (Matthew 13:47-50)." *Vox Reformata* 48 (1987): 3-14.

Arens, Edmund. *Kommunikative Handlungen. Die paradigmatische Bedeutung der Gleichnisse Jesu für eine Handlungstheorie.* Düsseldorf: Patmos, 1982.

Argyle, A. W. "Wedding Customs at the Time of Jesus." *ExpTim* 86 (1975): 214-15.

Arnal, William E. "The Parable of the Tenants and the Class Consciousness of the Peasantry." Pages 135-57 in *Text and Artifact in the Religions of Mediterranean Antiquity.* Waterloo: Wilfrid Laurier University Press, 2000.

Aune, David. "Oral Tradition and the Anaphorisms of Jesus." Pages 211-65 in *Jesus and the Oral Gospel Tradition.* Ed. Henry Wansbrough. JSNTSup 64. Sheffield: Sheffield Academic, 1991.

———. "The Significance of the Delay of the Parousia for Early Christianity." Pages 87-95 in *Current Issues in Biblical and Patristic Interpretation.* Ed. Gerald F. Hawthorne. Grand Rapids: Eerdmans, 1975.

Aus, Roger David. "Luke 15:11-32 and R. Eliezer Ben Hyrcanus's Rise to Fame." *JBL* 104 (1985): 443-69.

———. *Weihnachtsgeschichte, Barmherziger Samariter, Verlorener Sohn. Studien zu ihrem jüdischen Hintergrund.* Berlin: Institut Kirche und Judentum, 1988.

Austin, Michael R. "The Hypocritical Son." *EvQ* 57 (1985): 307-15.

Baarda, Tjitze. "'Chose' or 'Collected': Concerning an Aramaism in Logion 8 of the Gospel of Thomas and the Question of Independence." *HTR* 84 (1991): 373-97.

———. "Luke 12,13-14: Text and Transmission from Marcion to Augustine." Pages 107-62 in *Christianity, Judaism and Other Greco-Roman Cults.* Ed. Jacob Neusner. Leiden: Brill, 1975.

Baasland, Ernst. "Zum Beispiel der Beispielerzählungen. Zur Formenlehre der Gleichnisse und zur methodik der Gleichnisauslegung." *NovT* 28 (1986): 193-219.

Bailey, Kenneth Ewing. *Finding the Lost: Cultural Keys to Luke 15.* St. Louis: Concordia, 1992.

———. "'Inverted Parallelisms' and 'Encased Parables' in Isaiah and Their Significance for Old and New Testament Translation and Interpretation." Pages 14-30 in *Literary Structure and Rhetorical Strategies in the Hebrew Bible.* Ed. L. J. de Regt, J. de Waard, and J. P. Fokkelman. Assen: Van Gorcum, 1996.

———. "Jacob and the Prodigal: A New Identity Story: A Comparison between the Parable of the Prodigal Son and Gen. 27–35." *Theological Review* 18 (1997): 54-72.

———. *Jacob and the Prodigal: A Study of the Parable of the Prodigal Son in the Light of the Saga of Jacob.* Downers Grove: InterVarsity, 2003.

———. *Jacob and the Prodigal: How Jesus Retold Israel's Story.* Downers Grove: InterVarsity, 2003.

———. *Poet and Peasant: A Literary-Cultural Approach to the Parables in Luke.* Grand Rapids: Eerdmans, 1976.

———. "Psalm 23 and Luke 15: A Vision Expanded." *IBS* 12 (1990): 54-71.

———. *Through Peasant Eyes: More Lucan Parables, Their Culture and Style.* Grand Rapids: Eerdmans, 1980.

Bailey, Mark L. "The Parable of the Mustard Seed." *BSac* 155 (1998): 449-59.

———. "The Parable of the Tares." *BSac* 115 (1998): 266-79.

Bainton, Roland. "Religious Liberty and the Parable of the Tares." Pages 95-121 in *The Collected Papers in Church History*. Volume 1. Boston: Beacon, 1962.

Balabanski, Vicky. *Eschatology in the Making: Mark, Matthew and the Didache*. SNTSMS 97. Cambridge: Cambridge University Press, 1997.

———. "Opening the Closed Door: A Feminist Rereading of the 'Wise and Foolish Virgins' (Mt. 25:1-13)." Pages 71-97 in *The Lost Coin: Parables of Women, Work and Wisdom*. Ed. Mary Ann Beavis. Sheffield: Sheffield Academic, 2002.

Ball, Michael. "The Parables of the Unjust Steward and the Rich Man and Lazarus." *ExpT* 106 (1994-95): 329-30.

Ballard, Paul. "Reasons for Refusing the Great Supper." *JTS* 23 (1972): 341-50.

Baltensweiler, Heinrich. "Das Gleichnis der selbstwachsenden Saat (Markus 4,26-29) und die theologische Konzeption des Markusevangelisten." Pages 69-75 in *Oikonomia. Heilsgeschichte als Thema der Theologie, Festschrift für Oscar Cullmann*. Ed. Felix Christed. Hamburg-Bergstadt: Reich, 1967.

Banning, E. B. "Towers." *ABD* 6:622-24.

Barclay, William. *And Jesus Said*. Philadelphia: Westminster, 1970.

Barrett, C. K. *Jesus and the Gospel Tradition*. Philadelphia: Fortress, 1968.

Barth, Gerhard. "Auseinandersetzungen um die Kirchenzucht im Umkreis des Matthäusevangelium." *ZTK* 69 (1978): 158-77.

Barth, Karl. *Church Dogmatics*. Trans. G. W. Bromiley. Edinburgh: T. & T. Clark, 1958.

Barth, Markus. "The Dishonest Steward and His Lord: Reflections on Luke 16:1-13." Pages 65-74 in *From Faith to Faith*. Ed. Dikran Y. Hadidian. Pittsburgh: Pickwick, 1979.

Bartlett, David L. "An Exegesis of Matthew 25:31-46." *Foundations* 19 (1976): 212.

Bartsch, Hans-Werner. "Eine bisher übersehene Zitierung der LXX in Mark 4,30." *TZ* 15 (1959): 126-28.

Batten, Alicia. "Dishonor, Gender, and the Parable of the Prodigal Son." *TJT* 13 (1997): 187-200.

Bauckham, Richard. "The Delay of the Parousia." *TynBul* 31 (1980): 3-36.

———. "Descent to the Underworld." *ABD* 2:145-59.

———. "For Whom Were Gospels Written?" Pages 9-48 in *The Gospels for All Christians: Rethinking the Gospel Audiences*. Grand Rapids: Eerdmans, 1998.

———. "The Future of Jesus Christ." *SBET* 16 (1998): 97-110.

———. "The Parable of the Royal Wedding Feast (Matthew 22:1-14) and the Parable of the Lame Man and the Blind Man (Apokryphon of Ezekiel)." *JBL* 115 (1996): 471-88.

———. "The Rich Man and Lazarus: The Parable and the Parallels." Pages 97-118 in *The Fate of the Dead*. NovTSup 93. Leiden: Brill, 1998.

———. "The Scrupulous Priest and the Good Samaritan: Jesus' Parabolic Interpretation of the Law of Moses." *NTS* 44 (1998): 475-89.

———. "Synoptic Parousia Parables and the Apocalypse." Pages 92-117 in *The Climax of Prophecy*. Edinburgh: T. & T. Clark, 1993.

———. "The Two Fig Tree Parables in the Apocalypse of Peter." *JBL* 104 (1985): 269-87.

———. "Visiting the Places of the Dead in the Extra-Canonical Apocalypses." Pages 81-96 in *The Fate of the Dead*. NovTSup 93. Leiden: Brill, 1998.

Baudler, Georg. "Das Gleichnis vom 'betrügerischen Verwalter' (Lk 16,1-8a) als Ausdruck der 'inneren Biographie' Jesu." *TGW* 28 (1985): 65-76.

———. *Jesus im Spiegel seiner Gleichnisse*. Stuttgart: Calwer, 1986.

Bauer, Johannes B. "Gnadenlohn oder Tageslohn (Mt 20,8-16)?" *Bib* 42 (1961): 224-28.

Baumgarten, Joseph M. "4Q500 and the Ancient Conception of the Lord's Vineyard." *Journal of Semitic Studies* 4 (1989): 1-6.

Beardslee, William A. "Listening to the Parables of Jesus: An Exploration of the Uses of Process Theology in Biblical Interpretation." Pages 201-18 in *Texts and Testaments: Critical Essays on the Bible and Early Church Fathers*. Ed. W. Eugene March. San Antonio: Trinity University Press, 1980.

Beare, Francis W. *The Gospel According to Matthew*. San Francisco: Harper & Row, 1981.

———. "The Parable of the Guests at the Banquet: A Sketch of the History of Its Interpretation." Pages 1-14 in *The Joy of Study: Papers on the New Testament and Related Subjects*. Ed. S. E. Johnson. New York: Macmillan, 1951.

Beasley-Murray, George R. *Jesus and the Kingdom of God*. Grand Rapids: Eerdmans, 1986.

———. *Jesus and the Last Days: The Interpretation of the Olivet Discourse*. Peabody: Hendrickson, 1993.

Beavis, Mary Ann. "Ancient Slavery as an Interpretive Context for the New Testament Servant Parables with Special Reference to the Unjust Steward (Luke 16:1-8)." *JBL* 111 (1992): 37-54.

———. "The Foolish Landowner (Luke 12:16b-20)." Pages 55-68 in *Jesus and His Parables*. Ed. V. George Shillington. Edinburgh: T. & T. Clark, 1997.

———. "Joy in Heaven, Sorrow on Earth: Luke 15.10." Pages 39-45 in *The Lost Coin: Parables of Women, Work and Wisdom*. Ed. Mary Ann Beavis. Sheffield: Sheffield Academic, 2002.

———. "'Making Up Stories': A Feminist Reading of the Parable of the Prodigal Son (Lk. 15.11b-32)." Pages 98-122 in *The Lost Coin: Parables of Women, Work and Wisdom*. Ed. Mary Ann Beavis. Sheffield: Sheffield Academic, 2002.

———. *Mark's Audience: The Literary and Social Setting of Mark 4:11-12*. Sheffield: JSOT, 1989.

———. "Parable and Fable." *CBQ* 52 (1990): 473-98.

Beirnaert, Louis. "The Parable of the Prodigal Son, Luke 15:11-32, Read by an Analyst." Pages 197-210 in *Exegesis: Problems of Method and Exercises in Reading (Genesis 22 and Luke 15)*. Ed. François Bovon and Grégoire Rouiller. Trans. Donald G. Miller. Pittsburgh: Pickwick, 1978.

Bendemann, Reinhard von. "Liebe und Sündenvergebung. Eine narrative-traditionsgeschichtliche Analyse von Lk 7,36-50." *BZ* 44 (2000): 161-82.

Bengel, John Albert. *Gnomon of the New Testament*. Trans. James Bandinel. Edinburgh: T. & T. Clark, 1877.

Benjamin, Don C. "The Persistent Widow." *The Bible Today* (1990): 213-19.

Berger, Klaus. *Formen und Gattungen im Neuen Testament*. Tübingen: A. Francke, 2005.

———. "Hellenistiche Gattungen im Neuen Testament." *ANRW* 25/2:1031-1432.

———. *Identity and Experience in the New Testament*. Trans. Charles Muenchow. Minneapolis: Fortress, 2003.

———. "Materialien zu Form und Überlieferungsgeschichte neutestamentlicher Gleichnisse." *NovT* 15 (1973): 1-37.

Berry, Wendell. *Life Is a Miracle: An Essay against Modern Superstition*. Washington: Counterpoint, 2000.

———. "Property, Patriotism, and National Defense." Pages 98-111 in *Home Economics.* San Francisco: North Point, 1987.

Betz, Hans Dieter. *The Sermon on the Mount.* Hermeneia. Minneapolis: Fortress, 1995.

Betz, Otto. "The Dichotomized Servant and the End of Judas Iscariot." *RevQ* 5 (1964): 43-58.

———. "Jesu Lieblingspsalm: Die Bedeutung von Psalm 103 für das Werk Jesu." *TBei* 15 (1984): 253-69.

Binder, Hans. "Das Gleichnis vom barmherzigen Samariter." *TZ* 15 (1959): 176-94.

Birdsall, J. N. "Luke XII.16ff. and the Gospel of Thomas." *JTS* 13 (1962): 332-36.

Bishop, E. F. F. "The Parable of the Lost or Wandering Sheep." *ATR* 44 (1962): 44-57.

Bittner, Wolfgang. "Lasset beides miteinander wachsen bis zur Ernte. . . ." Pages 15-35 in *Basileia.* Ed. Hans Dürr and Christoph Ramstein. Basel: Mitenand, 1993.

Black, Matthew. *An Aramaic Approach to the Gospels and Acts.* 3d ed. Oxford: Clarendon, 1967.

———. "The Parables as Allegory." *BJRL* 42 (1959-60): 273-87.

Blickenstaff, Marianne. *"While the Bridegroom Is with Them": Marriage, Family, Gender and Violence in the Gospel of Matthew.* JSNTSup 292. London: T. & T. Clark, 2005.

Blinzler, Josef. "Die letzte Gnadenfrist. Lk 13,6-9." *BL* 37 (1963-64): 155-69.

Blomberg, Craig L. *Contagious Holiness: Jesus' Meals with Sinners.* NSBT 19. Downers Grove: InterVarsity, 2005.

———. *Interpreting the Parables.* Downers Grove: InterVarsity, 1990.

———. "Interpreting the Parables of Jesus: Where Are We and Where Do We Go from Here?" *CBQ* 53 (1991): 50-78.

———. "Midrash, Chiasmus, and the Outline of Luke's Central Section." Pages 217-61 in *Gospel Perspectives III: Studies in Midrash and Historiography.* Ed. R. T. France and David Wenham. Sheffield: JSOT, 1983.

———. "The Parables of Jesus: Current Trends and Needs in Research." Pages 231-54 in *Studying the Historical Jesus: Evaluations of the State of the Current Research.* Ed. Bruce Chilton and Craig A. Evans. Leiden: Brill, 1994.

———. "Poetic Fiction, Subversive Speech, and Proportional Analogy in the Parables." *HBT* 18 (1996): 115-32.

———. *Preaching the Parables: From Responsible Interpretation to Powerful Proclamation.* Grand Rapids: Baker, 2004.

———. "Tradition and Redaction in the Parables of the Gospel of Thomas." Pages 177-205 in vol. 5 of *Gospel Perspectives: The Jesus Tradition outside the Gospels.* Ed. David Wenham. Sheffield: JSOT, 1985.

———. "When Is a Parallel Really a Parallel? A Test Case: The Lukan Parables." *WTJ* 46 (1984): 78-103.

Boers, Hendrikus. *Theology Out of the Ghetto.* Leiden: Brill, 1971.

Bonhoeffer, Dietrich. *The Cost of Discipleship.* New York: Touchstone, 1995.

Borg, Marcus J. *Conflict, Holiness, and Politics in the Teachings of Jesus.* Studies in the Bible and Early Christianity 5. New York: Edwin Mellen, 1984.

Boring, Eugene M., Klaus Berger, and Carlsten Colpe, eds. *The Hellenistic Commentary to the New Testament.* Nashville: Abingdon, 1995.

Bornkamm, Günther. "Der Lohngedanke im Neuen Testament." Pages 69-92 in *Studien zu Antike und Urchristentum.* Munich: Kaiser, 1970.

————. "Die Verzögerung der Parusie." Pages 46-55 in *Geschichte und Glaube*. BEvT 48. Munich: Kaiser, 1968.

Bornkamm, Günther, Gerhard Barth, and Heinz Joachim Held. *Tradition and Interpretation in Matthew*. Trans. Percy Scott. Philadelphia: Westminster, 1963.

Borsch, Frederick Houk. *Many Things in Parables: Extravagant Stories of New Community*. Philadelphia: Fortress, 1988.

Bosley, Harold A. *He Spoke to Them in Parables*. New York: Harper & Row, 1963.

Boucher, Madeleine. *The Mysterious Parable*. CBQMS 6. Washington: The Catholic Biblical Association of America, 1977.

————. *The Parables*. Wilmington: Michael Glazier, 1981.

Bovon, François. *Das Evangelium nach Lukas*. EKKNT. Zurich: Benziger, 1989-.

————. *Luke 1: A Commentary on the Gospel of Luke 1:1–9:50*. Trans. Christine M. Thomas. Minneapolis: Fortress, 2002.

————. "The Parable of the Prodigal Son (Luke 15:11-32): First Reading." "The Parable of the Prodigal Son: Second Reading." Pages 43-73, 441-66 in *Exegesis: Problems of Method and Exercises in Reading (Genesis 22 and Luke 15)*. Ed. François Bovon and Grégoire Rouiller. Trans. Donald G. Miller. Pittsburgh: Pickwick, 1978.

Bowker, John W. "Mystery and Parable: Mark 4:1-20." *JTS* 25 (1974): 300-317.

Boyarin, Daniel. "History Becomes Parable: A Reading of the Midrashic *Mashal*." Pages 54-71 in *Mapping of the Biblical Terrain: The Bible as a Text*. Ed. Vincent L. Tollers and John Maier. Lewisburg: Bucknell University Press, 1990.

————. *The Parables*. Wilmington: Michael Glazier, 1981.

Brandenburger, E. *Das Recht des Weltenrichters. Untersuchung zu Matthäus 25,31-46*. Stuttgart: Katholisches Bibelwerk, 1980.

Brändle, R. *Matth. 25.31-46 im Werk des Johannes Chrysostomos*. Tübingen: Mohr-Siebeck, 1979.

Braumann, Georg. "Die Schuldner und die Sünderin, Luk. VII. 36-50." *NTS* 10 (1964): 487-93.

————. "Tot — lebendig, verloren — gefunden (Lk 15,24 und 32)." Pages 156-64 in *Wort in der Zeit. Festschrift für K. H. Rengstorf*. Ed. W. Haubeck and M. Bachmann. Leiden: Brill, 1980.

Braun, Willi. *Feasting and Social Rhetoric in Luke 14*. SNTSMS 85. Cambridge: Cambridge University Press, 1995.

————. "Symposium or Anti-Symposium? Reflections on Luke 14:1-24." *TJT* 8 (1992): 70-84.

Breech, James. *The Silence of Jesus: The Authentic Voice of the Historical Man*. Philadelphia: Fortress, 1983.

Bretherton, Donald J. "Lazarus of Bethany: Resurrection or Resuscitation?" *ExpTim* 104 (1993): 169-73.

Bridge, Steven L. *Where the Eagles Are Gathered: The Deliverance of the Elect in Lukan Eschatology*. JSNTSup 240. Sheffield: Sheffield Academic, 2003.

Broadhead, Edwin K. "An Example of Gender Bias in the USB[3]." *BT* 40 (1989): 336-38.

Brodie, Thomas. *The Birthing of the New Testament*. Sheffield: Sheffield Phoenix, 2004.

————. "Luke 7,36-50 as an Internalization of 2 Kings 4,1-37: A Study of Luke's Rhetorical Imitation." *Bib* 64 (1983): 457-85.

Broer, Ingo. "Die Gleichnisexegese und die neuere Literaturwissenschaft. Ein Diskussionsbeitrag zur Exegese von Mt 20,1-16." *BN* 5 (1978): 13-27.

———. "Das Gleichnis vom verlorenen Sohn und die Theologie des Lukas." *NTS* 20 (1974): 453-62.

Brokhoff, John R. *Preaching the Parables: Cycle B, Texts from Common, Lutheran, and Roman Catholic Lectionaries.* Lima: C.S.S., 1987.

———. *Preaching the Parables: Cycle C, Texts from Common, Lutheran, and Roman Catholic Lectionaries.* Lima: C.S.S., 1988.

Brooke, George J. "4Q500 1 and the Use of Scripture in the Parable of the Vineyard." *Dead Sea Discoveries* 2 (1995): 268-94.

Brown, Colin. "The Parable of the Rebellious Son(s)." *SJT* 51 (1998): 391-405.

———. "The Unjust Steward: A New Twist?" Pages 121-45 in *Worship, Theology and Ministry in the Early Church.* Ed. Michael J. Wilkins and Terence Paige. Sheffield: JSOT, 1992.

Brown, Francis, S. R. Driver, and Charles A. Briggs, eds. *A Hebrew and English Lexicon of the Old Testament.* Oxford: Clarendon, 1962.

Brown, Raymond. "Parable and Allegory Reconsidered." Pages 321-33 in *New Testament Essays.* Garden City: Doubleday, 1968.

———. *The Semitic Background of the Term "Mystery" in the New Testament.* Philadelphia: Fortress, 1968.

Brown, Schuyler. "Faith, the Poor and the Gentiles: A Tradition-Historical Reflection on Matthew 25:31-46." *TJT* 6 (1990): 171-81.

Brownlee, William H. "Messianic Motifs of Qumran and the New Testament." *NTS* 3 (1957): 195-210.

Bruce, A. B. *The Parabolic Teaching of Christ: A Systematic and Critical Study of the Parables of Our Lord.* 3d ed. New York: A. C. Armstrong and Son, 1887.

Bruce, F. F. "Justification by Faith in the Non-Pauline Writings of the New Testament." *EvQ* 24 (1952): 66-69.

Brunner, Emil. *Sowing and Reaping.* Trans. Thomas Wieser. Richmond: John Knox, 1946.

Bryan, Steven M. *Jesus and Israel's Traditions of Judgment and Restoration.* SNTSMS 117. Cambridge: Cambridge University Press, 2002.

Búason, Kristján. "The Good Samaritan, Luke 10:25-37: One Text, Three Methods." Pages 1-35 in *Luke-Acts: Scandinavian Perspectives.* Ed. Petri Luomanen. Göttingen: Vandenhoeck & Ruprecht, 1991.

Bultmann, Rudolf. *The History of the Synoptic Tradition.* Rev. ed. Trans. John Marsh. New York: Harper & Row, 1976.

———. *Theology of the New Testament.* Trans. Kendrick Grobel. New York: Charles Scribner's Sons, 1951.

Bussby, F. "Did a Shepherd Leave Sheep upon the Mountains or in the Desert?" *ATR* 45 (1963): 93-94.

Buth, Randall, and Brian Kvasnica. "Temple Authorities and Tithe Evasion: The Linguistic Background and Impact of the Parable of *the Vineyard, the Tenants, and the Son.*" Pages 53-80 in *Jesus' Last Week: Jerusalem Studies in the Synoptic Gospels — Volume One.* Ed. R. Steven Notley, Marc Turnage, and Brian Becker. Leiden: Brill, 2006.

Buttrick, David. *Speaking Parables: A Homiletic Guide.* Louisville: Westminster John Knox, 2000.

Buttrick, George A. *The Parables of Jesus.* Garden City: Doubleday, 1928.

Cadbury, Henry J. "The Single Eye." *HTR* 47 (1954): 69-74.

Cadoux, Arthur Temple. *The Parables of Jesus: Their Art and Use.* New York: Macmillan, 1931.

Cahill, Michael. "Not a Cornerstone! Translating Ps 118,22 in the Jewish and Christian Scriptures." *RB* 106 (1999): 345-57.

Caird, G. B. *The Gospel of St. Luke.* New York: Seabury, 1968.

———. *The Language and Imagery of the Bible.* Philadelphia: Westminster, 1980.

———. *New Testament Theology.* Compiled and ed. L. D. Hurst. Oxford: Clarendon, 1994.

Calvin, John. *Commentary on a Harmony of the Evangelists: Matthew, Mark, and Luke.* Trans. William Pringle. Grand Rapids: Eerdmans, 1949.

Cameron, Ron. "Matthew's Parable of the Two Sons." *FFF* 8 (1992): 191-209.

Camery-Hoggatt, Jerry. *Irony in Mark's Gospel: Text and Subtext.* SNTSMS 72. Cambridge: Cambridge University Press, 1992.

Campbell, Denis. "The Leaven." *ExpTim* 104 (1993): 307-8.

Cantinat, Jean. "Les Paraboles de la Misericorde." *TD* 4 (1956): 120-23.

Cantrell, Richard A. "The Cursed Fig Tree." *The Bible Today* 29 (1991): 105-8.

Capon, Robert Farrar. *Parables of Grace.* Grand Rapids: Eerdmans, 1988.

———. *Parables of Judgment.* Grand Rapids: Eerdmans, 1989.

———. *Parables of the Kingdom.* Grand Rapids: Eerdmans, 1985.

Carey, W. Gregory. "Excuses, Excuses: The Parable of the Banquet (Luke 14:15-24) within the Larger Context of Luke." *IBS* 17 (1995): 177-87.

Carlston, Charles Edwin. *The Parables of the Triple Tradition.* Philadelphia: Fortress, 1975.

———. "A *Positive* Criterion of Authenticity." *BR* 7 (1962): 33-44.

Carothers, J. Edward. *Living with the Parables: Jesus and the Reign of God.* New York: Friendship, 1984.

Carroll, John T. *Response to the End of History: Eschatology and Situation in Luke-Acts.* SBLDS 92. Atlanta: Scholars, 1988.

Carson, D. A. "The ΟΜΟΙΟΣ Word-Group as Introduction to Some Matthean Parables." *NTS* 31 (1985): 277-82.

Carter, Warren. "Construction of Violence and Identities in Matthew's Gospel." Pages 81-108 in *Violence in the New Testament.* Ed. Shelly Matthews and E. Leigh Gibson. London: T. & T. Clark, 2005.

———. "Resisting and Imitating the Empire: Imperial Paradigms in Two Matthean Parables." *Int* 56 (2002): 260-72.

Carter, Warren, and John Paul Heil. *Matthew's Parables: Audience Oriented Perspectives.* CBQMS 30. Washington: Catholic Biblical Association of America, 1998.

Catchpole, David. "Eine Schaf, eine Drachme und ein Israelit. Die Botschaft Jesu in Q." Pages 89-101 in *Die Freude an God. Unsere Kraft.* Ed. Johannes J. Degenhardt. Stuttgart: Katholisches Bibelwerk, 1991.

———. "Jesus, John the Baptist and the Parable of the Tares." *SJT* 31 (1978): 557-70.

———. "Q and 'the Friend at Midnight' (Luke xi.5-8/9)." *JTS* 34 (1983): 407-24.

———. "Q, Prayer, and the Kingdom: A Rejoinder." *JTS* 40 (1989): 377-88.

———. "The Son of Man's Search for Faith (Luke XVIII 8b)." *NovT* 19 (1977): 81-104.

Cave, C. H. "Lazarus and the Lukan Deuteronomy." *NTS* 15 (1969): 319-25.

Charette, Blaine. *The Theme of Recompense in Matthew's Gospel*. JSNTSup 79. Sheffield: Sheffield Academic, 1992.

Charlesworth, James H. "Jesus as 'Son' and the Righteous Teacher as 'Gardener.'" Pages 140-75 in *Jesus and the Dead Sea Scrolls*. Ed. James E. Charlesworth. New York: Doubleday, 1992.

———. "Jesus' Concept of God and His Self-Understanding." Pages 131-64 in *Jesus within Judaism: New Light from Exciting Archaeological Discoveries*. New York: Doubleday, 1988.

Cheong, C.-S. Abraham. *A Dialogic Reading of the Steward Parable (Luke 16:1-9)*. Studies in Biblical Literature 28. New York: Peter Lang, 2001.

Chilton, Bruce D. *A Galilean Rabbi and His Bible*. Wilmington: Glazier, 1984.

———. "(The) Son of (the) Man, and Jesus." Pages 259-87 in *Authenticating the Words of Jesus*. Ed. Bruce D. Chilton and Craig A. Evans. Leiden: Brill, 1999.

Christian, P. *Jesus und seine geringsten Brüder. Mt. 25,31-46 redaktionsgeschichtlich untersucht*. Leipzig: St. Benno, 1975.

Coats, George W. "Parable, Fable and Anecdote." *Int* 35 (1981): 368-82.

Collins, R. F. "The Man Who Came to Dinner." Pages 151-72 in *Luke and His Readers*. Ed. R. Bieringer, G. Van Belle, and J. Verheyden. Leuven: Leuven University Press, 2005.

———. "The Story of the Seed Growing by Itself: A Parable for Our Times." *Emmanuel* 94 (1998): 446-52.

Combrink, Hans J. B. "A Social-Scientific Perspective on the Parable of the Unjust Steward." *Neot* 30 (1996): 281-306.

Cope, Lamar. "Matthew XXV:31-46: 'The Sheep and the Goats' Reinterpreted." *NovT* 11 (1969): 32-44.

Cortés, Juan B. "The Greek Text of Luke 18:14a: A Contribution to the Method of Reasoned Eclecticism." *CBQ* 46 (1984): 255-73.

Cosgrove, Charles H. "A Woman's Unbound Hair in the Greco-Roman World, with Special Reference to the Story of the 'Sinful Woman' in Luke 7:36-50." *JBL* 124 (2005): 675-92.

Cotter, Wendy J. "The Parable of the Feisty Widow and the Threatened Judge (Luke 18:1-8)." *NTS* 51 (2005): 328-43.

———. "The Parables of the Mustard Seed and the Leaven: Their Function in the Earliest Stratum of Q." *TJT* 8 (1992): 37-51.

Craddock, Fred B. *Overhearing the Gospel*. Nashville: Abingdon, 1978.

Cranfield, C. E. B. "Diakonia." Pages 97-111 in *If God Be for Us*. Edinburgh: T. & T. Clark, 1985.

———. "The Parable of the Unjust Judge and the Eschatology of Luke-Acts." *SJT* 16 (1903): 297-301.

———. "St. Mark 4:1-34." *SJT* 4 (1951): 398-414.

———. "Who Are Christ's Brothers? Matthew 25.40." *Metanoia* 4 (1994): 31-39.

Crawford, Robert G. "A Parable of the Atonement." *EvQ* 50 (1978): 2-7.

Crespy, Georges. "The Parable of the Good Samaritan: An Essay in Structural Research." *Semeia* 2 (1980): 27-50.

Crook, Zeba Antonin. "The Synoptic Parables of the Mustard Seed and the Leaven: A Test Case for the Two-Document, Two-Gospel, and Farrer-Goulder Hypotheses." *JSNT* 78 (2000): 23-48.

Crossan, John Dominic. *Cliffs of Fall: Paradox and Polyvalence in the Parables of Jesus.* New York: Seabury, 1980.

———. *Finding Is the First Act: Trove Folktales and Jesus' Treasure Parable.* Philadelphia: Fortress, 1979.

———. *The Historical Jesus: The Life of a Mediterranean Jewish Peasant.* San Francisco: Harper, 1991.

———. *In Fragments.* San Francisco: Harper & Row, 1983.

———. *In Parables: The Challenge of the Historical Jesus.* New York: Harper & Row, 1973.

———. "Parable." *ABD* 5:148-49.

———. "Parable, Allegory, and Paradox." Pages 247-81 in *Semiology and the Parables.* Ed. Daniel Patte. Pittsburgh: Pickwick, 1976.

———. "Parable and Example in the Teaching of Jesus." *NTS* 18 (1971-72): 285-307.

———. "The Seed Parables of Jesus." *JBL* 92 (1973): 244-66.

———. "Structuralist Analysis and the Parables of Jesus." *Semeia* 1 (1974): 192-221.

Crump, David Michael. *Jesus the Intercessor: Prayer and Christology in Luke-Acts.* WUNT 2. Tübingen: Mohr-Siebeck, 1992.

———. *Knocking on Heaven's Door: A New Testament Theology of Petitionary Prayer.* Grand Rapids: Baker, 2006.

Culbertson, Philip L. "Reclaiming the Matthean Vineyard Parables." *Encounter* 49 (1988): 257-83.

———. *A Word Fitly Spoken: Context, Transmission, and Adoption of the Parables of Jesus.* Albany: State University of New York Press, 1995.

Curkpatrick, Stephen. "Dissonance in Luke 18:1-8." *JBL* 121 (2002): 107-21.

Dahl, Nils. "The Parables of Growth." Pages 156-66 in *Jesus in the Memory of the Early Church.* Minneapolis: Augsburg, 1976.

Dalman, G. *Arbeit und Sitte in Palästina.* 2: *Der Ackerbau.* Hildesheim: Georg Olms, 1964-2001.

———. *The Words of Jesus.* Trans. D. M. Kay. Edinburgh: T. & T. Clark, 1902.

Daniélou, Jean. "Le Bon Samaritain." Pages 457-65 in *Mélanges Bibliques rédigés en l'honneur de André Robert.* Paris: Bloud & Gay, 1956.

Danker, Frederick W. *Jesus and the New Age: A Commentary on St. Luke's Gospel.* Philadelphia: Fortress, 1985.

Daube, David. "Inheritance in Two Lukan Pericopes." *Zeitschrift der Savigny-Stiftung für Rechtsgeschichte* 72 (1955): 326-44.

———. "Neglected Nuances of Exposition in Luke-Acts." *ANRW* 25/3:2329-56.

———. "Shame Culture in Luke." Pages 355-72 in *Paul and Paulinism: Essays in Honour of C. K. Barrett.* Ed. Morna D. Hooker and S. G. Wilson. London: SPCK, 1982.

Davies, W. D., and Dale C. Allison. *A Critical and Exegetical Commentary on the Gospel according to Saint Matthew.* 3 vols. ICC. Edinburgh: T. & T. Clark, 1988-97.

DeBoer, Martinus. "Ten Thousand Talents? Matthew's Interpretation and Redaction of the Parable of the Unforgiving Servant (Matt 18:23-35)." *CBQ* 50 (1988): 214-32.

Degenhardt, Joachim. *Lukas. Evangelist der Armen.* Stuttgart: Katholisches Bibelwerk, 1965.

de Goedt, Michel. "L'explication de la parabole de l'ivraie (Mt. XIII,36-43)." *RB* 66 (1959): 32-54.

Deidun, Thomas. "The Parable of the Unmerciful Servant (Mt 18:23-25)." *BTB* 6 (1976): 203-24.

Deissmann, Adolf. *Light from the Ancient Near East.* Trans. Lionel R. M. Strachan. Reprint of the 4th ed. Grand Rapids: Baker, 1965.

Delling, Gerhard. "Das Gleichnis vom gottlosen Richter." *ZNW* 53 (1962): 1-25.

Delormé, Jean, ed. *Les Paraboles évangéliques. Perspectives nouvelles.* Lectio Divina 135. Paris: Cerf, 1989.

de Meeûs, X. "Composition de Lc., XIV et genre symposiatique." *ETL* 37 (1961): 847-70.

De Moor, Johannes C. "The Targumic Background of Mark 12:1-12: The Parable of the Wicked Tenants." *JSJ* 29 (1998): 63-80.

Dempke, Christoph. "Rengstorf, Karl Heinrich. Die Re-Investitur des Verlorenen Sohnens in der Gleichniserzählung Jesu Luk. 15, 11-32." *TLZ* 94 (1969): 762-63.

Derrett, J. Duncan M. "Ambivalence: Sowing and Reaping at Mark 4,26-29." *Estudios bíblicos* 48 (1990): 489-510.

———. "ΉΣΑΝ ΓΑΡ ΆΛΙΕΙΣ (Mk. I:16): Jesus's Fishermen and the Parable of the Net." *NovT* 22 (1980): 108-37.

———. "Figtrees in the New Testament." Pages 148-64 in *Midrash in Action and as a Literary Device.* Vol. 2 of *Studies in the New Testament.* Leiden: Brill, 1978.

———. "Fresh Light on St. Luke XVI: II. Dives and Lazarus and the Preceding Sayings." *NTS* 7 (1961): 364-80.

———. "Fresh Light on the Lost Sheep and the Lost Coin." *NTS* 26 (1979): 36-60.

———. "The Friend at Midnight: Asian Ideas in the Gospel of St. Luke." Pages 78-87 in *Donum Gentilicum: New Testament Studies in Honour of David Daube.* Ed. E. Bammel, C. K. Barrett, and W. D. Davies. Oxford: Clarendon, 1978.

———. *Law in the New Testament.* London: Darton, Longman, and Todd, 1976. Pages 1-16: "The Treasure in the Field." Pages 17-31: "The Parable of the Talents and Two Logia." Pages 32-47: "The Parable of the Unmerciful Servant." Pages 48-77: "The Parable of the Unjust Steward." Pages 100-125: "The Parable of the Prodigal Son." Pages 125-55: "The Parable of the Great Supper." Pages 208-27: "The Parable of the Good Samaritan." Pages 266-85: "The Anointing at Bethany and the Story of Zacchaeus." Pages 296-312: "Fresh Light on the Parable of the Wicked Vinedressers."

———. "'Love Thy Neighbor as a Man like Thyself'?" *ExpTim* 83 (1971): 55-56.

———. "Nisi Dominus Aedificaverit Domum: Towers and Wars (Lk XIV 28-32)." *NovT* 19 (1977): 241-61.

———. "The Parable of the Two Sons." *ST* 25 (1971): 109-16.

———. "The Rich Fool: A Parable of Jesus Concerning Inheritance." Pages 99-120 in *Midrash in Action and as a Literary Device.* Vol. 2 of *Studies in the New Testament.* Leiden: Brill, 1978.

———. "'Take Thy Bond . . . and Write Fifty' (Luke XVI.6): The Nature of the Bond." Pages 1-3 in *Studies in the New Testament I.* Leiden: Brill, 1977.

———. "Workers in the Vineyard: A Parable of Jesus." Pages 48-75 in *Studies in the New Testament I.* Leiden: Brill, 1977.

De Ru, G. "The Conception of Reward in the Teaching of Jesus." *NovT* 8 (1966): 202-22.

De Silva, David A. "Renewing the Ethic of the Eschatological Community: The Vision of Judgment in Matthew 25." *Koinonia* 3 (1991): 168-94.

Dewey, Joanna. *Markan Public Debate: Literary Technique, Concentric Structure, and Theology in Mark 2:1–3:6.* SBLDS 48. Chico: Scholars, 1980.

Dietzfelbinger, Christian. "Das Gleichnis vom ausgestreuten Samen." Pages 80-93 in *Der*

Ruf Jesu und die Antwort der Gemeinde. Ed. E. Lohse. Göttingen: Vandenhoeck & Ruprecht, 1970.

———. "Das Gleichnis von den Arbeitern im Weinberg." *EvT* 43 (1983): 126-37.

Dmitri, Archbishop. *The Parables: Biblical, Patristic, and Liturgical Interpretation.* Crestwood: St. Vladimir's Seminary Press, 1996.

Dodd, C. H. *The Parables of the Kingdom.* London: Nisbet, 1936.

Donahue, John R. *The Gospel in Parable: Metaphor, Narrative, and Theology in the Synoptic Gospels.* Philadelphia: Fortress, 1988.

———. "The 'Parable' of the Sheep and the Goats: A Challenge to Christian Ethics." *TS* 47 (1986): 3-31.

———. "Tax Collector." *ABD* 6:337-38.

———. "Tax Collectors and Sinners: An Attempt at Identification." *CBQ* 33 (1977): 39-61.

Donfried, Karl Paul. "The Allegory of the Ten Virgins (Matt 25: 1-13) as a Summary of Matthean Theology." *JBL* 93 (1974): 415-28.

Dormeyer, Detlev. "Literarische und Theologische Analyse der Parabel Lukas 14,15-24." *BibLeb* 15 (1974): 206-19.

———. *The New Testament Among the Writings of Antiquity.* Trans. Rosemarie Kossov. Sheffield: Sheffield Academic, 1998.

Downey, Glanville. "Who Is My Neighbor? The Greek and Roman Answer." *ATR* 47 (1965): 3-15.

Downing, Gerald. "The Ambiguity of 'The Pharisee and the Toll-Collector' (Luke 18:9-14) in the Greco-Roman World of Late Antiquity." *CBQ* 54 (1992): 80-99.

Doyle, B. Rod. "The Place of the Parable of the Labourers in the Vineyard in Matthew 20:1-16." *ABR* 42 (1994): 39-58.

Drexler, Hans. "Die grosse Sünderin Lucas 7:36-50." *ZNW* 59 (1968): 159-73.

Drury, John. "The Origins of Mark's Parables." Pages 171-89 in *Ways of Reading the Bible.* Ed. Michael Wadsworth. Totowa: Barnes and Noble, 1981.

———. *The Parables in the Gospels.* New York: Crossroad, 1985.

———. "The Sower, the Vineyard, and the Place of Allegory in the Interpretation of Mark's Parables." *JTS* 24 (1973): 367-79.

Dschulnigg, Peter. "Positionen des Gleichnisverständnisses im 20. Jahrhundert." *TZ* 45 (1989): 335-51.

———. *Rabbinische Gleichnisse und das Neue Testament. Die Gleichnisse der PesK im Vergleich mit den Gleichnissen Jesu und dem Neuen Testament.* Judaica et Christiana 12. Bern: Peter Lang, 1988.

Dunkerly, R. "Lazarus." *NTS* 5 (1959): 321-27.

Dunn, James D. G. "Altering the Default Setting: Re-Envisaging the Early Transmission of the Jesus Tradition." *NTS* 49 (2003): 139-75.

———. *Jesus Remembered.* Vol. 1 of *Christianity in the Making.* Grand Rapids: Eerdmans, 2003.

———. "Jesus, Table Fellowship, and Qumran." Pages 254-72 in *Jesus and the Dead Sea Scrolls.* Ed. James H. Charlesworth. New York: Doubleday, 1992.

Du Plessis, I. J. "Philanthropy or Sarcasm? Another Look at the Parable of the Dishonest Manager." *Neot* 24 (1990): 1-20.

Dupont, Jacques. "Le couple parabolique du sénevé et du levain, Mt 13,31-33; Lc 13,18-21." Pages 331-45 in *Jesus Christ in Historie und Theologie. Neutestamentliche Festschrift für Hans Conzelmann zum 60. Geburtstag.* Ed. Georg Strecker. Tübingen: Mohr-Siebeck, 1975.

———. "Encore la parabole de la Semence qui pousse toute seule (Mc 4,26-29)." Pages 96-108 in *Jesus und Paulus. Festschrift für Werner Georg Kümmel zum 70. Geburtstag.* Ed. E. Earle Ellis and Erich Grässer. Göttingen: Vandenhoeck & Ruprecht, 1975.

———. "Les implications christologiques de la parabole de la brebis perdue." Pages 331-50 in *Jesus aux Origines de la Christologie.* BETL 40. Leuven: Leuven University Press, 1975.

———. "La parabole de la semence qui pousse toute seule." *RSR* 55 (1967): 367-92.

———. "Le point de vue de Matthieu dans le chapitre des paraboles." Pages 221-59 in *L'Evangile selon Matthieu. Redaction et theologie.* Ed. M. Didier. Gembloux: J. Duculot, 1972.

Durber, Susan. "The Female Reader of the Parables of the Lost." *JSNT* 45 (1992): 59-78.

Eakin, Frank E., Jr. "Spiritual Obduracy and Parable Purpose." Pages 89-99 in *The Use of the Old Testament in the New and Other Essays.* Ed. James M. Efrid. Durham: Duke University Press, 1972.

Eckstein, Hans Joachim. "Pharisäer und Zöllner. Jesu Zuwendung zu den Sündern nach Lukas 18,9-14." Pages 143-51 in *Der aus Glauben Gerechte wird leben. Beiträge zur Theologie des Neuen Testaments.* Beiträge zum Verstehen der Bibel 5. Münster: Lit, 2003.

Eckstein, Richard. "Die von selbst wachsende Saat, Matthäus 4:26-29." Pages 139-45 in *Gleichnisse aus Altem und Neuem Testament.* Stuttgart: Klotz, 1971.

Edwards, James R. *The Gospel According to Mark.* Grand Rapids: Eerdmans, 2002.

Eissfeldt, Otto. *Der Maschal im Alten Testament.* Giessen: Alfred Töpelmann, 1913.

Elliot, John H. "Matthew 20:1-15: A Parable of Invidious Comparison and Evil Eye Accusation." *BTB* 22 (1992): 52-65.

Ellis, E. Earle. "How the New Testament Uses the Old." Pages 199-219 in *New Testament Interpretation.* Ed. I. Howard Marshall. Exeter: Paternoster, 1977.

The Entrevenes Group. *Signs and Parables: Semiotics and Gospel Texts.* Trans. Gary Phillips. Pittsburgh: Pickwick, 1978.

Erlemann, K. *Das Bild Gottes in den synoptischen Gleichnissen.* Stuttgart: W. Kohlhammer, 1988.

Ernst, Josef. "Gastmahlgespräche: Lk 14,1-24." Pages 57-78 in *Die Kirche des Anfangs. Für Heinz Schürmann.* Ed. Rudolf Schnackenburg, Josef Ernst, and Joachim Wanke. Freiburg: Herder, 1978.

Ernst, Michael. "Hellenistischen Analogien zu ntl. Gleichnissen. Eine Sammlung von Vergleichstexten sowie Thesen über die sich aus der parabolischen Redeweise ergebenden gesellschaftspolitischen Konsequenzen." Pages 461-80 in *Ein Gott, Eine Offenbarung. Beiträge zur Biblische Exegese, Theologie und Spiritualität. Festschrift für Nokter Füglister.* Ed. Friedrich von Reiterer. Würzburg: Echter, 1991.

———. ". . . verkaufte alles, was er besass, und kaufte die Perle (Mt 13, 46). Der ἔμπορος im Neuen Testament und in dokumentarischen Papyri." *Protokolle zur Bibel* 6 (1997): 31-46.

Esler, Phillip Francis. *Community and Gospel in Luke-Acts.* SNTSMS 57. Cambridge: Cambridge University Press, 1987.

———. "Jesus and the Reduction of Intergroup Conflict: The Parable of the Good Samaritan in the Light of Social Identity Theory." *BibInt* 8 (2000): 325-57.

Evans, C. F. "The Central Section of St. Luke's Gospel." Pages 37-55 in *Studies in the Gospels*. Ed. D. E. Nineham. Oxford: Blackwell, 1955.

———. "Uncomfortable Words — V." *ExpTim* 81 (1969-70): 228-31.

Evans, Craig A. "Do This and You Will Live": Targumic Coherence in Luke 10:25-28." Pages 377-93 in *Jesus in Context*. Ed. Bruce Chilton and Craig A. Evans. Leiden: Brill, 1997.

———. "God's Vineyard and Its Caretakers." Pages 381-406 in *Jesus and His Contemporaries: Comparative Studies*. AGJU 25. Leiden: E. J. Brill, 1995.

———. "How Septuagintal Is Isa 5:1-7 and Mark 12:1-9?" *NovT* 45 (2003): 105-10.

———. "Jesus and Rabbinic Parables, Proverbs, and Prayers." Pages 251-97 in *Jesus and His Contemporaries: Comparative Studies*. Ed. Craig A. Evans. Leiden: Brill, 1995.

———. "Jesus' Parable of the Tenant Farmers in Light of Lease Agreements in Antiquity." *JSP* 14 (1996): 65-83.

———. "Luke 16:1-18 and the Deuteronomy Hypothesis." Pages 121-39 in *Luke and Scripture*. Ed. Craig A. Evans and James Sanders. Minneapolis: Augsburg/Fortress, 1993.

———. *Mark 8:27–16:20*. WBC 34B. Nashville: Thomas Nelson, 2001.

———. *Noncanonical Writings and New Testament Interpretation*. Peabody: Hendrickson, 1992.

———. "A Note on the Function of Isaiah VI,9-10 in Mark IV." *RB* 88 (1981): 234-35.

———. "On the Isaianic Background of the Sower Parable." *CBQ* 47 (1985): 464-68.

———. "The Pharisee and the Publican: Luke 18:9-14 and Deuteronomy 26." Pages 342-55 in *The Gospels and the Scriptures of Israel*. Ed. Craig A. Evans and W. Richard Stegner. Sheffield: Sheffield Academic, 1994.

———. "The Recently Published Dead Sea Scrolls and the Historical Jesus." Pages 547-65 in *Studying the Historical Jesus*. Ed. Bruce Chilton and Craig A. Evans. Leiden: Brill, 1994.

———. *To See and Not Perceive: Isaiah 6.9-10 in Early Jewish and Christian Interpretation*. JSOTSup64. Sheffield: Sheffield Academic, 1989.

Farris, Michael. "A Tale of Two Taxations (Luke 18:10-14b): The Parable of the Pharisee and the Toll Collector." Pages 23-33 in *Jesus and His Parables: Interpreting the Parables of Jesus Today*. Ed. V. George Shillington. Edinburgh: T. & T. Clark, 1997.

Fay, Greg. "Introduction to Incomprehension: The Literary Structure of Mark 4:1-34." *CBQ* 51 (1989): 65-81.

Feldman, Asher. *The Parables and Similes of the Rabbis: Agricultural and Pastoral*. 2d ed. Cambridge: Cambridge University Press, 1927.

Fenton, John C. "Expounding the Parables IV: The Parables of the Treasure and the Pearl (Mt. 13:44-46)." *ExpTim* 77 (1966): 178-80.

Feuillet, André. "Les épousailles messianiques et les références au Cantique dans les évangiles synoptiques." *Revue Thomiste* 84 (1984): 399-424.

———. "La parabole des vierges." *La Vie spirituelle* 75 (1946): 667-77.

———. "La parabole du mauvais riche et du pauvre Lazare (Lc 16, 19-31) antithèse de la parabole de l'intendant astucieux (Lc 16,1-9)." *NRTh* 101 (1979): 212-23.

———. "La signification christologique de Luc 18, 14 et les références des Evangiles au Serviteur souffrant." *Nova et vetera* 15 (1980): 188-229.

Fichtner, Joseph. *Many Things in Parables: Reflections for Life*. New York: Alba House, 1988.

Fiebig, Paul. *Altjüdische Gleichnisse und die Gleichnisse Jesu.* Tübingen: Mohr-Siebeck, 1904.

———. *Die Gleichnisreden Jesus in Lichte der rabbinischen Gleichnisse des neutestamentlichen Zeitalters.* Tübingen: Mohr-Siebeck, 1912.

Fienzy, David. *The Social History of Palestine in the Herodian Period.* Lewiston: Mellen, 1991.

Findlay, J. Alexander. *Jesus and His Parables.* London: Epworth, 1957.

Firmage, Edwin. "Zoology." *ABD* 6:1146.

Fisher, Neal. *The Parables of Jesus.* New York: Crossroad, 1990.

Fitzmyer, Joseph A. *The Gospel According to Luke I–IX.* AB 28. Garden City: Doubleday, 1983.

———. *The Gospel According to Luke X–XXIV.* AB 28B. Garden City: Doubleday, 1985.

———. "The Languages of Palestine in the First Century A.D." *CBQ* 32 (1970): 501-31.

———. "The Story of the Dishonest Manager (Lk 16:1-13)." Pages 161-84 in *Essays on the Semitic Background of the New Testament.* Missoula: Scholars, 1974.

Fleddermann, Harry T. "The Householder and the Servant Left in Charge." Pages 17-26 in *Society of Biblical Literature Seminar Papers, 1986.* Ed. Kent Harold Richards. Atlanta: Scholars, 1986.

———. "Mustard Seed and Leaven in Q, the Synoptics, and Thomas." *Society of Biblical Literature 1989 Seminary Papers.* Ed. David J. Lull. Atlanta: Scholars, 1989.

———. "Three Friends at Midnight (Luke 11,5-8)." Pages 265-82 in *Luke and His Readers.* Ed. R. Bieringer, G. Van Belle, and J. Verheyden. Leuven: Leuven University Press, 2005.

Fletcher, Donald R. "The Riddle of the Unjust Steward: Is Irony the Key?" *JBL* 82 (1963): 15-30.

Flusser, David. "Aesop's Miser and the Parable of the Talents." Pages 9-25 in *Parable and Story in Judaism and Christianity.* Ed. Clemens Thoma and Michael Wyschogrod. New York: Paulist, 1989.

———. "Jesus' Opinion about the Essenes." Pages 150-68 in *Judaism and the Origins of Christianity.* Jerusalem: Magnes, 1988.

———. "A New Sensitivity in Judaism and the Christian Message." Pages 469-92 in *Judaism and the Origins of Christianity.* Jerusalem: Magnes, 1988.

———. "The Parable of the Unjust Steward: Jesus' Criticism of the Essenes." Pages 176-97 in *Jesus and the Dead Sea Scrolls.* Ed. James H. Charlesworth. New York: Doubleday, 1992.

———. *Die rabbinischen Gleichnisse und der Gleichniserzähler Jesus. 1: Das Wesen der Gleichnisse.* Bern: Peter Lang, 1981.

Foerster, Werner. "Das Gleichnis von den anvertrauten Pfunden." Pages 37-56 in *Verbum Dei Manet in Aeternum. Eine Festschrift für D. Otto Schmitz.* Ed. Werner Focrstcr. Witten: Luther, 1953.

Forbes, Greg W. *The God of Old: The Role of the Lukan Parables in the Purpose of Luke's Gospel.* JSNTSup 198. Sheffield: Sheffield Academic, 2000.

Ford, J. Massingberde. "The Parable of the Foolish Scholars." *NovT* 9 (1967): 107-23.

Ford, Mary. "Towards the Restoration of Allegory: Christology, Epistemology and Narrative Structure." *St. Vladamir's Theological Quarterly* 34 (1990): 161-95.

Ford, Richard Q. *The Parables of Jesus: Recovering the Art of Listening*. Minneapolis: Fortress, 1997.

Fortna, Robert. "Reading Jesus' Parable of the Talents through Underclass Eyes: Matt 25:14-30." *FFF* 8 (1992): 211-27.

————. "You Have Made Them Equal to Us." *JTSA* 72 (1990): 66-72.

Foster, Paul. "A Parable of Two Sons: But Which One Did the Far, Far Better Thing? A Study of Matt 21.28-32." *NTS* 47 (2001): 26-37.

Fowler, Robert M. *Let the Reader Understand: Reader-Response Criticism and the Gospel of Mark*. Minneapolis: Fortress, 1991.

France. R. T. *The Gospel of Mark: A Commentary on the Greek Text*. NIGTC. Grand Rapids: Eerdmans, 2002.

————. *Matthew: Evangelist and Teacher*. Grand Rapids: Zondervan, 1989.

————. "On Being Ready (Matthew 25:1-46)." Pages 177-95 in *The Challenge of Jesus' Parables*. Ed. Richard N. Longenecker. Grand Rapids: Eerdmans, 2000.

Fränkel, Hermann. *Die homerischen Gleichnisse*. Göttingen: Vandenhoeck & Ruprecht, 1921.

Franz, Gordon. "Text and Tell: The Parable of the Two Builders." *Archaeology in the Biblical World* 3 (1995): 6-11.

Freud, Sigmund. *Civilization and Its Discontents*. Trans. and ed. James Strachey. New York: Norton, 1962.

Freyne, Seán. *Galilee from Alexander the Great to Hadrian, 323 B.C.E. to 135 C.E.: A Study of Second Temple Judaism*. Wilmington: Glazier, 1980.

Frick, Frank S. "Palestine, Climate of." *ABD* 5:119-26.

Fridrichsen, A. "Exegetisches zum Neuen Testament." *SO* 13 (1934): 38-46.

Friedrich, J. *Gott im Bruder? Eine methodenkritische Untersuchung von Redaction, Überlieferung und Traditionen in Mt. 25,31-46*. Stuttgart: Calwer, 1977.

Friedrichsen, Timothy A. "The Temple, a Pharisee, a Tax Collector, and the Kingdom of God: Rereading a Jesus Parable (Luke 18:10-14a)." *JBL* 124 (2005): 89-119.

Fuchs, Ernst. *Hermeneutik*. 2 vols. 2d ed. Bad Cannstatt: R. Mullerschön, 1958.

————. "The Parable of the Unmerciful Servant (Matt. 18:23-25)." Pages 487-94 in *Studia Evangelica*. Ed. Kurt Aland. Berlin: Akademie, 1959.

————. *Studies of the Historical Jesus*. Trans. Andrew Scobie. SBT 42. Naperville: Allenson, 1964.

————. "Was heisst: 'Du sollst deinen Nächtsen lieben wie dich selbst'?" Pages 1-20 in *Gesammelte Aufsätze II. Zur Frage nach dem historischen Jesus*. Tübingen: Mohr-Siebeck, 1960.

————. "Das Zeitverständnis Jesu." Pages 304-76 in *Gesammelte Aufsätze II: Zur Frage nach dem historischen Jesus*. Tübingen: Mohr-Siebeck, 1960.

Funk, Robert W. "Beyond Criticism in the Quest of Literacy: The Parable of the Leaven." *Int* 25 (1971): 149-70.

————. "The Good Samaritan as Metaphor." *Semeia* 2 (1974): 74-81.

————. *Language, Hermeneutic, and Word of God*. New York: Harper & Row, 1966.

————. "The Looking-Glass Tree Is for the Birds." *Int* 27 (1973): 3-9.

————. "The Old Testament in Parable: The Good Samaritan." *Encounter* 26 (1965): 251-67.

————. *Parables and Presence*. Philadelphia: Fortress, 1982.

Funk, Robert W., Roy W. Hoover, and the Jesus Seminar, eds. *The Five Gospels: The Search for the Authentic Words of Jesus*. New York: Macmillan, 1993.

Funk, Robert W., Bernard Brandon Scott, and James R. Butts. *The Parables of Jesus: Red Letter Edition*. Sonoma: Polebridge, 1988.

Furnish, Victor Paul. *The Love Command in the New Testament*. Nashville: Abingdon, 1972.

Fusco, V. "'Point of View' and 'Implicit Reader' in Two Eschatological Texts (Lk 19,11-28; Acts 1,6-8)." Pages 1677-96 in *The Four Gospels 1992: Festschrift Frans Neirynck*. Ed. F. Van Segbroeck, et al. Leuven: Leuven University Press, 1992.

Gächter, Paul. "The Parable of the Dishonest Steward after Oriental Conceptions." *CBQ* 12 (1950): 121-31.

Galilea, Segundo. *The Music of God: Parables of Life and Faith*. Oak Park: Meyer Stone, 1988.

Ganschinietz, R. "Katabasis." PW 10/2:2359-2449.

Garcia, M. A. "Committed Discipleship and Jesus' Lordship: Exegesis of Luke 6:46-49 in the Context of Jesus' Discourse in the Plain." *African Christian Studies* 9 (1993): 3-10.

Garland, David E. *Reading Matthew: A Literary and Theological Commentary on the First Gospel*. New York: Crossroad, 1993.

Garnet, Paul. "The Parable of the Sower: How the Multitudes Understood It." Pages 39-54 in *Spirit within Structure*. Ed. Edward J. Furcha. Allison Park: Pickwick, 1983.

Gerhardsson, Birger. "The Earthly Jesus in the Synoptic Parables." Pages 49-62 in *Christology, Controversy, and Community: New Testament Essays in Honor of David R. Catchpole*. Ed. David G. Horrell and Christopher M. Tuckett. Leiden: Brill, 2000.

————. *The Good Samaritan, the Good Shepherd?* ConBNT 16. Lund: Gleerup, 1958.

————. "If We Do Not Cut the Parables Out of Their Frames." *NTS* 37 (1991): 221-35.

————. "Illuminating the Kingdom: Narrative Meshalim in the Synoptic Gospels." Pages 266-309 in *Jesus and the Oral Gospel Tradition*. Ed. Henry Wansbrough. JSNTSup 64. Sheffield: Sheffield Academic, 1991.

————. "The Narrative Meshalim in the Old Testament Books and in the Synoptic Gospels." Pages 289-304 in *To Touch the Text: Biblical and Related Studies in Honor of Joseph A. Fitzmyer*. Ed. Maurya P. Horgan and Paul J. Kobelski. New York: Crossroad, 1989.

————. "The Narrative Meshalim in the Synoptic Gospels: A Comparison with the Narrative Meshalim in the Old Testament." *NTS* 34 (1988): 339-63.

————. "The Parable of the Sower and Its Interpretation." *NTS* 14 (1968): 165-93.

————. "The Secret of the Transmission of the Unwritten Jesus Tradition." *NTS* 51 (2005): 1-18.

————. "The Seven Parables in Matthew XIII." *NTS* 19 (1972): 16-37.

Gibbs, Jeffrey A. "Parables of Atonement and Assurance: Matthew 13:44-46." *CTQ* 51 (1987): 19-43.

Gibson, J. "Hoi Telonai kai hai Pornai." *JTS* 32 (1981): 429-33.

Glancy, Jennifer A. *Slavery in Early Christianity*. Oxford: Oxford University Press, 2002.

————. "Slaves and Slavery in the Matthean Parables." *JBL* 119 (2000): 67-90.

Glen, J. Stanley. *The Parables of Conflict in Luke*. Philadelphia: Westminster, 1962.

Glombitza, Otto. "Der Perlenkaufmann. Eine exegetische Studie zur Matth. XIII.45-6." *NTS* 7 (1960-61): 153-61.

————. "Der reiche Mann und der arme Lazarus." *NovT* 12 (1970): 166-80.

Glover, F. C. "Workers for the Vineyard." *ExpTim* 86 (1975): 310-11.

Gnilka, Joachim. *Jesus of Nazareth: Message and History.* Trans. Siegfried S. Schatzmann. Peabody: Hendrickson, 1997.

———. *Die Verstockung Israels. Isaias 6,9-10 in der Theologie der Synoptiker.* Munich: Kösel, 1961.

Gollwitzer, Helmut. *Das Gleichnis vom barmherzigen Samariter.* Neukirchen: Neukirchener, 1962.

Gordon, Edmund I. "A New Look at the Wisdom of Sumer and Akkad." *Bibliotheca Orientalis* 17 (1960): 122-52.

———. "Sumerian Animal Proverbs and Fables: 'Collection Five.'" *Journal of Cuneiform Studies* 12 (1958): 1-75.

Gorringe, T. "A Zealot Option Rejected? Luke 12:13-14." *ExpTim* 98 (1987): 267-70.

Goulder, Michael D. "Characteristics of the Parables in the Several Gospels." *JTS* 19 (1968): 58-62.

———. *Luke: A New Paradigm.* 2 vols. JSNTSup 20. Sheffield: JSOT, 1989.

———. *Midrash and Lection in Matthew.* London: SPCK, 1974.

Gourges, Michel. "Faire confiance à la grâce de Dieu. La parabole du blé qui pousse tout seul (Mc 4,25-29)." *NRTh* 117 (1995): 364-75.

———. "Regroupement Littéraire et Équilibrage Théologique. Le Cas de Lc 13,1-9." Pages 1591-1602 in *The Four Gospels 1992: Festschrift Frans Nierynck.* 3 vols. Ed. F. Van Segbroeck, C. M. Tuckett, G. Van Belle, and J. Verheyden. Leuven: Leuven University Press, 1992.

Gowler, David. *What Are They Saying about the Parables?* Mahwah: Paulist, 2000.

Graffy, Adrian. "The Literary Genre of Isaiah 5,1-7." *Bib* 60 (1979): 400-409.

Granskou, David M. *Preaching on Parables.* Philadelphia: Fortress, 1972.

Grässer, Erich. *Das Problem der Parusieverzögerung in den synoptischen Evangelien und in der Apostelgeschichte.* BZNW 22. 2d ed. Berlin: Töpelmann, 1960.

Graves, Mike. "Luke 10:25-37: The Moral of the 'Good Samaritan' Story?" *RevExp* 94 (1997): 269-75.

Gray, A. "The Parable of the Wicked Husbandmen." *HibJ* 19 (1920-21): 42-52.

Gray, Sherman W. *The Least of My Brothers, Matthew 25:31-46: A History of Interpretation.* SBLDS 114. Atlanta: Scholars, 1989.

Green, Barbara. *Like a Tree Planted: An Exploration of Psalms and Parables Through Metaphor.* Collegeville: Liturgical, 1997.

Green, Joel B. *The Gospel of Luke.* NICNT. Grand Rapids: Eerdmans, 1997.

Green, Lowell C. "Justification in Luther's Preaching on Luke 18:9-14." *Concordia Theological Monthly* 43 (1972): 732-47.

Greeven, Heinrich. "*plēsion.*" TDNT 6:311-18.

———. "Wer unter Euch . . . ?" *WD* 3 (1952): 86-101.

Gregg, Robert C. "Early Christian Variations on the Parable of the Lost Sheep." *Duke Divinity School Review* 41 (1976): 85-104.

Grensted, L. W. "The Use of Enoch in St. Luke xvi.19-31." *ExpTim* 26 (1915): 333-34.

Gressmann, Hugo. *Vom reichen Mann und armen Lazarus. Eine literargeschichtliche Studie.* Abhandlungen der königlich preussischen Akademie der Wissenschaften 7. Berlin: Königlich Akademie der Wissenschaften, 1918.

Greswell, Edward. *An Exposition of the Parables and Other Parts of the Gospels.* 6 vols. Oxford: Rivington, 1834-35.

Gribble, Richard. *The Parables of Jesus: Applications for Contemporary Life, Cycle A.* Lima: C.S.S., 1998.

Grobel, K. ". . . Whose Name Was Neves." *NTS* 10 (1964): 373-82.

Gryglewicz, Felix. "The Gospel of the Overworked Workers." *CBQ* 19 (1957): 190-98.

Guelich, Robert A. *Mark 1–8:26.* WBC. Dallas: Word, 1989.

Gundry, R. "In Defense of the Church in Matthew as a Corpus Mixtum." *ZNW* 91 (2000): 153-65.

———. *Mark: A Commentary on His Apology for the Cross.* Grand Rapids: Eerdmans, 1993.

———. *Matthew: A Commentary on His Literary and Theological Art.* Grand Rapids: Eerdmans, 1982.

Guy, Laurie. "The Interplay of the Present and the Future in the Kingdom of God (Luke 19:11-44)." *TynBul* 48 (1997): 119-37.

Haaker, Klaus. "Das hochzeitliche Kleid von Mt. 22,11-13 und ein palästinisches Märchen." *ZDPV* 87 (1971): 95-97.

———. "Mut zum Bitten: Eine Auslegung von Lukas 11,5-8." *TBei* 17 (1986): 1-6.

Habershon, Ada R. *The Study of the Parables.* Grand Rapids: Kregel, n.d.

Haenchen, E. "Das Gleichnis vom grossen Mahl." Pages 135-55 in *Die Bibel und Wir. Gesammelte Aufsätze.* Tübingen: Mohr-Siebeck, 1968.

Hagner, Donald. *Matthew.* 2 vols. WBC. Dallas: Word, 1993.

———. "Righteousness in Matthew's Theology." Pages 101-20 in *Worship, Theology and Ministry in the Early Church: Essays in Honor of Ralph P. Martin.* Ed. Michael J. Wilkins and Terence Paige. JSNTSup 87. Sheffield: Sheffield Academic, 1992.

Hahn, Ferdinand. "Das Gleichnis von der ausgestreuten Saat und seine Deutung (Mk iv.3-8, 14-20)." Pages 133-42 in *Text and Interpretation.* Ed. Ernest Best and R. Wilson. Cambridge: Cambridge University Press, 1979.

———. "Das Gleichnis von der Einladung zum Festmahl." Pages 51-82 in *Verborum Veritas. Festschrift für Gustav Stählin.* Ed. Otto Bocher and Klaus Haaker. Wuppertal: Brockhaus, 1970.

Hallo, William W., and K. Lawson Younger Jr., eds. *The Context of Scripture.* 3 vols. Leiden: Brill, 2003.

Hamm, Dennis. "The Tamid Service in Luke-Acts: The Cultic Background behind Luke's Theology of Worship (Luke 1:5-25; 18:9-14; 24:50-53; Acts 3:1; 10:3, 30)." *CBQ* 65 (2003): 215-31.

Hammershaimb, Erling. "Om Lignelser og Billedtaler i de Gammeltestamentlige Psuedepigrafer." *SEÅ* 40 (1975).

Hanhart, Karel. *The Intermediate State in the New Testament.* Groningen: V.R.B., 1966.

Harmansa, H.-Konrad Von. *Die Zeit der Entscheidung. Lk 13,1-9 als Beispiel für das lukanische Verständis der Gerichtspredigt Jesu an Israel.* Erfurter Theologische Studien 69. Leipzig: Benno, 1995.

Harnisch, Wolfgang. "Der bezwingende Vorsprung des Guten. Zur Parabel von den bösen Winzern." Pages 22-38 in *Der Sprache der Bilder. Gleichnis und Metaphor in Literatur und Theologie.* Ed. Hans Weder. Gütersloh: Gerd Mohn, 1989.

———. *Die Gleichniserzählungen Jesu. Eine hermeneutische Einführung.* 3d ed. Göttingen: Vandenhoeck und Ruprecht, 1995.

—. *Gleichnisse Jesu: Positionen der Auslegung von Adolf Jülicher bis zur Formgeschichte.* Darmstadt: Wissenschaftliche Buchgesellschaft, 1982.

—. "Language of the Possible: The Parables of Jesus in the Conflict between Rhetoric and Poetry." *ST* 46 (1992): 41-54.

—. "The Metaphorical Process in Matthew 20:1-15." Pages 231-50 in *Society of Biblical Literature Seminar Papers, 1977.* Ed. Paul J. Achtemeier. Missoula: Scholars, 1977.

—. *Die neutestamentliche Gleichnisforschung im Horizont von Hermeneutik und Literaturwissenschaft.* Darmstadt: Wissenschaftliche Buchgesellschaft, 1982.

—. "Die Sprachkraft der Analogie." *ST* 28 (1974): 1-20.

—. *Die Zumutung der Liebe. Gesammelte Aufsätze.* Ed. Ulrich Schoenborn. FRLANT 187. Göttingen: Vandenhoeck & Ruprecht, 1999.

Harrill, James A. *Slaves in the New Testament.* Minneapolis: Fortress, 2006.

Harrington, Wilfrid. "The Prodigal Son." *Furrow* 25 (1974): 432-37.

Haubeck, Wilfrid. "Zum Verständnis der Parabel von den Arbeitern im Weinberg (Mt 20,1-15)." Pages 95-107 in *Wort in der Zeit.* Ed. Wilfrid Haubeck and Michael Bachmann. Leiden: Brill, 1980.

Hawkins, Peter S. "Parable as Metaphor." *CSR* 12 (1983): 226-36.

Hays, Richard B. *The Moral Vision of the New Testament: Community, Cross, New Creation: A Contemporary Introduction to New Testament Ethics.* San Francisco: Harper, 1996.

Hearon, Holly, and Antoinette Clark Wire. "Mt. 13.33; Lk. 13.20, 21; Gos. Thom 96; Mt. 6.28-30; Lk. 12.27-28; Gos. Thom. 36." Pages 136-57 in *The Lost Coin: Parables of Women, Work and Wisdom.* Ed. Mary Ann Beavis. London: Sheffield Academic, 2002.

Hedrick, Charles W. *Many Things in Parables: Jesus and His Modern Critics.* Louisville: Westminster John Knox, 2004.

—. *Parables as Poetic Fictions: The Creative Voice of Jesus.* Peabody: Hendrickson, 1994.

—. "Prolegomena to Reading Parables: Luke 13:6-9 as a Test Case." *RevExp* 94 (1997): 179-97.

—. "The Treasure Parable in Matthew and Thomas." *FFF* 2 (1986): 41-56.

—. "An Unfinished Story about a Fig Tree in a Vineyard, Luke 13:6-9." *PRSt* 26 (1999): 169-92.

Heichelheim, F. M. "Roman Syria." Pages 178-82 in vol. 4 of *An Economic Survey of Ancient Rome.* Ed. Tenney Frank. 6 vols. Paterson: Pageant, 1959.

Heil, John Paul. "The Double Meaning of the Narrative of Universal Judgment in Matthew 25.31-46." *JSNT* 69 (1998): 3-14.

—. "Reader-Response and the Narrative Context of the Parables about Growing Seed in Mark 4:1-34." *CBQ* 54 (1992): 278-86.

Heininger, Bernhard. *Metaphorik, Erzählstruktur und szenisch-dramatische Gestaltung in den Sondergutgleichnissen bei Lukas.* NTAbh 24. Münster: Aschendorff, 1991.

Henaut, Barry W. *Oral Tradition in the Gospels: The Problem of Mark 4.* JSNTSup 82. Sheffield: Sheffield Academic, 1993.

Hendrickx, Herman. "A Man Had Two Sons: Lk 15:11-32 in Light of the Ancient Mediterranean Values of Farming and Household." *East Asian Pastoral Institute* 31 (1994): 44-66.

—. *The Parables of Jesus.* San Francisco: Harper & Row, 1986.

Hengel, Martin. "Die ganz andere Gerechtigkeit." *TBei* 5 (1974): 1-13.

————. "Das Gleichnis von den Weingärtnern. Mc 12,1-12 im Lichte der Zenonpapyri und der rabbinische Gleichnisse." *ZTK* 59 (1968): 1-39.

Herbert, A. S. "The Parable (Māšāl) in the Old Testament." *SJT* 7 (1954): 180-96.

Hermaniuk, Maxime. *La Parabole Evangélique Enquête exégétique et critique.* Louvain: Bibliotheca Alfonsiana, 1947.

Herrenbrück, Fritz. *Jesus und die Zöllner. Historische und neutestamentlich-exegetische Untersuchungen.* WUNT 2/41. Tübingen: Mohr-Siebeck, 1990.

Hester, J. D. "Socio-Rhetorical Criticism and the Parable of the Wicked Tenants." *JSNT* 45 (1992): 27-57.

Herzog, William R., II. *Jesus, Justice, and the Reign of God: A Ministry of Liberation.* Louisville: Westminster John Knox, 2000.

————. *Parables as Subversive Speech: Jesus as Pedagogue of the Oppressed.* Louisville: Westminster John Knox, 1994.

Hezser, Catherine. *Lohnmetaphorik und Arbeitswelt in Mt 20,1-16.* NTOA 15. Göttingen: Vandenhoeck & Ruprecht, 1990.

Hicks, John Mark. "The Parable of the Persistent Widow (Luke 18:1-8)." *ResQ* 33 (1991): 209-23.

Hiers, Richard H. "Friends by Unrighteous Mammon: The Eschatological Proletariat (Luke 16:9)." *JAAR* 38 (1970): 30-36.

Hill, David. *The Gospel of Matthew.* London: Oliphants, 1972.

————. *Greek Words and Hebrew Meanings.* Cambridge: Cambridge University Press, 1967.

Hills, Julian. *Tradition and Composition in the Epistula Apostolorum.* Minneapolis: Fortress, 1990.

Himmelfarb, Martha. *Tours of Hell.* Philadelphia: University of Pennsylvania Press, 1983.

Hintzen, Johannes. *Verkündigung und Wahrnehmung. Über das Verhältnis von Evangelium und Leser am Beispiel Lk 16,19-31 im Rahmen des lukanischen Doppelwerkes.* BBB 81. Frankfurt: Hain, 1991.

Hirschfeld, Yizhar. *The Palestinian Dwelling in the Roman-Byzantine Period.* Studium Biblicum Franciscanum, Collection Minor 34. Jerusalem: Franciscan, 1995.

Hock, Ronald F. "Lazarus and Micyllus: Greco-Roman Backgrounds to Luke 16:19-31." *JBL* 106 (1987): 447-63.

————. "Romancing the Parables of Jesus." *PRSt* 29 (2002): 11-37.

Hoeren, Thomas. "Das Gleichnis vom Ungerechten Verwalter (Lukas 16:1-8a). Zugleich ein Beitrag zur Geschichte der Restschuldbefreiung." *NTS* 41 (1995): 620-29.

Hofius, Otfried. "Alttestamentliche Motive im Gleichnis vom verlorenen Sohn." *NTS* 24 (1977): 240-48.

Holgate, David A. *Prodigality, Liberality and Meanness: The Prodigal Son in Greco-Roman Perspective.* Sheffield: Sheffield Academic, 1999.

Holladay, John S., Jr. "House, Israelite." *ABD* 3:308-18.

Hollenbach, Bruce. "Lest They Should Turn and Be Forgiven: Irony." *BT* 34 (1983): 312-21.

Holmgren, Fred. "The Pharisee and the Tax Collector: Luke 18:9-14 and Deuteronomy 26:1-15." *Int* 48 (1994): 252-61.

Holst, Robert. "The One Anointing of Jesus: Another Application of the Form-Critical Method." *JBL* 95 (1976): 435-46.

Hooker, Morna D. *The Gospel According to St. Mark.* BNTC. Peabody: Hendrickson, 1991.

———. "Mark's Parables of the Kingdom (Mark 4:1-34)." Pages 79-101 in *The Challenge of Jesus' Parables*. Ed. Richard N. Longenecker. Grand Rapids: Eerdmans, 2000.

Hoppe, Rudolf. "Gleichnis und Situation. Zu den Gleichnissen von guten Vater (Lk 15,11-32) und gütigen Hausherrn (Mt 20,1-15)." *BZ* 28 (1984): 1-21.

Horst, J. "μακροθυμία, μακροθυμέω, ktl." *TDNT* 4:374-87.

Hough, Graham. "The Allegorical Circle." *The Critical Quarterly* 3 (1961): 199-209.

Hubaut, Michel. *La Parabole des vignerons homicides*. Cahiers de la Revue biblique 16. Paris: Gabalda, 1976.

Huffard, Evertt W. "The Parable of the Friend at Midnight: God's Honor or Man's Persistence?" *ResQ* 21 (1978): 154-60.

Huffman, Norman. "Atypical Features in the Parables of Jesus." *JBL* 97 (1978): 207-10.

Hughes, Frank W. "The Parable of the Rich Man and Lazarus (Luke 16.19-31) and Graeco-Roman Rhetoric." Pages 29-41 in *Rhetoric and the New Testament: Essays from the 1992 Heidelberg Conference*. Ed. Stanley E. Porter and Thomas H. Olbricht. Sheffield: Sheffield Academic, 1993.

Hultgren, Arland J. *The Parables of Jesus: A Commentary*. Grand Rapids: Eerdmans, 2000.

Hunter, A. M. *Interpreting the Parables*. London: SCM, 1960.

———. *The Parables Then and Now*. Philadelphia: Westminster, 1971.

Hunzinger, Claus-Hunno. "σίναπι." *TDNT* 7:287-91.

———. "Unbekannte Gleichnisse Jesu aus dem Thomas-Evangelium." Pages 209-20 in *Judentum-Urchristentum-Kirche*. Ed. W. Eltester. Berlin: Töpelmann, 1964.

Ingelaere, Jean-Claude. "La 'parabole' du jugement dernier (Matthieu 25/31-46)." *RHPR* 50 (1970): 23-60.

Instone-Brewer, David. "The Eighteen Benedictions and the Minim Before 70 CE." *JTS* 54 (2003): 25-44.

———. *Traditions of the Rabbis from the Era of the New Testament.* 1: *Prayer and Agriculture*. Grand Rapids: Eerdmans, 2004.

Ireland, Dennis J. *Stewardship and the Kingdom of God: An Historical, Exegetical, and Contextual Study of the Parable of the Unjust Steward in Luke 16:1-13*. NovTSup 70. Leiden: Brill, 1992.

Jacob, Irene, and Walter Jacob. "Flora." *ABD* 2:816.

———. *Flora and Fauna of the Bible*. 2d ed. London: United Bible Societies, 1980.

Jacobs, Joseph. "Aesop's Fables among the Jews." Pages 221-22 in *The Jewish Encyclopedia*. Ed. Isidore Singer. New York: Funk & Wagnall, 1906.

Jacobson, Delmar. "An Exposition of Matthew 13:44-52." *Int* 29 (1975): 277-82.

Jarvis, Peter G. "Expounding the Parables V: The Tower-builder and the King Going to War (Luke 14:25-33)." *ExpTim* 77 (1966): 196-98.

Jeremias, Joachim. "Die Deutung des Gleichnisses vom Unkraut unter dem Weizen." Pages 261-65 in *Abba*. Göttingen: Vandenhoeck & Ruprecht, 1966.

———. *Golgotha*. Vol. 1. Leipzig: Pfeiffer, 1926.

———. *Jerusalem in the Time of Jesus: An Investigation into the Economic and Social Conditions during the New Testament Period*. Trans. F. H. and C. H. Cave. Philadelphia: Fortress, 1969.

———. "Lampades in Matthew 25:1-13." Pages 83-88 in *Sola Deo Gloria*. Ed. J. McDowell Richards. Richmond: John Knox, 1968.

————. *New Testament Theology* 1: *The Proclamation of Jesus.* Trans. John Bowden. London: SCM, 1971.

————. "Palästinakundliches zum Gleichnis vom Sämann (Mark IV.3-8 par)." *NTS* 13 (1966-67): 48-53.

————. *The Parables of Jesus.* Trans. S. H. Hooke. 2d ed. New York: Charles Scribner's Sons, 1963.

————. "Tradition und Redaktion in Lukas 15." *ZNW* 62 (1971): 172-89.

Jeske, Richard. "Wisdom and the Future in the Teaching of Jesus." *Dialogue* 11 (1972): 108-17.

Johnson, Alan. "Assurance for Man: The Fallacy of Translating *Anaideia* by 'Persistence' in Luke 11:5-8." *JETS* 22 (1979): 123-31.

Johnson, Luke T. *The Literary Function of Possessions in Luke-Acts.* SBLDS 39. Missoula: Scholars, 1977.

————. "The Lukan Kingship Parable (Lk. 19:11-27)." *NovT* 24 (1982): 139-59.

Johnston, Robert M. "Greek Patristic Parables." Pages 215-29 in *Society of Biblical Literature Seminar Papers, 1977.* Ed. Paul J. Achtemeier. Missoula: Scholars, 1977.

————. "Parabolic Interpretations Attributed to Tannaim." Ph.D. diss. The Hartford Seminary Foundation, 1977.

Jones, Geraint Vaughn. *The Art and Truth of the Parables.* London: SPCK, 1964.

Jones, Ivor Harold. *The Matthean Parables: A Literary and Historical Commentary.* NovTSup 80. Leiden: Brill, 1995.

Jones, Peter Rhea. *Studying the Parables of Jesus.* Macon: Smyth & Helwys, 1999.

Juel, Donald H. "Encountering the Sower: Mark 4:1-20." *Int* 56 (2002): 273-83.

Jülicher, Adolf. *Die Gleichnisreden Jesu.* 2 vols. Freiburg i. B.: J. C. B. Mohr, 1888, 1889. Reprint in one vol. Darmstadt: Wissenschaftliche Buchgesellschaft, 1963.

————. "Parables." Pages 3563-67 in *Encyclopedia Biblica.* New York: Macmillan, 1902.

Jüngel, Eberhard. *Paulus und Jesus.* Tübingen: Mohr-Siebeck, 1962.

Kahlefeld, Heinrich. *Gleichnisse und Lehrstücke im Evangelium.* Frankfurt: Josef Knecht, 1964. ET: *Parables and Instructions in the Gospels.* Trans. Arlene Swidler. New York: Herder and Herder, 1966.

Kähler, Martin. *The So-Called Historical Jesus and the Historic Biblical Christ.* Trans. Carl E. Braaten. Philadelphia: Fortress, 1964.

Kamlah, Ehrhard. "Die Parabel vom ungerechten Verwalter (Luk. 16, 1ff.) im Rahmen der Knechtsgleichnisse." Pages 276-94 in *Abraham Unser Vater.* Ed. Otto Betz, et al. Leiden: Brill, 1963.

Karris, Robert J. "Poor and Rich: The Lukan *Sitz im Leben.*" Pages 112-25 in *Perspectives on Luke-Acts.* Ed. Charles H. Talbert. Danville: Association of Baptist Professors of Religion, 1978.

Käsemann, Ernst. "'The Righteousness of God' in Paul." Pages 168-82 in *New Testament Questions of Today.* Trans. W. J. Montague. NTL. London: SCM, 1969.

Katz, Steven T. "Issues in the Separation of Judaism and Christianity after 70 C.E.: A Reconsideration." *JBL* 103 (1984): 43-76.

Keener, Craig S. *A Commentary on the Gospel of Matthew.* Grand Rapids: Eerdmans, 1999.

Kennedy, Gerald. *The Parables.* New York: Harper and Brothers, 1960.

Kerr, A. J. "Matthew 13:25, Sowing Zizania among Another's Wheat: Realistic or Artificial?" *JTS* 48 (1997): 108-9.

Khoo, Jeffrey. "The Reality and Eternality of Hell: Luke 16:19-31 as Proof." *Stulos Theological Journal* 6 (1998): 67-78.

Kierkegaard, Søren. *Christian Discourses.* Trans. Walter Lowrie. New York: Oxford University Press, 1961.

———. *Purity of Heart Is to Will One Thing.* Trans. Douglas V. Steere. New York: Harper & Row, 1938.

———. *Søren Kierkegaard's Journals and Papers.* 6 vols. Ed. and trans. Howard V. Hong and Edna H. Hong. Bloomington: Indiana University Press, 1967.

———. *Works of Love.* Edited and trans. Howard V. and Edna H. Hong. Princeton: Princeton University Press, 1946.

Kilgallen, John J. "Forgiveness of Sins, Luke 7:36-50." *NovT* 40 (1998): 105-16.

———. "Luke 15 and 16: A Connection." *Bib* 78 (1997): 369-76.

———. "The Plan of the 'NOMIKOS' (Luke 10.25-37)." *NTS* 42 (1996): 615-19.

———. "A Proposal for Interpreting Luke 7:36-50." *Bib* 72 (1991): 305-30.

Kimelman, Reuven. "*Birkat Ha-Minim* and the Lack of Evidence for an Anti-Christian Prayer in Late Antiquity." Pages 226-44 in *Jewish and Christian Self-Definition* 2: *Aspects of Judaism in the Greco-Roman Period.* Ed. E. P. Sanders with A. I. Baumgarten and Alan Mendelson. Philadelphia: Fortress, 1981.

Kingsbury, Jack Dean. "The Parable of the Wicked Husbandmen and the Secret of Jesus; Divine Sonship in Matthew: Some Literary-Critical Observations." *JBL* 105 (1986): 643-55.

———. *The Parables of Jesus in Matthew 13: A Study in Redaction-Criticism.* Richmond: John Knox, 1969.

———. "The Title 'Kyrios' in Matthew's Gospel." *JBL* 94 (1975): 246-55.

Kinman, Brent. "Lukan Eschatology and the Missing Fig Tree." *JBL* 113 (1994): 669-78.

Kissinger, Warren S. *The Parables of Jesus.* Metuchen: Scarecrow, 1979.

Kistemaker, Simon J. *The Parables of Jesus.* Grand Rapids: Baker, 1980.

Kjargaard, Mogens Stiller. *Metaphor and Parable: A Systematic Analysis of the Specific Structure and Cognitive Function of the Synoptic Similes and Parables qua Metaphors.* Acta Theologica Danica 20. Leiden: Brill, 1986.

Klauck, Hans-Josef. *Allegorie und Allegorese in synoptischen Gleichnistexten.* NTAbh 13. Münster: Aschendorff, 1978.

Klemm, Hans Gunther. *Das Gleichnis vom barmherziger Samariter. Grundzüge der Auslegung im 16./17. Jahrhundert.* Stuttgart: Kohlhammer, 1973.

Kloppenborg, John. "The Dishonoured Master (Luke 16,1-8a)." *Bib* 70 (1989): 134-59.

———. "Egyptian Viticultural Practices and the Citation of Isa 5:1-7 in Mark 12:1-9." *NovT* 44 (2002): 134-59.

———. "Isa 5:1-7 and Mark 12:1-9 Again." *NovT* 46 (2004): 12-19.

———. "Isa 5:1-7, The Parable of the Tenants and Vineyard Leases on Papyrus." Pages 111-34 in *Text and Artifact in the Religions of Mediterranean Antiquity.* Waterloo: Wilfrid Laurier University Press, 2000.

———. "Self Help or *Deus ex Machina* in Mark 12:9?" *NTS* 50 (2004): 495-518.

———. *The Tenants in the Vineyard: Ideology, Economics, and Agrarian Conflict in Jewish Palestine.* WUNT 195. Tübingen: Mohr-Siebeck, 2006.

Knowles, Michael P. "Abraham and the Birds in *Jubilees* 11: A Subtext for the Parable of the Sower." *NTS* 41 (1995): 145-51.

Koehler, Ludwig, and Walter Baumartner. *The Hebrew and Aramaic Lexicon of the Old Testament.* Leiden: E. J. Brill, 1995.

Kogler, Franz. *Das Doppelgleichnis vom Senfkorn und vom Sauerteig in seiner traditionsgeschichtlichen Entwicklung. Zur Reich-Gottes-Vorstellung Jesu und ihren Aktualisierungen in der Kirche.* FB. Würzburg: Echter, 1988.

Kollmann, Bernd. "Jesus als jüdischer Gleichnisdicter." *NTS* 50 (2004): 457-75.

Kosmala, Hans. "The Parable of the Unjust Steward in the Light of Qumran." *ASTI* 3 (1964): 114-21.

Kossen, H. B. "Quelques Remarques sur l'ordre des Paraboles dans Luc XV et sur la Structure de Matthieu XVIII 8-14." *NovT* 1 (1956): 75-80.

Krämer, Michael. *Das Rätsel der Parabel vom ungerechten Verwalter, Lk 16,1-13. Auslegungsgeschichte — Umfang — Sinn. Eine Diskussion der Probleme und Lösungsvorschläge der Verwaltereparabel von den Vätern bis heute.* Biblioteca di scienze religiose 5. Zurich: PAS, 1972.

Kreitzer, Larry. "Luke 16:19-31 and 1 Enoch 22." *ExpTim* 103 (1992): 139-42.

Kuhn, Heinz-Wolfgang. *Ältere Sammlungen im Markusevangelium.* SUNT 8. Göttingen: Vandenhoeck und Ruprecht, 1971.

Kümmel, W. G. "Das Gleichnis von den bösen Weingärtnern (Mark 12,1-9)." Pages 120-31 in *Aux sources de la tradition chrétienne. Mélanges offerts à Maurice Goguel.* Neuchâtel: Delachaux & Niestle, 1950.

———. *Promise and Fulfillment: The Eschatological Message of Jesus.* Trans. Dorthea M. Barton. SBT 23. Naperville: Allenson, 1957.

Kuss, Otto. "Zum Sinngehalt des Doppelgleichnisses vom Senfkorn und Sauerteig." *Bib* 40 (1959): 641-53.

Kvalbein, Hans. "Jesus and the Poor: Two Texts and a Tentative Conclusion." *Themelios* 12 (1987): 80-87.

Ladd, George Eldon. *The Presence of the Future: The Eschatology of Biblical Realism.* Grand Rapids: Eerdmans, 1974.

———. *A Theology of the New Testament.* Rev. ed. Don Hagner. Grand Rapids: Eerdmans, 1993.

LaHurd, Carol Schersten. "Rediscovering the Lost Women in Luke 15." *BTB* 24 (1994): 66-76.

Lambrecht, Jan. *Once More Astonished.* New York: Crossroad, 1981.

———. *Out of the Treasure: The Parables in the Gospel of Matthew.* LTPM 10. Louvain: Peeters; Grand Rapids: Eerdmans, 1992.

Lampe, Peter. "Die markenische Deutung des Gleichnisses vom Sämann, Markus 4:10-12." *ZNW* 65 (1974): 140-50.

Lamsa, G. *Gospel Light: Comments on the Teachings of Jesus from Aramaic and Unchanged Eastern Customs.* Philadelphia: A. J. Holman, 1936.

Landry, David, and Ben May. "Honor Restored: New Light on the Parable of the Prudent Steward (Luke 16:1-8a)." *JBL* 119 (2000): 287-309.

Lane, Thomas J. *Luke and the Gentile Mission.* Frankfurt: Peter Lang, 1994.

Laufen, Rudolph. "BASILEIA und EKKLHSIA. Eine traditions- und redaktiongeschichtliche Untersuchung des Gleichnisses vom Senfkorn." Pages 105-40 in *Begegnung mit dem Wort. Festschrift für Heinrich Zimmermann.* Ed. Josef Zmijewski and Ernst Nellessen. BBB 53. Bonn: Peter Hanstein, 1979.

Lausberg, Heinrich. *Handbook of Literary Rhetoric: A Foundation for Literary Study.* Ed. David Orton and R. Dean Anderson. Trans. Matthew T. Bliss, Annemiek Jansen, and David Orton. Leiden: Brill, 1998.

Lebacqz, Karen. "Justice, Economics, and the Uncomfortable Kingdom." *ASCE* (1983): 27-53.

Leenhardt, F. J. "La Parabole du Samaritain." Pages 132-38 in *Aux sources de la tradition chrétienne.* Neuchâtel: Delachaux & Niestlé, 1950.

Legasse, Simon. "La Parabole des Dix Vierges (Mt 25,1-13). Essai de synthèse historico-litteraire." Pages 349-60 in *Les Paraboles Evangeliques. Perspectives Nouvelles.* Ed. Jean Delorme. Lectio divina 135. Paris: Cerf, 1989.

Lehnert, Volker A. *Die Provokation Israels. Die paradoxe Funktion von Jes 6,9-10 bei Markus und Lukas.* Neukirchener Theologische Dissertationen und Habilitationen 25. Neukirchen-Vluyn: Neukirchener. 1999.

Lehtipuu, Outi. "Characterization and Persuasion: The Rich Man and the Poor Man in Luke 16.19-31." Pages 73-105 in *Characterization in the Gospels: Reconceiving Narrative Criticism.* Ed. David Rhoads and Kari Syreeni. Sheffield: Sheffield Academic, 1999.

Lemcio, Eugene. "External Evidence for the Structure and Function of Mark 1:1-20, 6:14-23 and 8:14-21." *JTS* 29 (1978): 324-38.

―――. "The Parables of the Great Supper and the Wedding Feast: History, Redaction, and Canon." *HBT* 8 (1986): 1-26.

Léon-Dufour, Xavier. "La Parabole des vignerons homicides." *ScEccl* 17 (1965): 365-96.

Lewis, Theodore J. "Dead, Abode of the." *ABD* 2:101-5.

Liebenburg, Jacobus. *The Language of the Kingdom and Jesus: Parable, Aphorism, and Metaphor in the Sayings Material Common to the Synoptic Tradition and the Gospel of Thomas.* BZNW 102. Berlin: Walter de Gruyter, 2001.

Liefeld, Walter L. "Parables on Prayer (Luke 11:5-13; 18:1-14)." Pages 240-62 in *The Challenge of Jesus' Parables.* Ed. Richard N. Longenecker. Grand Rapids: Eerdmans, 2000.

Lightfoot, John. *Hebraicae et Talmudicae.* 4 vols. Reprint. Oxford: Oxford University Press, 1859.

Lindenberger, J. M. "Ahiqar." *OTP* 2:479-93.

Linnemann, Eta. *Historical Criticism of the Bible: Methodology or Ideology?* Trans. Robert W. Yarbrough. Grand Rapids: Baker, 1990.

―――. *Parables of Jesus: Introduction and Exposition.* Trans. John Sturdy. London: SPCK, 1966.

Little, J. C. "Parable Research in the Twentieth Century." *ExpTim* 87 (1976): 356-60; 88 (1977): 40-44, 71-75.

Ljungvik, H. "Zur Erklärung einer Lukas-Stelle." *NTS* 10 (1963): 289-94.

Llewelyn, S. R. "Self-Help and Legal Redress: The Parable of the Wicked Tenants." *NewDocs* 6:86-105.

―――. "Tax Collection and the τελῶναι of the New Testament." *NewDocs* 8:47-86.

Loader, William. "Jesus and the Rogue in Luke 16,1-8a, the Parable of the Unjust Steward." *RB* (1989): 518-32.

Lohfink, Gerhard. "Die Metaphorik des Aussaat im Gleichnis vom Sämann (Mk 4,3-9)." Pages 211-28 in *À Cause de L'Évangile. Études sur les Synoptics et les Actes.* Lectio Divina 123. Paris: Cerf, 1985.

Lohmeyer, Ernst. *Das Evangelium des Matthäus*. KEK. Ed. Werner Schmauch. 2d ed. Göttingen: Vandenhoeck & Ruprecht, 1958.

Longenecker, Richard N., ed. *The Challenge of Jesus' Parables*. Grand Rapids: Eerdmans, 2000.

Lorenzen, Thorwald. "A Biblical Meditation on Luke 16:19-31." *ExpTim* 87 (1976): 39-43.

Louw, J. "The Parables of the Tower-Builder and the King Going to War." *ExpTim* 48 (1936-37): 478.

Lövestam, Evald. *Spiritual Wakefulness in the New Testament*. Trans. W. F. Salisbury. LUÅ 55. Lund: Gleerup, 1963.

Lowe, Malcom. "From the Parable of the Vineyard to a Pre-Synoptic Source." *NTS* 28 (1982): 257-63.

Lundin, Roger, Clarence Walhout, and Anthony C. Thiselton. *The Promise of Hermeneutics*. Grand Rapids: Eerdmans, 1999.

Luomanen, Petri. "Corpus Mixtum — An Appropriate Description of Matthew's Community?" *JBL* 117 (1998): 469-80.

———. *Entering the Kingdom of Heaven: A Study on the Structure of Matthew's View of Salvation*. WUNT 2/101. Tübingen: Mohr-Siebeck, 1998.

Luz, Ulrich. "The Final Judgment (Matt 25:31-46): An Exercise in 'History of Influence' Exegesis." Pages 271-310 in *Treasures New and Old: Recent Contributions to Matthean Studies*. Ed. David R. Bauer and Mark Allan Powell. Atlanta: Scholars, 1996.

———. *Matthew 1–7: A Commentary*. Trans. Wilhelm C. Linss. Minneapolis: Augsburg, 1985.

———. *Matthew 8–20: A Commentary*. Trans. James E. Crouch. Minneapolis: Fortress, 2001.

———. *Matthew 21–28: A Commentary*. Trans. James E. Crouch. Minneapolis: Fortress, 2005.

———. *The Theology of the Gospel of Matthew*. Cambridge: Cambridge University Press, 1995.

———. "Vom Taumellolch im Weizenfeld." Pages 154-71 in *Vom Urchristentum zu Jesus*. Ed. Hubert Frankemölle and Karl Kertelge. Freiburg im Breslau: Herder, 1989.

Maccoby, Hyam. "How Unclean Were Tax-Collectors?" *BTB* 31 (2002): 60-63.

Mack, Burton L. "Teaching in Parables: Elaboration in Mark 4:1-34." Pages 143-60 in *Patterns of Persuasion in the Gospels*. Sonoma: Polebridge, 1989.

Mackay, John A. *God's Order: The Ephesian Letter and This Present Time*. New York: Macmillan, 1953.

Macky, Peter W. *The Centrality of Metaphors to Biblical Thought*. Lewiston: Mellen, 1990.

Maddox, Robert. "Who Are the 'Sheep' and the 'Goats'? A Study of the Purpose and Meaning of Matthew xxv:31-46." *ABR* 13 (1965): 19-28.

Magass, Walter. "Zur Semiotik der Hausfrömmigkcit (Lk 12,16-21). Die Beispielerzahlung 'Vom reichen Kornbauer.'" *LB* 4 (1971): 2-5.

Maier, Gerhard. "Verteilt Jesus die Güter dieser Erde?" *TBei* 5 (1974): 149-58.

Maisch, Ingrid. "Das Gleichnis von den klugen und torichten Jungfrauen." *BibLeb* 11 (1970): 247-59.

Major, H. D. A., T. W. Manson, and C. J. Wright. *The Mission and Message of Jesus*. New York: Dutton, 1938.

Malherbe, Abraham. "The Christianization of a *Topos,* Luke 12:13-34." *NovT* 38 (1996): 123-35.

Mann, Jacob. "Jesus and the Sadducean Priests: Luke 10:25-37." *JQR* 6 (1915-16): 415-22.

Manson, T. W. *The Sayings of Jesus as Recorded in the Gospels According to St. Matthew and St. Luke Arranged with Introduction and Commentary.* London: SCM, 1949.

————. *The Teaching of Jesus: Studies of Its Form and Contents.* Cambridge: Cambridge University Press, 1939.

Manson, W. "The Purpose of the Parables: A Re-Examination of St. Mark in iv.10-12." *ExpTim* 68 (1956-57): 132-35.

Marcus, Joel. "Blanks and Gaps in the Markan Parable of the Sower." *BibInt* 5 (1997): 247-62.

————. "The Intertextual Polemic of the Markan Vineyard Parable." Pages 211-27 in *Tolerance and Intolerance in Early Judaism and Christianity.* Ed. Graham N. Stanton and Guy G. Strousma. Cambridge: Cambridge University Press, 1998.

————. *Mark 1–8: A New Translation with Introduction and Commentary.* AB 27. New York: Doubleday, 2000.

————. *The Mystery of the Kingdom of God.* SBLDS 90. Atlanta: Scholars, 1986.

————. *The Way of the Lord: Christological Exegesis of the Old Testament in the Gospel of Mark.* Louisville: Westminster John Knox, 1992.

Mare, W. Harold. "The Smallest Mustard Seed — Matthew 13:32." *Grace Theological Journal* 9 (1968): 3-11.

Marguerat, Daniel. *Le jugement dans L'Évangile de Matthieu.* 2d ed. Le Monde de la Bible 6. Geneva: Labor ct Fides, 1995.

Marshall, I. Howard. *Beyond the Bible: Moving from Scripture to Theology.* Grand Rapids: Baker, 2004.

————. *Eschatology and the Parables.* London: Tyndale, 1963.

————. *The Gospel of Luke: A Commentary on the Greek Text.* NIGTC. Grand Rapids: Eerdmans, 1978.

Martens, Allan W. " 'Produce Fruit Worthy of Repentance': Parables of Judgment against the Jewish Religious Leaders and the Nation (Matthew 21:28–22:14 par.; Luke 13:6-9." Pages 157-76 in *The Challenge of Jesus' Parables.* Ed. Richard N. Longenecker. Grand Rapids: Eerdmans, 2000.

Mathews, Edward, Jr. "The Rich Man and Lazarus: Almsgiving and Repentance in Early Syriac Tradition." *Diakonia* 22 (1988-89): 89-104.

Mathewson, Dave L. "The Parable of the Unjust Steward (Luke 16:1-13): A Reexamination of the Traditional View in Light of Recent Challenges." *JETS* 38 (1995): 29-39.

Matthews, Mary W., Carter Shelly, and Barbara Scheele. "Proclaiming the Parable of the Persistent Widow (Lk. 18.2-5)." Pages 46-70 in *The Lost Coin: Parables of Women, Work and Wisdom.* Ed. Mary Ann Beavis. London: Sheffield Academic, 2002.

Mattill, A. J., Jr. "The Good Samaritan and the Purpose of Luke-Acts: Halévy Reconsidered." *Encounter* 33 (1972): 359-76.

————. *Luke and the Last Things: A Perspective for the Understanding of Lukan Thought.* Dillsboro: Western North Carolina, 1979.

Mazamisa, Llewellyn Welile. *Beatific Comradeship: An Exegetical Hermeneutical Study of Luke 10:25-37.* Kampen: Kok, 1987.

McArthur, Harvey K. "The Parable of the Mustard Seed." *CBQ* 33 (1971): 198-210.

McArthur, Harvey K., and Robert M. Johnston. *They Also Taught in Parables.* Grand Rapids: Zondervan, 1990.

McCall, Marsh H., Jr. *Ancient Rhetorical Theories of Simile and Comparison.* Cambridge: Harvard University Press, 1969.

McCane, Byron R. "Is a Corpse Contagious? Early Jewish and Christian Attitudes toward the Dead." Pages 378-88 in *Society of Biblical Literature Seminar Papers, 1992.* Ed. Eugene H. Lovering Jr. Atlanta: Scholars, 1992.

McDonald, J. Ian H. "Alien Grace (Luke 10:30-36): The Parable of the Good Samaritan." Pages 35-51 in *Jesus and His Parables.* Ed. V. George Shillington. Edinburgh: T. & T. Clark, 1997.

McFayden, J. F. "The Parable of the Unjust Steward." *ExpTim* 37 (1925-26): 235-39.

McGaughy, Lane C. "The Fear of Yahweh and the Mission of Judaism: A Postexilic Maxim and Its Early Christian Expansion in the Parable of the Talents." *JBL* 94 (1975): 235-45.

———. "Pagan Hellenistic Literature: The Babrian Fables." Pages 205-14 in *Society of Biblical Literature Seminar Papers, 1977.* Ed. Paul J. Achtemeier. Missoula: Scholars, 1977.

McIver, Robert K. "One Hundred-Fold Yield — Miraculous or Mundane? Matthew 13.8, 23; Mark 4:8, 20; Luke 8:8." *NTS* 40 (1994): 606-8.

———. "The Parable of the Weeds among the Wheat (Matt 13:24-30, 36-43) and the Relationship between the Kingdom and the Church as Portrayed in the Gospel of Matthew." *JBL* 114 (1995): 643-59.

McKnight, Scot. "Jesus and Prophetic Actions." *BBR* 10 (2000): 197-232.

———. *The Jesus Creed: Loving God, Loving Others.* Brewster: Paraclete, 2004.

———. *A New Vision for Israel.* Grand Rapids: Eerdmans, 1999.

Meier, John P. *A Marginal Jew: Rethinking the Historical Jesus.* 3 vols. Anchor Bible Reference Library. New York: Doubleday, 1991-2001.

Meinertz, Max. "Die Tragweite des Gleichnisses von den zehn Jungfrauen." Pages 94-106 in *Synoptische Studien.* Ed. Alfred Wikenhauser. Munich: Kösel, 1954.

Mell, Ulrich. *Die "anderen" Winzer. Eine exegetische Studie zur Vollmacht Jesu Christi nach Markus 11,27–12,34.* WUNT 77. Tübingen: Mohr-Siebeck, 1994.

———. "Der barmherzige Samaritaner und Gottes Gerechtigkeit. Eine Auslegung von Lk 10:30-35 in Anknüpfung an Adolf Jülicher." Pages 113-48 in *Die Gleichnisreden Jesu 1899-1999. Beiträge zum Dialog mit Adolf Jülicher.* Ed. Ulrich Mell. BZNW 103. Berlin: Walter de Gruyter, 1999.

———. *Die Gleichnisreden Jesus 1899-1999: Beiträge zum Dialog mit Adolf Jülicher.* Berlin: Walter de Gruyter, 1999.

———. *Die Zeit der Gottesherrschaft. Zur Allegorie und zum Gleichnis von Markus 4:1-9.* Beiträge zur Wissenschaft vom Alten und Neuen Testament 8/4. Stuttgart: Kohlhammer, 1998.

Menzies, Robert. "The Lost Coin." *ExpTim* 64 (1953): 274-76.

Merkel, Helmut. "Das Gleichnis von den 'ungleichen Söhnen' (Matth. XXI.28-32)." *NTS* 20 (1974): 254-61.

Metzger, Bruce M. *A Textual Commentary on the Greek New Testament.* 2d ed. New York: United Bible Societies, 1994.

Meye, R. P. "Mark 4,10: 'Those about Him with the Twelve.'" Pages 211-18 in *Studia Evangelica II.* Ed. F. L. Cross. Berlin: Akademie, 1964.

Meyer, Ben F. *The Aims of Jesus*. London: SCM, 1979.

———. *Critical Realism in the New Testament*. Allison Park: Pickwick, 1989.

———. "Many (= All) Are Called, But Few (= Not All) Are Chosen." *NTS* 36 (1990): 89-97.

Michaels, J. Ramsey. "Apostolic Hardships and Righteous Gentiles." *JBL* 84 (1965): 27-37.

———. "The Parable of the Regretful Son." *HTR* 61 (1968): 15-26.

Milavec, Aaron A. "Mark's Parable of the Wicked Husbandmen as Reaffirming God's Predilection for Israel." *JES* 26 (1989): 289-312.

Mitton, C. Leslie. "Expounding the Parables: The Workers in the Vineyard (Matthew 20:1-16)." *ExpTim* 77 (1966): 307-11.

———. "Present Justification and Final Judgment: A Discussion of the Parable of the Sheep and the Goats." *ExpTim* 68 (1957): 46-50.

Monselewski, Werner. *Der barmherzige Samariter. Eine auslegungsgeschichtliche Untersuchung zu Lukas 10,25-37*. Tübingen: Mohr-Siebeck, 1967.

Montefiore, Claude G. *The Synoptic Gospels*. 2d ed. 2 vols. London: Macmillan, 1927.

Moore, George Foot. *Judaism in the First Centuries of the Christian Era: The Age of the Tannaim*. 3 vols. Cambridge: Harvard University Press, 1950.

Moore, Marianne. "Poetry." Pages 176-77 in *Twentieth Century American Poetry*. Ed. Conrad Aiken. New York: Random, 1944.

Morrice, William G. "The Parable of the Dragnet and the Gospel of Thomas." *ExpTim* 95 (1984): 269-73.

Mottu, Henry. "The Pharisee and the Tax Collector: Sartrian Notions as Applied to the Reading of Scripture." *USQR* 29 (1974): 195-213.

Moule, C. F. D. "Mark 4:1-20 Yet Once More." Pages 95-113 in *Neotestamentica et Semitica: Studies in Honor of Matthew Black*. Ed. E. E. Ellis and Max Wilcox. Edinburgh: T. & T. Clark, 1969.

———. *The Phenomenon of the New Testament*. London: SCM, 1967.

Mournet, Terence C. *Oral Tradition and Literary Dependency*. WUNT 2/195. Tübingen: Mohr-Siebeck, 2005.

Mussner, Franz. "1Q Hodajoth und das Gleichnis vom Senfkorn (Mk 4:30-32 Par.)." *BZ* 4 (1960): 128-30.

Neusner, Jacob. *Fellowship in Judaism: The First Century and Today*. London: Vallentine Mitchell, 1963.

———. *Rabbinic Literature and the New Testament: What We Cannot Show, We Do Not Know*. Valley Forge: Trinity, 1994.

———. *Rabbinic Narrative: A Documentary Perspective*. 4 vols. The Brill Reference Library of Judaism. Leiden: Brill, 2003.

———. "Sanders's Pharisees and Mine: *Jewish Law from Jesus to the Mishnah*." Pages 247-73 in *Judaic Law from Jesus to the Mishnah: A Systematic Reply to Professor E. P. Sanders*. Atlanta: Scholars, 1993.

Newell, Jane E., and Raymond R. "The Parable of the Wicked Tenants." *NovT* 14 (1972): 226-37.

Neyrey, Jerome. "Ceremonies in Luke-Acts: The Case of Meals and Table-Fellowship." Pages 361-87 in *The Social World of Luke-Acts: Models for Interpretation*. Ed. Jerome H. Neyrey. Peabody: Hendrickson, 1991.

Nickelsburg, George W. E. "Riches, the Rich, and God's Judgment in 1 Enoch 92–105 and the Gospel According to Luke." *NTS* 25 (1978): 324-44.

Nolland, John. *The Gospel of Matthew: A Commentary on the Greek Text*. NIGTC. Grand Rapids: Eerdmans, 2005.

———. *Luke 1–9:20*. WBC 35A. Dallas: Word, 1989.

———. *Luke 9:21–18:34*. WBC 35B. Dallas: Word, 1993.

Norwood, Frederick A. "'Compel Them to Come In': A History of Luke 14:23." *Religion in Life* 23 (1954): 516-27.

Nouwen, Henri J. M. *The Return of the Prodigal Son*. New York: Doubleday, 1992.

Nygren, Anders. *Agape and Eros*. Trans. Philip S. Watson. London: SPCK, 1954.

Oakman, Douglas E. "Jesus and Agrarian Palestine: The Factor of Debt." Page 71 in *Society of Biblical Literature Seminar Papers, 1985*. Ed. Kent Harold Richards. Atlanta: Scholars, 1985.

———. *Jesus and the Economic Questions of His Day*. Lewiston: Mellen, 1986.

———. "Was Jesus a Peasant? Implications for Reading the Samaritan Story, Luke 10:30-35." *BTB* 22 (1992): 117-25.

O'Callaghan, José. "New Testament Papyri in Qumrān Cave 7?" *Supplement to JBL* 91 (1972): 1-14.

Oden, Thomas C., ed. *Parables of Kierkegaard*. Princeton: Princeton University Press, 1978.

Oesterley, W. O. E. *The Gospel Parables in the Light of Their Jewish Background*. New York: Macmillan, 1936.

Ogawa, Akira, "Paraboles de l'Israel Véritable? Reconsidération Critique de Mt. XXI 28–XXII 14." *NovT* 21 (1979): 121-49.

Oldenhage, Tania. *Parables for Our Time: Rereading New Testament Scholarship after the Holocaust*. Oxford: Oxford University Press, 2002.

Olmstead, Wesley G. *Matthew's Trilogy of Parables: The Nation, the Nations and the Reader in Matthew 21:28–22:14*. SNTSMS 127. Cambridge: Cambridge University Press, 2003.

Olson, Daniel C. "Matthew 22:1-14 as Midrash." *CBQ* 67 (2005): 435-53.

O'Neill, J. C. "The Source of the Parables of the Bridegroom and the Wicked Husbandmen." *JTS* 39 (1988): 485-89.

O'Rourke, John J. "Some Notes on Luke XV.11-32." *NTS* 17 (1971-72): 431-33.

Osei-Bonsu, J. "The Intermediate State in Luke-Acts." *IBS* 9 (1987): 115-31.

Ott, Wilhelm. *Gebet und Heil. Die Bedeutung der Gebetsparänese in der lukanischen Theologie*. Munich: Kösel, 1965.

Oudersluys, Richard C. "The Parable of the Sheep and Goats (Matthew 25:31-46): Eschatology and Mission, Then and Now." *Reformed Review* 26 (1973): 151-61.

Painter, John. *Mark's Gospel: Worlds in Conflict*. New Testament Readings. London: Routledge, 1997.

Palmer, Humphry. "Just Married, Cannot Come." *NovT* 18 (1976): 241-57.

Parker, Andrew. *Painfully Clear: The Parables of Jesus*. Sheffield: Sheffield Academic, 1996.

Parrott, Douglas. "The Dishonest Steward (Luke 16.1-8a) and Luke's Special Parable Collection." *NTS* 37 (1991): 499-515.

Parsons, Mikeal C. "Landmarks along the Way: The Function of the 'L' Parables in the Lukan Travel Narrative." *SwJT* 40 (1997): 33-47.

———. "The Prodigal's Elder Brother: The History and Ethics of Reading Luke 15:25-32." *PRSt* 23 (1996): 147-74.

Patte, Daniel. "Bringing Out of the Gospel-Treasure What Is New and What Is Old: Two Parables in Matthew 18–23." *Quarterly Review* 10 (1990): 79-108.

————. *The Gospel According to Matthew: A Structural Commentary on Matthew's Faith.* Philadelphia: Fortress, 1987.

————. "Parable, Allegory and Paradox." Pages 247-81 in *Semiology and Parables.* Pittsburgh: Pickwick, 1976.

Patten, Priscilla. "The Form and Function of Parables in Select Apocalyptic Literature and Their Significance for Parables in Mark." *NTS* 29 (1983): 246-58.

Patterson, Stephen J. *The Gospel of Thomas and Jesus.* Sonoma: Polebridge, 1993.

Pavur, Claude. "The Grain Is Ripe." *BTB* 17 (1987): 21-23.

Payne, Philip Barton. "The Authenticity of the Parable of the Sower and Its Interpretation." Pages 163-207 in *Gospel Perspectives* 1: *Studies of History and Tradition in the Four Gospels.* Ed. R. T. France and David Wenham. Sheffield: JSOT, 1980.

————. "Jesus' Implicit Claim to Deity in His Parables." *TJ* 2 (1981): 3-23.

————. "The Order of Sowing and Ploughing in the Parable of the Sower." *NTS* 25 (1979): 123-29.

————. "The Seeming Inconsistency of the Interpretation of the Parable of the Sower." *NTS* 26 (1980): 564-68.

Pearce, Keith. "The Lucan Origins of the Raising of Lazarus." *ExpTim* 96 (1985): 359-61.

Peisker, Carl Heinz. "Konsekutives ἵνα in Markus 4:12." *ZNW* 59 (1968): 126-27.

Pentecost, J. Dwight. *The Parables of Jesus.* Grand Rapids: Zondervan, 1982.

Perkins, Pheme. *Hearing the Parables of Jesus.* New York: Paulist, 1981.

Perpich, Sandra Wackham. *A Hermeneutic Critique of Structuralist Exegesis, with Specific Reference to Luke 10:29-37.* Lanham: University Press of America, 1984.

Perrin, Nicholas. *Thomas and Tatian: The Relationship between the Gospel of Thomas and the Diatessaron.* Academia Biblica 5. Atlanta: Society of Biblical Literature, 2002.

Perrin, Norman. *Jesus and the Language of the Kingdom.* Philadelphia: Fortress, 1976.

————. *Rediscovering the Teaching of Jesus.* London: SCM, 1967.

Pesch, Rudolf. *Markusevangelium.* 2d ed. HTKNT. Freiburg: Herder, 1977.

Pesch, Rudolf, and Reinhard Kratz. *So liest man synoptisch. Anleitung und Kommentar zum Studium der synoptischen Evangelien.* 4: *Gleichnisse und Bildreden aus der dreifachen Überlieferung.* 5: *Gleichnisse und Bildreden aus der zweifachen Überlieferung.* Frankfurt am Main: Knecht, 1978.

Peterson, William. "The Parable of the Lost Sheep in the Gospel of Thomas and the Synoptics." *NovT* 23 (1981): 128-47.

Petzhold, Martin. *Gleichnisse Jesu und christliche Dogmatik.* Göttingen: Vandenhoeck & Ruprecht, 1984.

Pilch, John J. "Separating the Sheep from the Goats." *Professional Approaches for Christian Educators* 20 (1992): 215-18.

Piper, Ronald A. "Social Background and Thematic Structure in Luke 16." Pages 1637-62 in *The Four Gospels: Festschrift Frans Neirynck.* Ed. F. Van Segbroeck, et al. 3 vols. Leuven: Leuven University Press, 1992.

Plummer, Alfred. *A Critical and Exegetical Commentary on the Gospel According to Luke.* 4th ed. ICC. Edinburgh: T. & T. Clark, 1901.

Pöhlmann, Wolfgang. "Die Abschichtung des Verlorenen Sohnes (Lk 15:12f.) und die erzählte Welt der Parabel." *ZTK* 70 (1979): 194-213.

————. *Der verlorene Sohn und das Haus. Studien zu Lukas 15,11-32 im Horizont der antiken Lehre von Haus, Erziehung und Ackerbau.* WUNT 68. Tübingen: Mohr-Siebeck, 1993.

Pokorný, Petr. "Lukas 15, 11-32 und die lukanische Soteriologie." Pages 179-92 in *Christus Bezeugen. Festschrift für Wolfgang Trilling zum 65 Geburtstag.* Ed. Karl Kertelge, et al. Erfurter theologische Studien 59. Leipzig: St. Benno, 1989.

Polk, Timothy. "Paradigms, Parables, and *Měšālîm:* On Reading the *Māšāl* in Scripture." *CBQ* 45 (1983): 564-83.

Porter, Stanley. "The Parable of the Unjust Steward (Luke 16:1-13): Irony *Is* the Key." Pages 127-53 in *The Bible in Three Dimensions.* Ed. David J. A. Clines, et al. Sheffield: JSOT, 1990.

Potterie, Ignace de la. "La parabole du prétendant à la royauté (Lc 19,11-28)." Pages 613-41 in *À Cause de L'Évangile. Études sur les Synoptiques et les Actes.* Paris: Cerf, 1985.

Praeder, Susan Marie. *The Word in Women's Worlds: Four Parables.* Wilmington: Michael Glazier, 1988.

Pregeant, Russell. *Christology beyond Dogma: Matthew's Christ in Process Hermeneutic.* Philadelphia: Fortress, 1978.

————. "The Matthean Undercurrent: Process Hermeneutic and 'The Parable of the Last Judgment.'" Pages 143-59 in *Society of Biblical Literature Seminar Papers, 1975.* Vol. 2. Ed. George MacRae. Missoula: Scholars, 1975.

Preiss, Theo. *Life in Christ.* Trans. Harold Knight. Chicago: Allenson, 1954.

Price, Robert M. *The Widow Traditions in Luke-Acts: A Feminist-Critical Scrutiny.* SBLDS 155. Atlanta: Scholars, 1997.

Priest, J. "A Note on the Messianic Banquet." Pages 222-38 in *The Messiah: Developments in Earliest Judaism and Christianity.* Ed. James H. Charlesworth. Minneapolis: Fortress, 1992.

Przybylski, Benno. *Righteousness in Matthew and His World of Thought.* SNTSMS 41. Cambridge: Cambridge University Press, 1980.

Puig i Tarrech, Armand. *La parabole des dix vierges. Mt. 25:1-13.* Analecta Biblica 102. Rome: Biblical Institute Press, 1983.

————. "La Parabole des Talents (Mt 25,14-30) ou des Mines (Lc 19,11-28)." Pages 165-93 in *À Cause de L'Évangile. Études sur les Synoptiques et les Actes.* Lectio Divina 123. Paris: Cerf, 1985.

————. "Une parable à l'image antithétique." Pages 681-93 in *The Sayings Source Q and the Historical Jesus.* Ed. Andreas Lindemann. Leuven: Leuven University Press, 2001.

Purdy, John C. *Parables at Work.* Philadelphia: Westminster, 1985.

Puzicha, M. *Christus Peregrinus. Die Fremdenaufnahme (Mt. 25,35) als Werk der privaten Wohltätigkeit im Urteil der Alten Kirche.* Münster: Aschendorff, 1980.

Quarles, Charles Leland. "The Authenticity of the Parable of the Warring King: A Response to the Jesus Seminar." Pages 409-29 in *Authenticating the Words of Jesus.* Ed. Bruce D. Chilton and Craig A. Evans. Leiden: Brill, 1999.

Quispel, Gilles. "Jewish-Christian Gospel Tradition." Pages 112-16 in *Gospel Studies in Honor of Sherman Elbridge Johnson.* Ed. Massey H. Shepherd, Jr., and Edward C. Hobbs. AThRSS 3. Evanston: Anglican Theological Review, 1974.

Rackham, H. J. *The Fable as Literature.* London: Athlone, 1985.

Rahner, Karl. "Anonymous Christianity and the Missionary Task of the Church." Pages

161-78 in vol. 12 of *Theological Investigations*. Trans. David Bourke. 23 vols. London: Darton, Longman, and Todd, 1974.

———. "Anonymous Christians." Pages 390-98 in vol. 6 of *Theological Investigations*. Trans. K. H. and B. Kruger. 23 vols. London: Darton, Longman, and Todd, 1969.

Räisänen, Heikki. "The Prodigal Gentile and His Jewish Christian Brother, Lk 15,11-32." Pages 1617-36 in *The Four Gospels 1992: Festschrift Frans Neirynck*. Ed. F. Van Segbroeck, C. M. Tuckett, G. Van Belle, and J. Verheyden. Leuven: Leuven University Press, 1992.

Rau, Eckhard. "Jesu Auseinandersetzung mit Pharisäern über seine Zuwendung zu Sünderinnen und Sündern. Lk 15,11-32 und Lk 18,10-14a als Worte des historischen Jesu." *ZNW* 89 (1998): 5-29.

———. *Reden in Vollmacht. Hintergrund, Form, und Anliegen der Gleichnisse Jesu*. FRLANT 149. Göttingen: Vandenhoeck & Ruprecht, 1990.

Ravens, D. A. S. "The Setting of Luke's Account of the Anointing: Luke 7.2–8.3." *NTS* 34 (1988): 282-92.

Reicke, Bo. "Synoptic Prophecies on the Destruction of Jerusalem." Pages 121-34 in *Studies in New Testament and Early Christian Literature*. Ed. David Aune. Leiden: E. J. Brill, 1972.

Reid, Barbara E. "Beyond Petty Pursuits and Wearisome Widows: Three Lukan Parables." *Int* 56 (2002): 284-94.

———. "'Do You See This Woman?' Luke 7:36-50 as a Paradigm for Feminist Hermeneutics." *BR* 40 (1995): 37-49.

———. "Violent Endings in Matthew in Matthew's Parables and Christian Nonviolence." *CBQ* 66 (2004): 237-55.

Reiser, Marius. *Jesus and Judgment: The Eschatological Proclamation in Its Jewish Context*. Trans. Linda Maloney. Minneapolis: Fortress, 1997.

Rengstorf, Karl Heinrich. *Die Re-Investitur des Verlorenen Sohnes in der Gleichniserzählung Jesu Luk. 15,11-32*. Arbeitsgemeinschaft für Forschung des Landes Nordrhein-Westfalen, Geistgewissenschaften 137. Cologne: Westdeutscher, 1967.

———. "Die Stadt der Mörder." Pages 106-29 in *Judentum, Urchristentum, Kirche*. Ed. W. Eltester. Berlin: Töpelmann, 1960.

Resenhöfft, Wilhelm. "Jesu Gleichnis von den Talenten, ergänzt durch die Lukas-Fassung." *NTS* 26 (1980): 318-31.

Richardson, Peter. *Building Jewish in the Roman East*. Waco: Baylor University Press, 2004.

Ricoeur, Paul. "Biblical Hermeneutics." *Semeia* 4 (1975): 29-148.

———. *The Conflict of Interpretations: Essays in Hermeneutics*. Ed. Don Ihde. Evanston: Northwestern University Press, 1974.

———. *Interpretation Theory: Discourse and the Surplus of Meaning*. Fort Worth, Texas: Texas Christian University Press, 1976.

———. "Listening to the Parables of Jesus." Pages 239-45 in *The Philosophy of Paul Ricoeur: An Anthology of His Work*. Ed. Charles E. Reagan and David Stewart. Boston: Beacon, 1978.

———. *The Rule of Metaphor: Multi-Disciplinary Studies of the Creation of Meaning in Language*. Toronto: University of Toronto Press, 1977.

Ringe, Sharon H. *Jesus, Liberation, and the Biblical Jubilee*. Philadelphia: Fortress, 1985.

———. "Solidarity and Contextuality: Readings of Matthew 18:21-35." Pages 199-212 in vol.

1 of *Reading from This Place*. Ed. Fernando F. Segovia and Mary Ann Tolbert. Minneaplis: Fortress, 1995.

Robinson, J. A. T. "The Parable of the Sheep and the Goats." Pages 76-93 in *Twelve New Testament Studies*. Naperville: Allenson, 1962.

———. "The Parable of the Wicked Husbandmen: A Test of Synoptic Relations." *NTS* 21 (1975): 443-61.

Robinson, James M. "Jesus' Parables as God Happening." Pages 134-50 in *Jesus and the Historian*. Ed. F. Thomas Trotter. Philadelphia: Westminster, 1968.

Rohrbaugh, Richard L. *The Biblical Interpreter: An Agrarian Bible in an Industrial Age*. Philadelphia: Fortress, 1978.

———. "A Dysfunctional Family and Its Neighbors (Luke 15:11b-32)." Pages 141-64 in *Jesus and His Parables*. Ed. V. George Shillington. Edinburgh: T. & T. Clark, 1997.

———. "A Peasant Reading of the Parable of the Talents or Pounds: A Text of Terror?" *BTB* 23 (1993): 32-39.

———. "The Pre-Industrial City in Luke-Acts: Urban Social Relations." Pages 137-47 in *The Social World of Luke-Acts*. Ed. Jerome H. Neyrey. Peabody: Hendrickson, 1991.

Roloff, J. "Das Kirchenverständnis des Matthäus im Spiegel seiner Gleichnisse." *NTS* 38 (1992): 337-56.

Ross, J. M. "Talents." *ExpTim* 89 (1978): 307-9.

Rüger, Hans Peter. "μαμωνᾶς." *ZNW* 64 (1973): 127-31.

Ruzer, Serge. "The Double Love Precept in the New Testament and the *Community Rule*." Pages 81-106 in *Jesus' Last Week: Jerusalem Studies in the Synoptic Gospels — Volume One*. Ed. R. Steven Notley, Marc Turnage, and Brian Becker. Leiden: Brill, 2006.

Safrai, Samuel. "Home and Family." *JPFC* 2:728-40.

———. "Pilgrimage to Jerusalem at the End of the Second Temple Period." Pages 12-21 in *Studies on the Jewish Background of the New Testament*. Ed. O. Michel, et al. Assen: Van Gorcum, 1969.

———. "Religion in Everyday Life." *JPFC* 2:814-16.

———. "Spoken and Literary Languages in the Time of Jesus." Pages 225-44 in *Jesus' Last Week: Jerusalem Studies in the Synoptic Gospels — Volume One*. Ed. R. Steven Notley, Marc Turnage, and Brian Becker. Leiden: Brill, 2006.

———. "The Temple." *JPFC* 2:885-90.

Saldarini, Anthony. "Pharisees." *ABD* 5:289-303.

Sanday, W. "The Parable of the Labourers in the Vineyard." *Expositor* 1/3 (1876): 81-101.

Sanders, E. P. *Jesus and Judaism*. Philadelphia: Fortress, 1985.

———. *Jewish Law from Jesus to the Mishnah*. Philadelphia: Trinity, 1990.

———. *Tendencies of the Synoptic Tradition*. SNTSMS 9. Cambridge: Cambridge University Press, 1969.

Sanders, Jack T. "The Parable of the Pounds and Lucan Anti-Semitism." *TS* 42 (1981): 660-68.

———. "Tradition and Redaction in Luke XV.11-32." *NTS* 15 (1969): 433-38.

Sanders, James A. *Christianity, Judaism, and Other Cults*. Ed. Jacob Neusner. Leiden: Brill, 1975.

———. "The Ethic of Election in Luke's Great Banquet Parable." Pages 245-71 in *Essays in Old Testament Ethics*. Ed. James L. Crenshaw and John T. Willis. New York: Ktav, 1974.

———. "From Isaiah 61 to Luke 4." Pages 75-106 in *Christianity, Judaisim, and Other Cults.* Ed. Jacob Neusner. Leiden: Brill, 1975.

———. "Sins, Debts, and Jubilee Release." Pages 84-92 in *Luke and Scripture: The Function of Sacred Tradition in Luke-Acts.* Ed. Craig A. Evans and James A. Sanders. Minneapolis: Fortress, 1993.

Scharlemann, Martin H. "The Parables of the Leaven and the Mustard Seed: A Suggested Methodological Model." Pages 335-54 in *Studies in Lutheran Hermeneutics.* Ed. John Reumann. Philadelphia: Fortress, 1979.

———. *Proclaiming the Parables.* St. Louis: Concordia, 1963.

Schippers, R. "The Mashal-Character of the Parable of the Pearl." Pages 236-41 in vol. 2 of *Studia Evangelica.* Ed. F. L. Cross. TU 87. Berlin: Akademie, 1964.

Schlatter, Adolf. *The History of the Christ: The Foundation of New Testament Theology.* Trans. Andreas J. Köstenberger. Grand Rapids: Baker, 1997.

Schlosser, Jacques. "Le Pharisien et le Publicain (Lc 18,9-14)." Pages 271-88 in *Les Paraboles Évangélique. Perspectives nouvelles.* Ed. Jean Delormé. Paris: Cerf, 1989.

Schmeller, Thomas. "Der Erbe des Weinbergs: Zu den Gerichtsgleichnissen Mk 12,1-12 und Jes 5,1-7." *MTZ* 46 (1995): 183-201.

Schmidt, Thomas E. *Hostility to Wealth in the Synoptic Gospels.* JSNTSup 15. Sheffield: Sheffield Academic, 1987.

Schnackenburg, Rudolf. *God's Rule and Kingdom.* New York: Herder and Herder, 1963.

Schneider, G. *Parusiegleichnisse im Lukas-Evangelium.* Stuttgarter Bibelstudien 74. Stuttgart: Katholisches Bibelwerk, 1975.

Schnider, Franz. "Ausschliessen und ausgeschlossen werden. Beobachtungen zur Struktur des Gleichnisses vom Pharisäer und Zöllner." *BZ* 24 (1980): 42-56.

Schnider, F., and W. Stenger. "Die Offene Tür und die unüberschreitbare Kluft." *NTS* 25 (1979): 273-83.

Schoedel, William R. "Parables in the Gospel of Thomas: Oral Tradition or Gnostic Exegesis?" *Concordia Theological Monthly* 42 (1972): 548-60.

Schottroff, Luise. "Die Erzählung vom Pharisäer und Zöllner als Beispiel für die theologische Kunst des Überredens." Pages 439-61 in *Neues Testament und christliche Existenz.* Ed. H. Betz and L. Schrottroff. Tübingen: Mohr-Siebeck, 1973.

———. "Das Gleichnis vom grossen Gastmahl in der Logienquelle." *EvT* 47 (1987): 192-211.

———. "Das Gleichnis vom verlorenen Sohn." *ZTK* 68 (1971): 27-52.

———. "Human Solidarity and the Goodness of God: The Parable of the Workers in the Vineyard." Pages 129-47 in *God of the Lowly.* Ed. Willy Schottroff and Wolfgang Stegemann. Trans. Matthew J. O'Connell. Maryknoll: Orbis, 1984.

———. *Let the Oppressed Go Free: Feminist Perspectives on the New Testament.* Trans. Annemarie S. Kider. Louisville: Westminster John Knox, 1993.

———. *The Parables of Jesus.* Trans. Linda M. Maloney. Minneapolis: Fortress, 2006.

Schrage, Wolfgang. *Das Verhältnis des Thomas-Evangelium zur synoptischen Tradition und zu den koptischen Evangelienübersetzungen.* BZNW 29. Berlin: Töpelmann, 1964.

Schramm, Tim, and Kathrin Löwenstein. *Unmoralische Helden. Anstössige Gleichnisse Jesu.* Göttingen: Vandenhoeck & Ruprecht, 1986.

Schultze, Bernard. "Die ekklesiologische Bedeutung des Gleichnisses vom Senfkorn (Matth. 13,31-32; Mk. 4,30-32; Lk. 13,18-19)." *Orientalia Christiana Periodica* 27 (1961): 362-86.

Schürer, Emil. *The History of the Jewish People in the Age of Jesus Christ (175 B.C.–A.D. 135)*. Rev. ed. Ed. Geza Vermes, Fergus Millar, and Matthew Black. 4 vols. Edinburgh: T. & T. Clark, 1973-87.

Schweitzer, Albert. *On the Edge of the Primeval Forest*. Trans. C. T. Campion. New York: Macmillan, 1931.

Schweizer, Eduard. *The Good News According to Matthew*. Trans. David E. Green. Atlanta: John Knox, 1975.

———. "The Significance of Eschatology in the Teaching of Jesus." Pages 1-13 in *Eschatology and the New Testament*. Ed. W. Hulitt Gloer. Peabody: Hendrickson, 1988.

Scott, Bernard Brandon. *Hear Then the Parable: A Commentary on the Parables of Jesus*. Minneapolis: Fortress, 1989.

———. *Jesus, Symbol-Maker for the Kingdom*. Philadelphia: Fortress, 1982.

———. *Re-Imagine the World: An Introduction to the Parables of Jesus*. Santa Rosa: Polebridge, 2001.

Scott, R. B. Y. "The Parable of the Unjust Steward (Luke xvi.1ff.)." *ExpTim* 49 (1937-38): 284-85.

Seccombe, David Peter. *Possessions and the Poor in Luke-Acts*. Studien zum Neuen Testament und seiner Umwelt 6. Linz: Fuchs, 1983.

Sellew, Philip. "Interior Monologue as a Narrative Device in the Parables of Luke." *JBL* 111 (1992): 239-53.

Sellin, Gerhard. "Lukas als Gleichniserzähler. Die Erzählung vom barmherzigen Samariter (Lk 10:25-37)." *ZNW* 65 (1974): 166-89.

———. "Lukas als Gleichniserzähler. Die Erzählung vom barmherzigen Samariter, Lk 10:25-37." *ZTK* 66 (1975): 19-60.

Senft, Christophe. "Ferdinand Christian Baur, Methodological Approach and Interpretation of Luke 15:11-32." Pages 77-96 in *Exegesis: Problems of Method and Exercises in Reading (Genesis 22 and Luke 15)*. Ed. François Bovon and Grégoire Rouiller. Trans. Donald G. Miller. Pittsburgh: Pickwick, 1978.

Seng, Egbert W. "Der Reiche Tor." *NovT* 20 (1978): 136-55.

Sevrin, Jean-Marie. "Saving Life and Keeping Sabbath (Matt 20:1b-15)." Pages 87-101 in *Jesus and His Parables: Interpreting the Parables of Jesus Today*. Ed. V. George Shillington. Edinburgh: T. & T. Clark, 1997.

———. "Un groupement de trois paraboles contre les richesses dans L'Évangile selon Thomas. EvTh 63, 64, 65." Pages 425-39 in *Les Paraboles L'Évangéliques. Perspectives Nouvelles*. Ed. Jean Delorme. Paris: Cerf, 1989.

Short, Robert L. *The Parables of Peanuts*. San Francisco: Harper, 1968.

Sibinga, Joost Smit. "Zur Kompositationstechnik des Lukas in Lk. 15,11-32." Pages 97-113 in *Tradition and Re-Interpretation in Jewish and Early Christian Literature*. Ed. J. W. Van Henten, et al. Leiden: Brill, 1986.

Sider, John W. "Interpreting the Hid Treasure." *CSR* 13 (1984): 360-72.

———. *Interpreting the Parables: A Hermeneutical Guide to Their Meaning*. Grand Rapids: Zondervan, 1995.

———. "Proportional Analogy in the Gospel Parables." *NTS* 31 (1985): 1-23.

Siebald, Manfred, and Leland Ryken. "Prodigal Son." Pages 640-44 in *A Dictionary of Biblical Tradition in English Literature*. Ed. David Lyle Jeffrey. Grand Rapids: Eerdmans, 1992.

Sim, David C. *Apocalyptic Eschatology in the Gospel of Matthew.* SNTSMS 88. Cambridge: Cambridge University Press, 1996.

———. "The Dissection of the Wicked Servant in Matthew 24:51." *Harvard Theological Studies* 58 (2002): 172-84.

———. "The Man without a Wedding Garment (Matthew 22:11-13)." *HeyJ* (1990): 165-78.

———. "Matthew 22:13a and 1 Enoch 10:4a: A Case of Literary Dependence." *JSNT* 47 (1992): 15-18.

Simon, Uriel. "The Poor Man's Ewe-Lamb: An Example of a Juridical Parable." *Bib* 48 (1967): 207-42.

Singer, Christophe. "La difficulté d'être disciple. Luc 14/25-35." *ETR* (1998): 21-36.

Smalley, Stephen S. "The Delay of the Parousia." *JBL* 83 (1964): 41-54.

Smith, B. T. D. *The Parables of the Synoptic Gospels.* Cambridge: Cambridge University Press, 1937.

Smith, Charles W. F. *The Jesus of the Parables.* Philadelphia: United Church Press, 1975.

———. "The Mixed State of the Church in Matthew's Gospel." *JBL* 82 (1963): 149-68.

Smith, Morton. *Tannaitic Parallels to the Gospels.* JBLMS 6. Philadelphia: Society of Biblical Literature, 1951.

Snodgrass, Klyne. "*Anaideia* and the Friend at Midnight (Luke 11:8)." *JBL* 116 (1997): 505-13.

———. "Common Life with Jesus: The Parable of the Banquet in Luke 14:16-24." Pages 186-201 in *Common Life in the Early Church: Essays Honoring Graydon F. Snyder.* Ed. Julian V. Hills. Valley Forge: Trinity, 1998.

———. *Ephesians: The NIV Application Commentary.* Grand Rapids: Zondervan, 1996.

———. "From Allegorizing to Allegorizing: A History of the Interpretation of the Parables of Jesus." Pages 3-29 in *The Challenge of Jesus' Parables.* Ed. Richard N. Longenecker. Grand Rapids: Eerdmans, 2000.

———. "The Gospel of Jesus." Pages 31-44 in *The Written Gospel: Festschrift for Graham Stanton.* Ed. Markus Bockmuehl and Donald A. Hagner. Cambridge: Cambridge University Press, 2005.

———. "The Gospel of Thomas: A Secondary Gospel." *SecCent* 7 (1990): 19-38.

———. "A Hermeneutics of Hearing Informed by the Parables, with Special Reference to Mark 4." *BBR* 14 (2004): 59-79.

———. "Justification by Grace to the Doers: An Analysis of the Place of Romans 2 in the Theology of Paul." *NTS* 32 (1986): 72-93.

———. "Matthew and the Law." Pages 536-54 in *Society of Biblical Literature Seminar Papers, 1988.* Ed. David J. Lull. Atlanta: Scholars, 1988.

———. "Modern Approaches to the Parables." Pages 177-90 in *The Face of New Testament Studies: A Survey of Recent Research.* Ed. Scot McKnight and Grant Osborne. Grand Rapids: Baker, 2004.

———. *The Parable of the Wicked Tenants.* WUNT 27. Tübingen: J. C. B. Mohr, 1983.

———. "Parables and the Hebrew Scriptures." Pages 164-77 in *To Hear and Obey: Essays in Honor of Frederick Carlson Holmgren.* Ed. Bradley J. Bergfalk and Paul E. Koptak. Chicago: Covenant, 1997.

———. "Prophets, Parables, and Theologians." *BBR.* Forthcoming.

———. "Reading and Overreading the Parables in *Jesus and the Victory of God.*" Pages 61-76 in *Jesus and the Restoration of Israel: A Critical Assessment of N. T. Wright's "Jesus and the Victory of God."* Ed. Carey Newman. Downers Grove: InterVarsity, 1999.

————. "Reading to Hear: A Hermeneutics of Hearing." *HBT* 24 (2002): 1-32.

————. "Recent Research on the Parable of the Wicked Tenants: An Assessment." *BBR* 8 (1998): 187-216.

————. "The Use of the Old Testament in the New Testament." Pages 209-29 in *Interpreting the New Testament: Essays on Methods and Issues*. Ed. David Alan Black and David S. Dockery. Nashville: Broadman and Holman, 2001.

Spencer, F. Scott. "2 Chronicles 28:5-15 and the Parable of the Good Samaritan." *WTJ* 46 (1984): 317-49.

Spencer, William David, and Aida Besançon Spencer. *The Prayer Life of Jesus: Shout of Agony, Revelation of Love: A Commentary*. Lanham: University Press of America, 1990.

Spicq, Ceslaus. *Agape in the New Testament*. Trans. Marie Aquinas McNamara and Mary Honoria Richter. St. Louis: Herder, 1963.

Sproule, John A. "The Problem of the Mustard Seed." *Grace Theological Journal* 1 (1980): 37-42.

Stagg, Frank. *Studies in Luke's Gospel*. Nashville: Convention, 1965.

Stählin, G. "χήρα." *TDNT* 9:441-48.

Stanton, Graham N. "Once More: Matthew 25.31-46." Pages 207-31 in *A Gospel for a New People: Studies in Matthew*. Edinburgh: T. & T. Clark, 1992.

Steele, E. Springs. "Luke 11:37-54 — a Modified Hellenistic Symposium?" *JBL* 103 (1984): 379-94.

Stegemann, Ekkehard W., and Wolfgang Stegemann. *The Jesus Movement: A Social History of Its First Century*. Trans. O. C. Dean, Jr. Minneapolis: Fortress, 1999.

Stegner, William Richard. "The Parable of the Good Samaritan and Leviticus 18:5." Pages 27-38 in *The Living Text*. Ed. Dennis E. Groh and Robert Jewett. Lanham: University Press of America, 1985.

Stein, Robert H. "The Genre of the Parables." Pages 35-50 in *The Challenge of Jesus' Parables*. Ed. Richard Longenecker. Grand Rapids: Eerdmans, 2000.

————. "The Interpretation of the Parable of the Good Samaritan." Pages 278-95 in *Scripture, Tradition, and Interpretation*. Ed. W. Ward Gasque and William Sanford LaSor. Grand Rapids: Eerdmans, 1978.

————. *An Introduction to the Parables of Jesus*. Philadelphia: Westminster, 1981.

————. *Luke*. NAC 24. Nashville: Broadman, 1992.

Steinmetz, David. "Calvin and the Irrepressible Spirit." *Ex Auditu* 12 (1996): 94-107.

Steinmetz, Franz-Josef. "'Unkraut unter dem Weizen' (Mt 13,24-30). Ein aktuelles, aber nichtssagendes Gleichnis?" *Geist und Leben* 66 (1993): 1-9.

Stendahl, Krister. *The School of St. Matthew and Its Use of the Old Testament*. Acta Seminarii neotestamentici upsaliensis 20. 2d ed. Lund: Gleerup, 1968.

Stern, David. "Jesus' Parables from the Perspective of Rabbinic Literature: The Example of the Wicked Husbandmen." Pages 42-80 in *Parable and Story in Judaism and Christianity*. Ed. Clemens Thoma and Michael Wyschogrod. New York: Paulist, 1989.

————. *Parables in Midrash: Narrative and Exegesis in Rabbinic Literature*. Cambridge: Harvard University Press, 1991.

————. "Rhetoric and Midrash: The Case of the Mashal." *Prooftexts* 1 (1981): 261-91.

Stern, Ephraim. "Buried Treasure: The Silver Hoard from Dor." *BAR* 24 (1998): 46-51, 62.

Strack, Herman L., and Paul Billerbeck. "Das Gleichnis von den Arbeitern im Weinberg. Mt 20,1-16 u. die altsynagogale Lohnlehre." *Str-B* 4:484-500.

Strecker, Georg. *The Sermon on the Mount: An Exegetical Commentary.* Trans. O. C. Dean, Jr. Nashville: Abingdon, 1988.

Streeter, Burnett Hillman. *The Four Gospels: A Study of Origins.* New York: Macmillan, 1964.

Stroker, William D. "Extracanonical Parables and the Historical Jesus." *Semeia* 44 (1988): 95-120.

Stuhlmacher, Peter. *Biblische Theologie des Neuen Testaments. Grundlegung von Jesus zu Paulus.* Göttingen: Vandenhoeck & Ruprecht, 1992.

Stuhlmann, Ranier. "Beobachtungen und Überlegungen zu Markus IV.26-29." *NTS* 19 (1972): 153-62.

Sutcliffe, Edmund F. "Many Are Called but Few Are Chosen." *ITQ* 28 (1961): 126-31.

Suter, David Winston. *Tradition and Composition in the Parables of Enoch.* SBLDS 47. Missoula: Scholars, 1979.

Swaeles, R. "L'Arrière-fond scripturaire de Matt. XXI.43 et son lien avec Matt. XXI.44." *NTS* 6 (1959-60): 310-13.

Swartley, Willard M. "Unexpected Banquet People (Luke 14:16-24)." Pages 177-90 in *Jesus and His Parables.* Ed. George V. Shillington. Edinburgh: T. & T. Clark, 1997.

Talbert, Charles H. *Reading Luke: A Literary and Theological Commentary on the Third Gospel.* New York: Crossroad, 1982.

————. "The Redaction Critical Quest for Luke the Theologian." Pages 171-222 in *Jesus and Man's Hope.* Ed. D. G. Buttrick. Pittsburgh: Pittsburgh Theological Seminary, 1970.

Tan, Betty O. S. "The Parable of the Pharisee and the Tax-Collector in Luke 18:9-14: A Study on the Practice of Prayer." *Asia Journal of Theology* 14 (2000): 286-303.

Tanghe, Vincent. "Abraham, son fils et son envoyé." *RB* 91 (1984): 557-77.

Tannehill, Robert C. "The Lukan Discourse on Invitations (Luke 14,7-24)." Pages 1603-16 in *The Four Gospels: Festschrift Frans Neirynck.* Ed. F. Van Segbroeck, C. M. Tuckett, G. Van Belle, and J. Verheyden. Leuven: Leuven University Press, 1992.

Taylor, Carl L. "Jesus, the Prodigal Son." *Covenant Quarterly* 57 (1999): 36-48.

Taylor, Vincent. *The Gospel According to St. Mark.* London: Macmillan, 1957.

Telford, William R. *The Barren Temple and the Withered Tree: A Redaction-Critical Analysis of the Cursing of the Fig-Tree Pericope in Mark's Gospel and Its Relation to the Cleansing of the Temple Tradition.* JSNTSup 1. Sheffield: JSOT, 1980.

TeSelle, Sallie McFague. *Speaking in Parables.* Philadelphia: Fortress, 1975.

Tevel, J. M. "The Labourers in the Vineyard: The Exegesis of Matthew 20:1-7 in the Early Church." *VC* 46 (1992): 356-80.

Theissen, Gerd. "Der Bauer und die von selbst Frucht bringende Erde. Naiver Synergismus in Mk 4:26-29?" *ZNW* 85 (1994): 167-82.

Theissen, Gerd, and Annette Merz. *The Historical Jesus: A Comprehensive Guide.* Trans. John Bowden. Minneapolis: Fortress, 1998.

Thiebeaux, Evelyn R. "'Known to Be a Sinner': The Narrative Rhetoric of Luke 7:36-50." *BTB* 23 (1993): 151-60.

Thielicke, Helmut. *The Waiting Father.* Trans. John W. Doberstein. New York: Harper & Row, 1959.

Thiselton, Anthony. "The Parables as Language Event: Some Comments on Fuchs's Hermeneutics in the Light of Linguistic Philosophy." *SJT* 23 (1970): 437-68.

Thoma, Clemens, and S. Lauer. *Die Gleichnisse der Rabbinen*. 4 vols. Judaica et Christiana 10. Bern: Peter Lang, 1986-.

Thoma, Clemens, and Michael Wyschogrod, eds. *Parable and Story in Judaism and Christianity*. New York: Paulist, 1989.

Thompson, William G. *Matthew's Advice to a Divided Community: Mt. 17,22–18,35*. Rome: Biblical Institute Press, 1970.

Thomson, Clarence. *Parables and the Enneagram*. New York: Crossroad, 1996.

Thorion-Vardi, Thalia. *Das Kontrastgleichnis in der rabbinischen Literatur*. Judentum und Umwelt 16. Frankfurt am Main: Peter Lang, 1986.

Tissot, Yves. "Patristic Allegories of the Lukan Parable of the Two Sons (Luke 15:11-32)." Pages 362-409 in *Exegesis: Problems of Method and Exercise in Reading (Genesis 22 and Luke 15)*. Ed. François Bovon and Grégoire Rouiller. Trans. Donald G. Miller. Pittsburgh: Pickwick, 1978.

Tolbert, Mary Ann. *Perspectives on the Parables*. Philadelphia: Fortress, 1979.

———. *Sowing the Gospel: Mark's Gospel in the Literary-Historical Perspective*. Minneapolis: Fortress, 1989.

Tooley, W. "The Shepherd and Sheep Image in the Teaching of Jesus." *NovT* 7 (1964-65): 15-25.

Trench, Richard Chenevix. *Notes on the Parables of Our Lord*. 9th ed. London: Macmillan, 1864.

Trilling, Wolfgang. *Das wahre Israel. Studien zur Theologie des Matthäus Evangeliums*. SANT 10. 3d ed. Munich: Kösel, 1964.

Tripp, David H. "Zizania, Matthew 13:25: Realistic, If Also Figurative." *JTS* 50 (1999): 628.

Trudinger, Paul. "Exposing the Depth of Oppression (Luke 16:1b-8a): The Parable of the Unjust Steward." Pages 121-37 in *Jesus and His Parables*. Ed. V. George Shillington. Edinburgh: T. & T. Clark, 1997.

———. "Ire or Irony? The Enigmatical Character of the Parable of the Dishonest Steward (Luke 16:1-13)." *The Downside Review* 116 (1998): 85-102.

———. "A 'Lazarus Motif' in Primitive Christian Preaching?" *Andover Newton Quarterly* 7 (1966): 29-32.

Tucker, Jeffrey T. *Example Stories: Perspectives on Four Parables in the Gospel of Luke*. Sheffield: Sheffield Academic, 1998.

Tuckett, Christopher M. "Q and Thomas: Evidence of a Primitive 'Wisdom Gospel'?" *ETL* 67 (1991): 346-60.

———. "Q, Prayer, and the Kingdom." *JTS* 40 (1989): 367-76.

———. "Thomas and the Synoptics." *NovT* 30 (1988): 132-57.

Turner, David L. "Matthew 21:43 and the Future of Israel." *BSac* 159 (2002): 46-61.

Turner, H. E. W., and Hugh Montefiore. *Thomas and the Evangelists*. London: SCM, 1962.

Turner, Nigel. *Grammatical Insights into the New Testament*. Edinburgh: T. & T. Clark, 1965.

Ukpong, Justin S. "The Parable of the Shrewd Manager (Luke 16:1-13): An Essay in Inculturation Biblical Hermeneutic." *Semeia* 73 (1996): 189-210.

Uriel, Simon. "The Poor Man's Ewe-Lamb: An Example of a Juridical Parable." *Bib* 48 (1967): 207-42.

Uro, Risto. "'Secondary Orality' in the Gospel of Thomas?" *FFF* 9 (1993): 305-29.

Vallet, Ronald E. *Stepping Stones of the Steward*. Grand Rapids: Eerdmans, 1994.

Van Elderen, Bastiaan. "Another Look at the Parable of the Good Samaritan." Pages 109-19 in *Saved by Hope*. Ed. James I. Cook. Grand Rapids: Eerdmans, 1978.

———. "The Purpose of the Parables According to Matthew 13:10-17." Pages 180-90 in *New Dimensions in New Testament Study*. Ed. Richard Longenecker and Merrill C. Tenney. Grand Rapids: Zondervan, 1974.

Van Iersel, B. M. F. *"Der Sohn" in den synoptischen Jesusworten*. Leiden: Brill, 1961.

Van Staden, P. "A Sociological Reading of Luke 12:35-48." *Neot* 22 (1988): 337-53.

Van Tuyll, Hendrik. *The Parables: The Forgotten Message*. Pelham: Middle Street, 1993.

Verhey, Allen. *Reading the Bible in the Strange World of Medicine*. Grand Rapids: Eerdmans, 2003.

Verhoef, Eduard. "(Eternal) Life and Following the Commandments: Lev 18,5 and Luke 10,28." Pages 571-77 in *The Scriptures in the Gospels*. Ed. C. M. Tuckett. Leuven: Leuven University Press, 1997.

Vermes, Geza. *The Gospel of Jesus the Jew*. Newcastle upon Tyne: University of Newcastle upon Tyne, 1981.

———. *Jesus and the World of Judaism*. Philadelphia: Fortress, 1983.

Via, Dan Otto, Jr. "Ethical Responsibility and Human Wholeness in Matthew 25:31-46." *HTR* 80 (1987): 79-100.

———. "Matthew on the Understandability of the Parables." *JBL* 84 (1965): 430-32.

———. "Parable and Example Story: A Literary-Structuralist Approach." *Semeia* 1 (1974): 105-33.

———. "The Parable of the Unjust Judge: A Metaphor of the Unrealized Self." Pages 1-32 in *Semiology and Parables*. Ed. Daniel Patte. Pittsburgh: Pickwick, 1976.

———. *The Parables: Their Literary and Existential Dimension*. Philadelphia: Fortress, 1967.

———. "The Prodigal Son: A Jungian Reading." *Semeia* 9 (1977): 21-43.

Vogels, Walter. "Having or Longing: A Semiotic Analysis of Luke 16:19-31." *EgT* 20 (1989): 27-46.

Vögtle, Anton. *Gott und seine Gäste. Das Schicksal des Gleichnisses Jesu vom grossen Gastmahl*. Biblische-theologische Studien. Neukirchen-Vluyn: Neukirchener, 1996.

Volf, Miroslav. *Exclusion and Embrace: A Theological Exploration of Identity, Otherness, and Reconciliation*. Nashville: Abingdon, 1996.

von Gemünden, Petra. *Vegetationsmetaphorik im Neuen Testament und seiner Umwelt*. NTOA 18. Göttingen: Vandenhoeck & Ruprecht, 1993.

Vorster, Willem S. "Meaning and Reference: The Parables of Jesus in Mark 4." Pages 161-97 in *Speaking of Jesus*. Ed. Eugene Booths. Leiden: Brill, 1979.

Vouga, François. "Formgeschichtliche Überlegungen zu den Gleichnissen und zu den Fabeln der Jesus-Tradition auf dem Hintergrund der Hellenistischen Literaturgeschichte." Pages 173-87 in *The Four Gospels 1992: Festschrift Frans Neirynck*. Ed. F. Van Segbroeck, C. M. Tuckett, G. Van Belle, and J. Verheyden. Leuven: Leuven University Press, 1992.

Waetjen, Herman C. "The Subversion of 'World' by the Parable of the Friend at Midnight." *JBL* 120 (2001): 703-21.

Wailes, Stephen L. *Medieval Allegories of Jesus' Parables*. Berkeley: University of California Press, 1987.

Wall, Robert W. "Martha and Mary (Luke 10:38-42) in the Context of a Christian Deuteronomy." *JSNT* 35 (1989): 19-35.

Waller, Elizabeth. "The Parable of the Leaven: A Sectarian Teaching and the Inclusion of Women." *USQR* 35 (1979-80): 99-109.

Walvoord, John F. "Christ's Olivet Discourse on the End of the Age: The Judgment of the Nations." *BSac* 129 (1972): 307-15.

———. "Christ's Olivet Discourse on the End of the Age: The Parable of the Virgins." *BSac* 129 (1972): 99-105.

Wansey, J. C. "The Parable of the Unjust Steward: An Interpretation." *ExpTim* 47 (1935-36): 39-40.

Watson, Duane F. "Gehenna." *ABD* 2:927-28.

Watts, Rikki. *Isaiah's New Exodus and Mark*. WUNT 2.88. Tübingen: Mohr-Siebeck, 1997.

Weber, Kathleen. "The Image of Sheep and Goats in Matthew 25:31-46." *CBQ* 59 (1997): 657-78.

———. "Is There a Qumran Parallel to Matthew 24,51//Luke 12,46?" *RevQ* 16 (1995): 657-63.

Weder, Hans. *Die Gleichnisse Jesu als Metaphern. Traditions- und redaktionsgeschichtliche Analysen und Interpretationen*. 4th ed. Göttingen: Vandenhoeck & Ruprecht, 1990.

Weeden, T. *Mark — Traditions in Conflict*. Philadelphia: Fortress, 1971.

Weinert, Francis D. "The Parable of the Throne Claimant (Luke 19:12, 14-15a, 27) Reconsidered." *CBQ* 39 (1977): 505-14.

Weiser, Alfons. *Die Knechtsgleichnisse der synoptischen Evangelien*. SANT 29. Munich: Kösel, 1971.

Weiss, K. "Der westliche Text von Lc 7:46 und sein Wert." *ZNW* 46 (1955): 241-45.

Wendland, Ernst. "'Blessed Is the Man Who Will Eat at the Feast in the Kingdom of God' (Lk 14:15): Internal and External Influence on the Interpretation of Christ's Parable of the Great Banquet." *Neot* 31 (1997): 159-94.

———. "Finding Some Lost Aspects of Meaning in Christ's Parables of the Lost — and Found (Luke 15)." *TJ* 17 (1996): 19-65.

Wengst, Klaus. "Wie aus Böcken Ziegen wurden (Mt 25,32f)." *EvT* 54 (1994): 491-500.

Wenham, David. "The Interpretation of the Parable of the Sower." *NTS* 20 (1974): 299-319.

———, ed. *The Rediscovery of Jesus' Eschatological Discourse*. Vol. 4 of *Gospel Perspectives*. Sheffield: JSOT, 1984.

———. "The Structure of Matthew XIII." *NTS* 25 (1979): 516-22.

Westermann, Claus. *The Parables of Jesus in the Light of the Old Testament*. Ed. and trans. Friedemann W. Golka and Alastair H. B. Logan. Minneapolis: Fortress, 1990.

White, K. D. "The Parable of the Sower." *JTS* 15 (1964): 300-307.

Wielenga, Bastiaan. "The Rich Man and Lazarus." *Reformed World* 46 (1996): 109-16.

Wierzbicka, Anna. *What Did Jesus Mean? Explaining the Sermon on the Mount and the Parables in Simple and Universal Human Concepts*. Oxford: Oxford University Press, 2001.

Williams, James G. *Gospel Against Parable: Mark's Language of Mystery*. Sheffield: Almond, 1985.

Williams, Ronald J. "The Fable in the Ancient Near East." Pages 3-26 in *A Stubborn Faith: Papers on the Old Testament and Related Subjects Presented to Honor William Andrew Irwin*. Ed. Edward C. Hobbs. Dallas: Southern University Press, 1956.

Wilmshurst, S. M. B. "The Historic Present in Matthew's Gospel: A Survey and Analysis Focused on Matthew 13:44." *JSNT* 25 (2003): 269-87.

Wilson, Stephen G. *The Gentiles and the Gentile Mission in Luke-Acts.* SNTSMS 23. Cambridge: Cambridge University Press, 1973.

Wimmer, Joseph F. *Fasting in the New Testament.* New York: Paulist, 1982.

Wink, Walter. "The Parable of the Compassionate Samaritan: A Communal Exegesis Approach." *RevExp* 76 (1979): 199-217.

Winterhalter, Robert, with George W. Fisk. *Jesus' Parables: Finding Our God Within.* New York: Paulist, 1993.

Wohlgemut, Joel R. "Entrusted Money (Matthew 25:14-28): The Parable of the Talents/ Pounds." Pages 103-20 in *Jesus and His Parables.* Ed. V. George Shillington. Edinburgh: T. & T. Clark, 1997.

Wood, H. G. "The Use of ἀγαπάω in Luke vii. 42, 47." *ExpT* 66 (1954-55): 319-20.

Wright, N. T. *Jesus and the Victory of God.* Vol. 2 of *Christian Origins and the Question of God.* Minneapolis: Fortress, 1996.

———. *The New Testament and the People of God.* Vol. 1 of *Christian Origins and the Question of God.* Minneapolis: Fortress, 1992.

Wright, Stephen Irwin. "Parables on Poverty and Riches (Luke 12:13-21; 16:1-13; 16:19-31)." Pages 217-39 in *The Challenge of Jesus' Parables.* Ed. Richard N. Longenecker. Grand Rapids: Eerdmans, 2000.

———. *The Voice of Jesus: Studies in the Interpretation of Six Gospel Parables.* Cumbria: Paternoster, 2002.

Wuellner, Wilhelm H. *The Meaning of "Fishers of Men."* Philadelphia: Westminster, 1967.

Yee, Gale. "A Form Critical Study of Isaiah 5:1-7 as a Song and a Juridical Parable." *CBQ* 43 (1981): 30-40.

Young, Brad H. *Jesus and His Jewish Parables: Rediscovering the Roots of Jesus' Teaching.* New York: Paulist, 1989.

———. *Jesus the Jewish Theologian.* Peabody: Hendrickson, 1995.

———. *The Parables: Jewish Tradition and Christian Interpretation.* Peabody: Hendrickson, 1998.

Young, Franklin W. "Luke 13:1-9." *Int* 31 (1977): 59-63.

Young, Norman H. "The Commandment to Love Your Neighbor as Yourself and the Parable of the Good Samaritan (Luke 10:25-37)." *AUSS* 21 (1983): 265-72.

Zerwick, Maximilian. *Biblical Greek.* Rome: Scripta Pontifici Instituti Biblici, 1963.

———. "Die Parabel vom Thronanwärter." *Bib* 40 (1959): 654-74.

Ziegler, Ignaz. *Die Königsgleichnisse des Midrasch beleuchtet durch die römische Kaiserzeit.* Breslau: Schottlaender, 1903.

Zimmermann, Ruben. "Das Hochzeitsritual im Jungfrauengleichnis. Sozialgeschichtliche Hintergruende zu Mt. 25:1-3." *NTS* 48 (2002): 48-70.

Zohary, Michael. *Plants of the Bible.* Cambridge: Cambridge University Press, 1982.

Index of Authors

Index of Ancient Sources

JEWISH SOURCES

QUMRAN